NEGLECTED BARBARIANS

STUDIES IN THE EARLY MIDDLE AGES

Previously published volumes in this series are listed at the back of this book

VOLUME 32

NEGLECTED BARBARIANS

Edited by

Florin Curta

BREPOLS

British Library Cataloguing in Publication Data

Neglected barbarians. – (Studies in the early Middle Ages ; v. 32)
    1. Ethnohistory – Europe. 2. Ethnology – Europe – History – To 1500. 3.
Ethnoarchaeology – Europe. 4. Civilization, Medieval – Research. 5. Europe –
Antiquities.
I. Series II. Curta, Florin.
940'.04-dc22

ISBN-13: 9782503531250

© 2010, Brepols Publishers n.v., Turnhout, Belgium

D/2010/0095/219
ISBN: 978-2-503-53125-0

Printed in the USA on acid-free paper

Contents

ACKNOWLEDGEMENTS

This book developed out of two sessions organized for the 40th International Congress on Medieval Studies in Kalamazoo (May 5–8, 2005). I am grateful to the Medieval Institute at Western Michigan University, the organizer of the congress, for its continuous support. Over the six years during which this book has taken — and changed — shape, I have acquired a number of debts. My largest thanks go to the authors of the essays included here. They stuck with the project despite many obstacles and disappointments. As all of us (including those who dropped out along the way) came to realize, the study of the 'neglected barbarians' takes a great deal of time, commitment, and perseverance.

The School of Historical Studies at the Institute for Advanced Study in Princeton provided the time, resources, and a genial and supportive atmosphere for bringing this project to fruition during the Spring semester of 2007. I wish to thank Carolyn Walker Bynum for encouragement and helpful suggestions. I am also grateful to those students who helped me with the translation and editing of several chapters in this book: Andrew Holt, Anna Lankina, and Reid Weber.

Gavritukhin and Kazanski, 'Bosporus, the Tetraxite Goths, and the Northern Caucasus'

Nagy, 'A Hun-Age Burial'

Tóth, 'A Fifth-Century Burial from Old Buda (Budapest)'

Harhoiu, 'Where Did All the Gepids Go?'

Kharalambieva, 'Gepids in the Balkans'

Jiřík, 'Bohemian Barbaria'

López Sánchez, 'Suevic Coins and Suevic Kings'

Berndt, 'Hidden Tracks: On the Vandal's Paths to an African Kingdom'

Plates

INTRODUCTION

Florin Curta

Barbarus hic ego sum, qui non intellegor ulli,
Et rident stolidi uerba Latina Getae.[1]

The history of ancient and medieval barbarians is a topic of perennial interest. It is witnessed by the constant flow of scholarship, popular histories of colourful barbarian leaders, and television programming in such venues as the History Channel.[2] The vast majority of books on the barbarians, whether monographs or surveys, single author or multi-author collections, concentrate on a small number of barbarian groups for which continuous narrative histories can be constructed, with however varying degrees of plausibility. The Goths, Franks, Anglo-Saxons, and Huns are subjected to a new treatment in one of the main scholarly languages every year or two, the Alamanni and the Lombards only slightly less regularly, while the Vandals and the early Slavs have only begun to emerge from years of relative invisibility in the past half decade.[3] Around this core of extensively

---

[1] Ovid, *Trista* 5.10.37–38: 'I'm the barbarian, no one understands me; | My Latin speech the stupid Getae mock' (translation from A. D. Melville, *Ovid, 'Sorrows of an Exile'* (Oxford, 1992), p. 109).

[2] See, for example, the seven-hour-long series entitled 'Barbarians', first aired in 2004, which features 'Vikings, Mongols, Huns, Saxons, Lombards and their savage brethren'.

[3] Michael Kulikowski, *Rome's Gothic Wars: From the Third Century to Alaric* (Cambridge, 2007); Christina Lee, *Feasting the Dead: Food and Drink in Anglo-Saxon Burial Rituals* (Woodbridge, 2007); *Des Goths aux Huns: le nord de la Mer Noire au Bas Empire et à l'époque des Grandes Migrations*, ed. by Mark B. Shchukin, Michel Kazanski, and Oleg Sharov (Oxford, 2006); John F. Drinkwater, *The Alamanni and Rome 213–496 (Caracalla to Clovis)* (Oxford, 2007); *Die Langobarden: Herrschaft und Identität*, ed. by Walter Pohl and Peter Erhart (Vienna, 2005); Nicoletta Francovich Onesti, *I Vandali: Lingua e storia* (Rome, 2002); Paul M. Barford, *The Early Slavs: Culture and Society in Early Medieval Eastern Europe* (Ithaca, 2001).

studied barbarian groups, however, shimmers a penumbra of many others, of greater and lesser accessibility in the literary and archaeological evidence.[4] Though diverse enough within their early medieval world, those barbarians share one fundamental characteristic: neglect by modern scholars.

There are several reasons for that neglect. One, obviously, is the relative paucity of sources. To be sure, the 'neglected barbarians' were still 'barbarians' inasmuch as they existed in relation to the Roman Empire, even if at a great distance from its frontiers.[5] They could thus catch, if only occasionally, the attention of Roman authors. But perhaps more important for the relative lack of interest in their history have been two other factors. First, the barbarians who have most suffered from neglect are those who had no 'national' historian like Jordanes or Gregory of Tours, upon whose narrative framework the modern historian can build. What we know about the 'neglected barbarians' often comes from sources written either by those who eventually conquered them or by outsiders with often indifferent, if not altogether hostile, attitudes towards those who did not appear as the winners of the day. Modern historians tend to see the periphery of the Mediterranean world through the eyes of those at its centre.[6] Second, the history of those barbarians can usually not be read as developing into that of one or another of the great medieval kingdoms. Most 'neglected barbarians' built ephemeral polities that left no significant political traditions and symbols for posterity. Indeed, the neglect with which

---

[4] As Walter Goffart, *Barbarian Tides: The Migration Age and the Later Roman Empire* (Philadelphia, 2006), p. 192, puts it, most barbarian peoples 'were snuffed out and did not survive into the Middle Ages'. According to Goffart, while only such names as Goths, Franks, Vandals, or Saxons are household words, with a little practice Sarmatians and Gepids can also become familiar to scholars interested in barbarians.

[5] To some, the dichotomy between barbarians and (Roman) civilization established by the works of ancient ethnography is a difficult thing to grasp. According to Michel Kazanski, 'Les Barbares à Chersonèse (Vᵉ–VIᵉ siècles)', in *Eupsychia: Mélanges offerts à Hélène Ahrweiler*, ed. by Michel Balard and others (Paris, 1998), pp. 329–44 (p. 329), there were barbarians in Chersonesus (Crimea) in Late Antiquity, and their presence is apparently betrayed, among other things, by 'objets de la *civilisation* de Černjahov' (emphasis added). As if to reinforce his incongruous notion of a barbarian civilization, Kazanski has barbarians coming to Chersonesus in Crimea as members of Roman military units stationed in the city, many of them being (so Kazanski) Ostrogoths and Danubian 'Germans'.

[6] Walter Pohl, 'Die Namen der Barbaren: Fremdbezeichnung und Identität in Spätantike und Frühmittelalter', in *Zentrum und Peripherie: gesellschaftliche Phänomene in der Frühgeschichte. Materialien des 13. internationalen Symposiums 'Grundprobleme der frühgeschichtlichen Entwicklung im mittleren Donauraum', Zwettl, 4.–8. Dezember 2000*, ed. by Herwig Friesinger and Alois Stuppner (Vienna, 2004), pp. 95–104 (p. 102).

such barbarian groups are commonly treated has much to do with the fact that their history has nothing interesting to offer to nationalist narratives created in the more recent past. Unlike the Franks, the Gepids are not claimed by any modern nation in Europe, while the Sueves, Crimean Goths, or Mauri even pose somewhat difficult problems of interpretation to scholars based in countries now occupying the lands once controlled by those barbarians. Ever since its discovery in the late nineteenth century, the so-called Olsztyn group in north-eastern Poland (Mazuria), a group of cemeteries whose sudden appearance in the late fifth century marks the implementation of an amazing network of long-distance relations with Merovingian Gaul, Crimea, and the Lower Danube region, posed insurmountable problems of interpretation.[7] With no written sources to help archaeologists put an ethnic name on the people burying their dead in Mazurian cemeteries, different scholars picked different names of other 'neglected barbarians' to fill in the gap. From Herules to Galindians, the Olsztyn group (previously known as 'masurgermanische Kultur') has continuously served as an illustration of how limited our understanding of the 'barbarian world' truly is.[8] Elsewhere, with no written sources at hand offering easy explanations for archaeological assemblages dated to the late antique or early medieval period, scholars do not hesitate to apply much later sources, thus pushing back in time the antiquity of groups that *can* be used for the nationalist discourse. This is certainly the case of Lithuania, where fifth- to sixth-century assemblages are attributed to groups whose existence is first documented in the twelfth century.[9] A certain kind of historiography has long associated the

[7] Wojciech Nowakowski, 'Die Olsztyn-Gruppe (masurgermanische Kultur) in der Völkerwanderungszeit: Das Problem ihrer chronologischen und territorialen Grenzen', in *Die spätrömische Kaiserzeit und die frühe Völkerwanderungszeit im Mittel- und Osteuropa*, ed. by Magdalena Maczyńska and Tadeusz Grabarczyk (Łódź, 2000), pp. 168–90.

[8] Bruno Ehrlich, 'Germanen, Balten und Slaven in Ostdeutschland in vor- und frühgeschichtlicher Zeit', *Vergangenheit und Gegenwart*, 19 (1929), 321–49; Carl Engel and Wolfgang La Baume, *Kulturen und Völker der Frühzeit in Preussenlande* (Königsberg, 1937); Eduard Šturms, 'Die ethnische Deutung der "masurgermanischen" Kultur', *Contributions of the Baltic University*, 31 (1947), 1–12; Józef Kostrzewski, 'Koniec legendy o kulturze mazursko-germańskiej', *Z otchłani wieków*, 21 (1952), 105–06; Fryda D. Gurevich, 'Iz istorii iugo-vostochnoi Pribaltiki v I. tysiacheletii n. e.', in *Drevnosti severo-zapadnykh oblastei RSFSR* (Moscow, 1960), pp. 328–449; Wojciech Nowakowski, *Od Galindai do Galinditae: Z badań nad pradziejami bałtyjskiego ludu z Pojezierza Mazurskiego* (Warsaw, 1995).

[9] I. Jonynas, 'Les Peuplades lithuaniennes jusqu'au XIVᵉ siècle', in *Pirmā Baltijas vēsturnieku konference. Rīga, 16.–20.VIII.1937. Runas un referāti* (Riga, 1938), pp. 46–61; Adolfas Tautavičius, 'Baltskie plemena na territorii Litvy v I tysiachel. n. e.', in *Iz drevneishei istorii baltskikh narodov (po*

Gepids, Crimean Goths, and *Gothi minores* in the Balkans with the *Ostgermanen*, the 'lost tribe' of a much greater family to be reunited either by linguistic paleontology or by military force.[10] But even the *germanische Altertumskunde* now discredited by the grotesque abuses of the Nazi regime did not regard either the Sueves in the West or the Gepids in the East as anything more than outliers, too 'exotic' to play any role in the master narrative of Germanic history. Moreover, the archaeology of both Gepids and Sueves was never a particular branch of the 'national' school of archaeology in either Hungary or Portugal, which greatly contributed to the further marginalization of the topic. With no 'national' historian to write their history, the 'neglected barbarians' are of no use to the 'imagined communities' of the more recent past, as apparently nothing links the Gepids, Sueves, or Frexes to modern Hungarians, Portuguese (or Spaniards), and Tunisians, respectively. As a consequence, even the remarkable resistance, in certain cases, of a group identity under foreign rule (such as that of the Gepids under the Avars or that of the Crimean Goths under the Khazars) appears as unremarkable to historians otherwise interested in the construction of group identities in the past. In fact, the recent focus of much early medievalist scholarship on ethnicity and 'ethnogenesis' — in such projects as the 'Transformation of the Roman World' conferences and elsewhere — has effectively sidelined barbarian groups for whom the literary evidence is too scant to contribute to theoretical debates on ethnicity.[11]

Studying neglected barbarians has a number of advantages. First, it allows one to reject the temptation of reproducing the stereotypes of the ancient ethnographers, who classified barbarians as 'absolute', 'primary', and 'secondary' on the

dannym arkheologii i antropologii), ed. by R. I. Denisova, F. A. Zagorskis, and Ē. Mugurēvičs (Riga, 1980), pp. 80–88; Valdemaras Šimėnas, 'Ob etnokul'turnoi situatsii v V–VIII vv. v nizov'iakh Nemana', *Arkheologiia i istoriia Pskova i Pskovskoi zemli*, 1987, 72–73; Regina Volkaitė-Kulikauskienė, 'Etnicheskaia situatsiia na territorii Litvy v I i nachale II tys. n. e.', in *VI Mezhdunarodnyi kongress slavianskoi arkheologii, g. Prilep, Iugoslaviia, 1990 g. Tezisy dokladov, podgotovlennykh sovetskimi issledovateliami*, ed. by V. V. Sedov (Moscow, 1990), pp. 14–16.

[10] Gustaf Kossinna, *Die ethnologische Stellung der Ostgermanen* (Strasbourg, 1896); Ludwig Schmidt, *Die Ostgermanen*, vol. I of *Geschichte der deutschen Stämme bis zum Ausgange der Völkerwanderung* (Munich, 1941; repr. 1969).

[11] This is particularly true for such volumes as *Kingdoms of the Empire: The Integration of Barbarians in Late Antiquity*, ed. by Walter Pohl (Leiden, 1997) or *Strategies of Distinction: The Construction of Ethnic Communities, 300–800*, ed. by Walter Pohl and Helmut Reimitz (Leiden, 1998); or *Regna and gentes: The Relationship Between Late Antique and Early Medieval Peoples and Kingdoms in the Transformation of the Roman World*, ed. by Hans-Werner Goetz, Jörg Jarnut, and Walter Pohl (Leiden, 2003).

basis of their exposure to and assimilation of various elements of civilization.[12] The basis for such a classification is the idea that barbarians from particular areas were fundamentally all the same, no matter how they changed their names.[13] Such an ingrained bias can still be recognized in what Walter Goffart has recently condemned as an obsessive preoccupation of the modern historians with 'Germanic' peoples and their futile effort to distinguish a presumably Hunnic, Gothic, or Frankish 'alternative' to the Roman Empire.[14] Second, precisely because of the lack of sufficient information from the written sources, the 'neglected barbarians' invite a re-examination of the relation between the historical and the archaeological evidence. As has recently been noted, 'Roman depictions of barbarians are not part of a dialogue between "us" and "them" (*we* are like this whereas *you* are like that), but between "us" and "us", between Romans (*we* are [or more often ought to be] like this because *they* are like that)'.[15] At the very least, this implies that when not useful for the dialogue between 'us' and 'us', particular groups are simply ignored and never show up in our sources. Nothing is known from the written sources about such groups as those associated with sixth- to seventh-century sites in Mazuria (Poland) or the so-called Nevolino culture in the foothills of the Ural Mountains in Russia. Yet the archaeological evidence is unambiguous about the relations those groups maintained with distant communities in Merovingian Gaul, Ostrogothic Italy, Byzantium, or Sassanian Persia.[16] But even in cases where there

---

[12] Yves Albert Daugé, *Le Barbare: recherches sur la conception romaine de la barbarie et de la civilisation* (Brussels, 1981), pp. 444–45, 488, and 490–91. Most 'primary' barbarians were isolated groups of population living on the fringes of the *oikoumene*.

[13] Procopius of Caesarea, *Wars*, 3.2.2–5. See also Guy Halsall, *Barbarian Migrations and the Roman West, 376–568* (Cambridge, 2007), p. 48.

[14] Goffart, *Barbarian Tides*, p. 198: 'Neither the Huns nor the Goths nor any other is "representative".'

[15] Halsall, *Barbarian Migrations*, p. 56.

[16] For the Olsztyn group in Mazuria, see Felix E. Peiser, 'Eine byzantinische Scheibenfibel', *Sitzungsberichte der Altertumsgesellschaft Prussia*, 23 (1905–08), 373–76; Volker Hilberg, 'Die westbaltischen Stämme und die überregionale Kulturaustausch in der Ostseeregion zur Merowingerzeit', *Bodendenkmalpflege in Mecklenburg-Vorpommern: Jahrbuch*, 51 (2003), 295–319. For the Nevolino culture, see Igor O. Gavritukhin and A. G. Ivanov, 'Pogrebenie 552 Varninskogo mogil'nika i nekotorye voprosy izucheniia rannesrednevekovykh kul'tur Povolzh'ia', in *Permskii mir v rannem srednevekov'e*, ed. by A. G. Ivanov (Izhevsk, 1999), pp. 99–159; A. G. Ivanov, 'Prikam'e v sisteme vostochnoevropeiskoi torgovli v VII–VIII vv. (po arkheologicheskim materialam)', in *Khazary: Vtoroi Mezhdunarodnyi kollokvium. Tezisy*, ed. by V. I. Petrukhin and A. M. Fedorchuk (Moscow, 2002), pp. 38–40.

is a relatively good coverage of written sources, the archaeological evidence warns against taking seriously the perspective of the ancient authors, who were much too eager to impose simplifying umbrella-terms upon a much more complex political and ethnic reality.

The problem of neglect has been quite universal, running from one end of the Roman world to the other. This volume addresses this neglect in a series of chapters which systematically cover those less-known corners of the late antique and early medieval barbarian world. Moving from east to west, from the Baltic and the Caucasus region to Spain and North Africa, the book attempts to address three main themes. First, why is a particular barbarian group neglected? Is it a problem of the source base, or are there any deeper, perhaps historiographic reasons? Second, just how much can one learn about a particular group of neglected barbarians, and how does one go about finding out? Third, what sorts of future research are necessary to extend or fill out our understanding about a particular group of neglected barbarians? Some chapters treat those questions organically, while others look at case studies which have the effect of establishing what we know and how we can move forward.

Audronė Bliujienė concentrates on the use of amber within communities in late antique and early medieval Lithuania. The *Aesti* of Tacitus, who were rich in amber, resurface in the correspondence of King Theoderic the Great preserved in Cassiodorus's *Variae*. However, most amber-rich sites in the Baltic region were at that time on the coast, and not in the interior. With the disappearance of amber finds from most assemblages dated after 550, Lamata, a small region in western Lithuania, became the only part of the Baltic lands which still produced amber. By means of amber, the 'neglected barbarians' of Lamata were able to maintain relations with Merovingian Francia, the northern shores of the Black Sea, and the Balkans.

A similar theme is pursued by Wojciech Nowakowski in a chapter based on the evidence from burial assemblages and a few settlement sites attributed to the so-called Olsztyn group from Mazuria (also known as *masurgermanische Kultur*). Like Bliujienė, Nowakowski deals with a difficult problem: how to interpret the trans-European relations established by the sixth- and seventh-century inhabitants of Mazuria with distant cultural and political areas such as Merovingian Gaul, Crimea, or the Lower and Middle Danube region. Rather than seeing the process of remarkable cultural change signalled by the emergence of the Olsztyn group as a mirror of social transformation, Nowakowski embraces a migrationist interpretation, even though he is forced to acknowledge that 'there are very few, if any, finds that could be used to support the idea of a migration'.

Unlike Nowakowski, Bartłomiej Szymon Szmoniewski faces a somewhat different problem. His barbarians have a name (Antes), but their exact location is difficult to establish on the basis of the information from written sources. Whereas the Galindians to whom Nowakowski attributes the material culture of the Olsztyn group were eventually absorbed 'into the Prussian ethnic community' and did not survive into the modern era, a direct continuity between Antes, Rus', and Ukrainians, as formulated most clearly by Mykhailo Hrushevs'kyi, plays a prominent role in the Ukrainian nationalist discourse to this day. Unlike Nowakowski, Szmoniewski undercuts the simplistic notion of associating any ethnic name (such as the Antes) known from written sources with any archaeological culture (such as the Pen'kivka culture) 'discovered' by archaeologists through the study of burial or settlement assemblages. He finds no support in the evidence available for the assumption widely spread among Russian and Ukrainian archaeologists and historians that the Antes were Slavs. Instead, Szmoniewski notices a rather complex political and ethnic configuration in the steppe lands north of the Black Sea, where sixth-century written sources located the Antes.

Chronology and long-distance contacts are at the fore of Igor Gavritukhin and Michel Kazanski's chapter on the barbarian groups of northern Caucasus and their relations with Bosporus and the so-called Tetraxite Goths. Their detailed analysis of the metalwork, especially fibulae and belt buckles from the northern Caucasus region, reveals a complicated network of relations between elites of groups at relatively long distance from each other. While assemblages in the region of Krasnodar and the neighbouring Kuban River valley produced evidence of contacts with Bosporus at least since the Hunnic period, the Kislovodsk area, Kabardino-Balkaria, and northern Ossetia seem to have rejected such contacts in favour of stronger ties with Byzantium through Abkhazia and the mountain passes around Elbrus. If there was any Bosporan influence on the central region of the Northern Caucasus, then it was certainly mediated by communities living along the Lower and Middle Kuban River. The archaeological evidence thus suggests that some barbarians in the Caucasus region were 'neglected' primarily because of their political and military alliances.

The Huns tend to drop out of studies of the Migration period after the collapse of the Hunnic polity in the late 450s. Both archaeologists and historians pay more attention to the 'successor' polities of the Ostrogoths or Gepids. Post-Nedao Huns in the Middle Danube region are truly 'neglected barbarians'. Without any direct reference to Nedao, Margit Nagy deals with a mid-fifth-century burial of a young horseman found in Budapest-Zugló. She points out that the fall of the 'Hunnic Empire' was not immediately accompanied by the abandonment of the old traditions linked to the glorious times of Attila. From her detailed analysis of the grave goods from the Zugló burial, Nagy puts forward a powerful argument for the continuity, if only for a short while, of the material culture expressions of social rank, which had been typical for Attila's polity.

Ágnes B. Tóth's chapter likewise offers a less conventional approach, this time to the archaeology of the 'successor' barbarian polities in the Middle Danube region, while examining a female burial assemblage discovered almost thirty years ago in the old town of Budapest (Old Buda). As means of expressing high social status within a small group of barbarians who may have settled on the bank of the river Danube during or after the Hunnic period, the brooch and the buckle found with the female skeleton in Old Buda indicate a richly adorned dress very similar to those of other aristocratic women in communities in eastern Hungary or southern Germany which have adopted both the Hun-age ('mounted nomad') and the 'eastern Germanic' traditions.

Continuity of traditions is also the theme of Radu Harhoiu's chapter on the Bratei III cemetery in Transylvania. For the sequencing of the cemetery, Harhoiu employs a chorological analysis in order to avoid the interpretive pitfalls associated with extensive burial robbing. He distinguishes two separate phases, the earliest of which coincided in time with the female burial in Old Buda examined by Ágnes B. Tóth. By the late sixth century, a large number of inhumations in the Bratei III cemetery display signs of a strong Avar influence from the Middle Danube region, a phenomenon which Harhoiu interprets as a sign of the acculturation of the local Gepids into the early Avar society. That the cemetery continued to be used for another fifty years is an indication of the same 'multicultural society' of the early Avar qaganate which has been brought to light by recent studies of the burial assemblages in western Hungary.[17]

Identifying Gepids in the archaeological record is also the topic of Anna Khara-lambieva's contribution. A few bow fibulae and eagle-headed belt buckles found in Bulgaria show that the fashionable dress of Gepid aristocratic women in the lands along the Tisza River was imitated in the North Balkan provinces of the empire, south of the Danube, where some Gepids may have moved during the sixth century. As Kharalambieva points out, the 'Gepid fashion' remained in use among

---

[17] Tivadar Vida, 'Conflict and Coexistence: The Local Population of the Carpathian Basin under Avar Rule (Sixth to Seventh Century)', in *The Other Europe in the Middle Ages: Avars, Bulgars, Khazars, and Cumans*, ed. by Florin Curta (Leiden, 2008), pp. 13–46; Tivadar Vida, 'Germani e Romani nel regno degli Avari', in *Roma i Barbari: La nascita di un nuovo mondo*, ed. by J.-J. Aillagon (Venice, 2008), pp. 421–23.

members of the barbarian aristocracy in the northern Balkan provinces of the empire longer than any other fashion, a possible indication of group (arguably, ethnic) identity.

No single group (ethnic) identity may be associated with the interpretation, in Jaroslav Jiřík's chapter, of the archaeological record of fifth- and early sixth-century Bohemia. The Vinařice group displays a number of analogies with the 'east Germanic' fashions of the Middle Danube region, which has encouraged speculations about the possible migration into Bohemia of peoples from the Carpathian Basin. However, as Jiřík notes, 'a generation separates the advent of the eastern federates to Pannonia (*c.* 380) and the earliest assemblages in Bohemia that could be attributed to the Vinařice group and dated to the 410s or 420s'. Meanwhile, the native population of Bohemia continued to occupy the old sites, as in Plotiště nad Labem. Without excluding the possibility of an immigration of small groups from the Danube region, Jiřík thus favours a cultural explanation for the emergence of the Vinařice group, one based on the idea that there were groups of different origins in central Bohemia during the fifth century. After all, as he correctly points out, the 'Danube fashion' was a fashion of the multiethnic elite running the Hunnic Empire, and was not associated with any particular ethnic group.

According to Walter Goffart, 'the Herules exist for scholars as a nest of intractable, probably insoluble, but fascinating problems'.[18] Two chapters in this book are dedicated to those problems. Roland Steinacher's is a critique of scholarly attempts to read the history of the Herules as a continuous narrative of how a people wandered from Scandinavia to the Maeotis Lake, and then back home. Steinacher demonstrates that narrative to be a historiographic myth originating in the ethnographic bias of the ancient sources, which is also responsible for the bad press the Herules got during Justinian's reign, despite their extraordinary military service in the Roman army on all fronts. In his chapter, Alexander Sarantis goes against such prejudices in an attempt to highlight the key role the Herules played in the military and political life of the empire during Justinian's reign. Sarantis analyses the circumstances responsible for the ambiguous political, geographical, and cultural situation of the Herules on the northern border of the empire, which further triggered their mutiny and the civil war of the late 540s. While Steinacher insists that the Herules 'were no different from other *gentes*', Sarantis's claim is that 'their fate was determined by imperial policies to a greater extent than any other group's'. Unlike Anna Kharalambieva's Gepids, those Herules who moved south of the Danube were quickly absorbed by the empire as local provincials and thus

---

[18] Goffart, *Barbarian Tides*, p. 205.

disappeared from the radar of the written sources. Sarantis's conclusion is therefore a paradox: 'integrated' barbarians tend to be 'neglected' barbarians. But if truly integrated, were they still barbarians?

The significance of this problem for the understanding of both the later perception of non-Roman inhabitants of the empire and the historiography of barbarian alterity forms the subject of my own essay. An examination of the complex historiographic debate surrounding Fallmerayer's theories reveals that at stake was not so much the understanding of the ways in which barbarian polities (*Sklaviniai*) were gradually incorporated into the empire, but the creation of a barbarian Other, the Slavs, without which there could be no definition of the Hellenic nation. Much like the Antes, the Slavs in Greece are not regarded as a product of the ethnographic imagination, but as perennial barbarians, a 'Slavic problem'. In Ukraine, as well as in Greece, the nationalist discourse obscured the details of a picture which is both more complex and more interesting than the dichotomy between civilization and barbarians.

Very similar obstacles blocked for a long time the reassessment of the traditional views of the northern peoples of late antique Hispania. Santiago Castellanos shows that the stereotype of northerners as rebels had such a great force that it had even been adopted by some of those peoples, which in turn can explain the historiographic distortions of the recent decades. Astures, Cantabri, and Vascones may have been neglected. But as Castellanos notes, they were not barbarians, for the central-northern region of Hispania did not escape the influence of Roman culture, had cities and rural villas, and was fully integrated into the economic and fiscal structure of the province as a whole. 'The northern regions of the peninsula certainly had local peculiarities, but the idea of tribal societies permanently arrayed in battle against a predominantly urban society in the south is nothing more than a historiographic myth.'

A major problem, already raised earlier, and a theme running through many of the chapters in this book, is how some barbarians may be neglected because of being subordinated in one way or another to other barbarians. This problem is raised in his chapter by Fernando López Sánchez, discussing the coinage of the early Suevic kingdom. Although the Suevic polity has always been viewed in relation to the Visigothic kingdom, its coinage has been discussed only in relation to that of the imperial court in Ravenna. In fact, as López Sánchez demonstrates, striking coins in Braga was a matter of Suevic relations with Tolosa, and not with Ravenna. To the extant that Suevic kings struck coins for political and not economic reasons, they were eager to announce their intentions to work for the Visigothic kings, who regarded the rulers of Braga as their proxies in Hispania. The direct line of communication with Ravenna established by King Rechiar and his conversion to Catholicism signalled the first Suevic claims to independence, to which the Visigothic king Theoderic II responded by reversing all of Rechiar's initiatives and eventually replacing him with his son Remismund. López Sánchez thus suggests that the military conflicts between Visigoths and Sueves cannot be regarded as wars between barbarian groups, but as quarrels between 'two partners in a common enterprise'. Similarly, the main reason for the migration of Geiseric's Vandals to Africa, as Guido Berndt shows in his chapter, was their precarious situation in Hispania caused by the intensification of Roman authority in the region, coupled with increasing pressure from the Goths and the growing power of the Sueves. Never an ethnically homogeneous confederacy, a distinct *gens Vandalorum* did not come into being before 429. It is clear from the evidence presented by Berndt that the crossing of the Mediterranean under the leadership of Geiseric and the subsequent conquest of Roman Africa were crucial historical events, which fundamentally changed the composition of the group. In other words, the events of 429 represent the beginning of the Vandal ethnogenesis, a process which continued unabated until the collapse of the kingdom in 533/34.

Conversely, the emergence of the Moorish group known as the Frexes may have been ultimately caused by the late fifth-century crisis in the southern regions of the Vandal kingdom. The transformation of a provincial Roman society described by Philipp von Rummel in his chapter is one of the most interesting and illuminating cases of 'neglected barbarians' on the edges of the Roman Empire discussed in this book, which can be compared with Santiago Castellanos's Astures and Cantabri. While the exact nature of the crisis responsible for the major problems in the region remains a matter of discussion, von Rummel demonstrates that the 'Moors' of Guenfan and Antalas were not different from Roman provincials in terms of material culture, appearance, or warfare.

The many contributors to this volume have adopted a wide variety of approaches, from survey mode to more thematic approaches, either by examining particular aspects or by examining issues from a more comparative, methodological, or theoretical standpoint. As a consequence, this volume is meant to provide a range of perspectives with which to highlight the rich diversity of issues and ideas underlying a complex yet critical subject. In revealing new directions for future research, the book does not aim at reconciling the different interpretations indicated by different categories of evidence. Instead, bringing together a number of specialists in a single volume is a first step towards a new evaluation of some of the more significant ways in which the study of the 'neglected barbarians' could change our understanding of Late Antiquity.

THE BACKCOUNTRY BALTS (*AESTI*) AND THE 'NORTHERN GOLD' IN LATE ANTIQUITY AND THE EARLY MIDDLE AGES

Audronė Bliujienė

Introduction: Amber and the Aestiorum Gentes *During the First Four Centuries AD*[1]

Classical authors had good reasons to introduce the *Aestiorum gentes* to the educated elites of Antiquity. After all, they were the main suppliers of *glesum* (*glaesum*), the so-called northern gold. Tacitus was the first to mention the *Aestiorum gentes* in his *Germania* written *c.* 98. According to him, the Aesti were 'the only ones who ransacked the sea to gather amber, and they called it *glesum*'.[2] Since Tacitus referred to them in the plural (*Aestiorum gentes*), the suppliers of amber may well have been the various communities in the Sambian Peninsula now associated with the Dollkeim-Kovrovo culture. In fact, 'Aesti' is

---

[1] Not all *Aestiorum gentes* had access to the amber-rich coast. The richest in amber was (and still is) the Sambian Peninsula. The local archaeological culture coinciding in time with Tacitus writing his *Germania* is known as the Dollkeim-Kovrovo culture (later replaced by the 'Prussian' culture). Some amounts of drift amber were also available on the eastern coast of the Baltic Sea, in Lithuania and Latvia, where first-century archaeological assemblages are attributed to the Western Lithuanian Stone Circle Grave culture. In Latvia proper, burial assemblages of the *Tarand* Grave culture produced small amounts of amber most likely from the Curonian Peninsula. By contrast, in the north-eastern region of present-day Poland (Mazuria), amber was mined (as opposed to collected) ever since prehistory. Amber may have also been mined within a small region on the Lower Nemunas River known as Lamata.

[2] Tacitus, *Germania*, 45, ed. by R. P. Robinson (Hildesheim, 1991).

now thought to be an umbrella-term for all inhabitants of the eastern and south-eastern Baltic shores, east from the mouth of the Vistula to that of the Narva.[3] The tendency is therefore to see as 'Aesti' not only the local Balts, but also the population linguistically and archaeologically defined as Finno-Ugrian. People of the Wielbark culture from the Vistula estuary region, which many archaeologists identify as 'Goths', were neighbours of the 'Aesti'. The *Aestiorum gentes* were therefore of mixed ethnic origin.[4] Before Tacitus, Pliny the Elder has paid some attention to amber in his *Natural History* written in 77. He knew that an expedition had been sent during the reign of Emperor Nero at some point between 60 and 63 to bring amber to Rome.[5] The expedition was led by a member of the equestrian order and aimed at reaching the Amber Coast on the Baltic Sea shore. In the mid-first century, that area was indeed experiencing something of a demographic boom, with many settlements, which may have been viewed as marketplaces (*commercia et litora*) in terms of size and role. The largest marketplaces were in the Vistula Delta, and they have all produced evidence of the Wielbark culture. In any case, the expedition is said to have encountered the *Aestiorum gentes* on the shores of the 'Suebian Sea' and did not fail to note their penchant for luxurious dress accessories, especially for those made of *glesum*.

Tacitus and other classical authors viewed the right side of the 'Suebian Sea' as part of the Central European *barbaricum*, an issue of much greater significance in political terms than the presence of amber. Tacitus knew that the Aesti 'had no use for it themselves'. Whatever his source of information, Tacitus's remark is confirmed by archaeology, as very little amber has so far been found on first- to second-century sites in Lithuania (Figure 1.1).[6] In the eastern Baltic region, the quantity of amber

---

[3] E. Gudavičius, *Lietuvos istorija: Nuo seniausių laikų iki 1569 metų* (Vilnius, 1999), p. 25; Rasa Banytė-Rowell and Anna Bitner-Wróblewska, 'From Aestii to Eesti: Connections Between the ·Western Lithuanian Group and the Area of Distribution of *Tarand*-graves', in *Interarchaeologia, I – Culture and Material Culture: Papers from the First Seminar of the Baltic Archaeologists (BASE), Held at the University of Tartu, Estonia, October 17th–19th, 2003*, ed. by Valter Lang (Tartu, 2005), pp. 105–20 (pp. 116–17).

[4] Wilhelm Gaerte, 'Das Ostgrenze der gotischen Weichselmündung-Kultur in römischen Kaiserzeit', *Mannus*, 24 (1932), 561–63, map 1; Wojciech Nowakowski, *Das Samland in der römischen Reich und der barbarischen Welt* (Marburg, 1996), p. 62.

[5] Pliny the Elder, *Naturalis Historiae*, 45, ed. by Carl Mayhoff (Leipzig, 1897).

[6] Wojciech Nowakowski, 'Od Galindai do Galinditae: Z badań na pradziejami bałtyjskiego ludu z Pojezierza Mazurskiego', *Barbaricum*, 4 (1995), 5–89 (pp. 81–82); Audronė Bliujienė, 'Lithuanian Amber Artifacts in the Middle of the First Millennium and their Provenance within the Limits of Eastern Baltic Region', in *Baltic Amber: Proceedings of the International Interdisciplinary*

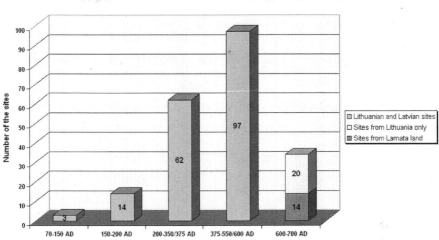

Figure 1.1. The distribution of first- to eighth-century amber artefacts
in Lithuania and southern Latvia.

artefacts in archaeological assemblages began to increase only during the second quarter of the third century.[7] The largest cluster of sites with amber is on the Baltic Sea shore between Liepāja and the mouth of the Nemunas River. A considerable increase in amber finds is visible in central and eastern Lithuania in the late 300s.[8] In Latvia, the largest number of amber artefacts was found on sites in the Liepāja region, especially at Mazkatuži and Kapsēde. Farther to the north along the coast, the quantity of amber finds decreases dramatically, and only twenty amber beads are so far known from third- and fourth-century burials on Saaremaa (Tõnija and Lepna) and northern Estonia (Lehmja-Loo, Kurna, Lagedi, and Proosa).[9]

Conference, Baltic Amber in Natural Sciences, Archaeology and Applied Arts, ed. by A. Butrimas (Vilnius, 2001), pp. 171–86 (p. 173).

[7] Ernst Wahle, 'Die Ausgrabungen in Rutzau und Bauske', in *Piemineklu valdes materialu krājumi: Archaiologias raksti* (Riga, 1928), pp. 10–29; Evdards Šturms, 'Mazkatuži Liepājas aps. Rucavas pag. 1942', unpublished manuscript in the archive of the Latvian Museum of History, Riga, no. 302; P. Stepiņš, 'Izrakiemiem Liepājas raj. Rucavas c. p/s Rucava zemē pie Mazkatuźu mājm', unpublished manuscript in the archive of the Latvian Museum of History, Riga, no. 342.

[8] Audronė Bliujienė, *Lietuvos priešistorės gintaras* (Vilnius, 2007), pp. 283–308.

[9] Personal information, Mirja Ots, Institute of History of Estonia, Tallinn.

Aesti (Hestii) and Amber during Theoderic the Great's Lifetime

Both Aesti (Hestii) and amber resurface in the sixth century, first in Cassiodorus's collection of letters known as *Variae*.[10] Apparently the Aesti were still collecting and trading amber. A little later, Jordanes mentioned them in his *Getica*.[11] Both Cassiodorus and Jordanes place the Aesti on the 'Ocean shore', but Jordanes gives them the Vidivar(r)i as western neighbours living around the mouth of the Vistula. If the two sources are to be trusted at all, then it appears that the territory of the Aesti has remained the same throughout the Migration period.

The letter of Theoderic, the king of the Ostrogoths, has long raised suspicions, and many now see it as fictional. Theoderic assumingly acknowledged a shipment of amber arriving to Ravenna with envoys from the Aesti. He viewed this diplomatic gift as a gesture of goodwill and as an attempt to restore commercial relations. If the letter is something more than a way for Theoderic to brag about contacts with faraway peoples, then it is difficult to understand under precisely what circumstances the diplomatic gift could have been sent to Ravenna. Some have even assumed that the addressees of Theoderic's letter of response were Gothic communities that may have remained behind at the mouth of the Vistula River and engaged in trade with amber.[12] However, such an interpretation takes at face value Jordanes's account of Gothic migration, which has been recently seen more as a literary strategy than as an authentic description of what had actually happened.[13]

Beginning with the late fourth century, the territory of present-day Lithuania and the surrounding regions experienced serious upheaval. The archaeological record clearly indicates dramatic cultural change taking place in the late fifth and early sixth centuries. Too often such changes have been attributed to the Great Migration, including the 'internal migration' of Baltic tribes. Such conclusions now seem too farfetched, even if it is also true that during this period important contacts were established between local communities and those in the Middle Danube region or in southern and central Scandinavia.[14] Besides the traditional

---

[10] Eugenija Ulčinaitė, 'Karaliaus Teodoriko laiškas aisčiams', in *Baltų mitologijos ir religijos šaltiniai*, ed. by Norbertas Vėlius, I (Vilnius, 1996), pp. 155–57.

[11] Eugenija Ulčinaitė, 'Jordanas VI a.', in *Baltų mitologijos*, ed. by Vėlius, pp. 159–61.

[12] Przemysław Urbańczyk, 'The Goths in Poland: Where Did They Come From and When Did They Leave?', *European Journal of Archaeology*, 1 (1998), 397–410.

[13] Walter Goffart, *Barbarian Tides: The Migration Age and the Later Roman Empire* (Philadelphia, 2006), pp. 56–72.

[14] Adolfas Tautavičius, 'Taurapilio "kunigaikščio" kapas', *Lietuvos archeologija*, 3 (1979), 23–32; Valdemaras Šimėnas, *Etnokultūriniai procesai Vakarų Lietuvoje pirmojo mūsų eros tūkstantmečio*

trade route along the Vistula, maritime communications across the Baltic Sea or land routes along the Daugava and Dnieper rivers were activated at that time. Amber artefacts now reached eastern Lithuania on local branches of the eastern route, and new groups of population may have moved into the area from that same direction. The amber found in central and south-eastern Lithuania came from the region of the Mazurian Lakes across Sudovia. Finally new fashions appeared in eastern Lithuania from such distant territories to the south-east as the Chernyakhov culture during the first quarter of the fifth century, when wealthy females were buried with large quantities of silver artefacts and with necklaces of multiple beads of various materials, including numerous amber specimens (Figure 1.2).[15]

Amber in Eastern Baltic Fashions of the Fifth and Sixth Centuries

During the so-called Migration period, amber beads of standard size and shape spread widely within *barbaricum*.[16] In Lithuania, the number of amber artefacts dated to this period increased considerably. Artefacts found in burials point to the widespread use of amber for dress accessories, particularly in the case of necklaces of exclusively amber beads, or of amber beads combined with glass, metal, leather,[17]

---

viduryje (Vilnius, 2006), pp. 44–72; Anna Bitner-Wróblewska, *From Samland to Rogaland: East–West Connections in the Baltic Basin during the Early Migration Period* (Warsaw, 2001); Audronė Bliujienė, 'Lokalių Europos puošybos stilių įtaka I tūkstantmečio vidurio baltų genčių ornamentikai', in *Iš baltų kultūros istorijos, skiriama Adolfo Tautavičiaus 75-mečiui*, ed. by Vytautas Kazakevičius and others (Vilnius, 2000), pp. 99–111 (pp. 101–07).

[15] Elzara Khairedinova, 'Die Tracht der Krimgoten im 6. und 7. Jahrhundert', in *Unbekannte Krim: Archäologische Schätze aus drei Jahrtausende*, ed. by Thomas Werner (Heidelberg, 1999), pp. 84–93; Mark B. Shchukin and Oleg V. Sharov, 'K probleme finala Cherniakhovskoi kul'tury', *Stratum+*, 4 (2000), 369–93 (p. 369); Audronė Bliujienė, 'Watershed between Eastern and Western Lithuania during the Early and Late Migration Period', *Archaeologia Lituana*, 7 (2006), 123–43 (pp. 125–31 with figs 2 and 4).

[16] Anna V. Mastykova, 'Amber Beads with Incised Linear Decoration in the Great Migration Period', in *International Connection of the Barbarians of the Carpathian Basin in the 1st–5th Centuries A.D. Proceedings of the International Conference Held in 1999 in Aszód and Nyíregyháza*, ed. by Eszter Istvánovits and Valéria Kulcsár (Aszód, 2001), pp. 341–58 with figs 1–9; Florin Curta, 'The Amber Trail in Medieval Eastern Europe', in *Paradigms and Methods in Late Ancient and Early Medieval Studies*, ed. by Celia Chazelle and Felice Lifshitz (New York, 2007), pp. 61–79.

[17] A detailed examination by Elona Končienė (Lithuanian National Museum) revealed that five beads from grave 190 of the Plinkaigalis cemetery in central Lithuania were made of tightly twisted leather strips, not of clay, as published by Vytautas Kazakevičius, 'Plinkaigalio kapinynas', *Lietuvos archeologija*, 10 (1993), 1–218 (pp. 98 and 156).

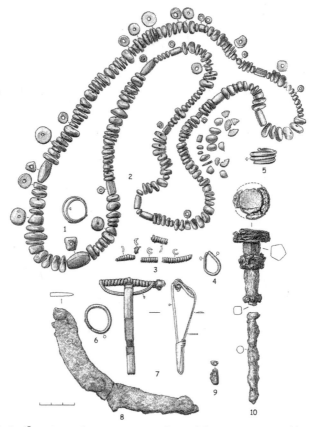

Figure 1.2. Baliulai (Švenčionys district, eastern Lithuania), barrow 12, grave 1 (first quarter of the fifth century). Grave goods found together with the female skeleton: (1, 3–6) bronze; (2) amber, glass, and bronze; (7) silver; (8, 9) iron; (10) iron and pewter. Drawing by Izolda Maciukaitė after Vida Kliaugaitė. Courtesy of the Lithuanian National Museum in Vilnius.

or coral beads, as well as with bronze spirals (Figures 1.2–4). More amber artefacts were found in assemblages of the fifth and early sixth centuries than in any other period before or after that. This was in many respects the golden age of the northern gold (Figure 1.1). By contrast, glass beads, though still in use, were not as fashionable as they had been during the Roman period. All over Lithuania, they were now replaced by beads of amber or of other materials.

Amber finds cluster in four main areas, all linked to the main routes of access to and from the present-day territory of Lithuania (Figure 1.5). The longest and most fashionable necklaces of amber beads were not found on coastal sites but on the Lower Nemunas, as well as in central and eastern Lithuania (Figures 1.2–4). A few amber beads also appear in burial assemblages from the region of the rivers

Figure 1.3. Kalniškiai (Raseiniai district, central Lithuania), grave 250 (fifth century). Grave goods found together with a child skeleton: (1) amber; (2–5) bronze; (6–6a) amber and iron. After Vytautas Kazakevičius. Courtesy of the Vytautas the Great Museum in Kaunas.

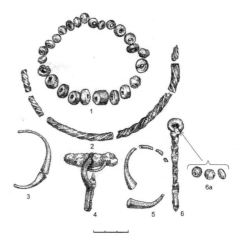

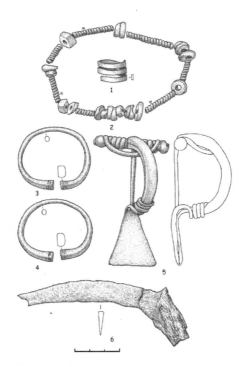

Figure 1.4. Riklikai (Anykščiai district, eastern Lithuania), barrow 12, grave A (first half of the fifth century). Grave goods found together with a female skeleton: (1, 3–5) bronze; (2) amber and bronze; (6) iron. Drawing by Izolda Maciukaitė. Courtesy of the Lithuanian National Museum in Vilnius.

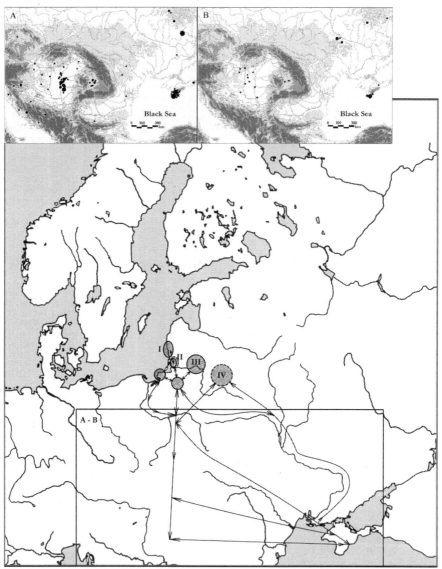

Figure 1.5. Cultural links and trade relations between the eastern Baltic region and Eastern Europe between the fifth and the seventh centuries: areas with amber finds (circle); (I) Lithuanian coast; (II) Lower Nemunas region; (III) central Lithuania; (IV) eastern Lithuania. (A) Distribution of fifth- to sixth-century amber artefacts in Eastern Europe; (B) distribution of seventh-century amber artefacts in Eastern Europe. Schematic map drawn by Audronė Bliujienė referring to Curta, 'Amber Trail'.

Nevėžis-Daugava and Jūra, the so-called Samogitian cemeteries. All of them are of a standard size and shape, namely of the Basonia type, which is the most common on contemporary sites in *barbaricum*.

During the fifth and early sixth centuries, the female fashion in central and eastern Lithuania required several necklaces of amber beads or in which amber beads were in greater numbers than any other kind of beads. Such necklaces appear in burials of both adult females and children, presumably girls (Figures 1.2–3). Amber necklaces with five to twenty beads have also been found in some male burials. However, throughout the fifth and early sixth centuries, males were more often buried with single amber beads. Such beads were commonly attached to the sword or dagger hilt.

Barrow cemeteries in eastern Lithuania also produced a large quantity of amber beads, often in necklaces of between 44 and over 230 specimens, sometimes in combination with glass and enamelled beads (Figure 1.2).[18] Such an impressive display of beads was part of a conspicuous pectoral ornament, which is consistently associated with burials of elite females in Central Europe.

The Sambian Peninsula produced so far the greatest quantity of amber finds in the entire region.[19] In addition, in that same region archaeological excavations also unearthed workshops for the manufacturing of amber beads. During the late fourth and early fifth centuries, Sambian workshops produced both delicately lathed beads (the so-called *paukenförmige*) and handmade beads of irregular shape, in addition to partially lathed, barrel-shaped beads. Such beads appear in great quantities with contemporary cremations in the region.[20]

Most finds of amber dated to *c.* 500 come from coastal sites.[21] Such burial sites in coastal areas as Užpelkiai, Lazdininkai-Kalnalaukis, and Rūdaičiai I stand out by virtue of the large number of small, simple, spherical, barrel-shaped, or conical

---

[18] Bliujienė, *Lietuvos priešistorės gintaras*, pp. 344–46 with figs 199–200.

[19] Vladimir I. Kulakov, *Prussy V–XIII vv.* (Moscow, 1994), p. 113 and fig. 4; Evgenii A. Tiurin, 'Pogrebeniia V veka n. e. s koniami mogil'nike Gora Velikanov (Hünenberg)', *Rossiiskaia arkheologiia*, 2006.1, 142–50.

[20] Nowakowski, *Das Samland*, pl. 26; Vladimir I. Kulakov, 'Istoki kul'tury prussov', in *Vakarų baltai: etnogenezė ir etninė istorija*, ed. by Irena Balčiūnenė and others (Vilnius, 1997), pp. 113–14 with fig. 2.

[21] Raimundas V. Sidrys, 'Vakarų baltų gintaro įkapės geležies amžiuje', in *Acta Historica Universitatis Klaipedensis II. Klaipėdos miesto ir regiono archeologijos ir istorijos problemos*, ed. by Alvydas Nikžentaitis and Vladas Žulkus, II (Klaipėda, 1994), pp. 59–106 (pp. 75–78); Bliujienė, *Lietuvos priešistorės gintaras*, fig. 195.

beads of amber. Drift amber collected on the coast was most likely the object of trade with the neighbouring regions in the interior (Figure 1.1). Drift amber from the Lithuanian and Latvian coast was used primarily for locally made, small beads of conical or spherical shape. Handmade or half-lathed, barrel-shaped beads (Mączyńska's classes 395a–b, 396, 433, and 434) were the commonest of all amber finds from burial assemblages dated to the Migration period.[22] Delicately lathed, step-cut amber beads (Mączyńska's classes 449 and 450a–b) were also found on sites of the West Lithuanian coastal cemeteries. In these cemeteries, short necklaces with amber beads appear mostly in female burials, which are otherwise gender-marked by a standard set of artefacts: miniature cups, sandstone spindle-whorls, and one or two crook-like iron pins for the attachment of the bead necklace. Necklace rings or fibulae were occasionally found in such burials.[23]

By contrast, the new forms of lathed or half-lathed beads, which appear before AD 500 have been found only on sites on the Lower Nemunas and in Central Lithuania. But such beads were in fact produced in workshops located in Kujavia and in south-eastern Poland.[24] The amber workshops in Świlcza (south-eastern Poland) and Konary (Kujavia) were still active in the mid-fifth century.[25] Both produced half-lathed and lathed beads of the same shape and size as those found on burial sites in central Lithuania and in the Lower Nemunas region. Such beads disappear from Lithuanian assemblages during the first half of or in the mid-sixth century.

Necklaces strung of Basonia-type beads (Mączyńska's classes 430, 437, 438, 440–43, and 451) with or without incised linear decoration were also common on burial sites in central Lithuania and the Lower Nemunas region.[26] Beads of

---

[22] Magdalena Tempelmann-Mączyńska, *Die Perlen der römischen Kaiserzeit und der frühen Phase der Völkerwanderungszeit im mitteleuropäischen Barbaricum* (Mainz, 1985), pp. 68 and 75, with pls 15, 16, 61, 67.

[23] Bliujienė, *Lietuvos priešistorės gintaras*, figs 202–03.

[24] Przemysław Wielowiejski, 'Pracownie obróbki bursztynu z okręgu wpływów rzymskich na obszarze kultury przeworskiej', *Kwartalnik historii kultury materialnej*, 39 (1991), 330–60; Przemysław Wielowiejski, 'Bernstein in der Przeworsk-Kultur', *Bericht der Römisch-Germanischen Kommission*, 77 (1996), 238–343.

[25] Aleksandra Gruszczyńska, 'Amber-workers of the Fourth and Fifth Centuries AD from Świlcza near Rzeszów', in *Investigations into Amber: Proceedings of the International Interdisciplinary Symposium 'Baltic Amber and Other Fossil Resins 997 Urbs Gyddanycz-1997 Gdańsk', 2–6 September 1997, Gdańsk*, ed. by Barbara Kosmowska-Ceranowicz and Henryk Paner (Gdańsk, 1999), pp. 185–90 with figs 3–5.

[26] Šimėnas, *Etnokultūriniai procesai*, figs 35–37 and 39; Bliujienė, *Lietuvos priešistorės gintaras*, pp. 349–54 and fig. 207.

Mączyńska's classes 440, 441, and 443 may have originated in the western Baltic region, where they may have been manufactured of local amber in fourth- and early fifth-century workshops.[27] Whether lathed or half-lathed, Basonia-type beads from Lithuania were produced in more than one workshop. The territory of present-day Lithuania is in fact the northernmost area of widespread distribution for the Basonia-type beads with or without incised linear decoration. Specimens with incised linear decoration dated between 430 and 480/90 have been found in numerous assemblages from Central and East Central Europe.[28] Most typical for barrows in eastern Lithuania, such as excavated at Baliuliai, Pavajuonis-Rėkučiai, Liūlinė, and Žvirbliai, are amber beads of irregular shape (Figures 1.2 and 1.4). Either singly or in necklaces of multiple specimens, such beads appear mostly in assemblages dated to the early 400s.

Much like elsewhere in contemporary *barbaricum*, in the Baltic lands amber beads worn in necklaces were part of the fashionable dress of elite females and as such may have served to mark social status. Single beads found in male burials may have had a similar function. In any case, Lithuania was on the northern periphery of that area of *barbaricum* in which amber beads were fashionable during the Migration period.

Amber in Eastern Baltic Fashions of the Late Sixth and Seventh Centuries

At some point after AD 550, amber bead sets disappear from burial assemblages in the eastern Baltic region (Figure 1.1). After *c*. 600 only single amber beads appear in burial assemblages. Between the seventh and the ninth centuries, only a few communities continued to use such dress accessories as necklaces of glass beads, bronze spirals, and occasional amber beads. Prior to the Viking Age, only a handful of communities in the area continued the late antique tradition of attaching single amber beads to fibulae (in the case of the male dress) or to pins (in the case of the female dress).[29] A very different image emerges from the examination of

---

[27] Przemysław Wielowiejski, 'Skarb bursztynu z pożniego okręsu rzymskiego odkryty w miejscowości Basonia, woj. Lubelskie', *Prace museum ziemi*, 41 (1990), 109–17 with fig. 3 and pls 1–2; Raimundas V. Sidrys, 'Gintaro įkapės senojo ir viduriniojo geležies amžiaus kapuose', in *Vidurio Lietuvos archeologija: Konferencijos medžiaga, 1994 m.*, ed. by Audrius Astrauskas (Vilnius, 1994), pp. 36–41 with figs 10–11.

[28] Mastykova, 'Amber Beads', pp. 341–60.

[29] Bliujienė, *Lietuvos priešistorės gintaras*, Appendix 14.2–14.5.

assemblages from the Sambian Peninsula that could be dated to or after the sixth century. Even though cremation was the main burial rite in the region throughout the early Middle Ages, grave goods, including amber beads, present no traces of fire and may have been detached from the body before cremation and then deposed in the grave pit together with the ashes. Amber beads may have also been deposed as additional offerings within the grave pit. This may indeed explain the survival of so many amber beads recuperated from assemblages in the Sambian Peninsula.

Amber also appears in some quantity in assemblages of the so-called Olsztyn group in Mazuria (north-eastern Poland), which have been dated to the sixth and seventh centuries.[30] Only a few amber beads are known from burial assemblages of the Olsztyn group, notwithstanding the fact that the wealth of those communities was based on the control of the amber trade and possibly also on the mining of the northern gold.[31] Much more popular were glass beads, of which there are substantially more specimens than of amber beads.[32] The archaeological record of the Mazurian Lake region shows multiple and diverse relations with distant communities in western, central, and south-eastern Europe.[33] The Olsztyn group certainly had relations with communities in Lamata, on the Lower Nemunas River (Figure 1.5), which may have involved trade with raw amber. However, amber beads typical for Lamata (Figure 1.6) have not so far been found on sites of the Olsztyn group in Mazuria. Some of the artefacts of foreign origin found in Lamata may have nonetheless been obtained through the intermediary of that group (Figure 1.7).

Lamata, a small region of just under 900 square miles in western Lithuania between the present-day towns of Šilutė, Priekulė, and Švėkšna, is the only part of the eastern Baltic area in which the quantity of amber finds did not diminish during the early Middle Ages (Figures 1.1 and 1.6).[34] Large numbers of lathed and half-lathed amber beads were produced in this region between the late sixth and the ninth centuries. Over one thousand specimens have been so far recorded in several museums in Lithuania as found on fourteen different sites. By contrast, the

---

[30] Jacek Kowalski, 'Chronologia grupy elbląskiej i olsztyńskiej kręgu zachodniobałtyskiego (V–VII w.): Zarys problematyki', *Barbaricum*, 6 (2000), 203–36 (pp. 230–36).

[31] The cemeteries that produced evidence of amber beads are Miętkie, Kosewo, Leleszki, and Tumiany. See Vladimir I. Kulakov, 'Mogil'niki zapadnoi chasti Mazurskogo poozer'ia kontsa V–nachala VIII vv. (po materialam raskopok 1878–1939 gg.)', *Barbaricum*, 1 (1989), 148–275 (pp. 174–75). See also Wojciech Nowakowski's contribution to this volume.

[32] Kulakov, 'Mogil'niki', figs 12.1 and 2, 22.3, 24.3, 25.5, 29, 39.4, 41.1, 46.1, 52, and 55.

[33] Kulakov, 'Mogil'niki', pp. 167–70; figs 12.2 and 12.3, 20.3, 26.6.

[34] Vladas Žulkus, *Kuršiai Baltijos jūros erdvėje* (Vilnius, 2004), p. 45.

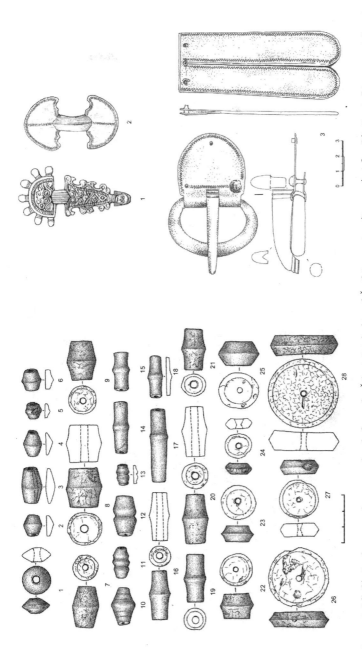

Figure 1.6 (left). Sixth- to ninth-century beads from the Šilutė-Priekulė and Švėkšna region (Lamata). After Bliujienė, *Lietuvos priešistorės gintaras*, p. 377 fig. 229.

Figure 1.7 (right). Sixth- to seventh-century 'exotic' artefacts in Lamata: (1) 'Slavic' bow fibula from Linkuhnen; (2) equal-armed fibula from Jurgaičiai; (3) silver belt buckle and strap end from Švėkšna. After Voigtmann, 'Zwei ostpreussische Fibeln'; Tautavičius, 'Prekybiniai-kultūriniai ryšiai'; and courtesy of the Lithuanian National Museum in Vilnius.

amount of amber found on nineteen contemporary cemeteries excavated in other parts of Lithuania is remarkably small (Figure 1.1).[35] Most if not all beads from Lamata have been found during field surveys or are stray finds, possibly from destroyed burial assemblages.[36] Judging from their peculiar shape, early medieval amber beads from Lamata may be divided into six groups (Figure 1.6).[37] In addition to hair pins or amber beads directly sewn onto a headdress, female fashions in early medieval Lamata required very long necklaces of amber beads attached to typical crossbow fibulae with slightly widened foot.[38]

Lamata was strategically positioned at a major crossroads linking the Sambian Peninsula to the Mazurian Lake region, central Lithuania, and the Baltic Sea coast. The region seems to have experienced considerable prosperity during the Baltic 'Dark Ages' (sixth to seventh centuries), at a time of much social and economic stress in Lithuania. The source of that prosperity was certainly amber, either manufactured or in raw form. That amber continued to be mined results from the sharp contrast between the quantity of amber finds in Lamata and their almost complete absence from the neighbouring regions. Amber may also explain the significant number of artefacts pointing to long-distance contacts between Lamata, the Middle Danube region, Merovingian Francia, the northern shores of the Black Sea, and the Balkans. For example, a gilded silver belt set with animal-shaped terminals was found in Vilkyčiai together with artefacts dated to the sixth century. The belt set has good analogies in fifth- and sixth-century assemblages in the Middle Danube region, which have been attributed to either Ostrogoths or Gepids.[39] Similarly, a silver belt buckle with a double strap end from Švėkšna (Figure 1.7.3) has good

---

[35] Bliujienė, *Lietuvos priešistorės gintaras*, Appendix 14.2–14.5.

[36] Many sites in Lamata, the southern part of what was once called the Memel Land, were excavated in the late nineteenth century by German scholars. The archaeological material from those excavations was taken to the Prussia Museum in Königsberg, the building of which was badly destroyed during World War II. As a consequence, many artefacts and excavation reports have been lost. See Christine Reich, 'Archäologie einer vorgeschichtlichen Sammlung: Die Bestände des ehemaligen Prussia-Museum im Berliner Museum für Vor- und Frühgeschichte', *Archäologisches Nachrichtenblatt*, 8 (2003), 14–23.

[37] Bliujienė, *Lietuvos priešistorės gintaras*, pp. 376–78, 381 and figs 223 and 229–34.

[38] Audronė Bliujienė, 'A Microregion between Šilutė-Priekulė and Švėkšna in Western Lithuania or Alternatively Lamata According to Archaeological Data', *Archaeologia Lituana*, 4 (2003), 122–37 (pp. 125–27 with figs 6.5 and 8).

[39] Nils Åberg, *Ostpreussen in der Völkerwanderungszeit* (Uppsala, 1919), p. 108; Bliujienė, 'A Microregion', fig. 2.

analogies in fifth- and sixth-century assemblages in Central Europe and in the Balkans.[40] Two 'Slavic' bow fibulae of Werner's class I B were found before World War II at Linkuhnen (now Rzhevskoe near Sovetsk, in the Kaliningrad region of Russia) and Schreitlauken (now Šereitlaukis in the Šilutė district of Lithuania) (Figure 1.7.1).[41] Such fibulae have a widespread distribution across Eastern Europe, from Lithuania to Greece. The closest parallel to the decoration of the Linkuhnen fibulae is a fibula from Veţel near Deva (Romania).[42] Even though there are no direct links between fibulae found in Greece, Bulgaria, Hungary, Transylvania, and Lithuania, the dissemination of such fashionable dress accessories suggests contacts between communities located at a great distance from each other. Brooches may have been transported together with their owners from one community to the other, but it is equally possible that craftsmen carrying manufactured brooches or models moved between such communities. Those splendid artefacts were certainly luxurious items most appropriate for gift exchange.[43] Finally, 'Slavic' bow fibulae may have been passed through a number of middlemen as items of long-distance trade.

Several tinned bronze equal-armed fibulae with semicircular plates have been collected during field surveys in Jurgaičiai and Miesteliai, both in Lamata (Figure 1.7.2).[44] Such fibulae are known from sites in the Sambian Peninsula.[45] But almost identical fibulae have also been found in seventh-century burial assemblages in

---

[40] Renata Madyda-Legutko, 'Zu den Beziehungen der litauischen Gebiete zu dem mitteleuropäischen Barbaricum in der frühen Völkerwanderungszeit', *Archaeologia Lituana*, 7 (2006), 145–54 with fig. 2.

[41] Kurt Voigtmann, 'Zwei ostpreussische Fibeln mit menschlicher Maske als Fusskopf', *Alt-Preußen*, 3 (1939), 114–15 with figs 2–3; Joachim Werner, 'Slawische Bügelfibeln des 7. Jahrhunderts', in *Reinecke Festschrift zum 75. Geburtstag von Paul Reinecke am 25. September 1947*, ed. by G. Behrens and Joachim Werner (Mainz, 1950), pp. 150–72. For the chronology of Werner's I B class of 'Slavic' bow fibulae, see now Florin Curta, 'Female Dress and "Slavic" Bow Fibulae in Greece', *Hesperia*, 74 (2005), 101–46 (pp. 107–17 with figs 7.10 and 9.16).

[42] See Florin Curta, 'On the Dating of the "Veţel-Coşoveni" Group of Curved Fibulae', *Ephemeris Napocensis*, 4 (1994), 233–65.

[43] Curta, 'Female Dress', pp. 124–25.

[44] Adolfas Tautavičius, 'Prekybiniai-kultūriniai ryšiai V–VIII amžiais', in *Lietuvos gyventojų prekybiniai ryšiai Lietuvoje II–XII a.*, ed. by Mykolas Michelbertas (Vilnius, 1972), pp. 126–52 (p. 149 with fig. 18); Linas Tamulynas, 'Miestelių kapinyno spėjamosios vietos (Miestelių k. Saugų sen., Šilutės raj.) archeologinių žvalgomųjų tyrinėjimų ataskaita 2001', unpublished archaeological report in the archive of the Institute of Lithuanian History, Vilnius, no. 3789.

[45] Kulakov, *Prussy*, p. 50 with fig. 24; Kulakov, 'Istoki kul'tury prussov', fig. 3a, g.

western France.[46] Similarly, long bronze pins with diamond-shaped heads or heads in the form of knitting needles have good analogies in Merovingian assemblages of the so-called *Reihengräberkreis*.[47]

That amber may have been the reason behind all those long-distance contacts that communities in Lamata established in the early Middle Ages results from the distribution of amber in contemporary Europe. Amber beads are particularly abundant in sixth- and seventh-century assemblages in Hungary and Crimea.[48] In both regions, amber beads were found in particularly rich burials together with luxurious silver dress accessories or artefacts of foreign origin. Florin Curta has noted that 'contacts between elites of those two regions at a great distance from each other have been documented, and newly published materials indicated that throughout the sixth century each area maintained relations with the northerly regions near the source of amber'.[49] Some of the amber sent to the Middle Danube region or to Crimea may have passed through communities of the Olsztyn group in the Mazurian Lake region. If so, then it is remarkable that only a few amber beads were retained for local use.

Conclusion

Throughout the early Middle Ages, Lithuania was the northern part of *barbaricum* from which amber came to various parts of Europe in great quantity. The number of artefacts found in the eastern Baltic region in burial assemblages of the Migration period is a direct consequence of the adoption of a fashionable female dress with long necklaces of exclusively amber beads or of beads of amber combined with beads of glass or metal, as well as with bronze spirals. During the fifth and early sixth centuries, the eastern Baltic area witnessed an unprecedented popularity of amber, now found in larger quantity than in any period before or after that. Amber beads were in fashion everywhere in Lithuania, where they replaced beads of glass and other materials. Amber finds cluster in four areas indicating different routes of access to amber sources. The longest and most fashionable necklaces have been

[46] Mechthild Schulze-Dörrlamm, 'Gleicharmige Bügelfibeln der Zeit um 600 aus dem Byzantinischen Reich', *Archäologisches Korrespondenzblatt*, 33 (2003), 437–44 with fig. 1.2–3.

[47] H. Neumayer, 'Schmucknadeln', in *Merowingerzeit: Die Altertümer im Museum für Vor- und Frühgeschichte*, ed. by Marion Bertram and Klaus Göken (Mainz, 1995), pp. 78–79 with pl. 59.

[48] Curta, 'Amber Trail', pp. 62 map 4.1 and 70 map 4.2.

[49] Curta, 'Amber Trail', p. 67.

found not on the coast, but inland, in the Lower Nemunas region, as well as in central and eastern Lithuania. In all those areas, amber artefacts did not originate from Lithuanian coastal sites.

After *c*. 550, amber bead sets disappeared from most sites in the eastern Baltic region. Only single amber beads appear occasionally in burial assemblages dated between the late sixth and the ninth centuries. In sharp contrast to this picture of diminishing access to or use of amber, early medieval assemblages in Lamata, a small region on the Lower Nemunas, abound in amber beads. From the sixth to the eighth centuries, prosperous communities in Lamata maintained relations with distant lands in western, central, and south-eastern Europe. It may well be that at the source of that prosperity was the northern gold.

THE MYSTERIOUS BARBARIANS OF MAZURIA: THE RIDDLE OF THE OLSZTYN GROUP

Wojciech Nowakowski

Located in the north-eastern part of modern Poland, Mazuria has a turbulent and complex history. After World War II the north-eastern region of the former Polish state was annexed by the Soviet Union, and Poles from that area flocked to Mazuria. They occupied the land, which was largely deserted by its former inhabitants, who until 1945 had lived within the borders of the East Prussian province of Germany, a region long associated in their own country with the rise of both the Second and the Third Reichs. During the sixteenth and seventeenth centuries, Mazuria was a protestant duchy held as a fief from the Catholic Kingdom of Poland. Its rulers, all members of the Hohenzollern dynasty, brought in from the neighbouring Mazovia a great number of Polish peasants called *Mazurs* in order to settle the much depopulated region in the south, the so-called Polish departments of Ducal Prussia (in German, *die polnischen Ämter*). The Mazurs gave the area its name, Mazuria (in German *Masuren*). As a matter of fact, the lay dukes of Prussia were acting much in the same spirit as the Grand Masters of the Teutonic Order who, back in the fourteenth century, had populated the Galindian Forest (the *Galindische Heide*) with Mazovian peasants, after the region was depleted of its native Prussians named Galindians, largely as a consequence of the Polish, Yatvingian, and Russian raids of the 1100s.

With so many migrations shaping the history of the region, there is no surprise that archaeological finds from Mazuria dated to the sixth and seventh centuries (the so-called Late Migration period) have been quickly interpreted as evidence of

This paper was prepared for a research project of the Ministry of Science of the Polish Republic, no. N109 016 31/0933. It was translated into English by Beata Furga.

some (other) alien group arriving in the area. Such an interpretation was primarily based on the presence within assemblages excavated in Mazuria of artefacts with no analogies in the local traditions of the preceding Roman period, which were more likely the result of the interregional communication between the 'Germanic' elites of the Late Migration period. However, 'exotic' artefacts such as those were sometimes associated within one and the same site with items of local clothing or with pottery of Baltic tradition. This gave the strong impression of a blending of local traditions with foreign 'Germanic' influences. As a consequence, in the early twentieth century, the sixth- to seventh-century assemblages from Mazuria were lumped together under the name '*masurgermanische Kultur*'.[1] After World War II, Polish archaeologists adopted a much more neutral label and began referring to such assemblages as the 'Olsztyn group' (Figure 2.1).[2]

The Origins of the Olsztyn Group

During the first centuries AD, Mazuria thrived and was densely populated, as indicated by numerous cemeteries located within close distance from each other. The climax seems to have been reached between the late first and the mid-third century.[3] The affluence of the time had its roots in the trade with amber, which ensured a continuous supply of Roman goods. The Roman interest in the region may explain the fact that Ptolemy knew about the name of the inhabitants of Mazuria at that time, the Galindians (*Galindai*).[4]

---

[1] See Nils Åberg, *Ostpreußen in der Völkerwanderungszeit* (Uppsala, 1919) pp. 70–71; Carl Engel, *Aus ostpreußischer Vorzeit* (Königsberg, 1935), pp. 98–99 with fig. 54; Ernst Petersen, *Der ostelbische Raum als germanisches Kraftfeld im Lichte der Bodenfunde des 6.–8. Jahrhunderts* (Leipzig, 1939), pp. 206–14; Eduard Šturms, 'Zur ethnischen Deutung der masurgermanischen Kultur', *Archaeologia Geographica*, 1 (1950), 20–22.

[2] Jerzy Okulicz, *Pradzieje ziem pruskich od późnego paleolitu do VII w. n. e.* (Wrocław, 1973), pp. 476–91.

[3] Archaeological finds from Mazuria dated to the first centuries AD (the Roman period) are attributed to the Bogaczewo culture. See Wojciech Nowakowski, *Die Funde der römischen Kaiserzeit und der Völkerwanderungszeit aus Masuren* (Berlin, 1998), pp. 14–16; see also the papers in *Kultura bogaczewska w 20 lat później*, ed. by Anna Bitner-Wróblewska (Warsaw, 2007).

[4] For the location of Ptolemy's Galindians in Mazuria and for the possibility of identifying them as the people of the Bogaczewo culture, see Nowakowski, *Funde*, pp. 16–18; Wojciech Nowakowski, 'Galinder', in *Reallexikon der germanischen Altertumskunde*, X, ed. by Heinrich Beck, Dieter Geunich, Heiko Steuer, and Dieter Timpe (Berlin, 1996), pp. 329–30.

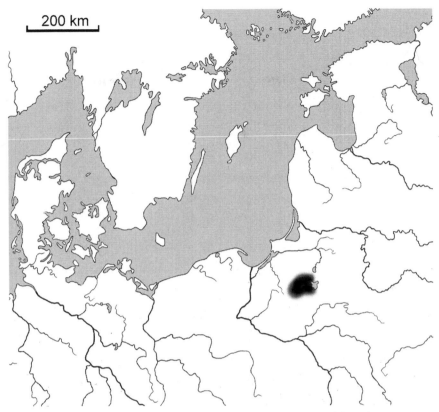

Figure 2.1. The Olsztyn group in the south-eastern region of the Baltic Sea.
Map drawn by the author.

There are definitely fewer archaeological finds in Mazuria dating back to the early fourth century, and their number is even smaller for the subsequent period between *c.* 350/75 and *c.* 450/75. Most importantly, none of the cemeteries in use during the previous period continued into the late fourth and early fifth centuries, and very few cemeteries were opened during that period. The conclusion seems inescapable: Mazuria experienced a dramatic decline in population. To be sure, such a conclusion needs qualification, given the poor state of research for the period under discussion. Much of what we know about late fourth- and fifth-century Mazuria comes from nineteenth-century excavations, which did not show any awareness of finds within the ploughed soil, or of shallow pit cremations, which seem to have been quite frequent at that time.[5] Nonetheless, it is significant that even recent finds lack the spectacular character of contemporary assemblages in other parts of the East Baltic region. Thus the scarcity of finds from Mazurian sites may not be just the result of the state of research, but also a consequence of the ongoing crisis at the time. Similar circumstances may now be observed to the west and to the south from Mazuria, in Warmia, Pomerania, and Mazovia. During the fourth century the settlements which had existed there since the Late Roman period, and which have been attributed either to the Goths or to the Gepids, became extinct, as in Warmia, or thinned out, as in Mazovia and a good portion of Pomerania, a phenomenon often interpreted as indicating a large-scale migration of the local population to the south and to the east.[6] A similar decrease in population is likely to have taken place in Mazuria as well, which may be observed in the archaeological record as a remarkable scarcity of grave goods. This in turn may be interpreted as an understandable unwillingness to discard by means of funerary deposition objects otherwise viewed as valuable, which were perceived as needed more by the living than by the dead. Most likely the cultural model of that time was viewed as inadequate. This led to the emergence of a new cultural form, the Olsztyn group.

The most conspicuous change taking place at the onset of the new structures was a return to lavish grave furnishings. The change must have been introduced gradually, for the earliest finds of the Olsztyn group are relatively rare. Prominent among them are three-knobbed bow fibulae dated to the late fifth or early sixth century, which were often the only goods deposited together with the cremated remains of the dead.[7] The only truly rich assemblage known for this period, namely

---

[5] In this respect, see Anna Bitner-Wróblewska's remarks on the quantitative and qualitative changes taking place as a result of the application of modern research techniques for the study of the Mazurian Lake district during the fourth and the fifth centuries: Anna Bitner-Wróblewska, 'Early Migration Period in the Mazurian Lakeland: Phantom or Reality?', in *Probleme der spätrömischen Kaiserzeit und der Völkerwanderungszeit im mitteleuropäischen Barbaricum*, ed. by Magdalena Mączyńska and Tadeusz Grabarczyk (Łódź, 2000), pp. 153–67.

[6] See Kazimierz Godłowski, *Frühe Slawen in Mitteleuropa* (Neumünster, 2005), fig. 18.

[7] Jerzy Okulicz, 'Problem ceramiki typu praskiego w grupie olsztyńskiej kultury zachodniobałtyjskiej (VI–VII w. n.e.)', *Pomerania antiqua*, 13 (1988), 103–33 (pp. 107–08); Jacek Kowalski, 'Z badań nad chronologią okresu wędrówek ludów na ziemiach zachodniobałtyjskich (faza E)', in *Archeologia bałtyjska*, ed. by Jerzy Okulicz (Olsztyn, 1991), pp. 67–85; Jacek Kowalski, 'Chronologia grupy elbląskiej i olsztyńskiej kręgu zachodniobałtyjskiego (V–VII w.): Zarys problematyki', *Barbaricum*, 6 (2000), 203–66; Wojciech Nowakowski, 'Ostpreußen als Brücke zwischen Ost- und

grave 14 of the Kosewo cemetery, produced an antler comb with a bell-like handle (Figure 2.2.1), two bronze spurs (Figure 2.2.3–4), and lancet-shaped strap-ends, along with two rectangular belt mounts decorated in the same style (Figure 2.2.5–8).[8] However, the most spectacular find from that assemblage is a Snartemo-type glass beaker of Frankish origin and make (Figure 2.2.9), which could be dated to the third quarter of the fifth century.[9]

It appears that the Olsztyn group had not fully developed before the end of the first quarter of the sixth century. Not until then did numerous cremation graves dated to the Late Migration period begin to appear within cemetery sites known for the Late Roman period, on which such graves either occupied a separate part within the cemetery or were planted in shallower pits above assemblages of the Late Roman period. The new burial assemblages produced typical combinations of bow fibulae of non-local origin, some with five knobs (Figure 2.3.1), others with rectangular head-plates, as well as crossbow fibulae of local tradition, especially later variants with wide silver-panelled bows (Figure 2.4.1).[10] Such dress accessories are often accompanied by belt sets with cross-on-tongue buckles (Figures 2.4.3 and 2.5.9), lancet-shaped strap-ends (Figures 2.3.4–5, 2.4.4, and 2.5.11–12), and belt mounts with open-work ornament (Figures 2.3.4–5 and 2.4.2). Male burials had no weapons but produced instead horse gear: spurs with plates for rivetting onto

Westeuropa: Funde des 5. bis 8. Jahrhunderts', in *Merowingerzeit: Europa ohne Grenzen. Archäologie und Geschichte des 5. bis 8. Jahrhunderts*, ed. by Wilfried Menghin (Berlin, 2007), pp. 145–55. See also Herbert Kühn, 'Das Problem der masurgermanischen Fibeln in Ostpreußen', in *Documenta archaeologica Wolfgang La Baume dedicata*, ed. by Otto Kleemann (Bonn, 1956), pp. 79–108; Herbert Kühn, *Die germanischen Bügelfibeln der Völkerwanderungszeit in Mitteldeutschland* (Graz, 1981).

[8] The width of the metal fittings suggests that the leather straps tying the spurs to the feet were rather narrow. See Max Weigel, 'Das Gräberfeld von Kossewen, Kreis Sensburg, Ostpreußen', *Nachrichten über deutsche Altertumsfunde*, 2 (1891), 24–25 with fig. 14; Nowakowski, *Die Funde*, p. 112 with pl. 9.139–48.

[9] Vera I. Evison, 'Glass Cone Beakers of the Kempston Type', *Journal of Glass Studies*, 14 (1972), 48–66; John Hunter and David Sanderson, 'The Snartemo/Kempston Problem', *Fornvännen*, 77 (1982), 22–28. For the date of the Kosewo 14 assemblage, see also Sigrid Thomas, 'Studien zu den germanischen Kämmen der römischen Kaiserzeit', *Arbeits- und Forschungsberichte zur Sächsischen Bodendenkmalpflege*, 8 (1960), 54–215 (p. 199); Kazimierz Godłowski, *The Chronology of the Late Roman and Early Migration Periods in Central Europe* (Cracow, 1970), p. 55.

[10] Šturms, 'Zur ethnischen Deutung', fig. 1.

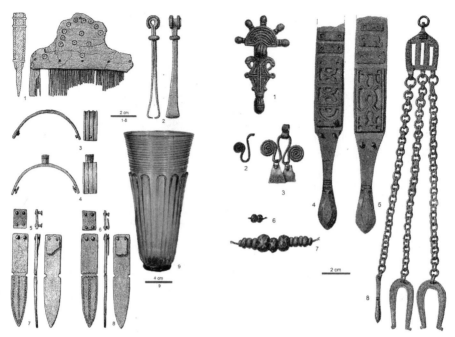

Figure 2.2 (left). Grave goods found with cremation 14 in Kosewo (district of Mrągowo, Poland):
(1) comb; (2) tweezers; (3, 4) spurs; (5, 6) belt mounts; (7, 8) strap ends; and (9) glass beaker. After
Nowakowski, *Die Funde*.

Figure 2.3 (right). Grave goods found with cremation 30 in Tumiany (district of Olsztyn, Poland):
(1) bow fibula; (2, 3) copper-alloy pendants; (4, 5) belt mounts and strap ends; (6, 7) glass beads;
and (8) pectoral ornament with chains and horseshoe-shaped pendants. After Heydeck, 'Das
Gräberfeld von Daumen'.

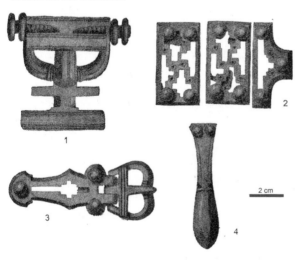

Figure 2.4. Grave goods found
with cremation 87 in Tumiany
(district of Olsztyn, Poland):
(1) crossbow brooch; (2) belt
mounts; (3) belt buckle; and
(4) strap end. After Heydeck,
'Das Gräberfeld von Daumen'.

the boots (Figure 2.5.8) and bridle bits.[11] Occasionally, the cremated remains of the horseman were buried on top of the non-cremated skeleton of his horse.[12] The burial assemblages of the Olsztyn group graves also produced urns in the form of pots with rectangular holes ('windows') beneath the rim (so-called *Fensterurnen*),[13] as well as hollow-stemmed cups with stamped decoration.[14]

Despite its clearly unique features, the exact boundaries of the territorial expansion of the Olsztyn group cannot so far be delineated with any precision. While it is clear that the centre was situated in the Olsztyn and Mrągowo Lake districts,[15] it appears that vast, deserted tracts of land surrounded this group of population to the south and to the west. Moreover, the eastern frontier remains elusive, given that such typical features as *Fensterurnen* or bow

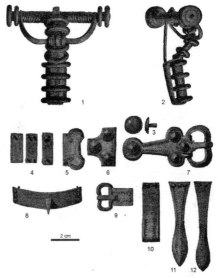

Figure 2.5. Grave goods found with cremation 141 in Tumiany (district of Olsztyn, Poland): (1, 2) crossbow brooches; (3–6 and 10) belt mounts; (7, 9) belt buckles; (8) spur; and (11, 12) strap ends. After Heydeck, 'Das Gräberfeld von Daumen'.

[11] See Johann Heydeck, 'Das Gräberfeld von Daumen und ein Rückblick auf den Anfang einer deutsch-nationalen Kunst', *Sitzungsberichte der Altertumsgesellschaft Prussia*, 19 (1893–95), 41–80; Emil Hollack, 'Das Gräberfeld bei Kellaren im Kreis Allenstein (I.)', *Sitzungsberichte der Altertumsgesellschaft Prussia*, 21 (1896–1900), 160–86; Adalbert Bezzenberger, 'Das Gräberfeld bei Kellaren im Kreise Allenstein (II.)', *Sitzungsberichte der Altertumsgesellschaft Prussia*, 21 (1896–1900), 186–95; Vladimir I. Kulakov, 'Mogil'niki zapadnoi chasti Mazurskogo poozer'ia konca V–nachala VIII vv. (po materialom raskopok 1878–1938 gg.)', *Barbaricum*, 1 (1989), 148–275.

[12] Carl Engel and Wolfgang La Baume, *Kulturen und Völker der Frühzeit im Preußenlande* (Königsberg, 1937), pp. 191–92 with fig. 42.

[13] Kurt Voigtmann, 'Die westmasurischen Loch- und Fensterurnen', *Alt-Preußen*, 6 (1940–41), 36–46.

[14] Wojciech Nowakowski, 'Studia nad ceramiką zachodniobałtyjską z okresu wędrówek ludów', *Barbaricum*, 1 (1989), 101–47.

[15] Engel, *Aus ostpreußischer Vorzeit*, fig. 54.

fibulae appear not only within the region of the Mazurian Lakes, but also in the Suwałki district.[16] Judging from the existing evidence, it appears that to the east, the Olsztyn group gradually blended into the native Baltic population.

Alien Elements in the Olsztyn Group

Among all artefacts associated with the Olsztyn group, bow fibulae have always attracted the greatest interest. They were cast in moulds using the lost-wax technique, which allowed the decoration of the entire surface of the fibula with an extensive chip-carved ornament cut out in the soft wax matrix (so-called *Kerbschnitt*).[17] For the Late Migration period, finds of such artefacts cluster on the Rhine and the upper Danube, the area under the control of the Merovingian kingdoms, on the middle and lower course of the Danube, as well as on the hillsides of the northeastern Carpathians and in the Dniester River Basin.[18] Further to the east they can be found in the Crimea and on the middle Dnieper River, the area recognized as the primary location of the Antes, who most probably were a Slavic tribe.[19] Besides

---

[16] Kurt Voigtmann, 'Neues zu den westmasurischen Loch- und Fensterurnen und eine Berichtigung', *Alt-Preußen*, 6 (1940–41), 64; Marian Kaczyński and others, in *Die Balten, die nördlichen Nachbarn der Slawen*, ed. by Gerd Biegel and Jan Jaskanis (Freiburg im Breisgau, 1987), p. 154 with fig. 636.

[17] E. A. Shablavina, 'Pal'chataia fibula iz kollektsii E. A. Goriunova', in *Kul'turnye transformatsii i vzaimovliianiia v Dneprovskom regione na iskhode rimskogo vremeni i v rannem Srednevekov'e: Doklady nauchnoi konferentsii, posviashchennoi 60-letiiu so dnia rozhdeniia E. A. Goriunova (Sankt-Peterburg, 14–17 noiabria 2000 g.)*, ed. by Valentina M. Goriunova and Olga A. Shcheglova (St Petersburg, 2004), pp. 244–53 (p. 246, figs 5 and 7–11). See also Helmut Franke, 'Zur Herstellung der Kerbschnittfibel von Groß Köris, Kr. Königs Wusterhausen', *Veröffentlichungen des Museums für Ur- und Frühgeschichte Potsdam*, 21 (1987), 237–41.

[18] Liudmil Vagalinski, 'Zur Frage der ethnischen Herkunft der späten Strahlenfibeln (Finger- oder Bügelfibeln) aus dem Donau-Karpaten-Becken (M. 6.–7. Jh.)', *Zeitschrift für Archäologie*, 28 (1994), 261–305 with figs 1 and 3–7. For the Upper Danube region, see Herbert Kühn, *Die germanischen Bügelfibeln der Völkerwanderungszeit in der Rheinprovinz* (Bonn, 1940). For the Middle and Lower Danube, see Joachim Werner, 'Slawische Bügelfibeln des 7. Jahrhunderts', in *Reinecke Festschrift zum 75. Geburtstag von Paul Reinecke am 25. September 1947*, ed. by G. Behrens and Joachim Werner (Mainz, 1950), pp. 150–72 with figs 4–5; Vagalinski, 'Zur Frage', figs 1–2 and 6–7; Uwe Fiedler, 'Die Slawen im Bulgarenreich und im Awarenkhaganat: Versuch eines Vergleichs', in *Ethnische und kulturelle Verhältnisse an der mittleren Donau vom 6. bis zum 11. Jahrhundert: Symposium Nitra 6. bis 10. November 1994*, ed. by Darina Bialeková and Jozef Zábojník (Bratislava, 1996), pp. 195–214 (pp. 202–05 with fig. 5).

[19] For Antes in Antiquity, see Godłowski, *Frühe Slawen*, pp. 162–65, with fig. 15. For the location of the sixth-century Antes, see Michał Parczewski, *Die Anfänge der frühslawischen Kultur*

those regions, there is no major concentration of finds of bow fibulae other than Mazuria, a region in which assemblages of the Olsztyn group producing bow fibulae cluster within a limited area surrounded by vast tracts of land devoid of any such finds. Only isolated finds are known from other parts of the Baltic lands[20] or from the region of the Oder and Vistula rivers, said to have been occupied at that time by the Slavs.[21]

Most finds of bow fibulae from sites associated with the Olsztyn group are not artefacts obtained from a distance, but local imitations of specimens procured from the Rhine, Danube, or Black Sea regions. The latest study dedicated to the Mazurian bow fibulae, based on the preserved specimens in the collections of the Prussia-

in Polen (Vienna, 1993), figs 32 and 34. It is commonly accepted that non-Slavic peoples, predominantly Iranians, might have been Antes. See Joachim Werner, 'Zur Herkunft und Ausbreitung der Anten und Sklavenen', in *Actes du VIII° Congrès international des sciences préhistoriques et protohistoriques Beograd 9–15 septembre 1971*, ed. by Grga Novak, I (Belgrade, 1971), pp. 243–52; Dan Gh. Teodor, 'Unele considerații privind originea și cultura anților', *Arheologia Moldovei*, 16 (1993), 205–13. For the Antes, see also Bartłomiej Szymon Szmoniewski's chapter in this volume. For Crimea, see Werner, 'Slawische Bügelfibeln', fig. 5; Vagalinski, 'Zur Frage', figs 1–2, 4, and 6; Aleksandr I. Aibabin, 'Khronologiia mogil'nikov Kryma pozdnerimskogo i rannesrednevekovogo vremeni', *Materialy po arkheologii, istorii i etnografii Tavrii*, 1 (1990), 5–68 (pp. 20–22 with figs 15–21 and pls 2–7); V. E. Rodinkova, 'Dneprovskie fibuly s kaimoi iz ptich'ikh golov', in *Kul'turnye transformatsii i vzaimovliianiia v Dneprovskom regione na iskhode rimskogo vremeni i v rannem Srednevekov'e*, ed. by Goriunova and Shcheglova, pp. 233–43 with fig. 2. For the Middle Dnieper region, see Werner, 'Slawische Bügelfibeln', figs 4–5; Vagalinski, 'Zur Frage', figs 1, 3, and 5–7; Rodinkova, 'Dneprovskie fibuly', fig. 2.

[20] In Sambia, only a few of the earliest bow fibulae have been found, all of them three-knobbed. See Herbert Kühn, *Die germanische Bügelfibeln der Völkerwanderungszeit im Süddeutschland* (Graz, 1974), pp. 728–30, 742–46, 874–75, with maps 24–25 and 36. No five-knobbed fibulae or square-headed brooches have so far been known from that region, see Werner, 'Slawische Bügelfibeln', figs 4–5. The alleged find from Rauschen-Cobjeiten turned out to be an antiquarian import: Kurt Voigtmann, 'Ein fränkisch-alamanischer Grabfund im Samland (Cobjeiten Gr. 86)', *Alt-Preußen*, 7 (1942), 8–9 with figs 1 and 3; Holger Göldner, 'Ein Bügelpaar vom Typ Andernach-Kärlich aus dem ehemaligen Ostpreußen?', *Archäologisches Korrespondenzblatt*, 15 (1985), 245–47. A few more specimens from Lithuania, Latvia, and Estonia may be added here: see Werner, 'Slawische Bügelfibeln', figs 4–5; Jānis Ciglis, 'Some Notes on the Chronology of Latgallian and Selonian Artifacts in the Middle Iron Age', *Archaeologia Lituana*, 2 (2001); 48–64, at p. 53 with p. 58, fig. 7/2; Adolfas Tautavičius, 'Prekybiniai-kultūriniai ryšiai V–VIII amžiais', in *Lietuvos gyventojų prekybiniai ryšiai Lietuvoje II–XII a.*, ed. by Mykolas Michelbertas (Vilnius, 1972), pp. 126–52 (pp. 144–46 with fig. 16); Lembit Jaanits and others, *Eesti esiajalugu* (Tallinn, 1982), pp. 295 and 231 fig. 158.1.

[21] This is the area in which Parczewski places the so-called Prague culture. *Die Anfänge*, pp. 9–72 with figs 19.2 and 20.9.

Museum in Königsberg,[22] has confirmed that only a few specimens, mostly those of Merovingian provenance and made of silver, can be treated as imports. The vast majority of finds were imitations locally produced by means of the lost-wax technique.[23] The production of bow fibulae of South-east European origin might have been different. According to Florin Curta, Werner's class I D originated in Mazuria, and then spread into the Middle and Lower Danube, as well as the Middle Dnieper and Black Sea areas.[24] Be that as it may, the range of interpretations currently advanced for this type of dress accessory illustrates well the extent of the long-distance connections established by communities of the Olsztyn group, as well as the complexity of the problems posed by Mazurian bow fibulae. A satisfactory solution to those problems is to be expected from a thorough investigation of all bow fibulae from the collections of the former Prussia-Museum, some of which are now in Berlin, others in Kaliningrad.[25]

The Olsztyn group sites produced relatively few other imports, noticeably a scarce number of Frankish glass vessels. Besides the aforementioned Snartemo beaker (Figure 2.2.9), there is only one small goblet painted in colorful stripes (Figure 2.6.1).[26] Two cicada fibulae may be added to the list. One of them was found on the north-eastern periphery of the Olsztyn group (Figure 2.6.3).[27] The other one

[22] For the history of the Prussia-Museum, and the postwar fate of its collections, see Christine Reich, 'Archäologie einer vorgeschichtlichen Sammlung: Die Bestände des ehemaligen Prussia-Museums im Berliner Museum für Vor- und Frühgeschichte', *Archäologisches Nachrichtenblatt*, 8 (2003), 14–23.

[23] Volker Hillberg, 'Die westbaltischen Stämme und der überregionale Kulturaustausch in der Ostseeregion zur Merowingerzeit', *Jahrbuch der Bodendenkmalpflege in Mecklenburg-Vorpommern*, 51 (2003), 295–319 (pp. 308–14 with figs 14–15).

[24] Florin Curta, 'Slavic Bow Fibulae? Werner's Class I D Revisited', *Acta Archaeologica Academiae Scientiarum Hungaricae*, 57 (2006), 423–74 (pp. 446–48, 450, 459–60, and figs 4–5). However, in what concerns bow fibulae from Mazuria, Curta's study relies exclusively on the published information (as opposed to a *de visu* examination of the artefacts). His conclusions should therefore be treated with caution. For Werner's class I D, see Werner, 'Slawische Bügelfibeln', p. 153 with pl. 29.25–29.

[25] Reich, 'Archäologie einer vorgeschichtlichen Sammlung'; Vladimir I. Kulakov, 'Istoriia obnaruzheniia chasti kollektsii Muzeia "Prussiia"', *Rossiiskaia Arkheologiia*, 2000.4, 206–17. See also Hillberg, 'Die westbaltischen Stämme', pp. 295–96 with n. 6.

[26] The goblet was found in Popielno, district Mrągowo (former Popielnen, Kreis Sensburg). See Max Ebert, *Truso* (Berlin, 1926), p. 74; Wilhelm Gaerte, *Urgeschichte Ostpreußens* (Königsberg, 1929), fig. 160c.

[27] Widryny, district Kętrzyn (former Widrinen, Kreis Rastenburg). See Åberg, *Ostpreußen*, p. 101.

was found even farther to the east (Figure 2.6.2),[28] practically outside the area associated with the Olsztyn group, but through which such artefacts may have had to go in order to reach their final destinations.

Moreover, the Olsztyn group assemblages did not produce any significant quantity of artefacts pointing to extensive contact with the regions on the northern coast of the Black Sea. The only undisputed import from that region is a silver eagle-headed buckle, similar to buckles found on the sixth- and seventh-century cemetery sites in Crimea (Figure 2.6.4).[29]

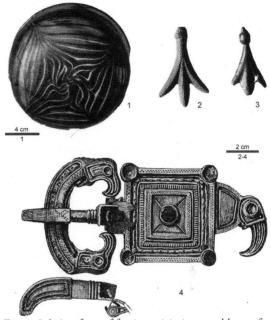

Figure 2.6. Artefacts of foreign origin in assemblages of the Olsztyn group: (1) glass goblet from Popielno (district Mrągowo, Poland); (2, 3) cicada fibulae from Czerwony Dwór and Widryny; and (4) eagle-headed belt buckle from grave 368 in Kosewo (district of Mrągowo, Poland). After Gaerte, *Urgeschichte Ostpreußens*; Nowakowski, 'Ostpreußen als Brücke'; and Åberg, *Ostpreußen*.

The Decline of the Olsztyn Group

The decline of the Olsztyn group (known as phase E_3) is marked by the gradual disappearance of artefacts signalling interregional contacts, which makes it difficult to establish its chronology.[30] The beginning of the decline is usually placed at *c.* 600, mostly on the basis of flat bow fibulae, on which the chip-carved decoration has been replaced by rows of

---

[28] Czerwony Dwór, district Gołdap (former Rothebude, Kreis Goldap). See Åberg, *Ostpreußen*, p. 101 with fig. 142.

[29] Kosewo, district Mrągowo (former Alt-Kossewen, Kreis Sensburg), site 2, grave 368. See Åberg, *Ostpreußen*, pp. 117–19 with figs 169–70. For analogies, see Aibabin, 'Khronologiia mogil'nikov', pp. 32–35 with figs 29–36.

[30] So far, all attempts to build up a chronology for the Olsztyn group have been based on 'imported' bow fibulae, with little reference to local artefacts. See Kowalski, 'Z badań nad chronologią', pp. 67–85; Kowalski, 'Chronologia grupy elbląskiej i olsztyńskiej', pp. 213–18 and 221–24.

embossed triangles along the edges.[31] Local crossbow fibulae also changed, as later specimens display a false bow cut from sheet metal.[32] One such fibula was found in a small cemetery in Prützke (Brandenburg, Germany) in association with an urn cremation with a handmade pot of the so-called Prague type. The assemblage has been linked to the earliest Slavic presence in the area and can consequently be dated to the middle or second half of the seventh century.[33] Also typical for the final stage of the Olsztyn group are urns imitating the previous window urns, on which the rectangular windows have been replaced by much smaller holes.[34]

Most conspicuously, the end of the Olsztyn group is marked by the cessation of burial on many of its cemetery sites, although it should be noted that the process did not unfold steadily within the whole area at the same time, and some of the sites must have existed longer than others. A number of sites might have come to be used only towards the end of the phase, and they were still occupied in the early eighth century.[35] Conspicuously absent from assemblages excavated in Wólka Prusinowska are artefacts typical for the 'classic' Olsztyn group. Not a single window urn has been found, but there are numerous imitations with small

---

[31] Kühn, 'Das Problem der masurgermanischen Fibeln', pls 26.V.13–V.18, V.20–V.21; 27.VI.12–VI.16; Kowalski, 'Z badań nad chronologią', p. 81 with fig. 2.

[32] Åberg, *Ostpreußen*, pp. 125–28 with fig. 182.

[33] Petersen, *Der ostelbische Raum*, pp. 51–52 and 106–08 with fig. 124; Wilhelm Unverzagt and Joachim Herrmann, 'Das slawische Brandgräberfeld von Prützke, Kr. Eberswalde', *Ausgrabungen und Funde: Nachrichtenblatt für Vor- und Frühgeschichte*, 3 (1958), 107–10 with pl. 15; Wilhelm Unverzagt, 'Zur Armbrustsprossenfibel von Prützke, Kr. Brandenburg-Land', *Ausgrabungen und Funde: Nachrichtenblatt für Vor- und Frühgeschichte* 5 (1960), 145–47; Sebastian Brather, 'Die Armbrustsprossenfibel von Prützke: Eine baltische Fibelvariante und die frühen slawischen Brandgräber', in '… *trans Albim fluvium*': *Forschungen zur vorrömischen, kaiserzeitlichen und mittelalterlichen Archäologie. Festschrift für Achim Leube zum 65. Geburtstag*, ed. by Michael Meyer (Rahden, 2001), pp. 479–92; Marek Dulinicz, *Frühe Slawen im Gebiet zwischen unterer Weichsel und Elbe: Eine archäologische Studie* (Neumünster, 2006), pp. 140–41 with fig. 52.2; 267–68 with fig. 201; 275–87; and 346–47.

[34] Carl Engel, 'Das jüngste heidnische Zeitalter in Masuren', *Prussia: Zeitschrift für Heimatkunde und Heimatschutz*, 33 (1939), 45–51 with figs 1a–b, 2d, and 5–6; Okulicz, 'Problem ceramiki typu praskiego', pp. 108–09 and 122–24 with fig. 9.

[35] For example, Wólka Prusinowska, in the district of Mrągowo (former Pruschinowen Wolka, Kreis Sensburg). At the turn of the twentieth century this burial site was examined by E. Hollack and then by F. E. Peiser. Each one of them used his own system of numbering the graves. Cf. Wojciech Nowakowski, 'Schyłek grupy olsztyńskiej – próba nowego spojrzenia: "Nowe" materiały z cmentarzyska w Wólce Prusinowskiej w powiecie mrągowskim', *Komunikaty Mazursko-Warmińskie*, 4 (2004), 407–17.

holes.[36] Instead of bow fibulae with chip-carved decoration, the cemetery produced only specimens decorated with embossed triangles.[37] They were sometimes accompanied by bird-shaped fibulae (so-called *Taubenfibeln*),[38] which bear a passing resemblance to late sixth- and seventh-century bird-shaped fibulae from the Alpine region.[39] However, it is difficult to establish at this moment whether *Taubenfibeln* from Mazuria were an imitation of bird-shaped fibulae from the southern parts of Central Europe or, as Niels Åberg has long maintained, from Scandinavia.[40]

However, Wólka Prusinowska also produced such rare testimonies of inter-regional exchange as equal-armed fibulae of Frankish origin. One of them has trapeze-shaped plates (Figure 2.7.3), very similar to Thörle's class V B originating in Italy, but otherwise well attested in assemblages north of the Alps dated to the first half of the seventh century,[41] as well as to his much later class V D. The latter appears especially in the Baltic Sea region no earlier than the late eighth century.[42]

---

[36] Engel, 'Das jüngste heidnische Zeitalter', pp. 50–51 with figs 5.b, 6.a; Voigtmann, 'Die westmasurischen Loch- und Fensterurnen', p. 45, no. 32; Nowakowski, 'Schyłek grupy olsztyńskiej', fig. 2.

[37] Åberg, *Ostpreußen*, p. 170 with fig. 117; Kühn, 'Das Problem der masurgermanischen Fibeln', pp. 98–99 with pl. 26.V.15, V.17; Nowakowski, 'Schyłek grupy olsztyńskiej', fig. 3a–c.

[38] Grave 27, excavated by Hollack produced a *Taubenfibel* and a late bow fibula decorated with rows of embossed triangles. See Adalbert Bezzenberger, *Analysen vorgeschichtlicher Bronzen Ostpreussens* (Königsberg, 1904), p. 91, fig. 118; Nowakowski, 'Schyłek grupy olsztyńskiej', fig. 3d–h. *Taubenfibeln* found in assemblages of the Olsztyn group are different from other bird-shaped fibulae, such as the so-called *Hahnfibeln*, for which see Maja Bausovac, 'Poznoantični kovinski predmeti z Gradce pri Prapretnem', *Arheološki Vestnik*, 54 (2003), 313–24 (pp. 315–16 with fig. 1.2).

[39] Volker Bierbrauer, s. v. 'Romanen', in *Reallexikon der germanischen Altertumskunde*, XXV, ed. by Heinrich Beck, Dieter Guenich, and Heiko Steuer (Berlin, 2003), pp. 223–24 with fig. 23; Volker Bierbrauer, 'Fibeln als Zeugnisse persönlichen Christentums südlich und nördlich der Alpen im 5. bis 9. Jahrhundert', *Acta Praehistorica et Archaeologica*, 34 (2002), 212–13 with fig. 2; Volker Bierbrauer, 'Die Keszthely-Kultur und die romanische Kontinuität in Westungarn (5.–8. Jh.): Neue Überlegungen zu einem alten Problem', in *Von Sachsen bis Jerusalem: Menschen und Institutionen im Wandel der Zeit. Festschrift für Wolfgang Giese zum 65. Geburtstag*, ed. by Hubertus Seibert and Gertrud Thoma (Munich, 2004), p. 59 with figs 3c and 69; see also Attila Kiss, *Avar Cemeteries in County Baranya* (Budapest, 1977), pp. 106–07, pl. 43.30.

[40] Åberg, *Ostpreußen*, pp. 100–01 with figs 140–41.

[41] Nowakowski, 'Schyłek grupy olsztyńskiej', pp. 407–18 (p. 414 with fig. 5a). See also Stefan Thörle, *Gleicharmige Bügelfibeln des frühen Mittelalters* (Bonn, 2001), pp. 106 and 113–14 with pls 29.7–15, 30.1–4, and 60.

[42] Nowakowski, 'Schyłek grupy olsztyńskiej', p. 414 with fig. 5b. See Thörle, *Gleicharmige Bügelfibeln*, pp. 110–11 and 118–19 with pls 30.18, 31.1–12, and 60; Mechtilde Schulze-

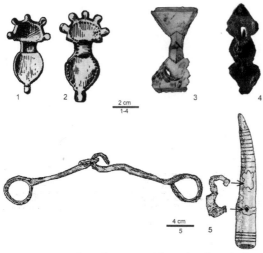

The other equal-armed fibula from Wólka Prusinowska has a small round shield on the bow (Figure 2.7.4), a feature most typical for Thörle's class VII A 3, which is dated to the late Merovingian or the early Carolingian period, that is, around 750.[43] Other artefacts of a late date include a diamond-shaped disc-fibula, a necklace, and a bracelet with rectangular section, as well as a clasp and rectangular belt mounts. The evidence from the Wólka Prusinowska cemetery strongly suggests that some, at least, of the people in the Olsztyn group remained in contact with the Rhine and upper Danube regions of Europe. Conversely, such ties are attested by finds of Baltic crossbow fibulae from the lands beyond the river Oder to the west.[44]

Figure 2.7. Artefacts from assemblages dated to the last stages of the Olsztyn group: (1, 2) bow fibula from grave 120 in Wólka Prusinowska (district Mrągowo, Poland); (3, 4) equal-armed brooches from graves 102 and 27 in Wólka Prusinowska; (5) bridle bit with antler cheek piece from the horse burial 2 in Tumiany. After Kühn, 'Das Problem der masurgermanischen Fibeln'; Nowakowski, 'Schyłek grupy olsztyńskiej'; and Baranowski, 'Pochówki koni'.

Later assemblages of the Olsztyn group suggest that contacts southwards of the Carpathian Basin should also be considered, although there is little evidence to prove their lengthy existence. The ties with the Middle Danube region in the sixth and seventh centuries are indicated by artefacts typically recognized as Avar imports or their imitations. This is the case with a wooden bucket from Miętkie (district of Szczytno), with metal mounts with embossed decoration around the edges.[45] Buckets with similarly decorated mounts are known from Early Avar as

Dörrlamm, 'Gleicharmige Bügelfibeln der Zeit um 600 aus dem Byzantinischen Reich', *Archäologisches Korrespondenzblatt*, 33 (2003), 437–44.

[43] Thörle, *Gleicharmige Bügelfibeln*, pp. 132 and 137–38 with pls 35.8–15 and 60.

[44] Brather, 'Die Armbrustsprossenfibel von Prützke', pp. 479–92.

[45] Gaerte, *Urgeschichte Ostpreußens*, p. 293, pl. X.a.

well as Merovingian assemblages.[46] Contacts with the Avar milieu are also signalled by bridle bits with antler cheek-pieces.[47] However, it is worth pointing out that typically Avar-age stirrups are absent from assemblages of the Olsztyn group, although they are otherwise present on contemporary sites in the Sambian Peninsula.[48]

Avar imports may have reached the Mazurian Lake district through the intermediary of Slavic populations occupying the Vistula Basin in the sixth and seventh centuries. However, in the absence of cemetery sites in the area north of the Carpathian Mountains, there is only limited archaeological evidence to support that idea.[49] Some have traced the Slavic influence to the S-shaped sections of simple pots found in ceramic assemblages of the Olsztyn group.[50]

The finds discussed here provide evidence that in its final stages dated to the seventh or even eighth century, the Olsztyn group did not become isolated, a phenomenon which could have allegedly led to rapid decline. Nor was Mazuria depopulated at the time. The gradual abandonment of the Olsztyn group cemeteries suggests that the existing burial rites were replaced by forms of disposing of the body of the deceased which left little, if any, traces in the archaeological record. In any case, it seems likely that some of the settlements within the territory of the Olsztyn group continued to exist for some time after most cemeteries were

[46] Sarolta Szatmári, 'Das Gräberfeld von Oroszlány und seine Stelle in der frühawarenzeitlichen Metallkunst', *Acta Archaeologica Academiae Scientiarum Hungaricae*, 32 (1980), 97–116 (pp. 102–10 with figs 7–14, and pp. 115–16). For somewhat later specimens, see Kiss, *Avar Cemeteries*, pp. 147 and 149 with pls 59.16 and 129.3; Éva Garam, *Das awarenzeitliche Gräberfeld von Tisza-füred* (Budapest, 1995), p. 373. For Merovingian specimens, see Joachim Werner, *Münzdatierte austrasische Grabfunde* (Berlin, 1935), p. 55 with n. 2, and p. 92 with pl. 18; Otto Doppelfeld, 'Das fränkische Knabengrab unter dem Chor des Kölner Domes', *Germania*, 42 (1964), 156–88 (p. 178 with fig. 13b and pl. 42.2).

[47] For example, that from the horse grave 2 in Tumiany, district of Olsztyn (former Daumen, Kr. Allenstein). See Tadeusz Baranowski, 'Pochówki koni z Tumian, w woj. Olsztyńskim', *Archeologia Polski*, 46 (1996), 65–120 (pp. 84–85 with figs 6–7). For Avar parallels, see Garam, *Das awarenzeitliche Gräberfeld von Tiszafüred*, pp. 354 and 357–58 with fig. 214.4; 424 with pls 175 and 178. See also Attila Kiss, *Das awarenzeitliche-gepidische Gräberfeld von Kölked-Feketakapu A* (Innsbruck, 1996), pp. 240 and 284–85 with pl. 87.

[48] Otto Kleemann, 'Samländische Funde und die Frage der ältesten Steigbügel in Europa', in *Documenta Archaeologica Wolfgang*, ed. by Kleemann, pp. 109–22 (p. 115 with pl. 32).

[49] Dulinicz, *Frühe Slawen*, pp. 266–67. For a few bow fibulae from the 'intermediary area', see Parczewski, *Die Anfänge*, pp. 69–73 with fig. 20.9–10, 12.

[50] Okulicz, 'Problem ceramiki typu praskiego', pp. 103–33; Parczewski, *Die Anfänge*, pp. 26–65.

abandoned. For example, a number of settlement sites existed in the early eighth century at Wyszembork, on the shore of Lake Sałęt near Mrągowo, for which no chronologically corresponding burials have been found within the nearby cemetery.[51] Moreover, a hillfort was identified within the same area on Lake Sałęt.[52] Judging from the existing evidence, it appears that an entirely new settlement pattern emerged in the area at some point during the eighth century, the centre of which was not the communal cemetery, but a ringwork. The fact that the earliest ringworks of Mazuria appeared during the last stages of the Olsztyn group suggests that by AD 700 the cultural landscape of the Mazurian Lake district came to resemble more closely the pattern in existence in other parts of early medieval Europe.[53]

Who Were the People of the Olsztyn Group?

There is no simple ecological or economic explanation for the three hundred year–odd history of the Olsztyn group in Mazuria, a period during which people in the Mazurian Lake district maintained contacts with distant areas of Europe to the west and to the south, from which dress accessories were procured, which were completely foreign to the local traditions. No evidence exists of any substantial changes in the landscape during this period, and so far no particularly unusual features have been identified within the economic profile of communities in the region. To be sure, such natural resources and products of the Mazurian Lake

[51] The date of site IV b at Wyszembork is secured by the discovery of a spur with attachment hooks bent inwards, which is dated to the late seventh century at the earliest, but may well be of an eighth-century date. See Wojciech Nowakowski, 'Zum Problem der Besiedlungsfortdauer in der Masurischen Seenplatte im 1. Jahrtausend u.Z. im Lichte von Forschungsergebnissen hinsichtlich der Mikroregion der Sałęt Seeufer', *Archaeologia Polona*, 19 (1980), 49–69 (pp. 60–63 and fig. 3h). See also Parczewski, *Die Anfänge*, pp. 84–88.

[52] See Wojciech Wróblewski, 'Czarny Las: wczesnośredniowieczne grodzisko w Szestnie, woj. Olsztyńskie', in *CONCORDIA: Studia ofiarowane Jerzemu Okuliczowi-Kozarynowi w sześćdziesiątą piątą rocznicę urodzin*, ed. by Wojciech Nowakowski (Warsaw, 1996), pp. 227–28.

[53] See Jerzy Antoniewicz and Jerzy Okulicz, 'Sprawozdanie z prac wykopaliskowych, przeprowadzonych w latach 1951–1954 w Jeziorku, pow. Giżycko', *Materiały Starożytne*, 3 (1958), 7–69; Romuald Odoj, 'Wyniki badań grodziska z VI–VIII w. n.e. w Pasymiu, pow. Szczytno, a problemy kultury mazurskiej', *Rocznik Olsztyński*, 7 (1968), 113–50. The new excavations within the ringwork at Jeziorko confirm that conclusion: Agnieszka Jaremek, 'Brązowa zawieszka zoomorficzna z Jeziorka', *Barbaricum*, 7 (2004), 291–93.

district as amber,[54] furs, or beeswax[55] may have been traded at high prices to other parts of contemporary Europe, and that trade may have theoretically financed the welfare of the Olsztyn group, as well as explained the presence of foreign goods of Frankish or south-east European origin. But if accepting that premise, one is immediately confronted with much more troubling questions, such as why the affluence did not spread to other parts of the south-eastern Baltic region. A prime candidate for that would have been the Sambian Peninsula or the western coast of Latvia, both of which had larger resources of drift (as opposed to mined) amber, as well as more convenient sea-lane connections to the northern and western parts of Europe. While economic development may have strengthened the position of the Olsztyn group against its neighbours, it cannot be used as an explanation for the appearance of that group in the first place.

In the absence of any simple and monocausal explanation for the rise of the Olsztyn group, most scholars turned to migration. Initially responsible for the rise of the Olsztyn group were the Gothic refugees from the Middle Danube region, who were fleeing their country in the aftermath of the collapse of Attila's Hunnic Empire. That few if any weapons have been found in male burial assemblages of the Olsztyn group seems to have encouraged speculations in that direction, given that the deposition of weapons in burials was known throughout the Roman period in the Baltic region, but not practised within the cultural areas associated with the Goths (and is not attested in burial assemblages of the Sântana de Mureş-Chernyakhov culture).[56] Others suggested that the immigrants were the Herules returning to Thule in the early sixth century, as reported by Procopius of Caesarea.[57]

[54] For the amber deposits of Mazuria, see Barbara Kosmowska-Ceramowicz and Teresa Pietrzak, *Znaleziska i dawne kopalnie bursztynu w Polsce* (Warsaw, 1982). Only a few beads or raw pieces of amber have been found so far found in assemblages of the Olsztyn group graves. See, for example, graves 49 and 106 in Tumiany; Heydeck, 'Das Gräberfeld von Daumen', pp. 51 and 60. For amber in the Baltic region, see also Audronė Bliujienė's contribution in this volume.

[55] On the production capacities of Mazurian bee-keepers, see Friedrich Mager, *Der Wald in Alt-preußen als Wirtschaftsraum*, I (Cologne, 1960), pp. 287–327, and p. 282 for hunting. The evidence for the early medieval trade with wax was collected by Charlotte Warnke: 'Der Handel mit Wachs zwischen Ost- und Westeuropa im frühen und hohen Mittelalter', in *Der Handel der Karolinger- und Wikingerzeit: Bericht über die Kolloquien der Kommission für die Altertumskunde Mittel- und Nordeuropas in den Jahren 1980 bis 1983*, ed. by Klaus Düwel (Göttingen, 1987), pp. 545–69.

[56] Heydeck, 'Das Gräberfeld von Daumen', pp. 70–73.

[57] Kühn, 'Das Problem der masurgermanischen Fibeln', pp. 103–08; Kühn, *Die germanischen Bügelfibeln der Völkerwanderungszeit in Mitteldeutschland*, pp. 14–24. For Procopius's reports on the Herules, and his account of their trek back to Thule, see Ronald Steinacher and Alexander Sarantis's chapters in this volume.

Another idea, first put forward in the 1920s, was to identify the inhabitants of Roman-age Mazuria with Ptolemy's Galindians.[58] A few personal names, whose pronunciation was likened to that of names known from Visigothic Spain, were supposed to prove that a group of the Galindians had accompanied the Visigoths to the Iberian Peninsula.[59] However, the majority of them were believed to have remained in the Balkans alongside other groups, such as the Ostrogoths and the Gepids, both supposedly originating from an area in the Baltic region close to the Galindian homeland.[60] Following the collapse of the Hunnic Empire in the mid-fifth century, the Galindian émigrés decided to return home to Mazuria. According to this scenario, the Galindian repatriates from the Carpathian Basin must therefore have been responsible for the emergence of the Olsztyn group. The archaeological argument most often cited in support of this idea was that most Olsztyn-group cemeteries appear on sites previously occupied during the Late Roman period.[61] The grandsons of those who had migrated to the south now used the graveyards of their ancestors, the location of which must have been kept in the collective memory of several generations of Galindian migrants.

There are of course several problems with such a reading of the archaeological evidence. First, the Galindians in first- to second-century Mazuria seem to have been quite isolated from the nearest sites attributed to the Wielbark culture in

---

[58] Tadeusz Lehr-Spławiński, 'Galindia', in *Słownik starożytności słowiańskich*, ed. by Władysław Kowalenko, Gerard Labuda, and Tadeusz Lehr-Spławiński, II (Wrocław, 1964), p. 78.

[59] Reinhard Wenskus and Dietrich Timpe, 'Galinder', in *Reallexikon der germanischen Altertumskunde*, X, ed. by Beck, Geunich, Steuer, and Timpe, p. 329. The presence of Galindians on the Iberian Peninsula is not attested by any historical sources. The idea, for which there is absolutely no archaeological confirmation, is simply a historiographical myth. Needless to say, the search for an archaeological correlate of that putative migration is misguided. After all, the well-known migration of the Vandals did not leave any archaeological trace, and the only trace of a Vandal presence on the Iberian Peninsula is the name (V)Andalusia. See Christian Courtois, *Les Vandales et l'Afrique* (Paris, 1955); Gerd G. Koenig, 'Wandalische Grabfunde des 5. und 6. Jahrhunderts', *Madrider Mitteilungen*, 22 (1981), 299–360. See also Guido Berndt's chapter in this volume.

[60] Jerzy Okulicz, 'Das Gräberfeld von Weklice zur Besiedlungsgeschichte des Weichseldeltaraums in der römischen Kaiserzeit', *Archeologia*, 40 (1989), 115–27; Volker Bierbrauer, 'Gepiden in der Wielbark-Kultur (1.–4. Jahrhundert n.Chr.)? Eine Spurensuche', in *Studien zur Archäologie des Ostseeraumes: Von der Eisenzeit zum Mittelalters. Festschrift für Michael Müller-Wille*, ed. by Anke Wesse (Neumünster, 1998), pp. 389–403.

[61] With the notable exception of a number of cemeteries located on the western border of the territory associated with the Olsztyn group, beyond the area of the Baltic settlement of the Late Roman period. See Engel, *Aus ostpreußischer Vorzeit*, pp. 98–99 with fig. 54.

Pomerania, which was attributed to the Goths.[62] The isolation continued through the third century, until the Wielbark groups (the 'Goths') began expanding across the Vistula River into Mazovia, Podlasia, and the Lublin Uplands.[63] It was only from that moment onwards that common elements appeared both in Mazuria and within the territory of the Wielbark culture, especially crossbow fibulae with a folded stem (Almgren's classes 161–62)[64] and champlevé enamel ornamentation.[65] This may well be a sign of close contacts, even of close cooperation, which could have resulted in the alleged Galindian participation in migrations to south-eastern Europe. However, there are very few, if any, finds that could be used to support the idea of a migration, and in any case that may well have been the migration of a few individuals, not of well-defined groups concerned with preserving their cultural and ethnic identity for almost a hundred years away from the homeland.

Strong arguments against the idea of a migration were already put forward in the late 1930s by the Prussian archaeologist Carl Engel. He noted that most so-called 'alien' artefacts within the Olsztyn group have analogies in different parts of Europe, which makes very difficult the task of identifying precisely the region from which the Galindians returned to Mazuria. He also pointed out that most barbarians in the Danube and Rhine regions from which such analogies are known had already been converted to Christianity at the time of the alleged migration and had been practising inhumation for a relatively long time. If so, then it is difficult to explain the use of cremation as the exclusive burial rite of the Olsztyn group.[66]

---

[62] Wojciech Nowakowski, 'Kultura wielbarska a zachodniobałtyjski krąg kulturowy', in *Kultura wielbarska w młodszym okresie rzymskim*, ed. by Jan Gurba and Andrzej Kokowski, II (Lublin, 1989), pp. 143–59.

[63] Ryszard Wołągiewicz, 'Kultura wielbarska – problemy interpretacji etnicznej', in *Problemy kultury wielbarskiej*, ed. by Tadeusz Malinowski (Słupsk, 1981), pp. 86–87 and 100–02 with fig. 3; Andrzej Kokowski, *Grupa masłomęcka: Z badań nad przemianami kultury Gotów w młodszym okresie rzymskim* (Lublin, 1995), pp. 61–65.

[64] See Wojciech Nowakowski, 'Żelazne zapinki kuszowate z podwiniętą nóżką w europejskim Barbaricum', *Wiadomości Archeologiczne*, 44 (1999–2001), 129–46.

[65] Anna Bitner-Wróblewska, 'Elementy bałtyjskie w kulturze wielbarskiej', in *Kultura wielbarska w młodszym okresie rzymskim*, ed. by Gurba and Kokowski, pp. 161–65 with maps 1–2; Anna Bitner-Wróblewska, 'Z badań nad ozdobami emaliowanymi w kulturze wielbarskiej: Na marginesie kolekcji starożytności Paula Schachta z Malborka', *Wiadomości Archeologiczne*, 52 (1991–92), 115–31; Andrzej Kokowski, *Schätze der Ostgoten* (Stuttgart, 1995), pp. 68–69 with fig. 45.

[66] Carl Engel, 'Das Geheimnis der masurgermanischen Kultur', in *Masurischer Volkskalender 1938* (Allenstein, 1937), pp. 39–43.

Despite all objections, there is so far no alternative to the idea of a return migration to the Mazurian homeland of a Baltic group.[67] Moreover, migration is so far the only explanation that can account for a number of consecutive developments. Thus, the sharp decline in settlement in Mazuria during the fourth and early fifth centuries mentioned above cannot be explained but as the migration of a significant group of the local population, possibly to the south, along with Gothic or Gepidic groups moving to south-eastern Europe. Those who remained must have had a hard time coping with the situation, and the accelerated decline may have encouraged others to leave the region. On the other hand, the archaeological evidence clearly shows that the earliest assemblages of the Olsztyn group coincided in time with the dramatic events taking place in the Middle Danube region and leading to the demise of the Hunnic Empire. The explosion of settlement in Mazuria during the subsequent decades, which is clearly reflected in the archaeological record, may well be the correlate of a large-scale immigration, possibly from the same region of the Middle Danube. The scouting phase of that migration may be represented by the groups who buried their dead during the second half of the fifth century, while the full-scale migration took place only in the early 500s. This led to the establishment of new burial grounds on the south-eastern border of the Baltic lands. The newcomers most certainly mixed with the local people who had continued to bury their dead in the old cemeteries. The archaeological correlate of such political and ethnic cleavage is the hybrid culture of the Olsztyn group.

The arguments in favour of this scenario have been based on weak premises, and the weaknesses themselves have already been presented. The proposed scenario has been predicated upon the most famous example of a return migration, namely that of the Herules mentioned by Procopius. A cremation cemetery recently discovered north of the Carpathian Mountains has been hastily linked to the returning Herules in an attempt to show that long after living within the Middle Danube region and after being converted to Christianity, the Herules did not abandon

---

[67] I have embraced that idea on a number of occasions, most explicitly in Wojciech Nowakowski, 'Die Olsztyn-Gruppe (masurgermanische Kultur) in der Völkerwanderungszeit: Das Problem ihrer chronologischen und territorialen Grenzen', in *Die spätrömische Kaiserzeit und die frühe Völkerwanderungszeit im Mittel- und Osteuropa*, ed. by Magdalena Mączyńska and Tadeusz Grabarczyk (Łódź, 2000), pp. 168–90; and 'Rückkehr in die Heimat? Die Olsztyn-Gruppe in Nordostpolen in der Völkerwanderungszeit', in *Atti del XIII Congresso della Unione internazionale delle scienze preistoriche e protoistoriche: Forli, Italia, 1996, 8–14 settembre*, V (Forlì, 1998), pp. 41–45.

their ancestral burial rites based on cremation.[68] But those returning to Mazuria brought back not just new styles and new fashions, such as the dress with bow fibulae, but also the awareness of the social and political significance of such styles for the barbarian elites on the northern frontier of the Roman Empire. It is quite possible that such versatility and the profound knowledge of the social and political etiquette of the barbarian world in both Western and Eastern Europe turned the emerging Olsztyn group into the most important, if not the only, partner at the same time of the Frankish kings in the West, of the Gepid kings in the Carpathian Basin, and of the Sclavene chieftains in the Lower Danube or Middle Dnieper regions. Isolated from its neighbours by vast tracts of uninhabited land, the Olsztyn group may have capitalized not only on local resources such as amber, wax, or fur, but also on its geopolitically strategic position between West and East. Various groups in both areas vied with each other to obtain the alliance of the Mazurian elites, for which they may have paid with gifts of luxuries. But the situation soon changed. By 570, the Avars had smashed the Gepid kingdom and forced the Lombards to migrate to Italy, while in the early seventh century the Slavic polity under the leadership of Samo emerged in Central Europe.[69] The Olsztyn group was now not in the middle, but on the peripheries of the important developments taking place in Central Europe. Building alliances with the Mazurian elites does not seem to have been that appealing anymore. Slowly but surely, the inhabitants of Mazuria moved away from the cultural model of the past and adopted the ways of living of their immediate, Slavic neighbours: the handmade pottery of the so-called Prague type, the ringworks, and burial customs mixing cremation with inhumation.[70] It is not altogether clear what made the Slavic culture so appealing, but the sunken-featured building with a fireplace in one of the four corners was certainly better adapted than any aboveground house to the harsh winter conditions of Mazuria. Along with liquid foodstuffs mostly prepared in and consumed from relatively tall pots with S-shaped section, the sunken-featured building of East

[68] Barbara Niezabitowska, 'Die Heruler', in *Die Vandalen. Die Könige. Die Eliten. Die Krieger. Die Handwerker,* ed. by Andrzej Kokowski and Christian Leiber (Nordstemmen, 2003), pp. 387–94.

[69] Walter Pohl, *Die Awaren: Eis Steppenvolk in Mitteleuropa, 567–822* (Munich, 1988). For Samo, see Gerard Labuda, *Pierwsze państwo słowiańskie: Państwo Samona* (Poznań, 1949).

[70] Parczewski, *Die Anfänge,* pp. 96–100 and 115–18. For ringworks, see Jerzy Nalepa, 'Grody', in *Słownik starożytności słowiańskich,* ed. by Kowalenko, Labuda, and Lehr-Spławiński, II, 163–64. To be sure, no Slavic ringworks have so far been found that could be dated before 600 (Parczewski, *Die Anfänge,* p. 105).

European tradition provided a much more comfortable accommodation at a much smaller price in material and energy than aboveground houses with open hearths.

Judging from the existing evidence, the adoption of this new cultural model coincided in time with the abandonment of the old cemeteries and the rise of ringworks. By the same token, that most settlement sites of the previous period continued to be used, while new ways of preparing and eating food were adopted, strongly suggests that the new changes were not linked to any migration of a new population, but instead must be interpreted as a deliberate rejection of the 'old ways'. The final result seems to have been the absorption of the Olsztyn group people into the Prussian ethnic community. During the ninth and tenth centuries, the material culture of the inhabitants of Mazuria differed very little from that of the neighbouring communities in the Prussian region.

Final Remarks

The above argument should by no means be treated as a definitive explanation. Nor was it meant to support the ongoing debate about the archaeological visibility of migrations or the application of evolutionary theory to the cultural changes taking place during the so-called 'Great Migration' period.[71] Instead, my intention has been to advance an explanatory model which could account for as much archaeological evidence as possible. My goal was to explain the rise of the mysterious barbarians of the Olsztyn group in Mazuria. The evidence available so far does not fit the idea of full-scale migration of a completely foreign group to Mazuria. Nor is it possible to tease out the specific features of the Olsztyn group from the local traditions of the Late Roman period by means of evolutionary theory. The idea put forward almost eighty years ago that a fraction of the Galindians returned to their homeland from south-eastern Europe remains the most convincing explanation, in that it does justice to the existing archaeological evidence. One can only hope that future excavations will produce more evidence for testing that hypothesis.

---

[71] Roland Prien, *Archäologie und Migration: Vergleichende Studien zur archäologischen Nachweisbarkeit von Wanderungsbewegungen* (Bonn, 2005).

THE ANTES: EASTERN 'BROTHERS' OF THE SCLAVENES?

Bartłomiej Szymon Szmoniewski

The Historiography of the Problem

Given that they often appear in written sources in association with the Sclavenes, it comes as no surprise that from the onset of historical writing on the subject, scholars have associated the Antes with the Slavs. The first to do so was the Polish poet and historian, Adam Naruszewicz (1733–96), who listed the Antes among the common ancestors of all Slavic-speaking nations. In his multivolume *History of the Polish Nation*, written at the behest of King Stanisław August Poniatowski (1794–95), Naruszewicz placed the Sclavenes, Antes, and Venethi mentioned by Jordanes on the territory of Poland and regarded all three as the ancestors of the Poles.[1] A few years later, the German philologist Johann Casper Zeuss (1806–56) saw things differently. According to him, the Sclavenes were Western Slavs, and the Antes an admixture of South and Eastern Slavs. That no source mentioned the Antes after *c.* 600 was simply due to the fact that the

I am greatly indebted to Albrecht Diem (Syracuse), Carmen Konzett (Innsbruck), Maya Maskarinec (Princeton), and Walter Pohl (Vienna) for helping me to bring order into chaos. The editor Florin Curta deserves many thanks for his splendid and dedicated work.

[1] Adam Naruszewicz, *Historya narodu polskiego*, new edn, IX (Leipzig, 1837), p. 134 with note. A Jesuit and titular bishop of Smoleńsk and Łuck, Naruszewicz was something of a court poet for King Stanisław Poniatowski. For his life and historiographic output, see Neomisia Rutkowska, 'Bishop Adam Naruszewicz and his History of the Polish Nation' (unpublished doctoral dissertation, Catholic University of America, 1941).

Antes had left their homeland. Zeuss believed that many old names disappeared and new ones were created in the circumstances surrounding the great migration of the Slavs.[2] Zeuss's contemporary, Pavel Josef Šafařík (1795–1861) equally believed the Antes to be a southern branch of the Eastern Slavs, but could not decide whether their name was of Slavic origin or not. According to him, the Byzantine authors mentioning the Antes had learned the name from Germanic tribes in Eastern Europe; the disappearance of the Antes from the historical record was thus a result of the Germanic migration to Western Europe.[3]

During the second half of the nineteenth century, the interest in things Antian was almost exclusively Russian. Unlike Zeuss and Šafařík, Russian scholars not only listed Antes among the Eastern Slavs, but also turned them into the ancestors of such tribes mentioned in the *Russian Primary Chronicle* as the Ulichi, Tivertians, and Viatichi.[4] Only Arist A. Kunik (1814–99) thought them to be a ruling family of Asian (Cherkes) origin, who had conquered the Slavs and gave them their name.[5] The idea that the Antes were of Caucasian origin was first developed by a Danish ethnographer, Axel Olrik (1864–1917), largely under the influence of the Nart epos and other Circassian folk tales published by the Kabardin poet Shora Bekmurzin Nogmov (1794–1844).[6] Ever since Olrik pointed out the similarity, the Circassian story of Duke Dauo and his oldest son Baksan being killed together with eighty noblemen by the kings of the Goths has been cited in parallel to

[2] Johann Kaspar Zeuss, *Die Deutschen und die Nachbarstämme* (Munich, 1837), pp. 597, 604, and 605. A professor of history in Munich, Zeuss was the founder of Celtic philological studies.

[3] Pavel Jozef Šafařík, *Slovanské starožitnosti* (Prague, 1837), pp. 459–64. For Šafařík's concept of Slavic ethnogenesis, see Jozef Kudláček, 'P. J. Šafařík a jeho koncepcia pôvodu Slovanov', *Historický časopis*, 5 (1957), 59–81.

[4] Tivertians: Evgenii E. Golubinskii, *Istoriia russkoi tserkvi*, I (Moscow, 1901), p. 15. Viatichi: Mykhailo Hrushevs'kyi, 'Anty: Uryvok z istorii Ukrainy i Rusy', *Zapysky Naukovoho tovarystva imeny Shevchenka*, 21 (1898), 1–16 (p. 7).

[5] Arist Kunik and Viktor R. Rozen, *Izviestiia al-Bekri i drugikh avtorov o Rusi i slavianakh*, I (St Petersburg, 1878), p. 147. A German scholar of Silesian origin and education, Ernst-Eduard (Arist A.) Kunik moved in 1842 to St Petersburg, where he remained for the rest of his life. Two years later, he published the first volume of his *Die Berufung der schwedischen Rodsen durch die Finnen und Slawen* (St Petersburg, 1844–45), one of the foundation stones for the Normannist historiography in Russia.

[6] Axel Olrik, *Ragnarök, die Sagen vom Weltuntergang* (Berlin, 1922), p. 467. See Shora Begmurzin Nogmov, *Die Sagen und Lieder des Tscherkessen-Volkes* (Leipzig, 1866). The Antes are also mentioned together with the Goths and Attila in Georges Wlastoff, *Ombres du passé: souvenirs d'un officier du Caucase* (Paris, 1899).

Jordanes's story of Boz, the king of the Antes, who was crucified together with his sons and seventy noblemen by Vinitharius.[7] However, as the Polish Henryk Łowmiański has long demonstrated, the similarity is simply due to the bookish influence of Jordanes on the Circassian folk tales, via Nikolai Karamzin's *History of the Russian State*, which replaces Boz with Boks.[8]

In spite (or perhaps because) of such literary reworking of Jordanes's story, the 'Caucasian thesis' was further developed by the Slovenian ethnographer and anthropologist Niko Županić, who first associated the Antes to a Lezgin tribe named Andias and concluded that the Antes were a mixture of Indo-European Slavs, Caucasian people, and, naturally, Serbian, Croat, and Czech tribes.[9] The leading elite of the Antes was of Circassian (Cherkes) origin. According to Županić, between the first and the fourth century, the Slavs within their homeland were under the influence of Sarmatian, Hunnic, and Avar tribes.[10] George Vernadsky adopted Kunik and Županić's ideas and thought that the Antes were Alans (As).[11] In the philological tradition of Zeuss, Vernadsky gathered all the sources mentioning ethnic names similar to the Antes, beginning with the An-tsai of the Chinese annals (140–127 BC) and ending with the Yassi (Alans) of the Russian medieval chronicles.[12] The 'Alan thesis' was also embraced by Francis Dvornik.[13] In Poland, as early as the 1970s, Tadeusz Sulimirski believed that the Antes were Alans (or Sarmatians) who by 500 underwent a process of rapid Slavicization. Remnants of

[7] Nogmov, *Die Sagen*, p. 30; Jordanes, *Getica*, 247, ed. by Fr. Giunta and A. Grillone (Rome, 1991).

[8] Hernyk Łowmiański, *Początki Polski: Z dziejów Słowian w I tysiącleciu n. e.*, I (Warsaw, 1963), p. 405. See Nikolai M. Karamzin, *Istoriia gosudarstva Rossiiskogo*, I (St Petersburg, 1818), p. 17.

[9] Niko Županić, 'Prvi nosilci etničnih imen Srb, Hrvat, Čeh i Ant', *Etnolog*, 2 (1928), 74–79 (p. 78); Niko Županić, 'Der Anten Ursprung und Name', in *Actes du III-e Congrès international d'études byzantines (session d'Athènes, octobre 1930)* (Athens, 1932), pp. 331–39; Niko Županić, 'Boz rex Antorum', *Situla*, 4 (1961), 91–122 (p. 101). The Lezgins are an ethnic group in southern Dagestan and north-eastern Azerbaidjan.

[10] Županić, 'Boz rex Antorum', pp. 101–03.

[11] George Vernadsky, 'On the Origins of Antae', *Journal of the American Oriental Society*, 59 (1939), 56–66; George Vernadsky, 'Sur l'origine des Alains', *Byzantion*, 16 (1942–43), 81–86 (p. 81); George Vernadsky, *Ancient Russia* (New Haven, 1943), pp. 82–83.

[12] Vernadsky, 'On the Origins of Antae', pp. 60–62.

[13] Francis Dvornik, *The Making of Central and Eastern Europe* (London, 1949), pp. 277–83; Francis Dvornik, *The Slavs: Their Early History and Civilization* (Boston, 1956), p. 23.

that old Sarmatian tradition were the *tamghas* supposedly surviving on the coats of arms of Polish noble families.[14]

In Russia, Kunik's idea of an Asian origin of the Antes was vehemently opposed by the Ukrainian historian Mykhailo Hrushevs'kyi (1866–1934). Against Kunik's emphasis on dynasty, Hrushevs'kyi insisted upon the importance among the early Slavs of the institution of popular assembly. According to him, the Antes were the ancestors of the southern branch of the Eastern Slavs and, as such, the direct ancestors of the present-day Ukrainians.[15] Hrushevs'kyi and other Russian scholars of the late nineteenth century who saw the Antes as ancestors of the Slavs (especially of the Ukrainians) received a sharp critique from Lubor Niederle, who instead placed the Antes in Volhynia, the region to which Niederle thought that the Arab geographer al-Masudi referred when writing about a certain king named Madzhak, the ruler of the tribe of the Waliniana. According to Niederle, Madzhak was the same as the 'king' of the Sclavenes named Musocius and mentioned by Theophylact Simocatta.[16]

A particularly strong influence on the study of the Antes and their relation to the Slavs was the Marrist monogenetic theory of language.[17] A Georgian linguist and philologist with significant contributions to the study of Caucasian languages, Nikolai Ia. Marr (1865–1934) believed that linguistic changes were brought about by the same social phenomena as those responsible for the Marxist transition from one mode of production to another.[18] Marr's ideas had a great influence on such Soviet scholars as Boris A. Rybakov, Mikhail A. Artamonov, Petr N. Tret'iakov,

---

[14] Tadeusz Sulimirski, *Sarmaci* (Warsaw, 1979), p. 179. For the fascination of the Polish nobility with things 'Sarmatian', see Maria Bogucka, *The Lost World of the 'Sarmatians'* (Warsaw, 1996).

[15] Hrushevs'kyi, 'Anty', pp. 1–16. See also Taras Kuzio, 'Nation Building, History Writing and Competition Over Legacy of Kyiv Rus in Ukraine', *Nationalities Papers*, 33 (2005), 29–58 (pp. 33–34).

[16] Lubor Niederle, 'Antové', *Věstník Královské české společnosti nauk*, 1909, 9–12 (p. 12); Lubor Niederle, *Manuel de l'antiquité slave: l'histoire* (Paris, 1923), p. 192. For Madzhak as Musocius, see Lubor Niederle, *Slovanské starožitnosti: Původ a počátky slovanů východních*, I (Prague, 1924), p. 79. See also Theophylact Simocatta, *History*, 6.9.1 and 56, ed. by C. de Boor and P. Wirth (Stuttgart, 1972).

[17] For Marr, his ideas, and the ethnonationalism of the Stalinist period, see Gisela Bruche-Schulz, 'Marr, Marx and Linguistics in the Soviet Union', *Historiographia Linguistica*, 20 (1993), 455–72; Yuri Slezkine, 'N. Ia. Marr and the National Origins of Soviet Ethnogenetics', *Slavic Review*, 55 (1996), 826–62.

[18] See Tadeusz Lehr-Spławiński, 'Zagadnienie pochodzenia Słowian w świetle nauki polskiej i rosyjskiej', *Światowit*, 20 (1948), 25–58 (p. 39).

and Aleksandr N. Udal'tsov.[19] The former squarely placed the Antes at the origin of Kievan Rus'. According to Rybakov, the 'Antian antiquities' (so called by Aleksander A. Spitsyn) dated to the sixth and seventh centuries paved the road for the rich and exuberant culture of Kievan Rus'. The Antes were thus not just the ancestors of the Eastern Slavs, but also the originators of their specific, 'national' culture.[20] Like Rybakov, Petr Tret'iakov believed that the Antes were the ancestors of the Rus' tribes: the name Antes had been simply replaced by Rus' (Ros) as a generic term for all Eastern Slavs.[21] This was obviously an attack on Hrushevs'kyi's earlier idea that the Antes were the ancestors *only* of Ukrainians, an idea Tret'iakov promptly condemned as nothing less than 'Chinese walls placed between Russians and Ukrainians'.[22] Aleksandr Udal'tsov approached the problem in a somewhat different way. For him, the Antes were in fact a conglomerate of different tribes — Slavs, Sporoi, Carpi, Costoboci, Roxolani, and Alano-Sarmatians — who had come together into a single ethnic entity during their fourth-century wars with the Goths mentioned by Jordanes.[23]

The explosion of archaeological research in the 1950s further fueled the development of the idea of a native, Slavic origin of the Antes. Initially, the Antes were associated with finds of what later came to be known as the Sântana de Mureș-Chernyakhov culture, as well as with the archaeological culture 'discovered' during excavations of the Romen hillfort in Left-Bank Ukraine.[24] Particularly relevant in that respect are the excavations carried out by D. T. Berezovets' and V. P. Petrov

---

[19] Lehr-Spławiński, 'Zagadnienie pochodzenia Słowian', p. 39. For the influence of Marr's ideas (as well as that of their rejection by Stalin), see Florin Curta, 'From Kossinna to Bromley: Ethnogenesis in Slavic Archaeology', in *On Barbarian Identity: Critical Approaches to Ethnicity in the Early Middle Ages*, ed. by Andrew Gillett (Turnhout, 2002), pp. 201–18 (pp. 207–09).

[20] Boris A. Rybakov, 'Anty i Kievskaia Rus'', *Vestnik Drevnei Istorii*, 1939.1, 319–37 (p. 337).

[21] Petr N. Tret'iakov, *Vostochnoslavianskie plemena* (Moscow, 1948), p. 113.

[22] Tret'iakov, *Vostochnoslavianskie plemena*, p. 111.

[23] Aleksandr D. Udal'tsov, 'Osnovnye voprosy etnogeneza slavian', *Sovetskaia Etnografiia*, 1947.6–7, 3–13 (p. 13); Aleksandr D. Udal'tsov, 'Proishozhdenie slavian', *Voprosy Istorii*, 1947.7, 95–100.

[24] Sântana de Mureș-Chernyakhov culture: Mikhail I. Artamonov, 'Spornye voprosy drevnei istorii slavian i Rusi', *Kratkie soobshcheniia Instituta istorii material'noi kul'tury*, 6 (1940), 3–14; Petr N. Tret'iakov, 'Anty i Rus'', *Sovetskaia Etnografiia*, 1947.4, 71–83; Mykhailo Iu. Braychevs'kyi, 'Anstkii period v istorii skhidnih slov'ian', *Arkheolohiia*, 1952.7, 21–42; Mykhailo Iu. Braychevs'kyi, 'Pro etnichny prinalezhnist' cherniakhivs'koi kul'turi', *Arkheolohiia*, 1957.10, 11–24; Boris A. Rybakov, 'Drevnie rusi: K voprosu ob obrazovanii iadra drevnerusskoi narodnosti v svete trudov I. V. Stalina', *Sovetskaia Arkheologiia*, 17 (1953), 23–104 (pp. 40–42). Romen culture: Rybakov, 'Anty i Kievskaia Rus'', p. 319.

in the vicinity of the village of Pen'kivka near Svitlovods'ke (region of Kirovohrad, Ukraine) and on the banks of the Tiasmin River, a right-bank tributary of the Dnieper.[25] Berezovets' initially attributed the materials discovered in Pen'kivka to the Eastern Slavs, from the Chernyakhov culture to Kievan Rus', with a broad dating between the fifth and the ninth century.[26] However, subsequent excavations allowed Petr N. Tret'iakov to endorse P. I. Khavliuk's earlier idea that the newly discovered assemblages were Antian.[27] Others were of a different opinion. According to Irina P. Rusanova, the newly discovered Pen'kivka culture was a complex of different elements with a fairly significant nomadic component.[28] Csanád Bálint also raised doubts about the ethnic attribution of the Pen'kivka culture favoured by Soviet archaeologists.[29]

According to Mikhail Artamonov, the pottery found at Pen'kivka, the finds from the neighbouring hillfort at Pastyrs'ke, as well as the hoards of silver and bronze known as 'Antian antiquities' were all elements of a separate culture, which he called Martynivka (after the find spot of a large hoard of silver) and located within a vast area of the steppe and forest-steppe lands between the Lower Danube and Left-Bank Ukraine.[30] The settlements of the population producing the Pen'kivka pottery were nomadic seasonal camps, with a main, administrative centre within the hillfort at Pastyrs'ke.[31] The Antes were also an important

---

[25] D. T. Berezovets', 'Poseleniia ulichei na r. Tiasmine', in *Slaviane nakanune obrazovaniia Kievskoi Rusi*, ed. by B. A. Rybakov (Moscow, 1963), pp. 145–208; V. P. Petrov, 'Stetsovka, poselenie tret'ei cherverti I tysiacheletiia n.e. (po materialam raskopok 1956–1958 v Potiasmine)', in *Slaviane nakanune*, ed. by Rybakov, pp. 209–33.

[26] Berezovets', 'Poseleniia ulichei', p. 208.

[27] Petr N. Tret'iakov, *Finno-ugry, balty i slaviane na Dnepre i Volge* (Moscow, 1966), p. 247. See P. I. Khavliuk, 'Ranneslavianskie poseleniia v srednei chasti Iuzhnogo Pobuzh'ia', *Sovetskaia Arkheologiia*, 1961.3, 187–201; P. I. Khavliuk, 'Ranneslavianskie poseleniia Semenki i Samchintsy v srednem techenii Iuzhnogo Buga', in *Slaviane nakanune*, ed. by Rybakov, pp. 320–50.

[28] Irina P. Rusanova, *Slavianskie drevnosti VI–VII vv. Kultura prazhskogo tipa* (Moscow, 1976), pp. 103–12.

[29] Csanád Bálint, *Die Archäologie der Steppe: Steppenvölker zwischen Volga und Donau vom 6. bis zum 10. Jahrhundert* (Vienna, 1989), pp. 84–88.

[30] Mikhail I. Artamonov, 'Etnicheskata prinadlezhnost i istoricheskoto znachenie na pastirskata kultura', *Arkheologiia*, 11 (1969), 2–7; Mikhail I. Artamonov, 'Pervye stranitsy russkoi istorii v arkheologicheskom osveshchenii', *Sovetskaia Arkheologiia*, 1990.3, 271–90 (p. 274).

[31] Mikhail I. Artamonov, 'Nekotorye voprosy otnosheniia vostochnykh slavian s bolgarami i baltami v protsesse zaseleniia zemli srednego i verkhnego Podneprov'ia i Podvin'ia', *Sovetskaia Arkheologiia*, 1974.1, 245–54 (p. 249).

research topic for Mykhailo Iu. Braychevs'kyi, who believed the sixth- to seventh-century 'Antian antiquities' (which he regarded as typical for the post-Zarubintsy period) to be the 'missing link' between the Chernyakhov and the early Rus' cultures.[32] Braychevs'kyi worked out a periodization of Eastern Europe between 106 and 965 with no less than ten stages, the third to the sixth of which he assigned to the 'Antian Empire' (270 to 635). The Antes and their 'empire' came into being during the third and fourth stages (270–451 and 451–569, respectively). The 'empire' reached the peak of its development during the fifth (451–568) and declined during the sixth stage (568–635). However, Braychevs'kyi and many other Ukrainian archaeologists believed that Chernyakhovian traditions survived well into the seventh period (635–744).[33]

Another prominent Soviet archaeologist who dealt with the problem of the Antes was Valentin V. Sedov. Sedov unequivocally declared that the Antes were a group of Eastern Slavs formed on a Chernyakhov basis with some Iranian elements.[34] The very non-Slavic (Iranian) name of the Antes was a sign of the relation

---

[32] Mykhailo Iu. Braychevs'kyi, 'Arkheologichni materialy do vyvchennia kul'tury skhidnoslov'ians'kykh plemen VI–VIII st.', *Arkheolohiia*, 1950.4, 27–55 (p. 54); Mykhailo Iu. Braychevs'kyi, 'Ob "antakh" Psevdomavrikiia', *Sovetskaia Etnografiia*, 1953.2, 23–33. The archaeological culture known as Zarubintsy (named after the eponymous site near Kaniv, region of Cherkasy, in Ukraine) spread in the Middle Dnieper region during the first two centuries AD. In Ukraine and in Russia, it has long been viewed as the culture of the 'prehistoric Slavs'. See V. N. Danilenko, 'Slavianskie pamiatniki I tysiacheletiia n. e. v baseine Dnepra', *Kratkie soobshcheniia Instituta Arkheologii Akademii Nauk SSSR*, 4 (1955), 27–29; Evgenii A. Goriunov, *Rannie etapy istorii slavian Dneprovskogo Levoberezh'ia* (Leningrad, 1981); E. V. Maksimov, 'Etnokul'turna sytuatsyia na Ukraini v I tys. n. e. (za arkheologichnymy materialamy)', in *Problemy pokhodzheniia ta istorichnogo rozvytky slov'ian: Zbirnyk naukovykh statey prysviachenyy 100-richchiu z dnia narodzhennia Viktora Platonovycha Petrova*, ed. by Volodymyr D. Baran, Rostislav V. Terpilovs'kyi, and N. S. Abashina (Kiev, 1997), pp. 26–35.

[33] Mykhailo Iu. Braychevs'kyi, 'Periodyzatsyia istorychnoho rozvytku skhidnoi Evropi v I tis. n. e.', *Arkheolohiia*, 1994.3, 13–18 (pp. 15–16). For the 'Antian Empire', see also Mykhailo Iu. Braychevs'kyi, 'Ants'ka problema v konteksti vizantiyskoi istorii', *Arkheolohiia*, 1991.2, 122–33; and 'Problema antiv', *Ukrains'kyi istoryk*, 34 (1997), 56–60.

[34] Valentin V. Sedov, 'Slaviane srednego Podneprov'ia (po dannym paleoantropologii)', *Sovetskaia Etnografiia*, 1974.1, 16–31 (pp. 21, 27–28, and 31); Valentin V. Sedov, 'Anty', in *Problemy sovetskoi arkheologii*, ed. by V. V. Kropotkin (Moscow, 1978), 164–73 (p. 173); Valentin V. Sedov, 'Slaviane i irantsy v drevnosti, istoriia, kul'tura, etnografiia i fol'klor slavianskikh narodov', in *VIII Mezhdunarodnyi săezd slavistov, Zagreb-Ljubljana, sentiabr' 1978 g.* (Moscow, 1978), pp. 227–40; Valentin V. Sedov, *Vostochnye slaviane v VI–XIII vv.* (Moscow, 1982), p. 28; Valentin V. Sedov, 'Anty', in *Etnosotsial'naia i politicheskaia struktura rannefeodal'nykh slavianskikh gosudarstv i*

established between the Slavs and speakers of Iranian languages within communities of the Chernyakhov culture. At that time, the strongest influence on the Slavs was that of the Alans, which was replaced in the early Middle Ages by that of the Turks.[35] Sedov distinguished between Antes on the Danube and Antes in the Middle Dniester and Middle Dnieper region. The Middle Dniester Antes were allies of Byzantium, an alliance which survived until 612.[36]

However, no other scholar in the former Soviet Union dedicated more time and energy to the study of the Antes than Oleg M. Prykhodniuk. Prykhodniuk initially insisted upon the idea that the Antes were Slavs, but then endorsed Braychevs'kyi's theory of an Antian large political entity (an 'empire' of sorts), while at the same time exploring the relations between the Antes and the steppe nomads.[37] Prykhodniuk also adopted Hrushevs'kyi's theory about the Antes being the ancestors of the present-day Ukrainians. According to him, the Polanian nobility was of Antian origin.[38] Among Ukrainian scholars in the diaspora, mention must be made of the Harvard-based, Polish-born linguist Bohdan Strumins'kyi, who regarded the Antes as related to the Goths in the northern Black

---

narodnostei, ed. by G. G. Litavrin (Moscow, 1987), pp. 16–22; Valentin V. Sedov, 'Anty', in *Ischeznuvshie narody: polovtsy, pechenegi, khazary, skify, anty, burtasy, avary, siunnu, tairona, chavin, mochika, maiia*, ed. by P. I. Puchkov and S. S. Neretina (Moscow, 1988), pp. 77–83.

[35] Valentin V. Sedov, *Slaviane* (Moscow, 2005), p. 193.

[36] Valentin V. Sedov, *Drevnorusskaia narodnost': Istoriko-arkheologicheskoe issledovanie* (Moscow, 1999), pp. 36–37.

[37] Slavic Antes: Oleg M. Prykhodniuk, 'K voprosu o prisutstvii antov v Karpato-Dunaiskikh zemliakh', in *Slaviane na Dnestre i Dunae: Sbornik nauchnykh trudov*, ed. by V. D. Baran, R. V. Terpilovs'kyi, and A. T. Smilenko (Kiev, 1983), pp. 180–91; Oleg M. Prykhodniuk, 'Anty i Pen'kovskaia kul'tura', in *Drevnie slaviane i Kievskaia Rus'*, ed. by P. P. Tolochko (Kiev, 1989), pp. 58–69. Antian 'Empire': Oleg M. Prykhodniuk, 'Anty ta Vizantyia', *Arkheolohiia*, 1991.2, 133–41; Oleg M. Prykhodniuk, *Stepove naselennia Ukrainy ta skhidni slov'iany: druga polovyna I tys. n.e.* (Kiev, 2001), pp. 49–60. Antes and nomads: Oleg M. Prykhodniuk, 'Anty ta avary', in *Problemy pokhodzhennia ta istorychnogo rozvytku slov'ian*, ed. by Baran, Terpilovs'kyi, and Abashina, pp. 142–48; Oleg M. Prykhodniuk, 'Arkheologicheskie dannye o sviazakh slavian v stepnogo naseleniia v VII–VIII vv.', *Materialy po arkheologii, istorii i etnografii Tavrii*, 5 (1996), 114–25 and 518–24; Oleg M. Prykhodniuk, 'Voenno-politicheskii soiuz antov i tiurkskii mir (po dannym istoricheskikh i arkheologicheskikh istochnikov)', *Materialy po arkheologii, istorii i etnografii Tavrii*, 7 (2000), 134–67.

[38] Oleg M. Prykhodniuk, 'Anti, sklavini ta venedi v svitli istorichnikh ta arkheolohichnykh dzherel', in *Etnogenez ta rannia istoriia Slov'ian: novi naukovi kontseptsii na zlami tisiacholit'*, ed. by V. D. Baran (L'viv, 2001), pp. 47–58 (p. 55).

Sea region (i.e. the ancestors of the Crimean Goths), 'rather than Slavs, let alone Eastern Slavs'.[39]

Most recently, Oleg B. Bubenok, a Ukrainian scholar specializing in Iranian studies, returned to the idea of a Slavic-Iranian alliance in the region to the northeast from the Lower Danube.[40] According to him, the ethnic name *Anti* derives from the Greek word *nautai*, which means 'watermen, sailors, wanderers', and as a result of a scribal misspelling appeared as *Antes* in Jordanes work. In Bubenok's opinion, Jordanes and Byzantine historians used the term *Antai*, for which no explanation is provided, as a common name for the territory settled by Slavs and Iranian-speaking people.[41]

Outside Ukraine, however, Vernadsky's ideas had a strong influence on the Romanian historian George I. Brătianu, and, more recently, on the Moldovan archaeologist Igor Corman.[42] According to Corman, the Antes were an alliance of several tribes led by Alans at a time the Goths acted as proxies for Attila within the region between the Carpathian Mountains and the Dniester River. After the fall of the Hunnic Empire and the migration of the Ostrogoths, the Antes remained sole rulers of that region, into which the Sclavenes began to infiltrate in the early 500s. Ruling over the Antes was an elite of Iranian origin: much like Vernadsky, Corman insisted upon the identity — linguistic and otherwise — between Antes and Alans (As).[43] An equally strong influence of Vernadsky's ideas may be detected

---

[39] Bohdan Strumins'kyj, 'Were the Antes Eastern Slavs?', *Harvard Ukrainian Studies*, 3–4 (1979), 786–96 (p. 795).

[40] Oleg B. Bubenok, 'Anti: slov'iany chi irantsi', *Skhidnii svit*, 2005.2, 9–33; and *Alani-Asi u skladi seredn'ovichnikh etnopolitichnikh ob'iednan' evraziis'koho stepu* (Kiev, 2006), pp. 22–23.

[41] Bubenok, *Alani-Asi*, p. 22.

[42] George I. Brătianu, *Marea Neagră: De la origini pînă la cucerirea otomană*, I (Bucharest, 1988), p. 253; Igor Corman, 'Migrațiile din teritoriul dintre Carpați și Nistru în sec. V–VII: Problema "anților"', *Revista Arheologică*, 1 (1993), 93–100 (republished in *Spațiul nord-est carpatic în mileniul întunecat*, ed. by V. Spinei (Iași, 1997), pp. 67–77).

[43] Igor Corman, 'L'Origine ethnique des Antes fondée sur les découvertes archéologiques dans l'espace d'entre Prout et Dniester', *Arheologia Moldovei*, 19 (1996), 169–89; Igor Corman, *Contribuții la istoria spațiului pruto-nistrian în epoca Evului Mediu timpuriu* (Chișinău, 1998), pp. 100–13. For a critical assessment of Corman's ideas, see Florin Curta's review of his book in *Archaeologia Bulgarica*, 4 (2000), 99–101. Corman's revival of Vernadsky's ideas is not politically innocent. It is in fact a response to claims by Russian-speaking archaeologists in Moldova that the earliest inhabitants of Moldova were Slavic-speaking Antes, not the Romance-speaking ancestors of Moldovans (Romanians). Corman's ideas were met with enthusiasm in certain circles in Romania; see Dan Gh. Teodor, 'Unele considerații privind originea și cultura anților', *Arheologia Moldovei*, 16 (1993), 205–13.

in Robert Werner's thorough analysis of the historical and linguistic sources pertaining to the Antes. According to him, there were traces of Antes among large groups of Iranian, Altaic, and Mongolian nomads. Werner believed that by the sixth century Slavic and Iranian elements in the southern parts of present-day Ukraine and Russia formed a new political and ethnic identity known as Antes, a name of Alanic origin.[44]

Worth mentioning in this context is also the tendency among Bulgarian archaeologists and historians to identify the earliest Slavs in the northern Balkans as Antes. Stefka Angelova classified the pottery found in sunken-featured buildings excavated in northern Bulgaria as Pen'kivka and attributed that to the first Slavs who crossed the Danube to settle in the Balkans.[45] In a later article published together with Rumiana Koleva, Angelova analysed both the remains of handmade pottery and the so-called 'Slavic' fibulae from Bulgaria and northern Dobrudja to conclude that most such finds come from early Byzantine fortified sites in the area. Nonetheless, she attributed all of them to the Pen'kivka culture, that is, to the Antes, who came to Dobrudja and northern Bulgaria in two waves, during the 530s and 630s, respectively.[46] Such views go back in fact to those espoused by Zhivka Văzharova in the 1960s, when it was fashionable to maintain that the Slavs had come to Bulgaria in the sixth century.[47] In her monograph of the Garvan settlement site near Silistra, Văzharova attributed the first occupation phase to Slavic settlers and associated the ceramic assemblages found on the site with the sixth-century Prague and Pen'kivka cultures.[48]

---

[44] Robert Werner, 'Zur Herkunft der Anten: Ein ethnisches und soziales Problem der Spätantike', *Kölner historische Abhandlungen*, 28 (1980), 573–95 (p. 590).

[45] Stefka Angelova, 'Po văprosa za rannoslavianskata kultura na iug i na sever ot Dunav prez VI–VII v.', *Arkheologiia*, 12 (1970), 1–12.

[46] Stefka Angelova and Rumiana Koleva, 'Arkheologicheski danni za rannoto slaviansko zaselvane v Bălgariia', *Godishnik na Sofiiskiia Universitet 'Sv. Kliment Okridski': Istoricheski fakultet – spetsialnost arkheologiia*, 2 (1995), 159–85. See also Stefka Angelova and Rumiana Koleva, 'Za niakoi osobenosti na rannoslavianskata keramika ot severozapadna Bălgariia', in *Prinosi kăm bălgarskata arkheologiia: Dekemvriiski dni na bălgarskata arkheologiia 'Prof. dr. Stancho Vaklinov'*, ed. by D. Ovcharov and I. Shtereva, I (Sofia, 1992), pp. 173–79.

[47] Zhivka Văzharova, 'Slavianite na iug ot Dunava (po arkheologicheski danni)', *Arkheologiia*, 6 (1964), 23–33.

[48] Zhivka Văzharova, *Srednovekovnoto selishte s. Garvan, silistrenski okrăg VI–XI v.* (Sofia, 1986), p. 70.

Antes in the Historical Sources: Selected Problems

The first to mention the Antes is Jordanes, who wrote in the mid-sixth century and was perhaps of Gothic or Alan origin.[49] According to Jordanes, the Antes were an offshoot of the ancient Venethi, but he also lists the Venethi alongside Antes and Sclavenes.[50] The Antes are described as living between the rivers Dniester and Dnieper, in close proximity to the Sclavenes, whose abode Jordanes describes as extending 'from the city of Noviodunum and the lake Mursianus to the Danaster, and northward as far as the Vistula'.[51] Judging from Jordanes's description, it seems that he thought of Antes as inhabiting the territories to the north from the nomads of the steppe lands in the northern Black Sea region. However, he also mentions that the Antes were attacked by the Goths at a point in time which may be placed in the late fourth century, perhaps the 370s.[52] Vinitharius killed Boz, the king of the Antes, together with his sons and seventy noblemen.[53] Much has been made of

[49] Andrew Kalmykow, 'Iranians and Slavs in South Russia', *Journal of the American Oriental Society*, 45 (1925), 68–71 (p. 68): 'Iornandes [*sic*!] was an Iranian himself from the Alan tribe, one of the chief division of the Sarmatae'. However, Jordanes himself claimed to be of Gothic descent (*Getica*, 265 and 315). See Lech A. Tyszkiewicz, *Słowianie w historiografii antycznej do połowy VI wieku* (Wrocław, 1990), pp. 132–33; Arne Søbe Christensen, *Cassiodorus, Jordanes, and the History of the Goths: Studies in a Migration Myth* (Copenhagen, 2002), pp. 84 and 123. Jordanes's assertion is viewed by some with suspicion. See Walter Goffart, *Barbarian Tides: The Migration Age and the Later Roman Empire* (Philadelphia, 2006), p. 70.

[50] The pair *Itites et Chimabes* mentioned by the Ravenna Geographer in the early 600s may well be a corrupted form of the pair *Antes et Vinedes* taken from Jordanes. See the Ravenna Geographer, *Cosmographia*, 1.12, ed. by J. Schnetz (Stuttgart, 1940). See also Marian Plezia, *Greckie i łacińskie źródła do najstarszych dziejów Słowian*, I (Poznań, 1952), p. 126; Zeuss, *Die Deutschen*, p. 668; Lujo Margetić, 'Etnogeneza Slavena', *Rad Hrvatske Akademije znanosti i umjetnosti*, 492 (2005), 89–143 (p. 102).

[51] Jordanes, *Getica*, 35; see also *Getica*, 30 and 119. For the identification and location of Lacus Mursianus, see Alexandru Madgearu, 'About Lacus Mursianus (Jordans, Getica, 30 and 35)', *Byzantinoslavica*, 57 (1997), 87–89. For the location of both Sclavenes and Antes on Jordanes's (imaginary) map, see Florin Curta, 'Hiding Behind a Piece of Tapestry: Jordanes and the Slavic Venethi', *Jahrbücher für Geschichte Osteuropas*, 47 (1999), 321–40 (pp. 324–26).

[52] Jordanes, *Getica*, 36. See Tyszkiewicz, *Słowianie w historiografii antycznej*, p. 147 with n. 115. According to Tyszkiewicz, the Antes must have been under Hunnic rule, which could explain why Balamber intervened on the side of the Antes and asked Gesimund for assistance. For the entire episode as a reworking of a story taken from Ammianus Marcellinus, see Curta, 'Hiding Behind a Piece of Tapestry', pp. 331–32.

[53] Jordanes, *Getica*, 246–48; Tyszkiewicz, *Słowianie w historiografii antycznej*, p. 147.

Boz's name. Some believed it to be of Slavic origin, derived from the word employed to refer to a deity. Šafařík suggested that the original name was Bože, while the Polish ethnologist Kazimierz Moszyński (1887–1959) insisted that the word for god (*bog*) was of Iranian origin and initially meant 'master' or 'chief'. The idea that the name was of Slavic origin was also advocated by Stanisław Raspond, but both Bohdan Struminskij and Niko Županić argued against it and claimed instead that the name was either Germanic or a word from the language of the Huns.[54] The fact that seventy noblemen were executed together with King Boz was also viewed as an indication of a peculiarly Antian social organization.[55] Henryk Łowmiański saw Boz as the leader of a large tribal unit; to him, that was the first Slavic state in history.[56] By contrast, Lech A. Tyszkiewicz believed that the *primates* of the Antes mentioned by Jordanes were chiefs of rather small tribes.[57]

The Antes are also mentioned by Jordanes's contemporary, Procopius of Caesarea.[58] Procopius had firsthand information about the Antes, most likely from mercenaries recruited for Belisarius's troops in Italy or from Antian soldiers in Constantinople.[59] Much like Jordanes, Procopius mentions the Antes together with the Sclavenes and even claims that they were both called Spori (Σπόροι) in ancient times. Unlike Jordanes, however, Procopius places the Antes within the

---

[54] Stanisław Raspond, 'Słowiańskie imiona w źródłach antycznych', *Lingua Posnaniensis*, 12–13 (1968), 99–117 (p. 102); Strumins'kyj, 'Were the Antes Eastern Slavs?', p. 789; Županić, 'Boz rex Antorum', p. 115. All efforts to etymologize King Boz's name assume that that (Boz) was truly his name. However, several manuscripts of Jordanes's *Getica* give slightly different spellings (*box* or even *booz*), which leaves room for many other possible interpretations.

[55] Tyszkiewicz, *Słowianie w historiografii antycznej*, p. 160.

[56] Henryk Łowmiański, *Podstawy gospodarcze formowania się państw słowiańskich* (Warsaw, 1953), p. 13.

[57] Tyszkiewicz, *Słowianie w historiografii antycznej*, p. 161.

[58] Procopius of Caesarea, *Wars*, 5.27.2, 7.14, 7.22, 7.40, and 8.4.8; *Secret History*, 11.11, 18.20, and 23.6. For a detailed analysis of those passages, see Lech A. Tyszkiewicz, *Słowianie w historiografii wczesnego średniowiecza od połowy VI do połowy VII wieku* (Wrocław, 1994), pp. 7–33; Florin Curta, *The Making of the Slavs: History and Archaeology of the Lower Danube Region, ca. 500–700* (Cambridge, 2001), pp. 36–43; Margetić, 'Etnogeneza Slavena', pp. 95–97.

[59] Robert Benedicty, 'Prokopios' Berichte über die slavische Vorzeit: Beiträge zur historiographischen Methode dés Prokopios von Kaisareia', *Jarbuch der österreichischen byzantinischen Gesellschaft*, 14 (1965), 51–78 (p. 73); Henryk Łowmiański, *Religia Słowian i jej upadek (w VI–XII w.)* (Warsaw, 1979), p. 85; Franziska E. Schlosser, 'The Slavs in Sixth-Century Byzantine Sources', *Byzantinoslavica*, 61 (2003), 75–82 (p. 76).

lands to the north from the region occupied by the Utigurs.[60] Lech A. Tyszkiewicz believed that the imprecise location of the Antes in Procopius's account may be seen as an indication that their abodes were widely known in Constantinople, but others have insisted on Procopius's ignorance of the geography of the region north of the Lower Danube and the Black Sea.[61] He was more concerned with the Slavic raids into the Balkan provinces of the empire, but seems to have envisioned the Antes as living somewhere to the north-east from the Lower Danube. The Antes were clearly not too far from the Danube frontier of the empire, for some of them were recruited for the Byzantine troops, which Emperor Justinian sent against the Ostrogoths in Italy. Antian soldiers are mentioned, together with Bulgars and Sclavenes, in Belisarius's troops of 536/37. Three hundred of them were instrumental in defeating the Gothic warriors led by Totila. Equally revealing for Procopius's familiarity with things Antian is his story of the 'phoney Chilbudius', an Antian POW impersonating the then deceased *magister militum per Thraciam*, Chilbudius.[62]

Agathias of Myrina did not write about the Antes as a whole. However, he mentioned an officer of Antian origin named Dabragezas, who in 554 was a commander of Roman troops on the eastern front, against the Persians. Dabragezas also commanded the Roman fleet in Crimea, which besieged Phasis in 555.[63] By contrast, Menander the Guardsman knew much about the conflict between Antes and Avars.[64] The exact date of their military confrontation and the nature of the relations between Antes and Avars after the Avar victory are two issues still debated. According to Wolfgang Fritze, the episode must be placed at some point

---

[60] Procopius of Caesarea, *Wars*, 8.4.8. For Procopius's description of the Sclavenes and the Antes as part of a broader polemic with Jordanes on the issue of barbarians in general, see Curta, 'Hiding Behind a Piece of Tapestry', pp. 326–27.

[61] Tyszkiewicz, *Słowianie w historiografii wczesnego*, p. 11; Florin Curta, 'The North-western Region of the Black Sea During the 6th and Early 7th Century AD', *Ancient West & East*, 7 (2008), 149–85 (pp. 149–51).

[62] For barbarian mercenaries in Italy, see J. L. Teall, 'The Barbarians in Justinian's Army', *Speculum*, 40 (1965) 294–322. For the story of the 'phoney Chilbudius', see Gennadii G. Litavrin, 'O dvukh Khilbudiakh Prokopiia Kesariiskogo', *Vizantiiskii Vremennik*, 47 (1986), 24–30.

[63] Agathias of Myrina, *History*, 3.6.9, 3.7.2, and 3.21.6, ed. by R. Keydell (Berlin, 1967). For historical commentary, see Tyszkiewicz, *Słowianie w historiografii wczesnego*, pp. 34–35; Curta, *Making of the Slavs*, p. 83 with n. 35; Margetić, 'Etnogeneza Slavena', p. 98.

[64] Menander the Guardsman, *fr.* 6, ed. and trans. by R. Blockley (Liverpool, 1985). For historical commentary, see Tyszkiewicz, *Słowianie w historiografii wczesnego*, pp. 35–49.

between 558 and 568, but Tibor Živković has recently proposed a date around 562.[65] It is interesting to note the participation in this conflict of an unknown Cutrigur (chieftain?), who apparently had good knowledge of the internal strife in the Antian society and advised the qagan of the Avar to kill the envoys of the Antes and attack their lands. The Cutrigur (chieftain) was so well informed about the Antes most likely because before the Avar onslaught, the Cutrigurs and the Antes lived side by side. But what was the status of the Antes after being defeated by the Avars? Did they remain independent or were they subject to the Avars? Tibor Živković pointed out the fact that the Antes may have felt protected by their alliance with Justinian and, as a consequence, even though they were defeated by the Avars, they appear as independent in subsequent events in the Lower Danube region.[66] The episode is also interesting for the details it offers on the Antian society. According to Menander the Guardsman, the leaders of the Antes decided to send to the Avars an envoy named Mezamer, who was 'the son of Idariz and brother of Kelagast'. Mezamer was apparently 'the most powerful of all amongst the Antes'.[67]

The last author to write about the Antes is Theophylact Simocatta. According to him, in 602 Avar troops under the command of Apsich moved against the Antes, but the outcome of the expedition is not known. Consequently, Gennadii Litavrin maintained that only a group of Antes was defeated and destroyed by the Avars. That as late as 612 the imperial title still included the epithet *Anticus* is an indication (so Litavrin) that the Antes were still the allies of the empire. However, as Florin Curta has shown, imperial epithets such as *Anticus* (a title first attested

[65] Wolfgang H. Fritze, 'Die Bedeutung der Avaren für die slavische Ausdehnungsbewegung im frühen Mittelalter', *Zeitschrift für Ostforschung*, 28 (1979), 498–545 (p. 519); Tibor Živković, 'Prilog hronologij avarsko-slovenskih odnosa 559–578. godine', *Istorijski časopis*, 42–43 (1997), 227–36 (English version in Tibor Živković, *Forging Unity: The South Slavs Between East and West: 550–1150* (Belgrade, 2008), pp. 7–16 (p. 10)).

[66] Živković, *Forging Unity*, p. 10.

[67] Menander the Guardsman, *fr.* 3. Too much has been made of the names of Mezamer, Idariz, and Kelagast, which some viewed as Slavic, others as Germanic, or Iranian. See Raspond, 'Słowiańskie imiona', pp. 106–07; V. Chaloupecký, 'Considerations sur Samon, le premier roi de Slaves', *Byzantinoslavica*, 11 (1950), 223–39 (p. 230); Wincenty Swoboda, 'Mezamir', in *Słownik starożytności słowiańskich*, ed. by Władysław Kowalenko, Gerard Labuda, and Zdzisław Stieber, III (Wrocław, 1967), pp. 202–03 (p. 202); Strumins'kyj, 'Were the Antes Eastern Slavs?', p. 793; Marian Plezia, 'Idaridzios', in *Słownik starożytności słowiańskich*, ed. by Władysław Kowalenko, Gerard Labuda, and Tadeusz Lehr-Spławiński, II (Wrocław, 1964), p. 239.

under Emperor Justinian) referred to imperial victories over barbarians, not to whatever temporary alliance the Romans may have established with any of them.[68]

An equally later source, the prologue to the 643 Edict of the Lombard king Rothari known as *Origo gentis Langobardorum*, contains a rather vague piece of information, which some scholars believe may be associated with the Antes. According to the *Origo*, at the beginning of their 'national' history, the Lombards took possession of a number of territories, such as Anthaib, Bainaib, and Burgundaib. The pair Anthaib and Banthaib also appears in Paul the Deacon's *History of the Lombards*, which used *Origo* as a source.[69] Exactly what was meant by Anthaib and Banthaib, or even whether those were truly place names, remains unknown. Nineteenth-century scholars, however, claimed that Anthaib was the 'land of the Antes', although no other source mentions any contacts between Antes and Lombards.[70]

The Archaeology of the Antes

Most scholars currently attribute the Pen'kivka culture to the Antes mentioned by historical sources (Figures 3.1–2).[71] The results of the archaeological excavations at Pen'kivka near Svitlovods'ke and on the Tiasmin River have immediately been compared to the so-called Prague culture and the two archaeological cultures promptly attributed to Antes and Sclavenes, respectively. The origin of the Pen'kivka culture is still a matter of much debate, with two interpretations most

---

[68] Gennadii G. Litravin, *Vizantiia i slaviane (sbornik statei)* (St Petersburg, 1999), pp. 574–77; Curta, *Making of the Slavs*, p. 105 with n. 93. Csaba Farkas, 'Megyegyzések a steppe 603 körüli történetének forrásaihoz', in *A Kárpát-medence és a steppe*, ed. by Alfréd Márton (Budapest, 2001), pp. 61–65 (pp. 61–62) redates the episode to 603 and associates the Avar concern with destroying the Antes with the rise of Great Bulgaria in the steppe lands north of the Black Sea.

[69] *Origo gentis Langobardum*, 2, in *Monumenta Germaniae Historica, Scriptores rerum Langobardicarum et Italicarum, saec. VI–IX*, ed. by G. Waitz (Hannover, 1878); Paul the Deacon, *History of the Lombards*, 1.21, ed. by G. Waitz (Hannover, 1878).

[70] Zeuss, *Die Deutschen*, p. 472; Šafařík, *Slovanské starožitnosti*, p. 424; Niederle, *Manuel*, p. 190.

[71] F. Conte, *Les Slaves: aux origines des civilisations d'Europe centrale et orientale* (Paris, 1986), p. 163; Dan Gh. Teodor, 'Slavii la nordul Dunării de Jos în secolele VI–VII d. H.', *Arheologia Moldovei*, 17 (1994), 223–51 (p. 230); Kazimierz Godłowski, *Pierwotne siedziby Słowian* (Cracow, 2000), p. 114; Michel Kazanski, 'La Zone forestière de la Russie et l'Europe centrale à la fin de l'époque des grandes migrations', in *Die spätromische Kaiserzeit und die frühe Völkerwanderungszeit im Mittel- und Osteuropa*, ed. by Magdalena Mączyńska and Tadeusz Grabarczyk (Łódź, 2000), pp. 406–59 (p. 409 with n. 3); Prykhodniuk, *Stepove naselennia*, p. 49.

Figure 3.1. The location of the Antes on a map of Central and Eastern Europe, based on the written sources pertaining to the second half of the sixth century. After Michał Parczewski, 'Beginnings of the Slavs' Culture', in *Origins of Central Europe*, ed. by Przemysław Urbańczyk (Warsaw, 1997), pp. 75–90 with fig. 5, modified.

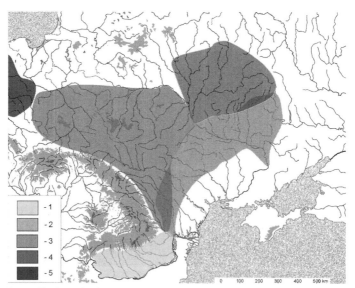

Figure 3.2. The Pen'kivka and other contemporary archaeological cultures in Central and Eastern Europe (late sixth to early seventh centuries): (1) Ipoteşti-Cândeşti culture; (2) Pen'kivka culture; (3) Prague culture; (4) Kolochin culture; (5) Dziedzice culture. After Prykhodniuk, *Pen'kovskaia kul'tura*, figs 1 and 2; Parczewski, 'Beginnings of the Slavs' Culture', fig. 4; Godłowski, *Pierwotne siedziby Słowian*, fig. 15, modified.

clearly articulated. According to one of them, the Pen'kivka culture grew organically out of the Chernyakhov culture in the Middle Dnieper area and in parts of the forest-steppe region between the Dnieper and the Dniester rivers.[72] Advocates of the other interpretation argue instead that the Pen'kivka culture is simply a continuation of the Kiev culture.[73] The current tendency is to accept both a Chernyakhov and a Kiev foundation for the Pen'kivka culture, but some now insist upon the role of the nomads in both cases.[74] Most scholars have by now rejected the idea of the German archaeologist Joachim Werner, according to which the Pen'kivka culture originated in the Upper Dnieper region within a Tushemlia-Kolochin milieu.[75]

Most assemblages assigned to the Pen'kivka culture have been found in Left-Bank Ukraine, especially along the rivers Seim, Sula, and Psel to the north-east and the Donets and the Oril' to the south-east. A series of settlement sites have been found deep into the steppe zone around the city of Zaporizhzhia, while the westernmost expansion of the Pen'kivka culture is believed to have covered the

[72] Valentin V. Sedov, *Slaviane verkhnego Podneprov'ia i Podvin'ia* (Moscow, 1970), pp. 68–69; Alla T. Smilenko, *Slov'iany ta ikh susidy v stepovomu Podniprov'i (II–XIII st.)* (Kiev, 1975), p. 65; Rusanova, *Slavianskie drevnosti*, pp. 106–12, Valentin V. Sedov, *Slaviane v drevnosti* (Moscow, 1994), p. 316.

[73] Oleg M. Prykhodniuk, *Arkheologichni pam'iatky seredn'ogo Prydniprov'ia VI–IX st. n. e.* (Kiev, 1980), pp. 113–22; Evgenii A. Goriunov, *Rannie etapy istorii slavian*, p. 59; Rostislav V. Terpilovs'kyi, 'Do problemy pokhodzhennia rann'oseredn'ovichnykh kul'tur Podniprov'ia', in *Problemy pokhodzhennia ta istorychnogo rozvytku slov'ian.*, ed. by Baran, Terpilovs'kyi, and Abashina, pp. 111–18 (pp. 114–15). The archaeological culture known as Kiev developed at the same time as the Sântana de Mureş-Chernyakhov culture (third to fifth century) in south-western Ukraine. For details, see Evgenii V. Maksimov and Rostislav V. Terpilovs'kyi, 'Kievskaia kul'tura', in *Slaviane i ikh sosedi v konce I tysiacheletiia do n.e.-pervoi poloviny I tysiacheletiia n.e.*, ed. by I. P. Rusanova and E. A. Symonovich (Moscow, 1993), pp. 106–22; Rostislav V. Terpilovs'kyi, 'Nasledie kievskoi kul'tury v V–VI vv.', in *Archeologia o początkach Słowian: Materiały z konferencji, Kraków, 19–21 listopada 2001*, ed. by Piotr Kaczanowski and Michał Parczewski (Cracow, 2005), pp. 387–402.

[74] Igor O. Gavritukhin and A. M. Oblomskii, *Gaponovskii klad i ego kul'turno-istoricheskii kontekst* (Moscow, 1996), pp. 116–19; Mark Shchukin, 'O trekh putiakh arkheologicheskogo poiska predkov ranneistoricheskikh slavian: Perspektivy tret'ego puti', *Arkheologicheskii sbornik Gosudarstvennogo Ermitazha*, 28 (1987), 103–18 (p. 115).

[75] Joachim Werner, 'Zur Herkunft und Ausbreitung der Anten und Sklawenen', in *Actes du VIIIᵉ Congrès international des sciences préhistoriques et protohistoriques: Beograd, 9–15 septembre 1971*, ed. by Grga Novak, I (Belgrade, 1971), pp. 243–52; Joachim Werner, 'K proiskhozhdeniiu i raspostraneniiu antov i sklavinov', *Sovetskaia Arkheologiia*, 1972.4, 102–15.

lower and middle course of the Prut and Dniester rivers in present-day Moldova.[76] Archaeologists claim to have identified zones of contact with the Kolochin culture to the north, the Prague culture to the west, and the nomads to the south.[77] However, it is important to note that most assemblages regarded as typical for all those cultures have in fact been found in 'zones of contact'. For example, the large cemetery excavated at Sărata-Monteoru in south-eastern Romania is in fact located on the border between the Prague and the Pen'kivka culture, or as Chavdar Bonev put it, between the Sclavenes and the Antes.[78] This is also true for the most spectacular find of craftsman tools (including moulds for the production of dress accessories) from the Bernashivka settlement, near Sokiryany (region of Chernivtsi) in south-western Ukraine.[79]

Distinguishing between Pen'kivka- and Prague-type pottery from assemblages found south of the Danube, in the northern Balkans, is very difficult. Handmade pottery hastily attributed to both cultures has been found on early Byzantine fortified sites and dated to the late sixth or early seventh century.[80] This has been

---

[76] Oleg M. Prykhodniuk, 'Pen'kovskaia kul'tura', in *Etnokul'turnaia karta territorii Ukrainskoi SSR v I tys.*, ed. by V. D. Baran, R. V. Terpilovs'kyi, and E. V. Maksimov (Kiev, 1985), pp. 85–93 (p. 85); Oleg M. Prykhodniuk, *Pen'kovskaia kul'tura: kul'turno-khronologicheskii aspekt issledovaniia* (Voronezh, 1998), pp. 21 and 78 fig. 1.

[77] Prykhodniuk, *Pen'kovskaia kul'tura*, p. 21.

[78] Chavdar Bonev, 'La Nécropole slave des VIᵉ–VIIᵉ siècles de Sărata Monteoru (Roumanie)', *Études Balkaniques*, 3–4 (1995), 183–95 (pp. 188–89).

[79] Ion S. Vynokur, 'Sotsial'no-ekonomichnyi rozvytok rann'oseredn'ovichnikh skhidnikh slov'ian u svitli novikh arkheologychnikh danikh', in *Istoriia Rusi-Ukrainy: Istoryko-arkheologichnii zbirnyk*, ed. by A. P. Motsia, Ia E. Borovs'kyi, and A. P. Tomashevs'kyi (Kiev, 1998), pp. 20–26 (p. 24).

[80] For the problems of classifying the early medieval pottery of Eastern Europe as Slavic, see Florin Curta, 'The Prague Type: A Critical Approach to Pottery Classification', *Archaeologia Bulgarica*, 5 (2001), 73–106; Florin Curta, 'Pots, Slavs, and "Imagined Communities": Slavic Archaeology and the History of the Early Slavs', *European Journal of Archaeology*, 4 (2001), 367–84. For 'Slavic' pottery in Dobrudja, see Maria Comșa, 'Contribution la question de la pénétration des Slaves au sud du Danube durant les VIᵉ–VIIᵉ siècles d'après quelques données archéologiques de Dobroudja', in *I. Międzynarodowy kongres archeologii słowiańskej: Warszawa 14–18 IX 1965*, ed. by Witold Hensel (Wrocław, 1970), pp. 320–30 (pp. 322–30); Aurelian Petre, 'Contribuția culturii romano-bizantine din secolele VI–VII e.n. la geneza culturii feudale timpurii din spațiul balcano-ponto-danubian', in *2050 de ani de la făurirea de către Burebista a primului stat independent și centralizat al geto-dacilor* (Bucharest, 1980), pp. 193–214; Maria Comșa, 'La Province de la Scythie Mineure (Dobroudja) et les Slaves pendant les VI–VII ss.', in *Istoriia i kul'tura drevnikh i srednevekovykh slavian*, ed. by Valentin V. Sedov (Moscow, 1999), pp. 301–13.

interpreted as 'the earliest evidence of a Slavic presence in the strongholds along the Danube and the main roads leading to Constantinople and Thessalonica', although there is no agreement as to whether the Slavs in question were members of the garrisons stationed in forts, those attacking and sacking the same forts, or the inhabitants of settlements subsequently established near the ruins of the destroyed forts.[81] In fact, the picture is far from being that simple. Morphologically, some of the pottery forms found on sites in Dobrudja are without any doubt similar to those from Pen'kivka assemblages. On the other hand, excavations in Capidava have produced pottery remains, the forms of which are typical for burial assemblages attributed to the nomadic horsemen of the steppe lands north of the Black Sea.[82] Such characteristic forms of decoration as finger impressions on the rim are known from assemblages not just of the Pen'kivka culture, but also from the earliest stages of the slightly later Volyntsevo culture.[83]

According to Oleg Prykhodniuk, settlement sites of the earlier phase of the Pen'kivka culture produced sunken-featured buildings of square plan, each one of them with only one posthole. Buildings in later settlement sites each have multiple

[81] Rumiana Koleva, 'Slavic Settlement on the Territory of Bulgaria', in *Actes du XII-e Congrès international des sciences préhistoriques et protohistoriques, Bratislava, 1–7 septembre 1991*, ed. by J. Pavuj (Bratislava, 1993), pp. 17–19 (p. 17). For Slavs as soldiers in the garrison, see Zofia Kurnatowska, 'Słowianie Południowi', in *Wędrówka i etnogeneza w starożytności i średniowieczu*, ed. by Maciej Salamon and Jerzy Strzelczyk (Cracow, 2004), pp. 203–18 (p. 205). Slavs as aggressors: Comşa, 'La Province', p. 303. Slavic settlers near the ruins of destroyed forts: Petre Diaconu, 'Autour de la pénétration des Slaves au sud du Danube', in *Rapports du III-e Congrès international d'archéologie slave, Bratislava 7–14 septembre 1975*, ed. by Bohuslav Chropovský (Bratislava, 1979), pp. 165–69.

[82] Ioan C. Opriş, *Ceramica romană târzie şi paleobizantină de la Capidava în contextul descoperirilor de la Dunărea de Jos, sec. IV–VI p.Chr.* (Bucharest, 2003), figs 27.252a, 39.256–257a, and 40.260a–262; M. V. Liubichev, 'Pen'kivs'ka kul'tura: shche raz pro terytoriiu ta etnichnu prynalezhnist", in *Etnokul'turni protsesy v Pivdenno-Skhidniy Evropi v I tysiacholitti n.e. Zbirnyk naukovykh prats'*, ed. by R. V. Terpilovs'kyi, N. S. Abashina, L. E. Skiba, and V. I. Ivanovs'kyi (Kiev, 1999), pp. 123–31 (p. 127 fig. 2.1–3 and 7–8).

[83] Prykhodniuk, 'Pen'kovskaia kul'tura', p. 120 with fig. 22.22–27. For the chronology of the Volyntsevo culture, see O. V. Sukhobokov, 'K khronologii slavianskikh pamiatnikov Dneprovskogo Levoberezh'ia poslednei chetverti I tys.', in *Istoriia Rusi-Ukrainy*, ed. by Motsia, Borovs'kyi, and Tomashevs'kyi, pp. 49–57; Iurii Iu. Shevchenko, 'K khronologii materialov volyntsevskogo tipa v Nizov'iakh Desny', in *Seminar 'Iuvelirnoe iskusstvo i material'naia kul'tura': Tezisy dokladov uchastnikov sed'mogo kollokviuma, 8–14 aprelia 1999 goda*, ed. by N. A. Zakharova (St Petersburg, 2000), pp. 103–06.

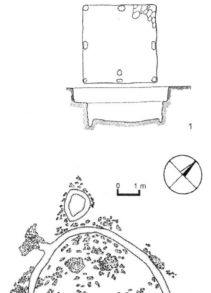

Figure 3.3. Examples of sunken-featured (1) and circular, tent-like buildings found in the settlements of the Pen'kivka culture: (1) Pen'kivka-Lug 1, house 1; (2) Stetsivka, house 8. After Berezovets', 'Poseleniia ulichei', fig. 28.5; and Petrov, 'Stetsovka, poselenie tret'ei cherverti I tysiacheletiia n.e.', fig. 3.3.

postholes, as well as heating facilities, either hearths or ovens (Figure 3.3.1).[84] Villages of Pen'kivka communities occasionally included buildings of circular plan (and possible tent-like appearance), which archaeologists believe to be typical for the nomadic camp sites and consequently, but wrongly, call yurts (Figure 3.3.2).[85]

---

[84] Prykhodniuk, *Pen'kovskaia kul'tura*, pp. 24–25 and 86–88 with figs 12–16; Andrei Măgureanu and Bartłomiej Szymon Szmoniewski, 'Domestic Dwellings in Moldavia and Wallachia in the Initial Phases of the Early Middle Ages', *Acta Archaeologica Carpathica*, 38 (2003), 111–36 (pp. 114–20 with fig. 4).

[85] Sedov, 'Anty', pp. 166 and 168; Prykhodniuk, *Pen'kovskaia kul'tura*, pp. 26–27 and 89 with fig. 17. For tent-like dwellings on camp sites associated with the medieval nomads, see L. G. Nechaeva, 'O zhilishche kochevnikov iuga Vostochnoi Evropy v zheleznom veke (I tys. do n.e.-pervaia polovina II tys. n.e.)', in *Drevnee zhilishche narodov vostochnoi Evropy*, ed. by M. G.

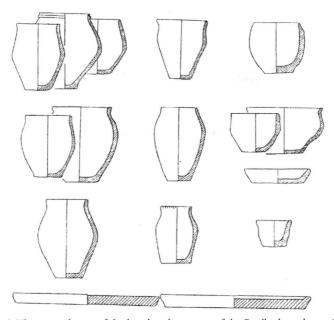

Figure 3.4. The main shapes of the handmade pottery of the Pen'kivka culture. After
Prykhodniuk, *Pen'kovskaia kul'tura*, fig. 21.

The handmade pottery found on Pen'kivka sites is quite simple, with some pots of
a typically barrel-like shape (Figure 3.4).[86] In addition to handmade pottery,
ceramic assemblages associated with the Pen'kivka culture occasionally produce
wheel-made pottery, which some archaeologists believe to be of nomadic origin.[87]

Rabinovich (Moscow, 1975), pp. 7–49; Valerii S. Flerov, 'Iurtoobraznye zhilishcha prabolgar v
Vostochnoi Evrope', in *Voprosy etnicheskoi istorii Volgo-Don'ia: Materialy nauchnoi konferentsii*, ed.
by A. V. Rastoropov and A. Z. Zinnikov (Penza, 1992), pp. 25–31. The Turkic word yurt means
'territory' or 'camp site' and has nothing to do with tent-like dwellings. See Uwe Fiedler, 'Bulgars
in the Lower Danube Region: A Survey of the Archaeological Evidence and of the State of Current
Research', in *The Other Europe in the Middle Ages: Avars, Bulgars, Khazars, and Cumans*, ed. by
Florin Curta (Leiden, 2008), pp. 151–236 (p. 200 with n. 231).

[86] Rusanova, *Slavianskie drevnosti*, pp. 93–98 and fig. 34. For a survey of the state of research
on Pen'kivka pottery up to 1995, see Gavritukhin and Oblomskii, *Gaponovskii klad*, pp. 111–16.

[87] Rusanova, *Slavianskie drevnosti*, p. 101. Besides a few fragments of early Byzantine amphorae
or jugs, the wheel-made pottery from Pen'kivka ceramic assemblages has not been sufficiently
studied: neither its chronology nor its provenance can be established with any degree of certainty,
in spite of such labels as 'Pastyrs'ke pottery', which are sometimes attached to it. Stefka Angelova
and Liudmila Doncheva-Petkova, 'Razprostranenie na t. nar. "pastirska keramika" v Bălgariia',

Most Pen'kivka burial assemblages are urn cremations, with occasional inhumation graves being attributed to the nomads.[88]

Oleg Prykhodniuk attributed to the Pen'kivka culture two fortified sites: Budyshche, near Cherkasy (Ukraine), and Seliște, near Orhei (Moldova).[89] Neither one of them has been properly published. Seliște, at least, may be a simple open settlement inside a much earlier, probably Iron-Age (Scythian), fortification, which had no military function in the early Middle Ages.[90] The same, however, is not true about the stronghold excavated at Pastyrs'ke, near Smila (region of Cherkasy, Ukraine) (Figure 3.5). Although its cultural affiliation is still debated — either Slavic (Pen'kivka) or nomadic (Turkic or Bulgar) — there seems to be no doubt as to its early medieval date, even though the site was previously occupied and fortified during the Iron Age.[91] Pastyrs'ke is located on the right bank of the middle Dnieper, on the border between the forest-steppe and the steppe belts. The partially preserved ramparts, which reach up to two or three metres in height, and the accompanying ditches enclose a 25-hectare area of a pear-shaped plan. On top of the still-standing ramparts, recent excavations have revealed postholes from what have been interpreted as elements of a reinforcing structure consisting of two

---

Arkheologiia, 24 (1992), 14–21; Ion Tentiuc, 'Siturile din secolele V–VII de la Moleşti-Ialoveni (Republica Moldova)', *Arheologia Moldovei*, 21 (1998), 201–12; Dan Gh. Teodor, 'Elemente nomade din secolele VI–VIII în regiunile de la est și sud de Carpați', *Mousaios*, 5 (1999), 71–90. See also V. M. Goriunova and Ol'ga A. Shcheglova, 'Spor dlinoiu v chetvert' veka: M. I. Artamonov i P. N. Tret'iakov o "pastyrskoi kul'ture"', in *Skify, khazare, slaviane, drevniaia Rus': Mezhdunarodnaia nauchnaia konferenciia, posviashchennaia 100-letiiu so dnia rozhdeniia professora Mikhaila Illarionovicha Artamonova. Sankt-Petersburg, 9–12 dekabria 1998 g. Tezisy dokladov*, ed. by A. D. Stoliar (St Petersburg, 1998), pp. 130–36.

[88] Helena Zoll-Adamikowa, 'W kwestii genezy słowiańskich praktyk pogrzebowych', in *Miscellanea archaeologica Thaddaeo Malinowski dedicata*, ed. by Franciszek Rożnowski (Słupsk, 1993), pp. 377–85 (pp. 377 and 380 fig. 1); E. V. Synytsia, 'Rann'osredn'ovichni ingumatsii v areali pen'kivs'koi kul'tury', *Vita antiqua*, 2 (1999), 98–110. For a critique of the stereotypical association of cremations with the Slavs and inhumations with the nomads, see Curta, 'North-western Region', pp. 151–63.

[89] Prykhodniuk, *Pen'kovskaia kul'tura*, p. 84 with pl. 9.

[90] Corman, *Contribuții*, p. 150.

[91] See now Oleg M. Prykhodniuk, *Pastyrs'ke gorodyshche* (Kiev, 2005). For Pastyrs'ke as a Pen'kivka site, see Smilenko, *Slov'iany ta ikh susidy*, pp. 69–70; Sedov, *Vostochnye slaviane*, p. 24. For Pastyrs'ke as a Turkic or Bulgar site, see Artamonov, 'Etnicheskata prinadlezhnost', p. 8; Olg'a A. Shcheglova, 'O dvukh gruppakh "drevnostei antov" v srednem Podneprov'e', *Materialy i issledovaniia po arkheologii Dneprovskogo Levoberezh'ia*, 1 (1990), 162–204 (p. 180).

wooden fences with a clay mixture between them or, more likely, as remains of two rows of palisade. A stream flowing through the site divided the fortification into two uneven sections.[92] The general layout of the Pastyrs'ke stronghold is very different from that of such contemporary fortified sites as Szeligi and Haćki in Poland, Zimno in Ukraine, and Nikadzimava in Belarus.[93] Pastyrs'ke is much larger than any of the other sites and, unlike all of them, produced evidence of living quarters within the enclosure. During excavations conducted on the site since 1898, some fifty

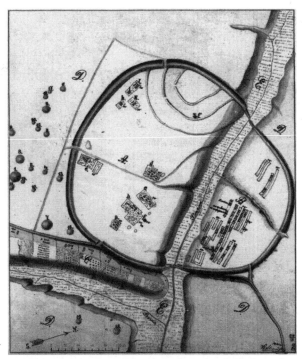

Figure 3.5. The map of the Pastyrs'ke stronghold, drawn by Vikentiy V. Khvoyka. After Prykhodniuk, *Pastyrs'ke gorodyshche*, fig. 2.

sunken-featured buildings have been found, some with hearths, others with stone ovens. Much like contemporary strongholds in Ukraine, Poland, or Belarus, Pastyrs'ke produced evidence of industrial activities, including a smithy, complete

[92] Oleg M. Prykhodniuk, 'Oboronni sporudy ta viys'kove sporiadzhennia Pastirs'kogo gorodyshcha', in *Etnokul'turni protsesy v Pivdenno-Skhidnyi Evropi*, ed. by Terpilovs'kyi, Abashina, Skiba, and Ivanovs'kyi, pp. 240–52; Prykhodniuk, *Pastyrs'ke gorodyshche*, pp. 12–20.

[93] Zbigniew Kobyliński, 'Early Medieval Hillforts in Polish Lands in the 6th to the 8th Centuries: Problems of Origins, Function, and Spatial Organization', in *From the Baltic to the Black Sea: Studies in Medieval Archaeology*, ed. by David Austin and Leslie Alcock (London, 1990), pp. 147–56; Marek Dulinicz, 'Miejsca, które rodzą władzę (najstarze grody slowiańskie na wschód od Wisły)', in *Człowiek, sacrum, środowisko: Miejsca kultu we wczesnym średniowieczu*, ed. by Sławomira Moździoch (Wrocław, 2000), pp. 85–98; Marek Dulinicz, 'Najstarsze grody wczesnośredniowieczne', in *Wspólnota dziedzictwa kulturowego ziem Bialorusi i Polski*, ed. by Aleksander Kośko and Alena Kalecyc (Warsaw, 2004), pp. 305–07.

with smelting furnaces.[94] A large number of artefacts — anthropo-zoomorphic and bow fibulae, brooches with circular plates, earrings with star-shaped pendants, and belt buckles — including miscasts testify to a local production of dress accessories.[95] Besides being a production centre for a relatively large area in Eastern Europe, Pastyrs'ke may have also been a political power centre, the seat of a ruler with territorial authority. At least that seems to be the most likely interpretation of one of the long structures found inside the ramparts, which may have been destroyed after a raid by steppe nomads. Exactly how artefacts produced in Pastyrs'ke reached distant regions to the north or to the east remains unknown. Nor is it clear what kind of political structure had its centre in Pastyrs'ke, or whether or not the ruler(s) presumably residing inside the stronghold may have been related to the very powerful Mezamer mentioned by Menander the Guardsman.[96]

'Antian Antiquities'

The regions known for assemblages attributed to the Prague, Pen'kivka, and Kolochin cultures have produced a relatively large number of silver and bronze artefacts, many of which have been found in hoards, which the Russian archaeologist Aleksander A. Spitsyn (1858–1931) called 'Antian antiquities' (Figures 3.6–7).[97]

[94] Oleg M. Prykhodniuk, 'Tekhnologiia vyrobnytstva ta vytoki iuvelirnogo styliu metalevykh prykras Pastyrs'kogo gorodyshcha', *Arkheolohiia*, 1994.3, 61–77; Prykhodniuk, *Pastyrs'ke gorodyshche*, p. 14.

[95] Oleg M. Prykhodniuk, 'Fibuly Pastyrskogo gorodischa', in *Arkheologiia vostochnoevropeiskoi lesostepi: Evraziiskaia step' i lesostep' v epokhu rannego srednevekov'ia*, ed. by A. D. Priakhin (Voronezh, 2000), pp. 48–73; Prykhodniuk, *Pastyrs'ke gorodyshche*, pp. 206–23, pls 10–29, 48–53, and 241–43; Bartłomiej Szymon Szmoniewski, 'Stronghold at Pastirs'ke (Ukraine), Centre of Power in the Forest-steppe Belt', in *Herrschaft und Sozialstrukturen im Mittelalter östlich der Elbe*, ed. by A. Paroń, S. Rossignol, B. Sz. Szmoniewski, and G. Vercamer (Wrocław, 2008), pp. 103–08.

[96] For power structures in early Slavic society, see Florin Curta, 'Feasting with "Kings" in an Ancient Democracy: On the Slavic Society of the Early Middle Ages (Sixth to Seventh Century A.D.)', *Essays in Medieval Studies*, 15 (1999), 19–34; Curta, *Making of the Slavs*, pp. 311–34.

[97] Aleksander A. Spitsyn, 'Drevnosti antov', in *Sbornik statei v chest' akademika Alekseia Ivanovicha Sobolevskogo*, ed. by V. N. Perettsa (Leningrad, 1928), pp. 492–95; Shcheglova, 'O dvukh gruppakh "drevnostei antov"'; Volodymr D. Baran, 'Skarby VI–VIII st. Anty chy Rus'?', *Arkheolohiia*, 1998.1, 15–28; Florin Curta, 'The Archaeology of Identities in Old Russia (*ca.* 500 to *ca.* 650)', *Russian History*, 34 (2007), 31–62 (pp. 37–42); Bartłomiej Szymon Szmoniewski, 'Two Worlds, One Hoard: What Do Metal Finds from the Forest-steppe Belt Speak About?', in *The Other Europe in the Middle Ages*, ed. by Curta, pp. 263–96.

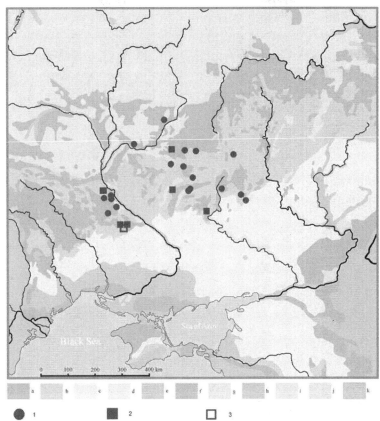

Figure 3.6. The distribution of the 'Antian antiquities' in the forest-steppe region of Eastern Europe: (1) Shcheglova's first group of hoards; (2) Shcheglova's second group of hoards; (3) location of the Pastyrs'ke Stronghold. From Szmoniewski, 'Two Worlds, One Hoard', fig. 1.

Spitsyn's catchphrase has been so influential that until recently no study of those artefacts has been written that was not concerned with their ethnic attribution. Spitsyn's own reason for labelling them 'Antian' was that the distribution of hoards containing such artefacts within the region of the Middle Dnieper coincided with what he believed to be the old homeland of the Antes. However, the same class of artefacts formed the basis for what the Hungarian archaeologist Nándor Fettich (1900–71) called the 'Martynovka culture' after one of the most important hoards

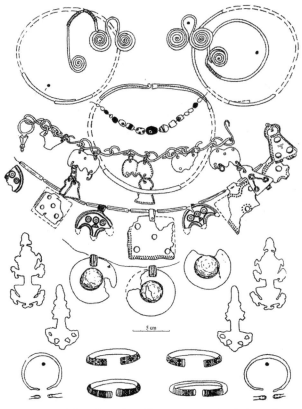

5 cm

Figure 3.7. Selected artefacts ('Antian antiquities') from the Koziivka hoard Ukraine. After Shcheglova, 'O dvukh gruppakh "drevnostei antov"', fig. 7.

containing 'Antian antiquities'.[98] In his foreword to Fettich's book on the 'late Hunnic metalwork', the Hungarian philologist János Harmatta (1917–2004) explicitly linked to the Turkic aristocracy, particularly to the Cutrigurs, the artefacts which Spitsyn had previously attributed to the Antes. Harmatta explained that the silver used for the production of such artefacts was part of the subsidies paid by Emperor Justinian to the Cutrigur chieftains in order to obtain the peace. That the 'Antian antiquities' were in fact dress accessories of nomadic fashions resulted also from the mixture of geometric and animal motifs employed for their decoration.[99]

---

[98] Nándor Fettich, _Archäologische Studien zur Geschichte der späthunnischen Metalkunst_ (Budapest, 1951), pp. 131–33. Unlike Spitsyn, Fettich attributed the Martynovka culture to the early medieval nomads and linked hoards of bronze and silver from Ukraine to such Central European finds as Čađavica in Croatia. See Nándor Fettich, 'Der Fund von Čadjavica', _Vjesnik Hrvatskoga arheološkoga društva_, 23 (1941), 55–61. For the Martynivka (Martynovka) hoard, see now Ljudmila V. Pekarskaja and Dafydd Kidd, _Der Silberschatz von Martynovka (Ukraine) aus dem 6. und 7. Jahrhundert_ (Innsbruck, 1994).

[99] János Harmatta, in Fettich, _Archäologische Studien_, pp. 99–105. In the early 1950s, the Cutrigurs were a popular theme in the Hungarian archaeology of the early Middle Ages. See Dezső Csallány, 'A Bácsújfalusi avarkori hamvasztásos lelet: Adatok a kuturgur-bolgárok (hunok) temetési szokásához és régészeti hagyatékához', _Archaeologiai Értesítő_, 80 (1953), 133–40.

Fettich's ideas were met with skepticism. Joachim Werner had already decided in favour of the idea that the 'Martynovka culture' was an essentially Slavic phenomenon resulting from contact with Byzantium, while in the Soviet Union the influential archaeologist Boris Rybakov bluntly dismissed any interpretations not in line with the idea that the Martynovka hoard — and, implicitly, the 'culture' named after it — was Antian.[100] Rybakov's main reason for embracing Spitsyn's concept of 'Antian antiquities' was his idea of an uninterrupted cultural continuity from prehistory to Kievan Rus', an approach ultimately inspired by Nikolai A. Marr's monogenetic theory of language. Instead of a critique of the 'bourgeois' ideas and the essentially culture-historical approach of Aleksander Spitsyn, which would have been normally expected in the political climate of the Soviet Union in the early 1950s, Rybakov adapted what was essentially Marrism tout court to the new Stalinist policies of encouraging a specifically Russian form of nationalism. As a consequence, Rybakov went much farther than Spitsyn. He boldly argued that the hoards of 'Antian antiquities' from the Middle Dnieper area, which had been previously attributed to the Antes, must be viewed as Rus'. According to Rybakov, the Rus' — the early medieval ancestors of modern Russians — were a 'tribe' within the Antian tribal confederacy.[101] On the basis of this new attribution, Rybakov redated all hoards of silver and bronze to the seventh and early eighth centuries, in order to link them to the metalwork of Kievan Rus'.[102] Despite Rybakov's extraordinary administrative and political powers throughout the last thirty years of the Soviet regime, his ideas had little if any influence, because the excavation in the 1950s of several settlement sites in the Middle Dnieper region shifted the emphasis from the 'Antian *antiquities*' to the Pen'kivka *culture*.[103] It is against that background that Galina Korzukhina's different take on the 'Antian

---

[100] Joachim Werner, 'Slawische Bügelfibeln des 7. Jahrhunderts', in *Reinecke Festschrift zum 75. Geburtstag von Paul Reinecke am 25. September 1947*, ed. by G. Behrens (Mainz, 1950), pp. 150–72 (pp. 168–72). Werner's reason for assigning the Martynovka hoard to the Slavs was of course that the hoard assemblage include a pair of so-called 'Slavic' bow fibulae (called so by Werner himself). See also Rybakov, 'Drevnie rusi', pp. 76–89. For Rybakov's endorsement of Stalin's policies, see Anatolii P. Novosel'tsev, '"Mir istorii" ili mif istorii?', *Voprosy istorii*, 1 (1993), 23–31.

[101] Boris A. Rybakov, *Remeslo Drevnei Rusi* (Moscow, 1948), pp. 75–90; Rybakov, 'Drevnie rusi', pp. 7–24. Ever since the beginning of World War II, Rybakov was at work attempting to establish the identity between Antes and Rus'(sians). See Rybakov, 'Anty i Kievskaia Rus''.

[102] Rybakov, 'Drevnie rusi', pp. 59 and 68.

[103] Khavliuk, 'Ranneslavianskie poseleniia', pp. 320–50; P. I. Khavliuk, 'Ranneslavianskie poseleniia v basseine Iuzhnogo Buga', in *Rannesrednevekovye vostochnoslavianskie drevnosti*, ed. by Petr N. Tret'iakov (Leningrad, 1974), pp. 181–215.

antiquities' must be understood.[104] Unlike Rybakov, Korzukhina did not take at
face value the written sources pertaining to the early medieval history of the
Middle Dnieper region. She also treated hoards as 'closed finds', and consequently
had little interest in drawing ethnic or tribal boundaries on the map. In the process,
she distinguished two kinds of assemblages labelled 'Antian antiquities': hoards in
the forest-steppe region, and graves in the steppe lands. Nonetheless, her goal was
to write history on the basis of the archaeological finds. Indirectly endorsing
Rybakov's dating (but not his historical conclusions), Korzukhina concluded that
most hoards were buried in the early 700s, most probably in connection with the
military events associated with the expansion of the early Khazar qaganate.[105]
According to her, the hoards were a testimony of the complex cultural and political
processes taking place in the forest-steppe zone of Eastern Europe during the late
seventh and first half of the eighth century. After Korzukhina's study, nothing of
significance was published about the hoards for over thirty years, until Ol'ga
Shcheglova's seminal study.[106] Shcheglova's approach was essentially different from
that of Korzukhina. First, she took into consideration only hoard and not burial
assemblages. Second, instead of topography, she concentrated on a thorough
analysis of hoard composition, and thus distinguished between two chronologically
different groups of hoards. She dated one of them to the late sixth and early
seventh centuries and placed the other chronologically between the early 600s and
the early 700s. Since then, Shcheglova has refined her chronology in a contribution
to the monograph of the Gaponovo hoard, a publication which in many ways has
changed the way in which scholars have come to look at such assemblages.[107] The
year 1996, in which the Gaponovo monograph appeared, was also the year of the
posthumous publication of Galina Korzukhina's comprehensive catalogue of
hoards, which set the entire scholarly discussion of such assemblages on a new,
much firmer basis, the more so that some of the artefacts included in that extensive

---

[104] Galina F. Korzukhina, 'K istorii srednego Podneprov'ia v seredine I tysiacheletiia n.e.',
Sovetskaia Arkheologiia, 22 (1955), 61–82.

[105] Korzukhina, 'K istorii srednego Podneprov'ia', p. 78.

[106] Shcheglova, 'O dvukh gruppakh "drevnostei antov"'.

[107] Ol'ga A. Shcheglova, in Gavritukhin and Oblomskii, *Gaponovskii klad*, pp. 47–53. See also
Ol'ga A. Shcheglova, 'Zhenskie ubor iz kladov "drevnosti antov": gotskoe vliianie ili gotskoe
nasledie?', *Stratum+*, 5 (1999), 287–312; Ol'ga A. Shcheglova and and V. E. Rodinkova, 'Krymskie
motivy v "drevnostiakh antov"', in *Bospor Kimmeriiskii i varvarskii mir v period antichnosti i
srednevekov'ia: Sbornik nauchnykh materialov IV Bosporskikh chtenii, Kerch', 20–24 maia 2003 g.*,
ed. by V. N. Zin'ko (Kerch', 2003), pp. 295–98.

corpus had meanwhile disappeared.[108] Together with the Gaponovo monograph, Korzukhina's catalogue has quickly become the standard point of reference for anyone studying the early medieval archaeology of the forest-steppe zone of Ukraine and Russia. Without any doubt, both publications were a catalyst for the current state of research, but their impact enhanced an already growing interest in the last fifteen years or so in early medieval hoards of bronze and silver.[109]

My own contribution to this topic has been twofold: the typological analysis of the selected artefacts from hoards, and the comparison of its results with contemporary cultural traditions.[110] Hoards with 'Antian antiquities' reflect a very complicated political and ethnic situation in the early medieval forest-steppe region. Artefacts from a variety of cultural milieus are combined in a manner which is certainly symbolic, although it is not easy to decipher just what those symbols mean. At any rate, it has by now become clear that the hoards of 'Antian antiquities' — mounts with human or animal decorations, belt sets, gold and silver dress accessories — cannot be divorced from the cultural traditions of communities of nomads in the steppe. On the other hand, ornaments made of tin- and lead-based

[108] Galina F. Korzukhina, 'Klady i sluchainye nakhodki veshchei kruga "drevnostei antov" v srednem Podneprov'e. Katalog pamiatnikov', *Materialy po arkheologii, istorii i etnografii Tavrii*, 5 (1996), 352–435 and 586–705.

[109] V. M. Goriunova, 'Novyi klad antskogo vremeni iz srednego Podneprov'ia', *Arkheologicheskie vesti*, 1 (1992), 126–40; Pekarskaja and Kidd, *Der Silberschatz*; Oleg M. Prykhodniuk, V. A. Padin, and N. G. Tikhonov, 'Trubchevskii klad antskogo vremeni', in *Materialy I tys. n.e. po arkheologii i istorii Ukrainy i Vengrii*, ed. by I. Erdélyi and others (Kiev, 1996), pp. 79–102; Curta, 'Archaeology of Identities'; Szmoniewski, 'Two Worlds, One Hoard'.

[110] Bartłomiej Szymon Szmoniewski, 'Anthropomorphic Brooches of the Dnepr Type in Initial Phases of the Early Middle Ages: The Migration of a Style-Idea-Object', in *Wędrówki rzeczy i idei w średniowieczu: Spotkania Bytomskie V*, ed. by Slawomir Możdzioch (Wrocław, 2004), pp. 301–12; Bartłomiej Szymon Szmoniewski, 'Cultural Contacts in Central and Eastern Europe: What Do Metal Beast Images Speak About?', in *Ethnic Contacts and Cultural Exchanges North and West of the Black Sea from the Greek Colonization to the Ottoman Conquest*, ed. by Victor Cojocaru (Iaşi, 2005), pp. 425–42. A typological approach to fibulae found in hoards is also adopted by V. E. Rodinkova, 'Dneprovskie fibuly s kaimoi iz ptich'ikh golov', in *Kul'turnye transformatsii i vzaimovliianiia v Dneprovskom regione na iskhode rimskogo vremeni i v rannem Srednevekov'e: Doklady nauchnoi konferentsii, posviashchennoi 60-letiiu so dnia rozhdeniia E. A. Goriunova (Sankt-Peterburg, 14–17 noiabria 2000 g.)*, ed. by Valentina M. Goriunova and Ol'ga A. Shcheglova (St Petersburg, 2004), pp. 233–43; V. E. Rodinkova, 'K voprosu o tipologicheskom razvitii antropozoomorfnykh fibul (slozhnye i dvuplastinchatye formy)', *Rossiiskaia Arkheologiia*, 2006.4, 50–63; V. E. Rodinkova, 'K voprosu o tipologischekom razvitii antropozoomorfnykh fibul (prostye formy)', *Rossiiskaia Arkheologiia*, 2006.3, 41–51.

alloys point without any doubt to the cultural traditions of sedentary populations in the forest zone of Eastern Europe.[111]

Conclusion

If anything, this survey of the current state of research on the Antes should convince the reader that very little from what the previous generation of scholars viewed as already established has remained unchallenged. Despite the past and current desire of many to recruit the Antes for Slavic history, there is currently no agreement as to the Slavic origin of the Antes. Recent studies in fact have moved away from the identification of a discrete, ethnically homogeneous entity and have revealed, if only partially, a highly complex political reality behind the late antique phenomenon known to sixth-century Byzantine authors as 'Antes'. Equally difficult seems to be to accept a simple equation between the Antes of the written sources and what Ukrainian and Russian archaeologists alike call the Pen'kivka culture. Leaving aside problems of ethnic attribution recently blamed for the political misuse of archaeology, the Pen'kivka culture is a territorially much larger entity than the largest territory to be assigned to the Antes on the basis of the written sources. The consensus among archaeologists seems to be that the population in Pen'kivka villages was a mixture of Slavic and nomadic, most likely Bulgar (Cutrigur), elements, but of course both 'Slavs' and 'nomads' need to be carefully defined before any agreement is reached on how to interpret the archaeological phenomenon known as the Pen'kivka culture.[112] The notable differences between that culture and the so-called Prague culture, especially the presence of metalwork most typical for the nomadic milieu, deserve more study.

---

[111] Szmoniewski, 'Two Worlds, One Hoard'.

[112] In that respect, my position is theoretically closer to that of Wojciech Szymański, *Słowiańszczyzna Wschodnia* (Wrocław, 1973), p. 34, and of Mikhail I. Artamonov, 'Slaviane i bolgary v Podneprov'e', in *Berichte über den II. internationalen Kongre für slawische Archäologie, Berlin, 24.–28. August 1970*, ed. by Joachim Herrmann and Karl-Heinz Otto (Berlin, 1970), pp. 121–30.

BOSPORUS, THE TETRAXITE GOTHS, AND THE NORTHERN CAUCASUS REGION DURING THE SECOND HALF OF THE FIFTH AND THE SIXTH CENTURIES

Igor O. Gavritukhin and Michel Kazanski

The peoples of the northern Caucasus region during the 'Great Migration' period undoubtedly belong to the large group of 'neglected barbarians'. There are various reasons for that. For one thing, written sources pertaining to that region were more often than not written very far from local realities, their coverage being so patchy as to discourage any hopes of piecing together the local history. Consequently, much is left out of the historical narrative. In fact, most studies based exclusively on written sources offer little more than a discussion of controversial points of interpretation.[1] Nor did the situation change as a consequence of large-scale archaeological excavations, because the analysis of the written sources has imposed on archaeologists the task to produce those materials which could illustrate the conclusions historians dealing only with written sources had already drawn.[2] Although the researches dealing with individual periods,

---

[1] This is particularly true for the so far most complete account of the ethnic history of the northern Caucasus region during the early Middle Ages, that of Aleksander V. Gadlo, *Ethnicheskaia istoriia Severnogo Kavkaza v IV–X vv.* (Leningrad, 1979). For a new approach (with new points of view and bibliography), see Constantin Zuckerman, 'A propos du Livre des ceremonies, II 48', in *Travaux et mémoires du Centre de recherches d'histoire et civilisation byzantines*, 13 (2000), 312–33.

[2] See, for example, Vladimir A. Kuznetsov, *Alanskie plemena Severnogo Kavkaza* (Moscow, 1962); Vladimir A. Kuznetsov, *Ocherki istorii alan* (Vladikavkaz, 1992); Vera B. Kovalevskaia, 'Severokavkazskie drevnosti', in *Stepi Evrazii v epokhu srednevekov'ia*, ed. by Svetlana A. Pletneva (Moscow, 1981), pp. 83–97; Vera B. Kovalevskaia, *Kavkaz, Skify, Sarmaty, Alany v I tys. do n. e.–I tys. n. e.* (Moscow, 2005).

territories, or peoples provide more detailed studies of sources, as a rule, they get over only a part of the shortcomings indicated above.[3]

The problem, in our opinion, is that, much like with many other regions, too many studies, some by very talented authors, dealing with the northern Caucasus region appear to be handicapped by two key factors. One of them is the lack of a systematic publication of the fundamental archaeological assemblages in a manner consistent with the current development of the discipline. Despite the fact that several such assemblages were excavated more than a century ago and that the artefacts found therein have meanwhile entered museum collections all over the world, the work of publication has just begun.[4] The other reason for the poor state

---

[3] Particularly significant in this respect are Mikhail I. Artamonov, *Istoriia khazar* (Leningrad, 1962; repr. 2002); Anatolii P. Novosel'tsev, *Khazarskoe gosudarstvo i ego rol' v istorii Votochnoi Evropy i Kavkaza* (Moscow, 1980); Maia P. Abramova, *Rannie alany severnogo Kavkaza III–V vv.* (Moscow, 1997). For a general view of the most important works, see also Michel Kazanski and Anna Mastykova, *Les Peuples du Caucase du Nord: le début de l'histoire (Ier–VIIe siècle apr. J.-C.)* (Paris, 2003).

[4] A few examples may substantiate this conclusion. Fifty years after its excavation, the sixth- to early eighth-century cemetery in Chir-Yurt, one of the most important sites for the archaeology of the early Middle Ages in the north-eastern Caucasus region, is still known only through the less-than-informative plates published without any text or explanation by Kovalevskaia, *Kavkaz*, figs 41–74. Similarly, the very rich cemetery excavated in Chmi (northern Ossetia) more than a century ago is known only from the publication of a rather small collection of artefacts now in the Naturhistorisches Museum in Vienna, as well as of a few catacombs discovered by Maia P. Abramova. See Igor O. Gavritukhin and A. M. Oblomskii, *Gaponovskii klad i ego kul'turno-istoricheskii kontekst* (Moscow, 1996), pp. 79–81 and 264–65; Abramova, *Rannie alany*, pp. 78 and 89–92. The situation in the Kislovodsk region is better than in any other part of the Caucasus region, largely because of the activity of Andrei P. Runich, for which see Iakov B. Berezin and Sergei N. Savenko, *Runich Andrei Petrovich* (Armavir, 1996). For a survey of assemblages in the Kislovodsk region, see Gennadii E. Afanas'ev, Sergei N. Savenko, and Dmitrii S. Korobov, *Drevnosti Kislovodskoi kotloviny* (Moscow, 2004). Only the cemetery in Mokraia Balka has so far been systematically published (Gennadii E. Afanas'ev and Andrei P. Runich, *Mokraia Balka* (Moscow, 2001)), but the published illustrations of artefacts are much too schematic, especially when compared to those in Igor O. Gavritukhin and Vladimir Iu. Malashev, 'Perspektivy izucheniia khronologii rannesrednevekovyi drevnostei Kislovodskoi kotliny', in *Kul'tury evraziiskikh stepei vtoroi poloviny I tysiacheletiia n.e. (voprosy khronologii): Materialy II Mezhdunarodnoi arkheolo-gicheskoi konferentsii, 17–20 noiabria 1997 g.*, ed. by Dmitrii A. Stashenkov, Anna F. Kochkina, and L. V. Kuznetsova (Samara, 1998), pp. 28–86; or Vladimir Iu. Malashev, *Keramika rannesred-nevekovogo mogil'nika Mokraia Balka* (Moscow, 2001). Kovalevskaia, *Kavkaz*, figs 85–103, published some general plans of catacombs and a few artefacts from Mokraia Balka. From over four hundred burial assemblages (some of which, in fact, may be dated to the early Iron Age — the Koban culture — or to the Sarmatian period of the first centuries AD) excavated in Klin-Iar, only twenty-eight have so far been published in Valerii S. Flerov, *Alany Tsentralnogo Predkavkaz'ia*

of research is the lack of any analysis of the archaeological sources. There are practically no typological studies of individual artefact categories, such as those traditionally used for building relative chronologies and for tracking cultural influences — fibulae or belt buckles. Very few local chronologies have so far been created.[5] All this means that little work has been done which could offer a new historical interpretation of the archaeological evidence, and what there is can be regarded as mere attempts to frame the question. This is certainly the case for such issues as the beginning of the power centres, which may be identified by means of clusters of rich or very rich assemblages,[6] the second- to fifth-century proto-urban

---

V–VIII vekov: obriad obezvrezhivaniia pogrebennykh (Moscow, 2000). A few other burial assemblages (graves 341 to 387) excavated by Andrei B. Belinskii and Heinrich Härke in the 1990s await publication in English. For a preliminary report on those excavations, see Heinrich Härke and Andrei B. Belinskii, 'Nouvelles fouilles de 1994–1996 dans la nécropole de Klin-Jar', in *Les Sites archéologiques en Crimée et au Caucase durant l'Antiquité tardive et le haut Moyen Âge*, ed. by Michel Kazanski and Vanessa Soupault (Leiden, 2000), pp. 193–210. From cemeteries excavated on the eastern Black Sea coast (Borisovo, with some 200 graves; Diurso, with 500 graves; and Bzhid, with some 150 graves), only a few assemblages are known, in addition to several illustrative artefacts, which have been published primarily in *Krym, Severo-Vostochnoe Prichernomor'e i Zakavkaz'e v epokhu srednevekov'ia IV–XIII veka*, ed. by Tat'iana I. Makarova and Svetlana A. Pletneva (Moscow, 2003). For other assemblages, see Kazanski and Mastykova, *Les Peuples*; Abramova, *Rannie alany*; Kovalevskaia, *Kavkaz*; Dmitrii S. Korobov, *Sotsial'naia organizatsiia alan severnogo Kavkaza IV–IX vv.* (Moscow, 2003); Dmitrii S. Korobov, 'K voprosu o rasselenni alanskikh plemen severnogo Kavkaza po dannym arkheologii i pis'mennykh istochnikam', *Rossiiskaia Arkheologiia*, 2009.3, 64–76; Musa Kh. Bagaev, *Kul'tura gornoi Chechni i Dagestana v drevnosti i srednevekov'e* (Moscow, 2008).

[5] However, some progress seems to have been recently made in that direction. Most important in this respect is the analysis of the pottery found in Mokraia Balka (Malashev, *Keramika*) and Klin-Iar (Vladimir Iu. Malashev, *R annesrednevekovaia keramika mogil'nika Klin-Iar III* (Moscow, 2000)). Equally significant are recent attempts to build chronologies based not on intuitive criteria, but on specific analogies. See Michel Kazanski, 'Die Chronologie der Anfangsphase des Gräberfeld von Djurso', in *Probleme der frühen Merowingerzeit im Mitteldonauraum,* ed. by Jaroslav Tejral (Brno, 2002), pp. 137–57; Igor O. Gavritukhin, 'Khronologiia epokhi stanovleniia Khazarskogo kaganata (elementy remennoi garnitury)', in *Khazary*, ed. by V. Petrukhin, W. Moskovich, and A. Fedorchuk (Jerusalem, 2005), pp. 378–426.

[6] Michel Kazanski and Anna V. Mastykova, 'Tsentry vlasti i torgovye puti v Zapadnoi Alanii v V–VI vv.', in *Severnyi Kavkaz: Istoriko-arkheologicheskiie ocherki i zametki. Sbornik statei*, ed. by Maia P. Abramova and Vladimir I. Markovin (Moscow, 2001), pp. 138–61; Michel Kazanski and A. Mastykova, 'Le Caucase du Nord et la région méditerranéenne aux 5e–6e siècles: à propos de la formation de la civilisation aristocratique barbare', *Eurasia antiqua*, 5 (1999), 523–73; Tamerlan A. Gabuev and Vladimir Iu. Malashev, 'Elementy pogrebal'nogo obriada Brutskogo gorodishcha', in *Severnyi Kavkaz*, ed. by Abramova and Markovin, pp. 458–71; Tamerlan A. Gabuev, 'Komu prinadlezhat kurgany u sela Brut?', in *Tri chetverti veka. D. V. Deopiku – druz'ia*

centres in the Caucasus region,[7] and the characteristics of the tradition and innovation mirrored by the dress employed by various ethno-cultural and social groups.[8] An important direction of research in this respect is the analysis of artefact circulation and of the underlying cultural relations. Much emphasis has been recently laid on the Byzantine (or, in more general terms, Mediterranean) and Sassanian influences.[9] However, equally important is the configuration of relations within the barbarian world. Our goal in this paper is to examine a component of that configuration which is defined by relations with the cultural area of the north-eastern Black Sea region (Bosporus, Tetraxite Goths), the strong western influence from the Mediterranean and Danube region, and the relations with other barbarians in the eastern parts of the northern Caucasus region.[10] Our purpose is to highlight the contacts between those areas in an attempt to outline a possible network of political ties. Given the complexity of the problem, we will focus on selected artefact categories over a period of slightly more than a century. The collapse of Attila's Hunnic Empire in the 450s, on the one hand, and the incorporation of the northern Caucasus region into the First Turkic qaganate in the 560s, on the other hand, constitute the chronological limits of this study.

i ucheniki, ed. by Nadezhda N. Bektimirova (Moscow, 2007), pp. 473–81; Tamerlan A. Gabuev and Vladimir Iu. Malashev, *Pam'atniki rannih alan tsentral'nyh raionov Severnogo Kavkaza* (Moscow, 2009). (Forthcoming is the book on the Brut elite cemetery by Tamerlan A. Gabuev.)

[7] Irina Arzhantseva, Dega Deopik, and Vladimir Malashev, 'Zilgi: An Early Alan Proto-city of the First Millennium AD on the Boundary Between Steppe and Hill Country', in *Les Sites archéologiques en Crimée*, ed. by Kazanski and Soupault, pp. 210–50; Vladimir Iu. Malashev, 'Kul'turnaia situatsiia v tsentral'nykh raionakh severnogo Kavkaza', in *Tri chetverti veka. D. V. Deopiku*, ed. by Bektimirova, pp. 487–501; Igor O. Gavritukhin, 'K voprosu o verkhnei date gorodishcha Zilgi', in *Tri chetverti veka. D. V. Deopiku*, ed. by Bektimirova, pp. 482–86. For contemporary cities in the eastern Caucasus region, see now Murtuzali S. Gadzhiev, *Drevnii gorod Dagestana* (Moscow, 2002).

[8] Anna V. Mastykva, *Zenskii Kostium Tsentralnogo I Zapadnogo Predkavkaz'a v kontse IV – seredine VI v. n.e.* (Moscow, 2009).

[9] For a bibliography of recent studies, see Kazanski and Mastykova, 'Le Caucase du Nord'; Dieter Quast, 'Mediterrane Scheibenfibel der Völkerwanderungszeit mit Cloisonnéverzierung: eine typologische und chronologische Übersicht', *Archäologisches Korrespondenzblatt*, 36 (2006), 259–78; Iurii A. Prokopenko, *Istoriia severokavkazskikh torgovykh putei IV v. do n.e.–XI v. n. e.* (Stavropol, 1999); Murtuzali S. Gadzhiev, *Mezhdu Evropoi i Aziei* (Makhachkala, 1997). The Iranian influence has been so far studied in a highly specialized fashion (coins, gems, certain types of buckles) with little concern for the overall picture.

[10] This chapter is an expanded version of a paper originally published in Russian, together with a catalogue of finds, as Igor O. Gavritukhin and Michel Kazanski, 'Bospor, tetraksity i Severnyi Kavkaz vo vtoroi polovine V–VI vv.', *Arkheologicheskie vesti*, 13 (2006), 297–344.

Figure 4.1. Sheet bow fibulae of the local variants of Levice or Székely series from the northern Caucasus region with associated artefacts (1–16, 18) and from Bosporus (17): (1–4) grave 510 in Diurso; (5) 'Northern Caucasus'; (6) Saniba; (7) Kamunta; (8–16) Khabl'; (17) Kerch'; (18) Krasnodar Reservoir. Scale a for 1–2, 5–16, and 18; scale b for 3 and 4. The Kerch' fibula is known only from a drawing by A. A. Spitsyn, without scale.

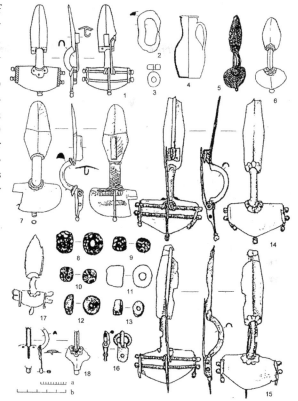

Sheet Bow Fibulae

An accidental find from the eroded the banks of the Krasnodar Reservoir (Figure 4.1.18), to the east of the main city in the region by the same name, is a specimen of a local, Kuban-Black Sea variant of bow fibulae originating from the Danube region.[11] Most typical for such fibulae are mushroom-shaped knobs and mounts

---

[11] During the period of the Hunnic Empire (c. 420/30–453/54), several series of sheet bow fibulae appeared in the barbarian milieu of the Middle Danube region (Figure 4.3). One can distinguish between at least four series known as Levice (fibulae with mounts in the shape of wide petals; Figure 4.2.10 and 14–15), Székely (fibulae with mounts in the shape of perforated petals; Figure 4.2.1–4), Grocka (fibulae with mounts in the shape of pointed petals; Figure 4.5.23), and Hochfelden (fibulae with mounts of varied width; Figure 4.5.51). While allowing for variations in ornamentation, all those fibulae share a number of morphological features, such as massive plates with mounts, cast, mushroom-shaped knobs, which are often refined for additional detail. Specimens of the four series served as models for local imitations from various parts of Europe, both East and

in the form of petals decorated with cells or imitations of cells. The earliest specimens (Figures 4.2.1–4; 4.3.1–2) are very similar to fibulae from the barbarian milieu in the Middle Danube region, especially to those from Székely (north-eastern Hungary; Figure 4.2.4–6). It is therefore appropriate to call this the 'Székely series'. Székely fibulae may be dated on the basis of the established chronology between *c.* 430/40 and *c.* 470/80.[12] Their imitations found in the Kuban-Black Sea region, especially in burial assemblages of the cemetery excavated in Diurso near

West. In some cases, craftsmen worked out technologically much more simplified solutions, such as casting mounts through the lost-wax procedures with imitation petals subsequently etched onto the surface (as in Figure 4.11.35). During the second half of the fifth century, a new series of sheet bow fibulae, this time with animal head–shaped knobs and pressed triangular mounts, in addition to bow fibulae with chip-carved decoration appeared in the Middle Danube region. Out of the former, a local series of fibulae developed in northern France, no doubt under the influence of the Danubian fashions. See Michel Kazanski and Patrick Périn, 'Les Barbares "orientaux" dans l'armée romaine en Gaule', *Antiquités nationales*, 29 (1997), 201–17. Another series of sheet bow fibulae developed in Spain as imitations of the Grocka series, possibly introduced into the area by the Ostrogothic refugees led by Vidimir. See Wolfgang Ebel-Zepezauer, 'Frühe gotische Blechfibeln aus Spanien', *Madrider Mitteilungen*, 35 (1994), 380–97; Patrick Périn, 'L'Armée de Vidimer et la question des dépôts funéraires des Wisigoths en Gaule et en Espagne (Vᵉ–VIᵉ siècles)', in *L'Armée romaine et les barbares du IIIᵉ au VIIᵉ siècle*, ed. by Françoise Vallet and Michel Kazanski (Paris, 1993), pp. 411–23, with fig. 26.7. The north-eastern region of the Black Sea was another area in which the Danubian sheet bow fibulae were imitated. Two distinct series with pressed mounts appear around the city of Bosporus and the area believed to have been inhabited at the time by the Tetraxite Goths. One of them is distinguished by triangular, the other by semicircular mounts. On the basis of analogies from Central and Western Europe, assemblages with sheet bow fibulae in the north-eastern region of the Black Sea (Figures 4.11, 4.8, 4.9 and 4.6.1–26) may be dated to the second half of the fifth century and the first decades of the sixth, but the use of sheet bow fibulae continued in the area well into the 550s (Figure 4.13). See Michel Kazanski, 'Khronologiia nachal'noi fazy mogil'nika Diurso', *Istoriko-arkheologicheskii al'manakh*, (Armavir) 7 (2001), 41–58; Michel Kazanski, 'Goty na Bospore Kimmeriiskom', in *100 let cherniakhovskoi kul'ture: Sbornik statei*, ed. by M. I. Hladykh (Kiev, 1999), pp. 277–97 (p. 286). Results of studying these fibulae are presented in more detail in the unpublished manuscript Igor O. Gavritukhin, *Dvuplasinchatye fibuly podgruppy II* (Archive of the Group of Archeology of Migration Period, Institute of Archeology RAS, Moscow).

    [12] Jaroslav Tejral, 'Zur Chronologie der frühen Völkerwanderungszeit im mittleren Donauraum', *Archaeologia Austriaca*, 72 (1988), 223–304; Jaroslav Tejral, 'Neue Aspekte der frühvölkerwanderungszeitlichen Chronologie im Mitteldonauraum', in *Neue Beiträge zur Erforschung der Spätantike im mittleren Donauraum: Materialien der internationalen Fachkonferenz 'Neue Beiträge zur Erforschung der Spätantike im mittleren Donauraum', Kravsko, 17.–20. Mai 1995*, ed. by Jaroslav Tejral, Herwig Friesinger, and Michel Kazanski (Brno, 1997), pp. 321–92.

Figure 4.2. Sheet bow fibulae of the Danubian variants of Levice and Székely series and associated artefacts: (1) Diegardt collection in the Roman-German Museum in Mainz; (2) 'Hungary'; (2a) Alba Iulia; (3) Borki; (4–6) Székely; (7–10) Szabadbattyán; (11–15) grave 5 in Levice. Scale a for 1–11 and 13–15; scale b for 12.

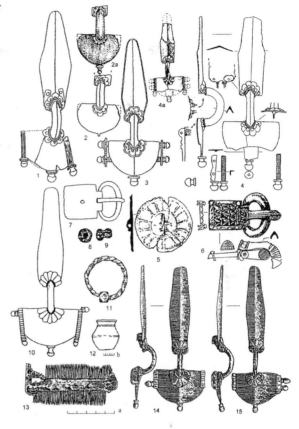

Novorossiisk (Figures 4.1.1 and 4.4.16) are of clearly local manufacture.[13] Some, at least, of the grave goods found in grave 300 of that cemetery may equally be dated between 430/40 and 470/80, thus making that assemblage coincide in time with those in the Middle Danube region marked with 'archaic' specimens of the Székely series (Figure 4.4). However, the excavator of the cemetery has attributed the site to the Tetraxite Goths, whom, mainly on the basis of Procopius of

[13] Aleksander V. Dmitriev, 'Rannesrednevekovye fibuly iz mogil'nika na r. Diurso', in *Drevnosti epokhi velikogo pereseleniia narodov V–VIII vekov: Sovetsko-vengerskii sbornik*, ed. by Anatolii K. Ambroz and István Erdélyi (Moscow, 1982), pp. 69–106; Anatolii K. Ambroz, *Khronologiia drevnostei Severnogo Kavkaza* (Moscow, 1989), pp. 47–48; Igor O. Gavritukhin and Aleksei V. P'iankov, 'Dvuplastinchatye fibuly iz novykh postuplenii Krasnodarskogo muzeia', *Drevnosti Bospora*, 4 (2002), 86–94.

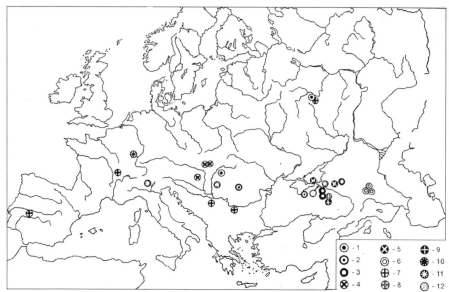

Figure 4.3. Distribution of sheet bow fibulae with semicircular mounts and mushroom-shaped knobs and of their imitations: (1–3) Székely series (1, 2 = Danubian variants, 3 = Kuban-Black Sea variants); (4–5) Levice series (4 = Danubian variants, 5 = Kuban-Black Sea variants); (6) North-Caucasian imitations of the Székely or Levice series; (7) Grocka series; (8–9) imitations of the Grocka series (Diurso, graves 289 and 483); (10) Hochfelden series; (11) variants with engraved mounts; (12) fibulae of undefined series.

Caesarea, he believed to have come to the Caucasus region in the company of the Huns withdrawing from Europe. If so, then grave 300 can certainly not be earlier than 455/60.[14] One may date grave 510 (Figure 4.1.1–4) to the same period or, possibly, a little later, between 450 and 480/90.[15] At any rate, all specimens of the Székely series found in the Kuban-Black Sea region seem to be dated to the second half of the fifth century. The sudden appearance of large sheet bow fibulae in Bosporus and, at the same time, in the northern Caucasus region is without any doubt the result of the adoption by local elites of the barbarian fashions developed in the Middle Danube region. Most typical for such fashions is the so-called Smolín group of burial assemblages, which some have attributed to the Gepid, Gothic, or

[14] Aleksander V. Dmitriev, 'Mogil'nik epokhi pereseleniia narodov na r. Diurso', *Kratkie soobshcheniia Instituta Arkheologii Akademii Nauk SSSR*, 158 (1979), 52–57; Ambroz, *Khronologiia*, pp. 45–46; Kazanski, 'Khronologiia nachal'noi fazy', pp. 41–58.

[15] Kazanski, 'Khronologiia nachal'noi fazy', p. 46.

Figure 4.4. Diurso, grave 300. Scale a for 2–24; scale b for 25 and 27–31; scale c for 26 – imitation of a Roman coin.

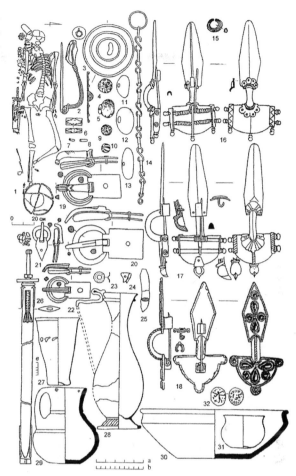

Scirian elites in Attila's entourage. Given that in the aftermath of the collapse of Attila's empire, several barbarian groups, especially the Angiskiri, withdrew together with the Hunnic refugees to the steppes of Eastern Europe, it is quite possible that members of the old barbarian elites in Attila's service reached Bosporus, where the local Tetraxite Goths quickly adopted their fashions.[16]

[16] Michel Kazanski, 'L'Influence danubienne dans la steppe pontique pendant la seconde moitié du Vᵉ siècle: le rôle des Angiskires', in *Medieval Europe 1992: Death and Burial* (York, 1992), pp. 139–44; Michel Kazanski, 'The Sedentary Elite in the "Empire" of the Huns and its Impact on Material Civilisation in Southern Russia During the Early Middle Ages (5th–7th

A find from Saniba near Vladikavkaz, in northern Ossetia, illustrates the presence of the Székely series in the Caucasus region (Figure 4.1.6). The Saniba fibula occupies a somewhat intermediary position between the Middle Danube and the Kuban-Black Sea specimens. According to Anatolii Ambroz, the Saniba fibula had been 'clipped', which would explain its rounded head plate and shortened foot. However, the same features appear on a number of other fibulae manufactured in Bosporus or in the Caucasus region (Figures 4.1.1, 5, 7, 17; 4.5.24; 4.6.28; 4.7.44–45, 47, 49, 54, 57–58, etc.). Another pair of sheet bow fibulae from the northern Caucasus was found in Khabl', near Abinsk in the Krasnodar region, in a destroyed, possibly female grave (Figure 4.1.14–15). Both fibulae belong to another group of Danubian origin, the Levice series, which is distinguished from the Székely series by the absence of either grooves or perforations on the mounts. The specimens found in the Middle Danube region (Figures 4.2.10, 14–15; 4.3) have all been dated between 430/40 and 470/80, mainly on the basis of assemblages from the cemetery excavated in Levice near Nitra (southern Slovakia) and of stylistic similarities with the Székely series. The Khabl' fibulae stand out among specimens of the Levice series by their simplified mounts, knobs of smaller size, and especially the extra layer underneath the thin plate of the foot, all features pointing to local imitations of original specimens from the Danube region. Moreover, the pentagonal shape of the head-plate suggests a later date for the Khabl' fibulae than for the specimens in the Middle Danube region (Figures 4.8.26; 4.9.20 and 30; 4.10.1). On the other hand, the relatively large size and elongated foot suggest that the North Caucasian specimens cannot be dated too late after the earliest fibulae of the Levice series. At any rate, the glass bead with mosaic-like ornamentation found together with the pair of sheet bow fibulae in Khabl' (Figure 4.1.8) does not contradict the idea of dating the assemblage to the second half of the fifth century.[17]

The fibula from Kamunta, near Ozagir, in North Ossetia, has a relatively small mount, an indication of further simplification in the process of imitating specimens of either the Székely or Levice series (Figure 4.1.7). All other features of the Kamunta fibula appear on other specimens from Bosporus and the northern Caucasus region

Centuries AD)', in *Cultural Transformations and Interactions in Eastern Europe*, ed. by John Chapman and Pavel Dolukhanov (Aldershot, 1993), pp. 211–35; Michel Kazanski, 'Les Germains orientaux au nord de la Mer Noire pendant la seconde moitié du Vᵉ s. et au VIᵉ s.', *Materialy po arkheologii, istorii i etnografii Tavrii*, 5 (1996), 324–37 and 567–81.

[17] Kazanski and Mastykova, 'Tsentry vlasti', pp. 139–45.

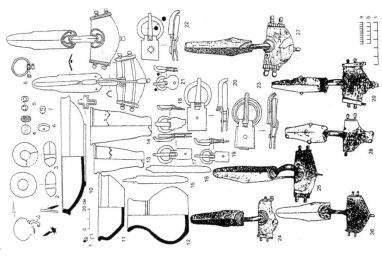

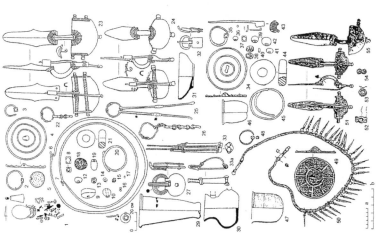

Figure 4.5 (left). Sheet bow fibulae from Diurso (with associated artefacts), Western Europe, South Crimea: (1–32) grave 483 in Diurso; (33–45) grave 298 in Diurso; (46–54) Hochfelden; (55) 'Suuk-Su'. Scale a for 29–31 and 46–47; scale b for 2–28, 32–45, and 48–55.

Figure 4.6 (right). Sheet bow fibulae from the northern Caucasus (and associated artefacts) and Bosporan regions, Western Europe, South Crimea: (1–23) grave 517 in Diurso; (24, 29) 'Southern Russia'; (25) Kerch'; (26) 'Maikop'; (27) Strasbourg; (28) 'Suuk-Su'. Scale a for 15–16; scale b for 10–14; scale c for 2–9 and 17–29.

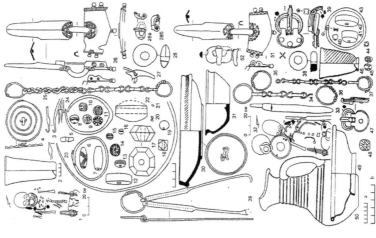

Figure 4.7 (left). Sheet bow fibulae with three knobs and other types of fibulae from the northern Caucasus, Bosporan, and Volga-Ural regions and associated artefacts: (1–25) grave 21 in Kushnarenkovo; (26) Kamunta; (27) Niznia Rutkha; (28) Kislovodskoe ozero 2; (29–41) Bylym-Kudinetovo; (42) Krasnodar Reservoir; (43) grave 5/1948 in Pashkovskyi 1; (44–45) grave 173 in Borisovo; (46) Soporu de Câmpie; (47) Donifars; (48) 'Kamunta or Kumbulta' (Ol'shevskii collection); (49) Kumbulta; (50–54) barrow 20 in Palasa-syrt; (55–58) grave 67/1987 in Iluraton (55 = coin struck for Emperor Arcadius, 395–408, which is used as a pendant). Scale a for 1; scale b for 56; scale c for 2–54 and 57–58.

Figure 4.8 (right). Sheet bow fibulae from Diurso and associated artefacts: (1–31) grave 516; (32–52) grave 408. Scale a for 2, 30–31, 33, 46, and 49–50; scale b for 3–29, 34–45, 47–48, and 51–52.

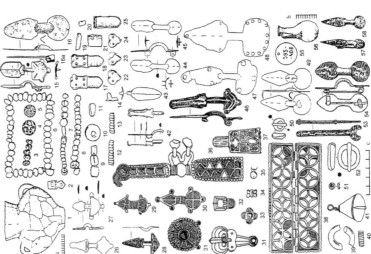

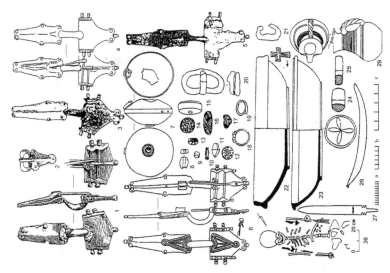

Figure 4.9 (left). Sheet bow fibulae from Diurso and associated artefacts: (1–27) grave 259; (28–43) grave 410. Scale a for 22–25 and 40–43; scale b for 1–21, 26–27, and 29–39.

Figure 4.10 (right). Sheet bow fibulae from the northern Caucasus with associated artefacts and from Bosporus: (1–2) Kerch'; (3) 'Chokrak'; (4) 'Maikop'; (5) 'Gurzuf'; (6–29) grave 420 in Diurso. Scale a for 27–29; scale b for 22–23; scale c for 1–21 and 24–25.

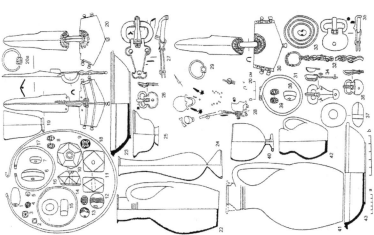

as well. This is particularly true for a fibula 'from the North Caucasus region' in the Ol'shevskii collection (Figure 4.1.5).[18]

The sheet bow fibula found in the village of Lenin, not far from Krasnodar, and another said to be 'from Maikop' have pressed semicircular mounts (Figures 4.11.1 and 4.6.26).[19] They both have good analogies among fibulae from Diurso and Bosporus (Figures 4.11.37; 4.8.26 and 51; 4.9.20 and 30; 4.6.8 and 24–25), the design of all of which was inspired by fibulae from the Middle Danube region, such as that from the Bákodpuszta.[20] Imitations of such fibulae from the Middle Danube region were quite common in Western Europe between the last third of the fifth century and the first third of the sixth.[21] According to Aleksander Dmitriev and Anatolii Ambroz, a number of features, such as small size, extra layers underneath fragile plates, or small round knobs, strongly suggest that the specimens from the Kuban-Black Sea region have all been manufactured locally. Most fibulae from Diurso have been found in assemblages dated to the third phase of the cemetery, namely to the last third of the fifth century and the early sixth century (graves 259, 408, 410, 516, and 517). Only one grave (291) with such fibulae may be dated to the first or second phase of the cemetery, that is, during the second half of the fifth century. With the exception of the pair of fibulae from grave 291, all other specimens from Diurso have a footplate widened in the middle and pointed at the end, not unlike that of similar fibulae from assemblages in Western Europe dated to the last quarter of the fifth century and the first third of the sixth.[22]

[18] It is impossible to read the details of the mounts on the published illustration of the fibula. See E. Chantre, *Recherches anthropologiques dans le Caucase*, III (Paris, 1886), pl. 17.3. However, judging from better drawings in the archives of the Institute for the History of Material Culture (Q503. 38, no. 326), it is quite clear that the fibula in the Ol'shevskii collection belongs to the same group as the Kamunta specimen.

[19] Oil was discovered in the environs of Maikop as early as 1901. Prior to the Bolshevik revolution of 1917, several European oil companies sent workers and experts to Maikop. Many of the artefacts those people purchased from local dealers (who had in turn obtained them from looted sites in the Kuban and Taman region) ended up on the antique market in Western Europe, especially in Germany. Those purchased by local museums are therefore commonly labelled as 'from Maikop,' although they may have well been from other sites in the northern Caucasus region.

[20] Attila Kiss, 'Die Skiren im Karpatenbecken, ihre Wohnsitze und ihre materielle Hinterlassenschaft', *Acta Archaeologica Academiae Scientiarum Hungaricae*, 35 (1983), 95–131 with fig. 8. Such fibulae appear also in the Lower Danube region: Ivan Velkov, 'Völkerwanderungszeitliche Grabfunde aus Bulgarien', *Germania*, 26 (1942), 48–50 with fig. 10A.

[21] Volker Bierbrauer, 'Les Wisigoths dans le royaume franc', *Antiquités nationales*, 29 (1997), 167–200 with pl. 1.1 and 2; Kazanski and Périn, 'Les Barbares "orientaux"', fig. 5.4 and 5.

[22] Kazanski, 'Khronologiia nachal'noi fazy', pp. 48–50.

Specimens with protruding mounts on the foot- and head-plates decorated with semispherical rivet heads are an altogether different line of development of the sheet bow fibulae. A pair of such fibulae are known from an assemblage said to be 'from Maikop' (Figure 4.10.4). An imitation of such developments is also the foot of the fragmentary fibula obtained from the eroded banks of the Krasnodar Reservoir (Figure 4.7.42). The earliest specimens with semispherical rivet heads are known from assemblages of the early Hunnic age.[23] Several early variants of specimens are known from a vast area between the Baltic Sea to the north, the Middle Danube region to the west, the Bosporus to the east, and the territory of the present-day Republic of Moldova to the south

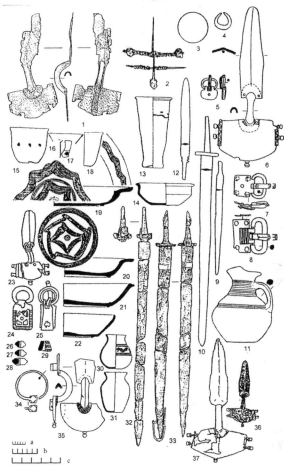

Figure 4.11. Sheet bow fibulae from the northern Caucasus and the Bosporan regions and associated artefacts: (1) Lenin; (2) Kumbulta; (3–14) grave 291 in Diurso; (15–34) grave 50 in Phanagoria; (35) Myskhako; (36) Kerch'; (37) 'Taman'. Scale a for 9–12 and 30–33; scale b for 13–22 and 26–29; scale c for 1–8, 23–25, and 34–37.

[23] Judging by the associated finds from grave 28 of the late Chernyakhov-culture cemetery excavated in Lazo (Republic of Moldova) and from the hoard found in Traprain Law (Scotland), such fibulae may have appeared as early as the late fourth or early fifth century. See A. N. Levinskii, 'Lazo: mogil'nik final'noi fazy cherniakhovskoi kul'tury v Moldove', *Stratum+*, 2 (1999), 121–67 (p. 145 with fig. 28); Alexander O. Curle, *The Treasure of Traprain: A Scottish Hoard of Roman Silver Plate* (Glasgow, 1923), p. 106 and pl. 32.

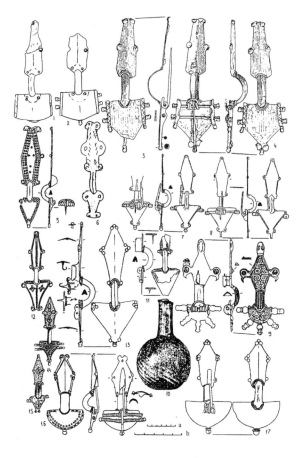

Figure 4.12. Sheet bow fibulae decorated with semispherical rivet from Bosporus and their prototypes: (1–2, 5–6, 14, and 17) Kerch', stray finds; (3–4) 'Southern Russia'; (7–10) burial chamber 11B/1905 in Kerch'; (11) Chersonesus; (12) Vajuga; (13) Untersiebenbrun; (15) Tápé-Lebö; (16) Lazo grave 28. Scale a for 10; scale b for 1–5, 7–9, and 11–17. Fibula 6 is known only from a drawing by A. A. Spitsyn, without scale.

(Figure 4.12.11–17).[24] While by the mid-fifth century such fibulae were replaced in Western Europe by other classes, in the north-eastern region of the Black Sea, two local series were developed and used during the subsequent decades.

One of them is characterized by a triangular head-plate and a pentagonal foot-plate (Figure 4.12.7–8).[25] The burial chamber 11B found in 1905 in Kerch' produced two burials, one with a pair of such fibulae, the other with a pair of fibulae of the Kerch type (Figure 4.12.9). The latter, despite the current controversy sur-

---

[24] Igor O. Gavritukhin, 'Final traditsii kul'tur rimskogo vremeni v Vostochnom Prikarpat'e', in *Die spätrömische Kaiserzeit und die frühe Völkerwanderungszeit im Mittel- und Osteuropa*, ed. by Magdalena Mączyńska and Tadeusz Grabarczyk (Łódź, 2000), pp. 262–324.

[25] For a complete list of finds (up to 1990), see Gavritukhin, 'Final traditsii', appendix 3.

rounding the details of its chronology, appeared only after 500. Irina Zasetskaia has advanced the idea that earlier versions without foot-plate knobs in the form of bird-heads may have been already in existence in the late fifth century.[26] On the other hand, the sheet bow fibulae with knobs are without any doubt imitations of Hunnic-age specimens. It is therefore likely that such fibulae of the first Black Sea series were in use between the mid-fifth and the early sixth centuries.

Specimens of the second Black Sea series are considerably larger and have pentagonal head-plates, a double spring, and two or three pairs of semispherical rivet heads (or imitations thereof) on the foot-plate. There are of course variations in the form of the head-plate, the type or even the presence of mounts, as well as the use of either true rivet heads or imitations (Figures 4.6.28–29; 4.10.1, 3–6; 4.12.1–4, 6). That the second series displays a much wider variety than the first series suggests that it remained in use for a comparatively longer time, no doubt because of its greater popularity. Unlike all other series of sheet bow fibulae, those of the second series appear singly in well-dated assemblages (Figure 4.10.6–29). One such fibula is known from grave 420 in Diurso, which belongs to the second phase of that site's chronology, and could thus be dated between 450 and 480/90. Most other specimens of the series are very similar to sheet bow fibulae with mounts discussed above and, judging by finds from Diurso and Khabl', could be dated between the second half of the fifth and the beginning of the sixth century. A fibula now in the collection of the British Museum is said to have been found within one and the same burial assemblage as a buckle with triangular plate (Figure 4.10.1–2), which has a good analogy in Diurso (Figure 4.9.30 and 34). It appears that the second Black Sea series of sheet bow fibulae with semispherical rivet heads coexisted during the second half of the fifth century (perhaps also during the first decades of the sixth century) with the first Black Sea series.

A key assemblage for the study of the sheet bow fibulae, their chronology, and coincidence in time with bow fibulae with chip-carved decoration is the burial vault 78 excavated in 1907 in Kerch' (Figure 4.13). In the eastern niche, a pair of fibulae of the Kerch type with a pair of bird-heads decorating the foot-plate was found in grave 12 (Figure 4.13.42). The entrance into the eastern niche was blocked by another grave (no. 1), which produced two bow fibulae with chip-carved decoration of Danubian inspiration, dated to the first third of the sixth

---

[26] For a survey of the controversy, see Irina P. Zasetskaia, 'Datirovka i proiskhozhdenie pal'chatykh fibul bosporskogo nekropolia rannesrednevekovogo perioda', *Materialy po arkheologii, istorii i etnografii Tavrii*, 6 (1997), 394–478.

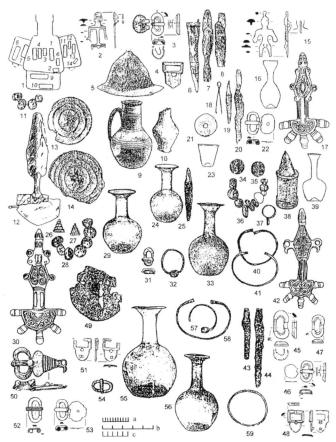

Figure 4.13. Kerch', grave goods from burial vault 78/1907: (1) plan of the vault; (2–10) grave 5; (11–14) grave 4; (15) grave 6; (16) by the right wall of the *dromos*; (17) grave 1; (18–23) grave 2; (24–25) niche over the left room; (26–30) grave 8; (31–32) grave 7; (33) niche over the right room; (34–42) grave 12; (43–48) grave 13; (49–56) grave 9; (57–59) grave 10. Scale a for 9–10, 16, 23, and 39; scale b for 2–4, 11–15, 17, 22, 26–28, 30–32, 34–38, 40–42, 45–54, and 57–59; scale c for 5–8, 18–21, 24–25, 29, 33, 43–44 and 55–56. After Zasetskaia, 'Datirovka i proiskhozhdenie' with additions from Aibabin, *Etnicheskaia istoriia*, and from originals (drawn by Igor O. Gavritukhin).

century (Figure 4.13.17). This strongly suggests that grave 12 is of an earlier date, which has considerable implications for the dating of the accompanying pair of fibulae of the Kerch type.[27] A fibula of the Udine-Planis type (Figure 4.13.30) was

---

[27] Kazanski, 'Les Germains orientaux', pp. 329 and 331.

found in grave 8 within the western niche. That type most likely originated in Bosporus at some point between the second quarter and the middle of the sixth century (see below for more details). The entrance into the western niche is blocked by grave 4, where a pair of sheet bow fibulae was found. Both fibulae appear to have mounts (Figure 4.13.12). This further suggests that sheet bow fibulae may have remained in use in Bosporus until the mid-sixth century. Finds in the burial vault thus fall into two groups, one linked to the Bosporan traditions of the late fifth or early sixth century, the other to later fashions. The glassware, the small buckles, and the other artefacts from the burial assemblages in the rooms and in the middle of the burial chamber are very similar to each other, which suggests a relatively short period of time for the complete filling of the burial vault within the first half or the mid-sixth century. During that same time, bow fibulae of the local Kerch type replaced the latest specimens of sheet bow fibulae as dress accessories for the local elites.

The examined sheet bow fibulae from the northern Caucasus region may be divided into two groups. The first group includes local imitations of Danubian specimens dated between 430/40 and 470/80. Such imitations cluster around Krasnodar and in the Kuban valley, on one hand, and in northern Ossetia, on the other hand (Figure 4.14). Finds from around Krasnodar are primarily imitations of the Levice and Székely series (Figure 4.1.14–15 and 18). The pair of fibulae and the associated grave goods from Khabl' (Figure 4.1.8–16) have close analogies in assemblages from Diurso and Kerch'.[28] The evidence strongly suggests the presence within the Krasnodar region of immigrants from the north-eastern Black Sea region, primarily women. It is commonly known that in archaic societies, the female costume or any part of it (with the exception of the princely costume) were not objects of trade, but moved more often together with the owner.[29] In this case, we may speak either of a relatively small colony or of exogamous relationships. Either situation evinces rather stable contacts of a group of the Kuban population with the inhabitants of Bosporus or with the closest territories inhabited by barbarians with connections with the Middle Danube region.

[28] Anna V. Mastykova, 'Sotsial'naia ierarkhiia zhenskikh mogil severokavkazskogo nekropolia Diurso (po materialam kostiuma)', *Istoriko-arkheologicheskii al'manakh*, (Armavir) 7 (2001), 58–69.

[29] Joachim Werner, 'Zur Verbreitung frühgeschichtlicher Metallarbeiten (Werkstatt-Wander-handwerk-Handel-Familienverbindung)', *Antikvariskt arkiv*, 38 (1970), 65–81; Vladimir Ia. Petrukhin, 'Ob osobennostiakh slaviano-skandinavskikh etnicheskikh otnoshenii v rannefeodal'nyi period (IX–XI vv.)', *Drevneishie gosudarstva na territorii SSSR*, 1981 (1983), 174–81.

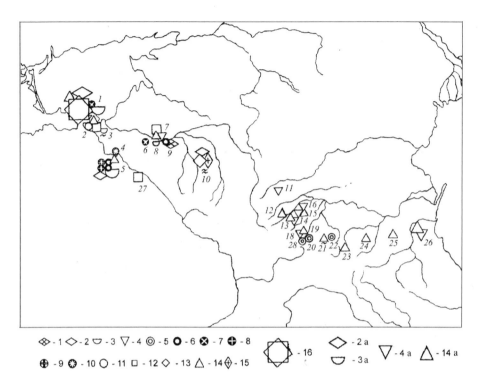

Figure 4.14. Distribution of fibulae and buckles of Bosporan and Tetraxite Goths inspiration or origin in the northern Caucasus region: (1–2) fibulae with semispherical rivet heads of the second Black Sea series or imitations; (3) sheet bow fibulae with mounts of the Diurso-Kerch' series; (4) sheet bow fibulae with three knobs of the northern Caucasus series; (5) North-Caucasian imitations of sheet bow fibulae of the Székely or Levice series; (6) Kuban-Black Sea variants of sheet bow fibulae of the Székely series; (7) Kuban-Black Sea variants of sheet bow fibulae of the Levice series; (8–9) imitations of the Grocka series; (10) variants of sheet bow fibulae with engraved mounts; (11) sheet bow fibulae of undefined series; (12) Black Sea series of bow fibula of the Udine-Planis type; (13) bow fibulae with chip-carved decoration of the Kerch' type; (14) cicada-brooches of the Dyerken type; (15) buckles of the Mačvanska Mitrovica-Noşlac type; (16) bow fibulae with chip-carved decoration from Kerch' (2a, 3a, 4a, 14a = three or more finds). Sites: *(1)* Kerch'; *(2)* Phanagoria; *(3)* 'Taman'; *(4)* Myskhako; *(5)* Diurso; *(6)* Khabl'; *(7)* Pashkovskyi; *(8)* Lenin; *(9)* Krasnodar Reservoir; *(10)* 'Maikop'; *(11)* Kislovodskoe ozero; *(12)* Tyrnyauz; *(13)* Bylym (Kudinetovo and Ozorukovo); *(14)* 'Baksan or Chegem'; *(15)* 'Chegem'; *(16)* Bachil-aul; *(17)* Mukulan; *(18)* Niznia Rutkha; *(19)* Kumbulta; *(20)* Kamunta; *(21)* 'Northern Ossetia'; *(22)* Saniba; *(23)* Kharachoi; *(24)* Martan-Chu; *(25)* Berduty; *(26)* Chir-Yurt; *(27)* Bzhid; *(28)* 'Kamunta or Kumbulta'.

The fibulae found in northern Ossetia were imitations of the same series (Figure 4.1.5–7), but with typically round head-plates and shorter foot-plates. Such features suggest that those were either imitations of Bosporan specimens (such as those on Figure 4.7.57–58) or altogether local variants of the general series.[30] The latter seems more probable, given the existence in northern Ossetia, already during the Hunnic period, of artefacts manufactured after Middle Danubian models.[31] The appearance in the northern Caucasus region of local centres for the production of such dress accessories is the result of the influence upon local elites of prestigious aristocratic fashions through the network of political connections across Europe.[32] Bosporus at that time was not only a centre for the formation of local styles but, apparently, also played a leading role in mediating contacts between communities in the Caucasus region and the barbarian polities of the Danube region.

Finds from the second group include fibulae dated to the second half (or perhaps last third) of the fifth century and the first third of the sixth, which are modelled after distinctively Danubian specimens, but are not their direct imitations. Such fibulae cluster in the Kuban region between Krasnodar and Maikop (Figures 4.11.1; 4.6.26; 4.10.4; 4.7.42; and 4.14). It follows that this group represents the continuation of the traditional contacts mentioned above in relation to fibulae of the first group. The assemblages in Diurso show that fibulae of the second group are later than those of the first group, even though the two groups may have coexisted for a brief period of time. This is evident from the fact that fibulae from both groups appear in assemblages of the first and second phases of the chronology of the Diurso cemetery, while only fibulae of the second group are known from assemblages of the third phase (graves 259, 408, 410, 516, and 517).

---

[30] Vladimir A. Khrshanovskii, 'Pozdneantichnye pogrebeniia na nekropole Ilurata', in *Nauchno-ateisticheskie issledovaniia v muzeiakh: Sbornik nauchnykh trudov*, ed. by V. A. Khrshanovskii (Leningrad, 1988), pp. 16–27. For local fibulae of the Hunnic period in Dagestan, see Figure 4.7.54; for other Caucasian finds, see Figure 4.7.47 and 49. See also Liudmila B. Gmyria, *Prikaspiiskii Dagestan v epokhu velikogo pereseleniia narodov* (Makhachkala, 1993).

[31] Michel Kazanski and Anna V. Mastykova, 'Germanskie elementy v kul'ture naseleniia Severnogo Kavkaza v epokhu velikogo pereseleniia narodov', *Istoriko-arkheologicheskii al'manakh*, (Armavir) 4 (1998), 102–35.

[32] Jaroslav Tejral, *Mähren im 5. Jahrhundert* (Prague, 1973); Tejral, 'Neue Aspekte'; Michel Kazanski, 'Les Tombes "princières" de l'horizon Untersiebenbrunn, le problème de l'identification éthnique', in *L'Identité des populations archéologiques: Actes des rencontres, 19–20–21 octobre 1995* (Sophia-Antipolis, 1996), pp. 109–26; Michel Kazanski, 'Les Tombes des chefs militaires de l'époque hunnique', in *Germanen beiderseits des spätantiken Limes*, ed. by Thomas Fischer, Gundolf Precht, and Jaroslav Tejral (Brno, 1999), pp. 293–316.

Bow Fibulae with Chip-carved Decoration

Bow fibulae are not particularly numerous in the Caucasus region. Volutes decorating head-plates and foot-plates with concentric diamond-shaped ornaments are a feature signalling the influence of the workshops in the Black Sea region. Two such fibulae, which have been classified by Herbert Kühn as the Gurzuf type, are said to be 'from Maikop' (Figure 4.15.1 and 18).[33] Judging by the unique features of their ornamenting style, as well as by the distribution of their closest analogies, both fibulae must be associated with Crimean influences. However, they may very well have been manufactured locally or in some cases, there is no doubt, in Bosporus.[34] At any rate, most scholars currently embrace the opinions expressed by Bernhard Salin and Anatolii Ambroz, according to which bow fibulae appeared in Crimea as a result of a cultural impulse from the Danube region.[35]

One may take such views a step further. The appearance of bow fibulae with chip-carved decoration within the Hunnic-age barbarian milieu of the Danube region was the result of an increasing influence of the traditions of late Roman craftsmanship. A good case in point is the fibula from the Úherce cemetery.[36] The bow fibulae with three head-plate knobs, which appear in the Middle Danube region in the mid-400s, are a direct outgrowth of that development. The earliest specimens of that kind have no projections on either side of the foot-plate.[37] Particularly interesting in this respect are fibulae with a large, cast head-plate knob in the middle and with two side knobs prolonging the axis of the brooch spring. To this group belong, for example, the fibulae from Sokolnice, the brooches of the Záhony class from the Upper Tisza region, as well as an 'import' from Taman' and the fibula found in 1973 in Chersonesus (Figure 4.15.30).[38] In parallel to those fibulae, much simpler imitations were produced, such as Bákodpuszta and Cífer-Pác, on which all knobs were cast together with the head-plate.[39]

---

[33] See above, note 19. See also Kazanski, 'Les Germains orientaux', p. 326.

[34] Igor O. Gavritukhin, 'Bospor i Podneprov'e v IV–VII vv. (k izucheniiu severopontiiskikh iuvelirnykh shkol)', in *Mezhdunarodnaia konferentsiia 'Vizantiia i Krym', Sevastopol', 6–11 iunia 1997 g. Tezisy dokladov* (Simferopol, 1997), pp. 27–32; Zasetskaia, 'Datirovka i proiskhozhdenie'.

[35] For a brief survey of this problem, see Aleksandr I. Aibabin, 'Khronologiia mogil'nikov Kryma pozdnerimskogo i rannesrednevekovogo vremeni', *Materialy po arkheologii, istorii i etnografii Tavrii*, 1 (1990), 5–68 (pp. 20–21).

[36] Tejral, 'Neue Aspekte', fig. 27.7.

[37] Gavritukhin, 'Bospor i Podneprov'e'.

[38] For Sokolnice, see Tejral, 'Neue Aspekte', fig. 28.13–14.

[39] Tejral, 'Neue Aspekte', fig. 28.12 and 15–16.

Figure 4.15. Bow fibulae with chip-carved decoration from the northern Caucasus region and from Bosporus and their analogies: (1 and 18) 'Maikop'; (2–5, 8, 16, 22–23, 25, and 28) 'Kerch'; (6) Prague-Podbaba; (7) grave 27 in Szentes-Berekhát; (9) Suuk-Su, stray find; (10–11 and 20–21) grave 155 in Suuk-Su; (12–17) burial vault 14/1914 in Chersonesus; (19) burial vault 3/1975 in Chersonesus; (24) Kursk; (26) Velký Pesek-Sikenica; (27) grave 88 in Kiszombor; (29) Grunajki; (30) Chersonesus, stray find.

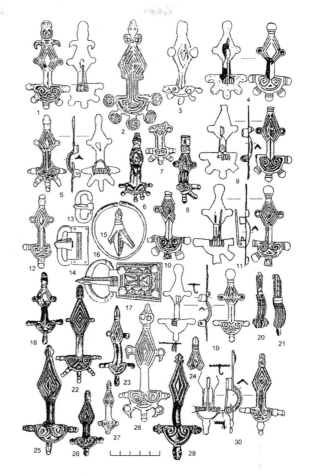

The finds from the Middle Danube region, the apparent centre for the diffusion of such dress accessories, describe all the phases in the development of the bow fibulae with chip-carved decoration. However, echoes of that development are also apparent in finds from the Baltic region, the forest belt of Eastern Europe (Figure 4.15.24), and Crimea, all of which may be interpreted as 'imports' from the Danube area[40] or 'close imitations'. The 'imports' became the basis for the development of a local type of bow fibula with chip-carved decoration, known as the Gurzuf type, early specimens of which have been found, besides Chersonesus, in

[40] For the Baltic region, see Herbert Kühn, *Die germanischen Bügelfibeln der Völkerwanderungszeit in Süddeutschland* (Graz, 1974), pl. 261.64, 5.

Velký Pesek-Sikenica (Slovakia), Grunajki (former Gruneiken, in north-eastern Poland), and Kursk (Russia) (Figure 4.15.24, 26, 29, and 30).[41] Very similar fibulae or local imitations of the Gurzuf type have been attributed to the Gepid (or barbarian, in general) milieu of the Carpathian Basin, to the material culture of the barbarian federate troops in Italy and the Balkans, on the Rhine, and on the northern coast of the Black Sea, including Kerch'.[42] Most such fibulae can be dated to the second half of the fifth and the early sixth centuries.[43] One of them, found in grave 88 of the Gepid cemetery excavated in Kiszombor (Hungary) together with a knife of a characteristic shape, dated not earlier than the first third of the sixth century, is a much simplified version of the Gurzuf type (Figure 4.15.27).[44]

The development of the Gurzuf type cannot therefore be separated from the appearance of local variations, their reciprocal influences, as well as stylistic influences from other types of bow fibulae. This is particularly true for the appearance of foot-plate knobs already during the second half of the fifth century (Figure 4.15.12–17), such as that found in Ártánd in north-eastern Hungary.[45] The pentagonal head-plate of such fibulae is reminiscent of various types of sheet bow

[41] For Velký Pesek-Sikenica, see Tejral, 'Neue Aspekte', fig. 28.8–9.

[42] Dezső Csallány, *Archäologische Denkmäler der Gepiden im Mitteldonaubecken (454–568 u.Z.)* (Budapest, 1961), pl. 134.2; Volker Bierbrauer, *Die ostgotischen Grab- und Schatzfunde in Italien* (Spoleto, 1975), pl. 39.8; Teodora Kovacheva and Anna Kharalambieva, 'Fibuli ot epokhata na Velikoto preselenie na Narodnite v Plevenskiia Muzei', *Izvestiia na Muzeite v Severozapadna Bălgariia*, 18 (1992), 47–51 with pl. 1.3; Gheorghe Mănucu-Adameşteanu, 'Un mormînt germanic din necropola cetăţii Argamum', *Studii şi cercetări de istorie veche şi arheologie*, 31 (1980), 311–20 with fig. 4; Spas Mashov, 'Rannosrednovekovni fibuli ot Avgusta pri s. Khărlets, Vrachanski okrăg', *Arkheologiia*, 18 (1976), 35–39 with fig. 1a and b; Kühn, *Die germanische Bügelfibeln der Völkerwanderungszeit im Süddeutschland*, pls 261.64,3, 6, 10–13, and 26; 262.64,36, 37, and 48.

[43] Ioan Glodariu, 'Ein Grab aus dem 5. Jahrhundert in Slimnic (Rumänien)', *Germania*, 52 (1974), 483–89 with fig. 2.4–5; Attila Kiss, 'Germanischer Grabfund der Völkerwanderungszeit in Jóbbagyi', *Alba Regia*, 19 (1982), 167–85 with fig. 1.7.

[44] Csallány, *Archäologische Denkmäler*, pl. 134. A similar knife was found in grave 146 of the same cemetery together with a belt buckle with a club-shaped tongue. It has wrongly been assumed that such buckles had gone out of use in Western and Central Europe by 530 or 540. See Helmut Roth and Claudia Theune, *Zur Chronologie merowingerzeitlicher Frauengräber in Südwestdeutschland* (Stuttgart, 1988), no. 23; Ursula Koch, *Das alamannisch-fränkische Gräberfeld bei Pleidelsheim* (Stuttgart, 2001); René Legoux, Patrick Périn, and Françoise Vallet, *Chronologie normalisée du mobilier funéraire mérovingien entre Manche et Lorraine* (Saint-Germain-en-Laye, 2006), no. 109.

[45] The Ártánd fibula has not been published. Many thanks are due to Eszter Istvánovits for the information regarding this artefact.

fibulae, including the Bratei type. This is particularly true for the fibula from a grave in Argamum, where it was associated with another of the Bratei-Vyškov class.[46] Fibulae of the Bratei-Vyškov class have been dated to the first half of the fifth century, but they undoubtedly were in use at a later date as well, as demonstrated by the specimen found in Buschberg, which has been dated between 430/40 and 470/80.[47] Apparently, the Argamum assemblage may also be dated to the third quarter of the fifth century, which suggests that alterations of the Gurzuf type were already taking place at that time.

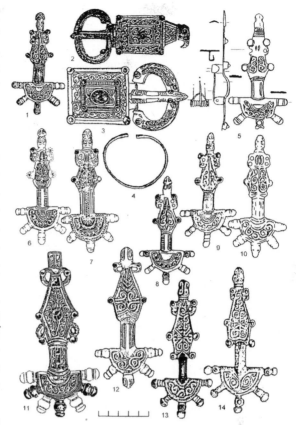

Figure 4.16. Bow fibulae with chip-carved decoration from Bosporus and associated artefacts, and their analogies: (1–4 and 8) Kerch'; (5) Artek; (6) Pećinska Reka; (7) Lörrach-Tumringerstrasse; (9) Vojnikovo; (10) Cherkasy region; (11) 'Hungary'; (12) Belgrade-Čukarice; (13) 'Bulgaria'; (14) Archar.

Another such alteration was the addition of no less than five knobs to the head-plate. Various other kinds of fibulae with five or even seven knobs were already known in the Danube region by the last half of the fifth century (e.g. Figure 4.16.11). However, specimens of the Gurzuf type with five knobs cannot be dated in that region before 500, as shown by the fibula from grave 1 in Dravlje, in which

[46] Mănucu-Adameşteanu, 'Un mormînt germanic', fig. 3.

[47] Erik Szameit, 'Ein völkerwanderungszeitliches Werkzeugdepot mit Kleinfunden aus Niederösterreich', in *Neue Beiträge zur Erforschung der Spätantike im mittleren Donauraum*, ed. by Tejral, pp. 233–57 with pl. 5.1–3. See also Gavritukhin, 'Final traditsii'.

it was associated with an early sixth-century buckle of the so-called Ljubljana-Dravlje type.[48]

In a number of cases, one can single out local series and variations of the Gurzuf type by means of a combination of characteristic features. Features such as a rounded head-plate, often of a small size, in combination with elongated knobs, as well as the tendency to the ornament consisting of a pair of volutes into a half-oval with points turned inward, single out the 'Gepid' series of Gurzuf type fibulae with five knobs (e.g. Figure 4.15.7–8).[49] Very similar features appear on 'Gepid' fibulae with three knobs, which often display short, chunky foot-plates (e.g. Figure 4.15.27).[50] Fibulae, reminiscent of the Gurzuf type but manufactured in accordance with local traditions, have also been found in the valley of the Elbe river (e.g. Figure 4.15.6).[51] Specimens from Italy display features which are otherwise typical for 'Ostrogothic' fibulae of different types.[52] Fibulae with five knobs and foot-plates without projections on the sides also appear in the Lower Danube region.[53] An interesting fibula of the Gurzuf type from Spas-Pereksha with closely twisted volutes has good analogies among buckles from the Upper Dnieper region, all of which are decorated in the tradition of the Middle Danube barbarian milieu of the second half of the fifth century.[54]

---

[48] Marijan Slabe, *Dravlje: Grobišče iz časov preseljevanja ljudstev* (Ljubljana, 1975), pl. 1.1–2; for the dating of the buckles of the Ljubljana-Dravlje class, see Bierbrauer, *Die ostgotischen Grab- und Schatzfunde*, p. 131.

[49] Csallány, *Archäologische Denkmäler*, pls 79.17 and 159.5; Dušan Mrkobrad, *Arheološki nalazi seobe naroda u Jugoslaviji* (Belgrade, 1980), pl. 36.1 and 4; Kühn, *Die germanische Bügelfibeln der Völkerwanderungszeit im Süddeutschland*, pl. 261.64,19, 21, 23, and 25.

[50] Csallány, *Archäologische Denkmäler*, pls 226.5 and 7; 159.5; Kühn, *Die germanische Bügelfibeln der Völkerwanderungszeit im Süddeutschland*, pl. 261.64,14 and 27.

[51] Kühn, *Die germanische Bügelfibeln der Völkerwanderungszeit im Süddeutschland*, pl. 261.64,30; Berthold Schmidt, *Die späte Völkerwanderungszeit in Mitteldeutschland* (Halle, 1961), fig. 31h.1.

[52] Bierbrauer, *Die ostgotischen Grab- und Schatzfunde*, figs 2.4, 52.1, and 73.3.

[53] Uwe Fiedler, *Studien zu Gräberfeldern des 6. bis 9. Jahrhunderts an der unteren Donau* (Bonn, 1992), fig. 17.11–13.

[54] Equally good analogies are the buckles from Blučina in Moravia (Czech Republic) and the chape of a sword of Danubian origin found in a warrior burial in Taurapilis (Lithuania). See Anatolii K. Ambroz, 'Iuzhnye khudozhestvennye sviazi naselenie verkhnogo Podneprov'ia v VI v.', in *Drevnie slaviane i ikh sosedi*, ed. by Iurii V. Kukharenko and Petr N. Tret'iakov (Moscow, 1970), pp. 70–74; Gavritukhin, 'Bospor i Podneprov'e'; Michel Kazanski, 'La Zone forestière de la Russie et l'Europe centrale à la fin de l'époque des Grandes Migrations', in *Die spätrömische Kaiserzeit*, ed. by Maczyńska and Grabarczyk, pp. 406–59 (p. 419).

Figure 4.17. Sheet bow fibulae with three knobs from the northern Caucasus with associated artefacts and from Bosporus and their analogies and prototypes: (1) 'Baksan or Chegem'; (2) Bachil-aul; (3) Pashkovskyi 1, stray find; (4–31) grave 15/1948 in Pashkovskyi 1; (32) Moschenka; (33–35 and 39–42) Kerch'; (36) Lalići; (37) Sveti Lambert pri Prstavi nad Stično; (38) 'Maikop'; (43) 'region of Kiev' (British Museum collection). Fibula 34 is known only from a drawing by A. A. Spitsyn, without scale.

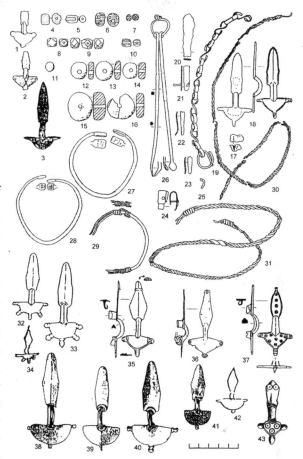

The complex network of mutual influences and relationships between 'imports' and local series is best represented by finds from Crimea and Eastern Europe. A number of very stylish specimens of the Gurzuf type from Chersonesus are undoubtedly imports, perhaps very early. Simpler fibulae with three knobs and foot-plates without projections on the sides are known from a vast territory in the southern part of Eastern Europe (Figure 4.15.25). Judging by their features, most of them are not different from specimens known from the Middle Danube region or from the Balkans. Only a few finds from Kursk and 'Southern Russia' display a uniquely pointed end of the foot-plate (Figures 4.15.24; 4.17.35). However, despite such a peculiar feature, there does not seem to be any basis for advancing the idea of a local production.

The same may be said about more 'developed' variations. A fibula with three knobs and a foot-plate without projections on the sides ending in a stylized animal-head terminal lobe is known from the local museum collection in Kerch'.[55] Its

[55] Aibabin, 'Khronologiia mogil'nikov', fig. 14.10.

closest analogies are from the Lower Danube region. There are also similar fibulae with five knobs, one of which, from the collection of the British Museum, has a foot-plate most typical for the Danubian specimens. The foot-plate of another fibula from the Grempler collection (Figure 4.15.22) reminds one of the East European finds with pointed foot-plates (Figure 4.15.24). Most East European finds cannot be dated with any degree of precision. However, because of their similarity to Danubian finds, it is possible to advance with some caution the idea that they too must be dated between the second half of the fifth century and the first decades of the sixth. East European finds are either imports or singular, local imitations. A fibula from the collection of the National Museum in Stockholm, which is said to be from Kerch', displays the typical features of the Danubian specimens of the series, which also became the hallmark of the Bosporan production of bow fibulae: a foot-plate decorated with concentric diamonds and the chain-like ornament of the head-plate (Figure 4.15.23).[56]

On the other hand, there is another group of East European finds which are clearly local variants of the Gurzuf type. A number of standardized specimens are known only from Kerch' and may have been an attempt to blend features of the Gurzuf and Kerch types (Figure 4.15.18).[57] Although no such fibulae have so far been found in 'closed-find' assemblages, it is likely that they were already in use in the early 500s, judging by the date of their models, such as that from the Kerch' burial chamber 78 discussed above.

Fibulae with three knobs and foot-plate ending in an elongated terminal lobe represent another local series (Figure 4.15.12 and 18).[58] The latter feature appears on fibulae of the Levice-Tokary class from Bulgaria.[59] However, on the fibulae of the Gurzuf type that feature may be noted only on specimens from Southern Crimea, 'Southern Russia', and 'from Maikop'. The chronology of this local series of the Gurzuf type is based on the finds from burial chamber 14 excavated in 1914 in Chersonesus (Figure 4.15.12–17).[60] This particular assemblage produced buckles of different types, the combination of which is typical for the entire period between the second half (or late decades) of the fifth century and the first half of

---

[56] Kühn, *Die germanische Bügelfibeln der Völkerwanderungszeit im Süddeutschland*, pl. 261.64,4.

[57] Zasetskaia, 'Datirovka i proiskhozhdenie', p. 404.

[58] Zasetskaia, 'Datirovka i proiskhozhdenie', p. 405.

[59] Igor O. Gavritukhin, 'Prichernomorskaia seriia fibul gruppy Levitse-Tokari (k izucheniiu vostochnogermanskogo kul'turnogo naslediia)', *Bosporskii sbornik*, 4 (1994), 32–42 with fig. 2.19.

[60] Aibabin, 'Khronologiia mogil'nikov', pp. 29–30.

the sixth.[61] There was also a cicada-brooch with good analogies in the Buschberg hoard dated between 430/40 and 470/80.[62] Apparently, burial chamber 14 in Chersonesus must be dated to the second half (possibly, even the last decades) of the fifth century, which constitutes a benchmark for the chronology of the Gurzuf-type fibulae with three knobs and foot-plate ending in an elongated terminal lobe.

Several other finds fall within the other local Black Sea series of the Gurzuf type (Figure 4.15.3–5, 9–11, and 19). They all display ornamental features which can otherwise be found on other artefacts of local manufacture. Fibulae of all three series may thus be regarded as signalling the beginning of a local production in Crimea, which was based on the imitation of 'imports' or singular, local replicas. The beginning of a local production may be dated shortly before or after AD 500, although, judging by finds from south-western Crimea, such fibulae may have re-mained in use until AD 600. For example, the finds from burial chamber 77 excavated in Luchistoe near Alushta (Figures 4.18, 4.19) may be dated to the late sixth or early seventh century.[63] A similar date may be advanced for the finds from grave 155 of the Suuk-Su cemetery, which also produced the belt buckle with the image of a lion, the buckle of 'heraldic' style, and two byzantian fibulae (Figure 4.15.10–11, 20–21).[64]

One of the fibulae said to be 'from Maikop' (Figure 4.15.18) best illustrates the first attempts in the late fifth century at creating a local series of the Gurzuf type imitating specimens from the Balkans or the Danube region. There are no exact parallels in Bosporus, but every detail has analogies on fibulae from this series, especially on those from Kerch'. On the other hand, there are no traces of direct contact during the second half of the fifth and the sixth centuries between South Crimea and the Kuban region, bypassing Bosporus. It is also important to note the paucity of available specimens for this series, as well as the uncertainty of prove-nance for many of them. Evidently, the fibula 'from Maikop' may well have arrived to the northern Caucasus region from Bosporus.

[61] Michel Kazanski, 'Les Plaques-boucles méditérranéennes des Vᵉ–VIᵉ siècles', *Archéologie médiévale*, 24 (1994), 137–98.

[62] Szameit, 'Ein völkerwanderungszeitliches Werkzeugdepot', fig. 5.4.

[63] Aleksandr I. Aibabin and Elzara A. Khairedinova. 'Novyi kompleks s pal'chatymi fibulami s nekropol'ia u s. Luchistoe', *Materialy po arkheologii, istorii i etnografii Tavrii*, 5 (1996), 85–93 and 496–506; Gavritukhin and Oblomskii, *Gaponovskii klad*, figs 67–72 and 90 (artefacts most typical for the second phase of the Suuk-Su culture).

[64] N. I. Repnikov, 'Nekotorye mogil'niki oblasti krymskikh gotov', *Zapiski Odesskogo obshchestva istorii i drevnostei*, 27 (1907), 101–48 (pp. 117–18).

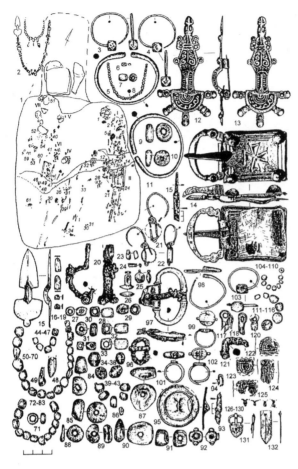

Figure 4.18. Bow fibulae with chip-carved decoration from burial chamber 77 in Luchistoe (Crimea) and associated artefacts: (1) plan of the chamber (I, II, ... VII – number of the grave); (2) reconstruction of the breast ornaments according to Elzara Khairedinova); (3–14) grave 1; (15–120) grave 2; (121–32) grave 2 or 3. See also Figure 4.19.

The size, the proportions, the unique features of the head-plate, and a number of other minute details underline the similarity between the second Gurzuf-type fibula 'from Maikop' (Figure 4.15.1) and the Black Sea series of fibulae with five knobs and foot-plates ending in rounded terminal lobes (Figure 4.15.3, 4, and 9–11).[65] The only features of the fibula 'from Maikop' which distinguish it from other specimens of that series are the animal head–shaped terminal lobe with two reversed bird-head beaks on either side, at the end of the foot-plate. Similar fibulae from Kerch' and South Crimea (Figure 4.15.5, 22, 25, and 28) display a very different treatment of the foot-plate end. In that respect, the fibula 'from Maikop'

---

[65] Gavritukhin, 'Bospor i Podneprov'e'. This is subtype 4B of the Kerch fibulae, according to Irina Zasetskaia's classification (Zasetskaia, 'Datirovka i proiskhozhdenie').

reminds one of specimens of the 'Gepid' series or of fibulae from northern Bulgaria (e.g. Figure 4.16.13–14). It appears that the fibulae 'from Maikop' represent the peculiar combination of an attempt to create a local variant of standard Bosporan fibulae with stylistic influences from the Danube region. This is by no means a unique example. A similar synthesis of Bosporan traditions and additional Danubian impulses is apparent also on a fibula from the Diergardt collection in the Römisch-Germanisches Museum in Mainz, which is also said to have been found in Kerch' (Figure 4.15.2). To this one can add another fibula from Kerch', a brooch with five knobs, which is a typical specimen of the 'Gepid' series (Figure 4.15.8).[66] Responsible for this new 'injection' of cultural influence from the Danube region may be the arrival in Crimea and Bosporus of more military units from

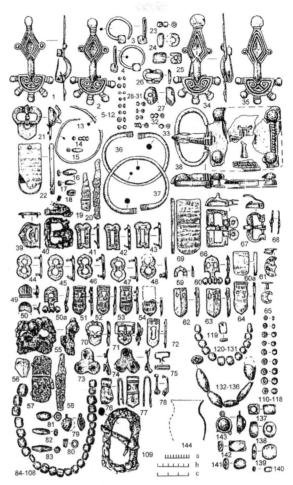

Figure 4.19. Bow fibulae with chip-carved decoration from burial chamber 77 in Luchistoe and associated artefacts: (1–18, 21–22) grave 6; (19–20 and 23–38) grave 7; (39–58) grave 4; (59–69) grave 5; (70–109) grave 3; (110–43) near the north-western wall of the chamber; (144) grave 1. Scale a for 144; scale b for 19–20 and 58; scale c for 1–18, 21–57, and 59–143. See also Figure 4.18

[66] Kühn, *Die germanische Bügelfibeln der Völkerwanderungszeit im Süddeutschland*, pl. 261.64,55.

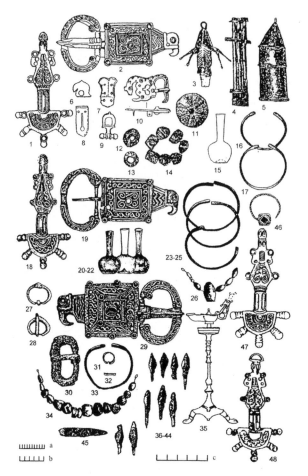

Figure 4.20. Bow fibulae with chip-carved decoration from Kerch' (Bosporus) and associated artefacts: (1–17) vault 180/1904, grave 7; (18–45) vault 152/1904 (18–26 = upper-level graves; 27–45 = lower-level graves); (46–47) grave 1/1977; (48) 'Southern Russia'. Scale a for 15, 20–22, and 35; scale b for 16–17 and 36–45; scale c for 1–14, 18–19, 23–34, and 47–48.

that region during the early years of Emperor Justinian's reign.[67] If so, then the most likely date for the Bosporan fibulae in question (Figure 4.15.1–2), including that 'from Maikop', is the second third to second half of the sixth century.

A bow fibula with chip-carved decoration appears among a number of stray finds from the cemetery of Pashkovskyi 1, now in Krasnodar. It belongs to a group of Bosporan imitations of the Udine-Planis type (Figure 4.20.1, 18, 47, and 48; 4.16.1 and 8–10), known as Zasetskaia's type III.[68] The models for such imitations were lavishly decorated fibulae from the Danube region dated to the second half of the

---

[67] Kazanski, 'Les Germains orientaux', p. 328; Kazanski, 'Les Tombes des chefs militaires', p. 286.
[68] Zasetskaia, 'Datirovka i proiskhozhdenie'.

fifth century (as in Figure 4.16.11–12). There are a great number and variety of imitations.[69] The Udine-Planis type appeared in the Ostrogothic milieu of Italy, most likely during the reign of Theoderic (471/73–526). The type comprises a number of series distinguished by the decoration of the central panel of the head-plate.[70] For example, Udine-Planis fibulae with head-plates decorated with half-circles filled with chip-carved stars or vertical lines (as in Figure 4.16.7) appear in Italy and the western Balkans, as well as north of the Alps.[71] The Black Sea series displays a different decoration of the head-plate, with a half-circle filled not with stars or vertical lines, but only with relief arcs. Such a decorative option is already apparent on fibulae from the Middle Danube dated to the second half of the fifth century (e.g. Figure 4.16.11) and must have been adopted in the Black Sea area as a consequence of a cultural influence from that direction.[72] If, as generally accepted, the Udine-Planis type originated in the Ostrogothic milieu of the Lower Danube region or in Italy, then it is likely that its Black Sea series appeared through the mediation of the barbarian milieu in the Middle Danube region (e.g. Figure 4.16.6) or in the Balkans.

The chronology of the Black Sea series of the Udine-Planis type is based on a number of Kerch' assemblages, in which such fibulae are consistently associated with eagle-headed buckles of the Kerch' series, later variants of Bosporan glassware, and belt sets with open-work ornamentation (Figures 4.20.1–2, 6–10, 15, and 18–22; 4.16.1–2). According to Irina Zasetskaia, such assemblages must be dated between the mid-sixth and the early seventh century. Comparable assemblages outside Bosporus do not contradict Zasetskaia's conclusion, for they all point to a date between the last decades of the sixth and the first decades of the seventh century (Figures 4.18, 4.19).[73] On the other hand, according to Anatolii Ambroz and

---

[69] Gavritukhin, 'Bospor i Podneprov'e', pp. 28–29 and 32.

[70] Gavritukhin, 'Bospor i Podneprov'e'.

[71] Gavritukhin, 'Bospor i Podneprov'e', figs 51–53. Volker Bierbrauer has attributed the specific development of this series to the general area of Ostrogothic cultural influence. See Volker Bierbrauer, 'Zu den Vorkommen ostgotischer Bügelfibeln in Raetia II', *Bayerische Vorgeschichtsblätter*, 36 (1971), 133–47.

[72] Gavritukhin, 'Bospor i Podneprov'e', figs 18, 20–23, 43, 49, 50; Igor O. Gavritukhin, 'Palchatye fibuly prazhskikh pamiatnikov Podnestrov'ia', in *Drevnosti Severnogo Kavkaza i Prichernomor'ia*, ed. by A. P. Abramov and others (Moscow, 1991), pp. 127–41 (p. 135 with pls 1.1–3, 2.1–8 and 10–12, and the comments on the map in appendix 1).

[73] This is further confirmed by the date of the burial assemblage in grave 144 of the cemetery excavated in Bzhid near Dzhubga, on the Black Sea coast of the Krasnodar region. We are grateful to Aleksei V. P'iankov for the details of his unpublished excavations in Bzhid.

Aleksandr Aibabin, various components of such assemblages may have remained in use for much longer time.[74] In any case, the earliest assemblage with Udine-Planis fibulae of the Black Sea series is burial chamber 78 excavated in 1907 in Kerch' (Figure 4.13), which seems to have been filled at some point during the first half or the middle of the sixth century. Taking into account the prototypes from the Balkan and Danube regions, it seems entirely justified to associate the appearance of the Black Sea series of the Udine-Planis fibulae with the abovementioned events of the early years of Emperor Justinian's reign, namely the arrival to Crimea and Bosporus of military units made up of Goths from the Balkans.

Buckles with Diamond-shaped Plates and Chip-carved Decoration

A buckle from the Diergardt collection of the Römisch-Germanisches Museum in Mainz, which is said to be 'from Maikop', is the Caucasian specimen of an otherwise well-known group of finds (Figure 4.21.1). Buckles with diamond-shaped plates and scrollwork have already been the object of many studies.[75]

The earliest examples of buckles with diamond-shaped plates with raised borders can be dated to the Hunnic age. Their appearance in the barbarian milieu of the Middle Danube region must be attributed to the influence of late antique craftsmanship (e.g. Figure 4.21.11). The spread of styles and the greatest diversity of forms taken by such buckles occurred approximately between 450 and 500 in connection to a number of production centres in the Danube region. Belt buckles with diamond-shaped plates were part of the female dress, which also included such accessories as fibulae, earrings, necklaces, bracelets, mirrors, and a variety of pendants. Especially representative in this respect are sheet bow fibulae with 'knobs'

---

[74] Aleksandr I. Aibabin, *Etnicheskaia istoriia rannevizantiiskogo Kryma* (Simferopol, 1999), p. 271.

[75] Giuseppe Annibaldi and Joachim Werner, 'Ostgotische Grabfunde aus Acquasanta, Prov. Ascoli Piceno (Marche)', *Germania*, 41 (1963), 356–73; Anatolii K. Ambroz, 'Dunaiskie elementy v rannesrednevekovoi kul'ture Kryma (VI–VII vv.)', *Kratkie soobshcheniia Instituta Arkheologii Akademii Nauk SSSR*, 113 (1968), 10–23; Bierbrauer, *Die ostgotischen Grab- und Schatzfunde*, pp. 134–42; Joachim Werner, 'Der Grabfund von Taurapilis, Rayon Utna (Litauen) und die Verbindung der Balten zum Reich Theoderichs', in *Archäologische Beiträge zur Chronologie der Völkerwanderungszeit*, ed. by Georg Kossack and Joachim Reichstein (Bonn, 1977), pp. 87–92; Evgenii V. Veimarn and Anatolii K. Ambroz, 'Bol'shaia priazhka iz Skalistinskogo mogil'nika', *Sovetskaia Arkheologiia*, 1980.3, 247–69; Attila Kiss, 'Über eine silbervergoldete gepidische Schnalle aus dem 5. Jahrhundert von Ungarn', *Folia Archaeologica*, 35 (1984), 57–76.

Figure 4.21. Buckles with diamond-shaped plates and chip-carved decoration: (1) 'Maikop'; (2) Metropolitan Museum collection; (3) grave 149 in Mačvanska Mitrovica; (4 and 6) 'Hungary'; (5) Noşlac; (7) Dombóvár; (8) surroundings of Mainz; (9) Kiskunfelégyháza; (10) Gava; (11) Zagorzyn; (12) Pekari; (13) Kosino; (14) Tiszalök; (15) Košice.

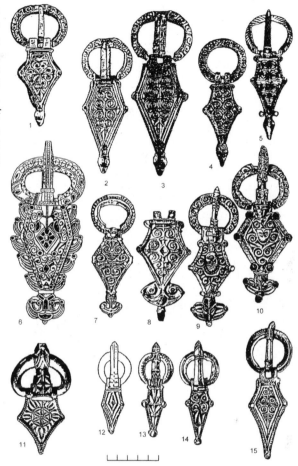

in the shape of animal heads and triangular mounts (Kosino, Tiszalök, Kiskun-felégyháza) and large bow fibulae with scrollwork ornamentation (Karavukovo, Domolospuszta, Gava), which are the closest stylistic analogies to the buckles in question.

There are several types of buckles with diamond-shaped plates. The simplest are specimens such as those of the Tiszalök-Košice type, which can be dated between 430/50 and 500. They are all small, with a round loop and with plates decorated with geometric chip-carved (Figure 4.21.12–13) or, more often, scrollwork orna-ment (Figure 4.21.14–15). While specimens of the first variant have been found both in the Middle Danube region and in Eastern Europe (Kerch', the Dnieper

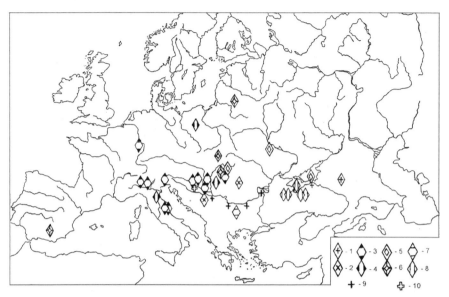

Figure 4.22. Distribution of buckles with diamond-shaped plate and chip-carved decoration: (1) 'Maikop'; (2) Mačvanska Mitrovica-Noşlac type; (3) Gava-Acquasanta and Domolospuszta-Karavukovo types; (4) Forli-Gyula type; (5–6) Tiszalök-Košice type (5 = with geometric chip-carved ornament, 6 = with scrollwork ornament); (7) Sadovsko Kale; (8) Black Sea series of the Forli-Gyula type; (9) bow fibulae with chip-carved decoration of the Archar series; (10) Domolospuszta series.

area),[76] the distribution of a second variant is restricted to the Middle Danube region, from which two specimens travelled north as far as Lithuania (Figure 4.22). The two specimens (initially parts of the female dress) were however turned into fasteners with strap directors for a sword of Danubian origin. The distribution and recycling of specimens of buckles of the Tiszalök-Košice type thus match those of the Levice-Tokary fibulae, which shortly after coming into being during the period of the Hunnic Empire, spread from the Middle Danube region to various parts of Eastern Europe, where some of them were imitated during the second half of the fifth century for the production of local series.[77]

Another series of the buckles with diamond-shaped plates, which Volker Bierbrauer further subdivided into the Gava-Acquasanta and Domolospuszta-

[76] Aibabin, 'Khronologiia mogil'nikov', fig. 23.11; Gavritukhin, 'Prichernomorskaia seriia', fig. 1; Kazanski, 'Les Germains orientaux', fig. 2.9.

[77] Gavritukhin, 'Prichernomorskaia seriia'; Gavritukhin, 'Final traditsii'.

Karavukovo types, respectively, is distinguished by a terminal lobe at the end of the plate, which is shaped as an animal head flanked by two bird heads (Figure 4.21.6–10).[78] Most finds of this type come from the barbarian milieu in the Middle Danube region and in Italy (Figure 4.22.3). Their chronology points to the times of Odoacer and Theoderic, that is, the second half of the fifth and the first quarter of the sixth century. The earliest is the buckle from a grave excavated in Dombóvár, which has been dated to the third quarter of the fifth century (Figure 4.21.7).[79] Indeed, the Dombóvár buckle was found in association with fifth-century earrings with polyhedral pendant with openwork ornamentation and a fibula reminiscent of the Prša-Levice type and Bratei-Vyškov subgroup.

Figure 4.23. Buckles of the Forli-Gyula type and their analogies: (1) burial chamber 98 in Chufut-kale; (2) burial chamber 288 in Skalistoe; (3) burial chamber 3 in Chufut-kale; (4) Forli; (5) Gyula; (6) Konarzew; (7) Szécsény; (8) Sadovsko Kale.

Buckles of the so-called Forli-Gyula type display pairs of animal heads on either side of the front part of the plate (Figures 4.23.1–6; 4.22.4 and 8), a detail clearly inspired by fifth- to early sixth-century Scandinavian fibulae.[80] The earliest specimens of this type were

[78] Bierbrauer, *Die ostgotischen Grab- und Schatzfunde*, pp. 134–42.

[79] Kiss, 'Über eine silbervergoldete gepidische Schnalle', fig. 4.4.

[80] Ambroz, 'Dunaiskie elementy', pp. 17–18.

manufactured in the Middle Danube region during the second half of the fifth century (Figure 4.23.6). Repaired specimens are also known from Ostrogothic Italy (late fifth and the first half of the sixth century) (Figure 4.23.4). Specifically South Crimean series, which remained in use until the seventh century, are in fact imitations of specimens of precisely that type (Figure 4.23.1–3).

Of Danubian origin are also buckles with a terminal lobe in the form of an animal head with a somewhat sharpened nose (Figures 4.21.1–5; 4.22.1–2), which Attila Kiss called the Mačvanska Mitrovica-Noşlac type.[81] Specimens of this type are known from the Carpathian Basin, but one such buckle has been found near Klaipėda, in western Lithuania.[82] To the same type belongs the buckle said to be 'from Maikop', which was mentioned at the beginning of this section. No such buckle has so far been found in a well-dated or published assemblage.[83] However, they are all stylistically related to buckles and fibulae dated to the second half of the fifth century. The ornamental styles that came into being during the second half of the fifth century continued to be employed for the decoration of artefacts produced after 500. This is particularly the case of the Forli-Gyula type of buckles, the South Crimean series of which were still manufactured in the 600s. Similarly, a buckle from the early Byzantine hillfort at Sadovsko Kale (Figure 4.23.8), which was built under Emperor Justinian, reminds one of specimens of the Karavukovo type.[84] Furthermore, the buckle may have belonged to the same set of dress accessories as a pair of silver bow fibulae, the decoration of which is stylistically related to that of the buckle, and with a pair of silver earrings.[85] The archaeological context strongly suggests that those luxury artefacts were lost in the circumstances surrounding the destruction of the fort in the 580s. If, as suggested by Syna Uenze, the artefacts belonged to a family jewellery case, the very fact that they have been kept together for some time is significant. Therefore, one can consider the possibility that they were used as models for the manufacturing of new products.

Let us now return to the buckle 'from Maikop'. Attila Kiss has already noted that the pattern of its scrollwork ornamentation is different from that of similar

[81] Kiss, 'Über eine silbervergoldete gepidische Schnalle', pp. 58–60.

[82] Werner, 'Der Grabfund von Taurapilis', fig. 4.4.

[83] Kiss, 'Über eine silbervergoldete gepidische Schnalle', p. 62.

[84] Syna Uenze, *Die spätantiken Befestigungen von Sadovec: Ergebnisse der deutsch-bulgarisch-österreichischen Ausgrabungen 1934–1937* (Munich, 1992), pp. 183 and 159–60.

[85] Uenze, *Die spätantiken Befestigungen*, pp. 161 and 183.

buckles from the Middle Danube region, Transylvania, or Italy.[86] The ornament is however to be found on fibulae of the Archar type, specimens of which appear in the Lower Danube region (Figures 4.16.13–14; 4.22.9).[87] One such fibula occurs also among stray finds from Kerch'.[88] Those finds also include a bow fibula with a foot-plate ending in a terminal lobe very similar to that of the buckles of the Mačvanska Mitrovica-Noşlac type (Figure 4.15.2). As mentioned above, that fibula displays stylistic features which reflect the cultural influence of the Danube region upon the craftsmen in Bosporus during the early years of Emperor Justinian's reign. This strongly suggests that the buckle 'from Maikop' was also manufactured in the Lower Danube region at some point between the last decades of the fifth and the early decades of the sixth century. The buckle apparently reached the Caucasus region via Bosporus during the second third of the sixth century.

All Caucasian finds of bow fibulae with scrollwork decoration and buckles with diamond-shaped plates cluster in a limited area between Krasnodar and Maikop. This distribution matches the picture already drawn on the basis of the analysis of sheet bow fibulae. While a Bosporan influence may be traced for the sheet bow fibulae found in the northern Caucasus, the bow fibulae with scrollwork decoration and the belt buckles with diamond-shaped plates are directly related to Bosporan fashions and styles. It is telling that no such finds are known from the Diurso cemetery. Contacts between communities in the north-western region of the Caucasus Mountains, on the one hand, and that which buried its dead in Diurso, on the other hand, are documented for the sixth and seventh century with artefacts, which were either rare or altogether unknown in Bosporus (fibulae with tubular foot, sword blades with 'blood grooves', etc.).[89] The late fifth- and early sixth-century distribution points to intensive contacts between Bosporus and the Tetraxite Goths to the north from the Novorosiisk Bay, which were then interrupted at some point between the second quarter and the middle of the sixth century. As

[86] Kiss, 'Über eine silbervergoldete gepidische Schnalle', p. 60.

[87] One such fibula was found in a late fifth-century grave of the cemetery excavated in Singidunum (modern Belgrade). See Vujadin Ivanišević and Michel Kazanski, 'La Nécropole de l'époque des grandes migrations à Singidunum', in *Singidunum 3*, ed. by Marko Popović (Belgrade, 2002), pp. 101–57 with fig. 9.

[88] Anatolii K. Ambroz, 'Iugo-zapadnyi Krym. Mogil'niki IV–VII vv.', *Materialy po arkheologii, istorii i etnografii Tavrii*, 4 (1994), 31–88 with fig. 5.7.

[89] Igor O. Gavritukhin and Aleksei V. P'iankov, 'Rannesrednevekovye drevnosti poberezh'ia', in *Krym i Kavkaz v epokhu srednevekov'ia*, ed. by Tat'iana I. Makarova and Svetlana A. Pletneva (Moscow, 2004), pp. 186–95.

Iurii G. Vinogradov has recently demonstrated, during the last decades of the fifth century (in any case after the departure of both Huns and Tetraxites in the 450s), a pro-Byzantine dynasty was restored to power in Bosporus, and by 520 the city was under the rule of Grod, the equally pro-Byzantine 'king' of the Huns, whose seat of power must have been somewhere to the east from Bosporus.[90] It appears that the Tetraxite Goths, whose Orthodox Christianity and pro-Byzantine sympathies are specifically mentioned by Procopius of Caesarea, easily found common ground both with the Bosporus rulers and with Grod.[91] The situation changed dramatically when the newly baptized Grod with the zealotry of a neophyte began to destroy the pagan idols of the Huns. A revolt ensued, and the Huns killed Grod and sacked Bosporus as well as other cities in the Taman' region. In Bosporus, they slaughtered the Roman garrison stationed there, which consisted of soldiers recruited from Hispania under the command of a tribune named Dalmatian.[92] In 534 or 535, Justinian sent an army, which landed at Bosporus and forced the barbarians to abandon the city. However, the relations with the Huns remained tense. Until 548, when Emperor Justinian received their embassy, the Tetraxites, who had been allied with the Huns, were cut off from any contact either with Byzantine Bosporus or with Constantinople. Interestingly, the situation thus created does not seem to have caused any interruption of contacts between the north-western region of the Caucasus Mountains, Bosporus, and the Tetraxite Goths.

The models which were imitated for the production of buckles and bow fibulae with scrollwork decoration found in the Caucasus region originated in the Lower Danube and the northern Balkan area. In Bosporus, this tradition is represented by imported items and local series which could be associated with a cultural impulse coinciding with the Justinianic takeover by troops most likely recruited in the Balkans.

---

[90] Iurii G. Vinogradov, 'Pozdneantichnye Bospor i ranniaia Vizantiia', *Vestnik Drevnei Istorii*, 1998.1, 233–47. For the withdrawal of both Huns and Tetraxites in the 450s, see Kazanski, 'Goty na Bospore'. For the location of Grod's seat of power, see Artamonov, *Istoriia khazar*, pp. 89–92.

[91] Procopius of Caesarea, *Wars*, 4.4.12–13, ed. by Z. V. Udal'tsova (Moscow, 1950).

[92] The presence of the Spaniards is betrayed also by a sword from Taman' with a guard most typical for weapons from the Western Mediterranean region dated to the second half of the fifth and first half of the sixth century. See Kazanski, 'Les Germains orientaux', p. 329; Michel Kazanski. 'Les Épées "orientales" dans l'armée romaine en Gaule', in *International Connections of the Barbarians of the Carpathian Basin in the 1st–5th Centuries A.D.: Proceedings of the International Conference Held in 1999 in Aszód and Nyíregyháza*, ed. by Eszter Istvánovits and Valéria Kulcsár (Nyíregyháza, 2001), pp. 389–418 (p. 408).

Three-knobbed Sheet Bow Fibulae

The first to notice the peculiar character of three-knobbed fibulae from the northern Caucasus region was Anatolii Ambroz, who classified them along with Caucasian and Volga sheet bow fibulae believed to have been manufactured under Bosporan influence.[93] Such fibulae appear to have been a crossing between sheet bow fibulae and regular bow fibulae (Figure 4.17.32–37 and 43).[94] The earliest specimens are those from the Pashkovskyi cemetery, which are however stylistically closer to plain bow fibulae with five knobs, such as those found in Kerch' and in the Dnieper region (Figure 4.17.32–34).[95] Kerch' also produced examples of plain bow fibulae with three knobs (e.g. Figure 4.17.35, possibly also 42), the models of which seem to have been sheet bow fibulae of the Villafontana type, otherwise well documented in Bosporus (e.g. Figure 4.17.38–41, possibly also 42).[96]

The earliest bow fibulae with three knobs in the northern Caucasus are those from Kabardino-Balkaria and the Pashkovskyi 1 cemetery in the Kuban region (Figure 4.17.1–3 and 18). Those are specimens of variants 5 and 6 of Gavritukhin's general typology of northern Caucasian bow fibulae with three knobs. Only one them is known to have been found in a 'closed-find' assemblage, namely in grave 15 excavated in 1948 in the Pashkovskyi 1 cemetery (Figure 4.17.4–31). The fibula found in that burial assemblage as well as another stray find from that same cemetery (Figure 4.17.3 and 18) are both specimens of Gavritukhin's variant 6, which is otherwise known only from the Krasnodar area. Fibulae of that variant were apparently manufactured either in Bosporus or under the influence of Bosporan styles.

The mapping of chronologically distinct artefacts delineates two areas of interments within the Pashkovskyi 1 cemetery, as excavated in 1948 and 1949 by

---

[93] Anatolii K. Ambroz, *Fibuly iuga evropeiskoi chasti SSSR* (Moscow, 1966), pp. 88–91; Anatolii K. Ambroz, 'Birskii mogil'nik i problemy khronologii Priural'ia v IV–VII vv.', in *Srednevekovye drevnosti evraziiskikh stepěi: Sbornik statei*, ed. by Svetlana A. Pletneva (Moscow, 1980), pp. 3–56 (pp. 8–10).

[94] Anatolii K. Ambroz, 'O dvukhplastinchatykh fibulakh s nakladkami-analogii k stat'e A. V. Dmitrieva', in *Drevnosti epokhi velikogo pereseleniia narodov*, ed. by Ambroz and Erdélyi, pp. 107–21 (p. 120); Igor O. Gavritukhin, 'Srednedneprovskie ingumatsii vtoroi poloviny V–VI v.', in *Kul'turnye transformatsii i vzaimovliianiia v Dneprovskom regione na iskhode rimskogo vremeni i v rannem srednevekov'e: Doklady nauchnoi konferentsii, posviashchennoi 60-letiiu so dnia rozhdeniia E. A. Goriunova (Sankt-Peterburg, 14–17 noiabria 2000 g.)*, ed. by Valentina M. Goriunova and Olga A. Shcheglova (St Petersburg, 2004), pp. 208–20; Gavritukhin, 'Final traditsii', fig. 6.19–29.

[95] Gavritukhin, 'Srednedneprovskie ingumatsii'.

[96] Kazanski, 'Goty na Bospore', p. 279.

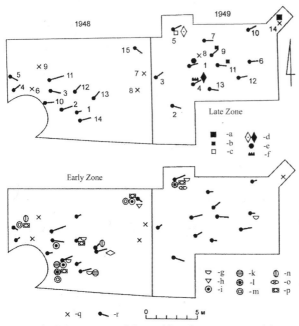

Konstantin F. Smirnov (Figure 4.24).[97] The first area is marked by mosaic glass and large rock-crystal beads. In Diurso, such a combination is most typical for graves with sheet bow fibulae dated between the second half of the fifth and the beginning of the sixth century.[98] Grave 15 in the Pashkovskyi 1 cemetery with the bow fibula with three knobs was located in the first area. The grave produced a mosaic glass bead (Figure 4.17.6), which is to be dated between the second half of the fifth and the first decades of the sixth century. Of about the same date or somewhat later must also be Gavritukhin's variant 5 (similar to variants 6 and 1 in morphological details), documented by two finds from Kabardino-Balkaria (Figure 4.17.1–2) showing influences from the Kuban region or perhaps directly from Bosporus.

Figure 4.24. Sequencing of the Pashkovskyi 1 cemetery: (a) Ж-shaped mounts; (b) buckles with open-work ornament; (c) high hollow buckles; (d) sheet bow fibulae; (e) fibulae with 'tubular' foot; (f) fibulae with longitudinal ribs on the bow; (g) fibulae with 'semi-tubular' foot; (h) sheet bow fibulae with three knobs; (i) mosaic glass beads; (k) beads decorated with multicolour longitudinal strips; (l) large faceted rock-crystal beads; (m) globular carnelian beads; (n) bulla-shaped rock-crystal beads; (o) spindle-shaped beads decorated with intersecting strips; (p) 14-faceted blue glass or rock-crystal beads; (q) mixed bones; (r) inhumation.

Later fibulae with three knobs are especially numerous in the cemetery excavated in Chir-Yurt, on the outskirts of Kiziliurt, in Dagestan (Figures 4.25, 4.26). The fibula from grave 17a belongs to Gavritukhin's variant 1, although it is

[97] Igor O. Gavritukhin, and others, 'Alany Severnogo Kavkaza i stepi Evrazii', in *Gumanitarnaia nauka v Rossii: Sorosovskie laureaty: istoriia, arkheologiia, kul'turnaia antropologiia i etnografiia*, ed. by A. R. Viatkin (Moscow, 1996), pp. 219–31.

[98] Dmitriev, 'Rannesrednevekovye fibuly', fig. 11; Kazanski, 'Khronologiia nachal'noi fazy'.

Figure 4.25. Sheet bow fibulae with three knobs from Chir-Yurt and associated artefacts: (1–19 and 22) grave56a; (20–21) grave 56b; (23–29) grave 56c; (30–41) grave 53; (42–50) grave 144a; (51–55) grave 72 (52 = perforated imitation of a Sassanian coin minted between 613 and 625); (56) grave 58; (57–60) grave 15. Scale a for 44, 49, and 58–59; scale b for 1–43, 45–48, 50–51, 53–57, and 60.

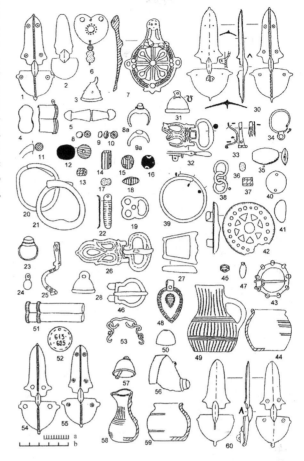

of a somewhat smaller size and with a longer bow (Figure 4.26.64). Larger fibulae with shorter bows belong to variant 2, which is very similar to variant 1 in minute morphological details (Figure 4.26.4–6 and 60–62). Outside Chir-Yurt, fibulae stylistically similar to specimens of variants 1 and 2 have been found in Niznia Rutkha in northern Ossetia (Figure 4.7.27). Specimens of variant 3 have very short bows, barely raised above the foot- and head-plates, and with 'deformed' details (Figures 4.25.2; 4.26.3 and 38–39). By contrast, variant 4 includes specimens of higher manufacturing standards. Those are larger fibulae, often decorated with raised ribs visually enhancing the longitudinal axis of the brooch, and with circles (Figure 4.25.1, 30, 54–55, and 60).

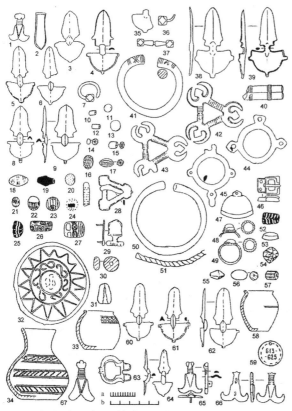

Figure 4.26. Sheet bow fibulae with three knobs and cicada-brooches from Chir-Yurt and associated artefacts: (1–3) grave 114; (4) grave 24; (5–6) grave 28a; (7–34) grave 13; (35–59) grave 40 (59 = perforated imitation of a Sassanian coin minted between 613 and 625); (60–61) grave 21a; (62) grave 28b; (63–66) grave 17a; (67) grave 140. Scale a for 33–34 and 58; scale b for 1–32, 35–57, and 60–67.

Let us now examine briefly the chronology of later fibulae with three knobs from northern Caucasus. A variant 1 specimen appears in a grave of the first phase of the Chir-Yurt cemetery, which also produced belt mounts with open-work ornament (so-called Martynivka mounts), which are also associated with phase 2a. The latter is characterized not only by the presence of fibulae of variant 2, but also by a greater diversity of 'Martynivka mounts' and by the presence of strap ends with curved sides, which in the Caucasus appear in the mid-seventh century.[99] Fibulae of variants 3 and 4 appear in phase 2b, which is dated by means of a Caucasus series of hinged buckles imitating Byzantine buckles of the second third of the seventh century, trapeze-shaped and lyre-shaped buckles (Figure 4.25.26–27, 32, 46), belt buckles with lyre-shaped plates (variants of the Boly-Želovce type; Figure 4.25.26 and 32), rare specimens of buckles and belt mounts with open-work ornament ('Martynivka mounts'), and coins struck for the Sassanian king Khosro II (591–628) or imitations thereof,

[99] Gavritukhin and Oblomskii, *Gaponovskii klad*, fig. 80.N5–7, N9–10, N14–15, N18–19, N20, N22, and N28; Gavritukhin and Malashev, 'Perspektivy izucheniia', p. 61.

some of which were pierced to be worn as pendants.[100] Phase 1 in Chir-Yurt may therefore be dated to the first half of the seventh century, with the subsequent phases 2a and 2b falling in the middle and in the second half of that century, respectively. This in turn gives us the date of the later variants of bow fibulae with three knobs.[101]

As for the chronology of the fibulae of Gavritukhin's variant 1, a key specimen is that from the cemetery Kislovodskoe ozero 2, excavated on the shore of Lake Kislovodskoe (Figure 4.7.28). The shape of its foot-plate reminds one of fibulae in polychrome style, such as those from Bylym-Kudinetovo, not far from Tyrnyauz, in Kabardino-Balkaria (Figure 4.7.29–30). Equally relevant in this respect is another analogy, namely the aforementioned imitation of a fibula with semi-spherical rivet heads found on the eroded banks of the Krasnodar Reservoir (Figure 4.7.42). The latter was dated between the second half of the fifth and the early sixth century. If so, then the lower limit for the chronological bracket advanced for fibulae of variant 1 in the northern Caucasus region cannot be later than the first half or the middle of the sixth century.

To sum up, the development of the North Caucasian fibulae with three knobs appears to be as follows. The earliest are fibulae of variant 6, so far known only from the Krasnodar area (Figure 4.17.3 and 18), which cannot be dated later than the first decades of the sixth century and may signal either Bosporan imports or a direct influence of Bosporan craftsmanship. Judging by many typologically unique features, fibulae of variant 5, which are found in Kabardino-Balkaria, may be dated to the same period and are probably a signal of contacts with Bosporus or of an influence from the Kuban region (Figure 4.17.1–2). Fibulae of variant 1, which are similar to those of variants 5 and 6, appear during the first half or in the middle of the sixth century, especially in the central and eastern parts of the northern Caucasus region (Figures 4.26.64; 4.7.28). Over the course of the seventh century, this variant will serve as model for fibulae of classes 2–4 manufactured in the region stretching from northern Ossetia to Dagestan.

Early fibulae with three knobs were also found in a princely grave under a late fifth- or early sixth-century barrow in Bylym-Kudinetovo (Figure 4.7.29–41).[102] The semispherical rivet heads of those fibulae (Figure 4.7.29 and 30) do not appear

---

[100] Gavritukhin and Oblomskii, *Gaponovskii klad*, figs 80 and 81.

[101] Gavritukhin and Oblomskii, *Gaponovskii klad*, fig. 90.

[102] For the dating of this assemblage, see Kazanski and Mastykova, 'Le Caucase du Nord', pp. 539–40.

to be connected with any Bosporan influence, for such semispherical rivet heads are known for fibulae of other types. A series equally far from any Bosporan influences is represented by a number of imitations of fibulae with semispherical rivet heads from the Caucasus region (Figure 4.7.47–48). The closest analogies for the head-plates of the Kudinetovo fibulae are the rounded and kidney-shaped buckle plates with cloisonné decoration of the Hunnic age.[103] The Kudinetovo head-plates also recall certain West Mediterranean fibulae dated to the same period, namely to the second third of the fifth century.[104] It is quite possible that the Kudinetovo fibulae signal a direct influence of the Mediterranean aristocratic fashions.[105] They certainly led to a distinct line of development in the Caucasus region. This is readily clear from the examination of the Kamunta imitation of a fibula with round head-plate and three knobs (Figure 4.7.26 and 30). Outside the Caucasus region, such artefacts may have been responsible for such unique fibulae as those from the cemetery excavated in Kushnarenkovo (Bashkortostan), which are to be regarded as imitations of Caucasian fibulae with three knobs (Figure 4.7.15).

Cicada-brooches

Sites known for finds of North Caucasian fibulae with three knobs have also produced cicada-brooches.[106] Herbert Kühn, though distinguishing several unique

---

[103] Ambroz, 'Iuzhnye khudozhestvennye sviazi', p. 73; Kazanski, 'Les Plaques-boucles méditérranéennes', figs 1.1, 14.10.

[104] E.g. Pistoin and Barbing-Irlmaut: Michel Kazanski and Patrick Périn, 'La Tombe de Childéric et la question de l'origine des parures du style cloisonné', *Antiquités nationales*, 28 (1996), 203–09 with figs 3–5.

[105] Kazanski and Mastykova, 'Le Caucase du Nord', pp. 593–94.

[106] J. de Baye, 'Note sur des bijoux barbares en forme de mouches', *Mémoires de la Société Nationale des Antiquaires de France*, 4 (1894), 1–22. Fundamental for the study of cicada-brooches remains Herbert Kühn, 'Die Zikadenfibeln der Völkerwanderungszeit', *Jahrbuch für prähistorische und ethnographische Kunst*, 22 (1935), 85–106, even though some of Kühn's conclusions cannot be accepted any more. See also Zdenko Vinski, 'Zikadenschmuck aus Jugoslawien', *Jahrbuch des Römisch-Germanischen Zentralmuzeums*, 4 (1957), 136–60; Günter Fitz, 'Römisch-kaiserzeitliche und völkerwanderungszeitliche Zikadenfibeln aus österreichischen Privatsammlungen', *Römische Österreich*, 13 (1986), 169–268; Aibabin, 'Khronologiia mogil'nikov', pp. 26–27; Kovacheva and Kharalambieva, 'Fibuli ot epokhata na Velikoto preselenie', pp. 45–46; Michel Kazanski and Patrick Périn, 'Les "Fibules-mouches" de l'époque des Grandes Migrations découvertes en Gaule', in *Les Sites archéologiques en Crimée*, ed. by Kazanski and Soupault, pp. 15–28. See also Margit Nagy's contribution to this volume.

features of such fibulae, treated them all as one group of dress accessories which appeared during the Roman period, but became popular only during the so-called Migration period. Similarly, Zdenko Vinski rejected the idea of an evolutionary development of the series and emphasized the fact that various types of cicada-brooches coexisted between the fifth and the early sixth centuries. Burchard Brentjes, on the other hand, drew a general typology and attributed variants to different chronological stages and cultures.[107] It is Brentjes's approach to typology that will be used in this section.

Most cicada-brooches known from the northern Caucasus share a number of distinctive features: standard size, similarly stylized head, and 'wings' in the form of massive plates, with terminal lobes and stylized curved ends. However, several unique features in the execution of details allow the separation of several variants. Specimens of the first variant are about four centimetres long, with a diamond-shaped head with prominent eyes and a small, pointed lobe between the 'wings' (Figure 4.27.45–46). The fragmentary brooch from Berduty near Shali, in Chechnia, also belongs to this or some other, similar variant (Figure 4.27.43). Brooches of the second variant are somewhat shorter (about three centimetres), with stylized heads, the front part of which is elongated (Figures 4.28.1 and 4.27.48). Specimens of the third variant are between three and four centimetres long, with a head with prominent eyes or in the form of a little crown (Figure 4.26.1 and 65–67). By contrast, brooches of the fourth variant are distinguished by the long neck, which is often larger than the rest of the fibula (Figure 4.27.50–52). There are, of course, cases for which the existing classification does not work. Finds from Martan-Chu in western Chechnia or those said to be 'from Chegem' in southern Kabardino-Balkaria (Figure 4.27.3 and 49) have good analogies among specimens of both the second and the fourth variants. Another from Kharachoi in south-eastern Chechnia imitates brooches of the first and third variants (Figure 4.27.44). The brooch from Kumbulta in the south-western part of northern Ossetia (Figure 4.27.47), though decorated in polychrome style, reminds one of specimens of the first and fourth variants.

The first variant may be dated between the second half of the fifth and the sixth century on the basis of finds from a destroyed cemetery in Ozorukovo near Bylym in Kabardino-Balkaria, which include Mediterranean buckles and brooches, as well

---

[107] Burchard Brentjes, 'Zur Typologie, Datierung und Ableitung der Zikadenfibel', *Wissenschaftliche Zeitschrift der Martin-Luther-Universität Halle-Wittenberg*, 3 (1954), 901–14.

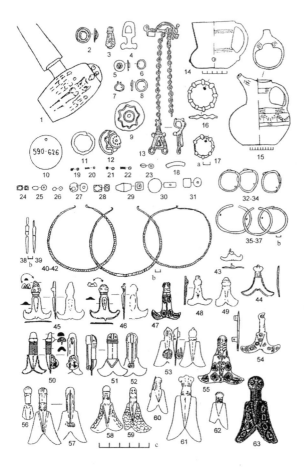

Figure 4.27. Cicada-brooches from the northern Caucasus region and associated artefacts, and their analogies and prototypes: (1–42) grave 7 in Martan-Chu (10 = perforated Sassanian coin minted between 590 and 626); (43) Berduty; (44) grave 47 in Kharachoi; (45) 'Northern Ossetia'; (46) 'Nal'chik'; (47) Kumbulta; (48) Mukulan; (49) 'Chegem'; (50) Pashkovskyi 1; (51) grave 373 in Diurso; (52) grave 390 in Diurso; (53) Chersonesus; (54) 'La Hillère'; (55) Beaurepaire; (56–57 and 60) 'Southern Russia'; (58) 'Hungary'; (59) Bivolare; (61) 'Taman'; (62) Maladière; (63) Dyerken. Scale a for 16–17; scale b for 33–42; scale c for 2–9, 11–13, 18–31, and 43–63.

as a coin struck for the Sassanian ruler Khosro I (531–79).[108] A brooch similar to specimens of the first variant has also been found among finds from another destroyed cemetery in Berduty and has been tentatively dated to the sixth and seventh centuries.[109] The brooch of the second variant, which was found within a burial chamber excavated in Tyrnyauz (Kabardino-Balkaria), may be dated between the late fifth and the sixth century on the basis of the associated grave goods

---

[108] Kazanski and Mastykova, 'Le Caucase du Nord', pp. 540 and 542; Kühn, 'Die Zikadenfibeln', p. 94.

[109] Khamid M. Mamaev, 'Khronologiia katakombnykh mogil'nikov Checheno-Ingushetii kontsa IV–pervoi poloviny VIII v.', in *Problemy khronologii pogrebal'nykh pamiatnikov Checheno-Ingushetii*, ed. by Vitalii B. Vinogradov (Groznyi, 1986), pp. 44–70 (pp. 59 and 61 with fig. 5.5–70).

(Figure 4.28). Cicada-brooches of the third variant from Chir-Yurt have been found in assemblages belonging to the first phase of that cemetery, which is dated to the first half of the seventh century, at the latest (see above). The specimen of the fourth variant from a number of destroyed graves from the Pashkovskyi 1 cemetery can be dated between the late fifth century and the early seventh century, that is, no later than the graves within that cemetery. Similar brooches from Diurso have been dated to the third phase of the cemetery, that is, between the last third of the fifth and the early sixth century.[110] A date within the first half of the seventh century (or *c.* 650) for the fragmentary brooch from grave 7 of the

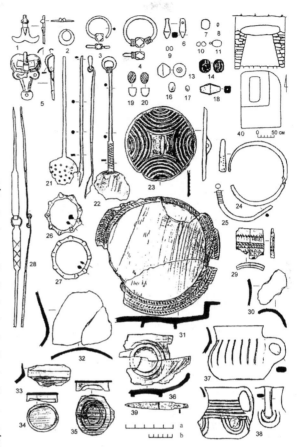

Figure 4.28. Cicada-brooch from Tyrnyauz and associated artefacts. Scale a for 1–28; scale b for 29–39.

Martan-Chu 2 cemetery, which has good analogies among specimens of the second and fourth variants, is also supported by the associated coins of the Sassanian ruler Khosro II (591–628), which have been perforated in order to be worn as pendants.[111]

---

[110] Dmitriev, 'Rannesrednevekovye fibuly', fig. 11; Kazanski, 'Khronologiia nachal'noi fazy', pp. 45 and 56. According to Michel Kazanski, such fibulae may also be attributed to the first two phases of the cemetery.

[111] Mamaev, 'Khronologiia katakombnykh mogil'nikov', pp. 61 and 63; Gavritukhin and Oblomskii, *Gaponovskii klad*, fig. 90.

Brentjes included most North Caucasian finds in his third ('North Caucasus') type, but a closer examination of the series suggests that they are in fact closer to his second type, which Brentjes himself called the 'Dyerken type' and which are in fact a local series. Several series of that type have been found in the Middle Danube region, in the Balkans, in Western Europe, as well as in the Black Sea area (Figures 4.27.53–63; 4.29). Judging by the grave goods from a number of burial assemblages from Levice, the fibula found there may be dated *c.* 450, while the one from grave 3 excavated in 1891 in Chersonesus cannot be later than the second half of the fifth century.[112] Fibulae of the Dyerken type seem to imitate brooches of the first half of the fifth century (Figure 4.29.II.1–3), which strongly suggests that the type itself appears during the first half of the fifth century or around 450. Several series of the Dyerken type may then be dated to the sixth century or as late as the first half of the seventh century.

Dyerken-type cicada-brooches similar to the North Caucasus series have been found in Bosporus and southern Russia. Particularly interesting in this respect is the brooch from Taman', with its prominent eyes, which is very similar to specimens of the third variant from Chir-Yurt (Figure 4.27.61). Equally relevant are the elongated necks of brooches from Kerch', which remind one of the fourth variant (Figure 4.27.56–57), as well as the ribbed neck of a brooch from Southern Russia (Figure 4.27.60), which may be compared to fibulae of the third variant and to those from Pashkovskyi (Figure 4.26.65–66 and 4.27.50). It appears, therefore, that cicada-brooches from the northern Caucasus are in fact imitations of Bosporan or Tetraxite fibulae of the Dyerken type.[113]

Cicada-brooches of the first variant and their imitations are found only within the central part of the northern Caucasus, from Kabardino-Balkaria to Chechnia. The second variant appears only within a restricted area between Baksan and Chegem in southern Kabardino-Balkaria. Specimens of the third variant cluster in

---

[112] Kazanski and Périn, 'Les "Fibules-mouches"', p. 20.

[113] North Caucasian cicada-brooches are strikingly similar to a number of specimens from France (Figure 4.27.54, 55, and 62). There is yet no satisfactory explanation for such parallels, but it appears that a number of dress accessories, including cicada-brooches, often decorated in the polychrome style, appear in significant numbers along the Roman frontiers, from Scotland to Bosporus, as well as within the Empire, in areas where barbarian troops in Roman service were stationed (such as southern Gaul). This seems to be linked to the creation of a 'frontier style'. See Michel Kazanski, 'Les Objets orientaux de l'époque des Grandes Migrations découvertes dans le couloir rhodanien', *Antiquités nationales*, 25 (1993), 119–27 (pp. 120, 124, and 125); Kazanski and Périn, 'Les "Fibules-mouches"', p. 26).

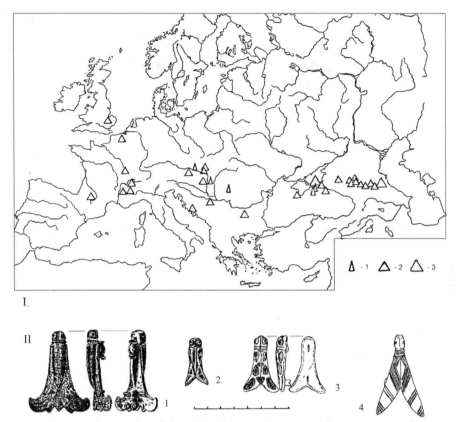

Figure 4.29. Distribution of cicada-brooches of the Dyerken type and their prototypes. I: (1) proto-types from the Hunnic period; (2–3) Dyerken type and derivatives (3 = three or more finds); II: Hunnic-age cicada-brooches: (1) Saromberke; (2) Csömör; (3) Kerch'; (4) Untersiebenbrunn.

the eastern, those of the fourth variant in the western part of the northern Caucasus region. This distribution overlaps that of variants of fibulae with three knobs, which can sometimes be dated to the same period as the respective variants of cicada-brooches. This is particularly true for the latest cicada-brooches, which have been found in Chir-Yurt and Martan-Chu, in the eastern part of the northern Caucasus region, which also produced the latest fibulae with three knobs.

Conclusion

The artefacts examined in this paper indicate a strong influence from both Bosporus and the region inhabited at that time by the Tetraxite Goths upon the northern Caucasus region. This influence was not uniform, and various artefacts have distinct distributions within the region. One cluster of finds showing the Bosporan-Tetraxite influence is within the region of Krasnodar and the nearest parts of the Kuban valley (Figure 4.14). Some, at least, of the artefacts found in that region — especially fibulae with three knobs and cicada-brooches of the North Caucasus series — must have been manufactured locally as imitations of original dress accessories from the Bosporan-Tetraxite region. Others were clearly imports from Bosporus (e.g. bow fibulae with scrollwork ornamentation). Bosporus thus had a rather intense and constant influence upon the aristocratic fashions in the Krasnodar region, an influence which seems to date back to the Hunnic period.[114] There are also reasons to suppose that some barbarians from the northern coast of the Black Sea, possibly Tetraxites, moved into the area. Although during the first half of the sixth century, as a consequence of dramatically changing political circumstances, the Tetraxites and Bosporus became increasingly isolated one from another, contacts with the northern Caucasus were not interrupted. Unfortunately, finds said to be 'from Maikop' are known only from museum collections or the antique market. Their provenance is therefore not secured and their position within the archaeological context of the region remains unclear. Nonetheless, finds 'from Maikop' display many similarities to those from the Krasnodar area. Only the excavation and publication of new assemblages may clarify such similarities.

Late antique and early medieval assemblages from the Kislovodsk region in the foothills of the Caucasus Mountains have been so far studied against the backdrop of other regions, particularly the northern Caucasus. The fact that the several hundred assemblages excavated in the Kislovodsk area produced only one of the dress accessories examined in this chapter is therefore significant. Apparently, unlike the northern Caucasus, there were very few direct or mediated contacts with Bosporus in that area. By contrast, a relatively large number and variety of dress accessories originating in the Black Sea area or even in the Mediterranean flowed into the Kislovodsk area, bypassing both Bosporus and the adjacent territories.[115] At the

---

[114] Gavritukhin and P'iankov, 'Dvuplastinchatye fibuly'.

[115] Anna V. Mastykova, 'K izucheniiu roli Kavkaza v sisteme vostochnoevropeiskikh torgovykh sviazei vtoroi poloviny I tysiacheletiia n. e.', *Istoriko-arkheologicheskii al'manakh*, (Armavir) 3

time, the Kislovodsk area was apparently included in a barbarian polity, which controlled the routes across the Caucasus Mountains and maintained strong ties to Byzantium through Abkhazia.[116] Lavishly furnished, fifth-century warrior graves in the area produced ceremonial Byzantine swords, while many accessories of Mediterranean origin have been found in contemporary female burials.[117]

The same conclusion applies to the region of the Upper Kuban, which is devoid of any of the dress accessories discussed in this chapter, but produced many Mediterranean imports, all of which apparently came from Abkhazia.[118] Moreover, the female adornments of Mediterranean origin which appear in the Kislovodsk area and in the valley of the Upper Kuban — bird-shaped fibulae, disc- and multi-petal fibulae — are rarely found in contemporary cemeteries in the Lower or Middle Kuban region or on the coast.[119]

Cicada-brooches and fibulae with three knobs cluster in the central area of the northern Caucasus region (Figure 4.14), in the southern part of Kabardino-Balkaria, between Baksan and Chegem, as well as in northern Ossetia, mainly in Digoria. Bosporan imports are not known from this area. Furthermore, local elites emulated the aristocratic fashions of the Danube region and the Mediterranean. In the Baksan valley, for example, the princely finds from barrows excavated in Bylym-Kudinetovo and Bylym-Ozurokovo strongly suggest the existence of a local polity, in contact with Byzantium through Abkhazia and the mountain passes around Elbrus.[120] Despite the Bosporan origin of cicada-brooches and fibulae with three knobs, finds from the central area of the northern Caucasus are only indirectly related to Bosporan ones, and instead reflect in more general terms the local fashions and styles, to the formation of which contributed also the influence of the Bosporan culture. The mediating factor in channeling that influence towards the

---

(1997), 80–88; Kazanski and Mastykova, 'Le Caucase du Nord', pp. 523–73; Kazanski and Mastykova, 'Tsentry vlasti'.

[116] Kazanski and Mastykova, 'Tsentry vlasti', pp. 139–46.

[117] Kazanski, 'Les Épées "orientales"'; Anna V. Mastykova, 'Sredizemnomorskie elementy v zhenskom u naseleniia Severnogo Kavkaza (V–VI vv.)', in *Evraziiskaia step' i lesostep' v epokhu rannego srednevekov'ia*, ed. by A. D. Priakhin (Voronezh, 2000), pp. 31–47; A. V. Mastykova, 'Sredizemnomorskii zhenskii kostium s fibulami-broshami na Severnom Kavkaze v V–VI vv.', *Rossiiskaia Arkheologiia*, 2005.1, 22–36.

[118] Kazanski and Mastykova, 'Tsentry vlasti', pp. 151–52.

[119] Kazanski and Mastykova, 'Le Caucase du Nord'; Mastykova, 'Sredizemnomorskie elementy'.

[120] Kazanski and Mastykova, 'Tsentry vlasti', pp. 148–51.

central area of the northern Caucasus region seems to have been the population of the Lower and Middle Kuban valley.

It is no accident that fibulae with three knobs and cicada-brooches appear in the eastern area of the northern Caucasus region, especially in burial chambers of the Martan-Chu, Berduty, and Chir-Yurt cemeteries (Figure 4.14). They signal an influence from territories farther to the west, which was channelled through political alliances, perhaps within the same kin groups. In any case, that influence alone can explain why such typical dress accessories remained fashionable in the region for so much longer than anywhere else.

In the northern Caucasus, fibulae and buckles can be used to trace cultural trends and political alliances, especially when examining in detail the chronology, not just of closed-find assemblages, but also of stray finds. It goes without saying that the Bosporan and Tetraxite influence in the northern Caucasus region cannot be reduced to the dress accessories examined in this chapter.[121] Equally significant are chains with 8-shaped links attached to wire rings, which appear in large quantities in Diurso (Figures 4.4.14; 4.5.22 and 26; 4.8.25 and 34–37; 4.9.32), but also in Pashkovskyi (Figure 4.17.19). In the northern Caucasus, bracelets, mirrors, and pendants or appliqués may also signal the influence of centres on the north-eastern coast of the Black Sea. The examination of the development and distribution of such artefacts, which have so far been regarded as less expressive and more difficult to date precisely, requires a detailed analysis of several archaeological assemblages. That, however, will only be possible after a complete publication of assemblages, in accordance with the standards of modern archaeology.

[121] Figures 4.1.18; 4.2.4; 4.7.27, 42, 44–45, and 49; 4.11.35; 4.12.11 and 13; 4.13.3, 15, 22, 45–48, and 51–53; 4.15.19 and 30; 4.16.5; 4.17.35 and 37; 4.27.50 and 53 — drawn by Igor O. Gavritukhin from originals; figures 4.1.7; 4.7.47–48; 4.12.7–9; 4.15.5 and 9–11; 4.25.30–34, 38–39, and 60; 4.26.4, 8–9, 29, 39, 61–62, and 63–66; 4.27.45–46; 4.28.1–39 — drawn by Anatolii K. Amboz from originals (the most part unpublished).

A HUN-AGE BURIAL WITH MALE SKELETON AND HORSE BONES FOUND IN BUDAPEST

Margit Nagy

The province of Valeria was created by Emperor Galerius (293–311) on a narrow strip of land along the river Danube in the eastern part of Pannonia. Beginning with the early fifth century, this territory remained unprotected and was constantly under barbarian attack — Vandals, Quadi, and Visigoths, and later Attila's empire.[1] According to the most recent studies, the abandonment of Valeria by the government of Ravenna to the Huns took place in the 430s as a reward for continuous military support.[2] The archaeological evidence points to a considerable population decline in Aquincum, the capital of the province, in the early fifth century. However, sporadic groups of graves of the resident inhabitants have been found next to the old military and civilian cemeteries.[3]

Aquincum (now within Óbuda, or district III of the city of Budapest) and the smaller Roman settlements along the Danube remained in the hands of the Huns from the first decades of the fifth century until the collapse of Attila's empire in the aftermath of the battle at the river Nedao (AD 454).[4] Stray finds — most likely from

---

[1] András Mócsy, s. v. 'Pannonia', in *Paulys Real-Encyclopedie der klassischen Altertumswissenschaft*, Suppl. IX (Stuttgart, 1962), pp. 579–82; András Mócsy, *Pannonia a késői császárkorban* (Budapest, 1975), pp. 103–05.

[2] Tibor Nagy, György Györffy, and László Gerevich, *Budapest története az őskortól az Árpád kor végéig* (Budapest, 1973), pp. 185–216; Endre Tóth, 'Provincia Valeria Media', *Acta Archaeologica Academiae Scientiarum Hungaricae*, 31 (1979), 197–226.

[3] Margit Nagy, 'Kora népvándorláskori sírleletek Budapest területéről,' *Budapest Régiségei*, 40 (2006), 95–115 (pp. 112–13).

[4] Nagy, Györffy, and Gerevich, *Budapest története*, pp. 186–87.

destroyed graves or hoards — show that Aquincum was in fact occupied by the Huns and, moreover, that persons of high social status were buried there as well.[5] The left bank of the river Danube has never been under direct imperial administration. Instead, it remained under the authority of barbarian chieftains, either of the Quadi or of the Sarmatians. Those barbarian groups, which were allowed to settle as *foederati* on land immediately opposite Aquincum across the Danube, appear to have abandoned their settlements before the first raids of the Huns. During the first half of the fifth century, the occupation of the left bank of the Danube is attested by finds from the territory of present-day Budapest. A map distribution of the archaeological finds dated to the D2 and D3 periods (390/400–430/40 and 430–60, respectively) in the Middle Danube region shows a continuous occupation of ruined buildings in the formerly Roman city, the river banks, and to the east, the sand dunes along the Rákos Creek.[6] It is against this background that the Budapest-Zugló burial discussed in this chapter becomes particularly significant, given that the analysis of the burial rite, the grave goods, and the human bones indicates that the assemblage may be directly linked to the Hun conquerors. Despite being excavated fifty years ago, this very important burial assemblage remained largely unknown, with the exception of a few finds mentioned in the archaeological literature published after 1962.[7] The following analysis of the Zugló grave of a young Hun buried with the head of his horse and its accompanying harness may

[5] Nagy, Györffy, and Gerevich, *Budapest története*, pp. 189–90; István Bóna, *Das Hunnenreich* (Stuttgart, 1991), pp. 163 and 288 with pl. 101; Margit Nagy, 'Óbuda a népvándorlás korban', *Budapest Régiségei*, 30 (1993), 353–95 with figs 1–3; Margit Nagy, 'Zwei spätrömische Waffengräber am Westrand der *canabae* von Aquincum', *Acta Archaeologica Academiae Scientiarum Hungaricae*, 56 (2005), 473–78; Nagy, 'Kora népvándorláskori sírleletek', pp. 133 and 155 with fig. 19.1–2.

[6] Nagy, 'Kora népvándorláskori sírleletek', pp. 95–155 with fig. 19.4. For the archaeological record of the D2 and D3 periods, see Jaroslav Tejral, 'Zur Unterscheidung der vorlangobardischen und elbgermanisch-langobardischen Nachlasses', in *Die Langobarden: Herrschaft und Identität*, ed. by Walter Pohl and Peter Erhart (Vienna, 2005), pp. 112–23.

[7] The burial was first described by Tibor Nagy, 'Buda régészeti emlékei III: Népvándorláskor', in *Budapest Műemlékei II*, ed. by Frigyes Pogány (Budapest, 1962), p. 265. See also Nagy, Györffy, and Gerevich, *Budapest története*, pp. 189–90; Bóna, *Das Hunnenreich*, pp. 102–04 and 282 with pl. 73.1–5. For the first detailed description and discussion of the burial, see Margit Nagy, 'Hunkori férfisír Budapest-Zuglóból', in *Vándorutak – Múzeumi örökség: Tanulmányok Bodó Sándor tiszteletére*, ed. by Gyula Viga, Szilvia Andrea Holló, and Edit Cs. Schwalm (Budapest, 2003), pp. 297–325. A few grave goods have been published by Michel Kazanski, 'Schnell – gefährlich – käuflich', in *Archäologie in Deutschland, Sonderheft 2005*, ed. by Matthias Knaut and Dieter Quast (Stuttgart, 2005), pp. 28–37 (pp. 36–37).

therefore be seen as an attempt to restore the historical significance of a group of 'neglected barbarians'.

Human and horse bones, as well as metal artefacts, were accidentally found on 1 December 1961 in Budapest, during construction work on the large plot at the south-western corner of the intersection of Vezér Street and Egressy Road (Zugló, District XIV). After inspecting the site, Tibor Nagy drew up a report, in which he noted that the construction workers first discovered the foot end of the grave pit in the bedding trench of building B/3.[8] They then uncovered a horse skull placed upside down, a few horse vertebrae, and an iron bell. The workers collected bronze and iron articles, as well as two gold mounts from the sand, which had been removed earlier. Mounts were also found at the foot end of the grave pit. The undisturbed, upper part of the human skeleton was then excavated by Tibor Nagy on 1 and 2 December 1961.

The site lies on the right bank of the Rákos Creek. Taking into consideration the hydrological conditions of the site, the discovery was made on the edge of a ridge between the largest left-bank tributary of the Danube and the Rákos Creek (Figure 5.1).[9]

The report of the rescue excavation and its plan documentation were themselves fortuitously discovered in June 2006 among the papers Tibor Nagy had left behind in the Aquincum Museum.[10] The first brief publication of the grave was based on the report drawn up during the inspection of the site, the laconic excavation report, and the photographs taken by Péter Füredi, who worked as a

[8] According to the report written in the Vezér Street office of the Construction Company No. 42 on 1 December 1961 (Archives of the Budapest Historical Museum, inv. no. 1002–79), the following finds were handed over: an iron bit (broken into two), a side-bar covered with gold foil, a diamond-shaped pendant of bronze sheet, two gold mounts (one with three cells set with red stones, of which one was missing, the other with a single stone), and a conical bronze object. The report does not mention the other finds, which came to light during the actual excavation of the burial. Tibor Nagy (1910–95), was a historian of Antiquity, archaeologist, and honorary lecturer at University Pázmány Péter in Budapest. He worked at the Aquincum Museum of the Budapest Historical Museum between 1937 and 1973. His scholarly interest and excavations covered the history of Budapest from prehistory to the tenth century, although his main interest was in Roman Pannonia and its military and religious history, in the inscriptions and iconography of that period.

[9] Tibor Nagy, 'Budapest XIV, Zugló, Ecke Egressy u. und Vezér u.', *Archaeologiai Értesítő*, 89 (1962), 265; Nagy, Györffy, and Gerevich, *Budapest története*, pp. 185–216. The map supplement was drawn by Tibor Nagy and Ernő Nagy. The site is marked as Site 7 of the Migration Age.

[10] The papers were found by László Schilling and István Sós, to whom I owe a special debt of gratitude for their assistance.

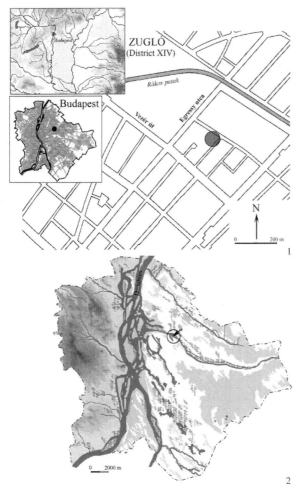

Figure 5.1. Budapest-Zugló, Vezér Street. (1) find spot; (2) location of the site on a map of the water system in the area. After Nagy, Györffy, and Gerevich, *Budapest története*.

photographer in the Archaeological Department at the time.[11]

The human skeleton came to light at a depth of 112.22 cm. The discoloured patch of the grave was 170 cm long and 90 cm wide in the enlargement of the bedding trench, with a slightly widened corner to the north-west. Its orientation (calculated from the N sign on the drawing and the photos) was north-east to south-west (26–58).[12] The 80 to 90 cm–wide grave contained the well-preserved, undisturbed skeleton of a twenty- to twenty-five-year-old Euro-Mongolid male.[13] Only the

[11] The photos are in the archive of the Aquincum Museum, Roman collection (inv. no. 4616–24).

[12] According to Bóna, *Das Hunnenreich*, p. 282, the grave orientation was north-west to south-east.

[13] Olga Bottyán, 'Data to the Anthropology of the Hun Period Population in Hungary', *Annales Historico-Naturales Musei Nationalis Hungarici, Pars Anthropologica*, 50 (1967), 455–64 (pp. 455–57 with plate 1). The skeletal remains are in the collection of the Anthropological Department of the Natural History Museum. Nothing is known about the whereabouts of the horse skull.

leg bones and the feet, which had most probably been discarded after discovery by the construction workers, were missing.[14] The skull was tilted to the right side; the lower arms rested on the pelvis. The precise position of the grave goods has been established on the basis of a careful examination of both grave drawing and photos (Figure 5.2). Next to the human skeleton were the B-shaped iron buckle (on the sacrum), seven gold mounts with garnet incrustations (between the thighs), and a small, oval iron buckle (on the inner side of the left thigh).

Appearing on the grave drawing are three artefacts, which are not mentioned in the report and cannot be found in the museum storeroom: a vessel fragment behind the skull; a 12 cm–long, single-edged knife; and a disc-shaped 'button' next to the lower ribs on the right side of the skeleton. Interestingly enough, the iron knife does not appear on the photos, despite the fact that the iron buckle can be clearly recognized in the pelvic area.

According to the report and the grave drawing, a horse skull placed upside down and three horse vertebrae were found close to the human skeleton's feet in the south-western corner of the grave pit. The construction workers found several other artefacts in this part of the grave and in the soil they had removed from the

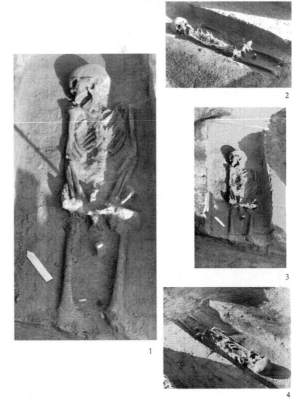

Figure 5.2. Budapest-Zugló, Vezér Street. The horseman burial. Photographs by Péter Füredi.

---

[14] Bóna, *Das Hunnenreich*, p. 282, believed that the burial had been disturbed in Antiquity ('wahrscheinlich schon früher beraubt'). However, there is nothing on either photos or drawings to suggest that to be the case.

pit: an iron bell, a bronze bell, a horse bit, the fragment of an iron bar covered with gold foil, and a diamond-shaped harness ornament.

Judging from the excavation report, there were two groups of grave goods, those placed by the human skeleton and those clearly associated with the horse bones.[15] An iron buckle lay by the pelvis of the human skeleton. The loop is flat, its middle is slightly curved (Figure 5.3.9). The tip of the tongue rests on the ring. Two pairs of round settings lined with gold foil were recessed into the iron ring and one into the base of the buckle tongue. Three of the gold cells on the ring have survived; the fourth has fallen out. The place of the cells can be seen on the X-ray photo made before the buckle's restoration (Figure 5.4.1a).[16] The sides of the cells were made from 0.4–0.5 mm–thick gold foil, whose edges were folded over each other. A double layer of wax covers the sides and the bottom of the cells. The outer wax layer is darker; the inner one is lighter and was probably colored with some mineral pigment. The glass inlay has survived in two cells: an iridescent, light mauve glass plate in one of the cells of the ring and a translucent mauve glass plate in the gold cell at the base of the tongue. The photo of the cell revealed that the edges of the glass plates had been carefully chipped off. A very thin, silver foil was placed between the two wax layers.[17] There is no silver foil between the wax layers in

[15] The grave goods are now in the Albertfalva storeroom of the Roman Collection in the Budapest Historical Museum. I found the box with grave goods in 1976. When registering the finds, I used the numbers already given by Tibor Nagy (Budapest Historical Museum, Migration period collection, inv. no. 76.2.1–13). According to the original numbering, the burial must have had thirteen grave goods, as follows: (1) an iron bit; (2) an iron bar covered with gold foil; (3) a diamond-shaped bronze pendant; (4–5) two gold mounts, found by the construction workers; (6) a bronze bell; (7) an iron buckle; (8) a small iron buckle; (9–13) five gold mounts, brought to light during the excavation of the human skeleton. A total of seven garnet-inlaid gold mounts reached the museum. As it turned out, the two gold mounts found earlier were re-placed in the grave by the lower end of the thigh bones (where they had originally been found), for the sake of photography. The iron bell found by the horse skull was not given any number by Tibor Nagy. I found the bell in another box in 1984 (inv. no. 84.3.1). Without any documentation, I could only assume that the bell came from the Zugló burial. This assumption was confirmed when István Bóna requested in 1989 permission from Tibor Nagy to take pictures of a few grave goods (see Bóna, *Das Hunnenreich*, pp. 102–04 with pl. 73.1–5). The recently discovered grave plan confirms that the bell (now marked as no. 14) had indeed been one of the burial's grave goods. Two other finds, an iron knife and the flat 'button', which appear on the grave plan, have not been identified and may have meanwhile disappeared.

[16] The buckle was restored by Katalin T. Bruder in March 2003. The X-ray photos were made by Gábor Hutai from the Hungarian National Museum.

[17] Tamás Fegyvári, 'A Budapest-Zugló, Vezér úti sírlelet berakásainak értékelése', in *Vándorutak – Múzeumi örökség*, ed. by Viga, Holló, and Schwalm, pp. 329–33 (pp. 329–30).

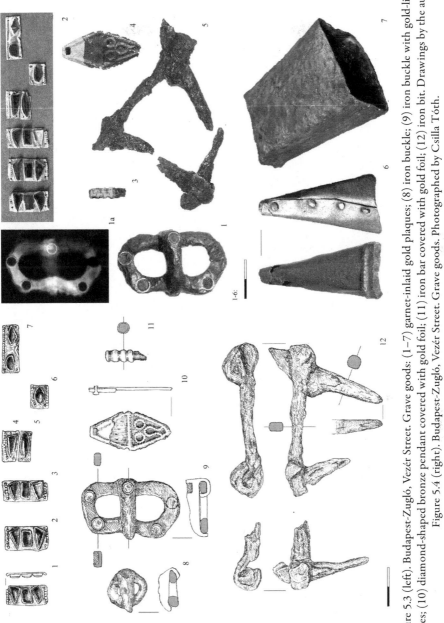

Figure 5.3 (left). Budapest-Zugló, Vezér Street. Grave goods: (1–7) garnet-inlaid gold plaques; (8) iron buckle; (9) iron buckle with gold-lined recesses; (10) diamond-shaped bronze pendant covered with gold foil; (11) iron bar covered with gold foil; (12) iron bit. Drawings by the author. Figure 5.4 (right). Budapest-Zugló, Vezér Street. Grave goods. Photographed by Csilla Tóth.

the cell of the buckle ring. Another smaller, oval iron buckle lay on the inner side of the left thigh (Figure 5.3.8).

Two gold mounts (Figures 5.3.3, 5.3.6 and 5.5.3) lay on the inner side of the left thighbone (nos 3 and 6 on the grave drawing). The large, rectangular gold mount was recovered from the grave pit's fill. It is decorated with pressed bead-row motifs along the short sides and three cells: a rectangular cell flanked by two triangular ones. The stone is missing from one of the latter; the other two are inset with a flat, polished, dark red, translucent plate garnet. The smaller one is set with an oval cabochon garnet (Figure 5.3.6). One long side is edged with a pressed bead-row, the other has the remains of two other cells, which were originally triangular or diamond-shaped. The corners are perforated.

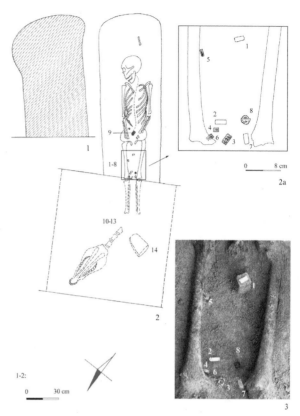

Figure 5.5. Budapest-Zugló, Vezér Street: (1) the discoloured patch indicating the grave pit; (2) grave plan; (2a) detail of the grave plan; (3) detail of the grave photo.

Two other gold mounts were found between the thighbones (nos 1 and 5 on the grave drawing) and three gold mounts around the knees (nos 2, 4, and 7). One gold mount (1) is decorated with three garnet inlaid cells: a rectangular cell flanked by two triangular ones (Figure 5.3.1). The four corners are perforated. It was found face down between the thighbones. Lying by the inner side of the right thighbone with the face upward was a rectangular gold mount (5) with a single oval, slightly pointed, garnet-inlaid cell (Figure 5.3.5). The corners of the mount are perforated. Another rectangular gold mount (7) lay face down by the lower end of the left thighbone, on its inner side (Figure 5.3.7). It is decorated with two cabochon garnets, one set in a semicircular, the other in a diamond-shaped cell. One of the long sides is edged with a bead-row punched from the reverse. The flattened side of another cell lies along the other long side. The four corners are perforated.

Two gold mounts were found by the lower end of the right thighbone, one of which (4) lay face up. It is decorated with a garnet inset with triangular cell and a bead-row edging along one of the long sides (Figure 5.3.4). The sides of this mount and of mount no. 5 fit perfectly together, indicating that the two garnets had originally been set beside each other. Yet another rectangular gold mount (2) was found face down by the inner side of the left knee (Figure 5.3.2). It is inset with three plate garnets arranged in a pattern of two triangular cells flanking a rectangular one.

Among the artefacts found by the remains of the horse skeleton, there were two oxidized fragments of an iron bit folded together (the two fragments do not match) (Figure 5.3.12). The mouthpieces are similarly fragmentary. The upper end of one of the bars curves inward just before breakage (its continuation cannot be accurately reconstructed). The other bar is oxidized to the inner surface of the loop at an oblique angle. Its lower end is pointed and traces of a ribbed pattern can be made out on its inner side.

The upper end of a fragment of a ribbed iron bar with round section (Figure 5.3.11) is covered with gold foil along a 1.5 cm section. It was perhaps part of a side-bar from another bit.

The diamond-shaped bronze pendant covered with gold foil, pressed from the reverse is framed with a slightly prominent rib and divided in two by a horizontal rib (Figure 5.3.10). The gold foil covering the plain half is damaged. The other half bears a pressed pattern of two circles combined with a loop motif. The edges of the gold foil were folded over the side to the back. The two parts of the pendant are held together with a bronze rivet. The back is plain without any trace of a suspension loop.[18] A cone of bronze sheet with edges folded over each other and held in place by four bronze rivets is most probably a bell (Figure 5.6.1). A pressed bead-row pattern encircles the base. The fragment of an iron clapper has survived in its interior.[19]

A conical iron bell was covered with bronze and iron oxide (Figure 5.6.3). It was cut from a thick iron sheet, folded lengthwise and riveted together (the contours

[18] Bóna, *Das Hunnenreich*, p. 282 with pl. 73.3. His remark concerning the suspension loop ('Seine Ergänzung ist vermutlich nicht ganz gut gelungen') is misplaced, for the bell was never restored.

[19] Bóna, *Das Hunnenreich*, pp. 104 and 282 with pl. 73.4–5.

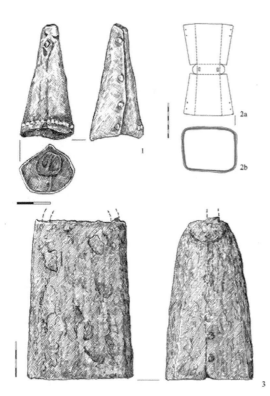

Figure 5.6. Budapest-Zugló, Vezér Street. Grave goods: (1) bronze bell; (2a–b) design of the iron bell; (3) iron bell. Drawings by the author.

of the two lower rivet heads can still be seen). The top, where the clapper was attached, is damaged. The stubs of a *c.* 1.5 cm wide loop have survived on the two sides. The clapper is missing.[20]

The Burial Rite

The grave dug on the island-like sand ridge surrounded by water was undoubtedly a solitary burial (Figure 5.1.2).[21] The grave orientation was north–south, with a slight inclination to the east. Early fifth-century burials in the steppe lands of southern Russia and in the Carpathian Basin have a typically north-west to south-

---

[20] Bóna, *Das Hunnenreich*, p. 102 with pl. 73.1. The bell was restored by Éva Várnai in April 2003.

[21] It seems likely that the museum organized the monitoring of the construction site after the discovery of the grave. István Bóna described the burial as a solitary grave, based on Tibor Nagy's personal communication.

east orientation.[22] Nothing is known about the original topography of the area, and as a consequence it remains uncertain whether or not there was any mound over the burial. However, it is altogether not impossible that a barrow was erected over the grave dug into the sandy soil, since this was a solitary burial.[23]

On the testimony of the report and the grave drawing, a horse skull placed upside down with a west–east orientation as well as three horse vertebrae were all found by the feet of the human skeleton, at an unknown depth. Given that the foot end of the grave pit was destroyed during the construction, it is also unclear whether the pit's southern end had been enlarged to accommodate the horse skull placed in the south-western corner. The iron harness bell (Figure 5.5.2) was found to the south-east from the horse skull and vertebrae. It was placed across the horse remains. The construction workers were unable to describe the exact position of the other artefacts belonging to the horse harness. Since the bit had oxidized in folded position, it seems likely that the bit, the bronze bell, and the diamond-shaped pendant had been placed beside the severed horse head by the feet of the human skeleton, together with the iron bell.

Burying a horse skull with or without severed legs, all wrapped in the hide, as a symbolic substitute for the entire animal, is a custom of East European origin, well documented in Sarmatian- and Hun-age assemblages.[24] According to Valéria Kulcsár, horse bones and skulls were often deposited in Sarmatian-age barrows,

---

[22] For the north–south orientation of Sarmatian burials, see Valéria Kulcsár, 'A kárpát-medencei szarmaták temetkezési szokásai', *Múzeumi Füzetek*, 49 (1998), 16–20. Most Hun-age graves in the Carpathian Basin have a north–south orientation. This is true for both female burials, such as that found at Csorna (Ilona Kovrig, 'Das Diadem von Csorna', *Folia Archaeologica*, 36 (1985), 107–48 (p. 107)) and male burials, such as that uncovered at Lengyeltóti (Kornél Bakay, 'Bestattung eines vornehmen Kriegers vom 5. Jahrhundert in Lengyeltóti (Komitat Somogy, Kreis Marcali)', *Acta Archaeologica Academiae Scientiarum Hungaricae*, 30 (1978), 149–72 (pp. 149–50)). For a discussion of grave orientation, see Joachim Werner, *Beiträge zur Archäologie des Attila-Reiches* (Munich, 1956), pp. 102–06. For the burial customs of the Hun age, see Dezső Csallány, 'Hamvasztásos és csontvázas hun temetkezések a Felső-Tisza vidékén', *Hermann Ottó Múzeum Évkönyve*, 2 (1958), 83–99 (pp. 86–87); Péter Tomka, 'A sztyeppei temetkezési szokások sajátos változata: A hun halotti áldozat', *Arrabona*, 22–23 (1986), 35–55; Péter Tomka, 'Hun temetkezés és hitvilág', in *Hunok, Gepidák, Langobardok,* ed. by István Bóna (Szeged, 1993), p. 20.

[23] Some elements of the burial rite noted in the case of Childeric's grave seem to originate in the Hun age. See Michel Kazanski and Patrick Périn, 'La Tombe de Childéric: un tumulus oriental?', in *Mélanges Jean-Pierre Sodini*, ed. by F. Baratte and others (Paris, 2005), pp. 287–98.

[24] Bóna, *Das Hunnenreich*, pp. 150–52; Irina P. Zasetskaia, *Kul'tura kochevnikov iuzhno-russkikh stepei v gunnskuiu epokhu (konets IV–V. vv.)* (St Petersburg, 1994), pp. 17–21.

usually in male burials.[25] Mihály Kőhegyi uncovered a partial horse burial in the
upper level of Mound 256 at Madaras-Halmok. The horse's head, the neck, the
right foreleg, and a part of the torso were placed in the grave. The skull rested on
the limb.[26] Grave 30 of the Sarmatian-age cemetery at Szentes-Sárgapart, a disturbed
burial of a female, contained a horse skull with the iron bit still in its mouth.[27]

A Sarmatian variant of the Hun-age partial horse burial was observed in grave
5 of the Kobiakovo burial mound cemetery in the Don region: in addition to cattle
and bird bones, a horse skull, a bit, and various harness mounts were placed by the
feet of the human skeleton (Figure 5.7.1).[28] A horse head was found above the
human skeleton during the excavation in 1904 of a Hun-age burial in Levice.[29]
While noting that the deposition of the horse skull and leg bones wrapped in the
animal's hide is typical for the Hunnic period, Irina Zasetskaia added more
examples from the steppe lands north of the Black and Caspian Seas (Verkhne
Pogromnoe, Pokrovsk, Crimea, and Kubei). Horse skulls and various horse bones
were recovered from the burials uncovered at Zdvizhenskoe in the Caucasus and
Alioshki by the southern reaches of the Dnieper.[30] However, none of the currently
known burials in the eastern Hunnic territories contained just a horse skull, as in
the case of Zugló. The only other cases of a horse head placed in a human burial are
a Sarmatian-age burial at Szentes-Sárgapart and a later, Gepid-age burial at
Hódmezővásárhely-Kishomok, in which the skull had been placed on the pelvis of
the human skeleton. On the basis of the associated pot, the burial was dated to the
middle third of the sixth century and may therefore be interpreted as reminiscent
of a practice most popular during the Sarmatian and Hunnic ages.[31]

[25] Kulcsár, 'A kárpát-medencei szarmaták temetkezési szokásai', pp. 72–74.

[26] Mihály Kőhegyi, 'Előzetes jelentés a Madaras-Halmok későszarmata-hunkori temetőjének
ásatásáról', *Archaeologiai Értesítő*, 98 (1971), 210–15 (pp. 214–15 with fig. 7). See also Mihály
Kőhegyi and Gabriella Vörös, 'Bestattungsbräuche in dem sarmatischen Gräberfeld von Madaras',
in *International Connection of the Barbarians of the Carpathian Basin in the 1st–5th Centuries A.D.:
Proceedings of the International Conference Held in 1999 in Aszód and Nyíregyháza*, ed. by Eszter
Istvánovits and Valéria Kulcsár (Aszód, 2001), pp. 195–200 (p. 199).

[27] Mihály Párducz, *A szarmatakor emlékei Magyarországon III.* (Budapest, 1950), p. 11 with
pl. 19.2–4; Kulcsár, 'A kárpát-medencei szarmaták temetkezési szokásai', p. 73.

[28] V. K. Guguev and S. I. Bezuglov, 'Vsadnicheskoe pogrebeniie pervykh vekov nashei ery iz
kurannogo nekropolia Kobiakova gorodishcha na Donu', *Sovetskaia Arkheologiia*, 1990.2, 164–75.

[29] Bóna, *Das Hunnenreich*, p. 280.

[30] Zasetskaia, *Kul'tura kochevnikov*, pp. 12–13 and 198–99.

[31] István Bóna and Margit Nagy, *Gepidische Gräberfelder im Theissgebiet I* (Budapest, 2002),
pp. 42 and 93.

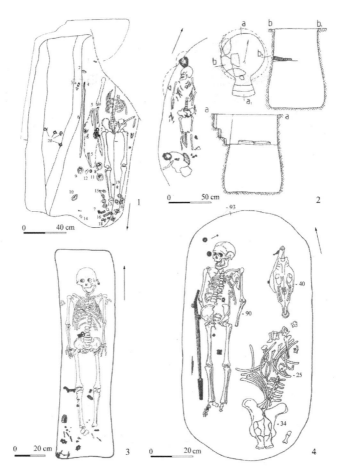

Figure 5.7. Hun-age partial horse burials: (1) Kobiakovo, burial mound 5; (2) Beliaus (1991); (3) Beliaus (1967); (4) Sopka II, grave 688. After Guguev and Bezuglov, 'Vsadnicheskoe pogrebeniie'; Aibabin, *Etnicheskaia istoriia*; and Molodin and Chikisheva, 'Pogrebenie voina'.

The upside-down position of the horse skull in Zugló is another characteristic feature of Hun-age burials. A similar case is known from grave 688 of the Sopka II site in the Baraba steppe land between the rivers Om' and Tartas (western Siberia). The grave contained various parts of a butchered horse placed on the left side of the human skeleton. The various parts were deposited in anatomical order, but at differing depths. The lower mandible with the bit lay deepest; above it was the horse skull, the pelvic bones were placed slightly higher, and the ribs and the middle vertebrae were on top, although the position of the latter suggests that those too had been butchered into larger chunks (Figure 5.7.4). Vyacheslav I. Molodin points to a comparable horse bone deposition case in burial IV at Bulan-Koba, in the Altai region.[32] The custom of placing horse remains in the grave-pit in reversed anatomical order may then be traced westwards all the way to Silesia. A horse placed on its back was deposited behind the skull of the warrior equipped with a lance at Ługi in Poland.[33] Those parallels from Siberia and Silesia suggest that the upside-down position of the horse skull in the Zugló burial must not be taken as a mere accident of excavation. Since there was no mention of other horse bones aside from the skull and the three neck vertebrae, it seems likely that the Zugló grave contained a partial horse burial: the severed horse head placed upside down by the feet of the deceased, in an attempt to represent symbolically a(n entire) horse offering. It is unclear whether the horse and the human skeletal remains lay at the same depth or, as noted in the abovementioned examples, the horse bones had been placed slightly higher than the human skeleton.

According to the construction workers, the bit lay near the horse vertebrae. Judging by their declarations, the oxidized, folded bit, the diamond-shaped mount, and the bronze bell were all between the head of the horse and the right foot of the human burial. The practice of burying the horse harness in a separate pit or depositing it in a small heap inside the horseman's grave was quite widespread in the Hunnic period. Horse harness sets deposited at the same level as the body are known from several graves excavated at Beliaus in the Crimea. In a grave uncovered in 1967, the horse head and legs were wrapped in the hide and placed by the human skeleton, a Mongoloid boy, while the harness set (a bit, silver strap distributor mounts, and an iron bell) was placed beside the right foot. In addition, there was a small horse figurine covered with gold foil by the right knee (Figure 5.7.3). Another child grave uncovered in 1991 contained the skeleton of a six- to nine-year-old boy laid to rest in a grave pit with access steps. A long bone from a horse skeleton and a dog mandible were placed on the flat stones above the lowermost step. The true horse offering consisted of the horse's tail placed across the child's legs. The bit made up of bronze and iron parts was folded in two and placed by the feet (Figure 5.7.2).[34] Burials of boys in the Crimea display two kinds of horse

[32] Vyacheslav I. Molodin and T. A. Chikisheva, 'Pogrebenie voina IV–V v. v n. e. v Barabe', in *Voennoe delo drevnego i srednevekogo naselenia Severnoi i Tsentral'noi Azii*, ed. by Iu. S. Khudiakov and Iu. A. Plotnikov (Novosibirsk, 1990), pp. 161–79 (pp. 162–63 with fig. 1).

[33] Magdalena Mączyńska, 'Das Ende der Przeworsk-Kultur', in *Die Vandalen. Die Könige. Die Eliten. Die Krieger. Die Handwerker*, ed. by Andrzej Kokowski and Christian Leiber (Holzminden, 2003), pp. 185–201 with fig. 6; Kazanski and Périn, 'La Tombe de Childeric', p. 293 with fig. 6.

[34] For a recent discussion of the Beliaus burials, see Aleksandr I. Aibabin, *Etnicheskaia istoriia rannevizantiiskogo Kryma* (Simferopol, 1999), pp. 73–75 with figs 27 and 28. The nature and

offerings, either with the head and legs wrapped in the hide or with just the tail. However, it is interesting to note that harness sets deposited by the feet appear in both cases.

It is important to note at this point that symbolic horse burials with harness sets, but without horse bones, are known from the late Roman military burials in Pannonia, though such burials are not very numerous. An iron bit was placed by the feet of the skeleton in grave 27 of the Intercisa cemetery;[35] another bit as well as bronze spurs were found in grave 4 of the Zengővárkony II cemetery, which has been coin-dated to the late fourth or early fifth century.[36] Formal analogies between late Roman military burials in Pannonia and those of Hun-age warriors, in terms of the precise location of the harness set deposition within the grave pit, suggest that Roman burial practices in Pannonia may have been under a strong influence from the East European steppe lands.

The Zugló burial stands out among similar assemblages because of the two bells found by the horse skull. The bronze bell was probably near the right foot of the human skeleton, while according to the construction workers, the large iron bell was found to the south-east from the horse skull. It is therefore possible to interpret the small bell, which was made from bronze sheet and had an iron clapper, as part of the harness set. By contrast, the larger and heavier iron bell without clapper may have been a cattle bell.

Horse bells buried together with horse bones and harness sets are very rare in Merovingian Europe. It has been noted that bells hanging from the necks of grazing animals (horses, cattle, sheep, or pigs) may have served not just for signalling the location of the animals, but also as a kind of ward-off amulet against thieves. Bells with possibly apotropaic functions may be seen hanging from the necks of horses depicted on bracteates. It may well be that the deposition of a bell in a burial had the same ritual significance.[37]

---

position of the animal remains (horse tail vertebrae) in the 1991 burial exactly match those of the animal remains (sheep sacrum and tail vertebra) found in the fifth-century grave of a young male excavated in Árpás. See Péter Tomka, 'Az árpási 5. századi sír', *Arrabona*, 39 (2001), 161–81 (p. 164 with fig. 3). The practice of depositing horse tails in burials seems to have been an exclusively Hun-age custom.

[35] László Barkóczi and others, *Intercisa (Dunapentele-Sztálinváros) története a római korban*, I (Budapest, 1954), pp. 55–56.

[36] János Dombay, 'Későrómai temetők Baranyában', *A Pécsi Janus Pannonius Múzeum Évkönyve*, 1957, 181–330 (pp. 274–78).

[37] Robert Reiß, 'Reiter, Pferd und Glocke im Spiegel frühmittelalterlicher Grabfunde', *Acta Praehistorica et Archaeologica*, 25 (1993), 272–88.

There is little evidence for the deposition of iron bells in Late Roman burials of Pannonia. In addition to a bronze mount, grave 4 in Pilismarót-Öregek dűlője produced an iron bell, which was found together with other artefacts (iron chain, iron knife, iron needle) by the right foot of the male skeleton (Figure 5.8.8). There were no remains of a harness set.[38] A cylindrical case of bronze sheet (Figure 5.9.9) came to light from a disturbed burial (grave 1106/a) of the Intercisa cemetery. The dolphin-headed buckle, the propeller-shaped mounts, and the round ornamental buttons that studded a military belt are among the latest finds of the cemetery (Figure 5.9.1–8).[39] The bronze case is very similar to the Zugló bronze bell, in terms of both form and size. Unfortunately, the Intercisa grave was disturbed and little can thus be known about its specific burial features.

In the Alföld (the Great Hungarian Plain), female and child burials of the Sarmatian age often contain small, cast bronze bells of an elongated, semispherical shape. Two such bells cast in iron and found in grave 8 from Törökszentmiklós-Surján-Újtelep were covered with bronze (Figure 5.8.1–2).[40] A bronze bell was part of a Hun-age assemblage from Hejőkeresztúr-Homokbánya on the Upper Tisza, which also included cremated bones, a silver buckle, silver earrings, a willow leaf–shaped silver pendant, two clay vessels, and a bell made from a bronze vessel (Figure 5.9.10–15). According to Dezső Csallány, this must have been a Hun-age cremation burial.[41] The child burial uncovered at Mártély in 1975 may be dated to the Hunnic period on the basis of the dark blue speckled beads. Though there

[38] László Barkóczi, 'Későrómai temető Pilismaróton', *Folia Archaeologica*, 12 (1960), 111–32 (pp. 113–14 with fig. 30).

[39] Eszter B. Vágó and István Bóna, *Der spätrömische Südostfriedhof: Die Gräberfelder von Intercisa* (Budapest, 1976), pp. 75–76 with pl. 18.10; Markus Sommer, 'Die Gürtel und Gürtelbeschläge des 4. und 5. Jahrhunderts im römischen Reich', *Bonner Hefte zur Vorgeschichte*, 22 (1984), 1–165 (pp. 24–25 and 125).

[40] Andrea H. Vaday, 'Die sarmatischen Denkmäler des Komitats Szolnok: Ein Beitrag zur Archäologie und Geschichte des sarmatischen Barbaricums', *Antaeus*, 17–18 (1988–89), 9–290 (p. 289 with pl. 147.12).

[41] Csallány, 'Hamvasztásos és csontvázas', pp. 83–84 with plates 1.1–4 and 2.1–3. Even though the specific rite of the Hejőkeresztúr burial cannot be reconstructed with any degree of certainty, it may have been a variant of Irina Zasetskaia's Group 1 (Zasetskaia, *Kul'tura kochevnikov*, p. 12). The Hejőkeresztúr small, semispherical bronze vessel decorated with three engraved lines under its rim has good analogies among the silver vessels from the Aquincum hoard. See Margit Nagy, 'Óbuda a népvándorlás korban', *Budapest Régiségei*, 30 (1993), 353–71 (pp. 356–57 with fig. 6.1–2, and pl. 6.1, 5). The analogy strongly suggests that the earliest artefacts in the hoard, such as the silver vessels, may be dated to the Hunnic age.

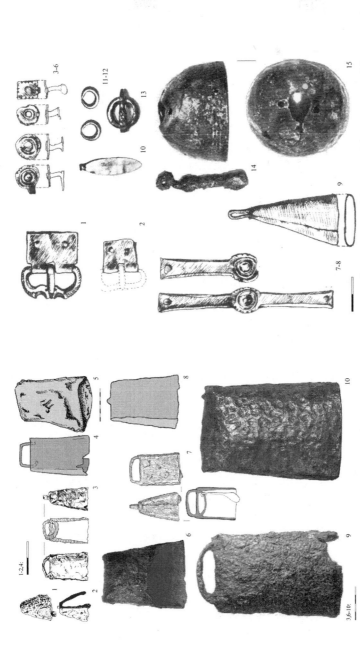

Figure 5.8 (left). Late Roman and Hun-age iron bells: (1–2) Törökszentmiklós-Surján-Újtelep, grave 8; (3) Beliaus; (4) Zamiatino 7; (5) Antonovka; (6) Ulcisia Castra/Szentendre; (7) Mártély; (8) Pilismarót-Öregek dűlője, grave 4; (9) Gorsium/Tác; (10) Budapest-Zugló. After Vaday, 'Die sarmatischen Denkmäler'; Zasetskaia, Kul'tura kochevnikov; Oblomskii, 'Poselenie Zamiatino-7'; Nagy, 'A Fővárosi Régészeti és Ásatási Intézet'; Nagy, 'Kora népvándorlás kori gyermeksír'; Barkóczi, 'Későrómai temető'; and Fitz, 'Gorsium'.

Figure 5.9 (right). Late Roman and Hun-age bells and other artefacts: (1–9) Intercisa, grave 1106/a; (10–15) Hejőkeresztúr-Homokbánya. After Vágó and Bóna, Der spätrömische Südostfriedhof; and Csallány, 'Hamvasztásos és csontvázas'.

was no harness set in that burial, it did produce a gilded bronze bell, which was found by the right hand of the skeleton, together with bone and boar-tusk pendants (Figure 5.8.7).[42]

On the other hand, the burial deposition of bells together with horse skeletons seems to have been a practice of conspicuously Central Asian origin, as documented, for example, in burial mound 3 excavated in 1954 in Noin-Ula (Mongolia).[43] According to István Bóna, the Levice and Zugló burials must be viewed as a variant of the partial horse burials of the Hunnic age, in which the head of the horse was placed either above the head or by the feet of the human skeleton.[44] In addition, the existing evidence strongly suggests that the Zugló burial is also the earliest Migration-period example of a horse buried with a bell.

It is noteworthy that although the twenty-five-year old man laid to rest in the Zugló grave may have been a warrior, his burial had no weapons. The absence of weapons can hardly be explained in terms of the destruction at the foot end of the grave pit. A more likely explanation is that no weapons were supposed to be deposited in the grave in the first place. Péter Tomka has already suggested that during the Hunnic age, weapons and harness sets were buried in separate pits next to the main graves.[45]

The Harness

The small bit from the Zugló burial was folded in two before deposition, and it oxidized in that position (Figure 5.4.5). The side-bars are passed through the rings of the bit; there is no trace of a side-ring on any of them. The upper part of each side-bar is broken, with a pointed lower end. The breakage surface on the upper part of the shorter bar bends inward, which suggests a bar with curved end. However, this reconstruction must be rejected, for the other bar is in fact straight. Such bits with side-bars are rather rare during the Hunnic period. Traces of ribs on the inner side of the right side-bar (Figure 5.3.12) suggest that the side-bars were initially covered with gold foil. The Zugló bit is different from specimens with ribbed straight or curved side-bars in that the latter were usually fitted to the ring

---

[42] Margit Nagy, 'Kora népvándorlás kori gyermeksír amulettekkel Mártélyról (Csongrád megye)', *Zalai Múzeum*, 14 (2005), 97–127 (pp. 97–98 with fig. 2).

[43] Bóna, *Das Hunnenreich*, p. 282.

[44] Bóna, *Das Hunnenreich*, p. 150.

[45] Tomka, 'Az árpási 5. századi sír', p. 169.

of the bit by means of a circular or rectangular link, as illustrated by several finds from large cemeteries in the Caucasus region.[46] Irina Zasetskaia has convincingly demonstrated that the tradition of ringed side-bars can be traced to the late La Tène period. Bits with ringed side-bars were buried with members of the second- or third-century Alan military aristocracy in the Zolotoe kladbishche on the River Kuban.[47] The only known analogy for the Zugló bit that could be dated to the Hunnic period is a poorly preserved specimen with side-bars found in grave 4 of the Giliach cemetery in the northern Caucasus.[48] The bit and the associated crescent-shaped harness mounts were by the feet of a male with artificially deformed skull, who had been buried together with his sword and spear.[49]

Bits with straight side-bars such as found in Zugló may have been more common in the Danube region in the mid-400s. The bits from the Apahida II burial resemble the one from Zugló in that the straight side-bars were passed through the outer ring. Additional rings were added to the outer side at the junction of the side-bar and the ring for the heavy, gold-ornamented straps of the head-stall.[50]

---

[46] Iu. N. Voronov and N. K. Shenkao, 'Vooruzhenie voinov Abkhazii IV–VII vv.', in *Drevnosti epokhi velikogo pereseleniia narodov V–VIII vekov*, ed. by Anatolii K. Ambroz and István Erdélyi (Moscow, 1982), pp. 121–65 (p. 135 with fig. 6); A. V. Dmitriev, 'Pogrebeniia vsadnikov i boevykh konei v mogil'nike epokhi pereseleniia narodov na r. Diurso bliz Novorossiiska', *Sovetskaia Arkheologiia*, 1979.4, 219–31.

[47] Zasetskaia, *Kul'tura kochevnikov*, pp. 40–41; Irina I. Gushchina and Irina P. Zasetskaia, '*Zolotoe kladbishche' rimskoi epokhi v Prikuban'e* (St Petersburg, 1994), pp. 50 with pl. 14, and 77 with pl. 56.

[48] Ilia R. Akhmedov, 'New Data about the Origin of Some Constructive Parts of the Horse-harness of the Great Migration Period', in *International Connection of the Barbarians*, ed. by Istvánovits and Kulcsár, pp. 363–88 (pp. 367 and 378 with fig. 3.7), describes the specimen as 'unique'.

[49] T. M. Minaeva, 'Raskopki sviatilishcha i mogil'nika vozle gorodishcha Giliach v 1965', in *Drevnosti epokhi velikogo pereselenia narodov*, ed. by Ambroz and Erdélyi, pp. 222–34 (pp. 228–30 with fig. 5). For the dating of grave 5, see Anatolii K. Ambroz, *Khronologiia drevnostei Severnogo Kavkaza V–VII vv.* (Moscow, 1989), pp. 30–33.

[50] Kurt Horedt and Dumitru Protase, 'Das zweite Fürstengrab von Apahida (Siebenbürgen)', *Germania*, 50 (1972), 174–220 (p. 185 with fig. 7); Michael Schmauder, *Oberschichtgräber und Verwahrfunde in Südosteuropa im 4. und 5. Jahrhundert: Zum Verhältnis zwischen den spätantiken Reich und der barbarischen Oberschicht aufgrund der archäologischen Quellen* (Bucharest, 2002), pp. 52–53 and pls 26–29; Ilia R. Akhmedov, 'Cheek-pieces and Elements of Harness with Zoomorphic Decoration in the Great Migration Period', in *Probleme der frühen Merowingerzeit im Mitteldonauraum*, ed. by Jaroslav Tejral (Brno, 2002), pp. 18–23 with fig. 6.1.

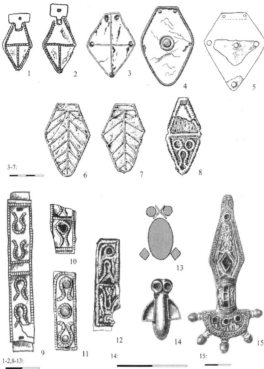

It is not clear what was the function of the ribbed iron bar covered with gold foil (Figure 5.4.3). In any case, the piece is too thin to have been a side-bar. Similar side-bars of the Pannonhalma type, which belong to Akhmedov's class I, are nonetheless thicker and with widened ends.[51] It is possible that there were two bits in the Zugló burial, and that the thinner bar was perhaps the inward-curving part of a Beliaus-type bit (Akhmedov's class 2, type 12).[52] However, even this seems unlikely, since all known side-bars of that type have widened extremities ending in polyhedral knobs.[53]

The pressed bronze pendant covered with gold foil (Figure 5.10.8) is a harness ornament most typical for the Hunnic period. Comparable pendants are known from Nizhniaia Dobrinka on the Lower Volga (Figure 5.10.5 and 9), Novohryhor'evka on the Lower Dnieper (Figure 5.10.4), Gora Klement'evka (Feodosiia) (Figure 5.10.1–2), and Kalinin in

Figure 5.10. Hun-age harness ornaments: (1–2) Gora Klement'evka; (3) Kalinin; (4) Novohryhor'evka; (5) Nizhniaia Dobrinka; (6–7) Pécs-Nagykozár-Üszögpuszta; (8) Budapest-Zugló; (9) Nizhniaia Dobrinka; (10) Conceşti; (11) Zdvizhenskoe; (12) Pannonhalma-Szélsőhalom; (13) Tiligul; (14) Mezőberény; (15) Ártánd-Lencsésdomb, grave 1. After Zasetskaia, *Kul'tura kochevnikov*; Bóna, *Das Hunnenreich*; Tomka, 'Der hunnische Fürstenfund'; Damm, 'Goldschmiedearbeiten der Völkerwanderungszeit'; Prohászka, 'A mezőberényi kora népvándorlás kori sír (1884)'; and Cseh and others, *Gepidische Gräberfelder*.

[51] Péter Tomka, 'Der hunnische Fürstenfund von Pannonhalma', *Acta Archaeologica Academiae Scientiarum Hungaricae*, 38 (1986), 423–88 (p. 427).

[52] Akhmedov, 'New Data', p. 378 with fig. 7.9.

[53] E.g. the specimen from grave 88 in Luchistoe (Crimea). See Akhmedov, 'New Data', p. 378 with fig. 6.5.

the Crimea (Figure 5.10.3).[54] Only one analogy is known from the Middle Danube region, namely the specimen from Pécs-Nagykozár-Üszögpuszta (Figure 5.10.6–7).[55] Irina Zasetskaia was able to reconstruct the head-stall of a Hun-age horse harness on the basis of the gem-inset harness mounts from burial mounds VIII and IX in Novohryhor'evka. The diamond-shaped pendants adorned the middle of the brow band, as well as the nose band.[56] Her reconstruction is confirmed by the discovery in several assemblages of pairs of similar pendants.

The ornamental pattern of the Zugló pendant consists of two circles and a loop-like line, a so-called 'omega motif'. This pattern is fairly common on many artefacts from steppe assemblages, which also display combinations of lines and circles, wavy and zig-zag lines, interlace patterns, and loops.[57] A necklace around the neck of the male skeleton found under burial mound 3 at Shipovo included stone-inset, omega-shaped pendants.[58] The pressed variant of the 'omega motif' appears in first- to third-century Alanic mound burials in the Caucasus foreland. The 'omega motif' on gold mounts has been interpreted as a zoomorphic design, namely as a symbolic depiction of ram heads.[59] Fifth-century cloisonné dress accessories from the northern region of the Black Sea include several examples of omega-shaped earring and necklace pendants.[60] A variant of this motif with stone inlay occurs on a buckle from Baamorto/Monforte de Lemos in western Spain.[61]

The loop was a popular motif on Hun-age harness mounts covered with gold foil. The motif occurs some times set in a row, and other times in antithetic pairs.

---

[54] Zasetskaia, *Kul'tura kochevnikov*, pp. 183 with pl. 30.4; 162–63 with pl. 1.5; 178 with pl. 26/3; and 176 with pl. 22.5.

[55] Bóna, *Das Hunnenreich*, p. 121 with fig. 48.

[56] Zasetskaia, *Kul'tura kochevnikov*, pp. 44–45 with fig. 8.1.

[57] Anatolii K. Ambroz, 'Kochevnicheskie drevnosti Vostochnoi Evropy i Srednei Azii V–VIII vv.', in *Vostochnoevropeiskie i sredneaziatskie stepi V-pervoi poloviny VIII v. stepi Evrazii v epokhu srednevekov'ia*, ed. by Svetlana A. Pletneva (Moscow, 1981), p. 12.

[58] Werner, *Beiträge*, pp. 103–05 and pl. 7.1; Zasetskaia, *Kul'tura kochevnikov*, p. 189 with pl. 40.8.

[59] Gushchina and Zasetskaia, 'Zolotoe kladbishche', pp. 14–15 with pl. 55.

[60] Inciser Gürçay Damm, 'Goldschmiedearbeiten der Völkerwanderungszeit aus dem nördlichen Schwarzmeergebiet: Katalog der Sammlung Diergardt 2', *Kölner Jahrbuch für Vor- und Frühgeschichte*, 21 (1988), 65–210 (p. 114 with n. 8 and 125–26).

[61] Alexander Koch, 'Zum archäologischen Nachweis der Sueben auf der Iberischen Halbinsel: Überlegungen zu einer Gürtelschnalle aus der Umgebung von Baamorto/Monforte de Lemos (Prov. Lugo, Spanien)', *Acta Praehistorica et Archaeologica*, 31 (1999), 156–98 (pp. 158–62 with fig. 2).

Examples include the mounts from Nizhniaia Dobrinka and Zdvizhenskoe (Figure 5.10.9, 11).[62] The motif is combined with a stone inlay on a fragmentary specimen from Conceşti (Figure 5.10.10)[63] and with a circle motif on the Pannonhalma harness mounts (Figure 5.10.12).[64] It also occurs three times on one and the same pressed gold strap end from an Avar-age burial at Kékesd. According to István Bóna, the Kékesd strap end must have been a Hun-age artefact, re-employed for an Avar-age burial.[65] Péter Tomka suggested that the circles framed by a grooved imitation of filigree decoration above the loop motif on the Pannonhalma harness mount were in fact an imitation of stone inlays. A unique variant of the 'omega motif' appears in the decoration of a pair of late fifth-century fibulae from Ártánd-Lencsésdomb. No less than three 'omega motifs' with glass inlays of decreasing size decorate the foot-plate of each one of the two silver gilt brooches (Figure 5.10.15).[66]

The 'omega motif'[67] is combined with two circles on the Zugló harness pendant. The circles flank the rounded upper part of the loop (Figure 5.10.8). This brings to mind the shape of a cicada, with the two circles possibly marking the eyes. The stylized representation of the insect and the emphasis on the eyes is unusual but by no means unique in the Hunnic period. A combination of stone inlays and an engraved, oblique cross in the centre of the diadem from Tiligul (Figure 5.10.13) was interpreted as a cicada.[68] A stylized representation of a cicada also appears on other Hun-age dress accessories in polychrome style. Most remarkable in that respect is the gold cicada-fibula from Mezőberény with its combination of an oval shape for the body and two round inset stones for the eyes (Figure 5.10.14).[69] The curved linear motif on the Zugló pendant also brings to mind a small, gem-inlaid cicada-brooch from Kerch'.[70]

---

[62] Zasetskaia, *Kul'tura kochevnikov*, pp. 183 with pl. 30.4; 168–69 with pl. 11.7.

[63] Zasetskaia, *Kul'tura kochevnikov*, pp. 174–75 with pl. 12.

[64] Tomka, 'Der hunnische Fürstenfund', pp. 429–30 with figs 6.5–9 and 10.1–8.

[65] Bóna, *Das Hunnenreich*, pp. 174 and 209 fig. 109.

[66] János Cseh and others, *Gepidische Gräberfelder im Theissgebiet II* (Budapest, 2005), pp. 54–55 and pl. 1.1–2.

[67] Zasetskaia, *Kul'tura kochevnikov*, contains no discussion of the 'omega motif', which does not even appear on any of figs 13 to 16 in that book.

[68] Damm, 'Goldschmiedearbeiten der Völkerwanderungszeit', p. 114 and fig. 56.5.

[69] Péter Prohászka, 'A mezőberényi kora népvándorlás kori sír (1884)', *Folia Archaeologica*, 51 (2003–04), 115–38 (p. 120 with fig. 2.1a).

[70] Damm, 'Goldschmiedearbeiten der Völkerwanderungszeit', p. 142.

The map distribution of pressed harness ornaments decorated with the 'omega motif' suggests that the cicada originated in the region between the Caspian and Black Seas (Figure 5.11.1). The motif was first used for the decoration of harness sets.[71] A recent study of the Hun-age religious beliefs in the Carpathian Basin views the reverence of winged insects (bees, crickets, and gad-flies) as a widespread phenomenon and points to ethnographic analogies. In Mongol mythology, for example, the human soul is believed to turn into an insect after death.[72] Sozomenus records a probably much deformed story originating in the steppe lands, according to which the Huns were led through a bog by an ox tormented by a gad-fly.[73] It is therefore no accident that Hun-age harness ornaments in both the Volga-Don and the Middle Danube regions were decorated with cicada motifs.[74] The best analogies for the Hun-age cicada-ornamented harness ornaments are the garnet-inlaid gold

[71] To be sure, the cicada motif first appears in the Scythian period. See Zdenko Vinski, 'Zikadenschmuck aus Jugoslawien', *Jahrbuch der Römisch-Germanischen Zentralmuseums Mainz*, 4 (1957), 136–60 (pp. 145–48). According to Bóna, *Das Hunnenreich*, pp. 196–97, the cicada motif was an ancestral symbol, which the Huns first brought to Europe. Zdenko Vinski's suggestion that the Huns adopted the motif from the Sarmatian and Alanic population of the Black Sea area seems to be borne out by the example of a harness set laid in the Brut I burial of an Alan warrior, the wealthiest so far found in the Caucasus. The Brut I head-stall was adorned with heart-shaped gold mounts resembling cicadas. See Michel Kazanski, 'Les Tombes des chefs militaires de l'époque hunnique', in *Germanen beiderseits des spätantiken Limes*, ed. by Thomas Fischer, Gundolf Precht, and Jaroslav Tejral (Brno, 1999), pp. 293–316 (p. 310 with fig. 13). See also Igor Gavritukhin and Michel Kazanski's contribution to this volume. During the early Migration period, an equally popular motif for the decoration of horse harness mounts was the bird of prey. On the testimony of the Apahida II assemblage, the eagle was a recurring motif on mid-fifth-century cloisonné-decorated harness mounts and saddle ornaments. See Horedt and Protase, 'Das zweite Fürstengrab', pp. 201–02 with figs 8–9; Radu Harhoiu, 'Chronologische Fragen der Völkerwanderungszeit in Rumänien', *Dacia*, 34 (1990), 169–208 (pp. 173–83). In fifth-century *barbaricum*, winged creatures seem to have been conceptually associated with warhorses.

[72] Ágnes Aszt and Ágnes Kovács, 'A Kárpát-medencei hunok vallásáról', in *A népvándorláskor fiatal kutatói 8. találkozójának előadásai (Veszprém, 1997. november 28–30)*, ed. by Ágota S. Perémi (Veszprém, 1999), pp. 47–67 (pp. 49–51).

[73] Sozomenus, *Ecclesiastical History*, 6.37, ed. by Joseph Bidez (Paris, 2005). See also Gyula Moravcsik, 'A csodaszarvas mondája a bizánci íróknál', *Egyetemes Philologiai Közlöny*, 38 (1914), 280–92; Sándor Eckhardt, 'Attila a mondában', in *Attila és hunjai*, ed. by Gyula Németh (Budapest, 1940; repr. 1986), pp. 143–216 (pp. 150–51); Aszt and Kovács, 'A Kárpát-medencei hunok vallásáról', pp. 49–50.

[74] For the pressed cicada-shaped strap ends of the Levice assemblage, see Bóna, *Das Hunnenreich*, fig. 65. Cloisonné-decorated strap ends with cicada wings are also known from Szeged-Nagyszéksós (Bóna, *Das Hunnenreich*, figs 80 and 83).

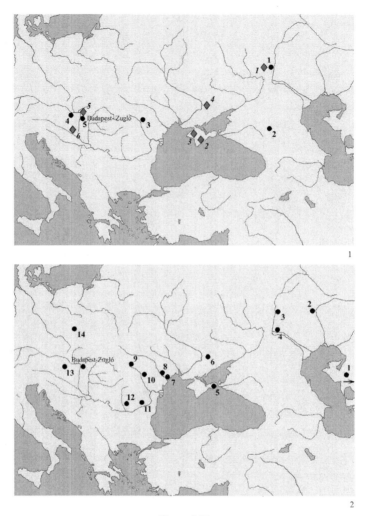

Figure 5.11.
1. Distribution of Hun-age pressed (circle) and diamond-shaped (diamonds) horse harness mounts. Pressed mounts: (1) Nizhnaia Dobrinka; (2) Zdvizhenskoe; (3) Conceşti; (4) Pannonhalma-Szélsőhalom; (5) Budapest-Zugló. Diamond-shaped mounts: *(1)* Nizhnaia Dobrinka; *(2)* Feodosiia; *(3)* Kalinin; *(4)* Novohryhor'evka; *(5)* Budapest-Zugló; *(6)* Pécs-Üszögpuszta. Data after Zasetskaia, *Kul'tura kochevnikov*; and Tomka, 'Der hunnische Fürstenfund'.
2. Distribution of Hun-age, gem-encrusted diadems with no filigree decoration: (1) Koktal; (2) Shipovo; (3) Berezovka; (4) Verkhne Pogromnoe; (5) Kerch'; (6) Tiligul; (7) Nikopol; (8) Antonovka; (9) Surbanec; (10) Buhăeni; (11) Dulceanca; (12) Gherăseni; (13) Csorna; (14) Jędrzychowice. Map drawn by the author after Kovrig, 'Das Diadem von Csorna'; and Zasetskaia, *Kul'tura kochevnikov*.

mounts from Childeric's burial in Tournai. The gold cicadas and the bull-head pendants had probably decorated the harness of the King's horse.[75] Cicadas were depicted in a stylized form on many pressed harness ornaments found in the vast region between the Middle Don and the Middle Danube rivers. It may well be that the 'magnificent' harness straps mentioned by Priscus were in fact adorned with bronze mounts covered with gold foil.

The Zugló burial produced a small bell made from bronze sheet and a larger one made from iron sheet. The body of the bronze bell was riveted together on the backside; the base has a band of bead-like ornaments. A part of the iron clapper survived in its interior. The loop of the iron bell was broken and its clapper was already missing when it was placed in the grave.

The bronze and the iron bells were both made from metal sheet and are therefore different from the cast bronze bells so popular both within the Roman province of Pannonia and in *barbaricum*.[76] Besides the already mentioned bronze-sheet bell from grave 1106 in Intercisa, a conical artefact resembling a bronze bell was also found in a Sarmatian-age burial in Szentes-Nagyhegy-Horváth Imre-szőlő. Much like the Zugló specimen, it was made of bronze sheet and was even of similar size.[77]

---

[75] *Die Franken: Wegbreiter Europas 5. bis 8. Jahrhundert*, ed. by Alfried Wieczorek and others, 2nd edn (Mainz, 1997) pp. 880–82. Childeric had been a former ally of the Huns and a king of the Salian Franks settled in the northern part of Belgica II province. István Bóna even believed that some of Childeric's weapons and ornaments were gifts from Attila. If true, this must also apply to the horse harness, even though Bóna, under the influence of Jean-Jacques Chiflet (who first published the Tournai assemblage) believed the cicadas to have decorated a cloak (Bóna, *Das Hunnenreich*, p. 128). Vinski, 'Zikadenschmuck', pp. 151–52, also believed that the cicadas from Childeric's grave had been made in southern Russia or in Hungary. The bee-shaped ornaments are now regarded as harness ornaments. See Patrick Périn and Michel Kazanski, 'Das Grab Childerichs I.', in *Die Franken*, ed. by Wieczorek and others, pp. 173–82 with fig. 128; Ursula Koch, Karin von Welck, and Alfried Wieczorek, 'Das Grab des Frankenkönigs Childerich I.', in *Die Franken*, ed. by Wieczorek and others, pp. 880–82 with fig. 118. For a good overview, see Michael Müller-Wille, 'Königtum und Adel im Spiegel der Grabfunde', in *Die Franken*, ed. by Wieczorek and others, pp. 206–10. It must here be noted that the 'bull-head' mounts from Childeric's burial may also be associated with Sozomenus's story about the origin of the Huns.

[76] In view of the increasing number of bell finds from this period, the use of bells as musical instruments, much as in the case of the Roman ones, must now be taken into consideration. For Roman cast bells as musical instruments, see Judit Topál, 'Musikalische Denkmäler in der römischen Sammlung von Aquincum (Budapest)', *Studia Musicologica Academiae Scientiarum Hungaricae*, 42 (2001), 275–89.

[77] Párducz, *A szarmatakor emlékei*, p. 25 with plate 78.22.

Unfortunately, little else is known about that burial, and the precise position of the bronze cone in the grave was not recorded.

A bronzed iron bell resembling the iron bell from Zugló was found in Mártély among numerous and various amulets placed in an infant grave. A date within the Hunnic period has been advanced for that burial on the basis of dark blue amulet beads.[78] By contrast, no date could be assigned to the bronzed iron bells found in a robbed female burial from the Sarmatian-age cemetery in Törökszentmiklós-Surján-Újtelep (Figure 5.8.1–2).[79] The East-European analogies of the Zugló bell dated to the Hunnic period have already been discussed by István Bóna. An iron bell was found by the right foot of the male skeleton in a grave uncovered in 1967 in Beliaus (Crimea), together with a bit and harness ornaments (Figure 5.8.3). As mentioned above, the grave also produced the skull and legs of a horse, all wrapped in the hide. Another iron bell was found by the feet of a female skeleton in a burial excavated in Antonovka near Odessa in 1965 (Figure 5.8.5). The associated grave goods include a diadem, but no horse harness.[80] Iron bells are relatively common in late Roman assemblages in Pannonia, as well as in Gaul: a specimen is known from Pilismarót (Figure 5.8.8), another from grave 2/13 in Intercisa, and a third one from Hermes in northern Gaul.[81] An iron bell was found together with iron hooks, a knife, a whetstone and other iron artefacts in the Hun-period settlement of Zamiatino 7 in the Don region (Figure 5.8.4).[82]

The conical form and the curved ear of the Hun-period iron bells imitate the Roman-age bells of Ágnes Salamon's class 1. The Törökszentmiklós-Surján bells belong to Salamon's class 2, which is by far the commonest of the entire Roman period. The riveted Roman bells made from sheet iron were coated with copper

[78] Nagy, 'Kora népvándorlás kori gyermeksír', pp. 103–04 and fig. 5.8.

[79] Vaday, 'Die sarmatischen Denkmäler', pp. 288–89 with plate 147.12.

[80] Bóna, *Das Hunnenreich*, p. 282 with fig. 73; Zasetskaia, *Kul'tura kochevnikov*, pp. 167 with pl. 8.4–6 (Antonovka) and 178–80 and pl. 27.3 (Beliaus).

[81] Pilismarót: Barkóczi, 'Későrómai temető', fig. 30.12. Intercisa: Ágnes Salamon, 'Gebrauch-gegenstände und Werkzeuge aus Eisen', in *Intercisa (Dunapentele): Geschichte der Stadt in der Römerzeit*, ed. by Maria R. Alföldi, II (Budapest, 1957), p. 376 with pl. 72/3. Hermes: Françoise Vallet, 'Regards critiques sur les témoins archéologiques des Francs en Gaule du Nord à l'époque de Childéric et de Clovis', *Antiquités nationales*, 29 (1997), 219–44 (p. 231 fig. 13.15).

[82] A. M. Oblomskii, 'Poselenie Zamiatino-7', in *Ostraia Luka Dona v drevnosti: Zamiatinskii arheologicheskii kompleks gunskogo vremeni*, ed. by A. M. Oblomskii (Moscow, 2004), p. 42 and fig. 81.9.

before the attachment of the clapper.[83] The coating protected the bell from corrosion while rendering the surface shiny and bright and making the tone more pleasant.

Good analogies to the large iron bell from Zugló can be found among Roman-age iron finds from Pannonia. Four similar bells were unearthed together with a sickle-like implement in the sacred precinct at Gorsium.[84] The largest of them is 19 cm long (Figure 5.8.9). Another, somewhat smaller, iron bell is known from the uppermost, Late Roman archaeological layer by the *porta decumana* of the Ulcisia Castra/Szentendre camp (Figure 5.8.6), in which it was associated with pottery with smoothed-in decoration.[85] Roman bells of Salamon's class 1 have come to light on various sites along the Roman *limes* in Pannonia (Intercisa, Szentendre, Budakalász, Leányfalu, and Nógrádverőce), as well as in the interior of the province (Baláca, Pogánytelek, and Balatonfűzfő). Close similarities between the specimens from Szentendre, Leányfalu, and Intercisa suggest that they were all produced within one and the same workshop.[86] Fragments of comparable *tintinabula* have been found within the Late Roman fort at Tokod.[87] In addition, dozens of conical iron bells have been reported from settlement sites elsewhere within the West European provinces of the empire.[88]

The nineteenth- to twentieth-century technique of manufacturing copper-coated bells has been described in great detail in the Hungarian ethnographic literature. As a consequence, we now know that even in modern times, bell-making was a complicated operation, with multiple work stages, each requiring years of experience and a tight coordination of several craftsmen. One of the key phases in the process was the addition of copper coating, which required good-quality clay for plastering. Clay sources therefore needed to be located close to the manufacturing workshops. Bells made in the nineteenth century in Jolsva (now Jelšava, in

[83] Salamon, 'Gebrauchgegenstände', pp. 373–74 with pl. 42.1–2.

[84] Jenő Fitz, 'Gorsium: Első jelentés a táci római település feltárásáról, 1958/59', *Alba Regia*, 1 (1960), 154–64 (pp. 160–61 with fig. 9). Traces of bronze coating can be recognized on one of the bells. See also Jenő Fitz, *Gorsium: A táci római kori ásatások* (Székesfehérvár, 1960), p. 38.

[85] Tibor Nagy, 'A Fővárosi Régészeti és Ásatási Intézet jelentése az 1938–1942 évek között végzett kutatásairól', *Budapest Régiségei*, 13 (1943), 379–99 (pp. 393–97 with fig. 39).

[86] Salamon, 'Gebrauchgegenstände', p. 374 and n. 123.

[87] Mária R. Pető, 'Eisenfunde aus der Festung', in *Das spätrömische Festung und das Gräberfeld von Tokod*, ed. by András Mócsy (Budapest, 1981), pp. 145–47 (p. 146 with figs 7–8).

[88] Nagy, 'Kora népvándorlás kori gyermeksír', pp. 106–07 with n. 24.

Slovakia) were taken to national markets and reached as far south as Serbia.[89] The ethnographic evidence also indicates that the most delicate production phase was tuning, for which experienced craftsmen employed special tuning hammers with which bits of metal were chipped off the inside surface. Such delicate operations required many years of training, and it consequently comes as no surprise that bell-tuning skills were passed down from father to son.[90]

The large number of Late Roman iron bells so far known from the Roman provinces suggests that bell-making had already been a long tradition in the empire. It seems likely that there were just a few workshops for each province, in which iron bells were made that could be used either for herd animals or as musical instruments. Close manufacturing similarities between Late Roman iron bells and the specimens from Zugló and Mártély suggest that during the early fifth century, the goods manufactured in Roman workshops were also available, perhaps through trade, beyond the limits of the Roman provinces.[91] Good-quality bells were no doubt a much-prized commodity in the Hun-age *barbaricum*, known for its large herds of animals, especially horses.

The ethnographic evidence also indicates that specific bells were often chosen very carefully for specific animals. Nineteenth-century herdsmen in Hungary associated different bell tunes with different animal species or with different herd owners. Bells were therefore a highly prized commodity, which may explain why cattle thefts were commonly accompanied by bell thefts. The same may have been true for the early Middle Ages. We learn from the Salian Lawcode that the bell of a herd leader was particularly valuable and that the highest fine was imposed for stealing the bell from a horse.[92]

[89] Mihály Márkus, 'Jolsvai kolomposok', in *Emlékkönyv Kodály Zoltán hatvanadik születésnapjára*, ed. by Béla Gunda (Budapest, 1943), pp. 245–64.

[90] As was still the case in central Germany in the early twentieth century. See Konrad Hörmann, 'Herdengeläute und seine Bestandteile', *Hessische Blätter für Volkskunde*, 12 (1913), 1–99 (p. 45); Márkus, 'Jolsvai kolomposok', p. 249.

[91] István Bóna (*Das Hunnenreich*, p. 282) has suggested that the iron bells from Tanais were also produced in some Late Roman workshop. His description of 'iron-coated' bells of the Hunnic period is nevertheless based on a misunderstanding. The aggressive iron oxide has the tendency to penetrate through and then cover the thin copper coating, a phenomenon which could easily be misinterpreted as an indication that bells were made entirely of iron.

[92] *Pactus legis Salicae*, 37.1–3 and 38, ed. by Karl August Eckhardt, MGH Leges nationum Germanicarum, 4.1 (Hannover, 1962; repr. 2002).

Prompted by the abundant ethnographic evidence, I decided to send photographs and drawings of the iron bells from Zugló and Mártély to Gyula Hodossy from Edelény (Borsod-Abaúj-Zemplén County), the only remaining craftsman in Hungary still employing the traditional bell-making techniques. According to Hodossy, bells in demand among herdsmen are still made from hammered and rivetted iron sheet. A copper coating is needed to prevent the build-up of fat from contact with the skin of the animal. Small flat bells are commonly used for sheep and goat, larger ones for cattle and horses. Horsemen from Hortobágy used to attach bells to their saddle-horses in order to be able to identify them quickly within the herd.

Hodossy's remarks bring to mind Kálmán Szabó's study on bells used by Kecskemét herdsmen. According to Szabó, larger bells were always employed for horse herds. A few old horses with bells around their necks could keep together the entire herd. Bells were also used around the farmstead on horses and foals, in order for the owner to identify quickly his saddle-horse or for the mare to find her foal.[93] The ethnographic evidence thus strongly suggests that iron bells found in Hun-age horse burials or burials with horse skeleton parts were employed on saddle-horses.

Dress Accessories and Ornaments

The function of the small, elongated elliptical iron buckle found by the left knee of the skeleton in the Zugló burial is not very clear. It may well have been part of the footwear. A similar buckle with an obviously different function was found on the waist of the skeleton in grave 31 of the Hun-age cemetery excavated in Nagydém-Középprépáspuszta.[94]

No analogies are so far known for the large, oval belt buckle. The loop and the tongue were decorated with round glass plates set into gold cells recessed into the iron. Four cells adorned the loop and another the upper end of the tongue (Figure 5.12.6). The sides of the cells were lined with gold foil bent into a cylindrical shape with overlapping edges. The base of the cells was filled with two layers of a wax-like substance, and the glass plates were set on top.[95] It seems unlikely that the cells had originally been inlaid with stones, with glass plates replacing the presumably lost

---

[93] Kálmán Szabó, 'Csöngettyű és kolomp a kecskeméti pásztorság kezén', *A Magyar Nemzeti Múzeum Néprajzi Tárának Értesítője*, 24 (1932), 68–75 (pp. 70–72).

[94] Gábor Ilon, 'Hun kori temető részlete Nagydém-Középprépáspusztán', in *A népvándorláskor fiatal kutatói 8. találkozójának előadásai*, ed. by Perémi, pp. 28–46 (p. 30 and fig. 4.31).

[95] Fegyvári, 'A Budapest-Zugló', p. 329 with figs 1–2.

Figure 5.12. Gem-encrusted artefacts
of the Hun period: (1) Kerch' (1904);
(2) Beja; (3) Kirchheim unter Teck;
grave 100; (4) Regöly-Pénzesdomb;
(5) Lavoye, grave 319; (6) Budapest-
Zugló; (7) Basel-Kleinhüningen, grave
108. After Aibabin, 'Khronologiia
mogil'nikov'; Kazanski, 'Les Tombes
des chefs militaires'; Menghin, *Das
Schwert*; Mészáros, 'A regölyi'; *Die
Franken*, ed. by Wieczorek and others;
and Moosbrugger-Leu, *Die Schweiz*.

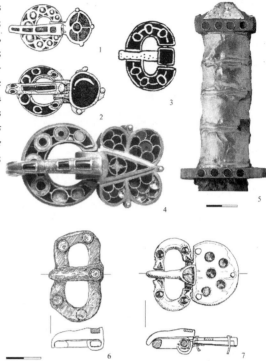

stones. The glass plates have most likely been there from the very beginning, as an
imitation of precious stones (probably garnets).

The Zugló buckle is a specimen of a common Late Roman and early medieval
type of buckle known as 'B-shaped buckle with incurving centre'. Several cast
bronze specimens, such as particularly fashionable in Late Antiquity, have been
found both inside and outside the Late Roman provinces.[96] Iron specimens with

---

[96] Alice Sz. Burger, 'The Late Roman Cemetery at Ságvár', *Acta Archaeologica Academiae Scientiarum Hungaricae*, 18 (1966), 99–234 (pp. 99 with fig. 100, 127 with fig. 102, and 141 with fig. 103). See also Vera Lányi, 'Die spätantiken Gräberfelder von Pannonien', *Acta Archaeologica Academiae Scientiarum Hungaricae*, 24 (1972), 53–213 with fig. 52.4.11; László Barkóczi, 'Beiträge zur Geschichte der Provinz Valeria im IV–VI. Jh. I. Soldatengürtel, Binnenfestungen und befestigte Siedlungen', *Specimina Nova Universitatis Quinqueecclesiensis*, 1994, 57–135 with figs 13.2 and 17.2; Ágnes Salamon and László Barkóczi, 'Pannonien in nachvalentinianischer Zeit (376–476): Ein Versuch zu Periodisation', in *Severin zwischen Römerzeit und Völkerwanderung: Ausstellung des Landes Oberösterreich, 24. April bis 26. Oktober 1982 im Stadtmuseum Enns*, ed. by Dietmar Straub (Linz, 1982), pp. 147–78 with fig. 3.46 (from Csákvár).

no buckle plate have been found in many fifth-century burial assemblages in Moravia (e.g. Velatice, Vyškov, Novy Šaldorf).[97] According to Irina Zasetskaia, B-shaped buckles were not very common in Eastern Europe during the Hunnic age, but several comparable specimens are known from fifth-century assemblages in the Carpathian Basin, such as Palkonya-Hőerőmű or Csongrád-Kenderföldek.[98]

Setting stones and enamel into a recessed surface was a technique most likely adopted from Late Roman jewellery.[99] Round settings can be seen on the so-called emperor's brooch, the earliest brooch in the second hoard from Şimleu Silvaniei (Romania) on which the round almandine plates were set into the polished onyx.[100] Stones set into embedded cells, either as symbols of animal eyes or as part of a geometric design, sometimes occur on one and the same piece of jewellery.[101] Stone inlay is very rare on Roman buckles,[102] for the practice of embedding cells into the buckle ring or plate first appears with the polychrome style of the fifth century. Round cells may be seen on some of the most lavishly decorated buckles of that period. For example, the ring of the Regöly buckle, the largest and most splendid piece of its time, is covered with concentric settings: the outer ones were filled with light green glass, the inner ones with red garnet plates (Figure 5.12.4).[103]

---

[97] Jaroslav Tejral, *Morava na sklonku antiky* (Prague, 1982), pp. 211 with fig. 89.4, 208 with fig. 83.5, 226 with fig. 105.5, and 224 with figs 100.2 and 103.1.

[98] Zasetskaia, *Kul'tura kochevnikov*, p. 96 with fig. 19v (Zasetskaia's type 38). For the goods associated with the Palkonya-Hőerőmű grave with side shaft, see Csallány, 'Hamvasztásos és csontvázas', pp. 84–85 with plate 9. Traces of grooving may be seen on the larger Palkonya-Hőerőmű buckle, which may have initially had a niello ornamentation. The grave also produced a mirror, for which see now Eszter Istvánovits and Valéria Kulcsár, 'Tükrök a császárkori és a kora népvándorlás kori barbár népeknél a Kárpát-medencében', *A Miskolci Herman Ottó Múzeum Évkönyve*, 30–31 (1993), 9–58 (p. 32 with plate 7.5). For Csongrád-Kenderföldek, see Mihály Párducz, 'Archölogische Beiträge zur Geschichte der Hunnenzeit in Ungarn', *Acta Archaeologica Academiae Scientiarum Hungaricae*, 11 (1959), 309–98 (p. 313 and pl. 8.13).

[99] Alois Riegl, *Spätrömische Kunstindustrie*, 4th edn (Darmstadt, 1987), pp. 344–46.

[100] Attila Kiss and Alfred Bernhard-Walcher, *Szilágysomlyó: A gepida királyok aranykincsei* (Budapest, 1999), pp. 54–55.

[101] Şimleul Silvaniei, brooch pair 50–51 and 58–59 (Kiss and Bernhardt-Walcher, *Szilágysomlyó*, pp. 60–61 and 63).

[102] A notable exception is the cabochon-inlaid buckle from grave 905 of the Samtavro cemetery in Armenia, which may be dated to the later second century. See Vanessa Soupault-Becquelin, 'IMITATIO IMPERII: le cas des mounts-boucles du style polychrome (du IIIᵉ au IVᵉ s. ap. J.-C.)', *Germania*, 77 (1999), 294–306 (pp. 300–01 with fig. 2.2).

[103] Gyula Mészáros, 'A regölyi korai népvándorlás kori fejedelmi sír', *Archaeologiai Értesítő*, 97 (1970), 66–92 (pp. 74–75 with fig. 10).

Similar cells adorn the heart-shaped hilt of the Oros sword.[104] The ring of a small buckle found in 1908 in a Kerch' catacomb has eight round recesses (Figure 5.12.1). The slightly narrower inlays on the ring of a buckle from Beja (Portugal) suggest that such stone inlays were sometimes used to mark animal eyes (Figure 5.12.2).[105]

The ring of the Regöly buckle is decorated with an ornamental pattern consisting of circles connected with a line. During the later decades of the fifth century, this pattern of probably eastern origin erupted in the repertoire of Late Roman decorative sculpture.[106] The later popularity of the motif may be associated to its symbolism most evident on the ring of the Regöly buckle. That the motif may be interpreted as a highly stylized image of a bird is suggested by the pairs of eyes on the tip of the buckle tongue and the buckle plate, respectively.[107] A sixth-century variant of the same stylized image is known from a male burial in the Kirchheim unter Teck cemetery in south-western Germany. The almandine-inlaid bronze buckle found in that assemblage had a similar motif, though without any further details of the animal's anatomy (Figure 5.12.3).[108]

---

[104] Jaroslav Tejral, 'Die spätantiken militärischen Eliten beiderseits der norisch-pannonischen Grenze aus der Sicht der Grabfunde', in *Germanen beiderseits des spätantiken Limes*, ed. by Fischer, Precht, and Tejral, pp. 217–92 (p. 270 with fig. 38.1).

[105] For Oros, see Aleksandr I. Aibabin, 'Khronologiia mogil'nikov Kryma pozdnerimskogo i rannesrednevekovogo vremeni', *Materialy po arkheologiii, istorii i etnografii Tavrii*, 1 (1990), 5–68 with fig. 22.26. For Beja, see Kazanski, 'Les Tombes des chefs militaires', p. 297 with fig. 2.12.

[106] Arne Dehli, *Architektonische und ornamentale Details hervorragender Bauwerke Italiens im byzantinischen Styl* (Berlin, 1890), p. 29 (an example from San Apollinare in Classe). Variants of the 'linked circles' motif can be traced to the Avar period. Throughout the seventh century, the motif appears on cloisonné-decorated artefacts. See Margit Nagy, 'Ornamenta Avarica I. Az avar kori ornamentika geometrikus elemei', *Móra Ferenc Múzeum Évkönyve – Studia Archaeologica*, 4 (1998), 377–459 (pp. 413–14). The pressed variant of the motif of the linked circles first appears on Hun-age artefacts, such as the harness ornaments from Nizhniaia Dobrinka or a mount from burial 3 in Shipovo (Zasetskaia, *Kul'tura kochevnikov*, pls 30.6–7 and 40.11). During the fifth century, the fashion of decorating various artefacts with this particular ornamental pattern spread quickly over a vast area, from Kerch' to northern Africa. See Christoph Eger, 'Vandalische Grabfunde aus Karthago', *Germania*, 79 (2001), 347–90 (pp. 354–59 with fig. 4.1–2 and fig. 6).

[107] According to István Bóna (*Das Hunnenreich*, p. 242), the closest parallel to this stylized representation of a bird of is the bird-shaped mount from a lavishly furnished burial of the Hunnic period found in Conceşti.

[108] Wilfried Menghin, *Das Schwert im frühen Mittelalter: Chronologisch-typologische Untersuchungen zu Langschwertern aus germanischen Gräbern des 5. bis 7. Jh. n. Chr.* (Stuttgart, 1983), p. 233.

The ornate buckles with cloisonné inlay, which often appear in male burials with weapons, were most likely manufactured in Mediterranean workshops. Joachim Werner believed that such buckles were modelled on Hun-age specimens from the Danube region. The round recessed cells were set with cabochon stones. But round and teardrop-shaped cells appear mostly on *plates* of cast buckles made of silver or bronze. They rarely occur on buckle *rings*.[109] An almandine-inlaid, iron buckle with teardrop-shaped settings was found in a warrior burial in Taurapilis (Lithuania). Werner believed that buckle to have been related to a group of buckles most popular in the mid- to late fifth-century Middle Danube region, as well as in Ostrogothic Italy.[110] Another specimen from a female burial of the Szolnok-Zagyvapart cemetery shows that such buckles remain in use after *c.* 500. The stones on the ring of the Szolnok-Zagyvapart specimen were set into recesses lined with gold foil, while those on the iron-framed plate had bronze settings.[111] Gold-lined recesses for holding stones appear not only on buckles, but also on many other artefacts, such as the hilt and cross-bar of a sword found in grave 319b of the fifth- to sixth-century Frankish cemetery at Lavoye (Figure 5.12.5). The Lavoye sword is decorated with a row of stones set into cells whose size matches that of the cells on the Zugló buckle. Judging from the associated grave goods, the Lavoye burial may be dated to the very end of the fifth century.[112]

The ornamental design on the silver buckle from grave 108 of the Basel-Kleinhüningen cemetery may help us understand why the ring of the Zugló buckle had four recessed settings for stones. The ring of the buckle found in the Basel-Kleinhüningen male burial was decorated with two antithetic animal heads, whose eyes were highlighted with garnets. The plate was adorned with five cells inset with

[109] Joachim Werner, 'Zu den donauländischen Beziehungen des alamannischen Gräberfeldes am Alten Gotterbarmweg in Basel', in *Helvetia Antiqua: Festschrift für Emil Vogt*, ed. by Rudolf Degen (Zürich, 1966), pp. 283–92 (pp. 283–87 with figs 1–2).

[110] Joachim Werner, 'Der Grabfund von Taurapilis, Rayon Utna (Litauen) und die Verbindung der Balten zum Reich Theoderichs', in *Archäologische Beiträge zur Chronologie der Völkerwanderungszeit*, ed. by Georg Kossack and Joachim Reichstein (Bonn, 1977), pp. 87–92 (p. 88 with fig. 2). A very similar buckle with a circular inlay on the loop is known from Capraia in Italy. See Michel Kazanski, Anna Mastykova, and Patrick Périn, 'Byzance et les royaumes barbares d'Occident au début de l'époque mérovingienne', in *Probleme der frühen Merowingerzeit*, ed. by Tejral, pp. 159–93 (p. 180 with fig. 2.4).

[111] Cseh and others, *Gepidische Gräberfelder*, p. 19 with pl. 37. 3.

[112] *Die Franken*, ed. by Wieczorek and others, pp. 579 and 885.

garnet plates (Figure 5.12.7).[113] One of the earliest in the entire Basel-Kleinhüningen cemetery, grave 108 has been dated to the mid-400s.[114] Much like in Zugló, there were no weapons in grave 108, although judging by his age and rank, the man buried there may well have been a warrior. Indeed, weapons appear only in later burial assemblages of that same cemetery. Buckle rings similar to that in grave 108, with two opposite animal heads, are rather rare. Such double-headed buckles may have derived from four-headed ones popular in Gaul and Britain during the Late Roman period.[115]

In conclusion, the somewhat unique decoration of the B-shaped buckle from Zugló was an imitation of double-headed buckles, with glass inlays replacing garnet plates for highlighting animal eyes. The recessed settings were made using a technique commonly employed on Hun-period artefacts from the Carpathian Basin, as well as on cloisonné-decorated buckles or scabbards from assemblages found in Germany, France, or Italy.

Six garnet-encrusted gold mounts with perforated corners were found between the thighs of the man buried in Zugló, all arranged in a row down to the knees. The position of those mounts suggests a decorative trimming of the long side of a caftan-like dress hanging from the waist downward and perhaps cross-wise at the knees. Three of the thin, light mounts were found face down, a position which may indicate that the mounts were sewn onto a leather strap held together by the iron

---

[113] Rudolf Moosbrugger-Leu, *Die Schweiz zur Merowingerzeit: Handbuch der Schweiz zur Römer- und Merowingerzeit* (Bern, 1971), pp. 144–45 with plate 30.114; Ulrike Giesler-Müller, *Das frühmittelalterliche Gräberfeld von Basel-Kleinhüningen* (Derendingen, 1992), pp. 99–100 with pl. 21.2; *Die Alamannen: Begleitband zur Ausstellung*, ed. by Karlheinz Fuchs (Stuttgart, 1997), p. 211 with fig. 216.

[114] Moosbrugger-Leu, *Die Schweiz*, pp. 144–45; Giesler-Müller, *Das frühmittelalterliche Gräberfeld*, pp. 99–100. An excellent analogy for the Basel-Kleinhüningen buckle is the buckle with open-work decoration from a barrow excavated in Zdvizhenskoe (Zasetskaia, *Kul'tura kochevnikov*, pl. 11. 18). This strongly suggests that the goods associated with grave 108 in Basel-Kleinhüningen cannot be dated too late after the Hunnic period. This is further substantiated by the brooch found in what appears to have been a male burial. In the early 400s, brooches could still be worn by men, while after *c.* 450 they appear only in female burials. See Rudolf Moosbrugger-Leu, *Die frühmittelalterlichen Gräberfelder von Basel* (Basel, 1982), pp. 22–23.

[115] Sommer, 'Die Gürtel', p. 25 with pl. 5. 1–2; Horst Wolfgang Böhme, 'Das Ende der Römerherrschaft in Britannien und die angelsächsische Besiedlung Englands im 5. Jahrhundert', *Jahrbuch der Römisch-Germanischen Zentralmuseums Mainz*, 33 (1986), 469–574 (pp. 479 and 564 with fig. 9.11). A variant of the Basel buckle, with punched circles instead of stone inlay, is known from Mašov-Čertová in north-eastern Bohemia. See Bedřich Svoboda, *Čechy v době stěhování národů* (Prague, 1965), p. 253 and pl. 32.1.

buckle. They may have therefore decorated shoe straps (Figure 5.13.1).[116] But it is equally possible that the mounts decorated an additional belt, which had been placed into the grave. It has recently been demonstrated that it was customary during the Sarmatian age to place additional belts into male burials.[117]

The Zugló mounts are decorated with garnet cabochons. The ornamentation of the seven mounts resembles the ornamental pattern of Hun-age diadems of Kovrig's class 2, which appear within a vast area between Kazakhstan and southern Poland (Figure 5.11.2).[118] A particularly exquisite specimen is known from a female burial in Csorna, on the north-western fringes of

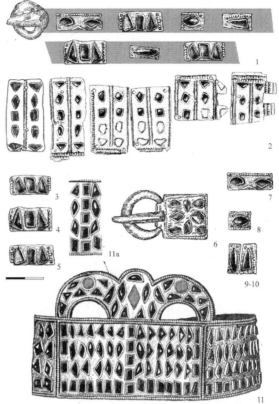

Figure 5.13. Garnet-encrusted artefact of the Hun period: (1, 3–5, and 7–10) Budapest-Zugló; (2) Jędrzychowice; (6) Kistokaj; (11–11a) Kerch' (?). After Werner, *Beiträge*; Bóna, *Das Hunnenreich*; and Ambroz, 'Kochevnicheskie drevnosti'.

the Carpathian Basin. The recycling of gold mounts, which is betrayed by perforations in the corners, was not an unusual practice during the Hunnic period.

---

[116] This interpretation has been offered by Jörg Kleeman during a visit to Aquincum on 12 October 2006.

[117] Gabriella Vörös, 'Övek a szarmata férfiak sírjaiban (A Hódmezővásárhely-kopáncsi sír leleteinek újraértelmezése)', *Móra Ferenc Múzeum Évkönyve – Studia Archaeologica*, 7 (2001), 319–31.

[118] Kovrig, 'Das Diadem von Csorna', pp. 122–26 with fig. 7; Bóna, *Das Hunnenreich*, pp. 147–49. See also Jaroslav Tejral, 'Zur Chronologie der frühen Völkerwanderungszeit im mittleren Donauraum', *Archaeologica Austriaca*, 72 (1988), 223–304 (p. 266).

The buckle and the supposed sword from the assemblage found in Jędrzychowice were both decorated with similar stone-inlaid mounts (Figure 5.13.2).[119] The gold mount encrusted with four rows of garnets, which was found in a male burial in Dulceanca (southern Romania), had originally been part of a diadem.[120]

In light of those observations, the Zugló mounts raise two important issues that need preliminary clarification. Were the mounts initially part of one or several different pieces of jewellery? And, if so, what was the function of the original piece(s)? In order to answer the first question, it is important to start from the fact that the mounts are all framed with bead-rows punched from the reverse side and are all encrusted with carefully polished garnets. The seemingly identical framing of all mounts suggests an originally larger mount from which each individual specimen was cut. However, a careful examination of the garnet shapes reveals that in reality the mounts came from different jewellery pieces, all made in 'diadem style'. Although goldsmiths of the Hunnic period seem to have been preoccupied with creating the optical illusion of randomly placed gemstones,[121] stones are in fact set according to certain patterns and with a definite care for symmetrical arrangements. A closer look to the Zugló mounts with similar inlays may therefore help us decide whether or not they actually came from the same artefact.

Three mounts are decorated with three pairs of garnets. Even though they do not exactly match, placing them next to each other suggests the reconstruction of a 2.1 to 2.3 cm–wide band with one end slightly tapering. The band was set with three rows of polished stones. The middle row with rectangular cells was flanked by two rows set with triangular cells. The long sides of the band were edged with a punched bead row (Figure 5.3.1–3). The three mounts probably came from the same frontlet. Indeed, the narrowest diadem-like frontlets known so far, such as those from Verkhne Iablochnoe and Staraia Igren', are no more than 2 cm wide.[122] The advanced reconstruction may be challenged on the grounds that the position of the cells in the horizontal rows does not conform to the style of diadem ornamentation. Triangular stones on narrow, frontlet-like diadems may point upward or downward, but never sideways. Triangular garnets pointing sideways appear only on scabbard mounts, such as those found in Novohryhor'evka (grave VIII),

[119] Werner, *Beiträge*, pp. 61–62; Bóna, *Das Hunnenreich*, p. 49 with fig. 16, and p. 242.

[120] Vladimir Dumitrescu, 'Ein neuer Beleg für die Anwesenheit der Hunnen in Muntenien: das Bruchstück eines hunnischen Golddiadems von Dulceanca', *Dacia*, 5 (1961), 537–42.

[121] Ambroz, 'Kochevnicheskie drevnosti', p. 12.

[122] Zasetskaia, *Kul'tura kochevnikov*, p. 203 with Annex 4.

Novo-Ivanovka, and Kalinin.[123] If the Zugló mounts are set in a vertical row (Figure 5.13.3–5), the position of the stone inlays matches the central zone of the bird-headed diadem from Kerch' (Figure 5.13.11–11a). It is possible that the diadem from which the Zugló mounts have presumably been cut out was itself assembled from small mounts framed with bead rows, very similar to those found in Verkhne Pogromnoe and Jędrzychowice (Figure 5.13.2).[124] The Csorna, Kerch', Buhăeni, and Jędrzychowice diadems have just one row of rectangular garnets, and so does the diadem from Nikopol.[125] Rectangular garnets arranged in a vertical row can only be found on the Kerch' diadem, whose central mount was divided in two by three vertical rows of rectangular garnets. Together with the lowermost horizontal row of rectangular garnets, they form a U-shaped frame enclosing the triangular garnets studding the surface of the mount. The style of the Zugló mounts and the position of their respective garnets closely resemble the Kerch' diadem.[126]

Each one of the smaller mounts from the Zugló burial has a single garnet. Two of them can be fitted together, a strong indication that they originally belonged to one and the same artefact (Figure 5.13.9–10). Their triangular garnets were polished in the same technique as those on the larger mounts, suggesting that the two matching mounts with single stones belonged to the upper part of a diadem similar to that from Kerch'. While garnets set in an identical position do not appear on the upper part of the Kerch' diadem modelled in the shape of opposing bird heads, the cells of the upper part may well have had a different arrangement in Zugló. It seems more likely that the longer mounts inlaid with larger garnets were cut out from some other artefact. A spectrographic analysis performed on the Zugló gold mounts in order to determine the composition of the gold alloy and the ratio of its silver and copper contents revealed in fact that they fall into two separate groups. Two of them (mounts 4 and 5) had a higher copper content (4.8 to 7.5 per cent), and were therefore made of a different alloy than the others.[127] The alloy composition

---

[123] Zasetskaia, *Kul'tura kochevnikov*, pl. 5.13–14; pl. 14.1, 4; pl. 23.6.

[124] For Verkhne Pogromnoe, see Kovrig, 'Das Diadem von Csorna', p. 123 with fig. 7 (class 2a, no. 6); Zasetskaia, *Kul'tura kochevnikov*, pl. 28.8; Bóna, *Das Hunnenreich*, p. 60 and fig. 20.5. For Jędrzychowice, see Werner, *Beiträge*, pp. 61–62 with pl. 64.1–4, and Kovrig, 'Das Diadem von Csorna', p. 126 with fig. 7 (class 2b, no. 23).

[125] Zasetskaia, *Kul'tura kochevnikov*, p. 180 with pl. 28.9.

[126] Ambroz, 'Kochevnicheskie drevnosti', fig. 7.2. The style of the gold mounts from Zugló was accurately identified and described by Kovrig, 'Das Diadem von Csorna', pp. 119 with fig. 6, and 125–30.

[127] Márta Járó, 'A Budapest-Zugló, Vezér úti sírlelet aranylemezeinek anyagvizsgálata', in *Vándorutak – Múzeumi örökség*, ed. by Viga, Holló, and Schwalm, pp. 327–28 with Table 3.

analysis thus substantiates the idea of two mounts being made of a material and in a style different from the other five. The best analogy for the size of the cells, as well as for the form and polishing technique of the garnets, on the five mounts is the diadem from Buhăeni (Romania).[128] The row of punched beads edging the long sides of the Zugló mounts suggests a diadem assembled from longitudinal parts.

The remaining two mounts have smaller garnets. The stones were removed from the cells of the next row on the original artefact and the cloisons were bent backwards. Two oblique cloisons remained on the smaller mount and one-half of a diamond-shaped cell on the larger one (Figure 5.13.7–8). The two mounts were clearly manufactured in the same style. The garnet inlay suggests that they were cut out from the gold mounts of an artefact smaller than a diadem. Exactly what kind of artefact that may have been is suggested by the similar form and disposition of garnets and cells on the plate of a buckle found in Kistokaj (Figure 5.13.6). Its diamond-shaped garnet flanked by two semi-oval garnets brings to mind the arrangement on the Zugló mounts.[129]

In conclusion, the mounts themselves offer little in the way of determining the nature of the artefact from which they had been cut. It appears that they had originally belonged to at least three objects made in different styles. It is unlikely that they had all been parts of diadems, even though three of them probably were, while others perhaps came from gold mounts covering a scabbard, a buckle, or a fibula. No indication exists that any one of them had been folded over a bronze article, a practice well documented for the Hunnic period. The disposition of the garnets brings to mind diadems of Kovrig's class 2b. The artefacts from which these mounts were cut out may be dated between *c.* 430 and *c.* 450. Diadems, as well as other gem-encrusted jewels of the Hunnic period, were crafted individually.[130] As a consequence, it is not always possible to reconstruct the original piece of jewellery from the few surviving fragments.

Conclusion

Shortly after the middle of the fifth century, a young Euro-Mongolid man was laid to rest in Zugló without his weapons in a grave pit with a north-east to south-west

---

[128] *Goldhelm, Schwert und Silberschätze: Reichtümer aus 6000 Jahren rumänischer Vergangenheit*, ed. by Alexandru Avram, Mircea Babeş, and Mihai Bărbulescu (Frankfurt a.M., 1994), p. 226.

[129] Bóna, *Das Hunnenreich*, fig. 40.2.

[130] Zasetskaia, *Kul'tura kochevnikov*, pp. 56–57.

orientation. He was accompanied in death by his horse, whose remains were symbolically placed in the grave according to a custom of East European origin. The folded bit and the head-stall were placed near the horse's head together with a bronze bell and an iron one. The man's belt was held together with an iron buckle, a somewhat unique artefact with gold recesses. His other belt or a leather strap (possibly part of his footwear) was adorned with garnet-inlaid gold mounts, which were cut out from diadems and other pieces of jewellery. Analogies for several grave goods discussed in this paper point to a date within the middle third of the fifth century. Since some, at least, of the accoutrements indicate a recycling of mid-fifth-century artefacts, the young man must have been buried during or shortly after the collapse of Hunnic rule in the Carpathian Basin.

The Zugló burial is so far the only known assemblage from Budapest which can be directly linked to the conquerors of the Hunnic period. In his overview of that period and discussion of the burial, Tibor Nagy suggested that the Danube Bend region of present-day Budapest had been occupied by a group known to Jordanes as Sadages (Sadagarii).[131] Even though far-reaching conclusions about the area's settlement history should not be drawn on the basis of a single burial alone, the Zugló burial is still a key burial assemblage of the Hunnic period, which offers new insights into the burial customs and beliefs of the mid-fifth-century Middle Danube region.

---

[131] Jordanes, *Getica*, 50 and 52, ed. by Theodor Mommsen, MGH AA, 5.1 (Berlin, 1882). See Nagy, Györffy, and Gerevich, *Budapest története*, p. 190. A Hun-age burial with the skull and leg bones of a horse skeleton wrapped in the animal's hide was recently found in Üllő, some 25–30 km south from Zugló. See 'Üllő 5.-Üllő 9. lelőhely', in *Régészeti kutatások másfél millió négyzetméteren: Autópálya és gyorsforgalmi utak építését megelőző feltárások Pest megyében 2001–2006*, ed. by László Simon and Edit Tari (Szentendre, 2006), pp. 42–43 and 46.

A FIFTH-CENTURY BURIAL
FROM OLD BUDA (BUDAPEST)

Ágnes B. Tóth

In 1980, a team of archaeologists from the Budapest Historical Museum conducted a salvage excavation by the western bridgehead of the Árpád Bridge in anticipation of its restoration. The burial described and discussed in this study came to light a few metres south of the bridgehead in the third district of Budapest (known as Old Buda), at the corner of Névtelen and Serfőző streets.[1]

The burial was discovered during the excavation of the Late Roman fort (Figure 6.1). Various buildings had been erected in the south-eastern part of the second-to third-century *canabae* of the Roman military fort prior to the construction of the Late Roman fort. To the east of the grave was the 'Porticoed Building', most likely a second- to third-century port warehouse. The apsidal wall remains west of the building had most likely been part of a bath. Both buildings were restored and perhaps joined under the same roof during the fourth-century occupation of the Late Roman fort. Even though several plan details of the buildings inside the fort, as well as their exact position relative to each other, remain unclear, judging by its size, the 'Porticoed Building' was undoubtedly one of the main buildings within the fort's

This study is an expanded version of the paper presented at the 2005 Kajdacs conference in memory of István Bóna. Drawings were made by Erzsébet Csernus, photographs by Csilla Tóth. The buckle was restored by Judit Dombóvári, who I also wish to thank for the photograph. I am also indebted to Margit Nagy for her generous help in preparing the illustrations and for her helpful comments on a draft version of this study. The manuscript was completed in November 2005.

[1] For the burial and the Roman buildings around it, see Ágnes B. Tóth, '55/2. Budapest III: Árpád fejedelem útja, Kulcsár u., Serfőző u., Lajos u., Korvin O. tér által határolt terület. 92. Budapest, III. Névtelen u.–Serfőző u.', *Régészeti Füzetek*, 34 (1981), 27–28 and 52.

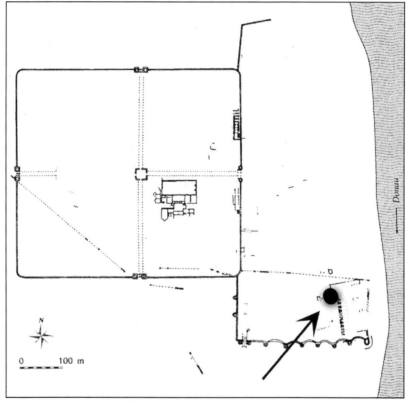

Figure 6.1. Budapest III (Old Buda), at the corner of Névtelen and Serfőző Streets.
The position of the grave within the Late Roman fort at Aquincum.

ramparts.[2] The burial was therefore within the ruins of a major Late Roman building compound, which had already been abandoned by the fifth century.

The grave pit was dug into the destruction layers of Late Roman date. The grave diggers stumbled upon a partially dismantled wall at the western end of the pit and decided not to dig any deeper. As a consequence, the head of the deceased was laid onto a stone taken from the neighbouring wall. The stone was moved by excavation workers during the clearing of the wall. The operation resulted in the right arm and legs of the skeleton being dislodged from their initial position (Figure 6.2).

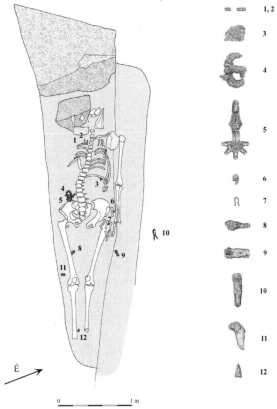

Figure 6.2. Budapest III (Old Buda), grave and grave goods.

The poorly preserved skeleton lay in a stretched position on the back. From the neck vertebrae to the end of the shin bone, it was about 140 cm long. The skeleton has a west–east orientation, with a slight deviation to the north (285–105°). Although the body itself was not disturbed, traces of a large, modern intrusion were noted in the northern trench wall. This may explain why neither the discolored patch of the grave nor the grave pit itself could be observed on the west–east section of the trench wall, which practically cut the grave lengthwise. The fifth-century occupation layer was also destroyed by modern building activity. As a

<hr />

[2] For a survey of the excavations within the Late Roman fort, see Klára Póczy, 'Aquincum: castra, canabae, colonia (Az 1976–1980. közötti időszak ásatási eredményeinek összefoglalása)', *Budapest Régiségei*, 25 (1984), 15–34; Margit Németh, 'Aquincum: Feltárások az 1981–1988 közötti időszakban. Aquincum', *Budapest Régiségei*, 28 (1991), 91–105.

consequence, the depth of the grave pit (3.7 m) could be measured only from the present-day ground level.

The Grave Goods in their Cultural Context

Between the upper ilium on the right and the vertebrae, there was a cast silver brooch with semicircular head-plate and a pentagonal foot-plate (Figures 6.2.5 and 6.3.3; Plate I.1.2a–b).[3] The five flat knobs were cast together with the brooch, as was also the foot-plate terminal in the shape of an animal head. The head-plate has a raised border frame and a finely engraved decoration. The main ornament is kidney-shaped, filled with an engraved scrollwork pattern. The bow is flat and has a median rib extending to the head-plate and the foot-plate. It is framed by ribbing, with slightly raised sections between the ribs. The foot-plate is wider by the bow with the lower part to terminal being slightly bent inward. The ornament of the foot-plate consists of a framework of opposing, punched triangles placed in pairs: ten pairs in the upper part of the foot-plate (between the bow and the line of maximum width) and twenty pairs in the lower part. The foot-plate ornament is perfectly symmetrical, with two pairs of acanthus scrolls springing from the centre and curling into a fourfold whirligig in the widest section, joined by two other scrolls towards the end of the foot-plate. The area between the scrollwork and the terminal in the shape of an animal head is filled with three longitudinal ribs, and a flat, horizontal rib separates the ornamental panel on the foot-plate from the terminal. The latter is shaped like a large, flat animal head with two sunken eyes and two oblique grooves starting from the nose. The fibula was gilded, with traces of gilding still within the recessed part of the decoration. Clear traces of wear and scratches are visible on the bow and the knobs. The spring was held in place by a single hook on the backside of the head-plate. The hook and the catchpin were cast together with the brooch. The iron spring and the corroded remains of the pin disintegrated during conservation. The catchpin had broken while the brooch was still in use, and the breakage surface was worn smooth.

Immediately beside the brooch was a B-shaped, iron buckle, badly preserved (Figures 6.2.4, 6.4.3a–b, 6.5.3a–b; Plate I.2).[4] The ring has an oval, the tongue a

---

[3] The fibula is 8.2 cm long and weighs 31.75 g.

[4] The buckle is 4.8 cm long. Only the front double curve of the ring and the tongue resting on it have been preserved. Missing was the back, straight section of the ring, as well as the attachment of the tongue.

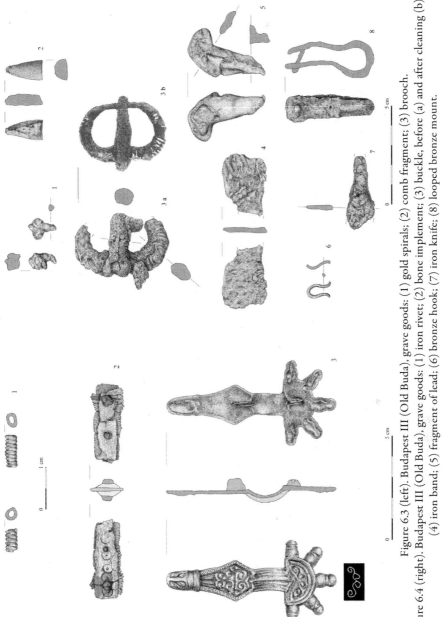

Figure 6.3 (left). Budapest III (Old Buda), grave goods: (1) gold spirals; (2) comb fragment; (3) brooch.

Figure 6.4 (right). Budapest III (Old Buda), grave goods: (1) iron rivet; (2) bone implement; (3) buckle, before (a) and after cleaning (b); (4) iron band; (5) fragment of lead; (6) bronze hook; (7) iron knife; (8) looped bronze mount.

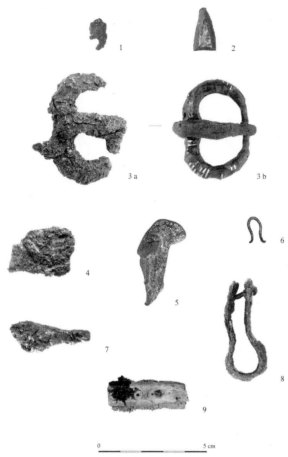

slightly rectangular section. After corrosion was removed, an ornamental pattern became apparent on the ring: pieces of copper wire have been hammered into furrows set perpendicularly to the curve of the ring, with only the section covered by the tongue left undecorated. The copper inlay survived only partially.

On the right side of the first neck vertebrae were two spirals of gold wire, one with nine, the other with six twists (Figures 6.2.1–2 and 6.3.1; Plate I.1.1).[5] No traces of fresh breakage were observed on the terminals, which had been hammered flat.

Between the left ilium and the left arm was a corroded iron rivet with broken head (Figures 6.2.6, 6.4.1, and 6.5.1). At about 10 cm from the finger bones of the left hand was a fragment of a double-sided comb (Figures 6.2.9, 6.3.2, and 6.5.9).[6] The 'sides' consist of two antler plates and of tooth segments, all held together by means of two rivets, one of bronze, the other of iron. The latter may well be the result of a later attempt to repair the comb. One

Figure 6.5. Budapest III (Old Buda), grave goods: (1) iron rivet; (2) bone implement; (3) buckle, before (a) and after cleaning (b); (4) iron band; (5) fragment of lead; (6) bronze hook; (7) iron knife; (8) looped bronze mount; (9) comb fragment.

[5] The gold wire is circular in section. The two spirals are 0.8 and 0.5 cm long, respectively, each with a diameter of 0.3 cm.

[6] The fragment is 3.65 cm long.

antler plate is covered with a circle-and-dot ornamental pattern, the other is strongly worn and damaged. Among the left hand bones was also a bronze hook with out-curving, tapered ends (Figures 6.2.7 and 6.5.6).[7] The fragment of a small knife was found under the inner side of the right thighbone (Figures 6.2.8, 6.4.7, and 6.5.7).[8] Another fragment of an iron object lay among the left ribs (Figures 6.2.3, 6.4.4, and 6.5.4).[9] Judging from the fact that a small section of the edge survived intact on one of its long sides, this may have been an iron band. Imprints of some organic substance were noted on one side. To the right of the right kneecap, there was a burnt, amorphous piece of flat lead with a vertical rib protruding from its surface (Figures 6.2.11, 6.4.5, and 6.5.5). A flat, triangular bone implement was found by the inner side of right shin bone (Figures 6.2.12, 6.4.2, and 6.5.2). Its pointed end was broken, while the two curved sides were polished.

A looped bronze mount was found in the loose soil from an animal burrow starting from the grave pit's ground (Figures 6.2.10, 6.4.8, and 6.5.8).[10] The mount consists of two trapeze-shaped plates joined by means of a rounded loop, which is slightly thicker and squatter but narrower than the plates. The plates were held together by means of two rivets, only one of which has been preserved: a round-headed rivet with traces of hammering.

The most chronologically sensitive artefact is the brooch, which is a specimen of a class most typical for the late fifth century ('pre-Lombard' period) in Hungary and the neighbouring regions.[11] The earliest known specimens of this class are the three-knobbed brooches from Szekszárd and Sokolnice. Both have two symmetrical S-scrolls on the head-plate and, on the foot-plate, an ornamental pattern with two pairs of opposing scrolls with outward-curving stem forming a four-armed whirligig

[7] The hook is 1.8 cm long.

[8] The fragment is 3.6 cm long.

[9] The fragment is 3.1 cm long.

[10] The mount is 4.6 cm long.

[11] The class is discussed in Jaroslav Tejral, 'Neue Aspekte der frühvölkerwanderugszeitlichen Chronologie im Mitteldonauraum', in *Neue Beiträge zur Erforschung der Spätantike im mittleren Donauraum: Materialen der internationalen Konferenz 'Neue Beiträge zur Erforschung der Spätantike im mittleren Donauraum', Kravsko, 17.–20. Mai 1995*, ed. by Jaroslav Tejral, Herwig Friesinger, and Michel Kazanski (Brno, 1997), pp. 321–62 (p. 350). Jaroslav Tejral, 'Beiträge zur Chronologie des langobardischen Fundstoffes nördlich der mittleren Donau', in *Probleme der frühen Merowingerzeit im Mitteldonauraum*, ed. by Jaroslav Tejral (Brno, 2002), pp. 313–58 (pp. 321–23) incorporates the conclusions drawn by Joachim Werner, Volker Bierbrauer, and Max Menke. For the Old Buda brooch, see also Margit Nagy, 'Bp. III. Óbuda, Névtelen Street', *Budapesti Történeti Múzeum*, 1995, 1–358 (pp. 124 and 153).

(*Vierpass*).[12] It has already been noted that this ornamental pattern recalls that displayed on a few belt buckles with chip-carved decoration, almost all of which have been found in the Middle Danube region.[13] At a close examination, there appears to be a slight difference between the ornamental patterns on the foot-plates of the Szekszárd and Old Buda brooches, in that on the latter the scroll stems are bent inwards. A similar detail may be observed on a brooch found in grave 9 at Rifnik (Slovenia; Figure 6.6.3), although the overall decoration of that fibula's head- and foot-plate is radically different from that of the Old Buda specimen.[14]

The four-spiral scrollwork pattern on the head-plate of the Old Buda brooch does not appear on either the Szekszárd or the Sokolnice brooches, but was quite often used for the decoration of slightly later brooches from the Middle Danube region.[15] According to Jaroslav Tejral, such brooches have a lot more in common with 'Gepid' and 'Ostrogothic' fibulae and, as a consequence, cannot be dated

---

[12] For the brooch from grave 217 in Szekszárd-Palánk, see Attila Kiss, 'Das Gräberfeld von Szekszárd-Palánk aus der zweiten Hälfte des 5. Jh. und der ostgotischen Fundstoff Pannonien', *Zalai Múzeum*, 6 (1996), 53–86, with fig. 11.9 and 11–12. For the brooch from grave 5 in Sokolnice, see Tejral, 'Beiträge', p. 321, who viewed the entire class as a hallmark of a typically Middle Danube fashion of the early Middle Ages. For a discussion of the ornamental patterns of the head- and foot-plate, respectively, see Margit Nagy, 'Ornamenta Avarica I. Az avar kori ornamentika geometrikus elemei', *Móra Ferenc Múzeum Évkönyve: Studia Archaeologica*, 4 (1998), 377–459 (pp. 378–79 with figs 1–3); Kiss, 'Das Gräberfeld von Szekszárd-Palánk', p. 59.

[13] The best known are the buckles from Tiszalök and Košice. See Ilona Kovrig, 'A tiszalöki és a mádi lelet', *Archaeologiai Értesítő*, 78 (1951), 113–20 with pl. 43.3; Jaroslav Tejral, *Morava na sklonku antiky* (Prague, 1982), p. 44 with fig. 30. A pressed variant of the scrollwork pattern is attested on large silver sheet brooches, such as those from Barabás and Kiskunfélegyháza. Volker Bierbrauer, 'Das Frauengrab von Castelbolognese in der Romagna (Italien): Zur chronologischen, ethnischen und historischen Auswertbarkeit des ostgermanischen Fundstoffs des 5. Jahrhunderts in Südosteuropa und Italien', *Jahrbuch des Römisch-Germanischen Zentralmuseums*, 38 (1991), 541–92 (pp. 545 and 572–81), dated both brooches between 440 and 450. He placed the Gyulavári brooch at an even earlier stage, during the second quarter of the fifth century. The ornamental pattern on the foot-plates of the Szekszárd and Sokolnice brooches appears on the plate of a buckle from Noşlac. See Radu Harhoiu, *Die frühe Völkerwanderungszeit in Rumänien* (Bucharest, 1997), pl. 91.B.

[14] For the Rifnik brooch, see Volker Bierbrauer, *Die ostgotische Grab- und Schatzfunde in Italien* (Spoleto, 1975), pl. 66.4. To be sure, the longitudinal grooves between the terminal in the form of an animal head and the scrollwork decoration of the foot-plate is also reminiscent of the Old Buda brooch.

[15] E.g., the Černín and Ladendorf brooches, for which see Tejral, 'Beiträge', pp. 325–26 with fig. 8.1–4.

Figure 6.6. The Old Buda burial in its cultural context: (1) Budapest III (Old Buda); (2) Monceau-le-Neuf-et-Faucouzy (after Werner, *Katalog*, pl. 5.15a–b); (3) Rifnik, grave 9 (after Bierbrauer, *Die ostgotische Grab- und Schatzfunde*, pl. 66.4); (4) Oradea (after Bóna, 'Daciától Erdőelvéig', pl. 29.9); (5) Szentes-Kökényzug, grave 29 (after Csallány, *Archäologische Denkmäler*, pl. 14.6); (6) Weingarten, grave 241 (after Roth and Theune, *Das frühmittelalterliche Gräberfeld bei Weingarten*, pl. 76.B.1); (7) Kistelek (after Nagy, 'Gepida viselet', fig. 26); (8) Dabronc-Ötvöspuszta (after Sági, 'Az ötvöspusztai V. századi sír', fig. 1.1–2); (9) Ladendorf (after Windl, 'Ein frühmerowingerzeitliches Frauengrab', pl. 1.1–2).

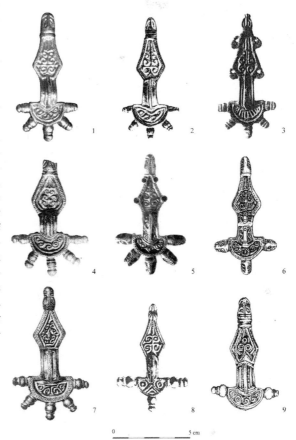

earlier than the last few decades of the fifth century.[16] But brooch head-plates with elaborate scrollwork decoration dated to the late fifth century are known not only from the Middle Danube region, but also from sites farther to the west. This is certainly the case of the specimens from Ladendorf in Lower Austria (Figure 6.6.9) and Weingarten on the Upper Danube (Figure 6.6.6).[17] Another analogy is offered

[16] In my opinion, the continuous scrollwork pattern on head-plates of smaller and humbler brooches derives from the larger, much more deeply engraved and carefully crafted scrollwork of luxurious fibulae such as Domolospuszta and Répcelak.

[17] Helmut Windl, 'Ein frühmerowingerzeitliches Frauengrab aus Ladendorf, VB Mistelbach, NÖ', in *Neue Beiträge zur Erforschung der Spätantike im mittleren Donauraum*, ed. by Tejral, Friesinger, and Kazanski, pp. 67–73, with pl. 1.1–2; Helmut Roth and Claudia Theune, *Das frühmittelalterliche Gräberfeld bei Weingarten (Kr. Ravensburg)* (Stuttgart, 1995), pl. 76.B.1. According

by a fibula found in grave 5 of the Hács-Béndekpuszta cemetery, a site within the borders of the former province of Pannonia. Although the design on the head-plate is made up of three scrolls only, the five knobs cast together with the head-plate and the wide, flat, undecorated bow match the corresponding features on the Old Buda brooch.[18] Brooch head-plates similarly decorated appear on late fifth-century sites in the eastern parts of the Carpathian Basin. The head-plate of the fibula from grave 29 of the Szentes-Kökényzug cemetery (Figure 6.6.5) has a pattern of five scrolls and is a somewhat more carefully crafted piece than a fibula from Oradea (Figure 6.6.4).[19]

An interesting aspect of the Old Buda fibula is that the diamond-shaped foot-plate is wider in its upper (towards the bow) than its lower part. The much longer lower part is also slightly bent inward. Such morphological details are typical for brooches found on late fifth- and early sixth-century sites in the eastern parts of the Carpathian Basin that have been associated with the Gepids. Such brooches lack the round stone inlays along the edge of the foot-plate.[20] The inspiration for this kind of foot-plate may have come from three-knobbed brooches such as found in

to Manfred Menke, 'Archäologische Befunde zu Ostgoten des 5. Jahrhundert in der Zone nord-wärts der Alpen', *Peregrinatio Gothica: Archaeologia Baltica*, 7 (1986), 239–81 (p. 256), the brooch from grave 241 in Weingarten is a 'Gepid' fibula produced somewhere in the eastern region of the Carpathian Basin.

[18] Attila Kiss, 'Das germanische Gräberfeld von Hács-Béndekpuszta (Westungarn) aus dem 5.–6. Jahrhundert', *Acta Archaeologica Academiae Scientiarum Hungaricae*, 36 (1985), 275–342 (p. 322) lists the Old Buda brooch among analogies for the Hács-Béndekpuszta fibula. According to Kiss, grave 5 in Hács-Béndekpuszta must be dated between 450 and 520 and may have been the burial of an Ostrogothic woman.

[19] Dezső Csallány, *Archäologische Denkmäler der Gepiden im Mitteldonaubecken (454–568 u. Z.)* (Budapest, 1961), pp. 27–28 and 110; pls 14.6 and 212.6. For the Oradea fibula, see also István Bóna, 'Daciától Erdőelvéig: A népvándorlás kora Erdélyben (271–896)', in *Erdély története*, ed. by Béla Köpeczi, I (Budapest, 1986), pp. 107–234 (p. 153 with pl. 29.9). Several other larger and more elaborate brooches with scrollwork and cloisonné decoration are known from Transylvania. See Harhoiu, *Die frühe Völkerwanderungszeit*, p. 182 and pl. 101c–f. Such brooches are only remotely related to the Old Buda fibula.

[20] They also have flat bows and scrollwork decorative patterns. Each one of the fibulae found in Kistelek (?) and grave 94 of the Hódmezővásárhely-Gorzsa cemetery was cast together with its five knobs. See Csallány, *Archäologische Denkmäler*, pp. 227 and 130; pls 195.9 and 228.8. By contrast, the unique piece said to be from Magyartés, but in fact found in Törökszentmiklós, had three knobs cast with the head-plate and four other knobs mounted one-by-one. See Csallány, *Archäologische Denkmäler*, p. 41 and pl. 109.3. An excellent parallel for the 'Magyartés' fibula is that from grave 5 of the cemetery found in Vienna on the Salvatorengasse. See Max Martin, '*Mixti Alamannis Suevi*? Der Beitrag der alamannischer Gräberfelder am Basler Rheinknie', in *Probleme der frühen Merowingerzeit im Mitteldonauraum*, ed. by Tejral, pp. 195–223 with fig. 14.1.

Transdanubia at Dabronc-Ötvöspuszta, which cannot be dated later than the middle third of the fifth century (Figure 6.6.8).[21] Furthermore, very good analogies to the foot-plate of the Old Buda brooch may be found on several sites farther to the west, such as Ladendorf or Weingarten.[22] The westernmost analogy is that from Monceau-le-Neuf (Figure 6.6.2).[23] Judging from the published photograph and drawing, this fibula is very similar to the Old Buda brooch, except that, on one hand, its knobs and animal-head terminal are smaller and less detailed, while, on the other hand, the scrollwork decoration on both head- and foot-plate is rather blurred. Unlike the Old Buda fibula, the punched triangle ornament of the Monceau-le-Neuf brooch also covers the bow.

Some of the above-mentioned analogies for the Old Buda brooch have a differing spring mechanism with two or three small hooks on the back of the head-plate. Brooches from Kistelek, Sikenica, Hemmingen (graves 14 and 24), and Ficarolo were equipped with two spring hooks, while those from Szentes-Kökényzug (grave 29) and Jobbágyi (grave 2) had three hooks.[24] On other specimens, such as another fibula from Jobbágyi, there are holes in the band framing the head-plate, most

---

[21] Károly Sági, 'Az ötvöspusztai V. századi sír', *A Veszprém Megyei Múzeumok Közleményei*, 17 (1985), 81–90 with fig. 1.1–2.

[22] Windl, 'Ein frühmerowingerzeitliches Frauengrab', pl. 1.1–2; Roth and Theune, *Das frühmittelalterliche Gräberfeld bei Weingarten*, pl. 76.1.

[23] Claude Boulanger, *Le Mobilier funéraire gallo-romain et franc en Picardie et en Artois* (Paris, 1902–05), pl. 22. 6. Herbert Kühn, *Die germanischen Bügelfibeln der Völkerwanderungszeit in Süddeutschland* (Graz, 1974), p. 763 with pl. 265.67,22, assigned this brooch to his Krainburg (Kranj) class, which he dated between 500 and 550. The brooch was also discussed briefly by Joachim Werner, *Katalog der Sammlung Diergardt. (Völkerwanderungszeitlicher Schmuck) 1. Die Fibeln* (Berlin, 1961), p. 15 and pl. 5.15a–b, who regarded it as an Ostrogothic import from Italy. Most recently, Alexander Koch, *Bügelfibeln der Merowingerzeit im westlichen Frankreich* (Mainz, 1998), pp. 241–42 and pl. 36.4, assigned it to his rather heterogeneous class III.3.6.4, in which the only feature shared by all class members is the absence of round settings along the edge of the foot-plate. Without any good analogies at hand, Koch thought that the Monceau-le-Neuf fibula had been produced in the Danube region and dated it shortly before or after 500 (early AM I).

[24] Hemmingen: Hermann F. Müller, *Das alamannische Gräberfeld von Hemmingen (Kreis Ludwigsburg)* (Stuttgart, 1976), pp. 30–31. Ficarolo: Herrmann Büsing, 'Die Dame von Ficarolo in ihrem historischen Kontext', *Kölner Jahrbuch*, 31 (1998), 253–76 (p. 262). Jobbágyi: Attila Kiss, 'Germanischer Grabfund der Völkerwanderungszeit in Jobbágyi (Zur Siedlungsgeschichte des Karpatenbeckens in den Jahren 454–568)', *Alba Regia*, 19 (1981), 167–85 (p. 167); Sikenica: Bohuslav Novotný, 'Ein völkerwanderungszeitliches Grab aus Sikenica-Velký Pesek, Bezirk Levice, Slowakei', *Mitteilungen der anthropologischen Gesellschaft in Wien*, 118–19 (1988–89), 305–12 with fig. 3.

obviously for the spring axis bar, a feature that Attila Kiss believed to be 'archaic'.[25] It can hardly be an accident that the construction of the Old Buda brooch spring mechanism resembles that of brooches from Monceau-le-Neuf, Weingarten (grave 41), and Eichstetten (grave 44).[26]

The Old Buda brooch is a worn piece, with traces of wear most conspicuous on the knob ends and the median rib on the bow. The bent-back part of the catchplate thinned from the heavy wear and eventually broke off. Before being deposited in the grave pit, therefore, the brooch had for some time ceased to serve as fastener. Other, similarly worn pieces were often repaired: a new catchplate was made for one of the brooches from grave 217 of the Weingarten cemetery, and the same is true for the brooch found in grave 3 at Mezőkeresztes-Cethalom. One of the brooches from Ladendorf was broken, but could still be worn as originally intended.[27]

The analogies cited above strongly suggest that the Old Buda brooch was manufactured in the Middle Danube region, perhaps in Pannonia. Tejral has recently argued for the existence of a workshop in the vicinity of the present-day Czech-Austrian border in southern Moravia or Lower Austria, which produced a wide range of brooches. The workshop may have operated during the last third of the fifth and the first decades of the sixth century.[28] That chronological span matches the date advanced for the Old Buda brooch, even though no evidence exists that it was produced in the workshop postulated by Tejral. Moreover, no indication exists of such a workshop in any other region of Pannonia.

Hermann F. Müller has long advanced another idea concerning the production of 'Pannonian-Ostrogothic' brooches such as found in Hemmingen. According to him, the astonishing variety of bow brooches found within a single region, as well as the remarkable similarities between brooches found at great distances from each other, called for a different explanation. The distribution of similar brooches

[25] This feature also appears on the brooches from Dabronc and Ladendorf.

[26] For Eichstetten, see Barbara Sasse, *Ein frühmittelalterliches Reihengräberfeld bei Eichstetten am Kaiserstuhl* (Stuttgart, 2001), p. 169. In many cases, not much is known about construction of the spring mechanism, because brooches were often published without any description of the backside. This is all the more regrettable since small technological details of this kind can contribute to the identification of possible workshops, if not even goldsmiths.

[27] Roth and Theune, *Das frühmittelalterliche Gräberfeld bei Weingarten*, p. 69 and pl. 76.B1a; Erika Simonyi, 'Gepida temető Mezőkeresztes-Cethalmon', in *A népvándorláskor fiatal kutatói 8. találkozójának előadásai (Veszprém, 1997. november 28–30)*, ed. by Ágota S. Perémi (Veszprém, 1999), pp. 74–75 and fig. 9; Windl, 'Ein frühmerowingerzeitliches Frauengrab', pl. 1.2.

[28] Tejral, 'Beiträge', p. 326.

suggests instead that such dress accessories were not mass-produced in workshops, but were more likely manufactured by itinerant craftsmen, who could easily carry their tools and molds and only needed raw material for casting various jewellery items. They plied their trade on the settlements of their potential customers, in the manors of the nobles. They blended decorative patterns and ornamental motifs according to their customers' taste. The region in which a particular craftsman was active did not necessarily coincide with any 'tribal' territory.[29] In a recent study on Slavic bow fibulae, Florin Curta examined the problem and concluded that 'linked specimens (fibulae) spread rapidly over wide distances, a phenomenon which could be explained by means of itinerant specialists or transmission of models. The dissemination of the ornamental patterns [...] is likely to indicate long-distance contacts between communities and to signal the rise of individuals having the ability both to entertain such contacts and to employ craft-persons experienced enough to replicate ornamental patterns and brooch forms [...] the absence of exact replications is a strong indication that each brooch or pair of brooches was produced as required, probably for only one occasion at a time'.[30] We will most likely never know where exactly the Old Buda fibula was made. It seems unlikely that it was in Aquincum, where no evidence exists so far of any large or particularly wealthy community in the late 400s, which could have called for the presence of an itinerant craftsman.

The fibula was found next to an iron buckle above the right ilium with its footplate pointing to the spine. Given the circumstances in which the burial was found, it is not impossible that there was another fibula, which may have then been accidentally thrown out together with the soil disturbed by modern intrusion. An overview of the similar finds certainly makes this a likely possibility.

There is little in the way of a detailed, comprehensive study on how brooches were worn in the Middle Danube region during the fifth and sixth centuries. Most late fifth-century female burials in northern and central Transdanubia produced pairs of brooches.[31] One of the few burials found undisturbed, which produced a

[29] Müller, *Das alamannische Gräberfeld von Hemmingen*, p. 102. The idea of 'itinerant craftsmen' goes back to Joachim Werner's interpretation of a passage in the *Vita S. Severini*. See Werner, *Katalog*, pp. 7–8. However, Werner's explanation is counterintuitive, since it must have been much easier for the itinerant craftsmen to produce similar fibulae on neighbouring sites than on sites located at a distance from each other.

[30] Florin Curta, 'Slavic Bow Fibulae? Werner's Class I D Revisited', *Acta Archaeologica Academiae Scientiarum Hungaricae*, 57 (2006), 423–74 (p. 460).

[31] E.g. graves 3, 18, 19, and 20 in Hács-Béndekpuszta; grave 210 and 217 in Szekszárd-Palánk; grave 150 in Balatonszemes-Szemesi berek; Miszla; grave 10 in Keszthely-Fenékpuszta; grave 1 in

single fibula, is grave 154 of the Tác-Fövenypuszta cemetery. The grave pit had been dug inside the ruins of a Late Roman building compound, and in that respect, as well as in terms of grave goods, the Tác-Fövenypuszta burial compares well with the Old Buda finds.[32]

Several studies have recently been devoted to how brooches were worn in different parts of early medieval Europe. The role of brooches in female dress among Goths and related peoples has received much attention,[33] as did the Merovingian brooch dress, especially in Max Martin's work. According to Martin, the women of the different Germanic peoples earlier wore a *peplos*-like garment which was fastened with two brooches at the shoulders. Aristocratic women in Merovingian Francia were among the first to abandon this particular dress in favour of a sleeved tunic stitched at the shoulders, for which there was therefore no need of brooches.[34] It may have been a fashion originating in the empire. Of all peoples of the early Migration period, the Goths appear to have been the most conservative in relation to the *peplos*-like garment, for pairs of brooches worn at the shoulders

Soponya; Intercisa-Öreghegy; and Dabronc-Ötvöspuszta. See Kiss, 'Das germanische Gräberfeld von Hács-Béndekpuszta', pp. 282–84; Kiss, 'Das Gräberfeld von Szekszárd-Palánk', pp. 54–56; Mária Bondár, Szilvia Honti, and Viktória Kiss, 'A tervezett M7 autópálya Somogy megyei szakaszának megelőző régészeti feltárása (1992–1999): Előzetes jelentés I', *Somogyi Múzeumok Közleményei*, 14 (2000), 3–24 (p. 7); Péter Straub, 'Die Hinterlassenschaft der Ostgoten in Fenékpuszta', 'Die archäologische Hinterlassenschaft der praelangobardischen Periode in Transdanubien', and 'Die Gräberfelder vor der Südmauer der Befestigung von Fenékpuszta', in *Germanen am Plattensee: Ausstellung des Balatoni Museums Keszthely im Museum für Frühgeschichte des Landes Niederösterreichs, Schloss Traismauer, vom 6. April bis 1. November 2002*, ed. by Róbert Müller (Traismauer, 2002), pp. 9–12 (pp. 9–10), 13–16, and 26–28; István Bóna, 'A népvándorlás kora Fejér megyében', in *Fejér megye története az őskortól a honfoglalásig 5*, ed. by J. Fitz (Székesfehérvár, 1971), pp. 221(5)–314(94) (p. 230); Sági, 'Az ötvöspusztai V. századi sír', pp. 82–84.

[32] Jenő Fitz, Vera Lányi, and Zsuzsa Bánki, 'Kutatások Gorsiumban 1973-ban', *Alba Regia*, 14 (1975), 289–333 (p. 292).

[33] Magdalena Tempelmann-Mączyńska, *Das Frauentrachtzubehör des mittel- und osteuropäischen Barbaricums in der römischen Kaiserzeit* (Cracow, 1989); Volker Bierbrauer, 'Archäologie und Geschichte der Goten vom 1.–7. Jahrhundert', *Frühmittelalterliche Studien*, 28 (1994), 51–171.

[34] For a detailed discussion, see Max Martin, 'Tradition und Wandel der fiebelgeschmückten frühmittelalterlichen Frauenkleidung', *Jahrbuch der Römisch-Germanischen Zentralmuseums*, 38 (1991), 629–80; Max Martin, 'Fibel und Fibeltracht', in *Reallexikon der germanischen Altertumskunde*, vol. VIII, ed. by Johannes Hoops and Heinrich Beck (Berlin, 1994), pp. 541–82. Martin insists that brooches were found in burial assemblages in the same position in which they were worn in life and that they could not have served for fastening funerary shrouds, as previously assumed. He also notes that a brooch with an extremely flat bow precludes its use as fastener.

remained in use longer in Ostrogothic Italy, Crimea, and Visigothic Spain than anywhere else. Adopting the sleeved tunic implied, on the other hand, the use of a *cingulum*, a wide belt originally restricted to the male dress. Having lost their original function as fasteners, brooches were now worn at the waist, most likely as a badge of social status. Pinned to the lower, hanging end of the *cingulum* were various artefacts, including items believed to have magical properties for averting evil. Later, smaller implements, such as knives, spoons, or needles, either in pouches adorned with metal mounts or simply pinned to ribbons, can also be found hanging from the *cingulum*, as were various amulets, such as beads made from a variety of materials, decorative balls, shells, snails, so-called 'Thor hammers', and the like. The cloak worn over the dress was still fastened with brooches of smaller size, first worn in pairs and, later, singly. This shift in fashions may be traced from the Franks to the Gepids, but the rate of change must have varied considerably from one area to the other. Martin has noted that since the influence of Mediterranean fashions spread throughout the entire area of Merovingian rule and influence, one cannot explain the change as a diffusion of western female fashions from western to central and eastern Europe.

In the light of Martin's remarks, it has become apparent that the female buried in Old Buda was placed in the grave in a most fashionable, sleeved tunic with a *cingulum* at the waist to which an otherwise useless brooch was attached. There are several other finds in Pannonia attesting the adoption of the new fashion by local women of high status. In female burials of the Hács-Béndekpuszta cemetery, brooches were sometimes found on the chest (graves 3, 5, 19), at other times in pairs on the pelvis, one on top of the other, pointing to the sacrum (graves 18, 20).[35] The brooch pair in grave 150 of the Balatonszemes-Szemesi berek cemetery was likewise found by the waist; a strap or ribbon adorned with amulets hanging from the belt was also part of the dress.[36] Grave 154 at Tác-Fövenypuszta produced a single brooch, found between the left elbow and the vertebrae. The comb lying at the end of the right thighbone and the iron knife found on the left thighbone were most likely fastened to a strap or ribbon hanging from the waist belt.[37] It is important to note at this point that the best analogies for the Balatonszemes and Tác brooches are from southern Germany.[38] Martin has pointed out that quite

---

[35] Kiss, 'Das germanische Gräberfeld von Hács-Béndekpuszta', pp. 297 and 305.

[36] Bondár, Honti, and Kiss, 'A tervezett M7 autópálya', p. 97. Amulets included barrel-shaped beads and smoky quartz beads strung on a silver ring, as well as a stone encased in a silver band.

[37] Fitz, Lányi, and Bánki, 'Kutatások Gorsiumban', p. 292.

[38] Straub, 'Die archäologische Hinterlassenschaft', p. 14 with fig. 15.

often the same popular brooches were used both for fastening the *peplos* and for adorning the tunic with *cingulum*. Brooches such as found in Szekszárd and Sokolnice are a case in point.[39]

The fashion of attaching brooches to the belt was quickly adopted by Gepids living in the eastern parts of the Carpathian Basin. Nonetheless, Gepid aristocratic women preferred single brooches to pairs.[40] Martin believes that the adoption of the new fashion took place around AD 500. Countless burial assemblages attest to the use of straps hanging from the belt and studded with metal fittings.[41] During the sixth century, this became the standard fashion among Gepid women, as attested, among others, by finds from the Szolnok-Szanda cemetery.[42]

Late fifth-century burial assemblages with grave goods similar to those found in the Old Buda grave are known from the Upper Danube region in southern Germany, the area that also produced the best analogies for the Pannonian brooches. Much like in the Middle Danube region, brooches found in burial assemblages of southern Germany usually lay on the pelvis, singly or in pairs (often in parallel or one on top of the other), with belt buckles immediately beside them. Judging from the position of knife scabbards and occasional amulets found in some graves, aristocratic females in southern Germany had already adopted the fashion of straps or ribbons hanging from the belt.[43]

[39] Martin, '*Mixti Alamannis Suevi?*', p. 216.

[40] Margit Nagy, 'Gepida viselet', in *Hunok, Gepidák, Langobardok,* ed. by István Bóna (Szeged, 1993), pp. 63–64.

[41] E.g. grave 19 in Szőreg; graves 49 and 50 in Szentes-Kökényzug; graves 5 and 22 in Szentes-Nagyhegy. See Csallány, *Archäologische Denkmäler*, pp. 154, 31, 45, and 49–50. In grave 19 of the Szőreg cemetery, the brooch was found in the waist region, beside an oval iron buckle with leather remains. The knife was pinned to the strap hanging from the belt, together with amber and chalk beads.

[42] See, for instance, graves 1, 18, 36, 73, 91, 118, and 145. See István Bóna and Margit Nagy, *Gepidische Gräberfelder im Theissgebiet I.* (Budapest, 2002), pp. 201–34. See also Margit Nagy's reconstruction of the female dress on the basis of finds from grave 77 of the Hódmezővásárhely-Kishomok cemetery (Bóna and Nagy, *Gepidische Gräberfelder*, pp. 128–29).

[43] For a survey of finds in southern Germany, see Martin, '*Mixti Alamannis Suevi?*'. Gisela Clauss, 'Die Tragsitte von Bügelfibeln: Eine Untersuchung zur Frauentracht im frühen Mittelalter', *Jahrbuch der Römisch-Germanischen Zentralmuseums*, 34 (1987), 491–603 (p. 523 fig. 26), points to comparable finds from the lavishly furnished grave 126 in Basel-Kleinhüningen. See also grave 75 from that same cemetery in Ulrike Giesler-Müller, *Das frühmittelalterliche Gräberfeld von Basel-Kleinhüningen* (Derendingen, 1992), p. 70 with pl. 13. The 'Pannonian-Ostrogothic' brooch from grave 24 in Hemmingen was found on the pelvis next to an iron buckle, much like the pairs of brooches from graves 14, 43, 52, and 59 of that same cemetery (see Müller, *Das alamannische*

Closer and more distant analogies thus suggest that brooches were worn singly or in pairs at the waist, perhaps attached to a belt fastened with an iron buckle or to one or more hanging straps or ribbons. The broken iron rivet found in the Old Buda burial on the left ilium may also have belonged to the belt (Figures 6.4.1 and 6.5.1).[44] If so, it may have fixed a strap or ribbon hanging from the belt. In southern Germany, cloaks worn over the dress were fastened at the chest with small brooches, but such brooches have not so far been found in contemporary burial assemblages in the Middle Danube region. Since the Old Buda burial was disturbed in the region of the chest by a modern intrusion, the possibility of one or two small brooches in that region cannot be ruled out.

The Old Buda brooch was found beside an iron buckle, a dress accessory most typical for the late fifth and early sixth centuries (Figures 6.4.3a–b and 6.5.3a–b; Plate I.2.1–2). Upon discovery, the buckle was probably viewed as not particularly interesting and was not cleaned. When eventually cleaned and re-examined, it turned out to be a very interesting piece.[45] The Old Buda buckle is a specimen of the so-called B-shaped class of buckles, also known as kidney- or lyre-shaped buckles. Comparable buckles without decoration are known from a few burials in the Middle Danube region. Good analogies for the Old Buda specimen are the buckles from grave 2 in Pécs-Málom and grave 2 in Sióagárd, both assemblages dated to the early or middle fifth century. Other analogies come from the region north of the Danube and from Lower Austria.[46] A somewhat larger specimen has been found

---

Gräberfeld von Hemmingen). Grave 44 in Eichstetten produced a pair of brooches of the Bittenbrunn-Dunaföldvár class, but also an iron buckle, which was found on the pelvis (see Sasse, *Ein frühmittelalterliches Reihengräberfeld*, p. 169 with pl. 13).

[44] A similar rivet was found in Ártánd-Nagyfarkasdomb beside a kidney-shaped shoe buckle. See Eszter Istvánovits and Valéria Kulcsár, 'Sarmatian and Germanic People at the Upper Tisza Region and South Alföld at the Beginning of the Migration Period', in *L'Occident romain et l'Europe centrale au début de l'époque des Grandes Migrations*, ed. by Jaroslav Tejral, Christian Pilet, and Michel Kazanski (Brno, 1999), pp. 67–94 (p. 87 with fig. 17.3).

[45] Much too often similarly corroded, fragmentary pieces receive little, if any attention, beyond being listed among small finds as 'oval buckle' or 'Migration period find'. Margit Nagy pointed out the need for having the Old Buda buckle examined by X-ray. Nonetheless, even the careful mechanical cleaning done by Judit Dombovári from the Hungarian National Museum produced surprising results. I take this opportunity to express my gratitude to both of them for their assistance.

[46] Erzsébet Nagy, 'V. századi népvándorláskori sírok Pécs-Málom lelőhelyen', *Janus Pannonius Múzeum Évkönyve*, 38 (1993), 95–102 (p. 95 with pl. 1.2.1); János. G. Ódor, '5. századi temető Sióagárdon', *Wosinszky Mór Múzeum Évkönyve*, 23 (2001), 39–50 (p. 39 with fig. 2.2.1). The Pécs-Málom buckle was found with a male skeleton, but it was not possible to establish the sex of the Sióagárd skeleton. B-shaped buckles are also known from Čataj near Bratislava (Slovakia) and Bad-

in a grave excavated on Berzsenyi Street in Csongrád, which is dated to the same period. The size and shape of the Csongrád buckle recall a bronze specimen from an unknown location in Hungary, with a ribbed ring and widened tongue base.[47]

Most early or mid-fifth-century B-shaped buckles from the Carpathian Basin were made of bronze or silver, not iron. Some have plain, others ribbed rings. They come in a variety of sizes, with larger ones probably used as belt buckles and smaller ones, usually found in pairs, apparently used as shoe buckles. Some small buckles are equipped with triangular plates, mostly made from bronze, although a few silver and gold pieces are also known. They are regarded as of eastern origin. German, Austrian, and Czech scholars have suggested that they were adopted from 'mounted nomads'.[48] Specimens without plates are also known from this period.[49] Plain B-shaped buckle rings were also made of non-ferrous metals.[50] Iron specimens covered with a non-ferrous or precious metal plate must be viewed as a cheaper

Pirawart (Lower Austria), but nothing is known about the sex of the associated skeletons. See Jozef Zábojník, 'Das völkerwanderungszeitliche Gräberfeld von Čataj', in *Neue Beiträge zur Erforschung der Spätantike im mittleren Donauraum*, ed. by Tejral, Friesinger, and Kazanski, pp. 77–82 (p. 80 with fig. 3.1); Herwig Friesinger, 'Das archäologische Fundmaterial aus dem Gräberfeld von Gaweinstal', *Archaeologia Austriaca*, 63 (1980), 135–237 (p. 135 with fig. 8).

[47] Grave 7 in Csongrád-Berzsenyi Street: Mihály Párducz, *Die ethnischen Probleme der Hunnenzeit in Ungarn* (Budapest, 1963), p. 20 with pl. 2.13.21 (male burial). For the bronze buckle from an unknown location in Hungary, see Csallány, *Archäologische Denkmäler*, p. 242 with pl. 216.9. According to Mechthild Schulze-Dörrlamm, that buckle belong to her class A5 dated between *c.* 480 and 520. See Mechthild Schulze-Dörrlamm, *Byzantinische Gürtelschnallen und Gürtelbeschläge im Römisch-Germanischen Zentralmuseum*, vol. I: *Die Schnallen ohne Beschläg, mit Laschenbeschläg und mit festem Beschläg des 6. bis 7. Jahrhunderts* (Mainz, 2002), pp. 12–14.

[48] Bronze specimens from female burials in Gencsapáti and Tamási-Adorjánpuszta: István Bóna, *Das Hunnenreich* (Stuttgart, 1991), pp. 107 with pl. 75.1–2 and 283 with pl. 76. Two silver specimens, perhaps shoe buckles, are known from Csorna: József Hampel, *Alterthümer des frühen Mittelalters in Ungarn*, II (Budapest, 1905), pl. 13.6–7. A gold buckle with a plain ring and a triangular plate was found at Árpás-Dombiföld: Péter Tomka, 'Az árpási 5. századi sír', *Arrabona*, 39 (2001), 161–82 (p. 164 with fig. 4.1). All those buckles have been dated to the Hunnic period, namely to the middle third of the fifth century.

[49] E.g. the silver buckles with ribbed rings from Dindeşti and Kővágószőlős, both dated to the third quarter of the fifth century. See István Németi, 'Descoperiri funerare din secolul al V-lea de lîngă Carei', *Acta Musei Napocensis*, 4 (1967), 499–504 with fig. 2.6; Olivér Gábor, '5. századi sírok Kővágószőlős határában', *Janus Pannonius Múzeum Évkönyve*, 43 (1998), 131–40 (p. 132 with pl. 2.6).

[50] E.g., the buckle from Arad-Micălaca (Csallány, *Archäologische Denkmäler*, p. 144 with pl. 212.8) and the shoe buckles from Ártánd-Nagyfarkasdomb (Istvánovits and Kulcsár, 'Sarmatian and Germanic people', p. 82 with fig. 17.3).

variant of the same class. The iron buckle found with a male skeleton in a grave of the Budapest-Gazdagrét cemetery was covered with a bronze plate decorated with a dotted pattern.[51] The shoe buckles from Drslavice in Moravia were made from iron covered with gold.[52] The buckle from grave 8 of the Břeclav-Líbivá cemetery represents yet another variant: a B-shaped bronze ring with an iron tongue. Analogies of the Břeclav-Líbivá buckle, as well as kidney-shaped specimens with ribbed rings, have been dated to the second and last thirds of the fifth century.[53] Silver or bronze B-shaped buckles commonly have ribbed rings, a decoration imitated with wire inlay on iron specimens. According to Tejral, the latter must be dated to the late fifth century.[54]

A magnificent lyre-shaped buckle with inlay ornament has been recently found at Ladendorf in Lower Austria. In both size and form it matches the Old Buda buckle. Moreover, the inlay ornament was similarly made with copper wire. The description and accompanying illustration indicate that the buckle had an iron plate, of which only a small fragment has survived. The excavator cites numerous examples of inlaid and plain iron buckles from the Upper Danube region, as analogies for the Ladendorf specimen.[55] An iron buckle with oval ring inlaid with copper is known from Drösing (Lower Austria).[56] Even though the above-mentioned

---

[51] Paula Zsidi, 'A Budapest XI. kerületi Gazdagréten feltárt 4–5. századi temető', *Communicationes Archaeologicae Hungariae*, 1987, 45–72 (p. 56 with fig. 10.1). Kidney-shaped iron buckles were recovered from other burials in that same cemetery (graves 37, 50, 71, and 81, the latter being a ribbed specimen). The decoration of a buckle made from precious metal was imitated on the B-shaped iron buckle from Budapest-Zugló. The cells lined with gold foil recessed into the buckle ring imitate animal eyes. See Margit Nagy's contribution to this volume.

[52] Tejral, *Morava*, p. 201 with fig. 8.2–3.

[53] Jiří Macháček and Evženie Klanicová, 'Die Gräber aus der Völkerwanderungszeit in Břeclav-Líbivá', in *Neue Beiträge zur Erforschung der Spätantike im mittleren Donauraum*, ed. by Tejral, Friesinger, and Kazanski, pp. 57–65 (pp. 58–60 with fig. 2.2).

[54] Tejral, 'Neue Aspekte', p. 351.

[55] Windl, 'Ein frühmerowingerzeitliches Frauengrab', p. 69. Comparable finds are known from Schletz, Horn, Straubing-Bajuwarenstrasse, Strass, Mitterhof, and Gaweinstal. For a discussion of those buckles in relation to the Schletz finds, see Helmut Windl, 'Völkerwanderungszeitliche Gräber aus Schletz, BH Mistelbach, Niederösterreich', *Archaeologia Austriaca*, 72 (1988), 203–06 (p. 203); Helmut Windl, 'Weitere völkerwanderungszeitliche Gräber aus Schletz, MG Asparn an der Zaya, VB Mistelbach, Niederösterreich', *Fundberichte aus Österreich*, 35 (1996), 377–87 (p. 381).

[56] Friedrich Jedlička, 'Drösing', *Fundberichte aus Österreich*, 33 (1994), 615 with fig. 946. In Lower Austria, oval iron buckles with copper inlay remained in use throughout the so-called 'Lombard period'. See Edeltraud Aspöck and Peter Stadler, 'Die langobardische Gräber von Brunn am Gebirge, Flur Wolfholz, NÖ', *Archaeologia Austriaca*, 87 (2003), 169–224 (p. 178 with pl. 1.2).

analogies may leave the impression that during the fifth century inlay decoration was only used in Lower Austria or the Upper Danube region, this is not in fact the case. Grave 38 of the Gazdagrét cemetery, which is located near Aquincum, produced an iron buckle with a B-shaped ring inlaid with silver.[57] In his discussion of the Tamási-Adorjánpuszta finds, István Bóna noted that while application of inlay ornament (*Streifentauschierung*) is known since Antiquity, it was rarely used for the decoration of dress accessories of the Hunnic period.[58] Iron buckles with inlay decoration appear in sixth-century burial assemblages of both western and eastern Hungary. Some, at least, of the much corroded buckles said to be just plain iron buckles may well turn out to have been decorated with an inlaid ornament.[59] It is therefore quite likely that B-shaped iron buckles decorated with metal inlay were manufactured in the Danube region during the last third or quarter of the fifth century, perhaps as humbler versions of fashionably ribbed specimens cast in non-ferrous or precious metals.[60] The list of known buckles contains more specimens with silver than with copper inlay.

[57] Zsidi, 'A Budapest XI. kerületi Gazdagréten feltárt 4–5. századi temető', p. 54 with fig. 7.38.2. Grave 38 is a disturbed, male burial, from which besides the buckle only a flint steel and a fragmentary knife were recuperated.

[58] Bóna, *Das Hunnenreich*, p. 283. A kidney-shaped, grooved iron buckle found in the Palkonya burial was most likely decorated with metal inlay. See Dezső Csallány, 'Hamvasztásos és csontvázas temetkezések a Felső-Tisza vidékén', *Herman Otto Múzeum Évkönyve*, 2 (1958), 83–99 (pp. 85 and 92 with pl. 1.9); Margit Nagy, 'Hunkori férfisír Budapest-Zuglóból', in *Vándorutak – Múzeumi örökség: Tanulmányok Bodó Sándor tiszteletére*, ed. by Gyula Viga, Szilvia Andrea Holló, and Edit Cs. Schwalm (Budapest, 2003), pp. 297–325 (p. 305 with n. 72). See also Margit Nagy's contribution to this volume.

[59] According to Orsolya Heinrich-Tamaska, *Studien zu den awarenzeitlichen Tauschierarbeiten* (Innsbruck, 2005), pp. 25–26, *Streifentauschierung* already appears on finds from the Mözs-Icsei dülő cemetery dated to the first and second thirds of the fifth century. But D-shaped, ribbed bronze buckles (an altogether different class from B-shaped buckles!) are first attested in burial assemblages in the eastern parts of the Carpathian Basin during the first two thirds of the sixth century, at about the same time as metal inlay began to be adopted as a common decorative technique. See Csallány, *Archäologische Denkmäler*, pls 16.15, 142.8, and 201.17. D-shaped buckles have also been classified differently by Mechthild Schulze-Dörrlamm, as members of her class A6. See Schulze-Dörrlamm, *Byzantinische Gürtelschnallen*, pp. 14–15.

[60] This type of buckle was quite popular in southern Germany. B-shaped and oval buckles with silver or copper inlay were found in several graves of the cemetery excavated on the Bajuwaren Street in Straubing. See Hans Geisler, *Das frühbairische Gräberfeld Straubing-Bajuwarenstrasse* (Rahden, 1998). For a similar find from Hemmingen, see Müller, *Das alamannische Gräberfeld von Hemmingen*, pp. 68–69.

A small, but luckily well-identifiable fragment of a comb was found by the left hand of the Old Buda skeleton (Figures 6.3.2 and 6.5.9). The original comb must have been heavily worn, as shown by the use of an iron instead of a bronze rivet to repair a cracked plate.[61] Double-layered combs first appear in Pannonia along with other types of combs in the late fourth century. Mária Bíró has advanced the idea that responsible for the appearance of this comb must have been *foederati*, even though the combs themselves were produced in Pannonia.[62] Given that the burial deposition of combs was not known before that, it is quite possible that the practice was introduced by barbarian newcomers, either as an expression of their religious belief or, more likely, as a new hairstyle fashion.[63]

The circle-and-dot motif was a quite popular ornamental pattern for Late Roman double-sided combs, second only to the simple linear decoration.[64] The short sides were usually moulded, and a few specimens decorated in that way are known from mid-fifth-century assemblages, such as Pécs-Málom.[65] A fragment of a moulded comb with circle-and-dot decoration recovered from a settlement feature in Cífer-Pác may be even later, namely of the late fifth century.[66] But combs

---

[61] For a similar repair procedure, see the comb in grave 1055 from Intercisa, in Mária Bíró, 'Combs and Comb-making in Roman Pannonia: Ethnical and Historical Aspects', in *Probleme der frühen Merowingerzeit*, ed. by Tejral, pp. 31–71 (pp. 32 and 67).

[62] Mária Bíró, 'Qualitative Analyse der Wechselwirkung der provinzialen und barbarischen Beinwerkstätte aufgrund der spätantiken Kämme', in *Gentes, reges und Rom: Auseinandersetzung, Anerkennung, Anpassung. Festschrift für Jaroslav Tejral zum 65. Geburtstag*, ed. by Jan Bouzek (Brno, 2000), pp. 167–71. Bíró's hypothesis is substantiated by combs with straight short sides found in Mágocs and dated to *c.* 400. Mágocs was the cemetery of a community whose ancestors may have been *foederati*, but which had meanwhile been assimilated into the Roman cultural environment. See Olivér Gábor, 'Későantik sírok Mágocson', *Janus Pannonius Múzeum Évkönyve*, 43 (1998), 113–30 (pp. 114–15 and 120 with pls 2.1 and 4.3). About 75 per cent of all known Pannonian combs are of the double-sided type.

[63] Jaroslav Tejral, 'Archäologisch-kulturelle Entwicklung im norddanubischen Raum am Ende der spätkaiserzeit und am Anfang der Völkerwanderungszeit', in *L'Occident romain et l'Europe centrale*, ed. by Tejral, Pilet, and Kazanski, pp. 205–71 (p. 222 with n. 26); Bíró, 'Combs and Comb-making', p. 180. Burial deposition of combs is well documented for assemblages of the Sântana de Mureș-Chernyakhov culture.

[64] About half of all known combs are decorated with linear designs, while about a third display the circle-and-dot motif. See Bíró, 'Combs and Comb-making', p. 181.

[65] Nagy, 'V. századi népvándorláskori sírok', p. 95 with pl. 1.2/2.

[66] The Cífer-Pác comb too had iron rivets. See Ivan Cheben and Matej Ruttkay, 'Objekt aus der Völkerwanderungszeit in Cífer-Pác', in *Neue Beiträge zur Erforschung der Spätantike im mittleren Donauraum*, ed. by Tejral, Friesinger, and Kazanski, pp. 89–99 (pp. 91–92 with fig. 2.2).

with circle-and-dot decoration were already in use after *c.* 450, as demonstrated by the straight-sided specimen from a grave in Szabadbattyán.[67] Two combs were found beside the head of a skeleton buried in the so-called Apsidal Building at Aquincum (Kiscelli Street); one of them had straight sides and a circle-and-dot decoration. Because of the lack of diagnostic types, the chronology of the cemetery excavated on the Kiscelli Street remains uncertain, but what little evidence there is points to a date within the fifth century.[68] The comb found in the Apsidal Building grave appears to be the closest analogy to the Old Buda comb, in terms of both dating and proximity.

Attila Kiss devoted two special studies to late fifth- and early sixth-century double-sided combs.[69] In his discussion of the Hács-Béndekpuszta finds, he noted that in Pannonia the custom of burial deposition of combs either by the head (in the hair, as probably worn during lifetime) or by the feet is attested only after the departure of the Goths. But János G. Ódor has meanwhile brought forward evidence that combs may have also been deposited in or by the hands.[70] Moreover, there is by now sufficient documentation to support the idea of a burial deposition of combs before *c.* 470,[71] even though the practice became popular only by the late fifth century. A similar phenomenon, involving mostly double-sided combs often with circle-and-dot decoration, is attested for burial assemblages in the eastern parts of the Carpathian Basin and in Moravia.[72] It is therefore very likely that the

[67] László Barkóczi and Ágnes Salamon, 'Das Gräberfeld von Szabadbattyán aus dem 5. Jahrhundert', *Mitteilungen des Archäologischen Instituts der Ungarischen Akademie der Wissenschaften*, 5 (1974–75), 89–111 (p. 99 with pl. 34.27, grave 14).

[68] Györgyi Parragi, 'Karéjos épület a Kiscelli utcában', *Budapest Régiségei*, 24 (1976), 160–61 and 177–83 (p. 179 with fig. 197).

[69] Kiss, 'Germanischer Grabfund', pp. 204–05; and 'Das germanische Gräberfeld von Hács-Béndekpuszta', pp. 313–14. Kiss did not include combs from the eastern parts of the Carpathian Basin.

[70] Ódor, '5. századi temető', pp. 40–41 (with examples from graves 6 and 8 from the Mözs-Icsei dűlő cemetery).

[71] See, for example, the burial assemblages from Pécs-Málom, Sióagárd, Kővágószőlős, and Keszthely-Fenékpuszta. For the latter, see Straub, 'Die Hinterlassenschaft der Ostgoten', p. 10 and fig. 2.

[72] For combs from assemblages in the eastern parts of the Carpathian Basin, see János Cseh, 'Adatok az V–VII. századi gepida emlékanyag egységéhez', *Szolnok Megyei Múzeumi Évkönyv*, 1984–88, 29–77 (pp. 31 and 55 with list 18); Ágnes B. Tóth, 'Kora népvándorlás kori sírok Tápé-Széntéglaégetőn', in *A kőkortól a középkorig: Tanulmányok Trogmayer Ottó 60. születésnapjára*, ed. by Gábor Lőrinczy (Szeged, 1994), pp. 285–309 (pp. 289–91); Bóna and Nagy, *Gepidische*

Old Buda comb was manufactured somewhere in northern Transdanubia in the late fifth century and was deposited by the left hand of the deceased woman as an offering.

When the Old Buda burial came to light, the two small gold spirals found between the dislodged right clavicle and the vertebrae were believed to have broken off some jewellery item at the time the burial was disturbed (Figure 6.3.1 and Plate I.1.1). However, no signs of a fresh breakage could be observed on their terminals and none was deformed. It seems more likely that the spirals were part of a necklace, possibly together with beads, which have meanwhile been lost. Such spirals were used in lieu of fashionable gilded beads, themselves an imitation of early Byzantine gold beads, which were worn by wealthy women in the fifth and sixth centuries. Such beads have also been found in some quantity in the Carpathian Basin, which suggests that they were made locally as imitations of Roman originals.[73] Beads made of sheet-gold were found in grave 29 of the Szentes-Kökényzug cemetery and in burials uncovered in Oradea, both sites mentioned above in relation to the brooch. Six small gold tubes lay around the neck of a female skeleton found in a lavishly furnished burial uncovered in Kapolcs (which, however, did not have any brooch). The tubes were not made of wire, but of ribbed sheet gold. About 10 mm long and 4 mm in diameter, they are nevertheless of the same size as the Old Buda spirals. Since they were found together with two gold pins on the neck, they may have been threaded onto the ribbon or the thread passed through the pins.[74]

Two other, slightly earlier analogies are known from early fifth-century assemblages in Rábapordány and Untersiebenbrunn (grave 1). Both produced necklaces strung of ribbed gold tubes with gold leaf pendants between them.[75] The gold tubes

---

Gräberfelder, pp. 95–98. Combs with circle-and-dot decoration are less frequent in the eastern region of the Carpathian Basin, but not altogether absent. See for instance the specimens from grave 81 in Szentes-Kökényzug, Tiszaeszlár-Jeges tanya, as well as sunken-floored building 10 in Moreşti (Csallány, *Archäologische Denkmäler*, pls 18.11, 198.34, and 268.2). For Moravia, see Tejral, *Morava*, pls 51.1 and 101.1 (Velatice and grave 1 in Vyškov).

[73] For gold beads in the Carpathian Basin, see Kiss, 'Das germanische Gräberfeld von Hács-Béndekpuszta', pp. 314–16; and Attila Kiss, 'Das germanische Frauengrab von Répcelak (Westungarn) aus der zweiten Halfte des 5. Jahrhunders', *Acta Archaeologica Academiae Scientiarum Hungaricae*, 52 (2001), 115–44 (p. 126).

[74] Margit Csabainé Dax, 'Keleti germán női sírok Kapolcson', *A Veszprém Megyei Múzeumok Közleményei*, 15 (1980), 97–106 (p. 97). The assemblage was dated to the last third of the fifth century.

[75] András Alföldi, *Leletek a hun korszakból és ethnikai szétválasztásuk* (Budapest, 1932), p. 73 with pl. 10; Wilhelm Kubitschek, 'Grabfunde in Untersiebenbrunn aus dem Marchfeld', *Jahrbuch*

from those burials are excellent parallels to the Old Buda spirals, as are the tiny spirals wound from gold wire, with which the gold leaf pendants were suspended from the Rábapordány necklace. A similar use for spirals may be assumed for a later period, but there are not sufficient finds dated to the later fifth century to support that hypothesis. It is equally possible that the Old Buda spirals adorned the woman's braided hair. However, glass beads adorning braids are so far known only from male burials.[76]

Even though the burial deposition of knives was a widespread custom both in Pannonia and among Sarmatians living in the Alföld, very few early fifth-century female burials produced knives. Such implements began to appear in graves of aristocratic women only from the mid-fifth century onwards.[77] By contrast, knives are very rare in poor burials of that same period.[78] Knives tend to appear in burial assemblages similar to that from Old Buda, such as grave 154 of the Tác-Fövenypuszta cemetery or grave 29 in Szentes-Kökényzug.[79] In such assemblages, the tool was found in a position suggesting that it may have been suspended from the belt, most likely in a leather scabbard. A small knife was found between the ankles of the skeleton on grave 10 of the Schletz cemetery, while the position of the knife found in the Ladendorf burial is not known.[80] Many more knives have turned out in burials of the so-called *Reihengräberkreis* dated to the late fifth and sixth

---

der k.-k. Zentral-Kommission für Erforschung und Erhaltung der Kunst- und historische Denkmale, 5 (1911), 32–74 with pl. 5.18.

[76] Such as the specimen most likely adorning the hair knot of a young male in burial from Iszkaszentgyörgy-Zsidóhegy. See Bóna, 'A népvándorlás kora', p. 228(12).

[77] Among the earliest instances of this practice are the Tiszalök burial and grave 2 of a cemetery recently excavated in Szentistván. See Kovrig, 'A tiszalöki és a mádi lelet', p. 113 with pl. 43.9; Emese Lovász, 'Hun és germán jellegű leletek Borsod megyében', *Herman Ottó Múzeum Évkönyve*, 37 (1999), 237–65 (p. 242 with pl. 2). In both cases, the knife was placed by the arms.

[78] Among such burials, see graves 8, 58, 63, 84, and 88 (all female burials) in the Singidunum necropolis, for which see Vujadin Ivanišević and Michel Kazanski, 'La Nécropole de l'époque des grandes migrations à Singidunum', in *Singidunum 3*, ed. by Marko Popović (Belgrade, 2002), pp. 101–57. Knives were also found in grave 14 of the Szabadbattyán cemetery (Barkóczi and Salamon, 'Das Szabadbattyán', p. 93 with pl. 34.28) and grave 19 of the Pilismarót cemetery (Ilona Kovrig, 'Nouvelles trouvailles du Vᵉ siècle découvertes en Hongrie (Szob, Pilismarót, Csővár, Németkér)', *Acta Archaeologica Academiae Scientiarum Hungaricae*, 10 (1959), 209–25 (p. 210 with pl. 3.7)).

[79] Fitz, Lányi, and Bánki, 'Kutatások Gorsiumban', fig. 1.5; Csallány, *Archäologische Denkmäler*, pl. 14.8.

[80] Windl, 'Weitere völkerwanderungszeitliche Gräber', p. 379 and pl. 3.5196; and Windl, 'Ein frühmerowingerzeitliches Frauengrab', pl. 3.9.

centuries. About 30 per cent of all female burials in the Hódmezővásárhely-Kishomok cemetery produced knives, which were found either near the thighbone or in the pelvic region.[81] Similarly, knives from Merovingian cemeteries in southern Germany were commonly found either between or around the thighbones.[82] Knives from female and children burials of the Hódmezővásárhely-Kishomok cemetery are all quite small instruments, much like the Old Buda knife. That knife too must have been attached to a strap or ribbon suspended from the belt, perhaps with the recuperated iron rivet (Figures 6.2.6, 6.4.1, and 6.5.1).

Looped bronze mounts similar to that found in Old Buda are rarely found in fifth-century burial assemblages (Figures 6.4.8 and 6.5.8). Given that the mount was not found in its original position, but in an animal burrow, it is even more difficult to assess its one-time function. Nevertheless, the mount served for holding some thick, hard material since the distance between the two bronze bands held together by rivets is 0.5–0.6 cm. The shank of the surviving rivet is also quite sturdy, suggesting that the material was a thick strap of leather or a piece of wood. The sturdiness of the mount section widening into a loop would again imply that some heavy item was suspended from it or that it was attached to an object with round section. Let us examine those possibilities.

In terms of shape, the Old Buda mount resembles another from Soporu de Câmpie, which served for the suspension of a spherical pendant encased in bronze bands.[83] We have seen that amulets pinned to straps or ribbons hanging from the belt are commonly found in the fifth-century burial assemblages in the Upper Danube region, which can only strengthen the value of that parallel. However, judging from the published illustration, the mount found with a late third-century urn cremation in Soporu de Câmpie appears to be thinner and smaller than the Old Buda mount. A somewhat better analogy was found in grave 787 of the

[81] Margit Nagy, 'A hódmezővásárhely-kishomoki gepida temető (elemzés)', *Móra Ferenc Múzeum Évkönyve: Studia Archaeologica*, 10 (2004), 129–239 (pp. 146–47).

[82] Roth and Theune, *Das frühmittelalterliche Gräberfeld bei Weingarten*, p. 69 and pl. 76.4 (Weingarten, grave 241, between the knees); Müller, *Das alamannische Gräberfeld von Hemmingen*, p. 31 (Hemmingen, grave 14); Giesler-Müller, *Das frühmittelalterliche Gräberfeld*, p. 70 with pl. 13.75.5 (Basel-Kleinhüningen, grave 75, by the inner side of the right thighbone); Clauss, 'Die Tragsitte von Bügelfibeln', p. 523 and fig. 26 (Basel-Kleinhüningen, grave 126, on a ribbon with amulet pendants).

[83] Kurt Horedt, *Untersuchungen zur Frühgeschichte Siebenbürgens* (Bucharest, 1958), p. 24 and fig. 1.3.

cemetery excavated in Straubing on the Bajuwaren Street.[84] The Straubing mount was the only artefact left behind after the burial had been robbed. Although made of iron, not bronze, it is of a similar size and, much like the Old Buda mount, its sides were held together by a single rivet. It probably served a similar function too, namely to support a hanging object. A looped bronze mount was also recovered from a richly furnished burial (grave 81) in Szentes-Kökényzug, but its exact position in the grave was not described.[85] Although slightly smaller and with just one rivet, the Szentes-Kökényzug is nevertheless very similar to the Old Buda mount. The brooches with which it was associated may be dated to about the same time as the Old Buda burial assemblage. Moreover, the Szentes-Kökényzug female burial produced a variety of articles (a spoon, tweezers, an amber bead, and a comb) attached to a strap or ribbon hanging from the belt. It is worth mentioning that looped mounts for suspension of objects have also been found in Late Roman burials of soldiers buried with their weapon belts. A recently published soldier grave from the *canabae* in Aquincum produced several belt fittings, including a tweezer-shaped silver strap end. In both size and form, the strap end resembles the Old Buda mount. Finally, an early fifth-century looped belt mount from Vieuxville may also be cited as analogy for the Old Buda mount.[86]

But the closest analogies are artefacts, the presence of which in the Old Buda burial assemblage would be very hard to explain. For example, the silver mounts of the Hun-age harness set from Coşovenii de Jos bear a striking resemblance to the Old Buda mount in terms of both shape and size. The looped section adjoining the ring is rather stout, the top of the Coşovenii de Jos mounts is rounded, a trait which can also be observed on the Old Buda mount. The sides of the mount are rectangular and widened at the ring. They were attached to the harness straps by means of three rivets.[87] Nothing supports the idea of a horse harness being deposited with the Old Buda burial. It is of course possible that the looped mount had served initially some other purpose, but when placed in the grave it was certainly used for suspension, even though it is not at all clear what exactly was the suspended object.

---

[84] Geisler, *Das frühbairische Gräberfeld*, p. 290 with pl. 287.787.1.

[85] Csallány, *Archäologische Denkmäler*, pp. 37–38 with pl. 18.2.

[86] Margit Nagy, 'Két késő római kori fegyveres sír az aquincumi canabae nyugati szélén', *Budapest Régiségei*, 38 (2004), 231–315 (p. 258 with figs 15.2 and 29.3). According to Nagy, the Aquincum burial contained the remains of a 'high-ranking soldier of barbarian origin'.

[87] Harhoiu, *Die frühe Völkerwanderungszeit*, pp. 172–73 with pl. 38.4–6 and 9. Comparable silver mounts have also been reported from other sites, such as a fourth-century burial in Berkasovo. See Nagy, 'Két késő római kori fegyveres sír', p. 257 with fig. 29.5.

On the other hand, we cannot rule out the possibility that the artefact entered the grave accidentally, when the soil was shovelled back into the grave pit, after the grave had been dug into a layer of debris from the Late Roman building.

Similarly, although the bronze hook was found among the bones of the left hand, it is not at all certain that it had originally been placed there (Figures 6.4.6 and 6.5.6). Several penannular earrings made from thin bronze wire are known from fifth-century cemeteries, such as Tokod, Letkés, Sikenica, and Ţaga.[88] A similarly shaped bronze wire was found in grave 271 of the Szentes-Berekhát cemetery, but neither the function of the artefact nor the sex of the skeleton in that grave could be established.[89] The Old Buda bronze hook may have been used for suspending something from the belt. It can perhaps be associated with the comb, which was also found on the left side of the skeleton

Like in Old Buda, many fifth-century burials produced fragments of corroded iron, whose function can hardly be reconstructed. Imprints of wood survive on the surface of the iron band from Old Buda; it may therefore have been a coffin mount (Figures 6.4.4 and 6.5.4).[90] The small bone implement was probably a scraper (Figures 6.4.2 and 6.5.2), but the purpose of the amorphous lead fragment remains unknown (Figures 6.4.5 and 6.5.5). It is of course possible that all those objects were accidentally mixed up with the earth shovelled back into the grave after burial.

Neglected Barbarians in Late Fifth- and Early Sixth-Century Aquincum

In contrast to the rich and varied record of Roman assemblages in Aquincum, fifth-century finds are rare. This may indeed indicate that the settlement was abandoned during the Hunnic period. On the testimony of the archaeological record, the *foederati* arriving to Aquincum in the Late Roman period were accompanied by civilian groups of barbarian origin. Perhaps only the poor, low-status inhabitants

---

[88] Vera Lányi, 'Das spätrömische Gräberfeld', in *Die spätrömische Festung und das Gräberfeld von Tokod*, ed. by András Mocsy (Budapest, 1981), pp. 169–221 (pp. 170–71 and 195 with fig. 4); László Papp and Ágnes Salamon, 'Gräber aus dem 5. Jh. In Letkés', *Mitteilungen des Archäologischen Instituts der Ungarischen Akademie der Wissenschaften*, 8–9 (1978–79), 85–92 (p. 85); Novotný, 'Ein völkerwanderungszeitliches Grab', p. 308; Harhoiu, *Die frühe Völkerwanderungszeit*, p. 192 with pl. 90.308.

[89] Csallány, *Archäologische Denkmäler*, p. 94 with pl. 83.7.

[90] The iron band fragments found beside the skull in grave 24 of the Hemmingen cemetery may be associated with the meticulously excavated coffin hollowed out from a tree trunk. See Müller, *Das alamannische Gräberfeld von Hemmingen*, p. 47 with fig. 22.

remained in Aquincum when the Huns arrived. Most Late Roman cemeteries had by then been abandoned, and throughout the fifth century they were no longer in use. Despite indications that the southern side of the Late Roman fort was still occupied, for this is where the Old Buda burial was found, the nature of that occupation remains unclear.[91]

Traces of fifth-century, intermittent occupation have been observed on several sites (former towns or forts) in Pannonia. Recent research has demonstrated that the former auxiliary camp at Arrabona continued to be occupied until the late fifth century, even though it has entirely lost its former character and was no different from contemporary barbarian settlements.[92] Only small clusters of barbarian burials could be found in the late fifth and early sixth centuries on the grounds of the former *villa* at Tác or inside the former Roman camp at Intercisa.[93]

Both written and archaeological sources give a very different picture for the situation in the southern parts of the Carpathian Basin to which the Ostrogoths moved between 455 and 473. Life was no doubt much more dynamic in the *civitates* and their hinterlands, with some settlements operating as episcopal sees and others as operational or supply bases for the *foederati*. In Noricum, along the Danube, the network of settlements survived until *c.* 488.[94]

The similarities between Old Buda and Tác are not restricted to apparently solitary burials or small groups of graves. At Tác, burials were dug into still extant

---

[91] Margit Nagy, 'Óbuda a népvándorlás korban', *Budapest Régiségei*, 30 (1993), 353–95 (pp. 353 and 363 with n. 16).

[92] Péter Tomka, 'Kulturwechsel der spätantiken Bevölkerung eines Auxiliarkastells: Fallbeispiel Arrabona', in *Zentrum und Peripherie: gesellschaftliche Phänomäne in der Frühgeschichte. Materialen der 13. internationalen Symposium 'Grundprobleme der frühgeschichtlichen Entwicklung im mittleren Donauraum', Zwettl, 4.–8. Dezember 2000*, ed. by Herwig Friesinger and Alois Stuppner (Vienna, 2004) pp. 389–409 (pp. 391–92 and 396). During the third phase of occupation on the site, there were few indications in the material culture record that would help us distinguish the surviving provincial population, forced into a life of self-subsistence, and the barbarian settlers.

[93] Bóna, 'A népvándorlás kora', pp. 229(13)–230(14): six graves at Tác and five graves at Intercisa. Meanwhile, another burial has been found in Tác, south of the walls of Building B, which may have had some religious function during Roman times. It is not clear whether the building was still standing at the time of the burial. See Fitz, Lányi, and Bánki, 'Kutatások Gorsiumban', pp. 291–92.

[94] Andreas Schwarz, 'Städte und Foederaten an der mittleren und unteren Donau im 5. und 6. Jahrhundert', in *Zentrum und Peripherie*, ed. by Friesinger and Stuppner, pp. 105–13 (p. 111). In the southern parts of the Carpathian Basin, the most important settlements were Sirmium, Singidunum, and Bassianae.

buildings, a practice wholly alien to Roman funerary customs. Since the overall ground plan of the so-called Porticoed Building in Old Buda is not known, it remains unclear whether the grave was dug inside the building or in its courtyard. A good parallel for the latter is known from Ficarolo, where two wealthy members of a small community, a man and a woman most likely coming to Italy from the Danube region, were buried in the courtyard of a *villa rustica*, which was still in use, at least partially. Both were buried there, instead of the local Christian cemetery, most likely because of their elevated status and, perhaps, because of their lineage.[95] Not a single 'communal' cemetery of the late fifth century has so far been discovered in Aquincum.[96]

The only assemblage of late fifth-century artefacts known from Aquincum is a small hoard retrieved from the main entrance of the amphitheatre in the military town. The hoard contained a pair of gilded silver brooches, silver cups, and silver beads, all worn and damaged to such an extent as to indicate that they had been concealed well after being manufactured, possibly in the early 500s. If the date of burial was indeed at some point during the first few years of the sixth century, the hoard may have been hidden in the circumstances surrounding the arrival of the Lombards.[97] On the basis of the hoard alone, István Bóna even suggested that a pre-Lombard, Suevic centre of power may have been located within the walls of the fort-like amphitheatre.[98] To be sure, it is quite clear that on the eve of the Lombard conquest of the area, Aquincum and its hinterland were inhabited by Sueves.[99] However, it is not at all clear when exactly the Sueves moved into this area from the region north of the Danube River, and where their settlement area bordered on that of the Ostrogoths between 455 and 473.[100] It is generally assumed that the

[95] Büsing, 'Die Dame von Ficarolo', pp. 255–56 and 275.

[96] Zsidi, 'A Budapest XI. kerületi Gazdagréten feltárt 4–5. századi temető', p. 69.

[97] Nagy, 'Óbuda a népvándorlás korban', p. 356.

[98] Bóna, 'Daciától Erdőelvéig', p. 121.

[99] Attila Kiss, 'Pannonien zur Zeit der Völkerwanderung: Ergebnisse und Probleme', in *L'Occident romain et l'Europe centrale*, ed. by Tejral, Pilet, and Kazanski, pp. 114–17 and 120–22. The Old Buda burial appears on Kiss's list of Suevic sites.

[100] Titus Kolník, 'Die Donausweben in der spätrömischen Kaiserzeit und in der Völkerwanderungszeit: Zum Ende der swebischen Besiedlung im mittleren Donauraum', *Anzeiger des Germanischen Nationalmuseums und Berichte aus dem Forschungsinstitut für Realienkunde*, 1988, 69–76 (p. 73), believed that as *foederati* the Sueves mut have already moved south of the Danube River in the early fifth century. István Bóna, 'Ungarns Völker im 5. und 6. Jahrhundert: Eine historisch-archäologische Zusammenschau', in *Germanen, Hunnen, und Awaren: Schätze der*

Sueves moved into northern Transdanubia immediately after the departure of the Ostrogoths in 473. The few references to Sueves in written sources seem to indicate that following the unsuccessful Gothic campaign, King Hunimund was unable to bring together the agrarian Suevic population living on both sides of the Danube in a militant and independent polity similar to that established by the Herules farther to the north-west.[101] But even if we accept that by 500 northern Transdanubia had come under Suevic rule or that it had been incorporated into the Suevic kingdom, it is unlikely that the only inhabitants of the region at that time were Sueves. Living side by side in northern Transdanubia were not only the descendants of the once provincial population, but also groups of barbarians (possibly even those of Eastern Germanic origin) who had settled there during or after the Hunnic period.[102]

The date of the Old Buda burial is relatively easy to establish on the basis of two distinctive grave-good categories, namely the brooch and the buckle. Analogies for both suggest a date within the last quarter of the fifth century, and perhaps the same holds true for the double-sided comb. The brooch and the comb were heavily worn and damaged by the time they were laid in the grave, which suggests that burial took place only a few decades after the artefacts had been manufactured, that is, shortly before or after AD 500. The woman buried in Old Buda must have been

---

Völkerwandgerungszeit. Germanisches Nationalmuseum, Nürnberg, 12. Dezember 1987 bis 21. Februar 1988, ed. by Wilfrid Menghin, Tobias Springer, and Egon Wamers (Nuremberg, 1988) pp. 116–29 (p. 121), argued that by 460 the Suevic territory extended south to Lake Balaton and then the Sueves all moved from the present-day Slovakia into Transdanubia in the last quarter of the fifth century. According to Kiss, 'Germanischer Grabfund', p. 177, the Sueves could not have moved into Pannonia before 473. However, Kiss, 'Pannonien zur Zeit der Völkerwanderung', p. 109, maintained that the Sueves extended their authority over northern Pannonia shortly after the collapse of Attila's Hunnic Empire in the mid-400s. The issue of the boundary between the Suevic and Ostrogothic settlement territories can hardly be solved by means of the archaeological evidence, since there are no sufficient finds to reconstruct the settlement territory of any particular *gens* in fifth-century Transdanubia.

[101] The Herules had settled in the region of Lake Fertő, in southern Moravia, and in Lower Austria. See Walter Pohl, 'Die Gepiden und die gentes an der mittleren Donau nach dem Zerfall des Attilareiches', in *Die Völker an der mittleren und unteren Donau im fünften und sechsten Jahrhundert: Berichte des Symposions der Kommission für Frühmittelalterforschung, 24.–27. Oktober 1978, Stift Zwettl, Niederösterreich*, ed. by Herwig Wolfram and Falko Daim (Vienna, 1980), pp. 239–305 (pp. 274–78).

[102] Women often moved from one cultural milieu to the other by virtue of marriage. At the same time, mobility is also assumed for many barbarian groups at this time, especially for members of the aristocracy.

dressed in richly adorned clothes, even though a later intrusion may have removed some of the grave goods. In any case, the surviving artefacts bespeak the high status of the deceased. In the late fifth century, difference in social status was neither necessarily nor exclusively marked in the nature of the clothes, but in the quality of the dress accessories in terms of material used, size, and craftsmanship.[103] The role the deceased woman may have played in her community may be judged from the more elaborate grave goods, such as the brooch, the buckle, and the gold spirals. It would appear that she was a free woman of some status, perhaps even a member of the local nobility, though by no means as affluent as women in the higher echelons of the aristocracy, some of whom owned riches illustrated by the hoard found in the amphitheatre. Nevertheless, the social position of the Old Buda female within her community was comparable to that of females whose burials have been often mentioned above in relation to the cultural context of the Old Buda grave goods (Ladendorf, grave 241 in Weingarten, grave 24 in Hemmingen, and grave 29 in Szentes-Kökényzug).

Northern Pannonia was probably already under Suevic rule when the grave was dug inside the 'Porticoed Building', although it is not known how far the militant kingdom of the Herules extended to the east. It is generally assumed that northern Pannonia was inhabited by Sueves at this time, and most assemblages dated after *c.* 450 are attributed to them. Whatever differences in material culture, if any, may have initially existed, judging by the archaeological record of the late fifth century, the local population had already adopted both Hun-age ('mounted nomad') and 'eastern Germanic' traditions, which explains the striking parallels that could be established between the Old Buda burial and assemblages farther to the west, within the lands at that time under the rule of the Herules (Ladendorf), or to the south-east, at that time within Gepid territory.[104]

During her lifetime, the woman buried in Old Buda must have worn her knife attached to a strap or ribbon hanging from the belt, a fashion with good analogies in burial assemblages from southern Germany. I have repeatedly pointed in this paper to links between finds from Alamannia and the Danube region. Such links have been explained in terms of the migration into southern Germany, after the mid-fifth century, of heterogeneous groups of population (which written sources

---

[103] Martin, 'Tradition und Wandel', p. 574.

[104] See Karol Pieta, 'Die Slowakei im 5. Jahrhundert', in *Germanen, Hunnen, und Awaren*, ed. by Menghin, Springer, and Wamers, pp. 385–97 (pp. 391–95).

describe as Sueves) from the Danube region.[105] However, it is equally possible that such similarities are due to 'the intensive exchange of various products and ideas', which transformed the material culture and customs of the peoples living in a broad region of Central Europe, which would in turn imply long-distance contacts between southern Germany and the Middle Danube.[106] It has also been suggested that many such similarities can be traced back to a 'common Mediterranean heritage'.

Men and women of some wealth were laid to rest in solitary graves or small grave groups in the Danube region.[107] Most contemporary burials in southern Germany or in the Alföld, which could be compared with the Old Buda burial, belong to an early phase of the *Reihengräberkreis*. Communities burying their dead in those cemeteries continued to do so for several subsequent generations. By contrast, the woman buried in Aquincum was most likely the member of a much smaller community, which did not settle in Aquincum for too long and, as a consequence, did not did not leave too many graves behind, dug into the ruined buildings of the former Roman fort.

[105] Martin, '*Mixti Alamannis Suevi?*', p. 219; Dieter Quast, 'Auf der Suche nach fremden Männern: Die Herleitung schmalen Langsaxe vor dem Hintergrund der alamannisch-donauländischen Kontakte der zweiten Hälfte des 5. Jahrhunderts', in *Germanen beiderseits des spätantiken Limes*, ed. by Thomas Fischer, Gundolf Precht, and Jaroslav Tejral (Brno, 1999), pp. 115–28.

[106] Tejral, 'Beiträge', pp. 317–18.

[107] The Old Buda grave may not after all have been a solitary burial. A second, most likely disturbed burial was found in the 'Porticoed Building' between 15 and 20 m from the first grave. The orientation of the grave pit was west–east, but the date of the burial could not be established for no grave goods have been found.

WHERE DID ALL THE GEPIDS GO? A SIXTH- TO SEVENTH-CENTURY CEMETERY IN BRATEI (ROMANIA)

Radu Harhoiu

When defeated, barbarians tend to be neglected. This is particularly true for the archaeology of the Gepids during the Avar age. The defeat of the Gepids by a Lombard-Avar alliance in 567 is regarded by many as a crucial event in the medieval history of East Central Europe. The migration of the Lombards to Italy and the subsequent conquest of the Carpathian Basin by the Avars play the role of a major historical watershed.[1] But what happened to the defeated Gepids? Were they annihilated, or did they melt into the ethnic conglomerate of the early Avar qaganate? Was there any sense of Gepid identity left in the aftermath of the Avar occupation of the Carpathian Basin? According to Theophylact Simocatta, there were still Gepids in Pannonia who lived in their own villages, when the Roman general Peter campaigned against the Avars in the region of the Lower Tisza River.[2] For a long time, however, the archaeological record appears to be at variance with the written sources, as it pointed to the discontinuity of occupation on many burial sites in the Tisza Plain, which had been occupied

---

[1] Walter Pohl, *Die Awaren: Ein Steppenvolk im Mitteleuropa 567–822 n. Chr.* (Munich, 1988), pp. 52–57.

[2] Theophylact Simocatta, *History*, 8.3.8–15, ed. by Carl de Boor and Peter Wirth (Stuttgart, 1972), pp. 288–89. There were Gepids in the Avar army which laid siege to Constantinople in 626. See Theophanes Confessor, *Chronographia*, AM 6117, ed. by Carl de Boor, vol. I (Leipzig, 1883), p. 315. See Walter Pohl, 'Die Gepiden und die Gentes an der mittleren Donau nach dem Zerfall des Attillareiches', in *Die Völker an der mittleren und unteren Donau im fünften und sechsten Jahrhundert: Berichte des Symposions der Kommission für Frühmittelalterforschung, 24.–27. Oktober 1978, Stift Zwettl, Niederösterreich*, ed. by Herwig Wolfram and Falko Daim (Vienna, 1980), pp. 239–305 (p. 300).

during the heyday of the sixth-century Gepid kingdom.[3] Some persisted in dating to the late sixth or even early seventh century several assemblages attributed to a 'Germanic' population and excavated in the early 1900s in Transylvania.[4] During the 1970s, the debate surrounding the interpretation of the finds from the Avar-age cemetery excavated in Környe in Hungary brought to the fore the issue of the Gepid survival in the aftermath of the Avar conquest.[5] The Hungarian archaeologist István Bóna first advanced the idea of a specifically Gepid culture of the Avar age, which according to him was illustrated primarily by finds from sites excavated in Transylvania.[6] Foremost among those sites is the cemetery excavated in Bratei.

The archaeological investigations in Bratei (Sibiu district, Transylvania, Romania) began in 1959 with a trial excavation at a site known as 'La Zăvoi', which is located on the left bank of the Târnava Mare River, at a distance of about 1 km to the east from the village. The results of the trial excavation proved to be so successful as to open no less than thirty years of continuous research of a 4 km stretch of the Târnava Mare river bank (Figure 7.1).

Systematic excavations were also carried out at the site of the sand quarry known as 'La Nisipuri' or 'Rogoaze' by Ion Nestor, accompanied by Eugenia Zaharia and Ligia Bârzu, as well as numerous students at the University of Bucharest. Those excavations led to the unearthing of two large settlements dated between the fourth and the thirteenth centuries, as well as of three cemeteries, of which the third one

---

[3] See, however, the remarks of Joachim Werner in his review of D. Csallány, *Archäologische Denkmäler der Gepiden im Mitteldonaubecken* (Budapest, 1961), in *Bonner Jahrbücher*, 167 (1967), 498–500 (p. 500).

[4] Kurt Horedt, 'Das Awarenproblem in Rumänien', *Študijné zvesti*, 16 (1968), 103–20 (p. 112); Kurt Horedt, 'Der östliche Reihengräberkreis in Siebenbürgen', *Dacia*, 21 (1977), 251–68 (p. 263); Kurt Horedt, 'Die Völker Südosteuropas im 6. bis 8. Jahrhundert: Probleme und Ereignisse', in *Die Völker Südosteuropas im 6. bis 8. Jahrhundert*, ed. by B. Hänsel (Berlin, 1987), pp. 11–26 (p. 13).

[5] Ágnes Salamon and István Erdélyi, *Das völkerwanderungszeitliche Gräberfeld von Környe* (Budapest, 1971). See also Max Martin, review of A. Salamon and I. Erdélyi, *Das völkerwanderungszeitliche Gräberfeld von Környe* (Budapest, 1971), in *Zeitschrift für schweizerische Archäologie und Kunstgeschichte*, 30 (1972), 110–12 (pp. 111–12); Hans Bott, 'Bemerkungen zum Datierungsproblem awarenzeitlicher Funde in Pannonien vorgelegt am Beispiel des Gräberfeldes von Környe', *Bonner Jahrbücher*, 176 (1976), 201–80 (p. 277).

[6] István Bóna, *Der Anbruch des Mittelalters: Gepiden und Langobarden im Karpatenbecken* (Budapest, 1976), pp. 20–21; István Bóna, 'Gepiden in Siebenbürgen – Gepiden an der Theiss (Probleme der Forschungsmethode und Fundinterpretation)', *Acta Archaeologica Academiae Scientiarum Hungaricae*, 31 (1979), 9–50 (pp. 37–44).

produced 294 inhumations over a period of six years (1964–69) (Figure 7.1). However, work in the sand quarry had already destroyed and continued to destroy large portions of both settlements and cemeteries. Knowledge of some one hundred graves of the third cemetery may thus have been lost in the process. Ligia Bârzu had begun the preparation of the monographic treatment of cemetery III for publication in the *Archaeologia Romanica* series but died

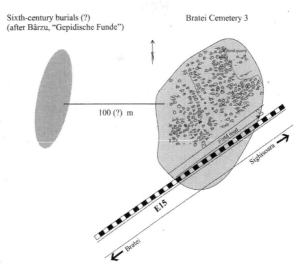

Figure 7.1. Bratei, cemetery III and sixth-century stray finds about 100 m away from the western edge of the cemetery (after Bârzu, 'Gepidische Funde').

before seeing the project through. It behooves the present author to bring that project to fruition.

Mortuary Practices

A common feature with most burials in the cemetery is single inhumation, with double burials recorded as exceptional. In certain areas, such as that in the northwest which is devoid of any graves, there is a clear discontinuity in burial activity. On the other hand, this is also to be explained at least in part as a consequence of the illegal quarrying of sand, which may have led to the destruction of many graves. Most surviving grave pits are over 1 meter deep, with skeletons lying in supine position, with arms stretched along the body. The only exception from the general west–east orientation are the horse graves, in which the animals have been deposed with heads to the east-north-east (Figure 7.2).

That the deceased were accompanied by food offerings results from the deposition of hand- and wheel-made ceramic containers, often either near the head or in the shoulder area. In fact, ceramic containers have been found in thirty-four cases near the head or in the shoulder area, whereas in another thirty-five cases pots were placed by the feet. These were small containers, such as pitchers, cups, or pots, most likely produced for the occasion. The rule seems to have been for a single-container

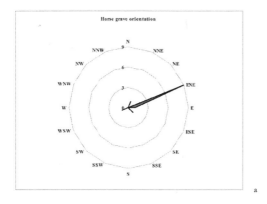

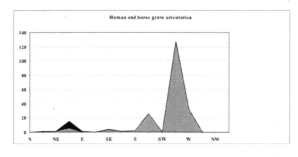

Figure 7.2. Bratei. Horse (a) and human and horse (b) grave orientation.

deposition, as indicated by the fact that while seventy-four graves had one ceramic container each, only seven graves produced pairs of containers. Equally common seems to have been the deposition of knives, which appear in seventy-two graves, and flint steels, which are documented in twenty-one graves. In addition, the graves in cemetery III produced six swords, four daggers, nine spear heads, and fifty-four arrow heads. A particularly interesting feature of this cemetery is the deposition of horse skeletons, sometimes accompanied by handmade pots.

Pottery thus occupied an important place among grave goods of cemetery III. Handmade pots are typically elongated, watermelon-shaped, oval, or slightly rounded vessels. The wheel-made wares are represented by large, flask-like, baggy vessels without handles or by pitchers and jugs.

Most personal accessories are combs, earrings with overlapping ends or with spiral ends, earrings with grape-shaped, bead-shaped, or star-shaped pendant, as well as diadems. Such earrings are often associated with necklaces, pendants, some of which are either trapeze- or diamond-shaped, medallions, or even pectoral crosses. Worth mentioning among accessories are also glass beads with eye-shaped inlays as well as amber beads. Worn in pairs were bow fibulae with three, five, or even seven knobs on the head-plate. Buckles come in different shapes and combinations: oval buckles with no plate, as well as buckles cast into a single piece or hinged specimens, the latter most likely of Byzantine origin. There are also buckles with elongated or heart-shaped plate, B-shaped loop and heart-shaped plate with ornament in the so-called Animal Style II, shield-shaped plate, and cross-shaped plate, as well as buckles of the Syracuse and Sucidava classes. Such buckles were employed for belts to which belonged also gag-shaped clasps (the so-called *Knebel-verschlüsse*),[7] strap ends and mounts, some of which are equally decorated with ornamental patterns in Animal Style II.

By far the most numerous among weapons are leaf-shaped, three-edged, or bifurcated arrow heads, followed at a distance by spear heads and swords. The horse gear is represented by rectangular or 8-shaped buckles with no plate, bridle bit rings or cheek pieces, some of which were carved in bone, and strap distributors. The stirrups have typically short loops.

The systematic robbing of the cemetery prevents a seriation of the burial assemblages, which may be further used to draw broad conclusions about chronology and social stratification. In order to circumvent this problem, I have tried to apply a chorological analysis focusing on specific details of ritual or on specific artefacts, in order to gain some understanding of the underlying structure of the cemetery and of its chronology. On the other hand, detailed excavation records and grave plans are of great assistance for the identification of the robbing methods employed for many graves. However, in the absence of such records the identification must remain tentative. On the fringes of cemetery III in Bratei, robbers operated by digging shafts closely following the contours of the grave pits (Figure 7.3). In the south-western sector of the cemetery, there is a cluster of robbing shafts dug into the central area of the grave pit. In any case, this robbing technique suggests that the robbing had taken place not long after burial, as the contour of the grave pit was still visible. A much broader distribution have the robbing shafts cutting across the grave pit (Figure 7.3). The cluster of such robbing pits in the south-western area of the cemetery may indicate that the robbed grave pits had been dug a long time before robbing took place. The south-western area of the cemetery is conspicuously marked by robbing pits dug into a limited part of the grave or along an axis different from that of the grave pit (Figure 7.4). The latter technique is also an indication that the contour of the much older grave pit was not visible anymore at the time of the robbing. On the other hand, one should not exclude the possibility that even burials that have been robbed by means of pits dug more or less along the contour of the grave were 'old' at the time of the robbing, but had been marked until then by some sign above the ground, the maintenance of which may have been the pious task of several members of the deceased person's family. In fact, no burial escaped robbing in some form or degree, and thoroughly robbed burials have

---

[7] Mechthild Schulze-Dörrlamm, 'Byzantinische Knebelverschlüsse des frühen Mittelalters', *Germania*, 80 (2002), 571–93.

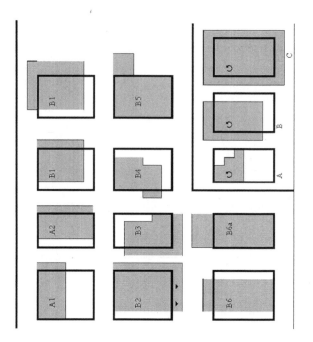

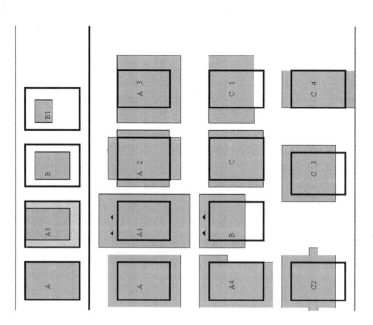

Figure 7.3 (left). Bratei, robbing shaft variation.
Figure 7.4 (above). Bratei, robbing shaft variation.

a random distribution all across the cemetery. By contrast, burials robbed in the upper part of the grave pit (down to the waist line of the skeleton) cluster in the southern and northern areas of the eastern and, to a lesser extent, of the western sectors of the cemetery.

Particularly interesting is the distribution of graves which have been robbed in the upper part (chest or waist) of the deposed skeleton. Together with robbed horse burials, male burials robbed in the chest area are to be found mainly on the fringes of the cemetery, while burials robbed around the waist region, although still peripheral, form a middle axis across the cemetery together with other burials. Whether this may be seen as a dividing line between the western and the eastern parts of the cemetery remains a hypothesis awaiting further confirmation. Burials robbed at the level of the groin cluster loosely in the north-eastern area and somewhat more compactly in the south-western part of the cemetery. Such difficulties in identifying patterns of burial robbing are only partially alleviated by the general state of skeleton preservation. Not many bones were found in anatomical position in any of the graves excavated in the cemetery. Only a few skeletons have been sufficiently well preserved to allow analysis. However, these are skeletons of humans and horses buried on the fringes of the cemetery and, as a consequence, offer little help in analysis. Skeletons without skulls are scattered randomly across the cemetery.

By contrast, there is a cluster in the south-eastern and south-western areas of the cemetery of graves with chest, arm, pelvis, and leg bones in anatomical position — a situation which points to a less thorough robbing of the burial — and, even more so, of those with only arm, pelvis, and leg bones in anatomical position, which indicates a much more thorough robbing of the burial at the level of the chest. Graves with only arm and leg bones in anatomical position, for which robbing seems to have concentrated in the groin area, have an equally random distribution across the cemetery. That the upper part of the burial pit was more often the target of the robbers is also indicated by the preservation in anatomical position of pelvis and leg bones. Such burials, however, do not cluster in any particular region of the cemetery, although there are slightly more examples in the south-east than in the south-west.

That the robbing took place soon after burial is also betrayed by bones found in anatomical connection, which appear in peripheral graves, especially in the south, and in which either the chest or the groin area was the target of the robbers. Worth mentioning at this point is also the strong association between robbing shafts closely following the contour of the grave pits and burials in which parts of the human or horse skeleton have been found in anatomical connection. The

ability of the robbers to follow precisely the contour of the grave pit and the anatomical connection are good indications that the reopening of the grave took place
shortly after burial. Nevertheless, a chorological analysis of the Bratei cemetery
produced no pattern and no regularities in the process or methods of robbing. I can
only suggest tentatively that, except cases in which the entire skeleton was so
thoroughly robbed that no bones survived, the majority of the graves have been
sounded by robbers at some point between the skull and the groin area and that
often the robbing took place shortly after burial. But the existing evidence does not
allow any distinction between robbing properly speaking (i.e. opening the grave in
order to plunder its content) and reopening of the grave for some other, perhaps
ritual reasons. On the other hand, the systematic robbing of practically all burials
in the cemetery suggests that this was by no means an exceptional practice in the
eyes of the surviving members of that community. It remains unclear whether the
robbing took place before that community abandoned its settlement in order to
move some place else and whether it was carried out by the very members of that
community.

A number of details stand out among the results of a careful analysis of burial
details: the purification of the grave pit, the layer of soil on the bottom of the pit,
and the use of wooden planks for some form of grave furniture. Even though the
thorough robbing of the graves deprived us of an understanding of social differences within the community, the cluster of all three details mentioned above in the
western area of the cemetery betrays clear differences between 'burial sectors' and
a differential treatment of the dead with possibly social implications (Figure 7.5).
This is further substantiated by the different orientation, with graves in the south-
west–north-west direction clustering in the western region of the cemetery. In the
east, besides horse graves with a north-east-north or east-north-east orientation,
graves were found in which skeletons were buried in a north-east-north, north-east,
or south-east direction (Figure 7.6). The contrast between the eastern and the
western halves of the cemetery is further strengthened by an examination of surviving grave goods. There are more graves in the west than in the east, which were
either completely empty or, in the absence of bones, produced only ceramic pots
and could thus be interpreted as cenotaphs. By contrast, most graves with no bones
or associated grave goods have been found in the east. Moreover, the east produced
all horse graves and six human burials with horse bones, as well as all other human
burials that also contained animal bones. In the west, such burials are either rare
or altogether absent, respectively.

In other respects, the contrast between east and west is not so stark. For example,
in regards to the specific position of ceramic pots inside the grave pit, there seems

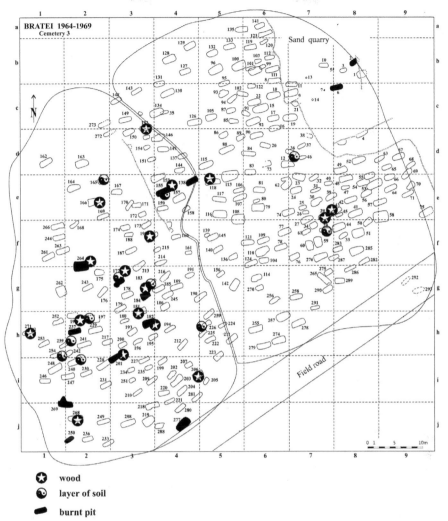

Figure 7.5. Bratei, grave pit structure.

to be no clear-cut pattern, except for a slight contrast between the deposition of pots by the head, which is much more uniformly distributed within the cemetery than deposition of the pot by the feet, which occurs primarily on the periphery. A similar conclusion may be drawn from the examination of weapon deposition. Burials with arrow heads are randomly distributed across the cemetery, but those with spear heads appear primarily on the periphery in direct association with horse graves, while graves with swords are to be found either in the south-east or in the south-west.

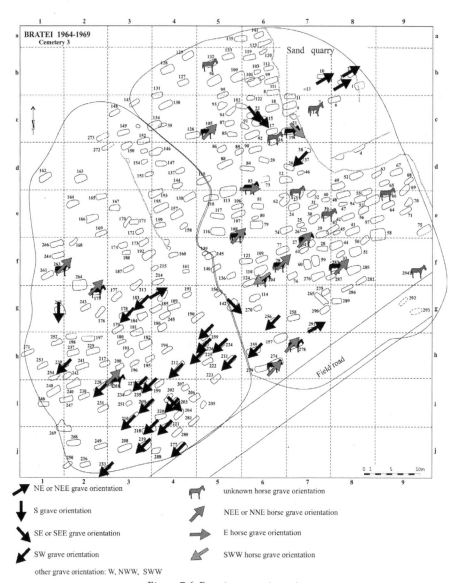

Figure 7.6. Bratei, grave orientation.

A more detailed analysis of the distribution of artefact categories may help us understand better the difference between the two areas of the cemetery. Unlike burials with wheel-made ceramic pots, those with handmade pots appear primarily in the east, again in association with horse graves. In the west, handmade pottery is only sporadically documented on the very edge of the cemetery. Together with horse graves, handmade pottery thus represents an important element of building a difference between the eastern and western regions of the cemetery. This is further substantiated by an examination of the distribution of pitchers and jugs, which have been recorded especially in the western half of the cemetery (Figure 7.7). The distributions of such vessels and of handmade pottery or horse graves are mutually exclusive. Combs appear especially in the eastern and only on the edges of the western region, another marker of difference.

This is also true for the distribution of earrings, with a clear concentration in the eastern region especially of those with blunt or spiral ends (Figure 7.8). Furthermore, glass beads with eye-shaped inlays and amber beads appear primarily in the east (Figure 7.9). By contrast, burials with bow fibulae are almost exclusively in the west. Further arguments for a west-east division of the cemetery may be found through the examination of the distribution of buckles and belt mounts. While buckles without plates, but with oval or U-shaped loops have been found especially in the east, buckles with massive round loops are more often found in graves located in the west (Figure 7.10). That buckles without plates but with rectangular or 8-shaped loops appear only in the east and in association with horse skeletons can only be explained as an indication that such buckles were part of the horse gear (Figure 7.11). However, they also appear in the east in human graves and may have therefore been a distinctive artefact category. By contrast, buckles with plates or with strap distributor, with stick-like plate or with gag-shaped clasp have no localized distribution. Nevertheless, much like bow fibulae, such buckles appear primarily in the west, or on the western edge of the eastern half of the cemetery.

Similarly, arrow heads with diamond-shaped blade have been documented more in the west, while in the east they occupy a peripheral position. There is a small number of other kinds of weapons, none of which has any significant distribution, although all have been documented in graves located in the southern regions of both halves. As already mentioned, despite systematic robbing of all horse graves, the deposition of horse gear is a particular feature of the eastern half of the cemetery. That conclusion is strengthened by the fact that in graves without much horse gear, the robbers left behind the spear heads, a situation which may indicate that the deposition of horse gear depended upon specific ritual requirements (Figure 7.12).

The chorological observations thus confirm the idea of a division of the cemetery into a western and an eastern half, each with specific burial rites and specific grave goods. Judging from the large number of horse graves, the deposition of handmade pottery, of buckles with rectangular loop, of earrings with spiral ends, or in direct relation to horse graves, of horse gear, burials in the eastern half of the

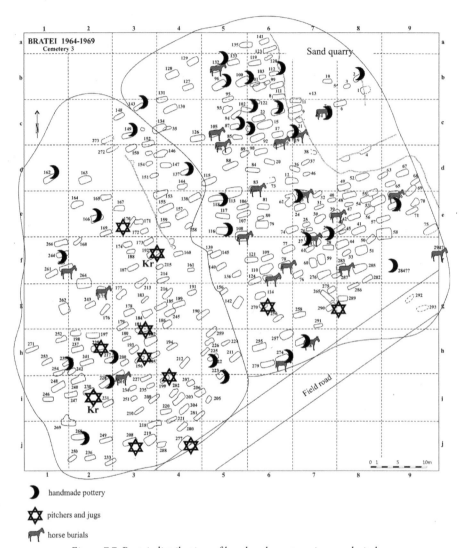

Figure 7.7. Bratei, distribution of handmade pottery, jugs, and pitchers
in relation to that of horse graves.

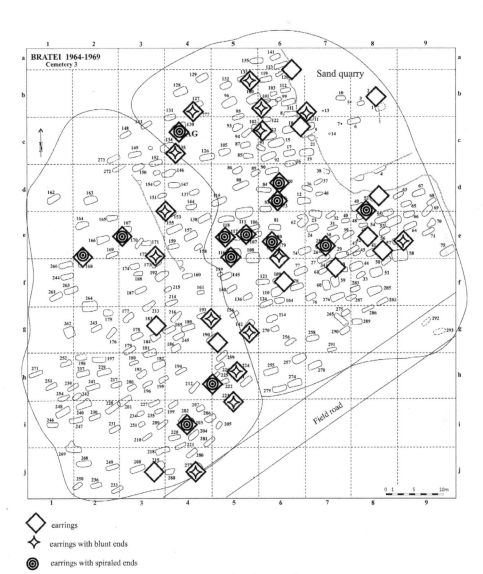

Figure 7.8. Bratei, distribution of earrings.

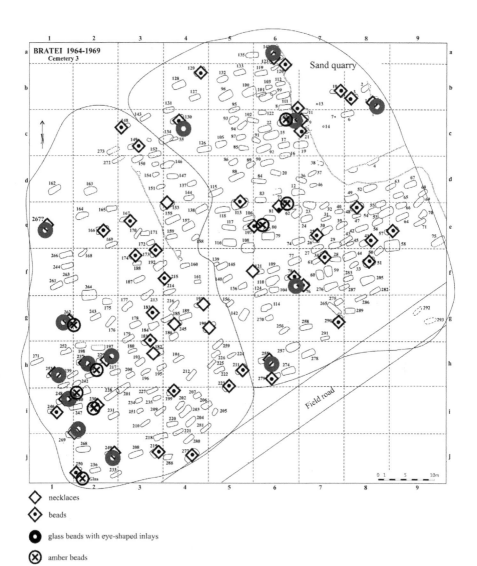

Figure 7.9. Bratei, distribution of beads.

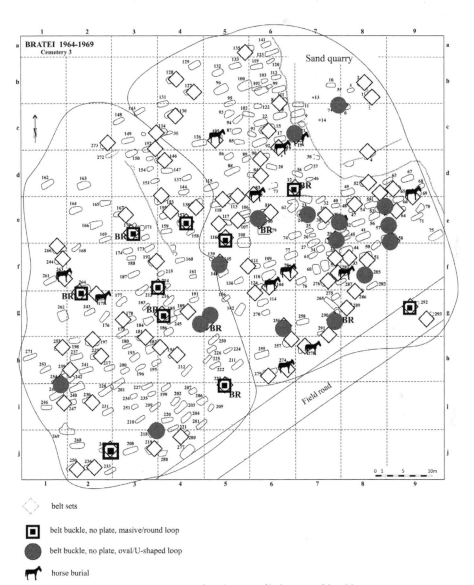

Figure 7.10. Bratei, distribution of belt sets and buckles.

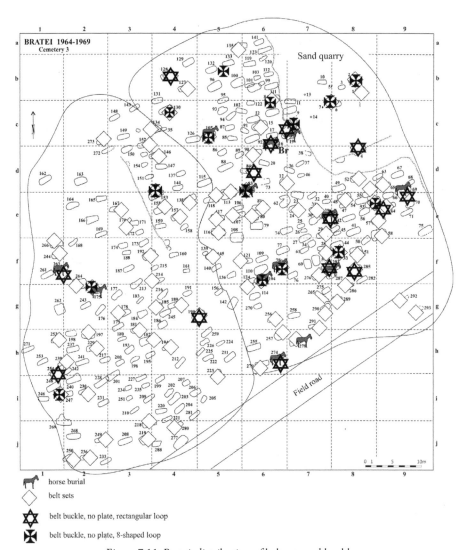

Figure 7.11. Bratei, distribution of belt sets and buckles.

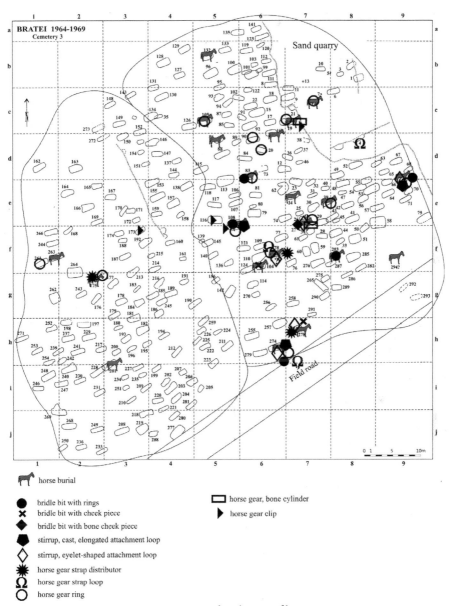

Figure 7.12. Bratei, distribution of horse gear.

cemetery may well be of a more recent date than those in the west. Burials in the western half produced evidence of a special treatment of the grave pit, pitchers and jugs, bow fibulae, and (Byzantine) buckles with plates of a variety of shapes. That Avar-age glass beads with eye-shaped inlays appear in the west only on the periphery may also be seen as an indication of an earlier date for the western half of the cemetery. If the coin struck for Emperor Justinian, which was found in grave 190, may be seen as chronologically significant, then it may be used to gauge the approximate date for the graves in the western half of the Bratei cemetery. It is important to note that there is no distinct border between the two halves of the cemetery (Figure 7.13). The lines of contrast drawn above are to be understood tentatively and not in absolute terms. In short, the cemetery seems to have developed gradually from west to east.

Chronology

In order to find an approximate date for the beginning of cemetery III at Bratei, it is necessary first to take a broader look at sixth- and seventh-century burial assemblages in Transylvania (see Figure 7.14 below). After the excavation of the Moreşti cemetery (Appendix, no. 29), it became clear that those assemblages can be divided into two chronological groups. The first to note the two groups was Kurt Horedt, whose studies later refined and strengthened that idea.[8] He assigned to the earliest group (Horedt's group III) a number of artefact types, such as bow fibulae with chip-carved or concentric-circle ornament, earrings with polyhedral pendant, eagle-headed buckles, buckles with rectangular plate and cloisonné ornament, weapons (swords, sax, shields, three-edged or leaf-shaped arrow heads, spear heads), tools (scrapers and scissors), double-layered combs, and a few ceramic pots.[9] Both artefact types and burial features display remarkable similarities with contemporary assemblages in the Tisza Plain, which have been interpreted as the archaeological

---

[8] Kurt Horedt, 'Die befestigte Ansiedlung von Moreşti und ihre frühgeschichtliche Bedeutung', *Dacia*, 1 (1957), 298–308 (p. 304); Kurt Horedt, *Untersuchungen zur Frühgeschichte Siebenbürgens* (Bucharest, 1958), pp. 97–107; Kurt Horedt, 'Der östliche Reihengräberkreis in Siebenbürgen', *Dacia*, 21 (1977), 251–68 (pp. 258–63 for his chronological groups III and IV); Kurt Horedt, *Moreşti: Grabungen in einer vor- und frühgeschichtlichen Siedlung in Siebenbürgen* (Bucharest, 1979), pp. 100–01. See also Radu Harhoiu, 'Quellenlage und Forschungsstand der Frühgeschichte Siebenbürgens im 6.–7. Jahrhunderts', *Dacia*, 43–45 (1999–2001), 97–158 (pp. 122–25).

[9] Horedt's group I is dated to the late Roman period, while his group II includes assemblages dated primarily to the late fourth and early fifth centuries.

correlate of the sixth-century Gepid polities on the basis of such things as the distribution of eagle-headed buckles.[10] As a consequence, Horedt's group III cannot be dated later than the destruction of the Gepid kingdom by the Avars in the late 560s.[11] New burial sites, which belong to Horedt's group IV, appear during the subsequent period. Those were cemeteries with large numbers of graves, many of which were warrior graves with new types of weapons (helmets and bifurcated arrow heads). Although, for example, the deposition of planes (*Hackmesser*) and scissors continued from group III, grave goods of Horedt's group IV are substantially different from those of the previous period. There are many more ceramic pots; buckles and belt mounts (strap ends, shield-on-tongue buckles, Byzantine

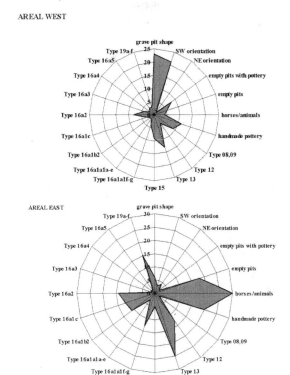

Figure 7.13. Bratei, the distribution of artefact categories in the two cemetery areas.

[10] István Bóna, *The Dawn of the Dark Ages: The Gepids and the Lombards in the Carpathian Basin* (Budapest, 1976). See also Margit Nagy, 'Die gepidischen Adlerschnallen und ihre Beziehungen', *Budapest Régiségei*, 36 (2002), 363–92. For burial assemblages in the Tisza Plain attributed to the Gepids, see now István Bóna and Margit Nagy, *Gepidische Gräberfelder am Theissgebiet*, I (Budapest, 2002) and János Cseh and others, *Gepidische Gräberfelder im Theissgebiet*, II (Budapest, 2005).

[11] Dezső Csallány, *Archäologische Denkmäler der Gepiden im Mitteldonaubecken (454–568 u.Z.)* (Budapest, 1961), pp. 320–21; Maria Comşa and Doina Ignat, 'Gräber aus dem 6. Jh. in Mediaş', *Dacia*, 15 (1971), 349–51 (p. 351); Dorin Popescu, 'Das gepidische Gräberfeld von Moreşti', *Dacia*, 18 (1974), 189–238 (pp. 213–14); István Bóna, 'Gepiden in Siebenbürgen – Gepiden an der Theiss (Probleme der Forschungsmethode und Fundinterpretation)', *Acta Archaeologica Academiae Scientiarum Hungaricae*, 31 (1979), 9–50 (p. 19).

buckles, buckles with damascened decoration), some of which were produced *au repoussé*; dress accessories ornamented in animal or dentil (*Zahnschnitt*) style; new earring types (such as earrings with bead or star-shaped pendant); and horse gear elements often associated with either entire skeletons or parts of horse bodies. Horedt dated his group IV to the seventh century, mostly to its first half,[12] but in any case no later than the middle or the third quarter of that century.[13]

For some time scholars did not seem to have noticed that Horedt's groups were separated by some thirty-odd years (*c.* 570 to 600). The gap was for the first time brought to light by the excavators of the large cemetery in Környe.[14] The damascened belt mounts found in Unirea-Vereșmort (Appendix, no. 44) and the dentil ornament of the finger ring found in grave 39 from the Band cemetery (Appendix, no. 5) bespeak a rather early dating, most likely to the second half of the sixth century or around AD 600. Max Martin has already shown the differences between those artefacts and their West European analogies pointing to a date around 600.[15] Similarly, Hans Bott wrote of exemplary products of a sixth- to seventh-century 'school' of damascened dress accessories.[16] Analysing the damascened belt mounts found in Kőlked-Feketekapu, Max Martin demonstrated that the mounts of his group A, to which one must also assign the Unirea-Vereșmort specimens, were manufactured in the Carpathian Basin, *c.* 600.[17]

---

[12] Many of the features listed by Horedt may be easily recognized at Bratei: large number of burials, warrior burials, deposition of ceramic pots in large numbers, belt sets (including Byzantine buckles), animal-style decoration, earrings with bead and star-shaped pendant, and deposition of horses or horse body parts, together with horse gear.

[13] Horedt, 'Das Awarenproblem', p. 112, where Band and Târgu Mureș may however be dated somewhat earlier, namely around 650; Horedt, 'Der östliche Reihengräberkreis', pp. 261–63.

[14] Salamon and Erdélyi, *Das völkerwanderungszeitliche Gräberfeld*.

[15] Max Martin, 'Awarische und germanische Funde in Männergräbern von Linz-Zizlau und Környe: Ein Beitrag zur Chronologie der Awarenzeit', *Wosinszky Mór Múzeum Évkönyve*, 15 (1990), 65–90 (pp. 69–70); see also Bott, 'Bemerkungen', p. 219.

[16] Bott, 'Bemerkungen', p. 214.

[17] Max Martin, 'Zu den tauschierten Gürtelgarnituren und Gürtelteilen der Männergräber von Kölked-Feketekapu A', in *Das awarenzeitlich gepidische Gräberfeld von Kölked-Feketekapu A*, ed. by Attila Kiss (Innsbruck, 1996), pp. 345–61 (pp. 346–50). See also Max Martin, 'Tauschierte Gürtelgarnituren und -beschläge des frühen Mittelalters im Karpatenbecken und ihre Träger', in *Ethnische und kulturelle Verhältnisse an der mittleren Donau vom 6. bis zum 11. Jahrhundert: Symposium Nitra 6. bis 10. November 1994*, ed. by Darina Bialeková and Jozef Zábojník (Bratislava, 1996), pp. 63–74. See also Orsolya Heinrich-Tamáska, *Studien zu den awarenzeitlichen Tauschierarbeiten* (Innsbruck, 2005).

The first to gather evidence against Horedt's idea of a chasm between his groups III and IV was the Hungarian archaeologist István Bóna.[18] He pointed out that the beginnings of the Band cemetery (Appendix, no. 5) are to be dated to the second half of the sixth century because of the earring with bead pendant from grave 141, a type which is also documented in grave 219 from Bratei and a number of other burial assemblages in the Tisza Plain, as well as western Hungary, Ukraine, and the Caucasus region. In the Middle Danube region, such earrings are coin-dated to the first half of the seventh century.[19] Equally datable to the second half of the sixth century is the fragment of the *au repoussé* belt mount from grave 150 in Band, as well as the padlock from grave 149 with good analogies in Poysdorf (Austria) and Tamási (Hungary), the bronze or silver belt mounts with four rivets, and the mount decorated in Animal Style I B from grave 174.[20] Nándor Fettich has already pointed out that the finger ring from grave 39 in Band (Appendix, no. 5) is an example of the 'Germanic' animal style to be dated after the conquest of Pannonia by the Avars.[21] Hans Bott viewed it as one of the best examples of the 'tooth-carved' ornament harking back to Germanic decorative patterns.[22] Even the articulated buckle with B-shaped loop and heart-shaped plate decorated in Animal Style II may be compared to the second group of dress accessories with Animal Style II decoration to be dated to the late sixth and early seventh centuries.[23] The

[18] Bóna, 'Gepiden in Siebenbürgen', pp. 37–40.

[19] István Kovács, 'A mezöbándi ásatások: Őskori telepnyomok és temető, La-Tène ízlésü temetkezés, népvándorláskori temető', *Dolgozatok az Erdélyi Nemzeti Múzeum Érem- és Régiségtárából*, 4 (1913), 265–329 (p. 346 fig. 66.4); Bóna, 'Gepiden in Siebenbürgen', p. 43; Attila Kiss, *Das awarenzeitlich-gepidische Gräberfeld von Kölked-Feketekapu A* (Innsbruck, 1996), p. 193; Éva Garam, 'Die münzdatierten Gräber der Awarenzeit', in *Awarenforschungen*, ed. by Falko Daim (Vienna, 1992), pp. 135–250 (pp. 148–49); Vera B. Kovalevskaia, 'Severokavkazkie drevnosti', in *Stepi evrazii v epokhu srednevekov'ia* (Moscow, 1981), pp. 83–97 and 173–87 (p. 169 fig. 62.133 and 143); Evgenii V. Veimarn and Aleksandr I. Aibabin, *Skalistinskii mogil'nik* (Kiev, 1993), p. 55 fig. 35.9–10.

[20] Bóna, 'Gepiden in Siebenbürgen', pp. 42–45. According to Günther Haseloff (*Die germanische Tierornamentik der Völkerwanderungszeit: Studien zu Salin's Stil I* (Berlin, 1981)), the Animal Style I B cannot be dated after *c.* 570.

[21] Nándor Fettich, *Az avarkori mûipár Magyarországon: Fogazási ornamentika és ötvöseszközleletek* (Budapest, 1926), pp. 47–48.

[22] Bott, 'Bemerkungen', p. 242.

[23] Margit Nagy, 'Frühawarenzeitliche Grabfunde aus Budapest: Bemerkungen zur awarenzeit-lichen Tierornamentik', in *Popoli delle steppe: Unni, Avari, Ungari*, I (Spoleto, 1988), pp. 373–407 (pp. 385–87). See also Kiss, *Das awarenzeitlich-gepidische Gräberfeld*, pp. 259–61.

finds of glass beads with eye-shaped inlays can also speak for a date in the Early
Avar period.[24] The silver trapeze-shaped pendant from grave 269 and the silver or
bronze diamond-shaped sheet pendants from graves 1 and 173 belong to a rather
common artefact-category of late sixth- and early seventh-century assemblages in
both the Middle Dnieper and the Middle Danube regions and may have been local
imitations of Byzantine dress accessories.[25]

Further indications of a date within the second half of the sixth century may be
obtained from the examination of fibulae. One of the commonest fibulae found in
burial assemblages in Transylvania is the so-called 'Slavic' bow fibula. Specimens
of this group of fibulae first identified and labelled 'Slavic' by Joachim Werner[26]
have been found on no less than eight sites in Transylvania. Cemetery III in Bratei
produced several specimens of Werner's classes I C, I D, I G, and I H.[27] Werner

[24] Horst W. Böhme, 'Der Awarenfriedhof von Alattyán, Kom. Szolnok', *Südost-Forschungen*,
24 (1965), 11–65 (pp. 6–7 and 41 map 2).

[25] Éva Garam, *Funde byzantinischer Herkunft in der Awarenzeit vom Ende des 6. bis zum Ende
des 7. Jahrhunderts* (Budapest, 2001), pp. 45–47 and 36 fig. 3; for Early Avar specimens in western
Hungary, see Garam, *Funde*, p. 275 pl. 24. 1–6. For a detailed discussion of the Ukrainian
specimens, see Igor O. Gavritukhin and A. M. Oblomskii, *Gaponovskii klad i ego kul'turno-
istoricheskii kontekst* (Moscow, 1996).

[26] Joachim Werner, 'Slawische Bügelfibeln des 7. Jahrhunderts', in *Reinecke Festschrift zum 75.
Geburtstag von Paul Reinecke am 25. September 1947*, ed. by G. Behrens and Joachim Werner
(Mainz, 1950), pp. 150–72; Joachim Werner, 'Neues zur Frage der slawischen Bügelfibeln aus süd-
osteuropäischen Ländern', *Germania*, 38 (1960), 114–20.

[27] Specimens found in Transylvania belong to different groups of Werner's classification. Those
found in Războieni-Cetate (Kurt Horedt, *Siebenbürgen im Frühmittelalter* (Bonn, 1986), p. 93 fig.
44.7), an unknown location in Transylvania (Horedt, *Untersuchungen*, pp. 93 and 91 fig. 28.5),
and Vețel (Horedt, *Siebenbürgen*, p. 93 fig. 44.7) are all specimens of Werner's group I B
(=Teodor's type 1.1; see Dan Gh. Teodor, 'Fibule "digitate" din secolele VI–VII în spațiul carpato-
dunăreano-pontic', *Arheologia Moldovei*, 15 (1992), 119–52 (p. 137)). This is Curta's Vețel-
Coșoveni class, for which see Florin Curta, 'On the Dating of the "Vețel-Coșoveni" Group of
Curved Fibulae', *Ephemeris Napocensis*, 4 (1994), 233–65. The fibulae found in Gâmbaș (Appendix, no. 22) and Cornești (Appendix, no. 12) belong to Werner's class I C (=Teodor's type 1.2.1;
see Teodor, 'Fibule "digitate"', p. 137). The fragmentary brooch found in Filiaș has been classified
as belonging to Curta's type Pietroasele (=Werner I F). See Zoltán Székely, 'Sud-estul Transilvaniei
în secolele VI–XIII', *Aluta*, 6–7 (1974–75), 57–71 (p. 39 with pl. 9.10); Florin Curta and Vasile
Dupoi, 'Über die Bügelfibel aus Pietroasele und ihre Verwandten', *Dacia*, 38–39 (1994–95),
217–38. Finally, the fibula from Sarmizegetusa is a specimen of Werner's class I G. See Csallány,
Archäologische Denkmäler, p. 196 with pl. 216.1–1a; Florin Curta, *The Making of the Slavs: History
and Archaeology of the Lower Danube Region, ca. 500–700* (Cambridge, 2001), pp. 247–45. For
Werner's class I H, see now Florin Curta, 'Werner's Class I H of "Slavic" Bow Fibulae Revisited',

thought that such dress accessories were index fossils for the migration of the Slavs to and across the Lower Danube in the course of the seventh century.[28] Later, he seems to have accepted an earlier date in the second half of the sixth century and the early 600s.[29] Dan Gh. Teodor also placed chronologically many fibulae of his type I into the first half of the seventh or the second half of the sixth century.[30] Uwe Fiedler narrowed the dating to the last quarter of the sixth century.[31] Florin Curta proposed a date as early as the first half of the sixth century, in any case excluding a dating to the seventh century, which seems to be right in the light of the existing evidence.[32]

A late sixth-century dating of cemetery III in Bratei is also supported by buckles of the Syracuse class,[33] by buckles with oval loop and U-shaped plate,[34] as well as by

Archaeologia Bulgarica, 8 (2004), 59–78. For Werner's class I D, see Florin Curta, '*Slavic* Bow Fibulae? Werner's Class I D Revisited', *Acta Archaeologica Academiae Scientiarum Hungaricae*, 57 (2006), 423–74.

[28] Werner, 'Slawische Bügelfibeln', p. 168.

[29] Werner, 'Neues zur Frage', p. 114, and even more clearly in Joachim Werner, 'K proiskhozhdeniiu i raspostraneniiu antov i sklavinov', *Sovetskaia Arkheologiia*, 1972.4, 102–15 (pp. 104–05 and 104 fig. 1).

[30] Teodor, 'Fibule "digitate"', pp. 124 (first half of the seventh century for Werner's class I B, which is Teodor's I.1), 126 (second half of the sixth century for Werner's class I C, which is Teodor's I.2.2), and 128–29 (sixth to seventh century for Werner's class I G, which is Teodor's I.4).

[31] Uwe Fiedler, *Studien zu Gräberfeldern des 6. bis 9. Jahrhunderts an der unteren Donau* (Bonn, 1992), p. 103; Uwe Fiedler, 'Die Slawen im Bulgarenreich und im Awarenkhaganat: Versuch eines Vergleichs', in *Ethnische und kulturelle Verhältnisse an der mittleren Donau vom 6. bis zum 11. Jahrhundert: Symposium Nitra 6. bis 10. November 1994*, ed. by Darina Bialeková and Jozef Zábojník (Bratislava, 1996), pp. 195–214 (pp. 202–05 with a dating to the first half of the sixth century).

[32] Curta and Dupoi, 'Über die Bügelfibel aus Pietroasele', p. 233; see also Curta, *Making of the Slavs*, pp. 260–61.

[33] Joachim Werner, 'Byzantinische Gürtelschnallen des 6. und 7. Jahrhunderts aus der Samm-lung Diergardt', *Kölner Jahrbuch für Vor- und Frühgeschichte*, 1 (1955), 36–48 (pp. 37, 45–47, and 46 fig. 1).

[34] For a Byzantine origin of this class of buckles, see the specimen from grave 132 in Callatis (Mangalia), which was associated with a solidus struck for Emperor Justinian between 538 and 545. See Constantin Preda, *Callatis: Necropola romano-bizantină* (Bucharest, 1980), pp. 38, 43–44, 55, 95, 164 pl. 34, and 195 pl. 65; Fiedler, *Studien*, p. 63. For more analogies, see Dan Gh. Teodor, 'Piese vestimentare bizantine din secolele VI–VIII în spaţiul carpato-dunăreano-pontic', *Arheologia Moldovei*, 14 (1991), 117–38 (p. 132 fig. 6.8). Such buckles also appear in late sixth- and early seventh-century assemblages in Crimea; see Aleksandr I. Aibabin, 'Khronologiia mogil'nikov

buckles with open-work ornament on the plate.[35] Chronologically sensitive artefact categories are also the buckles of the Salona-Histria[36] or Pápa classes,[37] as well
as the gag-shaped clasps,[38] copper-alloy, decorated strap ends,[39] or elongated rectangular strap ends with rounded tips.[40]

The conclusion to be drawn from those considerations regarding the chronology
of various artefact categories is that cemetery III, together with such other cemeteries as Band (Appendix, no. 5), Noşlac (Appendix, no. 30), Unirea-Vereşmort
(Appendix, no. 44), Bistriţa (Appendix, no. 6), and others, belongs to the latest

---

Kryma pozdnerimskogo i rannesrednevekovogo vremeni', *Materialy po arkheologii, istorii i
etnografii Tavrii*, 1 (1990), 5–68 with fig. 39.22. They also appear in Early Avar burial assemblages
in the Middle Danube region; see Garam, *Funde*, pp. 91–93, 95 fig. 11, and 307 pl. 56.1–2, 4.

[35] This is a variant of the much larger Sucidava class, which is dated to the sixth century. See
Werner, 'Byzantinische Gürtelschnallen', pp. 42–43 and pl. 8.6–11, 46 map 1; see also Joachim
Werner, 'Byzantinisches Trachtzubehör des 6. Jahrhunderts aus Heraclea Lyncestis und Caričin
Grad', *Starinar*, 40–41 (1989–90), 273–77 (pp. 274–76); Vladimir Varsík, 'Byzantinische Gürtelschnallen im mittleren und unteren Donauraum im 6. und 7. Jahrhundert', *Slovenská Archeológia*,
40 (1992), 77–103 (pp. 78–80, 90–91, and 104 pl. 6). Buckles with open-work decoration were
common in the sixth century at opposite ends of the Balkans, e.g. at Corinth but also in Dobrudja.
See Gladys R. Davidson, *The Minor Objects* (Princeton, 1952), no. 2187; Fiedler, *Studien*, p. 35
fig. 5.10.

[36] These buckles were a most common type in the Lower Danube region, in Crimea, and in
the Tisza region, but less so on the Dalmatian coast. See Syna Uenze, 'Die Schnallen mit Riemenschlaufe aus dem 6. und 7. Jahrhundert', *Bayerische Vorgeschichtsblätter*, 31 (1966), 142–81 (pp.
142–46, 166 fig. 13, and 178–79).

[37] Uenze, 'Die Schnallen', pp. 149–52, 166 fig. 12, and 179–80.

[38] In a similar position, the gag-shaped clasps appear also in burial assemblages in Noşlac, for
which see Mircea Rusu, 'Cimitirul prefeudal de la Noşlac', in *Probleme de muzeografie* (Cluj, 1965),
pp. 32–45 with pl. 1.5. The specimens from Bratei belong to the oldest gag-shaped clasps with
cross-shaped bar, which could be dated to the late sixth or early seventh century and may have been
the source of inspiration of an imitation, which was fashionable in Western Europe during the
seventh century. See Schulze-Dörrlamm, 'Byzantinische Knebelverschlüsse', pp. 571–73 and 572
fig. 1.

[39] The specimen from grave 6 belongs to the so-called Martynivka type, which is typically
decorated with engraved lines and appears in the late sixth or early seventh century on a variety of
sites from Central Asia to Italy. See Garam, *Funde*, pp. 124–26 and 341 pl. 90.1–7.

[40] Much like the similar specimens from Kölked-Feketekapu A, those could have been the main
strap ends of the belt. See Kiss, *Das awarenzeitlich-gepidische Gräberfeld*, pp. 224–25 (type 99) and
221 fig. 36.99. For similar specimens from Tiszafüred, see Éva Garam, *Das awarenzeitliche
Gräberfeld von Tiszafüred* (Budapest, 1995), p. 189 fig. 91.1–7.

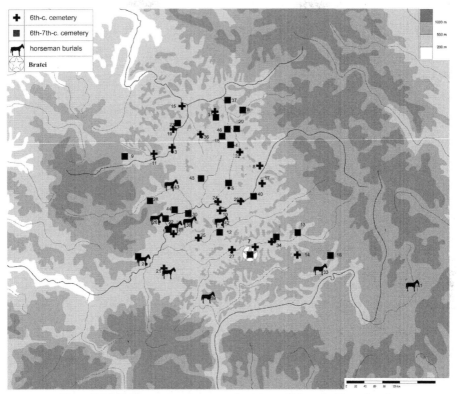

Figure 7.14. Sixth- to seventh-century burial assemblages in Transylvania.
The star marks the site of Bratei. All numbers refer to the appendix.

'row grave' (*Reihengräber*) cemeteries in East Central Europe, which could be dated to the late sixth or early seventh century (Figure 7.14 and Appendix). It is important to note at this point that the dress accessories found on the western edge of the cemetery, which Ligia Bârzu attributed to the sixth-century Gepid milieu, may be the earliest finds on the site and, as such, provide an approximate date for the beginnings of the cemetery.[41]

The grave goods found in the western half of the cemetery seem to point to an earlier date for those inhumations. The chorological analysis reveals that this area was predominantly marked by brooches and belt sets of Byzantine inspiration, if not origin. An earlier date of the western graves can be substantiated by comparing them with the horse deposition which is so conspicuous in the eastern part of the

---

[41] Ligia Bârzu, 'Gepidische Funde von Bratei', *Dacia*, 35 (1991), 211–14. That the artefacts were found at some 100 m away from the western edge of the cemetery has not been confirmed.

cemetery. Already in 1958 Kurt Horedt suggested that the deposition of horse bones and gear was the result of Avar influence.[42] He maintained that position over the years and continued to see the deposition of horse bones as a chronologically sensitive feature.[43] The same is true for István Bóna, who in 1990 thought that in the 630s, while the last dead were buried in the Band cemetery, most burials, including the Avar-age one, were reopened and plundered.[44] The idea of an acculturation process was in fact in the air. Ion Nestor spoke of 'Avaricized Gepids' and Bóna himself advanced, if only hypothetically, the idea of a replacement of the Gepid culture of Merovingian inspiration with an 'Avar-Germanic' culture.[45] This in fact was also brought up in connection with cemetery A in Kőlked-Feketekapu and its six Early Avar horse burials, although the stress in that case was laid on 'pure' Avars.[46]

To the same direction points the comparison between cemetery III in Bratei and that excavated in Gâmbaș. The twelve burials found there produced weapons, horse gear and bones, earrings (such as found in Bratei), as well as glass beads with eye-shaped inlays, all finds most typical for Early Avar assemblages. Further parallels may be established with grave 3 in Gâmbaș, in which beads, earrings with star-shaped pendant, and a wooden bucket were found in association with a pair of 'Slavic' bow fibulae of Werner's class I C, a situation remarkably similar to that documented in both Bratei and Kőlked. The latter parallel is even more remarkable, given that 'Slavic' bow fibulae are otherwise rare in eastern Pannonia. An important contribution to the clarification of those similarities between all those

---

[42] Horedt, *Untersuchungen*, p. 101.

[43] Horedt, 'Das Awarenproblem', p. 111; Kurt Horedt, 'Die Deutung des Gräberfeldes von Környe', *Jahrbuch des Römisch-Germanischen Zentralmuseums*, 18 (1971), 200–08 (p. 206): 'Weiter ist ersichtlich, daß sich die Awaren nicht gleich nach dem Zusammenbruch des gepidischen Reiches im Jahre 567 *auch in Bandu niederließen*' (emphasis added). A somewhat different view in Horedt, 'Der östliche Reihengräberkreis', p. 263: 'aus ihnen ist die Berührung der zeitlich und kulturell klar getrennten Fundgruppen ersichtlich, die sich aber nicht miteinander vermengen'. And again the sense of a migration, in Horedt, *Siebenbürgen*, p. 36: 'Man kann vermuten, daß Teile von ihnen [i.e. the Cutrigurs] sich auch nach Osten, nach Siebenbürgen wandten, wenn sie nicht bereits vorher schon hier waren. Ihren archäologischen Niederschlag finden diese Ereignisse im Ende des Gräberfeldes von Band, in dem Beginn der reiternomadischen Gîmbașgruppe im Miereschbogen und schließlich in der Verbergung des großen Münzschatzfundes auf dem Firtosch'. The events imagined in this way are believed to have taken place in *c.* 630.

[44] István Bóna, 'Völkerwanderung und Frühmittelalter (271–895)', in *Kurze Geschichte Siebenbürgens*, ed. by Béla Köpeczi (Budapest, 1990), pp. 62–106 (p. 94).

[45] Bóna, 'Gepiden in Siebenbürgen', p. 45.

[46] Kiss, *Das awarenzeitlich-gepidische Gräberfeld*, pp. 291–92.

assemblages is that of Attila Kiss, who, on the basis of his excavations in Kőlked-Feketekapu, advanced the idea of a close cultural affinity between the materials found in Kőlked, in Környe, and on various sites in Transylvania (Band, Unirea-Vereşmort, or Noşlac), on the one hand, and the assemblages of the Gepid culture in the Tisza Plain or in Transylvania (Horedt's group III), on the other hand. While stressing such similarities, he also indirectly pointed out the chronological distinction between the two groups.[47]

In this respect, the so-called Early Avar assemblages proved to be of crucial significance.[48] Unfortunately, the state of research as described by Kurt Horedt in the 1950s has changed very little in the last few decades.[49] Nevertheless, it became increasingly clear that the territory of the former 'Gepidia' was a part of the Avar qaganate in the seventh century. I shall return to the question of whether that also means that 'pure' Avars settled in territories previously inhabited by Gepids. Besides the finds mentioned by Kurt Horedt[50] and István Bóna,[51] one must now consider cemeteries that have produced horse skeletons or body parts, as well as horse gear.[52] It is important to note at this point that the Bistriţa cemetery shows that the deposition of horses appears also in the Someş valley, that is, within a region from which no Late Avar horseman burials are so far known. In any case, the absence of any indication of earlier materials of Horedt's group III from many of those cemeteries (Aiud, Măgina, Lopadea Nouă, Şpălnaca, and Stremţ) makes

[47] Kiss, *Das awarenzeitlich-gepidische Gräberfeld*, pp. 177–324, esp. pp. 184–285.

[48] Kurt Horedt, *Contribuţii la istoria Transilvaniei în secolele IV–XIII* (Bucharest, 1958), pp. 88–90. In Horedt, 'Das Awarenproblem', p. 110, this is called the Mureş group of assemblage, while in Horedt, *Siebenbürgen*, pp. 66–72, the group is rebaptized Gâmbaş. As Bóna, 'Gepiden in Siebenbürgen', p. 47 points out, these are in fact simply and plainly Early Avar assemblages.

[49] Horedt, *Contribuţii*, pp. 61–108.

[50] Corund (Horedt, *Contribuţii*, pp. 95 and 75 fig. 13.6–7), Dumbrăveni (Horedt, *Contribuţii*, pp. 102 and 84 fig. 18.11–19), Şura Mare (Appendix, no. 39), Rodbav (Horedt, *Contribuţii*, pp. 88 and 89 fig. 27.4), and Rupea (Appendix, no. 33).

[51] Turda (Appendix, no. 43), Alba Iulia (Appendix, no. 2), and Târnăveni (Appendix, no. 42).

[52] Aiud (Horedt, *Contribuţii*, pp. 91 and 93), Archiud (Appendix, no. 4), Band (Appendix, no. 5), Bistriţa (Appendix, no. 6), Bratei, Gâmbaş (Appendix, no. 22), Măgina (Appendix, no. 26), Noşlac (Appendix, no. 30), Lopadea Nouă (Appendix, no. 25), Şpălnaca (Appendix, no. 38), Stremţ (Horedt *Contribuţii*, p. 103), and Valea Largă (Appendix, no. 45). The chronological position of the horse burial (grave 3) in Cicău is uncertain. While Horedt, *Siebenbürgen*, pp. 66–67 placed it within the first half of the seventh century, Iudita Winkler, Matilda Tákács, and Gheorghe Păiuş, 'Necropola avară de la Cicău', *Acta Musei Napocensis*, 14 (1977), 269–83 (pp. 280–82), and Bóna, 'Völkerwanderung', p. 95, preferred a date in the early 700s.

it possible to regard them all as a single group. It is thus clear that the Transylvanian burial assemblages with horse deposition are to be directly associated to the Early Avar cemeteries in the Hungarian Plain. István Bóna suggested that the few cases of early deposition of horse bones be atrributed to the first generations of Avars in Pannonia (568 to 630).[53] His suggestion raises the question of whether the more recent row-grave cemeteries with horse deposition are in fact a final phase (perhaps of acculturation) of the same development. The peripheral position of the graves with horse deposition in Bratei seems to suggest that this was indeed the case.[54] If so, then in Bratei, as well as in many other Transylvanian row-grave cemeteries of a later date we may have an advanced process of acculturation of the seventh-century Gepids.[55]

The chorological analysis of the cemetery has thus revealed a chronological distinction between an earlier western and a later eastern sector. However, painting with a broad brush is not going to reveal the entire complexity of the situation, despite the somewhat clear-cut segregation of artefact categories (Figure 7.15). The sharp distinctions are obviously blurred in the case of fibulae or belt sets, which may be interpreted as an ongoing process of acculturation.

The historical interpretation of this archaeological situation must of course take into account the Avar conquest of the Carpathian Basin. The fall of the Gepid royal house in 567 was followed by a rapid collapse of all power structures in the kingdom. Much like the Sântana de Mureş-Chernyakhov cemeteries in the late fourth century, the late sixth-century row-grave cemeteries were abandoned. The archaeological reflex of this dramatic transformation is the later group of cemeteries identified in Hungary (Környe, Kőlked-Feketekapu), but also in Transylvania, which although still related somewhat to the earlier assemblages, obviously represents a much later phenomenon. It would, however, be a mistake to interpret those cemeteries as an indication of the presence of defeated Gepids fleeing the Avar onslaught.[56] Instead, everything points to the integration of those communities into the new political and cultural environment that appeared in the Carpathian Basin after 567.

---

[53] Bóna, 'Gepiden in Siebenbürgen', p. 42.

[54] Equally interesting in that respect is the situation in Band (Appendix, no. 5), where handmade pottery, spear heads, horse bones, *au repoussé* belt mounts, buckles with rectangular plates, and belt mounts with embossed decoration all have a peripheral distribution. See Horedt, *Siebenbürgen*, p. 35 fig. 15.

[55] Harhoiu, 'Quellenlage und Forschungsstand', pp. 130–33.

[56] An interpretation advanced by Popescu, 'Das gepidische Gräberfeld', p. 213.

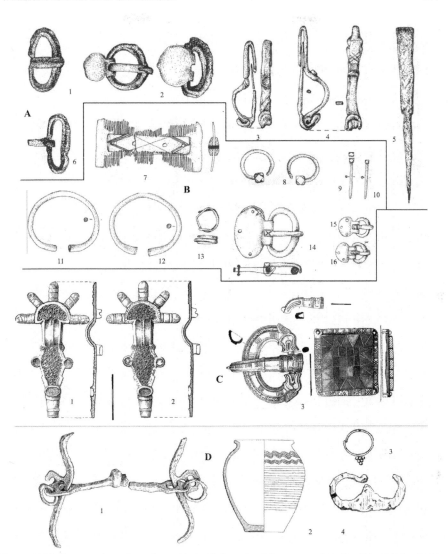

Figure 7.15. Bratei, selected artefacts. (A 1–6) from burials excavated in 'La Zăvoi' (after Ligia Bârzu, *Continuitatea populației autohtone în Transilvania în secolele 4–5: Cimitirul 1 de la Bratei* (Bucharest, 1973)); (B–D) from burials excavated in 'La Nisipuri'; (B 7–16) grave goods from the isolated burial found in 1964 (Ligia Bârzu, 'Monumente germanice descoperite la Bratei', *Studii și cercetări de istorie veche și arheologie*, 37 (1986), 89–101); (C 1–3) burials on the western periphery of the cemetery (Bârzu, 'Gepidische Funde'); (D 1–4) from burials excavated in cemetery II: (1) bridle bit from the Avar-age horseman burial; (2–3) grave goods from urn cremations and inhumation graves (Eugenia Zaharia, *Populația românească în Transilvania în secolele VII–VIII: Cimitirul nr. 2 de la Bratei* (Bucharest, 1977)).

Spatial Patterns

While the chronological division of the cemetery may thus be supported with solid arguments, other structures still remain to be identified. For the delineation of spatial groups it is necessary to locate the position of the graves within a system of coordinates covering the entire cemetery. The matrix thus obtained by plotting the average points of each grave may then be submitted for nearest-neighbour cluster analysis.[57] The resulting dendrogram shows seven groups, for the definition of which one may use five or four nearest-neighbour relations. We thus have four major groups (A–D, with four nearest neighbours) and 29 smaller groups (1–29, with five nearest neighbours). The dendrogram reveals the isolated position on the periphery of graves 292 and 293 (group E, with four nearest neighbours). When compared to the chronological division, it appears that, with the exception of six 'islands' (1–6) in the northern part of group A and of group D, all other 'islands' and groups fall neatly into one or the other of the two chronological divisions of the cemetery. The meaning of the smaller groups (with five nearest neighbours) is immediately apparent when considering that these were burials of children, young individuals, or women (burials with beads, as well as pairs of earrings and fibulae). It is perhaps not too farfetched to assume that the persons buried in those graves were in some way related to one another. They seem to have 'operated' as an important connection between graves within a larger spatial division of the cemetery. This is further substantiated by the presence of male burials with weapons and of burials with unsexed skeletons. There indeed seems to be some pattern underlying the spatial structuring of the cemetery. Each group contains burials of men, women, and children, while horse burials appear to have linked male burials together. A more advanced anthropological analysis of the human remains may confirm this interpretation in the future, but the large number of graves with unsexed skeletons (i.e. skeletons whose state of preservation does not unfortunately allow the identification of the individual's sex) prevents a deeper understanding of the spatial patterning of the cemetery. Nevertheless, it is possible at least to suggest

---

[57] For a description of the cluster analysis as a statistical method, see F. W. Wilmink and H. T. Uytterschaut, 'Cluster Analysis, History, Theory and Application', in *Multivariate Statistical Methods in Physical Anthropology: A Review of Recent Advances and Current Developments*, ed. by G. N. van Vark and W. W. Howells (Dordrecht, 1984), pp. 135–75. For an exemplary application to mortuary archaeology, see J. M. O'Shea, 'Cluster Analysis and Mortuary Patterning: An Experimental Assessment', *PACT: Revue du Groupe européen d'études pour les techniques physiques, chimiques et mathématiques appliquées à l'archéologie*, 11 (1985), 91–110.

that the patterning be interpreted as an indication of a clan structure of the Bratei community which buried its dead in cemetery III.

Conclusion

The cemetery excavated at 'La Nisipuri' ('Rogoaze') in the village of Bratei is one of the most interesting early medieval sites of Transylvania so far known from systematic archaeological excavations. During the second half of the fifth century, in the circumstances surrounding the Gepid takeover of the Tisza Basin and of Transylvania, a small group of graves appeared in Bratei, together with an isolated, but rich burial (Figure 7.15.B). By 500, more graves began to appear within the cemetery area and in its vicinity. Whether or not a number of isolated finds (Figure 7.15.C) have anything to do with cemetery III (perhaps with its earliest phase) cannot be established with certainty on the basis of the existing evidence. After *c.* 550 or somewhat earlier, regular burials began within the cemetery area. Later burials show a strong influence of the Early Avar culture, no doubt a sign of acculturation. The cemetery was probably abandoned by 650. There was in fact no continuity from the latest burials of cemetery III to those of the Late Avar cemetery II (late seventh to eighth century), which is located in the vicinity and produced evidence of radically different mortuary practices (Figure 7.15.D).

Appendix

Sixth- to Seventh-Century Cemeteries and Burial Finds in Transylvania

1. Aiud (Alba district); isolated find (before 1958); probable row-grave cemetery; Horedt, *Untersuchungen*, pp. 88 and 89 fig. 27.2, 4; Csallány, *Archäologische Denkmäler*, p. 197 and pl. 271.4, 7.

2. Alba Iulia (Alba district); a sixth- to seventh-century cemetery at Dealu Furcilor, signalled by a few isolated finds (before 1900) (see Horedt, *Untersuchungen*, pp. 90 and 84 fig. 27.3; Csallány, *Archäologische Denkmäler*, p. 197 and pl. 271.3); accidental finds of horseman burials with dress accessories from other unknown spots within the city (before 1900 and between 1900 and 1912) (see István Bóna, 'Über eine fruchtlose Polemik: Bemerkungen zur Abhandlung von Radu Harhoiu, "Die Beziehungen zwischen Romanen und Barbaren in Siebenbürgen in der Sicht einer ungarischen Geschichte Transilvaniens"', *Acta Archaeologica Academiae Scientiarum Hungaricae*, 40 (1988), 301–14 (p. 313); Éva Garam, *Katalog der awarenzeitlichen Goldgegenstände und der Fundstücke aus den Fürstengräbern im Ungarischen Nationalmuseum* (Budapest, 1993), p. 65 and pl. 40.3; Horedt, *Untersuchungen*, pp. 90 and 91 fig. 29; Csallány, *Archäologische Denkmäler*, p. 198); isolated ceramic find from a presumed cemetery with horseman burials on an unknown spot within the city (see Kurt Horedt, 'Ceramica slavă din Transilvania', *Studii şi cercetări de istorie veche*, 2 (1951), 182–204 (p. 192)).

3. Apahida (Cluj district); isolated finds from two different sixth-century cemeteries with two different locations (accidental excavations 1900–07 and 1880–1900, respectively); Horedt, *Untersuchungen*, pp. 72–73 and 88; Csallány, *Archäologische Denkmäler*, pp. 221 and 223.

4. Archiud (Teaca county, Bistriţa-Năsăud district); sixth- to seventh-century cemetery excavated between 1975 and 1981 at 'Hânsuri', with twenty inhumations, including warrior graves with weapons and deposition of horse bones; personal communication Corneliu Gaiu.

5. Band (Mureş district); sixth- to seventh-century cemetery excavated between 1906 and 1907 on a hill to the west from the village (186 inhumations with weapons, tools, horse bones and gear, as well as hand- and wheel-made pots); Kovács, 'A mezöbándi ásatások'.

6. Bistriţa (Bistriţa-Năsăud district); sixth- to seventh-century cemetery excavated in 1979 in the Târgul Roşu residential quarter ('Staţia 110KW/Poligon') with sixty burials; Corneliu Gaiu, 'Le Cimetière gépide de Bistriţa', *Dacia*, 36 (1992), 115–24.

7. Bratei (Sibiu district); sixth- to seventh-century cemetery excavated between 1961 and 1977 at 'La Nisipuri' ('Rogoaze'), with 293 burials; sixth-century isolated finds (1969) from several burials on the edge of cemetery III (Bârzu, 'Gepidische Funde').

8. Breaza (Mureş district); sixth-century isolated finds (before 1900); Horedt, *Untersuchungen*, pp. 88 and 91 fig. 28.3–4.

9. Căpuşul Mare (Cluj district); sixth- to seventh-century (?) cemetery excavated between 1949 and 1952; [no author], 'Şantierul "Aşezări slave în regiunile Mureş şi Cluj"', *Studii şi cercetări de istorie veche*, 3 (1952), 311–48 (pp. 312–17); Ion Russu and I. Roth, 'Rit de înmormîntare (sec. VII) (Pe baza săpăturilor de la Căpuşu Mare)', *Probleme de antropologie*, 2 (1956), 7–39.

10. Cipău, in Iernut (Mureş district); sixth-century cemetery partially excavated in 1954 at 'Gârle' (Pig Farm), with ten burials; [no author], 'Şantierul arheologic Moreşti (r. Tg. Mureş, reg. aut. maghiară)', *Studii şi cercetări de istorie veche*, 5 (1954), 199–232 (pp. 221–22); [no author], 'Şantierul arheologic Moreşti', *Studii şi cercetări de istorie veche*, 6 (1956), 643–87 (p. 660); Nicolae Vlassa, 'Cercetări arheologice în regiunile Mureş-Autonomă Maghiară şi Cluj', *Acta Musei Napocensis*, 2 (1965), 19–38 (pp. 28–31); Wanda Wolski and Dardu Nicolaescu-Plopşor, 'Două morminte gepidice descoperite la Cipău', *Studii şi cercetări de antropologie*, 9 (1972), 3–13.

11. Cluj-Napoca (Cluj district); cemetery with unknown number of burials excavated in 1958 at Cordoş (Crop and Fertilizer Plant); personal communication Ioana Hica (1978).

12. Corneşti (Adămuş county, Mureş district); grave accidentally found in 1970 or 1971 in a local backyard; A. Pálko, 'Descoperiri din secolul al VII-lea în valea Arieşului', *Studii şi cercetări de istorie veche*, 23 (1972), 677–79.

13. Cristuru Secuiesc (Harghita district); sixth- to seventh-century cemetery with three graves accidentally found by the post office; personal communication A. Székely (Cristuru Secuiesc), and Elek Benkö, *A középkori Keresztúr-szék régészeti topográfiája* (Budapest, 1992), p. 173 pl. 16.2–3.

14. Criţ (Buneşti county, Braşov district); sixth-century, isolated finds (1940–41); Kurt Horedt, ' Völkerwanderungszeitliche Funde aus Siebenbürgen', *Germania*, 25 (1941), 124 with pl. 21.5–6; Csallány, *Archäologische Denkmäler*, p. 198.

15. Dej (Cluj district); isolated find by the old bridge (before 1958); Horedt, *Untersuchungen*, p. 90.

16. Drăuşeni (Caţa county, Braşov district); late sixth- or early seventh-century, isolated find (1876 or 1877); Horedt, *Untersuchungen*, p. 90; Csallány, *Archäologische Denkmäler*, p. 208.

17. Ernei (Mureş district); sixth-century (?) isolated find (before 1958); Horedt, *Untersuchungen*, p. 90.

18. Fântânele (Matei county, Bistriţa-Năsăud district); sixth- to seventh-century cemetery excavated at 'Dâmbu Popii'; personal communication Corneliu Gaiu.

19. Fundătura (Iclod county, Cluj district); sixth-century, isolated find (1906); Mircea Rusu, 'Pontische Gürtelschnallen mit Adlerkopf (VI.–VII. Jh. u.Z.)', *Dacia*, 3 (1959), 485–523 (pp. 489–90).

20. Galaţii Bistriţei (Bistriţa-Năsăud district); sixth- to seventh-century cemetery excavated between 1972 and 1978 at 'La hrube', with thirty graves; Radu Harhoiu, 'Raport preliminar privind săpăturile arheologice de la Galaţii Bistriţei', *Materiale şi cercetări arheologice*, 13 (1979), 321–23.

21. Ghirbom (Berghin county, Alba district); fifteen sixth-century burials found between 1970 and 1975 at 'In Faţă' (see Adriana Stoia, 'Les Fouilles archéologiques en Roumanie', *Dacia*, 19 (1975), 269–307 (p. 287); personal communication Radu Heitel; Ioan Aldea, Ioan Alexandru, Eugen Stoicovici, and Mihai Blăjan, 'Cercetări arheologice în cimitirul prefeudal de la Ghirbom (com. Berghin, jud. Alba)', *Apulum*, 18 (1980), 151–77 (p. 151)); another cemetery with seven graves (some with horse bones) excavated between 1970 and 1975 at 'Gruiul Fierului' (see Aldea, Alexandru, Stoicovici, and Blăjan, 'Cercetări arheologice').

22. Gâmbaş, in Aiud (Alba district); late sixth- to early seventh-century cemetery with twelve graves excavated in 1913 in the Evangelical Cemetery; Horedt, *Contribuţii*, pp. 95–100.

23. Iclod (Cluj district); sixth- to seventh-century cemetery with five graves excavated at 'Pământul Vlădicii'; Ioana Hica-Cîmpeanu, 'Un grup de morminte din secolul VII e.n. la Iclod, jud. Cluj', *Acta Musei Napocensis*, 15 (1978), 287–93.

24. Lechinţa de Mureş (Iernut county, Mureş district); sixth-century cemetery with at least four graves accidentally excavated in 1925, 1950, 1951, and 1960, respectively, in 'Sălişte' (cemetery); [no author], 'Şantierul Moreşti', *Studii şi cercetări de istorie veche*, 4 (1953), 275–311 (p. 327).

25. Lopadea Nouă (Alba district); late sixth- to eighth-century cemetery with eleven graves, some of horsemen, excavated in 1905 and 1913 (?) in 'La şanţuri' ('La râpe'); Horedt, *Contribuţii*, p. 101.

26. Măgina, in Aiud (Alba district); burial with horse bones discovered in 1972 in a local backyard; Horia Ciugudean, 'Mormîntul unui călăreţ avar de la Măgina (jud. Alba)', *Studii şi cercetări de istorie veche şi arheologie*, 25 (1974), 457–59.

27. Mediaş (Sibiu district); sixth-century cemetery with four graves found in 1961 at Teba (see Comşa and Ignat, 'Gräber'); sixth-century grave accidentally excavated in 1969 at a different location (personal communication Mihai Blăjan and Gheorghe Togan).

28. Moldoveneşti (Cluj district); late sixth- or seventh-century grave accidentally excavated between 1970 and 1972 next to a local well; Pálko, 'Descoperiri', p. 678.

29. Moreşti (Ungheni county, Mureş district); sixth-century cemetery with eighty-one graves excavated between 1951 and 1956 at 'Hulă'; Popescu, 'Das gepidische Gräberfeld'; Horedt, *Moreşti*, pp. 156–205.

30. Noşlac (Alba district); sixth- to seventh-century cemetery with 122 graves excavated between 1960 and 1961 to the west from the village on the bank of the river Mureş; Mircea Rusu, 'The Prefeudal Cemetery of Noşlac (VI–VIIth Centuries)', *Dacia*, 6 (1962), 269–92; Rusu, 'Cimitirul prefeudal'.

31. Nuşeni (Bistriţa-Năsăud district); two sixth- to seventh-century burials found in 1936 and 1975, respectively, in a local backyard (see Gheorghe Marinescu, 'Cercetări şi descoperiri arheologice în jud. Bistriţa-Năsăud', *Arhiva someşană*, 3 (1975), 309–11); two sixth-century graves excavated in 1975 at 'Podul Ciorbii'; Adriana Stoia, 'Les Fouilles archéologiques en Roumanie. 1975', *Dacia*, 20 (1976), 273–86 (p. 280).

32. Ocniţa (Teaca county, Bistriţa-Năsăud district); sixth-century grave accidentally found in 1955 or 1956; Horedt, *Untersuchungen*, p. 92.

33. Rupea (Braşov district); possible burial with horse bones accidentally found between 1880 and 1888; Horedt, *Contribuţii*, pp. 102 and 75 fig. 13.13–14.

34. Sighişoara (Mureş district); sixth- to seventh-century with twenty graves excavated between 1986 and 2005 at 'Dealu Viilor' (Radu Harhoiu); sixth-century grave excavated at some point between 1905 and 1910 on the road to Stejăreni (see Csallány, *Archäologische Denkmäler*, p. 198); sixth-century grave accidentally found in 1973 at 'Herţeş'; Ioana Hica-Cîmpeanu and Ana Mureşan, 'Un mormînt din secolul al VI-lea e.n. la Sighişoara', *Marisia*, 7 (1977), 761–73.

35. Sînmiclăuş (Alba district); sixth-century cemetery with forty-three graves excavated in 1973 at 'Gruişor'; Gheorghe Anghel and Mihai Blăjan, 'Săpăturile arheologice de la Sînmiclăuş (com. Şona, jud. Alba)', *Apulum*, 15 (1977), 285–307.

36. Sucutard (Cluj district); isolated sixth-century find (before 1958); Horedt, *Untersuchungen*, p. 93.

37. Şintereag (Bistriţa-Năsăud district); sixth- to seventh-century grave excavated in 1973 at Hagău; Corneliu Gaiu, 'Descoperiri din epoca migraţiilor din nord-estul Transilvaniei', *Acta Musei Porolissensis*, 3 (1979), 541–42.

38. Şpălnaca (Hopârta county, Alba district); graves excavated in 1989 and 1990, some of them with horse bones; personal communication Mihai Blăjan and Mircea Rusu.

39. Şura Mare (Sibiu district); grave with horse bones accidentally found before 1928; Horedt, 'Völkerwanderungszeitliche Funde aus Siebenbürgen', p. 124 and pl. 21.11; Csallány, *Archäologische Denkmäler*, pl. 238.11.

40. Târgu Mureş (Mureş district); cemetery with six graves excavated in 1909 and 1910 on the street formerly named Kálmán Mikoszáth; István Kovács, 'A Marosvasárhely asatások', *Közlemenyék az Erdelyi Nemzéti Múzeum történeti-, müveszéti- és néprajázi tárából*, 6 (1915), 278–96 (pp. 278–93 and 317–24).

41. Târgu Secuiesc (Covasna district); grave with horse bones found in 1907 by the railroad near Breţcu; Horedt, 'Ceramica slavă', pp. 204–05.

42. Târnăveni (Mureş district), find from a cremation pit, together with horse bones; Bóna, 'Über eine fruchtlose Polemik', p. 312, and Bóna, 'Völkerwanderung', pl. 8.1–2.

43. Turda (Cluj district); isolated find before 1990, together with horse bones; Bóna, 'Völkerwanderung', pl. 8.7.–8.

44. Unirea-Vereşmort (Alba district); sixth- to seventh-century cemetery with nineteen graves partially excavated in 1914 on the bank of the Mureş river; Martin Roska, 'Das gepidische Gräberfeld von Veresmart', *Germania*, 18 (1934), 123–30.

45. Valea Largă (Mureş district); sixth- to seventh-century cemetery with sixteen graves excavated in 1973 at 'Capul Satului'; Ioana Hica, 'Un cimitir din sec. VII e.n. la Valea Largă (jud. Mureş)', *Studii şi cercetări de istorie veche şi arheologie*, 25 (1974), 517–26.

46. Vermeş (Lechinţa county, Bistriţa-Năsăud district); sixth- to seventh-century cemetery with several graves accidentally found before 1980 near the building of the local cultural association; personal communication, Corneliu Gaiu.

GEPIDS IN THE BALKANS:
A SURVEY OF THE ARCHAEOLOGICAL EVIDENCE

Anna Kharalambieva

A quick glimpse at Ludwig Schmidt, Herwig Wolfram, and Walter Pohl's studies on Gepids and other Germanic groups in south-eastern Europe will immediately lead to the conclusion that not much can be said about the Gepids without the assistance of the archaeological evidence.[1] To be sure, both older and more recent accounts of Gepid history are little more than a rehashing of Jordanes's version of events, here and there assorted with bits and pieces of archaeological information.[2] The Gepids, 'poorer' and 'stolid' relatives of the Goths, would have initially lived on the southern coast of the Baltic Sea in the region of the Vistula Delta. By the early third century, the bearers of the Wielbark culture (i.e. the Goths) began moving to the south-east in a migration that reached the northern shore of the Black Sea. According to Jordanes, being 'slow', the Gepids did not join their Gothic cousins, but preferred instead to stay behind in their Baltic homeland. Only later did they eventually decide to migrate to the south

---

[1] Ludwig Schmidt, *Die Ostgermanen*, vol. I of *Geschichte der deutschen Stämme bis zum Ausgange der Völkerwanderung* (Munich, 1941; repr. 1969); Herwig Wolfram, *Die Geschichte der Goten* (Munich, 1979); Walter Pohl, 'Die Gepiden und die Gentes an der mittleren Donau nach dem Zerfall des Attilareiche', in *Die Völker an der mittleren und unteren Donau im fünften und sechsten Jahrhundert: Berichte des Symposions der Kommission für Frühmittelalterforschung, 24.–27. Oktober 1978, Stift Zwettl, Niederösterreich*, ed. by Herwig Wolfram and Falko Daim (Vienna, 1980), pp. 239–305. The first monograph exclusively dedicated to Gepid history is that of Constantin C. Diculescu, *Die Gepiden: Forschungen zur Geschichte Daziens im frühen Mittelalter und zur Vorgeschichte des rumänischen Volkes* (Leipzig, 1923).

[2] For the use and abuse of Jordanes, see Walter Goffart, *Barbarian Tides: The Migration Age and the Later Roman Empire* (Philadelphia, 2006), pp. 56–72.

under the leadership of their legendary king Fastida.[3] In the course of their migration, the Gepids crossed the territory of the Luboszyce culture, which is attributed
to the Burgunds,[4] before reaching the densely forested slopes of the northern
Carpathian range on the border of the Roman province of Dacia. Jordanes claims
the Gepids won a victory over the Burgundians, but in the process 'unjustly
provoked the Goths'.[5] In the ensuing battle, they were defeated by Ostrogotha, the
king of the Goths. The battle between Goths and Gepids is said to have taken place
by an *oppidum* named Galtis, which was on the bank of the river Auha.[6] Following
their defeat at the hands of the Goths, the Gepids withdrew to the 'rugged mountains and forests' from which they had come and which historians hastened to
locate in the northern Carpathians, in the region of the Upper Tisza and Upper
Dniester rivers.[7] Moreover, Jordanes's story served others to date the events nar-
rated therein between 248 and 291. The Romanian archaeologist Kurt Horedt was
convinced that the battle could have taken place only between 249 and the withdrawal in the 270s of the Roman troops and administration from Dacia at the
orders of Emperor Aurelian.[8] Horedt used that argument to reject the legend
according to which the battle had taken place in Transylvania by a village named
Galt (the Saxon name of what is now known as Ungra in the district of Braşov) on
the river Olt, and instead proposed that Galtis be located somewhere to the east of
the Carpathian Mountains, that is, outside the Roman province of Dacia.

The Gepids are said to have participated in the barbarian coalition which Emperor Claudius II defeated in 269 in the Balkans. Groups of Gepid prisoners of war

---

[3] For a good illustration of a 'mixed argumentation' based on a peculiarly combined use of
archaeological evidence and historical narrative ultimately based on Jordanes, see Gerard Labuda,
'O wędrowce Gotów i Gepidów ze Skandynawii na Morze Czarne', in *Liber Josepho Kostrzewski
octogenario a veneratoribus dicatus*, ed. by Konrad Jażdżewski (Wrocław, 1968), pp. 213–36.

[4] Grzegorz Domański, *Kultura Luboszyca mięży laba a Odra w II–IV wieku* (Wrocław, 1979),
pp. 210–20.

[5] Jordanes, *Getica*, 96: 'male provocans'.

[6] Jordanes, *Getica*, 99: 'ad oppidum Galtis, iuxta quod currit fluuius Auha'.

[7] Jordanes, *Getica*, 100 and 98: 'montium [...] asperitate siluarumque'.

[8] Walter Pohl, s.v. 'Gepiden: Historisches', in *Reallexikon der germanischen Altertumskunde*,
XI, ed. by Johannes Hoops and Heinrich Beck (Berlin, 1998), pp. 131–40; Kurt Horedt, 'Zur
Geschichte der frühen Gepiden im Karpatenbecken', *Apulum*, 9 (1971), 705–12. The idea of a
Gothic-Gepid confrontation inside Transylvania is still looming large. See, for example, Volker
Bierbrauer, 'Gepiden im 5. Jahrhundert Eine Spurensuche', in *Miscellanea romano-barbarica: In
honorem septagenarii magistri Ion Ioniţă oblata*, ed. by Virgil Mihăilescu-Bîrliba, Cătălin Hriban,
and Lucian Munteanu (Bucharest, 2006), pp. 167–216 (p. 170 with n. 17).

were later settled in the Balkan provinces by Emperor Probus (276–82).[9] Whether or not this could indicate that the Gepids lived somewhere north of the Lower Danube frontier of the empire, no fourth-century source mentions them at all. This has been explained as an indication that the Gepids were not in fact living close to the Roman frontier and that their abodes may have been farther to the north, beyond the area of the so-called Sântana de Mureş-Chernyakhov culture, which most historians now associate with the Tervingi. Fourth-century Gepids are believed to have lived in the Upper Tisza region as well as between the Tisza and the Criş/Körös rivers.[10] While they may have shared the former area with the Vandals, they were most likely rubbing shoulders with the Goths in the latter region. Cemeteries excavated in north-eastern Hungary have produced a number of burials of warriors with swords, lances, and shields, which archaeologists attribute to the native Gepids. However, no essential difference exists between dress accessories found with female burials within the same cemeteries and those known from burial assemblages of the Sântana de Mureş-Chernyakhov culture attributed to the Goths, a fact perhaps too hastily interpreted as an indication of a mixed, Gepid-Gothic population. Rapid changes in fashion taking place in the late fourth and early fifth centuries make it possible to monitor the rise of a local identity, which may be called Gepid and is best illustrated by cemeteries excavated in northern Transylvania.[11] In any case, by the time of the Hunnic onslaught, some Gepids, at least, lived together with Vandals and Goths. Many Gepids thus followed the Gothic movement to the south-west. Those who remained in northern Transylvania seem to have become subjects of the Ostrogothic commanders in the Hunnic army and to have moved into the lands previously occupied by the Sântana de Mureş-Chernyakhov culture, where other Gepids may have previously lived along

---

[9] For a discussion of the written sources, see Schmidt, *Die Ostgermanen*, pp. 529–31.

[10] However, not everybody agrees with attributing assemblages of such an early date to the Gepids. E.g. Eszter Istvánovits and Valéria Kulcsár, 'Sarmatian and Germanic People at the Upper Tisza Region and South Alföld at the Beginning of the Migration Period', in *L'Occident romain et l'Europe centrale au début de l'époque des Grandes Invasions*, ed. by Jaroslav Tejral, Christian Pilet, and Michel Kazanski (Brno, 1998), pp. 67–94 (pp. 68–69): 'We do not have at our disposal any Gepidian material that can be dated to the 3rd century or first half of the 4th century.'

[11] Kurt Horedt, *Siebenbürgen im Frühmittelalter* (Bonn, 1986), pp. 1–6 and 8–57; Agnés B. Tóth, s.v. 'Gepiden: Archäologisches', in *Reallexikon der germanischen Altertumskunde*, XI, ed. by Hoops and Beck, pp. 118–19; Wilfried Menghin, 'Die Völkerwanderungszeit im Karpatenbecken', in *Germanen, Hunnen und Awaren: Schätze der Völkerwanderungszeit. Germanisches National-museum, Nürnberg, 12. Dezember 1987 bis 21. Februar 1988*, ed. by Wilfried Menghin, Tobias Springer, and Egon Wamers (Nuremberg, 1987), pp. 16–20.

with the Goths. In any case, the Gepid inhabitants of Transylvania were subjects of the Huns and of their warlords of Ostrogothic origin. They were thus part of Attila's Hunnic Empire. Archaeologists attribute to the circumstances surrounding these events a number of hoards of gold and silver found in northern Transylvania, especially those of Şimleu Silvaniei (Szilágysomlyó), now in the Kunsthistorisches Museum in Vienna.[12] The artefacts of Roman origin included in the Şimleu Silvaniei hoards bespeak the high honours bestowed by the emperor in Constantinople upon the local Gepid rulers. This will in fact become a hallmark of Gepid history for the subsequent century.

The troubling absence of any mention of Gepids in fourth-century sources is somewhat compensated by Jordanes's mention of the Visigoths 'preaching the Gospel both to the Ostrogoths and to their kinsmen' the Gepids at the time of Emperor Valens (364–78). However, Jordanes's remark is in fact part of his attempt to explain away Gothic Arianism as being no different from that of other 'rude and ignorant people', such as their 'kinsmen' and neighbours.[13]

On the testimony of Jordanes, the Gepids remained under Hunnic rule for over fifty years. Their chieftains were gradually adopted into the elite of Attila's empire, much like the rulers of the Ostrogoths, *Sciri*, Herules, Suebians, or *Rugi*. As a matter of fact, Attila praised Ardaric, the king of the Gepids, 'above all the other chieftains', except Valamir, the king of the Ostrogoths.[14] Within Attila's empire, the position of various vassals changed according to the needs and moods of the ruler.[15] Wars and raids brought much booty to the fighting men of one's own *gens*, while at the same time raising the prestige of that *gens* over others within the empire and placing its chieftain closer to Attila than other *reguli*. This is precisely what Jordanes describes as happening to the Ostrogothic Amali, to Edica, the

---

[12] Attila Kiss, 'Die Schatzfunde I und II von Szilágy Somlyó als Quellen der gepidischen Geschichte', *Archaeologia Austriaca*, 75 (1991), 249–60; Radu Harhoiu, *Die frühe Völkerwanderungszeit in Rumänien* (Bucharest, 1997), pp. 41–44 and 189–90. However, see the critical remarks of Bierbrauer, 'Gepiden im 5. Jahrhundert', pp. 195–96.

[13] Jordanes, *Getica*, 133: 'tam Ostrogothis quam Gepidis parentibus suis [...] euangelizantes'.

[14] Jordanes, *Getica*, 199: 'super ceteros regulos diligebat'. To Jordanes, Ardaric was the 'renowned' ('famosissimus') king of the Gepids.

[15] Jordanes, *Getica*, 200–01: 'Reliqua autem, si dici fas est, turba regum diuersarumque nationum ductores ac si satellites notibus Attilae attendebant, et ubi oculo annuisset, absque aliqua murmuratione cum timore et tremore unusquisque adstabat, aut certe, quod iussus fuerat, exequebatur. Solus Attila rex omnium regum super omnes et pro omnibus sollicitus erat.' Jordanes sets Ardaric and Valamir in sharp contrast to the other chieftains.

chieftain of the *Sciri*, as well as to the 'renowned' king of the Gepids, Ardaric.[16] They all took part in raids into the Balkan provinces of the empire, such as that of 447, which reached Thrace and Illyricum. They were also on the side of the Huns at the battle of Campus Mauriacum in which an army of Visigoths, Alans, and other *gentes* commanded by Aetius defeated Attila and his allies. Their shared experience as Attila's lieutenants may explain the alliance between Ardaric and other chieftains, which defeated Attila's sons at the battle on the Nedao River in Pannonia (454 or 455).[17] According to Jordanes, while the reason for Ardaric's revolt against the Huns was that 'he became enraged because so many nations were being treated like slaves of the basest condition', his rebellion 'freed not only his own tribe, but all the others who were equally oppressed'.[18]

The collapse of the Hunnic Empire seems to have greatly contributed to the disappearance of many fashions and customs that had left material remains in early fifth-century archaeological assemblages. No composite bows, bronze cauldrons, or golden diadems are known from assemblages dated after the battle at the river Nedao. Within the area which according to Jordanes had been the territory of the Huns, but which was now that of the Gepids, male burials were marked with swords instead of composite bows, while most prominent in burials of high-status females are not diadems, but gilded silver brooches with chip carving decoration. There are also signs of an activation of that 'poison of heresy', which Jordanes attributes to a Visigothic influence upon the late fourth-century Gepids. That Ardaric and his successors may have greatly benefited from the victory over the Huns on the banks of the river Nedao results from the examination of such incredibly rich assemblages as Apahida I–III or the Someşeni hoard, all of which have been dated to the second half of the fifth century.[19] The victory over the Huns

---

[16] Pohl, 'Die Gepiden', pp. 259–62.

[17] Wolfram, *Die Geschichte*, pp. 321–25.

[18] Jordanes, *Getica*, 260: 'indignatus de tot gentibus uelut uilissimorum mancipiorum condicione tractari'; 'nec solum suam gentem, sed et ceteras qui pariter praemebantur sua discessione absoluit'. Jordanes is quick to add, though, that the Gepids 'by their own might won for themselves the territory of the Huns', thus forcing the Ostrogoths out of Pannonia (Jordanes, *Getica*, 264).

[19] For Apahida I–III, see Rodica Marghitu, 'Männergrab II von Apahida, Kr. Klausenburg, Siebenbürgen/Transsylvanien, Rumänien', in *Das Gold der Barbarenfürsten: Schätze aus Prunkgräbern des 5. Jahrhunderts n. Chr. zwischen Kaukasus und Gallien*, ed. by Alfried Wieczorek and Patrick Périn (Stuttgart, 2001), pp. 147–55; Rodica Marghitu and Coriolan Opreanu, 'Grab des Omharus, Fürstengrab I von Apahida, Bez. Klausenburg, Siebenbürgen/Transsylvanien, Rumänien', in *Das Gold der Barbarenfürsten*, ed. by Wieczorek and Périn, pp. 1259–60; Rodica

must have put a premium on Ardaric and his successor's ability to further expand the area under their control and influence. It seems quite probable that the kings of the Gepids had under their control the region of and around the old seat of Hunnic power, which may be the reason for the archaeologically observable late fifth-century settlement shift from the uplands of Transylvania to the plain of the Tisza River and its tributaries. To be sure, both Jordanes and the archaeological evidence attest to the continuation of settlement in Transylvania, the 'ancient Dacia, which the race of the Gepids now possess'.[20] Jordanes even calls the region Gepidia, no doubt having in mind the political configuration of his own lifetime.[21] Within the western parts of Gepidia, István Bóna pointed to assemblages of the Poroshát-Malajdok-Csongrád group around the confluence of the Tisza and Maros rivers as the archaeological correlate of the Gepid expansion into the lowlands of the Tisza valley.[22]

The battle on the banks of the river Nedao may have also prompted a reorganization of the political and ethnic configuration of the Carpathian Basin. The Gepids and the Ostrogoths of Transylvania seem to have been staunch allies of Giesmos, a son of Attila who had married one of Ardaric's daughters. The existence of an independent centre of power in the region in the aftermath of the battle on the river Nedao is also confirmed by the rich burial and hoard assemblages from Apahida and Someşeni, as well as by numerous gold coin finds. Before *c.* 500, the Gepids seem to have expanded into the rest of the former province of Dacia,

---

Marghitu, 'Fund aus Grab III von Apahida, Bez. Klausenburg, Siebenbürgen/Transsylvanien, Rumänien', in *Das Gold der Barbarenfürsten*, ed. by Wieczorek and Périn, p. 16. For Someşeni, see Rodica Marghitu, 'Schatzfund von Cluj-Someşeni, Siebenbürgen/Transsylvanien, Rumänien', in *Das Gold der Barbarenfürsten*, ed. by Wieczorek and Périn, pp. 162–65.

[20] Jordanes, *Getica*, 73: 'Daciam dico antiquam, quam nunc Gepidarum populi possidere noscuntur'. In order to avoid any confusion with either Dacia Ripensis or Dacia Mediterranea (both Roman provinces *south* of the Danube created after the withdrawal of the Roman army and administration from Dacia under Emperor Aurelian), Jordanes adds that 'this country lies across the Danube within sight of Moesia, and is surrounded by a crown of mountains' (Jordanes, *Getica*, 74). For the archaeology of the Gepids in Transylvania, see Kurt Horedt, 'Der östliche Reihengräberkreis in Siebenbürgen', *Dacia*, 21 (1977), 251–68; Radu Harhoiu, 'Archäologische Kulturgruppen des 6.–7. Jahrhunderts in Siebenbürgen: Forschungsgeschichtliche Überlegungen', *Slovenská Archeológia*, 49 (2001), 139–63; Ioan Stanciu, 'Gepizi, avari şi slavi timpurii (sec. V–VII p.Chr.) în spaţiul vestic şi nord-vestic al României', *Ephemeris Napocensis*, 12 (2002), 203–36.

[21] Jordanes, *Getica*, 74: 'Daciam appellavere maiores, quae nunc, ut diximus, Gepidia dicitur.'

[22] István Bóna, 'Ein Vierteljahrhundert Völkerwanderungszeitforschung in Ungarn', *Acta Archaeologica Academiae Scientiarum Hungaricae*, 23 (1971), 265–336 (p. 274).

reaching the Lower Danube to the south and the Olt River to the south-east. They thus became neighbours of the Balkan provinces of the empire. On the other hand, the Ostrogoths under Valamir and his brothers had been on the side of the Huns under two of Attila's sons, Horminak and Dengizil. Soon after Nedao, the allies of the Huns found themselves not only at odds with the empire over the amount of the subsidies they were supposed to receive, but also in competition with their new neighbours, the *Sciri*, the Herules, and the Gepids.[23]

The Gepids were also involved, albeit occasionally, in intertribal conflicts in the Middle Danube region. According to Jordanes, a large coalition of Suebians, *Sciri*, and Gepids was defeated 'at the river Bolia in Pannonia' by the Ostrogoths under Thiudimer, an event commonly dated to 469.[24] However, a few years later, emboldened by their success against neighbouring tribes, Thiudimer and his son Theodoric, 'seeing prosperity everywhere awaiting' them, moved against the Balkan provinces of the empire. They eventually accepted the status of federates for themselves and their men, and never returned to Pannonia. As a consequence, the Gepids won the upper hand over the entire region of the Middle Danube. The kings of the Gepids will remain the most important political actors in that region for the subsequent century. In the process, they managed to occupy both the plain between the Danube and the Sava rivers, and the city of Sirmium, where the royal residence moved under one of Ardaric's sons named Thraustila.[25]

In 488, the Ostrogoths under Theodoric inflicted another defeat upon the Gepids near the river Ulca, when moving from Moesia to Italy. Thraustila was killed in that battle, and Sirmium subsequently fell to the Ostrogoths.[26] The new king of the Gepids, Thrasaric, son of Thraustila, is said to have ruled together with his mother from those parts of Gepidia farther to the north, which were controlled at that time by Gunderic, a chieftain of mixed Gepid-Hunnic heritage. To be sure, the Gepids attempted to retake Sirmium in 504, but without much success. Some of the Gepids involved in the attack on Sirmium chose to move into the empire, where they were granted the status of federates.[27] Twenty years later, Theodoric ordered the forceful resettlement to Gaul of the remnants of the Gepid population

[23] Pohl, 'Die Gepiden', pp. 268–72.

[24] Jordanes, *Getica*, 277: 'ad amnem Bolia in Pannoniis'. For the date of the battle, see Wolfram, *Die Geschichte*, pp. 326–35.

[25] Jordanes, *Getica*, 300.

[26] Pohl, 'Die Gepiden', pp. 291–92.

[27] Pohl, 'Die Gepiden', pp. 293–94.

in the hinterland of Sirmium. The archaeological evidence dated to the late fifth century in the Sirmium area is rather scarce and consists only of single finds.

However, the power of the Gepids rapidly increased after 500, when their kings established matrimonial alliances with more or less distant, but certainly powerful neighbours. The second wife of Wacho, king of the Lombards, was Austrigosa, the daughter of an unnamed Gepid king.[28] Their two daughters married into the Frankish royal family and later became Frankish queens. The eastern distribution of cemeteries of the so-called *Reihengräberkreis* so typical for areas of Western and Central Europe which were around 500 under Frankish rule or influence reaches far to the valley of the Tisza River and Transylvania.[29] In the early sixth century, the Gepids were neither 'poor' nor 'slow'. In fact, in the 540s they were quick to regain control of Sirmium, a city in which their king Cunimund would a few years later strike his own silver coinage.[30] During the middle third of the sixth century, Sirmium was also the seat of the Arian bishop of the Gepids.[31] The Gepid kingdom did not survive the Avar onslaught, and although Gepids continue to be mentioned in written sources of the late sixth and seventh centuries, the subsequent history of the Carpathian Basin is instead associated with their conquerors, the Avars.

Much of what we know about the archaeology of late fifth- and sixth-century Gepidia comes from a relatively large number of excavated cemeteries.[32] Those are the burial grounds of two or three generations of elite warriors, peasants, as well as craftsmen (as indicated by such graves of goldsmiths as that of Csongrád-Kenderföldek).[33] It is often assumed that most graves in those cemeteries are of Gepids, primarily warriors buried together with their weapons.[34] The Hun-age west–east orientation of graves apparently continued into the late fifth and early

[28] Paul the Deacon, *Historia Langobardorum*, 1.21. See also Eleonora Tabaczyńska and Stanisław Tabaczyński, 'Zarys kultury Longobardów: Studium archeologiczne', in *Italia*, ed. by Eleonora Tabaczyńska (Wrocław, 1980), pp. 9–22.

[29] Horedt, 'Der östliche Reihengräberkreis'.

[30] Margit Nagy, s.v. 'Gepiden', in *Reallexikon der germanischen Altertumskunde*, XI, ed. by Hoops and Beck, pp. 115–40 (p. 124).

[31] István Bóna, *Der Anbruch des Mittelalters: Gepiden und Langobarden im Karpatenbecken* (Budapest, 1976), pp. 86–90.

[32] Dezső Csallány, *Archäologische Denkmäler der Gepiden im Mitteldonaubecken (454–568 u.Z.)* (Budapest, 1961); István Bóna and Margit Nagy, *Gepidische Gräberfelder im Theissgebiet*, I (Budapest, 2002); János Cseh and others, *Gepidische Gräberfelder im Theissgebiet*, II (Budapest, 2005).

[33] Bóna, *Der Anbruch*, pp. 45–53.

[34] Nagy, 'Gepiden', pp. 127–28.

sixth centuries. Grave goods typically consist of dress accessories combining pagan and Christian symbols.

By contrast, very few assemblages south of the Lower Danube have been associated with groups of Gepids known from written sources to have chosen to move into the empire. One possible explanation for the scarcity of evidence comparable to that of the Tisza Plain is that, when the Gepid expansion southwards reached the Danube frontier of the empire, the lands on the other side had already been occupied by the Ostrogoths. However, less than a century later, the Gepids controlled the main fords across the Danube. Procopius knew that, in 551, they had required the Sclavenes returning from a particularly devastating raid in Thrace to pay one gold coin per person in exchange for being ferried across the Danube.[35] Burial assemblages attributed to the Gepids have been found in Serbia, both at Kostolac (Viminacium) and at Kamenovo (see below). By contrast, such assemblages are rare farther to the south-east, on the territory of present-day Bulgaria.[36] The available evidence is almost exclusively from single finds and consists of dress accessories, mainly bow fibulae and belt fittings, for which good analogies exist in contemporary burial assemblages in Gepidia and nowhere else.

Two silver bow fibulae (Figures 8.1 and 8.2) have been accidentally found on the territory of the late Roman town at Oescus, near the present-day village of Gigen in the district of Pleven. Both display a scrollwork ornament with a sequence of scrolls in the middle of the head-plate and around the diamond-shaped foot-plate. Such a decoration was produced by casting, with little if any additional engraving. Judging from the existing evidence, such brooches may well have been manufactured locally, by craftsmen attempting to imitate the splendid silver fibulae from the Middle Danube region. Another gilded silver brooch from the early Byzantine fort in Stărmen (district of Ruse; Figure 8.3) is similar to both the Oescus fibulae and to specimens from Hungary. According to István Bóna, such fibulae served as fasteners for the upper garments of aristocratic women.[37] In grave 19 of the Szöreg

---

[35] Procopius of Caesarea, *Wars*, 8.25.1–6, ed. by J. Haury (Cambridge, MA, 1914–28). Although it is not clear exactly where the crossing of the Danube had taken place, it is nevertheless possible that the Gepids had control over the entire stretch of the Danube valley between the Iron Gates and, at least, the mouth of the Olt River.

[36] Anna Kharalambieva, 'Gepidische Erbe südlich der unteren Donau', in *International Connection of the Barbarians of the Carpathian Basin in the 1st–5th centuries A.D.: Proceedings of the International Conference Held in 1999 in Aszód and Nyíregyháza*, ed. by Eszter Istvánovits and Valéria Kulcsár (Aszód, 2001), pp. 453–60.

[37] Bóna, *Der Anbruch*, pp. 40–45.

Figure 8.1 (left). Bow fibula from Oescus. Photo by the author.
Figure 8.2 (middle). Bow fibula from Oescus. Photo by the author.
Figure 8.3 (right). Silver bow fibula from Stărmen. Photo by the author.

cemetery and in grave 64 from Szentes-Kökényzug, similar fibulae were found in the abdominal region of the associated female skeletons.[38] But in grave 50 of the Szentes-Kökényzug cemetery, a pair of similar brooches was found on the shoulders of the female skeleton. This points to a *peplos*-like garment fastened at the shoulders in a manner similar to that of contemporary fashions documented for the Ostrogothic kingdom in Italy or for Gepidia in the Tisza Plain.

Besides silver brooches, bronze casts with typically 'Gepid' ornamentation have also been found in Bulgaria. A bronze fibula from Novgrad (district of Ruse; Figure 8.4) and another from the Kirika near Kalugerica (district of Shumen) have head-plates with embossed arches surrounding an empty, smooth, and semicircular field. One of the two fibulae has a foot-plate decorated with a similar ornamental pattern.

It has long been proposed that eagle-headed buckles be attributed to a specifically Gepid female fashion.[39] Ten such buckles, most of them in a fragmentary state

---

[38] Csallány, *Archäologische Denkmäler*, p. 154 and pl. 168.18; Herbert Kühn, *Die germanischen Bügelfibeln der Völkerwanderungszeit in Süddeutschland* (Graz, 1974), p. 617.

[39] Joachim Werner, 'Slawische Bügelfibeln des 7. Jahrhunderts', in *Reinecke Festschrift zum 75. Geburtstag von Paul Reinecke am 25. September 1947*, ed. by Gustav Behrens and Joachim Werner (Mainz, 1950), pp. 150–72 (p. 167); Mircea Rusu, 'Pontische Gürtelschnallen mit Adlerkopf

of preservation, are so far known from the territory of the northern Balkan provinces of the empire.[40] Most archaeologists dealing with this class of buckles assume that they are in fact local developments of buckles with bird heads dated to the second third of the fifth century.[41] These were small buckles typically associated with post-Hunnic burial assemblages with both male and female skeletons. They have been found in such culturally diverse areas as the northern Caucasus, the northern and western coasts of the Black Sea, the Balkans, as well as Central and Western Europe, all regions in which they were used to fasten the belt or auxiliary straps, such as shoe-, sword-, or pouch-straps.[42] In the lands south of the Lower Danube, buckles with bird heads have been found on early Byzantine fort sites, such as Cape Kaliakra on the Black Sea shore (Figure 8.5) or Chervena Skala near Zhivkovo (Figure 8.6).[43] Their closest analogies are buckles of Nagy's Mozs class.[44] However, a similar decorative pattern in

Figure 8.4. Bow fibula from Novgrad. Photo by the author.

the form of a bird's head and neck may be found on foot-plates of fibulae of the Bökénymindszent-Slimnic type dated to the third quarter of the fifth century.[45] In Central Europe, the distribution of the small buckles with bird heads is restricted to those areas known from historical sources to have been occupied by the

(VI.–VII. Jh. u. Z.)', *Dacia*, 3 (1959), 485–523; Zdenko Vinski, 'Adlerschnallfunde in Jugoslawien', in *Liber Josepho Kostrzewski*, ed. by Jażdżewski, pp. 314–25; Margit Nagy, 'Die gepidische Adlerschnallen und ihre Beziehungen', *Budapest Régiségei*, 36 (2002), 363–92.

[40] Lyudmil Vagalinski, Georgi Atanasov, and Dimităr Dimitrov, 'Eagle-headed Buckles from Bulgaria (6th–7th Centuries)', *Archaeologia Bulgarica*, 6 (2002), 78–91; Kharalambieva, 'Gepidische Erbe', pp. 455–58 with fig. 3.1–4.

[41] Rusu, 'Pontische Gürtelschnallen', pp. 508–09.

[42] Nagy, 'Die gepidische Adlerschnallen', p. 364. See also Igor Gavritukhin and Michel Kazanski's contribution to this volume.

[43] Vagalinski, Atanasov, and Dimitrov, 'Eagle-headed Buckles', pp. 87–88.

[44] Nagy, 'Die gepidische Adlerschnallen', pp. 364–65.

[45] Csallány, *Archäologische Denkmäler*, p. 42 with pl. 109.10; Radu Harhoiu, 'La Romania all'epoca degli Ostrogoti', in *I Goti*, ed. by Ermanno A. Arslan and Volker Bierbrauer (Milan, 1994), pp. 154–62 with fig. 3.19.c.

Figure 8.5. Buckle with bird head from Cape Kaliakra. After Bobcheva, *Srednovekovni nakiti ot Tolbukhinski okrăg*, pp. 37 and 18.

Figure 8.6. Buckle with bird head from Zhivkovo. After Vagalinski, Atanasov, and Dimitrov, 'Eagle-headed Buckles', pp. 89–90 with fig. 8a.

Ostrogoths. The same may be true for the two specimens found in Bulgaria, but it is also possible that such dress accessories may have been produced and worn by other 'neglected barbarians' settled, more or less as federates, on Roman soil, such as the Gepids.

The typically 'Gepid' eagle-headed buckles are of three main types.[46] Specimens of the same type have similar ornamental patterns and have all been found within one of three restricted areas: the Tisza valley, Transylvania, or the Lower Danube region. A buckle similar to those from the Lower Danube region is also known from Crimea. Lower Danube buckles have engraved ornaments with cabochons of almandines or encased, flat pieces of red glass, an ornamental pattern undoubtedly inspired by early fifth-century buckles with rectangular plates, encrusted decoration, and wedge-shaped engravings. On the basis of ornamental patterns and technological details, several scholars have advanced the idea of four 'workshops'. Mircea Rusu first proposed Crimea, while Margit Nagy argued in favour of two more in those areas of the Carpathian Basin which by 500 belonged to Gepidia. A fourth workshop may have existed in the northern Balkan provinces of the empire and produced mainly imitations of the buckles coming out of the workshops in the Carpathian Basin.

---

[46] Nagy, 'Die gepidische Adlerschnallen', p. 392 fig. 16.

The early sixth century was indeed a period of close contacts between Gepidia and the Lower Danube provinces of the empire. The Gepids took a relatively active part in barbarian raids into the Balkans, while Gepid troops from the Danube may have been recruited for the early Byzantine garrisons in Crimea, where the Gepid aristocratic women introduced the fashion of eagle-headed buckles. A local production of such dress accessories is attested by the fact that the Crimean buckles were commonly attached to the belt by means of a cover plate, instead of a hinge.

Imitations of eagle-headed buckles were also produced in the Lower Danube region, all with rounded bird heads and shoulders, as well as smaller, slightly bent, and sharpened beaks. Buckles from the Lower Danube region stand out among others by the seesaw-like engraved decoration of the eagle's neck. Moreover, the central field of the buckle plate is decorated with deeply engraved scrolls. Unlike Crimean buckles, those of the Lower Danube were attached by means of rivets to the belt (or strap) and the counter-plate on the other side. Some rivets have rounded heads imitating encased stones or pieces of flat glass, such as found on fifth-century buckles. The presence on many of them of additional rivets or holes strongly suggests that in the Lower Danube region eagle-headed buckles were reused several times for different belts or straps. This dovetails nicely with what is otherwise known about the survival in the northern Balkans of the aristocratic female dress in fashion among Gepids or other barbarian groups. Such resistance is difficult to interpret historically, but it may well be an indication of a group (arguably, ethnic) identity to which members of the barbarian aristocracy in the northern Balkan provinces of the empire clung longer than anywhere else.

Two of the eagle-headed buckles from Bulgaria have been found during the excavation of the early Byzantine fort at Krivina/Iatrus (Figures 8.7 and 8.8). Another buckle has been recuperated from treasure trove hunters operating on the site of the early Byzantine fort at Svishtov/Novae (Figure 8.9). A third specimen was found in the Rish Pass of the eastern Stara Planina range, possibly in another early Byzantine fort (Plate II.1). Its closest analogy is another buckle from Shumen, the site of yet another early Byzantine fort (Figure 8.10).[47] All those buckles are similar in size, with only minor differences in the decoration of the middle field of the plate. Three other buckles are known from the area of Veliko Tărnovo, which is known from written sources to have been devastated during the fourth

---

[47] Vera Antonova, 'Shumenskata krepost prez rannovizantiiskata epokha', *Godishnik na muzeite ot Severna Bălgariia*, 13 (1987), 53–68; Vera Antonova, *Shumen i shumenskata krepost* (Shumen, 1995); Dochka Vladimirova-Aladzhova, 'Shumenskata krepost', in *Rimski i rannovizantiiski gradove v Bălgariia*, ed. by Rumen Ivanov (Sofia, 2003), pp. 149–59.

Figure 8.7 (upper left). Eagle-headed buckle from Krivina. After Gomolka, 'Katalog der Kleinfunde', p. 320 with pl. 10.72.
Figure 8.8 (upper right). Eagle-headed buckle from Krivina. After Gomolka, 'Katalog der Kleinfunde', p. 326 with pl. 22.364.
Figure 8.9 (lower left). Eagle-headed buckle from Svishtov. After Vagalinski, Atanasov, and Dimitrov, 'Eagle-headed Buckles', p. 89 with fig. 7.
Figure 8.10 (lower right). Eagle-headed buckle from the Shumen district. After Vagalinski, Atanasov, and Dimitrov, 'Eagle-headed Buckles', pp. 88–89 with fig. 3.

and fifth centuries and later settled by Goths, Visgoths and *Gothi minores*, Ostrogoths, and perhaps Gepids (Figure 8.11).[48] The similarities between the buckles from the Lower Danube regions and those found in the Carpathian Basin are

[48] The *Gothi minores* were a group of Arian Goths fleeing the persecution of the Christians north of the Danube. Under their Bishop Ulfila (311–83) they settled in 348 in Lower Moesia under the protection of Emperor Constantius II.

evident. Their respective distributions are also
adjacent to each other (Figure 8.12). Everything
points to the conclusion according to which the
Lower Danube buckles were imitations of early
sixth-century 'Gepid' originals.

Excavations started a decade ago on the site
of the late antique cemetery in Izvor near
Kosharevo (district of Pernik).[49] The excavators
attributed the burial assemblages found there to
a group of Goths, but drew parallels to contemporary cemeteries otherwise associated with the
Gepids.[50] The grave goods of at least one assemblage show clear connections with 'Gepid' cemeteries in the Tisza valley. Similar finds farther to
the north-west display the same associations.
There were graves of possibly Gepid warriors in
the cemetery of the multiethnic frontier town of
Viminacium.[51] Two other assemblages with
similar grave goods have been found in the
hinterland of Viminacium, at Kamenovo.[52] It
may be assumed that the Gepids buried there
had been federates settled in the territory of the

Figure 8.11. Eagle-headed buckle from
Veliko Tărnovo. After Vagalinski,
Atanasov, and Dimitrov, 'Eagle-headed
Buckles', p. 89 with fig. 5.

Roman town or soldiers of fortune in the Roman army stationed in the area during
the last decade of Gepid political history, shortly before and after the destruction
of the Gepid kingdom by Lombards and Avars.

The archaeological record of the Gepid presence in the northern Balkan
provinces of the empire is still meagre, mostly because of the current state of

[49] Metodi Daskalov, 'Ein Grab der Völkerwanderungszeit aus Südwestbulgarien (2. Hälfte des
5. Jhs.–Anfang des 6. Jhs.)', *Archaeologia Bulgarica*, 2 (1998), 77–87; Metodi Daskalov and Katia
Trendafilova, 'Nekropol ot vremeto na gotskoto prisăstvie po bălgarskite zemi v m. "Izvor"', in
Gotite i starogermanskoto kulturno-istorichesko prisăstvie po bălgarskite zemi, ed. by Aleksandăr
Stanev and Rosen Milev (Sofia, 2003), pp. 97–99.

[50] Csallány, *Archäologische Denkmäler*, pp. 30–39 and 315–19; Ljubica Zotović, 'Die
gepidische Nekropole bei Viminacium', *Starinar*, 43–44 (1992–93), 183–99.

[51] Zotović, 'Die gepidische Nekropole', pp. 183–86.

[52] Katica Simoni, 'Dva priloga istraživanju germanskih nalaza seobe naroda u Jugoslaviji',
Vjesnik arheološkog muzeja u Zagreb, 10–11 (1977–78), 209–28.

Figure 8.12. Distribution of sixth-century finds in the lands south of the Lower Danube attributed to the Gepids. After Nagy, 'Die gepidische Adlerschnallen', with additions.

research in Bulgaria and Serbia, two countries in which the 'neglected barbarians' have long been ignored by both historians and archaeologists. More recently, more scattered pieces of information have surfaced, mainly because of the largely illegal activities of treasure trove hunters, metal detector fans, and antique dealers. In addition, museum collections in Bulgaria include a large number of still unpublished finds pertaining to the history of the 'neglected barbarians' of Late Antiquity. Meanwhile, archaeologists still rely on written sources in order to arrange this rather heterogeneous body of data into a chronologically meaningful sequence. Archaeological finds are still expected to illustrate what we already know from written sources. Nonetheless, the picture of a multiethnic and multicultural society in the northern Balkan provinces of the sixth-century empire is rapidly coming to light. Yet to be brought to the light of that picture is the shining almandine-color of the 'slow', but still much neglected Gepids.

Appendix

Sixth-Century Finds in the Northern Balkans Mentioned in the Text

Bow Fibulae

1–2. Gigen, Pleven district (*Oescus*); stray find; gilded silver; L=9.6 and 6.7 cm; Pleven Historical Museum, inv. 1167.1–2; Kharalambieva, 'Gepidische Erbe', pp. 453–55 with fig. 2.1–2. (Figures 8.1 and 8.2)

3. Kalugerica, Shumen district; stray find; copper alloy; fragment; L=2.0 cm; Shumen Historical Museum; Kharalambieva, 'Gepidische Erbe', pp. 453–59.

4. Novgrad, Ruse district; copper alloy; L=8.7 cm; Town Museum, Svishtov, inv. 937; Kharalambieva, 'Gepidische Erbe', pp. 453–59. (Figure 8.4)

5. Stărmen, Ruse district; stray find within the early Byzantine fort; gilded silver; L=8.8 cm; Ruse Historical Museum inv. C174; Kharalambieva, 'Gepidische Erbe', pp. 453–59. (Figure 8.3)

Buckles with Bird Heads

6. Zhivkovo, Shumen district; found by treasure trove hunters within the early Byzantine fort at Chervena Skala; copper alloy; L=5.6 cm; Shumen Historical Museum, uncatalogued; Vagalinski, Atanasov, and Dimitrov, 'Eagle-headed Buckles', pp. 89–90 with fig. 8a. (Figure 8.6)

7. Cape Kaliakra, Black Sea shore; stray find within the early Byzantine fort; copper alloy; Dobrich Historical Museum; Liudmila Bobcheva, *Srednovekovni nakiti ot Tolbukhinski okrăg* (Sofia, 1977), pp. 37 and 18. (Figure 8.5)

Eagle-headed Buckles

8. Gorski Goren Trămbesh, Veliko Tărnovo district; stray find; copper alloy; L=10.2 cm; private collection; Vagalinski, Atanasov, and Dimitrov, 'Eagle-headed Buckles', pp. 89–90 with fig. 4. (Figure 8.13)

9. Kostel, Veliko Tărnovo district; stray find from the Kulata site; silver alloy, gilded; fragment; L=4.1 cm; private collection; Vagalinski, Atanasov, and Dimitrov, 'Eagle-headed Buckles', pp. 89–90 with fig. 6. (Figure 8.14)

10. Krivina, Ruse district (*Iatrus*); found in 1958 during excavations within the early Byzantine fort; copper alloy; L=10.8 cm; Ruse Historical Museum (now lost); Gudrun Gomolka, 'Katalog der Kleinfunde', *Klio*, 47 (1966), 291–356 (p. 320 with pl. 10.72). (Figure 8.7)

11. Krivina, Ruse district (*Iatrus*); stray find from within the early Byzantine fort; copper alloy; fragment; L=4 cm; Ruse Historical Museum inv. 7037; Gomolka, 'Katalog der Kleinfunde', p. 326 with pl. 22.364. (Figure 8.8)

Figure 8.13 (left). Eagle-headed buckle from Gorski Goren Trămbesh. After Vagalinski,
Atanasov, and Dimitrov, 'Eagle-headed Buckles', pp. 89–90 with fig. 4.
Figure 8.14 (right). Eagle-headed buckle from Kostel. After Vagalinski, Atanasov, and
Dimitrov, 'Eagle-headed Buckles', pp. 89–90 with fig. 6.

12. Rish Pass, Shumen district; found by treasure trove hunters in 1986; copper
alloy; fragment; L=8.9 cm; Shumen Historical Museum, inv. 5206; Vagalinski,
Atanasov, and Dimitrov, 'Eagle-headed Buckles', p. 88 with fig. 2; Kharalambieva,
'Gepidische Erbe', pp. 458–59. (Plate II.1)

13. Unknown location, Shumen district; found by treasure trove hunters;
copper alloy; private collection; Vagalinski, Atanasov, and Dimitrov, 'Eagle-headed
Buckles', pp. 88–89 with fig. 3. (Figure 8.10)

14. Svishtov (Novae); found by treasure trove hunters within the early
Byzantine fort; copper alloy; fragment; L=3.7 cm; private collection; Vagalinski,
Atanasov, and Dimitrov, 'Eagle-headed Buckles', p. 89 with fig. 7. (Figure 8.9)

15. Veliko Tărnovo; found by treasure trove hunters south of the present-day
city; silver alloy, gilded; L=7.6 cm; private collection; Vagalinski, Atanasov, and
Dimitrov, 'Eagle-headed Buckles', p. 89 with fig. 5. (Figure 8.11)

Burial Assemblages

16. Kosharevo, Pernik district, grave 1; male skeleton with iron *sax* with
wooden scabbard with silver mounts decorated with garnets, and 'magic' chalk
bead; iron buckle; silver buckle; iron knife; silver ring; and bronze earring;
Daskalov, 'Ein Grab', pp. 77–87. (Plates II.2, III.1, III.2)

BOHEMIAN BARBARIANS:
BOHEMIA IN LATE ANTIQUITY

Jaroslav Jiřík

Introduction

The settlement of the Bohemian Basin passed through a very complicated development during Late Antiquity. During the fourth century it is possible to observe the evolution of the so-called Elbe-Germanic culture tradition which, for the Roman period, may be considered as native to the territory of Bohemia. Indeed, a major source of information regarding that tradition is the cremation cemeteries in Plotiště nad Labem near Hradec Králové, and Opočno by Louny. In Plotiště, Alena Rybová identified clear influences from the region of the Lower Elbe territory, which she further interpreted as evidence of Suebian immigrants.[1] Contacts with the territory of the Elbe-Germanic culture are also documented by a number of rich burials dated to the C3 (AD 300/20 to 380/400) and C3/D1 (AD 380/400 to 410/20) periods of the general chronology of Central and East Central Europe.[2] Some burials in north-western and central Bohemia which have been dated to the C3 period also point to contacts with present-day Bavaria. Considerable similarities may be established, for example, between the pottery found in Prosmyky and Neuburg an der Donau, respectively (Figure 9.1.A, C).

I wish to thank my colleague Dr Jiří V. Kotas, who read an earlier draft of this text and made several language corrections.

[1] Alena Rybová, 'Plotiště nad Labem: Eine Nekropole aus dem 2.–5. Jahrhundert u. Z. II. Teil', *Památky archeologické*, 71 (1980), 93–224 (pp. 196, 203, 209, and 213–14).

[2] Martina Beková and Eduard Droberjar, 'Bohatý ženský kostrový hrob z mladší doby římské ve Slepoticích (Pardubický kraj)', *Archeologie ve středních Čechách*, 9 (2005), 401–39.

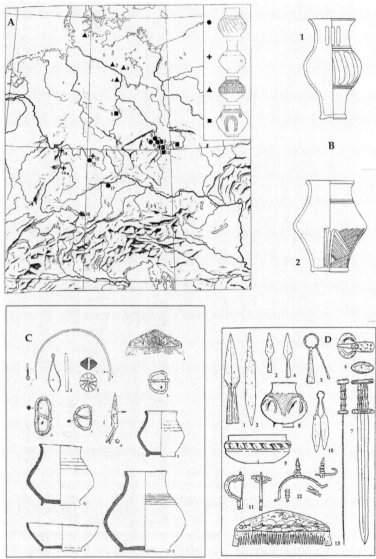

Figure 9.1. Pottery of Elbe-Germanic tradition: (A) distribution of the main types of Elbe-Germanic handmade pottery (after Keller, *Das spätromische Gräberfeld*, fig. 3); (B) handmade pottery of Elbe-Germanic tradition from Vienna (after Kronberger and Mosser, 'Spätrömisches Gräberfeld', pl. 7.8–9; (C) fourth-century finds of Elbe-Germanic tradition from Neuburg an der Donau (after Böhme, 'Zur Bedeutung', fig. 4); (D) selected grave goods from Beroun-Závodí (after Tejral, 'Die spätantiken militärischen Eliten', fig. 14).

Likewise, on account of miniature bronze weapons deposited in each one of them, the burials excavated in Litoměřice, Velké Žernoseky, and Beroun-Závodí (Figure 9.1.D) must be compared with that from Laisacker near Neuburg an der Donau.[3] More interesting parallels have recently come to light through the examination of pottery assemblages from contemporary settlements, some of which may have continued into the subsequent period (Figure 9.2).[4]

The archaeological record of fifth-century Bohemia is dominated by assemblages of the Vinařice group (Plate IV.A), so called by Bedřich Svoboda after the burials excavated in Vinařice near Kladno, which produced artefacts now dated to the D2 and D2/3 phases of the so-called early Migration period. The Vinařice group consists of a cluster of cemeteries, many of which are the best-known sites in Bohemia for this entire period. Nonetheless, only a few cemeteries have been properly excavated: Lužec nad Vltavou, Prague-Zličín, Vliněves, Zbuzany, and Litovice (Plate IV.B–F). The interpretation of the grave goods from those cemeteries has long been a subject of heated debate.[5] However, a much greater problem is the scarcity of contemporary settlement sites. Only a few remains have been identified on the hillfort site at Závist near Prague (Figure 9.3), and more sites are known from Jenštejn (Figure 9.4.A–B), Soběsuky (Figure 9.4.C), Prague-Dolní Liboc I–III

---

[3] Josef Kern, 'Germanische Miniaturbronzen des 3. Jahrhunderts n. Chr. aus Leitmeritz', *Sudeta*, 5 (1929), 148–55; Paul Reinecke, 'Ein spätkaiserzeitliches Germanengrab aus dem Neuburgischen', *Germania*, 10 (1934), 117–22; Erwin Keller, *Das spätromische Gräberfeld von Neuburg an der Donau* (Kallmünz, 1979), pp. 56 and 64 with pls 2.5–6 and 6.2–3; Jaroslav Tejral, 'Die spätantiken militärischen Eliten beiderseits der norisch-pannonischen Grenze aus der Sicht der Grabfunde', in *Germanen beiderseits des spätantiken Limes*, ed. by Thomas Fischer, Gundolf Precht, and Jaroslav Tejral (Brno, 1999), pp. 217–92 (p. 239 with fig. 14).

[4] Jaroslav Jiřík and Michal Kostka, 'Germánské sídliště v Dolních Chabrech', *Archeologie ve středních Čechách*, 10 (2006), 713–42; Jaroslav Jiřík, 'Vybrané sídlištní situace mladší doby římské až časné fáze doby stěhování národů v severozápadních Čechách', in *Archeologie barbarů 2006: Sborník příspěvků z II. Protohistorické konference, České Budějovice 21.–24. 11. 2006, Archeologické výzkumy v jižních Čechách, Supplementum 3*, ed. by Eduard Droberjar and Ondřej Chvojka (České Budějovice, 2007), pp. 535–64.

[5] Bedřich Svoboda, *Čechy v době stěhování národů* (Prague, 1965), pp. 78–126; Kazimierz Godlowski, 'Die Chronologie der jüngeren und späten Kaiserzeit in Mitteleuropa', in *Probleme der relativen und absoluten Chronologie ab Latènezeit bis zum Frühmittelalter: Materialen des III. Internationalen Symposiums 'Grundprobleme der frühgeschichtlichen Entwicklung im nördlichen Mitteldonaugebiet', Kraków-Karniowice, 3.–7. Dezember 1990*, ed. by Kazimierz Godlowski and Renata Madyda-Legutko (Cracow, 1992), pp. 23–54; Jaroslav Tejral, 'Vinařice Kulturgruppe', in *Reallexikon der germanischen Altertumskunde*, XXXII, ed. by Heinrich Beck, Dieter Geuenich, and Heiko Steuer (Berlin, 2006), pp. 414–23.

Figure 9.2. Archaeological finds from settlements in Bohemia dated to the C3 and C3/D1 periods. After Jiřík, 'Vybrané sídlištní situace', fig. 7.17–18 and 20–21; Jiřík and Kostka, 'Germánské sídliště', figs 3, 9, and 15.

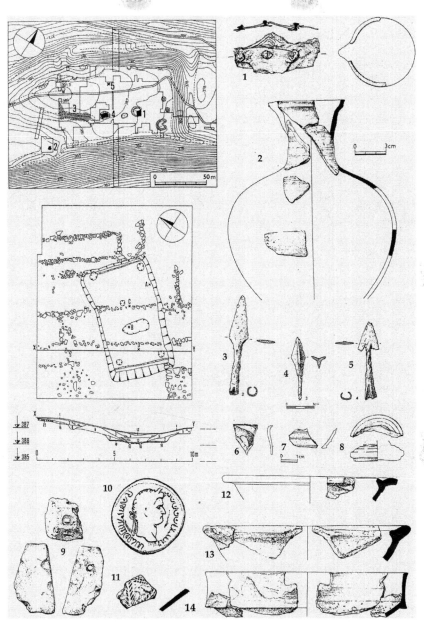

Figure 9.3. Závist near Prague: excavation plan, sunken-floored building, and associated artefacts. After Motyková, Drda, and Rybová, 'Some Notable Imports', figs 1–6; Motyková, Drda, and Rybová, *Závist*, fig. 50.1; Jansová, 'Hradiště nad Závistí', fig. 22.2–4.

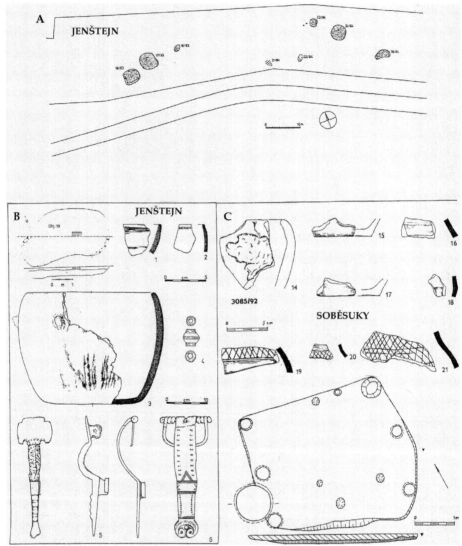

Figure 9.4. Jenštejn: plan of the fifth-century settlement (A) and archaeological finds from feature 19 (B) (after Droberjar and Turek, 'Zur Problematik', figs 3 and 7). Soběsuky: sunken-floored building and associated finds (C) (after Blažek, 'Die neuen unbekanten Funde', figs 4–5).

(Figure 9.5.C), Prague-Ruzyně, Žatec, and Siřem.[6] The most prominent features in Závist, Žatec, and Prague-Ruzyně are refuse pits, as well as sunken-floored buildings of square or rectangular plan and post construction. At the time those settlements were in existence, the southern and western parts of early fifth-century Bohemia witnessed the spread of the so-called Přešt'ovice-Friedenhain group (Figure 9.5.A), a cluster of sites with clear parallels on the other side of the present-day German-Czech border, in Bavaria.

'East-Germanic', Hunnic, and Sarmatian Foederati *in the Late Roman Army: The Material Culture of the Military Troops of Eastern Origin along the Danube and the Rhine, in Gaul, and in Britain*

In order to understand the explosion of cultural influences during the D1 and D2 phases of the early Migration period in Central Europe, it is important to turn to Late Roman military sites along the frontier, on which many artefacts have been found signalling contacts with the region occupied in the late fourth century by the so-called Sântana de Mureş-Chernyakhov culture. Emblematic for such contacts are the finds from the Roman fort at Iatrus, on the right bank of the Lower Danube, in Bulgaria: arrow heads, bone or antler reinforcement plates for composite bows, combs of Thomas's class 3,[7] large glass or basalt beads attached to sword

---

[6] Libuše Jansová, 'Hradiště nad Závistí v období pozdně římském a v době stěhování národů', *Památky archeologické*, 62 (1971), 135–76; Karla Motyková, Petr Drda, and Alena Rybová, 'Some Notable Imports from the End of the Roman Period at the Site of Závist', in *Archaeology in Bohemia 1985–1990*, ed. by Petr Charvát (Prague, 1991), pp. 56–63; Milan Kuchařík, Michal Bureš, Ivana Pleinerová, and Jaroslav Jiřík, 'Nové poznatky k osídlení západního okraje Prahy v 5. století', in *Barbarská sídliště: Chronologické a historické aspekty jejich vývoje ve světle nových výzkumů. Archeologie barbarů 2007. Sborník příspěvků z III. protohistorické konference, Mikulov 29.10.–3.11.2007*, ed. by Eduard Droberjar, Balázs Komoróczy, and Dagmar Vachůtová (Brno, 2008), pp. 341–72; Jan Blažek, 'Die neuen unbekanten Funde der späten römischen Kaiserzeit und der Völkerwanderungszeit in Nordwestböhmen', in *Neue Beiträge zur Erforschung der Spätantike im mittleren Donauraum: Materialien der internationalen Fachkonferenz 'Neue Beiträge zur Erforschung der Spätantike im mittleren Donauraum', Kravsko, 17.–20. Mai 1995*, ed. by Jaroslav Tejral, Herwig Friesinger, and Michel Kazanski (Brno, 1997), pp. 11–22 (p. 13 and figs 4–7); Eduard Droberjar and Jan Turek, 'Zur Problematik der völkerwanderungszeitlichen Siedlungen in Böhmen (Erforschung bei Jenštejn, Kr. Praha-východ)' in *Neue Beiträge zur Erforschung der spätantike im mittleren Donauraum*, ed. by Tejral, Friesinger, and Kazanski, pp. 99–118.

[7] Sigrid Thomas, 'Studien zu den germanischen Kämmen der römischen Kaiserzeit', *Arbeits- und Forschungsberichte zur sächsischen Bodendenkmalpflege*, 8 (1960), 54–215.

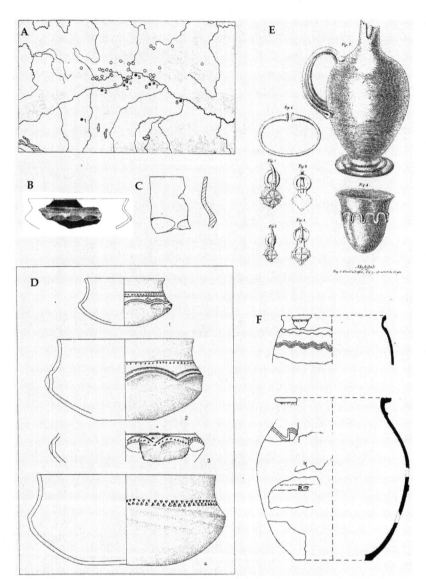

Figure 9.5. The early Migration period in Bohemia. (A) distribution of finds of the Přešťovice-Friedenhain group in southern and western Bohemia, as well as Bavaria (after Keller, 'Germanen-politik Roms', fig. 1); (B) carinated bowl from Prague-Dolní Liboc II (drawing by author); (C) fragment of a carinated bowl from Prague-Dolní Liboc I (after Svoboda, *Čechy v době*, fig. 9.2); (D) handmade carinated bowls from Bavaria (after Keller, 'Germanenpolitik Roms', fig. 5); (E) Fürst (Bavaria), grave goods (after Fehr, 'Bemerkungen', fig. 1); (F) Zbudov, settlement finds (after Droberjar, 'Od plaňanských pohárů', fig. 26).

pommels, sword scabbard mounts (very similar to finds in Vienna-Leopoldau or Novorossiisk-Diurso), as well as sheet fibulae with semicircular head-plates.[8]

Such artefacts have been interpreted as evidence for the presence at Iatrus, as well as elsewhere, of federates of East European origin. Equally relevant in that respect are finds of wheel-made pottery with burnished decoration from late fourth- or early fifth-century assemblages excavated in the Balkans on the territory of the formerly Roman provinces of Moesia inferior, Thracia, Dacia Ripensis, Dacia Mediterranea, Scythia Minor, and Rhodope.[9] Such pottery was found in large quantities on earlier sites north of the Lower Danube and is one of the most typical wares of Sântana de Mureş-Chernyakhov ceramic assemblages in that region. To the same direction point finds of combs of Thomas's class 2, which are typically decorated with horse heads (Figure 9.6.A7). Such combs are very similar to specimens of Thomas's class 3.3, which are equally decorated with animal pro-tomes, and have been found in some quantity on sites of the Sântana de Mureş-Chernyakhov culture (Figure 9.7.D4).[10] Such combs have also been found on contemporary sites within the border of provinces and empire and the close areas of barbaricum, in Budapest-Budafóki, Mingolsheim by Karlsruhe, Rommersheim by Oppenheim, and Ettringen by Tübingen.[11] Similarly, examples of combs of Thomas's class 2.3 are known from Late Roman military forts on the Lower and Middle Danube. One of the most important combs of that class is the specimen from a rich grave excavated in Lébény (Hungary; Figure 9.6.A), which is regarded by most scholars as typical for a Sântana de Mureş-Chernyakhov aspect of the Late Roman culture to be dated between 375 and 400. Among the grave goods associated with the Lébény grave is a ceramic pitcher with grooved decoration (Figure 9.6.A6), analogies for which belong to Magomedov's classes 1 or 6, most typical for a number of sites in southern Romania and in Left-Bank Dnieper Ukraine (Figure 9.6.B). The

---

[8] Gudrun Gomolka-Fuchs, 'Zur Militärbesatzung im spätrömischen Limeskastell Iatrus vom 4. bis zum zweiten Viertel des 5. Jahrhundert', *Eurasia antiqua*, 9 (2003), 509–22 (pp. 515–19 and figs 5.2–8 and 6.1–5).

[9] Ludmil Vagalinski, 'Spätrömische und völkerwanderungszeitliche Drehscheibenkeramik mit eingeglätter Verzierung südlich der unteren Donau (Bulgarien)', in *Die Sîntana de Mures-Černjachov-Kultur: Akten des Internationalen Kolloquiums in Caputh vom 20. bis 24. Oktober 1995*, ed. by Gudrun Gomolka-Fuchs (Caputh, 1999), pp. 155–77.

[10] Sofia Petković, 'Meaning and Provenance of Horse Protomes Decoration on the Roman Antler Combs', *Starinar*, 49 (1998), 215–28 with fig. 1.8–9.

[11] Jaroslav Tejral, 'Zur Chronologie der frühen Völkerwanderungszeit im mittleren Donauraum', *Archaeologia Austriaca*, 72 (1988), 223–304 with fig. 16.12.

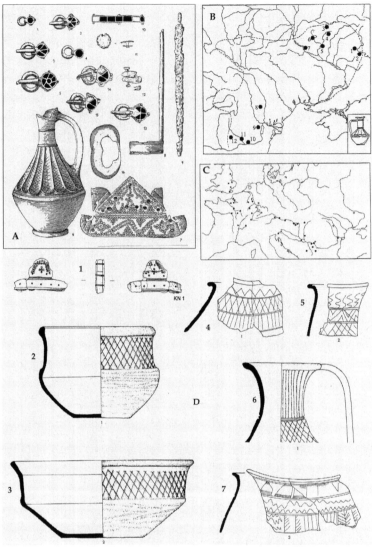

Figure 9.6. The material culture of barbarian federates on the frontier: (A) selected grave goods from Lébény (1–3, 5–9), Untersiebenbrunn (4, 10–13), and Mörbisch (14–16) (after Tejral, 'Zur Chronologie', fig. 21); (B) distribution of clay jugs with grooved decoration (after Magomedov, 'Zur Bedeutung', fig. 6); (C) distribution of combs of Thomas's class 3.3 (after Petković, 'Meaning and Provenance', map 1); (D) settlement finds from the *villa rustica* in Höflein-Aubüheln (1; after Kastler, 'Archäologie in Höflein', pl. 13: KN 1), the watchtower in Leányfalu (2–3), the fort in Pilismarót-Malompatak (4–5 and 7), and from Visegrád-Sibrik (6; after Soproni, *Die letzten Jahrzente*, pls 1–5).

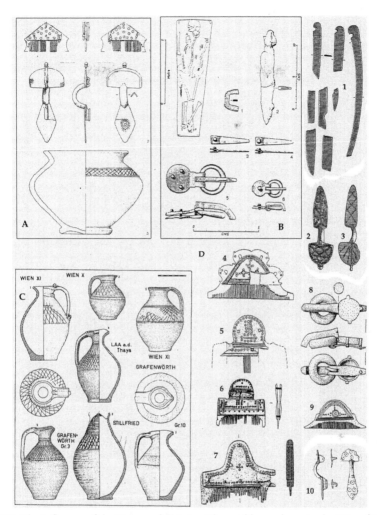

Figure 9.7. The influence of the Sântana de Mureş-Chernyakhov culture in the West: (A) grave goods from Götting (southern Germany; after Keller, 'Germanenpolitik Roms', fig. 3); (B) Gloucester (Great Britain), inhumation burial (after Böhme, 'Das Ende der Römerherrschaft', fig. 25); (C) finds of wheel-made jugs with burnished ornament from Austria (after Friesinger and Kerchler, 'Töpferöfen der Völkerwanderungszeit', fig. 24); (D) components of a composite bow (1), combs (4–7 and 9), fibulae (2–3 and 10), and buckle (8) from Intercisa (1), Oslip (2), Carnuntum (3), Mingolsheim (4), Geldersheim (5), Alzey (6 and 9), Neuburg an der Donau (7), 'Bürgle' bei Gundremmingen (8), and Geisfeld (10) (after Tejral, 'Zur Chronologie', fig. 12.1, 8–9; Petković, 'Meaning and Provenance', fig. 1.10; Pescheck, *Die germanischen Bodenfunden*, fig. 74.3; Kazanski, 'Les Barbares orientaux', fig. 3; Keller, *Das spätromische Gräberfeld*, pl. 12.5; Bernhard, 'Germanische Funde', pl. 35.2; and Haberstroh, 'Germanische Stammesverbände an Obermain und Regnitz', fig. 1.10).

distribution of such pitchers along the Middle Danube has been linked to the arrival in that region, after 380, of a group of 'East-Germanic', Hunnic, and Sarmatian federates under the leadership of Alatheus and Saphrax.[12] A similar interpretation has been applied to the distribution of combs of Thomas's class 2.3 along the Danube and Rhine frontiers, in Gaul, as well as in Britain (Figure 9.6.C).[13]

According to Sándor Soproni the barbarians under Alatheus and Saphrax, who are said to have been no less than one hundred thousand, settled north of the Drava River, along the frontier and in Valeria. Soproni's idea is substantiated by finds of wheel-made pottery with burnished decoration from many Late Roman forts or watchtowers in that area (Figure 9.6.D2–7). To the same group may also be attributed the cemeteries excavated in Cságvár and Szabadbattyán.[14] Finds on several sites in Lower Austria (Vienna-Simmering, Vienna-Leopoldau, Schiltern, Unterlanzendorf, Rannersdorf, Untersiebenbrunn, and the *villa rustica* in Höflein-Aubüheln) have also been linked to the presence of federates of East European origin (Figure 9.6.D1).[15] The cultural transformations in the Middle Danube region are fundamental for the understanding of developments taking place in Bohemia during the D2 period.

However, artefacts of eastern origin are also abundant in the western provinces of the Roman Empire. Connections with the Middle Danube may be illustrated by such artefacts as combs with semicircular handles, which are most typical for the Sântana de Mureş-Chernyakhov culture, but are also known from Carnuntum, Grafenwörth, and Cologne. In the West, such combs appear within the former

---

[12] Boris V. Magomedov, 'Do vyvchennia cherniakhovs'kogo goncharnogo posudu', *Arkheolohiia*, 1973.12, 80–87 with fig. 2; Boris V. Magomedov, 'Zur Bedeutung sarmatischer Kulturelemente in der Černjachov-Kultur', in *Kontakt, Kooperation, Konflikt: Germanen und Sarmaten zwischen dem 1. und dem 4. Jahrhundert nach Christus. Internationales Kolloquium des Vorgeshichtlichen Seminars der Philipps-Universität Marburg, 12.–16. Februar 1998*, ed. by Claus von Carnap-Bornheim (Neumünster, 2003), pp. 79–87 (p. 85 and fig. 6); Petković, 'Meaning and Provenance', p. 221.

[13] Petković, 'Meaning and Provenance', pp. 221–23.

[14] Sándor Soproni, *Die letzten Jahrzente des Pannonischen Limes* (Munich, 1986), pp. 86–93.

[15] Erich Polaschek, 'Wiener Grabfunde aus der Zeit des untergehenden römischen Limes', *Wiener prähistorischen Zeitschrift*, 19 (1932), 239–58; Eberhardt Geyer, 'Anthropologischer Befund', *Wiener prähistorischen Zeitschrift*, 19 (1932), 259–66; Gerhard Trnka, 'Spätrömische Funde des 4. und 5. Jahrhunderts vom Burgstall von Schiltern im Waldviertel, Niederösterreich', *Archaeologia Austriaca*, 65 (1981), 139–85; Peter Stadler, 'Völkerwanderungszeitliche Funde: eine Siedlung bei Unterlanzendorf und ein Gräberfeld bei Rannersdorf, Niederösterreich', *Archaeologia Austriaca*, 65 (1981), 239–85; Raimond Kastler, 'Archäologie in Höflein bei Bruck an der Leitha', *Carnuntum Jahrbuch*, 1993/94 (1995), 185–259 (p. 219 and pl. 13.KN1).

provinces of Raetia (Neuburg an der Donau, 'Bürgle' bei Gundremmingen, Lorenberg by Epfach, Frauenberg by Weltenburg, Regensburg, Abusina-Einig) (Figure 9.7.A and D7–8), Gaul (Ebersberg, Wiesbaden, Alzey, Bad Kreuznach, Eisenburg, Ruppertsberg, Worms, Beaucaire-sur-Baïse, Séviac et Bapteste, Rems, Strasbourg, Basel, Troyes, Montréal-Séviac, Mézin, Moncrabeau, grave 4607 in Krefeld-Gellep) (Figure 9.7.D4, 6, and 9), and Britain (Gloucester, Caerlon, and Traprain Law) (Figure 9.7.B). Assemblages from all those sites include brooches of several eastern types, combs of Thomas's class 3, belt buckles, 'Sarmatian' mirrors, 'Hunnic' kettles, and components of composite bows or of horse gear. There is also evidence of artificially deformed skulls and some elements of burial ritual believed to be of East European origin.[16] The eastern federates under the leadership of Alatheus and Saphrax were drawn from the Gothic cavalry forces mentioned as having participated in the battle at Adrianople (378). By 380 that group of eastern federates had moved to Pannonia. According to Walter Pohl, the move must be regarded as a Roman experiment in controlling groups of barbarians operating on Roman soil. As such, it must have typically combined various forms of contractual relations between the Roman government and the barbarian groups, ranging from outright *foedera* to ad hoc arrangements.[17]

On the other hand, Peter Heather has noted that no mention exists of Alatheus and Saphrax after 380. Their group must therefore have been among the barbarian losers of the early campaigns of Theodosius I, and could not possibly have prospered in Pannonia.[18] However, given that a complete annihilation of that group would have been impractical for a variety of reasons, its members could still have been recruited for Roman cavalry units stationed in the region. In any case, there is to

[16] Keller, *Das spätrömische Gräberfeld*, pp. 56–57, pl. 12.5, fig. 5.1–3 and 5–10; Erwin Keller, 'Germanenpolitik Roms im bayerischen Teil der Raetia Secunda während des 4. und 5. Jahrhunderts', *Jahrbuch des Römisch-germanischen Zentralmuseums Mainz*, 33 (1986), 575–92 (pp. 582–83 and fig. 4.1–2, 4, and 6); Michel Kazanski, 'Les Barbares orientaux et la défense de la Gaule aux IVe–Ve siècle', in *L'Armée romaine et les barbares du IIIe au VIIe siècle*, ed. by Françoise Vallet and Michel Kazanski (Paris, 1993), pp. 175–86 (pp. 175–78 with figs 1–3); Michel Kazanski, 'Les Barbares en Gaule du Sud-Ouest durant la première moitie du Ve siècle', in *L'Occident romain et l'Europe centrale au début de l'époque des Grandes Migration*, ed. by Jaroslav Tejral, Christian Pilet, and Michel Kazanski (Brno, 1999) pp. 15–23 (p. 15 with fig. 1.1–2); Horst W. Böhme, 'Das Ende der Römerherrschaft in Britannien und die Angelsächsische Besiedlung Englands im 5. Jahrhundert', *Jahrbuch des Römisch-germanischen Zentralmuseums Mainz*, 33 (1986), 469–574; Petković, 'Meaning and Provenance', pp. 227–28.

[17] Walter Pohl, *Die Völkerwanderung: Eroberung und Integration* (Stuttgart, 2002), pp. 50–51.

[18] Peater Heather, *The Goths* (Oxford, 1996), p. 137.

date no alternative explanation for the archaeological record of the Middle Danube region. For the purpose of this paper, it is more important to emphasize that cultural influences from Eastern Europe are not restricted to the area immediately adjacent to the Roman frontiers, but spread farther away into the neighbouring *barbaricum*, as, for example, in the valley of the Main River (Figure 9.7.D5 and 10).[19]

'East-Germanic' Influences and Late Antique Imports in Early Vinařice Assemblages

The Vinařice group seems to have emerged at some point during the D2 period, that is, between 410/20 and 440/50. Most significant for the chronology of the earliest Vinařice assemblages are metal, antler, glass, and ceramic artefacts (mostly from isolated finds) with numerous analogies in south-eastern Europe. Such is the case of cast, gilt bronze bow fibulae with embossed decoration from Lovosice and from an unknown location in Bohemia (Figure 9.8.2–3).[20] Both brooches have good parallels among bronze and silver specimens of Kokowski's class F, which are most typical for Sântana de Mureş-Chernyakhov assemblages.[21] Some of those parallels even have a similar embossed decorative pattern as that of the Lovosice fibula. Specimens from the Middle Danube area, especially on sites on the frontier such as Brigetio, Intercisa, Oslip, and Ternitz (Figure 9.7.D2–3) have been dated to the first half of the fifth century, although an earlier date within the D1 period may not be excluded.[22]

Equally 'eastern' may be the bow fibula found in Závist near Prague (Figure 9.8.14), for which many analogies are known from Sântana de Mureş-Chernyakhov

---

[19] Björn-Uwe Abels and Jochen Haberstroh, 'Burgellern, Stadt Scheßlitz (Lkr. Bamberg)', *Ausgrabungen und Funde in Oberfranken*, 11 (1997–98) 33–36 and 103–05 (p. 35 with fig. 28.2–3 and 11–12); Christian Pescheck, *Die germanischen Bodenfunde der römischen Kaiserzeit in Mainfranken* (Munich, 1978), pl. 113; Jochen Haberstroh, 'Germanische Stammesverbände an Obermain und Regnitz: Zur Archäologie des 3.–5. Jahrhunderts in Oberfranken', *Archiv für Geschichte von Oberfranken*, 75 (1995), 7–40 (p. 17 and fig. 1.10).

[20] Jan Blažek and Oldřich Kotyza, 'Další pohřebiště z doby stěhování národů v Lovosicích, okr. Litoměřice', *Litoměřicko*, 27–28 (1995), 7–11 (p. 8 with fig. 2.1); Blažek, 'Die neuen unbekanten Funde', pp. 11–22; Svoboda, *Čechy v době*, p. 81 and pl. 19.5.

[21] Andrzej Kokowski, 'O tak zwanych blaszanych fibulach z półokrągłą płytą na główce i rombowatą nóżką', *Studia Gothica*, 1 (1996), 153–79.

[22] Tejral, 'Zur Chronologie', pp. 244–45 and fig. 12.8–9.

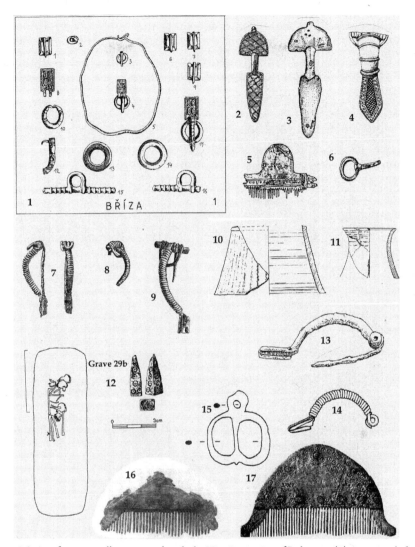

Figure 9.8. Artefacts typically associated with the Vinařice group of Bohemia: (1) grave goods from Bříza; (2) sheet fibula from an unknown location in Bohemia; (3) sheet fibula from Lovosice; (4) bow fibula of the Wiesbaden class from Vinařice; (5) comb of Thomas's class 3 from Vinařice; (6) golden buckle from Prague-Radotín; (7–9) crossbow fibulae from Prague-Veleslavín; (10–11) Murga ware from Závist; (12) 'Thor's pendant' from Lužec nad Vltavou; (13–14) crossbow fibulae from Závist; (15) iron pendant from grave 9 in Prague-Bubeneè; (16) comb from Litovice; (17) comb from Prague-Radotín. After Droberjar, 'Od plaòanských pohárù', pls 27.1–2 and 9–10, 28.1, 29.14; Droberjar, 'Praha germánská', pp. 791 and 795; Jansová, 'Hradiště nad Závistí', figs 20.7–9 and 22.1; Korený and Kytlicová, 'Dvě pohřebiště', fig. 13.1; Motyková, Drda, and Rybová, *Závist*, fig. 52.2; Pleinerová, 'Litovice (okr. Praha-západ)', fig. 9.1; and Svoboda, *Čechy v době*, pl. 32.18.

assemblages of the Late Roman period.[23] Three other fibulae from the Prague-Veleslavín cemetery (Figure 9.8.7–9) may belong to the same class, although they are different in minute details from the Závist brooch. Mechthild Schulze-Dörrlamm even called this group of brooches the 'Prague type' of crossbow fibulae and dated it to the mid-fifth century.[24]

Excavations in Závist also produced an iron crossbow fibula, possibly of eastern origin (Figure 9.8.13).[25] Undoubtedly East European are also the grave goods in a rich grave found in Bříza near Litoměřice: a sword, silver belt and footwear buckles, a golden torc, a kettle, and horse gear accessories (Figure 9.8.1).[26] The buckles with circular loop and rectangular plate are most typical for a group of burials known as Untersiebenbrunn, which is dated to phase D1/D2 and appears to derive directly from the Sântana de Mureş-Chernyakhov culture, especially from its variant documented in Crimea.[27] Golden buckles with similarly circular loop are known not only from a grave excavated in Prague-Radotín (Figure 9.8.6), but also from Western Europe (e.g. Gloucester in Britain), where they are usually treated as 'index fossils' of the early Migration period.[28] The sword and the golden torc

[23] Karla Motyková, Petr Drda, and Alena Rybová, *Závist: Keltské hradiště ve středních Čechách* (Prague, 1978), p. 182 with fig. 52.2. For analogies, see Anatolii K. Ambroz, *Fibuly iuga evropeiskogo chasti SSSR* (Moscow, 1966), pp. 71–72 with pl. 10.12–13; 'Săpăturile de la Poieneşti din 1949', in *Materiale Archeologice privind istoria veche a R.P.R.* (Bucharest, 1953), pp. 213–506 with fig. 251.1.

[24] It is nevertheless true that the Prague-Veleslavín and Závist brooches are somewhat different from most other Prague-type fibulae in that they both have twisted bows.

[25] Jansová, 'Hradiště nad Závistí', p. 147 and fig. 22.1; Eduard Droberjar, 'Od plaňanských pohárů k vinařické skupině (Kulturní a chronologické vztahy na území Čech v době římské a v časné době stěhování národů)', *Sborník Národního muzea v Praze, series A-Historie*, 53 (1999), 1–58 (p. 7).

[26] Svoboda, *Čechy v době*, pl. 21.

[27] Jaroslav Tejral, 'Naše země a římské Podunají na počátku doby stěhování národů', *Památky archeologické*, 76 (1985), 308–97 (pp. 365–66); Tejral, 'Die spätantiken militärischen Eliten', p. 250; Aleksandr I. Aibabin, 'Les Tombes des chefs nomades en Crimée', in *La Noblesse romaine et les chefs barbares du IIIᵉ au VIIᵉ siècle: Actes du Colloque International organisé par le Musée Antiquités Nationales, Saint-Germain-en-Laye, 16–19 mai 1992*, ed. by Françoise Vallet and Michel Kazanski (Saint-Germain-en-Laye, 1995), pp. 207–16; Bodo Anke, *Studien zur reiternomadischen Kultur des 4.–5. Jahrhunderts* (Weissbach, 1998), pl. 104. 3–5.

[28] Dieter Neubauer, 'Ostgermannen beiderseits des Rhein? Ein Beitrag zu völkerwanderungszeitlichen Schnallen in Mittel- und Westeuropa', in *Zeitenblicke: Ehrengabe für Walter Janssen*, ed. by Birgitt Berthold and others (Rahden, 1998), pp. 133–55 (pp. 144–45).

from Bříza were military insignia and symbols of rank in the Late Roman army. Torcs and bracelets were among the gifts the emperor's largesse bestowed on soldiers in the *scholae palatinae* or on the imperial bodyguards.[29] Torcs are known to have also been used as 'medals of valour' for units of federates, to which the men buried in Bříza may have belonged.

An 'East-Germanic' origin may also be postulated for antler combs with bell-shaped handles of Thomas's class 3, such as found in Vinařice, Prague-Podbaba-Juliska, grave 1 in Prague-Veleslavín, as well as graves 17 and 19 in Litovice (Figure 9.8.5).[30] The origin of such combs may be traced back to Sântana de Mureș-Chernyakhov assemblages, particularly those of the Dniester River valley.[31] Specimens of Thomas's class 3 are distributed along the Danube and Rhine frontiers and appear on sites that may have been occupied by federate troops. Combs of that class were manufactured in Intercisa, on the Danube.[32] Combs of Thomas's class 3 appear within the so-called Niemberg group of finds in East Central Germany, as well as in the Alemannian territories. In both regions, such combs appear in the mid-fifth century (later than on the Danube frontier) and with richer or much more elaborate ornamentation.[33] In the region of the Middle Danube, assemblages dated to an earlier period also produced combs with triangular handles and horse heads, which belong to Thomas's class 2.3. One such comb with stylized horse heads is known from a burial excavated in Litovice near Prague (Figure 9.8.16), with good analogies in Predjama, on the Danube, but also in Pohleheim-Holzeheim in

[29] Michael P. Speidel, 'Late Roman Military Decorations I: Neck- and Wristbands', in *Les Églises doubles et les familles: Antiquité tardive 4. Revue internationale d'histoire et d'archéologie (IVᵉ–VIIIᵉ s.)*, ed. by Jean-Michel Carrie (Turnhout, 1996), pp. 235–43.

[30] Svoboda, *Čechy v době*, p. 124, pl. 26.9; Tejral, 'Naše země', p. 365 and fig. 34.2; Ivana Pleinerová, 'Litovice (okr. Praha-západ): hroby vinařického stupně doby stěhování národů', in *Archeologie barbarů 2005: Sborník příspěvků z 1. protohistorické konference 'Pozdně keltské, germánské a časně slovanské osídlení', Kounice, 20.–22. září 2005*, ed. by Eduard Droberjar and Michal Lutovský (Prague, 2006), pp. 483–98 (p. 491 with figs 13.1 and 15.1).

[31] Galina F. Nikitina, 'Grebny cherniakhovskoi kul'tury', *Arkheolohiia*, 1969.1, 147–59 with fig. 1; Alexandru Levinschi, 'Gräberfeld der späten Sîntana de Mures-Černjachov-Kultur', in *Die Sîntana de Mures-Černjachov-Kultur*, ed. by Gomolka-Fuchs, pp. 23–32 (p. 28 with fig. 6).

[32] Mária R. Alföldi and others, *Intercisa II (Dunapentele): Geschichte der Stadt in der Römerzeit* (Budapest, 1957), pl. 84.10–11.

[33] Berthold Schmidt, *Die späte Völkerwanderungszeit in Mitteldeutschland* (Halle, 1961), pl. 52a; Jan Bemmann, 'Die Niemberger Fibeln und die Chronologie der Völkerwanderungszeit in Mitteldeutschland', *Slovenská Archeológia*, 49 (2001), 59–101 (p. 90); Ursula Koch, *Das alamanisch-fränkische Gräberfeld bei Pleidesheim* (Stuttgart, 2001), pp. 47–48 with fig. 12.X85.

Hessen.[34] A peculiar variant of Thomas's class I with a semicircular handle is also known from Prague-Radotín (Figure 9.8.17).[35] A similar comb was found in the Alzey fort on the Rhine (Figure 9.7.D9).[36]

Also made of antler is the pyramid-shaped pendant (of a type improperly known as 'Thor's pendant') from early fifth-century grave 29b in Lužec nad Vltavou (Figure 9.8.12).[37] An iron pendant from grave 9 in Prague-Bubeneč has a good analogy in Kosanovo (Ukraine) and may equally be viewed as an artefact of East European origin (Figure 9.8.15).[38] The same is true about the wheel-made pottery with burnished, zig-zag decoration, known as the Murga ware. Such a ware has been documented on a number of sites in Bohemia, at Zbuzany, Závist (Figure 9.8.10–11), and Holubice near Prague (all jugs), as well as in Prague-Podbaba (beaker).[39] A particularly problematic group of finds of this ware is known from Bohemia. The pottery with burnished decoration may well signal the presence of federates in the early 400s, but several assemblages in the Middle Danube region indicate that the Murga ware continued in use into the subsequent period, as shown by the artefacts associated with a burial in Veľký Pesek-Sikenica, especially the fibulae of the Gursuf-Bakodpuszta-Sokolnice class dated to phase D2/D3.[40] The later specimens

---

[34] Pleinerová, 'Litovice (okr. Praha-západ)', p. 491 with fig. 9.1. For analogies, see Petković, 'Meaning and Provenance', fig. 2.3; Berndt Steidl, *Die Wetterau vom 3. bis 5. Jahrhundert n. Chr.* (Wiesbaden, 2000), pl. 68.108.

[35] Svoboda, *Čechy v době*, pl. 32.18.

[36] Helmut Bernhard, 'Germanische Funde der Spätantike zwischen Straßburg und Mainz', *Saalburg Jahrbuch*, 28 (1982), 72–109 at fig. 35.2. Several other specimens of this type of comb are decorated with horse heads (see Petković, 'Meaning and Provenance', fig. 1.11–12).

[37] Rastislav Korený and Olga Kytlicová, 'Dvě pohřebiště z doby stěhování národů v Lužci nad Vltavou, okr. Mělník', *Archeologie ve středních Čechách*, 11 (2007), 423 and fig. 13.1. For the symbolism and distribution of this type of artefact, see Olg'a V. Bobrovs'ka, 'Zhynochi poiasni amulety cherniakhovs'koi kul'turi', *Arkheolohiia*, 1999.4, 89–95.

[38] Eduard Droberjar, 'Praha germánská', in *Praha pravěká*, ed. by Michal Lutovský and others (Prague, 2005), pp. 777–814 (pp. 790–91 with picture at p. 791.1).

[39] Svoboda, *Čechy v době*, pp. 106, 108 with fig. 32.4 and pl. 23.3; Jansová, 'Hradiště nad Závistí', fig. 20.7, 9. The Holubice jug is an unpublished find from the collection of the National Museum in Prague, but which originated from the excavations of Dr Vladimír Sakař. I am grateful to Dr Eduard Droberjar for directing my attention to this artefact.

[40] Jaroslav Tejral, 'Spätrömische und völkerwanderungszeitliche Drehscheibenkeramik in Mähren', *Archaeologia Austriaca*, 69 (1985), 105–45 (pp. 124 and 126); Tejral; 'Zur Chronologie', p. 277 with fig. 31.11; Karol Pieta, 'Neue Erkenntnisse zum Grab von Sikenica-Veľký Pesek', in *Probleme der frühen Merowingerzeit im Mitteldonauraum*, ed. by Jaroslav Tejral (Brno, 2002), pp. 237–45 (pp. 239–40 with fig. 1); Vagalinski, 'Spätrömische und völkerwanderungszeitliche', p. 165 with fig. 7.4.

of the Murga ware may still be regarded as 'imports', although direct proofs are missing. Runaways from the Middle and Lower Danube region into the Roman provinces are known for the mid-fifth century from written sources. The presence of the Murga type in Central Europe, as far as the Niemberg group of East Central Germany, may therefore perhaps be associated with the processes pushing splinter groups outside Attila's empire.[41]

Most artefacts associated with the Vinařice group appear to have been manufactured on sites on the empire's frontier on the Danube and the Rhine rivers. This is undoubtedly the case of the military belt sets with chip-carved decoration, such as the specimen from Prague-Vokovice (Figure 9.9.8). Such belt sets are particularly common along the Danube and Rhine frontier. As Horst Böhme has noted, their value as a symbol of military rank is well documented in the *Notitia Dignitatum*.[42] The buckle found in Kolín (Figure 9.9.11) belonged to one such belt set of western origin (probably from northern Gaul or from Britain).[43] The specimen from Prague-Radotín (Figure 9.9.10) is decorated with animal heads, and its analogies appear in northern Gaul and, less frequently, in Spain.[44] Also from Prague-Radotín is a buckle of Sommer's class 3e (Figure 9.9.6).[45] Another buckle loop with animal

[41] The Niemberg group is commonly identified as Thuringians, the local development of the Elbe-Gemanic environ with some elements and influences originating in Eastern Europe, but not the East-European refugees themselves. See Jan Bemmann, 'Zur Frage der Kontinuität von der jüngeren römischen Kaiserzeit zur Völkerwanderungszeit in Mitteldeutschland', in *Die spätrömische Kaiserzeit und die frühe Völkerwanderungszeit im Mittel- und Osteuropa*, ed. by Magdalena Mączyńska and Tadeusz Grabarczyk (Łódź, 2000), pp. 76–103; Christina M. Hansen, 'Frauengräber im Thüringerreich: Zur Chronologie des 5. und 6. Jahrhunderts n. Chr.', *Basler Hefte zur Archäologie*, 2 (2004), 88–90 with figs 109–13.

[42] Svoboda, *Čechy v době*, p. 114 and pl. 32.3; Bedřich Svoboda, *Čechy a římské impérium* (Prague, 1948), pl. 23.3; Tejral, 'Die spätantiken militärischen Éliten', pp. 228–31 with figs 7–10; Horst W. Böhme, *Germanische Grabfunde des 4. bis 5. Jahrhundert zwischen unterer Elbe und Loire* (Munich, 1974), p. 97 and pl. 11.

[43] Svoboda, *Čechy v době*, p. 115 and fig. 35.3–11; Böhme, *Germanische Grabfunde*, pp. 72–73 and pl. 16; Max Martin, 'Observations sur l'armement de l'époque mérovingienne précoce', in *L'armée romaine et les barbares du IIIᵉ au VIIᵉ siècle* ed. by Vallet and Kazanski, pp. 395–409 (p. 396 with fig. 4).

[44] Alexander Koch, 'Zum archäologischen Nachweis der Sueben auf der Iberischen Halbinsel: Überlegungen zu einer Gürtelschnalle aus der Umgebung von Baamorto/Monforte de Lemos (Prov. Lugo, Spanien)', *Acta Praehistorica et Archaeologica*, 31 (1999), 156–98 (pp. 169–70 with fig. 10); Droberjar, 'Od plaňanských pohárů', p. 8.

[45] Alena Rybová, 'Addenda zu dem Gräberfeld vom Beginn der Völkerwanderungszeit in Radotín', *Památky archeologické*, 79 (1988), 170–82 (p. 172 with figs 1 and 3.2).

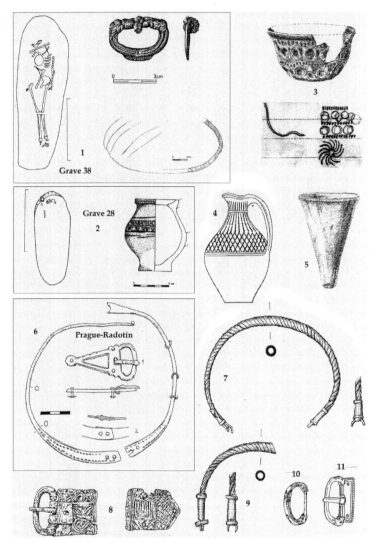

Figure 9.9. Roman frontier military culture in Bohemia: (1–2) graves 28 and 38 in Lužec nad Vltavou (after Korený and Kytlicová, 'Dvě pohřebiště', figs 12 and 15); (3 and 5) glass vessels from Vinařice (after Píč, *Starožitnosti*, pl. 2.11 and 13); (4) wheel-made jug from Prague-Kobylisy, most likely of Roman origin (after Droberjar, 'Od plaňanských pohárů', fig. 27.3); (6) grave goods from Prague-Radotín (after Droberjar, 'Od plaňanských pohárů', fig. 27.5); (7 and 9) bracelets from Prague-Malá Strana, Petřín, and Prague-Vokovice (after Droberjar, 'Praha germánská', p. 792); (8) military belt set with chip-carved decoration from Prague-Vokovice (after Droberjar, 'Od plaňanských pohárů', fig. 27.6); buckles from (10) Prague-Radotín (after Droberjar, 'Od plaňanských pohárů', fig. 27.7) and (11) Kolín-plynárna (after Droberjar, 'Od plaňanských pohárů', fig. 27.11).

heads from grave 38 in Lužec nad Vltavou (Figure 9.9.1) has been wrongly attributed to the Haillot or Krefeld-Gellep type.[46] In fact, this is more likely a barbarian imitation of a military belt buckle, for which several other examples are known from the Lower Main valley and from central Germany.[47] To the opposite direction, namely to Pannonia, point analogies for the bracelets found in Prague-Malá Strana, Petřín, and Prague-Vokovice (Figure 9.9.7 and 9), which are dated to c. 400.[48]

Of Roman origin must also be the glass bowl and conical beaker found in Vinařice (Figure 9.9.3 and 5). Similar glassware was found in abundance both within the Roman Empire and on sites of the Sântana de Mureş-Chernyakhov culture.[49] The bell-beaker from Prague-Podbaba may have been manufactured in the Middle Danube region, where such beakers appear in graves with weapons.[50] Ceramic jugs often with burnished decoration of undoubtedly Roman origin have been found in Prague-Podbaba-Juliska, grave 9 in Vinařice, Prague-Kobylisy,

[46] Korený and Kytlicová, 'Dvě pohřebiště', p. 422 and fig. 15.1. The wrong attribution was based on the peculiar form of the loop. In fact, that seems to be little more than a miscast, good analogies for which are known from other assemblages, e.g. grave 231 in Wenigumstadt (Germany) or grave 719B in Schleitheim (Switzerland). See Eva Stauch, *Wenigumstadt: Ein Bestattungplatz der Völkerwanderung und des frühen Mittelalters im nördlichen Odenwaldvorland* (Bonn, 2004), pl. 155.20; Anke Burzler and others, *Das frühmittelalterliche Schleitheim: Siedlung, Gräberfeld und Kirche* (Schaffhausen, 2002), pl. 89.719B/1.

[47] Kahl am Main, grave 125: Felix Teichner, *Kahl am Main: Siedlung und Gräberfeld der Völkerwanderungszeit* (Kallmünz, 1999), pl. 39. Butzow, Liebersee: Jan Bemmann, 'Romanisierte Barbaren oder erfolgreiche Plünderer? Anmerkungen zur Identität, Form und Dauer des provinzialrömischen Einflusses auf Mitteldeutschland während der jüngeren römischen Kaiserzeit und der Völkerwanderungszeit', in *Antyk i Barbarzyńcy*, ed. by Alexander Bursche and Renata Ciołek (Warsaw, 2003), pp. 53–108 (p. 59 with fig. 10.1–3).

[48] Droberjar, 'Praha germánská', pp. 833, 839, and 792 figs 1–2; Ellen Swift, *Regionality in Dress Accessories in the Late Roman West* (Montagnac, 2000), p. 124 and figs 148 and 167.

[49] Josef L. Píč, *Starožitnosti země české, díl III, svazek 1, Čechy za doby knížecí: Na základě praehistorické sbírky Musea království Českého a pramenů dějepisných* (Prague, 1909), pl. 2. 11 and 13; Svoboda, *Čechy v době*, pl. 28.8. For analogies, see Gudrun Gomolka-Fuchs, 'Gläser der Sîntana de Mures-Černjachov-Kultur aus Rumänien und der Republik Moldavien', in *Die Sîntana de Mures-Černjachov-Kultur*, ed. by Gomolka-Fuchs, pp. 129–40 (p. 132 with fig. 2.4–12). The conical beaker may have initially been made for a church chandelier; see *Die Welt von Byzanz: Europas östliches Erbe. Glanz, Krisen und Fortleben einer tausendjährigen Kultur*, ed. by Ludwig Wamser (Munich, 2004), p. 101 and figs 136 and 138.

[50] Svoboda, *Čechy v době*, pl. 28.5. See Jaroslav Tejral, 'Archäologisch-kulturelle Entwicklung im norddanubischen Raum am Ende der Spätkaiserzeit und am Anfang der Völkerwanderunszeit', in *L'Occident romain et l'Europe centrale*, ed. by Tejral, Pilet, and Kazanski, pp. 205–71 (pp. 248–49 with fig. 40).

Řísuty, grave 4 in Prague-Veleslavín (Figure 9.9.4), and grave 15 in Litovice.[51] Such jugs appear especially on Late Roman military sites of the D1 period, for example, in Rusovce, Carnuntum, Vindobona, and Klostenneuburg (Figure 9.7.C). This ceramic ware is dated between second half of the fourth and the second third of the fifth century.[52]

The settlement excavated in Závist has also produced fragments of green-glazed mortaria (Figure 9.3.12–13) of a kind most typical for the frontier provinces of Pannonia, Noricum, and Raetia.[53] Another interesting example of a jug with green-glazed and stamped ornament has been recently published from grave 28 in Lužec nad Vltavou, grave 28 (Figure 9.9.2). Similar jugs are known from the ceramic assemblages in Quadrata and Arrabona, two Roman sites on the Middle Danube frontier.[54]

The abundance of artefacts of Roman and eastern origin is not the only sign of dramatic changes taking place in the early 400s. Several settlements seem to have been located on well-protected hilltops, as is the case in Závist and Žatec. Within each one of those settlements, the most common feature is the sunken-floored building with post construction, which has no local traditions.[55] Important

---

[51] Svoboda, *Čechy v době*, pp. 106–08 and fig. 33; pls 22.2, 23.2, 25.10, 27.5 and 8; Pleinerová, 'Litovice (okr. Praha-západ)', p. 489 and fig. 7.1–3 and 12.

[52] Svoboda, *Čechy v době*, p. 107; Vilém Hrubý, 'Sídliště z pozdní doby římské ve Zlechově', *Archeologické rozhledy*, 19 (1957), 643–58 with fig. 212.9–13; Karol Pieta, 'Anfänge der Völker-wanderungszeit in der Slowakei (Fragestellungen der zeitgenössischen Forschung)', in *L'Occident romain et l'Europe centrale*, ed. by Tejral, Pilet, and Kazanski, pp. 171–89 (p. 175 with fig. 6.2–4); Herwig Friesinger and Helga Kerchler, 'Töpferöfen der Völkerwanderungszeit in Niederösterreich: Ein Beitrag zur völkerwanderungszeitlichen Keramik (2. Hälfte 4.–6. Jahrhundert n. Chr.) in Niederösterreich, Oberösterreich und dem Burgenland', *Archaeologia Austriaca*, 65 (1981), 193–266 (pp. 253–55 with figs 48, 49, and 57); Tejral, 'Archäologisch-kulturelle Entwicklung', p. 250 with fig. 41.

[53] Jansová, 'Hradiště nad Závistí', p. 158 and figs 3.1–2 and 20.1; Motyková, Drda, and Rybová, 'Some Notable Imports', pp. 60, 62 and figs 4.13 and 5.1. For analogies, see Doris Ebner, 'Die spätrömische Töpferei und Ziegelrei von Friedberg-Stätzling, Lkr. Aichach-Friedberg', *Bayerische Vorgeschichtsblätter*, 62 (1997), pp. 115–219 (pp. 153–62 and figs 22–30); Friesinger and Kerchler, 'Töpferöfen der Völkerwanderungszeit', p. 264 and figs 9–10.

[54] Luboš Rypka, 'Několik poznámek k nálezu římsko-provinciální glazované nádoby z Lužce nad Vltavou, okr. Mělník', in *Archeologie barbarů 2006, Sborník příspěvků z II.*, ed. by Droberjar and Chvojka, pp. 241–47.

[55] Milan Jančo, 'Príspevok k pravekým sídliskám v Čechách: Polozemnice typu Leube C2, C2/D2, D2 a D3', *Archeologie ve středních Čechách*, 6 (2002), 367–407; Miklós Takács, 'Der Haus-bau in Ungarn vom 2. bis zum 13. Jahrhundert n. Chr.: ein Zeitalter einheitlicher Grubenhäuser?',

changes were also noted in burial practices. Cremations in central and northern Bohemia completely disappeared, and the orientation of most inhumation graves was now west–south, instead of north–south. The only other fifth-century cremation cemetery situated in the peripheral part of eastern Bohemia is Plotiště nad Labem.[56] What exactly caused such changes remains unknown, but the changes themselves must have been linked to dramatic shifts in cultural patterns or religious representations, such as have been assumed for the Sântana de Mureş-Chernyakhov culture of the late Roman period.[57] Particularly suggestive for the presence within the Vinařice group of cultural features of East European origin, perhaps even of immigrants from that area, is, with few exceptions (Bříza, Radenice nad Ohří, Litovice, and Stehelčeves), the relative lack of weapons deposited in graves. The similar lack of weapons in graves excavated in Fenékpuszta and attributed to the Ostrogoths has been explained in terms of religious prohibitions.[58] A few skeletons with artificially deformed skulls are also known from northern Bohemia.[59] The custom first appeared in the Middle Danube region in the late 300s and early 400s in association with groups of Huns, Alans, and Goths settled as federates in Pannonia.[60]

So what caused the appearance of the Vinařice group in Bohemia? There are currently three different explanations. One of them is based on the idea of cultural diffusion. The 'East-Germanic' cultural elements spread to Central Europe

in *The Rural House from the Migration Period to the Oldest Still Standing Buildings: Ruralia IV. 8–13 September 2001*, ed. by Jan Klápště (Bad Bederkesa, 2002), pp. 272–90 (pp. 274–78 with pl. 1); Boris V. Magomedov, 'Siedlungen der Černjachov-Sîntana de Mures-Kultur', in *Die Sîntana de Mures-Černjachov-Kultur*, ed. by Gomolka-Fuchs, pp. 69–87 (pp. 70–71 with fig. 2.2–3).

[56] Rybová, 'Plotiště nad Labem', pp. 175–89.

[57] Ion Ioniţă, 'Römische Einflüsse im Verbreitungsgebiet der Sântana-de-Mureş-Černjachov-Kultur', *Arheologia Moldovei*, 17 (1994), 109–16 (p. 113); Levinschi, 'Gräberfeld der späten Sîntana', pp. 29–30; Gheorge A. Niculescu, 'Die sarmatische Kultur im Zusammenhang der kaiserzeitlichen Funde aus Muntenien: unter besondere Berücksichtigung der Funde von Tîrgşor', in *Kontakt, Kooperation, Konflikt*, ed. by von Carnap-Bornheim, pp. 177–205 (pp. 195–96).

[58] Péter Straub, 'Die Hinterlassenschaft der Ostgoten in Fenékpuszta', in *Germanen am Plattensee: Ausstellung des Balatoni Muzeums Keszthely im Museum für Frühgeschichte des Landes Niederösterreich, Schloss Traismauer vom 6. April bis 1. November 2002*, ed. by Róbert Müller (Traismauer, 2002), pp. 9–12 (p. 10).

[59] Korený and Kytlicová, 'Dvě pohřebiště', p. 420.

[60] Ágnes Salamon and István Lengyel, 'Kinship Interelations in a Fifth-Century "Panonian" Cemetery: An Archaeological and Palaeobiological Sketch of the Population Fragment Buried in the Mözs Cemetery, Hungary', *World Archaeology*, 12 (1980), 93–104 (p. 98).

(including northern Bohemia) only indirectly. The barbarians under the leadership of Alatheus and Saphrax and other chiefs may have engaged in relations with other barbarians across the frontier. Trade, matrimonial alliances, and political cooperation may thus explain the cultural transformations associated with the Vinařice group. The second explanation stresses migration. By 406, most Bohemian Suevi, Vandals, and Alans moved westwards to Gaul and Spain. The vacuum they left behind was filled with refugees from the Roman provinces. Several reasons could be offered as to why those people left the Roman Empire: anti-barbarian violence, especially as a result of the Stilicho affair,[61] or the raids of the Huns (especially that of 408 under Uldin's leadership)? An equally possible explanation along such lines would be the defeat of the usurper Constantine III. Coins struck for that usurper were found both in 'Bürgle' bei Gunnremingen, a Roman fort in Raetia with an abundant evidence of military frontier culture to be associated with the presence of federate troops, and in a rich grave in Měcholupy (Bohemia).[62] The main problem with the 'migrationist' explanation is that it does not really account for the many and significant parallels between the Vinařice group and assemblages of the Sântana de Mureş-Chernyakhov. A generation separates the advent of the eastern federates to Pannonia (*c.* 380) and the earliest assemblages in Bohemia that could be attributed to the Vinařice group and dated to the 410s or 420s. If so, then a generation may have been sufficient for the acculturation of the eastern federates, just as it was for the Vandals invading northern Africa, whose material culture had more in common with the Middle Danube barbarian elites than with assemblages of the Przeworsk culture, which some archaeologists believe to be Vandal.[63]

Finally, a third explanation for the rise of the Vinařice group combines elements of the other two interpretations: a small migratory group emulated local cultural practices. That at least a part of the old population continued to live on the same sites is demonstrated by the cremation cemetery found in Plotiště nad Labem, the fourth (and last) phase of which may be dated well into the fifth century. Handmade

---

[61] Pohl, *Die Völkerwanderung*, pp. 55–56.

[62] Svoboda, *Čechy v době*, p. 218. Keller, *Das spätromische Gräberfeld*, p. 57. Another coin struck for Constantine III was found also in Uherský Brod-Zběsná (Moravia), a site otherwise known for an early fifth-century grave with a skeleton with both artificially deformed and trephined skull, for which see Tomáš Zeman, 'Východomoravská periferie na prahu stěhování národů', in *Archeologie barbarů 2006, Sborník příspěvků z II.*, ed. by Droberjar and Chvojka, pp. 513–34 (p. 518).

[63] Dieter Quast, 'Völkerwanderungszeitliche Frauengräber aus Hippo Regius (Annaba/Bône) in Algerien', *Jahrbuch des Römisch-Germanischen Zentralmuseums*, 52 (2005), 237–315 (pp. 286–87 and especially 300).

pottery similar to that from Plotiště nad Labem has been identified in the ceramic assemblages of the Prague-Ruzyně settlement, especially in the assemblage from feature 618, which is clearly dated to the second half of the fifth century because of the associated crossbow fibula of the Rathewitz class.[64] It seems therefore possible to assume that central Bohemia was populated by groups of different origins.

The Rise and Decline of the Vinařice Group

The development of the Vinařice group has been dated in relative terms to the D2/D3 and D3 phases, that is, between 440/50 and 480/90.[65] In contrast to the period of its inception, the full development of this group is characterized by a shift from Middle Danube and East European to West European influences. Most prominent during this period were contacts with Alamannia, the Middle and Lower Main valley, and the western provinces of the empire. This is illustrated, among other things, by the distribution of silver and gilt silver bow fibulae of the Niderflorstad-Wiesloch (Figure 9.10.2) and Groß-Umstadt classes (Figure 9.10.4). Such fibulae were found, often in pairs, on several sites in the Bohemian basin (Plaňany, Prague-Michle, Vinařice, Prague-Podbaba-Juliska, Prague-Podbaba, and Prague-Zličín). They come in a variety of forms, mostly with semicircular or triangular head-plates and foot ending in the shape of an animal head. In Europe, there are two main clusters of finds besides Bohemia: one in Alamannia, the other in the region in Germany between the Rhine, the Main, and the Neckar rivers. Other finds are known from the Lower Elbe region, from northern Gaul, and from the region of the so-called Moravian Gate. By contrast, fibulae of the Niderflorstad-Wiesloch and Groß-Umstadt classes are almost absent from East Central Europe (Figure 9.10.1).[66]

[64] Alena Rybová, 'Brandgräberfelder des 5. Jahrhunderts in Böhmen', in *Germanen, Hunnen und Awaren: Schätze der Völkerwanderungszeit. Germanisches Nationalmuseum, Nürnberg, 12. Dezember 1987 bis 21. Februar 1988*, ed. by Wilfried Menghin, Tobias Springer, and Egon Wamers (Nuremberg, 1987), pp. 528–43 (p. 530); see also Jiří Zeman, 'Böhmen im 5. und 6. Jahrhundert', in *Germanen, Hunnen und Awaren*, ed. by Menghin, Springer, and Wamers, pp. 515–27 (p. 517). Kuchařík, Bureš, Pleinerová, and Jiřík, 'Nové poznatky', pp. 363–70 and fig. 16.6–24 and 17.

[65] Droberjar, 'Od plaňanských pohárů', p. 23; Jaroslav Tejral, 'Neue Aspekte der frühvölkerwanderungszeitlichen Chronologie im Mitteldonauraum', in *Neue Beiträge zur Erforschung der Spätantike im mittleren Donauraum*, ed. by Tejral, Friesinger, and Kazanski, pp. 321–92 (p. 351).

[66] Horst W. Böhme, 'Eine elbgermanische Bügelfibel des 5. Jahrhunderts aus Limetz-Villez (Yvelines, Frankreich)', *Archäologisches Korrespondenzblatt*, 19 (1989), 397–406 (pp. 398–400 with fig. 5).

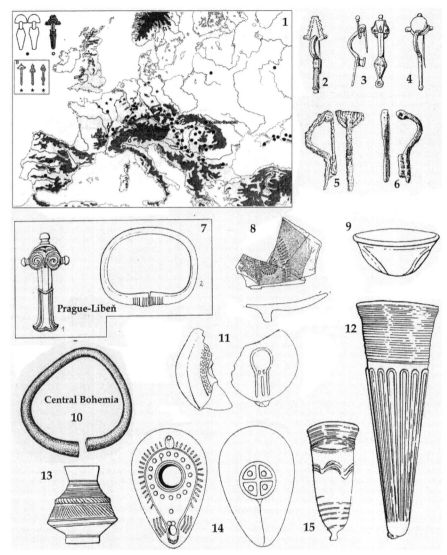

Figure 9.10. The development of the Vinařice group of Bohemia and its associated artefacts: (1) the distribution of bow fibulae of Niderflorstadt-Wiesloch and Groß-Umstadt, as well as Smolín classes (after Böhme, 'Eine elbgermanische Bügelfibel', fig. 5, and Müller-Wille, 'Prunkgräber', fig. 3, with additions); (2–6) bow brooches from Bohemia, dated to phase D2/D3; (7) grave goods from Prague-Libeň; (8) *terra sigillata* from Slavhostice (drawing by author); (9, 12, and 15) glass vessels from Úherce, Kobylisy, and Radonice; (10) bracelet with widened ends ('Kolbenarmringe') from central Bohemia; (11 and14) lamps from Slavhostice and Staré Čivice; (13) handmade pottery from Úherce. After Droberjar, 'Od plaňanských pohárů', pl. 29.2, 5, 7, 15, 18, 20, and 23–24; Droberjar, 'Zlatý náramek', fig. 4.4; and Jančo, 'Nálezy lámp', fig. 1.10–11.

There is no agreement as to the origin of such fibulae. Some believed them to have originated from Western provincial prototypes, such as the golden fibula from Pistoia with cloisonné decoration.[67] Others see the provincial crossbow brooches ('Zweibelknopffibel') as the model used for the production of Niderflorstad-Wiesloch and Groß-Umstadt classes.[68] Mechthild Schulze-Dörrlamm, while maintaining the general idea that such brooches were a barbarian imitation of provincial prototypes, nonetheless argues that the brooch of the Niderflorstadt-Wiesloch found in Alkofen must have been produced in a provincial workshop, as it morphologically resembles provincial bow brooches.[69] Finally, Alexander Koch further subdivided the Niderflorstadt-Wiesloch class into variants, one of which presents a diamond-shaped foot-plate (as, for example, the specimen found in Vinařice), which is otherwise typical for fibulae of the Bratei class.[70] Roman crossbow brooches of the 'Zweibelknopffibel' type were occasionally made of precious metal and may have been used to mark rank in the Roman army. Similarly, when worn by women, fibulae of the Niderflorstadt-Wiesloch and Groß-Umstadt classes may have been used to signal social distinction. Horst Böhme linked such fibulae with the Elbe-Germanic culture and assumed that their origin was with the Vinařice group. Specimens found in the Lower Main area and in northern Gaul are thus interpreted as evidence of migration from Bohemia, an idea otherwise substantiated by finds from the cemeteries of Eschborn (Figure 9.11.B),[71] Pleidesheim, Wenigumstadt (Figure 9.11.A) and others in south-western Germany. Böhme thus suggests that by the mid-fifth century, a relatively large number of the barbarian soldiers from the Vinařice and Niemberg groups were recruited in the Roman armies in the West.[72] By contrast, Alexander Koch attributed the fibulae of the Niderflorstad-

---

[67] Svoboda, *Čechy v době*, p. 86.

[68] Radu Harhoiu, 'Chronologische Fragen der Völkerwanderungszeit in Rumänien', *Dacia*, 34 (1990), 169–208 (p. 200).

[69] Mechthild Schulze-Dörlamm, 'Germanische Spiralplatenfibeln oder romanische Bügelfibeln? Zu den Vorbildern elbgermanisch-fränkischer Bügelfibeln', *Archäologisches Korrespondezblatt*, 30 (2000), 599–613 with fig. 6.4.

[70] Alexander Koch, *Bügelfibeln der Merowingerzeit im westlichen Frankreich* (Mainz, 1998), map 1. For the Vinařice fibula, see Svoboda, *Čechy v době*, p. 88 and pl. 24.10. For fibulae of the Bratei class, see Völker Bierbrauer, 'Bügelfibeln des 5. Jahrhunderts aus Südosteuropa', *Jahreschrift für mitteldeutsche Vorgeschichte*, 72 (1989), 141–60 (pp. 143–47 with fig. 1.4).

[71] Hermann Ament, *Das alamannische Gräberfeld von Eschborn (Main-Taunus-Kreis)* (Wiesbaden, 1992), p. 15 and pl. 2.2–3.

[72] Böhme, 'Eine elbgermanische Bügelfibel', p. 400.

Wiesloch and Groß-Umstadt classes to the Alamanni. In this interpretation, such fibulae spread from the Alamannian territory to Bohemia, and not the other way around. He further sees such fibulae as an indication of strong influences from the Elbe-Germanic culture, which, according to him, could explain their absence from the Frankish territory.[73] Nonetheless, more scholars seem now inclined to see the direction of influence from Bohemia to south-western Germany (Figure 9.11.C).[74]

Although in disagreement as to the direction of influence, both Horst Böhme and Alexander Koch attribute the fibulae of the Niderflorstad-Wiesloch and Groß-Umstadt classes to an Elbe-Germanic cultural tradition dating back to the Roman period. They thus favour an ethnic interpretation of material culture change. But the attentive examination of the distribution of several types of dress accessories in Central Europe during the second quarter of the fifth century suggests a very different approach. Particularly relevant in this context is the absence of fibulae of the Niderflorstadt-Wiesloch and Groß-Umstadt classes from the regions in East-Central Europe, in which finds of East European 'nomadic' or 'East Germanic' character are conspicuous. In such regions, the equivalent dress employed silver sheet fibulae of the Smolín class (Figure 9.10.1). There is a sharp contrast between the distribution of fibulae of the Niderflorstadt-Wiesloch and Groß-Umstadt classes, on the one hand, and that of specimens of the Smolín class, on the other hand.[75] Within the areas of the Vinařice and Niemberg groups, as well as in Alamannia, the Smolín class is unknown. Such fibulae were an essential part of a typically 'Danubian' fashion, which must have been associated with noble women within the Hunnic Empire. That fashion also stressed the use of double-layered combs, pins, earrings with polyhedral pendants, and diadems. Male accoutrements of that same region typically include swords, composite bows, three-edged arrow-heads, as well as dagger scabbard, sword, and saddle mounts made of gold or gilt bronze, with good analogies in a number of rich burials in Eastern Europe and

[73] Koch, *Bügelfibeln der Merowingerzeit*, pp. 541, 676 and pl. 1.

[74] Koch, *Das alamanisch-fränkische*, p. 391; Dieter Quast, 'Höhensiedlungen – donauländische Einflüsse – Goldgriffspathen: Veränderungen im archäologischen Material der Alamania im 5. Jahrhundert und deren Interpretation', in *Probleme der frühen Merowingerzeit*, ed. by Tejral, pp. 273–95 (p. 277 with fig. 6).

[75] Michael Müller-Wille, 'Prunkgräber der Völkerwanderungs- und Merowingerzeit', in *Herrschaft – Tod – Bestattung: Zu den vor- und frühgeschtlichen Prunkgräbern als archäologisch-historische Quelle Internationale Fachkonferenz, Kiel, 16.–19. Oktober 2003*, ed. by Claus von Carnap-Bornhaim (Bonn, 2006), pp. 127–45 (p. 131 with fig. 3).

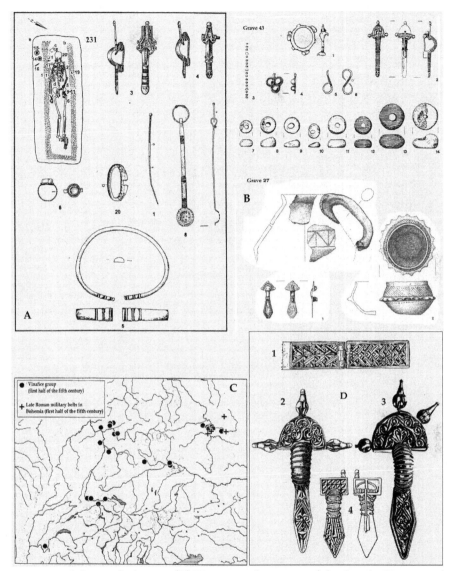

Figure 9.11. Bohemian barbarians? (A) Wenigumstadt, grave 231 (after Stauch, *Wenigumstadt*, pl. 155); (B) Eschborn, graves 43 and 18 (after Ament, *Das alamannische Gräberfeld*, pl. 4); (C) distribution of finds connected to the Vinařice group outside Bohemia (after Böhme, 'Zur Bedeutung', fig. 10); (D: 1, 4) Měcholupy, grave goods; (2) fibulae of the Wiesbaden class from Úherce (Droberjar, 'Od plaňanských pohárů', fig. 29.17); (3) fibula of the Wiesbaden class from Świelino (after Werner, 'Zu einer elbgermanischen Fibel', pl. 29.1).

Central Asia, all dated to the age of Attila.[76] Peter Heather advanced the idea that the 'Danubian fashion' emerged in the context of new social hierarchies created within the Hunnic Empire. The Huns, according to Heather, created new standards of ostentatious burial, which crisscrossed any ethnic boundaries that may have existed within that empire. The 'Danube fashion' was a fashion of the multiethnic elite running the Hunnic Empire, without being necessarily associated with any particular ethnic group.[77]

Such an interpretation of the 'Danubian fashion' invites a re-examination of the fibulae of Niderflorstadt-Wiesloch and Groß-Umstadt classes as symbols of social rank. If, as seems probable, the Vinařice group represents a political entity, however loosely defined, which was both independent from and outside the Hunnic Empire, much like Alamannia in the West, then a rejection of the symbols of rank used by elites in that empire may explain the adoption of completely different badges of social status. If this interpretation is correct, then the Vinařice group and its analogies in the West may represent a political alternative to the Hunnic Empire, which may have remained independent until Attila's western campaign in the 440s.

A similar explanation may be advanced for the distribution of fibulae of the Wiesbaden class with chip-carved ornaments in the Nydam style. Such fibulae were certainly produced in the north-eastern part of Central Europe. The best-known specimens of this class have been found in Weilbach, Groß Köris, Ártánd, Świelcza, and Świelino.[78] A slightly later, 'Burgundian' variant is known from grave 216 of the cemetery excavated in Yverdon-les-Bains (Switzerland).[79] In Bohemia, brooches of the Wiesbaden class have been found in Měcholupy (Figure 9.11.D4) and Úherce (Fig. 9.11.D2). The specimen from Úherce is quite similar to the brooch from the Świelino hoard (Fig. 9.11.D3) in which it was associated with other brooches with stamped ornament in the Sösdala-Untersiebenbrunn style dated to

---

[76] Tejral, 'Neue Aspekte', pp. 344–48; Tejral, 'Die spätantiken militärischen Eliten', pp. 266–67. For the 'nomadic' and 'East Germanic' styles of decoration employed for such dress accessories, see also Irina Zasetskaya, 'Les Steppes pontiques à l'époque hunnique', in *L'Occident romain et l'Europe centrale*, ed. by Tejral, Pilet, and Kazanski, pp. 341–56.

[77] Heather, *The Goths*, pp. 121–23.

[78] Tejral, 'Neue Aspekte', p. 349 and fig. 27.

[79] Gilbert Kaenel, *Archéologie du Moyen Âge: le canton Vaud du Vᵉ au XVᵉ siècle. Document du Musée Cantonal i archéologie et i histoire* (Lausanne, 1993), p. 30 and fig. 17; Dieter Neubauer, 'Das Maintal zwischen Würzburg und Karlburg: Eine neue entdeckte völkerwanderungszeitliche Siedlungskammer', *Beiträge zur Archäologie in Unterfranken*, 63 (1998), 129–45 (p. 143).

period D1/D2.[80] However, there are features connecting the Měcholupy burial assemblage to the rich grave found in Gáva on the Upper Tisza. Both assemblages produced golden pendants with encrusted stones (almandins). The shape of the brooch from Gáva is also reminiscent of fibulae of the 'Danubian fashion', but its geometrical chip-carved decoration executed in Nydam style is partly similar to the find from Měcholupy.[81] The Wiesbaden-type fibula from Świelca was found in an assemblage of the late phase of the Przeworsk culture, which has been dendrodated to AD 430±10.[82] Late fibulae of the Wiesbaden class, often made of precious metals and found within the territory of the Vinařice group and in southern Poland, within the area of the so-called Dębczyno group, suggest matrimonial alliances between the elites of the two groups, possibly with anti-Hunnic overtones. At any rate, the distribution of fibulae of the Niderflorstadt-Wiesloch, Groß-Umstadt, and Wiesbaden classes precludes any ethnic interpretation, but suggests the existence of political networks linking regional elites in different parts of Central Europe. The movement of goods from one region to the other could be explained in a similar way. Fibulae are definitely not the only reflection of such networks. Equally relevant are the silver bracelet from Prague-Libeň (Figure 9.10.7),[83] golden trefoil pendants with filigree decoration (Figure 9.11.B4),[84] some variants of the antler combs of Thomas's class 3,[85] or an antler, so-called 'Thor's pendant'.[86] Also very important are artefacts originating in the western provinces, particularly in the Rhine frontier region of Gaul. Glass beakers of Rhenish manufacture have been

[80] Joachim Werner, 'Zu einer elbgermanischen Fibel des 5. Jahrhunderts aus Gaukönigshofen, Ldkr. Würzburg: Ein Beitrag zu den Fibeln vom "Typ Wiesbaden" und zur germanischen Punzornamentik', *Bayerische Vorgeschichtsblätter*, 46 (1981), 224–54 (pp. 244–52); Kazimierz Godłowski, 'Das "Fürstengrab" des 5. Jhs. und der "Fürstensitz" in Jakuszowice in Südpolen', in *La Noblesse romaine et les chefs barbares du IIIe au VIIe siècle*, ed. by Vallet and Kazanski, pp. 155–79 (p. 156).

[81] Svoboda, *Čechy v době*, pp. 116–17 and pl. 29.4; Katalin Almássy and others, *Das Gold von Nyíregyháza (Archäologische Fundkomplexe mit Goldgegenständen in der Sammlung des Jósa-András-Museums Nyíregyháza)* (Nyíregyháza, 1997), pp. 62–63 and figs 47–48.

[82] Godłowski, 'Das 'Fürstengrab', p. 162.

[83] Svoboda, *Čechy v době*, pl. 33.6.

[84] Teichner, *Kahl am Main*, p. 225 and pl. 72; Alois Stuppner, 'Amulette und Anhänger vom Oberleiserberg bei Ernstbrunn, NÖ', in *Zwischen Rom und dem Barbaricum: Festschrift für Titus Kolník zum 70. Geburtstag*, ed. by Klára Kuzmová, Karol Pieta, and Ján Rajtár (Nitra, 2002), pp. 377–86 (pp. 381–82).

[85] Koch, *Das alamanisch-fränkische*, fig. 12.F5.

[86] Bemmann, 'Die Niemberger Fibeln', p. 90; Schmidt, *Die späte Völkerwanderungszeit*, p. 135; Droberjar, 'Od plaňanských pohárů', p. 8.

found in Prague-Kobylisy and Radonice (Figure 9.10.12 and 15). Another glass vessel is known from Úherce (Figure 9.10.9).[87] Shards of Argonne Ware or of pottery made in the *sigillata* technique have been recorded from Závist (Figure 9.3.11 and 14) and grave 76 in Prague-Zličín.[88] *Terra sigillata chiara* of North African production is also known from Závist and Slavhostice (Figure 9.10.8).[89] Perhaps from Slavhostice is also the fragment of a lamp of Hayes's type Ib, which was also produced in Northern Africa (Figure 9.10.11).[90]

Among the most important categories of evidence are also Roman gold coins. Almost two thirds of all Bohemian finds have been struck for the emperors Arcadius, Honorius, Constantine III, Valentinian III, and Theodosius II in the mints of Ravenna, Milan, and Rome, and not in Constantinople.[91] Finds from northern Bohemia also include three barbarian imitations of solidi. The coin finds within the area of the Vinařice group is in sharp contrast to the situation in Moravia and the neighbouring territories to the east, all the way to the Middle Danube, in which most coins were issues of the eastern mints, no doubt because of the tribute paid to the Huns.[92] The present-day border between Bohemia and Moravia thus represents the boundaries between the distributions of Roman gold coins struck in

[87] Svoboda, *Čechy v době*, pl. 31.17; Ursula Koch, *Die Glas- und Edelsteinfunde aus den Plangrabungen 1967–1983* (Heidelberg, 1987), pp. 111–13, 116–20 and figs 45, 47. The glass beakers from Prague-Kobylisy and Radonice belong to the Snartemo and Hammelburg classes.

[88] Motyková, Drda, and Rybová, 'Some Notable Imports', p. 62 and fig. 5.2; Jiří Vávra, Jaroslav Jiřík, Pavel Kubálek, and Milan Kuchařík, 'Pohřebiště z doby stěhování národů v Praze-Zličíně, ul. Hrozenkovská: průběžná zpráva o metodice a výsledcích výzkumu', in *Archeologie barbarů 2006, Sborník příspěvků z II*, ed. by Droberjar and Chvojka, pp. 565–77 (p. 570 and fig. 10). The fragment from Prague-Zličín is from a specimen of Chenet's form 319. See Raymond Brulet and Marc Feller, 'Recherches sur les ateliers de céramique gallo-romains en Argonne: 2. le site de production d'Avocourt 3 (Prix-Des-Blanches), zone fouillée', *Archaeologia Mosellana*, 5 (2003), 301–451 with figs 56.60–66 and 57.67–75.

[89] Jakub Halama, 'Nálezy terry sigillaty v Čechách', in *Archeologie barbarů 2006, Sborník příspěvků z II*, ed. by Droberjar and Chvojka, pp. 195–240 (p. 214 and fig. 12.4). Connections between eastern Gaul and Bohemia may also be demonstrated by means of the burial assemblage in grave 217 in Kahl am Main, which included a golden trefoil pendant and Argonne ware, as well as by that in grave 218 with a belt buckle of eastern origin associated with *terra sigillata chiara* of North African production. See Teichner, *Kahl am Main*, pl. 56.217 and 218.

[90] Milan Jančo, 'Nálezy lámp z doby rímskej v Čechách', *Památky archeologické*, 92 (2001), 165–83 (pp. 166 and 170).

[91] Jiří Militký, 'Finds of Roman and Early Byzantine Gold Coins on the Territory of the Czech Republic', *Slovenská numizmatika*, 17 (2004), 53–76 (pp. 61–64 and pl. 5).

[92] Radu Harhoiu, *Die frühe Völkerwanderungszeit in Rumänien* (Bucharest, 1997), pp. 143–47.

eastern and western mints, respectively. Moreover, several old Roman coins have been found in assemblages of the Vinařice group in the Bohemian basin: two denarii struck for Hadrian found in Závist (Figure 9.3.10), in addition to two pieces issued for Faustina junior and another for Commodus.[93] This is of course not a unique situation, as old Roman coins are known from other sites in *barbaricum* as well, such as Świelca in southern Poland, Runder Berg near Urach, and Glauberg in Germany.[94] Silver was minted only infrequently during Late Antiquity. However, soldiers were sometimes paid in silver, as in the disbursements on the occasion of the *Augustaticum* or *Quinquennium*, when each soldier received a pound of silver.[95] Older Roman coins must have been part of such payments during the early Migration period.

The impression one gets from the examination of the assemblages associated with the Vinařice group is one of intensive contacts with the world outside the Bohemian basin. Particularly important seem to have been contacts with Alamannia and the Lower Main valley. Specific conditions of the second quarter of the fifth century may have encouraged the establishment of such contacts. As a consequence, it is a mistake to regard the Vinařice group, the Main valley, and Alamania as sharing some 'Elbe-Germanic' tradition of the Roman age. Instead, we should envision a network of inter-elite relationships, if not an outright system of trade. Perhaps some artefacts, such as fibulae of the Niderflorstadt-Wiesloch class, indicate movement of people as well.[96] People, especially warriors, may have moved in the opposite direction, in search of employment in the Roman armies stationed in the West. The distribution of the artefact of an alleged 'Elbe-Germanic' tradition with origins in Bohemia within the valley of the river Main and in Alamannia should now be reconsidered as evidence of contacts between the Vinařice group and the West Roman Empire.[97]

[93] Motyková, Drda, and Rybová, *Závist*, p. 176 and fig. 50.1.

[94] Alexandra Gruszczyńska, 'Osada z wczesnego okresu wędrowek ludów w Świlczy, woj. Rzeszów', *Materiały i sprawozdania Rzeszowskiego Ośrodka Archeologicznego za lata 1976–1979* (1984), 103–29 (pp. 118–20); Godłowski, 'Das Fürstengrab', pp. 158–59; Steidl, *Die Wetterau*, p. 24.

[95] Wolfgang Hahn, *Die Ostprägung des Römischen Reiches im 5. Jahrhundert (408–491)* (Vienna, 1989), p. 17.

[96] Horst W. Böhme, 'Zur Bedeutung des spätrömischen Militärdienstes für die Stammesbildung der Bajuwaren', in *Die Bajuwaren: Von Severin bis Tassilo 488–788*, ed. by Walter Bachran and Hermann Dannheimer (Munich, 1988), pp. 23–37 (pp. 30–31).

[97] A comparative approach to the interpretation of the archaeological evidence is beyond the scope of this chapter. Such mutual oppositions are well known from other periods: the opposition between 'barbarian' and 'Roman,' as well as that between the late Merovingian and the 'early Slavic'

The late phase of the Vinařice group is dated to the D3/E1 period and thus synchronized with the developments taking place in the Carpathian Basin after the battle on the river Nedao. Dated to this period is the massive golden bracelet from an unknown location in central Bohemia (Figure 9.10.10). Such bracelets are known from contemporary assemblages in Tournai (Childeric's grave), Apahida I, Blučina, Großörner, Gáva, Pouan, Wolfsheim, and Fürst. In all such cases, the golden bracelet has been interpreted as a symbol of royal authority.[98] Such an interpretation may also be applied to the specimen from Central Bohemia, especially when we consider the independent position which the Vinařice group seems to have enjoyed in the past in relation to the Hunnic Empire. During phase D3/E1, fibulae previously in use disappeared, especially the Niderflorstadt-Wiesloch and Groß-Umstadt classes. They were partly replaced by fibulae of the Bákodpuszta-Sokolnice-Gursuf class, such as found in Horní Kšely by Kolín, Stehelčeves, grave 41 in Prague-Zličín, and an unknown location in Bohemia.[99] Those fibulae represent a new wave of influence from the Middle Danube. By contrast, the fibulae of the Krefeld and Rathewitz classes found in Vinařice,[100] that of the Weimar/Arcy-Sainte-Restitue class from Ratenice,[101] and that of the Pritzier-Perdöhl class from Liteň-Dolní Vlence,[102] are all reflections of contacts with the Thuringian kingdom during the early Merovingian period. Our knowledge of the late Vinařice group has

culture of the seventh century, are both predicated upon such dichotomies. For an even earlier example, see Wolfgang David, 'Südbayern als westliche Verbreitungsgrenze ostkarpatenländischer Nackenscheibenäxte der Mittel- und Spätbronzezeit', in *Popelnicová pole a mladší doba halštatská, Příspěvky z VIII. konference, České Budějovice 22.–24. 9. 2004*, ed. by Ondřej Chvojka (České Budějovice, 2004), pp. 61–89 (p. 76).

[98] Eduard Droberjar, 'Zlatý náramek typu Tournai-Blučina ze středních Čech', *Archeologie ve středních Čechách*, 5 (2001), 517–27; Almássy and others, *Das Gold*, pp. 61–63. For golden *Kolbenarmringe* within the empire, see Hubert Fehr, 'Bemerkungen zum völkerwanderungszeitlichen Grabfund von Fürst', *Bericht der Bayerischen Bodendenkmalpflege*, 43–44 (2002–03), 204–28 (p. 224 and fig. 12).

[99] Svoboda, *Čechy v době*, p. 81 and pl. 29.7–8; Bedřich Svoboda, 'Dva hroby z doby stěhování národů ve Stehelčevsi u Slaného', *Památky archeologické*, 66 (1975), 133–51; Jacek Kowalski, 'Chronologia grupy elbląskiej i olsztyńskiej kręgu zachodniobałtyjskiego (V–VII w.), Zarys problematyki', *Barbaricum*, 6 (2000), 203–66 (p. 213 with pl. 7.8).

[100] Svoboda, *Čechy v době*, p. 85, and Kowalski, 'Chronologia grupy elbląskiej i olsztyńskiej', p. 213 and pl. 7.8.

[101] Eduard Droberjar and Dan Stolz, 'Nové nálezy germánských a slovanských spon z 5. a 7. století ve středních Čechách', *Archeologie ve středních Čechách*, 9 (2005), 523–30 (p. 523 and fig. 1).

[102] Droberjar and Stolz, 'Nové nálezy', pp. 524–25 and fig. 2.

been considerably augmented by the recent excavation of the cemetery in Prague-Zličín with its 177 graves (Plate IV.C–D), one of the largest of its kind in Central Europe. Such a large number of graves is a strong argument against the idea that the hallmark of the period were small, 'princely' cemeteries with only a few graves. Although the majority of the graves were robbed, a number of golden and silver artefacts were found, which suggests that the cemetery was used by the élites of that time.[103] Finds of brooches of the Sokolnice-Bákodpuszta-Gursuf type as well as of Rhenish glass vessels with oblique grooves link the cemetery in Prague-Zličín to similar assemblages in Vel'ký Pesek-Sikenica and Bräunlingen.[104]

The Přešt'ovice-Friedenhain Group

The earliest knowledge of this group dates back to 1932, the year in which the Czech archaeologist Bedřich Dubský discovered and then excavated a cemetery with 522 cremations in Přešt'ovice (southern Bohemia). The characteristic that Dubský immediately recognized in the archaeological record of the Přešt'ovice cemetery was a number of handmade carinated bowls with oval faceting or oblique grooves (Figure 9.5). Other characteristics were identified later, during excavations on neighbouring sites in Bavaria, on the Regen, Naab, and Schwarzach rivers. The finds from Altenburg near Cham (eastern Bavaria) were dated to the D1/D2 period, but finds attributed to the Přešt'ovice-Friedenhain group have been identified not only in the environs of Regensburg, but also on Roman military sites on the frontier, for example, in Neuburg and Straubing. As a consequence, such finds were quickly interpreted as evidence of the presence of Germanic federates among the Roman troops on the frontier. More recently, settlement sites attributed to the

[103] Vávra, Jiřík, Kubálek, and Kuchařík, 'Pohřebiště z doby', pp. 565–77. The dominant grave orientation is west–east. In most graves, grave goods were placed in a special niche carved into the western pit wall. See also Jaroslav Jiřík and Jiří Vávra, 'Druhá etapa výzkumu pohřebiště z doby stěhování národů v Praze-Zličíně', in *Barbarská sídliště: Chronologické a historické aspekty jejich vývoje ve světle nových výzkumů*, ed. by Droberjar, Komoróczy, and Vachůtová, pp. 241–54 (pp. 242–46, and figs 2–6, 9–12).

[104] Jiřík and Vávra, 'Druhá etapa', pp. 250, 252 and figs 13 and 18; Gerhard Fingerlin, 'Bräunlingen, ein frühmerowingerzeitlicher Adelssitz an der Römerstraße durch den südlichen Schwarzwald', *Archäologische Ausgrabungen in Baden-Württemberg 1997*, 146–48 and pl. 14; *Das Gold der Barbarfürsten, Schätze aus Prunkgräbern des 5. Jahrhunderts n. Chr. Zwischen Kaukasus und Gallien*, ed. by Alfred Wieczorek and Patrick Périn (Stuttgart, 2001), pp. 61, 170–71 with figs 4.5.2.1, 4.15.1.2, 4.15.1.1, and 4.15.3.1.

Přešťovice-Friedenhain group have also been identified in southern (Zbudov, Zliv, and Sedlec), as well as western Bohemia (Nýřany, Plzeň-Radobyčice I and II, Vochov, and Plzeň-Vinice) (Figure 9.5.A).[105] Quite surprising is the presence of artefacts most typical for the Přešťovice-Friedenhain group within assemblages, which can otherwise be associated only with the Vinařice group, especially in Prague-Dolní Liboc I and II (Figure 9.5.B–C), grave 7 in Litovice, and Prague-Ruzyně.[106]

The development of the Přešťovice-Friedenhain group is not yet very clear. Most archaeologists seem to agree that a key component for the rise of the group were the local Elbe-Germanic and Thuringian traditions. But, as Michel Kazanski and Renaud Legoux have pointed out, the carinated bowls with oval faceting are strikingly similar to bowls known from ceramic assemblages of the Sântana de Mureş-Chernyakhov culture.[107] According to Günter Moosbauer, either the bowls in question appeared as an influence from Eastern Europe, or they are an independent, albeit similar, development ultimately based on the imitation of Roman glass bowls with faceted ornament.[108] A strong argument in favour of the latter possibility is that, while the Sântana de Mureş-Chernyakhov bowls are wheel-thrown, all Přešťovice-Friedenhain pots known so far are handmade. True, a certain influence from the Middle Danube region has been recently recognized for the settlement finds from Zliv, and especially Zbudov in southern Bohemia, which have produced wheel-made pottery of provincial and Middle Danubian production (Figure 9.5.F).[109] This has shifted the pendulum in the opposite direction, with a recent find of a brooch of the Bratei/Vyškov class in Vochov supporting Moosbauer's idea of a strong influence from Eastern Europe.[110] More evidence is surely needed before a firm solution to this problem will be offered.

---

[105] Svoboda, *Čechy v době*, fig. 15; Pavel Břicháček, 'Nové nálezy z Vochova', *Pěší zóna 10, Revue pro památkovou péči, archeologii, historii, výtvarné umění a literaturu* (2002), 15–16.

[106] Svoboda, *Čechy v době*, fig. 9.2; Pleinerová, 'Litovice (okr. Praha-západ)', fig. 10.1–2; Kuchařík, Bureš, Pleinerová, and Jiřík, 'Nové poznatky'.

[107] Michel Kazanski and Renaud Legoux, 'Contribution à l'étude des témoignages archéologiques des Goths en Europe orientale à l'époque des Grandes Migrations: la chronologie de la culture de Černjachov récente', *Archéologie médievale*, 18 (1988), 7–53 (p. 26 with pl. 3.46).

[108] Günter Moosbauer, *Kastell und Friedhöfe der Spätantike in Straubing: Römer und Germanen auf dem Weg zu den ersten Bajuwaren* (Passau, 2005), pp. 66 with n. 266, and 230–31.

[109] Petr Zavřel, 'Současný stav výzkumu doby římské a doby stěhování národů v jižních Čechách', *Archeologické rozhledy*, 51 (1999), 468–516 (p. 503 with figs 25.2, 26.3, and 27.9 and 11); Eduard Droberjar, *Věk barbarů* (Prague, 2005), p. 73.

[110] Břicháček, 'Nové nálezy', p. 16.

While waiting for new finds, though, another problem is the presence of élite graves. The only such finds known so far from the entire territory of the Přešťovice-Friedenhain group are those from Regensburg, as well as from a rich grave in Fürst (Figure 9.5.E).[111] The burial assemblage from Fürst included a glass jug, a glass beaker, three belt or footwear buckles with cloisonné ornament, and a massive golden bracelet with widened ends. Buckles are very typical for the 'Danubian fashion' of the D2 period, while bracelets were symbols of rank. Since no such finds are known from other assemblages of the Přešťovice-Friedenhain group, and since analogies for the Fürst finds may be found only in the Middle or Lower Danube region, it can be assumed that the burial was that of a nobleman of eastern, perhaps Danubian, origin who, together with his followers, may have served, probably as federates, in some unit of the Roman army stationed on the frontier in Bavaria. He may even have been, like the man buried in a mid-fifth-century grave in Pouan, the leader of a Hunnic unit in the Roman army. Be that as it may, there is no comparison between the Fürst and Regensburg finds and the assemblages attributed, on a much firmer basis, to the Přešťovice-Friedenhain group.

If we set the Fürst and Regensburg finds aside, then the only high-status warrior burial within the Přešťovice-Friedenhain group is that from Kemathen.[112] Even so, the Kemathen burial can hardly compare to the élite graves known from other parts of *barbaricum*. The Přešťovice-Friedenhain group thus appears as relatively poor in material culture correlates of social stratification. The only power centre known in Bohemia for the entire period of the early Migration period is outside the Přešťovice-Friedenhain group and within the territory of the Vinařice group. Bedřich Svoboda had long advanced the idea that the pottery of the Přešťovice-Friedenhain group and the Vinařice group were subject to mutual influence.[113] The settlement assemblages excavated in Prague-Dolní Liboc I–II and Litovice have confirmed the idea of a close contact between the Vinařice and the Přešťovice-Friedenhain groups.[114] Moreover, as Dieter Quast has noted, the influences of both within the Main River region or in Alamannia are intertwined, often on one and the same site, as in Kahl am Main.[115] In the absence of any power centre for the

[111] Fehr, 'Bemerkungen', pp. 204–28.

[112] Bernd Steidl, 'Zeitgenosse der Nibelungen: Der Krieger von Kemathen', in *Archäologie in Bayern: Fenster zur Vergangenheit*, ed. by C. Sebastian Sommer (Regensburg, 2006), p. 234.

[113] Svoboda, *Čechy v době*, pp. 101–03.

[114] Kuchařík, Bureš, Pleinerová, and Jiřík, 'Nové poznatky', pp. 363–64 and fig. 2.1, 5.

[115] Teichner, *Kahl am Main*, pp. 51, 111, pls 5.7 and 45.

Přešt'ovice-Friedenhain group, it is probably safer to assume that northern Bohemia was the political core of a multiethnic political formation.

Bohemia During the Early Merovingian Age (Phase E1) and the Politics of Interregional Relationships

In order to understand what happened during the final stage of the Vinařice group, it is necessary first to take a brief look at the historical circumstances and inter-regional relations across the European continent *c.* 500.[116] In the West, a number of so-called successor states had emerged at that time on the territory of formerly Roman provinces. In most cases, including those of the Ostrogoths in Italy and of the Thuringians in south-eastern and central Germany, those states were multiethnic formations. The first recorded contact between Thuringians and Ostrogoths dates back to 451, when both groups participated in Attila's campaign to Gaul. After defeating the Sueves, the Sciri, and the Sarmatians at the battle on the river Bolia, *c.* 469, the Ostrogoths moved into Pannonia Prima. After their migration to Italy, the border between the Ostrogoths and the Thuringians was established on the Upper Danube.[117] During Theoderic's rule, especially between 504 and 505, the Ostrogothic kingdom expanded into the Middle Danube region, besides already controlling, ever since the defeat of Odoacer, both Dalmatia and the province of Savia. Following his general's victory over the Gepids, the Ostrogothic king also won Pannonia Secunda, including the important city of Sirmium. Theoderic tem-porarily controlled the Visigothic kingdom of Spain and intervened in Vandal politics in northern Africa. In an effort to build an anti-Frankish coalition, he further developed diplomatic relations with the Thuringians, the Varni, and the Herules in the area north of the Alps. The Franks had emerged as a major power shortly after expelling the Visigoths from Aquitaine and defeating the Alamanni in 506. At about the same time, the Lombards defeated the Herules, occupied Moravia *c.* 508, and emerged as a new power in the northern region of the Carpathian Basin.

That in the meantime the Thuringians had moved into Raetia is known from written sources mentioning their attack and sack of Porta Batavia (Passau) in 480. Artefacts of Thuringian inspiration begin to show up in assemblages in Bavaria at

---

[116] For a more detailed account, see Guy Halsall, *Barbarian Migrations and the Roman West, 376–568* (Cambridge, 2007), pp. 284–319.

[117] Friedrich Lotter, 'Zur Rolle der Donausueben in der Völkerwanderungszeit', *Mittelungen des Instituts für Österreichische Geschichtsforschung*, 76 (1968), 275–98 (pp. 292–93).

about the same time, as with the pair of fibulae of the Niemberg class from a female burial excavated in Munich-Ramersdorf (Figure 9.12.A). A Thuringian influence may also be detected farther to the north in Upper Franconia, for example, the fibula of the Niemberg class from Saffelberg (Figure 9.12.E1). Thuringians may have been buried in Hirschlaid and Staffelstein (Figure 9.12.E2), two cemeteries dated to Schmidt's period IIB.[118] Excavations in Eggolsheim and Oberspitzheim suggest that during the second half of the fifth century, a number of hillforts in the area were reoccupied, probably by Thuringians. The presence of Thuringians has also been postulated for the cemetery excavated in Zeuzleben (Figure 9.12.B), and their traces have been discovered in local place names.[119] Such a prominent presence of Thuringians in Bavaria and Upper Franconia begs the question of what their influence was upon late fifth- and early sixth-century developments in Bohemia.

Until that question is properly dealt with in future studies, let us now turn to the other protagonists of the early sixth century, the Lombards. Most scholars have assumed that by 500, the Lombards ruled over Bohemia, but in more recent studies the archaeological assemblages previously attributed to Lombards have been re-attributed to Thuringians.[120] As Dušan Třeštík pointed out, the source explicitly mentioning Lombards ruling over Bohemia is a much later one, the *Chronicon Gothanum* written in 807–10. By contrast, from the little late fifth- or sixth-century sources have to say about Lombards at this stage, it appears that Bohemia may have been at the most a transit zone for Lombards moving farther to the south and south-east.[121] Conversely, a Thuringian influence, if not presence, seems to be supported by both written and archaeological sources. By 500 or so, contacts between the Thuringian and Ostrogothic kingdoms are specifically mentioned in the written sources, especially in connection with Hermenfrid's marriage to Theoderic's niece Amalaberga. At some point between 511 and 526 a treaty between Theoderic and the Thuringian king allowed for the settlement of barbarians, most likely of Bohemian origin, within the former province of Raetia. This barbarian

---

[118] Schmidt, *Die späte Völkerwanderungszeit.*

[119] Jochen Haberstroh, *Germanische Funde der Kaiser- und Völkerwanderungszeit aus Oberfranken* (Kallmünz, 2000), p. 134; Ludwig Wamser, *Eine thüringisch-fränkische Adels- und Gefolgschaftgrablege des 6./7. Jahrhunderts bei Zeuzleben* (Würzburg, 1984), pp. 1–2 and 4–6.

[120] Svoboda, *Čechy v době*, pp. 235–36. For Thuringians 'replacing' Lombards, see Droberjar, *Věk barbarů*, p. 153. For a slightly different interpretation, see Rastislav Korený, 'Čechy v 6. století: K problému konce germánského osídlení Čech', *Archeologie ve středních Čechách*, 9 (2005), 459–522 (p. 480).

[121] Dušan Třeštík, *Počátky Přemyslovců: Vstup Čechů do dějin (530–935)* (Prague, 1997), p. 36.

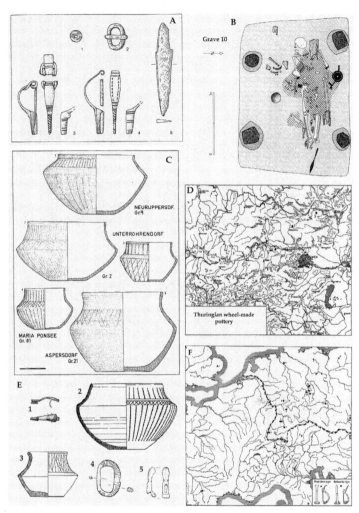

Figure 9.12. Thuringians on the Upper Danube in Bavaria. (A) Munich-Ramersdorf, female burial assemblage (after Keller, 'Germanenpolitik Roms', fig. 11); (B) Zeuzleben, grave 10 (after Wamser, *Eine thüringisch-fränkische Adels- und Gefolgschaftgrablege*, fig. 8); (C) Thuringian wheel-made pottery from Austria; (D) the distribution of Thuringian pottery in Austria (after Friesinger and Kerchler, 'Töpferöfen der Völkerwanderungszeit', figs 42 and 55); (E: 1) Saffelberg, fibula of the Niemberg class; (2) Staffelstein, Thuringian wheel-made pot (after Haberstroh, *Germanische Funde*, pls 112.17 and 119.6); (3) Regensburg, Thuringian handmade pot (after Koch, *Die Grabfunde*, pl. 34.10); (4–5) S. Antonio, buckle loop and tongue (after de Vingo and Fossati, 'Gli elementi da cintura', pl. 65.5–6); (F) the distribution of crossbow fibulae of the Rathewitz class (after Mechthild Schulze-Dörrlamm, 'Romanisch oder germanisch? Untersuchungen zu den Armbrust- und Bügelknopffibel des 5. und 6. Jhs. n. Chr. aus den Gebieten westlich des Rheins und südlich der Donau', *Jahrbuch des Römisch-Germanischen Zentralmuseums*, 33 (1986), p. 615 fig. 22).

group would later turn into a new ethnic group known as Baiuvars (Bavarians). In 531, the Thuringian kingdom, which may have exercised its influence upon Bohemia as well, was destroyed by the Frankish armies.[122] The archaeological record, which could be, with a certain degree of certainty, dated to this period, particularly that of the cemeteries excavated in Irlmaut and Straubing, is particularly interesting. According to Ursula Koch, specific types of fibulae, as well as the frequency of skeletons with artificially deformed skulls, all point to a number of parallels with other sites in the eastern Merovingian area, particularly in the Bohemian basin (Prague-Podbaba and Radovesice). Contacts between Bohemia and Bavaria may of course have been in both directions.[123]

On the other hand, contacts between Thuringians and Ostrogoths have been illustrated with fibulae of the Reggio Emilia (Figure 9.13.A) and with crossbow fibulae of Werner's class Gurina-Grepault (Figure 9.14.E) and Schulze-Dörrlamm's class Desana (Figure 9.14.F).[124] Thuringian-Ostrogothic contacts involving gift-giving may have been responsible for the presence of a helmet of Italian manufacture in Stößen. Early helmets of the Baldenheim type appear in Italy, in the Balkans, and in Alamannia (Figure 9.13.E), while later specimens are known from the area controlled in the sixth century by the Franks.[125] An Ostrogothic mediation has also been assumed in order to explain the deposition of early sixth-century solidi or of their 'barbarian' imitations in Thuringian burial assemblages. Ten coins are so far known from the eastern and central parts of Germany, nine of them struck for Roman emperors, from Anastasius to Justinian, and another being an imitative Ostrogothic issue of Athalaric.[126] A similar picture may be obtained from the examination of coin finds from neighbouring Bohemia.[127]

Under Theodoric, imitative gold coins were struck with countermarks copying old Roman bronze coins. On the other hand, the Ostrogoths must have also used coins struck within the imperial mints. That such coins reached the northern region of *barbaricum* via the Ostrogothic kingdom is demonstrated by the fact that hoards of gold solidi on the Baltic Sea shore and in southern Scandinavia end with

---

[122] Třeštík, *Počátky Přemyslovců*, pp. 38–39.

[123] Ursula Koch, *Die Grabfunde der Merowingerzeit aus dem Donautal um Regensburg* (Berlin, 1968), pp. 121–24.

[124] Hans Losert and Andrej Pleterski, *Altenerding in Oberbayern* (Berlin, 2003), pp. 88–89.

[125] Müller-Wille, 'Prunkgräber', p. 143 with fig. 15.

[126] Schmidt, *Die späte Völkerwanderungszeit*, pp. 157–59.

[127] Militký, 'Finds of Roman and Early Byzantine Gold Coins', pp. 64–65 with pl. 6. All coins are issues of Anastasius, Justin I, and Justinian.

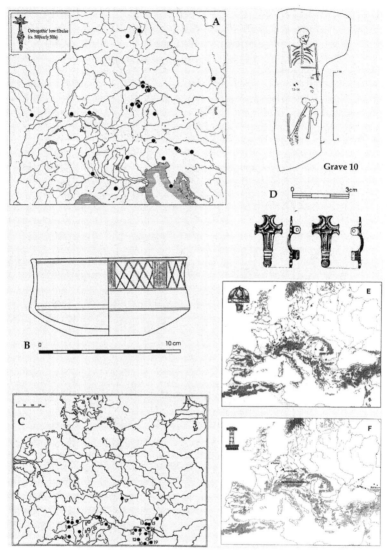

Figure 9.13. Interregional relations in the late fifth and the early sixth centuries. (A) the distribution of so-called Ostrogothic bow fibulae (after Böhme, 'Zur Bedeutung', fig. 13); (B) Krefeld-Stratum, bowl of the Altenerding-Aubing type; (C) the distribution of wheel-thrown pottery of the Kaschau 6 and Altenerding-Aubing types (after Fischer, 'Ein glätverziertes Knickwandschälchen', figs 1 and 2); (D) Lužec nad Vltavou, grave 10 (after Korený and Kytlicová, 'Dvě pohřebiště', fig. 7); (E) the distribution of helmets of the Baldenheim type (after Müller-Wille, 'Prunkgräber', fig. 15); (F) the distribution of *Goldgriffspatha* swords of the Althußheim type (after Müller-Wille, 'Prunkgräber', fig. 8).

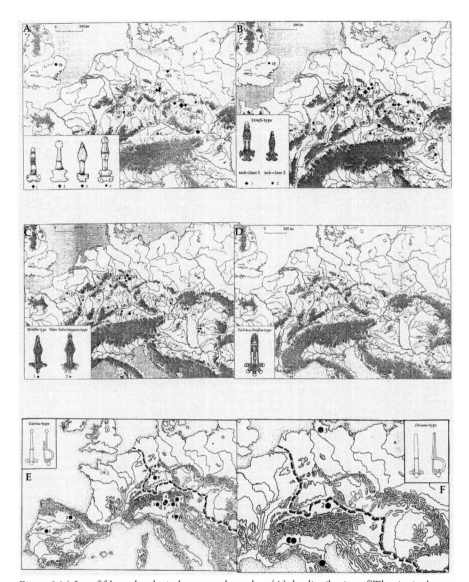

Figure 9.14. Late fifth- and early sixth-century brooches. (A) the distribution of 'Thuringian' tongs-shaped bow fibulae; (B) the distribution of bow fibulae of the Staß class; (C) the distribution of bow fibulae of the Mistřín class; (D) the distribution of bow fibulae of the Eisleben-Stößen class; (E) the distribution of crossbow brooches of the Gurina-Grepault class; (F) the distribution of crossbow brooches of the Desana class. After Losert and Pleterski, *Altenerding*, maps 3, 8–9, and 11; Schulze-Dörrlamm, 'Romanisch oder germanisch?', fig. 111.

coins struck for Emperor Justinian. In other words, no solidi reached the North after the destruction of the Ostrogothic kingdom by Justinian's armies.[128]

Interesting conclusions could further be drawn from the examination of the distribution of two particular types of pottery known as Kaschau 6 and Altenerding-Aubing (Figure 9.13.B), respectively. Most finds dated *c.* 500 cluster in the region of the Upper and Middle Danube, that is, along the frontier between Alamannia and the Ostrogothic kingdom (Figure 9.13.C). In this context the presence of pots of the Kaschau 6 type in Prague-Podbaba is significant. Thomas Fischer has even suggested that the pottery in question may have been produced in the area.[129] The political situation in Central Europe was indeed favourable to the development of a local trade network along the Danube, which could have occasionally expanded north of that river as well. After all, the production of wheel-made pottery with burnished decoration had by then a respectable tradition in the Middle Danube region.[130] The importance of the Danube frontier results from the efforts the Ostrogoths made to maintain the late antique military organization in the borderlands. Theoderic is said to have been *magister utrisque militae* in charge of the administration of Italy. It is therefore possible to regard the military units *comites civitatum* and *duces provinciarum* in Italy as successors of *comitatenses*, with the units in frontier forts in Raetia, Pannonia, Dalmatia, and Savia as a substitute for the now defunct units of *limitanei*. A soldier's pay was assessed in the form of the perquisite and in particular in monetary form during the campaign.[131] Much like in the fourth century, the presence of the military on the frontier may have stimulated the rise of local markets, which in turn encouraged the continuity of local manufacturing traditions.[132] Pottery of the Kaschau 6 and Altenerding-Aubing also appears in some quantity in Alamannia. It is known that Theoderic congratulated Clovis upon his victory over the Alamanni, and the archaeological evidence confirms that the important trade centre at Runder Berg near Urach was

---

[128] Georges Depeyrot, 'Les Monnayages barbares sont-ils la continuité du monnayage romain?', in *Coin Finds and Coin Use in the Roman World: The Thirteenth Oxford Symposium on Coinage and Monetary History 25.–27.3. 1993*, ed. by Cathy E. King and David G. Wigg (Berlin, 1996), pp. 129–37.

[129] Thomas Fischer, 'Ein glätverziertes Knickwandschälchen des Typs Altenerding-Aubing von Krefeld-Stratum', in *Probleme der frühen Merowingerzeit*, ed. by Tejral, pp. 125–27. See also Jiří Zeman, 'Na kruhu robená keramika z pozdní fáze doby stěhování národů v Čechách', *Praehistorica 21, Varia archaeologica*, 6 (1994), 53–68 (p. 63).

[130] Friesinger and Kerchler, 'Töpferöfen der Völkerwanderungszeit', fig. 57.

[131] Philippe Contamine, *Válka ve středověku* (Prague, 2004), p. 31.

[132] Edward James, *Frankové* (Prague, 1997), pp. 118–20 with fig. 14.

destroyed at about that time, no doubt in connection with the Frankish occupation of Alamannia north of the Upper Danube.[133] Prior to the Frankish onslaught,
Alamannia seems therefore to have had strong commercial ties to the south,
particularly to Italy. This is further substantiated by the find of a *Goldgriffspatha*
sword of the Althußheim type in Bräunlingen. Such swords were used to mark
high-status burials (one such sword was found in Childeric's tomb in Tournai), but
they must have been manufactured in the Mediterranean region, either within the
empire or in Ostrogothic Italy (Figure 9.13.F).[134]

A Thuringian influence, if not presence, in the region of the Danube frontier has
been documented through finds of fibulae with good analogies in eastern and central
Germany. This is the case of fibulae of the Mistřín class (Figure 9.14.C), of fibulae
with opposing bird-heads (Figure 9.15.A and B), of bow fibulae of the Straß (Figure
9.14.B), Eisleben-Stößen (Figure 9.14.D), and Weimar/Arcy-Restitue classes (Figure
9.15.C), as well as of 'Thuringian' tongs-shaped fibulae (Figure 9.14.A, all of which
have been found in assemblages in Bohemia to be dated to *c*. 500 or shortly
thereafter). An indirect link may even exist between the tongs-shaped fibulae and
fibulae from later assemblages of the Vinařice group. Conversely, the wheel-made
pottery believed to be of Thuringian origin appears as far south as Lower Austria
(Figure 9.12.C, D, and E3).[135] Judging by the existing evidence, Thuringians or barbarians under Thuringian political influence may have had a substantial contribution to the development of commercial networks on both sides of the Danube
frontier, as well as to the military infrastructure in that region. A Thuringian
political influence has also been assumed on the basis of the examination of 'exotic'
foreign goods associated with the family burial no. 5 within the Pleidesheim cemetery
in Alamannia.[136] In Bohemia, a strong Thuringian influence was recently advocated
by many archaeologists. However, there are serious problems of ethnic interpretation, not the least of which is that the so-called Lombard occupation of Moravia
begins *c*. 500 with assemblages typically including 'Thuringian' artefacts.[137]

---

[133] James, *Frankové*, p. 86.

[134] Fingerlin, 'Bräunlingen', pp. 147–48 and pl. 14.

[135] Friesinger and Kerchler, 'Töperöfen der Völkerwanderungszeit', figs 42 and 55; Koch, *Die Grabfunde*, pl. 34.10.

[136] Koch, *Das alamanisch-fränkische*, pp. 394–95.

[137] Jaroslav Tejral, 'Beiträge zur Chronologie des langobardischen Fundstoffes nördlich der mittleren Donau', in *Probleme der frühen Merowingerzeit*, ed. by Tejral, pp. 313–58 (pp. 328–33). For a historical interpretation of this phenomenon, see Třeštík, *Počátky Přemyslovců*, p. 36. Similarly, Bavarians may be associated with artefacts of 'Thuringian' origin.

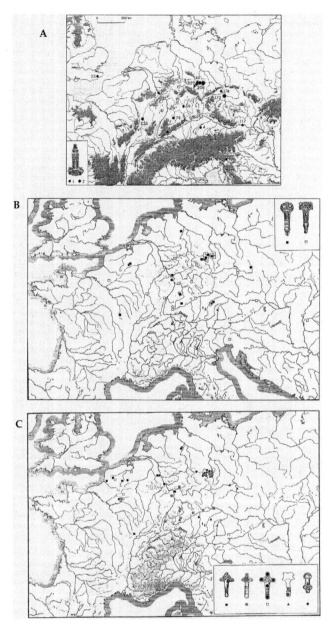

Figure 9.15. Late fifth- and sixth-century fibulae: (A) the distribution of fibulae with opposing bird-heads (after Losert and Pleterski, *Altenerding*, map 10); (B) distribution of fibulae with opposing bird-heads (after Koch, *Bügelfibeln der Merowingerzeit*, map 24); (C) fibulæ of the Weimar/Arcy-Restitue class (after Koch, *Bügelfibeln der Merowingerzeit*, map 25).

To be sure, such artefacts are also known from contemporary assemblages in Italy. According to the excavators, the tongue of a belt buckle with rigged loop found within the S. Antonio fort in Liguria (Figure 9.12.E5) has good analogies in southern and central Germany.[138] Similarly, 'Thuringian' crossbow fibulae of the Rathewitz class have been found as far south as Toulouse (Figure 9.12.F).[139]

The Identity of the Vinařice Group

Identifying the ethnic groups of the Migration period has traditionally been a problem of how to read the written sources of Late Antiquity. Identifying the polity in northern Bohemia, the territory of which corresponds to that of the Vinařice group, with any of the ethnic groups mentioned in those sources requires a re-examination of what is known about the location of the Central European barbarians. Of special importance appears to be the location of so-called Danube or Pannonian Sueves of the Migration period. They appear as a prominent group

[138] Paolo de Vingo and Angelo Fossati, 'Gli elementi da cintura', in S. Antonio, un insediamento fortificato nella Liguria bizantina, ed. by Tizziano Mannoni and Daniele Arobba (Bordighera, 2001), pp. 475–82 (pp. 477–79 with pl. 65.6). A very similar buckle tongue is also known from Crypta Balbi in Rome: Maria Stela Arena and others, Roma dall'antichità al medioevo: Archeologia e storia nel Museo Nazionale Romano, Crypta Balbi (Milan, 2001), p. 372 and pl. II.4.581. Another similar find comes from the isle of St Andrea in the Biotope 'Loppio Lake' (Trento, Italy), which is however dated to the early Lombard period: Barbara Murina, Carlo Andrea Postinger, and Maurizio Battisti, 'Ricerche archeologiche a Loppio, isola di S. Andrea (TN): Relazione preliminare sulla campagna di scavo 2004', Annali del Museo Civico di Rovereto, 20 (2004), 23–51 (p. 39 and fig. 20). The two fibulae of the Straß class (variant 2), which were found in Salona near Split (Croatia), also point to a possibly Thuringian influence. A 'Thuringian' fibula of the hybrid type is known from Ravenna, and a tongs-shaped one from Novi Banovci in Vojvodina (northern Serbia), a region controlled in the early sixth century by the Gepids. Zdenko Vinski, 'O rovašenim fibulama ostrogota i tirinžana povodomu rijetkog tirinškog nalaza u Saloni', Vjesnik arheološkog muzeja u Zagrebu, 6–7 (1972–73), 177–227 (pp. 178–79, 217, 226 with pls 1.1, 2, and 12.69); Zrinka Buljević, Sanja Ivčević, Jagoda Mardešić, and Ema Višić-Ljubić, 'Artes minores Salonae Christinae', in Salona Christiana: Izložba u povodu XIII. Međunarodnog kongresa za starokšćansku arheologiju, Split 25. 9.–31. 10. 1994, ed. by Emilio Marin (Split, 1994), pp. 213–90 (p. 222 with figs 20–21). It is possible to date the Split fibulae before 536, the year in which the city of Salona was retaken by Byzantium. See Milan Inaviševević, 'Povijesni izvori', in Salona Christiana: Izložba u povodu XIII, ed. by Marin, pp. 105–95 (p. 191). Procopius of Caesarea, Wars, 6.13 and 7.25 mentions the presence of the Thuringian royal family in Ostrogothic Italy; see also Schmidt, Die späte Völkerwanderungszeit, p. 176.

[139] Wolfgang Ebel-Zepezauer, Studien zur Archäologie der Westgoten vom 5.–7. Jh. n. Chr. (Mainz, 2000), p. 36.

in the much-discussed narrative of Jordanes's *Getica*, who, writing almost a century afterwards, presents them as the major rival of the Pannonian Goths in the events of AD 468, some fifteen years after Attila's death.[140] Friedrich Lotter rejected the idea of treating the Pannonian Suevi as descendants from the second-century Quadi mentioned by Roman sources as living in south-east Slovakia and Moravia. Thus Lotter distinguishes the Danube Suevi from Quadi-turned-Suevi, barbarians known to have been associated to the Vandals and Alans of AD 406, who participated in the 'great Rhine crossing' and the invasion of Gaul and Spain.[141]

The archaeological picture of the Suevi in Spain has been drawn primarily by Alexander Koch, with some recent additions by María Mariné Isidro, on the basis of comparison with the archaeological record of the Danube region.[142] As for the Danube Suevi, Friedrich Lotter regarded them as descendants of the Marcomanni mentioned in late fourth-century sources as ruled by a queen named Fritigil. Those barbarians lived since the early 300s in the Vienna Basin, as well as on the shores of the Neusiedler Lake in Lower Austria. Under Honorius, there were Marcomanni in *auxilia palatina* named *Honoriani seniores,* and *iuniores,* as well as in cavalry units stationed in Africa.

Whether or not we accept Lotter's idea, the barbarian presence around Vienna is attested by finds of fourth-century handmade pottery of Elbe-Germanic tradition (Figure 9.1.B).[143] After *c.* 400, there are significant changes in the settlement pattern of the region, which have been traditionally attributed to the arrival of Herules and Rugians by the mid-fifth century. Lotter places the Marcomanni-turned-Suevi in the former province of Savia, around Siscia, Neviodunum, Emona, Fines, Acervo, and Romula, primarily on the basis of a later source, the Ravenna Geographer. According to Friedrich Lotter's interpretation of Jordanes, Procopius,

[140] For Jordanes as a problematic source, see Walter Goffart, *The Narrators of Barbarian History, AD 550–800: Jordanes, Gregory of Tours, Bede, and Paul the Deacon* (Princeton, 1988), pp. 20–111.

[141] Lotter, 'Zur Rolle', p. 280. Jerome, *Epistolae*, 123.15, ed. J. Labourt, VII (Paris, 1949–63), pp. 91–92: 'Quadus, Vandalus, Sarmata, Halani, Gepides, Heruli, Saxones, Burgundiones, Alemanni, et, o lugenda respublica! hostes Pannonii.' For a cautionary note against taking Jerome's letter written from Bethlehem in 409 at face value, see Walter Goffart, *Barbarian Tides: The Migration Age and the Late Roman Empire* (Philadelphia, 2006), pp. 81–82.

[142] Koch 'Zum archäologischen Nachweis der Sueben', pp. 156–98; María Mariné Isidro, 'Fibulas romanas in Hispania: la Meseta', *Archivo español de arqueología*, 24 (2001), 272–73 with pls 186.1426–28 and 187.1429–30. See also Fernando Lopez Sánchez in this volume.

[143] Michaela Kronberger and Martin Mosser, 'Spätrömisches Gräberfeld Neuer Markt', *Fundort Wien*, 4 (2001), 158–221 with pl. 7.8–9.

and Cassiodorus, this is the region called *Suavia* (the land of the Sueves).[144] The mid-fifth-century Marcomanni-turned-Suevi are therefore located within a vast area stretching from the Neusiedler Lake to the north to the Sava River to the south. Other scholars demur, and if anything, the debate around the location of the Danube Suevi is far from closed.[145]

However, the problem may also be approached from a different angle. Adopting a proud ancient name, Suevi (first mentioned by Caesar and Tacitus), was a way to bring together, under a common identity, disparate groups of barbarians. This is clearly the case of the Silingi and Hasdingi, said to have come together as Vandals, the same people who would later invade Africa.[146] One should not of course exclude the possibility of small-scale migrations from northern *barbaricum*, but the 'rise' of the Danube Suevi is more a political than a demographic phenomenon. The Pannonian Suevi are mentioned by Sidonius Apollinaris as participating in Attila's army in the battle of the Catalaunian Fields (451). Following Attila's death, the Danubian Suevi were among those who successfully rebelled against and eventually defeated the Huns at the battle on the river Nedao (454). By 469, the Suevi were allied with Rugians and Sciri under the leadership of Edica, with Sarmatians, and with Gepids against the Pannonian Goths led by Thiudimer. However, Thiudimer prevailed over the anti-Gothic coalition with a great slaughter in the battle on the Bolia River.[147] Thiudimer then pursued the remaining Suevi, who were still under the leadership of a king named Hunimund. According to Jordanes, Thiudimer crossed the frozen Danube and fell upon the Suevi in their own country, a region described as having *Baibari* to the east, Franks to the west, Burgundians to the south, and Thuringians to the north.[148] Whether or not he

---

[144] Lotter, 'Zur Rolle', p. 278; Jordanes, *Getica*, 273, ed. by Theodor Mommsen, MGH AA, 5.1 (Berlin, 1882), p. 129: 'Dalmatia S u a v i a e vicina erat nec a Pannonis fines multum distabat, praesertim ubi tunc Gothi residebant'; Jordanes, *Romana*, 218, ed. by Mommsen, MGH AA, 5.1, p. 28; Procopius of Caesarea, *Wars*, 5.15.25 and 5.16.9, ed. by J. Haury (Leipzig, 1906); Cassiodorus, *Variae*, 4.49 and 5.14 and 15, ed. by Theodor Mommsen, MGH AA, 12 (Berlin, 1894).

[145] Max Martin, '*Mixti Alamannis Suevi*? Der Beitrag der Alamanischen Gräberfelder am Basler Rheinknie', in *Probleme der frühen Merowingerzeit*, ed. by Tejral, pp. 195–223 (pp. 218–19).

[146] Goffart, *Barbarian Tides*, pp. 82–87.

[147] Jordanes, *Getica*, 277–79, pp. 129–30. Bolia has been tentatively identified with the Sárvíz River in Hungary; see Attila Kiss, 'Der Goldene Schildrahmen von Sárvíz aus dem 5. Jahrhundert und der Skirenkönig Edica', *Alba Regia*, 26 (1997), 83–132.

[148] Jordanes, *Getica*, 280, p. 130. This is the earliest reference to Bavarians of certain date. See Goffart, *Barbarian Tides*, pp. 218–19.

found it in Cassiodorus, Jordanes's reference to the Suevian territory is not without problems.[149] He has the Suevi both in Pannonia and between Franks and Burgundians. In an attempt to solve the contradictions of Jordanes's text, Friedrich Lotter and other scholars suggested that a group of Suevi fleeing the Goths after the battle on the river Bolia moved westwards into Alamannia. Such an interpretation is substantiated by a passage in *Vita Severini* mentioning a certain leader named Hunumund who, together with his barbarians, sacked Porta Batavia (Passau). Hunumund is not called a 'king' in the *Vita Severini*, but some have identified him with Hunimund. Nonetheless, in the early 500s, the bulk of the Central European Suevi were in Pannonia.[150] A migration of a Suevic group to the west has been linked to the appearance of fibulae from the Middle Danube region in burial assemblages excavated around Basel (Switzerland) and dated to the second half of the fifth century.[151] But such artefacts could have reached the territory of present-day Switzerland by a number of other ways, such as trade or matrimonial alliances, without any migration of a large group of people. Dieter Quast has skilfully delineated a number of other links in the archaeological record of Alamannia and the Middle Danube region, respectively. No artefacts could therefore be assigned to the Danube Suevi, and only to them.[152]

Jordanes placed Hunimund's Suevi in the vicinity of Bavarians, Thuringians, Franks, and Burgundians. He apparently knew of no other barbarian polities in Central Europe. Most importantly, when locating the Suevian territory, Jordanes does not mention the Herules among its neighbours, perhaps because after the battle of the Bolia River, the Rugiland in Lower Austria had served as a launchpad for Thiudimer's punitive expedition. In other words, the location of the Suevian territory must be restricted to a stretch of land between Bohemia to the east and Frankish Gaul to the west. Moreover, Jordanes's account contains the first reference to Bavarians that could be dated with any degree of certainty. Archaeologists link the origin of those new barbarians to the Přešťovice-Friedenhain group of southern and western Bohemia. However, while information exists about the settlement pattern of that group, no power centre or structure has so far been identified. If the archaeological finds from Prague and Litovice are to be given any

---

[149] For a critique of the idea that Jordanes only copied Cassiodorus's now lost work, see Goffart, *Barbarian Tides*, pp. 59–61.

[150] Lotter, 'Zur Rolle', p. 277.

[151] Péter Straub, 'Die archäologische Hinterlassenschaft der praelangobardischen Periode in Transdanubien', in *Germanen am Plattensee*, ed. by Windl, pp. 13–15 (p. 14 with fig. 3).

[152] Quast, 'Höhensiedlungen', p. 279; Martin, '*Mixti Alamannis Suevi?*', pp. 218–19.

weight in this interpretation, then one will have to conclude that the political centre in the region was within the area covered by the Vinařice group. A one-to-one relation between Bavarians and the Přešťovice-Friedenhain group is fraught with other problems as well. No evidence exists for dating that group back into the second half of the fifth century, while southern Bohemia appears to have been deserted (or at least without any settlement sites) during the early 500s. If the Bavarians came from Bohemia in the early 500s, then they must have come from the northern district of that region. This, at least, is the picture drawn on the basis of written sources by Dušan Třeštík as well.[153]

Such an interpretation has the great advantage of indirectly offering an explanation for both continuity and discontinuity within the territory covered by the Vinařice group. 'Thuringian' tongs-shaped bow fibulae may have well derived from older fibulae commonly found in assemblages of the Vinařice group. In northern Bohemia, occupation of several sites dated to the early Migration period and attributed to that group continued well into the Merovingian period (early sixth century). Since the bulk of the evidence for that continuity comes from old or non-professional excavations of cemetery sites, the continuity thesis was initially established on the basis of artefacts alone. There are by now sufficient examples of well-excavated sites, such as Lužec nad Vltavou, Radonice nad Ohří, Zbuzany, perhaps also Litovice. The idea of settlement continuity is also confirmed by the results of the recent excavations in Prague-Zličín.[154] Continuity was also assumed indirectly on the basis of a family group of burials in the Pleidesheim cemetery in Alamannia. The fibulae of the Niderflorstadt-Wiesloch class from grave 65 are directly inspired from fibulae of the Vinařice group, while the bronze hoop from that same grave has a good analogy in Mochov, a burial site in northern Bohemia dated to the early Merovingian period.[155] Settlement continuity has recently been documented in Závist near Prague, a site which has produced a model for the casting of fibulae of the Taman class.[156]

In conclusion, the archaeological record of early sixth-century Bohemia seems to indicate at least some degree of continuity. There are also clear influences from the Niemberg group, while certain burial assemblages (e.g., those excavated in Lužec nad Vltavou) suggest the existence of finds and customs which can be

---

[153] Třeštík, *Počátky Přemyslovců*, pp. 37–38.

[154] Korený and Kytlicová, 'Dvě pohřebiště', pp. 428–30; Vávra, Jiřík, Kubálek, and Kuchařík, 'Pohřebiště z doby', p. 571; Jiřík and Vávra, 'Druhá etapa', pp. 251–53.

[155] Koch, *Das alamanisch-fränkische*, p. 391.

[156] Motyková, Drda, and Rybová, *Závist*, fig. 54; Droberjar, *Věk barbarů*, p. 185.

explained only in the context of the interregional contacts and, possibly, of Thuringian political control.

The Bavarian Language

The idea that Bavarians originated from barbarians settled in Bohemia, themselves of East Germanic origin, may also explain some features of their language. Old Bavarian is an unambiguously West Germanic language, but with some interesting East Germanic influences, particularly obvious at lexical level, with such words as *Ergetag* 'Tuesday' (from Gothic *arjausdags, 'the day of Arius'), *Pfinztag* 'Thursday' (from Gothic *pinta-dags, 'the fifth day'), *Maut* 'duty' (from Gothic *Mota*), *Dult* 'fair', *Pfoad* 'shirt', etc. Equally interesting in this respect is the so-called Bavarian dual which, if not a local feature, can only be of Gothic origin. No clear explanation has so far been offered for such parallels between Old Bavarian and Gothic. Some scholars believe that they originate in contacts with the population of the Middle Danube region (Rugians, Herules, and others), presumably speaking East Germanic languages, others that such parallels are simply an indication of linguistic influences from Ostrogothic Italy, possibly through a later, Lombard mediation.[157]

If a Bavarian identity was indeed formed among people from Bohemia whose material culture was of Elbe-Germanic tradition, with strong influences from groups of East European federates in the Middle Danube region, then the East Germanic features of Old Bavarian will have to be dated as early as the first decades of the fifth century. In any case, the new name shows that a territorial identification was preferred to the prestigious ancient name of Suevi: Baiuvari derives from **Bai(a)-haim-warjōz*, 'the warriors from Bohemia'.

---

[157] Heinrich Beck, 'Bajuwaren – Philologisches', in *Reallexikon der germanischen Altertumskunde*, I, ed. by Heinrich Beck and others (Berlin, 1973), pp. 601–06.

Appendix 1

In the late 1990s, a hoard of silver was found in a small cave in the Elbe canyon, not far from Hřensko, on the northern frontier of Bohemia. The hoard included a bow fibula of the Wiesbaden class, a crossbow brooch of Almgren's class 158, two bracelets with widened ends, and three small ingots (Plate V.1). The only non-metallic artefact is a glass bead of Temmpelmann-Mączyńska's type 300. Judging from its content, the assemblage may be dated to the first half of the fifth century.[158]

Its total weight (131.64 gr) represents two fifths of a Roman pound. According to the Theodosian Code (13.2.1) the ratio of gold to silver in the early 400s was 1 to 14.4, which means that a solidus was worth a fifth of a silver pound, that is, 12 *miliarense* or 30 *siliquae*.[159] The Hřensko hoard was therefore worth 2 solidi and was thus the equivalent in gold of the belt buckle from Prague-Radotín.[160] By comparison, a single golden bracelet of the Blučina/Tournai type from an unknown location in Central Bohemia was worth 36 solidi.[161] The high value of the dress accessories found on élite cemetery sites (such as Prague-Zličín) or local community 'headman' graves within more modest cemeteries in which members of the lower strata of society were buried (Lužec nad Vltavou) thus appears to have been considerable and points to the significant wealth differentials in existence within the local society.[162]

---

[158] Jaroslav Jiřík, Vladimír Peša, and Petr Jenč, 'Ein Silberdepot der frühen Phase der Völkerwanderungszeit aus der Elbe-Klamm bei Hřensko, Bz. Děčín, und seinem kulturellen Kontext', *Arbeits- und Forschungsberichte zur sächsischen Bodendenkmalpflege*, 50 (2008), 185–210. The site is at a distance of 70 km from the nearest known settlement site dated to the same period.

[159] Hahn, *Die Ostprägung*, pp. 15–17.

[160] In the 430s, 2 solidi could purchase 25 modii (i.e. 1135 gallons) of corn. See Edward A. Thompson, *Hunové* (Prague, 1999), p. 78.

[161] Droberjar, 'Zlatý náramek', p. 522.

[162] Korený and Kytlicová, 'Dvě pohřebiště', p. 419.

Appendix 2

An important site dated to the early Migration period has been discovered in the karst region of north-western Bohemia, namely at Čertova ruka (Devil's Hand) near the town of Semily (Plate V.2). The finds excavated between 1934 and 1935 at Nováková pec cavity included metal, glass, and amber artefacts. They can be divided into three groups in terms of the geographical direction of their analogies. The bridle belt, one of the belt buckles, and the three-edged arrowheads (Figure 9.16.2 and 5) may be attributed to the 'Danube fashion' of the early fifth century, while the fragments of bronze torcs, the two fibulae of the Niemberg class, together with the crossbow brooch with polyhedral bow knob, the glass and amber beads, the bronze ring with knuckles, and the fragmentary bronze bracelet (Figure 9.16.3–4, 6–8, 11, and 14–22) have good analogies within assemblages of the Niemberg group of central and eastern Germany and among finds from the Main River valley. Finally, the fragments of glassware and the buckle with animal heads are most likely of Roman origin (Figure 9.16.1 and 23–27). Judging from such analogies, the assemblage was most likely a one-time collection of artefacts dated to the second third of the fifth century.[163] If, as has been suggested, one should equate the Niemberg group with Thuringians, then the Čertova ruka find could well represent the wealth accumulate by Thuringian warriors who, according to Sidonius Apollinaris, served in Attila's army during the 451 expedition to Gaul. Nonetheless, such an interpretation would be based on a bluntly culture-historical approach to the archaeological record. The Čertova ruka finds may be regarded as evidence of cultural contacts that the native communities of north-western Bohemia maintained both with the neighbouring Roman provinces to the West and to the East and with other regions of *barbaricum* to the north.

---

[163] Jaroslav Jiřík, 'Ein Beitrag zur Erforschung der Besiedlung Ost- und Nordostböhmens während der späten Kaiserzeit und frühe Völkerwanderungszeit', in *The Turbulent Epoch: New Materials from the Roman Period and the Migration Period. Conference in Krasnobrod 18. 9.–22. 9. 2007*, ed. by Barbara Niezabitowska-Wiśniewska and others (Lublin, 2008), pp. 156–77.

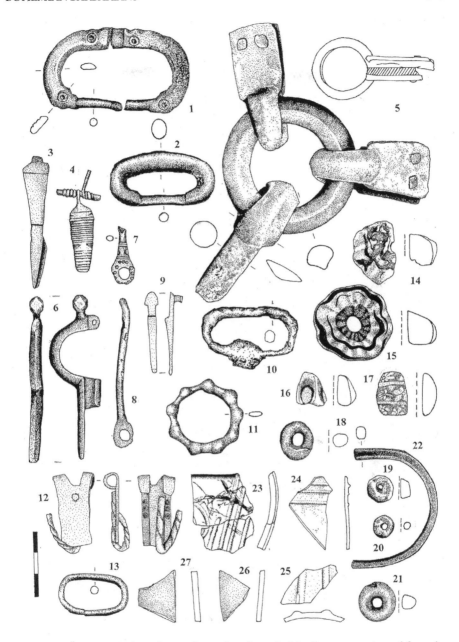

Figure 9.16. Čertova ruka (Devil's Hand), artefacts from the Nováková pec cavity and from the top of the crag: (1, 3–4, 6–9, 11–13, 22) bronze; (2, 5) copper-silver alloy; (10) iron; (14–20, 23–27) glass; and (21) amber. Drawing by author, courtesy of the Museum in Turnov.

THE HERULES: FRAGMENTS OF A HISTORY

Roland Steinacher

Some *gentes* — armed social units or peoples such as the Goths, Franks, Burgundians, or Vandals — became an intrinsic part of European history. Others like the Herules, Sciri, Gepids, and Rugi played their somewhat vague role, but disappeared from our sources without having had the opportunity to forge new medieval national identities or form any stable *regnum* on formerly Roman provinces. To be sure, historians did not hesitate to apply to the 'neglected barbarians' the concept of *Völkerwanderung*, complete with historical maps showing entire peoples wandering across the page.[1] The Herules, for example, appear on a map showing the 'Great Migration' published in a book that used to be very popular among German readers born in the 1940s. The map shows the Herules following a trail from southern Scandinavia, along the Danube, north of the sea of Azov, along the Lower Rhine, and finally into Italy.[2] In this essay I will not spend too much time discussing ideas of migration, even though it is important to be aware of numerous influential tales concerning the origin and migration of the Herules from the far North. The Herules have often been imagined more as a group of wandering warriors or as a band of Viking-like robbers than as a group with a distinctive ethnic identity. Other scholars even strove to reconstruct the history of the Herules as a people moving from Scandinavia all the way to the Maeotis Lake

I am greatly indebted to Albrecht Diem (Syracuse), Carmen Konzett (Innsbruck), Maya Maskarinec (Princeton), and Walter Pohl (Vienna) for helping me to bring chaos into order. The editor Florin Curta deserves many thanks for his splendid and dedicated work.

[1] Walter Goffart, *Barbarian Tides: The Migration Age and the Later Roman Empire* (Philadelphia, 2006), pp. 13–22; Walter Pohl, *Die Völkerwanderung: Eroberung und Integration* (Stuttgart, 2002), pp. 1–38.

[2] Emil Nack, *Germanien: Land und Volk der Germanen* (Vienna, 1958), pp. 359–60.

(Sea of Azov). It goes without saying that both positions conspicuously ignore the complexity of the historical sources available for writing Herul history. Nor does the older scholarship on the topic do justice to those sources, when attempting through a seemingly contiguous narrative to write the story of a people wandering from Scandinavia to the Maeotis Lake, and then back home. In Late Antiquity there were Gothic, Vandalic, and Alanic groups acting at various settings in time and space. The sources denominate those groups by the same name; for example, Silings and Hasdings are accepted as two Vandalic clusters. It is astonishing that the Herul groups acting in the East as in the West are not accepted as such. Most scholars discussed the idea of an East- and West-Herul people, each separated from the other in its history.[3] Discussing the very name Herules like other comparable phenomena is one aim of this text. It seems impossible to write a history of the Herules, even though a Herul identity existed, which was attached to a *regnum* established in Central Europe in the second half of the fifth century. Apart from that Herules were also part of the so-called 'Hunnic system', members of which joined Odoacar and fought in the armies of Justinian.[4] Procopius knew the Herules as fierce warriors, who could fight bravely in the Roman army. It seems therefore necessary to take into account different circumstances in order to get a complete picture of what we know about third- to sixth-century Herules. What is possible is to re-examine the sources available in an attempt to put together the fragments of Herul history. Delineating a Herul identity may be a much more difficult task. Sources have already been perused and analysed for almost five centuries now, and the end result is a wide variety of interpretations, editions, and commentaries. Besides source criticism, any new approach to Herul history will have to take into account the arguments put forward by generations of historians.[5]

[3] Goffart, *Barbarian Tides*, p. 206: 'The main scholarly problem they [the Herules] pose is whether "Herule" refers to one people, possibly in two branches, or two, possibly altogether distinct from each other.'

[4] Herwig Wolfram, *The Roman Empire and its Germanic Peoples* (Berkeley, 1997), p. 123. 'Hunnic Alternative' is the title of the book's fifth chapter. That refers to the Hunnic way of remaining outside the Roman borders and trying to get money from the Romans by means of tributes and other prosperities instead of entering the empire and becoming part of the Roman world, like the Goths did.

[5] Goffart, *Barbarian Tides*, pp. 205–10, gives a discussion of most sources related to the Herules as do Guenter Neumann and Matthew Taylor, s.v. 'Heruler', in *Reallexikon der germanischen Altertumskunde*, XIV, 2nd edn, ed. by Heinrich Beck, Dieter Geuenich, and Heiko Steuer (Berlin, 1999), pp. 468–74; Bruno Rappaport, s.v. 'Heruli', in *Realencyclopädie der classischen Altertumswissenschaft*, ed. by Wilhelm Kroll, Kurt Witte, Karl Mittelhaus, and Konrat Ziegler, VIII.1

The ethnic name 'Herules' first appears in Graeco-Latin literature during the third century. Groups of warriors identified by that name then resurface in different places and under different circumstances between the third and the sixth centuries, a phenomenon pointing to the complexity of ethnic identity in Late Antiquity. In 268, 'Scythians' are said to have attacked Greece and the Balkans, and among them were ῞Ερουλοι (*Eruloi*). Eighteen years later, the Emperor Maximian stopped barbarian intruders across the Lower Rhine. Among them were also *Eruli*. Some of those warriors eventually settled on Roman soil and were recruited for a newly formed auxiliary unit, the *numerus Erulorum*, which appears in several sources throughout the 300s. Herul raids into Gaul and down to the Spanish coast continued to AD 400. During the first half of the fourth century, the Herules attempted to establish a base of power north of the Sea of Azov. They were defeated and incorporated first into Ermanaric's Gothic kingdom and then into the Hunnic polity. During the 400s, it was apparently expected to find Herul warriors in Attila's troops.

Following the battle at the Nedao River (454 or 455), some Herules established a *regnum* on the river Morava, not far from the Roman frontier, while at the same time others joined Odoacar's army in Italy. The Herul kingdom in the Middle Danube region was an ephemeral polity, which came to an end after only a few decades. Herul warriors had to look for glory and booty elsewhere. According to Procopius, some Herules entered the empire as federates in Dalmatia, while others tried to reach Thule, in the Far North.[6] Procopius's story may have originated on account of the sudden interest of the Ostrogothic court in Italy for all things northern. In any case, one cannot take the story seriously, as proof of a supposed Scandinavian origin of the Herules (who now wanted to return 'home'). Instead, the story simply shows that elites in Constantinople (where Procopius may have written his *Wars*) knew about the image of the North created by and for the consumption of barbarian elites in Ostrogothic Italy. To be sure, Herul recruits fought in separate units within the Roman armies dispatched by Emperor Justinian to the eastern front against the Persians, to Africa against the Vandals, and to Italy against the Goths. After 550, the Herules completely disappear from the sources.

(Stuttgart, 1898; repr. 1992), pp. 1150–67. For a collection of sources concerning the Herules, see Pál Lakatos, *Quellenbuch zur Geschichte der Heruler* (Szeged, 1978). Two M.A. theses under Walter Pohl have been recently defended at the University of Vienna: Angelika Lintner-Potz, 'Die Eruler: Eine misslungene Ethnogenese' (2006); and Jürgen Flick, 'Die Integration barbarischer Randvölker an der mittleren Donau im 5. und 6. Jahrhundert: Am Beispiel der Rugier, Eruler und Langobarden' (2000).

[6] Procopius, *Wars*, 6.15, ed. by J. Haury and trans. by H. B. Dewing, III (London, 1954).

The Third Century: The Herules as Enemies or Partners of the Romans

Sources relating third-century events have the *Eruli* or ῞Εϱουλοι as one of the 'Scythian' groups attacking the eastern parts of the Roman Empire. Dexippus, for example, mentions a people named ῞Ελουϱοι, a name which he then explains as deriving from the swamps (in Greek ἕλος) around the Maeotis, in which those people supposedly lived.[7] Only Jordanes, writing in the mid-500s, linked Dexippus's swamp-dwelling ῞Ελουϱοι (*Eluri* in Jordanes's *Getica*) to contemporary Herules. Neither Jordanes nor Dexippus drew any explicit connection between Herules and the 'Scythian' invasion of 268–69.[8] Fourth- to sixth-century authors may have employed a name commonly used to describe third-century events, and not a specific ethnic name, even though it is theoretically possible that Herules participated in the invasion of 268–69 and that Dexippus's ῞Ελουϱοι were indeed in some way linked to the later Herules.[9]

Whatever the case, it can be no doubt that a sea-borne barbarian invasion of unprecedented size took place in the spring of 268. It is very difficult to reconstruct the exact chain of events, for there seem to have been many concurrent movements

[7] Publius Herennius Dexippus, *Fragmenta*, 5, in *Fragmente der griechischen Historiker*, ed. by Karl Müller, IIA (Paris, 1880), no. 100, p. 456; Thomas Gaisford, *Etymologicon magnum: seu verius Lexicon saepissime vocabulorum origines indagans e pluribus lexicis scholasticis et grammaticis anonymi cuiusdam opera concinnatum* (Oxford, 1848; repr. Amsterdam, 1994), no. 333, p. 952: Stephen of Byzantium, a contemporary of Procopius and Jordanes, also noted that Dexippus's ῞Ελουϱοι were a *gens Scythica*.

[8] Jordanes, *Getica*, 117, ed. by Theodor Mommsen, MGH AA, 5.1 (Berlin, 1882; repr. 1982), pp. 53–138; Andreas Schwarcz, 'Die gotischen Seezüge des 3. Jahrhunderts', in *Die Schwarzmeer-küste in der Spätantike und im frühen Mittelalter,* ed. by Renate Pillinger, Andreas Pülz, and Hermann Vetters (Vienna, 1992), pp. 47–57 (p. 52).

[9] All known variations of this ethnic name are discussed at length in Hermann Reichert, *Lexikon der altgermanischen Namen*, I (Vienna, 1987), pp. 254–58; Moritz Schönfeld, *Wörterbuch der altgermanischen Personen- und Völkernamen* (Heidelberg, 1911), pp. 78–80. The only doubts about the equivalence established between the two ethnic names were raised by Alvar Ellegård, 'Who Were the Eruli?', *Scandia*, 53 (1987), 5–34 (pp. 28–29): 'To summarize. Dexippos' Helouroi may have called themselves Eruli. In that case the later historians' identification of the two was in fact correct. On the other hand, Dexippos' form may be a correct rendering. In that case the identification of the Heluri and the Eruli was as mistaken as Jordanes' (and many others') identification of Gothi and Getae. We shall never know.' One can only add that Jordanes's (and, supposedly, Cassiodorus's) equation of Goths and Getae was not a 'mistake', but a central idea for the narrative strategy of the *Getica*. Roman authors interested in ethnography strove to classify barbarians, while at the same time supplying a credible version of history for their opponents and partners.

and battles. In addition, historians know the events from mostly later, not contemporary sources, primarily Zosimus, the *Historia Augusta*, Jordanes, John Malalas, George Synkellos, and Zonaras. Furthermore, all of them may have relied on the now lost works of Publius Herennius Dexippus, the author of a *Scythica* and of a Roman history from the beginnings to the reign of Claudius II Gothicus, which is often mentioned by the authors of the *Historia Augusta*.[10] 'Later literary sources provide only vague and disparate accounts of the Herul attack on Athens, and none which refers to it is earlier than the latter half of the fourth century. A further confusion arises from the fact that the episode apparently came at the very end of Gallienus's reign, and a decisive defeat of the Scyths was achieved only by Claudius.'[11]

Large numbers of warriors from among the 'Scythian' peoples ('Scytharum diversi populi, Peuci, Greutungi Austrogothi, Tervingi, Visi, Gipedes, Celtae etiam et Eruli')[12] left the shores of the Maeotis Lake (the region of the Sea of Azov) and the mouth of the Dniester on boats to cross the Black Sea. Zosimus claims five thousand boats while the *Historia Augusta* claims three thousand boats, and the total number of warriors is said to have been 320,000.[13] According to Ammianus Marcellinus, there were only two thousand boats and 'swarms of Scythian peoples' ('Scythicarum gentium catervae').[14] Those numbers appear as exaggerated as

[10] For a summary of the events, see John Wilkes, 'Provinces and Frontiers', in *Cambridge Ancient History*, 2nd edn, ed. by John Boardman, XII (London, 2005), pp. 212–68 (pp. 227–29); Emil Kettenhofen, 'Die Einfälle der Heruler ins Römische Reich', *Klio*, 74 (1992), 291–313; Herwig Wolfram, *Die Goten: Von den Anfängen bis zur Mitte des sechsten Jahrhunderts. Entwurf einer historischen Ethnographie*, 4th edn (Munich, 2001), pp. 62–65; Schwarcz, 'Die gotischen Seezüge', pp. 47–57; Rappaport, 'Heruli', pp. 1154–58.

[11] Fergus Millar, 'P. Herennius Dexippus: The Greek World and the Third-Century Invasions', *Journal of Roman Studies*, 59 (1969), 12–29 (p. 26). Older research assumed two separate invasions, one in the reign of Gallienus (267), the other in the reign of Claudius (269), and dated the sack of Athens and Dexippus's heroic defense of his homeland to 267. For the idea of two separate invasions, see Ludwig Schmidt, *Die Ostgermanen*, vol. I of *Geschichte der deutschen Stämme bis zum Ausgange der Völkerwanderung* (Munich, 1941; repr. 1969), pp. 215–20; Bruno Rappaport, *Die Einfälle der Gothen in das römische Reich bis auf Constantin* (Leipzig, 1899), pp. 67–92. For the theory of only one attack, dated to 268, see Wilkes, 'Provinces and Frontiers', p. 227; Schwarcz, 'Die gotischen Seezüge', p. 52 and n. 34.

[12] *Scriptores Historiae Augustae*, II, Divus Claudius 6.2, ed. by Ernst Hohl (Stuttgart, 1997).

[13] Zosimus, *Historia nova*, 1, 42, ed. by François Paschoud (Paris, 1989); *Scriptores Historiae Augustae*, II, Divus Claudius 6.4. For Zosimus, see Walter Goffart, 'Zosimus, the First Historian of Rome's Fall', *American Historical Review*, 76 (1971), 412–41.

[14] Ammianus Marcellinus, *Res gestae*, 31.5.15, ed. and trans. by John C. Rolfe, 3 vols (Cambridge, MA, 1935–58); Peter Heather, *The Goths* (Oxford, 1996), p. 47 and n. 35.

Ammianus's image of 'innumerae gentium multitudines' ('countless swarms of nations') pouring into the empire when the Goths arrived in Thrace in 376 in unexpected numbers. Herodotus had reported innumerable hordes of Persian barbarians invading Greece in the fifth century BC. According to Ammianus, what had happened in 376 confirmed the trustworthiness of the old stories of great numbers of barbarians living outside the known world.[15] In the region of the Sea of Azov and in the Crimea, along the northern border of the empire, barbarian warriors had taken over Greek cities and soon acquired from them the knowledge of how to operate ships and the manpower to do it.[16] This already announces the later takeover of Roman provinces by barbarians. In 268/69 the 'Scythians' caused a lot of havoc, and several land and sea operations by Roman forces had to be organized over the next few years in order to regain control of Greece and the Balkans. Several groups of Goths and Herules roamed freely in the area before the Romans were first able to intercept and destroy a large group of invaders on the river Nessos. Emperor Gallienus's new mobile field-army consisting of cavalry regiments (*tagmata*) are said to have killed three thousand men.[17] After that crushing defeat, the Herul chief Naulobatus surrendered to Gallienus in an act of *deditio* and received in turn the insignia of a Roman consul.[18] This was the earliest barbarian known to have received consular insignias.[19] It is quite possible that the defeated Herules, together with their chief, were immediately recruited into the Roman army, but that is nowhere explicitly mentioned in the sources. At any rate, the episode illustrates the speed at which defeated barbarians could be integrated into the Roman system immediately following their plundering of Roman provinces.

---

[15] Ammianus Marcellinus, *Res gestae*, 31.4.7–8.

[16] Alexander V. Podosinov, 'Am Rande der griechischen Oikumene: Geschichte des Bosporanischen Reichs', in *Das Bosporanische Reich*, ed. by Jochen Fornasier and Burkhard Böttger (Mainz, 2002), pp. 21–39 (pp. 36–38); Pohl, *Die Völkerwanderung*, p. 46.

[17] Zosimus, *Historia Nova*, 1, 43, 1–2; *Scriptores Historiae Augustae*, II, Vita Gallieni 13.9. See also Dietrich Hoffmann, *Das spätrömische Bewegungsheer und die Notitia Dignitatum*, I (Düsseldorf, 1969), pp. 247–49 and nos 406–09; Schwarcz, 'Die gotischen Seezüge', p. 53.

[18] Georgios Synkellos, *Chronographia*, 717, ed. by Wilhelm Dindorf (Bonn, 1829), p. 717, trans. by William Adler and Paul Tuffin, *The Chronography of George Synkellos: A Byzantine Chronicle of Universal History from the Creation* (Oxford, 2002), p. 78. See also s.v. 'Naulobatus', in *The Prosopography of the Later Roman Empire*, I, ed. by Arnold H. M. Jones, John Martindale, and John Morris (Cambridge, 1971), p. 618; Schwarcz, 'Die gotischen Seezüge', p. 53.

[19] Alexander Demandt, *Die Spätantike: Römische Geschichte von Diocletian bis Justinian 284–565 n. Chr.*, 2nd edn (Munich, 2007), pp. 320 and 323; Alexander Demandt, 'Der spätrömische Militäradel', *Chiron*, 10 (1980), 609–37 (p. 610).

Taking advantage of the chaotic situation, a group of Herules moved quickly to Athens and sacked the city. The story of Publius Herennius Dexippus gathering a group of two thousand companions from Athens and launching a counterattack is well known and needs no repetition.[20] One of the fragments surviving from his work is actually a patriotic speech associated with those events.[21] Another less-known episode is reported in a much later, Byzantine tradition. The Herules were about to set fire to a large pile of books in Athens, when one of them stepped forward urging that 'they should leave the Greeks something to occupy themselves in reading so that they would forget to exercise their armies and would be more easily vanquished'.[22] This episode illustrates a resistant stereotype about Herules: they were often depicted as violent, rude, and fierce warriors, while at the same time ruthless and strong, fascinating and horrible. Their image is that of an almost dehumanized human group marked by bestiality: they fought naked, were capable of killing their elders, and of forcing widows to commit suicide upon their husbands' deaths.[23] In reference to Pharas, a Herul officer who distinguished himself in Belisarius's army against the Persians and who laid siege to a fortress in the African mountains to which the Vandal king Gelimer had fled, Procopius mentions that

[20] Peter Heather, 'Disappearing and Reappearing Tribes', in *Strategies of Distinction: The Construction of Ethnic Communities, 300–800*, ed. by Walter Pohl and Helmut Reimitz (Leiden, 1998), pp. 95–112 (p. 97 and n. 6): 'Not only do they [Herules] find specific mention in Zosimus, but some surviving fragments of Dexippus' history (Zosimus's source) make it clear that Dexippus' famous defence of Athens was actually made against Herules, rather than against Goths or any other of the participating groups.' The *Scriptores Historiae Augustae* mentions Dexippus, but only Goths as his enemies. See *Scriptores Historiae Augustae*, II, Vita Gallieni 13.7–8, ed. by Hohl: 'Veneriano item duce navali bello Gothi superati sunt, cum ipse Venerianus militari perit morte. Atque inde Cyzicum et Asiam, deinceps Achaiam omnem vastarunt et ab Atheniensibus duce Dexippo, scriptore horum temporum, victi sunt. Unde pulsi per Epirum, Macedoniam, Moesiam pervagati sunt.'

[21] For the speech, see Publius Herennius Dexippus, *Fragmenta*, 28, in *Fragmente der griechischen Historiker*, ed. by Müller, IIA, 472 (for an English translation, see Millar, 'P. Herennius Dexippus', p. 26). See also Homer A. Thompson, 'Athenian Twilight: A.D. 267–600', *Journal of Roman Studies*, 49 (1959), 61–72 (pp. 61–66); Peter Heather and John Matthews, *The Goths in the Fourth Century* (Liverpool, 1991), pp. 2–3 and n. 5.

[22] Anonymus, *Continuatio Dii Cassii*, ed. by Karl Müller (Paris, 1885), p. 196; Zonaras, *Chronicon*, 12.26, ed. by Jacques-Paul Migne, *Patrologia Graeca*, CXXXIV (Paris, 1864), cols 401–14 and *Patrologia Graeca*, CXXXV, cols 9–326; George Cedrenus, *Compendium historiarum*, ed. by Immanuel Bekker (Bonn, 1838), p. 454. See also Thomas Burns, *A History of the Ostrogoths* (Bloomington, 1984), p. 29 and n. 34.

[23] Procopius, *Wars*, 2.27–28; 6.14.1–7; 6.14.36.

it is remarkable for a Herul not to be treacherous and drunken. Pharas is described as energetic and serious, *despite* being a Herul by birth.[24] Such patronizing comments come very close to the notion of racism as understood in more recent times, even if it is also true that Procopius and others may have been right in condemning the brutality of any Roman soldier, including those of Herul origin. Whatever the case, the stereotype about the Herules stuck and seems to have been reproduced in much later works of Byzantine authors.

In the spring of 269, an army under the Roman emperor Marcus Aurelius Claudius Augustus Gothicus inflicted a crushing defeat on both Goths and Herules near Naissus (modern Niš) in the province of Moesia Inferior. Following his victory, Claudius II assumed the triumphal epithet of *Gothicus*, the first Roman emperor to do so.[25] Another Herul chieftain named Andonnoballus is said to have switched sides.[26] However, 'Scythian' attacks from the northern shore of the Black Sea continued unabated until 276.[27]

In the West: Pirates and Soldiers in the Roman Army

In 286 Herules and Chaibones attacked Gaul. Emperor Maximian intercepted them and, according to a panegyric of Claudius Mamertinus, managed to kill them all. Modern commentators refused to take at face value Mamertinus's testimony and claimed instead that, following his victory, Maximian recruited barbarians for a Herul auxiliary unit.[28] During the fourth century, that Herul *auxilium* (*numerus*

---

[24] Procopius, *Wars*, 4.4.29. See also Averil Cameron, *Procopius and the Sixth Century* (London, 1985), p. 240 and n. 79; Felix Dahn, *Prokopius von Cäsarea: Ein Beitrag zur Historiographie der Völkerwanderung und des sinkenden Römerthums* (Berlin, 1865), pp. 121–22: 'Ganz besonders zuwider ist ihm der germanische Stamm der Heruler: er findet gar nicht Worte genug, sie herunterzusetzen, geräth in eine leidenschaftliche Heftigkeit.' Dahn assumes that Procopius had contacts with Herul warriors and did not like them because of his personal experience.

[25] Zosimus, *Historia nova*, 1, 45, 1; see Michael Kulikowski, *Rome's Gothic Wars: From the Third Century to Alaric* (Cambridge, 2007), p. 29 and n. 17; Wolfram, *Die Goten*, p. 65; Schmidt, *Die Ostgermanen*, pp. 216–17 and n. 7.

[26] Petrus Patricius, *Fragmenta*, p. 186; s.v. 'Andonnoballus', in *Prosopography of the Later Roman Empire*, I, ed. by Jones, Martindale, and Morris, p. 62.

[27] Schwarcz, 'Die gotischen Seezüge', p. 56.

[28] Claudius Mamertinus, *Panegyricus Maximiano Augusto dictus*, 2.5, ed. and trans. by Édouard Galletier (Paris, 1949), pp. 24–37 (pp. 28–29). See Hoffmann, *Das spätrömische Bewegungsheer*, pp. 156–57; Rappaport, 'Heruli', p. 1152; Schmidt, *Die Ostgermanen*, p. 558; Kaspar Zeuss, *Die Deutschen und die Nachbarstämme* (Munich, 1837; repr. 1925), p. 479.

Erulorum seniorum) was part of the *auxilia Palatina* in Italy. Several funerary inscriptions are known, which name the unit as a whole or some of its individual members. The unit was stationed near Concordia, an important military centre in Venetia.[29]

The *numerus Erulorum* was a troop of lightly equipped soldiers, who received much praise for their valour and was often mentioned together with the Batavians (*Batavi seniores*).[30] Ammianus Marcellinus mentions a Herul soldier named Vitalianus (*Erulorum e numero miles*), who began his career as *domesticus* under Emperor Jovian and later became *comes*.[31] Herules led by Charietto fought in January 366 against Alamannic marauders from across the Rhine. Charietto died in battle, and the Alamanni captured the standard of the Herul and Batavian unit, 'which the barbarians with insulting cries and dancing with joy frequently raised on high and displayed, until after hard struggles it was recovered'.[32] In 366, Julian sent the Herules against the Picts and the Scoti attacking Britannia, again accompanied by the Batavian *auxilium*. At the head of this corps was the *magister militum* Lupicinus. He crossed the channel from Gallia to Londinium,[33] only to learn that Constantius, jealous of Julian's military achievements, had ordered the transfer of the Herul and Batavian auxiliary troops to the eastern front under the pretext that they were needed for an attack against the Parthians the following spring.[34]

Herules had a good reputation as soldiers in the Roman army, but fifth-century sources depict them as fierce marauders and pirates. Jerome knew them as one of the barbarian groups crossing the Rhine and devastating Gaul in 406.[35] Herul raids are also reported as having targeted the coasts of Spain. Hydatius mentions seven

---

[29] *Notitia dignitatum*, Occ. 5.162; 7.13, in *Notitia dignitatum: Accedunt notitia urbis Constantinopolitanae et laterculi provinciarum*, ed. by Otto Seeck (Berlin, 1876). For inscriptions, see Hoffmann, *Das spätrömische Bewegungsheer*, pp. 77–79 and 88–91; Rappaport, 'Heruli', pp. 1152–53. See also Hoffmann, *Das spätrömische Bewegungsheer*, II, 272 (index).

[30] Ammianus Marcellinus, *Res gestae*, 20.1.3, 20.4.2, 27.1.6, and 27.8.7. See Hoffmann, *Das spätrömische Bewegungsheer*, pp. 156–58.

[31] Ammianus Marcellinus, *Res gestae*, 25.10.9.

[32] Ammianus Marcellinus, *Res gestae*, 27.1.6; Zosimus, *Historia nova*, 4, 9, tells the same story but mentions only Batavians.

[33] Ammianus Marcellinus, *Res gestae*, 20.1.3.

[34] Ammianus Marcellinus, *Res gestae*, 20.4.1–2; Rappaport, 'Heruli', p. 1153; Schmidt, *Die Ostgermanen*, p. 559.

[35] Jerome, *Ep*.123, ed. by Isidor Hilberg (Vienna, 1916), p. 92: '[...] quod Oceano Rhenoque concluditur, Quadus, Vandalus, Sarmata, Halani, Gypedes, Herules, Saxones, Burgundiones, Alamanni [...] vastaverunt'. See Friedrich Lotter, *Völkerverschiebungen im Ostalpen-Mitteldonau-Raum zwischen Antike und Mittelalter 375–600* (Berlin, 2003), p. 90 and n. 313.

ships and four hundred warriors attacking his native province, Gallaecia, and then moving to Cantabria.[36] Four years later an even stronger attack reached the coasts of Baetica.[37]

Scholars have traditionally treated those third- to fifth-century Herules as a separate 'West-Herul' group to be distinguished from the 'eastern Herules' mentioned in relation to the invasion of 268/69.[38] However, such a distinction is not mentioned by any late antique source. The idea of a separate 'West-Herul' group implies that the Herules were settled somewhere north of the Roman frontiers in the west. Ludwig Schmidt, for example, argued that such a settlement area was necessary to provide recruits for the *auxilium*. Further support for the idea of a Herul kingdom north of the Lower Rhine was found in a letter of Theoderic the Great contained in Cassiodorus's *Variae* and a cursory remark in one of Sidonius Apollinaris's letters. Theoderic's letter is addressed to the kings of the Thuringians, the Herules, and the Varni, without any specific names, and was meant to gather support for his attempt to negotiate a peace between Clovis and Alaric II. His request of assistance was apparently based on a precedent. Both Theoderic's letter and the short remark in Sidonius Apollinaris's letter have been taken as a proof for the existence of a Herul kingdom somewhere on the Lower Rhine.[39] However,

---

[36] Hydatius, *Continuatio Chronicorum*, 171, in *Chronica minora saec. IV. V. VI. VII.*, vol. II, ed. by Theodor Mommsen, MGH AA, 11 (Berlin, 1894; repr. Munich, 1981); English translation in Richard W. Burgess, *The Chronicle of Hydatius and the Consularia Constantinopolitana: Two Contemporary Accounts of the Final Years of the Roman Empire* (Oxford, 1993). See also Santiago Castellano's contribution to this volume.

[37] Hydatius, *Continuatio Chronicorum*, 194: 'Eruli maritima conventus Lucensis loca nonnulla crudelissime invadunt ad Baeticam pertendentes.'

[38] See for example Rappaport, 'Heruli', pp. 1152–55; Schmidt, *Die Ostgermanen*, pp. 548–64: 'Ostheruler; Westheruler'. The distinction between the 'European' or 'German' Herules and the 'Sarmatian' Herules can already be found in eighteenth-century encyclopaedias, such as *Grosses vollständiges Universallexikon aller Wissenschaften und Künste*, XII, ed. by Johann Heinrich Zedler (Leipzig, 1745), p. 1851, s. v. 'Heruli oder Eruli, Aeruli, Heluri': 'Ein altes Teutsches Volk Gothischen oder Vandalischen Geschlechts, welches von undencklichen Zeiten um und neben denen Rügen, Gothen und Wandlen gewohnet. [...] Einige von denen Herulis seyn in ihren alten Sitzen zurückblieben, die meisten aber haben sich bey denen grossen Wanderungen derer Völcker auch daraus begeben und zwar haben sie sich in 2 Hauffen getheilet. Deren einer sich gegen Osten, der andere gegen Westen gewendet. Daher man sie billig in 2 Aeste den in Teutschland und den in Sarmatia abtheilet. Jene sind die ältesten, obwohl ihre abkömmlinge, die Sarmatischen Heruli, denen Römern eher als sie bekannt worden, ihrer auch daher weder von Plinio noch von Tacito gedacht wird.'

[39] Cassiodorus, *Variae*, 3.3, ed. by Theodor Mommsen, MGH AA, 12 (Berlin, 1894; repr. Munich, 1981), pp. 79–80; English translation by S. J. B. Barnish (Liverpool, 1992), pp.

such an interpretation is not really necessary, for Theoderic may well have had in mind the Herul kingdom in the Middle Danube region, a point to which I shall shortly return. In fact, a Herul king in that region is the addressee of another letter written by Cassiodorus in the name of Theoderic ('regi Erulorum Theodericus rex').[40] Sidonius Apollinaris describes in his letter various envoys pressing upon one another at the court of the Visigothic king Euric. Among them is also a Herul: 'Here strolls the Herul with his glaucous cheeks, inhabitant of Ocean's furthest shore, and of one complexion with its weedy deeps.'[41] Sidonius's mention of the Herul's origin from the 'Ocean's furthest shore' has been interpreted as indicating a Herul kingdom at the mouth of the Rhine.[42] However, this may in fact be nothing more than a bookish reference to third-century accounts of Herules attacking from the sea. Indeed, a Parthian 'Arsacid' mentioned in the next line clearly points to a third-century historical context for Sidonius's allusions.[43] As a consequence, there is no support in either Theoderic's or Sidonius's letter for the idea of a 'West-Herul' group, which seems to have been concocted without much regard for sources. Neither a 'northern' kingdom, nor a specific settlement area is necessary in order to explain the presence of the Herules in the West as soldiers and pirates. Warriors who had started as soldiers in the Roman army could have easily turned into freebooters, and pirates may have easily become soldiers. Different Herul groups

47–48. According to Barnish, 'the Herules and Warni were probably the western branches of those tribes, between the lower Rhine and Elbe'. Elias Wessén, *De nordiska folkstammarna i Beowulf* (Stockholm, 1927), p. 86, wrongly believed that both letters of Theoderic had been sent to a Herul king in Scandinavia. Goffart discusses those sources in *Barbarian Tides*, p. 206 and nn. 93–96.

[40] Neumann and Taylor, 'Heruler', pp. 470–71. The second letter: Cassiodorus, *Variae*, 4.2.

[41] Sidonius Apollinaris, *ep.* 8.9, ed by Christian Lüetjohann, MGH AA, 8 (Berlin, 1887; repr. 1961), p. 136 ('Hic glaucis Herulus genis vagatur, imos Oceani colens recessus algoso prope concolor profundo'); English translation from *Sidonius, Poems and Letters with an English Translation*, trans. by William B. Anderson, William H. Semple, and Edward H. Warmington, II (Cambridge, MA, 1965), p. 145.

[42] Rappaport, 'Heruli', pp. 1153–54; Schmidt, *Die Ostgermanen*, p. 560; Andreas Schwarcz, 'Die Heruler an der Donau', in *Sprache als System und Prozess: Festschrift für Günter Lipold zum 60. Geburtstag*, ed. by Christiane M. Pabst (Vienna, 2005), pp. 504–12 (p. 508).

[43] Sidonius Apollinaris, *ep.* 8.9, ed by Lüetjohann: 'Ipse hic Parthicus Arsaces precatur, aulae Susidis ut tenere culmen possit foedere sub stipendiali. Nam quod partibus arma Bosphoranis grandi hinc surgere sentit apparatu, maestam Persida iam sonum ad duelli ripa Euphratide vix putat tuendam'. Ardashir I founded the Sassanian dynasty after defeating the last king of the Arsacid dynasty, Artabanus IV, in 226. See Jörg Wiesehöfer, s.v. 'Sāsāniden', in *Der Neue Pauly: Enzyklopädie der Antike*, ed. by Hubert Cancik and Helmuth Schneider, XI (Stuttgart, 2001), pp. 89–98.

appear to have operated in close proximity to the empire, but at different locations. To regard the Herules as 'pre-Vikings' from the North is based on nothing else than the association between their seaborne attacks and the Viking raids of later centuries, all in an ill-defined Scandinavian context inspired by Jordanes's and Procopius's accounts. Where sources fail to support such farfetched theories, linguistic speculations about ethnic names are called to the rescue.[44] In reality, there is nothing special about attacks from the sea: various marauders employed such tactics at various points in history. It is just easier and not too dangerous.

Gazing at the Dark Side of the Moon: *The Herules Choose, More or Less Voluntarily, the 'Hunnic Alternative'*[45]

Peter Heather has used the Herules to illustrate his idea of 'disappearing and reappearing tribes':

> No fourth-century text, however, mentions them [the Herules]. This could simply be a lacuna in the evidence, but contemporary sources make it clear that first Gothic and then Hunnic groups were politically dominant in the northern Pontic areas which Herules had occupied in the third century, and Herules certainly reappeared with a bang after the crash of the Hunnic Empire in the mid-fifth century. Their subsequent history is recorded in a number of sources.[46]

---

[44] For a particularly egregious example, see 'The Heruls', <http://www.gedevasen.dk/heruleng.html#C7> [accessed 1 April 2007]: 'We do not know a tribe called Wicinga and the word Viking is not known so early from other sources — long time before the Viking Ages. To the editor of Widsith in the 10th century a combination "Eorla cynn" would not make any sense in this line of names. Maybe he instead used "Wicinga" as a general word for Nordic warriors. If "wicinga" really was the original wording, this was probably a tribe giving name to the later Vikings, and as the Heruls were regarded as pirates in the Atlantic Ocean and the Black Sea they are probably in both cases the best candidates to the names "Wicingas" and "Lidwicingas" ("Lid" must be the old word for a private army used by the Vikings). Widsith also used the Herul-like "Herelingas" — probably covering at that position in Widsith a personal name and therefore unchanged by the authors of Widsith.'

[45] In his conclusion to session 613 entitled 'Neglected Barbarians' and organized for the 40th International Congress on Medieval Studies in Kalamazoo (8 May 2005), Thomas F. X. Noble used this striking metaphor to describe the confusion arising from the Greek and Roman ethnographic texts and our attempts to understand the world beyond the Roman borders: The territory north, east, and south of the Roman borders is the *dark side of the moon*. We know hardly more than names and archaeological material of the societies there. Our *bright side of the moon* is the empire with its texts and inscriptions. Wolfram, *The Roman Empire*, p. 123. 'Hunnic Alternative' is the title of the book's fifth chapter.

[46] Heather, 'Disappearing and Reappearing Tribes', pp. 97–98.

Before the mid-fourth century, the Herules appear in the region north of the Sea of Azov, but we do not know much about their political structures. That was certainly a region adjacent to territories under Roman control and with substantial urban structures. The Herules living in that area must have become part of a Gothic and, later, Hunnic confederation. Historians derive further information about the Herules from Jordanes, who wrote two centuries later. According to Jordanes, under their leader Alaric (*Halaricus*), the Herules were defeated by Ermanaric, the almighty Gothic king. It is important to note that in order to refer to the Herul leader, Jordanes avoids using the title of king: 'gentem Herulorum, quibus praeerat Halaricus' ('Alaric, who presided over the Herules').[47] Nothing is known about either a Herul king or a Herul kingdom, and all we have is what Jordanes has to offer:[48]

> He [Ermanaric] subdued many warlike peoples of the north and made them obey his laws, and some of our ancestors have justly compared him to Alexander the Great. [...] But though famous for his conquest of so many races, he gave himself no rest until he had slain some in battle and then reduced to his sway the remainder of the tribe of the Herules, whose chief was Alaric. Now the aforesaid race, as the historian Ablabius tells us, dwelt near Lake Maeotis in swampy places, which the Greeks call *hele*; hence they were named Heluri. They were a people swift of foot, and on that account were the more swollen with pride, for there was at that time no nation that did not choose from them its light-armed troops for battle. But though their quickness often saved them from others who made war upon them, yet they were overthrown by the slowness and steadiness of the Goths; and the lot of fortune brought it to pass that they, as well as the other tribes, had to serve Hermanaric, king of the Getae.[49]

---

[47] Jordanes, *Getica*, 117; Reinhard Wenskus, s.v. 'Alarich', in *Reallexikon der germanischen Altertumskunde*, I, 2nd edn, ed. by Heinrich Beck, Dieter Geuenich, and Heiko Steuer (Berlin, 1973), p. 129.

[48] Like many before and after him, Schmidt, *Die Ostgermanen*, p. 335, makes Alaric a king and assumes therefore that Ermanaric conquered a Herul kingdom.

[49] Jordanes, *Getica*, 116–18: 'Nam Gothorum rege Geberich rebus humanis excedente post temporis aliquod Hermanaricus nobilissimus Amalorum in regno successit, qui multas et bellicosissimas arctoi gentes perdomuit suisque parere legibus fecit. Quem merito nonnulli Alexandro Magno conparavere maiores. [...] Sed cum tantorum servitio clarus haberetur, non passus est nisi et gentem Herulorum, quibus praeerat Halaricus, magna ex parte trucidatam reliquam suae subegeret dicioni. Nam praedicta gens, Ablavio istorico referente, iuxta Meotida palude inhabitans in locis stagnantibus, quas Greci ele vocant, Eluri nominati sunt, gens quantum velox, eo amplius superbissima. Nulla si quidem erat tunc gens, quae non levem armaturam in acie sua ex ipsis elegeret. Sed quamvis velocitas eorum ab aliis crebro bellantibus evagaret, Gothorum tamen stabilitate subiacuit et tarditati, fecitque causa fortunae, ut et ipsi inter reliquas gentes Getarum regi Hermanarico servirent.'

After having beaten the Herules, Ermanaric turned against the Venethi. The much discussed equation of Venethi, Antes, and Sclaveni follows.[50] The Aesti, located on the farthest shore of the German Ocean, were also attacked and subdued by the great Gothic king. Finally, Jordanes remarks, Ermanaric ruled over all nations of Scythia and Germania.[51] Jordanes introduces Ermanaric as Theoderic's most important harbinger, equal to the great Alexander and 'raised into a mythical figure that has borrowed several characteristics from Attila'.[52] According to Ammianus, the mighty and famous *bellicosissimus rex* eventually committed suicide after having failed to resist the Hunnic onslaught. Ermanaric is the first Gothic king mentioned not only in Jordanes's *Getica*, but also in a contemporary, fourth-century source.[53] He was obviously a key character in the construction of a glorious past for the Amal dynasty. As a consequence, his deeds and merits were greatly exaggerated in Jordanes's account. Both Otto Maenchen-Helfen and Herwig Wolfram have suggested bringing Ermanaric's achievements to real size: instead of a large Gothic kingdom covering much of Eastern Europe, one should envision an area of trade relations and treaties, as well as intertribal conflicts.[54] Ermanaric was undoubtedly an important person in the 300s, but Jordanes described him as a Gothic Alexander, and the later medieval literature blew his image out of proportion even further.[55] As a consequence, as early as the mid-nineteenth century, German- and Slavic-speaking scholars began quarrelling over the true achievements

---

[50] See Florin Curta, 'Hiding Behind a Piece of Tapestry: Jordanes and the Slavic Venethi', *Jahrbücher für Geschichte Osteuropas*, 47 (1999), 321–40; Florin Curta, *The Making of the Slavs: History and Archaeology of the Lower Danube Region, ca. 500–700* (Cambridge, 2001), pp. 39–43; Roland Steinacher, 'Wenden, Slawen, Vandalen: Eine frühmittelalterliche pseudologische Gleichsetzung und ihre Nachwirkungen', in *Die Suche nach den Ursprüngen: Von der Bedeutung des frühen Mittelalters*, ed. by Walter Pohl (Vienna, 2004), pp. 329–53 (p. 329 and n. 3).

[51] Jordanes, *Getica*, 120: 'Idem ipse prudentia et virtute subegit omnibusque Scythiae et Germaniae nationibus ac si propriis lavoribus imperavit.'

[52] Ellegård, 'Who Were the Eruli?', p. 26.

[53] Ammianus Marcellinus, *Res gestae*, 31.3.1–2. See Heinrich Beck and Herwig Wolfram, s.v. 'Ermanarich', in *Reallexikon der germanischen Altertumskunde*, VII, 2nd edn, ed. by Heinrich Beck, Dieter Geuenich, and Heiko Steuer (Berlin, 1989), pp. 510–15 (p. 510); Kulikowski, *Rome's Gothic Wars*, pp. 111–12.

[54] Otto J. Maenchen-Helfen, *The World of the Huns: Studies in their History and Culture* (Berkeley, 1973), pp. 19–20; Beck and Wolfram, s.v. 'Ermanarich', pp. 511–12.

[55] Beck and Wolfram, s.v. 'Ermanarich', pp. 512–15; Walter Goffart, *The Narrators of Barbarian History, AD 550–800: Jordanes, Gregory of Tours, Bede, and Paul the Deacon* (Princeton, 1988), p. 79 and n. 283.

of Ermanaric and over the expanse of land he had under his rule. In his *Slavonic Antiquities*, Pavel Josef Šafarík (1795–1861), one of the founders of the discipline of Slavic studies, first raised doubts about the trustworthiness of Jordanes's account. In reply, Eduard von Wietersheim strove to demonstrate that, on the contrary, Jordanes's account must be taken seriously, and imagined a great Gothic Empire covering much of Eastern Europe.[56] To be sure, Jordanes's account is very imprecise, with no specific details about the location of the Herules. His etymological speculation connecting the Herules with the swamps and the Sea of Azov is entirely taken from Dexippus.[57] Ablabius is a problematic source, which is only mentioned by Jordanes. Theodor Mommsen first imagined Ablabius as the author of a now lost Gothic history, but more recent studies are much more reserved in that respect and some went so far as to raise doubts about the existence of Ablabius.[58]

In order to explain the Hunnic subjugation of the Goths, Jordanes introduces the story of the *Rosomonorum gens infida*. Following her husband's aborted revolt against the Gothic king, Queen Sunilda was tortured and eventually executed. According to Jordanes, her husband's treachery had aroused Ermanaric's rage. In return, Sunilda's brothers Ammius and Sarus assassinated Ermanaric, plunging a sword into his side.[59] The meaning of this episode for Jordanes's narrative strategy is obscure. The very name *Rosomoni* may be translated as either 'the quick ones' or 'people with red hair'. *Gens*, on the other hand, is a very ambiguous term, which can refer to a group of warriors regarded as a clan, to a family, or to a people. Herwig Wolfram viewed the *Rosomoni* as Herules living north of the Black Sea or as their *stirps regia*. He accordingly saw in Jordanes's episode the evidence for a Herul uprising taking advantage of the weakening of the Gothic rule. Others, however,

---

[56] Pavel Josef Šafarík, *Slawische Alterthümer*, I (Leipzig, 1844), p. 428: 'Nicht grundlos vermutet man, dass Jordanis die Thaten der Gothen, namentlich Ermanarich's, unverschämt übertrieben, ja dass seine ganze Geschichte von dem unermesslichen Reiche Ermanarich's auf Irrthum oder Lüge beruhe.' See also Eduard von Wietersheim, *Geschichte der Völkerwanderung*, IV (Leipzig, 1864), pp. 8–12. Ludwig Albrecht Gebhardi, *Geschichte aller Wendisch-Slavischen Staaten: Erster Band, welcher die älteste Geschichte der Wenden und Slaven, und die Geschichte des Reichs der Wenden in Teutschland enthält* (Leipzig, 1790), pp. 34–37, was more cautious and simply reproduced Jordanes's account.

[57] Ellegård, 'Who Were the Eruli?', pp. 28–29.

[58] See Goffart, *Narrators*, p. 62 with n. 208; Wolfram, *Goten*, p. 381 with n. 36; Norbert Wagner, *Getica: Untersuchungen zum Leben des Jordanes und zur frühen Geschichte der Goten* (Berlin, 1967), pp. 62–68; Theodor Mommsen, 'Prooemium', in Jordanes, *Getica*, ed. by Mommsen, pp. xxxvii–ix.

[59] Jordanes, *Getica*, 129; Maenchen-Helfen, *World of the Huns*, p. 17 and n. 23.

treat the *Rosomoni* as just another Gothic noble family. Both interpretations overstretch the evidence of Jordanes. In any case, name similarity is definitely not sufficient evidence for tracking down the 'disappearing Herules'.[60]

There is no mention of Herules throughout the entire period between *c.* 400 and 450. It is of course quite possible that Herul warriors fought alongside the Huns in Attila's army, but there were also Herules in Roman service. According to Sidonius Apollinaris, Herules marched into Gaul in 451 with Attila.[61] According to Peter Heather, they 'reappeared with a bang after the crash of the Hunnic Empire'.[62] Attila's death brought about the disintegration of the broad coalition of many different *gentes*, which had formed the Hunnic polity. The Hunnic leader had secured the constant supply of revenue extorted from the Roman Empire. His 'warriors could enjoy the benefits of the Roman world without having to enter it'.[63] But the Romans were also successful in fighting the Huns back, and a great Hunnic attack on the Eastern Empire, which was planned for 453, had to be abandoned. It was no longer possible either to wait in Pannonia for Roman supplies to be shipped or to organize successful raids across the borders into the neighbouring Roman provinces. This was the end of Attila's policies, aptly called the 'Hunnic alternative' by Herwig Wolfram, which the Herules, among others, had enjoyed.[64] At Attila's death in 453, his former allies and subjects were at each other's throats. The Hunnic leader's sons attemped to forge separate polities, which included selected *gentes* that may have remained loyal to them. If successful, this would have

---

[60] Wolfram, *Goten*, pp. 97–98: 'Die Bedeutung von Gens ist fließend; man kann darunter ebenso Völkerschaften, Kriegerverbände wie Großsippen verstehen, weil sich ihre Erscheinungsformen qualitativ kaum voneinander unterscheiden. Daher scheint es ziemlich gleichgültig zu sein, ob man die Rosomonen als Volk oder (königliches) Geschlecht bezeichnet, das "Ermanarich unter anderen (Völkern) in seiner Gefolgschaft hatte". Demnach wären die Rosomonen, deren Namen wie der der Eruler so viel wie die "Schnellen", die "Stürmischen" bedeuten könnte, mit der von Ermanarich unterworfenen Gens identisch gewesen.' For *Rosomoni* as a Gothic noble family, see Helmut Castritius and Guenter Neumann, s.v. 'Rosomonen', in *Reallexikon der germanischen Altertumskunde*, XXV, 2nd edn, ed. by Heinrich Beck, Dieter Geuenich, and Heiko Steuer (Berlin, 2003), pp. 353–58 (pp. 356–57).

[61] Sidonius Apollinaris, *ep.* 7.12 and 8.15; *carm.* 7.319–322. See Wolfram, *Goten*, p. 259 and n. 1; Schmidt, *Die Ostgermanen*, p. 473.

[62] Heather, 'Disappearing and Reappearing Tribes', p. 98.

[63] Walter Pohl, s. v. 'Huns', in *Late Antiquity: A Guide to the Postclassical World*, ed. by Glenn W. Bowersock, Peter R. L. Brown, and Oleg Grabar (Cambridge, MA, 1999), pp. 501–02 (p. 502).

[64] Wolfram, *The Roman Empire*, p. 139; Maenchen-Helfen, *World of the Huns*, pp. 137–42.

been the equivalent of a multitude of Hunnic rulers, each striving to maximize his version of the 'Hunnic alternative'. That alternative, however, was no longer viable. A coalition of forces was formed against those Hunnic petty kings, led by the Gepid king Ardaric. These men longed for a better apportionment. What actually happened after 453 is difficult to reconstruct, for the only source for the events that followed is again Jordanes, and since his purpose was to write a history of the Goths, he had no interest in documenting Gothic losses. Nevertheless, it is quite clear that the Goths of Valamir, Theodoric's grandfather, were on the side of Attila's sons and therefore entered the conflict with smaller groups attempting to evade the Hunnic rule. Jordanes did not have anything glorious to report about the generation of Goths before the great Theoderic. In 454 or 455, a coalition of Gepids, Sueves, Herules, and others obtained a decisive victory, the last one in a series, on the river Nedao in Pannonia. Attila's son Ellac died in battle.[65] 'Once again the same tribes fought on both sides; one thing is clear, though: the majority of the Hunnic Goths under Amal leadership were amongst the losers, while the Gepids led the victorious army.'[66] At this point in his narrative, Jordanes has a 'catalogue of nations' meeting on the battlefield, each one with its 'national' weapons, but it is not clear who was on what side.

> There an encounter took place between the various nations Attila had held under his sway. Kingdoms with their peoples were divided, and out of one body were made many members not responding to a common impulse. Being deprived of their head, they madly strove against each other. They never found their equals ranged against them without harming each other by wounds mutually given. And so the bravest nations tore themselves to pieces. For then, I think, must have occurred a most remarkable spectacle, where one might see the Goths fighting with pikes, the Gepidae raging with the sword, the Rugii breaking off the

[65] For a detailed analysis, see Walter Pohl, 'Die Gepiden und die gentes an der mittleren Donau nach dem Zerfall des Attilareiches', in *Die Völker an der mittleren und unteren Donau im fünften und sechsten Jahrhundert: Berichte des Symposions der Kommission für Frühmittelalterforschung, 24.–27. Oktober 1978, Stift Zwettl, Niederösterreich*, ed. by Herwig Wolfram and Falko Daim (Vienna, 1980), pp. 239–305 (pp. 254–62).

[66] Wolfram, *The Roman Empire*, p. 139; Martin Nagy, Walter Pohl, and Agnés B. Tóth, s.v. 'Gepiden', in *Reallexikon der germanischen Altertumskunde*, XI, 2nd edn, ed. by Heinrich Beck, Dieter Geuenich, and Heiko Steuer (Berlin, 2003), pp. 115–41 (pp. 133–34); Pohl, 'Gepiden', pp. 247–49. According to Pohl, the Ostrogoths and the Gepids were two rival groups vying for power under Hunnic rule. Valamir and Ardaric were both close companions of Attila (Jordanes, *Getica*, 199). The Gepids and the Huns were often mentioned together and sometimes even mistaken for one another. Attila, for example, is said to have been a Gepid in the *Chronicon Paschale* and in the *Chronographia* of John Malalas. See note 101 below.

spears in their own wounds, the Suevi fighting on foot, the Huns with bows, the Alani drawing up a battle-line of heavy-armed and the Herules of light-armed warriors.[67]

It is also not clear whether the Herules had been on the side of Attila's sons. There seems to have been a division of several *gentes* into warring parties. Edica, Odoacar's father, one of the most powerful followers of Attila who enjoyed much influence, was not capable of gathering all Scirians on his side.[68] According to Jordanes, not only did different *gentes* fight against each other, but also 'the bravest nations tore themselves to pieces' ('se ipsos discerperent fortissimae nationes'). Several splinter groups could thus appear out of a single ethnic group within a relatively short period of time. Ethnic identities were reinvented, and previously smaller groups rose to prominence. In Jordanes's words: 'Kingdoms with their peoples were divided, and out of one body were made many members not responding to a common impulse'. Several warlords may have gone their own way, with some Herul leaders fighting on the side of Attila's sons, others against them. Still others must have waited on the side, to see who would win in the final confrontation. There is therefore no room for the nineteenth-century idea of oppressed Germanic peoples freeing themselves from the Hunnic yoke through a liberation movement. Following this rather chaotic period, the Ostrogoths, but also some Sciri, Alans, Rugi, and many others ('vero aliaeque nationes nonnullae') asked the East Roman government for permission to enter the empire. They were settled as federates by Emperor Marcian. Given the subsequent developments, it seems likely that among the 'aliaeque nationes nonnullae' were also Herules.[69] To get a clear picture of them, it is necessary to understand the milieu in which they operated. One therefore needs to turn to the events taking place in the Middle Danube region, in Pannonia, and in Italy during the second half of the fifth century.

---

[67] Jordanes, *Getica*, 261: 'Illic concursus factus est gentium variarum, quas Attila in sua tenuerat dicione. Dividuntur regna cum populis, fiuntque ex uno corpore membra diversa, nec quae unius passioni conpaterentur, sed quae exciso capite in invicem insanirent; quae numquam contra se pares invenerant, nisi ipsi mutuis se vulneribus sauciantes se ipsos discerperent fortissimae nationes. Nam ibi admirandum reor fuisse spectaculum, ubi cernere erat contis pugnantem Gothum, ense furentem Gepida, in vulnere suo Rugum tela frangentem, Suavum pede, Hunnum sagitta praesumere, Alanum gravi, Herulum levi armatura aciem strui.' See Pohl, 'Gepiden', pp. 258–62; Helmut Castritius, s.v. 'Nedao', in *Reallexikon der germanischen Altertumskunde*, XXI, 2nd edn, ed. by Heinrich Beck, Dieter Geuenich, and Heiko Steuer (Berlin, 2002), pp. 49–51; Heather, *The Goths*, pp. 124–29.

[68] Jordanes, *Getica*, 277; Pohl, 'Gepiden', p. 261.

[69] Jordanes, *Getica*, 263–66, the citation from 266; Lotter, *Völkerverschiebungen*, p. 103, is certain that Herules were among the federates admitted into the Eastern provinces.

The Herul Regnum on the Roman Frontier

> After the battle the victorious tribes settled directly on the left bank of the Danube and established, between the Lower Austrian Wachau Valley and the Transylvanian Carpathians, a series of kingdoms linked as federates to Constantinople. At the threshold of a mighty *Gepidia* there arose, between the Danube and the Tisza, a Scirian, and a Sarmatian kingdom. West of them the Suebi had a *regnum*. The Herules and the Rugians resided at the March respectively north of the Danube. Evidently the victorious barbarians of the Danube had contractually guaranteed rights to the economic prosperity of the provincials on the right side of the Danube. To keep a rein on these claims, the defeated Goths were to be settled as federates of east Rome inside the empire.[70]

The place chosen by authorities in Constantinople for the Goths of Valamir and his brothers Thiudimir and Vidimir was Pannonia. There they controlled the Danube between Vindobona and Singidunum, a key area for both West and East, as well as for other barbarian groups emerging in the aftermath of the collapse of the Hunnic polity. Throughout the second half of the fifth century, the Pannonian Goths strove to obtain hegemony over all former subjects of Attila's Huns, either as an ally or as an enemy of the empire. The other *gentes* carried out attacks on the Goths either to enter the empire as a Roman *exercitus* or to force the Romans to pay them for maintaining the peace. By 473, however, the greater part of the Pannonian Goths left for the Balkans, and in 488 they entered Italy with an imperial mandate to fight Odoacar.[71] The second leading group emerging out of the Hunnic system were the Gepids, separated from the Goths by the old Roman frontier. The Gepids had occupied the territory between the Danube, the Tisza, and the Olt Rivers, on the one hand, and the Carpathian Mountains, on the other hand, an area which included the former province of Dacia. They had a contract of peace and friendship with the emperor, which lasted for nearly a century. As a consequence, they were paid *annua sollemnia*.[72] Between the Danube and the Tisza, a Scirian polity was established by Edica and his sons, Odoacar and Onoulf (Hunulf). Priscus had known Edica to be one of Attila's confidants.[73] This family,

---

[70] Wolfram, *The Roman Empire*, pp. 139–40. The situation is also described by Pohl, 'Gepiden', pp. 268–80; Herwig Wolfram, *Grenzen und Räume: Geschichte Österreichs vor seiner Entstehung 378–907* (Vienna, 1995), p. 34; Nagy, Pohl, and Tóth, 'Gepiden', p. 134; Lotter, *Völkerverschiebungen*, pp. 103–06.

[71] Jordanes, *Getica*, 264; Wolfram, *Die Goten*, pp. 261–67; Pohl, 'Gepiden', pp. 263–64.

[72] Jordanes, *Getica*, 264; Pohl, 'Gepiden', pp. 268–73.

[73] Walter Pohl, s.v. 'Edika', in *Reallexikon der germanischen Altertumskunde*, VII, 2nd edn, ed. by Heinrich Beck, Dieter Geuenich, and Heiko Steuer (Berlin, 1989), pp. 446–47.

having made themselves the Scirian *stirps regia*, was linked to several centres of power at that time. They established 'international' relations and soon became the main rivals of the Goths. Odoacar and Onoulf played important roles in barbarian society both inside and outside the empire. But the Scirian polity came to an end in *c.* 468, when the Ostrogoths defeated their rivals.[74] 'Thereupon the Goths proceeded to exact vengeance for the death of their king, as well as for the injury done them by the rebels. They fought in such wise that there remained of all the Scirian nation only a few who bore the name, and they with disgrace. Thus were all destroyed.'[75] Jordanes's report can be understood as a tale concerned with the end of an alternative. The Gothic solution was successful, the challengers had been beaten, and the Scirian ethnic coherence had become obsolete. The 'bearers of the Scirian name' can be understood as the royal family of Edica, Odoacar, and Onoulf, with enough warriors to act as a military power.[76] After all, they maintained an alternative to the powerful Goths by opening to other ethnic identification; the story of Odoacar in Italy demonstrates how that could actually happen. It took another twenty years for Theoderic to bring that alternative to an end.

In 470, with tacit Roman support, a broad coalition of Edica's Sciri, Sarmatians, Sueves, Gepids, and Rugi rose to challenge the Goths. There is no mention of Herules.[77] Edica died in the ensuing battle at the Bolia River, and his son Onoulf escaped to Constantinople, together with his retinue of warriors, where he entered

---

[74] Pohl, 'Gepiden', pp. 273–74; Helmut Castritius and Stefan Zimmer, s.v. 'Skiren', in *Reallexikon der germanischen Altertumskunde*, XXV, 2nd edn, ed. by Beck, Geuenich, and Steuer, pp. 353–58.

[75] Jordanes, *Getica*, 276: 'Gothi vero tam regis sui mortem quam suam iniuriam a rebellionibus exigentes ita sunt proeliati, ut pene de gente Scirorum nisi qui nomen ipsud ferrent, et hi cum dedecore, non remansissent: sic omnes extincti sunt.'

[76] Goffart, *Barbarian Tides*, p. 205: 'There is no evidence for the recruitment of Sciri into the Roman army until the days of Odoacer. [...] If they may be said to have a history at all, its most noticeable trait is that their final downfall as a people coincides with the prominence of two half-Scirians, sons of a famous father, in the military aristocracy of the Roman Empire.'

[77] Jordanes, *Getica*, 277: 'Quorum exitio Suavorum reges Hunimundus et Halaricus vereti, in Gothos arma moverunt freti auxilio Sarmatarum, qui cum Beuca et Babai regibus suis auxiliarii ei advenissent, ipsasque Scirorum reliquias quasi ad ultionem suam acrius pugnaturos accersientes cum Edica et Hunuulfo eorum primatibus habuerunt simul secum tam Gepidas quam ex gente Rugorum non parva solacia, ceterisque hinc inde collectis ingentem multitudinem adgregantes ad amnem Bolia in Pannoniis castra metati sunt.' Schwarcz, 'Die Heruler an der Donau', p. 509, suggests that Alaric, the king mentioned beside Hunimund, may have been a Herul because he had the same name as a fourth-century king. However, Jordanes specifically refers here to *Suavorum reges*.

Roman service and rose to the rank of *magister militum per Illyricum*. Some time later, in 479, he met his Gothic archenemies one more time, this time as a Roman officer.[78] Odoacar fled up along the Danube, met with St Severin who reputedly predicted him a great future, and then moved to Italy, where he was chosen leader by a great number of Herules, Sciri, Rugians, and Torcilingi eager to grab the opportunities opening for them in the West.[79] By their victory at the Bolia River, the Goths had taken revenge for the defeat at Nedao and established themselves as the uncontested hegemonial power at the gates of the empire in Pannonia.[80]

A Suevic *regnum* emerged in what is today southern Slovakia, established by those Sueves who had not left in 406 with the Vandals and the Alans. Their king Hunimund strove to establish a centre of power and to forge a strong Suevic identity. After several confrontations with the Goths, a separate Gothic strike crushed the Sueves at the Bolia River. Hunimund became a warlord with a few dozens of followers, a band mentioned in the *Vita Severini*.[81] Next to the Sueves, a Sarmatian polity had maintained itself, which the Goths soon also managed to destroy. Much like the Sciri and the Sueves, the Sarmatians were attacked by Theoderic in 471, who killed their king Babai in battle, captured his treasure, and occupied Singidunum.[82] Eliminating the royal *stirps*, capturing the treasury, and cutting off the ties to the empire were meant to deprive the barbarian elites of their basic needs.[83]

The Rugi established themselves north of the Middle Danube, with their royal seat around modern Krems on the Danube. Their short-lived polity was destroyed

---

[78] Malchus, *frg.* 8, in *Fragmente der griechischen Historiker*, ed. by Karl Müller, IV (Paris, 1885), p. 117; Pohl, 'Edika', p. 446; s.v. 'Edeco', and s.v. 'Onoulphus', in *The Prosopography of the Later Roman Empire*, II, ed. by Arnold H. M. Jones, John Martindale, and John Morris (Cambridge, 1980), pp. 385–86 and 806; Maenchen-Helfen, *The World of the Huns*, p. 388 and n. 104, rejects the idea that Edica, Attila's confident, was the same as the father of Odoacar.

[79] Eugippius, *Vita Sancti Severini*, 7, ed. by Theodor Nüßlein (Stuttgart, 1986); English translation in George W. Robinson, *The Life of Saint Severinus* (Cambridge, MA, 1914); Wolfram, *Die Goten*, p. 267 and n. 48; Goffart, *Narrators*, p. 355 and n. 88.

[80] Jordanes, *Getica*, 276; Pohl, 'Gepiden', pp. 260–62; Wolfram, *Die Goten*, pp. 266–68.

[81] Jordanes, *Getica*, 274–75, 277, and 281; Eugippius, *Vita Sancti Severini*, 22. See also Helmut Reimitz, s.v. 'Hunimund', in *Reallexikon der germanischen Altertumskunde*, XV, 2nd edn, ed. by Heinrich Beck, Dieter Geuenich, and Heiko Steuer (Berlin, 1989), pp. 245–46.

[82] Jordanes, *Getica*, 282; Martin Eggers and Ion Ioniţă, s.v. 'Sarmaten', in *Reallexikon der germanischen Altertumskunde*, XXVI, 2nd edn, ed. by Heinrich Beck, Dieter Geuenich, and Heiko Steuer (Berlin, 2004), pp. 503–12.

[83] Pohl, 'Gepiden', p. 276: 'Die geschilderte Operation des jungen Theoderich entspricht besonders gut der ostgotischen Praxis "wie zerstört man ein gentiles Herrschaftszentrum?".'

by Odoacar in 487.[84] By 454, a Herul polity was also established in the neighbour-hood, namely within the eastern *Weinviertel* and in southern Moravia. The Herul polity may have extended eastward to the Little Carpathians. The Herules ruled over a mixed population of local Sueves, Huns, Alans, and others.[85] The success of the Herul polity must have attracted other tribal groups as well, but its territorial expansion was primarily the work of Herul warriors. Procopius describes the situation as follows:

> But as time went on they became superior to all the barbarians who dwelt about them both in power and in numbers, and, as was natural, they attacked and vanquished them severally and kept plundering their possessions by force. And finally they made the Lombards, who were Christians, together with several other nations, subject and tributary to themselves, though the barbarians of that region were not accustomed to that sort of thing; but the Eruli were led to take this course by love of money and a lawless spirit.[86]

Local Suevic and (formerly) provincial farmers seem to have secured the relative prosperity of the Herul *regnum* well after 500.[87] The Herules were able to line up an impressive number of battle-seasoned warriors. The *Vita Severini* reports a Herul attack on Ioviaco (near Batavia/Passau) around 480. The holy man Severinus tried to warn the inhabitants of Ioviaco three separate times. During the night following the third warning, the Herules sacked the city and took many people captive. They hanged the local priest, Maximianus, on a cross. According to Eugippius, the Herules led many prisoners (*plurimos captivos*) away from Ioviaco.[88] This may indicate that

[84] Thomas Andersson and Walter Pohl, s.v. 'Rugier', in *Reallexikon der germanischen Alter-tumskunde*, XXV, 2nd edn, ed. by Beck, Geuenich, and Steuer, pp. 452–58; Pohl, 'Gepiden', pp. 278–80.

[85] Pohl, 'Gepiden', pp. 277–78; Jaroslav Tejral, 'Probleme der Völkerwanderungszeit nördlich der mittleren Donau', in *Germanen, Hunnen und Awaren: Schätze der Völkerwanderungszeit. Germanisches Nationalmuseum Nürnberg, 12. Dezember 1987 bis 21. Februar 1988*, ed. by Gerhard Bott (Nuremberg, 1987), pp. 351–67 (pp. 354–56), describes the rich variety of the archaeological evidence from this area. Schmidt, *Die Ostgermanen*, p. 562, has the Herul ruling class as a mixture of several 'East Germanic' groups. He conspicuously ignores any non-'Germanic' groups.

[86] Procopius, *Wars*, 6.14.8.

[87] Pohl, 'Gepiden', p. 278.

[88] Eugippius, *Vita Sancti Severini*, 24. Schwarcz, 'Die Heruler an der Donau', p. 505, interpreted the subsequent execution by hanging of a certain priest Maximianus as a ritual sacrifice to Wotan. However, the execution of the spiritual leader of a community may also be seen as an attempt to subdue that community and to prevent resistance. For the *Vita Sancti Severini*, see also Walter Goffart, 'Does the *Vita S. Severini* Have an Underside?', in *Eugippius und Severin: Der Autor, der Text und der Heilige*, ed. by Walter Pohl and Maximilian Diesenberger (Vienna, 2001), pp. 33–40.

the Herules were concerned with enlarging the population within their polity by means of prisoners of war from Noricum Ripense. From their core area north of the Danube, the Herules expanded into the territory south of that river, but north of Lake Balaton, taking advantage of the disappearance, one by one, of the Suevic and Scirian polities, both eliminated by the Pannonian Goths who soon after those struggles left for Italy, and then of the Rugians, destroyed by Odoacar in 488.[89]

Herules Trying to Make Odoacar their King in Italy

'Then as the spoil taken from one and another of the neighbouring tribes diminished', as Jordanes has it, warriors from the Danube region — Herules, Sciri, and Rugians — moved to Italy to participate in Odoacar's *exercitus* of *externae gentes*.[90] Herules were among the strongest in 'king Odoacar's whirlpool of peoples in which he made his career'.[91] Some sources even call him *rex Erulorum*. This underlines the key role Odoacar had in bringing at least some Herules to live the life of the rich and privileged in Italy. Odoacar himself originated from a mixed milieu at the meeting point between the Roman and Hunnic spheres of power. His brother Onoulf made his career in the East. Odoacar's career began in Italy under Ricimer. During the civil war fought by the *magister militum* Ricimer and Anastasius (471/72), he was on the side of the former. Onoulf, already a powerful man in Constantinople, joined Odoacar in Italy in 479 after having fallen out of favour with Emperor Zeno.[92]

Odoacar's unique opportunity arrived in 476, during the conflict between soldiers of the *externae gentes* and the *patricius* Orestes. Orestes had begun his career

[89] Demandt, *Die Spätantike*, pp. 212–14; Wolfram, *Grenzen und Räume*, p. 58.

[90] Jordanes, *Getica*, 283; Pohl, 'Gepiden', pp. 267–68.

[91] Robert L. Reynolds and Robert S. Lopez, 'Odovacer: German or Hun?', *American Historical Review*, 52 (1946), 36–53 (p. 37).

[92] See s.v. 'Odovacer', in *Prosopography of the Later Roman Empire*, II, ed. by Jones, Martindale and Morris, pp. 791–93; Wolfram, *The Roman Empire*, pp. 183–93; Herwig Wolfram, s. v., 'Odowakar', in *Reallexikon der germanischen Altertumskunde*, XXI, 2nd edn, ed. by Heinrich Beck, Dieter Geuenich, and Heiko Steuer (Berlin, 2002), pp. 573–75 (p. 574). Wolfram rejects the proposition that Odoacer was one and the same person as a Saxon leader in Gaul around 460 and criticizes the historians' obsession with prosopography ('prosopographischer Beziehungswahn'). For an example of what Wolfram criticizes, see Reynolds and Lopez, 'Odovacer', pp. 40–41; Timo Stickler, *Aëtius: Gestaltungsspielräume eines Heermeisters im ausgehenden Weströmischen Reich* (Munich, 2002), pp. 72, 97, and 122.

as Latin secretary to Attila, but soon became the rival of the Hunnic ruler's companion, Edika, Odoacar's father. Orestes was now opposed to the demand that
soldiers recruited from among the *externae gentes* be paid just like Roman soldiers
(a soldier of barbarian origin seems to have received much lower wages, perhaps as
a consequence of the constant supply of barbarians eager for recruitment). 'While
the Roman army had a vested legal claim to a third of the curial taxes, the economic
security of the federates of Italy was far less clearly established; they did not receive
"regular" pay but extraordinary monies, agreed upon by treaty, to be sure, but
revocable. In 476, the barbarians in Italy demanded to be given equal status with
the Roman army.'[93] When Orestes, as the highest magistrate present, refused to
yield to such demands, the soldiers turned to Odoacar who promised to fulfil their
requests, 'should he attain supramagisterial power'.[94] All in all, the impression one
gets from the sources makes one think of a coup d'état or a putsch performed by
armed forces.[95] According to Procopius, one third of the Italian land was thus given
to the barbarians, the same amount of land that Theoderic would grant to his
Goths in 491. This is not the place to enter the complex debate concerning the
'accommodation of the barbarians', whether by means of land or by means of tax
money.[96] Instead, it is worth re-examining our sources in order to identify those

[93] Wolfram, *The Roman Empire*, pp. 184–85.

[94] Wolfram, *The Roman Empire*, pp. 184–85.

[95] Goffart, *Narrators*, p. 355 and n. 88 gives an accurate idea how to understand the verb
invadere in Jordanes, *Romana*, 344, ed. by Theodor Mommsen, MGH AA, 5.1 (Berlin, 1882; repr.
1982): 'Jordanes spoke of Odoacer "invading" Italy supported by hordes of tribesmen; he probably
meant *invadere* in the sense of "to seize (from within, as by coup d'état)". [...] All in all, the
underpinnings for "Odoacer's barbarian conquest of Italy" were less flimsy than those for the lady
Digna and the Vandal plunder of the Campania.'

[96] Procopius, *Wars*, 5.1.5–8, trans. by Dewing, pp. 2–5: 'Now it happened that the Romans
a short time before had induced the Sciri and Alani and certain other Gothic nations to form an
alliance with them; [...] And in proportion as the barbarian element among them became strong,
[...] so that the barbarians ruthlessly forced many other measures upon the Romans much against
their will and finally demanded that they should divide with them the entire land of Italy. And
indeed they commanded Orestes to give them the third part of this, and when he would by no
means agree to do so, they killed him immediately. Now there was a certain man among the
Romans named Odoacer, one of the bodyguards of the emperor, and he at that time agreed to carry
out their commands, on condition that they should set him upon the throne. [...] And by giving
the third part of the land to the barbarians, and in this way gaining their allegiance most firmly, he
held the supreme power securely for ten years.' See Wolfram, 'Odowakar', p. 574, who sees in
Procopius the evidence for the fact that the wages to be paid to the troops were the main reason for
the conflict. The controversy regarding the accommodation of the barbarians in the later Roman

who raised Odoacar to power. According to Jordanes, although a Rugian by birth, he was the king of the Torcilingi, the Sciri, and the Herules, and of other *gentes*. The *Anonymus Valesianus* has Odoacar coming to Italy together with the Sciri.[97] But according to the *Auctarium Hauniense*, the Herul soldiers made Odoacar their king.[98]

To Felix Dahn, calling Odoacar a *rex Erulorum* was a mistake.[99] In reality, taking the account in the *Auctarium Hauniense* at face value implies accepting a version of history which is not at variance with what is otherwise known about barbarian identity in the fifth century. It also involves acknowledging the fact that several processes were at work at the same time. Proclaiming Odoacar their king

Empire is too complicated to be discussed in detail here. See however Goffart, *Barbarian Tides*, pp. 119–86; Walter Goffart, *Barbarians and Romans, A.D. 418–584: The Techniques of Accommodation* (Princeton, 1980); Jean Durliat, 'Le Salaire de la paix sociale dans les royaumes barbares Vᵉ–VIᵉ siècles', in *Anerkennung und Integration: Zu den wirtschaftlichen Grundlagen der Völkerwanderungszeit 400–600*, ed. by Herwig Wolfram and Andreas Schwarcz (Vienna, 1988), pp. 21–72; J. H. W. G. Liebeschuetz, 'Cities, Taxes and the Accommodation of the Barbarians: The Theories of Durliat and Goffart', in *Kingdoms of the Empire: The Integration of Barbarians in Late Antiquity*, ed. by Walter Pohl (Leiden, 1997), pp. 135–52.

[97] Jordanes, *Romana*, 344: 'Sed mox Odoacer genere Rogus Thorcilingorum Scirorum Herolorumque turbas [...] Italiam invasit.' Jordanes, *Getica*, 242: 'Augustulo vero a patre Oreste in Ravenna imperatore ordinato non multum post Odovacar Torcilingorum rex habens secum Sciros, Herulos diversarumque gentium auxiliarios Italiam occupavit et Orestem interfectum Augustulum filium eius de regno pulsum in Lucullano Campaniae castello exilii poena damnavit.' Anonymus Valesianus, 8.37, *Consularia Italica, Anonymi Valesiani pars posterior*, in *Chronica minora saec. IV. V. VI. VII.*, vol. I, ed. by Theodor Mommsen, MGH AA, 9 (Berlin, 1892; repr. Munich, 1981), pp. 306–28 (p. 308): 'superveniente Odovacre cum gente Scirorum'.

[98] *Consularia Italica, Auctarii Hauniensi ordo prior*, s.a. 476, 2, in *Chronica minora saec. IV. V. VI. VII.*, vol. I, ed. by Mommsen, pp. 307–21 (p. 309): 'Intra Italiam Eruli, qui Romano iuri suberant, regem creant nomine Odoacrem X k(alendas) Sept(embris), hominem et aetate et sapientia gravem et bellicis rebus instructum.' To say that the Herules were subject to Roman right implies that their subsequent actions were illegal. See Herwig Wolfram, 'Gotisches Königtum und römisches Kaisertum von Theodosius dem Großen bis Justinian I.', *Frühmittelalterliche Studien*, 13 (1979), 1–28 (p. 5 with n. 17); Herwig Wolfram, *Intitulatio I: Lateinische Königs- und Fürstentitel bis zum Ende des 8. Jahrhunderts* (Vienna, 1967), p. 54 and n. 103. *Consularia Italica, Auctarii Hauniensi ordo prior*, s.a. 487, p. 313: 'Fevva rex Rugorum adversum regem Erulorum Odoachrem bellum movet.'

[99] Felix Dahn, *Die Könige der Germanen: Das Wesen des ältesten Königthums der germanischen Stämme und seine Geschichte bis zur Auflösung des karolingischen Reiches*, vol. II: *Die kleineren gothischen Völker* (Munich, 1861), p. 2 and n. 8: 'Er [Odovakar] wird fälschlicherweise sogar Herulerkönig genannt.'

meant a lot to the Herules fighting with and for him. By raising him to that position, they entrusted him with the task of looking after the entire Herul *exercitus*. Herules in the army were in competition with other *gentes*, who also claimed Odoacar for themselves in order to obtain a hegemonic position within that army. The contemporary and parallel stories of the Vandals and Alans show clearly that different groups could split up at different moments, each taking on a new identity or reinventing itself on the basis of an already existing (but alternative) identity.[100] It is therefore not surprising that Odoacar bore many titles, as attested in our sources. He was *rex Gothorum, Rugorum*, but also simply *rex*, even *rex gentium* and *rex Italiae*. Similarly, Attila could become a Gepid in the eyes of John Malalas. Roman and Greek writers seem to have had a hard time grasping the bewildering variety of identity and names for all those whom they otherwise labelled simply 'Huns' or 'Scythians'. That they made mistakes and errors of interpretation in the process is only understandable.[101] An error is just one way of understanding those sources. We do not know much about Odoacar's self promotion during the political struggles in Italy. Perhaps he understood quite well how to manipulate different identities and ethnic affiliations to keep warriors on his side. If this was so, Roman and Greek authors just referred to a complex political situation and tried to do their best at transmitting what they knew. For sure Odoacar acted in different ways. The political symbols used to interact with Constantinople or the Roman Senate must have been very different from those used with the armed men in Italy. *Flavius* Odoacar adressed Roman aristocrats, a *rex Rugorum* the Rugian warriors. A Roman author made Odoacar the *rex gentium* to indicate the basis of his power.

If the Herules who proclaimed Odoacar their king had future dreams of a better life in Italy, their hopes were soon thwarted. Part of the problem seems to have been that they remained with Odoacar, and even when he started to slip, they did not hasten to Theoderic's side. Instead, they were together with Odoacar in Ravenna during its siege by Theoderic's troops. It is together with the Herules that Odoacar made his last-ditch attempt to break out of the besieged city in the night of 9 July 491. Livila, Odoacar's general and successor of Tufa, the former *magister militum* serving Odoacar who had deserted to Theoderic in 489, died in the

---

[100] Roland Steinacher, 'Gruppen und Identitäten. Gedanken zur Bezeichnung "vandalisch"', in *Das Reich der Vandalen und seine (Vor-)geschichten*, ed. by Guido Berndt and Roland Steinacher (Vienna, 2008), pp. 243–60.

[101] John Malalas, *Chronographia*, ed. by Johannes Thurn (Berlin, 2000) 19.5–12, p. 45: 'ἐκ τοῦ γένους τῶν Γηπέδων'. See also Pohl, 'Die Gepiden', p. 247 and n. 23.

ensuing battle, together with the best of Odoacar's Herul troops.[102] In Ennodius's words, 'quid Herulorum agmina fusa commemorem'.[103]

The Struggle in Pannonia at the Gates of Italy and the End of the Herul Regnum

Like Odoacar before him, the victorious Theoderic tried to secure the passage into Italy. Given the numerous eager and strong barbarian groups in that region, what Cassiodorus has to say about the *Raetiae* as protecting the gate to Italy ('Raetiae namque munimina sunt Italiae et claustra provinciae') also applies to the region of the Middle Danube and to Pannonia.[104] In 504, Theoderic conquered the 'former seeds of the Goths' from the Gepids, 'ad Sirmiensem Pannoniam, quondam sedem Gothorum'. It is from Pannonia that various leaders had entered Italy, the core of the Western Empire, from Alaric, Radagais, and Attila to Odoacar and Theoderic himself. Theoderic's capture of Sirmium brought him in direct conflict with the Romans, which in turn brought about the destruction of the Herul realm. Most likely Constantinople had granted Sirmium to the Gepids, and Theoderic acted against the plans of the imperial government.[105]

By 500, the Herules had established peaceful relations with the Goths, which may have encouraged Theoderic to treat them as potential allies. He made an unnamed Herul king his son-in-arms (*adoptio per arma*). Horses, shields, and *reliqua instrumenta bellorum* were sent to that king, who was now treated as the greatest barbarian ruler in the area.[106] Some have assumed that the unnamed king whom

---

[102] Cassiodorus, *Chronica*, 1326, in *Chronica minora saec. IV. V. VI. VII.*, vol. II, ed. by Mommsen, pp. 109–62 (p. 159): 'Hoc cons. Odovacar cum Erulis egressus Ravenna nocturnis horis ad pontem Candidiani a d(omi)n(o) nostro rege Theoderico memorabili certamine superatur'. Tufa: Anonymus Valesianus, *Consularia Italica, Anonymi Valesiani pars posterior*, 11.51, ed. by Mommsen, p. 316; see Wolfram, 'Odowakar', p. 576; s.v. 'Tufa', in *Prosopography of the Later Roman Empire*, II, ed. by Jones, Martindale, and Morris, p. 1131.

[103] Ennodius, *Panegyricus dictus clementissimo regi Theoderico*, ed. by Christian Rohr, MGH Studien und Texte, 12 (Hannover, 1995), p. 234 and n. 50. See also Rappaport, 'Heruli', pp. 1159–60; Wolfram, *Die Goten*, p. 283 and n. 9.

[104] Cassiodorus, *Variae*, 7.4.

[105] Cassiodorus, *Variae*, 3.23; Pohl, 'Die Gepiden', pp. 293–94; Wolfram, *Die Goten*, pp. 319–22.

[106] Cassiodorus, *Variae*, 4, 2, ed. by Mommsen: 'Damus tibi quidem equos enses clipeos et reliqua instrumenta bellorum: sed quae sunt omnimodis fortiora, largimur tibi nostra iudicia. summus enim inter gentes esse crederis, qui Theoderici sententia comprobaris.' See Wolfram, *Die Goten*,

Theoderic made his son-in-arms was Rodulf, a Herul leader mentioned by Procopius at the time when the reign of Emperor Anastasius (491–518) began, and by Paul the Deacon.[107] Jordanes had also a *Roduulf rex* seeking Theoderic's protection in Italy.[108] Some even went further and speculated about the kind of information about northern barbarians that Rodulf may have been able to supply to Cassiodorus for his history of the Goths.[109] Given the assumed influence of Cassiodorus's work upon Jordanes's *Getica*, Andrew Merrills's remarks are worth citing in full at this point:

> There are several problems with this interpretation, although none of them is substantial enough to warrant its complete rejection. Perhaps chief among these is the immmediate acceptance by later commentators that Roduulf's origins were precisely those claimed by the *Getica*. There is no reason to interpret Procopius's brief account of the king's background as an assertion that his homeland was in the far north of Europe or in Scandza. Indeed, the political and ideological implications of Theoderic's support for a northern exile would have been considerable in the early years of the sixth century, when his people began to assert their own affiliation with the northern parts of Europe. Roduulf's

p. 318; Procopius, *Wars*, 1.11.10–30, describes at length how the Byzantines used an *adoptio* to make peace with the Persians. According to him, 'the barbarians adopt sons not by a document, but by arms and armor'. Wolfram assumed that the Byzantine foreign policy used the *adoptio per arma* as one means to forge alliances. This would in turn mean that the *adoptio* of a Herul king by Theoderic followed Roman not barbarian customs. See Herwig Wolfram, s.v. 'Waffensohn', in *Reallexikon der germanischen Altertumskunde*, XXXIII, 2nd edn, ed. by Heinrich Beck, Dieter Geuenich, and Heiko Steuer (Berlin, 2006), pp. 49–51. According to Paul the Deacon, *History of the Lombards*, 1.23, in *Scriptores rerum Langobardicarum et Italicarum, saec. VI–IX*, ed. by Georg Waitz, MGH (Berlin, 1878; repr. 1988); English translation from Paul the Deacon, *History of the Lombards*, ed. by Edward Peters, trans. by William Dudley Foulke (Philadelphia, 1907; repr. 1975), 'it is not the custom among us that the son of the king should eat with his father unless he first receives his arms from the king of a foreign nation' ('nisi prius a rege gentis exterae arma suscipiat').

[107] Procopius, *Wars*, 6.14–15; Paul the Deacon, *History of the Lombards*, 1.20. See Claus Krag, s.v. 'Rodulf', in *Reallexikon der germanischen Altertumskunde*, XXV, 2nd edn, ed. by Beck, Geuenich, and Steuer, pp. 58–59; and s.v. 'Rodulfus', in *Prosopography of the Later Roman Empire*, II, ed. by Jones, Martindale, and Morris, p. 946.

[108] Jordanes, *Getica*, 24. Jordanes mentions Rodulf immediately after his account of *Dani* driving the Herules out of their lands: 'Sunt quamquam et horum positura Grannii, Augandzi, Eunixi, Taetel, Rugi, Arochi, Ranii, quibus non ante multos annos Roduulf rex fuit, qui contempto proprio regno ad Theoderici Gothorum regis gremio convolavit et, ut desiderabat, invenit. Hae itaque gentes, Germanis corpore et animo grandiores, pugnabant beluina saevitia.'

[109] Peter Heather, 'The Historical Culture of Ostrogothic Italy', in *Teodorico il Grande e i Goti d'Italia, Atti del XIII Congresso internazionale di studi sull'Alto Medioevo 1992* (Spoleto, 1993), pp. 317–53 (p. 347); Arne Søby Christensen, *Cassiodorus Jordanes and the History of the Goths: Studies in a Migration Myth* (Copenhagen, 2002), p. 256.

somewhat ambiguous origins may thus have been imposed, or accentuated retrospectively by Cassiodorus, in an effort to develop the political undertones of his own work. The *Getica* may, of course, be correct in its association of Roduulf with the far north, but the possibility that it merely reflects an ideological distortion should not be overlooked.[110]

The *adoptio per arma* of a Herul king in the Middle Danube region nicely dovetails with Theoderic's known political goals. There is therefore no need for an additional explanation concerning Rodulf's relation to the Ostrogothic court. Theoderic's second letter addressed to that same king may thus be understood better in such a light.

There is a third piece in Cassiodorus's *Variae* that historians have used to reconstruct the early sixth-century history of the Herules. The officials of the city of Pavia were enjoined to provide transport by boat between their city and Ravenna and to offer five days' provisions (*annonae*) to envoys from the Herules (*supplices Erulos*) travelling to Theoderic's court. Some have assumed that the *supplices* in question were Herul refugees taken in by Theoderic after the Lombard destruction of the Herul kingdom.[111] But those men were mere envoys, either members of a military unit in Italy or subjects of the Herul king north of the Danube. Cassiodorus uses *supplices* several times in his *Variae* and often in a rather general sense. The only basis for an interpretation favouring the idea of Herul refugees is the date of the letter, as proposed by Theodor Mommsen and Stefan Krautschik: 507 to 512. However, Andrew Gillett redated the letter to before September 527.[112] The former date suggests that the envoys were subjects of a Herul king ruling somewhere north of the Danube, the latter that they were members of a military unit in Italy. As a matter of fact, Paul the Deacon mentions Herul warriors in Italy, under Ostrogothic rule.[113]

---

[110] Andrew H. Merrills, *History and Geography in Late Antiquity* (Cambridge, 2005), p. 129.

[111] Cassiodorus, *Variae*, 4.45. See Andrew Gillett, *Envoys and Political Communication in the Late Antique West, 411–533* (Cambridge, 2003), pp. 183 and 189. For the Herul *supplices* as refugees, see Wolfram, *Die Goten*, p. 318; Schmidt, *Ostgermanen*, p. 553; Rappaport, 'Heruli', p. 1160.

[112] Stefan Krautschik, *Cassiodor und die Politik seiner Zeit* (Bonn, 1983), pp. 50–71, gives a detailed analysis of the chronology of the *Variae*. According to him, the third and fourth books must be dated between 507 and 511. Krautschik has nothing specific to say about the chronology of 4.45. For a general discussion of the chronology of the letters, see Gillett, *Envoys*, p. 241 and n. 85; Schwarcz, 'Die Heruler an der Donau', pp. 510–11 and n. 29.

[113] Paul the Deacon, *History of the Lombards*, 2.3, ed. by Waitz: 'Habuit nihilominus Narsis certamen adversus Sinduald Brentorum regem, qui adhuc de Herulorum stirpe remanserat, quos secum in Italiam veniens olim Odoacar adduxerat.'

It seems very likely that Roman diplomatic efforts were directed against the Herules by means of empowering the Lombards, in order to defeat Theoderic's attempts to create a system of alliances with other *gentes* of Central Europe.[114] Procopius and Paul the Deacon give different accounts of the Herul-Lombard conflict. However, neither of them mentions any Roman interference. According to Procopius, the reason for the war between Herules and Lombards was that 'the people being exceedingly vexed began to abuse their leader Rodolphus without restraint, and going to him constantly they called him cowardly and effeminate, and railed at him in a most unruly manner'. The king thus felt compelled to wage war on the Lombards, without any real reason.[115] This story is remarkably similar to what Jordanes has to say about the reasons the Ostrogoths left Pannonia. In both cases, one is left with the impression that war was a fundamental element of life in those societies. When individual warriors sought honour and booty, kings unable to meet their demands were in danger of losing face and power.[116] 'The cohesion of a group depended very largely on a leader's success.'[117] The Roman diplomacy must have been fully aware of such social and political mechanisms.

Paul the Deacon has a different reason for the Herul-Lombard conflict. Two hundred years after Procopius he 'gives the Herules a legitimate casus belli, but turns poor Rudolf into a fool'.[118] The Lombards stayed for three years in the formerly Rugian lands, and a war started up between the Lombard king Tato and Rodulf.[119] King Rodulf's brother had been sent as envoy to Tato, perhaps for the collection of tribute. During his stay at the Lombard court, a princess named Rumetruda deeply offended the Herul envoy, and this man defended his and his king's honour. Instead of smoothing the tension, however, Rumetruda's retainers murdered the Herul, thus causing a military conflict between Lombards and Herules. During the following battle Paul the Deacon depicts King Rodulf playing at draughts not at all wavering in his hope of victory. Two legends are then introduced about this king. In one of them, one of the King's followers is ordered to climb a tree, in order to tell the King more quickly about the victory of his troops. Rodulf threatened to cut off the man's head if he announced that the Herules were

[114] Wolfram, *Die Goten*, p. 322; Schwarcz, 'Die Heruler an der Donau', p. 511.

[115] Procopius, *Wars*, 6.14.11–13; see Goffart, *Barbarian Tides*, pp. 207–08.

[116] Pohl, 'Die Gepiden', pp. 285–86.

[117] Arnold H. M. Jones, *The Later Roman Empire, 284–602: A Social, Economic and Administrative Survey*, I (Oxford, 1964; repr. 1986), p. 195.

[118] Goffart, *Barbarian Tides*, p. 208.

[119] Paul the Deacon, *History of the Lombards*, 1.19.

not fighting bravely. Seeing that the Herules were losing the battle, the man asked heaven for help. The King now asked whether the Herules were fleeing, and the man was saved as the King himself had spoken the awful truth. In the second story, the fighting Herules saw the green-growing flax in the fields and thought it was water fit for swimming. Therefore they stretched out their arms as if to swim and were beaten by the enemy. Following the victory, Tato captured Rodulf's banner and helmet and the Herules lost their identity as a *gens*: Paul the Deacon subsumes the situation with the explanatory remark that the Herules had no king anymore ('Herules regem non habuerunt').[120] Kingship was a central part of ethnic tradition and self-awareness. After a defeat, an *exercitus* often disintegrated into small groups of warriors who kept on plundering or moved into the empire to find better employment. This seems to be exactly what happened to the defeated Herules. The failure of their king destroyed any faith that his warriors may have had in him. There was no purpose in re-establishing the *regnum*. Previous ethnic identities rapidly shifted, with some Herules becoming Lombards or looking for other solutions.

Herul Soldiers in Justinian's Wars and the Second (and Final) Disappearance of the Herules

Procopius did not like the Herules. But in his *Wars* they are mentioned quite often as participating in Justinian's campaigns against the Persians, the Vandals, and the Goths and were a key component of Justinian's military system. Procopius's Herul excursus is therefore meant to clarify who these people were and how they came into an alliance with the Romans. At the same time the excursus is full of stereotypes and negative attitudes towards this primitive people and its archaic conventions.[121]

---

[120] Paul the Deacon, *History of the Lombards*, 1.20; *Origo gentis Langobardorum*, 4, in *Scriptores rerum Langobardicarum et Italicarum, saec. VI–IX*, ed. by Waitz, pp. 1–6. See Ulrich Müller, s.v. 'Langobardische Sagen', in *Reallexikon der germanischen Altertumskunde*, XVIII, 2nd edn, ed. by Heinrich Beck, Dieter Geuenich, and Heiko Steuer (Berlin, 2001), pp. 93–102 (p. 95).

[121] Procopius, *Wars*, 6.14.1–7; trans. by Dewing, III, 403–05: 'Now as to who in the world the Eruli are, and how they entered into the alliance with the Romans, I shall forthwith explain. They used to dwell beyond the Ister River from of old, worshipping a great host of gods, whom it seemed to them holy to appease even by human sacrifices. And they observed many customs which were not in accordance with those of other men. For they were not permitted to live either when they grew old or when they fell sick, but as soon one of them was overtaken by old age or by sickness, it became necessary for him to ask his relatives to remove him from the world as quickly as possible. And these relatives would pile up a quantity of wood to a great height and lay the man at the top of the wood,

Within the Herul excursus Procopius gives some fragments of a history concerning Herules at the borders of the empire. He has the Herules beaten by the Lombards fleeing to formerly Rugian territory, where they were, however, hardly pressed by famine. 'Contrary to what is sometimes said (e.g., Schmidt, *Ostgermanen*, p. 503), the land of the Rugians to which Procopius has them momentarily withdraw is not the Rugian territory known from the *Vita S. Severini*, but the lands downstream (in Moesia or Dacia?) where the survivors from the Rugian defeat fled in 488.'[122] As a consequence, they were allowed into Gepid territory. But since the Gepids tried to subdue them, many Herules crossed the Danube, entered the Roman Empire, and were eventually settled by Emperor Anastasius in Illyricum, probably near Singidunum (Belgrade) around Bassiana, which was acquired in 510 from the

and then they would send one of the Eruli, but not a relative to the man, to his side with a dagger; for it was unlawful for a kinsman to be his slayer. And when the slayer of their relative had returned, they would straightaway burn the whole pile of wood, beginning in the edges. And after the fire had ceased, they would immediately collect the bones and bury them in the earth. And when a man of the Eruli died, it was necessary for his wife, if she laid claim to virtue and wished to leave a fair name behind her, to die not long afterward beside the tomb of her husband by hanging herself in a rope. And if she did not do this, the result was that she was in ill repute thereafter and an offence to the relatives to her husband. Such were the customs observed by the Eruli in ancient times.'

[122] Procopius, *Wars*, 6.14.24–25; Goffart, *Barbarian Tides*, p. 336, n. 104. For the following events, Procopius, *Wars*, 6.14.23–32 is our main source. The translation is Dewing's, III, 409–11: 'For this reason [the defeat at the hands of the Lombards] the Eruli were no longer able to tarry in their ancestral homes, but departing from there as quickly as possible they kept moving forward, traversing the whole country which is beyond the Ister River, together with their wives and children. But when they reached a land where the Rogi dwelt of old, a people who had joined the Gothic host and gone to Italy, they settled in that place. But since they were pressed by famine, because they were in a barren land, they removed from there not long afterwards, and came to a place close to the country of the Gepaedes. And at first the Gepaedes permitted them to dwell there and be neighbours to them, since they came as suppliants. But afterwards for no good reason the Gepaedes began to practise unholy deed upon them. For they violated their women and seized their cattle and other property, and abstained from no wickedness whatever, and finally began an unjust attack upon them. And the Eruli unable to bear all this any longer, crossed the Ister River and decided to live as neighbours to the Romans in that region; this was during the reign of the Emperor Anastasius, who received them with great friendliness and allowed them to settle where they were. But a short time afterwards these barbarians gave him offence by their lawless treatment of the Romans there, and for this reason he sent an army against them. And the Romans after defeating them in battle, slew most of their number, and had ample opportunity to destroy them all. But the remainder of them threw themselves upon the mercy of the generals and begged them to spare their lives and to have them as allies and servants of the emperor thereafter. And when Anastasius learned this, he was pleased, and consequently a number of the Eruli were left; however they neither became allies of the Romans, nor did they do them any good.'

Goths, now ruling Italy from Ravenna.[123] The Herul armed warriors shortly afterwards rose in rebellion, and a Roman army was dispatched against them. They were
obviously treated as an insurgent military unit and, as a consequence, decimated.
The survivors had to go through a *deditio* and were accepted as federates again.
Procopius further 'emphasizes the shrinkage of their numbers from successive
humblings by Lombards, Gepids, and Romans'.[124]

After Anastasius's strike against the insurgent Herules, Justinian abandoned
this policy and offered them a better deal in 527. According to Procopius, all
Herules converted to Christianity,[125] but Malalas reports that only a Herul king
called Grepes converted in 528 together with some nobles and twelve of his relatives. Justinian himself is said to have been the sponsor at Grepes's baptismal font

---

[123] Procopius, *Wars*, 6.14.23–28. See also Marcellinus Comes, *Chronicon*, AD a. 512.11, in
Chronica minora saec. IV. V. VI. VII., vol. II, ed. by Mommsen: 'Gens Herulorum in terras atque
civitates Romanorum iussu Anastasii Caesaris introducta.' See Goffart, *Barbarian Tides*, p. 208 and
n. 105; Wolfram, *Die Goten*, p. 322 and n. 103; Ernest Stein, *Histoire du Bas-Empire: de la disparition de l'Empire d'Occident à la mort de Justinien 476–565*, II (Paris, 1949; repr. 1968), pp. 156 and
305. Rappaport, 'Heruli', p. 1161, has the Herules settled in Illyricum without specifying the area:
'Wo die H[eruler] in Illyricum als Foederati zunächst angesiedelt wurden, läßt sich nicht genau
sagen. Als sie sich in ihren neuen Sitzen auf römischem Gebiet schwere Übergriffe erlaubten, mußte
Anastasius mit Waffengewalt gegen sie vorgehen und brachte ihnen eine schwere Niederlage bei.'

[124] Goffart, *Barbarian Tides*, p. 208 and n. 106; Procopius, *Wars*, 6.14.20–22, 27–28, 30–32.

[125] Procopius, *Wars*, 6.14.33–42; trans. by Dewing, III, 411–13: 'But when Justinian took over
the empire, he bestowed upon them good lands and other possessions, and thus completely succeeded in winning their friendship and persuaded them all to become Christians. As a result of this
they adopted a gentler manner of life and decided to submit themselves wholly to the laws of the
Christians, and in keeping with the terms of their alliance they are generally arrayed with the Romans
against their enemies. They are still, however, faithless toward them, and since they are given to
avarice, they are eager to do violence to their neighbours, feeling no shame at such conduct. And they
mate in an unholy manner, especially men with asses, and they are the basest of all men and utterly
abandoned rascals. Afterwards, although some few of them remained at peace with the Romans, as
will be told by me in the following narrative, all the rest revolted for the following reason. The Eruli,
displaying their beastly and fanatical character against their own "rex" one Ochus by name, suddenly killed the man for no good reason at all, laying against him no other charge that they wished
to be without a king thereafter. And yet even before this, while their king did have the title, he had
practically no advantage over any citizen whomsoever. But all claimed the right to sit with him and
eat with him, and whoever wished insulted him without restraint; for no men are less bound by
convention or more unstable than the Eruli. Now when the evil deed had been accomplished, they
were immediately repentant. For they said that they were not able to live without a ruler and
without a general; so after much deliberation it seemed to them best in every way to summon one
of their royal family from the island of Thule. And the reason for this I shall now explain.'

in Constantinople.[126] Malalas's account seems to be closer to reality and can serve as a good reminder that when our sources mention a 'people' in Late Antiquity, they often mean the ruling elite.[127]

For one generation, at least, the Herules remained in the Balkans as federates, and as such provided recruits for the Roman army. Herul warriors fought as separate units in the Roman armies that Emperor Justinian sent against the Persians, the Vandals, and the Goths.

> The pool of Herul manpower lay open to fill Justinian's armies. Procopius reports the presence of Herules under their own leaders in Persia, Africa, Italy, Thrace, and Lazica. A detachment even participated in the butchery of civilians at Constantinople that ended the Nika riots. Herule infantry receives a special description. A detachment of Herules under Pharas, whom Procopius personally praises, brought about the surrender of the Vandal king Gelimer (534). As Roman troops, Herules suffered casualties in Italy at the hands of the Gothic 'rebellion' of 541, and, at the great final battle of Narses against Totila, dismounted Herules stood alongside dismounted Lombards in the Roman centre (552). No other barbarian people compares with the Herules in contributing troops to Justinian's wars.[128]

'According to Jordanes, they were the finest light infantry in the world.'[129] The sixth-century authors Jordanes and Procopius even mention some peculiar equipment in use by those highly specialized Herul soldiers. Jordanes describes the respective weapons and tactics of various troops participating in the battle at the Nedao River. The Alans drew up a line of battle made up of heavily armed

---

[126] Malalas, *Chronographia*, 18.6; Theophanes Confessor, *Chronographia*, 6020, ed. by Johannes Classen (Bonn, 1841), pp. 174–75. See Goffart, *Barbarian Tides*, p. 208 with n. 107.

[127] I attempted to demonstrate the point in the case of the Vandals: Steinacher, 'Gruppen und Identitäten', pp. 244–49 and 256–60.

[128] Goffart, *Barbarian Tides*, p. 208. Some examples: Procopius, *Wars*, 1.13.19 (battle of Daras); 2.24.18; 2.25.20–22 (battle of Anglon); 3.11.11; 4.6.1–26 (a correspondance between the Herul officer Pharas and the besieged Vandal king Gelimer; see for this episode Steinacher, 'Gruppen und Identitäten', pp. 255–56); 4.14.12 (problems with Herul troops because of their Arian faith); 6.13.18 (two thousand Herules commanded by Visandus, Aluith, and Phanitheus join Narses); 8.33.19 (Herules take part in the assault of Rome). Goffart, *Barbarian Tides*, p. 337 and n. 108, and Rappaport, 'Heruli', pp. 1164–65 list all sources for Herul soldiers in Justinian's armies. See also Alexander Sarantis's contribution to this volume. Also in Agathias's histories Herul soldiers are mentioned quite often: Agathias, *The Histories*, ed. and trans. by Joseph D. Frendo (Berlin, 1975). The Herules are to be found at 1.11.3; 1.14.4–6; 1.18.8; 1.20.8; 2.7.2–7; 2.8.5–6; 2.9.7–13; 3.6.5; 3.20.10.

[129] Goffart, *Barbarian Tides*, p. 205 and n. 90. Jordanes, *Getica*, 117–18 as quoted above in note 49.

warriors, while the Herules lined up their lightly armed men.[130] Procopius describes Herul soldiers fighting against the Persians as having neither helmet nor corselet, nor indeed any other protective armor, except a shield and a thick jacket, 'which they gird about them before they enter into a struggle'.[131]

Apart from these structures and events modern scholarship has to deal with a part of Procopius's excursus which is harder to interpret. Some of the Herules beaten by the Lombards are said to have refused to enter the Roman Empire, and instead to have left their lands for 'the very extremity of the world' (τὰs ἐσχατιὰς τῆς οἰκουμένης). This problem will be discussed again in the final section of this chapter. Procopius further offers an amazing account of Herul attempts to find a new royal family in Thule, at the end of the world. The story may be interpreted as a post-factum rationalization of the sudden collapse of the Herul polity and an ironic comment regarding barbarian political structures.[132] The impression one

---

[130] Jordanes, *Getica*, 261: 'Alanum gravi, Herulum levi armatura aciem strui.'

[131] Procopius, *Wars*, 6.14.36. Edward A. Thompson, 'Early Germanic Warfare', *Past and Present*, 14 (1958), 2–29 (p. 4 with n. 17), notes the lack of defensive armour for other Germanic tribes.

[132] Procopius, *Wars*, 6.15.1–4; trans. by Dewing, III, 415: 'When the Eruli, being defeated by the Lombards in the above-mentioned battle, migrated from their ancestral homes, some of them, as has been told by me above, made their home in the country of Illyricum, but the rest were averse to crossing the Ister River, but settled at the very extremity of the world [τὰς ἐσχατιὰς τῆς οἰκουμένης]; at any rate, these men, led by many of the royal blood, traversed all the nations of the Sclaveni one after the other, and after next crossing a large tract of barren country, they came to the Varni, as they are called. After these they passed the nations of the Dani, without suffering violence at the hands of the barbarians there. Coming thence to the ocean, they took to the sea, and putting in at Thule, remained there on the island.' The story of the emigrating Herules is interrupted here (Procopius, *Wars*, 6.15.5–26) by a long ethnographic description of Thule. Procopius mentions the polar night, offers a lot of information on the *Scritiphini* (maybe the *Saami*) as well as other peoples and religions of Thule. Finally he remarks that the emigrated Herules had settled near the *Gautoi*. Rappaport, 'Heruli', p. 1161, and Schmidt, *Die Ostgermanen*, p. 553, as most other traditional interpretations, took this as a historical account as it seemed clear that a 'Germanic tribe' must have originated in Scandinavia. For a critical discussion, see the final section of this chapter and Goffart, *Barbarian Tides*, pp. 209–10 and n. 117. For an illustration of how widespread the traditional interpretation still is, see Barbara Niezabitowska, 'Die Heruler', in *Die Vandalen: Die Könige, die Eliten, die Krieger, die Handwerker*, ed. by Andrzej Kokowski and Christian Leiber (Nordstemmen, 2003), pp. 387–94 (p. 390). Niezabitowska has absolutely no doubts about Procopius's account of the wandering Heruls. She refers to the story as if it were a historical account: 'Nach diesem Ereignis kehrte ein Teil der Heruler in die alte Heimat zurück, ein anderer Teil schloß sich den Langobarden an. [...] Diese kurze Eintragung bei Procopius rief ein "Gewitter" in der archäologischen Welt hervor.' She adds in relation to a Polish excavation at Ulów near

gets from this account is that Procopius did not take any barbarian political structures too seriously. 'And as late as the sixth century there were peoples, like the Herules, over whom a king exercised a dominion that was as venerable as it was chaotic and ridiculous in the eyes of the Romans.'[133] If a people is in need of kings from 'the very extremity of the world' it cannot be very evolved or cultivated compared to the Romans. Walter Goffart accurately summarized the complex story and I will cite him again at this point.

> What became of the Herules is not easily deciphered from Procopius's account. Twenty years after baptism, King Grepes and his twelve relatives had vanished, possibly as victims of the great plague of 541–42. The Herules on imperial territory "display[ed] their beastly and fanatical character" by overthrowing their king Ochus and promptly ran out of royalty. They then remembered that there was much royal blood among their brethren who had trekked north early in the century and so sent an embassy to them. While the envoys were on their long mission, the fickle Herules asked Justinian for a king and were

Tomaszów Lubelski, 'Darf man diese Funde mit den Herulern in Verbindung setzen? — Hoffentlich ja.' Niezabitowska argues with nothing but the information from Procopius to classify that archaeological material. The following passage describing the Herul quest for a king in Illyricum is also connected with Procopius's Thule-excursus. Procopius, *Wars*, 6.15.27–36; trans. by Dewing, III, 421–25: 'On the present occasion, therefore, the Eruli who dwelt among the Romans, after the murder of their king had been perpetrated by them, sent some of their notables to the island of Thule to search out and bring back whomsoever they were able to find there of royal blood. And when these men reached the island, they found many there of the royal blood, but they selected the one man who pleased them most and set out with him on the return journey. But this man fell sick and died when he had come to the country of the Dani. These men therefore went a second time to the island and secured another man, Datius by name. And he was followed by his brother Aordus and two hundred youths of the Eruli in Thule. But since much time passed while they were absent on this journey, it occurred to the Eruli in the neighbourhood of Singidunum [Beograd] that they were not consulting their own interests in importing a leader from Thule against the wishes of the Emperor Justinian. They therefore sent envoys to Byzantium, begging the emperor to send them a ruler of his own choice. And he straightaway sent them one of the Eruli who had on time been sojourning in Byzantium, Suartuas by name. At first the Eruli welcomed him and did obeisance to him and rendered the customary obedience to his commands; but not many days later a messenger arrived with the tidings that the men from the island of Thule were near at hand. And Suartuas commanded them to go out to meet those men, his intention being to destroy them, and the Eruli, approving his purpose, immediately went with him. But when the two forces were one day's journey distant from each other, the king's men all abandoned him at night and went over of their own accord to the newcomers, while he himself took the flight and set out unattended for Byzantium. Thereupon the emperor earnestly undertook with all his power to restore him to his office, and the Eruli, fearing the power of the Romans, decided to submit themselves to the Gepides. This, then, was the cause of the revolt of the Eruli.'

[133] Wolfram, *The Roman Empire*, p. 69.

given Suartuas, a reliable man, long in imperial service. The envoys returning from Thule drew near with their candidate ruler, Datius, accompanied by his brother, Aordus, and two hundred youths. The new Herule king ordered his people to go to meet the challenger and eliminate him, but they promptly defected, and Suartuas fled back to Constantinople. "Thereupon the emperor earnestly undertook with all his power to restore [Suartuas] to his office, and the Eruli, fearing the power of the Romans, decided to submit themselves to the Gepaedes." So Procopius closes his narrative, leaving us with open mouths: does the story of the Herules really end so abruptly? There is a follow-up in the next book. Apparently the Herules split apart; only two-thirds went to join the Gepids, and the rest stayed loyal to Constantinople. While King Datius's brother Aordus was serving with the Gepids against the Lombards (547), he came upon a Roman detachment and was killed in the ensuing skirmish. Later than this, Narses must have performed some magic of Herule relations and somehow extracted a mounted force of three thousand for the climactic Italian campaign (551–52). The next we hear is that Justinian was negotiating with the Avars, newly arrived on the Roman Danubian frontier (ca. 561): he offered them the lands that the Herules had vacated. The Herules, it seems, had indeed gone away.[134]

The Herul captain Sinduald fought with Narses in Justinan's Italian war and was evidently one of the *magistri militum* serving under Narses. In 566, after the emperor Justinian had died, an insurgency of Herul soldiers in Northern Italy (the Trentino) is reported. Sinduald was proclaimed king by them, only to be defeated and executed shortly afterwards by Narses.[135] However, after the mid-sixth century,

---

[134] Goffart, *Barbarian Tides*, p. 209; see also s.v. 'Aordus', 'Datius', 'Ochus', 'Suartuas', in *The Prosopography of the Later Roman Empire*, III, ed. by John Martindale (Cambridge, 1992), pp. 94, 388, 1951, 1205; Walter Pohl, *Die Awaren: Ein Steppenvolk in Mitteleuropa 567–822 n. Chr.*, 2nd edn (Vienna, 2002), pp. 18–21.

[135] Agathias, *The Histories*, 2.7–9; Marius of Avenches, *Chronica*, a. 566, in *Chronica minora saec. IV. V. VI. VII.*, vol. II, ed. by Mommsen, p. 238: 'Eo anno Sindewala Erolus tyrannidem adsumpsit et a Narseo patricio interfectus est'; Paul the Deacon, *History of the Lombards*, 2.3, calls Sinduald a 'Brentorum rex'. See s.v. 'Sindual', in *Prosopography of the Later Roman Empire*, III, ed. by Martindale, pp. 1154–55; Richard Heuberger, *Rätien im Altertum und Frühmittelalter* (Innsbruck, 1932; repr. 1971, 1981), pp. 155–59; Evagrius, *Ecclesiastical History*, 4.24, ed. by Adelheid Hübner (Turnhout, 2007), p. 158. Evagrius gives Emperor Justin II the epithet of *Eroulikos* (*Ecclesiastical History*, 5.4). As most university professors in pre-war Austria embraced the cause of German nationalism, there have been several attempts to trace the national, 'Germanic' roots to the Alpine parts of Austria-Hungary, in sharp opposition to Italian scholars tracing their national roots to the Romans. Before World War I, the Tyrol had a mixed population speaking Italian, Ladinian, and German. Sinduald's title recorded by Paul the Deacon, 'Brentorum rex', was appropriately associated to the name of the river Brenta near Trento (although the supposed *Brenti* are nowhere to be found in the sources). As a consequence, the population of some Tyrolean valleys was given a Herul origin. See Josef Egger, 'Die Barbareneinfälle in die Provinz Rätien und deren Besetzung durch Barbaren', *Archiv für österreichische Geschichte*, 90 (1901), 214–15; Richard Heuberger, *Das*

there is no mention of the Herules in any source. They apparently lost their identity as a separate *gens*, much like the Vandals after 533.

Myths and Final Considerations

Few are the issues of late antique history that stirred and still stir more interest among scholars, as well as within the general public, than that of the origin of the barbarians. To write the history of the barbarians without approaching the question of their origin and migration back and forth is hardly acceptable.[136] The much-cited *Encyclopaedia Britannica* has the Herules as 'a Germanic people originally from Scandinavia',[137] thus reproducing Jordanes's and Procopius's migration myths, which have otherwise seeped through the boundaries of modern scholarship. Scandinavia (*Scandza*) as the womb of nations ('officina gentium aut certe velut vagina nationum')[138] is a very powerful image, whose appeal, as Walter Goffart recently noted, has not at all been eroded by decades of scholarly criticism.[139]

Burggrafenamt im Altertum (Innsbruck, 1935), p. 42: 'Nach der Vernichtung des italischen Ostgotenreiches legte nämlich der byzantinische Feldherr und Statthalter Narses anscheinend die 3000 von dem *magister militum* Sindual befehligten erulischen Reiter in das *territorium Tridentinum* und hier werden diese Leute auch nach der Niederwerfung des Aufstandes verblieben sein, den sie um 565 gegen den Vertreter des Kaisers unternommen hatten. Berichten die Quellen doch nur von einer Wiederunterwerfung, nicht aber von einer Vernichtung oder Verpflanzung der Aufrührer.' Schmidt, *Die Ostgermanen*, p. 558 and n. 3 mentioned but at the same time doubted the influence of Sinduald's Herules on 'the ethnographic situation in the Tyrolean valleys': 'Die hier vorgetragenen Argumente haben freilich, abgesehen etwa von den aus den Rechtsverhältnissen abgeleiteten, keine besondere Beweiskraft.'

[136] This is particularly true for the numerous websites dedicated to the problem that mushroomed in recent years. They all offer a bizarre mixture of scholarly opinion and non-academic penchant for sensationalism. All seem preoccupied with linking the Herules to the ancestry of some modern Scandinavian nation. See 'Heruli the History 268–568 AD', <http://freepages.history. rootsweb.ancestry.com/~catshaman/24erils4/0horse2.htm> [accessed 1 April 2007]; 'The Heruls', <http://www.gedevasen.dk/heruleng.html#C7> [accessed 1 April 2007]; 'New Northvegr Center', <http://www.northvegr.org/secondary%20sources/germanic%20studies/guthones/001.html> [accessed 1 April 2007].

[137] s.v. 'Herules', in *Encyclopaedia Britannica Online*, <http://www.britannica.com/ EBchecked/topic/263960/Heruli> [accessed 1 April 2007].

[138] Jordanes, *Getica*, 25.

[139] Walter Goffart, 'Jordanes's *Getica* and the Disputed Authenticity of Gothic Origins from Scandinavia', *Speculum*, 80 (2005), 379–98 (p. 398); Goffart, *Barbarian Tides*, pp. 14, 16, and 46.

When Konrad Peutinger first edited and published Jordanes's *Getica* in 1515, his volume also contained Paul the Deacon's *History of the Lombards*. Together with Tacitus's *Germania*, first published in a modern edition in Venice in 1470, those texts represent the starting point for the study of the 'Germanic' past as a source of inspiration for modern national identity and as a justification for territorial claims and war.[140] Felix Dahn (1834–1912) may have borrowed from Procopius the story of the Herul trek back 'home' to Thule and applied it to the Goths for his novel *A Struggle for Rome* in which a Viking jarl named Harald (*der Wiking*) arrives with a fleet of Viking drakkars (*Drachenboote*) to bring back to Scandinavia the remnants of the Gothic troops defeated by Justinian's armies around Naples. Together with them, he also returned to the northern homeland the body of the great Theoderic and the royal treasure. Dahn even strove to create the impression of an authentic Germanic *Stabreim*: 'Go on Freia's wise bird, fly, my falcon. And she threw the falcon in the air. "Show us the way to the north, to Thule!" Let's bring home the last of the Goths.'[141] At a time and within a generation mesmerized by Richard Wagner's music and obsessed with the reconstruction of a heroic Germanic past as a warranty for the present glory, Dahn's literary endeavours resonated with the political aspirations of the young German nation. But Dahn's novel is a constant reminder of the problems involved in the invention of a national identity out of sources several times removed, in terms of both time and space, from the real historical roots of the nineteenth-century German nation. This is, after all, still a challenge for contemporary scholarship.

Ever since the early sixteenth century, the idea of a Herul migration from the north into Europe and the Black Sea region was enthusiastically embraced by many scholars and never seriously doubted. At the root of this myth is Jordanes's account of how the Dani, who traced their origin to the same stock as the Suetidi he mentioned before, had driven the Herules from their homes, even though the Herules

---

[140] Heinz Heubner, 'Die Überlieferung der Germania des Tacitus', in *Beiträge zum Verständnis der Germania des Tacitus*, I, ed. by Dieter Timpe and Herbert Jankuhn (Göttingen, 1989), pp. 16–27; Ulrich Muhlack, *Geschichtswissenschaft im Humanismus und in der Aufklärung: Die Vorgeschichte des Historismus* (Munich, 1991), pp. 386–87. For the first printed version of Jordanes and Paul the Deacon, see *Jornandes, episcopus Ravennas, 'De rebus Gothorum'. Paulus Diaconus 'de gestis Langobardorum'*, ed. by Peutinger (Augsburg, 1515).

[141] Felix Dahn, *Ein Kampf um Rom* (Leipzig, 1888), p. 488: 'Auf, Freias kluger Vogel, flieg, mein Falke. Und hoch warf sie den Falken in die Luft, "weise den Weg nach Norden, gen Thuleland!" Heim bringen wir die letzten Goten.' The end of Dahn's novel is also discussed by Goffart, *Narrators*, p. 96 and n. 365.

had laid claim to pre-eminence among all the nations of *Scandza* for their tallness.[142]

A tradition described at length by Walter Goffart associated the Gothic origin with Britain. This points out the likelihood that Procopius's association of the Herules with Thule was something like the manifestation of a third myth of 'Gothic' origins. According to Goffart, Procopius used the account of the Herules wandering back to Thule, at the end of the world, in order to make a point about how the Goths should be treated after their expected defeat in Italy. The most likely source for this idea would have been Procopius's own interpretation of circulating Gothic (oral) traditions.[143] Recently Goffart added a remark concerning the story of a Herul migration to Thule: 'Intriguing though these and related questions are, they are more relevant to Procopius than to the Herules. Our information on the latter has enough substance to provide at least the whisper of a history.'[144] This is so far the most likely interpretation of Procopius's account of a Herul migration to Thule. According to Andrew Merrills, the idea of Goths originating in a large island of the Far North is an outgrowth of ancient geographical literature. The sole purpose of this idea was to find a place for the barbarians within the world as known to educated Romans. In other words, instead of a genuinely Gothic tradition, this idea is a by-product of Graeco-Roman ethnography.

Similarly, Merrills argues, 'it seems unlikely that the historic conflict between Dani and Herules would have been included in an oral mercantile source'.[145] One needs to take into consideration the tradition of the ethnographic literature written in both Greek and Latin when approaching Jordanes's account. Procopius and Jordanes certainly assumed a Scandinavian origin of the Herules, but this is nothing more or less than the story about Goths originating in the Far North: an explanatory device introduced by Roman ethnographers, not a genuinely 'native' tale of origins. (Further parallels, postulated quite often for example in religious — so called cultic — structures, between the history of Paul the Deacon and northern

---

[142] Jordanes, *Getica*, 23: 'Suetidi cogniti in hac gente reliquis corpore eminentiores, quamvis et Dani, ex ipsorum stirpe progressi, Herulos propriis sedibus expulerunt, qui inter omnes Scandiae nationes nomen sibi ob nimia proceritate affectant praecipuum.' See Georg Kappelmacher, s.v. 'Jordanes', in *Realencyclopädie der classischen Altertumswissenschaft,* ed. by Wilhelm Kroll and others, IX.2 (Stuttgart, 1916; repr. 1992), pp. 1908–29 (p. 1920).

[143] Procopius, *Wars*, 6.15.1–4. See Goffart, *Narrators*, pp. 88–96; Merrills, *History and Geography*, p. 126. *Contra*: Heather, *Goths*, p. 66 and n. 82.

[144] Goffart, *Barbarian Tides*, p. 210.

[145] Merrills, *History and Geography*, p. 152 and nn. 227–28.

sagas and Middle High German epic poems may thus be explained in terms of the diffusion of manuscripts containing the *History of the Lombards* and, by default, the dissemination of Paul the Deacon's work in medieval Central and Northern Europe. Writers and scholars working in Scandinavia or Iceland during the High Middle Ages like Snorri Sturluson were able to use manuscripts like we do.)[146] Attempts by several German and Scandinavian scholars to tie the Heruls known from late antique sources to Sweden are therefore futile.

There is nothing historically true about the story of a Herul wandering from, as well as returning to, a northern homeland. Equally problematic are attempts to present the Herules as a loose group of warriors, instead of a people, a *gens*. Some concluding remarks regarding such arguments are therefore needed at this point. According to Procopius, Herul warriors use neither helmet nor corselet nor any other protective armor, only a shield. He also mentions that Herul slaves go into battle without any shield at all. Upon proving themselves in combat, their masters allow them to carry shields in battles to come.[147] This account has been taken as evidence for 'Germanic' initiation rites and brotherhoods of warriors. In fact, denying the Herules the status of a *gens* implies turning them into a military brotherhood. This is exactly what Otto Höfler proposed in his work on Germanic secret societies.[148] Moreover, *Männerbünde* and brotherhoods of warriors (*Krieger-vereinigungen*) immediately invite comparison with the Vikings. At a closer examination, the only basis for such a line of reasoning appears to be etymological speculations about the name of the Herules and the rather loose use of sixth-century sources. The fact that the Herules had a reputation for good fighting is of course no indication of military brotherhoods. The Herules were a *gens* like any other, such as Goths or Vandals, different only on account of their smaller size. Nevertheless, the idea that the Herules were an association of warriors, not a *gens*,

---

[146] See Walter Pohl, *Die Germanen* (Munich, 2000), pp. 78–80; Heinrich Beck, 'Probleme einer völkerwanderungszeitlichen Religionsgeschichte', in *Germanische Religionsgeschichte: Quellen und Quellenprobleme*, ed. by Heinrich Beck, Detlev Ellmers, and Kurt Schier (Berlin, 1992), pp. 475–88.

[147] Procopius, *Wars*, 2.27–28.

[148] Otto Höfler, *Kultische Geheimbünde der Germanen*, I (Frankfurt am Main, 1934), pp. 267–69. See also Mischa Meier, s.v. 'Männerbund', in *Reallexikon der germanischen Altertums-kunde*, XIX, 2nd edn, ed. by Heinrich Beck, Dieter Geuenich, and Heiko Steuer (Berlin, 2001), pp. 105–10. Höfler also discussed the Taifalian manners mentioned by Ammianus Marcellinus, *Res gestae*, 31.9.5. According to Ammianus Marcellinus, among the Taifali, grown men have sexual relations with boys. Some act of bravery in hunting often seals such liaisons.

seems to be responsible for the peculiar position accorded to them in scholarship. It is striking that exactly in books defining 'Germanic' ethnicity as very severe, the Herules form an exception. But also in recent scholarship, such explanations were reused when they seemed to fit in new concepts. Beginning with their very name, allegedly meaning 'hero' or 'noble warrior' (on the basis of a contested comparison with such words as *erul*, *eorl*, or *jarl*, translated as 'hero' or 'noble warrior'), scholars have assumed that the Herules were initially groups of 'special' warriors known for their bravery or for particular military skills. According to Ellegård they may have been groups of warriors following a certain model rather than belonging to a well-defined people. As such, they appeared in different parts of Europe, but they eventually got together and formed both a people and a *regnum* on the river Morava.[149] This means telling the story of a *gens* while at the same time treating the Herules as a special case. One gets the impression that earlier scholarly debates subconsciously influenced Ellegård and thus resulted in a tautology.

It is of course far from clear exactly what Procopius had in mind when writing about Herul 'slaves'. But he surely provided plenty of evidence that any *gens* was open to newcomers. As in any other human community, both in the past and in the present, such newcomers had to prove themselves worthy before receiving full membership in that community. This must have been even truer for a community geared towards warfare. In other words, what Procopius has to say about Herul slaves earning their shields is perhaps no more than his (admittedly confused) description of a practice of accommodating new warriors within the already existing *gens*. An initiation rite, perhaps, but certainly not for admission into a military brotherhood. The Herules, therefore, were no different from other *gentes*. It is striking that tokens of *gentes* were and are used in the Herul case to define a special case in the rich field of identities in Late Antiquity. The discussion concerning the criteria of ethnic identity in Late Antiquity is ongoing, one of the most vivid in the field. Nothing justifies the neglect and at times distortion with which the Herules are currently treated in modern scholarship.

---

[149] Ellegård, 'Who Were the Eruli?', pp. 29–31; Wolfram, *Goten*, p. 62 and n. 32.

THE JUSTINIANIC HERULES:
FROM ALLIED BARBARIANS TO ROMAN PROVINCIALS

Alexander Sarantis

In comparison with other late antique Germanic groups that went on to form successor kingdoms in the provinces of the West Roman Empire, such as the Lombards and the Goths, the Herules have been the subject of very few academic works.[1] Articles by Ellegård, Schwarcz, and Brandt are exceptions.[2] The Herules have been referred to more frequently in discussions of the wars in which they fought or peoples with whom they came into contact. For example, Ernst Stein includes sections on the Herules in his history of the Late Roman Empire.[3]

---

[1] On the Goths, see, for example, Herwig Wolfram, *History of the Goths* (Berkeley, 1988); Peter Heather, *Goths and Romans 332–489* (Oxford, 1991) and Peter Heather, *The Goths* (Oxford, 1996); Michael Kulikowski, *Rome's Gothic Wars: From the Third Century to Alaric* (Cambridge, 2007); Patrick Amory, *People and Identity in Ostrogothic Italy, 489–554* (Cambridge, 1997). On the Lombards, see, for example, Neil Christie, *The Lombards: The Ancient Langobards* (Oxford, 1995); *Die Langobarden: Herrschaft und Identität*, ed. by Walter Pohl and Peter Erhart (Vienna, 2005); Walter Pohl, 'Die Langobarden in Pannonien und Justinians Gotenkrieg', in *Ethnische und kulturelle Verhältnisse an der mittleren Donau vom 6. bis zum 11. Jahrhundert: Symposium Nitra 6. bis 10. November 1994*, ed. by Darina Bialeková and Jozef Zábojník (Bratislava, 1996), pp. 27–35, and Walter Pohl, 'The Empire and the Lombards: Treaties and Negotiations in the Sixth Century', in *Kingdoms of the Empire: The Integration of Barbarians in Late Antiquity*, ed. by Walter Pohl (Leiden, 1997), pp. 75–134; Konstantinos Christou, *Byzanz und die Langobarden: von der Ansiedlung in Pannonien bis zur endgültigen Anerkennung (500–680)* (Athens, 1992).

[2] Troels Brandt, 'The Herules', <http://www.gedevasen.dk/heruleng.html> (2005); Alvar Ellegård, 'Who Were the Eruli?', *Scandia*, 53 (1987), 5–34. I have been unable to procure a copy of Andreas Schwarcz, 'Die Heruler an der Donau', in *Sprache als System und Prozess: Festschrift für Günter Lipold zum 60. Geburtstag*, ed. by Christiane M. Pabst (Vienna, 2005), pp. 504–12.

[3] Ernst Stein, *Histoire du Bas Empire: de la disparition de l'Empire d'Occident à la mort de Justinien 476–565* (Paris, 1949), pp. 305–08 and 529.

Authors of works on general barbarian history in this period have also discussed the Herules, for example, Peter Heather in his 'Disappearing and Reappearing Tribes', and Walter Goffart in the *Narrators of Barbarian History*.[4] Similarly, sections of books and entries in encyclopaedic works on Germanic barbarians have been devoted to the Herules. *Die Ostgermanen* by Ludwig Schmidt contains a chapter on the Herules, and the entries in the *Reallexicon der germanischen Altertumskunde* are well known.[5]

The reasons for this neglect are not hard to discern. Like most of the 'neglected barbarians' discussed in this book, the Herules never found themselves in a sufficiently powerful political and cultural position for it to be worth someone's while to produce a legitimizing history of their origins. With the exception of a relatively brief period in the late fourth and early fifth centuries, they never formed a powerful, independent political entity. Instead, what little is known of their history is characterized by political fragmentation, nomadic wandering, and a predilection to serve other barbarians or imperial authorities in a military capacity.

The principal trend in the limited historiography of the Herules has been to focus on their ethnogenesis, debating when and how they became Herules and, in particular, whether they originated in Scandinavia, as suggested by Jordanes's *Getica*, and when that could have happened.[6] This paper will largely steer clear of

[4] Peter Heather, 'Disappearing and Reappearing Tribes', in *Strategies of Distinction: The Construction of Ethnic Communities, 300–800*, ed. by Walter Pohl and Helmut Reimitz (Leiden, 1998), pp. 95–112 (pp. 97–99 and 108–09); Walter Goffart, *The Narrators of Barbarian History, AD 550–800: Jordanes, Gregory of Tours, Bede, and Paul the Deacon* (Princeton, 1988), pp. 94–96.

[5] Ludwig Schmidt, *Die Ostgermanen*, vol. I of *Geschichte der deutschen Stämme bis zum Ausgange der Völkerwanderung* (Munich, 1941; repr. 1969), pp. 548–64; Rudolf Much, s.v. 'Heruler', in *Reallexicon der germanischen Altertumskunde*, II, ed. by Johannes Hoops (Strassbourg, 1915), pp. 517–19; Matthew Taylor, s.v. 'Heruler', in *Reallexikon der germanischen Altertumskunde*, XIV, 2nd edn, ed. by Heinrich Beck, Dieter Geuenich, and Heiko Steuer (Berlin, 1999), pp. 470–74.

[6] Authors such as Schmidt, *Geschichte*, pp. 548–53, viewed Jordanes's reference to the Herules being expelled from Scandza by the Danes as evidence that the Herules originated in Scandinavia. Such authors asserted that the Herules must have subsequently migrated to the Sea of Azov area at the same time as the Goths, in the third century. Ellegård, 'Who Were the Eruli?', pp. 18–25, takes issue with this traditional view and argues instead that the Herules were more probably formed north of the Roman frontier in the third century between Castra Batava and Vindobona. He asserts that Jordanes's passage referring to their expulsion from Scandza by the Danes refers to a more recent event in the sixth century, probably the same episode that Procopius describes as the migration of a group of royal Herules to Illyricum to fill a leadership vacuum in the mid-540s. For a more elaborate summary of the historiographical debate, see Brandt, 'Herules', section 4, 'Sources and their Critics'.

these debates and will not seek to piece together an all-encompassing narrative of Herul history. Such an approach prioritizes issues of migration, long-term ethnic development, and 'tradition' at the expense of judging specific periods of Herul history on their own terms.[7] At the same time, such an approach runs the risk of assuming that the recycled ethnonym 'Herul' always refers to the same group, an assumption that is open to debate.[8]

Instead, the more limited aim of this chapter will be to home in on the best-documented group of Herules; those settled within the Roman province of Upper Moesia during the reign of Justinian. By piecing together the literary references to those Herules, this chapter sets out to demonstrate that they played key political and military roles within the Justinianic Empire that have not been stressed by modern historians, both as an important part of the Balkan defensive system and as a significant manpower resource in the wars of reconquest in the West and the wars with Persia in the East. By setting the Herules in a sixth-century context, and by placing them at the centre of the narrative, this paper will seek to answer questions regarding the political organization and ethnic identity of the Herules and their reaction to imperial policies, and what these factors tell us about the nature of Roman-barbarian relations in the Balkans in a period that has not received as much attention as those of Gothic, Hunnic, and Avar invasions.[9]

---

[7] For a thorough critique of the *Traditionskern* model of barbarian ethnogenesis and history, see *On Barbarian Identity: Critical Approaches to Ethnicity in the Early Middle Ages*, ed. by Andrew Gillet (Turnhout, 2002), especially Andrew Gillett, 'Introduction: Ethnicity, History, and Methodology', pp. 1–18; Walter Goffart, 'Does the Distant Past Impinge on the Invasion Age Germans?', pp. 21–37; and Charles Bowlus, 'Ethnogenesis: The Tyranny of a Concept', pp. 241–56. See also Roland Steinacher's contribution to this volume.

[8] Heather, 'Disappearing and Reappearing Tribes', pp. 97–99, concludes that the numerous references to Herules between the fourth and sixth centuries reflect the survival of the same ethnic group. However, Roland Steinacher, 'Rex oder Räuberhauptmann: Ethnische und politische Identität im 5. und 6. Jahrhundert am Beispiel von Vandalen und Herulern', in *Grenzen und Entgrenzungen: Der mediterrane Raum*, ed. by Beate Burtscher and others (Würzburg, 2006), pp. 2–21, is more sceptical. Steinacher argues that names such as Herul reflected formed and re-formed military groupings to a greater extent than they did biologically or culturally uniform peoples. Therefore, Odoacer was 'king of the Herules' simply on the basis of him being their commander in battle. Michael Kulikowski, 'Nation versus Army: A Necessary Contrast?', in *On Barbarian Identity*, ed. by Gillet, pp. 69–84 (pp. 81–84) takes issue with Heather's approach to Gothic history, arguing that there is insufficient evidence to speak of Gothic ethnogenesis given that the sources merely tell us about the actions of an army.

[9] For the Gothic migrations and invasions of the fourth and fifth centuries, see above, the references in note 1. For the Huns, see, for instance, E. A. Thompson, *The Huns* (Oxford, 1999); and Otto Maenchen-Helfen, *The World of the Huns: Studies in their History and Culture* (Berkeley,

The literary evidence for the Herules in this period is fragmentary, cursory, and composed by Romans. It consists largely of isolated references in Procopius's *History of the Wars*, Agathias's *Histories*, and the *Chronographia* of John Malalas. There is no need to rehearse the pitfalls of using such texts and the caution that is required when assessing the veracity and significance of their content.[10] The tendency of classicizing historians to use topoi and literary allusions in passages on barbarians, especially in ethnographic excurses and speeches, is the obvious concern. It must nevertheless be noted at the outset that the majority of those writers were contemporaries, who were composing their works not long after the events described and, in the case of Procopius, had almost certainly had dealings with the peoples to which he referred. They were writing history, not fiction, and could not entirely fabricate material on a group such as the Herules, members of which, at the time Procopius was writing, numbered among the Constantinopolitan military aristocracy.[11] Therefore, this chapter will judge the different types of information contained in the literary sources on their own merits. Their frequent use of precise numerical, prosopographical, and geographical information, especially in the discussion of military events, will be interpreted as an indication that they are based on written or oral sources. Meanwhile, the interpretative framework within which the narratives were constructed, often consisting of speeches, letters, and ethnographic discussions will be treated to the 'Goffart approach', viewed primarily as

1973). For the Avars, see Walter Pohl, *Die Awaren: ein Steppenfolk im Mitteleuropa, 569–822 n. Chr.* (Munich, 1988). For Roman-barbarian relations in the late sixth century, see Michael Whitby, *The Emperor Maurice and his Historian: Theophylact Simocatta on Persian and Balkan Warfare* (Oxford, 1988). The principal recent work on the Justinianic Balkans is that of Florin Curta, *The Making of the Slavs: History and Archaeology of the Lower Danube Region, ca. 500–700* (Cambridge, 2001), especially pp. 120–89. Articles such as Frank Wozniak, 'Byzantine Diplomacy and the Lombard-Gepidic Wars', *Balkan Studies*, 20 (1979), 139–58, and Pohl, 'The Empire and the Lombards', have discussed Justinianic diplomacy in Illyricum. Alexander Sarantis, *The Balkans during the Reign of Justinian* (forthcoming) will attempt to provide a comprehensive account of the history and archaeology of Roman-barbarian relations in the Justinianic Balkans.

[10] See, for instance, Roger Scott, 'The Classical Tradition in Byzantine Historiography', in *Byzantium and the Classical Tradition*, ed. by Margaret Mullett and Roger Scott (Birmingham, 1981), pp. 61–74; W. R. Conor, 'Narrative Discourse in Thucydides', in *Papers Presented to A. E. Raubitschek: The Greek Historians, Literature and History* (Stanford, 1985), pp. 1–17; Tim Rood, *Narrative and Explanation* (Oxford, 1988).

[11] See below on Suartas the Herul. Procopius composed his *History of the Wars* between AD 551 and 553. See Averil Cameron, *Procopius and the Sixth Century* (London, 1985), p. 9; Geoffrey Greatrex, 'The Dates of Procopius' Works', *Byzantine and Modern Greek Studies*, 18 (1994), 101–14.

good evidence for the ways in which a Roman audience perceived Herules and Herul-Roman relations.[12]

It must be admitted though that the limited evidence for the events and processes to be examined here means that certain conclusions may be considered overly speculative. For example, there is much less evidence for the military role of the Herules within the Balkan Peninsula than there is for their service in other parts of the empire. However, the nature of classicizing histories means that we have to look beyond what they tell us, as long as we have the additional evidence to fill in the gaps. Therefore, in the third section, the limited literary evidence for the military role of the Herules in the Balkans will be placed in the context of other literary, legislative, and archaeological evidence for the region in which they were settled, in order to highlight a strategic significance that cannot be ignored, even when this is not overtly spelt out in the sources.

Historical Background: The Kingdom of Rodulphus, the Defeat by the Lombards, and the Settlement within the Balkans Ordered by Emperor Anastasius

In order to understand Justinian's Herul policy, it will first be necessary to fill in the historical background to their settlement in the Middle Danube area. The Herules were a Germanic tribe that had been part of Attila's confederation and participated in the battle of Nedao in 454, in which Gepids and a number of tribes defeated the sons and successors of Attila.[13] In the late fifth century a large number of Herules were recruited to fight in the army of the Scirian general Odoacer.[14]

---

[12] Goffart, *Narrators*, pp. 3–20, summarizes his intention to treat the early medieval histories of the Lombards, Franks, and Goths to a literary analysis in which he would spend more time understanding what their content tells him about their authors than he would try to mine them for historical facts.

[13] Jordanes, *Getica*, 23.117–19, ed. by Theodor Mommsen, MGH AA, 5.1 (Berlin, 1882). On the battle of Nedao, see Walter Pohl, 'Die Gepiden und die Gentes an der Mittleren Donau nach dem Zerfall der Attillareiches', in *Die Völker an der mittleren und unteren Donau in fünften und sechsten Jahrhundert: Berichte des Symposions der Kommission für Frühmittelalterforschung, 24.–27. Oktober 1978, Stift Zwettl, Niederösterreich*, ed. by Herwig Wolfram and Falko Daim (Vienna, 1980), pp. 239–305 (pp. 252–63); Wolfram, *History*, pp. 258–59; Constantin Diculescu, *Die Gepiden: Forschungen zur Geschichte Daziens im frühen Mittelalter und zur Vorgeschichte des rumänischen Volkes* (Leipzig, 1923), pp. 60–69; and Steinacher, 'Rex oder Räuberhauptmann', p. 10.

[14] Stein, *Histoire*, p. 41.

Meanwhile, the Herul king Rodulphus had carved out a political entity in the Upper Danube region, apparently centred on the Lower Austrian and Moravian march.[15] Procopius and Paul the Deacon concur that the Herules had achieved a number of military successes, and Procopius states that they had come to dominate a series of other tribes, including the Lombards.[16] By 507, Rodulphus had achieved a position of sufficient pre-eminence in western Illyricum to be invited by the Gothic king of Italy, Theoderic, to be his son-in-arms, the traditional Germanic method of sealing a military alliance.[17] The Gothic Kingdom at this time not only included the Italian peninsula, but extended to the former West Illyrian provinces of Noricum, Pannonia, and Dalmatia, and presumably bordered the Herul territory along the Upper Danube (Figures 11.1 and 11.2).

The military and political success of the Herules ended with a crushing defeat by the Lombards. Procopius states that the battle occurred three years into the reign of Anastasius, that is, in 494.[18] However, Theoderic's letter to Rodulphus inviting him to be his son-in-arms is dated to *c.* AD 507. This suggests that historians such as Stein, Wolfram, and Christou have been right to prefer a date of *c.* AD 508 for the Herul-Lombard battle.[19] According to Procopius, this encounter resulted from Rodulphus's decision to give in to the restlessness of the Herul elites for further military conquests and to instigate hostilities with the Lombards.[20] Conversely, Paul the Deacon records that the dispute arose over the murder of Rodulphus's brother by the daughter of the Lombard king Tato during the course of a diplomatic visit by the Herules.[21] Given that Procopius was writing in the early 550s and Paul the Deacon in the early eighth century, the testimony of the former is to be preferred, even though the anecdotal nature of the two sources means that neither can be accepted as entirely reliable. Neither Procopius nor Jordanes provide much information regarding the course of the battle, although they generally concur regarding the outcome: the annihilation of the Herules and of their king.

[15] Christie, *The Lombards*, p. 22; Herwig Wolfram, *The Roman Empire and its Germanic Peoples* (Berkeley, 1997), pp. 279–80; Stein, *Histoire*, p. 53.

[16] Paul the Deacon, *History of the Lombards*, 20.1–7, ed. by G. Waitz (Hannover, 1878); Procopius of Caesarea, *Wars*, 6.14.8–10, ed. by J. Haury (London, 1918).

[17] Cassiodorus, *Variae*, 4.2, ed. by Theodor Mommsen, MGH AA, 12 (Berlin, 1894).

[18] Procopius, *Wars*, 6.14.10–11.

[19] Stein, *Histoire*, pp. 150–51; Wolfram, *History*, pp. 322–23; Christou, *Byzanz und die Langobarden*, pp. 54–55, on the date of the victory of the Lombards over the Herules.

[20] Procopius, *Wars*, 6.14.11–12.

[21] Paul the Deacon, *History of the Lombards*, 20.1–7.

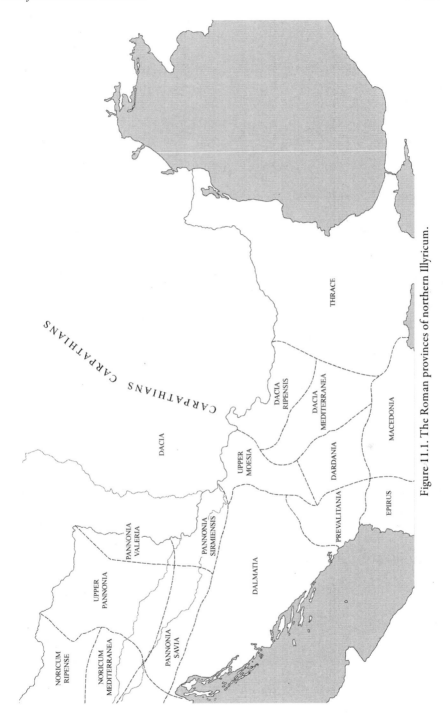

Figure 11.1. The Roman provinces of northern Illyricum.

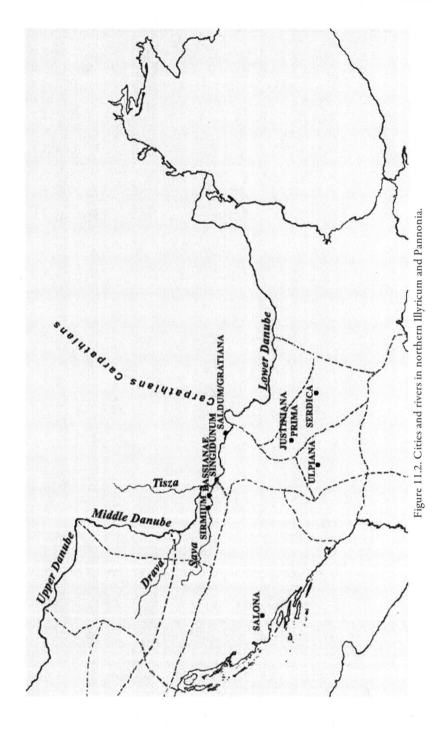

Figure 11.2. Cities and rivers in northern Illyricum and Pannonia.

The slaughter of the Herules precipitated the collapse of their kingdom and laid the foundation for their subsequent settlement in the Balkans. The Herules splintered into a number of groups. One seems to have migrated to Italy to serve Theoderic.[22] Another moved first to the area formerly settled by the Rugi, in the former Roman province of Noricum, and then migrated to the Dacian region east of the Middle Danube, where they became suppliants of the Gepid kingdom.[23] Procopius records that they were then forced out by the Gepids who had begun to plunder their property. This resulted in a further division. One group migrated northwards to Thule, widely believed to denote Scandinavia and, according to Jordanes, the ancestral home of the Herules.[24] In 512, the other group settled Roman territory in the north-western Balkans.[25] Stein convincingly argued that the Herules moved to the region surrounding the city of Bassianae in south-eastern Pannonia Sirmiensis, which had been ceded to the Roman Empire by the Gothic king Theoderic in AD 510.[26] His conclusion is to be preferred to that of Schmidt, who argued that they were located in Dacia Ripensis on the basis that the Gepids occupied Singidunum until 535.[27] The latter point has since been refuted by the majority of works on this subject.[28]

The basis on which the Herules settled in Illyricum is unclear. According to Marcellinus Comes, Emperor Anastasius instigated this movement, 'introducing them to the territories and cities of the Romans'.[29] Marcellinus's portrayal of this development as dictated by imperial policy is understandable given that he was a

---

[22] Wolfram, *History*, pp. 300–01.

[23] See Procopius, *Wars*, 6.14.23–29 and 15.1–4 on the migration and divisions of the Herules in this period.

[24] On the migration of the Herules to Thule, see Ellegård, 'Who Were the Eruli?', p. 9; Brandt, 'Herules', section 2.3; Goffart, *Narrators*, pp. 94–96. On Thule, see Andrew Robert Burn, 'Procopius and the Island of Ghosts', *English Historical Review*, 70 (1955), 258–61; Vincent H. de Cassidy, 'The Voyage of an Island', *Speculum*, 38 (1963), 595–602; E. A. Thompson, 'Procopius on Brittia and Britannia', *Classical Quarterly*, 30 (1980), 498–507; José Miguel Alonso-Núñez, 'Roman Knowledge of Scandinavia in the Imperial Period', *Oxford Journal of Archaeology*, 7 (1988), 47–64.

[25] Marcellinus Comes, *Chronicle*, s.a. 512, in *Chronica minora saec. IV. V. VI. VII.*, vol. I, ed. by Theodor Mommsen, MGH AA, 9 (Berlin, 1894).

[26] Stein, *Histoire*, pp. 305–06.

[27] Schmidt, *Geschichte*, p. 553.

[28] Pohl, 'Die Gepiden', pp. 300–05; Alexander Sarantis, 'War and Diplomacy in Pannonia and the North-west Balkans during the Reign of Justinian: The Gepid Threat and Imperial Responses', *Dumbarton Oaks Papers*, 63 (2009), 15–40.

[29] Marcellinus Comes, *Chronicle*, s.a. 512, trans. by B. Croke (Sydney, 1995), p. 37.

proud Roman Illyrian who had served in imperial armies against barbarian groups, left his homeland as a result of barbarian invasions in the 490s, and acquired the titles of *comes* and *vir clarissimus* while working for Anastasius's government in the 500s.[30] Conversely, Procopius, who did not have such an attachment to Illyricum or to the government of Anastasius, states that the Herules moved of their own accord into the Roman lands south of the Danube, a migration that was only subsequently ratified by Anastasius.[31] Given the imperial government's limited authority in the northern Illyrian provinces at this time, this is the more plausible version.

In the fifth century, direct Roman control over the Middle Danube area from the Iron Gates gorges to Pannonia had been eroded because of the migrations and invasions of Goths and Huns.[32] By the first decade of the sixth century, Roman authority in the province of Upper Moesia had been further restricted by Mundo, a Gepid warlord and ally of the Goths who controlled a significant group of barbarians in the vicinity of the confluence of the Morava and Danube rivers.[33] Anastasius had attempted to reinforce imperial authority in this area with the deployment of large armies in northern Illyricum, against the Bulgars in AD 499 and against Mundo and the Goths in 505.[34] However, the Romans' defeat in the latter engagement and the Gothic-Herul alliance of 507 confirmed the Gothic preeminence in western Illyricum and the barbarian threat to northern Illyricum. In light of this background, it was in Anastasius's interests to begin winning barbarian 'hearts and minds' in the area and accede to the settlement of the Herules from southern Pannonia in 512.

Nonetheless, Anastasius seems to have been quick to assert imperial authority over the group in subsequent years. Procopius vaguely recounts that on the pretext of the Herules' 'lawless treatment of the Romans living there' the Emperor sent an

---

[30] On the life of Marcellinus Comes, see Brian Croke, *Count Marcellinus and his Chronicle* (Oxford, 2005), pp. 17–77.

[31] Procopius, *Wars*, 6.14.28.

[32] For a discussion of the main historical developments in the Balkans in the fourth and fifth centuries, see the papers in *The Transition to Late Antiquity on the Danube and Beyond*, ed. by Andrew Poulter (Oxford, 2007), especially those of Andrew Poulter, 'The Transition to Late Antiquity', pp. 1–50 (pp. 4–15); Wolfgang Liebeschuetz, 'The Lower Danube Region under Pressure: From Valens to Heraclius', pp. 101–35 (pp. 101–10); Michael Whitby, 'The Late Roman Army and the Defence of the Balkans', pp. 135–63 (pp. 136–40); and Peter Heather, 'Goths in the Roman Balkans *c.* 350–500', pp. 163–90.

[33] Brian Croke, 'Mundo the Gepid: From Freebooter to Roman General', *Chiron*, 12 (1982), 125–35.

[34] Marcellinus Comes, *Chronicle*, s.a. 499 and 505.

army against them, which defeated them in battle and killed many of their number.[35] Because the passage provides no chronological reference, we can only conclude that the campaign took place at some point between 512 and 518. The
surviving Herules apparently submitted to Anastasius and agreed to be 'allies' and
'servants' of the Emperor thereafter. Whether they performed any important function during the remainder of Anastasius's reign or during that of his successor,
Justin I, is unclear given that they do not show up in the literary sources again until
early in the reign of Justinian.

The Role of the Herules Within Justinian's Defensive System in the Balkans

Procopius and Malalas provide evidence that Justinian established closer relations
with the Herules early in his reign. Malalas records that in 528 the Herul king
Grepes was baptized in Constantinople on Holy Epiphany along with his 'senators'
and twelve relatives, Justinian acting as his sponsor.[36] Malalas, at this time based in
Antioch, Syria, presumably acquired this information from an official dispatch.[37]
The decision of the Syrian chronicler to recount the baptism of the Herules
certainly advertises the empire-wide significance of the episode. Meanwhile,
Procopius's excursus on the Herules briefly outlines the changes in Roman-Herul
relations which took place in the aftermath of Justinian's accession.[38] Procopius's
narrative is typically short and general but emphasizes the main strands of Justinian's renegotiated Herul alliance. These included the provision of new lands to
the Herules and a missionary policy to convert them to Orthodox Christianity.
Procopius's sources for this information were likely Roman or Herul military officials he encountered while on campaign in Persia, Africa, or Italy, or possibly
diplomatic records of Roman-Herul relations.[39]

---

[35] Procopius of Caesarea, *Wars*, 6.14.29–32, trans. by H. B. Dewing (London, 1919), p. 411.

[36] John Malalas, *Chronographia*, 18.6, ed. by J. Thurn (Berlin, 2000); trans. by E. Jeffreys,
M. Jeffreys, and R. Scott (Melbourne, 1986), p. 247.

[37] Elizabeth Jeffreys, 'Malalas' Sources', in *Studies in John Malalas*, ed. by Elizabeth Jeffreys,
Brian Croke, and Roger Scott (Sydney, 1990), pp. 167–216.

[38] Procopius, *Wars*, 6.14.33–36.

[39] For Procopius's sources, see Cameron, *Procopius*, pp. 136–37; Geoffrey Greatrex, 'Recent
Works on Procopius and the Composition of *Wars* Book VIII', *Byzantine and Modern Greek
Studies*, 27 (2003), 45–67; Walter Kaegi, 'Procopius the Military Historian', *Byzantinische For-
schungen*, 15 (1990), 53–85; James Howard-Johnston, 'The Education and Expertise of Procopius',
Antiquité Tardive, 8 (2000), 19–30.

Therefore, Procopius and Malalas both demonstrate that Justinian's Herul policy in AD 527–28 involved a religious element. It is clear from Procopius's passages on the Herules in his *Vandalic Wars*, to be discussed below, that some of the Herules were Arian Christians.[40] Therefore, the symbolic conversion of King Grepes to Orthodox Christianity was presumably intended to encourage his people to follow suit. This can be placed in the context of Justin I and Justinian's drive to reform heretics and non-Orthodox Christian groups, including Arians, during the 520s and 530s.[41] Procopius states that Justinian's effort to convert 'all the Herules' had mixed results.[42] On the one hand, they were encouraged by their conversion to lead a gentler life and follow the laws of the Christians. On the other, they nevertheless remained faithless towards the Romans, avaricious, prone to violent deeds against their neighbours, and inclined to mate in an unholy manner. Historians have often taken those contradictory statements literally.[43] It would be better, however, to view Procopius as presenting two contrasting and exaggerated interpretations of the Herul conversion through the two statements, an approach he regularly adopts in his passages on Herules and other barbarian peoples. The first reflects an opinion, presumably derived from imperial propaganda, that the Christianization of barbarian settlers would enable their cultural integration and eventual acquisition of a Roman ethnicity. The second reflects a 'classicizing' and conservative viewpoint necessitating the portrayal of barbarians as uncivilized, base peoples.

Whether or not it was successful, the religious element of Justinian's Herul policy may be viewed as an attempt to integrate more closely the barbarian population of the Balkans, on a cultural as well as a political basis. This is understandable if one bears in mind the imperial authorities' loss of control over 'allied' and 'federate' barbarian groups in the area since the fifth century, best illustrated by the Gothic rebellions of the 470s and 480s.[44] Justinian's attempts to ensure the loyalty

---

[40] Procopius, *Wars*, 4.14.12.

[41] Alexander A. Vasiliev, *Justin I: An Introduction to the Epoch of Justinian* (Cambridge, MA, 1950), p. 213, on Theoderic's objection to Justin's treatment of Arian Christians. More generally on Justinian's religious policies, see Arnold H. M. Jones, *The Later Roman Empire, 284–602: A Social, Economic and Administrative Survey* (Oxford, 1964), pp. 542–65; Patrick Gray, 'The Legacy of Chalcedon', in *The Cambridge Companion to the Age of Justinian*, ed. by Michael Maas (Cambridge, 2004), pp. 215–38 (pp. 227–36); and James Allan Stewart Evans, *The Age of Justinian* (London, 1996), pp. 65–77, 183–92, and 240–51.

[42] Procopius, *Wars*, 6.14.33–36, trans. by Dewing, pp. 411 and 413.

[43] Stein, *Histoire*, pp. 305–06; Schmidt, *Geschichte*, p. 554.

[44] See above, note 32, as well as Heather, *Goths and Romans*, pp. 250–60.

of barbarian groups through religious conversion was also demonstrated by his baptism of Grod, king of the Bosporan Huns, in 528.[45]

The more specifically Illyrian context for his attempted conversion of the Herules is provided by his foundation of a new political and ecclesiastical capital of Illyricum in Dacia Mediterranea, near the border with Dardania. Judging by Procopius's description in the *Buildings*, a work which outlines Justinian's fortification and refortification efforts in the Balkans, Justiniana Prima was the jewel in the crown of Justinian's Balkan building plan.[46] Archaeological work at the site of Caričin Grad in modern Serbia, which is generally believed to be Justiniana Prima, has revealed a walled area of approximately eleven hectares that was dominated by ecclesiastical and administrative buildings and complexes.[47] Novel XI, promulgated in April 535, announces the movement of the archbishop from Thessalonica in Macedonia Prima, southern Illyricum, to Justiniana Prima in Dacia Mediterranea, farther to the north.[48] It also makes clear that by this point the Prefect of Illyricum had also moved to the city. The clear aim of this legislation was to project ecclesiastical authority within the Dacian diocese.

Both Malalas and Procopius concur that in addition to a religious angle, Justinian's Herul policy aimed to reinforce the military alliance which Anastasius struck with the Herules. Malalas records that Justinian sent Grepes and his force away with gifts, informing them 'whenever I want you, I will inform you', thereby implying a reiteration and possible augmentation of the military responsibilities of the Herules.[49] According to Procopius, the land which Justinian granted to the

[45] Malalas, *Chronographia*, 18.14.

[46] Procopius of Caesarea, *Buildings*, 4.1.19–27, ed. by J. Haury (London, 1918).

[47] *Caričin Grad I: les basiliques B et J de Caričin Grad, quatre objets remarquables de Caričin Grad, le trésor de Hajdučka Vodenica*, ed. by Noël Duval and Vladislav Popović (Belgrade, 1984); Noël Duval, 'L'Urbanisme de Caričin Grad: une ville artificielle et ses bâtiments d'apparat: une specificité locale ou une étape decisive dans la typologie des principia militaires', *Antiquité Tardive*, 4 (1996), 325–39; *Caričin Grad II: le quartier sud-ouest de la ville haute*, ed. by Bernard Bavant, Vladimir Kondić, and Jean-Michel Spieser (Belgrade, 1990); Bernard Bavant and Vujadin Ivanišević, *Justiniana Prima=Caričin Grad* (Belgrade, 2003); Bernard Bavant, 'Caričin Grad and the Changes in the Nature of Urbanism in the Central Balkans in the Sixth Century', in *The Transition to Late Antiquity on the Danube and Beyond*, ed. by Andrew Poulter (Oxford, 2007), pp. 337–74.

[48] *De privilegiis Archiepiscopi Primae Iustinianae*, in *Corpus Iuris Civilis: Novellae*, ed. and trans. by R. Schoell and G. Kroll (Berlin, 1954), p. 94. Whether or not the archbishop eventually moved to Justiniana Prima and how long he remained there, if at all, have been the subject of much debate. See Bavant, 'Caričin Grad', pp. 361–67, on the official buildings of the site.

[49] John Malalas, *Chronographia*, 18.6, trans. by Jeffreys, Jeffreys, and Scott, p. 247.

Herules consisted of the district around Singidunum on the Middle Danube (modern Belgrade).[50] Historians have surmised that the lands in question were located west of Singidunum and south of the river Sava.[51] This would mean that the Herules acquired additional lands bordering an initial area of settlement around Bassianae in Pannonia Sirmiensis. Procopius states elsewhere that the Herules were thereafter settled in this region as *xymmachoi*, military allies who received tribute from the emperor in return for the periodic provision of manpower for imperial military campaigns.[52] The confused nature of their relationship to the Roman Empire and the different bases on which they served the Roman army will be discussed in the following section. The military responsibilities expected of the Herul allies settled in this zone can be grouped in two categories.

The first of their roles was as a key part of Justinian's Balkan military system. The strategic significance of the Herul location becomes clear from a consideration of Justinian's Balkan fortification plan and military and diplomatic initiatives in the region. Novel XI justifies the creation of a new administrative and religious hub in northern, as opposed to southern, Illyricum. The novel recalls that until the Hun attack of 441, Sirmium, in Pannonia Sirmiensis, had been the Illyrian capital, and points to the recent reassertion of imperial control on both sides of the Middle Danube, at centres including Viminacium, Recidava, and Lederata.[53]

In spite of this rhetoric, the reality was that the new capital was created in neither Pannonia nor the Middle Danubian province of Upper Moesia, but further south, in the 'central-north' Illyrian province of Dacia Mediterranea (Figures 11.1 and 11.2). Together with Naissus, the base of the General of Illyricum, and Serdica, capital of Dacia Mediterranea, Justiniana Prima formed a triangle of cities controlling the routes into inner Illyricum to the south and the Balkan military highway leading to the diocese of Thrace and to Constantinople. That the Herules were settled just north of that triangle suggests that they operated as a buffer against possible barbarian incursions threatening those vital cities at a time of administrative reform in the area.

The literary and archaeological evidence for a Justinianic fortification plan in the Balkans reinforces this impression. Book IV of Procopius's *Buildings* and the

---

[50] Procopius, *Wars*, 7.33.13.

[51] Stein, *Histoire*, p. 305.

[52] Procopius, *Wars*, 6.14.34, refers to their *xymmachikon* with the Romans and 7.33.14 refers to their collection of tribute from Constantinople.

[53] *De privilegiis Archiepiscopi Primae Iustinianae*, p. 94.

archaeological evidence for fortifications demonstrate that the Balkan provinces were defended by a string of fortifications running from Singidunum to the Black Sea. This frontier was divided into two zones by the Carpathian Mountain range, which are dissected by the river Danube forming the Iron Gates gorges. From the Iron Gates gorges to the Danube Delta, the Lower Danube was defended by a large number of fortifications. Andrew Poulter's work at Nicopolis ad Istrum is perhaps the best-documented example of the militarization of the Lower Danube zone in Late Antiquity.[54] Literary evidence confirms that the provinces of Scythia Minor and Lower Moesia accommodated a large number of regular and federate troops and naval garrisons.[55]

[54] Andrew Poulter, 'Town and Country in Moesia Inferior', in *Ancient Bulgaria: Papers Presented to the International Symposium on the Ancient History and Archaeology of Bulgaria, University of Nottingham, 1981*, II (Nottingham, 1983), pp. 74–118; Andrew Poulter, 'The Use and Abuse of Urbanism in the Danubian Provinces During the Later Roman Empire', in *The City in Late Antiquity*, ed. by John Rich (London, 1992), pp. 99–135; Andrew Poulter, *The Roman, Late Roman and Early Byzantine City of Nicopolis ad Istrum: The British Excavations 1985–1992* (London, 1995); Andrew Poulter, *Nicopolis ad Istrum, a Roman to Early Byzantine City: The Pottery and the Glass* (London, 1999); and Andrew Poulter, *Nicopolis ad Istrum, a Late Roman and Early Byzantine City: The Finds and the Biological Remains* (London, 2007). See also *Transition to Late Antiquity on the Danube and Beyond*, ed. by Poulter. For an excellent survey of the archaeological evidence of the entire Danube basis, see John Wilkes, 'The Roman Danube: An Archaeological Survey', *Journal of Roman Studies*, 95 (2005), 124–225. For more archaeological evidence of Roman cities and fortresses in the Lower Danube area, see *Iatrus-Krivina, spätantike Befestigung und frühmittelalterliche Siedlung an der unteren Donau*, ed. by Gerda von Bülow (Berlin, 1995); Vencislav Dinchev, 'The Fortresses of Thrace and Dacia in the Early Byzantine Period', in *Transition to Late Antiquity on the Danube and Beyond*, ed. by Poulter, pp. 479–546; Vencislav Dinchev, 'Household Substructure of the Early Byzantine Fortified Settlements on the Present Bulgarian Territory', *Archaeologia Bulgarica*, 1.1 (1997), 47–63; Vencislav Dinchev, 'The Limits of Urban Area in the Late Antique Dioceses of Thrace and Dacia: The Overestimated Centres', *Archaeologia Bulgarica*, 4.2 (2000), 65–84; and Vencislav Dinchev, 'Zikideva: An Example of Early Byzantine Urbanism in the Balkans', *Archaeologia Bulgarica*, 1.3 (1997), 54–77; Florin Curta, 'Peasants as "Makeshift Soldiers for the Occasion": Sixth-Century Settlement Patterns in the Balkans', in *Urban Centres and Rural Contexts in Late Antiquity*, ed. by Thomas Burns and John Eadie (East Lansing, 2001), pp. 199–217; Peter Guest, 'Coin Circulation in the Balkans in Late Antiquity', in *Transition to Late Antiquity on the Danube and Beyond*, ed. by Poulter, pp. 295–310; Khristo Preshlenov, 'Urban Spaces in Odessus (6th C BC–7th C AD)', *Archaeologia Bulgarica*, 6.3 (2002), 13–43; and Khristo Preshlenov, 'A Late Antique Pattern of Fortification in the Eastern Stara Planina Mountain (the Pass of Djulino)', *Archaeologia Bulgarica*, 5.3 (2001), 33–43; Sergei Torbatov, 'The Roman Road Durostorum–Marcianopolis', *Archaeologia Bulgarica*, 4.1 (2000), 59–72; Andrzej B. Biernacki, 'A City of Christians: Novae in the 5th and 6th C AD', *Archaeologia Bulgarica*, 9.1 (2005), 53–74.

[55] Curta, *Making of the Slavs*, pp. 150–69. On the closed nature of the Lower Danube frontier from the 530s onward, see Florin Curta, 'Frontier Ethnogenesis in Late Antiquity: The Danube,

Novels XLI and L complement this evidence, describing the institution of the *quaestura exercitus*.[56] This new administrative unit was centred on the Lower Danube frontier provinces of Lower Moesia and Scythia Minor, but also included the Mediterranean provinces of Cyprus, Caria, and the Islands. It seems to have been a de facto military prefecture that was intended to make more efficient the provision of supplies to the military forces of the Lower Danube.[57] In addition to its large number of fortifications, military garrisons, and regular receipt of the *annona*, the Lower Danube was exceptionally well defended for geographical reasons. The main stretch of the river as it runs through what was once Lower Moesia is protected by heavily forested northern banks and, as it runs through what was once Scythia Minor towards the delta, by marshlands. Meanwhile, it would have been extremely difficult for barbarians to disembark in many places because of its steep southern banks.

Although also replete with fortifications along the Danube from Singidunum to Aquis, along the valleys and within the upland basins leading southward to Macedonia, the Prefecture of Illyricum was far more vulnerable to attack than the diocese of Thrace.[58] Rather than a linear frontier, it was protected by a more

the Tervingi, and the Slavs', in *Borders, Barriers and Ethnogenesis: Frontiers in Late Antiquity and the Middle Ages*, ed. by Florin Curta (Tunhout, 2005), pp. 173–204. For naval garrisons and troops along the Lower Danube, see Octavian Bounegru and Mihail Zahariade, *Les Forces navales du Bas Danube et de la Mer Noire aux Ier–VIe siècles* (Oxford, 1996). For Gothic, Hunnic, and Bulgar forces in the Lower Danube region, see Malalas, *Chronographia*, 16.16.

[56] *Constitutio ad Bonum Quaestorum exercitus data disponit de appellationibus ex quinque provinciis Caria et Cypro et Cyclasibus insulis et Mysia et Scthyia, apud quem examinandae sint*, in *Corpus Iuris Civilis*, ed. and trans. by Schoell and Kroll, pp. 263–65.

[57] On the *quaestura exercitus*, see Florin Curta, '*Quaestura Exercitus*: The Evidence of Lead Seals', *Acta Byzantina Fennica*, 1 (2002), 9–26; Sergei Torbatov, 'Questura Exercitus: Moesia Secunda and Scythia under Justinian', *Archaeologia Bulgarica*, 1.3 (1997), 78–87; Olga Karagiorgou, 'Lr2: A Container for the Military *Annona* on the Danubian Border?', in *Economy and Exchange in the East Mediterranean during Late Antiquity: Proceedings of a Conference at Somerville College, Oxford, 29th May, 1999*, ed. by Sean Kingsely and Michael Decker (Oxford, 2001), pp. 129–66.

[58] For fortifications in Illyricum, see Wilkes, 'The Roman Danube', pp. 189–92. For Caričin Grad, see above, note 47. For fortifications in the Iron Gates gorges, see Petar Petrović and Miloje Vašić, 'The Roman Frontier in Upper Moesia: Archaeological Investigations in the Iron Gate Area – Main Results', in *Roman Limes on the Middle and Lower Danube*, ed. by Petar Petrović (Belgrade, 1996), pp. 15–26; and Miloje Vašić, 'Le Limes protobyzantin dans la province de Mésie Première', *Starinar*, 45–46 (1994), 41–53. For Singidunum, see the serial publication *Singidunum*, especially Vujadin Ivanišević and Michel Kazanski, 'La Nécropole de l'époque des grandes migrations à Singidunum', in *Singidunum 3*, ed. by Marko Popović (Belgrade, 2002), pp. 101–57; and

permeable, less securely defended frontier 'zone'. Book IV of the *Buildings* confirms that Singidunum represented the limit of the Roman Danubian defences west of the Iron Gates (Figure 11.2).[59] This at least offered protection against possible invasions from the former Roman province of Dacia Inferior to the north. Further to the north, beyond Singidunum, the Danube cuts across the Hungarian plain, while the Sava and Drava rivers, both tributaries of the Danube, flow from the Julian Alps farther to the west. Moreover, the western borders of Upper Moesia and Prevalitana were vulnerable to attack from the regions of Pannonia Sirmiensis and Dalmatia, which lay south of the above-mentioned rivers (Figures 11.1 and 11.2). The Pannonian provinces and the rivers that run through them were controlled by various barbarian groups in the Justinianic period: first by the Gothic kingdom of Theoderic between 525 and 536; and thereafter by the Gepid and Lombard kingdoms. Consequently, those barbarians could potentially circumvent the Danube frontier zone and invade or facilitate invasions of Illyricum. This meant that northern Illyricum represented the Achilles' heel of the Balkan defensive system, a fact that casts further light upon the strategic importance of the Herules, who were settled at Singidunum in the vicinity of one of the main routes from Pannonia to Upper Moesia.

Procopius's narrative on the Gepid-Lombard crisis of the late 540s, to be discussed later in the paper, provides us with an insight into the approximate size of the Herul garrison in Upper Moesia. He records that a total of forty-five hundred Herules participated on both sides in the Herul-Roman military encounter of 549.[60] As will be seen in the next section, the largest Herul forces to fight outside the Balkans were the two thousand who accompanied Narses to Italy in 538 and the three thousand who participated in his invasion of the peninsula, fourteen years later. Therefore, we may assume that between fifteen hundred and two thousand Herules were based in the Balkans, although this number may have been

---

Vujadin Ivanišević, 'Le Début de l'époque des Grandes Migrations dans l'Illyricum du Nord', in *L'Occident romain et l'Europe centrale au début de l'époque des Grandes Migrations*, ed. by Jaroslav Tejral, Christian Pilet, and Michel Kazanski (Brno, 1999), pp. 95–107. See also the studies in *Villes et peuplement dans l'Illyricum protobyzantin: Actes du colloque organisé par l'École Française de Rome (Rome, 12–14 mai 1982)* (Rome, 1984), especially Bernard Bavant, 'La Ville dans le nord de l'Illyricum (Pannonie, Mésie I, Dacie et Dardanie)', pp. 245–88; Gilbert Dagron, 'Les Villes dans l'Illyricum protobyzantin', pp. 1–20; and Vladimir Kondić, 'Les Formes des fortifications protobyzantines dans la région des Portes de Fer', pp. 131–61.

[59] Procopius, *Buildings*, 4.5.12–17.

[60] Procopius, *Wars*, 7.34.42–43.

higher depending upon their overseas commitments. Even though this was not a very large force, it should be borne in mind that it was comparable in size with the Sclavene raiding parties mentioned by Procopius for this period.[61]

Indeed, the one example we have of the military role of the Herules in the Balkans during the reign of Justinian features a Sclavene raiding party.[62] Procopius relates that in 545, the eunuch general Narses was dispatched by Justinian to Illyricum to recruit Herul forces to aid Belisarius's war effort against the Goths in Italy. Having negotiated with the Herul *archontes* and mustered a force, Narses set out for Thrace. However, his journey was immediately interrupted and delayed when a Sclavene incursion took place across the Danube. The Herules engaged the Sclavenes and defeated them, expelling them from the Balkans. Procopius's text does not clarify whether the battle took place in Thrace or Illyricum. Whatever the case, the victory of the Herules over the Sclavenes and the indefinite postponement of their second Italian campaign point to the sort of military function they were accustomed to perform in the vicinity of Singidunum, the limit of the fortification system: defending the Balkans against incursions from Dacia Inferior and Pannonia.

Justinian's military and diplomatic efforts to apply pressure on barbarian groups in Pannonia beyond the Dacian diocese provide a more offensive military context within which we may understand his settlement of the Herules at Singidunum.[63] Although the Gothic kingdom of Italy was still in control of western Illyricum when Justinian came to power, it was facing a political crisis following the death of Theoderic in 526. Justinian seems to have exploited this weakness by adopting an aggressive Illyrian policy to apply pressure on Gothic-held Pannonia Sirmiensis. In addition to the renewed Herul alliance, he forged an alliance with the Gepids who inhabited the former province of Dacia, east of the Middle Danube. Justinian incited and perhaps aided the Gepids in a failed attack on Gothic-held Sirmium in 527, in which many Herules are believed to have participated.[64] Although the

---

[61] Procopius, *Wars*, 7.38.1–3, mentions three thousand Sclavenes crossing the Danube in 550, subsequently splitting into two groups, one of 1800, the other of 1200 warriors.

[62] Procopius, *Wars*, 7.13.21–26.

[63] For more details on Justinian's Illyrian policy, see Wozniak, 'Byzantine Diplomacy' and Sarantis, 'War and Diplomacy'.

[64] See Cassiodorus, *Variae*, 11.1, for a reference to the attack within an address to the Senate of Rome dated to 534. Historians, such as Wolfram, *History*, p. 335, have taken Procopius, *Wars*, 5.11.5 (a passage referring to the Gothic leader Vitiges's earlier service in Illyricum against the Gepids) to refer to the Gothic-Gepid conflict of the late 520s. However, because Procopius states that Vitiges's Illyrian tour took place during the reign of Theoderic, it should rather be associated

evidence for the involvement of the Herules is limited, it is not improbable that they played a part given their proximity to Sirmium.

Another element of Justinian's Illyrian policy was perhaps more crucial. In 529, the Gepid warlord Mundo, an erstwhile servant of the Gothic Kingdom and a key figure in local political and military matters in Upper Moesia and southern Pannonia, was received at Constantinople and appointed *magister militum per Illyricum*.[65] He proceeded to achieve a series of victories over Getic, Bulgar, and Hun forces in the following two years.[66] Given that the Herules were located close to Singidunum in the key border zone of Upper Moesia, it is likely that Mundo drew upon their manpower resources in his campaigns.[67] This is suggested by the fact that when he arrived in Constantinople in 532 (by simple accident, according to Procopius), the forces accompanying him happened to be composed entirely of Herules. Their subsequent role in putting down the Nika riot was one of many key military episodes to involve the Herules, as will be seen in the next section.

The dynamic of Justinian's Pannonian policy changed after his armies defeated the Goths in Dalmatia in 536 and forced their evacuation of western Illyricum. The key battles were fought by the Illyrian field army led first by Mundo and his son Mauricius and then, following their deaths in a series of bloody encounters in 535, by Constantiolus.[68] Since the Herules were in Mundo's service in the early 530s, it is probable that they participated in the Dalmatian campaign. Procopius relates that as soon as the Goths had been finally vanquished in 536, the Gepids took advantage of the absence of the Romans to occupy Sirmium.[69] Their occupation of the former Illyrian capital, which was of strategic importance, meant that they, rather than the Goths, were now Justinian's principal enemy in the region.

---

with the Gothic-Gepid war of 504. On the participation of the Herules and of Mundo in the Gepid attack, see Stein, *Histoire*, pp. 307–08.

[65] On Mundo's appointment and reception in Constantinople, see Malalas, *Chronographia*, 18.46. On Mundo, see Croke, 'Mundo the Gepid', and *The Prosopography of the Later Roman Empire*, III, ed. by John Robert Martindale (Cambridge, 1992), pp. 903–06.

[66] See Malalas, *Chronographia*, 18.46, for the victory over the Huns following arrival to take up post in Illyricum; Marcellinus Comes, *Chronicle*, s.a. 530, on victories over Getae and Bulgars.

[67] See Wozniak, 'Byzantine Diplomacy', p. 144, on the relationship between Mundo and the Herules since the early sixth century.

[68] See Procopius, *Wars*, 5.5.2, 5.7.1–10, 5.7.26–37, on the Roman campaigns in Dalmatia.

[69] Christou, *Byzanz und die Langobarden*, p. 69, argues that the Gepids moved into Sirmium either after the departure of the Romans from Sirmium or after Mundo's death. The idea originated in Diculescu, *Die Gepiden*, pp. 123–25.

Justinian responded to their annexation of Sirmium by putting a stop on the tributary payments they had been accustomed to receive, and by sending the new *magister militum per Illyricum*, Calluc, to attack them in 538.[70] The heavy defeat suffered by Calluc seems to have persuaded Justinian to seek a diplomatic solution. Procopius's text suggests that by the time Gepid and Lombard delegates arrived in Constantinople in 548 to petition Justinian for military support in their dispute, the Gepid-Roman alliance had long since been reinstituted.[71]

Along with the Gepids, Justinian also forged an alliance with the Lombards, another group that moved into the southern Pannonian region subsequent to the Romans' defeat of the Goths in 536. They settled an area bordering the Gepids to the west, encompassing sections of the former Roman provinces of Pannonia Prima, Pannonia Savia, and Noricum Mediterranea.[72] It is often believed that the Roman-Lombard alliance was arranged in 546, because the Lombard historian Paul the Deacon says as much.[73] However, given the late composition of his text, its dating cannot be considered infallible.[74] Paul could be referring to any of the numerous Lombard migrations that took place within the Pannonian region in the early sixth century. Further, Procopius provides evidence that the Roman-Lombard alliance had been arranged by AD 539. He records that in this year the Gothic leader Vitiges sounded out his Lombard counterpart Vaces regarding a possible alliance between their peoples, only to be rejected on the grounds that he had an existing

---

[70] Marcellinus Comes, *Chronicle*, s.a. 538, trans. by Croke.

[71] Procopius, *Wars*, 7.34.18–19 and 31–32.

[72] This is my conclusion, based on Procopius's assertion that they were settled 'not far from the Gepids' and in 'the city of Noricum and fortresses of Pannonia' (Procopius, *Wars*, 7.33.10). Given that no city of Noricum is known in the area, it seems likely that he was confused and is actually referring to the former Roman province. For a more elaborate argument, see Sarantis, *The Balkans*, and 'War and Diplomacy'. For various arguments on the location of Lombards and the nature of their settlement, see Christou, *Byzanz und die Langobarden*, pp. 79–80; Pohl, 'Die Langobarden', p. 29; and Neil Christie, 'The Survival of Roman Settlement Along the Middle Danube: Pannonia from the 4th to the 10th Century A.D.', *Oxford Journal of Archaeology*, 11 (1992), 317–39.

[73] Paul the Deacon, *History of the Lombards*, 2.22–23. The date of 546 has been advanced by Diculescu, *Die Gepiden*, p. 134; Stein, *Histoire*, p. 528; Christie, *The Lombards*, p. 35; and Schmidt, *Geschichte*, p. 580. A date between 545 and 546 is advocated by Wozniak, 'Byzantine Diplomacy', p. 148. For a date between 547 and 548, see Joachim Werner, *Die Langobarden in Pannonien: Beiträge zur Kenntnis der langobardischen Bodenfunde vor 568* (Munich, 1962), p. 140. See also Pohl, 'The Empire and the Lombards', p. 89, who proposes a date at any point after 543.

[74] On Paul the Deacon, see Walter Pohl, 'Paulus Diaconus und die *Historia Langobardum*: Text und Tradition', in *Historiographie im frühen Mittelalter*, ed. by A. Scharer and A. Scheibelreiter (Vienna, 1994), pp. 375–405.

agreement with the Romans.[75] Given that in 536 the Goths were defeated and the remnants of the bloodied Roman field army located on the Dalmatian coast, it would be remarkable had the Lombards waited another decade before moving into southern Pannonia. It seems much more likely that they took advantage of the political vacuum as did the Gepids in the years following 536. Indeed, had the Lombards not migrated at this time there would have been no one standing in the way of the Gepids occupying most of the former Pannonian diocese.

Therefore, although he had failed to recapture southern Pannonia, Justinian had ensured that it became an extended buffer zone formed by a 'three-tiered client state system' (Figure 11.3).[76] According to Procopius, the Gepid and Lombard kingdoms in southern Pannonia were *xymmachoi*, independent but allied states who received tribute from Constantinople in return for their loyalty and, in later years, irregular provision of military forces for individual campaigns. The status of the third group in this system, the Herules, is not as easy to define. They were also called *xymmachoi* by Procopius, received tribute from the emperor, and had their own leaders.[77] However, they were settled within the Roman provinces and, as has been demonstrated above, were subject to imperial attempts at cultural integration. The next section will explore further their ambiguous political status.

The Role of the Herules as a Manpower Resource for Wars Fought Throughout the Empire in the Justinianic Period

A significant proportion of the troops Justinian deployed throughout the empire, in wars with Persia in the East and in the wars of reconquest in Gothic Italy and Vandal Africa, were recruited from the Balkan Peninsula.[78] The archaeological evidence for the Balkans in this period confirms that this was a heavily militarized landscape that could well have accommodated large numbers of military forces, albeit in

---

[75] Procopius, *Wars*, 6.22.10–12.

[76] Through this client management, Justinian was projecting imperial influence beyond the actual frontiers of the empire in the same way as his fourth-century predecessors, prior to the era of the Great Migrations. See Peter Heather, 'The Late Roman Art of Client Management: Imperial Defence in the Fourth-Century West', in *The Transformation of Frontiers from Late Antiquity to the Carolingians*, ed. by Walter Pohl, Ian Wood, and Helmut Reimitz (Leiden, 2001), pp. 15–68.

[77] Procopius, *Wars*, 6.14.33–35.

[78] For example, Procopius states that the troops comprising Belisarius's army on the Vandalic campaign were 'almost all inhabitants from the land of Thrace' (Procopius, *Wars*, 3.11.10).

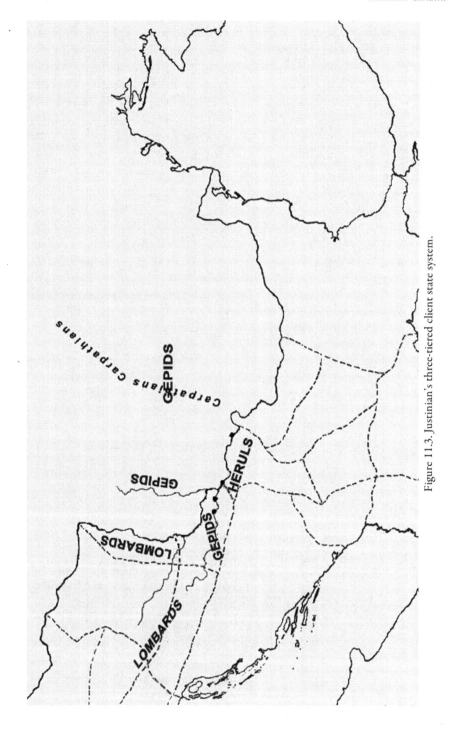

Figure 11.3. Justinian's three-tiered client state system.

dispersed locations.[79] That one of the Praesental forces and two of the field armies — those of Thrace and Illyricum — resided in the Balkans confirms that it accommodated the heaviest concentration of field troops in the East Roman Empire.[80]

In addition to provincial 'Roman' (Thracian and Illyrian) forces, Justinian could draw upon the services of the many barbarian groups settled in and in the vicinity of the Balkan provinces, as either allied or federate groups. The policy of absorbing barbarian groups and employing them in the Roman army had long been an important part of imperial policy in the Balkans, especially since the era of the Great Migrations in the late fourth and fifth centuries.[81] Indeed, the occupation of many frontier regions by elements of Attila's confederation in the 440s and 450s and the periodic settlement of the Ostrogoths in the 470s are prime examples of the developments that had led to the ethnic transformation of the frontier Balkan regions. The distinction between barbarian and Roman in such areas was not at all clear-cut.[82] Second-generation barbarians from such areas, like the children of Bessas, whom Procopius describes as a Roman general and a Goth, were most likely referred to as Illyrians or Thracians.[83]

As has already been explained, northern Illyricum had only recently been reabsorbed into the imperial realm by the early Justinianic era. By reinforcing the Herul alliance, Justinian was not only ensuring the support of a loyal group of barbarians in the defence of the Illyrian provinces, but was also acquiring an additional manpower resource for wars fought in other parts of the empire. By piecing together

[79] See notes 54, 55, and 58 above.

[80] Jones, *Later Roman Empire*, pp. 679–86; John Haldon, *Warfare, State, and Society in the Byzantine World, 565–1204* (London, 1999), pp. 67–72; Warren Treadgold, *Byzantium and its Army, 284–1081* (Stanford, 1995), pp. 43–86; Michael Whitby, 'The Army, c. 420–602', in *The Cambridge Ancient History*, XIV, ed. by Averil Cameron, Bryan Ward-Perkins, and Michael Whitby (Cambridge, 2000), pp. 289–313 (p. 292).

[81] On the blurring of Roman-barbarian distinctions due to the service of barbarians in the Roman army from the fifth century, see Geoffrey Greatrex, 'Roman Identity in the Sixth Century', in *Ethnicity and Culture in Late Antiquity*, ed. by Stephen Mitchell and Geoffrey Greatrex (London, 2000), pp. 267–92. On the increasing number of barbarians in Justinianic armies, perhaps as a result of the plague, see John Teall, 'The Barbarians in Justinian's Armies', *Speculum*, 40 (1965), 294–322.

[82] For a number of articles on the subjective and fluid nature of ethnic identities in this period, see *Strategies of Distinction*, ed. by Pohl and Reimitz; Patrick Geary, 'Ethnic Identity as a Situational Construct in the Early Middle Ages', *Mitteilungen der anthropologischen Gesellschaft in Wien*, 113 (1983), 15–26; and Amory, *People and Identity*.

[83] Procopius, *Wars*, 5.5.3 (from the lands of Thrace) and 5.16.2 (a Goth by birth).

the various fragments of literary evidence that refer to the Herules, mainly in Procopius's *Wars* and Agathias's *Histories*, it becomes clear that they occupied an important position in the Roman army and took part in all of the major theatres of war and in a large number of the major battles fought within them during the reign of Justinian. Before analysing in greater detail what those passages tell us about the nature of the Herules' deployment, it will first be important to recount briefly the numerous episodes they describe.[84]

In 530, a Herul force led by a man named Pharas occupied the left wing of the Roman army in the battle of Dara against the Persians.[85] In 532, the *magister militum per Illyricum* Mundo led a group of Herules to Constantinople where, along with a force led by Belisarius, he suppressed the Nika rioters in the Hippodrome.[86] The Herules next pop up in the *Vandalic Wars*, where Pharas once again accompanied Belisarius, this time with a force of four hundred men.[87] Having participated in Belisarius's conquest of Vandal Africa in 532–33, Pharas was appointed to keep guard of the Vandal king, Gelimer, who had sought refuge on Mount Papua.[88] According to Procopius, Pharas acted as the diplomatic link between Gelimer and Belisarius and, having made an unsuccessful attempt at storming the mountain, was instrumental in persuading Gelimer to surrender.

Although some of the Herules were left behind in Africa, where they participated in the mutiny of Stotzas in 536, others accompanied Belisarius to Italy in 535.[89] They feature in Procopius's account of the siege of Rome in 537–38, taking part in a sortie led by a general named Gontharis to seize the town of Albani from the Goths.[90] A different group of Herules numbering two thousand then arrived in Italy as part of General Narses's force of five thousand men in early 538.[91] They were

---

[84] Schmidt, *Geschichte*, pp. 556–57, runs through examples of the Herules serving abroad, but more briefly.

[85] Procopius, *Wars*, 1.14.33 and 39.

[86] Procopius, *Wars*, 1.24.41. For the Nika riot, see John Bagnell Bury, 'The Nika Riot', *Journal of Hellenic Studies*, 17 (1897), 92–119; Geoffrey Greatrex, 'The Nika Riot: A Reappraisal', *Journal of Hellenic Studies*, 117 (1997), 60–86 (pp. 79–80) argues that Procopius probably underplayed the role of Mundo and the Herules in suppressing the riot in order to emphasize Belisarius's contribution.

[87] Procopius, *Wars*, 3.11.11.

[88] Procopius, *Wars*, 4.6.1, 3, 15–30, and 31–34; 4.7.6–9.

[89] Procopius, *Wars*, 4.17.14–15.

[90] Procopius, *Wars*, 6.4.8.

[91] Procopius, *Wars*, 6.13.18.

commanded by Phanitheus, Visandus, and Aluith. The first of these leaders perished in an attack on Caesena later that year. Following the recall of Narses in 539, the Herules refused to serve Belisarius and instead set out first for Liguria and then for Venetia.[92] While Philemuth, Phanitheus's replacement, and Aluith set sail for Constantinople, Visandus remained in Venetia. In c. 540, Visandus and his Herul followers fought in the army of Vitalius that was defeated at Tarbesium by the forces of the Gothic leader Ildibad. Visandus and a number of his men lost their lives.[93]

Herules are next encountered in Procopius's narrative on the Persian wars of the early 540s. In c. 542, they took part in Belisarius's incursion into Mesopotamia, and in 543 they participated in the disastrous invasion of Persarmenia and defeat at the hands of the Persians in the battle at Anglon.[94] On the latter occasion, one group of Herules was commanded by Philemuth and Beros, while another served the Roman general Narses.

In c. 545, Narses recruited a force of Herules from Singidunum, led by Philemuth, among others, whom Justinian intended to send to Italy to aid Belisarius's campaign. This force defeated a Sclavene raiding party on its journey to Thrace with Narses, as discussed above. Although part of this force, including the General Philemuth, did not reach Italy until 552, another part, numbering three hundred, was sent to Italy in c. 547–48, under Beros.[95] This force was annihilated by Totila in the vicinity of Brindusium, shortly after it put in at Dryus. Although Beros survived, two hundred of his men were killed. It seems likely that another Herul force was already serving the Roman army in Italy, for Procopius relates that earlier in 547, the Herul leader Arufus had escaped to the hills at Lucania along with John, the nephew of Vitalian, following an attack by Totila's forces.[96]

Meanwhile, in c. 549, Philemuth and a force of fifteen hundred Herules participated in the Roman campaign against the Gepids, which will be discussed further in the next section.[97] Suartas, the Herul *magister militum praesentalis*, also led a force of Herules against the Gepids in 552.[98] Along with other Roman

---

[92] Procopius, *Wars*, 6.22.4–5 and 6–8.

[93] Procopius, *Wars*, 7.1.34–36.

[94] Procopius, *Wars*, 2.21.4 and 24.12, 14, and 18 on the Persarmenian campaign, and 2.24.10–35 on the battle of Anglon.

[95] Procopius, *Wars*, 7.27.3.

[96] Procopius, *Wars*, 7.26.23.

[97] Procopius, *Wars*, 7.34.42.

[98] Procopius, *Wars*, 8.25.11.

generals, he did not reach Gepid territory, but was forced to remain in Illyricum to suppress civil unrest at Ulpiana in Dardania.

Various groups of Herules featured in the Italian and Lazican campaigns of the 550s. Three thousand Herules led by Philemuth and another large Herul force led by Aruth participated in Narses's invasion of Gothic Italy in 552.[99] During the campaign, Herules killed and beheaded the Gothic leader, Usdrilas, at Ariminum, and lined up alongside the Lombards in the middle phalanx of the Roman army in the battle of Busta Gallorum.[100] Later on, Philemuth and his troops played important parts in the siege of Rome and, with John, the nephew of Vitalian, participated in the scouting expedition to Tuscany to ascertain the location of the Gothic leader Teias.[101] Agathias records that Philemuth died at some point in 553 and was replaced by Fulcaris.[102] In the same year, Fulcaris was placed in charge of a failed attack on the Franks at Parma where he was killed in the fighting.[103] His replacement, Sindual, led the Herules at the battle of the Volturnus River in which the Roman forces defeated the Franks of Butilinus in 554.[104] Sindual next appears in Italy in the mid-560s when, as the king of the Britti, he led a rebellion in the north of the peninsula. He was eventually defeated and killed by Narses.[105]

Meanwhile, in Lazica, the Herul general Uligagus was part of the force which put down the Abasgian rebels and captured the fort of Trachea in 550.[106] In 551, he was joint commander with Benilus of the largest Roman force in Lazica, the nine thousand men who retreated across the River Phasis, fleeing the Persian army of Mermeroes.[107] Agathias records that he was still in Lazica in 555, referring to him as the leader of the Herul contingent.[108] He mentions that another Herul leader, Gibrus, participated in the battle of the river Phasis in 556, in which the Romans repelled the Persian general Nachoragan.[109]

---

[99] Procopius, *Wars*, 8.26.13 and 17.

[100] Procopius, *Wars*, 8.28.10 and 8.31.5.

[101] Procopius, *Wars*, 8.34.22–24.

[102] Agathias, *Histories*, 1.11.3, ed. by R. Keydell (Berlin, 1967).

[103] Agathias, *Histories*, 1.14.4–15.5.

[104] Agathias, *Histories*, 2.7.2–10.9.

[105] Paul the Deacon, *History of the Lombards*, 3.1.

[106] Procopius, *Wars*, 8.9.5.

[107] Procopius, *Wars*, 8.13.9.

[108] Agathias, *Histories*, 3.6.5.

[109] Agathias, *Histories*, 3.20.10.

The episodes just described provide a number of clues regarding the military characteristics and the nature of Herul deployment in the imperial army. First of all, the regularity with which the Herules were called upon to serve in the Justinianic armies and the responsibility regularly given to their leaders points to their military prowess and flexibility. They took part in numerous campaigns, in a variety of geographical settings, and against a variety of opponents. The literary accounts of these events frequently praise the military ability of the Herules and extol the qualities of their leaders. For instance, Procopius refers to their 'wonderous display of valorous deeds' at the battle of Dara in 530 and later praises the 'orderly conduct', 'seriousness', and 'energetic nature' of Pharas and the Herules who besieged the Vandal king Gelimer on Mount Papua.[110] Similarly, Agathias praises Fulcaris's valour, skill, and many victories, and singles out the gallantry of Sindual and the Herules when celebrating the Romans' victory over the Franks at the battle of the Volturnus.[111] Such qualities seem to have enabled the Herules to contribute directly to a number of military successes. Pharas's brave charge into the Persians' right flank from the hillside at Dara in 530, Sindual's late arrival at the battle of the river Volturnus in 554, and the entry of Mundo's Herules into the Hippodrome through the Gate of Death in 532 — all contributed to major Roman military victories. Herules also took part in the conquest of Vandal Africa, the capture of Rome in 538, and the battles of Busta Gallorum in 552 and the river Phasis in 556.

Nevertheless, the literary texts also make clear that on certain occasions, the Herules suffered greatly in military defeats. Outstanding examples include the death of Visandus and his forces at the hands of Ildibad in Venetia in 540, the heavy losses the Herules suffered while serving Narses at the battle on Anglon in Persarmenia in 543, the defeat of Beros by Totila in 548, and the deaths of Fulcaris and his forces at the hands of the Franks at Parma in 553. The common explanation of these defeats is the propensity of the Herules to carry out fatally rash manoeuvres. Procopius stresses that Beros was a reckless drunkard whose spirit of daring resulted in the annihilation of his force by Totila after he took the foolish decision to leave the main Roman army led by John, the nephew of Vitalian.[112] Similarly, although Agathias highlights Fulcaris's bravery, he claims that he was let down by his wild character and impetuosity. Agathias blamed the defeat of the Herules at Parma almost entirely on Fulcaris's irrational decision to lead the charge

---

[110] Procopius, *Wars*, 1.14.39 and 4.4.28–31.

[111] Agathias, *Histories*, 1.14.3 and 2.7.2–10.9.

[112] Procopius, *Wars*, 7.27.3–11.

and then to turn down any opportunity of escape in order to die valiantly alongside his men.[113]

The cursory nature of the literary evidence for the Herules means that only general conclusions can be drawn regarding their military characteristics. The literary sources for the reign of Justinian corroborate those from the previous period in their suggestion that the Herules fought lightly armed.[114] The best example is found in Procopius's description of the Persarmenian campaign, in which he states that the Herules were not protected by armour, helmets, or corselets. Instead they apparently wore only a thick jacket and although most carried a shield, some went without.[115] The lightness of their arms seems to have contributed to their greatest assets, namely mobility and the ability to execute swift ambushes. At Dara, the Herules sought cover on higher ground before launching a sudden attack on the Persian right flank; near Brindisi they sought refuge in woodland when confronted by Totila; and at the river Volturnus they did not line up in the main phalanx, but arrived late in a sudden attack. Their lack of heavy armour was presumably compensated for by their impressive physique, which is suggested by Procopius in his discussion on Belisarius's Persian campaign of 542. He relates that Belisarius exaggerated the number of troops at his disposal before a Persian envoy by picking six thousand men of especially fine physique and stature to line a pavilion that he had erected especially for the occasion.[116] In addition to Vandals, Moors, Thracians, and Illyrians, those fine specimens included the Herules.

It should be noted that Herul cavalry troops are mentioned as well as infantry troops.[117] Philemuth's three thousand Herules who participated in Narses's invasion of Italy in 552 were cavalry troops. Procopius informs us that they had to dismount when forming part of the central phalanx of the Roman army at the battle of Busta Gallorum. Philemuth's fifteen hundred men who took part in the Gepid

---

[113] Agathias, *Histories*, 1.14.3–6.

[114] For instance, Jordanes, *Getica*, 50.261, refers to them as 'light-armed warriors'.

[115] Procopius, *Wars*, 2.25.27–28.

[116] Procopius, *Wars*, 2.21.4.

[117] Wolfram, *History*, p. 304, argues that Herules fought in all armies 'as light-armed troops'; Ellegård, 'Who Were the Eruli?', p. 28, argues that the Herules fought as infantry in the fourth and as cavalry in the sixth century. It is likely that neither is entirely correct and that the Herules consisted of both cavalry and infantry forces during all that time. See Walter Pohl, 'Telling the Difference: Signs of Ethnic Identity', in *Strategies of Distinction*, ed. by Pohl and Reimitz, pp. 17–70 (pp. 37–40), on the sources' stereotypical descriptions of the military characteristics of barbarian peoples and the likely reality that they were all similarly flexible.

campaign of 549 were part of a force that also included ten thousand Roman cavalrymen. Therefore, it seems likely that they too were mounted.

When assessing Procopius's treatment of the Herules, historians have tended to highlight his critical description of their anarchic and treacherous nature, as well as of their tendency to drunkenness and incest.[118] However, the above descriptions of the Herules in military service provide a more favourable impression.[119] It might be argued that Procopius's and Agathias's accounts of the Herules as lightly armed, valorous, and rash are stereotypical descriptions of barbarian groups.[120] Nonetheless, we cannot doubt that the Herules fought in and won or lost the battles described, given the precise prosopographical and numerical information supplied and the likelihood that Procopius at least was drawing on firsthand accounts. In fact, Procopius and Agathias employed barbarian stereotypes because of the genre within which they wrote. It might be argued that when they want to refer to Herul successes, they naturally employ the 'valorous barbarian' topos. Similarly, when discussing defeats, they employ the 'rash and irrational barbarian' topos. After all, most military victories are achieved in part as the result of brave deeds, and lost in part as the result of ill-advised tactical decisions. Generally speaking, the sources seem to illustrate the contemporary perception of the Herules as highly competent military troops who served in the majority of the Justinianic military campaigns and were for the most part extremely loyal to the Roman cause. Although Procopius asserts that loyal Herules, such as Pharas, were exceptions to the rule, he refers to such exceptions as frequently as he mentions Herules who conformed to type and launched rebellions. An underlying reason for the disparity between his rhetoric and the events he describes could be the ambivalent position of the Herules within the Roman army.

The bases on which the Herules were recruited to fight in campaigns around the empire seem to have varied, judging by the brief glimpses provided by the sources concerning their military service. On the one hand, in some campaigns they

[118] Stein, *Histoire*, p. 529, refers to their 'esprit inconstant'; Wolfram, *Roman Empire*, p. 69, states that the dominion of the Herul king 'was as venerable as it was chaotic and ridiculous in the eyes of the Romans'; Ellegård, 'Who Were the Eruli?', p. 9: 'Summing up, Procopius takes a rather dim view of these Illyrian Eruli'; Brandt, 'Herules', section 2.3, claims that Procopius was politically motivated to portray the Herules as drunkards and treacherous by his disappointment at their refusal to serve General Belisarius in 539.

[119] Schmidt, *Geschichte*, p. 564, admits that beneath the savage criticism, Procopius actually demonstrates the good qualities of the Herules.

[120] Gerhart Ladner, 'On Roman Attitudes toward Barbarians in Late Antiquity', *Viator*, 7 (1976), 1–26; Jonathan Hall, *Ethnic Identity in Greek Antiquity* (Cambridge, 1997).

fought under their own leaders, in units separate from the main Roman forces. Examples include the Herul force of Philemuth and Beros in the East in the campaign of 543. This force arrived in the vicinity of Citharizon after the force of Martinus, the *magister militum per Orientem*, and set up camp near to but away from the main army.[121] Similarly, Sindual's force seems to have operated independently from the rest of the Roman army prior to the battle of the Volturno River in 554. Following Narses's execution of a Herul who had murdered his servant, Sindual chose not to line up with the Roman force for battle against the Franks and only arrived after the Franks had made an inroad into the Roman front line.[122] The best example of a Herul force acting independently was that of the two thousand men who refused to serve Belisarius in Italy in 539.

Conversely, on other occasions, we hear of Herul contingents fighting under Roman generals, with no mention of Herul leaders. Examples include the Herules who served under the Armenian General Narses in Persarmenia in 543. Procopius also fails to mention a Herul leader in charge of Belisarius's Herul forces in Italy in the 530s or in the East in the early 540s. The Herules at Constantinople in 532 also seemed to have been directly commanded by the *magister militum per Illyricum* Mundo.

We also hear of Herules fighting under their own leaders, but within the armies of Roman generals of higher status. The Herules recruited by Narses apparently served their own leaders within his force: Philemuth, Aluith, Visandus, and Phanitheus in the late 530s, and Philemuth, then Fulcaris, and finally Sindual in the early 550s. Interestingly, Agathias claims that following the deaths of first Philemuth, and then Fulcaris, it was Narses who cast the deciding vote in the ensuing Herul leadership contests. This highlights the political and military authority that Narses had over his Herul forces.

Certain groups of Herules were loyal to particular Roman generals. Narses twice recruited Herules from the Balkans and, according to Procopius, they were extremely well disposed to the eunuch general, 'having been especially well treated by him'.[123] This is also apparent from their refusal to serve Belisarius in 539. At the same time, the Herules of Pharas seem to have followed the latter general from the East to Africa, while another group regularly operated under Mundo in the early 530s. Roman generals presumably rewarded the loyalty of the Herules with their patronage.

---

[121] Procopius, *Wars*, 2.24.12–14.

[122] Agathias, *Histories*, 2.7.2–7.

[123] Procopius, *Wars*, 8.26.17, trans. by H. B. Dewing (London, 1928), p. 333.

This would presumably explain how some Herul leaders rose sufficiently high in the Roman army to attain the position of general. Philemuth, Fulcaris, and Sindual all attained the title of *magister militum vacans* whilst serving Narses in Italy from 552, as did Beros in the late 540s. Suartas held the title of *magister militum praesentalis* from 548 to 552.[124] Whether those were honorary titles bestowed upon men who continued to command only their own Herul contingents or represented the high commands of Roman forces is not always clear. Uligagus is referred to variously as one of the commanders of the Roman army and as the leader of the Herul force in Procopius's and Agathias's narratives on the Lazican war after 548.[125] The high position and regular service of leaders such as Philemuth, Beros, and Suartas suggests the emergence of a Herul military aristocracy that had exploited and built upon patronage networks in time-honoured fashion. In some cases, it is clear that they were based in Constantinople.

Suartas, for example, resided in Constantinople for a number of years prior to the mid-540s.[126] Meanwhile, Aruth had 'from boyhood admired Roman ways' and married the grand-daughter of Mundo the Gepid.[127] How many other Herul forces actually resided in or around Constantinople is uncertain. While Herules were recruited by Narses from Singidunum in 545, those who departed from Italy in 539 set out for Constantinople. This was presumably either to receive further orders or because they were stationed there on a more permanent basis. Similarly, while the three hundred men commanded by Beros reached Italy in 548, it is unclear what happened to the remainder of the force recruited by Narses from northern Illyricum in 545, including the fifteen hundred men commanded by Philemuth. This force was apparently destined to winter in Thrace, but next shows up as part of the army Justinian sent against the Gepids in 549. Once again, we cannot say for certain whether this force spent the intervening years in Thrace or returned to the Herul lands in the vicinity of Singidunum.

This confusion regarding the status of the Herules can be understood in the context of the blurred distinctions between allied, federate, and regular Roman forces in the sixth century.[128] In the fourth century, federate troops had been forces

---

[124] *Prosopography of the Later Roman Empire*, III, ed. by Martindale, pp. 1154–55 (on Sindual), p. 1205 (on Suartas), pp. 1370–71 (on Beros), and pp. 1020–21 (on Philemuth).

[125] *Prosopography of the Later Roman Empire*, III, ed. by Martindale, pp. 1389–90.

[126] Procopius, *Wars*, 6.15.32.

[127] Procopius, *Wars*, 8.26.13.

[128] For the differences between allied and federate troops and the changing nature of the term *foederati*, see Hugh Elton, *Warfare in Roman Europe AD 350–425* (Oxford, 1996), pp. 91–96 and

provided by allies of the empire that were independent political entities without, or semi-independent groups within, its frontiers. They were typically recruited for individual campaigns and served their own military leaders, albeit within larger Roman armies. By the sixth century, the old type of federates were generally referred to as *xymmachoi*. As has already been stated, Procopius used this label to refer to the Herules, as well as to Gepids and Lombards.

However, on other occasions, he also refers to the Herules as *foederati* of the Roman army.[129] By the sixth century, *foederati* had become a regular part of the Roman armed forces. They were settled within the empire, received a regular salary, the *annona foederatum*, and could be called upon whenever the imperial government so decreed. Whilst on campaign, they would serve Roman generals on the same footing as Roman troops, albeit in separate divisions. In other words, they were not much different from Roman provincial frontier forces. Procopius refers to this blurring of the distinction between *foederati* and *stratiotai* in book III of the *Wars*: 'at the present time there is nothing to prevent anyone from assuming this name, since time will by no means consent to keep names attached to the things to which they were formerly applied'.[130] Indeed, when he reels off the forces at Belisarius's disposal during his eastern campaign of the early 540s, Procopius casually lists Herules, Vandals, and Moors along with Thracians and Illyrians. From the perspective that they originated in the Balkan provinces and rose to high military commands, the stories of Herules such as Suartas and Philemuth are little different from those of 'Romans' such as Marcellinus Comes, Emperor Justin, or Belisarius.

That the Herules served the Roman army as both *xymmachoi* and *foederati* can be explained by their ambiguous political and cultural relationship with the empire, discussed above. They were settled within the empire and could be summoned to Constantinople whenever required. On the other hand, they were politically independent to the extent that they had their own kings. Similarly, one group was

---

128; Evangelos Chrysos, 'Legal Concepts and Patterns for the Barbarians' Settlement on Roman Soil', in *Das Reich und die Barbaren*, ed. by Evangelos Chrysos and Andreas Schwarcz (Vienna, 1989), pp. 13–24 (p. 17); Evangelos Chrysos, 'Conclusion: *de foederatis iterum*', in *Kingdoms of the Empire*, ed. by Pohl, pp. 185–206 (pp. 192–200); Peter Heather, '*Foedera* and *feoderati* of the Fourth Century', in *Kingdoms of the Empire*, ed. by Pohl, pp. 57–74; Pohl, 'The Empire and the Lombards', pp. 78–87, on the various terms deployed by the literary sources to describe barbarian treaties and settlements with the empire. Interestingly, Procopius does not call the Herules *enspondoi*, the term he habitually uses for groups settled within Roman territory.

[129] Procopius, *Wars*, 3.11.3–4, on the status of soldiers on the Vandal expedition.

[130] Procopius, *Wars*, 3.11.3–4, trans. by Dewing, p. 103.

officially converted to Orthodox Christianity in the late 520s, although another was sufficiently proud to be Arian Christians that they joined Stotzas's rebellion in Africa in 536. When on military campaigns they either directly served Roman leaders as *foederati*, or served under their own leaders as *xymmachoi*. The consequences of this change of their status came to a head in the Herul rebellion and civil war of the mid-540s. It is to this episode that we now have to turn.

The Herul Rebellion of 545–48

Thus far, this chapter has looked mainly at the roles of the Herules in the Justinianic Empire from the perspective of 'what they did for the Romans' and why it was in the Romans' interests for them to carry out those functions. This is understandable given that our literary sources were all written by Romans. However, arguably the major episode to involve the Herules related by Procopius casts some light on how the Herules viewed and reacted to their position within the Roman Empire and Justinian's policies towards them.

According to Procopius, the Herul rebellion and civil war occurred 'not long before' the Gepid-Lombard dispute, which broke out in 548.[131] There is no suggestion that the Herules were in turmoil when Narses travelled to recruit his Herul force in 545, so we may assume that the events described by Procopius took place in the intervening years. He records that having murdered their king, Ochus, the Herules repented and sent to Thule for a replacement. On their second attempt, the Herul envoys succeeded in bringing back Datius, one of the Herul royal line, along with his brother Aordus and two hundred young Herules. Meanwhile, while the envoys were absent, the Herules near Singidunum changed their minds and requested that Justinian choose a successor to Ochus. He proceeded to send them Suartas, the Herul who had long resided in Constantinople. The Herules initially accepted Suartas as their king. When news reached him of the imminent return of the envoys to Thule, Datius, Aordus, and their followers, Suartas ordered his subjects to kill them. However, when they were one day from confronting the party from Thule, Suartas's men abandoned him and defected to Datius. When Justinian responded angrily by promising to use military force in order to reinstate Suartas, the majority of the Herules went over to the Gepids.

---

[131] Procopius, *Wars*, 7.34.43, on the chronological reference, and 6.15.27–36, on the Herul leadership dispute.

In the Roman campaign against the Gepids in 549, fifteen hundred Herules under Philemuth lined up with the Romans, while three thousand arrayed themselves alongside the Gepids.[132] Procopius relates that a detachment of the Roman army, who were on their way to join the Lombards, unexpectedly came across the Gepids' Herul allies and engaged them in a bloody battle.[133] The Romans were victorious and killed Aordus and many of the Herul rebels.

Procopius generally asserts that the murder of King Ochus was caused by the Herules' traditional lack of deference towards their rulers, and the decision to seek a replacement from Thule by their sudden realization that they did not wish to remain without a king. Subsequently, Procopius rationalizes their decision to demand a leader from Justinian as the consequence of an ad hoc realization that the Emperor's approval should be sought. Those inconsistent and imprecise explanations portray the Herules as typically illogical, anarchic barbarians. Too often modern historians have taken those vague explanations of the Herul rebellion at face value and placed the blame on the anarchic tendencies of the Herules.[134] Ellegård even goes so far as to speculate that the deposition of Ochus resulted from a drunken orgy that was repented once the effects of the alcohol had subsided.[135] However, Procopius's vague and anecdotal account owes much to his antibarbarian rhetoric and to the prejudices of his sources, perhaps 'loyalist' Herules encountered at Constantinople. His superficial statements mask the likely reality that the Herules were politically divided regarding the leadership issue and more broadly their relationship vis-à-vis the Roman Empire. It is probable that one group of *archontes*, responsible for the murder of Ochus, desired a king descended from traditional ruling elites and took the decision to send an embassy to Thule. This group presumably objected to Suartas, a Roman puppet, and defected with Datius and Aordus to the Gepids. Meanwhile, the faction of Herul leaders that remained loyal to the empire must have been responsible for requesting a leader from Justinian and were in favour of Suartas.

The decision of the majority of the Herules to cast off Roman control and throw in their lot with the Gepids, a group that was more independent and based in Pannonia, beyond the frontiers of the empire, can be attributed to their interactions with the Roman Empire during the reign of Justinian. We have already seen that Justinian sought to foster closer political, cultural, and military ties with the

---

[132] Procopius, *Wars*, 7.34.42–43.

[133] Procopius, *Wars*, 7.34.44–47.

[134] Stein, *Histoire*, p. 529; Schmidt, *Geschichte*, pp. 554–55.

[135] Ellegård, 'Who Were the Eruli?', p. 10.

Herules following his accession in 527. He clearly intended puppet leaders such as Grepes, Ochus, and Suartas to be agents through whom he might culturally assimilate the Herules and make them amenable to Roman control. However, a few isolated incidents cast light on the potentially negative Herul reaction to these policies. The participation of the Herules in the African mutiny of 536 is a particularly interesting example. According to Procopius, the rebellion had two causes: Justinian's harsh treatment of Arian Christians, and his decision to reclaim the Vandal lands as government 'property of the crown' from the Roman soldiers who had taken possession of them in the aftermath of the Roman victory.[136] Arian soldiers in the Roman army in Africa, including the Herules, were forbidden from receiving the sacraments. Arian Vandal priests were, therefore, able to incite them to rebellion. It seems likely, therefore, that a number of Herules at Singidunum would not have been pleased by Grepes's and perhaps Ochus's baptism in Constantinople.

The economic element of the mutiny in Africa is also relevant. The Herules participated in the mutiny partly because the central government wanted to acquire their spoils of war. They were presumably similarly limited in the Balkans regarding which economic assets — land or money — they were allowed to take or acquire, in contrast to the Gepids, who raided the empire from without and took what they wanted. Procopius vaguely states that the Herules at Singidunum 'overran and plundered the lands of the Illyrians and Thracians'.[137] Although this is clearly an exaggeration, it would not be surprising had the Herules at Singidunum grown restless and decided they wanted to throw off the economic and geographical shackles imposed upon them by Justinian. The Herul rebellion during the reign of Anastasius in the 510s was similarly triggered by the imperial government's objection to their 'lawless treatment of the Romans' in Illyricum.[138] Given that the Balkans was not the most economically prosperous region of the empire and that troops were not always enthusiastic to serve there, it might be speculated that the rebellious Herules consisted mainly of those regularly left behind to defend the Balkans, and the 'loyalists' those more regularly employed and paid by the Roman state in other regions.

[136] Walter Kaegi, 'Arianism and the Byzantine Army in Africa 533–546', *Traditio*, 21 (1965), 23–53, argues that although financial and political factors were ultimately more important than religious fervour in the uprising, Justinian's deprival of the Arians' rights caused sufficient consternation among the few thousand federate troops based in Africa to act as the initial trigger. See also Greatrex, 'Roman Identity', p. 277.

[137] Procopius, *Wars*, 7.33.13, trans. by Dewing, p. 441.

[138] Procopius, *Wars*, 6.14.29, trans. by Dewing, p. 411.

Indeed, the continued loyalty of certain Herul chiefs to the empire demonstrates a positive response to Justinian's attempted integration. We have already discussed their military service in great detail in the previous section, so there is no need to go into more detail on this subject. An outstanding example is Philemuth, who fought against his fellow Heruls in 549. He was clearly an especially loyal Herul leader who, as we have already seen, served in numerous campaigns throughout the empire. Similarly, Suartas, whose brief spell as leader of the Herules has been discussed, resided in the imperial capital and later commanded the *praesental* forces in Constantinople. The prestige, financial benefits, and land potentially accruing from the acquisition of such positions are likely factors behind the decision of one-third of the Herul allies to remain subservient to Justinian and seek their fortunes in alliance with the empire. In a number of speeches, Procopius casts light on these factors. The gist of the letter which the Herul leader Pharas sent to the Vandal king Gelimer in order to persuade him to come down from Mount Papua and give himself up to Justinian is that it is better to be a servant of the Roman Empire than a ruler of barbarian peoples such as the Moors: 'and they say that it is the wish of the Emperor Justinian to have you enrolled in the senate, thus sharing in the highest honour and being a patrician, as we term the rank, and to present you with lands both spacious and good and with great sums of money'.[139]

In his narrative on the battle of Busta Gallorum Procopius attributes to Totila a speech which casts doubts on the motivation of the barbarian allies of the Romans: 'And do not think that Huns and Lombards and Eruli, hired by them with I know not how much money, will ever endanger themselves for them to the point of death. For life with them is not so cheap as to take second place to silver in their estimation.'[140] Once again, it is important to acknowledge that those passages were fabricated by Procopius and represent in the first place his own perception of what it was that attracted such groups to the imperial banner. He had sufficient experience of groups such as the Herules to have a good idea of the issues involved. By describing the Romans' victory over Totila, he brushes aside the accusations of mercenary disloyalty to make clear that such groups played a vital role in the imperial army.

This is of course one of the reasons Justinian was keen to bring the Herules back in line in 549. Another was the problem of the hole in his Balkan defensive system created by their defection to an increasingly powerful Gepid kingdom in

---

[139] Procopius, *Wars*, 4.6.22, trans. by Dewing, p. 261.

[140] Procopius, *Wars*, 8.30.18–20, trans. by Dewing, pp. 367 and 369.

Pannonia.[141] The Roman forces' annihilation of the anti-Roman Herules demonstrates the gravity of those concerns. It was perhaps a more important aim of the military expedition of 549 than is suggested by Procopius's narrative, which portrays it as an accidental occurrence in the buildup to an expected confrontation with the Gepids. The defeat of the rebellious Herules seems to have limited their power. Thereafter, there is no mention of them as allies of the Gepids in the literary evidence. Schmidt speculated that they were absorbed by the Gepids and that the three thousand who accompanied Narses to Italy in 552 consisted of other groups that had subsequently entered the empire, in addition to the fifteen hundred loyal Herules under Philemuth. However, it seems more likely that the additional forces were drawn from the mutineers who had been reconscripted by the Roman army after 549. The survivors were presumably given the same choice as their predecessors had been by Anastasius in the 510s: submit or die. Assuming this was the case, approximately fifteen hundred of the mutinous Herul warriors were either killed by the Romans or joined the Gepids in 549.

Schmidt also claimed that the Herules left their lands about Singidunum during the 550s according to Menander Protector's account of Justinian's Avar negotiations of 562. Menander records that Justinian offered the Avars 'the land which the Herules had earlier inhabited, which is called Second Pannonia'.[142] However, this region represented the first area bestowed upon the Herules in 512. It did not necessarily include the lands about Singidunum, provided by Justinian. However long the Herules remained in Upper Moesia, they disappear from our literary sources after the reign of Justinian. It clearly became less and less worthwhile for subsequent generations of Herules to use their ethnonym given that they were essentially Roman provincials in the Balkans or subjects of the Lombard king in Italy.[143]

Conclusion

During the reign of Justinian, the geopolitical configuration north of the Danube was highly fragmented, with rival groups of Germanic, Hunnic, and Slavic barbarians competing with one another in Pannonia, modern Walachia, and the steppe

---

[141] On the threat posed by the Gepid king Thorisin, see Wozniak 'Byzantine Diplomacy', and Sarantis 'War and Diplomacy'.

[142] Menander the Guardsman, *fr.* 5.4, ed. and trans. by R. C. Blockley (Liverpool, 1985), p. 53. See also Schmidt, *Geschichte*, pp. 557–58.

[143] Ellegård, 'Who Were the Eruli?', p. 30.

lands north of the Black Sea. This contrasted with earlier and later periods when Attila and the Huns, on the one hand, and the Avars under the qagan Baian, on the other hand, united the barbarian world to form monolithic threats to the Balkans. Generally speaking, barbarians in this period had two choices: to remain outside the empire and compete for Roman resources in the shape of tributary payments and booty from periodic raiding on the Balkan provinces; or to settle within the Balkan provinces and serve the imperial armies, thereby receiving land, tribute, salaries, and in some cases, the prestige of Roman political status. The Herules are an interesting case study, because in a number of ways they fell between both stools.

They operated within a 'grey area' border zone, close to the section of the Danube frontier that was no longer guarded by Roman fortifications and within an area that had only recently been fundamentally reintegrated within Roman control. Further west, in Pannonia, the Goths before 536 and the Gepids and Lombards after that were politically independent from the Roman Empire, although the latter two groups were allies of the empire. Further east, in the Lower Danube area, the Gothic, Bulgar, and Hunnic federate forces mentioned in Malalas's discussion of Vitalian's rebellion of the 510s were more closely integrated within the political, economic, and military system of the empire.[144] The political organization of the Herules mirrored their geographical situation and fell somewhere between that of the Pannonian and Lower Danube barbarians just mentioned: they were semi-independent in that they had their own kings, but those kings were culturally initiated in Constantinople and at times appointed by Justinian. Further, although they had been given lands about Singidunum to inhabit, those lands actually fell within the borders of the empire. The Herules were also recruited for military service according to different arrangements, some fighting under their own leaders, a few of whom became high-ranking Roman generals, others directly serving Roman generals.

The ambivalent political, geographical, and cultural situation of the Herules resulted in the disparate tensions which provoked their mutiny and civil war of the late 540s. Where some Herules regularly served the Roman armies and acquired high-ranking military and, we may assume, social positions, others, possibly those who had not gained as big a share of the cake, rejected Justinian's attempts at cultural and political integration and chose to elect their own leaders from Scandinavia and throw their lot in with the Gepids, who lived outside the empire.

That Procopius's speeches and letters tend to emphasize a financial rationale for such actions is understandable given that his work was a political and military

---

[144] Malalas, *Chronographia*, 16.16.

history. Nonetheless, his inclusion of an ethnographic digression on the history and customs of the Herules, along with his references to their Arian Christianity, suggests that he at least considered that some of them were motivated by irrational feelings of ethnic and cultural belonging to assert their difference from the empire.[145] For instance, whether or not we accept at face value Procopius's reference to the decision the Herules took to summon a leader from Thule, that at the very least tells us that Procopius wished to present a group of Herules choosing for themselves a leader who had not been sent to them by Justinian and who was regarded as a member of their royal line.[146]

While Procopius frequently uses antibarbarian rhetoric to portray those cultural, independent, and anti-Roman elements of the Herules as anarchic, treacherous, and drunk, he simultaneously employs a different rhetoric to portray the Herul military leaders and forces who fought for the empire in a series of wars as valorous soldiers who were essentially not different from other provincial military forces. In other words, Procopius's text shows that he had the same concerns as modern historians have regarding Roman-barbarian relationships in this period. He was interested in the ways in which some barbarians acted for political and financial rewards, while others were motivated by more irrational, cultural motives. Similarly, his work describes the pros and cons of independence or Romanization, which were being weighed up by barbarians on the fringes of the empire. That Procopius eventually favoured the Romanized Herules should not surprise anyone.

Unfortunately, his fragmentary treatment of the Herules does not provide sufficient information with which we can answer questions relating to the demographic composition of the Herules and the socio-economic nature of their society.[147] We must not assume that they were simply a 'Heerschaft' as Schmidt had it, a warrior

---

[145] Procopius, *Wars*, 6.14.1–7, on the ethnographic characteristics of the Herules.

[146] Goffart, *Narrators*, pp. 94–96, argues that by portraying a group of Herules as having recently migrated to Thule, Procopius was demonstrating to his audience through such 'silly tales' that the empire could still be rid of the 'obnoxious proximity' of the barbarians. He portrays Jordanes's excursus on Scandza as a rebuke to Procopius, demonstrating the finality of the break between the Herules and their homeland. The problem with this argument is that Procopius proceeds to show that the Herules of Thule returned, an event taking place not many years before he was writing. In other words, however truthful his account, Procopius's intention, much like that of Jordanes, seems to have been to show a new connection between the lands of the north and groups now settled within the Balkan provinces.

[147] Kulikowski, 'Nation versus Army', pp. 70–84, is right to assert that speculative arguments regarding the precise political, social, and economic composition and workings of barbarian groups are futile when the evidence is limited.

aristocracy with few ties to the land and entirely motivated by war and hunting.[148] At the same time, there is no evidence for Herul women and children or the ratio of military to non-military members of the society.

Similarly, Procopius's text does not provide us with sufficient information to determine whether or not the nature of the Herul ethnicity or political organization played any role in the eventual disappearance of the Herules. The fact that they did not achieve the same success as the Gothic and Lombard groups means that it is less likely that they attracted people to their banner who wanted to become Herules for financial and political reasons.[149] Peter Heather has actually argued that they may ultimately have vanished from the history books because their identity was too strong and exclusive to attract the manpower necessary to survive, in contrast to the inclusive and flexible identities of more politically successful groups.[150] In contrast, Stein argued that their small size, religious disunity, and political weakness resulted in their demise.[151]

This brings us to the final conclusion. Whatever the ethnic and political characteristics of the Herules, it seems likely that their fate was determined by imperial policies to a greater extent than any other group's. As the work of Florin Curta on the Slavs has demonstrated, it was often the nature of imperial policies towards barbarian groups that could determine their political and ethnic development.[152]

---

[148] Schmidt, *Geschichte*, p. 562. Ellegård, 'Who Were the Eruli?', p. 32 with n. 18, moves even further from the notion of a territorial and genetically defined group, likening the Herules and similar groups to the supporters of modern football teams, such as Inter Milan and Real Madrid. Although such 'army' vs. 'nation' arguments threaten to 'throw the baby out with the bathwater', it certainly seems to be the case that the militarized nature of the Danube region resulted in social Darwinist competition. See, for example, Curta, 'Frontier Ethnogenesis in Late Antiquity', and Walter Pohl, 'Frontiers and Ethnic Identities: Some Final Considerations', in *Borders, Barriers and Ethnogenesis*, ed. by Curta, pp. 255–65 (p. 264).

[149] See Walter Pohl, 'Introduction', in *Strategies of Distinction*, ed. by Pohl and Reimitz, pp. 1–16 (pp. 5–6), on the relationship between political goals and 'ethnic' affiliation.

[150] Heather, 'Disappearing and Reappearing Tribes', p. 108.

[151] Stein, *Histoire*, p. 529.

[152] Curta, *Making of the Slavs*; Curta, 'Frontier Ethnogenesis in Late Antiquity'; Florin Curta, 'A Contribution to the Study of Bow Fibulae of Werner's Class I G', *Arheologia Moldovei*, 19 (1996), 93–123, which suggests that the Slavs were not an already extant *primordial* ethnic group, but emerged from a period of heightened political and economic competition north of the Danube, stimulated by the Roman militarization and closure of the Lower Danube frontier, as well as the predilection of the Romans to define externally barbarian groups in order to make sense of the confusing geopolitical situation on the northern world.

Unlike Curta's Slavs, excluded from the empire by a strong, heavily defended, and closed linear frontier — the Lower Danube — the Herules were located *within* the empire and subject to intense imperial efforts at integration. Rather than defining them as the 'other', Romans such as Procopius were coming to terms with the fact that the Herules were slowly becoming no different from Roman provincials.

Justinian's continuation of Anastasius's attempt to reintegrate the Danube frontier provinces reflects the realization of sixth-century emperors that barbarian groups in the Balkans had to be integrated on all levels as a matter of regional security. Justinian's baptism and/or ceremonial reception of barbarian leaders or generals whose peoples or troops occupied frontier regions, such as Grod, the king of the Bosporan Huns in 528, or Mundo, the *magister militum per Illyricum*, was part of an attempt to ensure the loyalty of barbarian leaders or generals. Such diplomatic initiatives were combined with a fortification policy and the aggressive deployment of military force.[153] Justinian's brutal and quick suppression of the Herul rebels in 549 highlights the importance of his Balkan policy. It can be no coincidence that the Herul rebellion is the only major barbarian rebellion in the Balkans to take place during his reign.

The 549 episode highlights the difference between the predicament of the 'neglected' Justinianic Herules and the oft-discussed Goths of the fourth and fifth centuries. Whereas the Tervingi who entered the Lower Danube provinces in 376 were very much 'strangers in a strange land', the Justinianic Herules were probably more at home in the Dacian diocese than were the Roman officials sent to administer the region from Justiniana Prima.

Like the Herules, the Goths of the late fourth and late fifth centuries were recruited to fight in Roman armies, and their leaders, Alaric and the two Theoderics, appointed *magistri militum*. At the same time, they inhabited Roman territory. However, the limits of this integration were that the imperial authorities acknowledged the Gothic leaders as leaders of the Goths and, as such, conceded that their peoples were semi-independent groups inhabiting Roman territory. Conversely, there is no evidence that the Herules were given the same chance to acquire the political cohesion and strong leadership of the Goths. Their rebellions,

---

[153] See Heather, 'The Late Roman Art of Client Management' for a comparable view of fourth-century imperial Balkan policy. Walter Pohl, 'Conclusion: The Transformation of Frontiers', in *The Transformation of Frontiers*, ed. by Pohl, Wood, and Reimitz, pp. 247–60 (p. 251), acknowledges the similarity of the picture Heather paints with the Justinianic situation. See Whitby, 'The Late Roman Army', pp. 151–54, on the expediency of imperial policy of barbarian recruitment as part of a Balkan military strategy.

although played up by Procopius, were not as damaging or politically significant as those of Theoderic's Goths, and were quickly put down. The existence of a stronger imperial government which had firmer control over the Balkans was also the reason why a larger proportion of the Herules were quite happy picking up their wages from the Roman military establishment and/or operating as a Balkan border defence force. Any that did not wish to comply had to seek new homes with the Gepids or the Lombards outside of the Balkan frontiers. The process of Gothic ethnogenesis, which, according to Peter Heather, was strengthened through an interaction with the Roman Empire within its frontiers, does not seem to have affected the Herul group, for which the opposite trend, of Romanization, was just as strong.[154] The lack of literary evidence for the Herules subsequent to the Justinianic period demonstrates that this trend reached its natural conclusion, the Herules south of the Danube being absorbed by the empire as Roman provincials.

Therefore, the case of the Herules reflects the fact that 'integrated' barbarians tend to be 'neglected' barbarians. By association, it must be noted that histories of barbarian-Roman interactions in the Balkans in Late Antiquity tend to focus on the disastrous periods of the late fourth to mid-fifth and late sixth to seventh centuries, in which powerful barbarian groups brought the Roman government of the Balkans to its knees.[155] Because these periods were naturally of particular interest to contemporary writers, modern histories of the period have the propensity to portray a series of disastrous barbarian invasions leading to the inevitable collapse of Roman authority in the region. However, it is important not to lose sight of the fact that there was also a long period in the late fifth to late sixth centuries in which the Romans were on the front foot in the area and had the upper hand in their dealings with certain barbarian groups.

---

[154] Heather, *The Goths*, pp. 85–93. See Pohl, 'Introduction', p. 2, on the role of Roman military service in creating the cohesive groups that later carved kingdoms out of the empire. However, in the case of the Herules, increasing service in the Roman armies was the precursor to internal tensions within the group and their disappearance from the sources.

[155] Very good and recent examples are Poulter, 'Transition to Late Antiquity', and Liebeschuetz, 'The Lower Danube Region Under Pressure'. By framing the chronological limits within which we understand this period as AD 300–600, the story inevitably veers towards theories of decline and fall. Whitby, 'The Late Roman Army' is generally more upbeat.

STILL WAITING FOR THE BARBARIANS?
THE MAKING OF THE SLAVS IN 'DARK-AGE' GREECE

Florin Curta

Why this sudden restlessness, this confusion?
(How serious people's faces have become.)
Why are the streets and squares emptying so rapidly,
everyone going home so lost in thought?
Because night has fallen and the barbarians have not come.
And some who have just returned from the border say
there are no barbarians any longer.
And now, what's going to happen to us without barbarians?
They were, those people, a kind of solution.
— Constantine Cavafy, *Waiting for the Barbarians*[1]

To say that the early Slavs are neglected in Greece would be to exaggerate — but not much. Four books have been published on the Slavs in Greece over the last fifteen years. Only two of them deal with the early period, one of which is the translation into Greek of a late nineteenth-century refutation of Jakob Philipp Fallmerayer, the German journalist who claimed that modern Greeks were descendants not of ancient Greeks, but of Slavs and Albanians, whose ancestors had settled in Greece during the Middle Ages and had learned to speak Greek from the Byzantine authorities.[2] Writing in the political climate created by the treaties of Adrianople (1829) and Constantinople (1832), which had placed the newly

---

[1] Constantine Cavafy, *Collected Poems*, ed. by George Savvidis, English trans. by Edmund Keeley and Philip Sherrard (Princeton, 1992), p. 19.

[2] Maria G. Nystazopoulou-Pelekidou, *Slavikes egkatastaseis stē mesaiōnikē Hellada: Genikē episkopēsē* (Athens, 1993); Carl H. F. J. Hopf, *Hoi Slavoi en Helladi: Aneskeuē tōn theoriōn Phallmeraur* (Athens, 1997); translation of *Die Slaweneinfälle in Griechenland* (Venice, 1872).

formed Greek state under the protection of the Great Powers, including Russia, and had vouchsafed its independence from the Ottoman Empire, Fallmerayer was not as concerned with the Slavs per se as he was with what he viewed as the catastrophic consequences of their migration into Greece.[3] Driven both by the political liberalism of the *Vormärz* years and by apprehensions about Russia's increasing influence in the Balkans, Fallmerayer saw the proclamation of an independent Greek state as a weakening of the Ottoman Empire and a strengthening of Russia. He was therefore enraged by the political naiveté of the European Philhellenes and attempted to prove that the Greeks and the Russians shared not only the same religion, but also the same ethnic origin.[4] His 'Slavs' were therefore primarily Russians, which may explain the extraordinary popularity of his views at the time of the Crimean War.[5]

[3] Fallmerayer first wrote about the Slavs in Greece in his *Geschichte der Halbinsel Morea während des Mittelalters: Ein historischer Versuch*, I (Stuttgart, 1830). He then dedicated special attention to the topic in his *Welchen Einfluß hatte die Besetzung Griechenlands durch die Slaven auf das Schicksal der Stadt Athen und der Landschaft Attika* (Stuttgart, 1835). He returned to the topic ten years later in his *Fragmente aus dem Orient* (Stuttgart, 1845). For Fallmerayer's sneering at Herder's views of the Slavs, see Reinhard Lauer, 'Jakob Philipp Fallmerayer und die Slaven', in *Jakob Philipp Fallmerayer: Wissenschaftler, Politiker, Schriftsteller*, ed. by Eugen Thurnher (Innsbruck, 1993), pp. 125–57 (p. 140).

[4] Fallmerayer, *Geschichte der Halbinsel*, p. iii–iv: 'Scythische Slaven, illyrische Arnaute, Kinder mitternächtlicher Länder, Blutsverwandte der Serbier und Bulgaren, der Dalmatiner und Moskowiten sind die Völker, welche wir heute Hellenen nennen, und zu ihrem eigenen Erstaunen in die Stammtafel eines Perikles und Philopömen hinaufrücken.' For Fallmerayer's anti-Russian political views, see Eugen Thurnher, *Jahre der Vorbereitung: Jakob Fallmerayers Tätigkeiten nach der Rückkehr von der zweiten Orientreise, 1842–1845* (Vienna, 1995), pp. 42–47; Ellē Skopetea, *Fallmerayer: Technasmata tou antipalou deous* (Athens, 1997), pp. 99–132. Fallmerayer's ideas were not entirely original. The first to speak about the 'Slavonization of Greece' was William Leake, *Researches in Greece* (London, 1814), pp. 61–63, 254–55, and 378–80. For Leake's influence on Fallmerayer, see Thomas Leeb, *Jakob Philipp Fallmerayer: Publizist und Politiker zwischen Revolution und Reaktion, 1835–1861* (Munich, 1996), p. 54.

[5] Reinhard Lauer, 'Gräkoslaven und Germanoslaven bei Jakob Philipp Fallmerayer', in *Die Kultur Griechenlands in Mittelalter und Neuzeit: Bericht über das Kolloquium der Südosteuropa-Kommission 28.–31. Oktober 1992*, ed. by Reinhard Lauer and Peter Schreiner (Göttingen, 1996), pp. 31–38. Karl Marx employed Fallmerayer's ideas for an article published in the *New York Daily Tribune* of 29 March 1854. The article dealt with the occupation of Piraeus by French and British forces in retaliation for the misguided policy of King Otto of Grece, who, taking advantage of the outbreak of the Crimean War, had proclaimed himself the champion of the Christian cause and encouraged the invasion by Greek irregulars of Thessaly and Epirus, at that time still under Ottoman rule. Georg Veloudis, 'Jakob Philipp Fallmerayer und die Entstehung des neugriechischen Historismus', *Südost-Forschungen*, 29 (1970), 43–90 (p. 65).

In Greece, those views had already stirred interest in the early Slavs, if only to combat Fallmerayer's increasingly pernicious influence. It was in reply to Fallmerayer that the Greek historian Constantine Paparrigopoulos (1815–91), then only twenty-eight years old, published the first Greek refutation of Fallmerayer's theories, which was also the first study published in Greek and dedicated to the problem of the early Slavs in Greece.[6] To Fallmerayer's racist theory, Paparrigopoulos opposed the idea of an immutable and timeless social organism, the Greek nation. The Slavs were neither sufficiently numerous nor culturally superior to be able to break the continuous progress through history of the *hellēnikon ethnos*.[7] Against Fallmerayer's emphasis on such late sources as the *Chronicle of Monemvasia*, Paparrigopoulos brought forward the evidence of contemporary authors, such as Theophylact Simocatta; against the idea of an early destruction of Greece by Slavic barbarians in the late sixth century, he argued that the historical evidence showed that the Slavs first moved to Greece peacefully after the plague of 746, when the Byzantine authorities allowed them to settle on deserted lands.[8]

Paparrigopoulos's arguments set the course for subsequent generations of Greek historians dealing with the problem of the Slavs in Greece. The canon established by him remains essentially unchanged to this day, with one or the other argument being simply refined or expanded, but not substantially modified. As Peter Charanis once noted, following Paparrigopoulos's lead, no Greek scholar writing in Grece has ever acknowledged that Slavs settled in Greece during the sixth century.[9]

---

[6] Konstantinos Paparrigopoulos, *Peri tēs epoikēseōs slavikōn tinōn phylōn eis tēn Peloponnēson* (Athens, 1843; repr. 1986). Paparrigopoulos's arguments were then repeated and much expanded in his multivolume *Historikai pragmateiai*, I (Athens, 1858), pp. 261–370. Outside Greece, Fallmerayer's theories had already received criticism by then from both linguists (Bartholomäus Kopitar) and historians (Johann Wilhelm Zinkeisen). See Leeb, *Jakob Philipp Fallmerayer*, pp. 62–63; Maria Nystazopoulou-Pelekidou, 'He ethnikē tautotēta tou mesaiōnikou ellēnismou stēn ellēnikē istoriographia tou 19ou ai.', in *Byzance et l'hellénisme: l'identité grecque au Moyen-Âge. Actes du Congrès International tenu à Trieste du 1er au 3e octobre 1997* (Paris, 1999), pp. 87–101 (pp. 98–101).

[7] For Paparrigopoulos's indifference towards ethnogenetic theories elaborated in comparative philology and ethnology, see Paschalis M. Kitromilides, 'On the Intellectual Content of Greek Nationalism: Paparrigopolous, Byzantium and the Great Idea', in *Byzantium and the Modern Greek Identity*, ed. by David Ricks and Paul Magdalino (Aldershot, 1998), pp. 25–34 (p. 29).

[8] Paparrigopoulos, *Peri tēs epoikēseōs slavikōn*, pp. 77–89; Paparrigopoulos, *Historikai pragmateiai*, I, 105–12.

[9] Peter Charanis, 'Observations on the History of Greece during the Early Middle Ages', *Balkan Studies*, 11 (1970), 1–34 (p. 26). To be sure, Charanis blamed Carl Hopf, and not Constantine Paparrigopoulos.

By contrast, the first work dedicated to the problem of the Slavs in Greece, and written outside Greece, rejected one by one all arguments which Paparrigopoulos had put forward. Alexander Vasiliev believed that the Slavs had begun to settle in Greece already at the end of the sixth century. That few Byzantine sources mentioned them after *c.* 600 did not mean in any way that they had entered Greece peacefully. After the plague of 746, a second wave of Slavic colonists arrived, who, in order to be distinguished from the native population of Greece, were now called *Helladikoi.*[10] Much, if not all, of the subsequent literature on the Slavs in Greece may be divided into two groups of studies: those who follow Paparrigopoulos, and those who follow Vasiliev. Almost all studies published in Greek fall into the former category. Like Paparrigopoulos, Greek historians for a long time maintained that the presence of the Slavs in Peloponnesus cannot be dated earlier than 700, and that the Slavs came to Greece not as invaders or hordes of barbarians to attack the country, but in family groups that sought out deserted areas in which to settle peacefully.[11] Most other historians dealing with the early history of the Slavs followed Vasiliev's lead (rarely, if ever, citing him) and argued instead that the earliest Slavic settlements in Greece must be dated back to the 580s.[12] In Greece proper,

---

[10] Aleksandr A. Vasil'ev, 'Slaviane v Gretsii', *Vizantiiskii Vremennik*, 5 (1898), 404–38 and 626–70 (pp. 669–70). Vasiliev's article also contains one of the first accounts of Fallmerayer's life and work (pp. 626–44). According to Speros Vryonis, it was Vasiliev's paper that opened the history of modern scholarship on the Slavs in Greece. See Speros Vryonis, Jr, Review of Michael W. Weithmann, *Die slavische Bevölkerung auf der griechischen Halbinsel: Ein Beitrag zur historischen Ethnographie Südosteuropas* (Munich, 1978), *Balkan Studies*, 22 (1981), 405–39 (pp. 438–39).

[11] Dionysios A. Zakythinos, *Hoi Slavoi en Helladi: Symvolai eis tēn historian tou mesaiōnikou Hellēnismou* (Athens, 1945); Ioannis Karagiannopoulos, 'Zur Frage der Slavenansiedlungen auf dem Peloponnes', *Revue des études sud-est-européennes*, 9 (1971), 443–60 (p. 460); Andreas N. Stratos, *Byzantium in the Seventh Century*, III (Amsterdam, 1975), p. 180; Maria Nystazopoulou-Pelekidou, 'Les Slaves dans l'Empire byzantin', in *The 17th International Byzantine Congress: Major Papers. Dumbarton Oaks/Georgetown University, Washington D.C., August 3–8, 1986* (New Rochelle, 1986), pp. 345–67 (p. 348); Ioannis Karagiannopoulos, 'Zur Frage der Slavenansiedlung im griechischen Raum', in *Byzanz und seine Nachbarn*, ed. by Arnim Hohlweg (Munich, 1996), pp. 177–218 (p. 189); Ilias Anagnostakis, 'Hoi peloponnēsiakoi skoteinoi khronoi: to slaviko problēma: Metamorphōseis tēs Peloponnēsou ē tes ereunas?', in *Hoi metamorphōseis tes Peloponnēsou (40s–150s ai.)*, ed by E. Grammatikopoulou (Athens, 2000), pp. 19–34 (p. 25). *Contra*: Phaedon Malingoudis, 'Za materialnata kultura na rannoslavianskite plemena v Gărtsiia', *Istoricheski pregled*, 41 (1985), 64–71 (p. 67).

[12] Lubor Niederle, 'Michal Syrský a dějiny balkánských Slovanů v VI. století', in *Sborník prací historických k šé. narozeninám Jaroslava Golla*, ed. by Gustav Friedrich and Kamil Krofta (Prague, 1906), pp. 48–54 (p. 51); Lubor Niederle, *Slovanské starožitnosti*, II (Prague, 1910), pp. 212, 215,

Paparrigopoulos's arguments were further reinforced during and especially in the aftermath of World War II and the subsequent Civil War. By then, Fallmerayer had been demonized to the point that, although actually an enemy of Russia, he came to be regarded as a Panslavist and an agent of the Tsar.[13] Long before its first translation into Greek, Fallmerayer's work was stigmatized as 'anti-Greek'.[14]

But during and after the Civil War, the 'Slavs' themselves became the national enemy. Throughout the Civil War, the Slav Macedonians of northern Greece provided an important contribution to the Communist cause. Following Comintern directives, Greek Communists had repeatedly promised Slav Macedonians an independent state of their own, which led to the idea that all Slav Macedonians were Communists, because both propaganda for an independent Macedonia and Communism came to be regarded as a threat to Greek territorial integrity.[15] A strong link was thus established between national identity and political orientation, as the Civil War and the subsequent defeat of the left-wing movement turned Slav Macedonians into the Sudetens of Greece.[16] By 1950, those embracing the

and 444 (see also Bohumila Zástěrová, 'Les Débuts de l'établissement définitif des Slaves en Europe méridionale: confrontation de la conception de L. Niederle avec l'état actuel des recherches', *Vznik a počátky Slovanů*, 6 (1966), 33–52 (pp. 44–45)); Peter Charanis, 'Ethnic Changes in the Byzantine Empire in the Seventh Century', *Dumbarton Oaks Papers*, 13 (1959), 25–44 (p. 40); Judith Herrin, 'Aspects of the Process of Hellenization in the Early Middle Ages', *Annual of the British School at Athens*, 68 (1973), 113–26 (p. 115); Bohumila Zastěrová, 'Zu einigen Fragen aus der Geschichte der slawischen Kolonisation auf dem Balkan', in *Studien zum 7. Jahrhundert in Byzanz: Probleme der Herausbildung des Feudalismus*, ed. by Helga Köpstein and Friedhelm Winkelmann (Berlin, 1976), pp. 59–72 (p. 62); Marilyn Dunn, 'Evangelism or Repentance? The Re-Christianisation of the Peloponnese in the Ninth and Tenth Centuries', *Studies in Church History*, 14 (1977), 71–86 (p. 72); John F. Haldon, *Byzantium in the Seventh Century: The Transformation of a Culture*, 2nd edn (Cambridge, 1997), p. 45.

[13] Vryonis, Review, p. 407; Ekkehard W. Bornträger, 'Die slavischen Lehnwörter im Neugriechischen', *Zeitschrift für Balkanologie*, 25 (1989), 8–25 (p. 9).

[14] Zakythinos, *Hoi Slavoi en Helladi*, p. 101. The first Greek translation of Fallmerayer's work is *Peri tēs katagōgēs tēn sēmerinon Hellēnōn*, trans. by Konstantinos P. Romanos (Athens, 1984).

[15] Even after the Greek Communist Party dropped its recognition of the Slav-Macedonian minority in Greece (1935), the perception remained that Slav Macedonians had turned against Greece siding with the Bulgarian occupation during World War II and with Yugoslav Communists during the Civil War. See Anastasia Karakasidou, 'Fellow Travelers, Separate Roads: The KKE and the Macedonian Question', *East European Quarterly*, 27 (1993), 459–61.

[16] John S. Koliopoulos, *Plundered Loyalties: World War II and Civil War in Greek West Macedonia* (New York, 1999), p. 283; Gerasimos Augustinos, 'Culture and Authenticity in a Small State: Historiography and National Development in Greece', *East European Quarterly*, 23 (1989),

ideology of the right saw their political rivals as the embodiment of everything that was antinational, Communist, and Slavic. To hold Fallmerayeran views thus became a *crimen laesae maiestatis*. Dionysios A. Zakythinos, the author of the first monograph on medieval Slavs in Greece, wrote of the Dark Ages separating Antiquity from the Middle Ages as an era of decline and ruin brought by Slavic invaders.[17] In the United States, Peter Charanis praised Emperor Nicephorus I for having saved Greece from Slavonicization.[18] A fomer student of Alexander Vasiliev, Charanis also believed that there could be little doubt that the Slavs had come and settled in the western part of Peloponnesus during the reign of Emperor Maurice (582–602).[19] Yet his critics noted that while Charanis seemingly held Fallmerayer up to opprobrium, his views were not 'unlike those entertained by Fallmerayer more than a

17–31 (p. 23); Loring M. Danforth, *The Macedonian Conflict: Ethnic Nationalism in a Transnational World* (Princeton, 1995), pp. 74 and 76.

[17] Zakythinos, *Hoi Slavoi en Helladi*, p. 72; Dionysios A. Zakythinos, 'La Grande Brèche dans la tradition historique de l'hellénisme du septième au neuvième siècle', in *Charisterion eis Anastasion K. Orlandon*, I (Athens, 1966), pp. 300–23 (pp. 300, 302, and 316). Echoes of Zakythinos's ideas can still be found in recent publications. See Anna Avramea, *Le Peloponnèse du IV-e au VIII-e siècle: changements et persistances* (Paris, 1997), p. 49. For Zakythinos's political activities during the Civil War, see Koliopoulos, *Plundered Loyalties*, p. 285.

[18] Peter Charanis, 'Nicephorus I, the Savior of Greece from the Slavs (810 AD)', *Byzantina-Metabyzantina*, 1 (1946), 75–92 (p. 86). After the Civil War, Charanis reassigned the role of saviour of Greece to the city of Thessalonica, 'for had she succumbed to their [the Slavs'] repeated attacks, the chances are that Greece would have been completely inundated by them'. See Charanis, 'Ethnic Changes', p. 41. Peter Charanis earned his PhD from the University of Wisconsin at Madison, with Alexander Vasiliev as his adviser. At the time of the Civil War in Greece, Charanis was a professor of History at Rutgers University, deeply involved in research on the ethnic history of the Byzantine Empire, particularly the problem of the Slavic presence in Greece. During that time, he published, among other things, 'On the Question of the Slavonic Settlements in Greece during the Middle Ages', *Byzantinoslavica*, 10 (1949), 254–58; and 'The Chronicle of Monemvasia and the Question of the Slavonic Settlements in Greece', *Dumbarton Oaks Papers*, 5 (1950), 141–66. He also reviewed favourably Zakythinos's book on the Slavs, which he regarded as 'the most significant study on the Slavs in Greece which has appeared in Greece since Paparrigopoulos' ('Review of Dionysios A. Zakythinos, *Hoi Slavoi en Helladi* (Athens, 1945)', *Byzantinoslavica*, 10 (1949), 94–96 (p. 94)). See John W. Barker, 'Peter Charanis: A Portrait', *Byzantine Studies*, 6 (1979), 1–24 (pp. 4 and 7); Norman Tobias, 'Peter Charanis', *Vyzantiaka*, 6 (1986), 163–67 (p. 166); Demetrios J. Constantelos, 'Peter Charanis, 15 August 1908–23 March 1985: A Pioneer in Byzantine Studies in the United States', in *Pioneers of Byzantine Studies in America*, ed. by John W. Barker (Amsterdam, 2002), pp. 85–92.

[19] Charanis, 'Review of Dionysios A. Zakythinos', p. 95. Charanis's position changed little during the decade following the end of the Civil War. See Charanis, 'Ethnic Changes', p. 40.

century ago'.[20] Charanis's interpretation of the written sources (especially of the *Chronicle of Monemvasia*) in favour of an early Slavic occupation of Greece (particularly of Peloponnesus) was accordingly criticized by Greek scholars.[21] Far from being neglected, the early Slavs had suddenly become a problem, *to slavikon zētēma*, which much like Fallmerayer's theory was to be treated as 'anti-Greek'.

As Dionysios Zakythinos correctly pointed out in 1945, this outburst of interest had been caused by a radical shift in emphasis, from historical sources to linguistics. The publication of Max Vasmer's study of place names of Slavic origin in Greece not only set a new course for the study of the Slavs in Greece, but also brought the scholarly research closer to the politics of the day. In his work, published shortly after the Nazi occupation of Greece, Vasmer claimed that the Slavs in Greece spoke a dialect closer to modern Bulgarian, given that several place names in Greece displayed linguistic features most typical for that language.[22] However,

---

[20] Kenneth M. Setton, 'The Emperor Constans II and the Capture of Corinth by the Onogur Bulgars', *Speculum*, 27 (1952), 351–62 (p. 351). The political overtones of the Setton-Charanis controversy of the early 1950s have been largely overlooked. The subtext of their respective papers published in the pages of *Speculum* invites an investigation that is beyond the scope of this paper. For example, according to Kenneth Setton, 'The Bulgars in the Balkans and the Occupation of Corinth in the 7th Century', *Speculum*, 25 (1950), 502–43 (p. 525), 'the Onogur Bulgars were in the plain of Monastir, in *continental Greece*' (my emphasis). While quoting Setton, Peter Charanis, 'On the Capture of Corinth by the Onogurs and its Recapture by the Byzantines', *Speculum*, 27 (1952), 343–50 (p. 344), added the following: 'Monastir is actually in Yugoslavia.' It is hard to believe that Setton did not know that Monastir (now Bitola) was in Macedonia. It is also significant that Charanis placed the city in Yugoslavia, and not in Macedonia.

[21] Stilpon P. Kyriakidis, *Vyzantinai Meletai VI: Hoi Slavoi en Peloponnēso* (Thessaloniki, 1947), pp. 5 and 7–8. See also Stilpon P. Kyriakidis, *Voulgaroi kai Slaboi eis tēn hellēnikēn istorian* (Thessaloniki, 1946). Kyriakidis's critique of Charanis is cited by Setton, 'Emperor Constans II', p. 354.

[22] Max Vasmer, *Die Slaven in Griechenland* (Berlin, 1941), especially p. 295. The reaction to Vasmer's book was immediate. Zakythinos, *Hoi Slavoi en Helladi* had an entire chapter (chap. 4) dedicated to Vasmer's study. Vasmer did not openly embrace Fallmerayer's theories. He prefaced his analysis of the linguistic material with a thorough examination of the written sources, but deliberately avoided choosing between Paparrigopoulos and Vasiliev's dating of the earliest presence of the Slavs in Greece. His ideas were nonetheless inspired by the racist concepts of his time. According to him, there was little, if any evidence of a full Slavonicization of Greece, 'sondern der Ausdruck ist [...] ähnlich aufzufassen, wie man heute jemand von einer deutschen Stadt behauptete, sie sei "ganz verjudet" gewesen' (*Die Slaven*, p. 15). For Vasmer's fundamental role in setting the scholarly tone for the linguistic and toponymic research on the Slavs in Greece, see Bornträger, 'Die slavischen Lehnwörter', p. 12. Despite a heavy barrage of criticism, many of Vasmer's arguments have been adopted by Greek linguists. See, for example, Phaedon Malingoudis, 'Frühe slawische Elemente im Namengut Griechenlands', in *Die Völker Südosteuropas im 6. bis 8. Jahrhundert*, ed. by B. Hänsel (Berlin, 1987), pp. 53–68.

his arguments resonated even more deeply with Greek scholars of the mid-twentieth century. In a country divided linguistically, as well as politically, by the diglossic opposition between *katharevousa* and *dimotiki*, the understanding of the Herderian tenet, according to which language was the quintessential feature of the national character, turned Vasmer's conclusions into a matter of national identity. On the other hand, language now became the means for exploring relations between native Greeks and speakers of Slavic in the past, which must have been largely peaceful and quite close in order to explain the influence of Slavic on Greek that Vasmer's study had revealed. Historians in postwar Greece therefore insisted upon Paparrigopoulos's old idea that the Slavs had entered Greece peacefully. There has never been any such thing as a Slavic conquest of Greece. 'The Slavs came, but they did not conquer.'[23] Instead of outright invasion, some now wrote of an insidious, yet peaceful infiltration of the Slavs into Greece.[24] Advancing with women, children, and livestock in tow, often in small bands, the Slavs established themselves in Greece, but were quickly 'domesticated' as a consequence of the beneficial, yet irresistible influence constantly exercised upon them by native Greeks and the Byzantine administration, which forced them to abandon their previously nomadic life of bandits.[25] The rapid process of assimilation explained why,

---

[23] Setton, 'Bulgars in the Balkans', p. 511. See also Antoine Bon, *Le Peloponnèse byzantin jusqu'en 1204* (Paris, 1951), p. 56; Stratos, *Byzantium*, p. 180; Avramea, *Le Peloponnèse*, p. 80.

[24] Setton, 'Bulgars in the Balkans', p. 510 ('peaceful penetration'); Antoine Bon, 'Le Problème slave dans le Péloponèse à la lumière de l'archéologie', *Byzantion*, 20 (1950), 13–20 (p. 14: 'avance progressive d'éléments non militaires'); Paul Lemerle, 'La Chronique improprement dite de Monemvasie: le contexte historique et légendaire', *Revue des études byzantines*, 21 (1963), 5–49 (p. 35: 'infiltration progressive'); Herrin, 'Aspects of the Process', pp. 115–16 ('an insidious infiltration', a 'disorganized invasion', 'unorganized infiltration'); Dunn, 'Evangelism or Repentance?', p. 73 ('a process of infiltration'); Michael F. Hendy, *Studies in the Byzantine Monetary Economy c. 300–1450* (Cambridge, 1985), p. 619 ('largely hesitant and piecemeal penetration'). For 'infiltration', 'penetration', and the wave metaphor used to describe the Slavic settlement in the Balkans, see Vasiliki Papoulia, 'To provlēma tēs eirēnikēs dieisdyseos tōn Slavōn stēn Hellada', in *Diethnēs symposio 'Vyzantinē Makedonia, 324–1430 m. Kh.', Thessalonikē, 29–31 Oktovriou 1992* (Thessaloniki, 1995), pp. 255–65; Florin Curta, *The Making of the Slavs: History and Archaeology of the Lower Danube Region, ca. 500–700* (Cambridge, 2001), pp. 74–75.

[25] Bon, *Le Peloponnèse*, p. 56; Panayotis A. Yannopoulos, 'La Pénétration slave en Argolide', in *Études argiennes* (Athens, 1980), pp. 323–71 (p. 353); Nystazopoulou-Pelekidou, *Slavikes egkatastaseis*, p. 23. For an example of 'domesticated' Slavs, see Nicholas Oikonomides, 'L'Archonte slave de l'Hellade au VIII-e siècle', *Vizantiiskii Vremennik*, 55 (1994), 111–18 (p. 115). The historiographic cliche of Slavs as bandits and nomadic pastoralists may go back to Civil War stereotypes. See Johannes Koder, 'Zur Frage der slavischen Siedlungsgebiete im mittelalterlichen Griechenland',

'in contrast with the Bulgar tribes in the north, the Slav settlements further south had no definite social form that can be clearly identified'.[26]

But when did the infiltration begin, which eventually opened the Dark Ages in the history of the Greek nation? In the absence of any sources unequivocally and conveniently dating the end of Antiquity and the beginning of the Middle Ages, scholars turned to archaeology. The first to do so were scholars writing in languages other than Greek, for in Greece the complete reliance on the historical record long prevented the use of archaeology for the study of the early Middle Ages.[27] Kenneth Setton and Peter Charanis 'infused the study of the texts with information from numismatics and archaeology' in a series of polemical articles on seventh-century Corinth, which were published in the American journal *Speculum*.[28] Apparently, the debate was about an obscure episode, the alleged conquest of Corinth by a group of nomads known to Byzantine sources as Onogur Bulgars. In fact, at stake was more than just the interpretation of a confusing passage in a late source, namely a letter of Isidore, the fifteenth-century metropolitan of Kiev, who had

---

Byzantinische Zeitschrift, 71 (1978), 315–31 (p. 327); Malingoudis, 'Za materialnata kultura', p. 65; Phaedon Malingoudis, *Slavoi stē mesaiōnikē Hellada* (Thessaloniki, 1988), pp. 15–18; Gennadii G. Litavrin, *Vizantiia i slaviane (sbornik statei)* (St Petersburg, 1999), pp. 539–45.

[26] Herrin, 'Aspects of the Process', p. 115.

[27] For the relative eclipse of interest in the (medieval) Dark Ages in Greek archaeology, see Kostas Kotsakis, 'The Past Is Ours: Images of Greek Macedonia', in *Archaeology under Fire: Nationalism, Politics, and Heritage in the Eastern Mediterranean and Middle East*, ed. by Lynn Meskell (London, 1998), pp. 44–67 (p. 45). For the complete reliance on the historical record in Greek (classical) archaeology, see Stephen L. Dyson, 'From New to New Age Archaeology: Archaeological Theory and Classical Archaeology', *American Journal of Archaeology*, 97 (1993), 195–202. For the relation between history and medieval archaeology, see Timothy C. Champion, 'Medieval Archaeology and the Tyranny of the Historical Record', in *From the Baltic to the Black Sea: Studies in Medieval Archaeology*, ed. by David Austin and Leslie Alcock (London, 1990), pp. 79–95. Until recently, all archaeological evidence pertaining to the Dark Ages in Greece consisted of stray or accidental finds, with no systematic excavation on any site. See W. Weithmann, 'Anthropologisches Fundgut zur Einwanderung der Slaven in Griechenland: Eine Materialzusammenstellung', *Homo*, 36 (1985), 102–09 (p. 104); Tatiana Štefanovičová, 'Slavic Settlement of Greece in the Light of Archaeological Sources', in *Etnogenez i etnokul'turnye kontakty slavian*, ed. by Valentin V. Sedov (Moscow, 1997), pp. 352–61 (p. 353).

[28] Vryonis, Review, p. 439. For the debate, see Setton, 'Bulgars in the Balkans'; Charanis, 'On the Capture of Corinth'; Setton, 'Emperor Constans II'. Peter Charanis, 'On the Slavic Settlement in the Peloponnesus', *Byzantinische Zeitschrift*, 46 (1953), 91–103 (p. 97), attributed to Antoine Bon 'the first general treatment' of the archaeological material pertaining to the 'Avaro-Slavic penetration of Peloponnesus'.

allegedly preserved (so Setton) 'a reminiscence of a Peloponnesian tradition'.[29] In
his first article, Setton reacted against Charanis's earlier work,[30] in which he had
treated the *Chronicle of Monemvasia*, one of the most controversial sources for the
early medieval history of Greece, as 'absolutely trustworthy'. According to Setton,
the *Chronicle* was no more than a 'medley of some fact and some fiction' that historians should use 'with caution'.[31] Charanis had taken the *Chronicle* at face value.
By contrast, Setton believed it was ludicrous to claim that the Peloponnesus could
have remained under Avar-Slavic domination for 218 years. According to Setton,
the 'Slavonization' of Greece was the result of a peaceful settlement: 'unknown
numbers of Slavs' came 'at unknown times and under unknown circumstances'.[32]
In response, Charanis wrote of Slavic domination and great numbers of settlers
coming to Greece during the entire period from 'just before the beginning of
Maurice's reign [582–602] to the early years of the reign of Heraclius [610–41]'.[33]

At a first glimpse, the Setton-Charanis debate was nothing new. Many of the
arguments used by both sides were by then almost a century old. But the controversy was substantially different from everything that had been published until
then on the subject of the 'Slavic problem'. Kenneth M. Setton and Peter Charanis
first used the archaeological evidence to support arguments derived from the interpretation of written sources. Following the attacks of the barbarians (according to
Setton, the Onogurs), Corinth must have been a deserted village. The barbarians
were eventually expelled by Emperor Constans II during his expedition of 657 or
658 against the Slavs.[34] Setton pointed out that the 'Bulgar buckles' found in

---

[29] Setton, 'Bulgars in the Balkans', p. 520. For the Onogur conquest of Corinth in Isidore's
letter, see Samuel Szádeczky-Kardoss, 'Eine unbeachtete Quellenstelle über die Protobulgaren am
Ende des 6. Jhs.', *Bulgarian Historical Review*, 11 (1983), 76–79 (p. 78 with n. 20).

[30] Charanis, 'Nicephorus I'.

[31] Setton, 'Bulgars in the Balkans', p. 517.

[32] Setton, 'Bulgars in the Balkans', p. 511.

[33] Charanis, 'On the Capture of Corinth', pp. 345–46.

[34] Setton, 'Bulgars in the Balkans', p. 523. For Constans II's expedition, see Theophanes Confessor, *Chronographia*, ed. by Carl de Boor, II (Leipzig, 1885), p. 347. The expedition is also mentioned by several Syrian sources and was followed by population transfers to Asia Minor. See Hans
Ditten, *Ethnische Verschiebungen zwischen der Balkanhalbinsel und Kleinasien vom Ende des 6. bis
zur zweiten Hälfte des 9. Jahrhunderts* (Berlin, 1993), pp. 210–11. See also G. G. Litavrin, 'Slavinii
VII–IX vv: Sotsial'no-politicheskie organizatsii slavian', in *Etnogenez narodov Balkan i severnogo
Prichernomor'ia: Lingvistika, istoriia, arkheologiia*, ed. by S. B. Bernshtein and L. A. Gindin (Mos-
cow, 1984), pp. 193–203. Needless to say, no evidence exists that Constans II's expedition reached

inhumation burials excavated in the 1930s represented the archaeological evidence of a barbarian presence in Corinth. According to him, 'if the Greeks wore Bulgarian buckles, so, a fortiori, did the Bulgars; if the French export perfume, they also use it'.[35] Because they produced weapons, the Corinthian burials must have been of soldiers, and the 'Bulgar buckles' showed that those were Bulgar (Onogur) soldiers killed in battle while attacking the city. Setton's conclusion was therefore that 'we must fit the Corinthian archaeological evidence as best we can into the historical pattern of events established for us by the literary and documentary record'.[36]

By shifting the emphasis from written to archaeological sources, Setton bequeathed to posterity not only his vision of the early medieval history of Greece, but also a powerful methodology for exploring its Dark Ages. It demanded that, in the absence of reliable written sources, archaeological data be used for historical reconstructions. Since the interpretation of the archaeological evidence relied on the 'historical patterns of events established for us by the literary and documentary record', such reconstructions quickly replaced traditional accounts based until then on historical and linguistic evidence, without however altering their fundamental thrust.[37] At stake, after 1950, was the ethnic attribution of artefacts found in burial or settlement assemblages from Greece. Through comparison with finds in Hungary, Gladys Davidson had already proposed that the Corinth burials dated to the late sixth and early seventh century be interpreted as the accoutrements of invading Avars.[38] Charanis too was convinced that the warriors buried in Corinth were

Corinth, an argument Charanis quickly directed against Setton's interpretation. See Charanis, 'On the Capture of Corinth', p. 345.

[35] Setton, 'Bulgars in the Balkans', pp. 523–24. Setton later explained the presence of such buckles in Athens as booty taken from the Onogurs by Emperor Constans II's soldiers during the 657/58 campaign against the Slavs. See Kenneth Setton, 'The Archaeology of Medieval Athens', in *Essays in Medieval Life and Thought, Presented in Honor of Austin Patterson Evans*, ed. by J. H. Mundy (New York, 1955), pp. 227–58 (p. 239); Robert Browning, 'Athens in the "Dark Age"', in *Culture & History: Essays Presented to Jack Lindsay*, ed. by B. Smith (Sydney, 1984), pp. 297–303 (p. 303).

[36] Setton, 'Bulgars in the Balkans', pp. 523 and 525.

[37] For a relatively early critique of hasty attempts to combine archaeological evidence and linguistic data (mainly, place names) for reconstructing the history of the Slavs in Greece, see Phaedon Malingoudis, *Studien zu den slawischen Ortsnamen Griechenlands*, I: *Slawische Flurnamen aus der messenischen Mani* (Wiesbaden, 1981), p. 177.

[38] Gladys R. Davidson, 'The Avar Invasion of Corinth', *Hesperia*, 6 (1937), 227–39. See also Gladys Weinberg Davidson, 'A Wandering Soldier's Grave in Corinth', *Hesperia*, 43 (1974), 512–21.

Avars, 'people who belonged to the same race that had occupied Hungary about the same time'. He further regarded the Corinth burials as confirming the evidence of the *Chronicle of Monemvasia*.[39]

Neither Charanis nor Setton mentioned the Slavs in relation to burial assemblages in Corinth. However, under their influence, most burial assemblages subsequently excavated in Greece were labelled 'Slavic' if associated with weapons or other artefacts regarded as 'barbarian' and similar to those found in Corinthian burials.[40] As a consequence, Greek archaeologists, especially Dimitrios Pallas, made every possible effort to challenge the idea that such artefacts were 'barbarian' and proposed instead that they were produced in Byzantine workshops.[41] Studies dedicated to the 'Slavic problem' in Greece typically concentrated on drawing lists

[39] Charanis, 'On the Question of the Slavonic Settlements', p. 257. Charanis's use of the word 'race' may have been deliberate. The Greek anthropometrist I. Koumaris had studied the skeletons from the burials published in 1937 by Gladys Davidson and concluded that their dolicocephalic skulls pointed to a human group of Mediterranean origin. If warriors buried in Corinth were Avars, Koumaris argued, one would have expected to see Mongoloid racial features. Such arguments were popular in Greece during the 1970s, despite the failure of contemporary attempts in Hungary to distinguish Mongoloid Avars. See Weithmann, 'Anthropologisches Fundgut', pp. 107–09; T. Tóth, 'Észak-dunántul avarkori népességének embertani problémái', *Arrabona*, 9 (1967), 55–65.

[40] Robert H. Hohlfelder, 'Migratory Peoples' Incursions into Central Greece in the Late Sixth Century: New Evidence from Kenchreai', in *Actes du XIV-e Congrès international des études byzantines, Bucarest, 6–12 septembre 1971*, ed. by Mihai Berza and Eugen Stănescu, III (Bucharest, 1976), pp. 333–38 (p. 335); Vera Hrochová, 'Problèmes des agglomérations slaves au Peloponnèse', *Études Balkaniques*, 12 (1976), 128–30 (p. 130); Tatiana Štefanovičová, 'Beitrag zur Frage der slawischen Ansiedlung Griechenlands', *Études Balkaniques*, 13 (1977), 126–28 (p. 127); Weithmann, 'Anthropologisches Fundgut', p. 104; Klaus Kilian, 'Archaiologikes endeixeis gia tēn slavikē parousia stēn Argolidokorinthia (60s–70s aiōnas m. Ch.)', *Peloponnesiaka*, 16 (1985–86), 295–304; Eric A. Ivison, 'Burial and Urbanism at Late Antique and Early Byzantine Corinth (c. AD 400–700)', in *Towns in Transition: Urban Evolution in Late Antiquity and the Early Middle Ages*, ed. by Neil Christie and S. T. Loseby (Aldershot, 1996), pp. 99–125 (pp. 118–19). In contrast, Anna Avramea has recently argued that, since the burials found in the Corinthian Agora coincide in time with the basilica excavated near the Temple of Apollo, they must be of Byzantine, not Avar or Slavic, warriors. See Avramea, *Le Peloponnèse*, p. 98.

[41] Dimitrios I. Pallas, 'Données nouvelles sur quelques boucles et fibules considerées comme avares et slaves et sur Corinthe entre le VI-e et le IX-e siècles', *Byzantinobulgarica*, 7 (1981), 295–318. According to Dimitrios I. Pallas, 'Ta archaiologika tekmēria tēs kathodou tōn varvarōn eis tēn Hellada', *Hellēnika*, 14 (1955), 87–105 (p. 102), there was no archaeological evidence of the presence of the Slavs in Greece. The first to advance the idea that the 'Bulgar buckles' were in fact Byzantine was Hans Zeiss, 'Avarenfunde in Korinth?', in *Serta Hoffileriana: Commentationes gratulatoria Victori Hoffiler sexagenario obtulerunt collegae, amici, discipuli A.D. XI kal. Mar. MCMXXXVII* (Zagreb, 1940), pp. 95–99.

of artefacts broadly accepted as 'barbarian' and Byzantine, respectively, and then deriving from their distribution a narrative tailored to fit the 'historical pattern of events' established on the basis of written sources. Despite an increasing number of archaeological finds pertaining to the seventh and early eighth centuries in Greece, as well as in other regions of the Balkans, the Setton-Charanis controversy brought historians into a cul-de-sac. Instead of innovative research programmes inspired by Setton and Charanis's use of the archaeological evidence, current research on Dark-Age Greece seems to be paralyzed by an obsessive concern with identifying ethnic groups in the archaeological record. Despite recognizing the ambiguity of the ethnic names employed by medieval sources, historians and archaeologists regard the Slavs as a monolithic, self-defined group identity. The Slavs are always an objective 'it' out there, in the medieval past, ready to be studied, measured, and identified by archaeological means. Only rarely has the fact been acknowledged that much of what we know about the early Slavs in general, and especially those in Greece, can be best described as ethnic stereotypes about barbarians, and not as ethnographic reports.[42] This applies even to ethnic names, such as 'Slavs' or 'Avars', which are too often taken to represent objective social realities of the medieval past.[43] While sorting out the polysemantism of ethnic names,

[42] For an excellent survey of Roman stereotypes about barbarians, in general, see Guy Halsall, *Barbarian Migrations and the Roman West, 376–568* (Cambridge, 2007), pp. 45–57. As Hallsall notes (p. 56), 'Roman depictions of barbarians are not part of a dialogue between "us" and "them" ("*we* are like this whereas *you* are like that") but between "us" and "us", between Romans ("*we* are [or, more often, ought to be] like this because *they* are like that").' This applies especially to such Byzantine sources on the Slavs in 'Dark-Age' Greece as Constantine VII Porphyrogenitus's *De administrando imperio* or the *Chronicle of Monemvasia*.

[43] See Walter Pohl, 'Die Namen der Barbaren: Fremdbezeichnung und Identität in Spätantike und Frühmittelalter', in *Zentrum und Peripherie: gesellschaftliche Phänomene in der Frühgeschichte. Materialien des 13. internationalen Symposiums 'Grundprobleme der frühgeschichtlichen Entwicklung im mittleren Donauraum', Zwettl, 4.–8. Dezember 2000*, ed. by Herwig Friesinger and Alois Stuppner (Vienna, 2004), pp. 95–104. For the Slavs, see John V. A. Fine, 'Croats and Slavs: Theories about the Historical Circumstances of the Croats' Appearance in the Balkans', *Byzantinische Forschungen*, 26 (2000), 205–18; Johannes Koder, 'Anmerkungen zum Slawen-Namen in byzantinischen Quellen', *Travaux et mémoires du Centre de recherches d'histoire et civilisation byzantines*, 14 (2002), 333–46. It is interesting to note that in Greece, the idea of a constructed identity has been used in studies of Vlach, but not Slavic ethnicity. See Konstantinos P. Christou, *Aromounoi: Meletes gia ten katagōgē kai tēn historia tous* (Thessaloniki, 1996). However, there is an increasing awareness that to look for the material culture correlates of the Slavic migration is to perpetuate old historiographic stereotypes about 'barbarity'. See Ilias Anagnostakis, 'He cheiropoiētē keramikē anamesa stēn Istoria kai tēn Archaiologia', *Vyzantiaka*, 17 (1997), 285–330.

historians have taken sources at face value and have reproduced their tendency to project into the past pseudo-ethnicities that existed only in the minds of those whose intention was to classify and dominate. As a consequence, 'Slav' has become the label for the Other, and the Slavs themselves — to use Cavafy's bon mot — 'a kind of solution'. The conceptual division of past peoples into 'civilized' and 'barbarian' thus obscures some of the fundamental questions that can now be rephrased in the light of both more evidence and current anthropological research on ethnicity.[44] Just who were the Slavs, who the Avars? What made them so difficult to identify by the traditional means of European archaeology and historiography? What were the historical conditions in which marking ethnic boundaries became important, and for what purpose? How was group identity represented in material culture terms and under what circumstances were certain cultural practices and items selected for marking ethnic boundaries? Above all, this chapter aims to provide plausible answers to some of those questions. My intention is to fashion a synthesis out of rather heterogeneous materials. I will first examine issues of chronology raised by the now fairly abundant archaeological evidence (Figure 12.1). My concern with chronology rather than ethnic or cultural attribution is the result of an effort to understand the social changes taking place in Dark-Age Greece that may have been reflected in material culture. Administrative and political changes will also be discussed in the second part in relation to the evidence of coins and seals. The third part of this paper presents the evidence of written sources. Issues of chronology and naming are the theme of that section. The forms of military and political organization in Dark-Age Greece are the focus of the last section, as various strands of evidence will be brought into a final conclusion.

The Archaeology of Dark-Age Greece

To many archaeologists, Greece appears as the ideal territory for testing hypotheses about the migration of the Slavs, because of the expected association of 'Slavic' or 'barbarian' artefacts with the well-datable contexts of early Byzantine sites. Unfortunately, the appealing culture-historical paradigm that most scholars have endorsed has prevented a serious archaeological analysis of the existing evidence. This is most obvious in the case of the French excavations at Argos. The ceramic

---

[44] Bernard Wailes and Amy L. Zoll, 'Civilization, Barbarism, and Nationalism in European Archaeology', in *Nationalism, Politics, and the Practice of Archaeology*, ed. by Philip Kohl and Clare Fawcett (Cambridge, 1995), pp. 21–38.

Figure 12.1. The distribution of the principal sites mentioned in the text.

assemblage from the ruins of Bath A was dated with surprising precision to AD 585. This has been done simply in reference to the date of the earliest Slavic raids into Greece known from narrative sources, the effects of which have in turn been 'extended' to Argos, although no source specifically mentions that city as conquered or even attacked by Slavs. Since, following the invasion, a settlement of the Slavs would have been inconceivable for a variety of reasons, the French archaeologist Pierre Aupert proposed that the 'Slavic ware' found in Argos be interpreted as evidence of a temporary camp that the Slavic marauders had established in the ruins of the city, right before returning to their homes north of the Danube River.[45] The relatively large quantity of 'Slavic ware' found at Argos and on various other sites in Greece sharply contradicts Aupert's interpretation. In addition, such views, which were rapidly embraced by others, are apparently based on a blatant error of dating. To be sure, the ceramic assemblage of Bath A at Argos is extremely difficult to date in the absence of any closed finds or a stratigraphically clear situation. In this particular case, it seems wiser to use pottery decoration for, at least, an approximate dating. A pot found in an area of the present-day city of Argos known as Koutroumbi as well as other fragments of pottery made on a tournette (a slow-turning wheel activated by hand) and discovered during the excavations of Bath A display a particular type of incised decoration with combed, vertical lines, sometimes cutting through the adjacent horizontal lines.[46] I will return shortly to this form of pottery decoration. For the moment, it is important to note that, should Aupert's line of reasoning be accepted, it must be acknowledged that absolutely no decoration of this kind was found on any category of pottery, either wheel- or handmade, on any sixth- or early seventh-century site north of the Danube River, where contemporary sources locate the Slavs.[47] On the other hand, the obsessive desire to illustrate by archaeological means what is already known from written sources is also responsible for the misdating, for a long period of time, of the cremation cemetery found in Olympia, which many regard as the only piece of 'hard'

---

[45] Pierre Aupert, 'Céramique slave à Argos (585 ap. J.-C.)', in *Études argiennes*, pp. 373–94; Pierre Aupert, 'Les Slaves à Argos', *Bulletin de Correspondence Hellénique*, 113 (1989), 417–19. For a critique of Aupert's approach, see Malingoudis, *Slavoi*, pp. 20–21; Timothy E. Gregory, 'An Early Byzantine (Dark-Age) Settlement at Isthmia: Preliminary Report', in *The Corinthia in the Roman Period Including the Papers Given at a Symposium Held at the Ohio State University on 7–9 March, 1991*, ed. by Timothy E. Gregory (Ann Arbor, 1993), pp. 149–60 (p. 152); Anagnostakis, 'He cheiropoiētē keramikē', pp. 298–300 and 317–23; Ilias Anagnostakis and Natalia Poulou-Papadimitriou, 'He protovyzantinē Messēnē (50s–70s aiōnas) kai provlēmata tēs cheiropoiētēs keramikēs stēn Peloponnēso', *Symmeikta*, 11 (1997), 229–322 (pp. 269–72); Ewald Kislinger, *Regionalgeschichte als Quellenproblem: Die Chronik von Monembasia und das sizilianische Demenna. Eine historisch-topographische Studie* (Vienna, 2001), pp. 74–77.

[46] Aupert, 'Céramique slave', pp. 380–81, nos 23–24 and figs 15–20, 22–24, and 30.

[47] Anastasis Oikonomou-Laniado, *Argos paléochrétienne: contribution à l'étude du Péloponnèse byzantin* (Oxford, 2003), p. 9, correctly remarks that such a decoration appears on the 'Slavic ware' of the Balkan region only at a comparatively later date.

evidence for the presence of the Slavs in Greece. Despite previous caveats by the Romanian archaeologist Ion Nestor and the French archaeologist Jean-Pierre Sodini, Speros Vryonis has dated the site to the late sixth and early seventh centuries, primarily on the basis of intuitive comparisons with the pottery of the so-called 'Prague type' in Bulgaria.[48] I have shown elsewhere the problems associated with using this ill-defined ceramic category as a benchmark. Meanwhile, on the basis of a thorough analysis of both beads and metal artefacts found in Olympia, Tivadar Vida and Thomas Völling have firmly established that the cemetery is to be dated at least one hundred years later than Vryonis initially assumed. The so-called 'Slavic ware' is now recognized as no more than the local pottery of household production, which may have been in use first in the mid-500s in such places as Thessalonica and Demetrias, but actually spread throughout Greece only after *c.* 600.[49] Moreover, doubts have already been raised about the possibility of using

[48] Speros Vryonis, 'The Slavic Pottery (Jars) from Olympia, Greece', in *Byzantine Studies: Essays on the Slavic World and the Eleventh Century*, ed. by S. Vryonis (New Rochelle, 1992), pp. 5–42 (p. 36). Vryonis's basis of comparison were the illustrations published in Liudmila Doncheva-Petkova, *Bălgarska bitova keramika prez rannoto srednevekovie (vtorata polovina na VI-krai na X v.)* (Sofia, 1977). For earlier caveats, see Ion Nestor, 'Les Éléments les plus anciens de la culture slave dans les Balkans', in *Simpozijum 'Predslavenski etnički elementi na Balkanu u etnogenezi južnih Slovena', održan 24–26. oktobra 1968 u Mostaru*, ed. by Alois Benac (Sarajevo, 1969), pp. 141–47 (p. 144); François Baratte, 'Les Témoignages archéologiques de la présence slave au sud du Danube', in *Villes et peuplement dans l'Illyricum protobyzantin: Actes du colloque organisé par l'École française de Rome (Rome, 12–14 mai 1982)* (Rome, 1984), pp. 164–80 (p. 170 with n. 33). Vryonis's was by no means the only approach to pottery classification inspired by the culture-historical paradigm. See Klaus Kilian, 'Zu einigen früh- und hochmittelalterlichen Funden aus der Burg von Tiryns', *Archäologisches Korrespondenzblatt*, 10 (1980), 281–90 (pp. 282–83 and 287); Sinclair Hood, 'Some Exotic Pottery from Prehistoric Greece', *Slovenská Archeológia*, 36 (1988), 93–97 (p. 93); Guy D. R. Sanders, 'Pottery from Medieval Levels in the Orchestra and Lower Cavea', *Annual of the British School at Athens*, 90 (1995), 451–57 (p. 454). For a critique of the culture-historical approach and the concept of 'Prague-type' pottery, see Florin Curta, 'The "Prague Type": A Critical Approach to Pottery Classification', in *Hoi skoteinoi aiōnes tou Vyzantiou (70s–90s ai.)*, ed. by Eleonora Kountoura-Galaki (Athens, 2001), pp. 171–88.

[49] John Hayes, 'Rapports régionaux: Grèce', in *70 Diethnes Synedrio Mesaiōnikes Keramikes tes Mesogeiou, Thessalonike, 11–16 oktovriou 1999. Praktika*, ed. by Charalambos Bakirtzis (Athens, 2003), pp. 529–36 (p. 533). That the involution in productive expertise signalled by handmade pottery cannot be attributed to barbarian invasions is demonstrated by the remarkably similar and concomitant return to part-time, semiprofessional, 'household-industry' production in southeastern Spain, a region with which early medieval Greece seems to have much in common. See Chris Wickham, *Framing the Early Middle Ages: Europe and the Mediterranean, 400–800* (Oxford, 2005), pp. 749–50.

handmade pottery for dating sites, given that such pottery also appears in much later archaeological assemblages and apparently remained in use until the fourteenth century.[50]

While research perspectives on the 'Slavic ware' remain unpromising, there has been a great deal of new work in the last ten years or so on sixth- and seventh-century buckles, including Setton's 'Bulgar buckles'.[51] Equally useful are numerous

[50] Tivadar Vida and Thomas Völling, *Das slawische Brandgräberfeld von Olympia* (Rahden, 2000); Anagnostakis, 'He cheiropoiētē keramikē'. For the lack of any ceramic means of dating Dark-Age sites, see Anagnostakis and Poulou-Papadimitriou, 'He protovyzantinē Messēnē', pp. 273–76; Joanita Vroom, *After Antiquity: Ceramics and Society in the Aegean from the 7th to the 20th Century A.C. A Case Study from Boeotia, Central Greece* (Leiden, 2003), pp. 107–10.

[51] Dan Gh. Teodor, 'Piese vestimentare bizantine din secolele VI–VIII în spațiul carpato-dunăreano-pontic', *Arheologia Moldovei*, 14 (1991), 117–38; Jozef Zábojník, 'Seriation von Gürtelbeschlaggarnituren aus dem Gebiet der Slowakei und Österreichs', in *K problematike osídlenia stredodunajskej oblasti vo včasnom stredoveku*, ed. by Zlata Čilinska (Nitra, 1991), pp. 219–321; Ursula Ibler, 'Pannonische Gürtelschnallen des späten 6. und 7. Jahrhunderts', *Arheološki vestnik*, 43 (1992), 135–48; Vladimír Varsik, 'Byzantinische Gürtelschnallen im mittleren und unteren Donauraum im 6. und 7. Jahrhundert', *Slovenská Archeológia*, 40 (1992), 77–103; Vladimír Varsik 'Zu manchen Problemen der Verbreitung byzantinischer Schnallen im mittleren und unteren Donauraum', in *Actes du XII-e Congrès international des sciences préhistoriques et protohistoriques, Bratislava, 1–7 septembre 1991*, ed. by Juraj Pavuj, IV (Bratislava, 1993), pp. 207–12; Brigitte Haas and Roland Schewe, 'Byzantinische Gürtelbeschläge im Germanischen Nationalmuseum', *Anzeiger des Germanischen Nationalmuseums und Berichte aus dem Forschungsinstitut für Realienkunde*, 6 (1993), 255–73; Igor O. Gavritukhin, 'Priazhki s korobchatoi petlei na iugo-vostoke Evropy', *Materialy po arkheologii, istorii i etnografii Tavrii*, 4 (1994), 201–14; Wolfgang Ebel-Zepezauer, '"Byzantinische" Gürtelschnallen auf der Iberischen Halbinsel', in *Festschrift für Otto-Herman Frey zum 65. Geburtstag*, ed. by C. Dobiat (Marburg, 1994), pp. 197–211; Ellen Riemer, 'Byzantinische Gürtelschnallen aus der Sammlung Diergardt im Römisch-Germanischen Museum Köln', *Kölner Jahrbuch für Vor- und Frühgeschichte*, 28 (1995), 777–809; Christoph Eger, 'Eine byzantinische Gürtelschnalle von der Krim in der Sammlung des Hamburger Museum für Archäologie', *Materialy po arkheologii, istorii i etnografii Tavrii*, 5 (1996), 343–48 and 584–85; Igor O. Gavritukhin and A. M. Oblomskii, *Gaponovskii klad i ego kul'turno-istoricheskii kontekst* (Moscow, 1996); Eleni Prokopiou, 'Vyzantines porpes apo tēn Amathounta kai tēn Palaia Syllogē tou Kypriakou Mouseiou', in *He Kypros kai to Aigaio stēn archaioteta apo tēn proistoriko periodo hos ton 70 aiōna m. Ch., Leukosia 8–10 Dekembriou 1995*, ed. by Dimos Christou and others (Nicosia, 1997), pp. 333–42; Alexandru Madgearu, 'The Sucidava Type of Buckles and the Relations Between the Late Roman Empire and the Barbarians in the 6th Century', *Arheologia Moldovei*, 21 (1998), 217–22; Isabella Baldini Lippolis, *L'oreficeria nell'impero di Costantinopoli tra IV e VII secolo* (Bari, 1999); Éva Garam, 'Über die Beziehung der byzantinischen Goldschnallen und der awarenzeitlichen Pseudo-schnallen', in *Kontakte zwischen Iran, Byzanz und der Steppe im 6.–7. Jahrhundert*, ed. by Csanád Bálint (Budapest, 2000), pp. 215–28; Éva Garam, *Funde byzantinischer Herkunft in der Awarenzeit*

contributions, mainly by Hungarian and Austrian scholars, to the refinement of the chronology of burial assemblages dated to the so-called Early Avar phase (*c.* 570–*c.* 650), which show a surprising number of good analogies with assemblages in Greece.[52] There are so far no large, Dark-Age cemeteries known from Greece,

vom Ende des 6. bis zum Ende des 7. Jahrhunderts (Budapest, 2001); Mechthild Schulze-Dörrlamm, *Byzantinische Gürtelschnallen und Gürtelbeschläge im Römisch-Germanischen Zentralmuseums*, I: *Die Schnallen ohne Beschläg, mit Laschenbeschläg und mit festem Beschläg des 6. bis 7. Jahrhunderts* (Mainz, 2002); Mücahide Lightfoot, 'Belt Buckles from Amorium and in the Afyon Archaeological Museum,' in *Amorium Reports II: Research Papers and Technical Reports*, ed. by C. S. Lightfoot (Oxford, 2003), pp. 81–103; Etleva Nallbani, 'Three Buckles From the Late Antique Period', in *Byzantine Butrint: Excavations and Surveys, 1994–99*, ed. by Richard Hodges, William Bowden, and Kosta Lako (Oxford, 2004), pp. 398–99; Valentin Pletn'ov, 'Buckles with Animal Images From North-east Bulgaria (9th–10th c. A.D.)', *Archaeologia Bulgarica*, 9 (2005), 75–86; Natalia Poulou-Papadimitriou, 'Les Plaques-boucles byzantines de l'île de Crète (fin IVᵉ–IXᵉ siècles)', in *Mélanges Jean-Pierre Sodini*, ed. by François Baratte and others (Paris, 2005), pp. 687–704; Etleva Nallbani, 'Précisions sur un type de ceinture byzantine: la plaque-boucle du type Corinthe au Haut Moyen Âge', in *Mélanges Jean-Pierre Sodini*, ed. by Baratte and others, pp. 655–72.

[52] The literature on the Early Avar period is enormous and grows exponentially by the year. Mention can be made here only of studies that are pertinent to a discussion of contemporary burial assemblages in Greece. For the Hungarian research, see László Simon, 'A tápéi korai avar kard', *Móra Ferenc Múzeum Évkönyve*, 1 (1991–92), 31–35; Adrien Pásztor, 'Typologische Untersuchung der früh- und mittelawarenzeitlichen Perlen aus Ungarn', in *Perlen: Archäologie, Techniken, Analysen. Akten des Internationalen Perlensymposiums in Mannheim vom 11. bis 14. November 1994*, ed. by Uta von Freeden and Alfried Wieczorek (Bonn, 1997), pp. 213–30; Gábor Lőrinczy, 'Kelet-európai steppei népesség a 6–7. századi Kárpát-medencében: Régészeti adatok a Tiszántúl kora avar kori betelepüléséhez', *Móra Ferenc Múzeum Évkönyve*, 4 (1998), 343–72; Tivadar Vida, *Die awarenzeitliche Keramik I. (6.–7. Jh.)* (Berlin, 1999); Éva Garam, 'Gürtelverzierungen byzantinischen Typs im Karpatenbecken des 6.–7. Jahrhunderts', *Acta Archaeologica Academiae Scientiarum Hungaricae*, 51 (1999–2000), 379–91; Csanád Bálint, 'Byzantinisches zur Herkunftsfrage des vielteiligen Gürtels', in *Kontakte zwischen Iran, Byzanz und der Steppe im 6.–7. Jahrhundert*, ed. by Bálint, pp. 99–162. For Austrian contributions, see Falko Daim, 'Die Awaren sitzen kurz ab. Diskussion zum Stand der österreichischen Awarenforschung im Milleniumsjahr', *Archäologie Österreichs*, 7 (1996), 8–20; Anton Distelberger, 'Import in die awarischen Westgebiete im 8. Jahrhundert', in *Reitervölker aus dem Osten: Hunnen + Awaren. Burgenländische Landesausstellung 1996. Schloß Halbturn, 26. April–31. Oktober 1996*, ed. by Falko Daim, Karl Kaus, and Péter Tomka (Eisenstadt, 1996), pp. 287–308; Peter Stadler, 'Quantitative Auswertung des awarenzeitlichen Gräberfeldes von Kölked-Feketekapu A mittels Seriation und Analyse der "N Nächsten Nachbarn"', in *Das awarenzeitlich gepidische Gräberfeld von Kölked-Feketekapu A*, ed. by Attila Kiss (Innsbruck, 1996), pp. 363–96; Falko Daim, 'Byzantine Belts and Avar Birds: Diplomacy, Trade, and Cultural Transfer in the Eighth Century', in *The Transformation of Frontiers: From Late Antiquity to the Carolingians*, ed. by Walter Pohl, Ian Wood, and Helmut Reimitz (Leiden, 2001), pp. 143–88; Peter Stadler, *Quantitative Studien zur Archäologie der Awaren I* (Vienna, 2005).

although Tigani, in Mani, may well be the first candidate to that title, if the excavators will decide some day to publish their finds properly in a monograph form.[53] By contrast, the cemetery around the Church of St Dionysius the Areopagite in Athens has been properly published, but the relatively small number of burials, some with multiple interments, prevents any analysis based on toposeriation that could lead to a refined chronology.[54] In the absence of any complete set of data, the following remarks and chronology must therefore be taken as no more than tentative.

A post-550 occupation phase in Olympia has only recently been documented, and several isolated finds confirm its dating.[55] So, for example, the belt buckle of the Sucidava class, with good analogies in grave C 62 in Piatra Frecăţei (Romania), grave 29 in Szentes-Nagyhegy (Hungary), and grave 1 in Veliki Tokmak (Ukraine) (Figure 12.2).[56] In some cases, such buckles were associated with perforated belt

---

[53] Consisting of inhumations inside the basilica built much earlier in the middle of the early Byzantine fort, the Tigani cemetery was excavated by Nikolaos V. Drandakis, Nikos Gkiolis, and Charalambos Konstantinidi between 1980 and 1983. See Christina Katsougiannopoulou, 'Einige Überlegungen zum byzantinischen Friedhof in Tigani auf dem Peloponnes', in *Archäologisches Zellwerk: Beiträge zur Kulturgeschichte in Europa und Asien. Festschrift für Helmut Roth zum 60. Geburtstag*, ed. by Ernst Pohl, Udo Recker, and Claudia Theune (Rahden, 2001), pp. 461–69.

[54] J. Travlos and A. Frantz, 'The Church of St. Dionysios the Areopagite and the Palace of the Archbishop of Athens in the 16th Century', *Hesperia*, 34 (1965), 157–202. For toposeriation and its applications, see François Djindjian, 'Seriation and Toposeriation by Correspondence Analysis', *PACT: Revue du Groupe européen d'études pour les techniques physiques, chimiques et mathématiques appliquées à l'archéologie*, 11 (1985), 119–35. An equally interesting, but poorly published, cemetery is Aphiona (on the northern coast of the island of Corfu), for which see Heinrich Bulle, 'Ausgrabungen bei Aphiona auf Korfu', *Mitteilungen des Deutschen Archäologischen Instituts: Athenische Abteilung*, 39 (1934), 147–240. Most other Dark-Age burial assemblages in Greece were found accidentally. See, for example, Ph. Petsas, 'Archaiotētes kai mnēmeia Kentrikēs Makedonias', *Archaiologikon Deltion*, 24 (1969), 302–11; Penelopi Agallopoulou, 'Palaiokastritsa', *Archaiologikon Deltion*, 28 (1973), 423–24. It is not known precisely how many of the twenty-three cist burials found in Meropi (near the Greek-Albanian border) could be dated between the seventh and the tenth centuries; see Ilias Andreou, 'Meropē kai Palēopyrgos Pōgōniou', *Archaiologikon Deltion*, 35 (1980), 303–07 (p. 303). Seven of them produced bronze finger-rings and iron bracelets, but none of them has been so far published to allow at least a tentative dating. See Ilias Andreou, 'Palēopyrgos Pōgōniou', *Archaiologikon Deltion*, 42 (1987), 307 and pls 166–67.

[55] For a wine press found in Olympia and coin-dated to the late sixth century, see Thomas Völling, '"Neuer Most aus alten Löwenköpfen": Ein frühbyzantinisches Gemach der alten Grabung in Olympia', *Mitteilungen des Deutschen Archäologischen Instituts: Athenische Abteilung*, 111 (1996), 391–410.

[56] Thomas Völling, 'Byzantinische Kleinfunde aus Olympia', in *ΜΟΥΣΙΚΟΣ ΑΝΗΡ: Festschrift für Max Wegner zum 90. Geburtstag*, ed. O. Brehm and S. Klie (Bonn, 1992), pp. 491–98

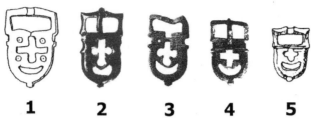

1   2   3   4   5

Figure 12.2. Belt buckles of the Sucidava class: (1) Olympia, stray find; (2) Piatra Frecăței, grave C 62; (3) Szentes-Nagyhegy, grave 29; (4) Szöreg, grave 11; (5) Veliki Tokmak, grave 1. After Völling, 'Byzantinische Kleinfunde'; Petre, *La Romanité*; Csallány, *Archäologische Denkmäler*; and Rashev, *Prabălgarite*.

mounts and strap ends commonly known as 'Martynivka mounts'. Recent studies by Péter Somogyi and Csanád Bálint have demonstrated that such mounts cannot be dated earlier than the mid-500s or later than *c.* 620.[57] In my opinion, the chronological bracket for the Olympia buckle may be further narrowed to the first

(pp. 491–92 with 494 fig. 4); Aurelian Petre, *La Romanité en Scythie Mineure (IIe–VIIe siècles de notre ère): Recherches archéologiques* (Bucharest, 1987), pp. 67–68 and pl. 122 bis fig. 189c; Desző Csallány, *Archäologische Denkmäler der Gepiden im Mitteldonaubecken (454–568 u.Z.)* (Budapest, 1961), pp. 50–51 and pl. 25.13 (Szentes-Nagyhegy, grave 29); Rasho Rashev, *Prabălgarite prez V–VII vek* (Sofia, 2000), pp. 19 and 122 fig. 16.4. For another, wrongly dated, specimen from a grave on the site of the episcopal palace in Louloudies near Pydna (northern Greece), see Euterpi Marki, 'Louloudies', *To Archaiologiko ergo stē Makedonia kai Thrakē*, 11 (1997), 289–96 (pp. 293 with 296 fig. 5). Similar buckles have been found in Syria and at Palmyra. See Michel Kazanski, *Qal'at Sem'an*, IV.3: *Les Objets métalliques* (Beirut, 2003), p. 40.

[57] Péter Somogyi, 'Typologie, Chronologie und Herkunft der Maskenbeschläge: zu den archäologischen Hinterlassenschaften osteuropäischer Reiterhirten aus der pontischen Steppe im 6. Jahrhundert', *Archaeologia Austriaca*, 71 (1987), 121–54 (p. 138); Csanád Bálint, 'Kontakte zwischen Iran, Byzanz und der Steppe: Das Grab von Üç Tepe (Sowj. Azerbajdžan) und der beschlagverzierte Gürtel im 6. und 7. Jahrhundert', in *Awarenforschungen*, ed. by Falko Daim, I (Vienna, 1992), pp. 309–496 (p. 405). For 'Martynivka mounts', see now Gavritukhin and Oblomskii, *Gaponovskii klad*, pp. 24–29. For the 'Martynivka mount' from Szentes-Nagyhegy (grave 29), see Csallány, *Archäologische Denkmäler*, pl. 25.14. For the specimens found together with the Veliki Tokmak buckle, see Rashev, *Prabălgarite*, p. 122 fig. 16.5–6. The Piatra Frecăței buckle was found together with an open-work mount similar to specimens found on fortified sites of the Justinianic age, especially in the central and northern Balkans. See Georgi Atanasov, 'Martyrium et hagiasmon dans le castel bas-byzantin près du village de Golech, région de Silistra (communication préliminaire)', in *Von der Scythia zur Dobrudža*, ed. by Khristo Kholiolchev, Renate Pillinger, and Reinhardt Harreither (Vienna, 1997), pp. 127–39 (pp. 127–29 with 138 fig. 5.7); Ivan Mikulčić, *Spätantike und frühbyzantinische Befestigungen in Nordmakedonien: Städte-Vici-Refugien-Kastelle* (Munich, 2002), pp. 157–58 with 156 fig. 47.6.

two decades or so after 550, given that such buckles appear in the Middle Danube region in association with bow or S-shaped fibulae.[58] To the same period may be dated a stone-lined grave accidentally found near a third-century burial chamber in Ladochori, near Igoumenitsa, in Epirus.[59] The associated short, dagger-like sword has good analogies in the same region of the Middle Danube, where such weapons were found together with S-shaped fibulae.[60] By contrast, the best analogy for the belt buckle with oval plate found in Ladochori is that found on skeleton 1 in burial chamber 495 of the large Crimean cemetery in Skalistoe, where it was associated with mid- to late sixth-century silver buckles with rectangular plates.[61] At least some of the robbed burials of the small cemetery excavated near the acropolis of the ancient city of Europos near Kilkis in Greek Macedonia may be of the same date. The only finds known from that site are two gold earrings with open-work, star-shaped pendant.[62] They may be compared to another pair found in Magnisi (Sicily) together with a coin struck for Emperor Tiberius II (578–82). Two other such earrings have been found in Piatra Frecăței together with a cast fibula with bent stem, for which good analogies are known from Bulgarian hoards with last coins struck for Emperor Justin II (565–78) (Figure 12.3).[63] The same date can be advanced for the belt buckle with shield-shaped end found in Corinth and the similar specimen from grave 13 in Porto Cheli (Halieis). One such buckle has been found in a house in the western portico of the street running from the circular plaza to the southern gate of the upper city in Caričin Grad (Serbia),

---

[58] Csallány, *Archäologische Denkmäler*, pp. 143–44 and pl. 233.13–15 (Pecica); 148–49 and pl. 188.2–3 (Szőreg, grave 11).

[59] Penelopi Agallopoulou, 'Ladochori Hēgoumenitsas', *Archaiologikon Deltion*, 30 (1975), 239.

[60] Várpalota, grave 1: Joachim Werner, *Die Langobarden in Pannonien: Beiträge zur Kenntnis der langobardischen Bodenfunde vor 568* (Munich, 1962), pl. 1. Jutas, grave 196: Gyula Rhé and Nándor Fettich, *Jutas und Öskü: Zwei Gräberfelder aus der Völkerwanderungszeit in Ungarn* (Prague, 1931), pp. 35–36 with pl. 10.7 and pl. 18.18.

[61] Evgenii V. Veimarn and Aleksandr I. Aibabin, *Skalistinskii mogil'nik* (Kiev, 1993), pp. 125–26 with 125 fig. 92.5, 30, and 31.

[62] Thomi Savvopoulos, 'Europos', *Archaiologikon Deltion*, 47 (1992), 389 with pl. 114 β.

[63] Magnisi: Baldini Lippolis, *L'oreficeria*, p. 101. Piatra Frecăței: Petre, *La Romanité*, p. 79 and pl. 145 fig. 239c, d. For cast fibulae with bent stem, see Nikola A. Mushmov, 'Izvorata Sv. Troitsa pri Bratsigovo', *Izvestiia na Bălgarskiia Arkheologicheskii Institut*, 5 (1928–29), 328–30 (pp. 328–29 with 329 fig. 191); Atanas Milchev and Georgi Draganov, 'Arkheologicheski ostanki v raiona na s. Koprivets, Rusensko', *Arkheologiia*, 24 (1992), 36–41 (p. 39 with fig. 5); Anna Kharalambieva and Dimităr Ivanov, 'Kăsnoantichni fibuli ot Muzeia v Ruse', *Godishnik na muzeite ot Severna Bălgariia*, 12 (1986), 9–20 (p. 10 with pl. 1.4).

Figure 12.3 (left). Earrings with open-work, star-shaped pendant: (1) Europos; (2) Piatra Frecăţei, grave E143. After Savvopoulos, 'Europos'; and Petre, *La Romanité*.
Figure 12.4 (right). Belt buckles with shield-shaped end: (1) Corinth; (2) Porto Cheli, grave 13; (3) Caričin Grad. After Davidson, *Minor Objects*; Rudolph, 'Excavations at Porto Cheli'; and Mano-Zisi, 'Iskopavanja na Caričinom Gradu'.

and associated with it was a cast fibula with bent stem (Figure 12.4).[64] At Nea Anchialos, on the site of the ancient city of Thebes, a burial chamber found between basilicas A and B produced a number of metal artefacts associated with scattered remains of several skeletons.[65] The bracelet with pointed ends has a good analogy in a certainly contemporary assemblage in Keramidi, near neighbouring Karditsa in Thessaly, which has also produced a pair of earrings similar to one of the eleven earrings found in Nea Anchialos.[66] Belt buckles similar to one of those found in Nea Anchialos are known from grave B45 in Piatra Frecăţei and a sixth-

[64] Gladys R. Davidson, *The Minor Objects* (Princeton, 1952), pl. 114.2210; Wolf W. Rudolph, 'Excavations at Porto Cheli and Vicinity. Preliminary Report V: The Early Byzantine Remains', *Hesperia*, 48 (1979), 294–320 (pp. 301 and 320 with fig. 14.57). For Caričin Grad, see Đorđe Mano-Zisi, 'Iskopavanja na Caričinom Gradu 1955 i 1956 godine', *Starinar*, 7–8 (1958), 311–28 (pp. 312–13 with 326 fig. 36). The Caričin Grad assemblage is crucial for the dating of this type of buckle. For a much later dating, based on finds from Merovingian Gaul, see Schulze-Dörrlamm, *Byzantinische Gürtelschnallen*, p. 224. A sixth- (as opposed to seventh-) century date is also suggested by the context of the buckle found in a female grave in Suuk Su (Crimea). See N. Repnikov, 'Nekotorye mogil'niki oblasti krymskikh gotov', *Izvestiia imperatorskoi arkheologicheskoi kommissii*, 19 (1906), 1–80 (pp. 22–23).

[65] Giorgios A. Sotiriou, 'Anaskaphai en Nea Anchialo', *Praktika tēs en Athēnais Archaiologikēs Hetaireias*, 111 (1956), 110–18 (pp. 113–15 with pl. 41β, for the buckle, the bracelet, and the earrings).

[66] Angelis G. Liankouras, 'Keramidi', *Archaiologikon Deltion*, 20 (1965), 321 with pl. 381α.

Figure 12.5. Belt buckles with open-work plate: (1) Nea Anchialos, burial chamber between basilica A and basilica B; (2) Piatra Frecăţei, grave B45; (3) Khats'ki. After Sotiriou, 'Anaskaphai en Nea Anchialo'; Petre, *La Romanité*; and Parczewski, 'Metalowe zabytki'.

1   2   3

to seventh-century hoard found in Khats'ki (Ukraine), in both cases associated with 'Martynivka mounts' (Figure 12.5).[67] The same association is decisive for the dating of another belt buckle found in Nea Anchialos, which has a good analogy in burial chamber 406 in Skalistoe, a context dated no later than *c.* 600, because of the associated Late Roman Ware C (Hayes's form 3).[68]

A date around AD 600 may be advanced for a large hoard of coins, copper-alloy vessels, and iron tools and implements found in 1877 in Olympia.[69] Unfortunately, no coins have been preserved from what seems to have been a fairly large collection. However, one of the copper jugs is remarkably similar to that from Horgeşti (Romania), which contained a hoard with the last coin struck in 597/98.[70] Whether

[67] Petre, *La Romanité*, pp. 69–70 with pl. 126 fig. 200d; Michał Parczewski, 'Metalowe zabytki naddnieprzańskie z VI–VIII w. w zbiorach Krakowskiego Muzeum Archeologicznego', *Archaeoslavica*, 1 (1991), 115–26 (pp. 119–20 with pl. 1.8). For the whole of the Khatski hoard, see G. F. Korzukhina, 'Klady i sluchainye nakhodki veshchei kruga "drevnostei antov" v srednem Podneprov'e. Katalog pamiatnikov', *Materialy po arkheologii, istorii i etnografii Tavrii*, 5 (1996), 353–435 and 586–705 (pp. 372–73).

[68] Veimarn and Aibabin, *Skalistinskii mogil'nik*, pp. 95 with 94 fig. 66.4 (for the buckle), 17, and 22 (for the associated Late Roman C Ware). An African Red Slip bowl of Hayes's form 99A found in a pit by the cemetery excavated in 1983 in the Papathanassiou area of present-day Argos may be dated as late as *c.* 620, but the type was popular mainly during the sixth century. Nothing else indicates that the cemetery was still in use after 600. See Oikonomou-Laniado, *Argos paléochrétienne*, pp. 32 and 35–36.

[69] Thomas Völling, 'Ein frühbyzantinischer Hortfund aus Olympia', *Mitteilungen des Deutschen Archäologischen Instituts: Athenische Abteilung*, 110 (1995), 425–59.

[70] Völling, 'Ein frühbyzantinischer Hortfund', pl. 93.1. For the Horgeşti jug, see Viorel Căpitanu, 'Tezaurul de monede bizantine descoperit la Horgeşti, jud. Bacău', *Carpica*, 4 (1971), 253–69 with fig. 1. Three similar jugs were found with another coin hoard in Zogeria, on the Spetsai island in the Argolid Bay, the latest coin of which was struck in 581/82. See *Kathēmerinē zoē sto Vyzantio: Thessalonikē, Leukos Pyrgos, Oktovrios 2001–Ianouarios 2002*, ed. by Dimitra Papanikola-Bakirtzis (Athens, 2002), pp. 148–49. Two other specimens have been found in the early Byzantine fort at Pece, in north-eastern Albania. See Luan Përzhita, 'Kështjella e Pecës në periudhën e antikitetit të

or not the Olympia hoard may be viewed as evidence of the Slavic invasions that supposedly devastated the city's hinterland in the late sixth or early seventh century (so Thomas Völling), it is so far one of the last pieces of evidence for any occupation of that ancient site. Slightly later must be the inhumation found in 1994 in the cemetery to the north-west from the Asklepieion in Messini, which produced a buckle with opposing animal protomes.[71] Two such buckles have been found in contemporary burials in Albania (graves 34 and 35 in Bukël), another is known from the Athenian Agora.[72] However, the chronology of those buckles can be established primarily on the basis of specimens found in Early Avar burial assemblages in Hungary, such as grave 59 in Nagyharsány and the so-called grave A in Alattyán, the cemetery that Ilona Kovrig used to postulate the existence of an Early Avar phase in Avar archaeology (Figure 12.6). Since such assemblages cannot be dated earlier than c. 600 and later than c. 650, the buckles with opposing animal protomes may also

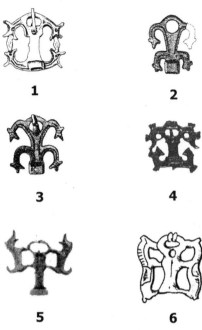

Figure 12.6. Belt buckles with opposing animal protomes: (1) Messini; (2) Bukël, grave 34; (3) Bukël, grave 35; (4) Athens; (5) Nagyharsány, grave 59; (6) Alattyán, grave A. After Anagnostakis and Poulou-Papadimitriou, 'He protovyzantinē Messēnē'; Anamali, 'Një varrezë'; Setton, 'Bulgars in the Balkans'; Papp, 'A nagyharsányi avarkori temető'; and Kovrig, *Das awarenzeitliche Gräberfeld*.

vonë dhe mesjetë (rrethi i Kukësit)', *Iliria*, 20 (1990), 201–41 (pp. 218–19 with 237 pl. 10.1 and 2). Finally, the Olympia hoard contains three other jugs with trefoil-shaped mouth with good analogies among finds from Sardis and Pergamon.

[71] Anagnostakis and Poulou-Papadimitriou, 'He protovyzantinē Messēnē', pp. 242–43 and 250, with fig. 9.

[72] Skënder Anamali, 'Një varrezë e mesjetës së hershme në Bukël të Mirditës', *Iliria*, 1 (1971), 209–25 (p. 217 with pl. 7.2 and 3); Setton, 'Bulgars in the Balkans', p. 522 and fig. For Early Avar specimens, see László Papp, 'A nagyharsányi avarkori temető', *Janus Pannonius Múzeum Évkönyve*, 9 (1963), 113–41 (pp. 130–31 with 131 fig. 24); Ilona Kovrig, *Das awarenzeitliche Gräberfeld von Alattyán* (Budapest, 1963), p. 60 and pl. 44.43.

be dated to the first half of the seventh century.[73] The same seems to be true for the burial chamber attached to the northern side of the apse in basilica Δ of Nea Anchialos.[74] The chamber contained four skeletons and produced a so-called 'Slavic' bow fibula and a hinged belt buckle with circle-and-dot decoration. Unfortunately, it is not known with which one of the four skeletons those artefacts had been found and whether or not they have been deposited at the same time. Hinged belt buckles are known from several sites in the eastern Mediterranean region, but the best analogy is from a female burial of the Early and Middle Avar cemetery excavated in Aradac (northern Serbia).[75] The Aradac buckle was attached to a bronze chain found on the left side of the skeleton's chest. A similar chain, but with a buckle of a different type, was found in grave 16 of that same cemetery, which also produced two silver earrings and a strap end with interlaced ornament, all good indications of a date within the Early Avar period (*c.* 600–50).[76]

[73] Syna Uenze, 'Die Schnallen mit Riemenschlaufe aus dem 6. und 7. Jahrhundert', *Bayerische Vorgeschichtsblätter*, 31 (1966), 142–81 (p. 156); Garam, *Funde*, p. 122; Schulze-Dörrlamm, *Byzantinische Gürtelschnallen*, p. 228. For other specimens, see Mechthild Schulze, 'Neuerwerbungen für die Sammlungen', *Jahrbuch des Römisch-Germanischen Zentralmuseums*, 32 (1985), 730–33 and 741–42 (p. 731 fig. 43); Sali Hidri, 'Materiale arkeologijke nga bazilika e Arapajt', *Iliria*, 21 (1991), 203–18 with pl. 11.12.

[74] Giorgios A. Sotiriou, 'Anaskaphai en Nea Anchialo', *Praktika tēs en Athēnais Archaiologikēs Hetaireias*, 97 (1939), 53–72 (pp. 62–63 with fig. 12); Nikolaos G. Laskaris, *Monuments funéraires paléochrétiens (et byzantins) de Grèce* (Athens, 2000), p. 37. Basilica Δ is also known as the 'cemetery basilica' for its location next to the largest late antique cemetery of Thebes, in use throughout the sixth century. The dates advanced for the basilica range widely, from the second half of the fifth century to the early seventh. At some point during the sixth century, the church was certainly turned into a *basilica coemeterialis*. See Johannes Koder and Friedrich Hild, *Tabula Imperii Byzantinii 1: Hellas und Thessalia* (Vienna, 1976), p. 271; Olga Karagiorgou, 'Demetrias and Thebes: The Fortunes and Misfortunes of Two Thessalian Port Cities', in *Recent Research in Late-Antique Urbanism*, ed. by Luke Lavan (Portsmouth, 2001), pp. 182–215 (pp. 189 and 194).

[75] Sándor Nagy, 'Nekropola kod Aradca iz ranog srednieg veka', *Rad Vojvodanskih Muzeja*, 8 (1959), 45–102 (p. 60 with pl. 12.9). For a complete list of analogies, see Vida and Völling, *Das slawische Brandgräberfeld*, p. 28. See also Florin Curta, 'Female Dress and "Slavic" Bow Fibulae in Greece', *Hesperia*, 74 (2005),101–46 (pp. 116–18).

[76] Sándor Nagy, 'Mečka – ein frühmittelalterliches Gräberfeld beim Dorfe Aradac', *Študijné zvesti*, 16 (1968), 165–74 (p. 167 fig. 1). For the interlaced ornament in dentil pattern (*Zahnschnitt*) as typically Early Avar, see Nándor Fettich, 'Zum Problem des ungarländischen Stils II', *Eurasia Septentrionalis Antiqua*, 9 (1934), 308–22; Orsolya Heinrich-Tamáska, 'Tier- und Zahnschnittornamentik im awarenzeitlichen Karpatenbecken', *Bericht der Römisch-Germanischen Kommission*, 87 (2006), 506–627.

Figure 12.7. Belt buckles of the Syracuse class: (1)
Edessa; (2) Athens, grave 10; (3) Plateia; (4) Das-
kaleio. After Petsas, 'Archaiotētes kai mnēmeia';
Travlos and Frantz, 'Church of St. Dionysios the
Areopagite'; and Avramea, *Le Peloponnèse*.

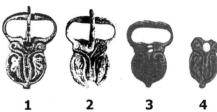

A small cemetery with stone-lined graves, some with pitched tile covers, was
accidentally found in the early 1970s on the Proussa Street in Edessa.[77] An isolated
find of a bell pendant reminds one of similar jingling accessories found in early
seventh-century Ukrainian hoards, as well as in Early Avar assemblages.[78] This is
not contradicted by what we know about finds from some of the burials excavated
in Edessa, such as the belt buckle of the Syracuse class found in association with
two 'Slavic' bow fibulae in grave A.[79] Similar buckles are known from a burial in
Athens, as well as from several islands near the Argolid coast (Figure 12.7).[80] Mechthild Schulze-Dörrlamm's recent study of the so-called 'Byzantine' belt buckles and
mounts in the collection of the Roman-Germanic Museum in Mainz shows that
the earliest specimens of this class of buckles cannot be dated earlier than the first
decades of Heraclius's reign.[81] Buckles of the Syracuse class remained in use

---

[77] M. Karamanoli-Siganidou, 'Edessa', *Archaiologikon Deltion*, 29 (1973–74), 709–10 (p. 710
with pl. 509).

[78] Korzukhina, 'Klady i sluchainye nakhodki', pp. 634 fig. 44.4–10 (Nova Odessa); 644 fig.
54.2–11 (Kozievka); 660 fig. 70.14–15 (Sudzha). For Early Avar specimens, see Lajos Roediger,
'Kora középkori lovas sírleletről Szeghegyen (Bács-Bodrog m.)', *Archaeologiai Értesítő*, 23 (1903),
272–76 (p. 273 fig. 1.1); Kovrig, *Das awarenzeitliche Gräberfeld*, pls 7.45, 14.70, and 17.65; Rhé
and Fettich, *Jutas und Öskü*, pl. 11.3.

[79] Petsas, 'Archaiotētes kai mnēmeia', p. 307 and fig. 320.

[80] Travlos and Frantz, 'Church of St. Dionysios the Areopagite', p. 167 and pl. 43a; Avramea,
Le Peloponnèse, pp. 89–90 and pl. 4a1 and 4c1. Of a similar date is also the equal-armed fibula from
the island of Daskaleio in the Argolid Bay (Avramea, *Le Peloponnèse*, p. 90 and pl. 4a3), a specimen
of Thörle's class I A2, dated shortly before or after 600. See Mechthild Schulze-Dörrlamm,
'Gleicharmige Bügelfibeln der Zeit um 600 aus dem Byzantinischen Reich', *Archäologisches
Korrespondenzblatt*, 33 (2003), 437–44 (p. 437); Stefan Thörle, *Gleicharmige Bügelfibeln des frühen
Mittelalters* (Bonn, 2001), pp. 21–23.

[81] Schulze-Dörrlamm, *Byzantinische Gürtelschnallen*, p. 179. Garam, *Funde*, p. 95, notes that
all specimens known from Hungary have been found in Early Avar assemblages. For an earlier
dating of specimens found in Sicily, see Ferdinando Maurici, 'Ancora sulle fibbie da cintura di età
bizantina in Sicilia', in *Byzantino-Sicula IV: Atti del I Congresso internazionale di archeologia della*

throughout the Early Avar period, but despite claims to the contrary, there is absolutely no indication that their chronology reaches the eighth century.[82] A date within the seventh century for the Edessa cemetery is confirmed by the buckle of the Boly-Želovce class found in grave Γ.[83] Unlike buckles of the Syracuse class, most Boly-Želovce specimens found in Hungary appear in Middle Avar assemblages of the second half of the seventh century. However, an early date may be supported by the association in the Kratigos (Mitilene) hoard of one such buckle with solidi struck for Emperor Heraclius.[84] A variant of the Boly-Želovce class has been found in excavations of the Hexamilion at Isthmia.[85] Its closest analogies are all Early Avar specimens, such as that from grave 510 in Zalakomár or, perhaps more significantly, that from the large cemetery in Zamárdi, where one such buckle was found in association with belt mounts decorated in the second animal style most typical for Early Avar dress accessories.[86] An early seventh-century date may

Sicilia bizantina (Corleone, 28 luglio–2 agosto 1998), ed. by Rosa Maria Carra Bonacasa (Palermo, 2000), pp. 513–57 (p. 515).

[82] Teodor, 'Piese vestimentare bizantine', pp. 129–30. Such claims seem to be based on a faulty chronology of assemblages from burial chambers in Crimean cemeteries, for which see Aleksandr I. Aibabin, 'Khronologiia mogil'nikov Kryma pozdnerimskogo i rannesrednevekovogo vremeni', *Materialy po arkheologii, istorii i etnografii Tavrii*, 1 (1990), 5–68. For a dating restricted to the first half of the seventh century, see Eger, 'Eine byzantinische Gürtelschnalle', p. 345; Riemer, 'Byzantinische Gürtelschnallen', p. 779. Such a narrow dating is based primarily on the association in burials from the Gymnasium in Samos of buckles of the Syracuse class with coins struck for emperors Heraclius and Constans II. See Wolfram Martini and Cornelius Steckner, *Das Gymnasium von Samos: Das frühbyzantinische Klostergut* (Bonn, 1993), pp. 125–26. There is no evidence of an eighth-century dating for any buckle of the Syracuse class known to have been found in a datable assemblage. See Ellen Riemer, *Romanische Grabfunde des 5.–8. Jahrhunderts in Italien* (Rahden, 2000), p. 152.

[83] Giorgos Gounaris, 'Chalkines porpes apo to oktagōno tōn Philippōn kai tēn Kentrikē Makedonia', *Vyzantiaka*, 4 (1984), 49–59 (pp. 57 and 56 fig. 2ε).

[84] Baldini Lippolis, *L'oreficeria*, pp. 37 and 229; Prokopiou, 'Vyzantines porpes', p. 339. For the latest coin in the Kratigos hoard, see Cécile Morrisson, Vladislav Popović, and Vujadin Ivanišević, *Les Trésors monétaires byzantins des Balkans et d'Asie Mineure (491–713)* (Paris, 2006), pp. 386–87. For a date within the Middle Avar period, see Ibler, 'Pannonische Gürtelschnallen', p. 140; Varsik, 'Byzantinische Gürtelschnallen', pp. 86–87; Garam, *Funde*, p. 101.

[85] Timothy E. Gregory, *The Hexamilion and the Fortress (Isthmia V)* (Princeton, 1993), pl. 25b.

[86] For the Zalakomár and Zamárdi specimens, as well as for other Early Avar analogies of the Isthmia buckle, see Garam, *Funde*, p. 101. For the Early Avar animal style (so-called 'second animal style'), see Nándor Fettich, 'Adatok az ősgermán állatornamentumok II. stílusának eredetéhez', *Archaeologiai Értesítő* 43 (1929), 68–110; Margit Nagy, 'Frühawarenzeitliche Grabfunde aus

Figure 12.8. Belt buckles of the Salona-Histria class: (1) Corinth; (2) Tiszaderzs; (3) Sakharna Golivka, burial chamber 52; (4) Sekić-Lovčenac. After Davidson, *Minor Objects*; Csallány, *Archäologische Denkmäler*; Veimarn, 'Arkheologichni roboti'; and Roediger, 'Kora középkori lovas sírleletről'.

1   2   3   4

also be advanced for the belt buckles of the Salona-Histria class found in Tiszaderzs (Hungary) and Sakharna Golivka (Crimea, Ukraine), the closest analogies I know for the specimen found in Corinth.[87] Indeed, an almost identical buckle was found in an Avar horseman burial in Sekić-Lovčenac (northern Serbia) together with a gold coin struck between 613 and 631 (Figure 12.8).[88] Belt buckles of the Balgota class, such as found in the Athenian Agora, are also dated to the Early Avar period.[89] The same is true for belt buckles with cross-shaped plates such as those from Athens or from several islands near the Argolid coast and in the Sea of Crete.[90]

Budapest: Bemerkungen zur awarenzeitlichen Tierornamentik', in *Popoli delle steppe: Unni, Avari, Ungari*, I (Spoleto, 1988), pp. 373–407; Margit Nagy, 'Kora avarkori sírleletek Budapestről: Megyegyzések az avarkori állatornamentikához', *Archaeologiai Értesítő*, 119 (1992), 1–42.

[87] Corinth: Davidson, *Minor Objects*, p. 271 and pl. 114.2211. Tiszaderzs, grave 3: Csallány, *Archäologische Denkmäler*, p. 216 and pl. 198.4. Sakharna Golivka, burial chambers 44 and 52: E. V. Veimarn, 'Arkheologichni roboti v raioni Inkermana', *Arkheologichni pam'iatky URSR*, 13 (1963), 15–89 (p. 46 fig. 5.15 and 16). For the chronology of belt buckles of the Salona-Histria class, see Uenze, 'Die Schnallen mit Riemenschlaufe', pp. 143–46; E. A. Goriunov and M. M. Kazanski, 'K izucheniiu rannesrednevekovykh drevnostei Nizhnego Podunav'ia (VI–VII vv.)', in *Slaviane na Dnestre i Dunae: Sbornik nauchnykh trudov*, ed. by V. D. Baran, R. V. Terpilovs'kyi, and A. T. Smilenko (Kiev, 1983), pp. 191–205 (p. 204).

[88] Roediger, 'Kora középkori lovas sírleletről', p. 273 fig. 1.5. For the Sekić solidus, see also Éva Garam, 'Die münzdatierten Gräber der Awarenzeit', in *Awarenforschungen*, ed. by Daim, I, 135–250 (p. 144).

[89] Setton, 'Bulgars in the Balkans', p. 522 and fig. (two specimens). All known buckles of the Balgota class that have been found in Hungary can be dated to the Early Avar period. See Garam, *Funde*, p. 99. By contrast, the buckle found in burial chamber 288 in Skalistoe together with a silver belt buckle with animal-style ornament that has good analogies in sixth-century burial assemblages in Italy may be dated even earlier. See Veimarn and Aibabin, *Skalistinskii mogil'nik*, p. 57 fig. 36.18; Riemer, *Romanische Grabfunde*, pp. 159–60.

[90] Travlos and Frantz, 'Church of St. Dionysios the Areopagite', pl. 43a (stray find and grave 9). For finds from islands near the Argolid coast, see Avramea, *Le Peloponnèse*, pp. 89–90, pls 3, 4e1 (Spetsai-Zogheria), 4b1–3 (Korakonissi), and 4c5–6 (Plateia). For a specimen from Antikythera, a small island to the north-west from Crete, see Nikoleta Pyrrou, Aris Tsaravopoulos, and Cătălin

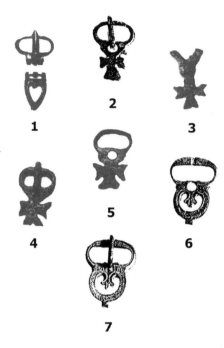

Figure 12.9. Belt buckles of the Bologna (1) and Pergamon (6, 7) classes and belt buckles with cross-shaped plates (2–5): (1) Athens; (2) Athens, grave 9; (3) Spetsai-Zogheria; (4) Korakonissi; (5) Plateia; (6) Athens, grave 13; (7) Athens, grave 23. After Setton, 'Bulgars in the Balkans'; Travlos and Frantz, 'Church of St. Dionysios the Areopagite'; and Avramea, *Le Peloponnèse*.

Another specimen has been found in association with three coins struck for Emperor Heraclius (the last one minted in 613/14) in Samos.[91] Of a somewhat later date may be the buckles of the Pergamon class found in two graves of the cemetery around the Church of St Dionysios the Areopagite in Athens (Figure 12.9).[92] One such buckle is known from burial 90 of the Italian cemetery in Castel

Ovidiu Bojică, 'The Byzantine Settlement of Antikythira (Greece) in the 5th–7th Centuries', in *The Society of the Living, the Community of the Dead (from Neolithic to the Christian Era): Proceedings of the 7th International Colloquium of Funerary Archaeology*, ed. by Sabin Adrian Luca and Valeriu Sîrbu (Sibiu, 2006), pp. 224–38 (pp. 226 and 234 pl. 5.2). For a specimen from Crete, see Poulou-Papadimitriou, 'Les Plaques-boucles byzantines', pp. 696 and 702 fig. 8. Such buckles have also been found in Cyprus, Sicily, and Syria; see Prokopiou, 'Vyzantines porpes', p. 335; Lippolis, *L'oreficeria*, p. 233; and Kazanski, *Qal'at Sem'an*, p. 46. Buckles with cross-shaped plates may have served not just as belt, but also as shoe or purse buckles. For their chronology, see Varsik, 'Byzantinische Gürtelschnallen', p. 85; Schulze-Dörrlamm, *Byzantinische Gürtelschnallen*, p. 197.

[91] Martini and Steckner, *Das Gymnasium*, pp. 127–28. In burial assemblages from Crimea, buckles with cross-shaped plates appear in association with others of the Bologna (Skalistoe, burial chamber 381), Pergamon (Eski Kermen, burial chamber 181), and Corinth classes (Skalistoe, burial chamber 625; and Suuk Su, grave 53). See Veimarn and Aibabin, *Skalistinskii mogil'nik*, pp. 87 fig. 60.18 and 140 fig. 103.4; Aleksandr I. Aibabin, 'Pogrebeniia kontsa VII-pervoi poloviny VIII v. v Krymu', in *Drevnosti epokhi velikogo pereseleniia narodov V–VIII vekov: Sovetsko-vengerskii sbornik*, ed. by Anatolii K. Ambroz and István Erdélyi (Moscow, 1982), pp. 165–92 (p. 175).

[92] Travlos and Frantz, 'Church of St. Dionysios the Areopagite', p. 167 and pl. 43a (graves 13 and 23). The specimen from grave 23 was associated with two other buckles of the Bologna and Boly-Želovce class, respectively. A third Pergamon specimen was found in the Athenian Agora; see Setton, 'Bulgars in the Balkans', p. 522 and fig.

Figure 12.10. Belt buckles of the Nagyharsány class: (1) Corinth, 'wandering soldier' grave; (2) Olympia, stray find. After Davidson, 'A Wandering Soldier's Grave'; and Völling, 'Byzantinische Kleinfunde'.

1   **2**

Trosino, where it was associated with belt mounts of the Civezzano class dated to the early 600s. However, another specimen was found in burial 67 of the Hungarian cemetery in Gyód together with buckles of the Oberpibing and Untereching classes most typical for Bavarian assemblages of the last third of the seventh century.[93] This suggests that some buckles may have been in use for longer time. This also seems to be the case of the Syracuse class, a specimen of which was found in Kenchreai together with two coins struck for Emperor Constans II (641–68).[94]

Finds of an Early Avar date are also known from excavations in Corinth. Most famous among them is the grave of the 'wandering soldier' found in 1938 in the colonnade of the southern Stoa.[95] The belt buckle of the Nagyharsány class has a good analogy in a fragmentary specimen from Olympia (Figure 12.10).[96] More precise details about its date may be obtained from the examination of the double-edged

[93] Riemer, 'Byzantinische Gürtelschnallen', p. 783. See also V. B. Kovalevskaia, *Poiasnye nabory Evrazii IV–IX vv. Priazhki* (Moscow, 1979), p. 23; J. Boube, 'Eléments de ceinturon wisigothiques et byzantins trouvés au Maroc', *Bulletin d'archéologie marocaine*, 15 (1983–84), 281–96 (pp. 290 and 292). The class has been named by K. Neeft, 'Byzantijnse gespen en riembeslag in Amsterdam', *Vereniging van Vrienden Allard Pierson Mus. Amsterdam: Mededelingenblad*, 43 (1988), 4–6.

[94] Pallas, 'Données nouvelles', p. 298. Another specimen was found together with coins minted for Emperor Constans II in a grave in the Gymnasium of Samos. See Martini and Steckner, *Das Gymnasium*, pp. 125–26. For late specimens of the Syracuse class as illustrating a standardization of buckles most typical for the seventh century, see Cornelius Steckner, 'Samos: der spätjustinianische Kirchenkomplex. Ost-westliche Beziehungen', in *Radovi XIII: Međunarodnog Kongresa za starokršćansku arheologiju. Split-Poreč (25.9.–1.10. 1994)*, ed. by Nenad Cambi and Emilio Marin, II (Vatican, 1998), pp. 173–88.

[95] Davidson, 'A Wandering Soldier's Grave', pp. 513–21. Two other buckles of the Nagyharsány class have been found in Corinth; see Davidson, *Minor Objects*, pl. 114.2209–10. Another was found on the island of Plateia in the Argolid Bay; see Avramea, *Le Peloponnèse*, p. 90 and pl. 4c 8.

[96] Davidson, 'A Wandering Soldier's Grave', pl. 110e; Völling, 'Byzantinische Kleinfunde', pp. 495–96 with 494 fig. 1. For the chronology of the Nagyharsány class of buckles, see Ibler, 'Pannonische Gürtelschnallen', p. 143.

sword with cross-bar, the closest analogy of which is that from a warrior grave in Aradac, in which it was accompanied by strap ends and mounts with dentil ornamentation most typical for the Early Avar period.[97] I do not know of any Hungarian analogy for the bronze trinket found in the right hand of the 'wandering soldier', but similar artefacts are known from seventh-century barrows in Latvia and Lithuania, as well as in the Smolensk region of Russia.[98] To the same period point the bronze chains found in Corinth, one in a grave within the square tower near the western gate of the Acrocorinth, the other in a burial within the southern Stoa.[99]

[97] Davidson, 'A Wandering Soldier's Grave', pp. 516 fig. 1; 518 fig. 3; 519 fig. 4; pl. 12a–c; Nagy, 'Nekropola kod Aradca', pp. 62 with 94 pl. 27.1. Because of its cross-bar, the Corinth sword is commonly viewed as 'Byzantine'; see Avramea, *Le Peloponnèse*, p. 97 (who offers nothing in the way of arguments); Vida and Völling, *Das slawische Brandgräberfeld*, p. 34 (who point to similar swords represented on fifth- and sixth-century ivory diptychs); Garam, *Funde*, pp. 158–59 (who takes the idea for granted). However, the first to express such opinions was Attila Kiss, 'Frühmittelalterliche byzantinische Schwerter im Karpatenbecken', *Acta Archaeologica Academiae Scientiarum Hungaricae*, 39 (1987), 193–210 (pp. 194–95 and 204), who was also the first to compare the Corinth to the Aradac sword. In sharp contrast to the 'Byzantine' cross-bar, the closest analogy for the cup-like guard of the Corinth sword is that of a long dagger from the seventh- to eighth-century Kudyrge cemetery in the Altai region of Central Asia. See Csanád Bálint, *Die Archäologie der Steppe: Steppenvölker zwischen Volga und Donau vom 6. bis zum 10. Jahrhundert* (Vienna, 1989), p. 254. The Corinth weapon is a two-edged sword, and the number of such weapons found in Early and Middle Avar assemblages has meanwhile increased considerably. E.g. grave 259 in Kölked (Hungary, dated to the Early Avar period on the basis of its association with a buckle of the Salona-Histria class; Attila Kiss, *Das awarenzeitlich-gepidische Gräberfeld von Kölked-Feketekapu A* (Innsbruck, 1996), pp. 230 and 232); grave 64 in Gyenesdiás (Hungary, associated with a solidus struck between 654 and 659; Róbert Müller, 'Das Gräberfeld von Gyenesdiás', in *Reitervölker aus dem Osten*, ed. by Daim, Kaus, and Tomka, pp. 411–16 (p. 411)). There are also examples of single-edged swords with similar cross-bars, e.g. grave 10 in Tarnaméra, dated to the mid-seventh century on the basis of the associated belt mounts. See János Győző Szabó, 'Az Egri múzeum avarkori emlékanyaga I: Kora-avarkori sírleletek tarnameráról', *Agria*, 3 (1965), 29–71 (pp. 42 and 47–48 with 69 pl. 8.1–3). For the mid-seventh-century transition from two- to single-edged swords, see Simon, 'A tapéi kora avar kard'; László Simon, 'Korai avar kardok', *Studia Comitatensia*, 22 (1991), 263–346 (p. 283); Éva Garam, 'A Tiszakécske-óbögi avarkori sírok: Adatok az avarkori szablyákhoz és az egyenes, egyélű kardokhoz', *Communicationes Archaeologicae Hungaricae*, 1991, 121–66 (p. 143).

[98] Wojciech Szymański, 'Niektóre aspekty kontaktów słowiańsko-bałtyjskich w świetle wyników badań w Szeligach, pow. Płock', *Archeologia Polski*, 13 (1968), 188–210 (pp. 205–06); Valentin V. Sedov, *Dlinnye kurgany krivichei* (Moscow, 1974), pp. 58; pl. 25.37–38 (Khotyn) and 39 (Iartsevo). For settlement finds from Belarus, see Ia. G. Zverugo, *Belaruskae Paville u zhaleznym veku i rannim siaredneviakoui* (Minsk, 2005), pp. 104 and 121 fig. 68.

[99] Davidson, 'Avar Invasion', pp. 230 and 232, with 231 fig. 2B; Ivison, 'Burial and Urbanism', pp. 117 and 115 fig. 5.6K.

Figure 12.11. Belt buckles of the Bologna class: (1) Corinth, grave II; (2) Athens, grave 26; (3) Thessaloniki, stray find; (4) Chinitsa. After Davidson, 'Avar Invasion'; Travlos and Frantz, 'Church of St. Dionysios the Areopagite'; Gounaris, 'Chalkines porpes'; and Avramea, *Le Peloponnèse*.

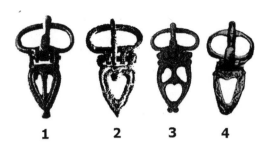

Such artefacts appear in seventh-century Ukrainian hoards and in Aradac, where a bronze chain was associated in grave 16 to a strap end with typically Early Avar plaited ornament.[100] The chain in the burial in the southern Stoa at Corinth was found together with two spear heads for which good analogies are known from Early Avar burials in Pécs and Csengele.[101]

A slightly later date may be advanced for another burial within the square tower by the western gate of the Acrocorinth.[102] The belt buckle of the Bologna class found in that grave has good analogies in Athens, Thessaloniki, and Chinitsa, a tiny island near the Argolid coast (Figure 12.11).[103] In Samos, buckles of the Bologna class were found together with two coins struck for Emperor Heraclius (611/12 and 613/14) in burial 3, and another minted for Emperor Constans II in burial 1 (652/53).[104] The belt buckles of the Boly-Želovce class that have been

[100] Korzukhina, 'Klady i sluchainye nakhodki', pp. 635 fig. 45.8 (Nova Odessa); 659 fig. 69.25 (Sudzha); Mikhailo Iu. Braichevs'kyi, 'K voprosu o geneticheskikh sviazakh iuvelirnogo remesla antov i Kievskoi Rusi', *Kratkie soobshcheniia Instituta Arkheologii Akademii Nauk SSSR*, 1 (1952), 43–49 (p. 48 fig. 2.1 for Iakhniki); Nagy, 'Nekropola kod Aradca', pl. 3.19 (Aradac, grave 16). For a complete list of Early Avar chain finds, see also Éva Garam, 'Ketten und Schüsseln in der Frühawarenzeit', *Communicationes Archaeologicae Hungariae*, 2002, 157–61.

[101] Ivison, 'Burial and Urbanism', pp. 117 and 115 fig. 5.6P and R; Attila Kiss, *Avar Cemeteries in County Baranya* (Budapest, 1977), pp. 94 and 96; pl. 37.30.6; Gyula Török, 'Avar kori temető Csengelén (Szeged-Csengele, Feketehalom)', *Móra Ferenc Múzeum Évkönyve*, 1 (1980–81), 43–62 with pl. 13.1.

[102] Davidson, 'Avar Invasion', pp. 230 and 232, with 231 fig. 2A.

[103] Travlos and Frantz, 'Church of St. Dionysios the Areopagite', p. 167 and pl. 43a (graves 23 and 26); Gounaris, 'Chalkines porpes', pp. 57 and 56 fig. 2γ; Avramea, *Le Peloponnèse*, p. 90 and pl. 4d1. For finds from Crete, see Poulou-Papadimitriou, 'Les Plaques-boucles byzantines', p. 700. For the chronology of the Bologna class of buckles, see Varsik, 'Byzantinische Gürtelschnallen', p. 84; Riemer, *Romanische Grabfunde*, p. 160.

[104] Martini and Steckner, *Das Gymnasium*, pp. 124–25.

Figure 12.12. Belt buckles of the Boly-Želovce class: (1, 2) Corinth; (3) Thessaloniki, stray find; (4) Athens, grave 23. After Davidson, *Minor Objects*; Gounaris, 'Chalkines porpes'; and Travlos and Frantz, 'Church of St. Dionysios the Areopagite'.

1   2   3   4

found in two burials within the church on the Acrocorinth point to a similarly broad chronological bracket.[105] Similar buckles are known from the hinterland of Thessaloniki, but also from a burial in Athens (Figure 12.12).[106] All specimens known from Hungary have been found in assemblages dated to the Middle Avar period, that is, to the second half or the last third of the seventh century.[107] The belt buckle of the Corinth class found in another burial within the square tower by the western gate of the Acrocorinth may be dated to the same period.[108] Three other specimens have been found in Corinth in the southern Stoa, the Hemicycle, and a burial excavated near Temple G in the south-western corner of the Roman Forum.[109] No less than seven specimens are known from burials within the Tigani basilica, four of which cluster within the southern aisle.[110] Isolated finds are also

[105] Davidson, *Minor Objects*, p. 272 and pl. 114.2186, 2188, and 2189; Ivison, 'Burial and Urbanism', pp. 117 and 116 fig. 5.7D, E. According to Ivison, those buckles were used for belts holding weapons, but no weapons have been found in grave GR26.15–18, while the skeleton in the other grave may have been that of a woman.

[106] Gounaris, 'Chalkines porpes', 57 and 56 fig. 2.ä; Travlos and Frantz, 'Church of St. Dionysios the Areopagite', p. 167 and pl. 43a (grave 23).

[107] Ibler, 'Pannonische Gürtelschnallen', p. 140; Varsik, 'Byzantinische Gürtelschnallen', p. 87; Garam, *Funde*, p. 101. In Slovakia, buckles of the Boly-Želovce class have been found in association with mid-seventh-century artefacts, such as a late Early Avar strap end in grave 88 in Radvaň nad Dunajom and a Middle Avar saber in grave 564 in Želovce.

[108] Davidson, 'Avar Invasion', p. 232 and fig. 3.

[109] Davidson, *Minor Objects*, p. 272 and pl. 114/2195 (grave III, skeleton A); Ivison, 'Burial and Urbanism', pp. 112 and 116 fig. 5.7C; Charles K. Williams, Jean Macintosh, and Joan E. Fisher, 'Excavation at Corinth, 1973', *Hesperia*, 43 (1974), 1–76 (p. 11 with pl. 2.8).

[110] Nikolaos V. Drandakis and Nikos Gkiolis, 'Anaskaphē sto Tēgani tēs Manēs', *Praktika tēs en Athēnais Archaiologikēs Hetaireias*, 135 (1980), 247–58 (pp. 253, 255, and pl. 149ε, for graves 13 and 25); Nikolaos V. Drandakis, Nikos Gkiolis, and Charalambos Konstantinidi, 'Anaskaphē sto Tēgani Manēs', *Praktika tēs en Athēnais Archaiologikēs Hetaireias*, 136 (1981), 241–53 (pp. 249, 251, and pl. 182γ, for graves 32, 40, 42, and 45); *Kathēmerinē zōē*, p. 293, no. 480. None of those

Figure 12.13. Belt buckles of the Corinth class: (1) Corinth, grave III; (2) Corinth, 1969 grave; (3) Tigani, grave 32; (4) Daskaleio. After Davidson, *Minor Objects*; Williams, Macintosh, and Fisher, 'Excavation at Corinth'; Drandakis, Gkiolis, and Konstantinidi, 'Anaskaphē sto Tēgani Manēs'; and Avramea, *Le Peloponnèse*.

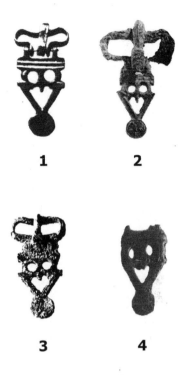

1   **2**

3   **4**

known from Corinth, Athens, and the islands of Korakonissi, Plateia, and Daskaleio (Figure 12.13).[111] Specimens from Hungary were accompanied by artefacts most typical for the Early Avar period, but in a grave of the Albanian cemetery in Kruje, a buckle of the Corinth class was found together with a pair of so-called 'Slavic' bow fibulae of Werner's class I C, dated to the second third of the seventh century.[112] The association of a buckle of the Corinth class with melon seed–shaped beads (*Melonenkern- perlen*) in a burial in Durrës also points to a date within the second half of the seventh century.[113]

assemblages produced any evidence allowing the interpretation of the accompanying buckles of the Corinth class as 'Orthodox "Byzantine" artifacts of the eighth century' (Sanders, 'Pottery from Medieval Levels', p. 456; see also Avramea, *Le Peloponnèse*, p. 91).

[111] Davidson, *Minor Objects*, p. 235 fig. 5 and pl. 114.2192; Setton, 'Bulgars in the Balkans', p. 522 and fig. (with two specimens); Avramea, *Le Peloponnèse*, pp. 89–90 and pl. 4a2, 4c2, and 4b6. For a buckle of the Corinth class from Delos, see Joachim Werner, 'Byzantinische Gürtelschnallen des 6. und 7. Jahrhunderts aus der Sammlung Diergardt', *Kölner Jahrbuch für Vor- und Frühgeschichte*, 1 (1955), 36–48 (p. 47). For specimens found on various sites in Crete, see Poulou-Papadimitriou, 'Les Plaques-boucles byzantines', pp. 698–99.

[112] Garam, *Funde*, p. 99; Skënder Anamali, 'Oreficerie, gioielli bizantini in Albania: Komani', *Corso di cultura sull'arte ravennate e bizantina*, 40 (1993), 435–46 (p. 445 fig. 4.2 for grave 28). See also Nallbani, 'Précisions', p. 668. For 'Slavic' bow fibulae of Werner's class I C, see Florin Curta, 'Some Remarks on Bow Fibulae of Werner's Class I C', *Slavia Antiqua*, 49 (2008), 45–98. For a late seventh-century date for the Corinth class of buckles, see also Varsik, 'Byzantinische Gürtelschnallen', p. 83; Aibabin, 'Pogrebeniia kontsa VII-pervoi poloviny VIII', p. 172.

[113] Fatos Tartari, 'Një varrezë e mesjetës së hershme në Durrës', *Iliria*, 14 (1984), 227–50 (p. 230 with pl. 2.28.6, for grave 28). For the chronology of *Melonenkernperlen*, see Vida and Völling, *Das slawische Brandgräberfeld*, pp. 85–86. Fur further specimens from Durrës, see Nallbani, 'Précisions', pp. 669–70.

Figure 12.14. Velestinon, selected mounts.
After Werner, *Slawische Bronzefiguren*.

Particularly difficult to place chronologically is the hoard accidentally found in the 1920s in Velestinon (Figure 12.14).[114] The hoard includes several bronze dies and lead models for mounts, some of them in the shape of dancing men. Such mounts most likely decorated the saddle and have been found in some quantity in

---

[114] Joachim Werner, *Slawische Bronzefiguren aus Nordgriechenland* (Berlin, 1953). The number of comparable finds has increased steadily since Werner's publication. See P. I. Khavliuk, 'Ranneslavianskie poseleniia v srednei chasti Iuzhnogo Pobuzh'ia', *Sovetskaia Arkheologiia*, 1961.3, 187–201 (p. 199 fig. 10.8); P. I. Khavliuk, 'Ranneslavianskie poseleniia Semenki i Samchintsy v srednem techenii Iuzhnogo Buga', in *Slaviane nakanune obrazovaniia Kievskoi Rusi*, ed. by Boris A. Rybakov (Moscow, 1963), pp. 320–50 (p. 321 fig. 2); Skënder Anamali and Hëna Spahiu, 'Varrëza e herëshme mesjëtare e Krujës', *Buletin i Universitetit shtetëror të Tiranës*, 17 (1963), 3–85 with pl. 8.8; Jane C. Waldbaum, *Metalwork from Sardis: The Finds Through 1974* (Cambridge, 1983), p. 117 and pl. 43.688; Ante Milošević, 'Mjesto nalaza i porijeklo ranosrednjovjekovne brončane matrice iz Arheološkog Muzeja u Zagrebu', *Vjesnik za arheologiju i historiju Dalmatinsku*, 83 (1990), 117–24; Valeri Iotov, 'Bronzova figura ot Iuzhna Dobrudzha', *Vekove*, 1991.1–2, 70–73. The Velestinon hoard certainly included pairs of bronze dies and lead models for the same mounts. All known lead models are in the collection of the Princeton Art Museum, including the lead replica of the 'votive hand' mentioned by Dafydd Kidd, 'The Velestínon (Thessaly) Hoard: A Footnote', in *Awarenforschungen*, ed. by Daim, I, 509–15. In addition to the existence of lead models, the main argument against the idea that the Velestinon bronze specimens are actual mounts is that, unlike other known mounts, none of them presents any perforations for attachment to the saddle or to any other background.

horseman burials in the northern Caucasus region.[115] In burial chamber 3 from Kugul, one such mount was associated with 'Martynivka mounts', and the same is true for another specimen from Pregradnaia.[116] On one of the Velestinon models in the shape of a lion, the mane is represented as a semicircular shield, much in the same way as on comparable mounts from the Martynivka and Cherkasy hoards.[117] If such analogies are allowed, then they confirm an early seventh-century date established for the Velestinon mounts on the basis of the stylistical analysis of some models, the crisp decoration of which is very similar to that of the 'Slavic' bow fibula from the burial chamber in Nea Anchialos discussed above.[118] A horse-shaped mount is known from Corinth, and another from Zogheria on the island of Spetsai near the Argolid coast.[119] Both mounts have analogies in the same region north from the Caucasus Mountains, specifically in a horseman burial assemblage from Galaity, in which such mounts were associated with gold sheet decorations of the saddle.[120] A saddle mount in the form of a stallion has also been found in the Ukrainian hoard at Martynivka, which also included a cup with four control stamps from the reign of Justin II, possibly from 577.[121]

---

[115] A. K. Ambroz, *Khronologiia drevnostei Severnogo Kavkaza V–VII vv.* (Moscow, 1989), pp. 78–80. For Velestinon-type mounts as used for decorating the saddle, see Attila Kiss, 'Archäologische Angaben zur Geschichte der Sättel des Frühmittelalters', *Alba Regia*, 21 (1984), 189–207 (p. 197); Witold Świętosławski, 'Die Elemente der fernöstlichen Bewaffnung im frühmittelalterlichen West- und Mitteleuropa', in *Actes du XII-e Congrès international des sciences préhistoriques et protohistoriques*, ed. by Pavuj, IV, 282–84 (p. 284); Françoise Vallet, 'Une tombe de riche cavalier lombard découverte à Castel Trosino', in *La Noblesse romaine et les chefs barbares du III*ᵉ *au VII*ᵉ *siècle: Actes du Colloque International organisé par le Musée Antiquités Nationales, Saint-Germain-en-Laye, 16–19 mai 1992*, ed. by Françoise Vallet and Michel Kazanski (Saint-Germain-en-Laye, 1995), pp. 335–49 (p. 335).

[116] Ambroz, *Khronologiia*, pp. 78–80.

[117] Bartłomiej Szymon Szmoniewski, 'Cultural Contacts in Central and Eastern Europe: What Do Metal Beast Images Speak About?', in *Ethnic Contacts and Cultural Exchanges North and West of the Black Sea from the Greek Colonization to the Ottoman Conquest*, ed. by Victor Cojocaru (Iaşi, 2005), pp. 425–42 (pp. 427 and 439 fig. 2).

[118] Kidd, 'The Velestínon (Thessaly) Hoard'.

[119] Davidson, *Minor Objects*, pl. 68.935; Avramea, *Le Péloponnèse*, p. 90 and pl. 4e2.

[120] Ambroz, *Khronologiia*, p. 80.

[121] Ljudmila V. Pekarskaja and Dafydd Kidd, *Der Silberschatz von Martynovka (Ukraine) aus dem 6. und 7. Jahrhundert* (Innsbruck, 1994), pl. 26.1–2; 27.1–2; 28.1; 29.1–2 (mounts) and 47–50 (cup). For the Martynivka mounts as shield decorations, see Dafydd Kidd and Ludmila Pekarskaya, 'New Insight into the Hoard of 6th–7th Century Silver From Martynovka', in *La Noblesse romaine et les chefs barbares du III*ᵉ *au VII*ᵉ *siècle*, ed. by Vallet and Kazanski, pp. 351–60 (p. 352).

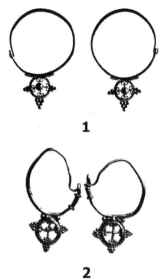

1

2

Figure 12.15. Earrings with open-work, star-shaped pendant: (1) Tigani, grave 25; (2) Halić. After Drandakis and Gkiolis, 'Anaskaphē sto Tēgani'; and Garam, 'VII. századi aranyékszerek'.

There seems to be some evidence to support a date within the second half of the sixth century for at least some of the burials excavated in the 1980s by Nikolaos Drandakis, Nikos Gkioles, and Charalambos Konstantinidi within the basilica inside the early Byzantine fort in Tigani. In other words, some burials, at least, may have coincided in time with the last building phase of the church. For example, the iron fibula with bent stem found in burial 8 is a dress accessory relatively common on sixth-century military sites in the Balkans.[122] A date around 600 may be advanced for the gold earrings with open-work, star-shaped pendant found in grave 25 in Tigani (Figure 12.15).[123] Several such earrings are known from a very rich burial in Golubić (Croatia), where they were associated with earrings with basket-shaped pendants most typical for late sixth- or seventh-century assemblages in the Alpine region and in western Hungary.[124] Two other such earrings are known from a little Early Avar hoard (or assemblage of

[122] Drandakis and Gkiolis, 'Anaskaphē sto Tēgani', p. 256. An iron fibula with bent stem was found together with a cast fibula with bent stem in house 26 of the sixth-century fort in Gabrovo (Bulgaria). The association suggests a date within the last third of the sixth century, given the relatively precise chronology of cast fibulae with bent stem established on the basis of the Bratsigovo and Koprivets hoards (see note 63 above). See Kina Koicheva and Anna Kharalambieva, 'Fibuli ot Istoricheskiia Muzeia v Gabrovo (III–VII vek)', *Godishnik na muzeite ot Severna Bǎlgariia*, 19 (1993), 57–72 (pp. 68, 69, and 71 with pl. 3.8). For iron fibulae with bent stem, see also Syna Uenze, *Die spätantiken Befestigungen von Sadovec: Ergebnisse der deutsch-bulgarisch-österreichischen Ausgrabungen 1934–1937* (Munich, 1992), pp. 149–50.

[123] Drandakis and Gkiolis, 'Anaskaphē sto Tēgani', pp. 250, 255, and 256, with pl. 148å.

[124] *Bizantini, Croati, Carolingi: Alba e tramonto di regni e imperi*, ed. by Carlo Bertelli and others (Milan, 2001), pp. 283 and 270 fig. For the chronology of earrings with basket-shaped pendant, see Volker Bierbrauer, *Invillino-Ibligo in Friaul I: Die römische Siedlung und das spätantik-frühmittelalterliche Castrum* (Munich, 1987), p. 147; Ellen Riemer, 'Byzantinische Körbchen- und Halbmondohrringe im Römisch-Germanischen Museum Köln (Sammlung Diergardt)', *Kölner Jahrbuch für Vor- und Frühgeschichte*, 25 (1992), 121–36 (p. 126).

grave goods) found in Halič (Slovakia).[125] The glass jugs found in Tigani in graves 18, 19, and 25 are similar to those found in Crimean burial chambers together with 'Martynivka mounts' and buckles of the Syracuse class.[126] Perhaps of the same date, if not slightly later, are graves 9 and 53 in Tigani, which produced bronze keys.[127] Such artefacts are known from Early Avar burial assemblages in Hungary.[128] While nothing indicates that the Tigani cemetery was in use after *c.* 700, some, at least, of its graves may be dated to the second half of the seventh century. We have seen that the cemetery produced six buckles of the Corinth class, some of which could be dated after *c.* 650. A seventh-century date may also be advanced for grave 11, which produced an iron hook of unknown function. Such artefacts appear frequently in both Early and Middle Avar assemblages.[129]

The last chronological phase of the Tigani cemetery coincides in time with the beginnings of another cemetery accidentally found in 1966 to the south-west of Ioannina.[130] Only a few artefacts are known from the twenty-one graves excavated there, none of which has been properly published. The bronze bracelets with widened ends have good analogies in burials found in Radolishte, on the north-western shore of Lake Ohrid, together with other artefacts dated to the late seventh or

---

[125] Éva Garam, 'VII. századi aranyékszerek a Magyar Nemzeti Múzeum gyűjteméneiben', *Folia Archaeologica*, 31 (1980), 157–74 (p. 172 and fig. 7).

[126] Drandakis and Gkiolis, 'Anaskaphē sto Tēgani', pp. 252–53 with pl. 148α and γ. For Crimean analogies, see Irina P. Zasetskaia, 'Datirovka i proiskhozhdenie pal'chatykh fibul bosporskogo nekropolia rannesrednevekovogo perioda', *Materialy po arkheologii, istorii i etnografii Tavrii*, 6 (1997), 394–478 (pp. 433 and 446 with 475 pl. 19.25, for burial chamber 170 in Kerch'); N. I. Repnikov, 'Nekotorye mogil'niki oblasti krymskikh gotov', *Zapiski Odesskogo obshchestva istorii i drevnostei*, 27 (1907), 101–48 (pp. 111–12 with 148 fig. 136, for burial chamber 131 in Suuk Su).

[127] Drandakis and Gkiolis, 'Anaskaphē sto Tēgani', p. 254 with pl. 149β; Drandakis, Gkiolis, and Konstantinidi, 'Anaskaphē sto Tēgani Manēs', p. 249.

[128] Garam, 'Ketten und Schlüssel', pp. 169 and 171.

[129] Drandakis and Gkiolis, 'Anaskaphē sto Tēgani', pp. 254–55 with pl. 149α. For Early Avar analogies, see Papp, 'A nagyharsányi avarkori temető', p. 119 and pl. 3.20; Kovrig, *Das awarenzeitliche Gräberfeld*, p. 50 and pl. 37.23; Arnold Marosi and Nándor Fettich, *Dunapentelei avar sírleletek* (Budapest, 1936), p. 31 and fig. 9.12. For Middle Avar analogies, see László Költő, 'A Kéthely-Melegoldali Keszthely-kultúrás temető (Előzetes jelentés)', *Móra Ferenc Múzeum Évkönyve*, 2 (1984–85), 171–85 (pp. 174 with 182 fig. 5.5); Éva Garam, 'Avar temetők Andocson', *Folia Archaeologica*, 23 (1972), 129–82 (pp. 162 with 161 fig. 22.14).

[130] Ioulia P. Vokotopoulou, 'Neochōropoulon Ioanninōn', *Archaiologikon Deltion*, 22 (1967), 342–44 with pl. 248/γ 1, 3–4 (bronze bracelets), γ 5 (bronze earring), δ 2 (finger-ring).

eighth century.[131] The finger-ring with encapsulated stone is similar to a specimen from Radolishte and to another from grave 2 in Igar, one of the most famous Middle Avar assemblages in Hungary.[132] The copper-alloy earring from Ioannina is also interesting, in that its analogies found in Keszthely and Alattyán (Hungary) also point to a date within the second half of the seventh century, as they were associated with artefacts typical for the Middle Avar period, such as melon seed–shaped beads (*Melonenkernperlen*).[133] While it remains unclear whether or not the Ioannina cemetery continued into the eighth century, a date after 700 can be firmly established for at least some of the graves in a cemetery excavated in Aphiona on the north-western coast of the island of Corfu.[134] To be sure, the fragment of a belt buckle of the Corinth class found in grave 2 suggests that the beginnings of that cemetery may well be placed within the first half of the seventh century. Similarly, the earrings with blue glass bead pendant found in graves 2, 7, and 14 show that the cemetery continued through the second half of the seventh century. Similar earrings were found together with melon seed–shaped beads in a burial of the Middle and Late Avar cemetery in Čoka (northern Serbia), and with a silver coin struck for Emperor Constantine IV in a burial chamber of the Crimean cemetery in Eski Kermen.[135] The isolated finds of pendants of the Koman class further point to a date *c.* 700, as such belt accessories became popular within a short period of transition from the Middle to the Late Avar period (Figure 12.16).[136] But the best

[131] V. Malenko, 'Ranosrednovekovnata materijalna kultura vo Okhrid i Okhridsko', in *Okhrid i Okhridsko niz istorijata*, ed. by Mihailo Apostolski, I (Skopje, 1985), pp. 269–315 (pp. 291–93 with pl. 21.1–5).

[132] Malenko, 'Ranosrednovekovnata materijalna kultura', pl. 20; Gyula Fülöp, 'Awarenzeitliche Fürstenfunde von Igar', *Acta Archaeologica Academiae Scientiarum Hungaricae*, 40 (1988), 151–90 (pp. 154–55 with 158 fig. 7.7, for grave 2 with a female skeleton).

[133] Ilona Kovrig, 'Ujabb kutatások a keszthelyi avarkori temetöben', *Archaeologiai Értesítő*, 87 (1960), 136–68 (p. 140 with 151 fig. 14.2, Keszthely, grave 3); Kovrig, *Das awarenzeitliche Gräberfeld*, pp. 24, 55, and 56, with pls 16.1–2, 41.9, and 42–43 (Alattyán, graves 187, 646, and 658).

[134] Bulle, 'Ausgrabungen bei Aphiona', pp. 219–20, 223, and 227; 222 fig. 26.24 (buckle of the Corinth class); 222 fig. 26.3, 4 (earrings), and 18 (pendant of the Koman class); 222 fig. 26.7 (beads).

[135] Ilona Kovrig and József Korek, 'Le Cimetière de l'époque avare de Csóka (Čoka)', *Acta Archaeologica Academiae Scientiarum Hungaricae*, 12 (1960), 257–97 (p. 262 with pl. 102.12 and 15, for grave 46); Aibabin, 'Pogrebeniia kontsa VII-pervoi poloviny VIII', pp. 186–87 with 185 fig. 10.7 (burial chamber 257, skeleton 4).

[136] Éva Garam, 'Spätawarenzeitliche durchbrochene Bronzescheiben', *Acta Archaeologica Academiae Scientiarum Hungaricae*, 32 (1980), 161–80 (pp. 174–75). In seventh- to eighth-century burial chambers of the Caucasus region, such pendants are more often associated with skeletons of

Figure 12.16. Pendant of the Koman class (1), belt buckle (2), and tongue (3) from eighth-century assemblages on Kerkyra: (1) Aphiona; (2, 3) Palaiokastritsa. After Bulle, 'Ausgrabungen bei Aphiona'; and Agallopoulou, 'Palaiokastritsa'.

1   **2**   **3**

indication of an eighth-century date is the pair of melon seed–shaped beads of blue color (Vida's class P 11) found in grave 10, which cannot be dated earlier than *c.* 700.[137] An eighth-century date may also be advanced for the neighbouring cemetery at Palaiokastritsa accidentally found in 1972.[138] The strap end from grave 1 is a typical specimen of Zabojník's class 108, with good analogies in cemeteries in Slovakia (Komárno, grave 79) and Austria (Mistelbach, grave 56), all of which have been dated to the last two subphases of the Late Avar period (i.e. to the second half of the eighth century).[139] Buckles similar to that found in grave 3 in Palaiokastritsa are known from Corinth, but an equally good analogy is the buckle from grave 145 in Devnia (Bulgaria), which has been dated to the late eighth or early ninth century on the basis of the associated earring with corkscrew-shaped pendant.[140]

In Greece proper, assemblages that can be safely dated to the eighth century are rare. Most notable among them are the urn cremations found in 1959 in Olympia.[141] Much like in Aphiona, there are some indications that the cemetery may have begun at some point during the second half of the seventh century (Figure 12.17). The flint steel found in burial 11 has a good analogy in a burial assemblage

relatively old women. See E. Kh. Albegova, 'Paleosotsiologiia alanskoi religii VII–IX vv. (po materialam amuletov iz katakombnykh pogrebenii Severnogo Kavkaza i Srednego Dona)', *Rossiiskaia Arkheologiia*, 2001.2, 83–96 (pp. 87 and 93).

[137] See Vida and Völling, *Das slawische Brandgräberfeld*, p. 88. For the Avar origin of the *Melonenkernperlen* found in the Balkans, see István Erdélyi, *Az avarság és kelet a régészeti források tükrében* (Budapest, 1982), p. 170.

[138] Agallopoulou, 'Palaiokastritsa', pp. 423–24 with pl. 385β (strap end and buckle).

[139] Zábojník, 'Seriation von Gürtelbeschlaggarnituren', p. 303 pl. 24.1, 2.

[140] Davidson, *Minor Objects*, pl. 114.2217–18; Uwe Fiedler, *Studien zu Gräberfeldern des 6. bis 9. Jahrhunderts an der unteren Donau* (Bonn, 1992), p. 507 and pl. 105.23.

[141] Nikolaos Gialouris, 'Periochē Olympias', *Archaiologikon Deltion*, 17 (1961–62), 105–07; Vryonis, 'Slavic Pottery', pp. 15–42; Vida and Völling, *Das slawische Brandgräberfeld*.

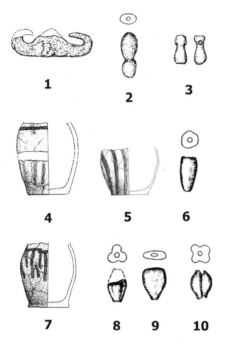

Figure 12.17. Olympia, chronologically sensitive
artefacts from the cremation cemetery: (1) grave
11; (2) grave 23; (3) grave 29; (4) grave 1; (5, 6)
grave 19; (7–9) grave 22; (10) grave 3. After Vida
and Völling, *Das slawische Brandgräberfeld*.

from one of the two annexes of the
Kenchreai basilica, in which it was associated with two coins struck for Constans II.[142] Equally early are the segment
beads found in Olympia in graves 23 and
29, for such beads appear only during the
last third of the seventh century in Middle Avar burial assemblages.[143] Slightly
later may be the urn in burial 1, with its
vertically incised decoration, similar to
pots deposited in graves of the Som-
merein cemetery in Austria that have
been dated on the basis of metal artefacts
to the late Middle and early Late Avar
periods.[144] A date within the seventh

[142] Vida and Völling, *Das slawische Brandgräberfeld*, pl. 10.11; Pallas, 'Données nouvelles', p. 299 fig. 5c. A similar flint steel was found in grave 7 in Aradac together with a strap end dated to the late Middle or early Late Avar period. See Nagy, 'Nekropola kod Aradca', p. 56 and pl. 2.3.

[143] Vida and Völling, *Das slawische Brandgräberfeld*, p. 89 and pl. 15.15 and 17.4. This dating is also supported by the association of such beads with two earrings with croissant-shaped pendant and a penannular brooch in grave 7 of the contemporary cemetery excavated in Mijele (Monte-negro). See O. Velimirović-Žigić, 'Mijele, près de Vir Pazar, nécropole du haut Moyen Âge', in *Époque préhistorique et protohistorique en Yougoslavie: Recherches et résultats*, ed. by Grga Novak and others (Belgrade, 1971), pp. 151–53 (p. 152 and fig.)

[144] Uwe Fiedler, Matthias Passlick, and Andreas Richter, 'Beiträge zur Formentwicklung der awarenzeitlichen Grabkeramik', *Archaeologia Austriaca*, 77 (1993), 243–75 (pp. 251 and 249 fig. 9, for graves 34, 37, and 218). Similarly decorated pots have been also found in late Middle and early Late Avar graves of the large cemeteries in Želovce (Slovakia) and Velika Gorica (Croatia). See Julius Béreš, 'Keramika na tzv. avarských pohrebiskách a sídliskách zo 7.–8. stor. na Slovensku', *Slovenská Archeológia*, 33 (1985), 15–70 (p. 20 with fig. 1); Katica Simoni, 'Zagreb i okolica u ranom srednjem vijeku', in *Arheološka istraživanja u Zagrebu i njegovoj okolici* (Zagreb, 1981), pp. 155–68 (p. 161 fig. 6.1). The decoration also appears on the pottery from contemporary cremation cemeteries and settlements in Slovakia. See Gabriel Fusek, *Slovensko vo včasnoslovanskom období*

century may also be advanced for the ceramic assemblages containing specimens with vertical incisions that have been found in Argos and Isthmia.[145] Even in Olympia, grave 19 with an urn decorated with vertical incisions also produced a melon seed–shaped bead of light green color, which is most typical for the Middle Avar period, a date confirmed by the associated iron torc.[146] On the other hand, grave 22 with an urn equally decorated with vertically incised lines produced melon seed–shaped beads of dark blue color dated to the Late Avar period, that is, after *c.* 700.[147] The same is true for the beads with four lobes found in grave 3.[148] It remains unclear how far into the eighth century one can stretch the chronology of the Olympia cemetery, but nothing indicates a date after 800.

Another contemporary but very different burial site was recently discovered in Agia Trias near Skliva (Ilia), during excavations of a Mycenaean cemetery.[149] Most interesting among the grave goods found together with the five cist inhumations so far excavated in Agia Trias is a pair of earrings, each with four attached loops and granulated, triangular ornaments. On the basis of supposed analogies from

(Nitra, 1994), pp. 249 with 374 pl. 60.3; Darina Bialeková, 'Staroslovanská osada v Siladiciach', *Archeologické rozhledy*, 12 (1960), 810–16, 827–28, and 833, with 815 fig. 290.4. It is important to note, however, that pottery with vertical incisions is also known from much earlier assemblages, such as that of a sunken hut in Dodești (Romania), which produced a buckle with three lobes dated to the Early Avar period. See Dan Gh. Teodor, *Continuitatea populației autohtone la est de Carpați: Așezările din secolele VI–XI e.n. de la Dodești-Vaslui* (Iași, 1984), p. 47 fig. 19.1–2.

[145] Aupert, 'Céramique slave', figs 15 and 16; Gregory, *Hexamilion*, pp. 41, 85, and 123 with pls 25d and 45c. See also Štefanovičová, 'Slavic Settlement', p. 355; Anagnostakis and Poulou-Papadimitriou, 'He protovyzantinē Messēnē', pp. 269–72 and 277–81; Vida and Völling, *Das slawische Brandgräberfeld*, pp. 23 and 88.

[146] Vida and Völling, *Das slawische Brandgräberfeld*, pl. 13.2 (bead), 4 (torc), 6 (urn).

[147] Vida and Völling, *Das slawische Brandgräberfeld*, pl. 14.11–13 (beads) and 18 (urn). The late dating of the dark blue beads is primarily based on the analysis of the biritual cemetery in Bratei (Romania), where such beads appear only with inhumations during the last phase of the cemetery. See Eugenia Zaharia, *Populația românească în Transilvania în secolele VII–VIII (cimitirul nr. 2 de la Bratei)* (Bucharest, 1977), pp. 87 fig. 35.1 (grave 237), 5 (grave 225), and 6 (grave 211); see also Vida and Völling, *Das slawische Brandgräberfeld*, p. 88.

[148] Vida and Völling, *Das slawische Brandgräberfeld*, p. 88 with pl. 7.8. Mostly typical for Late Avar assemblages, beads with three or four lobes cannot be dated earlier than *c.* 700.

[149] Olympia Vikatou, 'To christianiko nekrotapheio stēn Agia Triada Hēleias: Symvolē stē meletē tēs cheiropoiētēs keramikēs', in *Protovyzantinē Messēnē kai Olympia: Aktikos kai agrotikos choros stē Dytikē Peloponnēso. Praktika tou Diethnous symposiou, Athēna, 29–30 maiou 1998*, ed. by Petros G. Themelis and Voula Konti (Athens, 2002), pp. 238–39, with 259 figs 1–2; 260 fig. 3; 262 figs 5–6; and 265 fig. 11.

Corinth, the excavator proposed a sixth- to seventh-century date for the earrings from grave 3, which is not contradicted by what is otherwise known about the deposition in graves of one-handle jugs similar to that with which the earrings were associated.[150] Very similar earrings are also known from Abdera, Tigani (graves 10 and 54), as well as from a cist grave at the eastern end of the northern aisle of the Kraneion basilica near Corinth.[151] None of those analogies can be dated with any degree of precision, but similar earrings have also been found in southern Italy and Sicily, where they have been dated to the late seventh or eighth century.[152] In grave 10 in Tigani, such earrings were associated with a pair of golden buttons, good analogies for which are known from the Voznesenka burial assemblage in Ukraine, which has been dated to the eighth century.[153] Grave 10 was found in the middle of the nave of the three-aisled basilica, and its north–south orientation is in sharp contrast to all other neighbouring graves with a predominantly west–east orientation.[154] This strongly suggests for grave 10 a date much different from that of the

---

[150] Vikatou, 'To christianiko nekrotapheio', pp. 243 with 267 fig. 15 (jug) and 269 fig. 20 (earrings). One-handle jugs appear in sixth- to early seventh-century graves inside and around the basilica discovered in Stamata. See Eleni Gkini-Tsophopoulou and Eugenia Chalkia, 'Taphikē palaiochristianikē keramike apo tēn Attikē: hoi periptōseis tēs Stamatas kai tēs Anavysos', in *70 Diethnes Synedrio Mesaiōnikēs Keramikēs tes Mesogeiou*, ed. by Bakirtzis, pp. 755–57; Laskaris, *Monuments funéraires*, pp. 78–79. A one-handle jug with trefoil mouth was associated in grave 23 in Athens with a typically seventh-century buckle of the Boly-Želovce class. See Travlos and Frantz, 'Church of St. Dionysios the Areopagite', p. 167 with pl. 42e. The deposition of small jugs as funeral offering (perhaps used to pour wine or water over the corpse) is a custom that may have originated in Italy around 500 (Vroom, *After Antiquity*, pp. 139 and 141).

[151] 'Anaskaphē sta Abdera', *Praktika tēs en Athēnais Archaiologikēs Hetaireias*, 131 (1976), 131–37 (pp. 131 and 133–34; 132 fig. 1; pl. 97; fig. 99β); Drandakis and Gkiolis, 'Anaskaphē sto Tēgani', p. 254 with pl. 148δ; Drandakis, Gkiolis, and Konstantinidi, 'Anaskaphē sto Tēgani Manēs', p. 249; Demetrios Pallas, 'Anaskaphē tēs vasilikēs tou Kraneiou', *Praktika tēs en Athēnais Archaiologikēs Hetaireias*, 127 (1972), 205–50 (pp. 213 and 238 with pl. 222α).

[152] Lippolis, *L'oreficeria*, pp. 74 and 94 (with examples from San Lio and Chiaromonte). For other Sicilian examples, see also Paolo Orsi, *La Sicilia bizantina* (Rome, 1942), p. 145 and fig. 62; pl. 11.2, 7.

[153] V. A. Grinchenko, 'Pam'iatka VIII st. kolo s. Voznesenky na Zaporizhzhi', *Arkheolohiia*, 1950.2, 37–63 with pl. 5.6 and 7. For the dating and interpretation of the Voznesenka assemblage, see Anatolii K. Ambroz, 'O Voznesenskom komplekse VIII v. na Dnepre: vopros interpretatsii', in *Drevnosti epokhi velikogo pereseleniia narodov*, ed. by Ambroz and Erdélyi, pp. 204–22.

[154] Katsougiannopoulou, 'Einige Überlegungen', p. 462 fig. 2. The only other grave with a north–south orientation (no. 21) was cut by the southern wall of the nave and must therefore be considerably earlier. See Drandakis and Gkiolis, 'Anaskaphē sto Tēgani', p. 257. Equally early are

rest of the cemetery, but no conclusive evidence exists to place that date between 700 and 800. Nonetheless, a pair of gold earrings very similar to that from grave 10 has been found in a female burial of the cemetery in Kecel-Vádéi dűlő (Hungary), which cannot be dated earlier than *c.* 900.[155]

Whether or not the earrings from grave 10 may be dated after 700, there are several other indications of a late date for the cist inhumations excavated in Agia Trias. For example, the barrel-shaped bronze bead with which the earrings were associated in grave 3 has good analogies in Abdera, but also in eighth- to ninth-century burial assemblages in southern and north-eastern Bulgaria.[156] Similarly, segment beads such as found in Agia Trias in grave 15 are known from cemeteries in southern Bulgaria, but also, as mentioned above, from graves 23 and 29 in Olympia.[157] To further parallels with Olympia points a fragment of a handmade pot decorated with vertical incisions arranged in a manner very similar to that on the urns from graves 4, 10, 12, and 19 in Olympia.[158] It is therefore possible that Agia Trias and Olympia coexisted throughout the second half of the seventh and the first half of the eighth century. Much like in Olympia, it is impossible to tell how

graves 2 and 6, which may antedate the building of the basilica. See Laskaris, *Monuments funéraires*, pp. 58–59.

[155] István Fodor, *'Őseinket felhozád...' A honfoglaló magyarság: Kiállítási katalógus* (Budapest, 1996), pp. 323–24 with 323 fig. 1.

[156] Abdera: Charalambos Bakirtzis, 'Byzantine Thrace (AD 330–1453)', in *Thrace*, ed. by Vassiliki Papoulia and others (Athens, 1994), pp. 151–210 (p. 160). Kiulevcha (near Shumen), grave 89: Zhivka Văzharova, *Slaviani i prabălgari (po danni na nekropolite ot VI–XI v. na teritoriiata na Bălgariia)* (Sofia, 1976), pp. 137 with 139 fig. 86.2. Mishevsko (near Kărdzhali), grave 27: Văzharova, *Slaviani i prabălgari*, pp. 304 and 306; 305 fig. 189.8, 10. Tukhovishte (near Gotse Delchev): Dimka Stoianova-Serafimova, 'Die neuentdeckte mittelalterliche Nekropole beim Dorf Tuchovište, Kreis Blagoevgrad', in *Rapports du III-e Congrès international d'archéologie slave. Bratislava, 7–14 septembre 1975*, ed. by Bohuslav Chropovský, I (Bratislava, 1979), pp. 789–804 (p. 789 with 798 fig. 7.2). For a late seventh- to ninth-century date of the cemeteries in southern Bulgaria, see Stefka Angelova and Rumiana Koleva, 'Zur Chronologie frühmittelalterlicher Nekropolen in Südbulgarien', in *Karasura*, I: *Untersuchungen zur Geschichte und Kultur des alten Thrakien. 15 Jahre Ausgrabungen in Karasura. Internationales Symposium Čirpan/Bulgarien, 1996*, ed. by Michael Wendel (Weissbach, 2001), pp. 263–70.

[157] Ablanitsa (near Gotse Delchev), graves 10 and 23: Văzharova, *Slaviani i prabălgari*, pp. 275 and 278; 276 fig. 171; 277 fig. 172.1. Olympia, graves 23 and 29: Vida and Völling, *Das slawische Brandgräberfeld*, p. 89 with pl. 15.15 and 17.4.

[158] Vikatou, 'To christianiko nekrotapheio', p. 167 fig. 16; Vida and Völling, *Das slawische Brandgräberfeld*, pp. 119, 121, and 123 with pls 8.4, 10.10, 11.3, and 19.6. A parallel may also be drawn between the iron ring from grave 3 in Agia Trias and that found in grave 12 in Olympia.

far into the eighth century the chronology of Agia Trias may be stretched, but no indication exists of a date after 800.

In the absence of any securely dated artefacts, both the beginning and the end of other, possibly Dark-Age cemeteries with cist inhumations will remain unknown.[159] In some cases, there are clear parallels to cemeteries in southern Bulgaria, the precise chronology of which, however, remains unclear.[160] Only a few isolated assemblages are known for the ninth century, such as a number of inhumations in Thebes, Abdera, Philippi, Drymos, and Spilaion.[161] The earliest

[159] This is particularly true for the cemeteries excavated by Ilias Andreou in Meropi and Paliopyrgos (Epirus), near the Albanian-Greek border. See Andreou, 'Meropē kai Paleopyrgos Pōgōniou', pp. 303–07; Ilias Andreou, 'Meropē', *Archaiologikon Deltion*, 38 (1983), 229–30; Andreou, 'Paleopyrgos Pōgōniou', p. 307. According to Andreou, at least some of the graves in both cemeteries must be dated between the seventh and the tenth centuries, but not a single artefact has yet been published to support such a chronological bracket.

[160] E.g. the croissant-shaped silver earrings with pendants from the cemeteries excavated in Azoros and Milea (northern Thessaly) have a good analogy in grave 10 in Ablanitsa. Similarly, the pair of earrings with filigree-decorated pendants from Azoros may be compared to the pair found in grave 23 in Ablanitsa together with segment beads. The Azoros cemetery also produced a finger-ring with shield-shaped bezel decorated with the image of a bird, which has good analogies in Ablanitsa and on other sites in southern Bulgaria. See Lazaros Deriziotis and Spyridon Kougiomtzoglou, 'Anakalyptontas tēn agnōston christianikēn Perraibikēn Tripolin', in *Thorakion: Aphieroma stē mnēmē tou Paulou Lazaridē*, ed. by Isidoris Kakouris, Suzana Choulia, and Tzeni Albani (Athens, 2004), pp. 63–74 (pp. 68–69 and 72 with pls 25β, γ and 27); Văzharova, *Slaviani i prabălgari*, pp. 275, 278, and 289; 273 fig. 170.4; 278 fig. 173.1–2; 290 fig. 180.8. On the one hand, the earrings found in Ablanitsa have been dated between the seventh and the ninth centuries (Angelova and Koleva, 'Zur Chronologie frühmittelalterlicher Nekropolen', p. 265); on the other hand, the cemetery excavated in Milea produced a large quantity of eleventh- to thirteenth-century coins (Deriziotis and Kougiomtzoglou, 'Anakalyptontas', p. 72).

[161] Aspasia Kourenta-Raptaki, Chariklea Koilakou, and Mina Galani-Krikou, 'Nomos Voiotias: 1e Ephoreia Vyzantinōn Archaiotētōn', *Archaiologikon Deltion*, 49 (1994), 109–27 (pp. 116–17 with 116 fig. 20 and pl. 48); Bakirtzis, 'Byzantine Thrace', p. 160 fig.; Charalambos Pennas, 'Philippoi', *Archaiologikon Deltion*, 29 (1973–74), 843–46 (p. 843 with pl. 634δ); E. I. Mastrokostas, 'Palaiochristianikai vasilikai Drymou Vonitses', *Archaiologika analekta ex Athenōn*, 4 (1971), 185–95 (pp. 186–87 with 188 figs 4–5). The grave(s) in Abdera may be dated to the ninth century on the basis of the associated bronze beads, the best analogies of which have been found in grave 89 in Kiulevcha (Bulgaria) in association with a Carolingian disc-brooch. See Văzharova, *Slaviani i prabălgari*, pp. 137 with 139 fig. 86.2. The Spilaion grave produced a lead seal dated to 868/69. See Diamantis Triantaphyllos, 'Enas diachronikos tymbos sto Spēlaio Evrou', *To Archaiologiko ergo stē Makedonia kai Thrakē*, 11 (1997), 625–32 (pp. 628 with 632 fig. 15). The Thebes, Philippi, and Drymos inhumations may be of a later date, *c.* 900, because of the associated buckles with rectangular plates and animal decoration, examples of which are also known from several isolated

examples of clay pans found in Greece may also be dated to the ninth century.[162]

A tabulation of the preliminary results of this survey of the archaeological evidence shows a relatively large number of assemblages dated to the first half of the seventh century and a comparatively smaller number of sites for the second half of that century (Figure 12.18). Grave 10 in Aphiona, two inhumations in Agia Trias, four cremations in Olympia that produced melon seed–shaped beads of blue color and later date, as well as graves 1 and 3 in Palaiokastritsa are the only assemblages known so far that could be dated with some degree of certainty to the eighth century. The abrupt fall in numbers of assemblages after *c.* 650 may at a first glimpse be surprising, but it does dovetail nicely with what little is known about seventh-century settlements. The coarse ware pottery found on the rural site (possibly a farm) excavated in Pyrgouthi in the Berbati valley (Argolis) has its closest affinity with pottery from Corinth securely dated to the late sixth and early seventh centuries. However, the site seems to have already been abandoned by the mid-seventh century.[163] Similarly, the occupation of most military sites or 'isles of refuge' that could be dated to the early seventh century does not seem to have continued beyond the reign of Heraclius (610–41).[164] In Athens, the old colonnade of the

finds in the hinterland of Athens, Servia, and on the island of Ithaca. See Paulos Lazaridis, 'Anaskaphē Dagla para to Markopoulon Mesogeion,' *Archaiologikon Deltion*, 16 (1960), 69–72 (pp. 69 and 71 with pl. 57γ, with 2 specimens from Dagla); Nikolaos Ch. Kotzias, 'Anaskaphai tes basilikes tou Laureotikou Olympou', *Praktika tēs en Athēnais Archaiologikēs Hetaireias*, 107 (1952), 122, fig. 18 (Lauretikos Olympou); *Kathēmerinē zoē*, p. 393 no. 482 (Servia); Sarantis Symeonoglu, 'Anaskaphes Ithakes', *Praktika tēs en Athēnais Archaiologikēs Hetaireias*, 140 (1985), pl. 103δ (Ithaca). For this class of buckles, see now Pletn'ov, 'Buckles with Animal Images'.

[162] Kilian, 'Zu einigen früh- und hochmittelalterlichen Funden', p. 284 fig. 2.5. No clay pans are known to have been found in Greece in assemblages securely dated to the seventh or eighth century. For clay pans and the associated baking practices, see Joachim Herrmann, 'Getreidekultur, Backteller und Brot-Indizien frühslawischer Differenzierung', in *Zbornik posveten na Boško Babić: Mélange Boško Babić 1924–1984*, ed. by Mihailo Apostolski (Prilep, 1986), pp. 267–72. For clay pans found in assemblages clearly dated to the ninth century, see Marko Popović, *Tvrđava Ras* (Belgrade, 1999), pp. 147, 156, and 157; 143 fig. 89.12 and 13 (Pazarište-Gradina, house 23).

[163] Jenni Hjohlman, Arto Penttinen, and Berit Wells, *Pyrgouthi: A Rural Site in the Berbati Valley from the Early Iron Age to Late Antiquity. Excavations by the Swedish Institute at Athens, 1995 and 1997* (Stockholm, 2005), p. 241.

[164] The latest coins found on the island of Kephalos in the Ambracian Gulf suggest that any occupation ceased before the end of Heraclius's reign. The early Byzantine fort identified on the island of Dokos has two phases of occupation, one of which ends abruptly in the early 600s. Judging from the existing evidence the site remained unoccupied until the mid-seventh century. See

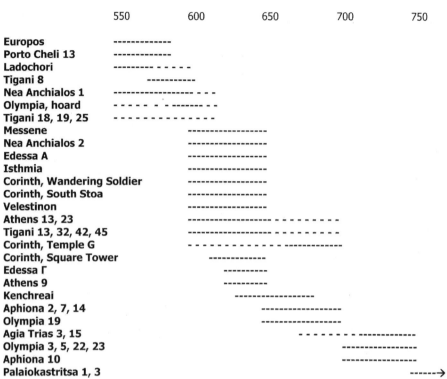

Figure 12.18. Chronology of Dark-Age archaeological assemblages from Greece. Continuous lines indicate firm date ranges; interrupted lines show date ranges possible, but not certain.

Stoa of Attalos lost its original architectural integrity and was subdivided into rooms at some point during the seventh century. In room 6, hundreds of teracotta roof tiles recovered from the fallen debris of the house destroyed sometime in the 630s were piled in neat rows for possible reuse. Those alterations have been coin-dated to the reign of Constans II (641–68).[165] Recent excavations in Isthmia

Charikleia N. Barla, 'Anaskaphai Kephalou Amvrakikou', *Praktika tēs en Athēnais Archaiologikēs Hetaireias*, 125 (1970), 90–97 (p. 97); William Bowden, *Epirus Vetus: The Archaeology of a Late Antique Province* (London, 2003), p. 188; Adonis K. Kyros, 'Periplaneseis hagiōn leipsanōn kai mia agnōste kastropoliteia ston Argoliko', *Peloponnēsiaka*, 21 (1995), 97–118 (p. 111). See also Sinclair Hood, 'Isles of Refuge in the Early Byzantine Period', *Annual of the British School at Athens*, 65 (1970), 37–44.

[165] T. Leslie Shear, 'The Athenian Agora: Excavations of 1972', *Hesperia*, 42 (1973), 359–407 (p. 397).

revealed a group of rooms in the north-western corner of the Bath, all built with walls of rough masonry. One of them had a cooking hearth, another an apsidal structure at the south end. The associated quern stones bespeak the rural character of the occupation.[166] The ceramic material found in those rooms has been quickly dubbed 'Slavic ware', but Tivadar Vida's detailed analysis of both forms and decoration suggests a date in the mid- to late seventh century.[167] Indeed, single-handled pots with similar decoration have been found on the south side of the North-eastern Gate at Isthmia, in association with a coin struck for Emperor Constans II in 655/56.[168] The so-called 'squatter' occupation at the Northern Bay of the Hexamilion has produced cooking pots, including one with a handle and obliquely and vertically incised ornament, as well as the belt buckle discussed above. If indeed the buckle was associated with the ceramic assemblage in question, this may be viewed as an indication of some occupation of the site between c. 600 and c. 650. Recent excavations in the Panagia Field of Corinth revealed the seventh- to eighth-century occupation of the city. The house built on top of a sixth-century bath produced fragments of cooking pots similar to those found in Constantinople and dated between the late seventh and the early ninth century, one-handled jugs with flat bases, and an early Abbasid coin.[169] In addition, the excavations in the Panagia Field produced evidence of Glazed White Ware, the early medieval alternative to

---

[166] Gregory, 'An Early Byzantine (Dark-Age) Settlement'.

[167] Gregory, 'An Early Byzantine (Dark-Age) Settlement', p. 151; Gregory, *Hexamilion*, p. 41; Vida and Völling, *Das slawische Brandgräberfeld*, p. 19.

[168] Gregory, *Hexamilion*, pp. 41, 85, and 123.

[169] Guy D. R. Sanders, 'An Overview of the New Chronology for 9th to 13th Century Pottery at Corinth', in *70 Diethnes Synedrio Mesaionikes Keramikes tes Mesogeiou*, ed. by Bakirtzis, pp. 35–44 with figs 10.1, 2, 4 and 12.1; Guy D. R. Sanders, 'Problems in Interpreting Rural and Urban Settlement in Southern Greece, AD 365–700', in *Landscapes of Change: Rural Evolutions in Late Antiquity and the Early Middle Ages*, ed. by Neil Christie (Aldershot, 2004), pp. 163–93 (pp. 185–86); Kathleen Warner Slane and Guy D. R. Sanders, 'Corinth: Late Roman Horizons', *Hesperia*, 74 (2005), 243–97 (pp. 246 with n. 12, and 273–80, where a seventh-century date is advanced, despite the presence of the Abbasid coin). The hand- and wheel-made cooking pots found in seventeen deposits in the orchestra and lower cavea of the ancient Theatre at Sparta have been dated to the eighth century, at the earliest, on the basis of their association with remains of globular amphorae, but one of the deposits also produced a coin struck for Emperor Constantine VII Porphyrogenitus (945–59), which strongly suggests a later date. See Sanders, 'Pottery from Medieval Levels', p. 454. Equally late must also be the fragment of Chinese Marbled Ware found in the castle at Methoni in south-western Peloponnesus. See Nikos D. Kontogiannis, 'A Fragment of a Chinese Marbled Ware Bowl from Methoni, Greece', *Bizantinistica: Rivista di studi bizantini e slavi*, 4 (2002), 39–46.

the Late Roman red-slip wares, which disappeared in the course of the seventh century. Made in Constantinople and derived from Roman monochrome glazed traditions, the Glazed White Ware is also attested in Athens, but only sporadically in the countryside.[170] Outside Athens and Corinth, there is very little evidence of occupation.[171] Extensive field surveys in northern Argolis (Berbati-Limnes) and Boeotia produced very little, if any, evidence of 'Slavic wares' and no remains that could be dated with any degree of certainty between 700 and 1000.[172]

The Numismatic and Sigillographic Evidence

This picture of severe contraction is confirmed by the numismatic evidence. There is a sharp break in coin accumulation in Greek hoards after the early 580s, and new coins appear briefly only after 600.[173] This is surprising, as coins struck in the meanwhile are known, albeit sporadically, from isolated and settlement finds.[174] A

[170] For fragments of Glazed White Ware chafing dishes from Athens, see Hayes, 'Rapports régionaux', figs 7–8 and 10–11. A single such fragment was found during the Berbati-Limnes survey of northern Argolis. See Margrete Hahn, 'The Early Byzantine to Modern Periods', in *The Berbati-Limnes Archaeological Survey, 1988–1990*, ed. by Berit Wells (Jonsered, 1996), pp. 345–451 (pp. 424 and 432).

[171] However, in Louloudies near Kitros in Pieria, archaeological excavations within the fortified episcopal compound abandoned in the late sixth century have revealed the existence of an eighth-century occupation phase. See Marki, 'Louloudies'; Euterpi Marki and Maria Cheimonopoulou, 'Céramique de l'époque paléochrétienne tardive de la fouille de Louloudies en Piérie', in *70 Diethnes Synedrio Mesaiōnikes Keramikēs tēs Mesogeiou*, ed. by Bakirtzis, pp. 703–12.

[172] Hahn, 'Early Byzantine to Modern Periods', p. 432; Vroom, *After Antiquity*, pp. 109–10; Frank R. Trombley, 'Early Medieval Boeotia (c. 580–1050 A.D.)', *Epetēris tēs Hetaireias Voiotikōn Meletōn*, 3 (2000), 990–1009 (p. 994).

[173] Florin Curta, 'Invasion or Inflation? Sixth- to Seventh-Century Byzantine Coin Hoards in Eastern and Southeastern Europe', *Annali dell'Istituto Italiano di Numismatica*, 43 (1996), 65–224 (pp. 84–87 and 221 fig. 44). The last Greek hoard of copper closed in the 580s is Pellene (with the latest coin struck in 584/85), the first hoard closed after 600, Chalkis (with the latest coin struck in 607/08). See Morrisson, Popović, and Ivanišević, *Les Trésors monétaires byzantins*, pp. 266 and 231. As a rule, hoards with the latest coins struck after 600 do not include coins struck before that date.

[174] Excavations in the Athenian Agora produced twenty-five coins minted for Emperor Maurice, two of which are folles struck in Nicomedia and Antioch in 587/88 and 595/96, respectively. See Margaret Thompson, *The Athenian Agora: Results of Excavations Conducted by the American School of Classical Studies at Athens*, II (Princeton, 1954), p. 104. Three folles (one struck in 586/87 and two others struck in 589/90) and a 10-nummia piece (struck in 586/87) have been

significant number of hoards of copper or gold have latest coins minted during Phocas's reign, but especially during Heraclius's early regnal years. Hoard finds from the first two decades of the seventh century are therefore in sharp contrast to those from the remainder of that century. Instead of a significant number of hoards of copper and gold, continental Greece has so far produced only three hoards, two of gold and one of copper, that could be dated after *c.* 630 and before *c.* 900.[175] All stray finds from that period are of copper. In the early 600s, hoards of gold were still buried in Greece, but after *c.* 630, gold finds disappear from the southern Balkans.[176] Moreover, copper coins of the last part of Heraclius's reign are very rare.[177] Michael Metcalf has proposed that responsible for the significant number of hoards with latest coins struck in the early 600s were the Slavic invasions of Greece at the beginning of Heraclius's reign years.[178] But small hoards of gold with five to ten solidi, such as Apidea, may represent payments to the army known as

found in Antikyra (Boeotia), another follis struck in 590/91 is known from Kephalos in the Ambracian Bay. See Ios Tsourti, 'Antikyra Voiōtias: Nomismatikē martyria', in *Thorakion*, ed. by Kakouris, Choulia, and Albani, pp. 123–28 (p. 126); Barla, 'Anaskaphai Kephalou Amvrakikou', p. 96. Bruno Callegher, 'La Circulation monetaire à Patras et dans les sites ruraux environnants (VIᵉ–VIIᵉ siècle)', in *Les Villages dans l'Empire byzantin, IVᵉ–XVᵉ siècles*, ed. by Jacques Lefort, Cécile Morrisson, and Jean-Pierre Sodini (Paris, 2005), pp. 225–35 (p. 229), mentions several coins from Patras, but without any details about their chronology.

[175] Athens, two hoards with the latest coins struck in 633/34 and *c.* 668, respectively: Morrisson, Popović, and Ivanišević, *Les Trésors monétaires byzantins*, p. 227; Mina Galani-Krikou and others, *Syntagma vyzantinōn 'thesaurōn' tou Nomismatikou Mouseion, (SBTh)* (Athens, 2002), pp. 74–76. Unknown location in Attiki, with the latest coins struck for Emperor Leo III: Speros Vryonis, 'An Attic Hoard of Byzantine Gold Coins (688–741) from the Thomas Whittemore Collection and the Numismatic Evidence for the Urban History of Byzantium', *Zbornik radova Vizantološkog Instituta*, 8 (1963), 291–300.

[176] Early seventh-century hoards of gold have been found in Malaisina, Paiania, Patras, Vasaras, and Solomos. See Morrisson, Popović, and Ivanišević, *Les Trésors monétaires byzantins*, pp. 255, 263, 265, 274, and 287.

[177] Only three such coins are known from Greece, one struck in 631/32 in Ravenna (a find from Athens) the other two struck in Constantinople in 633/34 (one from Athens, the other from Corinth). See Morrisson, Popović, and Ivanišević, *Les Trésors monétaires byzantins*, p. 227; Thompson, *Athenian Agora*, p. 70; Katherine Edwards, *Corinth: Results of Excavations Conducted by the American School of Classical Studies at Athens* (Cambridge, 1933), p. 131.

[178] D. M. Metcalf, 'The Aegean Coastlands under Threat: Some Coins and Coin Hoards from the Reign of Heraclius', *Annual of the British School at Athens*, 57 (1962), 14–23, but see also his 'Avar and Slav Invasions Into the Balkan Peninsula (c. 575–625): The Nature of the Numismatic Evidence', *Journal of Roman Archaeology*, 4 (1991), 140–48.

donativa. By 580, the accessional *donativum* was nine solidi, the quinquennial one five solidi. The practice of ceremonial payments to the army may have continued well into the seventh century, as late, perhaps, as the end of Heraclius's reign.[179] Late sixth- or early seventh-century hoards of five to ten solidi may therefore be interpreted as an example of the correlation between mint output and hoarding, on the one hand, and military preparations, on the other hand. Such hoards indicate the presence of the Roman army, not Slavic attacks. Their concealment is not necessarily the result of barbarian raids, because their owners may have kept their savings in cash in a hiding place *custodiae causa*, not *ob metum barbarorum*. Though the notable presence of the military in southern Greece is certainly to be associated with the turbulent years at the beginning of Heraclius's reign, as well as with the increasing raiding activity of both Slavs and Avars, signalled by such things as two sieges of Thessalonica (see below), the hoards themselves are an indication of accumulated wealth, not of destruction. To the presence of the military may also be attributed hoards of copper, despite the relatively small value of each one of the six Greek hoards dated to the first two decades of the seventh century.[180] The cluster of latest coins struck between 610 and 620 strongly suggests that those small collections of copper were never retrieved because of the general withdrawal of Roman armies from the Balkans. With a few exceptions,[181] there are no coins of Heraclius postdating the withdrawal of troops on any site in Greece.

By contrast, a great number of coins of Emperor Constans II are known from both Athens and Corinth.[182] In Athens alone, the number of coins of Constans is

---

[179] Hendy, *Studies in the Byzantine Monetary Economy*, pp. 188 and 646–47; Wolfgang Brandes, *Finanzverwaltung in Krisenzeiten: Untersuchungen zur byzantinischen Administration im 6.–7. Jahrhundert* (Frankfurt a. M., 2002), pp. 24–25. Light-weight solidi struck for Emperor Maurice may have been issued specifically for his quinquennial *donativum* of 587. See Wolfgang Hahn, 'A propos de l'introduction des solidi légers de 23 carats sous Maurice', *Bulletin de la Société Française de Numismatique*, 36 (1981), 96–97. For the correlation between mint output and military preparations, see D. M. Metcalf, 'Coinage and Coin Finds Associated with a Military Presence in the Medieval Balkans', in *Kovanje i kovnice antičkog i srednjovekovnog novca*, ed. by Vladimir Kondić (Belgrade, 1976), pp. 88–97.

[180] Chalkis (607/08), Pellene (602–10), Nea Anchialos (615/16), Politika-Psachna (615/16), Thasos 1 (617/18), and Thasos 2 (615–24): Metcalf, 'Aegean Coastlands', pp. 21–22; Olivier Picard, 'Trésors et circulation monétaire Thasos du IV-e au VII-e siècle après J.-C.', in *Thasiaca* (Athens, 1979), pp. 411–54 (pp. 451–52); Morrisson, Popović, and Ivanišević, *Les Trésors monétaires byzantins*, pp. 198, 231, and 267.

[181] See above, note 177.

[182] 817 in Athens, 127 in Corinth. See Thompson, *Athenian Agora*, pp. 70–71; Edwards, *Corinth*, pp. 132–33. D. M. Metcalf, 'Monetary Recession in the Middle Byzantine Period: The

four times larger than that of coins struck during the much longer reign of his father, Heraclius. Out of 817 coins of Constans II found in the Athenian Agora, 108 were struck in Constantinople in just one year (657). This unusually large number of coins has been explained in terms of the Emperor's visit of 662/63.[183] Relatively large numbers of coins of Constans have also been found in Corinth, and isolated finds are known from various parts of Greece.[184] The evidence thus suggests that in Athens, small change was suddenly put in circulation on the eve of Constans II's Italian campaign. Since a similar increase in numbers of coins struck for Constans has been noted elsewhere,[185] it is possible that the sudden infusion of copper coins was associated with the military preparations preceding the mobilization of the fleet for the war in Italy. The next surge in the number of coins took place during the very short reign of Philippikos (711–13).[186] Since among the thirty-one legible coins, only six obverse dies were represented, it has been suggested that these die-linked specimens formed a body of coin specifically transported from Constantinople and 'injected' into the circulating medium at Athens.[187] Responsible for this phenomenon must again have been the military. All these coins are low denominations, which are also known from a few isolated finds in Greece and in Dobrudja (Romania).[188] The distribution of coins struck for eighth-

Numismatic Evidence', *Numismatic Chronicle*, 161 (2001), 111–55 (p. 125), offers a tabulation of Athenian finds of coins struck for Constans II by *DOC* classes. His list has only 705 specimens, 146 of which belong to *DOC* classes 6 to 8, dated between 655 and 657/58.

[183] Hendy, *Studies in the Byzantine Monetary Economy*, p. 662. For coin finds from Corinth, see Vasso Penna, 'He zoē stis vyzantines poleis tēs Peloponnēsou: he nomismatikē martyria (80s–120s ai. m. Ch.)', in *Mnēme Martin J. Price*, ed. by A. P. Tzamalis (Athens, 1996), pp. 195–288 (p. 199).

[184] Kyros, 'Periplaneseis hagiōn leipsanōn', p. 112 fig. 5; Gregory, 'An Early Byzantine (Dark-Age) Settlement', pp. 151–53; Avramea, *Le Peloponnèse*, p. 74; Mina Galani-Krikou, 'Thēva 60s–150s aiōnas: He nomismatikē apo to Politistiko Kentro', *Symmeikta*, 12 (1998), 141–70 (p. 151).

[185] Ewald Kislinger, 'Byzantinische Kupfermünzen aus Sizilien (7.–9. Jh.) im historischen Kontext', *Jahrbuch der Österreichischen Byzantinistik*, 46 (1996), 25–36 (pp. 29–30).

[186] Margaret Thompson, 'Some Unpublished Bronze Money of the Early Eighth Century', *Hesperia*, 9 (1940), 358–80.

[187] D. M. Metcalf, 'How Extensive Was the Issue of Folles During the Years 775–820?', *Byzantion*, 37 (1967), 207–310 (p. 278).

[188] Monemvasia: Penna, 'He zoē stis vyzantines poleis', p. 201. Unknown location in Dobrudja: Gheorghe Poenaru-Bordea and Ion Donoiu, 'Contribuţii la studiul pătrunderii monedelor bizantine în Dobrogea în secolele VII–X', *Buletinul Societăţii Numismatice Române*, 75–76 (1981–82), 237–51 (p. 238). Unknown location(s) in north-eastern Bulgaria: Aleksandăr Peikov,

century emperors strongly suggests a connection between petty currency and coastal regions easily accessible by sea (Figure 12.19). The half-folles and deca-nummia found in Greece indicate the existence of local markets of low-price commodities, such as food in small quantities, serving a population that had direct access to both low-value coinage and sea-lanes.[189]

The role of the Byzantine navy in the seventh- and, especially, the eighth-century history of Greece is also betrayed by finds of seals.[190] To be sure, the earliest dated seals known so far are those of *kommerkiarioi*.[191] Anonymous seals of im-perial *kommerkia* are attested for Hellas on seals dated to 738/39, 748/49, and between 730 and 741, at a time such seals are also attested for the theme of Thrace and for the maritime 'gateways' of Thessalonica and Mesembria.[192] This nicely dovetails with what is otherwise known about an intensified military presence in the Balkans during most of the eighth century. Indeed, the state control of both commercial exchange and tax collection which became the hallmark of Leo III's reform of 730/31 responsible for the appearance of the anonymous seals of im-perial *kommerkia* survived longer in those provinces, such as Thrace, that were vital to the provisioning of the armies engaged in war against Bulgaria.[193] This is defi-nitely not the case of Hellas, where judging by the existing evidence both *kommer-kiarioi* and the imperial *kommerkia* disappeared by the mid-eighth century.[194]

'Moneti na imperator Filipik Bardan ot Severoiztochna Bălgariia', in *Kulturnite tekstove na minaloto: Nositeli, simvoli i idei. Materiali ot iubileinata mezhdunarodnata nauchna konferenciia v chest na 60-godishninata na prof. d.i.n. Kazimir Popokonstantinov. Veliko Tărnovo, 29–31 oktomvri 2003*, ed. by Vasil Giuzelev (Sofia, 2005), pp. 158–59.

[189] Florin Curta, 'Byzantium in Dark-Age Greece (the Numismatic Evidence in its Balkan Context)', *Byzantine and Modern Greek Studies*, 29 (2005), 113–46.

[190] Florin Curta, 'L'Administration byzantine dans les Balkans pendant la "grande brèche": le témoignage des sceaux', *Bizantinistica: Rivista di studi bizantini e slavi*, 6 (2004), 155–90.

[191] M. Mordtmann, 'Plombs byzantins de la Grèce et du Peloponnèse', *Revue archéologique*, 33 (1877), 289–98 (p. 291); Vitalien Laurent, *Les Sceaux byzantins du Médaillier Vatican* (Vatican City, 1962), pp. 128–29. For *kommerkiarioi* as high-ranking financial officers in charge of the collection of tax from various provinces, but actually residing in Constantinople, see Brandes, *Finanzverwaltung*, pp. 503–04.

[192] G. Zacos and A. Veglery, *Byzantine Lead Seals* (Basel, 1972), pp. 331–32; Nikolai P. Likhachev, 'Datirovannye vizantiiskie pechati', *Izvestiia Rossiiskoi Akademii Istorii Material'noi Kul'tury*, 3 (1924), 153–224 (p. 197). See also Brandes, *Finanzverwaltung*, pp. 365–68.

[193] Archibald Dunn, 'The *kommerkiairios*, the *apotheke*, the *Dromos*, the *vardarios*, and *The West*', *Byzantine and Modern Greek Studies*, 17 (1993), 3–24 (pp. 14–15).

[194] For the last seal of *kommerkiarios*, see Bon, *Le Peloponnèse*, p. 205; Curta, 'L'Administration byzantine', p. 164.

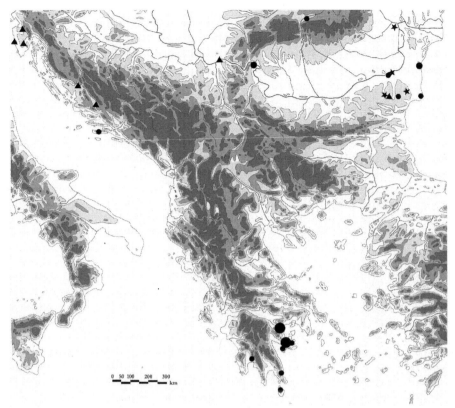

Figure 12.19. Distribution of eighth-century copper (circle), gold (triangle), and silver coins (star) in the Balkans. Circles of larger size indicate two and more than four coins. Data after Curta, 'Byzantium in Dark-Age Greece'.

Nonetheless, the number of seals of military officials, mainly of the navy, associated with Hellas is almost as large as that of seals of generals (*strategoi*) and officers of the land troops stationed in Thrace. The earliest mention of any military official in the Balkans refers to a general of Hellas named George, whose seal has been dated to the late seventh or early eighth century.[195] No less than three other *strategoi* of Hellas are mentioned on seals dated to the eighth century.[196] Two of

[195] Konstantinos M. Konstantopoulos, 'Vyzantiaka molyvdovoulla en to Ethniko Mouseio Athenōn', *Journal International d'Archéologie Numismatique*, 5 (1902), 149–64 (p. 160).

[196] Konstantinos M. Konstantopoulos, 'Vyzantiaka molyvdovoulla en to Ethniko Mouseio Athenōn', *Journal International d'Archéologie Numismatique*, 9 (1906), 161; Nikos A. Veis, 'Zur

them bore the title of *patrikios*, which suggests that they may have been of a rank equal to that of contemporary *kommerkiarioi*. Two *droungarioi* (navy commanders) of Hellas and Athens, respectively, appear in the eighth and early ninth centuries.[197] Turmarchs (navy colonels) appear in Hellas in the late eighth century and at the same time in Peloponnesus, but nowhere else in the Balkans.[198] It was a turmarch named Agallianos who led the rebellion of the Helladikoi against Emperor Leo III in 726.[199]

Much more difficult to interpret is the late seventh- or early eighth-century seal of a certain Peter, *archon* of Hellas.[200] No less than eight seals of *archontes* are so far known from the Balkans, six of which were associated with two cities, Mesembria and Debeltos.[201] *Archontes* seem to have been local officials with various degrees of autonomy, but the seal of one Theodore, *archon* of Vagenetia (the coastal region opposite the island of Corfu) suggests that the title may have also been accorded to local chieftains.[202] This may also be the case of Peter. Besides him, we know of

Sigillographie der byzantinischen Themen Peloponnes und Hellas,' *Vizantiiskii Vremennik*, 21 (1914), 90–110 and 192–235 (p. 198); Zacos and Veglery, *Byzantine Lead Seals*, p. 1406.

[197] Zacos and Veglery, *Byzantine Lead Seals*, pp. 1379 and 1733.

[198] B. A. Panchenko, 'Kollektsii Russkago Arkheologicheskago Instituta v Konstantinopole: Katalog molivdovulov', *Izvestiia Russkogo arkheologičeskogo instituta v Konstantinople*, 13 (1908), 78–151 (p. 133); *Prosopographie der mittelbyzantinischen Zeit*, ed. by Ralph-Johannes Lilie and others, IV (Berlin, 2001), pp. 559–60 and 669. Some turmarchs seem to have been important individuals, such as a certain Theophylact who bore the same title of *protospatharios* as two contemporary *strategoi* of Peloponnesos. The seal of a turmarch of Hellas named Leo was found in Constantinople, and it is quite possible that he was an officer of the navy stationed in Hellas. See Nikolai P. Likhachev, *Molivdovuly grecheskogo Vostoka* (Moscow, 1991), pp. 52–53.

[199] Theophanes Confessor, *Chronographia*, p. 405. See Oikonomides, 'L'Archonte slave', p. 111. Greek historians used to regard the revolt as the political crisis of which the Slavs took advantage to 'infiltrate' Greece. See I. K. Vogiatzidis, 'He thēsis tēs Kyrios Hellados entos tou Vyzantinou kratous', *Epēteris Hetaireias Vyzantinōn Spoudōn*, 19 (1949), 252–58 and 405–06 (p. 256). For Agallianos, see *Prosopographie der mittelbyzantinischen Zeit*, ed. by Ralph-Johannes Lilie and others, I (Berlin, 1999), pp. 35–36.

[200] *Catalogue of Byzantine Seals at Dumbarton Oaks and in the Fogg Museum of Art*, ed. by John Nesbitt and Nicholas Oikonomides, II (Washington, DC, 1994), p. 23. See Panagioti G. Papadimitriou, 'Thesmiske scheseis kai stadia ensōmatōses tōn Slavikōn plēthousmōn stē vyzantinē autokratoria kata to deutero miso tou 70u aiōna', *Vyzantina*, 24 (2004), 167–218 (pp. 214–16).

[201] Panchenko, 'Kollektsii Russkago Arkheologicheskago Instituta', p. 86; Zacos and Veglery, *Byzantine Lead Seals*, pp. 975, 1111–12, 1320, 1391, 1420.

[202] Nicolae Bănescu, 'O colecție de sigilii bizantine inedite', *Memoriile secției de științe istorice*, 3 (1938), 115–26 (pp. 116–17). See also Kristo Frashëri, 'Les Albanais et Byzance aux VIᵉ–XIᵉ

another *archon* of Hellas named Dargaskavos, a name presenting a Slavic pho-
netism that predates the metathesis of the liquids, a phenomenon that linguists
commonly date to *c.* 800.[203] Nicholas Oikonomides has proposed that both Peter
and Dargaskavos be viewed as *archontes* of the Slavs living in the immediate vicinity
of, or even within the theme of, Hellas, perhaps in the valley of the river Sper-
cheios.[204] Whether or not any group called itself 'Slavs' at that time, several other
seals of *archontes* which refer to tribes, and not territories, substantiate Oikonomides's interpretation. The Evidites had two *archontes*, Voidargos and John, mentioned on seals dated to the eighth and early ninth centuries.[205] Tichomiros appears
on another seal as *archon* of the Belegezites, a Slavic tribe otherwise known from
literary sources as living 'in the region of Thebes and Demetrias'.[206] A recently discovered seal of one Peter, *archon* of the Drugubites, points to the same literary
source: the Drugubites appear in the *Miracles of St Demetrius*, first as part of an
alliance of Slavic tribes bent on conquering Thessalonica in 677, then as subjects
of Emperor Constantine IV (668–85), who ordered them to feed the refugees
coming from the Avar qaganate under the command of Kuver and Mauros.[207]
Mauros's own seal describes him as *archon* of the Sermesianoi and the Bulgars, with
the former being the name given to the refugee group because their ancestors had

siècle', in *Hoi Alvanoi sto Mesaiōna*, ed. by Charalambos Gasparis (Athens, 1998), pp. 47–57 (p.
55). For Peter as a precursor to the *strategos* of Hellas, see Brandes, *Finanzverwaltung*, p. 211 with
n. 217.

[203] *Catalogue*, pp. 23–24; Werner Seibt, 'Siegel als Quelle für Slawenarchonten in Griechenland',
Studies in Byzantine Sigillography, 6 (1999), 27–36 (p. 29); Werner Seibt, 'Weitere Beobachtungen
zu Siegeln früher Slawenarchonten in Griechenland', in *Byzantium, State and Society: In Memory
of Nikos Oikonomides*, ed. by Anna Avramea, Angeliki Laiou, and Evangelos Chrysos (Athens,
2003), pp. 459–66. For the chronology of the metathesis of the liquids, see Henrik Birnbaum,
Common Slavic: Progress and Problems in its Reconstruction (Columbus, 1975), pp. 228 and 232.

[204] Oikonomides, 'L'Archonte slave'.

[205] Seibt, 'Siegel als Quelle', pp. 29–30; and 'Weitere Beobachtungen', pp. 463–64.

[206] Seibt, 'Siegel als Quelle', p. 28; O. V. Ivanova, 'Chudesa Sv. Dimitriia Solunskogo', in *Svod
drevneishikh pis'mennykh izvestii o slavianakh*, ed. by Sergei A. Ivanov, Gennadii G. Litavrin, and
V. K. Ronin, II (Moscow, 1995), pp. 91–211 (pp. 154 and 202).

[207] Alexandra Kyriaki-Wassiliou, 'Neue Siegel der 1. Hälfte des 9. Jh. aus Südostbulgarien: Mit
einem Appendix zu den Drugubiten', in *Numizmatichni i sfragistichni prinosi kăm istoriiata na
zapadnoto Chernomorie: Mezhdunarodna konferentsiia, Varna, 12–15 septemvri 2001 g.*, ed. by
Valeri Iotov and Igor Lazarenko (Varna, 2004), pp. 246–52 (p. 249). See also *Miracles of St
Demetrius*, 2.1, 2.4.255, and 2.5.289, ed. by Paul Lemerle (Paris, 1979). See also Ivanova, 'Chudesa',
p. 191. The Drugubites lived to the west of Thessalonica, around Veria.

initially been settled by the Avars in the region of Sirmium. The seal also mentions Mauros's title of *patrikios*, but according to the *Miracles of St Demetrius*, the emperor had bestowed upon him the lofty title of *hypatos*, whereby Mauros became equal in rank to the *archontes* of Mesembria and, more importantly, to his contemporary Peter, the *archon* of Hellas.[208]

So what does the numismatic and sigillographic evidence tell us about Dark-Age Greece? First, there can be no doubt any more as to the sustained Byzantine presence in eastern Greece between *c.* 600 and *c.* 800. Following the creation of the theme of Hellas, the introduction of *kommerkiarioi* coincided in time with a sharp decline in the number of coins found on the two main sites within the borders of the theme, namely Athens and Corinth. But the imperial *kommerkia* of Hellas did not exist in an economic environment completely devoid of coins. On the contrary, *kommerkiarioi* in Hellas witnessed, but most likely did not contribute to, unusual injections of copper coinage into local markets, such as during the reigns of Philippikos and Leo III. Judging by the existing evidence, the *kommerkiarioi* may have coexisted with a number of fiscal agents larger than in any other province in the Balkans, which confirms the idea that for Hellas, at least, *kommerkiarioi* served as tax collectors. Nothing indicates, though, that Hellas participated in any way in the sea trade network of which Thessalonica was a major link. The only fleet directly documented by seals of Hellas is the war fleet, initially the Karabisianoi, later the Kibyrrhaiotai. It is therefore no surprise that the number of seals of military officials, mainly of the navy, associated with Hellas is almost as large as that of seals of *strategoi* and officers of the land troops stationed in Thrace. In addition, a number of remarkable seals are known of *archontes* of loosely defined polities on what must have been the fringes of the theme, some of whom are specifically mentioned as 'of Hellas'. The distribution of those polities on the northern and north-eastern border of the theme reminds one of Procopius's description of the Justinianic ideal of an empire surrounded by 'barbarian' allies operating as 'buffer states' against the rest of *barbaricum*.[209] The *archontes* on the northern border of Hellas were subordinated directly to the emperor and often played an important role in the

[208] Maria Nystazopoulou-Pelekidou, 'Sceaux byzantins, improprement appelés protobulgares', *Vyzantiaka*, 11 (1991), 15–22 (pp. 16–17). See also *Miracles of St Demetrius*, 2.5.292. For the Sermesianoi, see Michel Pillon, 'L'Exode des Sermésiens et les grandes migrations des Romains de Pannonie dans les Balkans durant le Haut Moyen Âge', *Études Balkaniques*, 38 (2002), 103–41.

[209] Sergei A. Ivanov, 'Poniatiia "soiuza" i "podchineniia" u Prokopiia Kesariiskogo', in *Etnosotsial'naia i politicheskaia struktura rannefeodal'nykh slavianskikh gosudarstv i narodnostei*, ed. by Gennadii G. Litavrin (Moscow, 1987), pp. 27–32.

history of the region. During the siege of Thessalonica in 677, the Drugubites had 'kings'. A few years later, when, at the orders of the emperor, they provided supplies to the refugees from the Avar qaganate, the 'kings' had disappeared. The Drugubites seem to have rapidly turned into a client polity, and Peter may well have been their first *archon*. Even more prominent was the *archon* of the Belegezites, Akamiros, who in 799 allied himself with the Helladikoi and supported a son of Constantine V against Empress Irene.[210] He must have been a successor of that Tichomiros mentioned on an eighth-century seal, but his alliance with the Helladikoi cannot be an accident. The *archontes* of the Belegezites have been already drawn into the political developments of the theme of Hellas. Akamiros was no barbarian chieftain, but a client ruler with knowledge of and influence in local Byzantine politics.

Dark-Age Greece in Written Sources

The analysis of the archaeological, numismatic, and sigillographic evidence suggests that by AD 600, Greece entered a relatively long period of political instability. Barbarian attacks on the southern part of the Balkan Peninsula resumed during Heraclius's early regnal years. In distant Spain, Isidore of Seville knew that, at the beginning of the reign, the Persians had conquered Syria and Egypt, and the Slavs had taken Greece. It is difficult to visualize Isidore's source for this brief note, but his association of the Slavic occupation of Greece with the loss of Syria and Egypt to the Persians indicates that he was informed about the situation in the entire Mediterranean basin.[211] Peter Charanis believed that Isidore's notion of *Graecia*

[210] Theophanes Confessor, *Chronographia*, pp. 473–74. See Oikonomides, 'L'Archonte slave', p. 117. For the title of *archon*, see also Jadran Ferluga, 'Archon: Ein Beitrag zur Untersuchung der südslawischen Herrschertitel im 9. u. 10. Jh. in lichte der byzantinischen Quellen', in *Tradition als historische Kraft*, ed. by N. Kamp and J. Wollasch (Berlin, 1982), pp. 254–66; Hans Ditten, 'Prominente Slawen und Bulgaren in byzantinischen Diensten (Ende des 7. bis Anfang des 10. Jahrhunderts)', in *Studien zum 8. und 9. Jhr. im Byzanz*, ed. by Helga Köpstein and Friedhelm Winkelmann (Berlin, 1983), pp. 95–119 (pp. 110–11). Slavic archontes were apparently among the 'western commanders' whom Emperor Leo III ordered in 718 to assist in the suppression of the usurpation of Gregory-Tiberius in Sicily (Theophanes, p. 398). See also Tibor Živković, 'The Strategos Paul and the Archontes of the Westerners', *Symmeikta*, 15 (2002), 161–76.

[211] Isidore of Seville, *Chronicon*, in *Chronica minora saec. IV. V. VI. VII.*, vol. II, ed. by Theodor Mommsen, MGH AA, 11 (Berlin, 1894), p. 479. See Peter Charanis, 'Graecia in Isidore of Seville', *Byzantinische Zeitschrift*, 64 (1971), 22–25; Samuel Szádeczky-Kardoss, 'Die Nachricht des Isidorus Hispalensis und des spanischen Fortsetzers seiner "Historia" über einen Slaweneinfall in Griechenland', in *Szlávok-Protobolgárok-Bizánc*, ed. by Nino Nikolov, Samu Szádeczky-Kardoss, and

referred to what used to be known as Illyricum, not to Greece proper.[212] This might indeed be the case for Isidore, but certainly does not apply to the unknown author of Book II of the *Miracles of St Demetrius*. Writing in the late seventh century, he knew that before attacking Thessalonica, the Slavs had devastated Thessaly and its islands, the islands of Greece, the Cyclades, Achaia, Epirus, Illyricum, as well as parts of Asia. The reference to both Illyricum and Greece makes it clear that there is no confusion.[213] However, the first Slavic attack on Thessalonica is impossible to date with any precision. We are only told that it occurred under the episcopate of John, the author of Book I of the *Miracles of St Demetrius*. The description of the territories ravaged by Sclavenes before they turned against Thessalonica is viewed by many as fitting into the picture of Heraclius's early regnal years, snapshots of which are given by George of Pisidia and Isidore of Seville. In particular, the fact that the author of Book II specifically refers to maritime raids òn canoes reminds one of what George of Pisidia has to say about the 'Sclavene wolves'.[214] Historians agree, therefore, that the attack should be dated to the first decade of Heraclius's reign.

Unlike previous raids of the 580s, the Sclavenes of the early seventh century had brought with them families, for 'they had promised to establish them in the city

Teréz Olajos (Szeged, 1986), pp. 51–61 (pp. 53–54); José R. Marín, 'La "cuestión eslava" en el Peloponeso Bizantino (siglos VI–X)', *Bizantion: Nea Hellas*, 11–12 (1991–92), 205–44 (pp. 225 and 228); O. V. Ivanova, 'Isidor Sevil'skii', in *Svod drevneishikh pis'mennykh izvestii o slavianakh*, ed. by Ivanov, Litavrin, and Ronin, II, 353–58 (pp. 356–57). In the *Continuatio hispana*, written in 754, the raid is dated to Heraclius's fourth regnal year, but the source for that entry was not Isidore (Szádeczky-Kardoss, 'Die Nachricht des Isidorus', p. 54; Ivanova, 'Isidor Sevil'skii', p. 355). For *Sclavi* as an ethnic name originating in Constantinople, see Curta, *Making of the Slavs*, pp. 45–46.

[212] Charanis, 'Graecia in Isidore of Seville', pp. 22–25.

[213] *Miracles of St Demetrius*, 2.1.179. For Book II of the *Miracles of St Demetrius*, see Johannes Koder, 'Anmerkungen zu den *Miracula Sancti Demetrii*', in *Byzance: Hommage à André N. Stratos*, ed. by Nia A. Stratos, II (Athens, 1986), pp. 523–38 (pp. 530–31). For an unconvincing attempt to show that the Slavs could not have possibly reached the Cyclades on their canoes, see Karagiannopoulos, 'Zur Frage der Slavenansiedlung', p. 187; Xenophon Moniaros, 'Slavikes epidromes sto Aigaio stis archēs tou 70u ai: He periptōsē tēs Chiou', *Vyzantina*, 18 (1995–96), 285–302.

[214] *Miracles of St Demetrius*, 2.1.179; see also 2.4.253 and 254. For the 'Sclavene wolves', see George of Pisidia, *Bellum Avaricum*, 197–201, ed. by A. Pertusi (Ettal, 1959); Sergei A. Ivanov, 'Georgii Pisida', in *Svod drevneishikh pis'mennykh izvestii o slavianakh*, ed. by Ivanov, Litavrin, and Ronin, II, 65–74 (pp. 66–67). Frano Barišić, *Čuda Dimitrija Solunskog kao istoriski izvori* (Belgrade, 1953), pp. 86–95, dated the siege to 616. Paul Lemerle, *Les Plus Anciens Recueils des Miracles de Saint Démétrius et la penetration des Slaves dans les Balkans*, II: *Commentaire* (Paris, 1981), pp. 91–94, preferred to date the siege to 615. See also Ivanova 'Chudesa', p. 191.

after its conquest'.[215] This suggests that they were coming from the surrounding countryside, for the author of Book II used 'Sclavenes' as an umbrella-term for a multitude of tribes, some of which he knew by name: Drugubites, Sagudates, Baiunetes, Berzetes, and Belegezites.[216] We have seen that the latter are again mentioned in Book II as living in the region of Thebes and Demetrias. When did they establish themselves there? It is impossible to tell with precision, but it cannot have been earlier than the reign of Heraclius. Nevertheless, it is hard to believe that the Belegezites and the other tribes mentioned by the author of Book II were responsible for the devastation of the islands of Thessaly, the Cyclades, of most of Illyricum, and of parts of Asia. There are two other 'lists of provinces' in Book II of the *Miracles of St Demetrius*, one of which betrays an administrative source.[217] It is therefore likely that, in describing a local event — the attack of the Drugubites, Sagudates, Belegezites, Baiunetes, and Berzetes on Thessalonica — of relatively minor significance, the author of Book II framed it against a broader historical and administrative background, in order to make it appear as of greater importance. When all the other provinces and cities were falling, Thessalonica alone, under the protection of St Demetrius, was capable of resistance. When the Sclavenes failed to take the city and to establish themselves in Thessalonica, they called upon the Avars for assistance. They offered rich presents and promised much more provided that the qagan of the Avars would help them capture the city. Those Sclavenes were certainly not subjects of the qagan. They were negotiating an alliance with the Avars as equals. That other Sclavenes, however, were still obeying the orders of the qagan is shown by the composition of the army he eventually sent to Thessalonica.[218] The siege of Thessalonica was definitely not an event of major importance. Even the author of Book II was aware that nobody, not even the emperor, knew about it.[219] The emperor in question is not named, but he must have been Heraclius, for the siege occurred not long after the one described in the first homily of Book II. Indeed, two years after being offered the alliance of the

---

[215] *Miracles of St Demetrius*, 2.1.180.

[216] For the multitude of tribes, see *Miracles of St Demetrius*, 2.1.179. For the location of the various tribes, see Lemerle, *Les Plus Anciens Recueils*, pp. 89–90; Mitko B. Panov, 'On the Slav Colonization and the Ethnic Changes in Macedonia by the End of the 6th and the First Half of the 7th Century', *Balcanica Posnaniensia*, 11–12 (2001), 23–33 (pp. 26–27).

[217] *Miracles of St Demetrius*, 2.2.197 and 2.5.284.

[218] *Miracles of St Demetrius*, 2.2.197–98. The Sclavenes attacked on the fourth day (2.1.185) and the decisive confrontation took place on that same day.

[219] *Miracles of St Demetrius*, 2.2.210.

Sclavene tribes who had failed in capturing Thessalonica, the qagan marched against the city. The siege must have taken place in 617 or 618, at the latest, and lasted just over a month.[220] In the end, however, the qagan failed to take the city. He opened negotiations with the besieged, in order to obtain some form of monetary compensation for withdrawing his troops.

Shortly after that, *c.* 620, Heraclius moved all troops from the Balkans to the eastern front. This seems to have allowed the Avars a wider range of both raiding and control in the Balkans. In 623, they ambushed the Emperor himself near the Long Walls; three years later, the Avars put Constantinople under siege. Nothing else is known about developments in Greece until after the middle of the seventh century. In 662/63, on his way to Italy, Constans II stopped in Athens, perhaps for the winter months, an indication of the presence of troops at least in the eastern region of Greece.[221] The contemporary situation in northern Greece is well documented in Book II of the *Miracles of St Demetrius*. The fourth homily is an extremely valuable source for the seventh-century history of the Balkan Slavs, and without this text there would be very little to say about Dark-Age Greece. The unknown author of Book II describes a powerful polity under the rule of the 'king' of the Rynchines, Perbundos. Other groups of Sclavenes existed in the vicinity of Thessalonica. There were also Sclavenes in the Strymon valley by the time the king of the Rynchines was arrested and executed, and the Sagudates allied themselves with the Rynchines against Thessalonica. A third tribe, the Drugubites, joined the alliance. The ensuing siege of the city is to be dated to 25 July 677, because of a clear reference to 'July 25 of the fifth indiction'. The Sclavenes appear as better organized than in any of the preceding sieges, with an army of special units of archers and warriors armed with slings, spears, shields, and swords. In a long story

[220] *Miracles of St Demetrius,* 2.2.198. See Lemerle, *Les Plus Anciens Recueils,* pp. 99–100; Walter Pohl, *Die Awaren: Ein Steppenvolk im Mitteleuropa 567–822 n. Chr.* (Munich, 1988), pp. 242–43.

[221] *Liber pontificalis,* ed. by Theodor Mommsen (Berlin, 1898), p. 186: 'Huius temporibus venit Constantinus Augustus de regia urbe per litoraria in Athenas et exinde Taranto.' Paul the Deacon's account of Constans II's campaign is based on the biography of Pope Vitalian in the *Liber Pontificalis.* As a consequence, he too claims that the Emperor marched overland from Constantinople. See Paul the Deacon, *History of the Lombards,* 5.6, ed. by Georg Waitz (Hannover, 1878), p. 146. Since the communication by land between Constantinople and Thessalonica was re-established only under Constantine IV, it is unlikely that Constans crossed through southern Thrace and Macedonia to reach Athens. See also Stratos, *Byzantium,* p. 171; Yannopoulos, 'La Pénétration slave', p. 343; Herbert Hunger, 'Athen in Byzanz: Traum und Realität', *Jahrbuch der Österreichischen Byzantinistik,* 40 (1990), 43–61 (p. 49).

most likely derived from an oral account, the author of Book II mentions a Sclavene craftsman building a siege machine. There were also Sclavene tribes living at a considerable distance and not taking part in the Sclavene alliance against Thessalonica. The Belegezites, who lived near Thebes and Demetrias, even supplied the besieged city with grain.[222] The author of Book II also refers to Sclavene pirates raiding as close to Constantinople as the island of Proconnesus. The emperor (whose name is not given) eventually decided to send an army to Thrace and to the 'land on the opposite side', against the Strymonian Slavs. Since the siege can be dated to 677, and we are specifically told that prior to the siege the emperor was preparing for war against the Arabs, this expedition against the *Sklaviniai* of southern Macedonia must have been ordered by Constantine IV. The successful campaign took place in 678, shortly after the failure of the Arab blockade of Constantinople.[223] As a consequence, it was possible for the Archbishop of Thessalonica to participate in the Sixth Ecumenical Council in Constantinople (680/81), together with the bishops of Athens, Argos, Lacedaemona, and Corinth.[224]

With Book II of the *Miracles of St Demetrius* we come to the end of a long series of contemporary accounts on the early Slavs in the Balkans. None of the subsequent sources is based on autopsy and all could be referred to as 'histories', relying entirely on older sources. According to Theophanes, in 725, 'the inhabitants of Hellas and the Cyclades' rose against Leo III and proclaimed a new emperor, Cosmas. The rebels sent a large fleet to Constantinople under the command of the

---

[222] *Miracles of St Demetrius*, 2.3.219, 2.3.222, 2.4.231, 2.4.242, 2.4.255, 2.4.255, 2.4.262, 2.4.271–76. For supplies of grain from the Belegezites, see 2.4.254 and 268. The Drugubites too supplied food to Kuver and his people (2.5.289). For the execution of Perbundos, see Miroslaw Jerzy Leszka, 'Kilka uwag na temat śmierci Prebuda, ksiecia Rynchinów', *Slavia Antiqua*, 46 (2005), 57–62 (but with a faulty chronology of events). For the Sclavene army besieging Thessalonica, see Christos Zachopoulos, 'Hē polemikē ischys tōn "Sklavinōn" stēn "5e poliorkia" tēs Thessalonikēs kai hoi scheseis tous me to vyzantino kratos stēn idia periodo', in *12' Panellēnio Chistoriko Synedrio (29–31 Maiou 1992): Praktika*, ed. by Ioannis Karagiannopoulos (Thessaloniki, 1992), pp. 39–64.

[223] *Miracles of St Demetrius*, 2.4.277, 2.4.278, 2.4.232. For the date of Constantine IV's campaign, see Lemerle, *Les Plus Anciens Recueils*, pp. 131–33; Theodoros Korres, 'Paratēreseis schetikes me tēn pemptē poliorkia tēs Thessalonikēs apo tous Slavous (676–678): Palaiotēre ereuna kai neotēres ermēneies', *Vyzantiaka*, 19 (1999), 137–65 (p. 163).

[224] Rudolf Riedinger, *Die Präsenz- und Subskriptionslisten des VI. oekumenischen Konzils (680/81) und der Papyrus Vind. G. 3* (Munich, 1979), pp. 8 and 14. The presence of the five bishops in Constantinople is commonly interpreted as indicating that Corinth, Argos, Athens, and Lacedaemona were, like Thessalonica, under Byzantine control.

turmarch of the theme, Agallianos.[225] Much has been made of the mention of Monemvasia, at the southernmost tip of Peloponnesus, in the story of the pilgrimage of Bishop Willibald of Eichstätt to the Holy Land.[226] The author of the story was a nun, Hugeburc of Heidenheim, who wrote down what she had been told by Willibald himself 'in dictation from his own mouth'.[227] According to her, Willibald set out on his pilgrimage in 722. One year later, he sailed from Syracuse and 'reached the city of Monemvasia, in the land of Slavinia'.[228] That Willibald travelled directly from Sicily to Monemvasia is a clear indication that in the early eighth century, in order to reach Constantinople from the western provinces, one needed to circumnavigate Peloponnesus.[229] The sojourn in Monemvasia does not seem to have been long, but the fact that Hugeburc reports that the place was 'in the land of Slavinia' is often interpreted as an indication of a Slavic presence in the hinterland.[230] The Latin word *Slawinia* is a clear, though by no means unique, calque of the Greek form *Sklavinia*, which Theophanes used for the polities attacked by Constans II in 656 and by Justinian II in 688. A 'Sklavinia' was a more or less independent, but loosely organized barbarian polity beyond the borders of

---

[225] Theophanes Confessor, *Chronographia*, p. 405.

[226] *Vita Willibaldi episcopi Eischstetensis et vita Wynnebaldi abbatis Heidenheimensis auctore sanctimoniale Heidenheimensis*, ed. by O. Holder-Egger, MGH SS, 15.1 (Hannover, 1887; repr. 1992), pp. 80–117. For Hugeburc's life and work, see Bernard Bischoff, 'Wer ist die Nonne von Heidenheim?', *Studien zur Geschichte des Benediktinerordens*, 49 (1931), 387–88; Eva Gottschaller, *Hugeberc von Heidenheim: Philologische Untersuchungen zu den heiligen Biographen einer Nonne des 8. Jahrhunderts* (Munich, 1973); Claudio Leonardi, 'Una scheda per Ugeburga', in *Tradtion und Wertung: Festschrift für Franz Brunhölzl zum 65. Geburtstag*, ed. by Günter Bernt, Fidel Rädle, and Gabriel Silagi (Sigmaringen, 1989), pp. 23–26. For Willibald's pilgrimage, see K. Guth, 'Die Pilgerfahrt Willibalds ins Heilige Land (723–728/9): Analyse eines frühmittelalterlichen Reiseberichts', *Sammelblatt des Historischen Vereins Eichstätt*, 75 (1982), 13–28; Michael McCormick, *Origins of the European Economy: Communications and Commerce, A.D. 300–900* (Cambridge, 2001), pp. 129–34.

[227] *Vita Willibaldi*, p. 86; English translation by C. H. Talbot, in *Soldiers of Christ: Saints and Saints' Lives from Late Antiquity and the Early Middle Ages*, ed. by Thomas F. X. Noble and Thomas Head (University Park, PA, 1995), pp. 143–44.

[228] *Vita Willibaldi*, p. 93: 'Et inde navigantes, venerunt ultra mare Adria ad urbem Manafasiam in Slawinia terrae.' From Monemvasia, Willibald, his father, and his brother went to Chios, 'leaving Corinth on the port side'.

[229] McCormick, *Origins*, pp. 502–08.

[230] George Leonard Huxley, *Monemvasia and the Slavs: A Lecture on Some Works of Historical Geography in the Gennadius Library of the American School of Classical Studies at Athens* (Athens, 1988), p. 9; McCormick, *Origins*, pp. 131 and 508.

the empire. As such, the word was occasionally used in Carolingian sources as well. As Theophanes' usage of the word suggests, there was more than one Sklavinia at any one time. From the point of view of the Byzantine authorities in Constantinople, what mattered was not the precise description of the ethnic identities associated to any Sklavinia, but the fact that such polities were independent and potentially hostile. It is therefore important not to read too much in Hugeburc's mention of Monemvasia in the 'land of Slavinia'. What she probably meant was not that the city was surrounded by Slavs, but that the power of the Byzantine emperor or of his local deputy ended at the very walls of the city: beyond that, it was barbarian land.[231] In any case, the 'land of Slavinia' was most likely not the name that those living in the environs of Monemvasia employed to refer to their country. Instead, the phrase betrays the administrative nature of Hugeburc or Willibald's source of information about what was beyond Monemvasia. As a consequence, the phrase is little more than a stereotype, albeit of administrative, not bookish origin.

By contrast, the apocryphal *Life of St Pancratius*, the first bishop of Taormina, may have employed eyewitness accounts. Recent studies have demonstrated that its author, Evagrius, was writing shortly after the introduction of the thematic organization in Sicily (709/10), possibly before 695.[232] Evagrius placed the life of Pancratius, a disciple of St Peter who lived in the first century AD, in the context of his own lifetime. Pancratius's mission of conversion is thus set against the background of the first Arab attacks on Sicily, in the late seventh or early eighth century. One of Pancratius's converts was a local *hegemon* named Bonifatius. Portrayed as the *strategos* of the Sicilian theme residing in Taormina, Bonifatius was the supreme commander of the army, which he led in campaigns against 'tyrants'

---

[231] V. K. Ronin, 'Zhitie Villibal'da, episkopa Eikhshtettskogo', in *Svod drevneishikh pis'mennykh izvestii o slavianakh*, ed. by Ivanov, Litavrin, and Ronin, II, 439–40 (p. 440). For Sklavinia in Byzantine and Carolingian sources, see Stjepan Antoljak, 'Unsere "Sklavinien"', in *Actes du XIIe Congrès international des études byzantines, Ochride 10–16 Septembre 1961*, II (Belgrade, 1964), pp. 9–13 (pp. 11–12); Klaus Bertels, 'Carantania: Beobachtungen zur politisch-geographischen Terminologie und zur Geschichte des Landes und seiner Bevölkerung im frühen Mittelalter', *Carinthia*, 177 (1987), 87–190 (pp. 160–61).

[232] Cynthia Jean Stallman, 'The Life of S. Pancratius of Taormina' (unpublished doctoral dissertation, University of Oxford, 1986), pp. 156 and 247. Others went as far as to date the earliest redaction of the *Life* to the reign of Constans II. That early version was then reworked at some point during the first phase of the iconoclastic controversy, i.e. between 715 and 787. The terminus ante quem is given by the mention of the *Life* in three letters of Theodore of Stoudios, dated to 815/16, 816/18, and 826, respectively. See Wolfram Brandes, 'Das Gold der Menia: Ein Beispiel transkulturellen Wissentransfers', *Millenium*, 2 (2005), 175–226 (pp. 200–21 with n. 134).

in Sicily or barbarians abroad. At one time, he is described as organizing a seaborne expedition into the regions of Dyrrachium and Athens. Upon returning to Sicily, he is confronted by St Pancratius, who claims that his prisoners look like Christians. Bonifatius assures him they were Avars, who are to be distributed among the soldiers to be baptized, and are to be taught Greek and Latin, the languages in use at that time in Taormina.[233] Through the intermediary of a translator, the prisoners then declare that they worship fire, water, and their own swords.[234] It is hard to establish the possible source for this story, but there is no doubt about its

---

[233] Stallman, 'Life of S. Pancratius', p. 271. When Bonifatius presents his prisoners, the Taorminians declare that they will make the captives speak Greek and Latin and become Christians, as they have done before with Persians and Macedonians, a detail Stallman placed within the 'realm of the aetiological excursus', an example of Evagrius's 'intention of advancing the historical importance of Taormina'. According to her (p. 276 with n. 15), the reference to Athens in the Avar episode is a commonplace, representing an unspecific notion of a location across the Adriatic. Indeed, elsewhere in the *Life of St Pancratius* (p. 344) 'Athenians' is used as a generic term. Within the Avar episode, however, Athens does not stand alone, but in association with Dyrrachium, which does not support the idea of an 'unspecific location across the Adriatic'. This idea also contradicts Stallman's suggestion (p. 284) that the *Life* preserves some genuine evidence of a raid by Emperor Constans II from Sicily to Greece. Stallman (p. 287) also suggested that Evagrius got a version of Theophanes' notice of Constans's campaign against *Sklavinia* (Theophanes Confessor, *Chronographia*, p. 347) from some unknown source, reworked and adapted it for his own purpose, while attributing it to Bonifatius. However, there is no reference to *Sklavinia* in Evagrius, while Bonifatius's captives are Avars, not Slavs. The first to notice the importance of this source for the question of the Avar presence in Greece were Arnulf Kollautz and Hisyuki Miyakawa, *Geschichte und Kultur eines völkerwanderungszeitlichen Nomadenvolkes: Die Jou-Jan der Mongolei und die Awaren in Mitteleuropa*, I (Klagenfurt, 1970), p. 282. For a much later reference to Avars around Budva, north of Dyrrachium, see Jovan Kovačević, 'Avari na Jadranu', in *Referati sa simpozijuma praistorijske i srednjevjekovne sekcije Arheološkog Društva Jugoslavije*, ed. by Nikola Tašić (Belgrade, 1966), pp. 53–81 (p. 73).

[234] Stallman, 'Life of S. Pancratius', p. 271. The Avar episode appears in two eleventh-century manuscripts, one from Vienna, the other from Moscow. According to both, the Avar prisoners were captured in the provinces (*eparchiai*) of Dyrrachium and Athens. See Vasil'ev, 'Slaviane v Gretsii', p. 416; Mario Capaldo, 'Un insediamento slavo presso Siracusa nel primo millennio d. C.', *Europa Orientalis*, 2 (1983), 5–17 (p. 13); Teréz Olajos, 'Quelques remarques sur une peuplade slave', *Vizantiiskii Vremennik*, 55 (1994), 106–10 (pp. 107–08); Papadimitriou, 'Thesmiske scheseis', pp. 173–74; Florin Curta, 'Barbarians in Dark-Age Greece: Slavs or Avars?', in *Civitas divino-humana: V chest na profesor Georgi Bakalov*, ed. by Tsvetelin Stepanov and Veselina Vachkova (Sofia, 2004), pp. 513–50 (pp. 530–32). For Avars speaking Slavic, see Florin Curta, 'The Slavic Lingua Franca (Linguistic Notes of an Archaeologist Turned Historian)', *East Central Europe*, 31 (2004), 125–48 (pp. 143–44).

authenticity.[235] Though the translator employed to interrogate the Avar prisoners may well have been a member of a Slavic community from Syracuse mentioned in another passage, the author of the *Life of St Pancratius* clearly and carefully distinguished Avars from Slavs.[236]

That communication between Sicily and Peloponnesus was not disturbed by Arab raids in the early eighth century is confirmed by other, independent sources. According to Theophanes, the plague of 745/46 'travelled like a spreading fire' from Sicily and Calabria to Monemvasia, Hellas, 'and the adjoining islands', before reaching Constantinople. Ten years later, Emperor Constantine V brought families from the islands, Hellas, and 'the southern parts' to Constantinople, in an attempt to repopulate a city devastated by the plague.[237] In 766, he 'collected artisans from

---

[235] Nor is it possible to link this episode to the memories of Greek refugees from Peloponnesus, whom Evagrius allegedly met in Sicily. See Stallman, 'Life of S. Pancratius', p. 273; Vera von Falkenhausen, 'Arethas in Italien?', *Byzantinoslavica*, 56 (1995), 359–66 (p. 361). The fact that the Avar prisoners worshipped fire, water, and their own swords reminds one of what Menander the Guardsman had to say about Bayan, the qagan of the Avars, who took an oath on his own sword, on the heavenly fire, and on water. See Menander the Guardsman, *fr.* 25.1c, ed. and trans. by R. C. Blockley (Liverpool, 1985), p. 221; Olajos, 'Quelques remarques', p. 110. No evidence exists, however, that Evagrius read Menander. On the other hand, by casting the Avar episode as a parallel to Pancratius's later confrontation to Aculinus and to St Marcian's challenge to the pagans, Evagrius may have been encouraged to complete the *synkrisis* by attributing temples and idols to the Avars. See Stallman, 'Life of S. Pancratius', p. 271.

[236] For the Slavic settlement near Syracuse, see Stallman, 'Life of S. Pancratius', p. 355. Evagrius attributes the information about the Slavic settlement to a written source, the *historiographoi*, but as Stallman notes, this may well be just one of Evagrius's authenticating techniques. For Evagrius's distinction between Slavs and Avars, see Capaldo, 'Un insediamento slavo', pp. 8 and 13. *Contra*: Samuel Szádeczky-Kardoss, 'Der Awarensturm im historischen Bewusstsein der Byzantiner der 11.–13. Jahrhunderte', in *Actes du XV-e Congrès international d'études byzantines: Athènes, septembre 1976*, ed. P. Zepos, IV (Athens, 1980), pp. 305–14 (pp. 309–10); Olajos, 'Quelques remarques', p. 100.

[237] Theophanes Confessor, *Chronographia*, pp. 422 and 429. See Panagiotis A. Yannopoulos, 'Métropoles du Péloponnèse mésobyzantin: un souvenir des invasions avaro-slaves', *Byzantion*, 63 (1993), 388–400 (p. 391), who regards the transfer of population from Hellas to Constantinople as indicating a considerable growth of population in Greece. However, in the mid-eighth century, those settled in restored or newly built forts in the theme of Thrace were not inhabitants of the neighbouring theme of Hellas, but Christians deported from Germanicea, Sozopetra, Melitene, and other cities in Asia Minor taken by Constantine V from the Arabs. For the plague spreading along trade routes, see Ilse Rochow, *Byzanz im 8. Jahrhundert in der Sicht des Theophanes: Quellen-kritisch-historischer Kommentar zu den Jahren 715–813* (Berlin, 1991), p. 162; Ewald Kislinger, 'Lakedaimonia, Demenna kai to Chronikon tēs Monemvasias', *Vyzantines kai Metavyzantines Ereunes*, 3 (1992), 103–21 (pp. 105–06).

different places' and brought five hundred clay-workers from Hellas and the islands.[238] Apparently, by that time, a relatively large number of Slavs lived beyond, if not inside, the borders of the theme of Hellas, as well as in the vicinity of Thessalonica. In 783, an army led by the logothete of the Swift Course, Staurakios, moved from Constantinople to Thessalonica and Hellas, 'against the Sklavinian tribes', and forced them to pay tribute to the empire. According to Theophanes, Staurakios's army then moved into Peloponnesus and 'brought back many captives and much booty to the Roman Empire'.[239] It is important to note that although Staurakios is said to have moved against the Sclavenes, the exact ethnicity of his Peloponnesian prisoners is not mentioned. In any case, at least three important Peloponnesian centres were under imperial control in the 780s, as indicated by the participation of the bishops of Troizen, Monemvasia, and Patras in the Council of Nicaea that restored the cult of the icons (787).[240] On the other hand, Staurakios's campaign had no impact on the Slavic clients of northern Greece. We have seen that in 799, prompted by conspirators from the theme of Hellas, Akamiros, the *archon* of the Belegezites, attempted to release Constantine V's sons from their

---

[238] Theophanes Confessor, *Chronographia*, p. 440.

[239] Theophanes Confessor, *Chronographia*, pp. 456–57. The campaign is also mentioned by Michael the Syrian and the thirteenth-century chronicle of Gregory Barhebraeus, who adds that Staurakios left a garrison in 'the country of Peloponnesus'. According to Barhebraeus, those conquered by Staurakios were 'Arabs' (perhaps 'Avars'), not Slavs. See Bar Hebraeus, *Chronography*, ed. and trans. by E. A. Wallis Budge, I (London, 1932), p. 120; Teréz Olajos, 'Une source inob-servée concernant l'histoire des Slaves du Péloponnèse', in *La Méditerranée et l'Europe: histoire et politique*, ed. by György Kukovecz and Nourredine Abdi (Szeged, 1998), pp. 39–44. Staurakios celebrated his victory in January 784, an indication that his campaign in the Peloponnese may have lasted until November 783, most likely in order to force the Slavs out of the mountains. See Nicholas Oikonomides, 'A Note on the Campaign of Staurakios in the Peloponnese (783/4)', *Zbornik radova Vizantološkog Instituta*, 38 (1999–2000), 61–66. Following that campaign, the emphasis in Byzantine sources shifts from Thracian and Macedonian Slavs to those of Greece. See Vasmer, *Die Slaven*, p. 15; Huxley, *Monemvasia and the Slavs*, p. 9.

[240] Several other sees in continental Greece were represented at Nicaea, along with the sees of Salona, Dyrrachium, and Kotor. See Jean Darrouzès, 'Listes épiscopales du concile de Nicée (787)', *Revue des études byzantines*, 33 (1975), 5–76 (pp. 37–38). Shortly after that, Athens and Patras were elevated to metropolitan status. See Vitalien Laurent, 'L'Érection de la métropole d'Athènes et le statut ecclésiastique de l'Illyricum au VIIIe siècle', *Revue des études byzantines*, 1 (1943), 58–72 (pp. 69–70); Yannopoulos, 'Métropoles du Péloponnèse mésobyzantin', pp. 395 and 398–99; Browning, 'Athens in the "Dark Age"', p. 301; Avramea, *Le Péloponnèse*, p. 188.

exile in Athens and to proclaim one of them as emperor. The rebels were defeated and blinded and nothing else is known about the Slavic *archon*.[241]

There are several conclusions to be drawn from this examination of the written sources pertaining to the history of the southern Balkans between *c*. 600 and *c*. 800. First, no pattern exists of a unique, continuous, and sudden invasion of either Slavs or Avars. Moreover, until the siege of Thessalonica during Heraclius's early regnal years, there is no evidence at all for outward migration, in the sense of a permanent change of residence. The Sclavenes said to have besieged Thessalonica at some point during the 610s had brought with them their families, for they intended to establish themselves in the city following its conquest. This also indicates that they were not coming from afar, for the prisoners they had taken after the siege could return to Thessalonica carrying the booty taken by the Sclavenes from the inhabitants of the city.[242] Moreover, some of the tribes mentioned in Book II of the *Miracles of St Demetrius* are described as living in the immediate vicinity of the city. When did they settle there? Paul Lemerle argued that in the 610s a Slavic settlement around Thessalonica must have been a relatively recent phenomenon. How recent, however, is impossible to tell. The evidence of the late seventh century suggests that by then there were also Slavs in Thessaly, while Sclavene pirates raided the Thracian coast and the Straits as far as the island of Proconnesus. Judging from the existing evidence, a true migration could have taken place only during a relatively short period of time, namely not long after Heraclius's accession to power. The evidence for a Slavic settlement in southern Greece, however, cannot be dated earlier than *c*. 700. To the author of the *Life of St Willibald*, Monemvasia was 'in the land of Slavinia', but this only shows that in the 720s the imperial government in Constantinople, where the phrase *Sklavinia* was in use, had no control over the

---

[241] Theophanes Confessor, *Chronographia*, pp. 473–74. See Vasmer, *Die Slaven*, p. 16; Yannopoulos, 'La Pénétration slave', p. 350; Ditten, *Ethnische Verschiebungen*, p. 240; Oikonomides, 'L'Archonte slave', p. 117. Judging from the existing evidence, around the year 800, the most dangerous Slavs were those of Greece, not those of Thrace. In 784, Empress Irene toured Thrace in the company of her tagmatic troops. She rebuilt Beroe (modern Stara Zagora), rebaptized Irenopolis, and reached as far west as Philippopolis (modern Plovdiv), without encountering any opposition. Shortly following that visit, at some point after 790 but before 802, the theme of Macedonia was created in western Thrace, centred in Adrianople. See Ekaterini Christophilopoulou, 'Vyzantinē Makedonia: Schediasma gia tēn epochē apo ta telē tou 6' mechri ta mesa tou 9' aiōna', *Vyzantina*, 12 (1983), 9–63 (p. 48); Nikolai Sharankov and Dimităr Iankov, 'A 784 AD Inscription of Constantine VI and Irene from Beroe-Irenopolis (Modern Stara Zagora, South Bulgaria)', *Archaeologia Bulgarica*, 12 (2008), 77–86.

[242] *Miracles of St Demetrius*, 2.2.196. See Charanis, 'Ethnic Changes', p. 38.

hinterland of Monemvasia. We only learn about Slavs after the creation of the theme of Peloponnesus shortly before 800.[243]

On the other hand, and despite the general withdrawal of troops from the Balkans in *c*. 620, the empire seems to have maintained control over several coastal areas. In 662, Athens was large enough to accommodate for several months the emperor himself, together with his court. Moreover, the city had a bishop, who participated in the Sixth Ecumenical Council as papal legate. Under Justinian II, the first attempts were made to secure the safety of the ancient road linking Constantinople to Thessalonica, as military outposts were established near mountain passes north of Via Egnatia. The newly created theme of Thrace served first as a buffer against Bulgaria to the north and only later as the basis for further expansion into the central region of the Balkans. Similarly, the creation of the theme of Hellas in the late seventh century did not result in a gradual extension of the imperial authority inland from the outposts on the coast, for at least initially Hellas was little more than a naval base. Despite Constans II's and Justinian II's brief campaigns, the *Sklaviniai* remained outside the area of direct Byzantine control, though still in the orbit of the newly created themes. This may explain why the perspective on developments in the southern Balkans remained Constantinopolitan and why sources based on information originating in the capital, such as the *Life of St Willibald* and Theophanes' *Chronography*, spoke exclusively of *Sklaviniai* and Sclavenes. The author of Book II of the *Miracles of St Demetrius* was the first to introduce tribal names, such as Drugubites, Sagudates, Belegezites, Berzites, and Rynchines. In the mid-tenth century, Constantine VII Porphyrogenitus wrote of two other tribes, the Ezeritai and the Milingoi, fiercely defending their independence against Byzantine encroachment.[244] In both cases, the difference between various groups was important, because of differing political interests linked with various ethnicities. Some of the tribes described in Book II of the *Miracles of St Demetrius* besieged Thessalonica. They were viewed as savage, brutish, and heathen. Others, like the Belegezites, were friendly and, at times, potential and important allies who were able to supply the besieged city with food. To Constantine Porphyrogenitus, the Ezeritai and the Milingoi were different from all Slavs

---

[243] Tibor Živković, 'The Date of the Creation of the Theme of Peloponnese', *Symmeikta*, 13 (1999), 141–55.

[244] Constantine Porphyrogenitus, *De administrando imperio*, 50, ed. by Gyula Moravcsik and English translation by R. J. H. Jenkins (Washington, DC, 1967). See Henrik Birnbaum, 'Noch einmal zu den slavischen Milingen auf der Peloponnes', in *Festschrift für Herbert Bräuer zum 65. Geburtstag am 14. April 1986*, ed. by Reinhold Olesch and Hans Rothe (Cologne, 1986), pp. 15–26.

because of their successful resistance against various military governors of the theme. That the *Life of St Pancratius* used 'Avars', instead of 'Slavs', cannot be attributed to either confusion or the fluidity of the early medieval concept of ethnicity.[245] In the *Chronicle of Monemvasia*, those conquering and holding Peloponnesus for 218 years are Avars, while Slavs appear only later, when unsuccessfully opposing the army of the imperial *strategos* under Emperor Nicephorus I. In all those cases, ethnicity was a function of power in a very concrete and simple way. Ethnic groups were not classified in terms of language or culture, but in terms of their military and political potential. Names were important, therefore, because they gave meaning to categories of political classification.

Conclusion

Could the archeological evidence of the seventh century be attributed to either Slavs or Avars? Eric Ivison has interpreted the Corinth burials as indicating the presence of 'groups of Slavs invested with land by the State to defend the city and issued with military equipment, some of which accompanied them to the grave'. According to him, the warriors buried in Corinth were 'Slavic members of a military garrison'.[246] In my opinion, the archaeological evidence contradicts his interpretation. First, and if the culture-historical line of reasoning in the Charanis-Setton controversy is to be followed with any consistency, then it is very clear that analogies for the archaeological assemblages discussed in the first part of this paper point to other regions of Eastern Europe than those associated on the basis of

---

[245] Pohl, *Die Awaren*, pp. 107–08. Pohl believes that those who viewed themselves politically closer to the Avars chose to leave at the end of the raid, together with the qagan. Slavs became those who presumably remained and settled in Greece. The analysis of the written evidence shows this interpretation to be wrong. Stanisław Turlej, *The Chronicle of Monemvasia: The Migration of the Slavs and Church Conflicts in the Byzantine Source from the Beginning of the 9th Century* (Cracow, 2001), p. 52 with n. 89, categorically rejects the idea of the author of the *Chronicle* not knowing the difference between Avars and Slavs. On the other hand, Constantine Porphyrogenitus clearly associates the Slavs with 'other insubordinates', who rebelled 'and neither obeyed the military governor nor regarded the imperial mandate, but were practically independent and self-governing' (*De administrando imperio* 50, p. 233). To Emperor Constantine, 'Slavs' was the name for the barbarians in Greece (see *De administrando imperio*, 49), in general, while Milingoi and Ezeritai designated the troublesome barbarians. Some took that a step further and argued that neither Milingoi nor Ezeritai were speakers of Slavic. See J. Benos, 'Waren die peloponnesischen Melinger Vlachen?', *Thetis*, 2 (1995), 143–48.

[246] Ivison, 'Burial and Urbanism', p. 119.

written sources with the presence of the early Slavs. As Tivadar Vida and Thomas Völling have demonstrated, most known analogies for artefacts found in the cremation burials in Olympia are from Avar burials in Hungary or assemblages in the steppes north of the Black Sea associated with medieval nomads. Most other seventh-century archaeological assemblages in Greece are inhumations in burial chambers or stone-lined graves, and as such they are radically different from anything known in that respect from the archaeological evidence of the Lower Danube region, where late sixth- and early seventh-century sources placed the Sclavenes. On the other hand, the grave of the 'wandering soldier' in Corinth, as well as other similar assemblages in Greece, can hardly be interpreted in direct connection with Early Avar assemblages in Hungary or the neighbouring regions, in which *stone-lined* graves with weapons are unknown. By contrast, such graves are the preferred form of inhumation in sixth-century cemeteries of Balkan cities or forts and in the Mediterranean area during the 600s. At any rate, the stone lining of the 'wandering soldier' grave has much more in common with contemporary burial assemblages in Greece than the associated grave goods. In other words, the 'wandering soldier' grave stands out among burials with or without weapons that can be dated with some degree of accuracy to the early seventh century as prominently as the burials with 'Slavic' bow fibulae from Nea Anchialos and Edessa. In all three cases, the extraordinary status of the deceased is emphasized either by exceptional grave goods or by privileged location. The message encoded in burial dress combines cultural elements of very different origins in what seems to have been a statement about relative identity. The resulting emblemic style most likely had to do with the more or less imagined position of the deceased within the social network. Much like the 'wandering soldier' grave, the Edessa and Nea Anchialos graves reflect preoccupation with marking the exceptional by means of a few artefacts that may be viewed as 'quoting' fashions known from other regions of early medieval Europe.

The 'wandering soldier' may well have been a prominent Avar warrior, one of those who had defected to the Romans in 602, during the campaign of the Avar general Apsich against the Antes.[247] Or he may have been one of the Turks in the Persian army who were sent in 591 to the Romans, having on their foreheads the symbol of the cross tattooed in black, or, finally, an officer of the Kök Turk troops that Yabghu Xa'kan left with Heraclius in 627, after the siege of Tiflis.[248] But those who

---

[247] Theophylact Simocatta, *History*, 8.6, ed. by Carl de Boor and Peter Wirth (Stuttgart, 1972). For that campaign, see Litavrin, *Vizantiia i slaviane*, pp. 568–78.

[248] Theophanes Confessor, *Chronographia*, pp. 289 and 446–48. For the latter episode, see also Walter E. Kaegi, *Heraclius, Emperor of Byzantium* (Cambridge, 2003), pp. 144–45.

buried him in Corinth had no intention to stress his barbarian otherness. Buried in a stone-lined grave, like many others in Greece and the surrounding Mediterranean regions at that time, wearing a 'Byzantine' belt buckle that is more often associated with *female* burials, the 'wandering soldier' looks very different from his contemporaries buried in the Middle Danube region or in the steppes north of the Black Sea. Similarly, the women (if indeed they were women) buried in the chamber built next to the apse of the basilica Δ in Nea Anchialos or in a simple grave pit in Edessa may well have been barbarian wives of men in Byzantine service. They may even have been former members of the Slavic tribes that had settled in the region in the 620s or 630s. However, the privileged status of the Nea Anchialos woman was rendered visible by access to a Christian burial site, and in that respect her counterpart is the woman of equally high status buried in grave 25 inside the central nave of the Tigani basilica. Much like the 'wandering soldier', the burial of the Edessa woman displays a peculiar combination of a 'Byzantine' buckle more often associated with *male* burials and a pair of 'Slavic' bow fibulae. As such, the emblemic dress style of the Nea Anchialos and Edessa high-status females conveys the idea of *femme-reflet* mirroring the social position and privilege of her husband that Joëlle Beaucamp has brilliantly shown to be one of the main aspects of the sixth-century legislation and social practice in the empire.[249] The 'exotic' artefacts in seventh-century assemblages in Greece are therefore more likely to signal alliances with more or less distant barbarians than their destructive presence. This is certainly true also for the dress accessories found in graves of the seventh- to eighth-century cemeteries on the island of Corfu, such as pendants of the Koman class, earrings with corkscrew-shaped pendant, or cast strap ends with open-work ornament, all of which have good analogies in Middle or Late Avar assemblages in Hungary.

No eighth-century finds are so far known from mainland Greece that could match the Aphiona and Palaiokastritsa burial assemblages. When looking for the archaeological evidence pertaining to the 700s, we are left with the Olympia cremations and the Agia Trias inhumations. However, given the relative abundance of the numismatic and sigillographic evidence, the rarity of a significant number of eighth-century finds from mainland Greece could hardly be interpreted as indicating the disappearance of the Byzantine authority and troops. In my opinion, two other factors must be taken into consideration. First, there seems to be a strong correlation between the presence of land troops stationed more or less permanently together with their families and burial assemblages that could safely be dated to the

---

[249] Joëlle Beaucamp, *Le Statut de la femme à Byzance (4e–7e siècle): les pratiques sociales* (Paris, 1990), pp. 261 and 271.

eighth century. This is certainly the case of the two cemeteries on Corfu, which are otherwise part of a group of burial sites stretching further up the coast into northern Albania and inland into Macedonia and known, for lack of a better name, as the 'Komani culture'.[250] Those sites have much in common with contemporary cemeteries excavated in Sicily or Sardinia, which have also been attributed to Byzantine garrisons stationed at key points in the defence system of those two islands.[251] Finally, Bulgarian archaeologists have recently established solid links between the 'Komani culture' and a number of cemeteries around Gotse Delchev, Smolian, and Zlatograd, just north of the present-day Greek-Bulgarian border, which they attributed to Byzantine garrisons stationed on the northern frontier of Thrace, perhaps to control the access to Via Egnatia from across the Rhodopes.[252] To be sure, finds similar to those of Albania, Sardinia, and southern Bulgaria are known from several sites in Greece, such as Tigani, where a seventh-century cemetery cut through the floor of a sixth-century basilica. The relation between cemetery and church reminds one of the situation on such contemporary sites as Sv. Erazmo and Radolishte in Macedonia, Shurdhah in Albania, or Tharros in Sardinia, where seventh-century stone-lined graves cut through the floors of abandoned sixth-century churches.[253]

[250] The literature on the 'Komani culture' is considerable. See, more recently, William Bowden, 'The Construction of Identities in Post-Roman Albania', in *Theory and Practice in Late Antique Archaeology*, ed. by Luke Lavan and William Bowden (Leiden, 2003), pp. 57–78; Etleva Nallbani, 'Résurgence des traditions de l'Antiquité tardive dans les Balkans occidentaux: étude des sépultures du nord de l'Albanie', *Hortus Artium Medievalium*, 10 (2004), 25–42; Etleva Nallbani, 'Transformations et continuité dans l'ouest des Balkans: le cas de la civilisation de Komani (VIe–IXe siècles)', in *L'Illyrie méridionale et l'Epire dans l'Antiquité. IV. Actes du IVe colloque international de Grenoble, 10–12 octobre 2002*, ed. by Pierre Cabanes and Jean-Luc Lamboley (Paris, 2004), pp. 481–90.

[251] Orsi, *La Sicilia*, pp. 113–15 and 124–27; Pier Giorgio Spanu, *La Sardegna bizantina tra VI e VII secolo* (Oristano, 1998), pp. 127 and 150. See also Riemer, *Romanische Grabfunde*, p. 156.

[252] Stefka Angelova and Todor Marvakov, 'Über zwei Nekropolen aus Südwestbulgarien', in *Velká Morava meži východem a západem: Sborník příspěvku z mezinárodní vedécké konference. Uherské Hradiště, Staré Město 28.9.–1.10.1999*, ed. by Luděk Galuška, Pavel Kouřil, and Zdeněk Měřínský (Brno, 2001), pp. 13–27; Angelova and Koleva, 'Zur Chronologie frühmittelalterlicher Nekropolen'.

[253] Elica Maneva, 'La Survie des centres paléochrétiens de Macédoine au Haut Moyen Âge', in *Radovi XIII*, ed. by Cambi and Marin, II, 843–58 (pp. 846–47); Hëna Spahiu, 'La Ville haute-médiévale albanaise de Shurdhah (Sarda)', *Iliria*, 5 (1976), 151–67 (pp. 155–56); Spanu, *La Sardegna*, p. 85. For Tigani, see also Anna Avramea, 'Le Magne byzantin: problème d'histoire et de topographie', in *Eupsychia: Mélanges offerts à Hélène Ahrweiler*, ed. by Michel Balard and others, I (Paris, 1998), pp. 49–52 (p. 51). See also Boško Babić, 'Deneshnite teritorii na Republika

However, with the exception of Olympia and Agia Trias, no assemblages have been so far found in continental Greece that could be clearly dated between 700 and 800. That burial activity ended by 700 on such sites as Tigani and, perhaps, Ioannina may indicate that the garrisons stationed there were withdrawn or had meanwhile become irrelevant. This may have something to do with the dramatic military changes already taking place during the second half of the seventh century. If the surge in numbers of coins minted for Emperor Constans II and found in Athens can be associated with his preparations for the sea expedition to Italy, the presence and importance of the navy in Hellas during the reign of Constantine IV is highlighted in a passage from the second book of the *Miracles of St Demetrius*, in which we are told that a *strategos* of the navy named Sisinnios was sent to Thessalonica together with his troops to sort out things related to accusations of conspiracy levelled at Mauros and his men.[254] The creation of the theme of Hellas shortly before 700 and, in the course of the eighth century, of that of Cephallenia,[255] effectively made land troops stationed at key points in the interior unnecessary, as both administrative units existed almost exclusively in relation to the navy. It is perhaps no accident that the introduction of the maritime themes coincides with that of the 'Slavic' client polities on the northern border of the theme of Hellas, which operated as a 'buffer zone' against Avar and Bulgar attacks from the north. The *archontes* of Hellas are mentioned throughout the eighth century, but by 750 their seals began referring to individual tribal groups, such as Drugubites, Belegezites, or Evidites. The distinction seems to have been important, given that some of them were seriously involved in the imperial political struggles in the theme of Hellas.

No such clients existed on the western frontier of the theme of Hellas. Can the cremation cemetery in Olympia therefore be in any way associated with the 'Slavic problem'? Tivadar Vida's thorough analysis of both grave goods and their analogies has shown how comparisons consistently point to the Middle Danube region of the Avar qaganate. Iron torcs, for example, are unknown in the Balkans, but are

Makedonija i Republika Albanija vo VII i VIII veka', in *Tsivilizatsii na pochvata na Makedoniia* (Skopje, 1995), pp. 153–82.

[254] *Miracles of St Demetrius*, 2.5. Sisinnios was a *strategos* of the Karabisianoi.

[255] Nicolas Oikonomides, 'Constantin VII Porphyrogénète et les thèmes de Céphalonie et de Longobardie', in *Documents et études sur les institutions de Byzance (VIIᵉ–XVᵉ s.): Collected Essays of Nicolas Oikonomides*, ed. by Hélène Arhweiler (London, 1976), pp. 118–23; Tadeusz Wasilewski, 'Le Thème maritime de la Dalmatie byzantine dans les années 805–822 et sa reconstitution par l'empereur Michel III', *Acta Poloniae Historica*, 41 (1980), 35–49 (p. 36). Several seals of eighth-century *strategoi* of Cephallenia are known that antedate the earliest mention of the theme in written sources in the early ninth century.

particularly frequent on burial sites in Hungary and Slovakia during the Middle and Late Avar periods.[256] The specific decoration of many of the urns found in Olympia has good analogies in Middle and Late Avar assemblages, but it is also attested on contemporary sites in the western Balkans, such as Kašić in Croatia or Mušići in Bosnia.[257] But in the southern Balkans, the Olympia cemetery is unique, for no other cremation burials have so far been found in Greece, Albania, Macedonia, or southern Bulgaria. The Olympia cemetery began at some point during the second half of the seventh century. The community that used the cemetery must therefore have coexisted with the garrison in Tigani and with some of those who buried their dead in Corinth at some point before 700. Despite occasional links that could be established between grave goods found in all those burial assemblages (e.g. the flint steel in Olympia and its analogy in Corinth), Olympia represents an archaeological phenomenon fundamentally different from anything that was in existence at that time in Greece. In other words, everything points to an intrusive group, and not to the 'cohabitation of Byzantine peasants and Slavs'.[258] Whether or not we can call 'Slavs' those who buried their dead in Olympia is a matter of how the archaeological evidence is going to be interpreted. In any case, that evidence has nothing to do with what has so far been found in those regions of northern Greece in which the author of Book II of the *Miracles of St Demetrius* placed the Sclavene tribes of the Drugubites, Belegezites, Berzites, and Rynchines. Instead, most analogies point to the Middle Danube region of the Avar qaganate and to its southern periphery. Despite claims to the contrary, the Olympia urns have nothing to do with the so-called Prague-type pottery, while the handmade pot found in the 'wandering soldier's' grave in Corinth has much more to do with the pottery from Early and Middle Avar assemblages in Hungary than with the so-called 'Slavic pottery'. Setton was ultimately right: there was after all no such thing as a Slavic conquest of Greece: 'The Slavs came, but they did not conquer.'[259] But before coming they had to be invented: 'They were, those people, a kind of solution.'

---

[256] Vida and Völling, *Das slawische Brandgräberfeld*, pp. 61–76.

[257] Janko Belošević, 'Ranosrednjovjekovna nekropola u selu Kašić krai Zadra', *Diadora*, 4 (1968), 221–46; Irma Čremošnik, 'Die Untersuchungen in Mušići und Žabljak: Über den ersten Fund der ältesten slawischen Siedlung in Bosnien', *Wissenschaftliche Mitteilungen des bosnisch-herzegowinischen Landesmuseums*, 5 (1975), 91–176.

[258] Sanders, 'Pottery from Medieval Levels', p. 455; Avramea, *Le Peloponnèse*, p. 86.

[259] Setton, 'Bulgars in the Balkans', p. 511.

ASTURES, CANTABRI, AND VASCONES: THE PEOPLES OF THE SPANISH NORTH DURING THE LATE AND POST-ROMAN PERIOD

Santiago Castellanos

The idea of the northern peoples of Roman Hispania being rebels has become so common that it has been reduced to the level of historiographic topos. The landscape to the north of the Meseta, the central plateau in Spain, is dominated by the impressive Cantabrian Mountain range, which runs from western Galicia to Cantabria and the Basque region. Outsiders have also attached a certain romanticized image to the peoples who live deeply ensconced in those rugged mountains. They have sometimes adopted for themselves that image, which may explain its serious impact on the historiography of the region and its role in the perpetuation of such stereotypes as 'northerners-as-rebels'. Despite the fact that such stereotypes indirectly point to the mountains as a barrier separating 'subjects' from 'rebels', the Cordillera Cantábrica was actually not a clear-cut frontier during either Antiquity or the Iron Age. The peoples whom the Greeks and Romans called Astures and Cantabri lived not only within the mountain districts, but also well beyond them. People defined as Astures and Cantabri appear in the northern Meseta, in the present-day provinces of León, Palencia, and Burgos, and in the coastal regions of Asturias and Cantabria. Astures lived in the current Spanish provinces of Asturias and León and in parts of Zamora and Tras-os-Montes (Portugal), while Cantabri lived in Cantabria, northern Palencia, Burgos, and also La Rioja. The original abodes of the Vascones were in Navarre, but they appear during Late Antiquity in the present-day Basque region. In any case,

This chapter has been written as part of the research project ref. HUM2007–61826/HIS, funded by the Spanish Science Office.

such references to geographic locations must be viewed as approximate: for example, there is evidence of Cantabri in Álava, which today is part of the Basque country. The actual limits of the ethnic territories in the past were less clearly fixed or even defined than previously believed.

Useless Historiographic Topoi Replaced by New Perspectives

One can trace how the image of the people of the north has been transmitted through the years and into scholarly tradition. That image has by now been embraced by a variety of competing historiographic perspectives on both the right and the left wings of the political field in contemporary Spain. For a long while, the northerners were viewed as founders of the Spanish nation and initiators of the Reconquista. During the 1960s and 1970s, new concepts were introduced into the historical interpretation, most prominently by Abilio Barbero and Marcelo Vigil.[1] Both historians opened new avenues of research on Late Antiquity and the early Middle Ages, shifting the emphasis away from lists of kings and battles, through which several generations of Spanish school and university students have suffered. One of their leading ideas was that the northern indigenous societies were primarily tribal and kin-based, in sharp contrast to societies in southern Spain. Such ideas gained support from the then fashionable theory of the Roman *limes* in Northern Spain, an idea promoted not only by Antonio García y Bellido, Pedro de Palol, and José María Blázquez, but also by Abilio Barbero and Marcelo Vigil.[2] All those authors were among the most significant scholars in Spanish research from the 1960s through the 1980s, and the theory of the *limes* enjoyed a considerable popularity among Spanish historians. That theory was a key component of the late twentieth-century Spanish historiography.

In more than one sense, the idea of a Roman *limes* in northern Hispania was the direct result of the romanticization of the northern peoples. That idea worked in conjunction with the image of the mountain peoples being separated from communities in Late Roman Hispania and organized on the basis of their tribal structure and supposedly wild character. One of the main sources of evidence for the *limes* in northern Hispania is the *Notitia Dignitatum*, a complex and difficult

---

[1] Abilio Barbero and Marcelo Vigil Pascual, *Sobre los orígenes sociales de la Reconquista* (Barcelona, 1974).

[2] For a survey of the historiographic debate, see José Miguel Novo Güisán, *Los pueblos vasco-cantábricos y galaicos en la Antigüedad tardía, siglos III–IX* (Alcalá de Henares, 1992).

document. I shall refrain from engaging in any debates surrounding this text and limit myself to just two important points. First, it is worth mentioning that most references to the Western Empire are late additions, perhaps as late as the first quarter of the fifth century. Moreover, this is no homogeneous body of changes to the text, as different additions were made at different times. Second, one cannot be sure that at the time of the redaction, the military stations mentioned as being in Hispania have actually retained useful military functions. All the same, the *Notitia* was useful for the defenders of the *limes* theory because of a list of military garrisons said to have been in existence in Northern Hispania. When plotted on a map, those garrisons form a line from Galicia to the Basque country. They could be, and were therefore, interpreted as the *limes* separating the northern peoples (Astures, Cantabri, and Vascones) from the rest of Late Roman Hispania.

The problem is that the idea of a *limes* cannot find support either in the critical study of the *Notitia Dignitatum* or, more importantly, in the examination of the archaeological evidence. Arguments against the theory have been recently advanced by Javier Arce, José Miguel Novo Güisán, and others.[3] It has by now become clear that the *limes* theory is just one among many historiographic stereotypes that have come to shape the study of northern Spain in Late Antiquity. Like all others, this one is also linked to the image of an indigenous population of purely tribal organization. By way of analogy, it is perhaps worth recalling for a moment the parallel situation in England. There are plenty of archaeological sites with excellent presentations for those curious to learn about the interaction between Romans and the native population on the military frontier of Roman Britain. One can even send a humorous postcard abroad showing a local Briton being told by a Roman soldier, 'I expect you have heard about Roman roads'. In other words, both archaeology and the interpretative work involved in heritage tourism are predicated upon the idea that the northern peoples must have heard, seen, and even used Roman roads and, as a consequence, must have also been included in the Roman political system. Nonetheless, the humorous postcard may also serve as a reminder that the idea of recognizable difference is the key to the historiographic concept of *limes* and to scholarly views of northern barbarians. In fact, there is very little difference between such views and the stereotypes reproduced in classical literature about what

---

[3] Novo Güisán, *Los pueblos*; Javier Arce, 'Un *limes* innecesario', in *'Romanización' y 'Reconquista' en la Península Ibérica: Nuevas perspectivas*, ed. by Maria José Hidalgo, Dionisio Pérez, and Manuel J. Rodriguez Gervás (Salamanca, 1998), pp. 187–90. For the historical value of the *Notitia*, see now Michael Kulikowski, 'The *Notitia Dignitatum* as an Historical Source', *Historia*, 49 (2000), 358–77.

separated barbarians from either Greeks or Romans.[4] If anything, such views therefore perpetuate the idea that history must be understood in terms of a straight-
jacket of binary oppositions: assimilation vs. resistance, colonialism vs. indigenous,
urban vs. tribal societies, etc. Roman Hispania is always the first member of each
pair, and the northern peoples are believed to hide behind the second member. But
such dichotomies are spurious, for we now know much more about the archaeological evidence, while the written sources can no longer be studied with scholarly
naïve questions in mind.[5]

The old Romantic idea of the northern peoples has been discredited primarily
by new approaches to such classical texts as Pliny the Elder and Ptolemy, as well as
by studies published especially in the 1980s on the early and high imperial inscriptions of the central and northern regions of the Peninsula. Those studies have
demonstrated that the northern societies were, if not hierarchical, then certainly
complex and ranked, with local and powerful aristocracies.[6] The testimony of the

---

[4] Arnaldo Momigliano, *Sagesses barbares: les limites de l'hellénisation* (Paris, 1979). Setting
barbarians in sharp contrast to 'civilized' Greeks or Romans is a well-worn topos of classical
literature. For its use in Polybius, for example, see María Cruz González Rodríguez, 'El bárbaro y
lo bárbaro en la obra polibiana', in *Polibio y la Península Ibérica*, ed. by Juan Santos Yanguas and
Elena Torregaray Pagola (Vitoria, 2005), pp. 141–71. I have studied the late antique perception
of barbarians, and especially the changing attitudes of Christian authors, in Santiago Castellanos,
'Bárbaros y cristianos en el Imperio tardorromano: La adaptación de la intelectualidad cristiana
occidental', in *Cristianismo y poder en la Antigüedad* (Salamanca, 2006), pp. 237–56.

[5] A recent view about the traditional historiographic lines on the Northern peoples in Hispania
is in Carmen Fernández Ochoa and Angel Morillo Cerdán, 'Romanización y asimilación cultural
en el Norte Península: Algunas reflexiones sobre un topos historiográfico desde una perspectiva
arqueológica', in *Los poblados fortificados del Noroeste de la Península Ibérica: formación y desarrollo
de la cultura castreña. Coloquios de Arqueología en la Cuenca del Navia. Homenaje al Prof. Dr. José
Manuel González y Fernández-Valles*, ed. by Miguel A. de Blas Cortina and Angel Villa Valdés
(Navia, 2002), pp. 261–77.

[6] Juan Santos Yanguas, *Comunidades indígenas y administración romana en el noroeste hispánico*
(Bilbao, 1985); María Cruz González Rodríguez, *Las unidades organizativas indígenas del área
indoeuropea de Hispania* (Vitoria, 1986); José Manuel Iglesias Gil, 'Cántabros', in *Las entidades
étnicas de la Meseta Norte de Hispania en época prerromana*, ed. by José María Solana Sáinz
(Valladolid, 1991), pp. 41–58; Miguel Abilio Rabanal Alonso, 'Astures', in *Las entidades étnicas*,
ed. by Solana Sáinz, pp. 61–71; *Las estructuras sociales indígenas del norte de la Península Ibérica*,
ed. by María Cruz González Rodríguez and Juan Santos Yanguas (Vitoria, 1994); María Cruz
González Rodríguez, *Los astures y los cántabros vadinienses: problemas y perspectivas de análisis de
las sociedades indígenas de la 'Hispania' indoeuropea* (Vitoria, 1997); Joaquín González Echegaray,
Los cántabros (Santander, 1997); Inés Sastre Prats, *Las formaciones sociales rurales de la 'Asturia'
romana* (Madrid, 2001); Inés Sastre Prats, *Onomástica y relaciones políticas en la epigrafía del
'conventus Asturum' durante el Alto Imperio* (Madrid, 2002); Inés Sastre Prats, 'Los procesos de la

classical texts about Astures or Cantabri operated inside traditional intellectual parameters, which renders many of their conclusions problematic. Most authors from the Augustan age (e.g. Strabo) to the end of the Principate insisted upon the savagery and primitive lifestyles of the barbarians. The conquest of Astures and Cantabri, during Augustus's reign, provided an opportunity for an ethnographic treatment of northern Iberia within the framework of classical historiography. The image of the central northern peoples remained relatively the same throughout the first and second centuries, despite the fact, which has only recently been brought to the fore in Spanish scholarship, that the Roman administration eventually managed to include that region of Hispania into the *ciuitas* model in existence throughout the rest of the Peninsula. Some written sources hint at the complexity of those societies, but the most compelling evidence now available in that respect is that of archaeology.

Historians have by now accepted the idea of towns, *uillae*, and settlements in existence in central northern Hispania which were not different from those known elsewhere for the Late Roman period.[7] Luis Ramón Menéndez Bueyes has recently examined the archaeological evidence pertaining to that problem from the modern region of Asturias.[8] Moreover, there are several important archaeological projects currently underway, for example, in the coastal town of Gijón in Asturias under the direction of Carmen Fernández Ochoa, and in the nearby *uillae* of Veranes. Both those and other projects are a stern reminder of how misleading the old stereotypes are about the savagery of the northern barbarians in Late Antiquity, as well as in earlier periods. The existing evidence strongly suggests an intensification of the hierarchical divisions and social cleavage among the central northern peoples during the Iron Age and the early Roman period. Personal names recorded in inscriptions are often accompanied by references to sites (such as *castella*) and suprafamiliar entities (plural genitives). In spite of traditional interpretations linking such aspects to a tribal organization of society, it has by now been demonstrated

complejidad social en el Noroeste peninsular: arqueología y fuentes literarias', *Trabajos de prehistoria*, 61 (2004), 99–110.

[7] A. Fuentes Domínguez, 'La romanidad tardía en los territorios septentrionales de la Península Ibérica', in *Los finisterres atlánticos en la Antigüedad: Época prerromana y romana. Coloquio internacional*, ed. by Carmen Fernández Ochoa and Manuel Fernández Miranda (Madrid, 1996), pp. 213–21; Carmen Fernández Ochoa, 'La ciudad en la Antigüedad tardía en la cornisa cantábrica', in *Complutum y las ciudades hispanas en la Antigüedad tardía*, ed. by Luís A. García Moreno and Sebastián Rascón Marqués (Alcalá de Henares, 1999), pp. 73–86.

[8] Luis Ramón Menéndez Bueyes, *Reflexiones críticas sobre el origen del reino de Asturias* (Salamanca, 2001).

that they belong to a different order of things pertaining to complex societies, associated with such features as landed property, commercial relations, and territorial
control.[9]

The epigraphic evidence is very useful in showing that, instead of destroying the
indigenous hierarchical structure, Romans preserved it in order to use it to their
own advantage. Two recently discovered and published inscriptions are excellent
illustrations of this particular relation. The so-called Edict of Bierzo is a disposition
of Emperor Augustus for the area of the present-day district of Bierzo (in the León
province of north-western Spain), from which it is ascertainable how the Emperor
used the local settlements as fiscal entities.[10] The *castra* and local communities were
viewed as inside the Roman state and *ciuitas* model of administration. For the
region of the Cantabri, a first-century inscription mentions a certain Douiderus
as *princeps Cantabrorum*. It is of course not easy to establish exactly what kind of
leader he was, and what form of power a *princeps Cantabrorum* could have. Nonetheless, as Maria Cruz González Rodríguez has pointed out, it is quite clear that the
title must be understood against the background of the local, Cantabrian power
structure, one that was now recognized as such by the Roman authorities, in order
to ensure Roman control through local aristocracies.[11]

The Roman administration accelerated the process of securing Roman authority in the region, for the Romans developed their political power through the
incorporation of indigenous structures. This further undermines another historiographic stereotype, namely that local communities stood in sharp opposition to the
Roman power, an opposition best described by the dichotomy between assimilation and resistance. The Romans drew more advantage from dealing with the
complex societies of the northern peoples than from dealing with tribal and savage
groups. This is especially true for Roman relations with the Astures, and for the
Roman extraction of the region's gold, one of the richest sources of that precious
metal in the entire first- to third-century empire. The Roman extraction of the
gold, especially from the present-day archaeological region of Las Médulas (León)
followed the conquest of the Astures in the late first century BC by Augustus. The
quick implementation of Roman power was made possible, as recent studies have
shown, by Roman use of the local settlement pattern of *castra* and *castella*, as well

[9] See the works by Juan Santos Yanguas, María Cruz González Rodríguez, and Inés Sastre Prats
mentioned above in note 6, as well as elsewhere in this chapter.

[10] See below, note 14.

[11] María Cruz González Rodríguez, 'Anotaciones sobre las élites indígenas cántabras y su
integración por parte de Roma', *Veleia*, Anejos 17 (2002), 309–18.

as by harnessing local forms of aristocratic power.[12] The Romans, of course, created typically Roman structures, such as the town of Asturica Augusta, to serve as the administrative and political centre of the region. Indeed, Asturica became one of the main regional foci of development during Late Antiquity. Imperial control of the Astures, however, cannot be understood without taking into account the empire's relation to the local power structures, in particular to various sources of power and to the organization of the territory.

The local aristocracies quickly learned how to use the channels of the Roman administrative system. Particularly illustrative in that respect is the famous 'treaty of the *Zoelae*' applying to the southern region of the Astures, the area of the present-day district of Trás-os-Montes a Alto Douro in northern Portugal. Among other things, it is evident how across the two chronological periods covered in that document indigenous entities called *gentes* and *gentilitates* were transformed inside the *ciuitas*, the new generic scope of Roman power, but also of local adaptation.[13] The *gens Zoelarum* ceased to exist, to be replaced by a *ciuitas Zoelarum*, in which the traditional social segments were incorporated in order to promote the political and tributary interests of the empire, but also in order to support local powers. Similar arrangements were designed for those territories whose structures were the basis for Roman tributary exploitation. The Edict of Bierzo shows how Augustus used the local structures for the implementation of a tributary system.[14] In short, the overall picture is much more complex than that suggested by more or less humorous postcards, and that is also true for the particular period covered in this chapter, namely the fifth, sixth, and seventh centuries.

Inside and Outside Gallaecia and Hydatius's World: Neglected Northern Peoples during the Final Century of Roman Power

Much of what historians know about Late Antique Hispania relies primarily on the *Chronicle* of Hydatius, which covers a significant portion of the fifth century

---

[12] See the works of Inés Sastre Prats cited above, in note 6.

[13] In addition to the works of María Cruz González Rodríguez, Juan Santos Yanguas, and Inés Sastre Prats cited above, in note 6, see Estíbaliz Ortiz de Urbina Alava, *Las comunidades hispanas y el derecho latino: Observaciones sobre los procesos de integración local en la práctica político-administrativa al mundo romano* (Vitoria, 2000), p. 121.

[14] *El Edicto del Bierzo: Augusto y el noroeste de Hispania*, ed. by F. Javier Sánchez Palencia and Julio Mangas Manjarrés (Ponferrada, 2000).

up to *c.* 468/69. Hydatius, however, was from Gallaecia, the neighbouring province to the north-west. Some areas of the Astures were inside that province, such as the region around Asturica (today Astorga) and, in general, large territories in the current province of León and in the western Asturias. Most problematic for historians of the northern peoples is the fact that they lived outside Gallaecia and, therefore, outside the range of Hydatius's interests. Historians have therefore to content themselves with brief references to the peoples of the central northern area of the Iberian Peninsula, in addition to archaeological data. Only after the fifth century, during the Visigothic period, do those peoples appear with more defined roles in the texts, but these references are not without problems.

Besides Hydatius, references to those peoples are made in the fourth century, often in a poetic context, by Ausonius and his pupil Paulinus. Claudian, who died *c.* 404, also mentioned the northern peoples but was otherwise not particularly interested in the affairs of northern Hispania.[15] He did sometimes refer to the region, for example, in *Laus Serenae*, the praise of Serena, the wife of Stilicho, Emperor Honorius's strongman. Honorius and his brother Arcadius, the emperor in the East, were from Hispania much like their father Theodosius (d. 395). Claudian knew that very well, and most of his references to Hispania must be understood in that context. Thus in the *Laus Serenae*, he insists that the legacy and contribution of Hispania to the Roman Empire was precisely the reigning Augusti.[16] Serena, a niece of Theodosius who belonged to the imperial family, was also from Hispania. The *laus* has a single reference to the Astures, but it is to be understood entirely within the traditional poetic and political context, namely praising Serena's birth at the fortuitous time when the river Taxus (now Tajo, in central Spain) flooded the fertile fields, the Cantabrian sea deposited valuable stones on the coast, and the pale Astures did not wander around the mountains.[17] In other words, Claudian knew about the Cantabrian region and the Astures, and he wanted to highlight them in the poetic composition to Serena. Beyond that, however, there is no useful information about either the Cantabrian region or the Astures.

Another poet referring to the northern peoples was a younger contemporary of Claudian born in Hispania. Prudentius was from Calagurris (today Calahorra, in La Rioja), a middle-sized settlement in the Ebro valley. The town has been in the

---

[15] For this part of the chapter, I relied on *Claudii Claudiani Carmina*, ed. by J. B. Hall (Leipzig, 1985). It is essential, in whatever reference to Claudian, to take into account Alan Cameron's irreplaceable book, *Claudian: Poetry and Propaganda at the Court of Honorius* (Oxford, 1970).

[16] Claudian, *Laus Serenae*, 50.

[17] Claudian, *Laus Serenae*, 70–76.

orbit of the Keltiberoi of the Greek sources, the Celtic groups populating the Middle Ebro valley and the north-eastern Meseta during the Iron Age and the early Roman period, following the conquest of the Ebro region in the second century BC. After the civil wars of the late Republic, the town fell within the territory of the Vascones, and it remained so during Late Antiquity. Prudentius was a Christian but also a Roman poet who remained close to the classical tradition.[18] He employs generic references to the Vascones, calling them *bruta quondam gentilitas*.[19] Despite Prudentius's poetic license, his work is nonetheless important for our subject matter, because it confirms that during the Late Roman period, Prudentius's hometown, Calagurris, was believed to be part of Vasconia, and even the course of the Ebro had a 'Vasconian' part, the *Vasco Hiberus*.[20] Another reference to Vasconia in the same area appears a few decades later.

Finding information about the political, social, and religious life of the peoples living in the central-northern region during the last century of Roman power in Hispania is not without problems. The chief source is again Hydatius. However, his references to the northern peoples are always ranked second, if not third, after his main interest in reporting the religious problems created for the Catholic Church in north-west Hispania by, and the general consequences of, the Sueve, Vandal, and Alan invasion of 409. Hydatius's *Chronicle* focuses mainly on the battles between what he calls *Hispani* and barbarians, on conflicts between barbarians (especially those between the Sueves and the Visigoths, *foederati* of the Western Empire), and, finally, on conflicts between bishops. All references to the peoples of the central-northern region in Hydatius's *Chronicle* are therefore oblique because that region is thoroughly outside his core interest.

This is not the place for yet another overview of the last century of Roman power in northern Spain based on Hydatius's work. Instead, I will shift the emphasis to an examination of how the central-northern peoples appear in Hydatius's world.[21] The Sueves and the Vandals (until their move to Baetica and then to Africa, *c.* 429) settled in the north-western province of Gallaecia, although some barbarian groups

---

[18] About Prudentius's life and work, see Anne-Marie Palmer, *Prudentius on the Martyrs* (Oxford, 1989); Michael John Roberts, *Poetry and the Cult of the Martyrs: The Liber Peristephanon of Prudentius* (Ann Arbor, 1993); Luis Rivero García, *La poesía de Prudencio* (Huelva, 1996).

[19] Prudentius, *Peristephanon*, 1.94, in *Obras completas*, ed. by Isidoro Rodríguez and Alfonso Ortega (Madrid, 1981).

[20] Prudentius, *Peristephanon*, 2.537.

[21] For fifth-century Hispania, see now Michael Kulikowski, *Late Roman Spain and its Cities* (Baltimore, 2004); Javier Arce, *Bárbaros y romanos en Hispania, 400–507 A.D.* (Madrid, 2005).

may have also moved into the territory of the Astures.[22] In any case, one of the most dramatic aspects of the fifth-century history of the north-western region of the Iberian Peninsula was the Suevic expansion to the east and to the south, and the subsequent encroachment into the territory of the Astures and the Cantabri, respectively. At the onset of their expansion in *c.* 430, the Sueves were met with stiff resistance from the local communities of central Gallaecia, who locked themselves up in *castella tutiora*.[23] Such strongholds were part of a complex territorial organization in Gallaecia, which archaeologists have just begun to study.[24] Given that some parts of what during the Principate constituted the territory of the Astures were later, during the Late Roman period, included into the province of Gallaecia (e.g. Asturica and its territory), one can conclude that some, at least, of the *castella* mentioned by Hydatius must have been within the region of the Astures.

There are several other references in the chronicle to the expansion of the Sueves and to their disregard for treaties with the local communities.[25] Either in military confrontations or in peaceful negotiations, the new kingdom in the north-west is said to have dealt with local *potentes*, including bishops like Hydatius himself. Albeit brief, such hints at the local political landscape point to the existence of local leaders with sufficient power to make decisions, enter treaties, or travel to regional central places. In the aftermath of the disappearance of the imperial power from the region, local communities and their leaders had a good opportunity to fill the vacuum of power, which brought them into the spotlight of historical sources.[26] The expansion of the Sueves certainly affected such local communities. King Rechiarius even entered some kind of alliance with the leader of the *Bacaudae* in the Ebro valley, in order to attack a number of towns along the river, in southern Vasconia, and in other parts of central Tarraconensis. In 455–56, the Sueves also

---

[22] Hydatius, *Chronicle*, 41, ed. by Richard W. Burgess (Oxford, 1993). For the Vandal move to Africa, see Guido Berndt's contribution in this volume.

[23] Hydatius, *Chronicle*, 81.

[24] Jorge López Quiroga and Mónica Rodríguez Lovelle, 'Castros y *castella tutiora* en Galicia y norte de Portugal: ensayo de inventario y primeras propuestas interpretativas', *Hispania Antiqua*, 23 (1999), 355–74; Jorge López Quiroga, *El final de la Antigüedad en la Gallaecia: la transformación de las estructuras de poblamiento entre Miño y Duero (siglos V al X)* (La Coruña, 2004).

[25] E.g. Hydatius, *Chronicle*, 86, 91, and 105.

[26] For the valley of the Duero river, that is, at least in part in relation to the southern territories examined in this chapter, see Pablo C. Díaz, 'La ocupación germánica del valle del Duero: un ensayo interpretativo', *Hispania Antiqua*, 18 (1994), 457–76. See also *De Roma a los bárbaros: Poder central y horizontes locales en la cuenca del Duero*, ed. by Santiago Castellanos and Iñaki Martín Viso (León, 2008).

attacked their own territories in the Tarraconensis.[27] At that time, the Suevic kingdom must have been the most important source of instability in the entire southern section of central-northern Hispania. The attacks of the Sueves reached the southern parts of Asturia (already in a large measure inside the Suevic kingdom), Cantabria, and Vasconia. In addition, groups of Herules are said to have attacked the coast of the Cantabri and Vardulli in 456 and, following that, to have raided the coast around Lucus Augusti in northern Gallaecia.[28]

As it happened, it was the Suevic expansion that finally triggered the intervention of the imperial forces. Much like in the case of the *Bacaudae*, the imperial government relied on its proxies, the Visigoths, to deal with the Suevic threat. The Visigoths fully accomplished their task when defeating in 456 the Sueves in the battle of the Urbicus (today Órbigo) river, not far from Asturica.[29] The Visigothic victory over the Sueves did not put an end to the devastations of the southern part of the central-northern region of Hispania. Having finished off the Sueves, the Visigoths now attacked Asturica, where, according to Hydatius, they killed many, they destroyed churches, and they captured two bishops. Other cities in the southern area of the central-northern region, such as Palantia, also suffered from Visigothic depredations, while others, such as Castrum Couiacense, in the southern part of the ancient region of the Astures (within the present-day province of León), successfully resisted their attacks.[30] In all likelihood, the Visigoths were looking for booty as a reward for their efforts on behalf of the government in Ravenna, and local communities had to pay the price.

The Visigothic intervention may have been an effective way to put an end to the Suevic aggression, but it did not assuage the political and military hardships of the local *castra* and *ciuitates* under the control of local strongmen. In fact, and despite the increasing tension between Visigoths and Sueves in the region, the Suevic pressure on local communities continued after the battle on the Órbigo river. Indeed, a definite end of both the kingdom of the Sueves and of their depredations would come only with the conquest of 585 by King Leovigild. For more than a century, the history of the region thus continued to be dominated by now traditional tensions between the aristocracies (*aliquantis honestis natu*) in local communities and the central power the Suevic kings strove to consolidate.[31] Such

[27] Hydatius, *Chronicle*, 163.

[28] Hydatius, *Chronicle*, 164. See Roland Steinacher's chapter in this volume.

[29] Hydatius, *Chronicle*, 166.

[30] Hydatius, *Chronicle*, 179.

[31] Hydatius, *Chronicle*, 191.

conflicts involved the *Callici*, that is, the inhabitants of Gallaecia, now also incor-
porating the region of Asturica. Towards the end of the *Chronicle* of Hydatius, we
read of repeated Suevic attacks against Asturica to be dated at some point in the
late 460s.[32] Hydatius's references to Vascones also appear in the narrative context
of the Suevic expansion or of the movements of *Bacaudae*. For example, the Vascones are mentioned as victims of the Suevic king Rechiarius who attacked them
in 449, during his return from Visigothic Gaul, where he had taken in marriage
King Theoderic's daughter.[33] Those were years with considerable fighting in the
middle Ebro Valley in the southern part of Vasconia, which was part of Tarraconensis. The main problem in the region seems to have been the *Bacaudae* who
operated out of Aracelli, in what is today Navarre. Several imperial armies had been
sent against them under the command of such important generals as Asturius and
Merobaudes.[34]

In spite of older interpretations, the *Bacauda* was not a regional movement of
the Vascones.[35] It actually seems to have taken place mainly in southern Vasconia
and in other areas along the Ebro River and inside Tarraconensis. As a matter of
fact, and despite a considerable literature dedicated to the movement, we know
very little, if anything, about what the *Bacaudae* really wanted. In 449, they
attacked the town of Turiasso (modern Tarazona), fought against Visigothic
foederati, and killed the local bishop. There was also an apparent link between
Bacaudae and Sueves.[36] The alliance between the *Bacaudae* under the leadership of
Basilius and the Suevic king Recharius was formed for raiding outside Vasconia, as
witnessed by combined attacks on Caesaraugusta (Zaragoza) and Ilerda (Lérida)
on the Middle Ebro.[37] The end of the *Bacaudae* in Tarraconensis came only with
the Visigothic intervention of 454.[38]

Hydatius was also interested in ecclesiastical affairs, especially in disputes between bishops. There were numerous such disputes in the mid-fifth century, many
of them quite serious. As we have seen, Asturica, the ancient capital of the *Asturi-
censis conuentus iuridicus* and of the territory of the Astures during the Principate,

---

[32] Hydatius, *Chronicle*, 243.

[33] Hydatius, *Chronicle*, 132.

[34] Hydatius, *Chronicle*, 117 and 120.

[35] The literature on the *Bacauda* is abundant, but the most recent *mise-au-point* is that of Arce, *Bárbaros y romanos*, p. 159. In general, see below, note 66.

[36] Hydatius, *Chronicle*, 133.

[37] Hydatius, *Chronicle*, 134.

[38] Hydatius, *Chronicle*, 150.

had by now been incorporated into Gallaecia. Asturica was a typical administrative centre of the Augustan age, with a remarkably diverse social structure, as witnessed by inscriptions.[39] During Late Antiquity, the city's diversity was among other things illustrated in theological disputes. In 445, Hydatius, bishop of Aquae Flaviae, and Thoribius, bishop of Asturica, brought a group of Manicheans to the attention of the Bishop of Emerita (now Mérida), the capital of the *diocesis Hispaniarum* and the main administrative town in late Roman Hispania [40] Combatting Manichean ideas seems to have been high on the ecclesiastical agenda of that time, and even the pope got involved in local affairs by circulating many encyclicals and texts in Hispania.[41] Some of them were written by Leo I, the Roman pope otherwise more famous for his dealings with Attila. Hydatius and Thoribius reported to Emerita, leading to the condemnation of the Manichean refugee Pascentius by Antoninus, the bishop of Emerita.[42]

Most important for the topic of this paper is the fact that in Asturica, at the southern edge of the traditional territory of the Astures, heretical theological interpretations found a harsh critic in the person of the local bishop Thoribius, who led the persecution against Manicheism and Priscillianism.[43] The Bishop of Asturica acted according to his own understanding of Church hierarchy, bypassing the jurisdiction of neighbouring centres of ecclesiastical authority, such as Bracara (Braga, Portugal). It was in fact a deacon from Asturica who brought back Pope Leo's texts from Rome.[44] The episode seems to point to some conflict between the bishops of

---

[39] Manuel Abilio Rabanal Alonso and Sonia María García Martínez, 'Poder y sociedad en *Asturica Augusta*', in *Actas del I Congreso Internacional de Historia Antigua: La Península Ibérica hace 2000 años* (Valladolid, 2000), pp. 475–84.

[40] Hydatius, *Chronicle*, 122.

[41] Hydatius, *Chronicle*, 125.

[42] Hydatius, *Chronicle*, 130. For the texts and the relation between Antoninus and the Suevic king, see Purificación Ubric Rabaneda, *La Iglesia en la Hispania del siglo V* (Granada, 2004), p. 121. On the specific case of Pascentius, his Manicheism, and the possibility of identifying him with a person mentioned in an inscription from the region of Emerita, see J. San Bernardino, 'Exilio y muerte de un heterodoxo en la tardorromanidad: en torno al caso de Pascentius en Lusitania', in *Congreso Internacional 'La Hispania de Teodosio'*, ed. by Ramón Teja and Cesareo Pérez, I (Segovia, 1997), pp. 217–31.

[43] It is possible that Thoribius was a convert, which could explain the harshness of his dealings with the non-orthodox. See María Victoria Escribano Paño, 'Estado actual de los estudios sobre el priscilianismo', in *El Cristianismo: Aspectos históricos de su origen y difusión en Hispania. Actas del Symposius de Vitoria-Gasteiz, 25 a 27 noviembre de 1996*, ed. by Juan Santos Yanguas, Ramón Teja, and Elena Torregaray Pagola (Vitoria, 2000), pp. 263–87.

[44] Hydatius, *Chronicle*, 127.

the north-western region of the Peninsula, the details of which, however, are not at all clear.

The Visigothic Kingdom and the North (Sixth to Seventh Centuries)

Post-Roman sources tend to employ ancient names, such as Cantabri, Astures, Vascones, or Sappi, as lexical 'flags' in order to indicate ethnic groups. Although the evidence is too limited to allow for more than mere speculation, it seems clear that such ancient names appear far more often during the sixth and seventh centuries than they do in the later empire, perhaps because of the fragmentation and subsequent disappearance of Roman authority in the area.[45] In the political vacuum thus created, local communities and especially their leaders had multiple opportunities to assert social and territorial control. Names such as Aspidius, Honorius, or Abundantius appear within ethnic groups designated by old names in correlation with properties and positions of pre-eminence.

A quick glimpse at the sources reveals that a constant preoccupation of the Visigothic kings was to extend their control over the northern territories. Leovigild conquered the north-west in 585, an event that resuscitated the idea of central power in the region. Now the *sedes regia* was not Bracara (Braga, Portugal) any more, but Toledo. However, the victory over the Sueves was not accompanied by a complete cessation of the administrative mechanisms they had created in the area. In fact, both Leovigild and his successors seem to have maintained the administrative methods implemented by the Sueves, including the association of bishoprics and mints. As a consequence, the identification, first introduced by the Suevic kings, between minting as an activity under royal supervision and episcopal prerogatives and sees was maintained under Visigothic rule as well.[46]

---

[45] Pablo C. Díaz and Luis R. Menéndez Bueyes, 'The Cantabrian Basin in the Fourth and Fifth Centuries: From Imperial Province to Periphery', in *Hispania in Late Antiquity: Current Perspectives*, ed. by Kimberly Diane Bowes and Michael Kulikowski (Leiden, 2005), pp. 265–97.

[46] See the *Parrochiale Suevum*, in Corpus Christianorum, Series Latina, 175 (Turnhout, 1965), pp. 412–20. See also Pablo C. Díaz, 'El *Parrochiale Suevum*: organización eclesiástica, poder político y poblamiento en la Gallaecia tardoantigua', in *Homenaje a José María Blázquez*, ed. by Julio Mangas Manjarrés and Jaime Alvar (Madrid, 1998), pp. 35–47; Pablo C. Díaz, 'Acuñación monetaria y organización administrativa en la *Gallaecia* tardoantigua', *Zephyrus*, 57 (2004), 367–75; Jorge López Quiroga and Mónica Rodríguez Lovelle, 'Cecas y hallazgos monetarios de época suevo-visigoda: *Civitates* y vías de comunicación en el Noroeste de la Península Ibérica', in *Rutas, ciudades y moneda en Hispania: Actas del II Encuentro peninsular de numismatica antigua, Porto, marzo de 1997*, ed. by Rui Manuel Sobral Centeno, M. P. García-Bellido, and G. Mora (Madrid, 1999), pp. 433–39.

Things were somewhat different in other areas, such as the central-northern territories examined in this chapter. There are several mentions in the sources about campaigns of Visigothic kings against the Astures, the Cantabri, and the Vascones.[47] However, it would be a gross mistake to understand relations between the northern peoples and the *regnum Gothorum* as purely confrontational. First of all, it is not at all sure that the meaning of such terms as Astures or Cantabri remained unchanged throughout the Visigothic period. It is also possible that some form of political and military expansion in the northern territories triggered the military intervention of the court in Toledo.[48] In fact, the existing evidence strongly suggests that the process of political centralization in the northern territories was well on its way, in spite of both destabilizing military conflicts and historiographic stereotypes about northern barbarity.[49]

For instance, it is known that Leovigild conducted a war against the Cantabri in 574.[50] In the process he seems to have conquered an extensive area between the main Cantabrian Mountains and the territories as far south as the central parts of the modern provinces of Palencia, Burgos, and La Rioja, in the Upper Ebro valley. However, at a closer examination of the existing sources, the situation presents itself in a different light. We know that the Visigothic king had to destroy a nucleus of local resistance in the Upper Ebro region, which is mentioned as *senatus* by Bishop Braulius of Zaragoza who wrote about it more than fifty years after the events, in *c.* 630 or 640. Braulius was one of the most important bishops in the Visigothic kingdom, not only because of his political influence, but also, and to a greater extent, because of his cultural profile. Braulius could not have been either mistaken or careless when

---

[47] For a complete list of references, see Novo Güisán, *Los pueblos*.

[48] That, at least, is the conclusion of Amancio Isla Frez, 'Los astures: el *populus* y la *populatio*', in *La época de la monarquía asturiana: Actas del simposio celebrado en Covadonga, 8–10 de octubre de 2001* (Oviedo, 2002), pp. 17–42.

[49] This idea is further developed for the Visigothic period in Santiago Castellanos and Iñaki Martín Viso, 'The Local Articulation of Central Power in the North of the Iberian Peninsula (500–1000)', *Early Medieval Europe*, 13 (2005), 1–42.

[50] John of Biclaro, *Chronicon*, 32, ed. by C. Cardelle de Hartmann, Corpus Christianorum, Series Latina, 173A (Turnhout, 2001); Isidore of Seville, *Historia Gothorum*, 49, ed. by C. Rodríguez Alonso, in *Las historias de los godos, vándalos y suevos de Isidoro de Sevilla* (León, 1975); Braulius, *Vita Sancti Aemiliani*, 33, ed. by Ignacio Cazzaniga, 'La Vita di S. Emiliano scritta da Brauliusne vescovo di Saragozza: edizione critica', *Bollettino del Comitato per la preparazione della Edizione Nazionale dei Classici Greci e Latini*, 3 (1954), 7–44. The conquest of Cantabria was to be completed not under Leovigild (*a.* 574), but under Sisebut (612–21). See Juan José García González, 'Incorporación de la Cantabria romana al estado visigodo', *Cuadernos de Historia Burgalesa*, 2 (1995), 167–230.

using a word such as *senatus* to describe the power in the region of Cantabria.[51] Needless to say, the word does not have to be understood in its classical sense. Nonetheless, Braulius most clearly wished to convey to his audience the idea of a senate in the classical meaning of the term.[52] He seems to have aimed at giving the impression of aristocracies in Cantabria united against Leovigild. At any rate, it is important to emphasize that he indirectly pointed to the existence of such aristocracies, since for many years the existence of such aristocracies in Cantabria was denied in favour of an exclusively tribal basis for the medieval 'Reconquista'.[53] Moreover, both the archaeological evidence and an attentive reading of the written sources suggest that Leovigild had to fight not against tribal chiefs, but against local aristocracies.[54] Those aristocrats had Roman names and possessed lands, slaves, and social dependents.[55]

The official conversion of the Visigothic kingdom to Catholicism took place early in the reign of Reccared, at the third council of Toledo (589).[56] The council's enactments show that the central-northern region of the kingdom was associated with the central political power in Toledo to a greater degree than would have been possible if the Visigoths had simply imposed themselves upon some archaic tribal societies. This is particularly true when examining the number of bishoprics in the area, such as Auca in the area of present-day Villafranca de Montes de Oca

---

[51] I have discussed this issue in Santiago Castellanos, *Poder social, aristocracias, y hombre santo en la Hispania visigoda: La 'Vita Aemiliani' de Braulius de Zaragoza* (Logroño, 1998). See more recently Santiago Castellanos, *La hagiografía visigoda: Dominio social y proyección cultural* (Logroño, 2004).

[52] See Castellanos, *Poder social*.

[53] This was one of the central ideas of Barbero and Vigil Pascual, *Sobre los orígenes sociales*.

[54] For the archaeological record, see, for example, Julio Escalona Monge, *Sociedad y territorio en la Alta Edad Media castellana: la formación del Alfoz de Lara* (Oxford, 2002); Díaz and Menéndez Bueyes, 'Cantabrian Basin'. For the Meseta, whose northern part is included in the northern territorios examined in this chapter, see more recently Alexandra Chavarría Arnau, 'Dopo la fine delle ville: le campagne ispaniche in epoca visigota (VI–VIII) secolo', in *Dopo la fine delle ville: le campagne dal VI al IX secolo: 11 Seminario sul tardo antico e l'Alto Medioevo, Gavi, 8–10 maggio 2004*, ed. by Gian Pietro Brogiolo, Alexandra Chavarría Arnau, and Marco Valenti (Mantova, 2005), pp. 263–85.

[55] The issue is examined in greater detail in Castellanos, *Poder social*.

[56] Santiago Castellanos, *Los godos y la cruz: Recaredo y la unidad de Spania* (Madrid, 2007). That political context has significant consequences not only generally, but also on a local scale. One of the best examples in that respect is the important town of Mérida, in the south. For the ideological background of the hagiographical documentation on Mérida, see Santiago Castellanos, 'The Significance of Social Unanimity in a Visigothic Hagiography: An Ideological Screen', *Journal of Early Christian Studies*, 11 (2003), 387–419.

(province of Burgos), between the Upper Ebro and La Rioja. Although located in the mountains, Auca was not far from the lowlands of the northern Meseta, and the bishopric there may have been created at some point during the second half of the sixth century.[57] As early as the reign of Reccared, the local bishop served as a link between the *sedes regia* in Toledo and the local communities under Visigothic rule since the days of King Leovigild. An inscription dated to the reign of Reccared indicates that Asterius, bishop of Auca, consecrated a church dedicated to St Mary in present-day Mijangos (province of Burgos), within the region known as Cantabria during the entire Visigothic period. In his *Life of St Emilian*, Braulius called Cantabri the people of that region, as well as of what is today western Rioja. Asterius purposefully used regnal years to date an inscription which was certainly meant to be seen and read by locals. The Bishop may have therefore served as intermediary between Toledo, the aristocracies mentioned in the *Life of St Emilian*, the leaders of Cantabria, and whatever other social segments there were between them, the dependents mentioned by Braulius for the western Rioja. This hardly fits the model of a Visigothic power superimposing itself in the region. Instead, this rather points to an articulation of the central power in the northern region, through the intermediary of the local elites. The liturgy, the celebration of the Mass, and the reading of the *Life of St Emilian* (Braulius specifically mentions the recitation of his small work) were subtle means to project the image of a regional church associated with the royal power in Toledo. The incorporation of the region into the Visgothic kingdom was thus a dynamic process, which resulted in the creation of new administrative structures, such as the duchies of Cantabria and, possibly, Asturias.[58]

In the case of Vasconia and the people named Vascones, the historiographic positions have also been marked by the idea of a low level of Roman influence. In fact, that notion is more pronounced with the Basques than with any other people in the northern area. Although establishing definitive boundaries is rather difficult, late antique Vasconia covered the modern provinces of Navarre, Vizcaya, Alava, and Guipuzcoa.[59] Modern political debates about the status of the Basque country

---

[57] Iñaki Martín Viso, 'Organización episcopal y poder entre la Antigüedad tardía y el Medievo (siglos V–XI): las sedes de Calahorra, Oca y Osma', *Iberia: Revista de la Antigüedad*, 2 (1999), 151–90.

[58] Luis A. García Moreno, 'Estudios sobre la administración del reino visigodo de Toledo', *Anuario de Historia del Derecho Español*, 44 (1974), 5–155; Luis A. García Moreno, 'Estirpe goda y legitimidad del poder en tiempos de Sancho el Mayor', in *Ante el milenario del reinado de Sancho el Mayor: Un rey navarro para España y Europa* (Pamplona, 2004), pp. 271–99 (p. 296).

[59] For what follows, I am indebted to Iñaki Martín Viso, 'La configuración de un espacio de frontera: propuestas sobre la *Vasconia* tardoantigua', in *Comunidades locales y dinámicas de poder*

had unfortunate consequences on the scholarly discourse about Vasconia. The idea that Vasconia remained 'pure' and untainted by Roman influence is to a large extent the product of political interests and nationalist imagination. The idea of a limited Romanization of Vasconia could go unchallenged for a relatively long while because, until recently, very little archaeological evidence existed from the Basque country.[60] Such an idea has now been completely discredited, as it became clear that the Basque country had not only *ciuitates* and *uillae*, but more importantly, Roman forms of life and control of territory and revenue.[61] Both *ciuitates*, such as Pompaelo (present-day Pamplona) and seaport sites, such as Oiasso (on the Bidasoa River by the sea) were dynamic centres from which Romans controlled the hinterland and in which they collected taxes.[62] In short, Vasconia was not some kind of 'village of Astérix' always at war with the Roman legions. It was rather a diverse region with several peoples controlled by Rome from at least the late Republican period. Through Late Antiquity, the region appears as assembled around a dominant group, the Vascones, but other peoples are known as well, such as the Autrigones, Vardulli, and Caristi. The Vascones were never a problem for Rome, but they were a nuisance for the Visigothic kings.[63] On the other side of the Pyrenees the Vascones caused similar problems to the Merovingian kings of the Franks.[64]

Fifth-century Vasconia was, like most other northern regions, a territory with remarkable military forces. During the first quarter of the century, Emperor

en el norte de la Península Ibérica durante la Antigüedad tardía, ed. by Urbino Espinosa and Santiago Castellanos (Logroño, 2006), pp. 101–39.

[60] This is particularly true for Roger Collins, *The Basques* (Oxford, 1986).

[61] Agustín Azkarate Garai-Olaun, 'El País Vasco en los siglos inmediatos a la desaparición del Imperio Romano', in *Historia del País Vasco: Edad Media (siglos V–XV)*, ed. by Pedro Barruso Barés and José Angel Lema Pueyo (San Sebastián, 2004), pp. 30–32.

[62] For a list of archaeological sites, see Viso, 'La configuración'. For a critical approach to the archaeological record pointing to local communities on a small scale, see Juan Antonio Quirós Castillo and Alfonso Vigil-Escalera, 'Networks of Peasant Villages between Toledo and Velegia Alabense, Northwestern Spain (V–Xth Centuries)', *Archeologia Medievale*, 33 (2006), 79–128, who compare two very different regions, namely Madrid, in the Meseta, and the southern Basque country.

[63] Armando Besga Marroquín, 'Apuntes sobre la situación política de los pueblos del norte de España desde la caída del Imperio Romano hasta el reinado de Leovigildo', *Letras de Deusto*, 73 (1996), 84–87.

[64] Michel Rouche, *L'Aquitaine des Wisigoths aux Arabes, 418–781: naissance d'une région* (Paris, 1979).

Honorius wrote to soldiers stationed in Pompaelo, perhaps only for a brief while.[65] A little later, the *Bacaudae* made their appearance in southern Vasconia, as well as in Tarraconensis. Some have seen the *Bacaudae* as a sort of 'nationalist' movement of the local Vascones against the world around them.[66] But the *Bacaudae* also appeared in other regions outside Vasconia, such as Gaul, which clearly shows how misguided such nationalist interpretations truly are. This is not to say that there were not Vascones among the *Bacaudae* of Tarraconensis, but the movement most certainly had no 'nationalist' programme. Instead, it may have verged on social rebellion, as the *Bacaudae* repeatedly attacked properties and bishoprics, although the political dimension should not be excluded, particularly anti-imperial overtones in the Ebro River region.

During the post-Roman period, Vasconia served as a buffer zone between the Merovingian and Visigothic kingdoms. After the battle of Vouillé (507), in which the Franks of Clovis defeated the Visigoths, Vasconia found itself in the middle of the territories that were still not wholly tethered one way or another. A particularly disruptive event was the campaign which the Frankish kings Childebert and Chlotar led in 541 deep into Vasconia, up to Pompaelo (*Pampilone* of the late antique and medieval sources) and Caesaraugusta (Zaragoza).[67] The Merovingian

[65] For the letter, see Koldo Larrañaga Elorza, 'Glosa sobre un viejo texto referido a la historia de Pamplona: el *De laude Pampilone*', *Príncipe de Viana*, 201 (1994), 137–47. For the idea that Roman troops in Pompaelo were not permanent, see Arce, *Bárbaros y romanos*, p. 90.

[66] For scholarly expressions of such ideas, see E. A. Thompson, 'Revueltas campesinas en la Galia e Hispania bajoimperial', in *Conflictos y estructuras sociales en la Hispania antigua*, ed. by Antonio García y Bellido (Madrid, 1977), pp. 61–76; Gonzalo Bravo, 'Las bagaudas: vieja y nueva problemática', in *Ier congreso peninsular de Historia Antigua, Santiago de Compostella, 1–5 julio 1986*, ed. by Gerardo Pereira Menaut, III (Santiago de Compostela, 1988), pp. 187–96; Gonzalo Bravo, *Revueltas internas y penetraciones bárbaras en el Imperio* (Madrid, 1991); Raymond Van Dam, *Leadership and Community in Late Antique Gaul* (Los Angeles, 1985); John F. Drinkwater, 'The Bacaudae of Fifth-Century Gaul', in *Fifth-Century Gaul: A Crisis of Identity?*, ed. by John F. Drinkwater and Hugo Elton (Cambridge, 1992), pp. 208–17; Juan José. Sayas Abengochea, *Los vascos en la Antigüedad* (Madrid, 1994); Juan Carlos Sánchez León, *Los bagaudas: rebeldes, demonios, mártires. Revueltas campesinas en Galia e Hispania durante el Bajo Imperio* (Jaén, 1996); Armando Besga Marroquín, Domuit vascones, *El País Vasco durante la época de los reinos germánicos: La era de la independencia (siglos V–VIII)* (Bilbao, 2001).

[67] Gregory of Tours, *Historiarum libri decem*, 3.29, ed. by Bruno Krusch and Wilhelm Levison, MGH SS rer. Merov., 1.1 (Hannover, 1951); *Consularia Caesaraugustana*, 130ª, ed. by C. Cardelle de Hartmann, Corpus Christianorum, Series Latina, 173 A (Turnhout, 2001); Isidore of Seville, *Historia Gothorum*, 41.

expedition was not successful, and Vasconia, along with the other northern regions, eventually fell under Visigothic rule.

The first Visigothic attack on Vasconia was led by Leovigild, who managed to conquer the *partem Vasconiae* in 581.[68] The foundation of a new city, Victoriacum, may be viewed as a symbolic act of imposing tribute on the Vascones. As with other regions, the Visigothic king's goal seems to have been to extract a tribute as large as possible from the newly conquered lands. Similarly, on the other side of the Pyrenees, the Franks attacked the Vascones in the early 600s with the purpose of forcing them into paying tribute.[69] Leovigild, however, only conquered *partem Vasconiae*, as clearly indicated in John of Biclaro's *Chronicle*. The later history of the Vascones during the Visigothic period to the fall of the kingdom in 711 is marked by frequent military campaigns which Visigothic kings launched in order to assert their dominance over the region. Suintila, for example, attacked the region in the early seventh century and founded a *ciuitas Gothorum* named Ologicus. Ologicus (present-day Olite, in Navarre) was not only an administrative centre of the Visigothic power in the region, but, as Isidore of Seville noted a little later, it also served as a basis for collecting taxes and *stipendia*.[70] Finds of coins struck for King Suintila from Pampilona and Calagurris substantiate the idea of the Visigoths extracting tribute from Vasconia, which is otherwise based primarily on the evidence of Isidore. The foundation of Ologicus, like that of Victoriacum before it, may have been not only an attempt to create a basis for Visigothic control in the region, but also an attempt to shift the emphasis away from Pampilona, which had until then been the regional centre for the local elites.[71] During the second half of the seventh century, King Wamba also campaigned in Vasconia. Again, we are told that the Visigothic king's intention was to impose tribute payments (*tribute*) on the Vascones, who brought them directly to him. From Vasconia, Wamba moved against rebels in southern

[68] John of Biclaro, *Chronicon*, 60.

[69] Fredegar, *Chronicle*, 4.21, ed. by J. M. Wallace-Hadrill, in Olivier Devillers and Jean Meyers, *Frédégaire: Chronique des temps mérovingiens* (Turnhout, 2001): 'Eo anno Teudebertus et Teudericus exercitum contra Wasconis dirigunt ipsoque Deo auxiliante deiectus suae dominatione redegiunt et tributarius faciunt.'

[70] Isidore of Seville, *Historia Gothorum*, 63, written in the first part of the seventh century. I use the edition by Cristóbal Rodríguez Alonso, *Las Historias de los Godos, Vándalos y Suevos de Isidoro de Sevilla* (León, 1975).

[71] The functional contrast between Pampilona and Ologicus is developed by Viso, 'La configuración'.

Gaul.[72] It would, therefore, appear that the Vascones posed constant and serious problems to the Visigothic kings interested in controlling the northern regions of the Peninsula. Why were the Vascones such notorious trouble-makers?

The archaeological record may offer some explanation, as the region displays some unique characteristics, especially when compared to others discussed in this chapter. The Basque country has produced evidence of several cemeteries with what may be viewed as warrior graves.[73] Such graves have been so far excavated in Finaga (Basauri, Vizcaya), Aldaieta (Nanclares de Gamboa, Álava), Buzaga (Elorz, Navarra), San Pelayo (Alegría-Dulantzi, Álava), and even Pamplona.[74] They all produced more weapons than any other contemporary cemetery site in the Iberian Peninsula.[75] Significantly, those cemeteries show strong similarities with materials from the other side of the Pyrenees, which has allowed some scholars to suggest that they belong to Aquitanian or Frankish groups. Finally, recent anthropological studies have concluded that we are dealing with family groups with a hierarchical structure based on military leadership.[76] Texts from the Visigothic period help explain the situation with their frequent references to violence perpetrated by Vascones. In about 653, Bishop Taio of Zaragoza wrote to another bishop named Quiricus about Vascones joining the forces of the Visigothic rebel Froia, who was at war with King Reccesvinth, the son and successor of Chindasvinth. Taio described them in the terms of the old historiographic stereotypes about the savage

[72] Julian of Toledo, *Historia Wambae Regis*, 10, ed. by W. Levison, Corpus Christianorum, Series Latina, 115 (Turnhout, 1976).

[73] Agustín Azkarate Garai-Olaun, 'Nuevas perspectivas sobre la tardoantigüedad en los Pirineos occidentales a la luz de la investigación arqueológica', in *Visigoti e longobardi: Atti del seminario, Roma, 28–29 aprile 1997*, ed. by Javier Arce and Paolo Delogu (Firenze, 2001), pp. 37–55; Agustín Azkarate Garai-Olaun, '*Reihengräberfelder* al sur de los Pirineos occidentales?', *Sacralidad y Arqueología: Antigüedad y Cristianismo*, 21 (2004), 389–413; Viso, 'La configuración'.

[74] Finaga: Iñaki García Camino, *Arqueología y poblamiento en Bizkaia, siglos VI–XII: La configuración de la sociedad feudal* (Bilbao, 2002), pp. 66–76. Aldaieta: Agustín Azcarate Garai-Aldaun, *Aldaieta: Necrópolis tardoantigua de Aldaieta (Nanclares de Gamboa, Alava)*, I: *Memoria de la excavación e inventario de los hallazgos* (Vitoria, 1999). Pamplona: Maria Angeles Mezquíriz de Catalán, 'Necrópolis visigoda de Pamplona', *Príncipe de Viana*, 98–99 (1965), 107–31; Jorge de Navascués y de Palacio, 'Rectificaciones al cementerio hispano-visigodo de Pamplona', *Príncipe de Viana*, 142–43 (1976), 119–27.

[75] Gisela Ripoll, 'The Transformation and Process of Acculturation in Late Antique Hispania: Select Aspects from Urban and Rural Archaeological Documentation', in *The Visigoths: Studies in Culture and Society*, ed. by Alberto Ferreiro (Leiden, 1999), pp. 263–302.

[76] Azkarate Garai-Olaun, 'Nuevas perspectivas' and '*Reihengräberfelder*?'.

Vascones.[77] His episcopal predecessor Braulius noted the difficulties posed by marauders for the roads and safe environment of Caesaraugusta, a region that was a common target of Vasconian raids.[78] Iñaki Martín Viso has convincingly argued that the Vasconian military posturing made sense only on the periphery of the Visigothic kingdom, in other words in a frontier region, such as Vasconia was throughout the entire post-Roman period.[79]

The many references in the sources to Visigothic attacks on Vasconia suggest that the region was only partially under Visigothic control. Vasconia was certainly on the periphery of the kingdom. Only a few central places, such as Pampilona, or *ciuitates*, such as Calagurris, together with their hinterlands seem to have operated along the same lines as 'regular' towns inside the administrative structure of the kingdom meant to serve as tax-collecting centres and seats of bishops. Even though the Church was certainly present in Vasconia through such bishoprics as Pampilona and Calagurris, there is sufficient evidence to suggest that Christianity had failed to prevail over local pagan cults, which seem to have continued well into the early medieval period.[80] In fact, the very history of the bishopric of Pampilona is an illustration of the considerable obstacles the conversion to Christianity encountered in the region, as well as how difficult it was to maintain relations with the church organization centred upon the *sedes regia* of Toledo, where the general councils of the kingdom took place.[81]

In short, the Vascones may have appeared in post-Roman Hispania as savage barbarians, but this was nothing more than a stereotype. It is clear that Vasconia was a region which Visigothic kings found difficult to control, much like the Vascones were a nuisance for the Merovingian kings. However, it would be a gross mistake

[77] Taio, *Ep. ad Quiricum*, ed. by Jacques-Paul Migne, Patrologia Latina, 80 (Turnhout, 1986).

[78] Braulius attributed instability around Caesaraugusta to *latrones* in his *ep.* 24, which may refer to Vascones. See also his *ep.* 3.4–6, ed. by L. Riesco Terrero, *Epistolario de San Braulius: Introducción, edición crítica y traducción* (Sevilla, 1975): 'non modo sterilitatis uel inopie malo uerum etiam luis et hostilitatis quominus inquirerem orribili sum praepeditus incursu'.

[79] Viso, 'La configuración'.

[80] Koldo Larrañaga Elorza, 'Proceso cristianizador y pervivencia de rituales paganos en el País Vasco en la Tardo Antigüedad y Alta Edad Media', *Hispania Sacra*, 104 (1999), 613–21.

[81] Juan José Larrea, 'El obispado de Pamplona en época visigoda', *Hispania Sacra*, 97 (1996), 123–47; Juan José Larrea, 'De nuevo en torno a los primeros siglos del obispado de Pamplona', *Hispana Sacra*, 99 (1997), 319–26; Juan José Larrea, *La Navarre du IVᵉ au XIIᵉ siècle: peuplement et société* (Brussels, 1998); Koldo Larrañaga Elorza, 'Sobre el obispado pamplonés en época visigoda', *Hispania Sacra*, 99 (1997), 279–317; Koldo Larrañaga Elorza, 'A vueltas con los obispos de Pamplona de época visigoda: Apostillas a una réplica', *Hispania Sacra*, 101 (1998), 35–62.

to view Vasconia or the Vascones as a strange and barbarian entity completely iso-lated from the rest of Hispania. Taio of Zaragoza may have been fond of such stereotypes as *gens effera Vasconum*, but within one and the same letter, he depicted the Vascones as closely tied to Froia, a leader who, like so many other Visigothic usurpers, was striving to gain control over the central power in Toledo.[82] In other words, the Vascones were not that far removed from the general affairs of the kingdom. The region's peculiarity and singularity had much more to do with local social structures, which, unlike any other region in the Peninsula, were primarily geared towards warfare. Pampilona was the regional centre ever since the Roman conquest, but in the process of conquering at least parts of Vasconia, Visigothic kings developed alternative nuclei. The Visigothic encroachment, and especially the im-position of tribute payments, eroded the traditional organization of the local soci-ety along the lines of military hierarchy, as indicated by the archaeological evidence of burial assemblages. The reaction to the Visigothic encroachment and its conse-quences was also complex. On the one hand, Vasconian warlords decided to get involved in political and military affairs inside the kingdom, as in the case of their support for Reccesvinth's rival Froia. On the other hand, they sometimes directly confronted the Visigothic kings. It can be no accident that King Roderic was battling the Vascones at the time his kingdom collapsed under the attack of Muslim warriors.

Conclusion

The peoples of the central-northern region of the Iberian Peninsula, especially the Astures, the Cantabri, and the Vascones, were sometimes often depicted as bar-barians, and in that respect they could certainly be treated as 'neglected barbarians'. The background for such stereotypes as savagery and tribalism attached to them was, of course, the intellectual tradition of exclusivism projected by Greek and Roman authors for so many centuries. The idea that the north was basically savage was already established during the Republican age, in part as a consequence of the wars that took place towards the end of that age. This is readily evident at even a cursory reading of the sources written after Augustus and his generals' wars against the Cantabri and the Astures. By contrast, the Vascones played virtually no role in that early history. The stereotypes were applied to them first during Late Antiquity.

The greatest hurdle in the way of studying the late antique and early medieval history of the peoples in the central-northern region of the Iberian Peninsula is

---

[82] Taio, *Ep. ad Quiricum*, 2.

that the stereotypes produced and reproduced in ancient sources have also been adopted by modern historians. With new critical approaches developed towards ancient sources, such uncritical stances are untenable. It has become clear that the central-northern region was also touched by Romanization, the establishment of Roman forms of social and political control. There may not have been in the north an urban landscape as clearly defined as that from other regions of Hispania, but there can be no doubt by now about the Roman presence in the area or about the complex transformations of the local societies. Whatever the result of comparisons with regions of Hispania on which the Roman power had a much more profound impact, the model of the Roman *ciuitas* was certainly present in the north, and so was the rural system of *uillae*. As recently discovered sources indicate, taxes were collected from the northern regions just as they were from other regions of the Peninsula.

Much of the same is true for the late and post-Roman period, during which (and especially during the fifth century) the central-northern regions shared in the common fate of the Peninsula: local leaders emerged, sometimes with power over regional structures, whose names mentioned in the sources appear to be indigenous. The examination of such structures reveals not tribal forms of organization, but rather aristocratic power, as in the case of the Upper Ebro valley or of Aspidius in the north-west. The degree of cohesion within each one of those aristocratic structures varied from one area to the other. In Vasconia, local structures of power took on conspicuously military overtones, with good material culture parallels in south-western Gaul. The specifically military organization in Vasconia made it possible for local aristocrats to resist the encroachment of Visigothic power, something that had not been possible during the Roman age. Finally, the network of episcopal sees extended over the central-northern region as well, although to a lesser degree than elsewhere in Hispania. Wherever bishops were present, the central power in Toledo was able to implement its ideas and messages. The northern regions of the peninsula certainly had local peculiarities, but the idea of tribal societies permanently arrayed in battle against a predominantly urban society in the south is nothing more than a historiographic myth. Denouncing that myth implies the understanding that there were aristocracies, dependents, and power systems at both individual and collective levels in the central-northern regions which were not unlike those from other parts of Hispania. From this point onwards, historians must examine the developments of those structures not outside of, but rather within, the general political framework of the later Roman Empire and of the Visigothic kingdom.

SUEVIC COINS AND SUEVIC KINGS (418–456): THE VISIGOTHIC CONNECTION

Fernando López Sánchez

In the year 418, the Visigoths, ruled by a new king, Vallia, signed a second *foedus* with the Roman governor Constantius III. The terms of this treaty included a reward for their military support, and they received land for settlement in the provinces of Aquitania Secunda, Novempopulonia, and Narbonense Primera.[1] The Sueves, who were supposed to be eliminated according to the terms of an earlier treaty signed in the year 416, not only survived the treaty of 418, but even benefited from a Visigothic intervention on their behalf at the point where they were about to be defeated by the Vandals in the Nervasian Mountains.[2] Luis A. García Moreno believed that the real reason behind the Visigothic and imperial support

---

I would like to express my gratitude to Purificación Ubric Rabaneda. Without a careful reading of her substantial and valuable studies on the Church and the barbarians in fifth-century Hispania, these lines would have been more difficult to write. I would also like to thank Professor Fergus Millar and Nicolas Márquez Grant for their careful readings of earlier drafts of this chapter.

[1] Hydatius, *Chronicle*, 61 [69], in *The Chronicle of Hydatius and the Consularia Constantinopolitana: Two Contemporary Accounts of the Final Years of the Roman Empire*, ed. and trans. by Richard W. Burgess (Oxford, 1993). In what follows, chapter numbers from the *Chronicle* which appear between brackets are those of Theodor Mommsen's edition, in *Chronica minora saec. IV. V. VI. VII.*, vol. II, MGH AA, 11 (Berlin, 1894), pp. 13–36, followed by that of Alain Tranoy (Paris, 1974). See also Isidore of Seville, *Historia Gothorum*, 22, ed. by C. Rodríguez Alonso, in *Las historias de los godos, vándalos y suevos de Isidoro de Sevilla* (León, 1975).

[2] Hydatius, *Chronicle*, 63 [71] and 66 [74], and Isidore of Seville, *Historia Wandalorum*, 73, ed. by Rodríguez Alonso.

for the Sueves was that they were considered to be harmless if confined to Galicia.[3] This was, however, the first time the Suevic leader, Hermericus, gets a mention in the *Chronicle* of Hydatius as the king of the Sueves.[4] It is not hard to understand why Ravenna and Toulouse would set aside Galicia for a people like the Sueves. However, if the Sueves were believed to be harmless, why then were they promoted through the recognition of their leader as king (*rex*) in the year 419?

The departure of the Vandals to North Africa in 429 left the Sueves as the sole masters in Hispania. This event appears to have instilled in them a sense of great self-confidence, which in turn encouraged them to extend their power beyond the areas they had settled in Galicia in an attempt to occupy the territories which the Vandals had by now abandoned. During this period, Aetius, Emperor Valentinian III's *magister militum* in Gaul, adopted a diplomacy-based policy towards the Sueves, which was put into practice by *comes* Censorius, a member of Aetius's inner circle, and by Hydatius, a well-known and influential Galician bishop. In sharp contrast to Aetius, however, Valentinian III adopted a strong anti-barbarian (and anti-Aetius) policy, which proved anything but successful, as Suabian attacks on their Hispano-Roman neighbours in Galicia were contained for only a very limited period.[5] Between 430 and 456, the power of the Sueves expanded into Lusitania, Betica, and Cartaginense, while the empire was able to regain control only over some parts of the province of Cartaginense, which had been previously occupied by the Sueves.[6] In the end, the king of the Sueves agreed to a peace treaty with Ravenna in the year 453.[7]

During this entire period, and until Theodoric II launched his campaign against Rechiar in 456, the Visigoths, the empire's most trustworthy allies in the West, seem to have done nothing to prevent the consolidation of Suevic power in Hispania. On the contrary, all the evidence points to their having endorsed that power. Rechiar, against whom the Visigoths campaigned in 456, had been married since 449 to one of Theodoric I's daughters[8] and had visited the court of his father-

---

[3] Luis A. García Moreno, 'Nueva luz sobre la España de las invasiones de principios del s. V: La epístola XI de Consencio a S. Agustín', in *Verbo de Dios y palabras humanas* (Pamplona, 1988), pp. 153–74 (pp. 162–63).

[4] Hydatius, *Chronicle*, 63 [71]: 'rex Suevorum'.

[5] Hydatius, *Chronicle*, 88 [98] and 103 [111]. For Valentinian III's anti-barbarian and anti-Aetius attitude, see Giuseppe Zecchini, *Aezio: l'ultima difesa dell'Occidente romano* (Rome, 1983), p. 199.

[6] Hydatius, *Chronicle*, 147 [155] and 153 [161].

[7] Hydatius, *Chronicle*, 105 [113].

[8] Hydatius, *Chronicle*, 132 [140].

in-law.[9] As Luis A. García Moreno noted, Rechiar's visit to Theodoric's court must be seen in the broader context of an earlier and stronger alliance between the Visigoths and the Sueves.[10] A Suevic-Visigothic matrimonial alliance had in fact already been sealed as far back as the year 418, when a daughter of the Visigoth king Vallia was handed over in marriage to a Suevic aristocrat. The son born to that family was no other than Ricimer, the all-too-powerful figure in the political life of the Western Empire between 456 and 472.

Every modern historian's view of the fifth-century Suevic kingdom is thoroughly conditioned by the reading of the *Chronicle* of Hydatius, as all archaeological efforts of the last few decades have failed to identify the material culture correlates of the Suevic presence in Hispania. Similarly, the 150 to 200 fifth- to sixth-century Suevic coins known so far cannot compare with the 10,000 or so coins known from the entire history of the Visigothic kingdom between the fifth and the eighth centuries.[11] There is therefore no surprise that little if any attention has so far been paid to those firsthand historical records. This in turn may explain why, in comparison to the kings of the Visigoths, the Suevic rulers of Hispania have been largely neglected by modern historiography.

On the other hand, it is quite obvious that a power as central to the narrative of Hydatius as the Suevic kingdom could not have been as insignificant as some modern historians have claimed. The purpose of this paper is to demonstrate the contrary on the basis of a historical argument developed from some of the most characteristic Suevic coins that have been discovered. My goal is not to contrast the information provided by Hydatius or other ancient authors with data from surviving Suevic coins, but instead to offer a new interpretation of the only institutional and truly Suevic historical sources currently available to us. It is my hope that a painstaking reading of those neglected sources will throw some light upon the much neglected Suevic kingdom in fifth-century Hispania.

Chronological Problems in Suevic Numismatics

Although the total number of known specimens does not even reach two hundred, Suevic coins are believed to provide clues to many of the problems surrounding the

---

[9] Hydatius, *Chronicle*, 134 [142].

[10] Luis A. García Moreno, *Historia de la España visigoda* (Madrid, 1989), p. 59.

[11] Jesús Vico Monteoliva, María Cruz Cores Gomendio, and Gonzalo Cores Uría, *Corpus nummorum Visigothorum ca. 575–714 Leovigildus-Achila* (Madrid, 2006), p. 25.

fifth-century history of Hispania. There is therefore little surprise that those coins have come to the attention of many historians.[12] In sharp contrast to more general or historical studies, however, there are very few purely numismatic studies. The most recent and most complete work was published several years ago. With that book, J. M. Peixoto Cabral and David M. Metcalf produced a scholarly study of Suevic coins, with a particular focus on description, weight, measurements, and metal composition.[13]

Peixoto Cabral and Metcalf's study solved a number of problems, but broader questions, such as the chronology of most series or the reasons behind the icono-graphical and stylistic development of the coin types, still await an answer. The exact provenance of most single and hoard finds (except, of course, the Seville hoard found in 1972) remains unknown.[14] Perhaps because of the lack of a suffi-cient number of finds with known provenance, very few reliable dates have been established for the majority of Suevic coins. The only exception is the series of *Latina Munita* tremisses, which have been dated to the second half of the sixth century.[15] The chronology of the remaining series bearing the names Honorius or Valentinian is not certain. As a consequence, in order to identify coins which can safely be dated earlier than the *Latina Munita* tremisses, several authors have decided that, besides stylistic traits, one needs to take into consideration the historical context.[16]

The historical context has been reconstructed primarily by Peixoto Cabral and Metcalf by means of a few key dates. The most important among them is 453, the

---

[12] For a general bibliography on Suevic coins, see Antonio Roma Valdés, 'Los visigodos (Península Ibérica): Los años oscuros', in *A Survey of Numismatic Research 1996–2001*, ed. by Carmen Alfaro, Michel Amandry, and Andrew Burnett (Madrid, 2003), pp. 381–82 (nos 10, 11, 19, and 22); Stanisław Suchodolski, 'Early Middle Ages: Suevi and Visigoths', in *A Survey of Numis-matic Research, 1990–1995*, ed. by Cécile Morrisson and Bernd Kluge (Berlin, 2007), pp. 298–99 (nos 104, 110, and 113); J. M. Peixoto Cabral and David M. Metcalf, *A Moeda sueva: Suevic Coinage* (Porto, 1997), pp. 219–32. For further literature, see also Alberto Ferreiro, *The Visigoths in Gaul and Spain A.D. 418–711: A Bibliography* (Leiden, 1988) pp. 536–40, nos 6883–6929.

[13] Peixoto Cabral and Metcalf, *A Moeda sueva*.

[14] Peixoto Cabral and Metcalf, *A Moeda sueva*, p. 33: 'Of the 150 to 200 known gold coins, the great majority unfortunately lack any exact find-spot.'

[15] Peixoto Cabral and Metcalf, *A Moeda sueva*, pp. 94–96.

[16] Peixoto Cabral and Metcalf, *A Moeda sueva*, p. 70; Robert A. G. Carson, John P. C. Kent, and Andrew Burnett, *The Roman Imperial Coinage*, X: *The Divided Empire and the Fall of the Western Parts, AD 395–491* (London, 1994), p. 466 (nos 3787–88), who believe that Suevic minting began in 452, not 453–54.

year of a treaty between the Western Empire and the Suevic king Rechiar (448–56).[17] All tremisses bearing the name Valentinian (i.e. Emperor Valentinian III), without exception, would have been issued after that date. However, those coins began to circulate only after Emperor Valentinian's death in 455. The series with Valentinian's name would therefore have to coincide in time with the 'dark' century of the Suevic kingdom (455–559), at the end of which the *Latina Munita* tremisses began to be struck.[18] Another important date for Peixoto Cabral and Metcalf is 441, the year in which Seville was taken by Rechila. Since thirty Suevic solidi with the name Honorius were found here in 1972, Peixoto Cabral and Metcalf concluded that those coins were Suevic imitations minted in Seville, which circulated also within Hispania.[19] As with the 'Valentinianic' tremisses, the coin engravers chose to depict on the obverse an emperor who was already dead by the time the solidi began to circulate.

To be sure, the 'fossilization' of certain types and the minting of coins after the death of the emperor portrayed on their obverses are two quite common phenomena in the 400s. The Visigothic kings of Tolosa struck solidi in the name of Libius Severus (461–65) long after his death.[20] The Suevic silver coin bearing the inscription *Iussu Rechiari Reges* was struck by King Rechiar with the portrait of Emperor Honorius (395–425) on the obverse, even though that emperor had been dead for twenty-five years. Peixoto Cabral and David Metcalf's idea of Suevic obverses being later than the reign of the depicted emperors is therefore quite reasonable. However, there are other possible explanations for Rechiar choosing to depict Honorius on his silver coins besides the King's presumed rejection of Valentinian III.[21] Siliquae with the name of Rechiar are exceptional for several

---

[17] Peixoto Cabral and Metcalf, *A Moeda sueva*, p. 69: 'The choice of this prototype (the Valentinianic tremissis) is probably intended as a reference to the political allegiance of the Sueves following the treaty of 453.' See also p. 46 for 453/54 as a decisive date for establishing the chronology of siliquae. For the treaty of 453, see Hydatius, *Chronicle*, 147 [155] and 154 [161].

[18] Peixoto Cabral and Metcalf, *A Moeda sueva*, p. 69: 'we think that the Valentinianic tremisses belong largely or wholly to the so-called second Suevic kingdom'; see also p. 77.

[19] Peixoto Cabral and Metcalf, *A Moeda sueva*, pp. 53, 54, and 56.

[20] George Depeyrot, 'Émissions wisigothiques de Tolosa (Ve siècle)', *Acta Numismatica*, 16 (1986), 79–104 (pp. 96–97).

[21] Peixoto Cabral and Metcalf, *A Moeda sueva*, p. 46: siliquae 'were struck either before the treaty of 453' (for in the absence of a treaty between Ravenna and the Suevic kingdom, there would be no reason to refuse to put Valentinian's image on the coins) or 'after the death of Valentinian' in 454 (as Rechiar could now express hostility towards the deceased emperor). However, at the

reasons. First, those were coins struck in silver, a metal rarely used for coins at the time. Moreover, the appearance of Honorius in the series does not in any way imply a late date for the solidi.[22] In other words, Honorius on siliqua is no proof of a late date for the 'Valentinianic' tremisses.

The Municipal Issue Iussu Richiari Reges: Rechiar at the Service of Rome

Many view siliquae with the inscription *Iussu Richiari Reges* as the most surprising of all the coins minted by Sueves (Plate VI.1). Not only is Rechiar named on the reverse with the title *rex*, but *B* and *R* appear in the interior of the depicted crown as mint marks, with a letter at either side of the central cross. On the obverse, the inscription mentions Honorius (*DN. Honorius P. F. Avg*), not Valentinian III (425–55) who was at that time the ruling emperor. Stanisław Suchodolski interpreted the siliqua in question as an affirmation of independence and as a political challenge from the Suevic king Rechiar to the Roman government.[23] Rechiar, at odds with the reigning emperor Valentinian III, would have denied the use of Valentinian's effigy on his coins. According to Suchodolski, Rechiar chose instead the most prestigious sovereign of the fifth century. The choice of Honorius (so Suchodolski) must have been motivated by the Emperor's benevolent attitude towards the Sueves. Furthermore, the choice of a deceased emperor showed Rechiar's decision to break with the imperial monopoly over minting.[24] But if Rechiar's goal was to challenge the imperial authority, would he have chosen to have the inscription mentioning his name on the reverse, instead of the obverse of

same time Peixoto Cabral and Metcalf advocate the idea that the tremisses with the name of Valentinian began to be struck in 453–54.

[22] Peixoto Cabral and Metcalf, *A Moeda sueva*, pp. 52 (for siliquae), 54 (for solidi: 'it is easy to imagine that King Rechila [...] was the first to strike gold coins'), 69, and 77 (for tremisses).

[23] Stanisław Suchodolski, 'La silique du roi Rechiar et les autres monnaies des suèves', *Quaderni Ticinesi di Numismatica e Antichità Classiche*, 18 (1989), 353–62. There are four known specimens with the inscription *Iussu Richari Reges*. One of them weighs 1.785 grams and was described in the late 1700s by J. Eckhel. The specimen was bought in 1864 by the Cabinet des Médailles de Paris. The second coin was found at Castro de Lanhoso, near Braga in 1940. Finally, recent excavations in Casa do Infante (Porto) produced a third coin. See Suchodolski, 'La silique', pp. 353–54, and Peixoto Cabral and Metcalf, *A Moeda sueva*, pp. 45–46.

[24] Suchodolski, 'La silique', p. 361, writes of 'briser le monopole impérial dans le monnayage se servant d'un métal moins précieux'. See also Xavier Barral i Altet, *La Circulacion des monnaies suèves et visigothiques: contribution à l'histoire économique du royaume visigoth* (Munich, 1976), pp. 51–52.

the coin? Why was he happy with just an inscription, without his own portrait? The design of Rechiar's siliqua suggests a much more complex explanation than that offered by Stanisław Suchodolski.

An attentive examination of the epigraphical details suggests clear analogies between the inscription on the obverse (*DN Honorius PF Aug*) and that on the reverse (*Iussu Richiari Reges*).[25] Since both inscriptions must be read from left to right, starting at the position of eight o'clock and ending at four o'clock, there is deliberate overlap between the word *Richiari* on the reverse, and the name *Honorius* on the obverse. Moreover, and perhaps more significantly, *PF Aug* on the obverse juxtaposes *Reges* on the reverse.[26] Such details suggest that, far from seeking 'independence' from Honorius, Rechiar instead chose to present himself as a subordinate of the Roman emperor. *Iussu* on the reverse indicates that the coins were struck with the explicit consent of Rechiar. On the other hand, the coin was not struck in his name, and Rechiar appears as a highly ranked official in the service of the emperor. This has a number of very instructive parallels on the reverses of provincial coins from Africa dated between 21 and 23, on which five proconsuls put together their names in a similar formula, *Permissu*.[27] This association between the name of a high-ranking official and the epigraph *Permissu* is not unique. In fact, a *legatus Augusti* of consular rank named Q. Caecilius Metellus Creticus Silanus also appears in a series of first-century coins from Beirut.[28] Evidently, and as in

[25] For a detailed discussion of the inscriptions, see Alessia Bolis, 'Legende circolari, legende in circolo: un repertorio di scrittura numismatica', *Acme*, 58 (2005), 127–34 (p. 130 with n. 130). See also Philip Grierson and Mark Blackburn, *Medieval European Coinage with a Catalogue of the Coins in the Fitzwilliam Museum*, I (Cambridge, 1986) pp. 211–84.

[26] This is remarkably similar to the obverse legend *Fl (H)Annibaliano Regi* of the year 335, for which see Patrick M. Bruun, *Constantine and Licinius: AD 313–337* (London, 1966), p. 584, no. 100. According to Otto Seeck, *Geschichte des Untergangs der antiken Welt*, 4th edn, IV (Stuttgart, 1923), p. 25, the title shows that Hannibalianus was supposed to replace Shapur, an idea later endorsed by Timothy D. Barnes, *Constantine and Eusebius* (Cambridge, 1981), p. 259; and 'Constantine and the Christians of Persia', *Journal of Roman Studies*, 75 (1985), 126–36 (p. 132).

[27] Three of them in a single *colonia* (Paterna) within three years (AD 21–23). Most issues coincide in time with Tacfarinas's rebellion. See Andrew Burnett, Michel Amandry, and Pere Pau Ripollès Alegre, *Roman Provincial Coinage, from the Death of Caesar to Vitellius (44 BC to AD 69)*, I (London, 1998), p. 196 (nos 762–70).

[28] The coins were struck under Emperor Tiberius. For *Permissu Silani* (referring to Q. Caecilius Metellus Creticus Silanus), see Burnett, Amandry, and Ripollès Alegre, *Roman Provincial Coinage*, I.1, no. 4541 (see also *Perm Sil* in no. 4544). For other examples, see Burnett, Amandry, and Ripollès Alegre, *Roman Provincial Coinage*, I.2, p. 755.

other cases, *Permissu* refers to the authority of the emperor, in whose name the coins were in fact struck. The officials of consular rank whose names appear on the reverse of the coins were only delegates of the imperial authority, and the phrase *Richiari Reges* must be seen against the background of such a monetary tradition. In other words, on his silver coins struck in Braga, Rechiar appears as a mere official in the service of the Roman emperor. However, he is specifically said to be not a high-ranking official, but a *rex*. According to Procopius, that was the name barbarians often gave to their leaders.[29] The choice of *rex*, without any additional honorific titles, does not imply any particular distinction for Rechiar. This is, in fact, the only instance of such a low profile of the Suevic king, and no such inscription appears on any fifth-century coins. Had the choice of legend depended entirely on Rechiar, the King would have probably not chosen the formula *Richiari Reges* to refer to himself on silver coins struck in his capital at Braga.

Further insight into the significance of the title *rex* may be obtained from a passage in Jordanes distinguishing between two forms of power that Theoderic, king of the Ostrogoths, had over barbarians under his rule and over Romans.[30] As a highly successful ruler, it was only natural for Theoderic to strike imperial poses, even though Procopius notes that Theoderic never adopted the title of emperor, but instead called himself 'king', like most other barbarian leaders.[31] Procopius also insists that, although Theoderic was regarded as a usurper (that is, he was nothing more than a barbarian *rex*), in reality he behaved like an emperor. Theoderic's blending of imperial authority and power as a *rex* found its expression in the inscriptions on the Senigalla gold medallion: the obverse bears the inscription *Rex Theodericus Pius Princ(eps) I(nvictus) S(emper)*, while the inscription on the reverse reads *Rex Theodericus Victor Gentium* (Plate VI.2).[32] Both iconography and epigraphy contribute

---

[29] Procopius of Caesarea, *Wars*, 7.1.1.26, ed. by J. Haury and G. Wirth (Leipzig, 1963).

[30] Jordanes, *Romana*, 349, ed. by Theodor Mommsen, MGH AA, 5.1 (Berlin, 1882).

[31] Procopius, *Wars*, 7.1.1.26 and 27. When Jordanes, *Getica*, 295, describes Theoderic's position of ruler over Goths and Romans, the word he chooses is the rather neutral *regnator*. Any assertion of royal authority over the Romans would have been repugnant to Theoderic's Roman subjects. See also John the Lydian, *Powers*, 1.3, ed. by Anastasius C. Bandy (Philadelphia, 1983). Despite Gregory of Tours's claims to the contrary (*Historiarum libri decem*, 2.27, ed. by Bruno Krusch and Wilhelm Levison, MGH SS rer. Merov., 1.1 (Hannover, 1951), pp. 36–94), Syagrius hardly deserved the title of *Romanorum rex*. See in this respect Edward James, 'Childéric, Syagrius et la disparition du royaume de Soissons', *Revue archéologique de Picardie*, 3–4 (1988), 9–13 (p. 11): 'il est nécessaire de remettre en question l'existence même de ce royaume de Syagrius et l'importance de Syagrius dans l'histoire de la France'.

[32] Philip Grierson, 'The Date of Theoderic's Gold Medallion', *Hikuin*, 11 (1985), 19–26.

Figure 14.1. Copy of the lost ring of King Childeric. Second half of fifth century. Cabinet des Médailles et Antiques, Bibliothèque Nationale, Paris. Courtesy of Dominique Hollard, curator of Roman Numismatics.

to the formulation of imperial claims by a Germanic king. On the obverse, Theodoric is depicted frontally as a Germanic king, with a moustache and with long hair covering his ears. However, this 'Germanic' look is combined with a typically imperial gesture. Theoderic has his right hand half raised, while in his left hand he appears to be holding a globe on which stands *Victoria*, facing him and bearing a wreath and a palm-branch. The reverse of the coin is also more typical of an emperor than a king: an image of Victoria, facing towards the right, holding a wreath in her right hand and a palm-branch leaf in her left hand.[33]

The inscription *Richiari Reges* reminds one of *Childirici Regis*, which appears on the fifth-century signet ring found in Childeric's tomb at Tournai (Figure 14.1). It is believed that the ring symbolized the status bestowed upon the Frankish king by the East Roman emperor.[34] Similarly, Gregory of Tours sometimes refers

---

[33] The Senigalla medallion is not unique in that respect. The so-called last sesterces struck by Theodahad (AD 534–36) show the portrait of the King, beardless but with moustache. The legends on the obverse and reverse read *DN Theoda-hatus Rex/Victoria Principium*. The iconography of the reverse is very similar to that on the Senigalla medallion, with Victory in girdled chiton standing right on prow. She has a wreath on the right and a palm-branch on the left, alongside the letters SC in the field. See Warwick Wroth, *Catalogue of the Coins of the Vandals, Ostrogoths and Lombards and the Empire of Thessalonica, Nicaea and Trebizond in the British Museum* (London, 1911), pp. 75–76. Ostrogothic kings often mixed imperial and Germanic features on their coins.

[34] Helmut Roth, 'Childerichs Ring: Fremde Könige mit den Augen von Byzanz gesehen?', *Acta Praehistorica et Archaeologica*, 34 (2002), 129–34 (p. 129). According to Roth, the signet ring from the grave of Childeric in Tournai has no parallel in the Merovingian world. The hair style, the necklace, and the lance portrayed on it are attributes typically associated with supposedly Germanic warriors depicted as bodyguards of the Roman emperors in the East. Roth argues that such images are of foreign kings received as vassals at the imperial court and not of imperial bodyguards. At any rate, the choice of attributes for Childeric's portrait on his ring is not a peculiarly Frankish way to depict a king, but a deliberate attempt to represent his power by the means in place at the imperial court in Constantinople.

to Clovis as just a *rex*, while on occasion he describes him as consul or even Roman patrician. As Ralph Mathisen put it, it is quite possible that there was 'une grande incompatibilité entre les idées d'Anastase et celles de Clovis' with reference to the institutional status of a Frankish ruler in fifth-century Gaul.[35]

Such an 'incompatibility' of status may have also been at work in the case of Rechiar in Hispania, and in much the same way as in Clovis's and Theoderic's cases. If, as often believed, *rex* merely indicates that a military leader had jurisdiction over his people, but was not a 'territorial monarch', then it is rather unlikely that Rechiar would have chosen that title for himself. Hydatius first refers to Rechiar's grandfather, Hermericus, as *rex Suevorum* in 419, but not earlier.[36] If this was actually meant to say that Hermericus only got his title after the treaty of 418, then the choice of Honorius instead of Valentinian for the obverse of Rechiar's siliqua makes much more sense. The formula *Regis Richiari* back-to-back with *Honorius PF Aug* points in fact to that 'first instance' in which the status of *rex* was conferred *in obsequium* upon a Suevic military commander.

There are many examples of such an intitulature on earlier imperial coins. A sesterce issued between 140 and 144 attests the fact that the king of the Quadi received his power *in obsequium* from Antoninus Pius (Figure 14.2).[37] On that coin, Antoninus is on the right dressed with a toga, while the Quadian king — *Rex Quadis Datus* — appears on the left.[38] The meaning of the scene is crystal clear: the Quadian king held power in the Danube region thanks to a Roman emperor. However, the coin in question was not minted in the Danube region, but in Rome, most likely in commemoration of the investiture of the Germanic king in that city. The authority issuing the coin was in this case Rome, not the emperor himself. Similarly, the Suevic coin may well have been issued by the city of Braga, and not

[35] Ralph W. Mathisen, 'Clovis, Anastase et Grégoire de Tours: consul, patrice et roi', in *Clovis, histoire et mémoire,* ed. by Michel Rouche, I (Paris, 1997), pp. 395–405 (p. 404).

[36] Hydatius, *Chronicle,* 63 [71]. See also Dietrich Claude, 'Prosopographie des spanischen Suebenreiches', *Francia,* 6 (1978), 647–76 (p. 659).

[37] This was a common practice during Tacitus's lifetime; see *Germania,* 42.2, ed. by M. Hutton and E. H. Warmington (London, 1914): 'Marcomanis Quadisque [...] vis et potentia regibus ex auctoritate romana.' For the date of the sesterce, see Harold Mattingly and Edward Allen Sydenham, *The Roman Imperial Coinage,* III: *Antoninus Pius to Commodus* (London, 1930), p. 110 no. 620, pl. 5 no. 107.

[38] Robert Göbl, '*Rex ... Datus*: Ein Kapitel von der Interpretation numismatischer Zeugnisse und ihren Grundlagen', *Rheinisches Museum für Philologie,* 104 (1961), 70–80.

Figure 14.2. Sesterce of Antoninus Pius, 140–44 (Mattingly and Sydenham, *Roman Imperial Coinage*, III, pl. 5, no. 107). After *Zwischen Rom und dem Barbaricum: Festschrift für Titus Kolník zum 70. Geburstag*, ed. by Klara Kuzmová, Karol Pieta, and Ján Rájtar (Nitra, 2002), cover.

by Rechiar.[39] This would explain both the unique use of *Richiari Reges* only for these particular coins and the depiction of the Suevic king from a Roman, rather than 'Germanic', perspective.[40] Siliquae struck for Rechiar may therefore have been minted at the expense of the city of Braga, either from private or from ecclesiastical funds.[41] Moreover, this may also explain the abbreviation *BR* (for Braga) in a

[39] The choice of silver over gold also reminds one of the monetary practice in Rome, where bronze was reserved for ceremonial issues commonly struck when the ruling emperor entered the city. This is particularly the case of the *Int. Urb.* (*Intra Urbem* or *Introitus Urbis*) series struck for Aurelian in 274, for which see Michael Grant, *Roman Anniversary Issues: An Exploratory Study of the Numismatic and Medallic Commemoration of Anniversary Years 49 B.C.–A.D. 375* (Cambridge, 1950), pp. 140–43. For similar issues struck for Gallienus, see Carlo Poggi, '*Integra Urbe*: La *corona obsidionalis* nella monetazione di Gallieno', in *La tradizione iconica come fonte storica: Il ruolo della numismatica negli studi di iconografia*, *Atti del I Incontro di Studio del Lexicon Iconographicum Numismaticae, Messina, 6–8 Marzo 2003*, ed. by Maria Caccamo Caltabiano, Daniele Castrizio, and Mariangela Puglisi (Messina, 2004), pp. 449–56.

[40] Jean Lafaurie (private communication) has proposed that the obverse was struck with a die from an official workshop plundered during the sack of Rome and re-engraved after that. In support of Lafaurie's theory, Barral i Altet, *La Circulacion*, p. 52 with n. 230, has pointed to the coins from the burial found in Heilbronn-Böckingen (Swabia).

[41] Pablo C. Díaz, 'El reino suevo de Hispania y su sede en Bracara', in *Sedes regiae (ann. 400–800)*, ed. by Gisela Ripoll, José Maria Gurt Esparaguerra, and Alexandra Chavarría (Barcelona, 2000), pp. 403–23. That liturgical vessels may have been turned into coins is suggested, among other things, by the Traprain Law hoard found in Scotland, which, besides a great quantity of ingots, some of which were covered with lead, also produced coins of Valens, Valentinian II, and Honorius. See Alexander O. Curle, *The Treasure of Traprain: A Scottish Hoard of Roman Silver Plate* (Glasgow, 1923); François Baratte, 'Quelques remarques à propos des lingots d'or et d'argent du Bas Empire', in *Frappe et ateliers monétaires dans l'antiquité et moyen âge, Actes du symposium réuni du 30 au 1er février 1975 dans le Musée National de Belgrade*, ed. by Vladimir Kondić (Belgrade, 1976), pp. 63–71 (p. 64). It is well known that in 620–21, Emperor Heraclius ordered church-plate to be melted and later turned into gold and silver coins in order to pay the troops he needed for his campaign against Persia in 622–24. See Cyril Mango and Roger Scott, *The Chronicle*

position on the reverse exactly corresponding to the image of Honorius on the obverse.[42]

A detailed analysis of the reverse of the *Iussu Richiari Reges* siliqua further suggests that at stake with this coin was Braga, and not King Rechiar. The mint abbreviation *BR* is placed at the centre of the field, in association with the cross in the interior of the bay leaf wreath, and not in the exergue, as expected.[43] Normally on siliquae or tremisses with such an iconography, the mint mark appears in the exergue, as in the case of the inscription *Comob* on a tremissis of Marcian struck in Milan (Plate VI.3). When not shown in exergue, the mint mark is therefore given some special emphasis by the die engravers, as with the initials *BR* on Rechiar's siliqua. In doing so, the engravers deliberately put aside the longstanding tradition of placing the mint mark, even on solidi, within the monetary field flanking the main figure (see Figure 14.4 and Plates IX.1 and IX.2 below), and not inside a wreath (Plate VI.1). By contrast, on Rechiar's siliqua, the letters *BR* appear on the type of the reverse, in the middle of the crown. There must have therefore been some special reason for the engravers to stress the wreath, most likely because they also desired to highlight the mint mark *BR*. This is further substantiated by the presence on the reverse of a palm branch and of two additional garlands.

---

of Theophanes Confessor: Byzantine and Near Eastern History AD 284–813 (Oxford, 1997), p. 435. See also Walter E. Kaegi, *Heraclius Emperor of Byzantium* (Cambridge, 2003), p. 110. From the plate taken from pagan temples, Constantine was able to strike a great quantity of gold coins, for which see George Depeyrot, 'Economy and Society', in *The Cambridge Companion to the Age of Constantine,* ed. by Noel E. Lenski (Cambridge, 2006), pp. 226–52 (p. 237).

[42] During the first two centuries AD, several colonies and municipalities produced coins with wreaths of bay leaves on the reverse, as well as the name of the town in the centre. See, for example, the Julio-Claudian towns of Segobriga (Burnett, Amandry, and Ripollès Alegre, *Roman Provincial Coinage,* I.1, nos 473–77) and Ercavica (Burnett, Amandry, and Ripollès Alegre, *Roman Provincial Coinage,* I.1, no. 463). In other cases, it was also the rank of the city that was highlighted. See, for example, the rank of *colonia* for Colonia Patricia (Burnett, Amandry, and Ripollès Alegre, *Roman Provincial Coinage,* I.1, no. 129) and Acci (Burnett, Amandry, and Ripollès Alegre, *Roman Provincial Coinage,* I.1, nos 141–42); or that of *municipium* for Turiaso (Burnett, Amandry, and Ripollès Alegre, *Roman Provincial Coinage,* I.1, nos 405–06). For the monetary responsibilities of the curia and of the decurions, see Fergus Millar, 'Empire and City, Augustus to Julian: Obligations, Excuses and Status', *Journal of Roman Studies,* 73 (1983), 76–96, as well as the excellent work of Juan M. Abascal Palazón and Urbano Espinosa Ruiz, *La ciudad hispano-romana: Privilegio y poder* (Logroño, 1989), pp. 96, 113, 119, 136, 149, 155, and 199.

[43] Bolis, 'Legende circolari', p. 128: 'ogni moneta per se consente da comunicare un singolo coherente messagio sulle due facce, oppure una molteplicità di informazioni che mettono più o meno in relazione il dritto e il rovescio della moneta'.

Furthermore, many municipal coins of the early empire have the town name in the middle of the crown shown on the reverse, with the imperial portrait on the obverse. This monetary practice, which no doubt mirrors the urban growth in the Mediterranean region during the first three centuries AD, can still be recognized on the sixth-century civic issues of Rome, Ticinum, and Ravenna under Ostrogothic rule. It is therefore highly probable that the short-lived *Iussu Richiari Reges* issue had been struck at the expense of the city of Braga, which in turn may explain the choice of silver for minting the coin.[44] To have Rechiar's name inside the wreath on the reverse would have shifted the emphasis away from the city and onto the King himself, in the same way as the names of some Ostrogothic kings appearing on sixth-century coins struck in Rome (Plates VII.1 and VII.2).[45]

This series of siliquae bearing Rechiar's name must therefore be regarded as a commemorative issue celebrating the city of Braga as capital of the Suevic kings. However, the real meaning behind the striking of the coin has to be understood in terms similar to those applying to sesterces struck in Rome at some point between 140 and 144. The second-century coins celebrated the nomination by Emperor Antoninus Pius of a Quadian ('Suevic') king. Rechiar's siliqua bears no marks pointing to the transfer of *regalia* as shown on the second-century sesterce, but there can be little doubt as to the interpretation of the parallel between Honorius on the obverse and Rechiar on the reverse. If both are not found together within one and the same image, it is either because Rechiar did not receive kingship from Honorius himself, or because there was no physical contact with any other Roman emperor acting as his successor. At any rate, Honorius appears on the siliqua struck in Braga as the ruler who established Suevic royal authority. In conclusion, the siliqua in question must be regarded as an issue commemorating Rechiar's accession to the throne.

[44] Philip Grierson, 'The Role of Silver in the Early Byzantine Economy', in *Ecclesiastical Silver Plate: Papers of the Symposium Held May 16–18, 1986 at the Walters Art Gallery, Baltimore and Dumbarton Oaks, Washington D.C.*, ed. by Susan A. Boyd and Marlia Mundell Mango (Washington, DC, 1992), pp. 137–46 (p. 137): 'In times past the choice was between coin on the one hand, and silver plate or jewellery, on the other.'

[45] Such coins are known for Athanaric (526–34), Theodahad (534–36), Witigis (536–40), and Baduila (or Totila). See Wroth, *Catalogue*, pp. 67–68, 74–75, 77, 79, 86, and 88–91.

The Accession Issue Iussu Richiari Reges, *AD 449: Rechiar, King of the Sueves with the Consent of Theoderic I, King of the Visigoths*

In itself, the crown that surrounds the initials *BR* and the cross on the reverse of the siliqua constitutes evidence enough of the superior status of the city of Braga over the Suevic king Rechiar. However, neither the palm branch nor the two crowns depicted in the exergue of the reverse (Plate VI.1) can be explained away by such means. Both symbols were nevertheless viewed by the die engravers as of some significance, given the careful symmetry obtained for the lower part of the siliqua, as well as the corresponding formula *Iussu Richiari Reges* in the upper part.[46] Crowns had honorific connotations often used to distinguish a city in a monetary series. For instance, reverses of coins struck by Arles in the fourth century show crowns. Crowns were also employed to mark the distinction of a military unit, as is the case of some *vexillationes* which had participated in Victorinus's expedition of 270–71.[47] Pairs of crowns appear on reverses only when the purpose was to indicate the participation of two subjects in some common enterprise. For example, Valentinian I and Valens are both depicted with crowns in order to celebrate their joint rule on the *Virtus Romanorum* series of Valens struck in Constantinople in 364 (Plate VIII.1). Although several gold series also stressed the duality of the imperial government during the Valentinianic period, the *Virtus Romanorum* series of 364 is particularly interesting for commemorating Valens's accession to the throne. Similarly, the *Victores Augusti* solidi minted by Valentinian in Treveris celebrate the rise to the Augustan purple of Gratian in 367 (Figure 14.3). In this particular case, a senior Augustus (Valentinian) is described as raising to the purple a younger one (Gratian). The image on the obverse conveys the idea that Gratian's accession to the throne was in fact a co-optation, while on the obverse, the Emperor was depicted as wearing a star-shaped helmet and carrying a spear and a shield on the left. To drive the point home, the image of Valentinian on the reverse is considerably larger than that of Gratian, although both hold together the *globus mundi*. There are several other examples of such iconographic conventions throughout the Valentinianic and Theodosian period, and in all of

[46] Peixoto Cabral and Metcalf, *A Moeda sueva*, p. 45, view the design of the reverse as 'original, inventive, and elegant'. For some unknown reason, Juan R. Cayón, *Compendio de las monedas del imperio romano*, IV: *De Delmacio (335 d.C.) a Anastasio (491 d.C.)* (Madrid, 1985), p. 2871, no. 54, thinks the design is meant to represent a 'ram'.

[47] Bertrand Schulte, *Die Goldprägung der gallischen Kaiser von Postumus bis Tetricus* (Aarau, 1983), pp. 54–58.

Figure 14.3. Solidus, Treveris mint, 367, *DN Valen-s PF Aug/Victores Augusti/TR. Ob.*
After Cayón, *Compendio*, p. 2714, no. 30.

them crowns played a particularly significant role.[48] Those iconographic types were already well established during the reign of Diocletian, who in 293 began striking a series of *aurei* in Cyzicus, in order to celebrate the Tetrarchy. On the reverse, those coins showed two crowns distributed by Victoria, a hint at the pair of Augusti in the new form of imperial government (Plate VIII.2). The accompanying inscription in fact reads *Concordiae Augg NN* clearly pointing to two Augusti, even though the series were most likely intended to celebrate the accession to power of Maximin, the junior Augustus whom Diocletian had chosen to be his colleague.

Much of the symbolic language of the late third- and fourth-century coins was still at work in the 400s. To be sure, there is a tendency towards simplification, but the visual conventions remained the same. For example, tremisses were struck in 456–57 in Milan to celebrate the rise to power of the four emperors of Italy. What Guy Lacam has regarded as a small apex or a *chrism* on the cross shown on those tremisses is in fact the hand of God distributing the crowns. From a purely iconographic point of view, therefore, the Milan tremisses are therefore highly simplified versions of the solidi struck on a regular basis during the fifth century.[49] While on

[48] See, for example, the iconography of Gratian's solidi struck at some point between 378 and 383 in Thessalonica: J. W. E. Pearce, *The Roman Imperial Coinage*, IX: *Valentinian I–Theodosius I* (London, 1951), p. 179 no. 33ᵃ-R4 with pl. X, no. 3. The series may have been struck on the occasion of Theodosius's accession to power in 379.

[49] Guy Lacam, 'La Main de Dieu: son origine hébraïque, son symbolisme monétaire durant le Bas Empire romain', *Rivista Italiana di Numismatica*, 94 (1992), 143–61. Guy Lacam, *La Fin de l'empire romain et le monnayage d'or en Italie 45–493*, I (Lucerne, 1983), p. 147, mentions 'une sorte de crochet ou d'esse émanant du sommet de la Croix' for the tremisses of Marcianus struck in Milan in 456. See also the same explanation on p. 213 for the tremisses of Avitus, and on p. 307

a larger monetary flan, an emperor may be depicted standing between the cross and the crown (see Plate IX.2), on tremisses with a much smaller area of representation the crown is on top of a cross (Plate VI.3). At any rate, the crown shown on tremisses minted in Milan in 456–57 is a symbol of the proclamation by local troops of Avitus, Marcian (Plate VI.3), Leo, and Zeno as emperors.[50]

Although relatively rich in dual representations (Rome and Constantinople), the fifth-century coinage lacks any instance of two emperors being crowned by the same Victory. With the division of the empire in 395, the iconographic convention discussed here was abandoned on both eastern and western issues. However, it is not altogether impossible that the visual conventions of representing an imperial co-optation were the source of inspiration for the iconography of the *Iussu Richiari Reges* siliqua. On Rechiar's coin, one of the two crowns on the reverse may therefore be for the Suevic king. But for whom was the second crown, given that the idea of Rechiar's being co-opted by a Roman emperor is untenable? If we follow the conventions of the iconographic symbolism established in the fourth century, then that crown must have been for a person of a status almost equal to Rechiar's. In my opinion, that person can be no other than Theoderic I (419–51), king of the Visigoths at the time Rechiar was made king of the Suevi in 448/49. Theoderic I may have had a position higher than that of the Suevic king, since Rechiar travelled to Tolosa shortly after his accession to the throne in 448/49, in order to obtain recognition from Theoderic, in addition to the hand of a Visigothic king's daughter.[51] Had Rechiar been an independent and strong ruler, equal in status to the Visigothic king, he would have barely needed to travel to Tolosa in person in order to obtain an alliance. Quite the contrary seems to have been true: the Suevic king was in no way independent from the Visigothic kingdom of Tolosa. It is only in the light of such considerations that we can understand the true meaning of the 417 or 418 marriage of the Visigothic king Wallia's daughter to a Suevic nobleman. The matrimonial alliance established in that year is also the act of foundation for the royal house of Hermericus, for without the Visigothic alliance, the Sueves would not have been included in the *foedus* sealed between the Visigoths and the

---

for those of Maiorianus. Carson, Kent, and Burnett, *Roman Imperial Coinage*, x, 178–79, believe that the detail is just a 'flaw'.

[50] Fernando López Sánchez, 'Innovation et prestige dans le monnayage d'Avitus (455–456 ap. J.-C.)', *Cahiers Numismatiques*, 149 (2001), 23–36.

[51] Hydatius, *Chronicle*, 132 [140]. See also María Rosario Valverde, 'La monarquía visigoda y su política matrimonial: De Alarico I al fin del reino visigodo de Tolosa', *Aquitania*, 16 (1999), 295–315.

patricius Constantius.[52] From then on, however, the house of Hermericus owed loyalty to the Visigothic kings.

Rechiar's recognition as Suevic king by Theoderic I is indicated by more than just a matrimonial alliance.[53] While renewing the Suevic oath of allegiance to Theoderic, Rechiar obtained in return the Visigothic approval for his future actions, such as attacking the Basque area, as well as the Ebro Valley, the *Bacaudae*, raiding around Caesaraugusta, occupying Lerida, and taking a great number of prisoners. Since all those areas were close to the heart of the Visigothic kingdom in south-

[52] Hydatius, *Chronicle*, 63 [71]. For the significant role Hermericus had in shaping the Suevic military monarchy, see Javier Pampliega, *Los Germanos en España* (Pamplona, 1998), pp. 287–303. The treaty of 416 stipulated that Visigoths promised to fight against the barbarians that had settled in Hispania, to capture and deliver the usurper Priscus Attalus, and to return Galla Placidia. In exchange, they were to receive six hundred thousand measures of wheat. See Orosius, *History*, 7.43.12–13, ed. by Karl Friedrich W. Zangemeister (Vienna, 1882); Hydatius, *Chronicle*, 52 [60]; Prosper, *Chronicle*, a. 416, ed. by Theodor Mommsen, *Chronica Minora*, I (Berlin, 1892), pp. 341–499; Olympiodorus, *fr.* 30, ed. and trans. by Richard C. Blockley in *The Fragmentary Classicising Historians of the Later Roman Empire: Eunapius, Olympiodorus, Priscus and Malchus* (Liverpool, 1983), pp. 151–220. For a detailed analysis of the *foedus* of 416, see Pampliega, *Los Germanos*, pp. 178–82. Jordanes, *Getica*, 31 and 32, provides a very different view of the facts. He extols the leading role of the Visigoths and their own initiative in the confrontation with the Vandals. In Jordanes's version, the Visigoths appear as heroes with good intentions, who decide to free the inhabitants of Hispania of all sorrows caused by the Vandals. There has been much speculation about the reasons behind Constantius's decision to include the Sueves in the treaty. Some have argued that he feared that the Visigoths would become too strong after their defeat of the Alans and the Silingi in the relatively rich province of Baetica. Others pointed to a possible alliance between the Sueves and the Visigoths, given that Wallia had arranged the marriage of his daughter to a Suevic nobleman, a marriage from which the patrician Ricimer was born. See Sidonius Apollinaris, *Carmina*, 2.360–70, ed. by André Loyen, I (Paris, 1960); Andrew Gillett, 'The Birth of Ricimer', *Historia*, 44 (1995), 380–84. Other influencing factors may have been the usurpation of Maximus, who was supported by Gensericus, as well as a possible pact between Gensericus and the Visigoths. See Pampliega, *Los Germanos*, pp. 187–88. Finally, the inability of the empire to supply the *annona* to the Goths, as well as the concern with the growing influence of the *Bacaudae* movement may also have been on the mind of Constantius. For all these factors, see Purificación Ubric Rabaneda, *La Iglesia y los Estados bárbaros en la Hispania del siglo V (409–507)* (Granada, 2003), p. 106 with n. 413.

[53] García Moreno, *Historia*, p. 59, thinks that it was Theoderic I who wanted an alliance with the Sueves because of his fear about Attila's growing power. It is also rather logical to think that Rechiar travelled to see Theoderic in Tolosa because an alliance had already been in existence for some time. According to Pampliega, *Los Germanos*, pp. 319–20, when the daughter of King Theoderic I got married, Rechiar became his *Waffensohn* ('son of arms'), which would imply the existence of a pact between the Sueves and the Visigoths.

western Gaul, it is difficult to avoid the conclusion that Rechiar's actions may have been previously approved by the King in Tolosa.[54] Suevic raids in the foothills of the Pyrenees must have been the price for the renewal of Suevic oaths of allegiance to Theoderic I.

Given the connection between the Suevic military activity in the Ebro Valley and the Visigothic recognition of Rechiar as king of the Sueves, the palm branch between the two crowns shown on Rechiar's siliqua may be a subtle allusion to the Suevic expansion into north-eastern Spain. In this case, the palm branch did not point to any great military victory, such as that obtained by Victorinus upon the fall of Autun in 271, which caused the depiction of the palm branch on his coins of that same year.[55] Nor is the presence of a palm branch always a sign of a great military victory, as attested by the reverse on a denarius struck by the moneyer C. Marius in AD 13.[56] The palm branch on the *quadriga* shown on the reverse of that coin was meant as a symbol for Agrippa, who as Dio Cassius relates, did not consider himself worthy of a triumphal procession, since he had not completely defeated the Cimerii.[57] In the monetary tradition of Rome, the palm branch shown on coin reverses is not only a sign of victory, but also a symbol for any military campaign of some significance. This is certainly the case of the solidi struck early in AD 379 in Sirmium, and showing Gratian and Theodosius I seated, facing each other, and holding a globe between them with *Victoria* standing with her wings open (Plate VIII.3). The palm branch between the two Augusti points to a Roman victory, but the long sideburns depicted on the face of Gratian on the obverse are a symbol of mourning. Here, Gratian mourns his deceased uncle, namely Valens, who died at Adrianople in AD 378.

---

[54] Hydatius, *Chronicle* 132 [140]. According to Hydatius, *Chronicle*, 134 [142] and 163 [170], by the time Rechiar returned from the court of Theoderic, the Sueves had already ransacked Tarraconensis in alliance with the *Bacaudae*.

[55] Heinz-Joachim Schulzki, *Die Antoninianprägung der gallischen Kaiser von Postumus bis Tetricus: Typenkatalog der regulären und nachgeprägten Münzen* (Bonn, 1996), pl. 15, no. 6.

[56] C. H. V. Sutherland, *The Roman Imperial Coinage*, I: *From 31 BC to AD 69* (London, 1984), p. 72, no. 399. The empty *quadriga* on the denarius alludes to Agrippa's gesture of rejecting the triumph while, and very obviously, the palm branch is a symbol of the triumph itself.

[57] Dio Cassius, *Roman History*, 54.24, ed. by Earnest Cary (London, 1924): 'he did not succeed in subduing them until Agrippa arrived in Sinope to lead an expedition against them. Once they discovered this, they laid down their arms and surrendered to Polemon. [...] Sacrifices were offered in Agrippa's name on the occasion of these successes. [...] Agrippa formally declined to celebrate the triumph which was voted.'

During the fifth century, issues with palm branches on monetary reverse are frequently associated with military campaigns. In 422, Honorius struck in Ravenna a series of solidi with a palm branch on the reverse between the representations of Rome and Constantinople (Plate IX.1). The type of the obverse suggests that the palm branch must be linked with some important military activity ending in success for Honorius, perhaps the victory over the Spanish usurper Maximus, which is dated to the same period.[58] As a consequence, the palm branch on the *Iussu Richiari Reges* siliqua struck in Braga most likely hints at the Suevic military activity in the Ebro Valley region. If so, then the siliqua must have been struck in 449, shortly after Rechiar's coronation and trip to Tolosa. The iconography of the coin conveys the idea that although Honorius was ultimately responsible for the creation of a Suevic kingdom, such a polity would not have been possible without Visigothic protection. It was the Visigothic, and not the Suevic, king who in 418 entered an alliance with Ravenna, to which most Visigothic rulers remained loyal throughout the fifth century. As a consequence, the siliqua of Braga added two crowns and a victory palm branch to the iconography, which, despite several parallels in the imperial coinage, must be understood as symbols of Theoderic I's recognition of and alliance with Rechiar in 449.

The Suevic Solidi with Mint Marks MD: *The Suevic Kings as Guardians of Hispania*

As military commander in the service of Rome, Hermericus (418–41) had to make a demonstration of his skills in Hispania. His 429 campaign against the Vandals of Hermigiarius in Mérida most certainly served that purpose.[59] The campaign may be viewed as a continuation of that carried out by Visigothic troops in 416–18 against the Vandals in Betica and Gallaecia. Hermericus, a member of the noble line of Suevic kings, was acting on behalf of the Roman authority and, as a consequence, his men must have enjoyed the same status as the Visigoths of 418.[60] The

---

[58] Maximus was executed together with Jovinus in Italy in 422, on the occasion of Honorius's *tricennalia*. See Jordanes, *Romana*, 326; Ubric Rabaneda, *La Iglesia*, p. 59 with n. 182.

[59] Incidentally, judging from his name, Hermigiarius may have been a relative of Hermericus.

[60] The militaristic theory of J. H. W. G. Liebeschuetz, 'Alaric's Goths: Nation or Army', in *Fifth-Century Gaul: A Crisis of Identity*, ed. by John Drinkwater and Hugh Elton (Cambridge, 1992), pp. 75–84, can equally be applied to the Sueves in Spain.

Suevic king led a carefully planned campaign against the most important town in Hispania and the most powerful army in the Peninsula, that of the Vandals.[61]

As Luis A. García Moreno once noted, the *exercitus hispanicus* was nowhere to be found or, at least, remained completely inactive at the time of the barbarian invasion of 409. Instead the Roman government preferred to rely on barbarian allies. Most, if not all, of those during Honorius's and Valentinian III's reigns were Visigoths, but in Hispania Interior there were also Sueves from 411 onwards. It is against the background of the Sueves in the service of Rome that one needs to understand the importance of the military operation carried out on their behalf in the Nervasii Mountains.[62] This is also the background against which one needs to evaluate the significance of Hermericus's rise to the Suevic throne and of the relation of his house to the Visigothic kings in Tolosa. Much like the Franks of Childeric and Clovis were acting during the second half of the fifth century in lieu of the Rhine legions in Gaul, the Sueves of Hermericus were viewed as replacement for the long-absent Roman troops of north-western Spain. Braga was a provincial capital controlling access to the river Douro, to Gaul, and southwards to Mérida.[63] Not only did Honorius create a royal house with Hermericus, but Ravenna assigned a capital to the rising Suevic kings from which they could act militarily on behalf of the Roman authorities. In that respect, in 418–56 Braga was certainly the most important military centre in the entire Iberian Peninsula.[64]

As evidence that the Suevic expansion into Hispania started from Braga, J. M. Peixoto Cabral and David M. Metcalf cite thirty solidi found in 1972 in a well-recorded hoard from Seville. All had been freshly struck in the name of Honorius,

---

[61] Ubric Rabaneda, *La Iglesia*, pp. 194–211 and 222–34; Jorge López Quiroga and Mónica Rodríguez Lovelle, 'De los vándalos a los suevos en Galicia: una visión crítica sobre su instalación y organización territorial en el noroeste de la Península Ibérica en el siglo V', *Studia Historica: Historia Antigua*, 13–14 (1995–96), 405–20; Jorge López Quiroga and Mónica Rodríguez Lovelle, 'De los Romanos a los Bárbaros: la instalación de los Suevos y sus consecuencias sobre la organización territorial en el Norte de Portugal (411–469)', *Studi Medievali*, 38 (1997), 529–60.

[62] For Asterius's expedition to Gallaecia some time later, see Michael Kulikowski, 'The Career of the *Comes Hispaniarum* Asterius', *Phoenix*, 54 (2000), 123–41.

[63] From Braga one could monitor access to the strategic route linking Astorga to Bordeaux. See Gerd. G. König, 'Wandalische Grabfunde des 5 und 6 Jahrhunderts', *Madrider Mitteilungen*, 22 (1981), 299–360 (p. 355); Pampliega, *Los Germanos*, p. 214.

[64] Pío Beltrán Villagrasa, 'Las primeras monedas Suevas', *Caesaraugusta*, 7–8 (1957) 115–29 (p. 127), believed that around 420, at the time the Vandals left Gallaecia, the Sueves had already obtained from Emperor Honorius the right to strike their own coins.

and all were imitations of the *MD* series minted in Milan.[65] According to Peixoto Cabral and Metcalf, those solidi confirm not only that Suevic solidi were different from the model they imitated in respect to the type of *signifer* Honorius on the right side (an emperor crushing a barbarian) with a mint mark *MD*, but also that such solidi were minted in Seville in 441. This series of a purely military character must have been coined in order to commemorate the Suevic conquest of the city.[66] Whether the thirty hoard solidi were minted in Seville or in northern Portugal, as seems to be the case of most other Suevic coins known so far, remains unclear.[67] The collection of coins in the hoard found in Seville in 1972 was certainly assembled well after 441, given that it was buried after 527. The coins in that collection also belong to two very different groups, forty solidi and eighteen tremisses, all non-Suevic solidi being Visigothic imitations. The Visigothic coins must have been hoarded for their intrinsic value and not in any relation to the mint of origin. There is no reason to believe that this was in any way different from the thirty Suevic coins, which could well have been struck in Braga to be later hoarded in Seville.[68] No other Suevic solidus with the mint mark *MD* related to any Suevic campaign has been found in Mérida or in any other city in southern Hispania.[69]

Except the Seville hoard, most finds of Suevic solidi cluster around Braga and thus strongly suggest that the military capital of the kingdom was there, and not in Mérida or anywhere else in the Peninsula.[70] If, therefore, Braga had always been

[65] Peixoto Cabral and Metcalf, *A Moeda sueva*, p. 56: 'They are enough to remove any remaining doubt that the type is Suevic.'

[66] Peixoto Cabral and Metcalf, *A Moeda sueva*, p. 54: 'It is easy to imagine that King Rechila [...] was the first who wished to strike gold coins. That is pure speculation. But it might make good sense of the Seville hoard, particularly if the Honorian solidi in it are imitative. Perhaps they were struck in Seville, where skilled craftsmen were available. That, again, is pure speculation.'

[67] Many of those coins, now in Portuguese collections, are known to have been found in northern Portugal. See Peixoto Cabral and Metcalf, *A Moeda sueva*, pp. 55–56: 'they are now known to have been found in considerable numbers in Portugal and far more so than elsewhere'.

[68] The campaign against Seville does not seem to have been particularly difficult for the Sueves. As a matter of fact, the city surrendered without any major problem for the conquerors. See Purificación Ubric Rabaneda, 'La adaptación de la aristocracia hispanorromana al dominio bárbaro (409–507)', *Polis*, 16 (2004), 197–212; Ubric Rabandeda, *La Iglesia*, pp. 72–78.

[69] As Peixoto Cabral and Metcalf, *A Moeda sueva*, p. 56, rightly point out, had *MD* solidi been struck in the cities of Baetica or Cartaginensis, many more specimens would have been found in the southern region of the Peninsula than in northern Portugal.

[70] In 439 Rechila entered Mérida (Hydatius, *Chronicle*, 111 [119]), where he also died nine years later, when he was succeeded by his son Rechiar (Hydatius, *Chronicle*, 129 [137]). The idea

the military capital of the Sueves, as indicated, among others things, by the fact that their kingdom was brought down when the Visigoths attacked the city in 456, then the Suevic military strategy must have been very Roman in style. For it was very much in the Roman tradition to concentrate all troops available in a region within one and the same town away from the frontier, in order to have them ready in a secure location. Such a military strategy would explain very well why there are more Suevic solidi from Portugal than from either Seville or Mérida. It would also provide an explanation for choosing *MD* as a mint mark for the Suevic solidi (Plate VI.3). There is a wide variety of mint marks on Roman coins found in the Iberian Peninsula, but not many specimens displaying *MD* in reference to Milan.[71] To be sure, *RV* would have perhaps made more sense than *MD*, given that Ravenna, not Milan, was the capital of the Western Empire.[72] This, at least, is the case of the Visigothic coins struck in Tolosa, most likely in recognition of the special relationship between Ravenna and the Visigoths during the reign of Emperor Valentinian III. The strong position the Visigoths had within the Western Empire and the fact that their kings were well aware of their importance results, first of all, from the mint mark change appearing on Visigothic coins after the deaths of Aetius and Emperor Valentinian in 454 and 455, respectively. From this moment onwards, as if to point out the Visigothic autonomy to the government in Ravenna, Visigothic solidi would bear the mark *RA* for Arles, a clear reminder of the strong position the Visogothic kings had in southern Gaul.[73] The adoption of a mint abbreviation referring to Milan looks like a voluntary militaristic sphere of competence for the Sueves. Ever since the third century, Milan was a military centre of Italy, its location serving to protect the Italian Peninsula in all directions. While choosing *MD* as a mint mark on their coins, the Suevic kings must have thought of their position

that Mérida functioned for a while as a Suevic capital is nothing more than a tempting hypothesis, for which see Luís A. García Moreno, 'Mérida y el reino visigodo de Tolosa (418–507)', in *Homenaje a J. Sáenz de Buruaga* (Badajoz, 1982), pp. 227–40 (p. 230); García Moeno, *Historia*, p. 56. If the Sueves ever had any capital other than Braga, then that could only have been the result of their military role in the Peninsula.

[71] Peixoto Cabral and Metcalf, *A Moeda sueva*, p. 47.

[72] Peixoto Cabral and Metcalf, *A Moeda sueva*, pp. 54–55: 'MD mark [...] should have been regarded as a necessary part of a well recognized design. The practice of imitation was not haphazard in the barbarian kingdoms.'

[73] Depeyrot, 'Émissions wisigothiques', p. 85. For the Visigoths in southwestern Gaul, see Guy Lacam, 'Teodoric II et la mutation sur les solidi wisigoths R-V en R-A', *Nomismatika Chronika*, 9 (1990), pp. 33–42 (pp. 41–42).

in Braga as a city capital of a province from which they could have controlled a significant part of Hispania.[74] To the Sueves Braga seems to have been what Tolosa was to the Visigoths: the undisputed centre of their political and military power.

The Suevic *MD* solidus issue was short-lived: no such coins are known to have been struck in the name of Emperor Valentinian, despite the fact that there are quite a number of tremisses bearing his name. It is possible that the minting of solidi in Emperor Honorius's name continued after his death, alongside that of tremisses for Emperor Valentinian. Solidi for Honorius with the inscription *Oho* in exergue appear to be later than those with the mark *Comob* and may be compared with late Valentinianic tremisses bearing the same abbreviation.[75] The small production of tremisses in the name of Honorius suggests that replacing Honorius with Valentinian took place on Suevic tremisses, but not on solidi. Striking solidi in the name of Honorius at the same time as tremisses in the name of Valentinian is a phenomenon with Visigothic parallels.[76] The kings of Tolosa struck imitative coins in the name of Libius Severus during his reign, but also abundantly after his death, as well as during the reign of Antemius, Glycerius, and Olybrius. After the death of Romulus Augustulus, Tolosa began to strike imitative tremisses in the name of the emperors in Constantinople, Zeno and Basiliscus, but never solidi. There are many stylistic parallels between Visigothic tremisses in the name of Zeno and the solidi struck in the name of Severus, which highlight the fact that solidi and tremisses with divergent imperial inscriptions were in fact minted at the same time.[77] The main explanation for such a bizarre combination of denominations and imperial names lies in the decision the imperial government took to allow the Visigothic kings to mint coins. According to Procopius, there was much indignation

[74] Peixoto Cabral and Metcalf, *A Moeda sueva*, p. 54: 'solidi of Honorius were the last issues of imperial gold to reach Spain in quantity'.

[75] Peixoto Cabral and Metcalf, *A Moeda sueva*, pp. 57–58.

[76] The solidi in question must have been struck over a long period, since 'they show a wide range of style, from excellent imitations of a Milanese original to very crude copies on a reduced weight standard and of debased alloy' (Peixoto Cabral and Metcalf, *A Moeda sueva*, pp. 35 and 53–58).

[77] Depeyrot, 'Émissions wisigothiques', pp. 96–97: 'apparition d'une croix sur l'épaule de Sévère III (solidus 2 et solidus 3/9) sans doute à mettre en relation avec la croix frontale ou ponctuant certains *tremisses* de Zénon (*tremisses type* 6); adjonction d'un S à la légende de revers sur les *solidi* comme sur les *tremisses* de Zénon (*solidus* de Sévère n° 3/6, *tremisses* de Zénon n° 4). Sur les *tremisses*: influence de la césure du *solidus* sur celle des *tremisses*'. See also Cathy E. King, 'Roman, Local and Barbarian Coinages in Fifth-Century Gaul', in *Fifth-Century Gaul*, ed. by Drinkwater and Elton, pp. 184–95 (p. 191), which follows George Depeyrot.

at the court in Constantinople when news arrived that the Frankish king Theude-
bert (534–47) had decided to depict himself on gold coins.[78] This suggests that
even in the sixth century the monetary hierarchy was carefully monitored. Without
any doubt, such a supervision of monetary competence must have been even more
scrupulously observed in the fifth century. After the death of Severus in 467, kings
in Tolosa were not allowed to put the imperial effigy on their coins. This must of
course be understood as a sign that no relations existed between Ravenna and the
Visigothic kings during the final years of the Western Empire. The absence of contacts at the imperial court thus explains the lack of any new monetary inscriptions
on the Visigothic coins struck during the reign of Euric. Only after his envoys were
received by Emperor Zeno in Constantinople was there a renewal of the Visigothic
coin types in use since the death of Severus.[79] Emperor Zeno allowed Euric to strike
coins in his name, but only tremisses, not solidi. Such a careful distinction suggests
that the relations between the Visigoths and Constantinople were not very close,
since to strike one type or another and to receive one coin or another had always
been a matter of measuring status in Roman terms. Tremisses were viewed as of
second rank in comparison with solidi. Charity as practiced by women of the imperial house in Constantinople was measured in tremisses, while imperial *donativa*
were counted in solidi.[80] As a consequence, if the kings of Tolosa did not strike
solidi in the name of Zeno, it was most likely because they were not viewed as
worthy of being awarded that privilege by the emperors in Constantinople.[81]

By way of analogy, if the Suevic coinage was anything like the Visigothic one
after the death of Severus, then we must conclude that relations between Braga and
Ravenna must have been rather cool throughout the fifth century. The kings of the
Sueves could of course strike solidi in the name of Honorius ever since Hermericus

---

[78] Procopius of Caesarea, *Wars*, 8.33.

[79] Euric sent an embassy to Basiliscus to deal with Nepos: Michel Rouche, *L'Aquitaine des
Wisigoths aux Arabes (418–781): essai sue le phénomène régional* (Lille, 1977), p. 42.

[80] Pierre Bastien, *Monnaie et donativa au Bas-Empire* (Wetteren, 1988). For female charity
measured in tremisses, see Carson, Kent, and Burnett, *Roman Imperial Coinage*, X, 12.

[81] Following Wilhelm Reinhart, 'Die Münzen des tolosanischen Reiches der Wesgoten',
Deutches Jahrbuch für Numismatik, 1 (1938), 107–35, Carson, Kent, and Burnett, *Roman Imperial
Coinage*, X, 462, no. 3769, believe a series of solidi with the name Zeno to be a Visigothic imitative
coin. However, Reinhart's attribution remains uncertain. See Depeyrot, 'Émissions wisigothiques',
p. 97 with n. 52.

Figure 14.4. Suevic solidus with mark *MD*, 418–56, *DN Honori-us PF Aug.* After Peixoto Cabral and Metcalf, *A Moeda sueva*, p. 236, no. 2; pl. 1, no. 2.

was recognized as *rex Sueuorum*.[82] The treaty of 418 and the remarkable style of many Suevic solidi are strong arguments in favour of such a conclusion (Figure 14.4). But after 418, the position of the Suevic kings in relation to the Roman power was clearly following the model of the Roman-Visigothic relations. That is why Hydatius has no mention of any treaty before 453–54 between the Sueves and the imperial court or *magister militum*. As a consequence, the Suevic kings were not permitted to strike coins in the name of Valentinian, as no agreement with the court in Ravenna existed after 418. The new treaty was undertaken only due to a Visigothic intervention, and only a short time before the death of Valentinian; it therefore could not contribute to any rapprochement between the Sueves and Ravenna. Since its inception, the Suevic kingdom grew in the shadow of the Visigothic power. Although solidi in the name of Honorius were struck in Braga, the absence of Valentinian's name on tremisses points to the distancing of the Suevic kings from the imperial power in Ravenna. The issue of tremisses in the name of Valentinian must not be understood as a rapprochement between the Suevic kings and the imperial court. The imitative solidi struck in the name of Honorius with the mark *MD* minted provide evidence for the agreement between the imperial court and the Visigothic kings: the Sueves with their army had to defend Hispania for Ravenna.[83]

[82] Pío Beltrán Villagrasa may have been mistaken when considering that only silver coins were struck by the Sueves, while the striking of gold coins was restricted to the emperor. But he certainly was right when noting that different denominations could derive from different authorities in the fifth century. See Villagrasa, 'Las primeras monedas Suevas', p. 127.

[83] For the growing importance of the Hispania Interior during the fifth century, see Fernando López Sánchez, 'Coinage, Iconography and the Changing Political Geography of the Fifth-Century Hispania', in *Hispania in Late Antiquity: Current Perspectives,* ed. by Kim Bowes and Michael Kulikowski (Leiden, 2005), pp. 487–518.

The Suevic Tremisses in Relation to the Visigothic Solidi, AD 439 (and not 453–54): Rechila and Rechiar, reges totius Hispaniae

Beginning with 439 the Visigothic kings of Tolosa struck large quantities of solidi in imitation of the most common type at that time, the human-headed serpent.[84] Although similar in many details to the imperial solidi, the Visigothic coins have nonetheless less gold in composition,[85] in addition to a small crown above the portrait of Emperor Valentinian III (Plate IX.2). Small crowns with hands appear on obverses of fifth-century solidi issued for female members of the imperial family and have been interpreted as a symbol of those women's dependence upon their husbands.[86] This is why emperors were never depicted being crowned on *obverses*, although portraits of emperors crowned as military commanders often appear on reverses. A prominent exception to this rule is a bronze series AE2 with the name of Arcadius issued in 383. Arcadius is shown on the reverse with a spear in his left hand and a shield in the right, a clear sign that this particular coin struck by Theodosius was meant to present his son as the new Augustus in front of the eastern troops (Figure 14.5). Theodosius's *quinquennalia*, as well as the military and political events in the West, marked by the usurpation of Maximus, delineate the circumstances in which Arcadius was raised to the purple on 19 January 383.[87] The series of 383 is obviously not meant to depict Arcadius as a great sovereign, but as dependant upon the military support of his father. The crown above the portrait

---

[84] The type had been struck first in northern Gaul by a Roman authority, not by barbarians. See Depeyrot, 'Émissions wisigothiques', p. 86. The date 439 is that of the treaty with Aetius established in Tolosa, for which see Prosper 1338, ed. by Th. Mommsen, *Chronica Minora*, I, 477: 'Pax cum Gothis facta, cum eam post ancipitis pugnae lacrimabile experimentum humilius quam [unquam] antea poposcissent'. Jordanes, *Getica*, 177, has a different version of the event, but confirms the existence of the treaty.

[85] The Visigothic solidus has about 75 per cent gold, the remaining 25 per cent being silver. Since the Roman state prohibited the circulation of lightweight solidi within its territory, the Visigothic coins must have been in circulation only within those territories which were under Visigothic control. See Depeyrot, 'Émissions wisigothiques', p. 82.

[86] In her desire to reaffirm the power of the threatened Theodosian dynasty, Pulcheria closed the door on any military attempts to gain power. She imposed quasi-monastic, ascetic rules at the court and extolled the cult of virginity. See Kenneth G. Holum, *Theodosian Empresses: Women and Imperial Dominion in Late Antiquity* (Berkeley, 1982), p. 227.

[87] Harold Mattingly and others, *The Roman Imperial Coinage*, IX: *Valentinian I–Theodosius I* (London, 1968), p. xx.

Figure 14.5. AE2, Arcadius, Constantinople, 383–86. After
Philip Grierson and Melinda Mays, *Catalogue of Late Roman
Coins in the Dumbarton Oaks Collection and in the Whittemore
Collection: From Arcadius and Honorius to the Accession of Anas-
tasius* (Washington, DC, 1992), p. 347, no. 9; pl. 1, no. 9.

of Arcadius does not symbolize any special power
granted upon him, but simply the continuity of
power which Theodosius secured for his son.

The appearance of a crown above the portrait of
Valentinian III on Visigothic coins must be interpreted in the same way. The 439 treaty with Aetius
and Valentinian III reflected the inability of the Roman government to control the situation in Gaul.[88]
It also mirrored the increasing autonomy of Tolosa in
regard to Valentinian and, as a matter of fact, his own
reliance upon the Visigoths for the preservation and
continuity of imperial power in the West. As a con-

sequence, the little crown added on top of Valentinian III's portrait on the
Visigothic solidi is not a mere detail, but a subtle way to emphasize the authority
the kings in Tolosa exercised over the son of Galla Placidia. To underline even
more its de facto autonomy, Tolosa also abandoned the cross on the reverse of
tremisses struck in the name of the Visigothic kings and replaced it with an image
of the imperial Victoria. Since during the sixth century, Victoria was also adopted
by Leovigild in order to replace the cross on the Byzantine coins, as a sign of
independence from Constantinople, the image of the imperial Victoria on the
coins struck in Tolosa may be interpreted in the same way. Georges Depeyrot even
believed that both innovations (the crown on the solidi and the imperial Victoria
on the tremisses) effectively put an end to the Visigothic imitative issues and
turned them into a genuinely new coinage. According to Depeyrot, with both

[88] The exact date of the treaty is 19 January 439; see Prosper 1339, ed. by Mommsen, p. 477;
Hydatius, *Chronicle*, 155; *Adnotationes antiquoires ad cyclos dionysianos*, s.a. 439, ed. by Theodor
Mommsen, *Chronica minora*, I, 755; *Laterculus Regum Wandalorum et Alanorum*, s.a. 439, ed. by
Theodor Mommsen, *Chronica minora*, III, 456–60. See also Christian Courtois, *Les Vandales et
l'Afrique* (Paris, 1955), p. 171.

those innovations on solidi and tremisses,[89] the Roman-Visigothic treaty of 439 made it possible for Aetius to move his forces against the Vandals in Africa.[90] However, and despite their initial hostility, the Vandals managed to obtain a similar treaty from the Roman government in 442.[91]

Within such a political context, in which Ravenna seems to have been forced to acknowledge a number of barbarian kingdoms in existence within the borders of the empire, it is unlikely that the Sueves remained outside the new international order. Their opposition to the new political settlement would have provoked Aetius's intervention in Hispania, a campaign that never took place. As Juan C. Sánchez León rightly notes, the Suevic expansion in the 440s into the provinces of Lusitania, Baetica, and Cartaginensis was much favoured by the new international situation.[92] Since there is no mention in Hydatius of any Suevic treaty with the empire or with Aetius during those years, the autonomy of Visigothic kings in Hispania and its de facto recognition by the Roman government may have been the result of the Visigothic protection.[93] As a smaller branch of the royal family in Tolosa, the house of Hermericus, now represented by King Rechila (438–48), was protected by the stipulation of the Visigothic-Roman treaty of 439.[94] In other

[89] Depeyrot, 'Émissions wisigothiques', p. 86: 'nous ne sommes plus dans le cas des frappes serviles d'imitations, mais au contraire dans un contexte politique d'instauration d'un nouveau monnayage'.

[90] The Vandals had meanwhile occupied Carthage in a brilliant coup that surprised both Prosper and his contemporaries. See Prosper 1339, ed. by Mommsen, p. 477. See also Guido Berndt's contribution to this volume.

[91] Prosper 1342, 1344, 1346, 1347, ed. by Mommsen, pp. 478–79; Courtois, *Les Vandales*, pp. 172–73; Frank M. Clover, 'Geiseric the Statesman: A Study of Vandal Foreign Policy' (unpublished doctoral dissertation, University of Chicago, 1966), pp. 68–78.

[92] Juan C. Sánchez León, *Los bagaudas: rebeldes, demonios, mártires. Revueltas campesinas en Galia e Hispania durante el Bajo Imperio* (Jaén, 1996), p. 65. In 439 Rechila entered Emerita Augusta (Hydatius, *Chronicle*, 111 [119]). García Moreno, 'Mérida y el reino visigodo', p. 230; García Moreno, *Historia*, p. 56, believed that taking over the capital of Lusitania, which would later become the see of the Hispanic diocese, gave the Suevic king the opportunity to control what was left of the administrative Roman system in that province. According to Hydatius, *Chronicle*, 115 [123], after taking Hispalis, the Sueves were de facto rulers of both Baetica and Cartaginensis.

[93] As a consequence, there is in fact no such thing as Valentinianic politics in Hispania against the barbarians, only Aetian politics. See Zecchini, *Aezio*, pp. 191–99. However, Hydatius, *Chronicle*, 126 [134], attests to the existence of a Visigothic-Suevic alliance against Aetius.

[94] Relations with Aetius were therefore tougher than expected. Aetius ordered Rechila to kill *comes* Censorius, his own representative in Hispania, who was eventually murdered in Hispalis by

words, the Suevic kings followed their Visigothic protectors as minor partners in a barbarian alliance. It is therefore likely that the first Suevic tremisses in the name of Valentinian were first struck in or shortly after 439 and not at a later date, such as 453–54, as initially advanced by Peixoto Cabral and Metcalf.[95] According to them, only direct relations established between the Suevic kings and Ravenna could have justified the striking of tremisses in the name of Valentinian III. Given the stylistic variation between specimens of the Valentinianic tremissis series, Peixoto Cabral and Metcalf proposed wide chronological brackets for the entire issue, namely between 453 and the date of the *Latina Munita* series, *c.* 559.[96] In support of this late and rather long chronology, they also cite the argument of the tremisses with the inscription *Valentinianus* on the obverse and a corrupted mint mark abbreviation in the exergue (*Oho*), two features that also appear on mid- to late sixth-century specimens of the *Latina Munita* series.[97]

However, the vast majority of Valentinianic tremisses have a correctly rendered legend on the obverse (*Valentinianus*) and the conventional mint mark *Comob* or *Conob* in the exergue. There is therefore no reason to treat those coins as late along Metcalf's line of reasoning. Nor is it necessary to assume that the Valentinianic tremisses spread over the entire period between 453 and 559.[98] On the contrary, we should envision an intensive production over several, short periods of time, an interpretation otherwise supported by the existence of obverse and reverse die links

Agilulfus. See Hydatius, *Chronicle*, 113 [121] and 131 [139]. According to Hydatius, *Chronicle*, 106 [114], his deteriorating health had convinced Hermericus to pass the royal crown in 438 unto his son Rechila. Hermericus died three years later (Hydatius, *Chronicle*, 114 [122]). Nothing is known about his possible involvement, during the last years of his life, in the politics of the realm. For Rechila and his achievements, see Pampliega, *Los Germanos*, pp. 303–12.

[95] Peixoto Cabral and Metcalf, *A Moeda sueva*, pp. 77–78, regard much of the literature on the Valentinianic tremisses as of little if any value.

[96] Peixoto Cabral and Metcalf, *A Moeda sueva*, p. 77: 'Some of the Valentinianic tremisses are certainly late in date, and many of them may be. A survey of their style encourages that view.'

[97] According to Metcalf, the Valentinianic tremisses 'are not stylistic groups in the sense that all the coins in each group are related by style'. As a consequence, if some of them may be of a later date, all of them must be of that same date. As a consequence, 'the majority of the surviving tremisses (and the reduced-weight solidi) belong to the "second kingdom"'. There is an *R* on the reverse of the tremisses with the deformed inscription Valentinianus, which Metcalf compares to specimens of the sixth-century *Latina Munita* series. Equally late, according to him, must be the mark *N*. See Peixoto Cabral and Metcalf, *A Moeda sueva*, pp. 70 and 77; pls 13–15.

[98] Peixoto Cabral and Metcalf, *A Moeda sueva*, p. 77.

between various tremisses of the 'spear-head' type.[99] Since there is a good number of 'spear-head' or similar tremisses within the Valentinianic tremissis series, most, if not all of them must have been struck within a relatively short period of time.[100] The political circumstances explaining such a decision dovetail better with the reign of Valentinian III than with any later period.[101] The appearance of the name *Valentinianus* on Suevic tremisses has to be regarded as a parallel to the above-mentioned Visigothic monetary innovations of 439, especially if taking into consideration the political dependence of the Suevic kings upon the regime in Tolosa. That the Suevic kings issued no solidi with the name *Valentinianus* may therefore be interpreted as their recognition that that was an exclusive privilege of the Visigothic kings. The monetary mechanism adopted by Sueves and Visigoths mirrors those in use in Tolosa under King Euric. The least powerful partner (the Sueves) had the right to strike only tremisses in the name of the reigning sovereign. By contrast, the more powerful partner (the Visigoths) had the right to strike both tremisses and solidi.

Suevic tremisses present no innovations comparable to those on Visigothic issues after 439. To be sure, there is a final development of the 'butterfly wings' design, which initially appeared on coins struck in the name of Honorius (Figure 14.6b). The purpose of that design seems to have been to highlight the honorific nature of the central crown.[102] In the lower part of this design, the crown ribbons stretch across the monetary field to reach its border, forming a semicircle (Figure 14.6.a). The 'butterfly wings' design is in fact created by the repetition of the same motif in the upper half of the monetary field, with the ribbons of the small crown

---

[99] Peixoto Cabral and Metcalf, *A Moeda sueva*, p. 72: 'At least eight specimens with spear-head share an obverse die, and at least six of them are also from the same reverse die. [...] The dies in question were evidently heavily used.'

[100] Peixoto Cabral and Metcalf, *A Moeda sueva*, p. 57: 'close stylistic similarity would be a good argument for saying that a group of coins was produced in the same mint and at roughly the same date, but the opposite does not follow'. Given the great variety of styles among Valentinianic tremisses, it is difficult to know whether they were all late, as Peixoto Cabral and Metcalf would have it. Nor is it readily evident that they all coincide in time, for some could certainly be later copies of older specimens, as seems to have been the case for solidi struck in the name of Honorius. The only certainty is that a group of Valentinianic tremisses, which is much larger than Peixoto Cabral and Metcalf initially assumed, appears to be of an early date, which fits better the political circumstances of 439 than those of 453–54. For tremisses similar to the 'spear-head' coins, see Peixoto Cabral and Metcalf, *A Moeda sueva*, pp. 271–78.

[101] George Depeyrot, *Les Bas Empire Romain: économie et numismatique (284–491)* (Paris, 1987), p. 91, writes of 456 as a 'terme définitif aux émissions suèves'.

[102] Peixoto Cabral and Metcalf, *A Moeda sueva*, pp. 256–57.

Figure 14.6 (above, left (a) and right (b)). Suevic tremisses
(only reverses), 418–39, *DN Honori-us PF Aug*. After Peixoto
Cabral and Metcalf, *A Moeda sueva*, p. 256, no. 2; pl. 1, no. 2.

Figure 14.7 (right). Suevic tremissis with spear-head mark,
439–56, *DN Valentinianus PF Aug/Comob*. Peixoto Cabral
and Metcalf, *A Moeda sueva*, p. 260, no. 1; pl. 7, no. 1.

(Figures 14.6b and 14.7).[103] If the Valentinianic tremisses began to be struck in 439
or shortly after that, the introduction of the spearhead on the obverse may be a sign
of a strictly military task accomplished by the Suevic king(s) (Figure 14.7). The
association of a spear with a person from the royal house was a traditional symbol
for the situation in which a *princeps iuventutis* accomplished the military task
assigned to him, without interfering in politics at the highest level. Such symbolism
applies, for instance, to the Frankish king Childeric, whose spearhead may have
pointed to a particularly worthy army in Roman service and to himself as a military
legate of Roman power in the region (Figure 14.1). The king of the Lombards, who
exercised considerable military power in Italy in the late sixth and throughout the
seventh century, used spears as a symbol of their military authority, although they
preferred to call themselves *reges totius Italiae*, and never assumed, like Theoderic
the Great, the title of *Pius Princ(eps) I(nvictus) S(emper)*.[104] Perhaps they showed

---

[103] The meaning of the 'butterfly wings' design is always linked to the recognition of some
extraordinary service for Rome. Crowns are usually employed in Roman series to symbolize the
imperial reward for worthy troops, as in the case of Victorinus's legionary series, which was struck
in Colonia in 271. See Fernando López Sánchez, 'La Série légionaire de Victorin et ses emblèmes *ad
hoc*', in *Recherches et Travaux de la Société d'Études Numismatiques et Archéologiques (SÉNA) n° 1:
Actes de la journée d'études du 10 décembre 2005*, ed. by Dominique Hollard (Paris, 2006), pp. 37–49.

[104] Stefano Gasparri, 'Kinsghip and Ideology in Lombard Italy', in *Rituals of Power: From Late
Antiquity to the Early Middle Ages*, ed. by Frans Theuws and Janet L. Nelson (Leiden, 2000) pp.

in this way that they had understood the problems that lofty titles had created for the Ostrogothic kings, and chose instead to take symbolically an institutional backseat in relation to Constantinople.

The spearhead represented on Suevic coins may similarly be regarded as a symbol of the Suevic king's recognition that he had a secondary position in relation to the Visigothic ruler in Tolosa. In sharp contrast to the Visigothic crown, with its symbolism linked to higher political claims, the spearhead shows that the Suevic king was expected to perform some military service. In this respect, it was very similar to the *chrism* (*Chi-Rho* sign) which appears on some African inscriptions dated before 313. The *chrism* was inserted into the title of Constantine and nowhere else, which seems to symbolize the personal guard of Constantine, viewed as a military Caesar, with no significant civilian responsibilities.[105] Indeed, Augusti entrusted to Caesars mainly military occupations and reserved civilian attributions for themselves. The relation between Visigothic and Suevic kings was in many ways similar to that between an Augustus and his Caesar. By the mid-fifth century, though, that relation had rapidly deteriorated. Suevic coins with the name of Valentinian issued after 439 did not vary the purely military message that they had earlier transmitted. However, by 450, Rechiar had assumed a position of a *rex totius Hispaniae*, which was much more than just the military commander the king in Tolosa expected him to be. His conversion to Catholicism brought him closer to the whole of the population of Hispania, while his treaty with Ravenna in 453–54 provided him with a new and increased sense of political legitimacy.[106] That treaty marked the end of the political supremacy exercised for some time by the Visigothic kings over those ruling in Braga. Taking advantage of the death of Aetius and of the extinction of the Theodosian house in Ravenna, Theoderic II decided therefore to intervene and curb any Suevic claims to independence.[107]

95–114 (p. 107). While it is true that 'a crown offered by Agilulf to the church of Monza bore the inscription *Agilulf gratia Dei vir gloriossisimus rex totius Italiae*', nothing indicates that Agilulf saw himself as a ruler over the whole of Italy. 'The whole of Italy' must be understood here in reference to the sphere of competence of the Ostrogothic kings.

[105] Pierre Salama, 'Les Provinces d'Afrique et les débuts du monogramme constantinien', *Bulletin de la Société nationale des antiquaires de France*, 1998, 137–59 (pp. 153–57).

[106] García Moreno, *Historia*, p. 59; Luis A. García Moreno, 'La Conversion des Suèves au catholicisme et à l'arianisme', in *Clovis, histoire et mémoire,* ed. by Rouche, I, 199–216 (pp. 202–03).

[107] García Moreno, 'Mérida y el reino visigodo', p. 230, writes of an 'excessive' identification of the Suevic kings with Hispania, which provoked the Visigoths and precipitated the collapse of the Suevic kingdom.

A Neglected Suevic Monarchy

The rise and fall of the Suevic kingdom has always been regarded as a function of its relation to the Visigoths. However, the beginning and expansion of the Suevic coinage has been studied in connection to the political relations between Braga and Ravenna. The iconography and legends of the Suevic coins suggest that striking Suevic coins was a matter of Suevic relations with Tolosa, and not with Ravenna. The Suevic issues also indicated that coinage and political and military expansion are intimately related phenomena, which are not necessarily responding to any political decisions in Ravenna. As a consequence, the numismatic evidence must be interpreted in the light of the Suevic king's attempt to obtain recognition from Tolosa, after Hermericus was first recognized as a king after 418. From this moment onwards, Suevic kings viewed themselves as accomplishing the task of providing a military force for the Roman government in Hispania, a true *exercitus Hispanicus*.[108]

Suevic kings did not strike coins in response to an economic demand, but for reasons of political prestige.[109] Nevertheless, the Suevic series with the names of Honorius and Valentinian show that Braga opted for types with military connotations. This tendency was made clearer from 439 onwards, after the kings in Tolosa decided to stress the autonomy they had gained within the Western Empire. The different development of the Visigothic and Suevic coinages after 439 therefore have to be interpreted as divergent reactions to the Visigothic-Roman treaty of that same year. They also show the profound inequality in existence at that time between Braga and Tolosa.

The Suevic kings were never real 'kings' in the sense in which Theodor Mommsen once defined the term.[110] While certainly true, such a statement could however be applied to a long list of proxies, which the Roman imperial power used

---

[108] It is therefore possible to treat Hermericus's rise to power in 418 and his association with the Visigoths in Tolosa as a direct result of Roman policies of turning the Sueves into a substitute for the Roman armies in Hispania. Honorius certainly did not trust the *exercitus Hispanicus* at that time and may have chosen to rely on the Sueves instead. See Luis A. García Moreno, 'El ejército regular y otras tropas de guarnición', in *La Hispania del siglo IV: Administración, economía, sociedad cristianización,* ed. by Ramón Teja (Bari, 2002), pp. 267–83 (p. 282).

[109] The volume of the Suevic coinage was relatively high: about one million solidi with the name of Honorius, and just as many, if not more, tremisses in the name of Valentinian III. This suggests a quite active minting. See Peixoto Cabral and Metcalf, *A Moeda sueva,* p. 108.

[110] Theodor Mommsen, *Römisches Staatsrecht,* II (Leipzig, 1876), p. 911.

in the course of its history, a history which Gilbert Dagron rightly called 'une chaîne perpétuelle de délégations'.[111] Such a delegation of Roman power was a feature most common to barbarian polities, in which royal households had always relied on Roman support for their political survival. What is really extraordinary and unusual in the case of the Suevic kings of Braga is not only that the kingdom came into being with Visigothic approval, but that each and every one of the Suevic kings had to be subsequently approved first by the ruler in Tolosa. The specific links tying the Suevic to the Visigothic kings are expressed in the civic series *Iussu Richiari Reges* minted in Braga in 449. The rise of a Suevic kingdom in Hispania may be the indirect result of the problems the Visigothic kings had after 418 to control simultaneously Hispania and Gaul. The consolidation of the Visigothic power in Gaul, as well as the disappearance of Aetius and of Valentinian III freed the Visigoths of the obligations deriving from their treaties with the house of Theodosius. Such a favourable situation coincided in time with the first attempts in the mid-fifth century of the Suevic kings to turn their purely military leadership into civilian rule. The direct link established in 453–54 between the Suevic kings and Ravenna, as well as King Rechiar's conversion to Catholicism, were clear signals that Braga was looking for ways to obtain independence from Tolosa.

The Visigothic intervention of 456 reversed all political decisions previously taken by Rechiar, but at the same time he appointed his son as the new Suevic king eight years later.[112] Military conflicts between Visigoths and Sueves are not therefore to be interpreted as wars between two early medieval *gentes*. On the contrary, the wars between the Sueves and the Visigoths appear as quarrels of power between two partners in a common enterprise.

---

[111] Gilbert Dagron, *Empereur et Prêtre: étude sur le 'césaropapisme' byzantin* (Paris, 1996), p. 72.

[112] The Visigoths favoured the rise to power of their protégé Remismund (Hydatius, *Chronicle*, 219 [223], 215 [219], and 216 [220]). The new Suevic king took an oath of loyalty to the Visigothic king Theoderic II, thus recognizing his subordination to the ruler of Tolosa (Pampliega, *Los Germanos*, pp. 346–58). Once recognized as Suevic *rex* (see Hydatius, *Chronicle*, 219 [223]), he could exchange embassies with Theoderic. One of them brought to Remismund his future wife, in addition to weapons and other gifts. See Hydatius, *Chronicle*, 222 [226]; Isidore of Seville, *Historia Gothorum*, 33. To strengthen the dependency of the Suevic ruler, Theoderic dispatched an Arian mission to Gallaecia. Ajax, the Arian missionary, had the specific task of converting the inhabitants of Gallaecia to Arianism, while Remismund was expected to provide protection for the mission. See Hydatius, *Chronicle*, 228 [232]; Ubric Rabaneda, *La Iglesia*, p. 121.

HIDDEN TRACKS:
ON THE VANDAL'S PATHS TO AN AFRICAN KINGDOM

Guido M. Berndt

Introduction: New Approaches to the History of the Vandals

There are comparatively more scholarly studies on the history of the Vandals than on that of other *gentes*, such as Gepids, Herules, and other smaller groups discussed in this book.[1] However, in comparison to Goths, Lombards, and Franks, on which shelves of monographs have so far been produced, the Vandals have been rather neglected. To be sure, they were part of the master narrative focused on a selective group of *gentes*, which are central to both the European collective memory of modern times and to the history of Europe and of the Mediterranean world during the fifth and sixth centuries. However, our knowledge

This paper is an opportunity to present some of the conclusions drawn in my dissertation to an English-reading audience. I would like to thank Florin Curta for the opportunity to get these ideas published. Furthermore I would like to thank Verena Berndt and Andy Merrills for valuable support. As this chapter was already completed in the summer of 2007 I have not been able to take account of the research published since then. This applies in particular for the continued debates on the meaning of ethnicity and the implications of the term 'ethnogenesis'.

[1] 'Vandals' is the name given here to a heterogeneous, barbarian coalition, which appears to have coalesced *c*. AD 400 in the lands to the east of the Rhine River. The underlying assumption is that no distinctive Vandal *gens* existed (or could be proved to have existed) before the 429 migration to North Africa. Whenever possible, the name 'Vandals' will be accompanied by the name of the respective king, in order to avoid confusion. For more details, see Guido M. Berndt, *Konflikt und Anpassung: Studien zu Migration und Ethnogenese der Vandalen* (Husum, 2007). For new approaches to the history of the Vandals, see now the studies collected in *Das Reich der Vandalen und seine (Vor-)Geschichten*, ed. by Guido M. Berndt and Roland Steinacher (Vienna, 2008). It is important to stress that I do not use 'ethnogenesis' in a teleological sense but rather as an instrument to describe a certain form of creating new identities in Late Antiquity and the early Middle Ages.

of the Vandals is still fragmentary.[2] As a consequence, they deserve to be among the 'neglected barbarians' of Late Antiquity.[3]

In this chapter I will focus on some issues relating to the migration of the Vandals. Under the leadership of Godegisel, the Vandals came to be known as a group of fifth-century invaders heading for the *Imperium Romanum*. Starting with the crossing of the Rhine River in 406/07,[4] their migration took them across the whole of Western Europe, with a three-year stay in Gaul, and a further twenty-year long sojourn in the Iberian Peninsula. Ten years after their transition to North Africa, the Vandals managed to conquer Carthage. On 19 October 439, an army of Vandals, Alans, Sueves, Goths, and others made their entrance into the city, by far the second largest in the Western Empire and one of the most important cities in the Mediterranean area. Undergraduate textbooks as well as scholarly works emphasize this now classical account of a 'people on the move' at the expense of all other aspects of the Vandal migration. Such a simplifying description, however, does not do justice to the complexity of the process. A closer examination of the sources generates a number of difficult questions, the answers to some of which constitute the substance of this chapter. Movements of population on the fringes of the Roman Empire appear in Greek and Roman ethnography and historiography only when significant for Roman territorial interests.[5] This is the main reason for our fragmentary knowledge of late antique and early medieval migrations. Little information can be found in the marginal notes of the fifth-century chronicles about why the Vandals migrated. It seems appropriate, therefore, to integrate some results of the *historische Migrationsforschung* into the analysis of Vandal history.[6]

---

[2] Walter Pohl, 'The Vandals: Fragments of a Narrative', in *Vandals, Romans and Berbers: New Perspectives on Late Antique North Africa*, ed. by Andrew H. Merrills (Aldershot, 2004), pp. 31–47.

[3] Given the bad press the Vandals received in later centuries, I use ' barbarian' in a rather non-pejorative way, as an umbrella term for what is otherwise known as the 'Germanic peoples' around and within the Late Roman Empire.

[4] Michael Kulikowski, 'Barbarians in Gaul, Usurpers in Britain', *Britannia*, 31 (2000), 325–45, favours a slightly earlier date (405/06) for this invasion. For a rebuttal in favour of the older dating, see my arguments in Berndt, *Konflikt und Anpassung*, pp. 85–94.

[5] The literary motif of mass migration, which would later enjoy great popularity, already appears in Ammianus Marcellinus, *Historia Romana*, 31.4, ed. by Wolfgang Seyfarth, 4 vols (Berlin, 1968–71), at IV, 254: 'Nam postquam innumerae gentium multitudines per provincias circumfusae.'

[6] Herbert Graßl, 'Zur Logistik antiker Wanderbewegungen', in *'Troianer sind wir gewesen' – Migrationen in der antiken Welt: Stuttgarter Kolloquium zur Historischen Geographie des Altertums 8, 2002*, ed. by Eckart Olshausen and Holger Sonnabend (Stuttgart, 2006), pp. 14–19.

In an attempt to explain migrations, scholars distinguish between push factors and pull factors. Of all 'push factors', famine is most frequently mentioned in such key sources such as Procopius of Caesarea's *History of Wars*. Naturally, one has to treat those accounts with great caution. Food shortages certainly belong to some of the most popular topoi of stories of ancient migrations. In the case of the Vandals under Godegisel, the determining factor may have been the Hunnic *Wanderlawine* heading westwards and driving many other *gentes* into migration. Conversely, an important pull factor was the desire to participate in the achievements of the *Imperium Romanum*, concerning which the Vandals could have acquired knowledge by several different means. Throughout forty years of documented migration, intervals of peace and temporary settlement were often introduced by means of negotiation and treaties with the Romans, which secured land assignments in exchange for military support. This was certainly the case of Gerontius. This *magister militum* played a significant role in the turmoil in the Roman west at the beginning of the fifth century. He rebelled against Constantine III and proclaimed Maximus emperor. Following Zosimus he won the support of the troops in Spain against Constantine and also called for the help of the barbarians, the Vandals. A little later, he seems to have granted them land in Spain, money, and food supplies.[7]

Such contracts also served as pull factors. Settling a people required making special arrangements for those carrying the *Traditionskern*, to employ Reinhard Wenskus's bon mot.[8] In the case of the Vandals, just as in that of other groups, such carriers of traditions were first and foremost *reges* such as Godegisel, Gunderic, or Gaiseric. Judging by the existing evidence, the entire group appears to have been organized in a hierarchical structure with the members of the Hasding family at the top.[9] As for the migration properly speaking, no data is available to identify the participants. Simply put, everyone able to go was welcome to join. Such circumstances may have led to the creation of a motley crew on the move. One can only speculate as to the social and ethnic composition of the initial Vandal groups. The only hard evidence available concerns the move from Spain to Africa, which is

[7] For the problems identifying foreign soldiers in the archaeological record of late antique Spain, see Philipp von Rummel, *Habitus barbarus: Kleidung und Repräsentation spätantiker Eliten im 4. und 5. Jahrhundert* (Berlin, 2007), pp. 344–45.

[8] Reinhard Wenskus, *Stammesbildung und Verfassung: Das Werden der frühmittelalterlichen Gentes* (Cologne, 1961), p. 75. The term *Traditionskern* is not Wenskus's invention, but was in fact introduced in 1912 by H. Munro Chadwick, the first to speak of 'kernels of tradition'.

[9] Frank M. Clover, 'Timekeeping and Dyarchy in Vandal Africa', *Antiquité Tardive*, 11 (2003), 45–63.

Figure 15.1. Means of transportation: an oxcart. After Stefan Link and Joachim Molthagen, *Römisches Alltagsleben in Bildern* (Hamburg, 2001).

covered by both Victor of Vita and Procopius.[10] Such sources answer only indirectly questions concerning the logistics of the migration. Historians must take into consideration both land and sea routes, since different migration phases employed different means of transportation. The Vandals are known to have travelled on horseback and/or in wagons (Figure 15.1), but also by foot, as in *c.* 400, 406/07, 409, and then again in 429. At sea, they needed a sufficiently large fleet of boats (Figure 15.2), which the Vandals are said to have confiscated in Cartagena and other cities on the southern coast of Spain. Some boats must also have been built for the occasion. Finally, finding and maintaining constant supplies of food and fodder must have been no easy task.

The goals of the migration, to the extent that they could at all be identified in the case of the Vandals, must have varied considerably from one case to another. The Vandals do not seem to have preplanned to go anywhere. It would be inadequate to presume that those who crossed the Rhine in the winter of 406/07 were planning to move against Carthage in North Africa. Each migration phase

---

[10] Victor of Vita, *Historia persecutionis Africanae provinciae*, 1.2, ed. by Michael Petschenig (Vienna, 1881), p. 3; Procopius, *Wars*, 1.3.26, ed. by Jakob Haury, 4 vols (Leipzig, 1905–13) and trans. by H. B. Dewing, 6th edn (Cambridge, MA, 1990), p. 31.

Figure 15.2. Means of transportation: ships in the harbour of Ravenna. After Renzo Matino, *Ravenna: Stadt der Künste* (Ravenna, 2000).

therefore has a different goal, either booty or some negotiated arrangement in the form of a *foedus*. The ultimate goal of such movements of people was to get as deeply as possible into Roman territory, in order to find sufficient resources necessary for the survival of the group. As a consequence, any attempt at explaining the migration by emphasizing any one factor alone is fundamentally flawed.

Ethnogenesis has long been a controversial topic of research on the early Middle Ages. Earlier interpretations projected the image of a race or a people by employing such biological metaphors as birth, growth, maturity, and decline, usually under the assumption that all those groups were relatively homogeneous entities. In fact, the very term 'ethnogenesis' suggests comparison with the biological act of birth. It is therefore important to stress that ethnic groups are in fact the result of historical processes, based on many political, economic, and cultural factors. The concept of ethnogenesis therefore helps to describe the formation and establishment of an (early medieval) group under certain historical and cultural circumstances. The definition of that group from both inside and outside is determined by a variety of factors, ranging from belief in a common descent and history to common habits, uniform language and customs, as well as religious beliefs. Such factors induce an 'ethnic identity' that ultimately originates from a strong sense of community.[11] Group identities cluster around an internal core of identity. Anthropological and sociological studies show that such identities are neither homogeneous nor discrete. Ethnic boundaries are permanently negotiated, especially during migration.[12]

Ethnogenetic processes in the age of the *Völkerwanderung* has recently been the subject of a great number of studies.[13] Equally impressive is the number of studies dedicated to individual ethnogeneses. The Vandals, however, have not received the

---

[11] Sebastian Brather, 'Ethnische Identitäten als Konstrukte der frühgeschichtlichen Archäologie', *Germania*, 78 (2000), 139–77 (pp. 160–61). See now Sebastian Brather, *Ethnische Interpretationen in der frühgeschichtlichen Archäologie: Geschichte, Grundlagen und Alternativen* (Berlin, 2004).

[12] Patrick J. Geary, 'Ethnic Identity as a Situational Construct in the Early Middle Ages', *Mitteilungen der Anthropologischen Gesellschaft in Wien*, 113 (1983), 15–26.

[13] Allen A. Lund, *Die ersten Germanen: Ethnizität und Ethnogenese* (Heidelberg, 1998); Jörg Jarnut, 'Aspekte frühmittelalterlicher Ethnogenese in historischer Sicht', in *Entstehung von Sprachen und Völkern: Glotto- und ethnogenetische Aspekte europäischer Sprachen. Akten des 6. Symposiums über Sprachkontakt in Europa*, ed. by Per Sture Ureland (Tübingen, 1985), pp. 83–91; Jörg Jarnut, 'Die langobardische Ethnogenese', in *Typen der Ethnogenese unter besonderer Berücksichtigung der Bayern*, ed. by Herwig Wolfram and Walter Pohl (Vienna, 1990), pp. 97–102; Walter Pohl, 'Tradition, Ethnogenese und literarische Gestaltung: eine Zwischenbilanz', in *Ethnogenese und Überlieferung: Angewandte Methoden der Frühmittelalterforschung*, ed. by Karl Brunner and Brigitte Merta (Munich, 1994), pp. 9–26.

same degree of attention. It has by now become common knowledge that *Völker-wanderung* identities have nothing to do with the modern nations.[14] However, no precise definition exists for the term *ethnos*, even within the discipline of ethnology deriving its very name from that term.[15] Moreover, *ethnos* means different things to different people in different disciplines. In Germany, the term is used in substantially different ways by archaeologists (namely those involved in research on *Ur- und Frühgeschichte*), historians, sociologists, and biologists. An additional problem is the fact that, initially a metaphor, the term 'ethnogenesis' conveys the idea of some primordial state, a 'zero degree' of development, an idea which creates much ambiguity given that some ethnogenetic processes develop slowly. Ethnogenetic studies typically focus on the nature and characteristics of a particular group.[16] It is often forgotten that 'ethnogenesis' is a modern construct, which does not appear in any historical source. As long as it is understood as a Weberian ideal type, however, the concept can be helpful in the analysis of historical sources.

In ethnogenetic studies, perhaps more than in any other studies, terminology matters. The Latin word *gens* is the equivalent of the Greek word *ethnos*. However, late antique and early medieval sources also employ *natio* and *populus*, especially in political contexts.[17] Reinhard Wenskus used *ethnos* to indicate a group in which membership was linked to a *belief* in common descent. As a consequence, Herwig Wolfram further expounded the problems and implications of terms describing true descent such as *gens*, *genus*, or *natio*. The underlying idea is that an *ethnos* does not emerge from a biologically common origin of its members, but from historical circumstances.[18] Special attention needs to be paid in that respect to barbarian armies, the heterogeneous composition of which was very different from that of their members' groups. Wenskus's concept of *Traditionskern* has recently been the

[14] Walter Pohl, 'Conceptions of Ethnicity in Early Medieval Studies', *Archaeologia Polona*, 29 (1991), 39–49 (p. 39).

[15] Johannes Fried, '*Gens* und *Regnum*: Wahrnehmungs- und Deutungskategorien politischen Wandels im früheren Mittelalter', in *Sozialer Wandel im Mittelalter*, ed. by Jürgen Miethke and Klaus Schreiner (Sigmaringen, 1994), pp. 73–104 (p. 78).

[16] Falko Daim, 'Gedanken zum Ethnosbegriff', *Mitteilungen der anthropologischen Gesellschaft in Wien*, 112 (1982), 58–71 (p. 59).

[17] Wenskus, *Stammesbildung und Verfassung*, p. 47: 'Nach den Quellen der Wanderzeit ist eine *gens* also zugleich *natio*, Abstammungsgemeinschaft, und *populus*, Staatsvolk.'

[18] Herwig Wolfram, *Die Goten: Von den Anfängen bis zur Mitte des sechsten Jahrhunderts. Entwurf einer historischen Ethnographie*, 3th edn (Munich, 1990), pp. 17–18.

object of much criticism. As Wolfram pointed out, it is doubtful that changing 'kernel of tradition' to 'carriers of tradition' would solve the problem.[19]

The concept of ethnogenesis is one of several possible ways to approach historical developments and political thought in the early Middle Ages. As such, it privileges ethnic identities, particularly that of the so-called Germanic *gentes*, over any other form of identity. The concept essentially serves as the description of special historical processes ascertainable from the sources. Under what particular circumstances could new ethnic entities be forged out of heterogeneous peoples, which could be identified as marked by a belief in common origin and common traditions? Shifting the emphasis from biological descent to belief in common descent was a way to avoid taking tribes as discrete entities and opening the way for a deeper understanding of the political dynamics of Late Antiquity and the early Middle Ages.[20] By 1960, a consensus seems to have been reached on the importance of self-definition in the emergence of ethnic groups. This encouraged research in potential differences between the emic definition by members of the group and the ethic labelling by outsiders.[21] It also became clear that group identities are subject to constant change, often marked by discontinuity and transformation. Such an understanding, however, makes it very difficult, if not impossible, to isolate the 'origin' of any historically documented group. As a consequence, confidence in numerous scholarly attempts to discover the *Urgermanen* has quickly evaporated.

Rediscovery in the Twenty-first Century, or How Neglected Are the Vandals?

Research on the history of the Vandals has a long tradition, particularly in the German-speaking countries. The beginning of the scholarly research on the Vandals may be set at 1785, the year in which Conrad Mannert published his

---

[19] Herwig Wolfram, 'Auf der Suche nach den Ursprüngen', in *Die Suche nach den Ursprüngen: Von der Bedeutung des frühen Mittelalter*, ed. by Walter Pohl (Vienna, 2004), pp. 11–22 (p. 16).

[20] Walter Pohl, 'Ethnicity, Theory, and Tradition: A Response', in *On Barbarian Identity: Critical Approaches to Ethnicity in the Early Middle Ages*, ed. by Andrew Gillett (Turnhout, 2002), pp. 221–39 (p. 221).

[21] Siân Jones, *The Archaeology of Ethnicity: Constructing Identities in the Past and Present* (London, 1997). Jones attempted to reconcile different opinions of different scholars in different disciplines, in order to reach a sufficiently broad level of generalization to offer a definition of ethnic identity.

monograph dedicated to the Vandals.[22] Leaving aside the fact that today few would now endorse Mannert's labelling of the Vandals as a 'Germanic' people, he nevertheless succeeded in outlining the fundamentals of Vandal history in relation to the sources. In addition, he questioned the extent to which the Vandals could be made responsible for the fall of the Roman Empire,[23] an issue that almost all pertaining scholarship has featured since 1785. In the nineteenth century there were numerous researchers who paid attention to the history of the Vandals. Exemplary among them was Carl Meinicke with his history of the group up to the invasion of Northern Africa.[24] In 1837, Felix Papencordt published in German his *History of Vandal Rule in Africa*,[25] the French translation of which had just received an award from the *Académie des Inscriptions et Belles Lettres*. In the course of the French occupation of Algeria, the *Académie* created a commission to study of the history of the occupied territories and prepared a specific budget for a 'history of the Vandals'. Having just published his work in 1838, Louis Marcus decided to apply for the available funding.[26]

Felix Dahn included the Vandal kings, with little comment, in his study of the Germanic kings.[27] Responding to an increasing interest in national origins throughout Europe during the nineteenth century, Dahn's work gave special importance to the Vandals as ancestors of the modern Germans. Dahn is the author of most entries on Vandal kings in the *Allgemeine Deutsche Biographie*, a grandiose

---

[22] Conrad Mannert, *Geschichte der Vandalen* (Leipzig, 1785).

[23] This remains a controversial theme. See Peter Heather, *The Fall of the Roman Empire: A New History of Rome and the Barbarians* (Oxford, 2005); Bryan Ward-Perkins, *The Fall of Rome and the End of Civilization* (Oxford, 2005). Ward-Perkins and Heather argue in a similar way that at the beginning of the fifth century a number of catastrophic military defeats resulted in the decline of the Roman civilization. Such views remind one of Edward Gibbon's *Decline and Fall of the Roman Empire*. Other scholars, such as Chris Wickham and Walter Goffart argue instead that there had been a collapse of Roman imperialism but no downfall of the Roman world per se. See Chris Wickham, *Framing the Early Middle Ages: Europe and the Mediterranean, 400–800* (Oxford, 2005); Walter Goffart, *Barbarian Tides: The Migration Age and the Later Roman Empire* (Philadelphia, 2006).

[24] Carl E. Meinicke, *Versuch einer Geschichte der Vandalen bis zu ihrem Einfall in Afrika* (Prenzlau, 1830).

[25] Felix Papencordt, *Geschichte der vandalischen Herrschaft in Afrika* (Berlin, 1837).

[26] Louis Marcus, *Histoire des Wandales* (Paris, 1838).

[27] Felix Dahn, *Die Könige der Germanen: Das Wesen des ältesten Königthums der germanischen Stämme und seine Geschichte bis zur Auflösung des karolingischen Reiches. Erste Abtheilung: Die Zeit vor der Wanderung – Die Vandalen* (Munich, 1861).

'Who's Who' of the newly established German *Reich*. Ludwig Schmidt's monograph was first submitted for publication in 1901, and then republished, in a slightly modified version, in 1942. Schmidt's critical approach to sources had a considerable influence upon subsequent generations of scholars writing in German. Moreover, the work was translated into several other languages, which contributed to the expansion of Schmidt's influence in non-German scholarly circles. More than a century after its first publication, Schmidt's book remains the standard work in matters Vandalic.[28]

More than fifty years ago, Christian Courtois published his masterly book on the Vandals in Africa.[29] Despite unnecessarily stressing the dichotomy between Roman Africa and the 'forgotten' Africa of the nomads, the influence of this work upon subsequent studies has been considerable. Courtois took advantage of a considerable literature available at that time in French on the history and archaeology of North Africa during Late Antiquity.[30] His own book became the basis for all future studies on the Vandals. It has been recently suggested that Courtois brilliantly united the French tradition of the *Annales*, with its emphasis on the concept of region and with its use of geographical studies, with the best scholarship produced in the tradition of the *Germanenforschung*. (Be that as it may, Courtois's untimely death in 1956, just one year after the publication of his book, made it impossible to gauge his reaction to the fundamental changes taking place in German-speaking research brought by Reinhard Wenskus, Herwig Wolfram, and

---

[28] Ludwig Schmidt, *Geschichte der Wandalen* (Munich, 1901; repr. 1942 and 1970).

[29] Christian Courtois, *Les Vandales et l'Afrique* (Paris, 1955; repr. Aalen, 1964), pp. 20–21. For corrections to Courtois's views of North Africa, see now Andrew H. Merrills, 'Vandals, Romans and Berbers: Understanding Late Antique North Africa', in *Vandals, Romans and Berbers*, ed. by Merrills, pp. 3–28 (pp. 7–8). It is important to note that Courtois wrote his chapter on the 'préhistoire des Vandales' on the basis of Schmidt's book. The only difference is that, unlike Schmidt, he refused to employ such terms as *Volk* or *Urheimat* for such an early period: 'Mais il n'est pas possible, je crois, de pousser plus avant l'hypothèse et d'assigner aux Vandales telle ou telle patrie primitive (*Urheimat*), car c'est supposer résolue une question qui ne l'est pas, c'est-à-dire admettre que les Vandales formaient déjà, au cours de La Tène II (250–100), un peuple défini et cohérent. Plus raisonnable est de considérer comme un ensemble hétérogène, issu des îles danoises, du Jutland et des régions méridionales de la Suède et de la Norvège, aggloméré par on ne sait quel péril commun, ces tribus germaniques qui allaient s'installer dans les plaines de loess de l'Allemagne sud-orientale et de la Pologne méridionale.'

[30] E.g. Stéphane Gsell, *Histoire anciennne de l'Afrique du Nord*, 5 vols (Paris, 1920–28); Charles-André Julien, *Histoire de l'Afrique du Nord: Tunisie, Algérie, Maroc* (Paris, 1931).

the so-called Vienna school.)[31] Wenskus's work was particularly influential, given that much of the subsequent research on ethnogenetic processes was predicated upon its thesis.[32] Equally influential were the numerous works of Hans-Joachim Diesner, mainly published in the 1960s, including his brief monograph on the Vandal kingdom.[33]

After 1966, the Vandals almost completely disappear from the research agenda. Much therefore remains to be said about the Vandals particularly when compared to the other peoples of the 'Great Migration' period. Goths, Franks, and Lombards always offered and still offer more potential for modern nationalisms than the Vandals. The fact that no modern inhabitant of Tunisia would claim to be a descendant of the Vandals means that there is little popular interest in those very lands in which the Vandals eventually established their kingdom.

Anyhow a revival of interest in things Vandalic has taken place.[34] It is not easy to understand why, for such a long time after Courtois and Diesner, scholars of Late Antiquity and the early Middle Ages lost any interest in the Vandals. The large-scale research project entitled 'The Transformation of the Roman World' and funded by the European Science Foundation may have been partially responsible for their rediscovery, as the project was specifically aimed at re-evaluating the history of the 'Great Migration' period.[35] Equally significant is the number of young scholars interested in mapping out new territories for future research, away from the trodden paths of the previous historiography. Whatever the reason for

---

[31] Harsh criticism of Wenskus, Wolfram, and the Vienna school can be found in *On Barbarian Identity*, ed. by Gillett. For a reaction to such criticism from a student of Vandal history, see my review of *On Barbarian Identity* in *Das Mittelalter*, 8 (2003), 193–94.

[32] Wenskus, *Stammesbildung und Verfassung*. See Pohl, 'Tradition, Ethnogenese und literarische Gestaltung', p. 9: 'Das [the debates surrounding such terms as *populus, gens*, and *natio*] zeigt, daß die von Reinhard Wenskus vor über dreißig Jahren angeregten Forschungen noch keineswegs abgeschlossen sind.'

[33] Hans-Joachim Diesner, *Das Vandalenreich: Aufstieg und Untergang* (Stuttgart, 1966).

[34] Similarly, there has been much discontinuity in the scholarly and popular interest in things Lombard. See Jörg Jarnut, 'Zum Stand der Langobardenforschung', in *Die Langobarden: Herrschaft und Identität*, ed. by Walter Pohl and Peter Erhart (Vienna, 2005), pp. 11–19.

[35] Nonetheless, there is only one single contribution concerning the Vandals in the numerous volumes published in the series dedicated to that project. See J. H. Wolfgang G. Liebeschütz, '*Gens* into *regnum*: The Vandals', in *Regna and Gentes: The Relationship between Late Antique and Early Medieval Peoples and Kingdoms in the Transformation of the Roman World*, ed. by Hans-Werner Goetz, Jörg Jarnut, and Walter Pohl (Leiden, 2003), pp. 55–83.

such a rebound, the Vandals have recently made a spectacular comeback into the focus of historical and archaeological research.[36]

Digging in Fragments: Towards a Prehistory of the Vandals

The lack of sources may explain the uncertainty as to the precise moment in time in which a specific group of people began identifying themselves as 'Vandal'. Greek and Roman writers provide little information except the name, while testimonials concerned with the Vandals prior to their entry into the Roman Empire (406/07) may only be validated through archaeology. Such a procedure, however, has its own problems associated with the attribution of cultural assemblages, no matter how clearly delineated, to ethnic groups known from documentary sources. Of course, a history of the Vandals begins in the first centuries AD, but any search for a Vandal *Urheimat*, the point at which most older studies of the Vandals started, is in fact pointless.[37] Earlier studies insisted upon the archaeological evidence allegedly attesting that the earliest Vandal settlements were those of Scandinavia, but such interpretations in fact lacked any basis in scientific method.[38]

A handful of historians and geographers writing in the imperial period provide a handful of fragmentary references to the early Vandals.[39] On the basis of such accounts (and the use of a modern map of Europe), one is led to believe that the Vandals lived somewhere between the Vistula and the Oder Rivers. But how much

[36] Philipp von Rummel, 'Zum Stand der afrikanischen Vandalenforschung', *Antiquité Tardive*, 11 (2003), 13–19. The papers presented in two conferences on Vandal and Byzantine Africa taking place in Tunis and Paris, respectively, have been published in the tenth (2002) and eleventh (2003) volumes of the journal *Antiquité Tardive*. In addition, several sessions on the Vandals were organized at the International Medieval Congress in Leeds. See also Berndt, *Konflikt und Anpassung* and Helmut Castritius, *Die Vandalen: Etappen einer Spurensuche* (Stuttgart, 2007).

[37] For the problems associated with the search for *Urheimat* for any Germanic gens known from written sources, see Alexander Callander Murray, 'Reinhard Wenskus on "Ethnogenesis", Ethnicity, and the Origin of the Franks', in *On Barbarian Identity*, ed. by Gillett, pp. 39–68 (pp. 67–68). See also Brather, *Ethnische Identitäten*, p. 174: 'Die Suche nach einer vermeintlichen "Urheimat" ist von vornherein gegenstandslos, weil schon deren Existenz nicht gesichert werden kann, geschweige denn eine auch nur mehr als vage zeitliche und räumliche Ansetzung möglich ist.'

[38] Schmidt, *Geschichte der Wandalen*, p. 6, in a stance reminiscent of Gustaf Kossinna's ideas, who associated the name Hasdings to the half-mythical Norwegian dynasty of the Haddingjar in order to support the idea of a Scandinavian origin of the Vandals.

[39] Denis B. Saddington, 'Roman Attitudes to the *Externae Gentes* of the North', *Acta Classica*, 4 (1961), 90–102.

can one trust such accounts? Pliny the Elder lists five basic groups of peoples in the fourth book of his *Natural History*, the first of which he identifies as the Vandili, before dividing it into smaller units.[40] An almost identical statement may be found in the *Germania* of Tacitus, who regarded the *Vandilii* as a subgroup of the three 'Mannus tribes', without concealing his own uncertainty about their individual names.[41] It is therefore unclear which *gentes* were known as *Vandilii* to Tacitus. He made further remarks only about the Lugi, a group which scholars have long viewed as a cult community, to which the Vandals may also have belonged.[42] One is constantly reminded, however, that Tacitus's descriptions of exotic peoples were specifically tailored for his Roman audience. As a consequence, his *interpretation Romana* must be taken into consideration when attempting to understand his ethnography.[43] In the mid-second century AD, Ptolemy was familiar with the name of the Silings, apparently a separate group, which would resurface in the account of the fifth-century migration of the Vandals.[44]

No interpretation advanced so far has satisfactorily explained any of those names or the relation between them. It seems at least clear that contemporary authors regarded the *Vandili* or *Vandilii* as a distinct *gens*.[45] On the other hand, a stable and uniform picture was very likely to emerge from contemporary accounts, given the constantly changing alliances and confederacies, along with the always

---

[40] Pliny the Elder, *Naturalis Historiae*, 4.99, ed. by Gerhard Winkler (Munich, 1988): 'Germanorum genera quinque: Vandili, quorum pars Burgodiones, Varini, Charini, Gutones.'

[41] Tacitus, *Germania*, 2.3, ed. by Alfons Städele (Munich, 1991): 'Quidam, ut in licentia vetustatis, pluris deo ortos plurisque gentis appellationes, Marsos Gambrivios Suebos Vandilios, affirmant, eaque vera et antiqua nomina.'

[42] Ingeborg Masur, 'Die Verträge der germanischen Stämme' (unpublished doctoral dissertation, Berlin, Freie Universität, 1952), pp. 80–81 with n. 1; Klaus Tausend, 'Lugier – Vandilier – Vandalen', *Tyche*, 12 (1997), 229–36 (p. 233).

[43] Tacitus, *Germania*, 43.2: 'Dirimit enim scinditque Suebiam continuum montium iugum, ultra quod plurimae gentes agunt. Ex quibus latissime patet Lugiorum nomen in plures civitates diffusum.'

[44] Ptolemy, *Geography*, 2.11.10, ed. by Edward Luther Stevenson (New York, 1932; repr. Dover, 1991).

[45] Patrick J. Geary, 'Barbarians and Ethnicity', in *Late Antiquity: A Guide to the Postclassical World*, ed. by G. W. Bowersock, Peter Brown, and Oleg Grabar (Cambridge, MA, 1999), pp. 107–29 (p. 110): 'Ancient names could and did come to designate very different groups of people.' See also Jes Martens, 'The Vandals: Myths and Facts about a Germanic Tribe of the First Half of the 1st Millenium AD', in *Archaeological Approaches to Cultural Identity*, ed. by Stephen Shennan (London, 1989), pp. 57–65 (p. 57).

likely possibility that new generic labels could be created to refer to such groupings. Only the Marcomannic Wars brought the Vandals into the focus of Roman writing about the northern barbarians. After that, they again disappear for quite some time from the sources.[46]

A few Vandals were allowed to settle as *foederati* in the Roman province of Dacia in 180 or 181. Around the same time, small groups of Vandals began to raid Roman territory. Cassius Dio reports that negotiations were therefore opened with the Hasding Vandals under the leadership of Raus and Raptus. Little else is known about the two men besides their names. According to Cassius Dio, the Vandals wanted money and land.[47] The next bit of information refers to a victory Emperor Aurelian obtained against the Vandals, following which he settled the defeated barbarians on Roman territory, as *foederati* who were now expected to provide troops for Rome's wars, whenever needed. Dexippos knew about Emperor Aurelian's victory over a Vandal army and, through him, so did Jordanes in the sixth century. In addition, Jordanes knew of a Vandal king named Visimar from the Hasding.[48] The Vandals also appear in the *Origo gentis Langobardorum*, as a Lombard victory over the Vandals seems to have been a key component of the Lombard myth of origin.[49]

Around AD 400, the Vandals and the Alans broke through the frontiers of Pannonia pushing westwards. The *magister militum* Stilicho (Figure 15.3) succeeded in preventing their devastations and settling them in the province of Pannonia Prima. However, the Vandals soon moved out of Pannonia into Noricum and Vindelicia, where in the winter of 401/02 Stilicho again offered them a *foedus* in exchange for peace.[50]

[46] Herbert Schutz, *The Germanic Realms in Pre-Carolingian Central Europe, 400–750* (New York, 2000), p. 42. For the Marcomannic Wars, see Horst Wolfgang Böhme, 'Archäologische Zeugnisse zur Geschichte der Markomannenkriege (166–180 n. Chr.)', *Jahrbuch des Römisch-Germanischen Zentralmuseums Mainz*, 22 (1975), 153–217.

[47] Cassius Dio, *Historia Romana*, 71.12.1, in *Griechische und lateinische Quellen zur Frühgeschichte Mitteleuropas bis zur Mitte des 1. Jahrtausends u. Z.*, ed. by Joachim Herrmann, III (Berlin, 1988), pp. 266–335 (p. 326).

[48] Jordanes, *Getica*, 12, ed. by Theodor Mommsen, MGH AA, 5.1 (Berlin, 1882), p. 87: 'Primitias regni sui mox in Vandalica gente extendere cupiens contra Visimar eorum rege qui Asdingorum stirpe, quod inter eos eminet genusque indicat bellicosissimum, Deuxippo storico referente.'

[49] Walter Pohl, *Die Völkerwanderung: Eroberung und Integration* (Stuttgart, 2002), pp. 186–87.

[50] Claudian, *De bello Pollentio sive Gothico*, 363–65, in *Griechische und lateinische Quellen zur Frühgeschichte Mitteleuropas bis zur Mitte des 1. Jahrtausends u. Z.*, ed. by Joachim Herrmann, IV

Figure 15.3. *Magister militum* Stilicho on an ivory diptych. After Pontus Hultén, *The True Story of the Vandals* (Värnamo, 2001).

The literary sources do not allow a continuous narrative linking the early Vandals of the second century to those who established themselves in Northern Africa. Earlier studies have often attempted to fill in the gap of knowledge through recourse

(Berlin, 1988), pp. 164–87 (p. 182): 'Iam foedera gentes exuerant Latiique audita clade feroces Vindelicos saltus et norica rura tenebant.' See also Jaroslav Šašel, '*Antiqui Barbari*: Zur Besiedlungsgeschichte Ostnoricums und Pannoniens im 5. und 6. Jahrhundert nach den Schriftquellen', in *Von der Spätantike zum frühen Mittelalter: Aktuelle Probleme in historischer und archäologischer Sicht*, ed. by Joachim Werner and Eugen Ewig (Sigmaringen, 1979), pp. 125–39 (p. 127).

to archaeological 'cultural groups' in order to create the impression of a full-fledged, uniform *gens* moving from Scandinavia, through modern Poland, to Gaul, Spain, and finally to modern Tunisia. Walter Goffart's criticism of such an approach is of course justified, but hardly novel.[51] The idea of a Vandal *Urheimat* in Scandinavia has long been exposed as little more than late nineteenth- and early twentieth-century wishful thinking. A distinction was drawn relatively early between the 'archaeological Vandals' and those known from sources concerning the Marcomannic Wars.[52] As written sources have nothing to say about the composition or even the identity of those groups, prehistoric archaeology cannot be used either to confirm or to reject any ethnogenetic theories. This much has been recognized by Kazimierz Godłowski, one of the staunchest advocates of a culture-historical approach to the archaeology of the Przeworsk culture: 'Nonetheless, this does not justify the practice, which is still quite common, of regarding the Przeworsk culture as Vandalic or of automatically and completely equating Vandals and Lugi.'[53] Given the existing evidence, it is indeed wrong to equate the Lugi to the Vandals, and both to the 'bearers of the Przeworsk culture'. By contrast, no serious arguments currently stay in the way of associating the Vandili(i) of the first centuries AD with the Vandals of later times, even though no direct continuity existed between the two groups. The appearance, disappearance, and reappearance of tribal names has by now been recognized as a typical feature of the imperial and late antique ethnography.

It is possible that groups settling between the Oder and the Vistula Rivers also returned to the old and therefore prestigious name of the Vandals when the confederacy began moving out of that region. Such names may be understood to have applied initially to small 'family' units, later to groups getting larger as a result of military or political success, and finally to an entire *gens* as a marker of identity.

---

[51] Walter Goffart, 'Does the Distant Past Impinge on the Invasion Age Germans?', in *On Barbarian Identity*, ed. by Gillett, pp. 21–37 (pp. 25 with n. 17, and 27): 'By modern standards, the idea of an 'original home' (=*Urheimat*) is absurd.'

[52] Martens, 'The Vandals'.

[53] Kazimierz Godłowski, 'Die Przeworsk-Kultur', in *Beiträge zum Verständnis der Germania des Tacitus*, II: *Bericht über die Kolloquien der Kommission für die Altertumskunde Nord- und Mitteleuropas im Jahre 1986 und 1987*, ed. by Günter Neumann and Henning Seemann (Göttingen, 1992), pp. 9–90 (pp. 55–56): 'Jedoch reicht dies alles nicht aus, um, wie bisher üblich, die Przeworsk-Kultur restlos als wandalisch zu betrachten oder die Wandalen automatisch und vollständig mit den Lugiern zu identifizieren.'

Traitors and Collaborators: Precursors of Migrations

The Romans did not regard the Vandals as a threat as long as they remained outside the borders of the empire. This changed decisively with the Vandal-Alan coalition crossing the Rhine in 406/07. In the time between the crossing of that river and the crossing of the Pyrenees, sources document no diplomatic negotiations or agreements between Vandals and Romans. However, Gerontius seems to have negotiated with the Vandals before their migration to Spain.[54] The Vandals, in view of their precarious situation in Aquitaine, were able to offer Gerontius arms, aid, and protection.

Shortly after their arrival in North Africa, the Vandals under the leadership of Geiseric began battling the troops under the command of the *comes Africae*, Boniface. Despite the additional forces sent to his support, he was unable to expel the Vandals. The situation in North Africa was apparently too difficult for the (East) Roman troops under the command of Aspar and in 432 they were withdrawn. Soon after that, Boniface was recalled from Africa, only to be involved in serious conflict with Aetius in Italy. Geiseric's only two considerable opponents for control of North Africa were thus removed. Following his occupation of Hippo Regius, the power of the Vandal king rapidly stabilized. The Vandals created their kingdom on Roman soil approximately one generation after entering Roman territory, not unlike the Visigoths, Ostrogoths, Burgundians, and Franks before them.[55] Those realms were based primarily on the power of armies of barbarian origin, which needed land to settle and feed their families after military successes.[56] Since they did not receive that land from the Romans through *foedera*, they forcibly took possession of what was conquered. The groups themselves, in a constant process of formation and re-formation, may have employed names known from ethnographic works of the early imperial period, only slightly modified to fit the new needs: Goths instead of Gutones, and Vandals instead of Vandili. Such names were rooted in tradition and must have carried great importance in the eyes of those

---

[54] Olympiodorus, *Fragmenta*, 17.1, in *The Fragmentary Classicising Historians of the Later Roman Empire: Eunapius, Olympiodorus, Priscus and Malchus*, ed. by Robert C. Blockley, II (Liverpool, 1983), pp. 176 and 178.

[55] See, in general, *Kingdoms of the Empire: The Integration of Barbarians in Late Antiquity*, ed. by Walter Pohl (Leiden, 1997). For single *gentes*, see also Dietrich Claude, *Geschichte der Westgoten* (Stuttgart, 1970); Wolfram, *Die Goten*; Jörg Jarnut, *Geschichte der Langobarden* (Stuttgart, 1982); Dieter Geuenich, *Geschichte der Alemannen* (Stuttgart, 1997); Reinhold Kaiser, *Die Franken: Roms Erben und Wegbereiter Europas?* (Idstein, 1997); Patrick Amory, *People and Identity in Ostrogothic Italy, 489–554* (Cambridge, 1997); Reinhold Kaiser, *Die Burgunder* (Stuttgart, 2004).

[56] Pohl, 'Ethnicity', p. 225.

who proudly used them.[57] It is equally possible, however, that such names simply reflected Roman needs to classify groups living on the periphery of the empire. In order to bring more protection against the raids from outside the imperial frontiers, Stilicho removed a number of garrison troops from the Rhine frontier, as part of his wider campaign of preparation against Radagaisus. It is likely that the movements of the Roman troops were also known to barbarian groups on the opposite, right bank of the Rhine. Later, a campaign of demonizing Stilicho turned into treachery his measures aimed at providing protection for the Roman heartland. Orosius went as far as to claim that Stilicho had made a pact with the barbarians.[58] Similarly, Claudian believed that Stilicho removed all border troops in the winter of 401/02, because he needed soldiers for his war in Italy against Radagaisus.[59] A complete withdrawal of all troops from the frontiers of the empire is of course highly improbable, and Claudian was no neutral witness either. A very similar charge had been brought against Constantius II by Julian, who accused the Emperor of abandoning the cities and fortresses of the Rhine to the barbarians in 350/51.[60] That Stilicho removed part of the *comitatenses* need not be doubted, but the accusation that Stilicho had completely neglected the Rhine frontier or even betrayed Rome is without basis, especially since parts of the frontier army remained on the Rhine and furthermore because Frankish units were positioned for the protection of that frontier.[61]

In the years 406/07 a coalition had taken form from different confederacies to pursue a common goal. After three years in Gaul (Figure 15.4) the Vandals, Alans, and Sueves united to advance into the rich provinces of the Iberian Peninsula

---

[57] One should not loose sight of this 'antiquarian' approach when analysing the barbarian 'successor states'. See Walter Goffart, *The Narrators of Barbarian History, AD 550–800: Jordanes, Gregory of Tours, Bede, and Paul the Deacon* (Princeton, 1988).

[58] Orosius, *Historia adversus paganos*, 7.38.3, ed. by Carl Zangemeister (Vienna, 1882; repr. Hildesheim, 1967): 'Praeterea gentes alias copiis viribus intolerabiles, quibus nunc Galliarum Hispaniarumque provinciae premuntur, hoc est Alanorum, Suevorum, Vandalorum, ipsoque simul motu inpulsorum Burgundiorum, ultro in arma sollicitans, deterso semel Romani nominis metu suscitavit.'

[59] Claudian, *De bello Pollentino sive Gothico*, 419–29 (p. 184). See also Dietrich Hoffmann, 'Die Gallienarmee und der Grenzschutz am Rhein in der Spätantike', *Nassauische Annalen*, 84 (1973), 1–18 (p. 16): 'Man wird demnach in der Forschung künftig davon Abstand nehmen müssen, das Jahr 401/02 mit seiner vermeintlichen "Räumung der Rheingrenze" als ein Epochenjahr in der Geschichte der Römerzeit nördlich der Alpen zu betrachten.'

[60] Julian, *Orationes*, 1.35a, ed. by Wilmer Wright, 2nd edn (Cambridge, 1980).

[61] Hoffmann, 'Die Gallienarmee', p. 10.

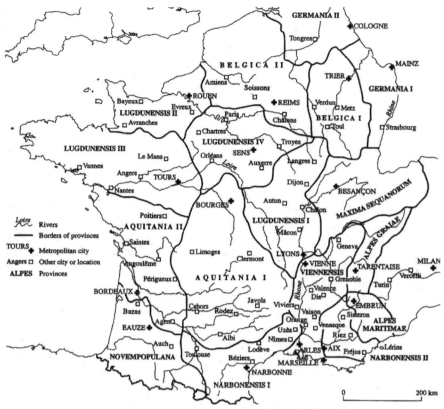

Figure 15.4. Late antique Gaul. Map drawn by the author.

(Figure 15.5). As previously mentioned, according to Olympiodorus, instead of confronting the barbarians, Gerontius chose to negotiate with them.[62] These negotiations resulted in an alliance between Gerontius and the Vandals, and directly led to their migration from Gaul to Spain. Most historians seem to have neglected this fundamental aspect. The Vandals advanced to Spain under the leadership of Gunderic only because that was part of a configuration of political affairs in the Western Empire. The usurper Maximus later played an important role in these events, but no reason exists to presume that the Vandals had no other choice but to raise Maximus to the purple.[63] To be sure, as rival emperor, Maximus became a

---

[62] Olympiodorus, *Fragmenta*, 17.1.

[63] As stated by Ralf Scharf, *Spätrömische Studien: Prosopographische und quellenkundliche Untersuchungen zur Geschichte des 5. Jahrhunderts nach Christus* (Mannheim, 1996), p. 84.

Figure 15.5. The Iberian Peninsula in the fifth century. After Arce, 'Enigmatic Fifth Century'.

puppet of the Vandal king Gunderic. The relationship was very similar to that existing in 412 between Priscus Attalus and the Gothic chieftain Ataulf. In the case of Maximus, he was taken prisoner by the *vicarius* of Maurocellus after a defeat of the Vandals at Bracara. Maximus was executed in 420, probably during Emperor Honorius's *tricennalia* celebrated in Ravenna (Figure 15.6).

Gerontius launched a rebellion from Tarragona, whose subsequent failure led to his replacement by a certain Justus, an event adding to the growing complexity of the situation in Spain and the other parts of the West still under imperial control.[64] Having learned about the Vandals and their precarious situation in Aquitaine, Gerontius had previously negotiated with them, offering land in Spain in return for military assistance against Constans and Constantine III, his former masters.[65]

---

[64] Sozomenus, *Historia Ecclesiastca*, 9.13.1, ed. by Günther Christian Hansen (Turnhout, 2004); Zosimus, *Historia Nova*, 6.5.1, ed. by Ludwig Mendelsohn (Leipzig, 1887).

[65] Javier Arce, 'The Enigmatic Fifth Century in Hispania: Some Historical Problems', in *Regna and Gentes*, ed. by Goetz, Jarnut, and Pohl, pp. 135–59 (p. 137).

Figure 15.6. Beheaded usurpers in a fragment of the Ravenna consular *fasti*.
After Bischoff and Köhler, 'Eine illustrierte Ausgabe'.

The invasion of Spain by Vandals, Sueves, and Alans , therefore, is a direct consequence of Gerontius's call for military assistance.[66] Entering Gaul, Gerontius also
defeated and executed Constans near Vienne. However, Gerontius was later forced
by the imperial troops to flee to Spain, where his own soldiers turned against him
and drove him into committing suicide.[67] When Maximus learned about those
developments, he is said to have fled to the barbarians. He was captured and sent
to Ravenna in the course of Asterius's campaign against the Vandals.[68] Since the
campaign is explicitly said to have been directed against the Vandals, it is likely that

[66] Kulikowski, 'Barbarians in Gaul', pp. 337–38.

[67] Roger Collins, *Early Medieval Spain: Unity in Diversity, 400–1000* (London, 1983), p. 17.
The main source for this episode is Olympiodorus, *Fragmenta*, 17.1. Gerontius was the victim of
a conspiracy organized by his own troops. Together with one of his slaves, a man of Alan origin,
Gerontius attempted to resist when the soldiers put his house under siege. When they put fire to
the house, without any way to escape, Gerontius killed his wife, then his slave, before committing
suicide. See also Sozomenus, *Historia Ecclesiastica*, 9.14; Orosius, *Historia adversus paganos*, 7.42.3;
and Prosper Tiro, *Epitoma Chronicorum*, 1243, in *Chronica minora saec. IV. V. VI. VII.*, vol. I, ed. by
Theodor Mommsen, MGH AA, 9 (Berlin, 1892), pp. 341–499.

[68] Michael Kulikowski, 'The Career of the *Comes Hispaniarum* Asterius', *Phoenix*, 54 (2000),
123–41.

the barbarians to whom Maximus went were Gunderic's Vandals.[69] In his chronicle, Hydatius writes of the allocation in 411 of Iberian land to the invaders of the previous years: Gallaecia to the Vandals and the Sueves, Lusitania and Carthaginensis to the Alans, Baetica to the 'Vandals called Silings'.[70] The implication is that for two years the barbarians now allotted different provinces in the peninsula had resided there without finding any solution to their problems. There have been several different interpretations of the arrangement mentioned by Hydatius. The settlement was either a consequence of a *foedus* or arranged with no Roman interference through the allotment of land according to barbarian customs.[71] According to Hydatius, the Hasding Vandals received eastern Gallaecia and the Siling Vandals Baetica, with the other provinces divided between Alans and Sueves.[72] Tarraconensis remained in Roman hands, possibly as a result of the treaty with Gerontius, since he had proclaimed Maximus the emperor in the provincial capital Tarragona, its political centre of power.[73] In the course of the land distribution, the invaders seem to have been assigned primarily fields that had been left fallow, which suggests that in this case the settlement was not reached by means of *hospitalitas* and that Roman landowners were not required to transfer a third of their property to the newcomers.[74] Some details seem to point to a possible settlement of the barbarians

---

[69] *Chronica Gallica 452*, 89, ed. by Richard W. Burgess, in *Society and Culture in Late Antique Gaul: Revisting the Sources*, ed. by Ralph M. Mathisen and Danuta Shanzer (Aldershot, 2001), pp. 52–84. See also Marcellinus Comes, *Chronicon*, 422.2, ed. by Theodor Mommsen, MGH AA, 9 (Berlin, 1894). A fragment of the Ravenna consular *fasti* preserved in an eleventh-century manuscript mentions the execution of Maximus in 412; see Bernhard Bischoff and Wilhelm Köhler, 'Eine illustrierte Ausgabe der spätantiken Ravennater Annalen', in *Medieval Studies in Memory of A. Kingsley Porter*, ed. by Wilhelm Köhler, I (Cambridge, 1939), pp. 125–38.

[70] Hydatius, *Chronicon*, 49, ed. by Richard W. Burgess (Oxford, 1993). Whether the Vandals settled in Hispania as *foederati* is still a matter of much scholarly dispute. The scarce sources, mainly chronicles, do not offer sufficient information to draw any conclusion in that respect. Nor can much be gained from later sources, such as Victor of Vita and Procopius, who had limited, if any, interest in Spanish affairs. See Paul S. Barnwell, *Emperor, Prefects, and Kings: The Roman West, 395–565* (London, 1992), pp. 114–15.

[71] Arce, 'Enigmatic Fifth Century', p. 139.

[72] Relevant sources for those problems are Orosius, *Historia adversus paganos,* 7.40.10, and Sozomenus, *Historia Ecclesiastica*, 9.12.3.

[73] Frank M. Ausbüttel, 'Verträge zwischen Vandalen und Römern', *Romanobarbarica*, 11 (1991), 1–20 (p. 4).

[74] For the debate on *hospitalitas*, see Jean Durliat, 'Le Salaire de la paix sociale dans les royaumes barbares (Vᵉ–VIᵉ siècles)', in *Anerkennung und Integration: Zu den wirtschaftlichen Grundlagen der Völkerwanderungszeit 400–600*, ed. by Herwig Wolfram and Andreas Schwarcz (Vienna, 1988),

as *foederati*, since after the regular Roman troops were removed from Spain, their place had to be taken by other troops. According to Edward Thompson, although the invaders did not arrive as *foederati* to Spain, they later entered contractual agreements with the Romans.[75] Their possible partners in such contracts may have been Gerontius and Maximus, both of whom controlled in 411 vast tracts of land in the Iberian Peninsula and were in dire need of military support. There is also the likely possibility that, following the fall of Gerontius, Maximus found shelter in Spain with those barbarians who had been his allies.[76]

The Western Mediterranean, by this time, was not under Roman rule any more. Both Vandals and Goths controlled important sea lanes. This, according to Javier Arce, was a relatively short period of time, which 'the two main components forming the initial settlements spent in the Peninsula' and which 'allows us to think that their impact on Roman society and structures was limited and without any visible consequences either for political administration, or for cultural matters, or as regards economic organization'.[77] Well into the seventh century, the administrative structure in the peninsula still looked Roman.[78]

An episode is reported in later sources which brings *comes Africae* Boniface into direct relation with the Vandal invasion of Africa.[79] He is said to have negotiated with Gunderic and his half-brother Geiseric about a threefold division of the North African provinces.[80] This arrangement between Boniface and the Vandals

---

pp. 21–72; Sam J. B. Barnish, 'Taxation, Land and Barbarian Settlement in the Western Empire', *Papers of the British School at Rome*, 54 (1986), 170–95; J. H. Wolfgang G. Liebeschuetz, 'Cities, Taxes and the Accommodation of the Barbarians: The Theories of Durliat and Goffart', in *Kingdoms of the Empire*, ed. by Pohl, pp. 135–52.

[75] Edward A. Thompson, 'The End of Roman Spain', *Nottingham Medieval Studies*, 20–23 (1976–79), 3–28 (p. 22).

[76] Collins, *Early Medieval Spain*, p. 17.

[77] Arce, 'Enigmatic Fifth Century', p. 156.

[78] Edward A. Thompson, 'The Barbarian Kingdoms in Gaul and Spain', *Nottingham Medieval Studies*, 7 (1963), 3–33 (p. 5); Michael Kulikowski, *Late Roman Spain and its Cities* (Baltimore, 2004).

[79] Hans-Joachim Diesner, 'Die Lage der nordafrikanischen Bevölkerung im Zeitpunkt der Vandaleninvasion', *Historia*, 11 (1962), 97–111 (p. 108): 'Der Hilferuf [of count Boniface] braucht nicht historisch zu sein, obwohl wir bis zum Gegenbeweis an seiner Möglichkeit oder sogar Wahrscheinlichkeit festhalten müssen.' For Boniface, see Johannes L. M. De Lepper, *De rebus gestis Bonifatii comitis Africae et magistri militum* (Tilburg, 1941).

[80] Procopius, *Wars*, 3.3.23–26. See Javier Arce, 'Spain and the African Provinces in Late Antiquity', in *Hispania in Late Antiquity: Current Perspectives*, ed. by Kim Diane Bowes and Michael Kulikowski (Leiden, 2005), pp. 341–61 (p. 348).

appears only in sixth-century sources.[81] The Roman failure to resist Geiseric, his Vandals, and their allies taking over the African provinces left Roman writers in search of an explanation.[82] There are many comparable examples of this scapegoat motif in the historiography of Late Antiquity. One obvious example is the 'call for assistance' in 455 from the emperor's widow Eudoxia to King Geiseric, in her efforts to combat the usurper Petronius Maximus.[83] The fact that following their sack of Rome, the Vandals took her hostage, along with her children and several other Roman aristocrats, makes it unlikely that there was ever an agreement of that kind between Eudoxia and the Vandal king.[84]

Surely the war between Boniface and Felix had destabilized the North African provinces, which almost guaranteed the lack of any significant resistance to the Vandal conquest. A strong argument against the idea of an agreement between Geiseric, Gunderic, and Boniface is the fact that Boniface defended Hippo Regius against the Vandals for a year, a detail that does not fit well with his supposed rebellion against the government in Ravenna. It is true that later Byzantine sources maintain that he changed his mind at this point. But why would that have been the case, given the increasing weakness of Valentinian III's position from the time of the supposed threefold division of North Africa to the siege of Hippo? The political position of the *comes Africae* Boniface was certainly peripheral, since he could hardly have had any influence at the court in Ravenna or in Rome. His was without any doubt a strong position, for he had gained control over considerable quantities of grain, the shipment or absence of which could indeed influence the developments in Italy. According to Prosper Tiro, the emperor tried in vain to bring the situation in Africa under control.[85] A campaign ordered by the *magister militum* Felix failed miserably. The only general who had any success against Boniface was Sigisvult, but he failed to capture and execute him.[86] Boniface withdrew into the interior of Mauretania Sitifensis. Only after long negotiations was his

---

[81] Jordanes, *Getica*, 167–69: 'Gizerichus rex Vandalorum iam a Bonifatio in Africam invitatus.'

[82] Possidius, *Vita Augustini*, 28, ed. by Jacques-Paul Migne, in Patrologia Latina, 32 (Paris, 1865); Procopius, *Wars*, 3.5.21.

[83] Roberto Cessi, 'La crisi imperiale degli anni 454–455 e l'incursione Vandalica a Roma', *Archivio della R. Società Romana di Storia Patria*, 40 (1917), 161–204.

[84] Alberto Gitti, 'Eudossia e Genserico', *Archivio Storico Italiano*, 4 (1925), 3–38.

[85] Prosper Tiro, *Epitoma Chronicorum*, 1295.

[86] Ralph W. Mathisen, 'Sigisvult the Patrician, Maximus the Arian, and Political Strategems in the Western Roman Empire c. 425–40', *Early Medieval Europe*, 8 (1999), 173–96 (pp. 176–77).

status as enemy of the state removed; by May 429 he was back in the service of Ravenna.[87]

In short, Procopius's description of the supposed agreement between the Vandals and Boniface for the division of the North African provinces cannot be taken at face value, because no such contract is known for the entire history of the empire and the agreement is not mentioned in any contemporary source. Moreover, the idea that Boniface called the Vandals to Africa to his assistance is nothing more than a myth, which as Ludwig Schmidt has shown was fabricated in Constantinople almost a century after the events.[88] Such contemporary authors as Hydatius, Possidius, the unknown author of the Gallic chronicle, and, somewhat later, Victor of Vita had no knowledge of any 'betrayal' by Boniface on the eve of the Vandal invasion.

Was There a Gens Vandalorum before the Migration to Africa?

Visigothic military pressure was one of the decisive factors behind the final Vandal migration to North Africa.[89] For the Vandals, Africa offered a better protection from Roman attacks than Spain. In May of 429, the last significant phase of the Vandal migration took place.[90] A comparatively late source indicates that the Vandals embarked at Julia Traducta.[91] Some have suggested however two other ports, Tarifa and Algeciras. In addition, the coastal town of Cartagena must have had a considerable merchant fleet, which the Vandals would now have had at their

---

[87] Augustine, *Epistulae*, 220.7 (dated 427/28), ed. by Alois Goldbacher (Vienna, 1911): 'Quis autem crederet, quis timeret Bonifacio domesticorum et Africae comite in Africa constituto cum tam magno exercitu et potestate, qui tribunus cum paucis foederatis omnes ipsas gentes expugnando et terrendo pacaverat.' According to Augustine, Boniface's return to the imperial favour may have caused some Berbers to react violently.

[88] Ludwig Schmidt, 'Bonifatius und der Übergang der Wandalen nach Afrika', *Historische Vierteljahrsschrift*, 2 (1899), 449–62.

[89] Christian Courtois, 'Rapports entre Wisigoths et Vandales', in *I Goti in Occidente: problemi* (Spoleto, 1956), pp. 499–507 (p. 502).

[90] At the most, Prosper Tiro's remark that in 427 'exinde gentibus, quae navibus uti nesciebant, dum a concertantibus in auxiliam vocantur' may be interpreted as referring to a raid to Africa by some Vandal troops, prior to the migration of 429.

[91] Gregory of Tours, *Historiarum libri decem*, 2.2, ed. by Bruno Krusch and Wilhelm Levison, MGH SS rer. Merov., 1.1 (Hannover, 1937; repr. 1951 and 1992): 'Post haec prosequentibus Alamannis usque Traductam, transito mare, Wandali per totam Africam ac Mauritaniam sunt dispersi.'

disposal. It is unlikely that the crossing could have taken place earlier in the year than the month of May, since the inclement weather of the winter months substantially curtailed any activity at sea.[92] In addition, during the first months of 429, Geiseric's Vandals are known to have briefly fought against the Sueves. This was the last in a series of military confrontations in the southern region of the Iberian Peninsula. Cassiodorus mentions a Gothic attack on the Vandals, shortly before their departure from Spain. This may however refer to two different campaigns that the historical sources have conflated.[93] If so, then the Goths almost certainly acted on behalf of the Roman government. By contrast, and despite Courtois's idea that the Sueves attacked the Vandals on Roman instruction, it seems more convincing that their activities were part of their broader plans to expand into the Iberian Peninsula.[94] Geiseric seems to have taken very seriously the Suevic threat, for following their defeat, he pursued them into the interior and managed to kill King Hermigar near Mérida (Augusta Emerita). The crossing to Africa could take place safely only after removing the Suevic threat. According to the chronicle of Prosper Tiro, the entire *gens* of the Vandals left the Spanish provinces to go to Africa.[95] Such a formulation alludes to the ethnogenetic process taking place since the early fifth century. Procopius includes all participants of the enterprise under the *gens* of the Vandals, while Hydatius insists that involved in the migration were all Vandals including warriors and families.[96] However, in his biography of Augustine, Possidius claims that this was a medley of people with different ethnic backgrounds.[97] Similarly, Procopius's account stresses the polyethnic character of the migrant group: 'However, after that time by their natural increase among themselves and by associating other barbarians with them they came to be an

[92] Lionel Casson, *Ships and Seamanship in the Ancient World* (Princeton, 1995), pp. 270–71.

[93] Cassiodorus, *Chronica*, 1203 and 1215, in *Chronica minora saec. IV. V. VI. VII.*, vol. II, ed. by Theodor Mommsen, MGH AA, 11 (Berlin, 1894), pp. 109–61.

[94] Courtois, *Les Vandales*, p. 56 with n. 5.

[95] Prosper Tiro, *Epitoma Chronicorum*, 1295: 'Gens Wandalorum ab Hispaniae ad Africam transiit.'

[96] Procopius, *Wars*, 1.5.21; Hydatius, *Chronicon*, 80: 'Gaisericus rex de Betice provinciae litore cum Vandalis omnibus eorumque familiis [...] transit.'

[97] Possidius, *Vita Augustini*, 28: 'Verum brevi consequenti tempore divina voluntate et potestate provenit, ut manus ingens diversis telis armata et bellis exercitata, immanium hostium Vandalorum et Alanorum commixtam secum habens Gothorum gentem aliarumque diversarum personas, ex Hispaniae partibus transmarinis, navibus Africae influxisset et irruisset.'

exceedingly numerous people. But the names of the Alani and all the other barbarians, except the Moors, were united in the name of Vandals.'[98]

Possidius mentions Goths among those joining the Vandals, possibly because
of choosing what appeared to be a more attractive life in North Africa. The alternative was to remain in the Iberian Peninsula only to be involved in endless military
conflicts, which marked the dissolution of the social structures in the provinces in
what amounted to little less than civil war.[99] A large number of people had been
driven away from their homes, while numerous slaves had escaped their masters
and had begun new lives as impoverished farmers. Many individuals facing such
difficult times may have been compelled to join the heterogeneous coalition of the
Vandals. Participation in that coalition may have in turn given a new sense of
Vandal identity. In other words, the *gens Vandalorum* said to have crossed into
Northern Africa was made up of bits and pieces of very different social and ethnic
backgrounds. Whatever unity existed behind that heterogeneous coalition, it
would be brought to light during the hardships of the crossing. This further highlights another factor behind the integration into the Vandal *gens*, namely membership in the Vandal army. The Vandals were never an ethnically homogeneous
confederacy. During its movements across the Western Empire, the group had expanded by accepting new social elements from each one of the territories through
which the migrants had moved. A Vandal elite emerged as a consequence of
military prowess, and not of an ethnic creed.[100]

According to Victor of Vita, the census ordered by Geiseric in the spring of 429
indicated a total population of eighty thousand, including elders, adolescents,
children, and slaves.[101] Most modern commentators have taken the figure at face
value.[102] A few decades after Victor of Vita, Procopius claimed that Geiseric had
arranged his army into eighty 'thousands', each placed under the command of a
millenarius, in order to mask its actual weakness. If one gives credit to Procopius,
this would then imply that the actual strength of the Vandal coalition was smaller

---

[98] Procopius, *Wars*, 1.5.21, trans. by Dewing, p. 53.

[99] Peter Heather, 'The Emergence of the Visigothic Kingdom', in *Fifth-Century Gaul: A Crisis of Identity?*, ed. by John Drinkwater and Hugh Elton (Cambridge, 1992), pp. 84–94 (p. 88).

[100] Andrew Gillett, 'Was Ethnicity Politicized in the Earliest Medieval Kingdoms?', in *On Barbarian Identity*, ed. by Gillett, pp. 85–121 (p. 121).

[101] Victor of Vita, *Historia persecutionis Africanae provinciae*, 1.2.

[102] E.g. Ludwig Schmidt, 'Zur Frage nach der Volkszahl der Wandalen', *Byzantinische Zeitschrift*, 15 (1906), 620–21; Courtois, *Les Vandales*, pp. 215–21.

than that indicated by Victor of Vita, perhaps as small as fifty thousand.[103] Jakob Haury, on the other hand, believed that it was altogether wrong to believe that the figure of eighty thousand given by Victor of Vita also included women.[104] Procopius's account suggests that the Vandals themselves, who wished to give the appearance of a much stronger army, may have been responsible for inflating the numbers.[105] On the other hand, there is no mention of women in Victor of Vita.[106]

Be that as it may, it is nonetheless clear that no source could be really trusted in terms of an accurate number of participants in the Vandal migration to Africa. Figures like that have always been problematic for the interpretation of the historical writing of Late Antiquity. Figures for entire groups must be carefully distinguished from those referring to armies.[107] A migrating confederacy of the 400s consisted of warriors accompanied by their family members and slaves. As a result, it is often very difficult to decide whether figures advanced by contemporary or later sources refer only to the group of warriors or to the entire confederacy. In addition, contemporary authors frequently employ numbers that are anything but reliable. For example, if we trust Jordanes, Radagaisus's army entering Italy had 200,000 men, a figure which Zosimus later doubled to 400,000. Such numbers must be regarded as little more than markers of a narrative strategy designed to convey the image of a multitude of barbarians.[108] However, the figure advanced for Geiseric's Vandals leaving Spain in 429 may not be too far from reality. Should one consider that the *gens Vandalorum* was in fact a coalition of groups of different origins, including Hasdings, Silings, Alans, Goths, Hispano-Romans, and possibly even runaway slaves, it appears clear how small was the number of people who may

---

[103] The Vandal *millenarii* (*chiliarchoi*) may be compared to the Gothic *thiufadi*. See Thompson, 'The Barbarian Kingdoms', p. 9 with n. 43. For a brief description of the Vandal military organization, see Hans Delbrück, *Geschichte der Kriegskunst* (Berlin, 1921; repr. 1966), pp. 315–16.

[104] Jakob Haury, 'Über die Stärke der Vandalen in Afrika', *Byzantinische Zeitschrift*, 14 (1905), 527–28.

[105] Procopius, *Wars*, 1.5.18.

[106] Victor of Vita, *Historia persecutionis Africanae provinciae*, 1.2: 'Transiens igitur quantitas universa callidate Geiserici ducis, ut famam suae terribilem facet gentis, ilico statuit omnem multitudinem numerari. [...] Qui reperti sunt senes, iuvenes, parvuli, servi vel domini, octoginta milia numerati. Quae opinio divulgata, usque in hodiernum a nescientibus armatorum tantum numerus aestimatur.'

[107] Michael Kulikowski, 'Nation versus Army: A Necessary Contrast?', in *On Barbarian Identity*, ed. by Gillett, pp. 69–84.

[108] Walter Goffart, *Barbarians and Romans, AD 418–584: The Techniques of Accommodation* (Princeton, 1980), p. 231 ('poetic number[s]').

have actually called themselves 'Vandals'. This also demonstrates the fallacy of any biological interpretation of ethnicity in Late Antiquity or the early Middle Ages, including that of the Vandals. Likewise, there is no support in the sources for any kind of 'Germanic sense of confraternity' supposedly binding such groups together. If one accepts the figure of eighty thousand as credible, then the number of Vandal warriors was probably no larger than twenty thousand.[109] The Vandals thus appear as a minuscule group, especially when compared to some 2.5 to 3 million inhabitants of the North African provinces of the empire.[110] Whether one believes Victor of Vita or Procopius, the Vandals who entered North Africa in 429 were actually a quite small army, an indication of how far removed was the military situation of the early fifth century from the great Roman armies of the previous centuries.

If considering the political conditions that led to the migration of Geiseric's Vandals, it becomes apparent that their previous position in the Peninsula was noticeably more precarious because of the intensification of Roman authority in the region. The increased pressure from the Goths, as well as the growing power of Hermigar's Sueves only added to an already difficult situation. The Alans and Silings were crushed by Valia's campaign, with the survivors being integrated as far as possible into the confederacy led by the Hasding family.[111] Furthermore, the isolation of the Vandals in the southern region of Hispania may have increased their supply problems. On the other hand, Africa, shaken by a series of civil wars, lent itself as a viable alternative. One was probably reminded of the failed attempts of Alaric to establish himself in Africa, after his invasion fleet sank off the coasts of Italy in a storm, or of the Visigothic attempt to conquer Africa in 415.[112] No barbarian invasion of North Africa (Figure 15.7) had been attempted since then, but over the intervening years internal conflicts had substantially reduced the efficacy of Roman power in the region. The Vandal leader may have been fully aware of all those factors.

It is important to note that, prior to 429, various constitutive groups had resisted fusion, since as late as 411, following the invasion of Hispania, the Vandal confederacy could still break into several fragments. A distinctive *gens Vandalorum*

---

[109] Helmut Castritius, 'Wandalen', in *Reallexikon der germanischen Altertumskunde*, XXXIII, ed. by Heinrich Beck, Dieter Geuenich, and Heiko Steuer (Berlin, 2006), pp. 168–209 (p. 188). The figure of eighty thousand is also advanced for the Burgundians by Orosius, *Historia adversus paganos*, 7.32.11.

[110] Durliat, 'Le Salaire', p. 39 with n. 95.

[111] Hydatius, *Chronicon*, 67.

[112] Herwig Wolfram, *Das Reich und die Germanen: Zwischen Antike und Mittelalter* (Berlin, 1990), p. 236.

Figure 15.7. North Africa in the fifth century.
After Andrzej Kokowski and Christian Leiber, *Die Vandalen* (Nordstemmen, 2003).

had not existed prior to the year 429. If in need of labels for the constitutive groups, then one could certainly speak of a Hasding *gens*, a *gens* of the Silings, as well as of an Alanic *gens*. The crucial historical event that fundamentally changed the composition of the group was the crossing of the Mediterranean under the leadership of Geiseric. From this moment onwards the Vandal *gens* began to grow, and its name, previously given by outsiders, now became a unifying element of the Vandal ethnogenesis.

The official title of the Vandal king (*rex Vandalorum et Alanorum*) can be ascertained only from sources dating to the reign of Huneric, although it may be assumed that the title was also employed by Geiseric. If specific evidence is missing, this is only because of a lacunose historical record.[113] For numerous internal affairs as well as for his foreign policy, Gaiseric needed such a title as self-evident. Two early medieval analogies are known for the Vandal royal title, with its characteristic combination of two ethnic names. The Berber Masuna in the realm of Altava

---

[113] Herwig Wolfram, *Intitulatio I: Lateinische Königs- und Fürstentitel bis zum Ende des 8. Jahrhunderts* (Graz, 1967), p. 82, distinguishes 'absolute' from 'ethnic' titles assumed by kings of barbarian successor-states. According to Wolfram, the presence of an ethnic attribute in the title implies some limitation of royal power, whereas an 'absolute' title shows no limitations. Courtois's idea that the Berber kingdoms were only ephemeral polities has been convincingly rejected by Camps. Modern studies have further shown that these were not just tribal confederacies, but complex systems in which indigenous and Roman elements were fused together. See Gabriel Camps, '*Rex Gentium Maurorum et Romanorum*: recherches sur les royaumes de Maurétanie des VIe et VIIe siècles', *Antiquités Africaines*, 20 (1984), 183–218; Andy Blackhurst, 'The House of Nubel: Rebels or Payers?', in *Vandals, Romans and Berbers*, ed. by Merrills, pp. 59–75 (p. 74).

called himself *rex gentium Maurorum et Romanorum*.[114] According to Herwig Wolfram, Masuna imitated the Vandal royal intitulature.[115] However, it may well have been the other way around, with the Vandals imitating Berber practices. Moreover, in Europe such practices are known only from much later times: following the conquest of the Lombard kingdom, Charlemagne assumed the title of *rex Francorum et Langobardorum*.[116] As for the Vandals, their kings continued to use the double ethnic attribute all the way to Gelimer, the last Vandal ruler, who is called *Geilamir rex Vandalorum et Alanorum* in an inscription on a silver bowl (Figure 15.8).[117]

The fact that the royal title remained unchanged for more than a century points to a certain continuity of political representations. On the other hand, the continuing exclusion of the Romans may have made acculturation very difficult. But was the use of the 'Alans' in the title an indication of some Vandal collective memory? In 406/07, the Alans had come to the rescue of the Vandals during the key military intervention on the Rhine frontier, just two generations before Geiseric's Vandals crossed into Northern Africa. The Hasdings had lost even their king Godegisel, a catastrophe that could easily have led to the dissolution, if not destruction, of the entire confederacy. The kings of the *gens* were regarded as 'carriers of tradition', the very embodiment of the identity of that *gens*. Later, the division of land within Spanish provinces shows the Alans to have been the strongest group in the coalition. They clearly received substantially more land than Sueves, Hasdings, or Silings. Only the Gothic army acting on behalf of the government in Ravenna was able to

---

[114] Courtois, *Les Vandales*, App. II, n. 95 (*Corpus inscriptionum Latinarum*, vol. VIII: *Inscriptiones Africae Latinae*, ed. by Gustav Wilmanns (Berlin, 1881), 9835). Courtois dated the inscription to 508, but other authors proposed different dates. See Yves Modéran, *Les Maures et l'Afrique romaine romaine (IVᵉ–VIIᵉ siècle)* (Rome, 2003), pp. 375–76.

[115] Wolfram, *Intitulatio I*, p. 82; Courtois, *Les Vandales*, pp. 333–34.

[116] Jarnut, *Geschichte*, p. 123. Gillett, 'Was Ethnicity Politicized?', p. 110 with n. 31, rejects the idea that the history of the Vandals offers a prime example of an early medieval ethnogenesis. See Gillett, 'Was Ethnicity Politicized?', p. 114: 'Of the kingdoms established in the first generations after the collapse of Roman power in the West, only Vandal and Moorish Africa provides more-or-less unambiguous evidence of ethnic titulature, though not as the exclusive or necessarily dominant royal titulature.'

[117] The inscription can be found in Courtois, *Les Vandales*, App. II, n. 111 (*Corpus inscriptionum Latinarum*, VIII, 17412). The bowl was probably made between 530 and 533 and arrived in Constantinople as part of the booty taken after Belisarius's conquest. It was later moved to Italy under unknown circumstances. See Theodor Mommsen, 'Vandalische Beutestücke in Italien', in *Gesammelte Schriften*, ed. by Theodor Mommsen, IV (Berlin, 1965), pp. 565–66.

Figure 15.8. Silver bowl of King Gelimer. After Hultén, *True Story*.

break the military pre-eminence of the Alans. It is quite possible that their later incorporation into the *gens Vandalorum* was the result of the Vandal-Alan relations established ever since the crossing of the Rhine. If the Vandals remembered that moment as defining for their history, especially in the light of them losing their king, then the Alans must have been regarded as a key actors in that history.

Conclusion: The Path to an African Kingdom

The ethnogenesis of the Vandals was a process with several stages, each one of which is directly linked to a particular leg in their migration: the settlement between the Vistula and the Oder Rivers, the Pannonian sojourn, the three-year stay in Gaul, then the Iberian Peninsula, and finally the hundred-year long kingdom in North Africa. Each stop marked a new phase in a process that culminated in the creation of a *gens Vandalorum*. Before the invasion of the North African provinces and the establishment of their *regnum*, the Vandals had already spent some thirty years within the empire. They must therefore have been familiar with many economic, social, and political structures of the Late Roman Empire. This was particularly the case of the Iberian Peninsula, whose cities the Vandals began to conquer, one by one, in the 420s. They found working systems of suitable Roman culture and an excellent infrastructure, including an economic system based on taxation.[118] In Hispania, the Vandals assimilated the knowledge they would later use in North Africa. The ethnogenesis of the Vandals and ultimately the creation of their realm in North Africa can only be understood with respect to their earlier migrations, since the experience accumulated while crossing the Western Empire was the very basis on which a *gens Vandalorum* took shape after 429, and a *regnum Vandalorum* was established. Survival was possible only through the unification of diverse barbarian groups under an old and prestigious name, such as that of the Vandals. The different stops of the Vandal migration had varying degrees of influence upon the later *gens*. The crossing of the Rhine is the first event that we know about for the 'historical Vandals' and is therefore to be regarded as an important stage of the Vandal migration.[119] Their history had just begun.[120] In other words, it marked the beginning of a new ethnogenetic process, from which later a Vandal *gens* would result; but this was not a result in a teleological sense, for the process of identity-building continued. The 'prehistory' of the Vandals can thus be treated as 'proto-ethnogenesis'. Only after 429 would a Vandal identity take shape, including the Alans, a phenomenon which continued up to the collapse of the realm in 533/34. These phenomena were highly dynamic processes, which can also be observed in other barbarian successor states.

---

[118] Michael Kulikowski, 'Cities and Government in Late Antique Hispania: Recent Advances and Future Research', in *Hispania in Late Antiquity*, ed. by Bowes and Kulikowski, pp. 1–70.

[119] Javier Pampliega, *Los germanos en España* (Pamplona, 1998), pp. 202–04.

[120] For a detailed analysis of many aspects of the history of the Vandals in Africa, see my *Konflikt und Anpassung*, pp. 175–254, and *Das Reich der Vandalen und seine (Vor-)Geschichten*, ed. by Berndt and Steinacher.

THE FREXES: LATE ROMAN BARBARIANS
IN THE SHADOW OF THE VANDAL KINGDOM

Philipp von Rummel

Research on the Late Roman barbarians usually focused on northern or, more often, Germanic groups and their role in the transformation of the Roman world. This is also true for research on barbarians in the non-European parts of the Roman Empire including the North African provinces. There, in spite of the existence of various barbarian tribes of African origin, the emphasis of research was laid primarily on the Vandals who conquered the African provinces in AD 429. Their establishment of a kingdom in the heart of the Roman Empire, until then undisturbed by northern barbarians, is undoubtedly one of the most impressive events in the period of the so-called Great Migrations. Yet, although much work remains to be done on the Vandals, they can no longer be regarded as neglected barbarians. The Vandals, their kingdom, and its Roman-barbarian conflict are now to be ranked with the better-examined barbarian tribes.[1]

During the last decades of their rule in North Africa the Vandals were confronted with increasing problems caused by other barbarians inside and near their kingdom. The growing activity of those people, generally called *Mauri* or *Maurousioi* in ancient sources, caused a paradoxical situation that transformed the former

---

[1] See the papers on 'L'Afrique vandale et byzantine' in *Antiquité Tardive*, 10 (2002) and 11 (2003), as well as *Vandals, Romans and Berbers: New Perspectives on Late Antique North Africa*, ed. by Andrew Merrills (Aldershot, 2004); John H. W. G. Liebeschuetz, '*Gens* into *regnum*: The Vandals', in *Regna and Gentes: The Relationships Between Late Antique and Early Medieval Peoples and Kingdoms in the Transformation of the Roman World*, ed. by Hans Werner Goetz, Jörg Jarnut, and Walter Pohl (Leiden, 2003) pp. 55–83; *Das Reich der Vandalen und seine (Vor-)Geschichten*, ed. by Guido Berndt and Roland Steinacher (Vienna, 2008); and Guido Berndt's contribution to this volume.

barbarian Vandals into defenders of the classical urban civilization of North Africa. Procopius, a Byzantine historian and a participant in Belisarius's 533/34 campaign against the Vandals, describes the differences between those groups of African barbarians:

> For of all the nations which we know that of the Vandals is the most luxurious, and that of the Moors the hardiest. For the Vandals, since the time they gained possession of Libya, used to indulge in baths, all of them, every day, and enjoyed a table abounding in all things, the sweetest and best that the earth and sea produce. And they wore gold very generally, and clothed themselves in the Medic garments, which now they call 'seric', and passed their time, thus dressed, in theatres and hippodromes and in other pleasurable pursuits, and above all else in hunting. And they had dancers and mimes and all other things to hear and see which are of a musical nature or otherwise merit attention among men. And the most of them dwelt in parks, which were well supplied with water and trees; and they had great numbers of banquets, and all manner of sexual pleasures were in great vogue among them. But the Moors live in stuffy huts both in winter and in summer and at every other time, never removing from them either because of snow or the heat of the sun or any other discomfort whatever due to nature. And they sleep on the ground, the prosperous among them, if it should so happen, spreading a fleece under themselves. Moreover, it is not customary among them to change their clothing with the seasons, but they wear a thick cloak and a rough shirt at all times. And they have neither bread nor wine nor any other good thing, but they take grain, either wheat or barley, and, without boiling it or grinding it to flour or barley-meal, they eat it in a manner not a whit different from that of animals.[2]

To Procopius, the Vandals, a tribe from whose name the synonym for barbarism was derived, became luxurious and effete 'Romans' in contrast to the ferocious Mauri. While the Vandal kings represented the successors of Roman imperial power, the Mauri were the 'real' barbarians of North Africa, and as such they are the subject of the following pages.

The term *Mauri*, however, is as vague as *Germani*. The only feature all Moors shared was that they were not Roman. In fact, they consisted of dozens of tribes in a steady process of formation, dispersal, and reorganization. As this situation in its entirety is too complex for this short paper, I shall use the tribe of the Frexes as an example to illustrate Roman-barbarian relations in late antique North Africa. Living inside the ancient Roman province of Byzacena and thus inside the official borders of the Vandal kingdom, they are a suitable subject for a case study.

---

[2] Procopius, *Wars*, 4.5–13, ed. by J. Haury and trans. by H. B. Dewing, II (London, 1954). For Procopius's participation in Belisarius's campaign, see Averil Cameron, *Procopius and the Sixth Century* (Berkeley, 1985), pp. 171–87.

The Moors: Neglected Barbarians?

One might wonder whether the Mauri are really 'neglected barbarians'. If we look at the thirty-six-page bibliography in Yves Modéran's recent monograph,[3] 'neglect' is surely not the first word that comes to mind. Research on the Moors does indeed have a long tradition. From an early medieval point of view, however, Moorish tribes never played a significant role in comparative research on Late Roman barbarians. Therefore, Moorish tribes are undoubtedly ignored in the modern public perception of ancient barbarians. This neglect of the Moors appears to stem from the fact that research on other barbarian groups was considered more suitable, and was easier as well. Some years ago, Michael Brett and Elisabeth Fentress actually spoke of a 'total ignorance' of the Berbers in both Great Britain and the United States due to the lack of literature available in English.[4] This gap may be almost closed now by their diachronical view on the Berbers and the preceding monographs in French, especially that of Gabriel Camps.[5]

In the French-speaking world, interest in the ancient and modern Berbers was always greater than in other European countries. Far from being neglected, the history of northern Africa became interesting to French scholars ever since the conquest of Algeria in 1830. The interest in North African history and archaeology survived the end of the French government in the Maghreb. In 1927, Stéphane Gsell published a fundamental study on the native kingdoms in pre-Islamic North Africa.[6] Later, the works of different scholars headed by Gabriel Camps and Jehan Desanges contributed considerably to the knowledge of North African tribes in Antiquity and of their material culture.[7] In the late 1970s, Marcel Bénabou's book

---

[3] Yves Modéran, *Les Maures et l'Afrique romaine (IVᵉ–VIIᵉ siècle)* (Rome, 2003).

[4] Michael Brett and Elisabeth Fentress, *The Berbers* (Oxford, 1996), p. 1.

[5] Gabriel Camps, *Les Berbères: mémoire et identité*, 3rd edn (Paris, 1995).

[6] Stéphane Gsell, *Histoire ancienne de l'Afrique du Nord*, V: *Les Royaumes indigènes: organisation sociale, politique et économique* (Paris, 1927).

[7] Jehan Desanges, *Catalogue des tribus africaines de l'Antiquité classique à l'ouest du Nil* (Dakar, 1962); Jehan Desanges, 'Une notion ambiguë: la *gens* africaine. Réflexions et doutes', *Bulletin archéologique du Comité des Travaux Historiques et Scientifiques*, 22 (1992), 169–76; William Seston and Maurice Euzennat, 'Un dossier de la chancellerie romaine: la Tabula banasitana', *Comptes-Rendus des Séances de l'Académie des Inscriptions et Belles-Lettres*, 1971, 468–90; Maurice Euzennat, 'Les Zegrenses', in *Mélanges d'histoire ancienne offerts à William Seston* (Paris, 1974), pp. 183–85; Maurice Euzennat, 'Les Structures tribales dans l'Afrique préislamique: un état de la question', in *Monuments funéraires: institutions autochtones. VIᵉ colloque international sur l'Afrique du Nord antique et médiévale 1993*, ed. by Pol Trousset (Paris, 1995), pp. 247–54; David J.

on the African resistance against Romanization initiated an intensive debate on the
definition of Romanization, its role, and the relationship between 'Romans' and
'non-Romans' in North African history.[8] The debate caused an intensive reconsideration of old ideas such as, for example, that of the 'Berber permanence'. The
notions of Berbers living in a cultural tradition that remained unchanged over the
last 2500 years; of the North African history being exclusively one of conquerors,
from Phoenicians and Romans to Vandals, Byzantines, and Arabs; and of Berbers as
a constantly obstreperous people, are now largely abandoned. It became obvious that
Numidians, Moors, or Berbers did change and that they were to be studied according
to different regional and chronological contexts.[9] In spite of this seminal discussion
that preceded other questions on the deeper sense of such concepts as 'acculturation' or 'Romanization', Moors or Berbers never played, according to Brett and
Fentress, the role of protagonists in their own history.[10] Yves Modéran called this
phenomenon a 'historiographic paradox': in spite of the central role of the Moors
in several works on late antique North Africa, they were never studied per se.[11]

'Neglect' is a more adequate term in respect to the archaeological research. It is
true that thanks to the pioneering work of Noël Duval and Paul-Albert Février,
global approaches to the material culture of late antique North Africa are nowa-
days common. However, the regions in which the Moorish kingdoms were located
in Late Antiquity are still largely unexplored outside a number of towns, in which
the emphasis is on particular monuments. Moreover, much of what is known relies
on late nineteenth- and early twentieth-century surveys of the French military. In

Mattingly, 'The Laguatan: A Libyan Tribal Confederation in the Late Roman Empire', *Libyan
Studies*, 14 (1983), 96–108; Yves Modéran, 'Les Premiers Raids des tribus sahariennes en Afrique
et la Johannide de Corippus', in *Histoire et archéologie de l'Afrique du Nord: Actes du IVe colloque
international, Strasbourg 1988* (Paris, 1991), pp. 479–90.

[8] Marcel Bénabou, *La Résistance africaine à la romanisation* (Paris, 1976); Yvon Thébert,
'Romanisation et déromanisation en Afrique: histoire décolonisée ou histoire inversée?', *Annales:
Économies, Sociétés, Civilisations*, 33 (1978), 64–82; Marcel Bénabou, 'Les Romains ont-ils conquis
l'Afrique?', *Annales: Économies, Sociétés, Civilisations*, 33 (1978), 83–88; Philippe Leveau, 'La Situation coloniale de l'Afrique romaine', *Annales: Économies, Sociétés, Civilisations*, 33 (1978), 89–92.

[9] Brett and Fentress, *The Berbers*, pp. 1–9.

[10] Brett and Fentress, *The Berbers*, p. 7.

[11] Modéran, *Les Maures*, p. 4. For works on late antique North Africa mentioning the Moors,
see Charles Diehl, *L'Afrique byzantine: histoire de la domination byzantine en Afrique (533–709)*
(Paris, 1896); Christian Courtois, *Les Vandales et l'Afrique* (Paris, 1955); William H. C. Frend, *The
Donatist Church: A Movement of Protest in Roman North Africa* (Oxford, 1952); Denys Pringle,
The Defence of Byzantine Africa, from Justinian to the Arab Conquest (Oxford, 1981).

spite of an archaeological record that is exceptional compared to most other parts of the Roman Empire, archaeological studies of the more rural regions in the southern parts of the African provinces are still rare. Archaeological research has mainly concentrated on urban centres with their impressive Roman monuments.[12] A number of archaeological surveys have indeed contributed a wealth of information on the African countryside,[13] but with the exception of Bruce Hitchner's project in the region of Cillium (Kasserine, Tunisia),[14] all those surveys avoided the regions of the late antique Moorish kingdoms in Numidia and Byzacena. Consequently, there can be little doubt that there is still a lot of work to be done. Compared to other groups of the late Roman period, the Moors and the archaeology of their homelands have certainly been neglected.

Such 'neglect' seems to play well with future researchers. A look at recent studies on the more prominent Germanic tribes shows that contemporary archaeology is mainly intent on discussing problems of ethnic interpretations advanced

[12] David J. Mattingly and R. Bruce Hitchner, 'Roman Africa: An Archaeological Review', *Journal of Roman Studies*, 85 (1995), 165–213.

[13] On Tripolitania, see Richard G. Goodchild, *Libyan Studies* (London, 1976); Olwen Brogan and David J. Smith, *Ghirza: A Romano-Libyan Settlement in Tripolitania* (Tripoli, 1985); Michel Reddé, *Prospection des vallées du nord de la Libye (1979–1980): la region de Syrte à l'époque romain* (Paris, 1988); Isabella Sjöstrom, *Tripolitania in Transition: Late Roman to Early Islamic Settlement* (Aldershot, 1990); David J. Mattingly, *Tripolitania* (London, 1995); Graeme Barker and David J. Mattingly, *Farming the Desert: The Unesco Libyan Valleys Archaeological Survey*, 2 vols (Paris, 1996). For Cherchell, see Philippe Leveau, *Caesarea de Maurétanie et son territoire* (Rome, 1984). For Segermes, see *Africa Proconsularis: Regional Studies in the Segermes Valley of Northern Tunisia,* ed. by Søren Dietz, Leila Ladjimi Sebaï, and Habib Ben Hassen (Copenhagen, 1995); *Africa Proconsularis: Regional Studies in the Segermes Valley of Northern Tunisia,* ed. by Peter Ørstedt and others, III (Aarhus, 2000). For Carthage, see Joseph A. Greene, 'Une reconnaissance archéologique dans l'arrière-pays de la Carthage antique', in *Pour Sauver Carthage: exploration et conservation de la cité punique, romaine et byzantine,* ed. by Abdelmajid Ennabli (Paris, 1992), pp. 195–97. For Dougga, see *Rus Africum: Terra, acqua, olio nell'Africa settentrionale. Scavo e ricognizione nei dintorni di Dougga (alto Tell tunisino),* ed. by Mariette de Vos (Trento, 2000). For the Tunisian coast, see *Le Littoral de la Tunisie: étude géoarchéologique et historique,* ed. by Hedi Slim and others (Paris, 2004). For the Sahel Pottery Survey, see David P. S. Peacock, Fathi Bejaoui, and Nejib Ben Lazreg, 'Roman Pottery Production in Central Tunisia', *Journal of Roman Archaeology*, 3 (1990), 59–84.

[14] R. Bruce Hitchner, 'The Kasserine Archaeological Survey, 1982–1986', *Antiquités Africaines,* 24 (1988), 7–41; R. Bruce Hitchner, 'The Kasserine Archaeological Survey 1987', *Antiquités Africaines,* 26 (1990), 231–60; R. Bruce Hitchner, 'Historical Text and Archaeological Context in Roman North Africa: The Albertini Tablets and the Kasserine Survey', in *Methods in the Mediterranean: Historical and Archaeological Views on Texts and Archaeology,* ed. by David B. Small (Leiden, 1995), pp. 124–42.

by previous generations of scholars.[15] In the case of the Mauri, the archaeological 'neglect' has brought about the positive byproduct that nobody seriously attempted to reconstruct late antique Moorish history by means of allegedly typical fibulae, buckles, or ceramics. This may be a good starting point for future studies of contemporary evidence in its entirety and a chance to gain knowledge of the *Mauri* and their way of life through comprehensive studies of the regions where the Moorish presence is confirmed by written sources.

The Frexes

One such region is located in the south-western part of the ancient province of Byzacena near the frontier of present-day Tunisia and Algeria. There, in the later Vandal period, a formerly insignificant tribal group[16] under the leadership of a certain Guenfan and his son Antalas became one of the most powerful factions in the territory of Vandal and later Byzantine Africa.[17] What we know from the written sources about this interesting group comes mainly from Procopius and Corippus, a sixth-century poet of African origin. Corippus's *Johannis*, an epic poem describing the campaign conducted against the insurgent *Mauri* by the Byzantine general John Troglita, is the only written source mentioning the tribal name of Antalas's group: they were called Frexes.[18]

From both authors we learn that the followers of Guenfan and Antalas lived in Byzacena, where Guenfan and his people became a powerful faction in the early 500s. When Antalas was young, an oracle of Ammon had told Guenfan about the great future of his young son.[19] When he reached seventeen, the young man started to pillage the local countryside and began to develop an impressive reputation among the local people.[20] The defeat of a Vandal army during the reign of the Vandal king

[15] Sebastian Brather, *Ethnische Interpretationen in der frühgeschichtlichen Archäologie: Geschichte, Grundlagen und Alternativen* (Berlin, 2004).

[16] Flavius Cresconius Corippus, *Johannis*, 3.153, ed. by Josef Partsch, MGH AA, 3.2 (Berlin, 1879): 'humilis gens'.

[17] Modéran, *Les Maures*, pp. 315–34.

[18] Corippus, *Johannis*, 2.42–46 and 184; 3.184–88; 7.383–84; and 8.647–49. See also Gabriel Camps, 'Antalas', in *Encyclopédie Berbère*, V (Aix-en-Provence, 1988), pp. 706–08; and Jehan Desanges, 'Frexes', in *Encyclopédie Berbère*, XIX (Aix-en-Provence, 1998), p. 2935.

[19] Corippus, *Johannis*, 3.152–54.

[20] Corippus, *Johannis*, 3.156–81.

Hilderic (523–30) was his first success in an open battle against the Vandals.[21] Corippus completes Procopius's report with the information that Antalas started to devastate African towns and countryside after a hundred years of Vandal rule, that is, in 529.[22] Corippus also informs us that Africa thrived until the thirtieth year of Antalas, who, therefore, must have been born around 499.[23]

When Belisarius entered Africa in 533, Antalas and his Frexes declared themselves loyal to the Byzantine government, a situation that lasted until 544. In that year, however, Antalas's brother Guarizila was killed at the order of the Byzantine general Solomon.[24] Moreover, the Levathae or Laguatan, a nomadic tribe from the Tripolitanian desert, moved into southern Byzacena. Enraged by the assassination of his brother,[25] Antalas allied himself to those nomads and went to war against the Byzantine troops. During the heavy fighting against the Byzantines, various sources of information about Antalas depict him as one of the important leaders of the Moorish coalition eventually defeated by the Byzantine general John Troglita in 547. Antalas survived the decisive battle near the town of Taparura (Sfax, Tunisia) and submitted again to the Emperor. After 547, both Antalas and the Frexes disappear from the radar of the written sources. It is unknown whether any connection or continuity can be established between the sixth-century Frexes and the third-century Fraxinenses, mentioned in inscriptions from Lambaesis (Algeria).[26] Some scholars believe that the modern seminomadic tribe of the Frechich, living in the region between Thala (Thala, Tunisia) and Thelepte (Medinet el-Kedima, Tunisia),[27] obtained its name from the ancient Frexes.[28]

[21] Procopius, *Wars*, 3.9. 3.

[22] Corippus, *Johannis*, 3.184–88. For the date, see Modéran, *Les Maures*, p. 315 with n. 2.

[23] Corippus, *Johannis*, 3.73–74. See Modéran, *Les Maures*, p. 316.

[24] Corippus, *Johannis*, 4.364–66.

[25] Corippus, *Johannis*, 2.28–31.

[26] *Corpus inscriptionum Latinarum*, VIII: *Inscriptiones Africae Latinae*, ed. by Gustav Wilmanns (Berlin, 1881) no. 2615 . See Modéran, *Les Maures*, p. 326 n. 5: 'il est peu probable que la tribu de Guenfan [...] ait eu une origine aussi lointaine'.

[27] Gabriel Camps and André Martel, 'Fraichich', in *Encyclopédie Berbère*, XIX, 2930–33.

[28] Diehl, *L'Afrique byzantine*, p. 303; Charles Monchicourt, *La Région du Haut Tell en Tunisie* (Paris, 1913), pp. 297–98; Courtois, *Les Vandales*, p. 346.

Where Were the Frexes?

Christian Courtois describes the region around Thala in the Dorsale Mountains as the centre of Antalas's power. His arguments for this location of the 'kingdom of the Dorsale' are that it is now the home of the Frechich; that the location corresponds to the distribution of Byzantine forts in the region; and that it was the *ignotae regiones* which, on his way to Sicca Veneria (El Kef, Tunisia), Fulgentius is said to have crossed after Moorish barbarians looted his monastery near Thelepte.[29] But François Châtillon and Yves Modéran rejected Courtois's location of the Frexes, arguing that the *ignotae regiones* mentioned in the *Life of Fulgentius* were not the homeland of Antalas's people but the Vandal lands in the Proconsular province.[30] Following a suggestion by Gabriel Camps, that the lands of the Frexes were in south-western Byzacena,[31] Modéran recently proposed to locate them on the basis of a number of clues from Corippus. According to Corippus, Antalas lived *in finibus Libycis*, which is the southern part of the Byzacena, and in a region of mountains.[32] Taking into consideration several alternatives in southern Byzacena, Modéran advanced the idea that Antalas lived in the mountains west of the route from Theveste (Tebessa, Algeria) via Thelepte (Medinet el-Kedima, Tunisia) to Capsa (Gafsa, Tunisia).[33] Had the Frexes been further to the east, there would be no way to explain why Solomon launched his attack on Antalas from Tebessa.[34] It would also be impossible to understand why in 544 the Tripolitanian Laguatan came to the region between Gafsa and Tebessa even though there was not much to be gained from raiding that region, at least not as much as one could expect from the much richer region to the north or on the coast. According to Procopius, the Tripolitanian *Mauri* probably took the route to Tebessa in order to meet their ally Antalas, instead of taking a much easier eastern route to Carthage.[35] There is a good deal of Byzantine fortification in the region west of the axis Theveste–Capsa,

---

[29] *Vita Fulgentii*, 5.13, ed. and trans. by Guillaume Lapeyre (Paris, 1932), pp. 32–33; Courtois, *Les Vandales*, pp. 345–46.

[30] François Chatillon, 'L'Afrique oubliée de C. Courtois et les "ignotae regiones" de la *Vita Fulgentii*', *Revue du Moyen Âge Latin*, 11 (1955 [1965]), 371–88. See also Modéran, *Les Maures*, pp. 316–21.

[31] Camps, 'Antalas', pp. 706–08.

[32] Corippus, *Johannis*, 2.34–35; 3.383; 3.176–78.

[33] Modéran, *Les Maures*, pp. 317–23 with map 12.

[34] Procopius, *Wars*, 4.21.19.

[35] Procopius, *Wars*, 2.21.17–19. See Modéran, *Les Maures*, pp. 316–23, esp. p. 321.

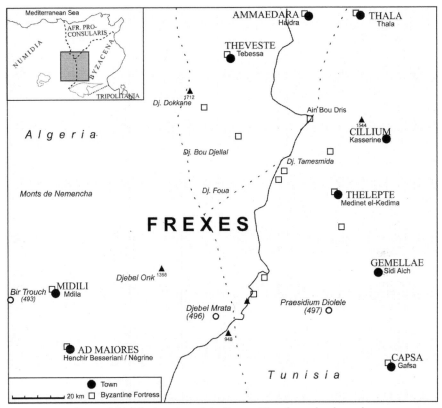

Figure 16.1. The location of the Frexes. Map drawn by the author.

which in itself is an indication of the Moorish presence in the vicinity.[36] This is further substantiated by one of Justinian's decrees installing the *dux* of Byzacena not in the old capital Hadrumetum (Sousse, Tunisia), but in Capsa and Theveste.[37] In light of such evidence, Modéran's idea of locating of the Frexes of Antalas near Thala in the Dorsale Mountains is quite plausible (Figure 16.1).

At first glance, this may appear as a surprising location for the Frexes. According to our sources, the barbarians of Antalas lived in a region that had belonged until then to the civilized, or Roman, parts of Africa. Not far from Thala, the so-called *Ostraka of Bir Trouch* were found in the Oued el-Mitta in 1965, which

[36] Modéran, *Les Maures*, pp. 321–22 with n. 28, and pp. 600–01 with map 20.

[37] *Codex Iustinianus*, 1.27.2.1 (534), ed. by P. Krueger (Berlin, 1895), p. 79; see also Modéran, *Les Maures*, pp. 322–23.

included five inscribed potsherds that had served as receipts of payments in agricultural products of a certain Massies. The potsherds were dated to the reign of the Vandal king Gunthamund.[38] The famous *Albertini Tablets*, a set of late fifth-century archival documents inscribed on wooden tablets and a singular proof of the continuity of the Roman tenure system from the first century AD into the Vandal period,[39] came from a mountainous region near the present-day Algerian-Tunisian border, a region that was most likely under the control of Antalas. As the tablets had been accidentally found by local people and then sold to a French administrator in Tebessa in 1928, the exact spot of their discovery remains unknown. However, it is possible to reconstruct the environment of their origin. According to the team of French scholars who published the tablets in 1952, they had been found in the region of Bir el-Horchane, Henchir ed-Debine, and Aïn Mrata.[40] If so, and if the tablets reflect the late fifth-century economic and social practices of the region in which they were found, then the inhabitants of the *fundus Tuletianos*, one of the four such *fundi* mentioned in the tablets dating contracts by the regnal years of the Vandal kings, not only lived at the same time as, but also in the vicinity of the abode of Antalas's father, Guenfan.[41]

Distinguishing between Moors, Vandals, and Romans

In spite of such proximity, the Frexes were ideologically in opposition to both Romans and Vandals. Corippus believed it was important to stress that the people of Antalas were not Romans, at least not in his eyes. While calling the war against the Roman rebel Stotzas a civil war (*bellum civile*), and the soldiers on both sides

[38] Jean-Pierre Bonnal and Paul-Albert Février, 'Ostraka de la région de Bir Trouch', *Bulletin d'Archéologie Algérienne*, 2 (1966–67), 239–49.

[39] Christian Courtois and others, *Tablettes Albertini: Actes privés de l'époque vandale (fin de Vᵉ siècle)* (Paris, 1952); David J. Mattingly, 'Olive Cultivation and the Albertini Tablets', in *L'Africa Romana*, VI (Sassari, 1989), pp. 403–15; Hitchner, 'Historical Text and Archaeological Context', pp. 124–42; Peter Ørstedt, 'From Henchir Mettich to the Albertini Tablets: A Study in the Economic and Social Significance of the Roman Lease System (*locatio-conductio*)', in *Landuse in the Roman Empire*, ed. by Jesper Carlsen, Peter Ørstedt, and Jens Erik Skydsgaard (Rome, 1994), pp. 115–25; Jonathan P. Conant, 'Literacy and Private Documentation in Vandal North Africa: The Case of the Albertini Tablets', in *Vandals, Romans and Berbers*, ed. by Merrills, pp. 199–224.

[40] Courtois and others, *Tablettes Albertini*, pp. 3–4.

[41] The other three estates are identified as *fundus magula*, *fundus capprarianus*, and *fundus gemiones*.

fellow Romans (*cognate*), Corippus always referred to Antalas as the leader of a distinct barbarian tribe. This invites us to consider who the 'Romans' and who the 'Moors' might have been in that region and during that period.

If taking at face value the idea that the African *Romania* was a land of urban civilization, then it becomes clear that the opposite of the 'Roman' town-dwellers were the 'Moorish' peasants of the hinterland.[42] While the 'Romans' were members of a *civitas* organized on the basis of Roman law and supporting public duties and constructions, the people who did not live in a city were automatically members of some *gens*, that is, *not cives* and, therefore, not 'Romans'.[43] To a sixth-century Roman, a *Maurus* was a man who lived in the countryside and belonged to a group without real political institutions.[44] However, several scholars rejected the idea of a sharp contrast between Roman plains and Moorish highlands, which was first introduced by Christian Courtois,[45] and argued instead that at least some mountain regions were just as influenced by the Roman civilization as the neighbouring plains.[46] This certainly applies to the lands of the Frexes in south-western Byzacena.[47] On the other hand, the production of olive oil and the practice of Christianity do not necessarily rule out the possibility of tribal identities surviving in the region.[48] Unfortunately, it is hard to find any clues as to what may have distinguished the people on the estates of Flavius Geminius Catullinus or the Massies mentioned in the Ostraka of Bir Trouch from the people under the leadership of Guenfan and Antalas.

Both Procopius and Corippus carefully distinguished between the people of Antalas and the nomadic tribes of Tripolitania. It is therefore likely that the Frexes were a settled community.[49] Thus their way of life may not have been very different from people living on Roman estates, perfectly integrated into the fiscal, legal, and economic mechanisms of the Late Roman state. The issue of how to distinguish

[42] Courtois, *Les Vandales*, p. 112; Modéran, *Les Maures*, pp. 418–21 and pp. 441–43.

[43] Modéran, *Les Maures*, pp. 417–21, here p. 441: 'Le contexte idéologique de la reconquête byzantine ne favorisait plus la prise en compte de ce type de nuances: la tribu était définie dans sa globalité comme un organisme foncièrement opposé à la cité.'

[44] Modéran, *Les Maures*, p. 443.

[45] Courtois, *Les Vandales*, pp. 118–26 and 144–49.

[46] Philippe Leveau, 'L'Opposition de la montagne et de la plaine dans l'historiographie de l'Afrique du Nord antique', *Annales de Géographie*, 86 (1977), 201–05; Thébert, 'Romanisation et déromanisation', pp. 67–69; Leveau, *Caesarea de Maurétanie*, pp. 473–500.

[47] For the archaeological evidence pertaining to that region, see below.

[48] Modéran, *Les Maures*, pp. 453–68.

[49] Modéran, *Les Maures*, pp. 65–66.

between different groups is therefore a complex matter that needs a detailed examination of differences between groups with very similar social and economic backgrounds.

Language

Traditionally, Greek and Roman authors used a set of criteria to describe the differences between the bearers of the classical civilization and the barbarians. Among these were language, religion, weaponry and ways of fighting, clothing, hairstyle, and body signs.[50] Language was probably one of the most important markers of foreign identity, but, unfortunately, no reliable information on Antalas's mother tongue survives. Writing in the early 390s, Ammianus Marcellinus also called Moors the followers of another African rebel, Firmus. As with Antalas, Romans regarded Firmus as a national enemy (*perduellis*), an insurgent (*rebellis*), and a brigand (*latro*). Like Antalas, he was the son of a powerful Moorish leader, of a *regulus per nationes Mauricas potentissimus*.[51] Both Ammianus and Corippus drew from a conventional pool of Barbarian stereotypes for their portrayal of the Moors and, as a consequence, depicted them as completely un-Roman.[52] Unlike Antalas, however, Firmus is known from more than one source. Several sources — Augustine, Jerome, and Claudius Claudianus, as well as inscriptions — reveal that the family of Nubel, Firmus's father, was far from being one of 'superficially Romanised Moorish kinglets'.[53] In fact, quite the contrary is true:[54] members of the family

---

[50] Walter Pohl, 'Telling the Difference: Signs of Ethnic Identity', in *Strategies of Distinction: The Construction of Ethnic Communities, 300–800*, ed. by Walter Pohl and Helmut Reimitz (Leiden, 1998), pp. 17–69.

[51] Ammianus Marcellinus, *Res gestae*, 29.5, ed. by Wolfgang Seyfarth (Leipzig, 1978).

[52] Timothy D. Barnes, *Ammianus Marcellinus and the Representation of Historical Reality* (Ithaca, 1998), pp. 107–19; John Matthews, *The Roman Empire of Ammianus* (London, 1989), pp. 304–82; Vincent Zarini, *Berbères ou Barbares? Recherches sur le livre second de la Johannide de Corippe* (Nancy, 1997), p. 22; Ilona Opelt, 'Barbarendiskriminierung in den Gedichten des Flavius Cresconius Corippus', *Romanobarbarica;* 7 (1982–83), 162–79; Joseph Mantke, 'Das Bild der Barbaren in der "Iohannis" des Corippus', *Philologus*, 140 (1996), 329–33.

[53] Zeev Rubin, 'Mass Movements in Late Antiquity: Appearances and Realities', in *Leaders and Masses in the Ancient World: Studies in Honor of Zvi Yavetz*, ed. by Irad Malkin and Zeev W. Rubinsohn (Leiden, 1995), pp. 129–87 (p. 136).

[54] Andy Blackhurst, 'The House of Nubel: Rebels or Players', in *Vandals, Romans and Berbers*, ed. by Merrills, pp. 59–75.

boasted in Latin inscriptions of being champions of the Roman culture and proudly displayed their position within the provincial Roman aristocracy. The rebellion of Firmus was therefore neither an 'ethnic uprising' nor a matter of 'tribal ambitions'.[55] There can be no doubt that Nubel and his kinsmen spoke Latin fluently. They were high officials of the empire, mentioned in different written sources, and related to important people. Their Roman-ness is indubitable, as is their African background.[56] The names of Nubel's legitimate and illegitimate children[57] point to that cultural ambivalence: three sons bore Libyan names (Gildo, Mascazel, and Sammac), two of them Latin names (Firmus and Dius), and one daughter of Nubel, Cyria, had a Greek name. Though having a Libyan name does not exclude in any way the idea of Roman-ness,[58] the thorough integration of Nubel's family into the Roman Empire cannot conceal its tribal background. This becomes obvious in an inscription in Latin hexameters found in Tubusuptu (Tiklat, Algeria):

> With prudence he establishes a stronghold of eternal peace, and with faith he guards everywhere the Roman state, making strong the mountain by the river with fortifications, and this stronghold he calls by the name of Petra. At last the tribes of the region, eager to put down war, have joined as your allies, Sammac, so that strength united with faith in all duties shall always be joined to Romulus' triumphs.[59]

Reading the first and last letters of each line vertically, the inscription gives the acrostic *Praedium Sammacis* (Sammac's estate). It is therefore a clear demonstration of Sammac's close links to Roman authority,[60] but at the same time an expression of his integration in the local tribal structure. Though they live inside the official borders of the empire, the tribes appear as allies of Sammac, and not of Rome.

Guenfan and his son Antalas had a similarly ambivalent role. It goes without saying that they cannot compare to the prominence of Nubel's family. Unlike

---

[55] Maureen A. Tilley, *The Bible in Christian North Africa: The Donatist World* (Minneapolis, 1997) p. 94; Matthews, *Roman Empire*, p. 375.

[56] Blackhurst, 'House of Nubel', pp. 59–75; Brett and Fentress, *The Berbers*, pp. 71–75.

[57] Matthews, *Roman Empire*, p. 372, argues that the term 'brother', when applied to several leaders in their relationship to Firmus, may have had a much broader meaning for the extended family of a Moorish prince than for that of a typically Roman family.

[58] The classical example in that respect is Monica, St Augustine's mother, but there are many other examples of North African Romans with 'native' names.

[59] *ILS*, no. 9351; English translation from Brett and Fentress, *The Berbers*, p. 72.

[60] Matthews, *Roman Empire*, p. 373, points to an inscription mentioning Nuvel (Nubel) in relation to the building of a church at Rusguniae and the dedication of a relic from the True Cross to the newly built church.

Firmus and his other brothers, major power brokers in their own time, Guenfan and Antalas wielded only a regionally limited power. As a consequence, they do not feature as prominently in our sources. In addition, the number of inscriptions diminished drastically in the 400s, especially when compared to the number of inscriptions known for the late 300s. That we know comparatively little about Antalas's sense of Roman-ness may therefore be only due to insufficient sources. If we keep in mind other contemporary Moorish princes, such as Masties, a *dux* who proclaimed himself *imperator* in the Aurès mountains,[61] or Masuna, a *rex gentium Maurorum et Romanorum* ruling in what is now western Algeria,[62] Antalas appears not as a savage barbarian from the highland district, but rather as one of those Mauro-Roman kinglets who expressed their power over Moorish tribesmen in Latin inscriptions. That much is true about his desire to declare himself a subject of the Emperor in the letter he sent to Justinian, the text of which was transmitted by Procopius.[63] Moreover, it appears that Antalas was among the Moorish leaders who received their insignia of power from Belisarius.[64]

Antalas must have communicated with the Byzantine leaders in either Latin or Greek, which suggests that he was, at least, bilingual.[65] Speaking of the embassy of Amantius to Antalas, Corippus mentions the Moors consulting each other in a broken and ugly tongue with barking and fizzling sounds.[66] Leaving aside the stereotypical view of foreign languages as non-human, it seems probable that the Moors of Antalas spoke a local Libyan (Berber) dialect. Augustine, Jerome, and Procopius confirm the survival of a Punic language in late antique North Africa.[67]

---

[61] Jérôme Carcopino, 'Un "empereur" maure inconnu d'après une inscription latine récemment découverte dans l'Aurès', *Revue des Études Anciennes*, 46 (1944), 94–120; Courtois, *Les Vandales*, p. 336; Jérôme Carcopino, 'Encore Masties, l'empereur maure inconnu', *Revue Africaine*, 100 (1956), 339–48; Pierre Morizot, 'Pour une nouvelle lecture de l'*elogium* de Masties', *Antiquités Africaines*, 25 (1989), 263–84; Pierre Morizot, 'Masties a-t-il été imperator?', *Zeitschrift für Papyrologie und Epigraphik*, 141 (2002), 231–40; Modéran, *Les Maures*, pp. 398–415.

[62] *Corpus inscriptionum Latinarum*, VIII, 9835 from Altava (Algeria). See Gabriel Camps, '*Rex Gentium Maurorum et Romanorum*: Recherches sur les royaumes de Maurétanie des VIe et VIIe siècles', *Antiquités Africaines*, 20 (1984), 183–218.

[63] Procopius, *Wars*, 4.22.7.

[64] Procopius, *Wars*, 3.25.5–8.

[65] Modéran, *Les Maures*, p. 334 with n. 76.

[66] Corippus, *Johannis*, 4.350–52: 'illi [i.e., the Moors] inter sese fracto sermone furentes | latratus varios, stridentibus horrida linguis | verba ferunt'.

[67] Procopius, *Wars*, 4.10.20. For Augustine, see William M. Green, 'Augustine's Use of Punic', in *Semitic and Oriental Studies: A Volume Presented to William Popper on the Occasion of his*

Some even believe in a Phoenician language surviving well into Late Antiquity.[68] Others have convincingly argued that the Punic language mentioned by Augustine is not the language of the ancient Carthaginians, but a Libyan-Berber dialect of Augustine's Numidian homelands.[69] Corippus, our main source for the history of Antalas and his people, employed Punic to refer to the inhabitants of the North African provinces.[70]

It has become evident that even within a thoroughly 'Romanized' region such as Augustine's diocese of Hippo Regius (Annaba, Algeria), the late Roman society was largely bilingual. How much more then should one assume that to be the case for the regions further to the south, where the role and influence of Latin was probably comparatively smaller? In any case, some of the people mentioned in the Albertini Tablets display a remarkable degree of Latin education, and it seems improbable that the command of Latin was lost during the next few decades. In fact, Corippus specifically mentions a certain Maccus, who was the envoy Antalas sent to Johannes, and who was able to speak Latin.[71] Cusina, another Moorish king ruling to the south from the lands of the Frexes, was the son of a Roman mother, and he too spoke Latin.[72] On the other hand, Libyan dialects were probably so widely spread in late Roman North Africa and so frequently used that language seems to be of little practical importance for distinguishing between 'Romans' and 'Moors.'

Religion

The history of Vandal Africa shows that religion and religious affiliation played a key role as distinguishing features during this period. Unfortunately, little is

---

Seventy-Fifth Birthday, October 29, 1949, ed. by Walter Joseph Fischel (Berkeley, 1951), pp. 179–90; Peter Brown, 'Christianity and Local Culture in Late Roman North Africa', *Journal of Roman Studies*, 58 (1968), 85–95. For Jerome and other sources, see Fergus Millar, 'Local Cultures in the Roman Empire: Libyan, Punic and Latin in Roman Africa', *Journal of Roman Studies*, 58 (1968), 126–34.

[68] Millar, 'Local Cultures'.

[69] William H. C. Frend, 'A Note on the Berber Background in the Life of Augustine', *Journal of Theological Studies*, 43 (1942), 188–91; Christian Courtois, 'S. Augustin et la survivance de la Punique', *Revue Africaine*, 94 (1950), 239–82; Brown, 'Christianity and Local Culture', p. 85.

[70] Corippus, *Johannis*, 3.277; 4.86.

[71] Corippus, *Johannis*, 1.466: 'Romanae fuerat facundia linguae.'

[72] Modéran, *Les Maures*, pp. 334–50.

known about the religion of Antalas. Corippus narrates a story in which Guenfan, Antalas's father, consulted an oracle of Ammon about the future of his son.[73] If this may be in any way taken as showing that Guenfan's family was pagan, then we have obtained a positive result in our quest for a discrete feature marking the difference between 'Moors' and Christian 'Romans'. There is in fact some evidence for the fourth-century survival of paganism in the Moorish territories of what is now Libya, particularly at the site of Ghirza in Tripolitania, and there is also evidence for the cult of Ammon.[74] This seems to have been a Libyan adaptation of the cult of the Egyptian god Amun, which was further conflated with that of Jupiter/Zeus. The cult of Amun may have spread out from the famous shrine of Amun in the Siwa oasis in Egypt to the Augila oasis in Libya,[75] reaching the Libyan tribes, especially the Austuriani and the Laguatan of the Syrte and Tripolitania.

Asking an oracle of Ammon about the future of Antalas may thus have been an expression of Guenfan's adherence to that god's cult. However, Corippus's description of the oracle of Ammon is not based on his own observations in the field. Instead, it is largely made up of literary borrowings from Lucan.[76] Moreover, the archaeological record strongly suggests that Christianity was at the time well established in the lands of the Frexes.[77] It appears therefore that the story of Ammon's oracle was nothing more than a narrative strategy, the purpose of which was to help Corippus build a dichotomy between Christian Byzantines and pagan Moors, without much regard for facts. There may certainly have been surviving pagan elements in the Christianity of Antalas's people, which received prompt condemnation from the Church hierarchy.[78] But, as Yves Modéran puts it, our ability to identify the religion of Antalas or to describe that religion in order to distinguish his group among others remains very limited.[79] Since some Moorish leaders were

[73] Corippus, *Johannis*, 3.91–140.

[74] Mattingly, *Tripolitania*, pp. 38–40; Modéran, *Les Maures*, pp. 235–44 and 513–14.

[75] Procopius, *Buildings*, 6.2 and 14–18, ed. by J. Haury and trans. by H. B. Dewing (London, 1961); Modéran, *Les Maures*, pp. 243–44.

[76] Averil Cameron, 'Corippus' *Iohannis*: Epic of Byzantine Africa', in *Papers of the Liverpool Latin Seminar 4*, ed. by F. Cairns (Liverpool, 1984), pp. 167–80 (pp. 173–74).

[77] Modéran, *Les Maures*, pp. 512–40 with pp. 532–33, map 17.

[78] Modéran, *Les Maures*, pp. 331–33.

[79] Modéran, *Les Maures*, p. 333 n. 74. Nor can the old idea be accepted any more, namely that African Donatism was a specifically Moorish movement (Frend, *The Donatist Church*). Donatists came from all levels of society and from all regions of North Africa. In addition, no difference existed between the liturgical furnishings of Catholic and Donatist churches, which means that the buildings themselves cannot reveal the specific beliefs of the associated congregations.

clearly pagans (Ierna) and others devout Christians (Masties), religion does not seem to be the critical feature expected for the definition of Moorish identity.

Clan Membership and Political Affiliation

In pre-Roman Africa, but also during the Roman period, tribal organization and clan membership seem to have been among the important factors of social identity.[80] Inside the African provinces of the Roman Empire, however, a specific African system of land management had continuously diminished the strength of tribal groups. The *lex Manciana* gave *coloni* (tenants) on estates the right to claim uncultivated land for their own needs. Financial security was further guaranteed to tenants by means of exemption from the regular dues for as long as newly planted trees needed to bear fruit. The *lex Hadriana* extended this system in giving the tenants the right to sell or bequeath the fig or olive trees and the vines they had planted, but not the land, which remained in the hands of the landowner. The two *leges* provided incentives for tenants to invest in uncultivated land, which led to a substantial growth in the production of olive oil and grain. The latter is well represented in the distribution of African amphorae across the Mediterranean area. At the same time, the laws established a growing community of small possessors whose holdings linked them to the large estates and drew them away from common tribal property and their tribal ties.[81]

Although a considerable number of Africans embraced a Roman identity when integrated into the successful, first- to third-century Roman system, many tribes seem to have persisted through the empire, particularly in Tripolitania, Numidia, and Mauretania, but also in the southern parts of what would later be known as Byzacena.[82] Some of those tribes, living inside the borders of the empire, are called federate tribes (*gens foederata*) and their leaders appear as princes (*principes*), while men like Sammac, Firmus, or Gildo used their power within the local tribes to acquire positions in the Roman provincial administration. The revival of tribal structure in Late Antiquity was therefore based on older structures, and the distribution in 533 of insignia of power to various Moorish kings simply continued well-established practices. P.-A. Février emphasized the importance of political

---

[80] Camps, *Les Berbères*, pp. 64–89.

[81] Brett and Fentress, *The Berbers*, pp. 55–61.

[82] Brett and Fentress, *The Berbers*, pp. 61–76; Matthews, *Roman Empire*, pp. 367–76; Modéran, *Les Maures*, pp. 421–43.

affiliation for the distinction between Moors and Romans. For him, a *Maurus* was primarily someone hostile to the Roman Empire.[83] It is true that hostility to the actual Roman ruler made people un-Roman, at least from a certain point of view. However, written sources clearly show that the acceptance of the Roman system did not make people automatically Roman in every sense. It was possible to embrace the Roman system and to stay inside Moorish tribal structures at the same time.[84] This is demonstrated by Firmus in the fourth century or in the time of Antalas by his neighbour, the *ductor Maurorum*[85] Cusina who was at the same time a 'leader of barbarians'[86] and a holder of a high rank in the Roman army.[87]

There are, unfortunately, no hints of prior tribal structures in the lands of the Frexes. But in the second and third centuries, the nearby region of Cillium (Kasserine, Tunisia) was the home of the *Musunii Regiani*.[88] According to the Albertini Tablets, in the late fifth century landowners and tenants still followed the old *lex Manciana*. Tenants had cultivation rights in perpetuity and access to the associated irrigation systems, while land ownership rights remained with Flavius Geminius Catullinus, a *flamen perpetuus*. Both the title and the dating of the tablets to the reign of the Vandal king Gunthamund (484–96) suggest that the people on the *fundi* recognized the ruler in Carthage as the supreme authority in matters of law.[89] As a consequence, from the little we know about them, it appears that the people of the Albertini Tablets were first owners, tenants, or neighbours of the *fundi*, then Romans, and finally subjects of the Vandal king. Some of their names are Latinized versions of African names.[90] The presence of names of Germanic origin is still

---

[83] Paul-Abert Février, 'Le Maure ambigue ou les pièges du discours', *Bulletin archéologique du Comité des Travaux Historiques et Scientifiques*, 19 B (1985), 291–304 (p. 301).

[84] See the example of Banasa, in Euzennat and Seston, 'Un dossier de la chancellerie romaine'.

[85] Corippus, *Johannis* 3.405–08.

[86] Procopius, *Wars*, 4.10.6.

[87] Corippus, *Johannis*, 8.268–70 (Cusina as *magister*); *Johannis*, 6.268: 'Cusina, Romanis semper fidissimus armis'. For Cusina, see also Modéran, *Les Maures*, pp. 334–50.

[88] Modéran, *Les Maures*, pp. 475–77.

[89] For the discussion of imperial or royal-Vandal references to the title of *flamen*, see Frank M. Clover, 'Emperor Worship in Vandal Africa', in *Romanitas-Christianitas: Festschrift für Johannes Straub*, ed. by Gerhard Wirth and Johannes A. Straub (Berlin, 1982) pp. 663–74; Noël Duval, 'Culte monarchique dans l'Afrique vandale: culte des rois ou culte des empereurs?', *Revue des Études Augustiennes*, 30 (1984), 269–73.

[90] Courtois and others, *Tablettes Albertini*, p. 206.

debated.[91] The tenants mentioned in the Albertini Tablets might thus have been integrated into a kind of Moorish tribal structure, which in turn might have served as a subgroup of what would later be known as Frexes.[92]

Everyday Life, Housing, and Economy

A recurrent problem for archaeologists and historians working in north-western Europe is that no direct correlation exists between material culture and ethnic identity. The essence of the problems is that material cultural distributions rarely have clear-cut boundaries. Similarly, 'Roman' material culture was not opposed to 'Moorish' identity, just like 'indigenous' cultural traits were not in contrast to 'Roman' identity. As already mentioned, the use of a Roman-style oil press must bear no significance as to the ethnic identity of the user. That is why the search for markers of ethnic distinction is primarily a historical, and not an archaeological, question. But the search for evidence of distinctive features in the written sources does not produce any satisfying results. There will probably never be an answer to the question of whether the ancestors of Guenfan and Antalas lived in south-western Byzacena as 'Romans' or as a distinctive *gens*, something like the *Musunii Regiani*, who settled in the region around Cillium in the second and third centuries AD.[93] There is therefore no way to tell whether or not the fifth- and sixth-century archaeological record from that area has anything to do with the Frexes. The only way to learn about the daily life of Antalas and his people is through comprehensive archaeological studies of the region in which the written sources locate the Frexes.

Until recently, however, the state of archaeological research was very poor for the high steppe west of the axis linking Theveste (Tebessa, Algeria) to Capsa (Gafsa, Tunisia), namely within the region in which Antalas lived with his people. Even larger Roman towns such as Thelepte (Feriana, Tunisia) remain beyond the scholarly reach, except of course the visible ruins. Thelepte has a number of prominent late antique monuments awaiting research, including one of the most interesting cases of Byzantine fortresses in North Africa, in addition to seven churches

[91] Conant, 'Literacy and Private Documentation', p. 202 n. 10. *Contra*: Courtois and others, *Tablettes Albertini*, p. 206.

[92] That much can be gleaned from Corippus mentioning a *gens* at the time of Antalas's early years (Corippus, *Johannis*, 3.153: 'namque humilis gens illa fuit').

[93] Modéran, *Les Maures*, pp. 475–77.

(Plate X.1).[94] The fact that no less than three bishops, one of Catholic and two of Donatist faith,[95] represented Thelepte at the council of 411 shows that the city must have been quite large in the early fifth century. Saint Fulgentius of Ruspe was born in Thelepte, became a *procurator* of the city, and began his life as a monk in the monastery of Faustus, which was not far from Thelepte.[96] Local bishops are attested well into the mid-seventh century.[97] The surrounding countryside is still an archaeological terra incognita, even though the Tunisian Department of Antiquities (Institut National du Patrimoine/INP) and especially Fathi Béjaoui have considerably expanded the accessible data to monuments in the environs of Thelepte, notably at Henchir el-Gousset and Henchir el-Erg.[98] There is a remarkably growing evidence of inscriptions from that region, which are dated to the reigns of the Vandal kings Thrasamund and Gunthamund and point to a late heyday of Vandal influence in a region that was not too far away from the land of the Frexes.[99] Thelepte, however, is not the place to search for the material culture

[94] For the churches of Thelepte, see Stéphane Gsell, *Édifices chrétiens de Thelepte et d'Ammaedara* (Tunis, 1933), pp. 5–55; Paul Gauckler, *Basiliques chrétiennes de Tunisie* (Paris, 1913), pls 20–25; Noël Duval, *Les Églises africaines à deux absides*, II: *Inventaire des monuments. Interprétation* (Paris, 1973), pp. 211–22; Fathi Bejaoui, 'Recherche archéologique à Thelepte et ses environs: note sur les récentes découvertes', in *Histoire des Hautes Steppes: Antiquité–Moyen-Âge. Actes du Colloque de Sbeitla, Session 2001*, ed. by Fathi Bejaoui (Tunis, 2003), pp. 147–61 (pp. 147–49).

[95] André Mandouze, *Prosopographie de l'Afrique chrétienne (303–533)* (Paris, 1982), pp. 138 (Bellicius, Donatist), 284–85 (Donatianus, Catholic), 266 (Datianus, Donatist). In 484, one Catholic bishop, Frumentius, is mentioned in Thelepte (Mandouze, *Prosopographie*, p. 506).

[96] Hans-Joachim Diesner, *Fulgentius von Ruspe als Theologe und Kirchenpolitiker* (Stuttgart, 1966); Yves Modéran, 'La Chronologie de la vie de saint Fulgence de Ruspe et ses incidences sur l'histoire de l'Afrique vandale', *Mélanges de l'École Française de Rome*, 105 (1993), 135–88.

[97] The last bishop, Stephanus Talaptensis, is mentioned for 646. See Jean-Louis Maier, *L'Épiscopat de l'Afrique romaine, vandale et byzantine* (Rome, 1973), p. 215.

[98] Bejaoui, 'Recherche archéologique à Thelepte', pp. 149–61. See also Jean-Marie Lassère, 'Les Cultures sur le *FVNDVS TVLETIANENSIS*: une société rurale en crise?', in *Histoire des Hautes Steppes*, ed. by Bejaoui, pp. 39–47; Mouna Hermassi, 'Quelques données sur les vestiges oléicoles autour de Thelepte', in *Histoire des Hautes Steppes*, ed. by Bejaoui, pp. 81–85; Fathi Bejaoui, 'Une église d'époque vandale à Henchir El-Gousset (région de Thélepte—Tunisie)', *Africa*, 13 (1995), 101–22; François Baratte and Fathi Bejaoui, 'Églises urbaines, églises rurales dans la Tunisie paléochrétienne: nouvelles recherches d'architecture et d'urbanisme', *Comptes-Rendus des Séances de l'Académie des Inscriptions et Belles-Lettres*, 2001, 1447–97.

[99] Fathi Bejaoui, 'Les Vandales en Afrique: témoignages archéologiques. Les récentes découvertes en Tunisie', in *Das Reich der Vandalen und seine (Vor-)Geschichten*, ed. by Berndt and Steinacher, pp. 197–212.

remains pertaining to the Frexes. Thelepte was not just a city, and as such a traditional symbol of 'Roman-ness', but also under Vandal and later Byzantine control,
up to the seventh century. The homeland of Antalas laid farther to the west, in the
rural regions of the steppe near the present-day border between Algeria and
Tunisia (Plate X.2).

Within that region, several place names comprising the word *Henchir*, an Arabic
term for ancient ruins, indicate a high concentration of old settlements. Topo-
graphical surveys carried out by the French military authority in the early 1900s
revealed a great number of settlements of various sizes, including farms, cisterns,
tombs, mosaics, inscriptions, streets, dams, cisterns, and wells, all of which strongly
suggests that the land of the *Frexes* had been thoroughly Romanized during the
preceding centuries. Olive oil production is well documented by many finds of oil
presses, while Christianization is attested by numerous small churches and inscriptions of Christian character.[100] Additional information is to be found in the
Albertini Tablets: in addition to olive trees (which represent 72 per cent of all trees
mentioned in the tablets), peasants in the regions produced figs and almonds, as
well as some pistachios and wine. The Kasserine Survey produced evidence of the
cultivation of cereals, probably barley.[101] According to Hitchner, pulses, in particular field peas and lentils, must also have been present.[102] Even if oak trees seem to
have grown there in the late fifth century,[103] the region is in fact a steppe land with
very few trees. Because of the very dry climate, agriculture on the southern border
of the steppe was inconceivable without irrigation. That much is clear both from
the Albertini Tablets and from the scarce archaeological record.[104] Judging from

---

[100] For the archaeological record of the region, see *Atlas Archéologique de la Tunisie*, feuille 52
(Feriana); Stéphane Gsell, *Atlas archéologique de l'Algérie* (Paris, 1911), maps 39 (Cheria), 40
(Feriana), 50 (Negrine), and 51 (Gafsa). For olive production, see Henriette Camps-Fabrer,
L'Olivier et l'huile dans l'Afrique romaine (Alger, 1953), p. 27; David J. Mattingly, 'Oil for Export?
A Comparison of Libyan, Spanish and Tunisian Olive Oil Production in the Roman Empire',
Journal of Roman Archaeology, 1 (1988), 33–56 (pp. 44–49). For Christianization, see Modéran,
Les Maures, pp. 532–40.

[101] Hitchner, 'Kasserine Archaeological Survey 1987', p. 245.

[102] Hitchner, 'Kasserine Archaeological Survey 1987', p. 245.

[103] Courtois and others, *Tablettes Albertini*, table no. 14.

[104] See, for example, the channels and dams observed in the region of Bordj Sbeika, for which
see Louis Carton, 'Travaux antiques d'irrigation et de culture dans la région du Djebel Onk', *Recueil
des notices et mémoires de la Société Archéologique du Département de Constantine*, 43 (1909),
193–225. See also R. Bruce Hitchner, 'Irrigation, Terraces, Dams and Aqueducts in the Region of
Cillium (mod. Kasserine)', in *Productions et exportations africaines: actualités archéologiques. VI*

the distribution of modern place names containing such terms as *Aïn* (source), *Bir* (well), and *Ogla* (well), water is not altogether absent from the region, and there is no reason to believe that the situation was any different in Late Antiquity.[105] Stock farming is not mentioned in the tablets, but cattle raising was undoubtedly another source of income and supply for the people in south-western Byzacena.[106] Both the Albertini Tablets and the French archaeological atlases of Algeria and Tunisia, with their frequent references to streets and bridges, indicate that the high steppe lands had an extended infrastructure during the Roman period. A *via de camellos* mentioned in tablet XXI[107] hints at a trading route to the south, as well as to the usual presence of nomads from the southern regions. According to Corippus, the region was quite prosperous during Antalas's early years,[108] and we may suppose that the ancient economic and infrastructural base was still in existence by 500, even if, as a result of increasing Moorish activity, there seems to have been a steady drop in the amount of agricultural produce. Unfortunately, next to nothing is known about the settlement pattern in the region and as a consequence about possible changes taking place as a result of the political upheavals of the late fifth century. There are no significant geographical or climatic differences between Kasserine and the region to the south-west from Thelepte. Moreover, the maps of the *Atlas archéologique de l'Algérie* for the regions of Cheria, Feriana, Negrine, and Gafsa[109] show settlement concentrations similar to that in the environs of Cillium. As a consequence, Hitchner's survey of that region[110] may give some idea of how the land of Antalas was organized. There, the American team found a large number of well-preserved but recently and severely looted sites scattered throughout the landscape, including two major towns as well as villages and farms of various sizes containing oil presses, terraces, wells, and irrigation works.

The region of Cillium shows some very interesting variations of rural sites. Hitchner subdivides the 'primarily Romanized settlement hierarchy' into large

---

colloque international sur l'Afrique du Nord antique et médiévale 1993, ed. by Pol Trousset (Paris, 1995), pp. 143–57. For the region farther to the west, but within the same climate zone, see the aerial photos of Jean Baradez, *Fossatum Africae: vue aerienne de l'organisation romaine dans le Sud Algérien* (Paris, 1949).

[105] Courtois and others, *Tablettes Albertini*, p. 191.

[106] Hitchner, 'Kasserine Archaeological Survey, 1982–1986', p. 17 with n. 19.

[107] Courtois and others, *Tablettes Albertini*, p. 278 line 6.

[108] Corippus, *Johannis*, 3.66–78.

[109] Gsell, *Atlas archéologique*, maps 39 (Cheria), 40 (Feriana), 50 (Negrine), and 51 (Gafsa).

[110] See note 14 above.

farms (sites between one and ten hectares serving as centres of agricultural production for the surrounding area), farm-houses (sites between one-half and one hectare
containing a series of independent units, one of which usually contains an olive
press), agricultural villages (sites comprising a series of farm-houses and associated
elements together to form a unitary settlement), and small structures (small complexes of around 500 square metres containing one or two units).[111] While the bulk
of the large farms are very 'Roman-looking' compounds with regular ground
plans,[112] some of them look more like the Roman villas of central and western
Europe. Some villages in the mountain district are characterized by an irregular
arrangement of building groups containing commercial sections as well as living
quarters.[113] The layout of such settlements may correspond to surviving features
of pre-Roman Africa. The little we know about pre-Roman settlements in non-
Punic North Africa, such as the Numidian royal town of Thugga (Dougga, Tunisia) for example, suggests that, in contrast to later Roman towns, such settlements
had an irregular layout.[114] Late Roman villages like those found by Hitchner may
be a reflection of the tribal organization of local society; and it may be no coincidence that such settlements were exclusively located in the mountain district of the
surveyed area. The villages near Cillium may therefore be an indication of some
indigenous cultural traditions that survived in the southern regions.

Another Moorish example of such surviving traditions are the *Djedars* near
Tiaret (Algeria), a group of large stepped pyramids serving as monumental tombs
for a sixth-century Moorish royal dynasty.[115] Like Theoderic's mausoleum in

---

[111] Hitchner, 'Kasserine Archaeological Survey, 1982–1986', p. 12.

[112] The Kasserine survey revealed several such compounds. The only main building excavated
in any compound is the one at Nador in Northern Algeria, for which see Lucilla Anselmino,
Mounir Bouchenaki, and Andrea Carandini, *Il Castellum del Nador: storia di una fattoria tra
Tipasa e Caesarea (I–VI sec. d. C.)* (Rome, 1989).

[113] Hitchner, 'Kasserine Archaeological Survey, 1982–1986', pp. 29–34.

[114] For Dougga, see Mustapha Khanoussi, Stefan Ritter, and Philipp von Rummel, 'The
German-Tunisian Project at Dougga: First Results of the Excavations South of the Maison du
Trifolium', *Antiquités Africaines*, 40–41 (2004–05), 43–66.

[115] Fatima K. Kadra, *Les Djedars: monuments funéraires berbères de la région de Franda (Wilaya
de Tiaret, Algérie occidentale)* (Aix-en-Provence, 1974); Fatima K. Kadra, 'Der Djedar A von Djebel
Lakhdar, ein spätes Berbermonument', in *Die Numider: Reiter und Könige nördlich der Sahara*, ed.
by Heinz Günter Horn and Christoph B. Rüger (Bonn, 1979), pp. 263–84; Alan Rushworth,
'From Arzurges to Rustamids: State Formation and Regional Identity in the Pre-Saharan Zone',
in *Vandals, Romans and Berbers*, ed. by Merrills, pp. 77–98 (pp. 79–86); Jean-Pierre Laporte, 'Les
Djédars, monuments funéraires berbères de la region de Tiaret', in *Identités et cultures dans l'Algérie
antique*, ed. by Claude Briand (Rouen, 2005), pp. 321–406.

Ravenna, those fairly neglected buildings belong to the most important monuments associated with barbarian kingdoms organized during Late Antiquity on previously Roman territory. Through their pyramidal structure, they clearly refer to the pre-Roman traditions of funerary architecture in North Africa. As Christian tombs, they are at the same time a symbol of the blending of different cultural traditions in sixth-century Africa. Gabriel Camps describes African handmade pottery as a 'living symbol of technical conservatism' and of 'North African aesthetics with prehistoric roots'. From Camp's point of view, these ceramics are an example of the 'Berber permanence', of the long-living cultural traditions of indigenous North Africa.[116] There are certainly some eye-catching traditional features in present-day Maghreb, such as the traditional production of *tabouna*-bread in small vertical ovens, according to a method reminiscent of Procopius's description of a Moorish woman preparing bread in the form of a flat cake baked in glowing ashes.[117] But handmade pottery with remarkably constant characteristics from the Numidian period well into Late Antiquity appears on almost every settlement in North Africa, even in large cities, an indication that pre-Roman aspects of North African material culture survived even in the most Romanized centres, without making the inhabitants of those places less 'Roman' than any other inhabitants of the empire. This is, of course, also true from an opposite point of view: a 'Roman' layout of a farm or the presence of African Red Slipware says nothing about the ethnic or political identity of the people, just as the consumption of *tabouna*-bread or the preparation of pancakes in a handmade, clay pan does not necessarily reveal the Berber identity or origins of modern Tunisians or Algerians. A local culture may have existed in a form which left no written records or datable artefacts, but, given the present state of research, it is almost impossible to distinguish between Frexes and Romans through their material culture and to identify their settlements by archaeological means.

Clothing, Hairstyle, and Body Signs

Not much is known about the physical appearance of Guenfan, Antalas, and their Frexes. This is mainly because pictorial representations and literary descriptions are

---

[116] Camps, *Les Berbères*, pp. 206–13, here p. 213: 'Elle est, cependant, le symbole vivant d'un conservativisme technique et esthétique nord-africain, qui plonge ses racines dans les siècles antérieures à l'Histoire. C'est donc un exemple de permanence berbère.'

[117] Procopius, *Wars*, 4.7.3.

rare,[118] while archaeological finds of textiles and other clothing accessories are completely absent. As a consequence, the debate over 'ethnic costumes', which is so prevalent in the archaeology of other barbarians, such as the African Vandals, has no meaning for the Frexes.[119] There is of course the possibility that Antalas sported the Byzantine royal insignia he may have received from Belisarius: a silver-gilt staff, a silver headdress, a white mantle attached to the right shoulder by means of a gold fibula, like a Thessalian chlamys, and gold shoes.[120] He may thus have looked like other barbarian leaders, wearing a Roman costume that imitated imperial robes but was, at the same time, clearly of a lower rank. Some steles from Algeria, initially believed to show late antique Moors, turned out to be of a Numidian (Hellenistic) date.[121] They cannot therefore have any implications for the reconstruction of the appearance of late antique Moors. According to Corippus, those taken captive during and after the battle of 548 did not all have the same color of skin: mention is made of a black mother and her children.[122] As the coalition against the Byzantines spanned a lot of different tribes, some of them from the far south, this bit of information says nothing about the physical appearance of the Frexes.

Weaponry and Ways of Fighting

Our knowledge of Moorish weaponry is poor as well. Whatever Corippus had to say about the equipment and tactics employed by Antalas's men, they certainly were no different from 'Roman' practices. The Frexes fought on horseback and on foot with lances, spears, swords, and various projectiles, and were protected by shields and helmets. In the battle against John Troglita, the Moorish coalition

[118] Paul Monceaux, 'Inscriptions chrétiennes du cercle de Tébessa', *Recueil des notices et mémoires de la Société Archéologique de Constantine*, 42 (1908), 234–36, mentions a Christian inscription from Tozeur showing a warrior with 'Libyan costume' and a lance in his left hand.

[119] For the 'ethnic costume' of the Vandals, see Philipp von Rummel, 'Habitus Vandalorum? Zur Frage nach einer gruppenspezifischen Kleidung der Vandalen in Nordafrika', *Antiquité Tardive*, 10 (2002), 131–41; Philipp von Rummel, 'Les Vandales ont-ils porté en Afrique en vêtement spécifique?', in *La Méditerranée et le monde mérovingien: témoins archéologiques*, ed. by Xavier Delester, Patrick Périn, and Michel Kazanski (Aix-en-Provence, 2005), pp. 281–91.

[120] Procopius, *Wars*, 3.25.5–8.

[121] Jean-Pierre Laporte, 'Stèles libyques figurées de Grande Kabylie', *Africa Romana*, 9 (1992), 389–423; Jean-Pierre Laporte, 'Les Chefs libyques sur les stèles figurées', in *L'Algérie au temps des royaumes numides: catalogue de l'exposition de Rouen, 2003*, ed. by Geneviève Sennequier and Cécile Colonna (Paris, 2003), pp. 33–35.

[122] Corippus, *Johannis*, 6.92–96.

under the command of Antalas arranged camels in a big circle.[123] This, however, seems to be a practice of southern Moors, the Tripolitanian Laguatan in particular, who are known to have formed several camel-walls in battle against both Vandals and Byzantines.[124] However, no noticeable differences seem to have existed between Moorish and Roman soldiers on the battle field, as Corippus mentions difficulties in distinguishing friend from foe on the battlefield in 548.[125]

In conclusion, and given the current state of research, there seems to be no way to distinguish the Frexes from the people that lived in the same region some years before as 'Romans'. It might thus be helpful to ask what happened in the southern regions of the Vandal kingdom in the late fifth century that could have triggered the creation of new, formerly unknown entities.

A Potential Crisis in Late Vandal North Africa and the Origin of the Frexes

Such considerations invite us to re-examine a well-known archaeological phenomenon, namely the gradual decline of economy ever since the late fifth and early sixth centuries, as well as the concomitant decrease in the number of rural settlements in the interior. That much, at least, has resulted from the Kasserine survey.[126] This is in contrast to the results of other surveys in the former Proconsular province further to the north, where a decline in the numbers of rural settlements does not seem to occur until the late sixth or even seventh century. On the other hand, the conclusions of the Kasserine survey match those of the Libyan Valleys survey.[127] It appears that at least some regions in the south went through turbulent times from the late fifth century onwards. Besides archaeological surveys, there are additional indications of growing problems in the late fifth century. Between 468 and 470, Tripolitania suffered under barbarian attacks from the south.[128] The last *ostrakon* of Bir Trouch dates from 493, the last Albertini Tablet from 496. Since not much

---

[123] Corippus, *Johannis*, 4.632–33.

[124] Procopius, *Wars*, 3.8.25–29 (against Thrasamund) and 4.11.122 (against Solomon).

[125] Corippus, *Johannis*, 5.355–57.

[126] Hitchner, 'Kasserine Archaeological Survey, 1982–1986', p. 40.

[127] Anna Leone and David Mattingly, 'Vandal, Byzantine and Arab Rural Landscapes in North Africa', in *Landscapes of Change: Rural Evolutions in Late Antiquity and the Early Middle Ages*, ed. by Neil Christie (Aldershot, 2004), pp. 135–62.

[128] Procopius, *Wars*, 3.6.9.

time must have separated the execution of the last juridical acts and the hiding of the documents at Bir Trouch and Djebel Mrata, both finds may point to troubles in the late 490s that induced the people to protect their documents. Both Corippus and Procopius report Moorish activities in this region in the late fifth century. Fulgentius of Ruspe left his monastery of Praesidium (probably *Praesidium Diolele* between Capsa and Thelepte) in 497 because of Moorish raids in the region.[129] The acute problems visible in the historical as well as in the archaeological record may well have been connected to Moorish activities.

But what caused the late fifth-century problems? The traditional approach blames everything on the rise of powerful Moorish tribes. Much like in the northern parts of the empire, barbarian migrations are believed to have triggered the late antique transformations. According to such an interpretation, the immigration of powerful tribes from the desert into the Roman provinces caused a significant change in the regional political and social structure.[130] However, this interpretation cannot be applied to the Frexes, who did not come from anywhere, but instead emerged within the Roman province itself. Moreover, alternative explanations are required for two other phenomena: the 'natural urge' of Berbers to revolt and the change in Vandal diplomacy.[131]

Some scholars believe that the main reason for decline was the Vandal conquest of 429 and 439 and the removal of the imperial tax system as the basic catalyst for continued agricultural prosperity and an important motivation for the population outside the desert to produce a surplus.[132] It is true that the revenue surplus from Africa was essential for balancing the imperial books, and that the emperors needed the surplus to afford its large armed forces. Thus, the loss of the richest African provinces was a disaster for the west Roman state.[133] It is also true that the Vandals' takeover profoundly affected social structure and local political relationships.[134]

[129] Modéran, 'La Chronologie', p. 149.

[130] For the history of research, see Modéran, *Les Maures*, pp. 131–52.

[131] Modéran, *Les Maures*, p. 554.

[132] For a general overview on this question and Africa's relation to Mediterranean economy, see Chris Wickham, *Framing the Early Middle Ages: Europe and the Mediterranean 400–800* (Oxford, 2005), pp. 708–13, 720–28, and 635–44.

[133] Peter Heather, *The Fall of the Roman Empire: A New History of Rome and the Barbarians* (Oxford, 2005), p. 281: 'With the arrival of Geiseric on the fringes of Numidia in the year 430, the sword of Damocles was hanging over the entire western Empire.'

[134] Guy Halsall, *Barbarian Migrations and the Roman West, 376–568* (Cambridge, 2007), p. 327.

However, these effects of the Vandal invasion do not explain the problems in southern Byzacena. Pressure on the rural population was certainly not absent in the Vandal kingdom, especially not in Byzacena, the province from which the Vandals collected their taxes.[135] Moreover, if Vandal presence and the end of the *annona* really was a reason for economic decline, then we should expect to see similar phenomena in other rural regions further to the north. One reason for the first Moorish opposition in the Aurès may have been the large-scale Vandal persecution of Catholics in 484. The traditional interpretation is predicated upon the assumption that the Moors caused the archaeologically visible economic decline. However, one should at least consider the alternative view, namely that the process of 'Moorization' was not the cause, but the result of decline.[136]

Even though probably not connected to the termination of the *annona* system, economic problems may have been one important factor in the development of the Moorish tribes. The Albertini Tablets do indeed suggest a problematic situation. Many of the documents bear witness to the sale of title to agricultural parcels of the *cultores* who appear mainly as vendors, not as buyers.[137] This seems to indicate a downward trend, perhaps caused by a regional economic crisis. Moreover, the prices mentioned in the tablets are very low and may therefore point to a seriously low demand.[138] The increase in the number of imported amphorae of eastern origin especially in Carthage and especially during the Vandal period[139] has been

[135] Yves Modéran, 'L'Établissement territorial des Vandales en Afrique', *Antiquité Tardive*, 10 (2002), 87–122.

[136] Modéran, *Les Maures*, p. 555.

[137] Yves Modéran, 'Documents vandales: les tablettes Albertini et les Ostraka de Bir Trouch', in *Algérie Antique: Catalogue de l'exposition à Arles*, ed. by Claudes Sintes and Ymouna Rebahi (Arles, 2003), pp. 249–53.

[138] Pierre Salama, 'Économie monétaire de l'Afrique du Nord dans l'antiquité tardive', in *Histoire et archéologie de l'Afrique du Nord: Actes du IIᵉ colloque international Grenoble 1983*, ed. by Serge Lancel (Paris, 1985), pp. 183–203 (pp. 195–200).

[139] John A. Riley, 'The Pottery from Cisterns 1977.1, 1977.2, 1977.3', in *Excavations at Carthage 1977 Conducted by the University of Michigan*, ed. by John H. Humphrey (Ann Arbor, 1981), pp. 85–124 (pp. 115–22); Clementina Panella, 'Le anfore di Cartagine: Nuovi elementi per la ricostruzione dei flussi commerciali del Mediterraneo in età imperiale Romana', *Opus*, 2 (1983), 53–73; Michael Fulford, 'The Long Distance Trade and Communications of Carthage, c. A.D. 400 to c. A.D. 650', in *Excavations at Carthage: The British Mission*, I.2: *The Avenue du Président Habib Bourgouiba, Salammbo: The Pottery and Other Ceramic Objects from the Site*, ed. by Michael G. Fulford and David P. S. Peacock (Sheffield, 1984), pp. 225–62 (p. 258); Lucilla Anselmino and others, 'Cartagine', in *Società Romana e Impero Tardoantico: Le merci, gli insediamenti*, ed. by

interpreted as a sign of economic problems in the later Vandal kingdom. Clementina Panella recognized in the Carthaginian finds an indication of loosening ties between town and countryside that made it necessary to obtain from abroad those foodstuffs which no longer flowed in sufficient quantities from inland to the port towns.[140] Others, however, regard the increasing number of amphorae as evidence of increasing wealth.[141] At any rate, it is unlikely that the importation into Carthage of Eastern wine and oil can in any way be associated with the decrease in oil-producing settlements in the Cillium area. When considering imports, one needs to recognize that at the same time African products were still shipped elsewhere in the Mediterranean region. The Keay 8B/Bonifay 38–39 amphora dated between the second half of the fifth and the early sixth centuries, which most likely transported oil from southern Byzacena,[142] was found not only in Carthage and on other sites in the western Mediterranean, but also in Alexandria and Constantinople.[143] The production of fine ceramics in south-western Byzacena continued well into the sixth century, in itself a sign of economic vigour.[144]

Jean-Marie Lassère rightly points out that Geminius Felix, whose name appears in the Albertini Tablets as buying titles to agricultural parcels, would not have done any of that without a certain trust in a better future. As a consequence, the alleged crisis may have had more a local than a general character.[145] Béjaoui's recent discoveries in the region of Thelepte of funerary inscriptions dated to the reigns of the Vandal kings Gunthamund and Thrasamund strongly suggest a consolidation

Andrea Giardina (Rome, 1986), pp. 163–95 (p. 177); Michael Mackensen, 'Spätantike Keramikensembles und Baumassnahmen in der südlichen Raumzeile der Insula E 218', in *Karthago III: Die deutschen Ausgrabungen in Karthago*, ed. by Friedrich Rakob (Mainz, 1999), pp. 545–65.

[140] Panella, 'Le anfore di Cartagine', pp. 62–73.

[141] Fulford, 'Long Distance Trade', p. 259.

[142] Michel Bonifay, *Études sur la céramique romaine tardive d'Afrique* (Oxford, 2004), p. 132; Lucinda Neuru, 'Appendix 2: The Pottery of the Kasserine Survey', *Antiquités Africaines*, 26 (1990), 255–59.

[143] Bonifay, *Études*, p. 132; John W. Hayes, *Excavations at Saraçhane*, II: *The Pottery* (Princeton, 1992), fig. 22 no. 1.

[144] Lucinda Neuru, 'Red Slipped Wares of Southwestern Central Tunisia: New Evidence', *Rei Cretariae Romanae Fautorum Acta*, 26 (1987), 175–88; Michael Mackensen and Gerwulf Schneider, 'Production Centres of African Red Slip Ware (3rd–7th c.) in Northern and Central Tunisia: Archaeological Provenance and Reference Groups Based on Chemical Analysis', *Journal of Roman Archaeology*, 15 (2002), 122–58; Kaouther Selmane, 'L'Artisanat en Byzacène à l'époque vandale', in *Histoire des Hautes Steppes*, ed. by Bejaoui, pp. 117–28.

[145] Lassère, 'Les Cultures sur le *FVNDVS TVLETIANENSIS*', p. 47.

of Vandal power in south-western Byzacena in the late fifth century.[146] Together with other inscriptions from the regions of Tebessa and Haïdra, the newly discovered ones point to a nucleus of Vandal authority in a region where no evidence of Vandal settlement exists for the period of the Vandal kings Geiseric and Huneric.[147] The inscriptions may therefore be seen as a result of reinforced Vandal power in a crisis-ridden region. If so, then the inscriptions are a symptom of the same crisis that accelerated the rise of the Frexes. This is, of course, just one possible interpretation. The letters of the epitaph of Fortunatiana in El-Erg have been carved in positive relief.[148] That method of stone-carving is known from other inscriptions from Haïdra, the region of Tebessa, Sétif, and El-Asabaa in Tripolitania; it may have been an imitation of grave mosaics.[149] However, this is no indication of the inability to commission mosaics, since the baptistery of El-Erg where the inscription of Fortunatiana was found is in fact decorated with an opulent mosaic pavement.[150] On the contrary, it appears that inscriptions carved in positive relief are in fact a sign of prosperity. In spite of all expected problems, cultural life, at least for Christians, seems to have continued unabated in late Vandal Byzacena.

In their search for explanations for growing insecurity, some scholars have also pointed to climate change. To be sure, geomorphologic and palaeobotanical studies indeed suggest that during the fifth and sixth centuries the climate was considerably drier. But in the absence of any synthetic overview of the different approaches and methods employed for the reconstruction of the climate history of North Africa during Late Antiquity, there is no way to reconcile the contradictory conclusions of various studies.[151] In 1981, Brent D. Shaw could not find any signs of

---

[146] Bejaoui, 'Les Vandales en Afrique'; Noël Duval, 'Les Systèmes de datation dans l'Est de l'Afrique du Nord à la fin de l'Antiquité et à l'époque byzantine', *Ktema*, 18 (1993), 189–211 (p. 199).

[147] For the Vandal settlement and the question of the *sortes Vandalorum*, see Modéran, 'L'Établissement territorial', pp. 87–122.

[148] Baratte and Bejaoui, 'Églises urbanes, églises rurales', pp. 1477–81 with fig. 24; Bejaoui, 'Les Vandales en Afrique'.

[149] Baratte and Bejaoui, 'Églises urbanes, églises rurales', pp. 1478–79 with nn. 39–43. For funerary mosaics, see Noël Duval, *La Mosaïque funéraire dans l'art paléochrétien* (Ravenna, 1976).

[150] Baratte and Bejaoui, 'Églises urbanes, églises rurales', p. 1475 fig. 22.

[151] This is particularly true for the current debate on the influence of climate change on the expansion of late antique settlements in the eastern Mediterranean. See Rehav Rubin, 'The Debate Over Climate Changes in the Negev, 4th–7th Centuries C.E.', *Palestine Exploration Quarterly*, 121 (1989), 71–78; Arie S. Issar, 'Climate Change: An History during the Holocene in the Eastern

climate change between the 'golden age' of Roman North Africa and the Arab invasions. According to him, the connection between climate change and economic decline was a historiographic myth.[152] Others, however, still foster that assumption.[153] According to Dominik Faust and Christoph Zielhofer, all studies of the Holocene morphodynamics in the entire region from the Maghreb to Southern Spain indicate that an abrupt change to much drier conditions was already taking place around 2850 BC. Geomorphologic investigations in the Medjerda valley in Northern Tunisia and the reconstructed water level amplitude of that important North African river (the Roman Bagradas) produced similar results.[154] The prehistoric dry period was followed by a more humid phase with weak soil formation between 2600 and 2000 BP (i.e. 650 to 50 BC), during the Punic and early Roman periods. This is now confirmed by a number of studies carried out in the Sahara and in the Baleares and by marine pollen profiles from the gulf of Gabes. Big flood events are clearly visible through the subsequent arid period in the Oued Medjerda in terms of the formation of high plain sediments from AD 150 onwards. Much like in other regions of the Mediterranean, such a strong morphodynamic activity during the Roman period may be associated with an intensive land use and, according to Faust, with the abandonment of agricultural fields during Late Antiquity.[155] In

Mediterranean Region', in *Water, Environment and Society in Times of Climatic Change: Contributions from an International Workshop within the Framework of International Hydrological Program (IHP) UNESCO, Held at Ben-Gurion University Sede Boker, Israel from 7–12 July 1996*, ed. by Arie S. Issar and Neville Brown (Dordrecht, 1998), pp. 113–28; Yizhar Hirschfeld, 'A Climate Change in the Early Byzantine Period? Some Archaeological Evidence', *Palestine Exploration Quarterly*, 136 (2004), 133–49.

[152] Brent D. Shaw, 'Climate, Environment, and History: The Case of Roman North Africa', in *Climate and History: Studies in Past Climates and their Impact on Man*, ed. by Tom M. L. Wigley and others (Cambridge, 1981), pp. 379–403.

[153] Madeleine Rouvillois-Brigol, 'Quelques remarques sur les variations de l'occupation du sol dans le sud-est algérien', in *Actes du IIIᵉ colloque international d'Histoire et d'Archéologie de l'Afrique du Nord, Montepellier 1985* (Paris, 1986), pp. 35–52; Jean-Louis Ballais and Mohamed T. Benazzouz, 'Données nouvelles sur la morphologie et les paléoenvironnements tardiglaciaires et holocènes dans la vallée de l'oued Cheria-Mezeraa (Nemencha, Algérie orientale)', *Méditeranée*, 3–4 (1994), 59–71; Dominik Faust and Christoph Zielhofer, 'Reconstruction of the Holocene Water Level Amplitude of the Oued Medjerda as an Indicator for Changes of the Environmental Conditions in North Tunisia', in *Environmental Change and Geomorphology*, ed. by Roland Baumhauer and Brigitta Schütt (Berlin, 2002), pp. 161–75.

[154] Faust and Zielhofer, 'Reconstruction of the Holocene Water Level', pp. 170–75.

[155] Faust and Zielhofer, 'Reconstruction of the Holocene Water Level', p. 171.

conclusion, the 'apparent contrast between the extensive and impressive ruins of the Roman period [...] and the desolation of the countryside about them'[156] appears to be manmade and not natural.

On the other hand, there can be no doubt that there were also natural reasons for economic and social problems in that period. Victor of Vita refers to a great drought followed by a famine in AD 484: 'At that time a famine occurred which was beyond belief, and it began to devastate the whole of Africa, laying it all waste. There was no rain then; not a single drop fell from heaven.'[157] Followed by a dramatic description of shrivelled vines, grain fields, and olive trees as well as desiccated rivers and wells, this account may serve as an example of the kind of event that could have conspicuously weakened an already fragile agricultural system. However, a famine like the one of 484 may not be an indication of long-term climatic change. A study carried out in the early 1900s showed a remarkable variation in rainfall and crops in Tunisia.[158] An unfortunate succession of dry years could thus have easily caused famine and social unrest. If it could be firmly established that drier conditions were particularly prominent in the fifth century, then that would perhaps become a possible trigger for the rapid political and economic transformations in the then Moorish territories. A region which highly depended upon constant water supply may have been extremely sensitive to climate changes. Nonetheless, our knowledge of Mediterranean climate history is still too fragmentary to evaluate local studies such as that of Madeleine Rouvillois-Brigol[159] and to draw definitive conclusions. Isabella Sjöström rightly concludes that, although a progressively drier climate cannot be excluded, it is at least as likely that less intensive farming in post-Roman Tripolitania was due to political and economic insecurity rather than to environmental causes.[160]

This is unfortunately also true for other aspects of life in late antique and early medieval south-western Byzacena. Information is still too scanty in general for any solid explanations. In this respect, intensified archaeological research in the lands of the Frexes may not only expand our knowledge of the people who lived there,

---

[156] Shaw, 'Climate, Environment, and History', p. 382.

[157] Victor of Vita, *History of the Vandal Persecution*, 3.55–60, ed. by Michael Petschenig (Vienna, 1881); English translation from John Moorhead, *Translated Texts for Historians*, X (Liverpool, 1992), p. 86.

[158] Gaston Loth, *L'Enfida et Sidi-Tabet: la grande colonisation française en Tunisie* (Tunis, 1910), p. 158.

[159] Rouvillois-Brigol, 'Quelques remarques sur les variations'.

[160] Sjöström, *Tripolitania in Transition*, p. 122.

but also of the reasons that pushed them to become *Mauri*. It may be expected that future research will allow greater and more precise insights into these questions.

Conclusion

While it may be impossible to isolate any single factor responsible for the crisis in the southern regions of the Vandal kingdom, one can still conclude that a crisis of agricultural production, perhaps caused by growing aridity, was responsible for the major problems in the region where Antalas was born in the late fifth century. Unfortunately, we know nothing about the conditions in which his grandparents lived. It seems, however, quite probable that they belonged to the provincial population of North Africa, which lived and worked under Roman law and within the social and economical framework of the empire. No way exists currently to establish whether or not those people described themselves as Romans, but we know from other cases that a combination of economic and social problems within a region with a strong indigenous background may well push a formerly peaceful rural population to accept the rule of a powerful warlord. Breaking with the Roman order and turning to a regional leader may have been the way in which the group of Guenfan and Antalas became a powerful Moorish tribe. Through this transformation from Roman provincials into barbarians, the Roman Empire had created another barbarian *gens*, a process with numerous parallels elsewhere in the empire. The transformation of the Frexes of Antalas from peaceful Roman provincials into a militarized group of barbarian looters seems to be a typical example of late antique ethnic processes. However, the complex set of reasons that led to this development in the North African province must be a subject of further, particularly archaeological research.

AFTERWORD: NEGLECTING THE BARBARIAN

Peter Heather

Neglecting the barbarians of first-millennium Europe is a pastime with a long pedigree, which directly reflects the pattern of surviving source materials. The original Greek word form carried connotations of massive and overwhelming inferiority, but even if we would not now accept this type of value judgement, 'barbarian' remains a useful collective term for all those elements of the landmass population who were not part of any of the great European empires of the era, whether Roman, Byzantine, or Frankish/Ottonian. To be specific, we are talking about large numbers of indigenous Germanic-speaking groups in central Europe of the first half of the millennium, although at that point many of them became incorporated into the new shape of 'imperial Europe' which emerged from the fall of the Roman west, as well as their Slavic-, Baltic-, and Finno-Ugric-speaking counterparts farther to the east and to the north. A succession of nomadic intruders into Europe from the great Eurasian steppe — Sarmatians, Huns, Avars, Bulgars, and Magyars — complete the catalogue. As Florin Curta rightly notes in his introduction, some of those barbarians are more neglected than others, but the total weight of writing on even the least neglected groups pales into insignificance next to the amount of scholarly ink expended on the imperial societies of first-millennium Europe. There is a very real sense, therefore, in which barbarian Europe as a whole has been thoroughly neglected over the years. The reasons for this are several.

Most obviously, one of the features which make those population groups barbarian is the fact that they were illiterate. Occasional inscriptions and other short pieces of writing turn up in barbarian contexts: enough, indeed, to show that barbarian populations were sometimes more familiar with different kinds of written communication than is usually assumed. The fourth-century Gothic Tervingi are quite unique, however, in having generated an extensive literature while occupying territory beyond the imperial frontier. And even here, the literary oeuvre consisted substantially of a Bible translation, which was composed by the descendants of Roman prisoners taken in the third century. At the very least, therefore, one has to consider it a semi-imperial production, and its value as a firsthand Gothic source is distinctly limited. Loan words and particularities of translation suggest certain things about Gothic social institutions, but because it is a Bible translation tied into materials which originated in the ancient Near East, those can only be suggestions, and, in that sense, even the existence of this text does not contradict the basic point.[1] A lack of literacy means that Europe's barbarians conspicuously lack their own voice, at least in the eras when they were barbarians. The only histories of any Germanic groups around the Roman Empire, as Florin Curta again notes, come from after they had created kingdoms on parts of the empire's former territory, and it is very unclear that texts such as Jordanes's *Getica*, the *Histories* of Gregory of Tours, or Paul the Deacon's *History of the Lombards* tell us anything at all profound about the deeper Germanic past before those kingdoms came into existence.[2]

It was only in mid-ninth-century Moravia, likewise, that the first written version of a Slavic language was developed by the Byzantine missionaries Cyril and Methodius, again to translate the Bible and other key Christian texts.[3] In the centuries which followed, even Latin and Greek literacy in the Slavic world remained largely restricted to religious contexts, and it was not until the early twelfth century that it started to generate its own accounts of the past: the *Chronicle* of Cosmas of Prague in Bohemia (written from *c.* 1120), Gallus Anonymus in Poland (*c.* 1115), and the *Russian Primary Chronicle* in Kiev (1116). Nearly half a millennium separates those first Slavic accounts of Slavic history from the period when Slavic domination was establishing itself over vast tracts of the European landscape, and

---

[1] For an introduction to Ulfilas and his work, see chaps 5 and 6 in Peter J. Heather and John F. Matthews, *The Goths in the Fourth Century* (Liverpool, 1991). Chap. 3 in Herwig Wolfram, *History of the Goths* (Berkeley, 1988) is a good attempt to use the evidence of the Gothic Bible to write social history.

[2] Walter Goffart, *The Narrators of Barbarian History (AD 550–800): Jordanes, Gregory of Tours, Bede, and Paul the Deacon* (Princeton, 1988) represents a minimizing scholarly tradition. However, one does not have to think those texts as quite so literary and/or deliberately misleading as Goffart in order to find their historical value only limited. On Jordanes, see for example the first two chapters in Peter J. Heather, *Goths and Romans 332–489* (Oxford, 1991). On Lombard historical traditions, see *Die Langobarden: Herrschaft und Identität*, ed. by Walter Pohl and Peter Erhart (Vienna, 2005).

[3] Francis Dvornik, *Les Légendes de Constantin et de Méthode vues de Byzance* (Prague, 1933; repr. 1969) remains an excellent introduction.

it is not really surprising that those historical texts are singularly uninformative on the subject. A fundamental reason for the historic neglect of barbarians, therefore, is the almost complete lack of firsthand access to their history.

Archaeological materials fill this gap in certain ways, and many of the contributions to this volume are exploiting either new materials or the exciting new opportunities that modern techniques and analytical insights have to offer. Indeed, if you step back from the detail of the many particular studies, what strikes you, when contemplating the bulk and quality of the relevant literature, is just how far the archaeological analysis of barbarian Europe has come in the last two scholarly generations. This results, as far as I can see, from an intersection of three separate or separable lines of intellectual development, although in practice they have tended to feed into one another. First, a vast amount of new evidence has become available: not least for central and eastern Europe where the slightly bizarre mix of Marxist and nationalist ideologies espoused by the old eastern bloc regimes of the Soviet era resulted in an intense interest in the deep past which provided plentiful resources by means of archaeological exploration.[4] Second, and in part facilitated by the plethora of new information that became available, hugely important technical advances became possible. There are far too many to cite here, but they range from unbelievably painstaking excavation methods which are now regularly capable of detecting the remains of disappeared wood (very important when studying a barbarian world which built fundamentally in wood) to the emergence of diverse and increasingly secure methods for establishing chronology, whether expensive and highly technical ones like dendrochronology and radiocarbon, or Godłowski's refinement of old stylistic dating techniques to depend upon whole assemblages rather than single items.[5] Third, again empowered by the sheer wealth of new information available, the last fifty years have seen a flourishing of much more theoretically informed debates on the kinds of subject areas upon which archaeological materials might be able to shed some light. As a result, knowledge of just about every aspect of barbarian Europe has been transformed out of all recognition, and everything has come under scrutiny, from evolving diet and agricultural

---

[4] Paul Barford, *The Early Slavs: Culture and Society in Early Medieval Eastern Europe* (London, 2001), especially the introduction and the first chapter.

[5] Kazimierz Godłowski, *The Chronology of the Late Roman and Early Migration Periods in Central Europe* (Cracow, 1970) was the great leap forward. But note that more secure dating resolved many old controversies, such as the association between the Chernyakhov culture and the Gothic power north of the Black Sea in the late third and fourth centuries. See Mark B. Shchukin, 'Das Problem der Černjachow-Kultur in der sowjetischen archaologischen Literatur', *Zeitschrift für Archäologie*, 9 (1975), 25–41.

Peter Heather

technique, to those broader facets of economic and social organization that might be illuminated by settlement hierarchies. It is simply the case, therefore, that much more is known about barbarian Europe of the first millennium in general terms than ever before.

All of this more than makes up for the one major negative finding simultaneously to emerge from these reconsiderations, but it is important to note its effect upon our capacity to study barbarian Europe. As has been discussed repeatedly in recent years, the initial and highly influential interpretive framework impressed upon the emergent discipline of archaeology by the work of Montelius and Kossinna in the late nineteenth and early twentieth centuries has proved incapable of bearing the weight put upon it. Montelius and Kossinna were working in the epoch of rampant European nationalism, and in that intellectual context it was entirely natural, when geographically coherent patterns of similarity and difference began to be identified among ancient remains, to suppose that this patterning reflected the remains of separate ancient 'peoples'. This — 'culture history' as it has come to be labelled — made it possible to extend the history of particular ancient European population groups back into a past where there were no actual written histories. It was built, however, upon the fundamental assumption that each ancient people would have its own material culture, and hence that patterns of material culture will be telling you something about the history of ancient peoples. But as anthropology and the social sciences have been exploring particularly since 1945, group identity is much more complex than this: people with different group identities can share the same material culture, people sharing the same group identity can show massive variations in their material culture, and more generally, people often have more than one group identity anyway. Correspondingly, archaeological theorists have shown that, while such patterns of similarity and difference do often exist, they may be generated by any kind of interconnection (cultural, economic, religious as well as the political, whereas culture history essentially assumed that material culture would always be closely correlated to politics) and cannot be read as reflecting the history of particular barbarian groups. As a result, the overall body of archaeological evidence can tell us a huge amount about barbarian Europe in general, but not about particular historically known groups of barbarians, except in particular cases, in which we can locate groups and relevant remains so precisely in time and space as to be sure that the latter belongs to the former.[6]

---

[6] Gustaf Kossinna, *Ursprung und Verbreitung der Germanen in vor- und frühgeschichtlicher Zeit* (Leipzig, 1928) is a clear statement of the culture-historical method. There are many introductions to evolving understandings of group identity, but see e.g. Azril Bacal, *Ethnicity in the Social Sciences:*

With no information of any substance from the barbarians themselves, therefore, and only a more general kind of information from archaeological materials,
those who want to study the non-imperial peoples of first-millennium Europe still
have to turn to what is written about them by authors writing in imperial contexts:
Roman, Byzantine, or Frankish. Occasionally, later in the millennium, Arab ethnographic writings also come into the picture. Barbarians of all kinds exercised a
certain fascination for these imperial societies, but for very particular reasons. We
are all used now to the idea, as Florin Curta's introduction again reminds us, that
barbarians represented the 'other' for Greeks and Romans, where they located the
antithetical vices of what they considered to be the virtues of their own societies.
In Greek geographical and ethnographic tradition, Scythia was often portrayed as
a chill wilderness, the archetypal 'other', the mirror image of Greek civilization.
And to the inhabitants of this world, every imaginable type of uncivilized beha-
viour was ascribed: blinding, scalping, flaying, tattooing, even drinking wine un-
mixed with water. Fundamentally, though, Greeks and Romans saw all foreigners
as lacking the divinely ordained and supported rational social order which reflected
the underlying blueprint of the Cosmos, and which was designed to bring human
beings to the maximum degree of rational perfection that it was possible for them
to achieve. Human beings alone of all the creatures in the universe combined the
rational and irrational — an irrational body and a rational spirit or mind — and,
according to the qualities of the society in which they lived, might go in either
direction. Barbarians represented all that was irrational — whether in the form of
the despotic slavery under which even elites suffered under Persian rule, for
instance, or the might-equals-right societies of barbarian Europe — whereas the
classical civilization of the Mediterranean basin alone could develop humanity's
rational potential to the full, even if different facets of this ideological construct
tended to be stressed at different moments. For classical Greeks of the fifth century
BC, education and the rational debate inherent in the process of arranging your affairs at town council meetings were the key paths to rationality. In the thoroughly
Roman world of Late Antiquity, the existence of written law — ordering society

A View and a Review of the Literature on Ethnicity (Coventry, 1991) with the essays in *On Barbarian Identity: Critical Approaches to Ethnicity in the Early Middle Ages*, ed. by Andrew Gillett
(Turnhout, 2002) for various early medieval case studies. Nonetheless, it remains possible
occasionally to make convincing associations between material remains and particular historically
documented groups, such as that between the Goths and the Chernyakhov culture (see previous
note), or between particular sixth-century fibula types and the Lombards and Gepids of the middle
Danube region, for which see chap. 3 in Florin Curta, *The Making of the Slavs: History and
Archaeology of the Lower Danube Region, ca. 500–700* (Cambridge, 2001).

and giving everyone their place — had become the key differentiating factor between civilized and barbarian. This tradition continued to be influential into the early Middle Ages, steadily transforming itself into a focus on the presence or absence of Christianity as the key defining factor of the civilized and the barbarian, although it still seems to have been pretty much de rigueur to issue a written law code to signal your emergence as a civilized Christian society.[7]

All this means that barbarians were in a certain sense of great interest to imperial commentators, and that barbarians could play some extremely significant roles in that crucial task of ideological self-justification. In particular, barbarians were liable to be trundled out whenever anything needed legitimating, from literary studies to the need to codify written law. Not least, again in the Roman era, the need to defend civilization from the barbarian threat played a hugely important role in justifying the tax collection which was used to support the army and other governmental structures of the empire. And, by extension, as is now very well understood in modern intellectual contexts where 'post-colonial' is such a buzz word, this means that any imperially generated writing about barbarians poses potential intellectual problems of considerable difficulty. Since barbarians had such a negative role to play in imperial self-justification, how likely is it that any particular statement about barbarians, or any particular group of them, will reflect anything close to reality rather than an ideologically convenient image?

But even this problem, I would argue, fades into relative insignificance next to a still more basic one. Although imperial commentators were interested in barbarians in a theoretical way, and happy enough to refer to them as and when important for their own purposes, there were very few who were that interested in barbarians in practice. Tacitus's *Germania* poses some wonderfully tricky problems of interpretation, but, frankly, it is a pleasure to have them. If we had even one monograph of that kind on barbarians per century of the first millennium, we would count ourselves, I think, hugely blessed. For the most part when studying barbarians, one is not faced with the problem of how to read 'colonial' texts in a

[7] On classical visions of the barbarian and their intersections with imperial ideologies, see e.g. Yves A. Dauge, *Le Barbare: recherches sur la conception romaine de la barbare et de la civilisation* (Brussels, 1981) and Francis Dvornik, *Early Christian and Byzantine Political Philosophy: Origin and Background* (Washington, DC, 1966). For introductions to the influence of those ideas in the post-Roman west, see e.g. Peter J. Heather, 'The Historical Culture of Ostrogothic Italy', in *Teoderico il grande e i Goti d'Italia: Atti del XIII Congresso internazionale di studi sull'Alto Medioevo 1992* (Spoleto, 1993), pp. 317–53, and the first chapter in Patrick Wormald, *The Making of English Law: King Alfred to the Twelfth Century*, I (Oxford, 1999), for the ideological significance of lawmaking.

post-colonial way, but with a deafening wall of silence. Even such a detailed text as the history of Ammianus Marcellinus, which devotes many thousands of words to various fourth-century barbarians, above all the Alamanni, never bothers to tell you even basic things about them. A few precious fragments of information emerge incidentally as his narrative unfolds, but Ammianus is never interested enough to describe the politics, society, or economy of the barbarians he knows in any detail, and his materials even on the Alamanni have generated substantially differing overall interpretations among modern commentators.[8] In all this, Ammianus is entirely representative of the broader run of imperial commentators on barbarian Europe. Not only is what they do tell us filtered through the lens of imperial self-justificatory ideologies, but, actually, they do not tell us very much at all.

In the face of such partial and non-user-friendly materials, even given the massive advances on the barbarian front, a general neglect of barbarians is to an extent unavoidable. It is just so much more difficult to write about them than imperial Europe where fruitful combinations of equally plentiful texts and archaeological evidence offer so many avenues for productive research. That said, there has always been a set of reasons beyond mere practical difficulty which have generated a relative lack of attention to Europe's barbarians. For if one looks at Europe in the broadest terms, the origins of the vast majority of the big ideas and overarching patterns of human organization, which are characteristic of its state structures, those at least that have any first-millennium roots, have to be traced back firmly to imperial Europe and not to the barbarian 'other' beyond the frontier. Courses in Western Civilization have long accustomed us to the classical roots of modern European philosophical and broader intellectual cultures, but the list of Europe's debts to its ancient empires is far longer than that. An obvious case in point is Christianity. This grew up in a Roman imperial context, and then went through further stages of evolution in the post-Roman Frankish imperial west and Byzantium before spreading, eventually, right across the European landscape. Similar patterns of dissemination are also visible in the histories of such important institutions as self-governing towns, written legal systems, bishoprics, and monasteries. These and many other major bulwarks of medieval and more modern European culture and society had their origins in imperial Europe, and their influence is still

---

[8] In my view (and that of many others in fact) Ammianus's evidence helps make the case that Germanic political society had changed substantially between the first century and the fourth. See chap. 2 in Peter Heather, *The Fall of The Roman Empire: A New History of Rome and the Barbarians* (Oxford, 2005). Others disagree: John F. Drinkwater, *The Alamanni and Rome 213–496 (Caracalla to Clovis)* (Oxford, 2007).

very broadly felt. In economic terms, likewise, the broader debt owed to imperial
Europe is enormous. Arguably the most important single development here was
the development of manorialized arable agriculture. This had huge limitations but,
in its own context, represented a massive step forward in the management of
landed resources, responsible for greatly increasing food production and hence
population size right across northern Europe. Most monarchical ideologies and
even bureaucratic habits and the other structures of government also moved
outwards from imperial Europe in the same way. There is a real sense in which it
has always been perfectly reasonable to argue, therefore, that what really matters
in the first millennium is a sequence of developments within imperial Europe, since
between them they provided the blueprint on which the whole of Europe — barbarian and imperial combined — would subsequently be based. 'Barbarian' has not
always been used with the kind of non-judgemental force that is increasingly the
case now. And, for many, the ancients were quite right. Barbarian societies were
inferior, and all the really interesting ideas and institutions with any future had
their origin in imperial Europe.

For much of the twentieth century, there were two big exceptions to this broader
pattern of intellectually generated neglect. First, some particular barbarian population groups of the first millennium were seen as directly ancestral to modern nation
states. As Florin Curta explores in the introduction to this volume, this goes some
way to explaining why some barbarians were less neglected than others. Again, as
with the emergence of culture history in archaeology, we are dealing here with an
idea-set which originated in the intellectual climate of high nationalism. This
assumed that distinctive modern population conglomerates had equally distinctive
ancestors from whom they were directly descended. And, in many cases, the supposed lines of ancestry ran out somewhere in the first millennium. In the late nineteenth century (although it is important to note that there were always dissenting
voices), many Englishmen thought of themselves and the state in which they lived
as directly descended from the people and institutions of the Anglo-Saxons of the
mid-first millennium, while Franks and Lombards were thought to have made
important, if not numerically so overwhelming, contributions to the creation of
France and Italy. In a similar vein, different units of ancestral Slavs were thought to
have set the histories of large parts of central and eastern Europe — whether Croatia,
Slovenia, or Poland among many others — off on a new trek towards historical
particularity which would culminate in at least a claimed right to set up a nation
state. Culture history, as has again been explored almost to death in the last scholarly
generation, carried within it an inherent tendency to explain archaeologically
visible change in terms of migration. As each 'people' had its own material culture,

then it was natural to explain any major change in patterns of material culture in terms of a new 'people' moving into a landscape. In visions of the past driven by nationalist imperatives, it was thus a central historical enterprise to search the past for the arrival of the ancestral community upon the soil of what would become its national homeland. A direct line of historical descent was an essential element in justifying those claims, and this served to power up one line of interest in first-millennium barbarians across large parts of the European landscape.

The second reason for taking barbarians seriously had quite different roots: classical Marxist understandings of historical development. In Marx and Engel's understanding of the past, at least the Germanic barbarians of first-millennium Europe had a crucial role to play. Their destruction of the Roman Empire was responsible for the elimination of the slave-based mode of production of the ancient world and for ushering in the military/feudal mode characteristic of medieval Europe, where a small militarized aristocracy exploited manorialized serfs rather than slaves living on plantations. In Marxist thought, of course, forces were at play beyond the power of individuals or even human conglomerates to manipulate and control, so that the barbarians were in a sense tools rather than empowered historical actors with an individual effect upon events. Nonetheless, the Marxist agenda did give a further, very real reason to examine barbarian Europe, and hence the potent combination of Marxism and nationalism (even though nationalism can only be a non-class and therefore 'false' consciousness in Marxist terms) which powered the archaeological bonanza in the old eastern bloc states whose fruits are still being reaped in modern archaeological research.

Neither of those old intellectual imperatives for studying Europe's barbarians, however, now carries much conviction. One specific dimension of the general reconsideration of the workings of group identity has been the debunking of the nationalist conceit that some essential unity links modern nations with any of the ancient 'peoples' who appear in the historical record during the first millennium. Nations have been shown to be human communities created at particular times in a particular set of circumstances, and cannot be seen as merely the latest expression of an ancient and enduring entity. And once it became understood that modern nations were new unities created out of diverse fragments of population in the modern era, and that they are inconceivable without, amongst other things, relatively modern systems of communication and levels of education, then searching the past for the arrival of the ancestral barbarians lost its central point. Indeed, at the same time, and for a variety of reasons, culture history's over-reliance on a very simple mass migration/ethnic cleansing model of material cultural progression was being rightly discredited.[9] As a result, much more real history has emerged, and I would not for a moment bemoan the passing of the old intellectual order. But it is the case that post-nationalist state structures are much less interested in the deeper past, as opposed to the present, and much less likely to accord its study substantial funds.

The idea that some of Europe's barbarians were ultimately responsible for moving Europe onwards to the feudal mode of production has also lost much of its force. For one thing, it has become clear that plantation slavery only operated in some highly restricted contexts in the ancient world — the Italian wine industry for instance in the century either side of the birth of Christ — but that, otherwise, it would simply not have been profitable. Concomitant with this, some late Roman estates in the well-documented province of Egypt mobilized their labour forces in a centrally directed fashion which looks remarkably like the classic medieval manor of the so-called feudal era. The fall of the Roman Empire certainly did see the emergence of militarized land-owning elites, but manors pre-existed this development in some places, it seems, and in others only emerged a number of centuries later.[10] Finding the roots now of deeply profound, epochal change of the Marxist type in something particular to do with Europe's barbarians qua barbarians and the process of Roman imperial collapse looks rather like a forlorn hope, and few would now look to uphold a properly Marxist interpretation of this process, even if, as I myself would, one sees it as marking a major sea-change in European history.

So if we cannot see any first-millennium barbarians as direct progenitors of the modern nations of Europe, and it is not at all clear that their intrusions moved the world clock from one epoch to the next, why should we bother to study them, especially given all the problems that the lack of firsthand source material generates? One answer, of course, is that everything is worth studying, and a central element of the general post-colonial agenda is certainly applicable here. All human

---

[9] The literature on nationalism is enormous, but Benedict Anderson, *Imagined Communities: Reflections on the Origin and Spread of Nationalism* (London, 1991) is a key document. For an introduction to developing archaeological theory, see Colin Renfrew and Paul G. Bahn, *Archaeology: Theories, Methods and Practice*, 4th edn (London, 2004) or *Reading the Past: Current Approaches to Interpretation in Archaeology*, ed. by Ian Hodder and Scott Hutson (Cambridge, 2003).

[10] For reviews of what can be retrieved of Marx's views on Rome's fall, see Chris Wickham, 'The Other Transition: From the Ancient World to Feudalism', *Past and Present*, 103 (1984), 3–36; and Chris Wickham, 'La Chute de Rome n'aura pas lieu: a propos d'un livre récent', *Le Moyen Âge*, 99 (1993), 107–26. Peter Sarris, *Economy and Society in the Age of Justinian* (Cambridge, 2006) is excellent on Egyptian estate organization. Guy Halsall, *Settlement and Social Organization: The Merovingian Region of Metz* (Cambridge, 1995) showed that manorial-type estates only appeared in north-eastern Francia in the seventh century.

activities have the same value and ought to be studied with the same intensity, not just those features of imperial societies which will eventually colonize larger land-scapes. Barbarians are worth studying in their own right, even those which were, in the long run, on that metaphorical historical road to nowhere.

I would certainly hold to this point of view, but would at the same time argue that there is a pressing reason to study barbarians, even for those whose interests lie in the broader metanarratives of European history. It emerges with clarity when one considers the broader historical development visible across the European land-scape in the course of the first millennium as a whole. Round about the birth of Christ, it is clear that we need to be thinking broadly in terms of a three-speed Europe. As far east as the river Rhine and north to the river Danube lay a zone which had or was just about to come under Roman rule, and which would show by far the quickest pace of economic, social, and political development in the next few centuries. Indeed, a good argument can be made that the geographical extent of this territory was no accident, since Roman conquest ran out of steam just a little beyond the boundaries of a key pre-existing divide in the European landscape, that between more-developed, largely Celtic-dominated La Tène Europe to the west and south and largely Germanic-dominated Jastorf and post-Jastorf Europe further north and east. Pre-Roman Celtic material culture is famous for a distinctive art style, expressed particularly in beautifully crafted metalwork. Celtic settlements of the period also shared a general sophistication in other aspects of material culture: amongst other things, technologically advanced wheel-turned pottery, substantial and often walled settlements (so-called *oppida*), and the considerable use of iron tools to generate a comparatively productive agriculture.[11]

The material remains generated by Germanic speakers in the same period, by contrast, were generally of a much less rich and developed kind. Typical finds from Germanic Europe consist of cremation burials in urns with few or no grave goods, only hand-worked rather than wheel-made pottery, no developed metalwork style, and no *oppida*. The general level of agricultural productivity in Germanic-dominated areas was also much less intense. It was precisely because the economy of Germanic Europe produced less of an agricultural surplus than neighbouring Celtic regions, of course, that there was smaller scope for the employment of the specialist smiths and artists required to produce sophisticated metalwork. And

---

[11] For an introduction to the pre-Roman world of the Celts, see e.g. Barry W. Cunliffe, *The Ancient Celts* (Oxford, 1997) or Simon James, *The Atlantic Celts: Ancient People or Modern Invention?* (London, 1999). On the equation between Roman expansion and profit, see e.g. Benjamin Isaac, *The Limits of Empire: The Roman Army in the East* (Oxford, 1992).

while the Romans never took a broad strategic decision to absorb just Celtic Europe, the narratives of attempted conquest indicate that Roman commanders on the ground eventually came to appreciate that the less developed economy of Germanic Europe just was not worth the effort of conquest. Traditional accounts of Rome's failure to conquer the *Germani*, as these Germanic speakers are now often called, emphasize the latter's destruction of Varus's three legions at the battle of the Teutoburger Wald in AD 7. Reality was more prosaic. The potential taxes from a conquered Germanic Europe would pay neither for the costs of conquest nor for its subsequent garrisoning.[12]

Still further east, beyond the river Vistula and west of the river Don (east of which rainfall levels are too low for conventional farming to be possible without irrigation), lay Europe's third zone.[13] Issues of ethnicity and language-spread among the populations of this region remain deeply contested, particularly the highly vexed question of where Europe's Slavic speakers might be found at this date, if, indeed, a recognizable Slavic language had yet split off from the common ancestor it shares with speakers of Baltic languages. Archaeologically, however, the general picture of the inhabitants of those wooded and forested zones of Eastern Europe around the birth of Christ is reasonably straightforward. Like that of the Germani to the west, it was a world of farmers, but farmers with an extremely simple material culture, considerably less developed even than that prevailing further west in Germanic Europe. The remains of its pottery, tools, and settlement are so simple, in fact, that they frustrate attempts at stylistic and hence chronological categorization, being extremely slow to change before the second half of the first millennium AD. This archaeological evidence suggests that Europe's third zone was a world of small, isolated farming settlements, operating at a still lower level of subsistence and with much lower population densities than the Germani, with little sign of any surplus, and none of the trade links with the richer world of the Mediterranean to the south.[14]

[12] Useful introductions to the early Germanic world are Rolf Hachmann, *The Germanic Peoples* (London, 1971); *Die Germanen: Geschichte und Kultur der germanischen Stämme in Mitteleuropa*, ed. by Bruno Krüger and others, I (Berlin, 1976); Walter Pohl, *Die Germanen* (Munich, 2000).

[13] This is a geographical simplification; west of the Don, there are various micro-regions producing habitats better suited to more nomadic agricultural strategies than traditional arable agriculture. On the southern parts of this region, see now the excellent study of Roger Batty, *Rome and the Nomads: The Pontic-Danubian Realm in Antiquity* (Oxford, 2007).

[14] Good introductions to the vexed question of Slavic origins are the introduction to Barford, *Early Slavs*, and the first chapter in Curta, *Making of the Slavs*. On the geography and ancient

The contrast between this situation and the year 1000 could not be more dramatic. In the winter of AD 999, the Holy Roman Emperor Otto III left the city of Rome. The Emperor had heard of the miracles being performed at the tomb of a recent Christian martyr, the bishop and missionary Adalbert, and resolved to pay the shrine a visit. First-millennium emperors, Roman and after, all thought they were appointed by God and hence had a vested interest in manifestations of divine power. Before turning to the brief and ill-fated missionary drive which led to his death, Adalbert had been Bishop of Prague in Bohemia, but Otto was setting off for Poland. There the latest representative of its ruling Piast dynasty, Boleslav Chobry, had ransomed Adalbert's body and built a magnificent tomb for it at Gniezno. What happened next is told by the contemporary chronicler, Thietmar of Merseburg:

> [Otto] was led into the church where, weeping profusely, he was moved to ask the grace of Christ's martyr. Without delay, he established an archbishopric there. [...] He committed the new foundation to Radim, the martyr's brother, and made subject to him Bishop Reinbern of Kolberg, Bishop Poppo of Krakow, and Bishop John of Wrocław. [...] And with great solemnity, he also placed holy relics in an altar which had been established there. After all issues had been settled, the duke [of Poland] honoured Otto with rich presents and, what was even more pleasing, three hundred armoured warriors. When the emperor departed, Boleslav and an illustrious entourage conducted him to Magdeburg, where they celebrated Palm Sunday with great festivity.[15]

At the start of the first millennium, Poland and Bohemia had been dominated by Germanic speakers, and the basic pattern of life involved clusters of wooden huts — some larger, some smaller — grouped together amidst prevailing woodlands. There were still plenty of trees at the end of the millennium, but the ruling Přemyslid and Piast dynasties of Bohemia and Poland were all Slavic speakers. The clusters of wooden huts had also been superseded by castles, cathedrals, and armoured knights, which had become pretty much standard appurtenances of power right across central and eastern Europe, and central Poland had become a destination fit for an emperor, and a suitable location for an independent province of the Christian Church. There could be no greater symbol that Poland had just been welcomed to the club of Europe's Christian states.

---

archaeological patterning of the society and economy of Europe's third region in this era, see Pavel M. Dolukhanov, *The Early Slavs: Eastern Europe from the Initial Settlement to the Kievan Rus* (London, 1996).

[15] Thietmar of Merseburg, *Chronicle*, 4. 45–46; English trans. from David A. Warner, *Ottonian Germany: The Chronicon of Thietmar of Merseburg* (Manchester, 2001), p. 185.

Nor was Poland alone. Prague also had a bishop, and although Bohemia did not yet rate an archbishopric, it too had its fair share of castles, cathedrals, and knights. Its ruling Přemyslid dynasty had definitively converted to Christianity in the person, no less, of Good King Wenceslas in the 920s. Subsequent members of the dynasty slipped in and out of Ottonian imperial favour, but this would be true of the rulers of Poland too, and does not alter the basic picture that both Slavic ruling lines were firmly members of the club of Christian Europe. The first Slavic entity to demand and be granted this kind of recognition was the so-called 'Great' Moravia, which emerged from the wreck of the old Avar Empire in the early ninth century. It was the first Slavic state to convert to Christianity, receiving, amongst other missionaries, the famous Byzantine Saints Cyril and Methodius in the 860s, who, as we have seen, were responsible for the first written form of a Slavic language.

In Scandinavia too, in the aftermath of ninth-century Viking chaos, matters were moving in a similar direction. From the middle of the tenth century, a powerful state structure began to emerge, based on Jutland and the Danish islands, dominated by successive members of the Jelling dynasty, named after the place of their most famous burial ground. Originally pagan, it converted to Christianity in the person of Harald Bluetooth and, even if maintaining a larger naval capacity than its continental Slavic counterparts, was soon putting up castles and cathedrals of similar kinds, and likewise alternately squabbling with or receiving favours from different Holy Roman emperors. Intermarriages between the Danish and Slavic, particularly the Polish, dynasties soon followed, and they were all part of the same broader diplomatic and cultural orbit.

Moreover, Scandinavian expansion had flowed as much eastwards as westwards in the Viking era, where one of its chief outcomes was the Riurikid-dominated Rus' state, centred on Kiev. This dynasty held on to its ancestral paganism for a little longer than its western counterparts and, reflecting the particularities of its origins, took a bit longer to get round to castles and cathedrals. Not, however, that much longer: Vladimir converted his state definitively to Christianity in the late 980s, and shortly after the year 1000 constructed in Kiev the famous Tithe Church dedicated to the Mother of God. Built of brick and stone, it measured 27 metres by 18, and could boast three aisles, three apses, and a cupola: the greatest structure yet seen so far east and north in the European landscape.[16]

---

[16] The classic treatment in English of all the Slavic kingdoms remains Francis Dvornik, *The Making of Central and Eastern Europe* (London, 1949) supplemented by Francis Dvornik, *The Slavs: Their Early History and Civilization* (Boston, 1956). The more recent bibliography is immense, but *Origins of Central Europe*, ed. by Przemysław Urbańczyk (Warsaw, 1997); *Early Christianity in Central and East Europe*, ed. by Przemysław Urbańczyk (Warsaw, 1997); *Europe*

By the end of the first millennium, therefore, the vast disparities in development that prevailed in the three-speed Europe of a thousand years before had given way to patterns of much greater uniformity and equality. It is important, of course, not to overstate the argument. Some Baltic-speaking regions, not least those where Adalbert had met his end, would not be brought into the European mainstream until the northern crusades were unleashed in all their venom, and the Elbe Slavs, likewise, remained beyond the Christian pale.[17] It is also the case that the new states of central and eastern Europe, and the societies that supported them, still lagged far behind more-developed parts of Europe in terms of advanced literacy, building in brick and stone, and more sophisticated aspects of economic development. Nonetheless, much of the divide of a thousand years before had been closed, and it would not be long before the Piast, Přemyslid, and Riurikid dynasts would be busy recruiting churchmen to run their bureaucracies and peasants and merchants from further west to kick-start their economies, although these were already showing considerable signs of life. For without economic surpluses and much larger populations all this state building would have been completely impossible.

This extraordinary contrast shows precisely why it remains imperative to study Europe's first millennium barbarians, both the more and the less neglected. For they are central, in fact, to what is surely the biggest story of the era: the creation of Europe itself. As has often been pointed out, Europe is not in fact a geographical entity. What we call Europe is no more than the western end of the great Eurasian landmass. What gives Europe an identity — even if its margins can certainly be debated and extended — is a substantial degree of religious and other cultural, economic, and political interaction among societies who all shared some commonalities. In a very real sense, then, Europe did not exist at the beginning of the first

---

around the Year 1000, ed. by Przemysław Urbańczyk (Warsaw, 2001); *Polish Lands at the Turn of the First and the Second Millennia*, ed. by Przemysław Urbańczyk (Warsaw, 2004); Barford, *Early Slavs*; *East Central and Eastern Europe in the Early Middle Ages*, ed. by Florin Curta (Ann Arbor, 2005); Simon Franklin and Jonathan Shepard, *The Emergence of Rus 750–1200* (Harlow, 1996); Elena A. Mel'nikova, *The Eastern World of the Vikings* (Gothenburg, 1996); Władysław Duczko, *Viking Rus: Studies on the Presence of Scandinavians in Eastern Europe* (Leiden, 2004) are particularly helpful in bringing matters up to date. Klavs Randsborg, *The Viking Age in Denmark: The Formation of a State* (London, 1980); Else Roesdahl, *Viking-Age Denmark* (London, 1982); Birgit Sawyer and Peter H. Sawyer, *Medieval Scandinavia: From Conversion to Reformation c. 800–1500* (Minneapolis, 1993) provide excellent introductions to developments in Scandinavia.

[17] On the Elbe Slavs, see e.g. Christian Lübke, *Regesten zur Geschichte der Slaven an Elbe und Oder (vom Jahr 900 an)* (Berlin, 1984–88), and on the Northern crusades, Erik Christiansen, *The Northern Crusades: The Baltic and the Catholic Frontier, 1100–1525* (London, 1980).

millennium, when the landmass was home to such huge disparities, and large parts of its population were in no contact whatsoever with the broader mainstream. By the end of the millennium, however, the situation was completely different. With the emergence of new state structures in the east and north in the ninth and tenth centuries, Europe first took on something of the outline shape which it has broadly retained to the present: a network of not entirely dissimilar, economically and culturally interconnected political societies clustering at the western end of the great Eurasian landmass. As a result of this process, one might say, barbarian Europe was barbarian no longer. The ancient world order of Mediterranean domination over a massively underdeveloped north and east had given way to cultural and political patterns which were much more directly ancestral to those of modern Europe. Studying Europe's first-millennium barbarians, therefore, is absolutely central to understanding the creation of Europe itself.

This is not, moreover, a process that should be taken remotely for granted as a natural and inevitable outcome that requires no further discussion. There is nothing so obviously great about dominant militarized elites living off the labour of a subjugated peasantry, it should be stressed, for us simply to assume that this kind of outcome was bound to be seized upon by all as an excellent end point for the transformations of the first millennium. Even the triumph of Christianity — perhaps the most durable of all first-millennium phenomena — should not be considered inevitable, although an overly narrow focus on just European events might lead one to think so. For one thing, even first-millennium European history throws up enough examples where the religion's exclusive and monolithic ideologies stimulated a significant degree of resistance. Around the year 1000, the Elbe Slavs remained resolutely pagan, an Ottonian imperialism which was closely associated with Christianity having sponsored a widespread rebellion in the marches which took an explicitly anti-Christian form. Earlier in the millennium, likewise, the Gothic Tervingi had deliberately looked to limit the religion's influence in their lands north of the Danube because it was too closely associated with Roman domination.[18] In the long run, those attempts to resist Christianity, the religion of Europe's first-millennium empires, were doomed to failure, but they did not necessarily have to be so, as the history of the Arabs, another set of barbarians on one of the other fringes of the Roman Empire, demonstrates so clearly. The only difference between Attila the Hun and Muhammad, arguably, is that Attila was not clever enough to come up with a sufficiently durable religious ideology to bind

---

[18] Elbe Slavs: Lübke, *Regesten*. For the fourth-century Tervingi, see chap. 4 in Heather and Matthews, *Goths*, as well as chap. 3 in Heather, *Goths and Romans*.

together his disparate and previously politically separate followers into a grouping tight enough to survive his own demise. Otherwise their careers look remarkably similar: effectively both added an extra dimension of unity to a context which was already producing political structures of greater size and stability in response to the various stimuli which had flowed over a series of centuries from their proximity to an imperial power. This extra unity then allowed the new grouping to predate upon that neighbouring empire with unprecedented effectiveness.[19]

In fact, Muhammad even used an adapted form of the imperial religion itself to achieve this effect (in the sense that his new faith drew substantially upon Judaeo-Christian idea-sets), so that the whole Islamic-Arab phenomenon makes no sense unless understood as some kind of broader reaction to imperial power. But as this example emphasizes, the reaction to imperial stimuli did not always have to take the form merely of straightforward acceptance. Any account of the spread of imperially generated ideas and institutions north and eastwards into barbarian Europe which does not take full account of the fact that the barbarians had a choice of whether to adopt them or not, or whether to adopt them in full or only in a form carefully adapted to their own needs, is a thoroughly insufficient one. The barbarians of first-millennium Europe had great powers of 'agency' as it would now be called in post-colonial rhetorical terms. The concept runs into difficulty when it comes to precise definition, but its general significance is straightforward. The barbarians were not just obeying orders but adopting and adapting imperial forms and ideologies for their own purposes, according to their own specific agendas.[20] What this clearly means, in terms of writing first-millennium history, is that, when studying the spread of similarities across the European landscape, it is not enough to study in detail merely the origin of those similarities in imperial Europe; one also needs to study with quite as much intensity exactly how and why they were adopted by the neighbouring barbarians. That subsequent process played just as large a role in the final outcome as the first emergence of the ideas and

---

[19] In my view, the pattern of political evolution in the Arab world of the fourth to the sixth century was, like that of the Germani of the first to the fourth, one moving towards structures of greater size and stability. This emerges clearly from studies such as Maurice Sartre, *Trois Études sur l'Arabie romaine et byzantine* (Brussels, 1982) and Robert G. Hoyland, *Arabia and the Arabs: From the Bronze Age to the Coming of Islam* (London, 2001). For an introduction to Attila, see chaps 7 and 8 in Heather, *The Fall of the Roman Empire*.

[20] Jon E. Wilson, 'Agency, Narrative, and Resistance', in *The British Empire: Themes and Perspectives*, ed. by Sarah E. Stockwell (Oxford, 2008), pp. 245–68, provides a very helpful review of the agency issue.

institutions that spread outwards from imperial Europe and was the result of a whole series of individual decisions and contingent outcomes. In other words, all of Europe's first-millennium barbarians, those who made it through to longer histories and those who did not, played key roles in the eventual outcome which was the creation of Europe, and it is necessary to take account of all their histories. In this sense, the overall effect of post-colonial agendas does not just have to amount to a splintering of the big picture into smaller, better-understood fragments, but can also help produce a much better quality metanarrative.

The story of how Europe's barbarians debarbarized themselves for their own reasons is obviously a huge one, and one that is not going to be easy to tell. It is bound to be full of twists and turns and historical dead ends ('might-have-beens' that did not quite come to long-term fruition) as groups and leaderships struggled to maximize their positions in political, economic, and cultural contexts that were undergoing dramatic transformation. The main crux points for discussion, however, are reasonably easy to identify and lay out in chronological order. One set of important processes unfolded around the fringes of the Roman Empire in the first half of the first millennium. The pulses of major migration onto Roman soil at the end of the fourth and beginning of the fifth centuries and the rise and fall of the Hunnic Empire represent another set of profoundly important and in my view intimately linked tipping points for the configuration of power and society in barbarian Europe. Just as important, subsequently, was the rise of Avar power at the heart of central Europe and the more or less simultaneous slavicization of large parts of central and eastern Europe which was clearly linked to it in some way. The destruction of Avar power at the hands of Charlemagne, and the processes towards state formation in central and eastern Europe which this somehow let loose, accompanied chronologically (though not in an obvious way causally) by the Viking diasporas from Scandinavia in the ninth and tenth centuries complete a quite obvious list of crunch points of transformation. How all of those processes unfolded in detail, however, how they interrelated, and why they should have resulted in the creation of Europe is not so easy to say, and much work is still required on all those fronts.

Viewed from this perspective, however, the contributions to this volume acquire a second significance. They can be understood not only as particular contributions detailing aspects of the history of individually neglected barbarians, but also collectively as a major contribution to the reconstruction of this far larger story. In range, this particular volume does not include any papers dealing with the Viking era, or the later stages of state formation in central and eastern Europe. The different contributions do have important things to say, however, about different aspects of all the other major transformative moments. The papers of von Rummel and Castellanos illuminate different case studies of the kinds of socio-political and economic transformations that tended to be generated amongst groupings who found themselves on the fringes of the Roman Empire in the first half of the millennium. As such they need to be thought about alongside the histories of better-known and slightly less neglected groups like the Gothic Tervingi north of the Danube or the Alamanni of the Rhine frontier region. Various aspects of the rise and fall of Hunnic power then concern a distinct cluster of papers. Two — those of Berndt and López Sánchez — deal with a subject close to my own heart, the effect upon intrusive outsiders of having to adapt to survive upon Roman soil and the effects of that struggle upon adjacent Roman provincial populations, and hence upon the central Roman state itself. The obvious parallels here are the creation of the Visigoths and Ostrogoths, and, to some extent, the Merovingian Franks, as coherent entities, although the latter really emerged only after the central Roman state had lost much of its capacity to act effectively.[21] The largest cluster of studies then illustrates different aspects of the rise and fall of the Hunnic Empire in central Europe. Three explore transformations at its very distant fringes whether in the north beside the Baltic (Bliujienė and Nowakowski) or in the far south-east (Gavritukhin and Kazanski). Others look much closer in, either at the Huns themselves (Nagy) or at one of the areas adjacent to its core (Bohemia: Jiřík), at the history of the empire's successor states (Tóth and in part Harhoiu), or at the history and archaeology of one of the great losers from the process: the Herules (Steinacher and Sarantis). Four further papers then deal with aspects of the rise and fall of the Avar Empire and with the initial slavicization of Europe (Harhoiu again, Kharalambieva, Szmoniewski, and Curta).

All of those papers, of course, have their individual contributions to make — whether in terms of information, methodology, or insight — and must be read, too, as their authors intended, as specific studies of the histories of particular neglected barbarian groups. To my mind, however, they also add up to a major contribution to a new type of history that still needs to be written, the overall tale of Europe's generally neglected barbarians. Only by studying those barbarians with as much intensity as the major empires of the first millennium, and by paying full attention to their autonomous responses to the developing world around them, methodologically demanding as this undoubtedly is, will it be possible to provide a more convincing account of the creation of Europe.

---

[21] The creation of the Visigoths and Ostrogoths was the subject of Heather, *Goths and Romans*.

CONTRIBUTORS

Guido M. Berndt is researcher at the Institute of Ancient History, University of Erlangen-Nuremberg (Germany). He has published several studies on Vandal history, for example, *Konflikt und Anpassung: Studien zu Migration und Ethnogenese der Vandalen* (Husum, 2007), and is the co-editor of *Das Reich der Vandalen und seine (Vor-)Geschichten* (Vienna, 2008). He has published a critical edition of the *Vita* of Meinwerk (Munich, 2009), an early eleventh-century Bishop of Paderborn. His current project deals with Gothic warriors in Late Antiquity.

Audronė Bliujienė is Senior Research Fellow at the Institute of Baltic Sea Region History and Archaeology, University of Klaipėda (Lithuania). Bliujienė's research interests include various aspects of the social, economic, and cultural history of the Baltic lands during Late Antiquity and the early Middle Ages. In relation to the excavations of such key sites as the Lazdininkai cemetery, her recent research has focused on gender representation in burial assemblages of the early Middle Ages. She is the author of *Vikingų epochos kuršių papuošalų ornamentika* (Vilnius, 1999) and *Lietuvos priešistorės gintaras* (Vilnius, 2007), as well as the co-editor of *Weapons, Weaponry, and Man: In Memoriam Vytautas Kazakevičius* (Klaipėda, 2007).

Santiago Castellanos is professor of Ancient History at the University of León (Spain). His books include *Poder social, aristocracias, y hombre santo en la Hispania visigoda: La 'Vita Aemiliani' de Braulius de Zaragoza* (Logroño, 1998), *La hagiografía visigoda: Dominio social y proyección cultural* (Logroño, 2004), and most recently, *Los godos y la cruz: Recaredo y la unidad de Spania* (Madrid, 2007). Castellanos has published extensively on Late Roman and post-Roman societies in Western Europe, especially in Visigothic Spain and Merovingian Gaul. He is the co-editor of *Comunidades locales y dinámicas de poder en el norte de la Península Ibérica durante la Antigüedad tardía* (Logroño, 2006) and *De Roma a los bárbaros:*

Poder central y horizontes en la cuenca del Duero (León, 2008). He currently works on a research project sponsored by the National Education Office of Spain about intellectual attitudes in Late Antiquity and the early Middle Ages.

Florin Curta is professor of Medieval History and Archaeology at the University of Florida. His books include *The Making of the Slavs: History and Archaeology of the Lower Danube Region, ca. 500–700* (Cambridge, 2001), which received the Herbert Baxter Adams Award of the American Historical Association, and *Southeastern Europe in the Middle Ages, 500–1250* (Cambridge, 2006). Curta is the editor of three collections of studies: *East Central and Eastern Europe in the Early Middle Ages* (Ann Arbor, 2005); *Borders, Barriers, and Ethnogenesis: Frontiers in Late Antiquity and the Middle Ages* (Turnhout, 2005); and *The Other Europe in the Middle Ages: Avars, Bulgars, Khazars, and Cumans* (Leiden, 2008). He is also the editor-in-chief of the Brill series 'East Central and Eastern Europe in the Middle Ages, 450–1450'. His most recent book is an economic and social history of Greece between *c.* 500 and *c.* 1050 to be published by the Edinburgh University Press.

Igor O. Gavritukin is archaeologist at the Institute of Archaeology of the Russian Academy of Sciences in Moscow. He is the co-author of *Gaponovskii klad i ego kul'turno-istoricheskii kontekst* (Moscow, 1996) and co-editor of *Drevnosti Severnogo Kavkaza i Prichernomor'ia* (Moscow, 1991) and *Vostochnaia Evropa v seredine I tysiacheletiia n. e.* (Moscow, 2007). Gavritukhin's research focuses on the archaeology of the early Middle Ages in Eastern Europe, especially on dress accessories (fibulae, belt buckles, and belt mounts) and 'Slavic' pottery.

Radu Harhoiu is senior researcher at the 'Vasile Pârvan' Institute of Archaeology in Bucharest (Romania). He is the author of *The Fifth-Century AD Treasure from Pietroasa, Romania* (Oxford, 1977) and *Die frühe Völkerwanderungszeit in Rumänien* (Bucharest, 1997). He has published extensively on the archaeology of the fourth, fifth, and sixth centuries in Romania, with a special emphasis on Transylvania. His long-time excavation of the settlements and cemeteries in Sighişoara-'Dealul Viilor' have been recently published in a two-volume monograph, *Sighişoara-Dealul Viilor: Monografie arheologică* (Bistriţa/Cluj-Napoca, 2006–07).

Peter Heather is professor of Medieval History at King's College London. His research interests lie in the Late Roman Empire and the early Middle Ages, with a focus on the fourth and fifth centuries. In recent years, that focus shifted to issues of migration and ethnicity. He is the author of *The Goths* (Oxford, 1996) and *The Fall of the Roman Empire: A New History of Rome and the Barbarians* (Oxford,

2005), as well as the editor of *The Visigoths from the Migration Period to the Seventh Century: An Ethnographic Perspective* (Woodbridge, 1999).

Jaroslav Jiřík is archaeologist at the Prácheň Museum in Písek (Czech Republic). He is currently a doctoral candidate at the Institute of Prehistory and Early History of the Charles University in Prague, working on a dissertation entitled 'Bohemia in the Early Stages of the Migration Period'. He participated in excavations of prehistoric sites, as well as of sites of the Roman and post-Roman age. One of his most recent projects is the excavation and complex study of a large cemetery of the Vinařice group in Prague-Zličín.

Michel Kazanski is Senior Research Fellow at the Centre for the History and Civilization of Byzantium, Collège de France in Paris (France). His publications include *Les Goths (Iᵉʳ–VIIᵉ s. ap. J.C.)* (Paris, 1991) and *Les Slaves: les origines (Iᵉʳ–VIIᵉ siècle après J.-C.)* (Paris, 1999). In addition, Kazanski is co-author of *La Nécropole gallo-romaine et mérovingienne de Breny (Aisne): d'après les collections et les archives du Musée des Antiquités Nationales* (Montagnac, 2002); *Les Peuples du Caucase du Nord: le début de l'histoire (Iᵉʳ–VIIᵉ siècle apr. J.-C.)* (Paris, 2003); *Qal'at Sem'an*, IV: *Les Objets métalliques* (Beirut, 2003), *Les Nécropoles de Viminacium à l'époque des Grandes Migrations* (Paris, 2006), and *Des Goths aux Huns: Le Nord de la Mer Noire au Bas-Empire et à l'époque des Grandes Migrations* (Oxford, 2006).

Anna Kharalambieva is senior curator at the Archaeological Museum in Varna (Bulgaria). She has studied late antique and early medieval dress accessories, especially fibulae from museum collections in Varna, Ruse, Dobrich, Shumen, and Gabrovo. Kharalambieva is the author of *The Roman Baths of Odessos* (Varna, 2003). Recently, her research interests have also included eleventh- to twelfth-century pectoral crosses as an indication of contact between Byzantium and Kievan Rus'.

Fernando López Sánchez is a full-time researcher at the Jaume I University in Castellón (Spain) and fellow of the Wolfson College in Oxford. He is the author of *Victoria Augusti: La representacion del poder del emperador en los reversos monetales de bronce del siglo IV d.C.* (Zaragoza, 2004). He is also the editor of a collection of studies entitled *The Coin and the City* to be published in the British Archaeological Reports International Series. Gaul and the Danube region during the third and fourth centuries have been López Sánchez's main area of research. His current project deals with the semantics of iconography on Roman coins from the third century BC to the sixth century AD.

Margit Nagy has been the head of the Migration-Age Department in the Budapest Historical Museum (Hungary) since 1968. She is the author of *Awarenzeitliche Gräberfelder im Stadtgebiet von Budapest I–II* (Budapest, 1998) and *Állatábrázolások és az I. germán állatstílus a Közép–Duna–vidéken (Kr. u. 3–6. század)* (Budapest, 2007). Nagy is also the co-author of the two volumes dedicated to the archaeology of the Gepids in Hungary, *Gepidische Gräberfelder im Theissgebiet* (Budapest, 2002 and 2005). She has published extensively on the archaeology of the early Middle Ages, with a special emphasis on finds from the city of Budapest and its environs.

Wojciech Nowakowski works at the Institute of Archaeology of the University of Warsaw (Poland). He is the author of *Od Galindai do Galinditae: Z badań nad pradziejami bałtyjskiego ludu z Pojezierza Mazurskiego* (Warsaw, 1995), *Die Funde der römischen Kaiserzeit und der Völkerwanderungszeit aus Masuren* (Berlin, 1998), and *Pogranicze trzech swiatów: Kontakty kultur przeworskiej, wielbarskiej i bogaczewskiej w świetle materiałów z badań i poszukiwan archeologicznych* (Warsaw, 2006). He is also the editor of two collections of studies dedicated to his professor, Jerzy Okulicz: *Concordia: Studia ofiarowane Jerzemu Okuliczowi-Kozarynowi w sześćdziesiątą piątą rocznicę urodzin* (Warsaw, 1996) and *Officina archaeologica optima: Studia ofiarowane Jerzemu Okuliczowi-Kozarynowi w siedemdziesiątą roznice urodzin* (Warsaw, 2001).

Philipp von Rummel is head of the editorial office at the German Archaeological Institute in Rome. He is the author of *Habitus barbarus: Kleidung und Repräsentation spätantiker Eliten im 4. und 5. Jahrhundert* (Berlin, 2007) and of a dozen articles on the Vandals and Vandal archaeology in Tunisia. Von Rummel served as director of excavation at Thugga (Dougga, Tunisia), one of the best preserved Roman towns of North Africa. His most recent research projects focus on the publication of the German-Tunisian excavations in Chemtou, Tunisia (the ancient Roman colony of Simitthus) and of the German excavations in Carthage.

Alexander Sarantis completed his PhD at the University of Oxford in 2006, with a dissertation about the Balkans during the reign of Justinian. He has recently authored articles on A. H. M. Jones and the Gepids, and is one of the editors of the Brill series on Late Antique Archaeology. His research interests include imperial military strategies and barbarian invasions, as well as settlement and integration in the East Roman Empire during Late Antiquity.

Roland Steinacher is Junior Scientist at the Institute for Medieval Studies of the Austrian Academy (OeAW) in Vienna (Austria). He is also a member of the

Institute for Austrian Historical Research. Currently he works as a fellow of the Gerda-Henkel Stiftung, Duesseldorf (Germany). Among his current research interests are the history of late antique North Africa, regional and provincial identities in the Mediterranean from the Principate to the end of the first millennium, and the history of the Vandals. He received his PhD from the University of Vienna (2002) with a dissertation on 'The Identification of the Ethnonyms Wenden, Slaws and Vandali from Early Medieval Sources to the 18th Century'. Steinacher is the author of several studies on barbarians in Late Antiquity, ancient history, and early modern scholarship and the co-editor of *Das Reich der Vandalen und seine (Vor-)geschichten* (Vienna, 2008).

Bartłomiej Szymon Szmoniewski works at the Institute of Archaeology and Ethnology of the Polish Academy of Sciences in Cracow. His publications include articles in *Acta Archaeologica Carpathica* and in *Ethnic Contacts and Cultural Exchanges North and West of the Black Sea from the Greek Colonization to the Ottoman Conquest*, ed. by Victor Cojocaru (Iaşi, 2005). He is co-editor of *Wczesnośredniowieczne odwazniki i ciezarki olowiane z Dabrowy Górniczej-Losnia* (Cracow, 2007) and *Władza a struktury społeczne w średniowieczu na wschód od Łaby: Materiały konferencyjne* (Wrocław/Göttingen, 2008).

Ágnes B. Tóth teaches Archaeology at the József Attila University in Szeged (Hungary). She received her PhD in Archaeology from the Eötvös-Loránd University in Budapest (1978) with a dissertation on the fourth- to sixth-century settlement pattern in eastern Hungary. She is the author of *Gepidische Siedlungen im Theissgebiet* (Budapest, 2006) and of many studies on the archaeology of the Tisza region during the sixth century.

STUDIES IN THE EARLY MIDDLE AGES

All volumes in this series are evaluated by an Editorial Board, strictly on academic grounds, based on reports prepared by referees who have been commissioned by virtue of their specialism in the appropriate field. The Board ensures that the screening is done independently and without conflicts of interest. The definitive texts supplied by authors are also subject to review by the Board before being approved for publication. Further, the volumes are copyedited to conform to the publisher's stylebook and to the best international academic standards in the field.

Titles in Series

Cultures in Contact: Scandinavian Settlement in England in the Ninth and Tenth Centuries, ed. by Dawn M. Hadley and Julian D. Richards (2000)

On Barbarian Identity: Critical Approaches to Ethnicity in the Early Middle Ages, ed. by Andrew Gillett (2002)

Matthew Townend, *Language and History in Viking Age England: Linguistic Relations between Speakers of Old Norse and Old English* (2002)

Contact, Continuity, and Collapse: The Norse Colonization of the North Atlantic, ed. by James H. Barrett (2003)

Court Culture in the Early Middle Ages: The Proceedings of the First Alcuin Conference, ed. by Catherine Cubitt (2003)

Political Assemblies in the Earlier Middle Ages, ed. by P. S. Barnwell and Marco Mostert (2003)

Wulfstan, Archbishop of York: The Proceedings of the Second Alcuin Conference, ed. by Matthew Townend (2004)

Borders, Barriers, and Ethnogenesis: Frontiers in Late Antiquity and the Middle Ages, ed. by Florin Curta (2006)

John D. Niles, *Old English Enigmatic Poems and the Play of the Texts* (2006)

Teaching and Learning in Northern Europe, 1000–1200, ed. by Sally N. Vaughn and Jay Rubenstein (2006)

Narrative and History in the Early Medieval West, ed. by Elizabeth M. Tyler and Ross Balzaretti (2006)

People and Space in the Middle Ages, 300–1300, ed. by Wendy Davies, Guy Halsall, and Andrew Reynolds (2006)

John D. Niles, *Old English Heroic Poems and the Social Life of Texts* (2007)

The Crisis of the Oikoumene: *The Three Chapters and the Failed Quest for Unity in the Sixth-Century Mediterranean*, ed. by Celia Chazelle and Catherine Cubitt (2007)

Text, Image, Interpretation: Studies in Anglo-Saxon Literature and its Insular Context in Honour of Éamonn Ó Carragáin, ed. by Alastair Minnis and Jane Roberts (2007)

The Old English Homily: Precedent, Practice, and Appropriation, ed. by Aaron J. Kleist (2007)

James T. Palmer, *Anglo-Saxons in a Frankish World, 690–900* (2009)

Challenging the Boundaries of Medieval History: The Legacy of Timothy Reuter, ed. by Patricia Skinner (2009)

Peter Verbist, *Duelling with the Past: Medieval Authors and the Problem of the Christian Era, c. 990–1135* (2010)

Reading the Anglo-Saxon Chronicle: Language, Literature, History, ed. by Alice Jorgensen (2010)

England and the Continent in the Tenth Century: Studies in Honour of Wilhelm Levison (1876–1947), ed. by David Rollason, Conrad Leyser, and Hannah Williams (2010)

In Preparation

Early Medieval Northumbria: Kingdoms and Communities, 450–1100, ed. by David Petts and Sam Turner

Conceptualizing Multilingualism in Medieval England, c. 800–c. 1250, ed. by Elizabeth M. Tyler

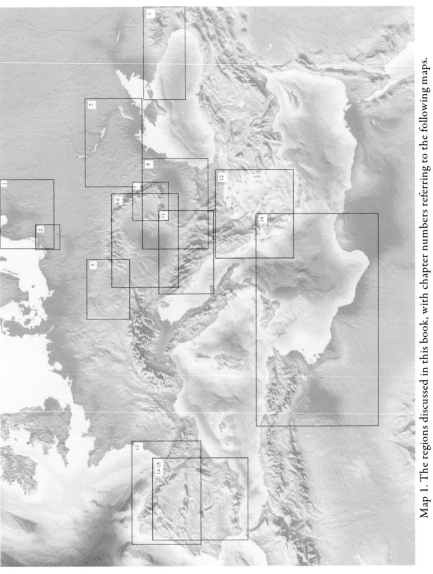

Map 1. The regions discussed in this book, with chapter numbers referring to the following maps.

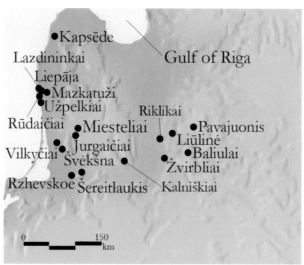

Map 2. The distribution of the principal sites mentioned in
(1) Bliujienė, 'Backcountry Balts'.

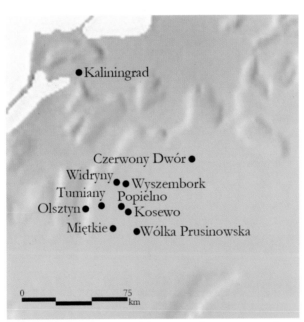

Map 3. The distribution of the principal sites mentioned in
(2) Nowakowski, 'Mysterious Barbarians of Mazuria'.

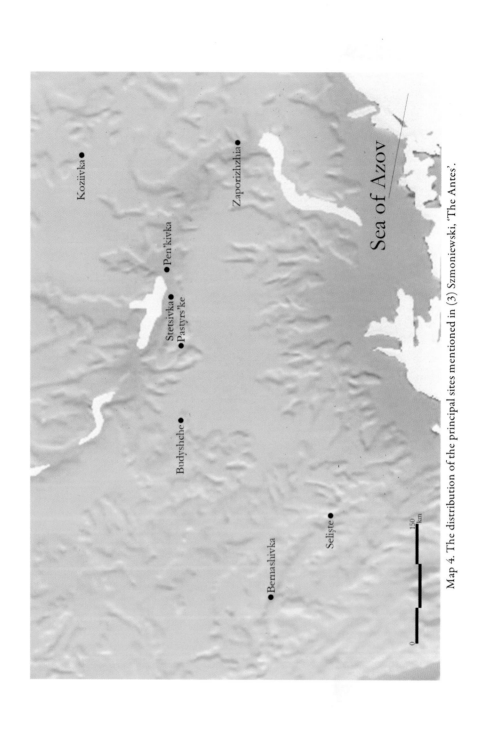

Map 4. The distribution of the principal sites mentioned in (3) Szmoniewski, 'The Antes'.

Map 5. The distribution of the principal sites mentioned in

(4) Gavritukhin and Kazanski, 'Bosporus, the Tetraxite Goths, and the Northern Caucasus Region'.

Map 6. The distribution of the principal sites mentioned in (5) Nagy, 'Hun-Age Burial with Male Skeleton and Horse Bones' and (6) Tóth, 'Fifth-Century Burial from Old Buda'.

Transylvanian Alps

Velatice
Vyškov
Břeclav
Drslavice
Ladendorf
Drösing
Untersiebenbrunn
Cifer
Levice
Oros
Letkés
Kistokaj
Hejőkeresztur
Tokod
Pilismarót
Jobbágyi
Mezőkeresztes
Rábapordány
Szentendre
Leányfalu
Budakalász
Budapest
Törökszentmiklós
Şimleu Silvaniei
Kapolcs
Tác
Szolnok
Arrand
Oradea
Taga
Balatonfüzfő
Csongrád
Mezőberény
Balatonszemes
Intercisa
Szentes
Apahida
Hács
Regöly
Csorna
Márély
Kistelek
Hódmezővásárhely
Zengővárkony
Szekszárd
Dabronc
Pécs
Madaras
Kékesd
Palkonya

0   150
         km

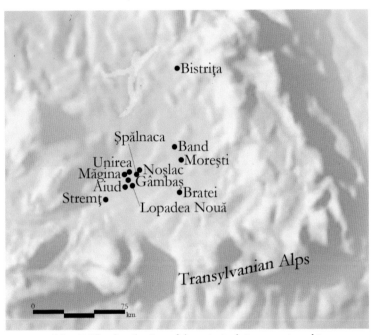

Map 7. The distribution of the principal sites mentioned in
(7) Harhoiu, 'Where Did All the Gepids Go?'.

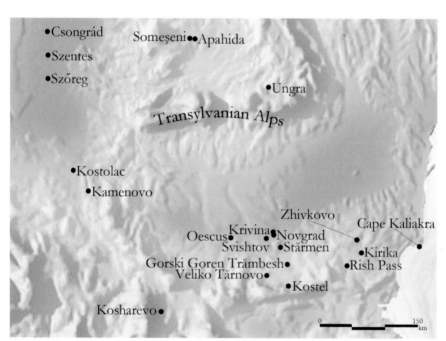

Map 8. The distribution of the principal sites mentioned in
(8) Kharalambieva, 'Gepids in the Balkans'.

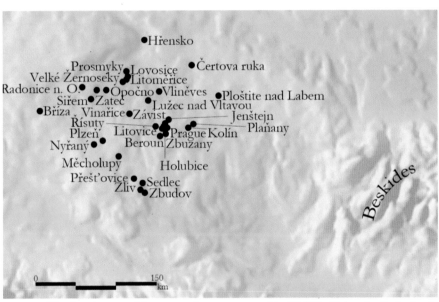

Map 9. The distribution of the principal sites mentioned in (9) Jiřík, 'Bohemian Barbarians'.

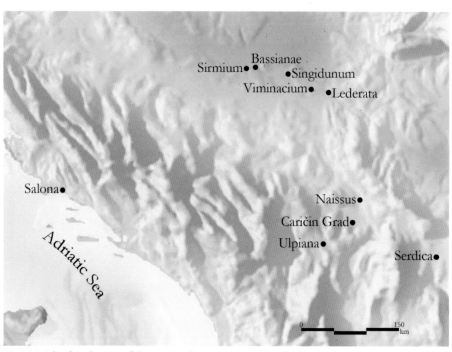

Map 10. The distribution of the principal sites mentioned in (11) Sarantis, 'Justinianic Herules'.

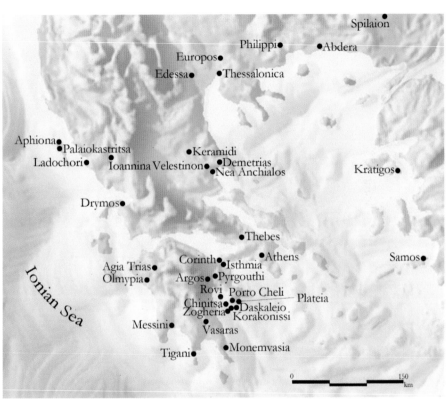

Map 11. The distribution of the principal sites mentioned in
(12) Curta, 'Still Waiting for the Barbarians?'.

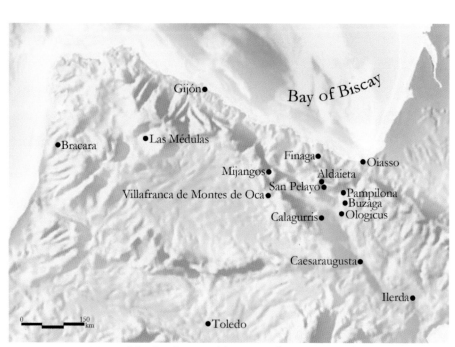

Map 12. The distribution of the principal sites mentioned in
(13) Castellanos, 'Astures, Cantabri, and Vascones'.

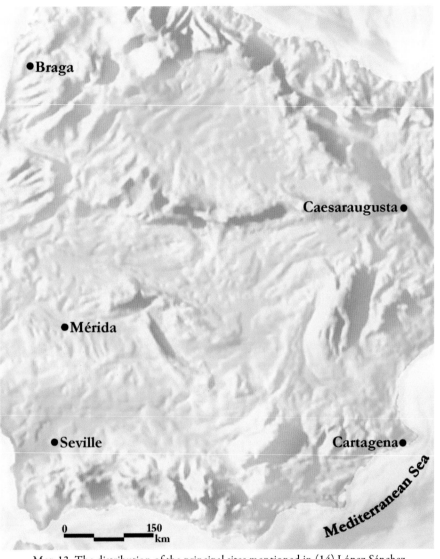

Map 13. The distribution of the principal sites mentioned in (14) López Sánchez,
'Suevic Coins and Suevic Kings' and (15) Berndt, 'Hidden Tracks'.

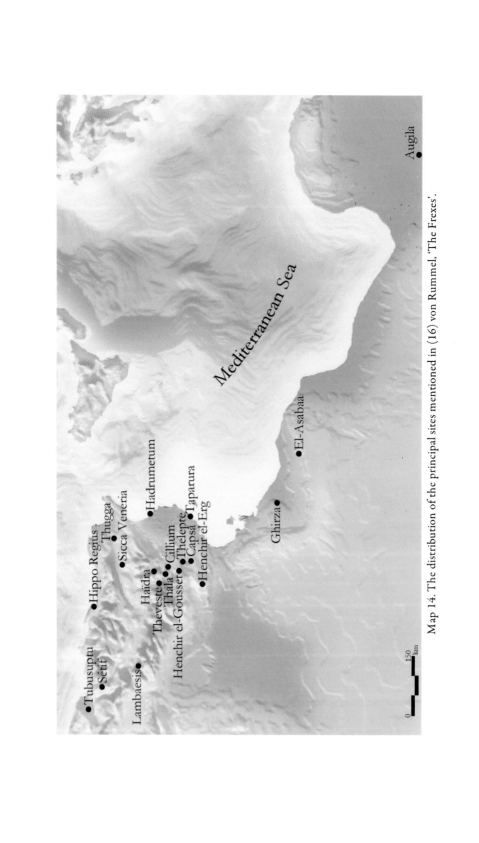

Map 14. The distribution of the principal sites mentioned in (16) von Rummel, 'The Frexes'.

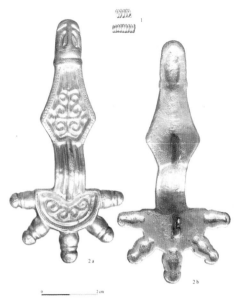

Plate I.1. Budapest III (Old Buda), gold spirals and brooch.

Plate I.2. Budapest III (Old Buda). Iron buckle before cleaning (1) and after cleaning and restoration (2), with a detail of the buckle ring (3).

Plate II.1. Eagle-headed buckle from the Rish Pass.
After Vagalinski, Atanasov, and Dimitrov, 'Eagle-headed Buckles', p. 88 with fig. 2.

Plate II.2. Kosharevo, grave 1: buckle. After Daskalov, 'Ein Grab'.

Plate III.1. Kosharevo, grave 1: scabbard silver mount. After Daskalov, 'Ein Grab'.

Plate III.2. Kosharevo, grave 1: iron sax. After Daskalov, 'Ein Grab'.

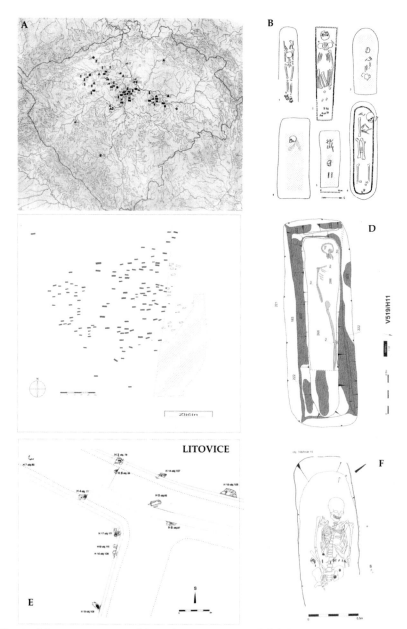

Plate IV. The Vinařice group of the early Migration period: (A) distribution of burial assemblages of the Vinařice group in Bohemia (after Svoboda, *Èechy v dobi*, fig. 78); (B) graves of the Vinařice group from Kolín (after Svoboda, *Èechy v dobi*, fig. 27); (C) the cemetery in Prague-Zličín, plan (as of 2006; after Vávra, Jiřík, Kubálek, and Kuchařík, 'Pohřebištì z doby'); (D) Prague-Zličín, grave 11 (after Vávra, Jiřík, Kubálek, and Kuchařík, 'Pohřebištì z doby'); (E) the Litovice cemetery (after Pleinerová, 'Litovice (okr. Praha-západ)', fig. 2); (F) Litovice, grave 19 (after Pleinerová, 'Litovice (okr. Praha-západ)', fig. 3.4).

Plate V.1. Hřensko, hoard of silver. Photo by author.

Plate V.2. Čertova ruka (Devil's Hand). Photo by Pavel Jiřík.

Plate VI.1 (above). Siliqua, Braga mint, 449, *DN Honori-us PF Aug/Iussu Richiari Reges*, Cabinet des Médailles et Antiques, Bibliothèque Nationale, Paris. Courtesy of Dominique Hollard, curator of Roman Numismatics.

Plate VI.2 (left). Senigalla medallion, 509, *Rex Theodoricu-s Pius Princis/Rex Theodoricus Victor Gentium/Comob*. After Wroth, *Catalogue*, frontispiece.

Plate VI.3 (below). Tremissis, Milan mint, Marcianus, 456–57, *DN Marcian-us PF AVG/Comob*. Cabinet des Médailles et Antiques, Bibliothèque Nationale, Paris. Courtesy of Dominique Hollard, Curator of Roman Numismatics.

Plate VII.1 (left). AE 3 (decanummium), Rome mint, 526–34, *Invict-a Roma/DN Athal-aricus*. After *Auction XI, The New York Sale. Wednesday, January 11, 2006. Greek, Roman, Byzantine and Mediaeval Coins. Indian Coins. Selection of World Coins* (London/New York/Washington, 2006), p. 79, no. 416.

Plate VII.2 (right). Quarter siliqua in the name of Justinian I, Rome mint, 526–34, *DN Iust-inian Aug/DN/Athal/aricus/Rex*. After *Auction XI*, p. 79, no. 413.

Plate VIII.1 (left). Solidus, Constantinople mint, 364, *DN Valens-PF Aug/Virtus Romanorum/ Cons. Münzauktion Tkaleg Ag. 1500 Jahre Münzprägekunst.* Zürich. 18 February 2002, no. 256.

Plate VIII.2 (right). Aureus, Cyzicus mint, 293, *Maximianus-Augustus/Concordi-ae Augg NN.* After *Auction 24: A Highly Important Collection of Roman and Byzantine Gold Coins, Property of an European Nobleman*, Numismatica Ars Classica Ag, 5 December 2002 (Zürich, 2002), p. 109, no. 243.

Plate VIII.3. Solidus, Sirmium mint, 379, *DN Gratian-nus PF Avg/Victor-ia Augg.* After *Triton IX: In Conjunction with the 34th Annual New York International*, 10–11 January 2006, Sessions 2–4, Classical Numismatic Group, Inc. (Lancaster/London 2006), p. 214, no. 1601.

Plate IX.1. Solidus, Ravenna mint, 422, *DN Honori-us PF Aug/Vot XXX-Mult XXXX/Comob/RV*. Cabinet des Médailles et Antiques, Bibliothèque Nationale, Paris. Courtesy of Dominique Hollard, curator of Roman Numismatics.

Plate IX.2. Visigothic solidus, Tolosa mint, 439–54, *DN Pla Valenti-nianus PF Aug/Victori-aauggg/Comob/RV*. Cabinet des Médailles et Antiques, Bibliothèque Nationale, Paris. Courtesy of Dominique Hollard, curator of Roman Numismatics.

Plate X.1. Thelepte (Feriana, Tunisia): collapsed wall of the Byzantine fortress.
Photo by the author.

Plate X.2. The Djebel Mrata region. Photo by the author.